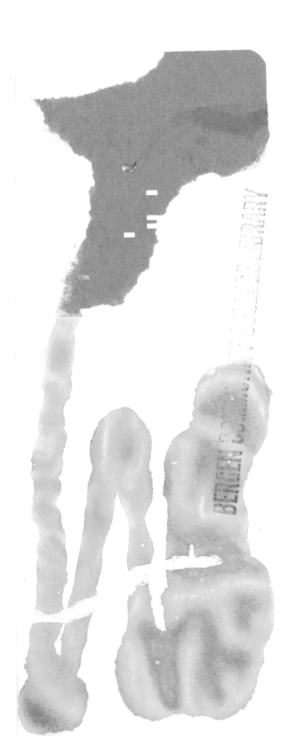

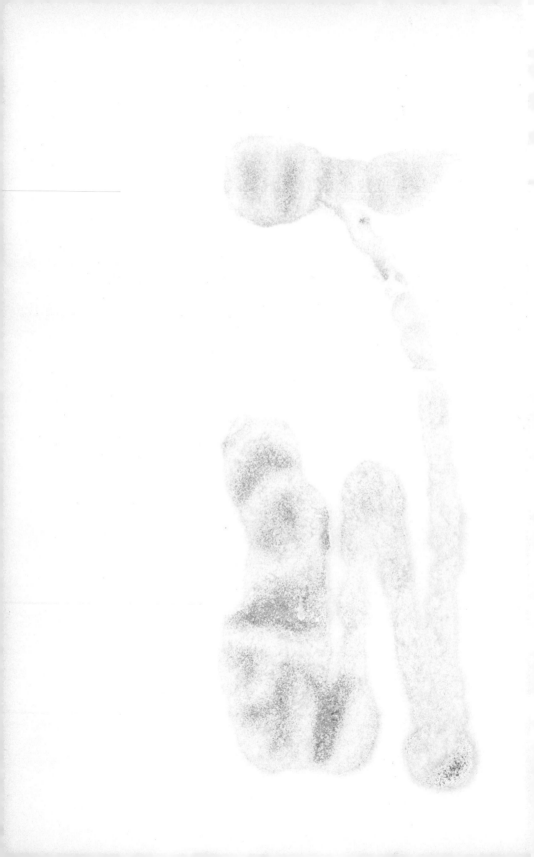

AMERICAN WOMEN

images and realities

AMERICAN WOMEN
Images and Realities

Advisory Editors
ANNETTE K. BAXTER
LEON STEIN

A Note About This Volume

Mary Simmerson Cunningham Logan (1838-1923) grew up in a southern Illinois pioneer community. Married at 17, she travelled with her husband, a state attorney, on his court circuit, then into the field while he served as colonel in the Union army, and finally on the campaigns that brought him to Congress and the Senate. Her home was a center of social life in Washington. She and her daughter, Mary Logan Tucker, prepared this compendium of lives of famous and not-so-famous women—with special sections on Catholic and Jewish women—between 1902 and 1909.

THE
PART TAKEN BY WOMEN
IN
AMERICAN HISTORY

[Mary S.] Logan

ARNO PRESS
A New York Times Company
New York • 1972

Reprint Edition 1972 by Arno Press Inc.

Reprinted from a copy in The State Historical
Society of Wisconsin Library

American Women: Images and Realities
ISBN for complete set: 0-405-04445-3
See last pages of this volume for titles.

Manufactured in the United States of America

- - - - - - - - - - - -

Library of Congress Cataloging in Publication Data

Logan, Mary Simmerson (Cunningham) 1838-1923.
    The part taken by women in american history.

    (American women: images and realities)
    Bibliography: p.
    1. Women in the United States--Biography. I. Title.
II. Series.
CT3260.L57 1972   920.72   72-2613
ISBN 0-405-04467-4

> *"No country seems to owe so much to its women as America*
> *—to owe to them so much of what is best in its social institutions,*
> *and in the beliefs that govern conduct."*—PROF. JAMES BRYCE.

THE
PART TAKEN BY WOMEN
IN
AMERICAN HISTORY

BY

MRS. JOHN A. LOGAN

WITH SPECIAL INTRODUCTIONS BY

MRS. DONALD McLEAN
Ex-President D. A. R.

MRS. HARRIET TAYLOR UPTON
Ex-Treasurer Suffrage Association of America.

MRS. M. M. NORTH
Nat. Special Press Correspondent Woman's Relief Corps.

MRS. CORNELIA B. STONE
Ex-President Daughters of the Confederacy.

MRS. MATTHEW T. SCOTT
President D. A. R.

MRS. C. E. SEVERANCE
President first Woman's Society ever organized and known as "The Mother of Clubs."

MRS. SARAH D. LaFETRA
President Woman's Christian Temperance Union of District of Columbia.

MRS. KATHARINE G. BUSBEY
Sketch of Author.

PUBLISHED BY
THE PERRY-NALLE PUBLISHING CO.
WILMINGTON, DEL., U. S. A.
1912

PREFACE.

In the preparation of this volume, the editor has gained infinite pleasure by reason of the fact that in making the research necessary, she has familiarized herself with the stupendous work performed by the women of America. Before taking up the work she labored under the impression that she knew something about the achievements of the women of her own country. Now she confesses she had no conception of the voluminous results they have achieved or the extent of their prodigious labors. She was not aware that women were the authors of so many movements for the welfare of mankind and the advancement of civilization.

To scan the meagre published records that have previously been made should awaken limitless pride in our countrywomen who have been so quick to discover the possibilities in the scope of woman's sphere and so indomitable in the prosecution of the development of those possibilities.

The writer has found that those women, who have done the most for the church, the state, in philanthropy, in charity, in education and in patriotism, have been the best wives and mothers. Their hearts have been full of love of God, of Country, and of mankind; they have not been idlers while the world moved on.

The only regret experienced is that the editor has not been able to secure the data for sketches of every woman who has done something for the betterment of mankind. She appreciates that very many have been omitted who are entitled to a place in this volume because of the impossibility of procuring names and information which it would have been a pleasure to present.

It is with profound gratitude that the editor acknowledges the extreme kindness of friends all over this broad land who have so generously furnished data for sketches herein; to Hon. Herbert Putnam, Librarian of the Library of Congress, and his able assistants who have so courteously allowed the use of the books of the Library, from which has been gathered much of the information

used, the editor desires to tender thanks.   Appended herewith is a
partial list of books consulted:

DISTINGUISHED WOMEN.—*Mrs. Hale.*
WOMEN OF THE REFORMATION.—*Mrs. Annie Wittenmeyer.*
LADIES OF THE WHITE HOUSE.—*Laura C. Holloway.*
QUEENLY WOMEN CROWNED AND UNCROWNED.—Ed. by *Prof.
  S. W. Williams.*
THE WORLD'S WOMEN.—*Richmond.*
THE WORLD'S CONGRESS OF REPRESENTATIVE WOMEN.—*M. W.
  Sewall.*
AMERICAN WOMEN.—*F. E. Willard.*
LITTLE PILGRIMAGES AMONG THE WOMEN WHO HAVE WRITTEN
  FAMOUS BOOKS.—*E. F. Harkins* and *C. H. L. John-
  ston.*
GIRLS WHO BECAME FAMOUS.—*Sarah K. Bolton.*
BIOGRAPHICAL AND CRITICAL STUDIES.—*Baskerville.*
THE YOUNGER AMERICAN POETS.—*Rittenhouse.*
SOUTHERN LITERATURE.—*Manly.*
KENTUCKY PIONEER WOMEN.—*Laney.*
REPRESENTATIVE SOUTHERN POETS.—*Hubner.*
SELECTIONS FROM THE WRITINGS OF CONNECTICUT WOMEN.
PROMINENT WOMEN OF TEXAS.—*Brooks.*
PIONEER WOMEN OF THE WEST.—*Ellet.*
WOMEN OF AMERICA.—*Larus.*
EMINENT MISSIONARY WOMEN.—*Mrs. J. T. Gracey.*
THE WOMEN OF AMERICA.—*McCracken.*
A BELLE OF THE FIFTIES.
QUEENS OF AMERICAN SOCIETY.—*Ellet.*
HISTORY OF AMERICAN STAGE.—*T. Allston Browne.*
THE HISTORY OF WOMAN SUFFRAGE.—*Stanton, Anthony* and
  Gage.
WHO'S WHO IN AMERICA.
CATHOLIC WHO'S WHO IN AMERICA.—*Miss Curtis.*
SEVEN GREAT FOUNDATIONS.—*Leonard P. Ayers.*
WHAT AMERICA OWES TO WOMEN.—Ed. by *Lydia Hoyt
  Farmer.*

FOREWORD.

American women and students of American history have long deplored the meagre credit which has been given to women for the part they have taken in the progress and achievements of America as a Nation.

The women citizens of our country—native and adopted—have worked with indefatigable energy, unswerving loyalty and marvelous intelligence for the betterment and progress of the people. Sections have not always agreed upon policies but the women of all sections have labored with untiring devotion for what seemed to them must bring the greatest good to the greatest number.

Appreciating the fact that scant tribute has been paid to the women of America and that no concrete record of their achievements existed, I have for several years, by conscientious and laborious research through all available sources, including the Congressional Library at Washington—one of the three greatest libraries in the world—endeavored, and, I believe, with success, to bring together the names of the women well known, and to rescue from oblivion those unheralded and unknown, and thus form a compendium of all names and achievements of the women who have taken a part in the vital affairs of our country.

The result of my efforts has been the writing of the book entitled "THE PART TAKEN BY WOMEN IN AMERICAN HISTORY."

I have, I believe, in this book, given an impartial portraiture of the part taken by women in American history, of those who have contributed to the development of our country in Art, Science, Literature, Music, Religion, Education, Philanthropy, Patriotism, Domestic Science, Club and Home Life, and to the various efforts women have made for the uplift of all mankind.

The names of paternal ancestors adorn the pages of history because of their wisdom in the adjustment of the affairs of peace, and their heroic deeds in time of war, but little is known of our maternal ancestors—of the women who shared so patiently and courageously the privations, struggles and sacrifices for the Republic, in war and in peace, from the landing of the Pilgrims from the Mayflower until the present time.

In cosmopolitan America, women of every race under the sun have had opportunity to "show the world the rarest excellence of woman in the exercise of the largest and truest liberty the world has ever known." It can be added that her achievements are unprecedented, enabling her to stand side by side with the noble men of the Nation in every onward and upward movement for the advancement of civilization and Christianity.

"THE PART TAKEN BY WOMEN IN AMERICAN HISTORY" begins with those women of our country's earliest days, giving a correct chronicle of their lives; followed by a true history of such of their descendants as have, to the present time, done anything in any line for the advancement of American civilization, enumerating them as follows:

Aboriginal women.

Women of the Mayflower.

Women of Colonial Days.

Women's part in the Revolution or War of Independence.

Women's endurance during the continual conflict with the Indians during the early days of the Republic.

Women's co-operation in building the pioneer churches, establishing schools and the laying of the foundation of our social relations.

Women's part in the extension of the spirit of humanity, philanthropy, Christianity and civilization to the uttermost parts of the earth.

Women's part in the pioneer's shibboleth "Westward the course of the empire takes its way," sharing in all the privations and hardships of the pioneers.

Women's part as missionaries of Christianity, morality and education.

Women's part in bringing about peaceful settlement of the conflict between the United States and Mexico in 1848.

The prodigious sacrifices of the women, north and south, during the Civil War.

Woman's part during the Reconstruction days, and her unprecedented heroism and nobility in helping to heal the wounds, efface the scars and happily restore union between the states.

Women's achievements in the Sciences, Arts, Education, Politics, and Religion.

Women of America lifting the yoke of oppression from the necks of women throughout the whole world.

Women as home builders and homekeepers.

Women as builders of churches, school houses and hospitals.

Women as patriots and teachers of patriotism.

Women's part along all lines in the wonderful achievements of the nineteenth century and the American woman's splendid equipment for the stupendous work of the twentieth century.

Women as co-partners in the guardianship of American institutions for the benefit of mankind.

Women's part in demonstrating the truthfulness of the axiom "In union there is strength" by organizing clubs, societies and associations in the interest of History, Charity, Culture and Society.

I have given to this work my love and enthusiasm. I believe that in this record of the achievements of the women of America we will find that which will spur on the women of the twentieth century, with their enlarged opportunities and high ambition, to the assuming of responsibilities and labors that would have appalled the bravest of the sex in the nineteenth century.

In offering you "THE PART TAKEN BY WOMEN IN AMERICAN HISTORY," I do so with the confidence that it will appeal to you and that every woman in this broad land of ours will derive benefit and encouragement from the reading of the wonderful achievements of those of our sex who have done so much for the advancement of civilization and progress and welfare of our beloved country.

Cordially yours,

Mrs John A Logan

Washington, D. C.

CONTENTS

	PAGE
PREFACE	v-vi
FOREWORD	vii-ix
CONCERNING THE AUTHOR—MRS. JOHN A. LOGAN	1-17
ABORIGINAL WOMEN OF AMERICA	18
WOMEN PIONEERS	22
WOMEN OF THE REVOLUTION	105
WOMEN FROM THE TIME OF MARY WASHINGTON	205
Women in the Civil War	305
Women Nurses of the Civil War	309
The Woman's Relief Corps, Auxiliary to the Grand Army of the Republic	340
Women of the Woman's Relief Corps	347
National Association of Army Nurses of the Civil War	357
Army Nurses of the Civil War, 1861-1865	360
Women of the New South	377
Introduction to Club Section	386
Federation of Women Clubs	389
Women's Clubs in Cincinnati	390
Arts and Crafts	391
Home Culture Clubs	393
The Washington Travel Club	395
The Woman's National Press Association	396
The Woman's National Rivers and Harbors Congress	397
Bunker Hill Monument Association	400
National Society Daughters of the American Revolution	421
WOMEN OF THE CONFEDERACY	485
The United Daughters of the Confederacy	486
WOMEN IN THE MISSIONARY FIELD	507
WOMEN AS PHILANTHROPISTS	523
WOMAN SUFFRAGE	548
History of Woman's Suffrage Organization	552

	PAGE
WOMEN REFORMERS	589
Women Sociologists	593
CATHOLIC WOMEN IN AMERICA	605
JEWISH WOMEN OF AMERICA	631
Jewish Women's Work for Charity	637
WOMEN AS TEMPERANCE WORKERS	653
WOMAN'S WORK FOR THE BLIND	696
CHRISTIAN SCIENCE	701
WOMEN EDUCATORS	706
WOMEN IN PROFESSIONS	736
Artists	749
Actresses	770
Lecturers	784
Playwrights and Authors	789
WOMEN INVENTORS	882
WOMEN IN CIVIL SERVICE	889
WOMEN IN BUSINESS	893

LIST OF ILLUSTRATIONS

Mrs. John A. Logan .... (Photogravure) *Frontispiece*

PAGE

Calumet Place—Home of Mrs. John A. Logan 1

Landing of the Pilgrim Fathers 24

Massacre at Fort Mimms 64

The Battle of Bunker Hill 105

Molly Pitcher at the Battle of Monmouth 176

Mary Washington House—Fredericksburg, Va. 205

Mary Washington Monument—Fredericksburg, Va. .. 224

Louisa May Alcott as a Hospital Nurse 357

Memorial Continental Hall, Washington, D. C. 421

Winnie Davis Monument in "Hollywood," Richmond,
    Virginia 485

Distinguished Women Orators 592

Distinguished Women Poets 800

CALUMET PLACE—HOME OF MRS. JOHN A. LOGAN.

Concerning the Author—Mrs. John A. Logan.

KATHERINE G. BUSBEY.

America is changing beneath our eyes. Yesterday's books of impressionalistic views concerning her are antiquated; descriptions of ten years ago are hopelessly out of date; between the writing of a book descriptive of America's national psychology and its publication half the conclusions should be changed. The only way, therefore, to really interpret America is through a study of the biographies of those who have lived and wrought and made America what she is.

From the biographies of America's strenuous sons the world would seem to conceive of America as a nation definitely organized for one purpose, straining every nerve and sinew to attain that end, until "business," the foreign critic tells us, is the all-absorbing interest, by the side of which nothing else counts at all. But, interwoven with the history of this nation joyously set out on the commercial conquest of the world, is the life of America's splendid womanhood—not always as the foreign eulogist would extol her for her physical superiority—but the American womanhood working in peace and quietness whether through the fierce energy of the pioneer mother or, later in our history, supplementing now by the subtlety of nature and now by gift of grace, man's material or martial labor for the country's welfare. In speaking of the higher existence above our industrial energy some one has said, "in America the women alone live," and certainly no better vision

of what American life stands for with all other interest ruthlessly swept aside, can be gained than that which comes in
looking through the biographies of American women.   But
to make these lives of value as a national interpretation—not
a mere unilluminated statistical array—the task must rest in
the hands of an American woman with the sympathy and
understanding which can come only from having touched at
first hand and at various points the typical life of American
womanhood.   And this is Mrs. John A. Logan's pre-eminent
qualification as the author of this volume.   With no attempt
at eulogy except such expressions as sincere admiration and
deepest personal affection must inspire, I shall present such
leading phases of Mrs. Logan's bravely wrought, richly-spent
career that they may illustrate how, apart from the prominence
which the reflected glory of her illustrious husband gives her
name, this American woman's mind, vitality, private tragedies,
and the strange and varied forces shaping her magnificent
character, all bear testimony to a life given to high causes
and to her ability unselfishly to appreciate and to portray so
that it may survive the inexorable years, the work—brave,
influential, patriotic, and imaginative—of other American
women in which our national pride exalts.

First then, Mrs. Logan even at an early age played her
heroic part as the child of pioneers in Southern Illinois. Her
father was often called from the hearthstone to meet the hostile
Indians in the northern part of the state, and when the Mexican
War broke out this spirited patriot, Captain John M. Cunningham, again gave his good right arm to his country's cause.
Mrs. Logan, then Mary S. Cunningham, was the eldest of
thirteen children, sheltered and loved in that pioneer homestead, and during the long absences of her father at the front
she shared with her mother all the hardships and dangers of
frontier life, relieving her parent of every task which was

within the range of her strength and forging in her own girlish body the steel fibres of character which were to stand her in such good stead in the stress of military and political life as co-worker with her distinguished husband, and in the temptations of that lighter world of diplomacy and wit into which her personal popularity placed her as a star.

An early biographer of Mrs. Logan has written, "Beyond a fine constitution, a comely presence, a tendency to a highly moral standard in childhood fostered by early beneficent influences, and an abiding faith in the goodness of God, Mary Logan cannot be said to have been specially endowed . . . she was simply a good, honorable girl, who early became imbued with the conviction that the secret of success in life is the faculty of seizing promptly an opportunity . . . Every opportunity for self-help that has passed her way she has been wise enough to improve to its uttermost and the consequence is that Mrs. Logan has played her prominent part in the drama of national life bravely and well, and will remain in the hearts of the many until the inexorable prompter rings down the curtain upon the last act of her well rounded career."

This, though undoubtedly a just estimate, can hardly be judged overgenerous, since it fails to mention the great asset that Mrs. Logan's charming personality has always been. Moreover, the pioneer girl, Mary S. Cunningham, became a strikingly handsome woman, a woman who has always commanded attention by her appearance and bearing as well as through her talents. And yet a glimpse of her earlier public life written by Mrs. Logan herself gives the following modest summary of that period:

"My father being made registrar of the Land Office at Shawneetown, Illinois, under the Pierce administration, we subsequently removed to that place. I attended school at the Convent of St. Vincent, near Uniontown, Kentucky, graduating at that school in 1855. I came home and soon after met my husband, General John A. Logan, who had served during the War with Mexico with my father, and to whom I am said to have been given by father when I was a child. We were married on the twenty-seventh day of November, 1855. My husband was at that time a promising young lawyer, and we removed to Benton, Franklin County, Illinois, when he was appointed prosecuting attorney for the third judicial district of the State of Illinois, which embraced sixteen counties. In those days we were not furnished with official blanks for everything, as is the case to-day, and I began to assist my husband in writing indictments for minor offenses, and in that way gradually drifted into taking part in everything he did. We had the same struggle that all young people without money had in those early days, but the fact that in 1858 my husband was elected to Congress shows that we were not altogether unsuccessful."

What lies between those modest lines is the fact that the young wife immediately on marriage installed herself in the place of companion and helpmeet to her ambitious husband, not only in the housewifely sense, but as secretary and assistant in his office work, and in this work she acquired that marvelous facility for handling large numbers of letters, briefs, etc., which enabled her years later to cope with the enormous correspondence of General Logan while he was representing his country in Congress, and at that critical time when the national crisis made secrecy in regard to the affairs of her public servants an imperative necessity. While, as for the "success" of the political career which it was Logan's ambition to achieve even in these incipient stages, as ever after, Mrs. Logan's personality was an asset too large to be accurately estimated. The superb strength of the young woman and her loyal resourcefulness were nowhere better illustrated than in the way she met the first great crisis of their united lives.

In 1860 General Logan was re-elected to Congress and Mrs. Logan spent that memorable winter of tension and dread in the affairs of state in Washington with him. Scarcely had they returned home when came the news of the fall of Sumter, and, in response to President Lincoln's Proclamation convening an extra session of Congress, General Logan was forced to hurry back to Washington. Mrs. Logan remained at their home in Marion, Williamson County, Illinois, realizing more and more acutely the difficulty, even the danger, of her position in that community, which was settled largely by southerners or persons of southern descent. These constituents were thoroughly in sympathy with the southern cause and grew more and more restive to know what Logan's course would be. His speeches in the House of Representatives revealed his determination to adhere to the Union, and when word was brought that at the Battle of Bull Run instead of remaining in Washington he had joined Colonel Richardson's Michigan Regiment and fought with it all day, these people of Southern Illinois were in a ferment of discontent over their Congressman's action. The day arrived for General Logan to reach home and so great was the excitement in Marion that all business was suspended. The adult population was about one thousand and every one of these people who could get about the streets roved to and fro with loud declamations against any course which would drive them to fight for the negroes. It was known that besides these excited but order-loving citizens, there had been a large accession of desperate characters, drawn thither by their anxiety to join in any sanguinary fray. Passion was at fever heat, and General Logan, speeding there, was the avowed victim. Trembling for the safety of her husband Mary Logan jumped into a buggy and drove to Carbondale, twenty-two miles distant, but the nearest railway station, where her husband must alight. Here she found that his train had missed connections and would not arrive for some hours. Desirous of informing the populace that the cause of delay was accidental, and not dilatory tactics on her husband's part, she turned her tired horse's head and drove rapidly back to Marion. Evening had fallen when she reached there and the crowds of the day had been increased by numbers of farmers from the outskirts. The atmosphere was charged with the dangerous explosive of revolt.

At first sight of her buggy the riotous crowds surrounded it and demanded to know why her husband had failed to appear. Her voice was inaudible above the din and Captain Swindell, Sheriff of the County, and Colonel White, then Clerk of the Court, exerted themselves unavailingly to pacify the mob. It was not until the Sheriff stood up in her buggy and urged the crowd to disperse, assuring them that Logan would be there to address them in the morning, that the deafening clamor could be quelled and Mary Logan released from her position of peril.

Then rejecting all offers of a substitute to convey to her husband the condition of affairs, as well as all her father's pleading to return to her home and rest for the night, Mrs. Logan trembling with fatigue and anxiety, once more set out alone on the long drive to Carbondale, twenty-two miles distant. At two in the morning the train arrived and Mrs. Logan rapidly reviewed the situation to her husband. "Very well," said he quietly as he got into the buggy, "Now, Mary, you get out and stay here and rest in Carbondale with friends for a few days. If there is any danger in Marion I don't want you to be there." But Mrs. Logan was not of that calibre; she smiled up at him, took the whip and reins and started the horse. "My dear, I did not marry you to share in the sunshine of life and desert you when clouds gathered above us," she said simply.

When General Logan rose to speak the next morning there were in the crowd who listened, more than a score of men who had sworn to take his life if he declared for the Union. But John A. Logan mounted the wagon drawn up in the public square and proceeded by the force of his eloquence, his reasoning, his persuasion and by the outpouring of the passionate patriotism to turn so completely the tide of feeling that on getting down he immediately enlisted one hundred and ten men for the first Company of the Regiment which he proposed raising for the defense of the Union.   Within ten days one thousand and ten men were enrolled as their country's defenders for three years, or until peace was declared, and he received from Governor Yates a commission as Colonel of the Thirty-first Illinois Infantry Volunteers.   During this period and while the regiment was being organized, Mrs. Logan acted as his aide-de-camp, carrying his dispatches from Marion and other points to Carbondale, the nearest telegraph station, alone during the day and at night accompanied by no more formal escort than a village lad named Willie Chew.

Logan saved Southern Illinois to the Union, but what measure of credit for that great exploit should be accorded his plucky wife, women of America may judge!

During his campaigns in the war which followed, Mrs. Logan took every opportunity offered to be near her husband. She followed him to many a well-fought field and endured the privations of camp life as thousands of other patriotic women did, without murmur, only too glad to share her husband's perils or to minister to the sick and wounded of his regiment for the sake of being near him.

When the troops were ordered from Cairo—on the expedition to Fort Donelson and Fort Henry—Mrs. Logan returned to Marion.   The pay of our Colonels and Officers of higher rank was at that time small and uncertain and perhaps one of what has been called, "the biggest little things" of Mrs. Logan's noble life was when she, in these hard war times, brought into play all her acuteness and economic skill to respond to the continual demands upon her for the relief of the families who found it impossible to live on the pay of their soldier husbands who had volunteered in defense of their country. With heart and soul, Mary Logan, the woman who had graced Washington society, and who had also known the excitement of war at the front, became a cultivator of the land, raising wheat, corn and cotton on their small farm in South Illinois. And no unusual sight during the cotton picking season was Mrs. Logan riding into town on a load of cotton, thus preventing, by her supervision, the loss by the wayside of a single pound of it, as it was sold in those days at one dollar per pound. Arriving at the cotton gin in town, she would peer over the shoulder of the weigher, and producing her memorandum book, would compare his figures with her own. Nobody ever swindled her and her cotton speculations "panned out" well. This labor was the least of her troubles. The constant anxiety for the safety of her husband during the hazardous campaigns of the war and the tax upon her sympathies in responding to the appeals of the soldiers' families, were burdens almost insupportable for the delicate woman Mrs. Logan then was.

The war over, General Logan returned home and shortly there ensued that exciting canvass for the successor to Governor Yates; John M. Palmer, ex-Governor Richard J. Oglesby and John A. Logan being the rival candidates. Three abler men it would be hard to find. All three had held military commands during the Civil War and all three had distinguished themselves. All three, therefore, had ardent friends who desired their election to the Senate, but, to quote from one of the Springfield, Illinois, newspapers of that day, " 'Black

Jack' Logan had one surpassing advantage over his competitors, that being Mrs. John A. Logan." Indeed, Mrs. Logan, ever passionately eager to assist her husband, had accompanied him to the Capital and there had begun her career as a potent factor in this, his first candidacy for the Senate. When upon the assembly of the Republican caucus, Logan was found to have more than three to one votes over his rivals and the announcement was made that John A. Logan was Senator, among the first to reach his late opponent's hand was Governor Oglesby and he followed his congratulations with a sly gallantry to the effect that perhaps it was not that the people loved Oglesby less, but Mrs. Logan more.

In 1877 occurred General Logan's next fight for the Senate, and again Mrs. Logan, assisted now by her beautiful and versatile daughter, displayed those admirable qualities of diplomacy, tact, and practicality which had always proved so potent. John A. Logan, himself, made more frequent reference than anyone else to his wife's diplomacy, affection and unwavering loyalty as a devoted wife and helpmate.

Great strength of character was now required on the part of Mrs. Logan to avert an occurrence which she, with her honest, sane view of life, would have regarded as a catastrophe —a severance of her individuality from that of her husband's. Mary Logan proved herself equal to the occasion; her conduct was admirable in its poise and self-effacement. When the public men of the day applauded her wifely enthusiasm, Mrs. Logan quietly remarked that she saw no reason why she should not be with the General in his political campaigns in the same capacity in which she had been near him at Belmont, Fort Donelson and Pittsburgh Landing—as a faithful helpmate and companion. She sent carefully worded regrets to all offers which came to her to lecture, to give readings, to contribute for the press on political subjects, and she indignantly denied that report—before the allure of which many a brilliant woman has fallen a victim to vanity—that she wrote her husband's speeches for him. And yet, despite all protests by Mrs. Logan, the sentiment of her influence in matters political—the General's military career was his own beyond dispute—grew to such an extent that it almost reached the point of a similar situation, a century earlier, when the old Scotchman, Davy Burns, who erected the first house in Washington, said testily to the immortal George:

"And prithee, Mr. Washington, who would you have been if you hadn't been lucky enough to marry the widow Custis?"

Mrs. Logan's life during the General's senatorial career in Washington, full of success, adulation and social prestige as it was, was not without its trials; bores, borrowers and false claimants of relationship being numerous; even cranks and fanatics were not unknown intruders in her home, while the cruel charges of wealth dishonestly obtained by Senator Logan, which often found publication in a certain class of newspapers, were a source of acute suffering to his sensitive and proud wife. But Mrs. Logan's loyalty kept her head high in noble patience and belief, and in seeking his vindication she was one with the General as in every other matter, and when he was triumphantly acquitted of any infamous connection with the Credit Mobilier enterprise even his accuser conceded, "All honor is due to Logan for his truly statesmanlike conduct, and all honor to his wife, who stood staunchly by her husband's side in his scruples of conscience."

It was at Mrs. Logan's suggestion that Senator Logan applied for the back pension for Mrs. Lincoln, which was granted to the martyred President's wife; and it was she who suggested the establishment of Decoration Day. The circumstances attending the issuance of Order No. 11—Commander-In-Chief G. A. R., are as follows:

Colonel Charles Wilson, editor of the Chicago *Journal*, and a party of prominent women from Boston and Chicago, came to Washington in February, 1868, and invited General and Mrs. Logan to go with them to Richmond to visit the historic ground around that city. His duties in Congress prevented General Logan from going, but Mrs. Logan went, and when she returned, she told her husband of the simple decoration on the Confederate graves. This touched him deeply, and he at once alluded to the custom, which prevailed among the Greeks, of honoring the graves of their dead with chaplets of laurel and flowers. As Commander-in-Chief of the G. A. R., he immediately issued the order for the annual decoration of the graves of the loyal deceased. He also interested himself in getting the bill through Congress, setting apart a day for the honoring of the graves of dead soldiers as a legal holiday, and he succeeded in accomplishing this design of his patriotic heart.

It was a terrible blow when this strong man, of whom she was so proud, was stricken down with illness, and after a short illness was taken from her, and Mrs. Logan was left alone in the stately colonial mansion which she had struggled so hard to possess, worked so long to adorn and joyfully opened to the public on all occasions in the hospitable régime of this statesman's career which now lay broken. Face to face with the misery of a broken tie, of a lost love, and a severed companionship, Mrs. Logan's strong heart and courage faltered. But quickly came that inspiration for work and constant occupation of mind which had impelled all her moves in life, and her achievements since General Logan's death have been of a character to mark Mrs. Logan one of America's foremost daughters even if naught of distinction had gone before. Mrs. Logan had children; other relatives too were dependent upon her and her financial circumstances were not easy, for General

Logan had enriched the nation's honor roll more than her statesman pay roll had enriched him. So Mrs. Logan bravely determined to test her talent in the literary world. While gathering her mental poise after the shock of General Logan's death, she took the two charming daughters of the late George M. Pullman, of Chicago, on a tour of Europe, but her serious work was taken up immediately upon her return. She began her literary career writing for a number of periodicals, and then for six years she edited, in Washington, *The Home Magazine,* almost a pioneer in that type of helpful, entertaining, literary journals devoted to the interests of the women of the country. In this work Mrs. Logan scored a success which left even her most ardent admirers breathless, working up an ardent patronage of three hundred thousand subscribers and giving it a standing by the absolute reliability of its household information, and literary merit which no magazine of that order has been able to outdo. Into this work Mrs. Logan threw herself with all the ardor of her vital, vigorous nature. In every one of the several departments of the *Home Magazine* she imprinted the stamp of her brilliant individuality. She herself worked indefatigably to make it a journal of the very highest class in its realm, and she gathered around her a corps of special writers who gave of their varied intellectual gifts to lend a charming variety of knowledge and color to its pages. Mrs. Logan's wonderful executive ability was ably evidenced in the office of the *Home Magazine,* and to work with and for her became a labor of love and enthusiasm. The *Home Magazine* was a phenomenal success during the half dozen years she remained at its helm, but when she gave up her place, for good and sufficient reasons, it suffered at other hands the natural reverses of fortune which inevitably attend neglect and mismanagement.

Mrs. Logan's specialty, however, in literary work has been

the essays and articles which she has published and is still publishing. These are splendid examples of the way in which a brilliant woman, free from the modern mania for hysterical viewpoint and hyperbolic phrase, can direct public attention to national wrongs and the teachings of history. Her style in these articles is crystal clear and gently didactic and the heart interest of a broad-minded, sympathetic woman lies as the undernote even in her most scathing arraignment of our national foibles.

Mrs. Logan's interest in the soldiers of our Civil War has never lapsed. To many people these soldiers have figured merely as old men in need of charity, but Mrs. Logan, remembering them as the brave, strong boys who went to the front in that terrible conflict to return broken and scarred, has always given them the admiration due exalted heroes as well as the material help which needy cases called for. A member of the Woman's Relief Corps, for many years she made it her sacred duty to attend the reunions of the Grand Army all over the country and her receptions at these gatherings have ever been enthusiastically warm. While visiting Boston to dedicate the post named in honor of her husband, a beautiful jeweled badge was given her and glorious speeches were delivered as sincere tributes to her as well as to her husband. The poet Whittier contributed the following stanza to his poem celebrating the occasion:

"What shall I say of her who by the side
Of Loyal Logan walked in love and pride,
Whose faith and courage gave a double power
To his strong arm in freedom's darkest hour?
Save that her name with his shall always stand
Honored alike throughout a grateful land."

At Milwaukee, August 27, 1889, fifteen thousand Grand Army veterans passed before Mrs. Logan in review and the enthusiasm caused by her presence in the city was so great that the remark was frequently heard to the effect that if Mary Logan were a man civic honors would be easy to her. Beloved of the common soldiers, even the greatest of generals found pleasure in her intellectual companionship. When asked if there was any truth in the story that General Grant had once given her a cigar during a conversation, Mrs. Logan replied with her serene smile and added, "It was as fine a tribute to the feminine intellect as was ever made to a woman. General Grant and I were discussing a political topic from different points of view. The General became absolutely absorbed, but recognizing that I had the best of him in the argument, he suddenly offered me a cigar in an absent-minded sort of way. When he realized what he had done he laughed and apologized, but I thanked him for the compliment and said I should look upon that cigar in the light of a surrender, man to man, as when an officer hands his sword to his captor."

Mrs. Logan's immense reception of the Knights Templars occurred in Washington, October 10, 1889, and it was estimated that between ten and twelve thousand persons passed by her as she stood at the head of a long line of prominent women who assisted her in greeting the honorable Sir Knights.

The great reception in the rotunda of the Capitol to the Union veterans occurred September 20, 1892, and at this wonderful gathering in the historic hall, Mrs. Logan and her family were the centers of attraction.

At the Hamline Church, February, 1893, Mrs. Logan delivered a strong address under the auspices of the colored Y. M. C. A., entitled "The Colored American in Industrial Pursuits." In this speech she urged the colored people to take advantage of their present great opportunities and thus secure good positions in life through their own talent and education.

President Harrison appointed Mrs. Logan one of the

women commissioners of the District of Columbia to the Columbian Exhibition held in Chicago, in 1893. She sat in the carriage beside the Duchess of Veragua in the great procession and was warmly received as a member of *American* Royalty wherever she appeared.

Moreover, Mrs. Logan had found time to carry out successfully the plans of one of the grandest charities of Washington, the Garfield Hospital, having been president of the board for many years, during which time she and the charitable people associated with her built up one of the best hospitals in this part of the country. In fact Mrs. Logan's public activities have been, to quote in all reverence that comprehensive summary, "too numerous to mention."

She was consulted at every step in the erection of the two statues of General Logan, one in Washington and one in Chicago, and they are both worthy expressions of what a nation's pride in a great chief should be. A touching feature of the ceremonies dedicating these memorials was the unveiling of the statues by Mrs. Logan's grandson. It was John A. Logan, 3rd, a tiny lad, then, wearing a sailor's uniform, who was the principal actor in the unveiling of the statue on the beautiful lake front in Chicago. At a given signal the child pulled the cords holding together the eight flags which had concealed the heroic figure, and, amid cheers from thousands of throats, the boy disclosed the statue of his grandfather. The child, a little appalled at the enthusiastic tumult, nestled to his grandmother's side again and asked, "Grandma was he as big as that?"

"Yes," answered Mrs. Logan in a tear-choked voice, "he was as big as that."

The Washington monument surmounting a wonderful base with the scenes of General Logan's life in bas relief, was unveiled by another grandson, little George E. Tucker, who has since passed to join his valiant soldier grandfather in the Great Beyond. The Chicago statue of General Logan is by St. Gaudens, and it is considered by many that the great sculptor, who was, like the great soldier he modeled, of humble origin, put the greatest vitality of his great art into that spirited figure. It was Mrs. Logan who suggested for the pose that psychological moment in the General's career when, having seized a flag from a color bearer, he waved it aloft as he dashed forward to meet the foe, on the 22nd of July, 1864, in the memorable battle in which the gallant McPherson lost his life. One of the greatest memorials to General Logan and his brave son, is the priceless collection of mementos now in the Logan Memorial Room in the Capitol Building, at Springfield, Illinois. The collection comprises General Logan's battle flags, swords, sashes, badges, engraved testimonials, autograph pictures of fellow-statesmen, of historic scenes, and many hundreds of other personal belongings and souvenirs of the great soldier. This collection of wonderful interest to the nation filled, for years, the private Memorial Hall in Mrs. Logan's Washington home. A few years ago, with beautiful generosity, she donated the bulk of this collection to the State of Illinois, and it is now sacredly housed in a memorial room in the Capitol at Springfield.

Mrs. Logan's own monument is the abiding affection and veneration in which she is held by those who have known her friendship in Illinois and Washington. No one who has ever come a stranger to Washington and at once felt Mrs. Logan's right hand of fellowship bidding them enter the enchanting circle of her home and friendship, but has gone forth feeling that the world was perhaps a kindlier place than they had imagined, and that if America can turn out women like Mrs. John A. Logan, American republicanism is a success whatever may be its material future. I know, because I was once one of the many so befriended.

Though many years have passed since the days of girl-hood, Mrs. Logan still retains much of the vivacity of her youth; with it is combined a most beautiful and ennobling dignity, the crown of her long active years before the public. The alertness of her carriage and the acuteness of her mentality give one the impression of indomitable youth, but the depth of grief which at times dims her dark sparkling eyes, the yearning sympathy of the lines in her fine face as others tell her of their sorrow, reveal the suffering that the storm of life has brought and that she has weathered so bravely and so well. The death of her only son in the Philippines, leading a gallant charge, tore the mother-heart asunder. But if her toll to the nation's glory seemed at that time ever-heavy, she never for one instant allowed it to depress her patriotic spirit. Strong, alert, sympathetic, Mrs. John A. Logan still dedicates her best thoughts and endeavors to her country and the women of that glorious land.

Aboriginal Women of America.

We find among all the accounts of the aboriginal women of North America that the status of these women was much better before the advent of the white settlers. The Indians were divided into what was known as jens, organized bodies of consanguineal kindred, and these into tribes. Different customs prevailed in the different tribes. The early settlers divided them into what was called the Five Nations, and in many of these the line of descent was through the mother. The father was so little considered that the children would not provide for him if he became disabled or too old to make proper provision for his family. The life of a woman was rated at a higher value than that of a man and we have Father Raguneau's statement that among the Hurons thirty-five gifts were considered compensation for the death of a man and forty for the death of a woman. Women frequently took part in the councils of their nation, and, we are told, frequently led the warriors to battle. There is even an account of a woman having been made chief of her tribe, "Queen of Pamunkey," who was the widow of Totapotamoi, a great Indian chief in the Virginias. She had been summoned to the council to give a promise of assistance, and is described as a woman of commanding appearance and of intellectual powers, remarkable in her race. We also read of "Queen Esther," who was a noted Indian woman and took a prominent part in the massacre of Wyoming, in 1788. She was a half-breed woman. Her mother, Catherine Montour, had been captured by the Senecas, and it is told that she was sent to the council of the Indian commissioners and delegates from the Sixth Nation, held at Lancaster, Pennsylvania, in 1744, and was made much of by the ladies of Philadelphia. During the Wyoming massacre the name of Mrs. Mary Gould, wife of James Gould, is mentioned for conspicuous heroism.

A noted character, and the one with which we are the most familiar, is Pocahontas, the daughter of Powhatan. Every one has read of her saving the life of John Smith. It remains a debatable question even to this day whether it was her love for him, or because she desired to adopt him as her brother—which was permitted in those days by the Indians to those captured—which made her exert herself so conspicuously in his behalf. Suspicion by many historians has been cast upon the wily chief Powhatan, who might through Smith's adoption have opened an avenue for the establishment of more friendly relations with the whites. Some years later Pocahontas was herself captured by one Captain Argall, who bought her from some Potomac Indians, and it is stated the price paid was a copper kettle. Soon after her capture she married John Rolfe, and was taken by him to England. Here she again met Captain Smith, who showed scant appreciation of her sacrifices for him. After she was presented at the Court of King James, she was given the name of Lady Rebecca. She died in England, in 1617, leaving one child, by Rolfe, and it is said that through this child her blood flows in the veins of some of the best families in Virginia.

In the Seminole War, Osceola, the great chieftain, was the son of an Indian woman by a white man by the name of Powell. Little is known of his mother except that she was a very remarkable character, and it is believed it was through her influence that her son was selected as chief.

Before the dawn of the last century the influence and power of these aboriginal women among their tribes was fast disappearing and the position of woman retrograding. To the lowering of the standard of morality was largely due her changed position. We find among the Pueblo Indians, however, that the matter of divorce was in the discretion of the woman. At the time of the occupation of North America by the English and French, there was a very remarkable Indian among the Ottawas, Pontiac, who was not only the chief of his own tribe, but had made other tribes acknowledge him as their leader. After the defeat of the French on the plains of Abraham, the English took possession of Detroit and the Indians were so harshly treated that great trouble arose and the Indians threatened to drive out their new rulers. The Indians proposed to capture Detroit, which was then a fort and not a city. The plans for the attack were fully agreed upon and Pontiac was to call a council with Major Gladwin who was in command of the fort at Detroit, and here by a signal from Pontiac all the officers were to be murdered and the entire garrison meet a like fate, or that of captivity. Among one of the tribes was a girl named Catherine, with whom Major Gladwin was in love. She, having heard of the plans of Pontiac and his followers, went to her lover, told him of the plot on the part of the Indians, and the entire garrison was saved, the Indians being taken instead. Through this girl's loyalty to her white friends, the English supremacy in North America was saved. We have a story of another Indian whose services to the white settlers were invaluable, that of Sacajawea, known as the "bird woman." She was made a captive by the Black Feet when a child and sold into slavery by them to a Frenchman, one Chabonneau. When Lewis and Clark reached the Mandan villages, they found this Indian woman, who acted as their guide and interpreter along the Upper Missouri across the divide into the mountains, until she finally again found her own people, the Shoshones, who through her gave their services to the explorers further on toward the Pacific. One of the most valuable services rendered by this woman was that of saving the valuable records and instruments of these explorers. The story which has lived in song and poetry of Hiawatha is supposed to have had its foundation in fact.

Women Pioneers.

The Guiding Hand of Deity, as in all things, can be seen in the ultimate landing of the Pilgrims at Plymouth, New England.

The persecutions inflicted by the bishops and zealots upon dissenters from the mother church, who were denominated "Separatists" caused them to seek a new field where they hoped to be allowed to worship God according to the dictates of their own consciences.

After many unsuccessful attempts, they finally left England, in 1608, and took up their abode in Amsterdam, Holland. There are many conflicting traditions and reports as to the welcome they received in Dutchland. There was, beyond question, disinclination on the part of the Ruler and the people to extend to them cordial hospitality, lest the friendly relations might be interrupted between England and Holland. They were, however, allowed to remain at Amsterdam until, of their own volition, they removed to Leyden, the principal manu-facturing town of the Netherlands. They hoped by this change to better their condition and secure employment for the artisans among them who had had training and experience in the factories in England. They endured unspeakable hardships, disappointments and the loss of many of their numbers in Holland. They had gained little but respite from persecution by leaving their homes in England.

Their saintly Bishop, John Robinson by name, hoped that at Leyden, with more lucrative resources, through the pos-sibility of securing employment, they might eventually obtain permanent homes and probably increase the number of followers of their creed. They soon found, however, that Leyden offered little encouragement.

Meanwhile, they heard marvelous stories of the American Continent and of the opportunities it offered for material prosperity, absolute freedom of conscience and perfect religious liberty.

It had been impossible, handicapped as they were by untoward environment, for them to save any money or extend their privileges in any manner. Chained by necessity to daily arduous labor for existence, and enfeebled by illness and misfortunes, they were well nigh exhausted when relief came in the form of agents seeking colonists for America, and "Merchant Adventurers" trying to procure settlers for rich plantations in the new country. The povery of these noble people is evident from the hard terms to which they were obliged to submit in their contracts with the agents and the "Merchant Adventurers" to procure passage to the Land of Hope and Liberty.

After months of negotiations, the Pilgrims finally embarked on the Speedwell, a craft scarcely sea-worthy for the voyage from Delfshaven to Southampton to join the proposed expedition. They reached that port after perilous experiences, which had the effect of discouraging very many of the party, causing the dispirited to abandon their leaders on their arrival at Southampton.

However, the indomitable spirits of such men as Robert Cushman, John Carver, and others were not to be dissuaded from their purpose. Hence, after another long period of waiting and tedious negotiations with the "Merchant Adventurers" and agents of companies interested in securing colonists for the New World, the Mayflower was chartered between the 12th and 22nd of June, 1620. Captain Thomas Jones was in command of the ship; John Clarke as first mate or pilot, an experienced navigator, having crossed the Atlantic many times previously; Robert Coppin was second mate or pilot—he had been once at least on a voyage to the New World; Master Williamson, purser; Dr. Giles Heale, from discovery by the Mayflower descendants, was, doubtless, surgeon of the Mayflower.

There were on board one hundred and two souls. The ship was poorly provided with means of defense, having but three pieces of ordnance and some small arms and ammunition. But these brave souls, some of them with families, and their meagre household effects, dared to set out for a land where they hoped to secure not only religious liberty but opportunity for amassing fortunes.

Alack! with all their religious fervor and heroism "a man's a man for a' that," and it required skilful management on the part of the wisest to adjust the many difficulties and dissolve the innumerable conspiracies that were continually being formed between the zealous but unreasonable religionists and the agents of the "Merchant Adventurers" to change the plans of the leaders of the sect, whose chief object was to establish a colony of their own faith.

Floating the English Union Jack, the Mayflower was piloted by Thomas English, the helmsman of the shallop of the Mayflower, into Plymouth harbor and safely anchored on the stormy night of Sunday, December 16, 1620, thus ending the long voyage of the Pilgrims from Plymouth, England, to Plymouth, New England, in one hundred and fifty-five days. Looking back across the centuries that have intervened, it would be difficult to imagine the emotions that swelled the hearts of those devout people as they stepped upon the soil of the promised land upon which they had builded so many bright hopes. From the Log of the Mayflower, given by Dr. Azel Ames, we learn

LANDING OF THE PILGRIM FATHERS.

"The breaking waves dash'd high,
On a stern and rock-bound coast."

that there disembarked from the Mayflower one hundred and three souls on that bleak Sunday, December 16, 1620,—seventy-five men and boys and twenty-eight women and girls. Sad to relate, one-half of that number were laid "beneath the sod of their new home before it was clothed by the Spring's verdure."

History and tradition have made heroes of many of the men, and they were entitled to far more glory than they have ever received for their heroic daring. Alas! of the women who shared the burdens and displayed equal courage with the men, little to their credit has been preserved by tradition or history. But when one recalls that in those days women had not the privileges they have now, one realizes that their self-denial, heroism, patience and long-suffering were accepted as a matter of course and no note was taken of it by their selfish liege lords.

In the enlightenment of the twentieth century, one recognizes that the women were the martyrs of that long and perilous voyage. It was the women who kept the weary vigils through sunshine and storm; it was the wives and mothers who were the nurses and comforters of their families; they cooked and cleaned and helped to keep the Mayflower habitable. There were, doubtless, times when weaker women would have been a burden to the men, who had hourly difficulties to overcome, which taxed their courage and strength almost to the point of exhaustion.

When at last they landed, they received a cold reception, not only on account of the inclemency of the midwinter weather, but because the natives were far from cordial in their greetings to strangers whom they suspected had designs upon what they considered their country. They had watched the inroads upon their domain and invasion of their rights by those who had preceded the Pilgrims, and regarded this new intrusion as boding ill for them. However, these brave people set to work religiously to win their way to the confidence and toleration of the savages to whose country they had fled for liberty.

History has long since told the story of the Puritan victories under the banner of the Cross, and of the constant additions to their numbers as soon as the news of the successful landing of the expedition and their auspicious prospects was wafted across the seas to the Old World. At the time, they did not fully appreciate the limitless scope of the blessings their labors, endurance and wisdom under the guidance of the Infinite would bring to the unborn millions of human souls of all lands who have continually, to this day, sought freedom of thought, personal rights, and religious liberty in our great American Republic, whose foundation was laid by the Pilgrims who came to our shores in the Mayflower.

It has long since been admitted that mothers have always had all to do with the instilling of principles and developing the character of children. Upon this hypothesis, it is easy to account for the sterling qualities which have characterized New England men and women and given them the leadership in the early days of the Republic in religious education and patriotism. Their Puritan mothers, with their deep religious convictions and conscientious scruples as to the discharge of every duty of life, instilled in their offspring their own exalted religious principles. These sons and daughters, as time has rolled on, have followed the course of the Empire and set up altars to Almighty God and their Country wherever they have halted to establish homes.

As civilization has step by step pushed forward its boundaries from the Atlantic to the Pacific, the same principles of religion and patriotism have inspired the succeeding generations until the American Republic represents the full fruition of the tree of liberty planted so firmly on Plymouth Rock by the Pilgrims.

Unless one has attempted a research of the records, they cannot possibly realize how little has been written of the achievements of the women of the American Nation, notwithstanding the fact that since the landing of the Pilgrims women have stood side by side with the men in the marvelous development of the resources of the New World and the advancement of modern civilization.

The correct explanation of this curious phenomenon lies in the indisputable truth that the brave women who embarked on the Mayflower as the wives and daughters of the adventurous Pilgrims had always been subservient to the male members of their families. The Pilgrim Fathers, laboring under the influence of fanaticism, believed that the Old and New Testaments placed women under the domination of men. Acting upon this conviction, they appropriated the fruits of their women companions' self-sacrifice, intuitive knowledge, inventive genius, wise suggestions and natural diplomacy as their very own, without giving the women any credit whatever or making any note or acknowledgment of the influence and aid of the women who shared in all of the trials and hardships of the perilous voyage across the seas and in establishing homes in the wilderness of the New World.

The examples of the Pilgrim Fathers were followed by their sons for generations. The men, in keeping the records and in handing down the traditions, naturally neglected to "render unto Cæsar that which was Cæsar's." The few women shared nobly in the indescribable hardships and suffering experienced by the indomitable spirits who made the first settlements on the shores of New England. Neither history nor tradition has accorded to these women the meed of praise so justly their due. It is left to one's imagination to picture their patience, forbearance, fortitude, quick perception, dauntless courage and intelligence in discharging the duties that fell upon these women as wives, mothers, nurses and companions of men imbued with the idea of their superiority and whose selfishness was prodigious. Trained in the rough school of pioneer struggles which required physical strength, brute force, daring courage, and contempt for weakness, one can readily understand that they were unmindful of the finer feelings and tenderness which are the natural fruits of civilization, and that the men accepted the help of the women as their legitimate rights.

When at last an era of success dawned, it was natural that the men as the leaders of the adventurous settlers of the New World should have all the glory and that the prodigious labors and sacrifices of the women should be overlooked. Half a century had passed before women were accorded any measure of their deserts. During the two-thirds of a century since women had any recognition, they have step by step won their way to equality in all respects, save perhaps physically, to the men, though the privilege of suffrage and representation is not accorded in every state because the women themselves disagree upon the expediency of being given the right of suffrage. With this exception, every avenue is open to women in this "land of the free and the home of the brave."

So well and intelligently have women improved their opportunities that to them belongs the credit of greatly expediting the progress of Christianity, education, and civilization. The natural intuitions of women in the discovery of the good in all things and their keen perception as to how to develop that good are admitted. Julia Ward Howe wrote in the preface of a book "Woman is primarily the mother of the human race. She is man's earliest and tenderest guardian, his life-long companion, his trusted adviser and friend. Her breath is the music of the nursery; the incense of the church." Woman's mission and sphere is thus graphically portrayed by the gifted pen of one of the noblest women of our race.

The majority of women have exemplified this aphorism by the faithful performance of their duties as wives, mothers and members of society. In three or four decades they have succeeded in demonstrating their abilities in fields other than domestic drudgery to which they were assigned in the earlier days of the Republic through the misconception of Bible truths, fanaticism and the prejudices of the unenlightened. The barriers erected by the Puritans have been broken down and women during the last half century in almost equal numbers with men have contested successfully for the honors in science, literature, music, art, political economy, education, the professions of law, medicine and theology, and also in many of the vocations of life which are based on industrial principles—to say nothing of her achievements in the higher realms of Christianity, humanity, philanthropy and in the solution of the problems of social purity, domestic science, municipal administration, cultivation and betterment of the conditions of mankind.

The majority of women as "mothers of the race" have the advantage in that they have the power to transmit to their offspring principles which inspire high ambitions, noble instincts, pure thoughts and inclination for right living. They have in their keeping the infant minds which they can mould and train for noble or ignoble lives. Unfortunately, the influence of mothers does not invariably abide in their children, but in most cases it is felt from the cradle to the grave by the children they have borne and reared properly.

The object of this book is to furnish examples worthy of emulation by future generations. It is the desire of the author to record the heroism, triumphs over adversity, and obstacles raised by ignorance and prejudice, and to emphasize the intellectual attainments, faithfulness, patience, tenderness, mercy, love and holy ministrations of the women of the American

Nation, and to accord full credit to individuals, as far as we possibly can, to those who have been instrumental in elevating women to the plane which is their rightful inheritance.

The Early Period of Settlement.

Jamestown was founded May 13, 1607, and the first woman of whom we have any mention in that settlement was Mistress Forest and her maid, Ann Burrs, and she is supposed to have been the first English woman married on American soil. The terrible sufferings of these settlers from starvation and want is a matter of history, and not more than sixty of the original five hundred souls remained after what is known as the "Starving Time," and it is a most remarkable fact that of these sixty survivors a large proportion were women. In 1621 it became evident that a new lot of settlers must be brought out to America if this new colony was to survive. Sir Edwin Sandys, at the head of the London Company, who had charge of the interests of the Virginia settlers, adopted the plan of sending out wives, respectable young women, to these planters, and in one year he sent over one thousand two hundred and sixty-one new settlers, and on one voyage ninety women were sent to become the wives of these hardy pioneers. Being of a thrifty turn this English company did not do this from a purely disinterested motive, as they required pay from each man who thus secured a wife, and the price fixed was one hundred and twenty pounds of tobacco, about eighty dollars of our present money. The contract, however, was permitted to be a free one on the part of the woman, and she could not be forced into contracting a marriage objectionable to her, but history tells us that no maiden remained unmarried out of this first venture.

In November, 1620, the Pilgrim fathers landed from "The Mayflower" at Plymouth Rock, Massachusetts, and Mary Chilton, it is said, was the first to place her foot upon American soil. The day after the arrival of these Pilgrims, the first child was born. The parents were William and Susanna White. The son was named Peregrine, which signifies Pilgrim. There are very few records of any women of conspicuous effort or influence at this time. Longfellow's poem, "The Courtship of Miles Standish" is familiar to us all and presents a more or less authentic picture of the lives of the women of that day in New England.

The wives of the Pilgrims were: Mrs. Katherine Carver, Mrs. Dorothy Bidford, Mrs. Elizabeth Winslow, Mrs. Mary Brewster, Mrs. Mary Allerton, Mrs. Elizabeth Hopkins, the two Mrs. Tilley, Mrs. Tinker, Mrs. Rigdale, Mrs. Rose Standish, Mrs. Martin, Mrs. Mullens, Mrs. Susanna White, Mrs. Sarah Eaton, Mrs. Chilton, Mrs. Fuller, and Mrs. Helen Billington. The daughters of these Pilgrim mothers were: Elizabeth Tilley, Remember Allerton, Mary Allerton, Constance Hopkins, Damaris Hopkins, Mary Chilton, and Priscilla Mullens, and Desire Minter may be listed as a "Mayflower" daughter. "Mrs. Carver's maid" must also be mentioned among the women of the Mayflower, and even the little "bound" girl, Ellen More, is worthy of place in this distinguished group.

KATHERINE CARVER.

Mrs. Katherine Carver, it has been supposed by some, was a sister of Pastor Robinson. This supposition rests, apparently, upon the expression in his parting letter to Carver, where he says: "What shall I say unto you and your good wife, my loving sister?" Neither the place of Mrs. Carver's nativity nor her age is known.

DESIRE MINTER.

Desire Minter was evidently a young girl of the Leyden congregation, between the ages of fourteen and seventeen, who, in some way (perhaps through kinship), had been taken into Carver's family. She returned to England early.

"MRS. CARVER'S MAID."

"Mrs. Carver's maid," it is fair to presume, from her position as lady's maid and its requirements in those days, was a young woman of eighteen or twenty years, and this is confirmed by her early marriage. Nothing is known of her before the embarkation. She died early.

MARY BREWSTER.

The wife of Elder Brewster, the "Chief of the Pilgrims," was about fifty-one years of age at the time of the landing of the Mayflower. She was the mother of three sons; the two younger, Love and Wrestling Brewster, accompanied their parents to the new land.

ELIZABETH (BARKER) WINSLOW.

Mrs. Elizabeth (Barker) Winslow, the first wife of the Governor, appears by the data supplied by the record of her marriage in Holland, May 27, 1618, to have been a maiden of comporting years to her husband's, he being then twenty-three. Tradition makes her slightly younger than her husband.

ELLEN MORE.

Ellen More, "a little girl that was put to him" (Winslow), died early. She was a sister of the other More children, "bound out" to Carver and Brewster.

MRS. DOROTHY (MAY) BRADFORD.

Mrs. Dorothy (May) Bradford's age (the first wife of the Governor) is fixed at twenty-three by collateral data, but she may have been older. She was probably from Wisbeach, England. The manner of her tragic death (by drowning, having fallen overboard from the ship in Cape Cod harbor), the first violent death in the colony, was especially sad, her husband being absent for a week afterward. It is not known that her body was recovered.

MARY (NORRIS) ALLERTON.

Mary (Norris) Allerton is called a "maid of Newberry in England," in the Leyden record of her marriage, in October, 1611, and it is the only hint as to her age we have. She was presumably a young woman. Her death followed (a month later) the birth of her still-born son, on board the Mayflower in Plymouth Harbor, February 25, 1621.

REMEMBER ALLERTON.

Remember Allerton, apparently Allerton's second child, was, no doubt, born in Holland about 1614. She married Moses Maverick by 1635, and Thomas Weston's only child, Elizabeth, was married from her house at Marblehead, to Roger Conant, the first "governor" of a "plantation" on the Massachusetts Bay territory.

MARY ALLERTON.

Mary Allerton, apparently the third child, could hardly have been much more than four years old in 1620. She was probably born in Holland about 1616. She was the last survivor of the passengers of the Mayflower, dying at Plymouth, New England, 1699.

SUSANNA (FULLER) WHITE.

Susanna (Fuller) White, wife of William, and sister of Dr. Fuller (?), was apparently somewhat younger than her first husband and perhaps older than her second. She must, in all probability (having been married in Leyden in 1612), have been at least twenty-five at the embarkation eight years later. Her second husband, Governor Winslow, was but twenty-five in 1620, and the presumption is that she was slightly his senior. There appears no good reason for ascribing to her the austere and rather unlovable characteristics which the pen of Mrs. Austin has given her.

ALICE MULLENS.

Mrs. Alice Mullens, whose given name we know only from her husband's will, filed in London, we know little about. Her age was (if she was his first wife) presumably about that of her husband, whom she survived but a short time.

PRISCILLA MULLENS.

Priscilla Mullens, whom the glamour of unfounded romance and the pen of the poet Longfellow have made one of the best known and best beloved of the Pilgrim band, was either a little older or younger than her brother Joseph—it is not certain which. But that she was over sixteen is probable.

ELIZABETH HOPKINS.

Nothing is known concerning Mrs. Elizabeth Hopkins, except that she was not her husband's first wife. Some time apparently elapsed between her husband's marriages.

CONSTANCE (OR CONSTANTIA) HOPKINS.

Constance (or Constantia) Hopkins was apparently about eleven years old in 1620, as she married in 1627, and probably was then not far from eighteen years old.

DAMARIS HOPKINS.

Damaris Hopkins, the younger daughter of Master Hopkins, was probably a very young child when she came in the Mayflower, but her exact age has not been ascertained. Davis, as elsewhere noted, makes the singular mistake of saying

3

she was born after her parents arrived in New England. She married Jacob Cooke, and the ante-nuptial agreement of his parents is believed to be the earliest of record in America, except that between Gregory Armstrong and the widow Billington.

HUMILITY COOPER.

Humility Cooper is said by Bradford to have been a "cosen" of the Tilleys, but no light is given as to her age or antecedents. She was but a child apparently. She returned to England very soon after the death of Mr. and Mrs. Tilley, and "died young."

BRIDGET (VAN DER VELDE) TILLEY.

Mrs. Bridget (Van der Velde) Tilley was her husband's second wife, concerning whom nothing is known, except that she was of Holland, and that she had, apparently, no child.

ELIZABETH TILLEY.

Elizabeth Tilley is said, by Goodwin and others, to have been fourteen years old at her parents' death in 1621, soon after the arrival in New England. She was the child of her father's first wife. She married John Howland before 1624. Historians for many years called her the "daughter of Governor Carver," but the recovery of Bradford's MS. "historie" corrected this, with many other misconceptions, though to some the error had become apparent before.

MRS. CHILTON.

Mrs. Chilton's given name is declared by one writer to have been Susanna, but it is not clearly proven. Whence she came, her ancestry, and her age, are alike unknown.

MARY CHILTON.

Mary Chilton was but a young girl in 1620. She married, before 1627, John Winslow, and was probably not over fourteen when she came with her parents in the Mayflower.

SARAH EATON.

Mrs. Sarah Eaton, wife of Francis, was evidently a young woman, with an infant, at the date of embarkation. Nothing more is known of her, except that she died in the spring following the arrival at Plymouth.

ELLEN (OR "ELEN") BILLINGTON.

Mrs. Ellen (or "Elen") Billington, as Bradford spells the name, was evidently of comporting age to her husband's, perhaps a little younger. Their two sons,

John and Francis, were lively urchins who frequently made matters interesting for the colonists, afloat and ashore. The family was radically bad throughout, but they have had not a few worthy descendants. Mrs. Billington married Gregory Armstrong, and their ante-nuptial agreement is the first such record known in America.

One of the most powerful influences exercised by the women pioneers was the influence for religion. Every pioneer woman was transfused with a deep, glowing, unwavering religious faith, and through all the terrible trials of those earliest days, as well as through those of the generations which followed, their faith never wavered, and at all times proved a bulwark of strength in seasons of trouble.

In 1630, we find the name of Lady Arabella Johnson, wife of Isaac Johnson, among those who came with the fleet of eleven ships to Massachusetts Bay, driven out of England by the religious persecution of the time. In this same colony of Pilgrims came one, Ann Dudley, the daughter of an old servant of the Count of Lincoln, father of Lady Arabella Johnson, and married to one Simon Bradstreet, who afterward became Governor of Massachusetts. She was a Puritan of the strictest Puritan type. She became quite famous as a poetess, and there were but few writers of that day. Governor Winthrop's wife was one of the early authors and when she lost her mind it was claimed by her Puritanical feminine friends that this was caused by her deserting her domestic duties and meddling with such things as were proper only for men.

Some idea of the severity of those days can be gained through the fact that in 1634, there was enacted a law which forbade any person, either man or woman, to make or buy any "woolen, silk, or linen with any lace on it, silver or gold thread, under the penalty of forfeiture of said clothes. Gold and silver girdles, hat bands, belts, ruffs, and beaver hats were prohibited, the planters being permitted to wear out such apparel as they were already provided with." Five years later another law prohibited "immoderate great breeches, knots of ryban, broad shoulder bands, and rayles, silk ruses, double ruffles and capes," and should any person wear such apparel they were fined ten shillings, or any tailor make a garment of these materials he was fined ten shillings. Notwithstanding the strict ideas of those days the story is told of one Agnes Surriage, a servant and mere drudge, scrubbing the floor of the tavern at Marblehead, attracting the attention of young Sir Harry Frankland, collector of the Port of Boston. He became so infatuated with her beauty that he had her educated by the best masters in Boston and instructed in religion by Dr. Edward Holyoke, president of Harvard College, but did not honor her with his name until the terrors of the earthquake in 1755, in Lisbon, brought him to a realization of her position, and they were married. She became Lady Frankland and was later received with great honor in England. He was appointed Consul-General at Lisbon, but died in 1768, in England, and Lady Frankland returned to America. During the Revolution she suffered exile as a Tory. She later married John Drew, a rich banker, and died at the age of fifty-eight, having been one of the most prominent figures in Colonial history.

In 1689, Mr. Paris came to Salem from the West Indies, bringing with him two colored servants, John an Indian, and Tituba his wife. Like all people of their race, they were full of superstitious belief in second sight, and so infected the village of Salem that many young girls were brought under their influence and learned to go into trances and prate all manner of foolishness. This brought about the belief that they were possessed of witches. Chief among these young people were Mary Walker, Mary Hubbard, Elizabeth Booth, Susan Sheldon, Mary Warren, and Sarah Churchill, young girls still in their teens, with Ann Putnam and Mary Lewis, the latter two being most prominent. Mrs. Ann Putnam, about thirty years of age, and, it is supposed now, of unsound mind, was a beautiful and well-educated woman. She became the leader in this mischief. Tituba, the Indian hag, had associated with her two old women by the name of Sarah Good and Sarah Osborne. They were finally brought to Boston for trial and they implicated two respectable women of the community, Martha Corey and Rebecca Nurse. This mania became almost an epidemic. Men were even accused and the best women were not saved from the accusations of this evil-minded coterie. Susan Martin was accused on the ground that she walked on a country road without getting her skirts and feet muddy and must be a witch. A special court finally had to be appointed by Sir William Phipps, the first Governor, to try these women, when nineteen suffered death. Charges were even brought against Lady Phipps, the wife of the Governor. The death blow to this panic was given when some people of Andover on being accused brought suit for defamation of character in the courts.

ANNE HUTCHINSON.

When the ship "Griffin" arrived in the port of Boston, on the 18th day of September, 1634, that band of Puritan settlers who set forth from the embryo town to meet and welcome the newcomers would have been very much disturbed and astonished if they had known that there was one among that ship's company who was to bring great trouble to the feeble Colony and still greater calamity upon herself. Anne Hutchinson was to play the most conspicuous part in a great religious controversy; it was something more vital than a mere theological dispute; it was the first of many New England quickenings in the direction of social, intellectual and political development; in fact New England's earliest protest against formulas. Its leader was a woman whose name should be written large as one of the very few women who have really influenced the course of events in American history. It is indeed curious that at that time, when women held such an inferior position in the intellectual world, heads of councils of state and hoary-headed ministers should have allowed themselves to be involved in controversy in which their chief adversary was a woman.

Anne Hutchinson was born at Alford, in Lincolnshire, not far from Boston, England, on the 28th of July, 1591, so that she must have been forty-three years old when she came to Boston, though her comely figure and attractive face and engaging manners gave her a much more youthful appearance. Her father was a college man and her mother was a great-aunt of the poet Dryden, and was also related to the family from which descended the famous writer, Jonathan Swift, so Anne from both parents inherited intellect and force. Her marriage with William Hutchinson was the result of pure and disinterested love, for he had no right to heraldic devices. Of this husband little need be said. He is described by contemporaries as a man of very mild temper and weak parts, and wholly guided by his wife. Perhaps this was fortunate, considering his wife's strong and dominant will.

Things might have gone well for Mistress Hutchinson in the Colony had she not fallen into some heated disputes on certain religious subjects with one of her fellow-voyagers on board the "Griffin." This resulted in her adversary's, the Rev. Zechariah Symmes, gaining a deep and bitter animosity toward her. No sooner had they landed than he took occasion to denounce her as a prophetess—a dangerous accusation in those days. Regardless of her "Reverend" foe she immediately began to teach her new strange doctrines to those about her. And almost all of Puritan Boston fell under the spell of her eloquence and her magnetic charm. The women crowded her home to hear her read from the Scriptures and explain texts, and, it must be admitted, criticised the preachers, for this powerful woman was not afraid to express her opinion with dangerous candor. Boston was really at that period under a religious despotism. Looking back upon those times, it seems strange that the early Puritan settlers, beset as they were with bodily danger and physical hardship, should have spent so much of their time in splitting hairs upon theological subjects. It was, nevertheless, significant of an intellectual unrest, which was to result in people doing their own thinking. This has always been a marked characteristic of the American—one of which we are justly particular, and it should be remembered that this young woman was its pioneer. Mistress Anne Hutchinson taught that the Gospel of Christ had superseded the law of Moses that no matter what sin overtook one who had received the gift of the "Crest of Love," he was still one of the elect; that the spirit of the Holy Ghost dwells in a "Justified Person," and other things that nobody understands and nobody is foolish enough to bother about in these days. In 1634, Mistress Hutchinson and her followers and the ministers of the Boston Church wrangled over these confusing and unnecessary doctrines until it is very likely they themselves became very much mixed up. It is what historians call the Antinomian Controversy. Antinomy being opposed to the law, Winthrop and Endicott considered it a very dangerous heresy. Mistress Anne was finally brought to trial for her teachings—a thing she could hardly have failed to expect, for though she was a gentle and patient nurse to the sick, a fond wife and mother, and a Godly woman, still she was transgressing her right in openly setting up a new creed among the people with whom she had chosen to dwell. Among the ministers there were two of whom she earnestly approved, the Rev. Mr. Cotton and Joseph Wheelwright, her brother-in-law. But the preachings and teachings of all the others she earnestly condemned, which made these narrow-minded spiritual ministers her mortal enemies. In 1637, the Rev. John Cotton, who had appeared to share Anne Hutchinson's opinions to some extent, changed his course and the way was prepared for her accusation and trial. This trial was before the Court of Magistrates, at Cambridge, November, 1637, and to quote from Jared Sparks, "It will be allowed by most readers to have been one of the most shameful proceedings recorded in the annals of Protestantism." The scene must have been an impressive one—the dignified Governor Winthrop, grave, strong, courteous, but already convinced of the culprit's guilt; Endicott, who, as Hawthorne says, "Would stand with his drawn sword at the Gate of Heaven and resist to the death all pilgrims thither except they traveled his own path"; Bradstreet, Nowell, Stoughton, Welde, all her judges and her enemies. As the biting north wind swept cold gusts through the bare room in which the assemblage sat on that November day, the defenseless woman must have felt that the cold gale that blew from the gloomy wilderness on the desolate shore was no more chilling than the hearts of her judges. She was ill and faint, but she was allowed neither food nor a seat during that long exhausting day, until she fell to the floor from weakness, while first one and then another of them plied her with questions. And, as Anne Hutchinson answered these questions clearly and sensibly, quoting passages from the Scriptures to prove that she had done nothing unlawful, nothing worthy of condemnation, perhaps she may have felt, even among her enemies and with no hand stretched out toward her, a thrill of pride in her heart that she, a woman without the influence of wealth or station, was pitting her intellect against that of the wisest men in the Colony. No matter what the issue should be the fact of her trial was an acknowledgment of her power and influence—a power and influence never before nor since equaled in this country.

Of an intensely spiritual nature and of rare elevation of purpose, Anne Hutchinson stood that day for the principle of liberty of speech, and the seed planted almost three hundred years ago has grown into the glorious religious and intellectual freedom of to-day.

At the conclusion of the trial, when she heard the verdict of banishment, Anne Hutchinson, turning to Winthrop said boldly, "I desire to know wherefore I am banished." He replied, with high-handed superciliousness, "Say no more, the court knows wherefore and is satisfied."

Joseph Welde was the brother of Rev. Thomas Welde, who had been her bitterest enemy, and he had called her the "American Jezebel," so she had little to expect in the way of consideration and comfort. But the banished woman had followers and the court found it expedient to issue an order that "All those whose names are under written shall upon warning give all such guns, pistols, swords, pewter shot and matches over to their custody upon penalty of 10 pounds." This shows that the magistrates feared violence from those who believed in Mistress Hutchinson and loved and revered their teacher.

Having been excommunicated from the Boston Church, and admonished for her grievous sins she was ordered to leave Massachusetts by the end of March. And on the twenty-eighth of that month Anne Hutchinson set forth upon her journey to Aquidneck, R. I., where she hoped to commune with God and her fellow-beings according to the dictates of her conscience. Many Bostonians followed her and amid the forests of Rhode Island she found for a little while a peaceful life. But even here she was not spared from her old persecutors, who still feared that a new sect might arise in their neighborhood. Mrs. Hutchinson, whose husband had died, determined to go into the Dutch Colony of the New Netherlands where the magistrates did not care quite so much what the colonists believed, and eventually she planned her settlement in the solitude of what is now called Rochelle. A swamp in the vicinity of her cottage still bears the name of Hutchinson's river and we may imagine how as the evening shades closed in upon them the settlers would gather around their leader, who read from the Scriptures and exhorted them to continue steadfast in the faith she had delivered to them. As the candle-lights shone and flickered on her strong face with its lines of struggle and of sorrow and was reflected in the deep, dark eyes, she seemed a woman who had fled away to this remote spot divinely inspired.

But she had chosen a bad time to come to this part of the country, for while safe from the men of her own race, who had given her nothing but injustice and persecution, she was surrounded by dangers from the natives. Governor Kieft, the Dutch Governor, had by cruel treatment aroused the Indians to sullen resentment. Not long after the arrival of Anne Hutchinson and her little colony, savage hostilities broke out. Suddenly, when the New Netherlanders were unprepared, an army of fifteen hundred swarthy warriors swept over Long Island, killing, burning and torturing the settlers on Manhattan Island and carrying their savage warfare to the very gates of the fort.

Far out across the Harlem River, Anne Hutchinson's weak settlement of sixteen souls was at the mercy of the merciless Indians. The chief who had entered the land of this section according to tribal laws had sent to find out the strength and weakness of the colony. The messenger was treated with the hospitality which it was a part of Anne Hutchinson's religion to show to the "Stranger" who came within her gates. But the Indian spy was the messenger of death, for that night the colony was attacked and every one of that little settlement perished by clubs or tomahawks. Anne Hutchinson and her children with the exception of one, perished in the flames of her cottage, the cries of the massacred mingling in her dying ears with the savage shouts of the fiendish murderers. The little girl eight years old, who escaped was sent back by the Dutch to New England, where a good many of her descendants live.

It was the custom of the Indians to take the name of a person they had killed, and the chief who led this attack called himself after the massacre, "Anne's Hoeck," which is ground for the belief that the great chief himself was her murderer. The neck of land at Pelham, N. Y., bears to this day the name of Anne's Hoeck or Anne's Hook.

This brave woman's death was the end of the theological tragedy of early Boston, but it was the beginning of that religious freedom we enjoy to-day.

MARGARET BRENT.

Not long after King Charles made the grant of land to his friend, Lord Baltimore, a woman of queenly daring and republican courage found her way to the new colony and into the councils of its leading men, and her name, Margaret Brent, stands for the most vigorous force in the early history of Maryland. She was born in England, about 1600, and died at Saint Mary's, Maryland, about 1661. A writer of this time has said about her, "Had she been born a queen she would have been as brilliant and daring as Elizabeth; had she been born a man she would have been a Cromwell in her courage and audacity."

However, she might not have exerted quite so much influence over these first Maryland colonies had she not stood in the relationship she did to the Governor of Maryland, Leonard Calvert, the brother of Lord Baltimore. There are some who think that Margaret Brent was an intimate friend or kinswoman of Leonard Calvert, and there are others who believe that she was his sweetheart. But at any rate an atmosphere of doubt and mystery still lingers about the names of Margaret Brent and Leonard Calvert and their old-time relationship.

It was in the year 1634, that Leonard Calvert came to America bringing over three hundred colonists, some twenty of them men of wealth and position. These three hundred English colonists sailed into wide Chesapeake Bay and up that broad river, the Potomac, till they reached the place where a little river joins the waters of the larger, and there they founded their city, calling both city and river Saint Mary's.

Four years after the coming of Leonard Calvert, Margaret Brent arrived in the city of Saint Mary's. It was in November, that Mistress Margaret first saw Maryland, then brilliant in the beauty of Indian Summer. The orioles were still singing in the forests, the red wild flowers were blooming in the crevices of the rocks and the trees still kept their foliage of red and gold, and the English woman is said to have remarked that the air of her new home was "Like the breath of Heaven;" that she had entered "Paradise."

Margaret, with her brothers and sisters, seem always to have had a prominent part in the affairs of the colony. Immediately after their arrival they took up land in the town and on Kent Island built themselves a Manor House and carried on a prosperous business. Margaret became as wise as her brothers or even wiser in the intricacy of the English law. We hear of her registering cattle marks, buying and selling property and signing herself "Attorney for My Brother." The early records of the American Colony afford rare glimpses of Mistress Margaret Brent as a person of influence and power. She was indeed a woman of pronounced courage and executive ability. She knew people and was able to manage them and their affairs with remarkable tact. Moreover, although she was no longer very young, she could still please and fascinate, and so it is not surprising that she became in effect if not in fact the woman ruler of Maryland. She is supposed to have shared the exile of Governor Calvert when rebellion drove him from the colony, but with fearlessness and daring she seems to have appeared in the colony at the time when her home was threatened by raids under Clayborne, the claimant of Kent Island. Two years passed before Governor Calvert was able to put down the rebellion and return to his colony and he did not live long to enjoy the peace that followed. He died in the summer of 1647, and there was wondering as to whom he would appoint his heir. Thomas Green, with a few others of the Governor's council, and Margaret Brent were with him just before he died. He named Thomas Green as his successor as Governor. Then his eyes rested upon Margaret Brent, perhaps with love, perhaps with confidence and admiration. There was no one in the colony so wise, so able, so loyal as she. Leonard Calvert had always known that. Pointing to her, so that all might see and understand, he made the will that has come down to us as the shortest one on record: "I make you my sole executrix," he said, "Take all, and pay all." And after he had spoken those words of laconic instruction, he asked that all would leave him except Mistress Margaret. One cannot know what passed between Leonard Calvert and Margaret Brent in this last interview, nor what they said, for Margaret Brent never told.

But, "Take all and pay all," he had said, and Margaret Brent determined to carry out his command to the letter. The first thing that she took was his house. There was some dispute as to her title to it, but Mistress Margaret did not wait for this dispute to close; she at once established herself in the Governor's mansion, for she was well acquainted with the old letter by which possession is nine points. Then having secured the house she collected all of Governor Calvert's property and took it under her care and management.

This would have been enough for most women but Mistress Margaret was not so easily satisfied. She was determined to have all that was implied in the phrase, "Take all and pay all," so we soon find her making claim that since she had been appointed "Executrix" of Leonard Calvert, she had the right to succeed Leonard Calvert as Lord Baltimore's attorney and in that character to receive all the profits and to pay all the debts of his lordship's estate and to attend to the state's reservation.

Her next step was more daring than all those that had gone before, being no less than a demand for vote and representation. This demand was made two centuries and a half ago, when talk of Woman's Rights was as unheard of as the steam engine or electricity. Certainly Margaret Brent was far in advance of her times. She might be known to history as the Original Suffragette! Her audacity carried her even further. She was Leonard Calvert's executrix, she told herself, and was entitled to vote in that capacity and so she concluded she had the right to two votes in the general assembly. No one but Margaret Brent would have meditated those two votes, one for a foreign Lord, who had never authorized her to act for him, and the other for a dead man whose only instruction to her had been, "Take all and pay all." We can only wonder at her ingenious reasoning, as did that biographer of hers who was moved to exclaim in admiration of her daring, "What woman would ever have dreamed of such a thing!"

Her astonishing stand for woman's rights was made on the 21st of January, 1648. At the first beat of the drum, that was used to call the assemblymen together in the early days of the Maryland colony, Mistress Margaret started on her way for Fort Saint John's, where the general assembly was to meet.

We may well believe there was determination in her eye and in her attitude as she sat erect upon her horse and rode over the four miles of snow-covered roads to the fort, for she was determined that at least she would have her say before the crowd and show the justice of her suit. Mistress Margaret would not let herself be disturbed by the cool reception with which she was met; for, although the court tried to hedge her about with rules and orders to keep her quiet, she remained firm in her intentions to speak. And finally when her opportunity came she rose and put forward for the first time in America the claims of a woman's right to seat and vote in a legislative assembly.

We can only imagine the scene that followed that brief and dangerous speech of hers in the court room at Fort Saint John's. A wave of startled wonder and amazement passed over the whole assembly and preposterous as her demand was to those first Maryland planters, there were some among them who moved by her persuasive eloquence would have been willing to grant her request. But Governor Green, who had always regarded Margaret Brent as his most dangerous rival, braced himself for prompt and autocratic action and promptly refused. The Maryland records attest, "The said Mistress Brent should have no vote in the house." The "said Mistress Brent" did not take her defeat without protest. She objected vehemently to the proceedings of the assembly and departed from the court room in anger and dignity. She had failed in her purpose but by her bold stand she had made for herself the signal record as the first woman in America to advocate her right to vote. It is to be noted, moreover, that the Governor Green who had denied her this right was the Governor who turned to her for help whenever an emergency arose.

Soon after the death of Leonard Calvert there threatened to be a mutiny in the army. The soldiers who had fought for

Governor Calvert when he was an exile in Virginia had been promised that they should be paid in full "out of the stock and personal property of his Lordship's plantation." Governor Calvert was dead, the pay was not forthcoming and the only course left to the soldiers seemed to be insurrection. Governor Green could think of nothing to appease the half-starved indignant troops, so he went to Margaret Brent for aid. As soon as Mistress Margaret heard of the trouble, she recalled the instructions which Leonard Calvert had given her to "pay all," so without hesitation she sold the cattle belonging to Lord Baltimore and paid off all the hungry soldiers. News traveled slowly in those early Colonial days and it was some time before Lord Baltimore heard of all that Margaret Brent was claiming and doing as his own attorney and executrix of his brother. And not really knowing Mistress Margaret he was inclined to look upon her as a person who had been "meddling" in his affairs and he wrote "tartly" and with "bitter invectives" concerning her to the general assembly. But the general assembly understood Margaret Brent better than Lord Baltimore did and they sent a spirited reply to him in gallant praise of Margaret Brent and her wise conduct. So we find the Maryland Assembly which could not give Mistress Margaret the right to vote defending her even against the Lord of their own colony and declaring her "the ablest man among them."

To the end of her days Margaret Brent continued to lead a life of ability and energetic action. There are occasional glimpses of her latter history as she flashes across the records of the Maryland colony—always a clear-cut, fearless, vigorous personality. At one time she appears before the assembly claiming that the tenements belonging to Lord Calvert's manor should be under her guard and management. Again she comes pleading her cause against one Thomas Gerard for five thousand pounds of tobacco. At another time she figures as an offender accused of stealing and selling cattle only to retort indignantly that the cattle were her own, and to demand a trial by jury. In all of these cases and many others she seems to have had her own way. The General Assembly never denied her anything but the right to vote. She had only to express a wish in her clear persuasive fashion and it was granted. In point of view Margaret Brent ruled the colony.

When she came for the last time before the General Assembly her hair must have been gray, but her speech no less eloquent, and her manner no less charming, than in the days of Leonard Calvert. We can imagine her in the presence of the court stating with dignity and frankness that she was the heir to Thomas White, a Maryland gentleman, who, dying, left her his whole estate as a proof of "his love and affection and of his constant wish to marry her." One would like to know more about this Thomas, but he appears only in the one role, that of Margaret Brent's lover. It has been suggested that possibly if Mr. White had lived, Mistress Margaret might have been induced at last to resign her independent state; that she had grown weary of her land operations and her duties as executrix and attorney and was willing to settle down to a life of domestic calm. But it is almost impossible to think of Margaret Brent as changing her business-like, self-reliant nature and meditating matrimony. It is more likely that this interesting and unusual Colonial dame died as she had lived, loving nothing but the public good and the management of her own and other people's affairs.

MOLLY BRANDT.

No pen picture has been left of Molly Brandt, and yet her influence had much to do with the colonists' success in subduing the most savage of the Indian tribes. She was the sister of

4

Joseph Brandt, that mysterious character who was supposed to have been born an Indian chief among the Mohawk tribe, and who was the young Nation's intermediary with the Indians. It was through her shrewdness and the influential position which Molly Brandt came to occupy in the family of Sir William Johnson that her brother came to the attention of those in authority and received his education. She arranged to have him sent to the Moor Charity School at Lebanon, Connecticut, in 1761. Through this training of his mind, and the cultivation of sympathy with the colonists, he became as valuable an assistant as many trained diplomatists have been in later years. We find, moreover, that in 1770, Sir William, after the decease of Lady Johnson, "took to his home as his wife, Mary Brandt, or Miss Molly." And this may be the first historic instance of an American girl marrying a title!

MARY MOORE.

The early history of West Virginia is filled with the same stories of privation, suffering, and horrors experienced by the settlers in Tennessee, Kentucky, and North Carolina. The privations of that time necessitated women taking upon themselves the hardest labors. They worked with their husbands clearing the land, and the rude provisions for domestic comfort were largely those acquired by their own efforts. The tableware of those days consisted of a few pewter plates and kettles which had survived long journeys from the East. They wove the cloth of which their own and their children's garments were made, spun the flax which made the linen, and in fact, the entire furnishings of their homes were the work of their own hands. It is said that the first settlers came into West Virginia in 1749, and in 1751 two settlers were sent in by the Green Brier Company to open up the lands, and the first settlement was made near Wheeling. As soon as the outposts were established, others followed in the train of these first venturesome pioneers. In 1761, Mrs. Dennis was taken captive from the James' settlement and taken to the Indian settlement near Chillicothe, Ohio. She became famous among the Indians as a nurse, and her medicines, prepared from herbs, were sought far and near, and through this medium she ultimately made her escape. In 1763, while gathering herbs she reached the Ohio River. Wandering alone through the woods and the forests, and rafting herself down the great Kanawha, she ultimately reached the Green Brier, but was so exhausted and worn by her long tramp and the exposure that she finally gave up and lay down expecting to die, but was discovered by some of the settlers and nursed and cared for. But for this act of kindness the settlers were made to pay dearly. They were attacked by the Indians, and all the men were killed and the women and children taken captives. In this attack a Mrs. Clendennin showed such courage that her name has been enrolled among the women heroes of that time. Early in 1778, an attack was made on one of the blockhouses on the upper Monongahela. In this hand to hand conflict, Mrs. Cunningham, the wife of Edward Cunningham, seeing her husband's strength almost spent, grabbed the tomahawk and finished the Indian who would have taken her husband's life. In an attack by the Indians on the house of William Morgan, in Dunker's Bottom, Mrs. Morgan was bound to a tree. She succeeded in untying herself with her teeth and escaping with her child. In March, 1781, an attack was made by the Indians on the house of Captain John Thomas, situated on one of the little streams tributary to the Monongahela. Captain Thomas was killed and Mrs. Thomas and her six children butchered by the savages, only one little boy escaping. While this bloody orgy was going on, a woman named Elizabeth Juggins, who had been attracted by the cries of the helpless victims, had come to their aid. On reaching the house, she realized her absolute helplessness and hid under one of the beds. When the Indians had left, supposing that they had completed their murderous work, Miss Juggins found that Mrs. Thomas was still alive, and succeeded in ultimately reaching other settlers and spreading the alarm. On the 29th of June, 1785, the house of Mr. Scott was attacked. Mrs. Scott witnessed the savages cutting the throats of three of her children and the murder of her husband, and then was carried into captivity by the Indians. The old chief seemed to have at least a drop of the milk of human kindness in his veins, and Mrs. Scott through the care of the old man succeeded in gaining her liberty. She wandered from the 10th of July to the 11th of August through the woods with nothing on which to sustain life but the juices of plants. Among this long list of names of the women who suffered Indian captivity and its attendant horrors were the names of Mrs. Glass, Mary Moore, Martha Evans, and other splendid women. James Moore, Mary Moore's brother, was taken captive by the Indians in 1784, and in 1786, a party of Indians made a hasty attack on the settlement before they were able to realize their danger, the settlers having been lulled into a feeling of security by the absence of any trouble for some time. Her father was killed in this attack, and her mother and three children—two brothers and a sister—were made prisoners. They were taken into the Scioto Valley, and here Mary Moore and her friend, Martha Evans, spent some time in captivity. They were ultimately sold to men in the neighborhood of Detroit, where they were employed as servants. In the invasion of Logan from Kentucky three years later, a young French trader took a great fancy to young James Moore, who was living among the Indians of the Pow Wow Society, and through this trader, James obtained information of his sister Mary, who was then near Detroit. Young Moore went to Stogwell's place, where he found his sister had been very cruelly treated and was then in the most frightful condition of poverty and suffering. James applied to the commanding officer of Detroit, who sent him to Colonel McKee, then superintendent for the Indians, and Stogwell was brought to trial through the complaint made against him by James Moore. It was decided that Mary Moore could be returned to her home when proper remuneration was made, and through the efforts of Thomas Evans, the brother of Martha who had accompanied Mary Moore into captivity, she obtained her liberty in 1789, after having suffered three years of captivity. Shortly after her return to Rockridge, Mary Moore went to live with her uncle, Joseph Walker, whose home was near Lexington, and she later became the wife of Rev. Samuel Brown, pastor of New Providence. She was the mother of eleven children, nine of whom survived her. Martha Evans married a man by the name of Hummer and resided in Indiana, rearing a large family of children.

During the attack of Cornwallis and his approach near Charlotte, a Mr. Brown sought protection in the home of James Haines, and while here the British plundered the house and made the owner a prisoner. Mrs. Haines' maiden name was Annie Huggins. She was the daughter of John Huggins, a Scotch Presbyterian, who had emigrated to America from the north of Ireland, in 1730. She had married, in 1788, James Haines, and in 1792, he with his two brothers had emigrated to a colony in North Carolina, and here they were neighbors to the hostile Cherokees and Kanawhas who gave the settlers of those days constant alarm and terror. Later Colonel Bird, of the British army, established Fort Chissel as a protection to these settlers, and still later Governor Dobbs, of North Carolina, established Fort Loudon in the very heart of the Cherokee Nation. These settlements grew rapidly, notwithstanding the close proximity of these savage Indians. One of the striking characteristics of almost all these settlers of that time was their strong religious faith, particularly the women, and certainly nothing else could have supported and sustained them through the daily horrors of their lives. Mrs. Haines died in 1790, having survived her husband only a few years.

ELIZABETH BARTHOLOMEW.

Born in Bethlehem, Hunterdon County, New Jersey, February 14, 1749, she was the sixteenth child of her parents, having even a younger sister. On her mother's side she was descended from the Huguenots of France. Her parents had removed to Germany after the Edict of Nantes, and later emigrated to America. In 1771 Elizabeth Bartholomew was married to Alexander Harper, of Harpersfield, New York. He was one of several brothers to enter the service at the outbreak of the Revolutionary War. Owing to the frequent visits of the Indians and Tories, the families of these Whig leaders were obliged to seek protection in Fort Schoharie. In moments of peace and quiet, Mrs. Harper lived with her children a short distance from the fort. In times of trouble, she spent her necessary imprisonment within the enclosure of the fort in baking bread for the soldiers and in making bullets. On one of these occasions the commander of the fort becoming discouraged by the tardy arrival of ammunition decided to surrender, and ordered a flag of truce hoisted. This brought forth such indignant protests from Mrs. Harper and the other women who had been working since early morning preparing ammunition for the poor wearied soldiers, that they determined to make one more effort to repel the enemy themselves. A soldier offered to fire on the flag of truce if hoisted, provided the women would conceal him, and as often as the flag was run up he fired at it, bringing down the wrath of the commander, who was unable to find the audacious person who treated his authority with such contempt. This delay and the insubordination of the soldiers prevented the truce being carried into effect and the reinforcement arrived in time to force the retreat of the enemy. In 1780, Captain Harper, finding no necessity, owing to the peaceful condition then prevailing, of his longer service, went to look after his property in Harpersfield. Here he was taken prisoner by the Indians and carried to Canada, Mrs. Harper being in ignorance of his capture. He was eventually released. In 1797, a company was formed in Harpersfield to purchase land in the far West, or what is better known as the Northwest Territory. The Connecticut Land Company was formed, and people were sent out to investigate the new country. On the 7th of March, 1798, Alexander Harper, William McFarland, and Ezra Gregory started for this new land of promise with their families. After a most difficult trip they reached, on the 28th of June, Cunningham's Creek, and near here Colonel Harper took up his location near Unionville. This little settlement was rapidly added to by their friends from the East. In March, Daniel Bartholomew brought out his family accompanied by Judge Griswold, and what is now Ashtabula was settled in a township called Richfield. In August an election was held for the purpose of sending an application to the convention to be held at Chillicothe the following winter preparatory to an effort for the admission of Ohio as a state into the Union. In the war of 1812, the country was exposed to all the dangers of the frontier. Mrs. Harper lived to the great age of eighty-five, dying on the 11th of June, 1833, retaining her remarkable intellect to the very last.

MARY DUNLEVY.

Mary Dunlevy was of Scotch parentage, being born on the voyage of her parents from Scotland to America, in 1765. The family name was Craig. They settled in New York and experienced the early oppressions which brought on the Revolution. Her father's death occurred soon after they reached this country, her mother being left with the care of a little family of three—two daughters and one son. At the time of the occupation of New York City by the British troops, Mrs. Craig expressed no little alarm for the safety of herself and children. Among her small circle of friends from the old country was a British officer, whom she married. This made a very uncomfortable home life for Mary Dunlevy, who soon sought a more friendly atmosphere in the home of Dr. Halstead, of Elizabethtown, New Jersey. She was a strong advocate of Independence and in this respect was in sympathy with those of her new home and felt deeply the separation from her family. Her sister married an Englishman and went to England to live, but Mary always felt the warmest friendship for her American friends, and frequently risked her life in efforts to save their property from destruction by appealing to the British Commander, and on one occasion a sword was drawn upon her threatening instant death if she did not leave the room of this austere commanding officer. She, however, persisted and did ultimately accomplish her purpose and save the property of her friends. Frequently she spent whole days and nights making bullets and tending the wounded and dying. She was one of the young girls who witnessed the triumphal march of General Washington and helped to strew the road with flowers as he passed. There was no more enthusiastic participant in the rejoicing over the establishment of independence than Mary Dunlevy. In 1789, she married James Carpenter, who had recently returned from a visit of exploration to the new Northwest Territory. He was so delighted with the new country that he determined to settle there, and thither they went after their marriage in 1789. They made their home near Maysville, Kentucky. Mary had been accustomed to hardship and exposure in her early days and proved her worth in this new home. But Carpenter's difficult labors of the winter in clearing the ground and raising the building which was to form their little home brought on a hemorrhage which two years later resulted in his death. Though urged by her friends to take up her home inside the borders which the settlers had erected, she preferred the solitude and independence of her own little home which her husband had made for her. It is said that she planned a way of protecting her little children in case of an attack by the Indians by digging out beneath the puncheon floor of her cabin a small cellar, and every night she lifted the timbers and placed her children on beds in this cellar, keeping a lonely vigil herself. Her fears were not groundless, her cabin being frequently surrounded by savages, and but for her careful provisions for protection, she and her little family no doubt would have been killed. Cincinnati became the headquarters of the army through the establishment of a garrison there known as Fort Washington. One of the first schools established in the Northwest Territory was that of young Francis Dunlevy who had served in many Indian campaigns, and came to Columbia, in 1792, and established his school. Hearing of Mrs. Carpenter's courage and sacrifices for her children, he sought her out and finding that none of them had been exaggerated he became a suitor for her hand, and they were married in January, 1793. Mr. Dunlevy became one of the most respected citizens of that section of the country, and was afterwards a member of the legislature of the Northwest Territory and the convention which formed the constitution of Ohio. He was also Judge of the Court of Common Pleas. Mrs. Dunlevy had two daughters by her first marriage and three sons and three daughters by her second, and after the death of her eldest child her health failed and she died in 1828, without any apparent cause but that of a broken heart.

RUTH SPARKS.

Ruth Sparks, whose maiden name was Ruth Sevier, was the daughter of General John Sevier by his second wife, Catherine Sherrill. General Sevier commanded his troops through the Indian wars, and proved the greatest friend and protector of the settlement. General Sevier was most successful in his dealings with the Indians, and during the intervals of peace, the chiefs of the tribes were often seen at his house. Ruth always manifested the greatest interest in the Indian history and lives. At one time General Sevier had thirty Indian prisoners at his house, whom he fed and cared for at his own expense, and through this kindness the greatest friendship was shown him by the neighboring tribes, and Ruth learned from them the Cherokee language. The Indians always predicted that she would some day be a chief's wife, and strange as it may seem, this was really fulfilled. In the early settling of Kentucky, many bloody conflicts had taken place between the Indians and the white settlers, and during one of these a white child four years of age was captured by the Indians and taken to the Shawnee settlement on the Kentucky River. The old chief of the Shawnees had two sons about the age of this young white captive, whom he immediately adopted as a son, and he was reared with them, his name changed to Shawtunte. After his release from captivity, he was given the name of Richard Sparks. Here he lived until he had reached the age of sixteen, becoming almost an Indian in his habits and, of course, knew no other language, he having been taken when so young among them. In 1794 he was released and returned to Kentucky just before the victories of General Wayne over the Indians. On his return none of his relatives recognized him, and he was only recognized by his mother by a small mark on his body. Sparks sought the aid and protection of

General Sevier, who found his knowledge and experience of the Indians most valuable. General Sevier used his influence to procure for him a military appointment, and he was given a captain's commission. He performed very valuable service for General Wayne, and stood very high among all the officers. He met Ruth Sevier, and won her love and the ultimate consent of the Governor for her marriage to this untutored young man. She found him a very apt scholar, and he was soon able to pass the examination which enabled him to be promoted to the rank of colonel in the United States army, being ordered to Fort Pickering on the Mississippi, now the beautiful city of Memphis. This was one of the chain of forts established to maintain peace among the Chickesaw Indians. After the purchase of Louisiana, Colonel Sparks was moved to New Orleans. Mrs. Sparks proved a most valuable helpmeet and aid to her husband, performing the duties of his secretary, keeping his accounts, writing his letters, and making out his reports to the War Department. Owing to his early life among the Indians and General Sevier's well-known reputation of humanity, both Colonel and Mrs. Sparks had a most beneficial influence over the Indians of the lower Mississippi. Colonel Sparks' health failed, and he was at first allowed to return to Mrs. Sparks' old home, but they finally removed to Staunton, Virginia, at which place he died in 1815. Mrs. Sparks married the second time a wealthy planter of Mississippi, and lived near Port Gibson in Mississippi. While on a visit in 1874 to some friends in Maysville, Kentucky, she died.

SARAH SHELBY.

Was the daughter of Mrs. Bledsoe who was so famous among the settlers of the first settlements of Tennessee. Sarah was quite young when her parents moved from Virginia to eastern Tennessee. Miss Bledsoe married in 1784, David Shelby. Mrs. Shelby's husband was said to be the first merchant in Nashville, in 1790. Mrs. Shelby suffered all the exposures and hardships incident to the life of the early settlers in Tennessee.

RUHAMA GREENE.

Ruhama Greene was born in Jefferson County, Virginia, and married Charles Builderback and they were among the first settlers on the Ohio near Wheeling. In an attack made by the Indians, in 1789, on this settlement, Mrs. Builderback and her husband were taken prisoners. She remained a prisoner about nine months, being condemned to the hardest labor in working for the squaws and their brutal masters. She was finally released by the commandant at Fort Washington, and restored to her family. After her husband's death, she married a Mr. John Greene, and removed to a settlement near Lancaster, where she resided at the time of her death in 1842.

REBECCA ROUSE.

Among the settlers to remove from New England, in 1788, to Ohio, we find the names of John Rouse and Jonathan Duvall. John Rouse's family consisted of a wife and eight children. Mrs. Duvall was the sister of Mrs. Rouse, and he was the "noble architect of the Mayflower," which conveyed the first detachment from Simrels Ferry, on the Yohoghany to the mouth of Muskingum and was among the first settlers to land on the 7th of April, 1788, in the state of Ohio. The large covered wagons which the settlers used in those days for conveying their families across the country were called schooners and frequently received nautical names. Teams of oxen were frequently preferred to horses by these Nw England emigrants and pioneers, they being more familiar with their use and, too, they were less likely to be captured by the Indians, as, owing to the slowness of their gait they were not considered desirable possessions by these warrior inhabitants. Thus outfitted, this little band of emigrants made their way from New England through New York, Pennsylvania, and over the mountain ranges to Ohio. As they approached the mountains the rains of November had set in and their progress was filled with the greatest difficulties and hardships particularly to the women and children, who were obliged to walk most of the way over the rocky and steep ascent of the mountain roads. Near the last of November when they reached the point where the Monongahela and the Alleghany meet in the waters of the Ohio, they rested after their terrible struggles through the mountains. The old garrison Fort Pitt was then standing as a protection to the few hundred inhabitants. While their boats in which they had come down the Monongahela were moored the waters rose, and the men rushing to the rescue, the entire party was carried down the river to a point called Fort Mackintosh at the mouth of the Beaver and to the new settlement at Muskingum. Here they embarked for a place known as Buffalo, to which point some of their friends from the East had preceded them. The following spring a company was formed and a settlement established on the Ohio River called Belpre, and here Captain Duvall, Mr. Rouse, and several other settlers, joined by many from New England, moved their families. In 1790, Bathsheba Rouse opened a school for boys and girls at Belpre, which is believed to be the first school for white children in the state of Ohio. Bathsheba Rouse married Richard Greene, the son of Griffin Greene, one of the Ohio Company's agents. Cynthia Rouse became the wife of Hon. Paul Fearing, the first delegate to Congress from the Northwest Territory and for many years a judge of the court. Levi Barber, a receiver of public moneys and a member of Congress for two sessions, was the husband of Elizabeth Rouse. These early settlers were the founders of the state of Ohio. Many of these settlers of the Northwest Territory were men in the prime of life who had exhausted their fortunes in the War of Independence, and being left in the most impoverished condition, had chosen to seek their fortunes in the new country west of the Alleghanies. Many of the young men were the descendants of the Revolutionary patriots who had given their lives for their country. The Moravian school at Bethlehem at this time enjoyed quite a reputation. We find among these early settlers one Colonel Ebenezer Sproat who had been a distinguished officer of the Revolution. His daughter, Sarah W. Sproat, was born in Providence, Rhode Island, on the 28th of January, 1782. Her grandfather was Commodore Abram Whipple, also a distinguished hero of that war, who impoverished himself for his country in fitting out vessels and men for its service. His son-in-law and he, finding their necessities great, joined the emigrants to the new settlement near Marietta. When but ten years of age, Miss Sproat was sent to Bethlehem school, and after three years to Philadelphia to complete her education. In 1797, her father went to Philadelphia to bring her home and brought with them a piano, the first taken west of the Alleghany Mountains. After the establishment of the Northwest Territory, they had what was called a general court, which met alternately at Cincinnati, Detroit, and Marietta. Among the young lawyers practicing before this court was one Mr. Sibley who had come from Massachusetts to Ohio in 1787, and resided at that time in Detroit. While attending one of the sessions of this court, he met Miss Sproat. Their friendship ripening into love, they were married in October, 1802. At that time the route from Marietta to Detroit was by way of the Ohio River to Pittsburgh, thence to Erie and across the lake to Detroit. This city was largely settled by Southerners and many French who were the descendants of noble families in France, making at that time a society of much refinement and polish. Colonel Sproat was one of the most distinguished men of that section of the country, and the family have in their possession a miniature of him painted by Kosciuszko, the distinguished Pole and himself having been intimate friends in the Revolution. In February, 1805, Colonel Sproat died, and in June of that year the city of Detroit was entirely destroyed by fire. Mrs. Sibley had been spending the winter with her father and mother, owing to his failing health. Colonel Sibley fitted up as soon as possible a very large old house which was then situated some distance from the town, now the very center of the city opposite the Biddle house, and here they made their home for many years. At the time of the war of 1812, Mrs. Sibley bore herself with great courage and rendered great assistance, making cartridges and scraping lint for the wounded. At the time of the news of the surrender the humiliation felt by these courageous women was shown by an incident of which Mrs. Dyson, a cousin of Mrs. Sibley, was the heroine. As the American soldiers marched out of the fort, Mrs. Dyson took all the clothing and belongings, tied them up in a bundle, and threw them out of the window, declaring that the British should not have them. Mrs. Sibley applied to General Proctor after the surrender for permission to go to her family in Ohio, and this was finally granted her, and in the spring when Detroit was again given up to the Americans, she returned to her home. On the death of her grandparents, Commodore and Mrs. Whipple, in 1819, Mrs. Sproat was left entirely alone, so Mrs. Sibley made the journey to Marietta most of the way on horseback to remove her mother to Detroit, where she remained until her death in 1832. Mrs. Sibley's husband, Solomon Sibley, was one of the judges of the Supreme Court of the early territory of Michigan, and on his removal to Detroit he was made one of the first members of the territorial legislature. He was also United States commissioner and helped General Cass to negotiate the treaty with the Indians in which they surrendered a large portion of the peninsula of Michigan. He was a delegate from the territory of Michigan in Congress, District Attorney of the United States, and Judge of the Supreme Court of Michigan. He died on April 4, 1846, one of the most highly respected citizens of Detroit.

ANN BAILEY.

The Scioto Company early in 1786 sent out a prospectus of their lands in the Northwest Territory. A glowing account was given of the opportunities for settlers, and an office for the sale of these lands was opened in Paris, France. Many of the French families had been driven out of their native country by the Revolution and this seemed to offer them an opportunity of regaining their fortune. Some five or six hundred emigrants including men of all professions who had purchased lands through the agent in Paris, sailed in February, 1790, from Havre de Grace for Alexandria, Virginia. Here they were received with a warm welcome, but soon discovered that the company had failed in their requirements by the United States Government, and that the lands had reverted to the Treasury Board and had been sold in 1787 pursuant to an act of Congress passed the July preceding. Realizing their situation, a meeting was called and a committee appointed to go to New York and demand indemnification from the acting agents of the Scioto Company, and another committee was appointed to appeal personally to General Washington to right their wrongs. Finally an agreement was reached that other lands should be secured to them and that the site of Gallipolis should be surveyed and parcelled out in lots, houses erected, and wagons and supplies furnished to convey the colonists to Ohio. But many had lost their faith in the company, and they removed to New York, Philadelphia, and elsewhere. The few who still held on to the hope of obtaining some foothold in the new country set out as soon as the wagons and necessary supplies could be secured, reaching their destination in October, 1790. Here they found cabins erected, block houses for the protection against an attack, and many other things for their comfort. They set to work at once clearing the land, and in 1791 a party

MASSACRE AT FORT MIMMS.

started out to explore the country adjoining and they hoped that on their return the Scioto Company would put them in possession of the lands which they had purchased, but being convinced of the hopelessness of this, they petitioned Congress for an appropriation of land, which resulted in twenty thousand acres being turned over to be equally divided among the French emigrants living at Gallipolis at a certain time under condition of their remaining there a certain number of years. Other grants were afterwards given to these colonists in Kentucky. In the history of this settlement we find the account of a most remarkable woman who received from the settlers the name of "Mad Ann." Her maiden name was Hennis. She was born at Liverpool, and married a man by the name of Richard Trotter. Richard Trotter volunteered as one of the men under General Lewis, who went out at the order of Lord Dunmore, the Governor of Virginia, in 1774, against the Indian towns on the Scioto, and while waiting for news from the commander-in-chief at Point Pleasant an engagement between the Indians and these troops took place in which the Virginians suffered great loss. Among those engaged in this battle were the well-known names of Shelby, Sevier, and James Robertson, spoken of in former accounts. Trotter was killed in this battle. From the time of the news of her husband's death, Ann Bailey seemed possessed of a wild spirit of revenge. She abandoned all female employment and even gave up female attire, clad herself in hunting shirt, moccasins, wore a knife and tomahawk, and carried a gun. Notwithstanding her strange conduct and the assumption of manly habits, she made a second alliance. She went with a body of soldiers which were to form a garrison at a fort on the great Kanawha where Charlestown is now located, and we find in many of the historical sketches she is spoken of as handling firearms with such expertness that she frequently carried off the prize. She became a trusted

5

messenger, taking long journeys on horseback entirely alone. One incident is told of how, when information of a supposed attack on a fort at Charlestown was threatened, and the commandant found it necessary to send to Camp Union near Lewisburg for supplies, as they were without ammunition, Ann Bailey offered to make this journey of one hundred miles through a trackless forest alone. Her offer was accepted and she reached Camp Union in safety, delivered her orders and returned as she had come, alone, laden with the ammunition. It is said that the commandant stated that the fort would not have been saved except for this act of heroism on the part of Mrs. Bailey, which hardly has a parallel. The services she rendered during the war endeared her to the people who overlooked her eccentricities and were ever ready to extend to her every kindness which their gratitude suggested. When her son settled in Gallipolis, she came with him and spent the remainder of her life wandering about the country, fishing and hunting. Her death took place in 1825.

Among the incidents of the early settlement of Kentucky none is more significant than the Rustic Parliament, which convened at Boonesborough, May 24, 1775. Without any warrant other than a common desire and reverence for justice, seventeen delegates convened. They were five hundred miles from any organized society or civil government. Nominally within the jurisdiction of Virginia, nominally subjects of the British crown, without knowledge of the battles of Lexington and Concord or even the Declaration of Independence, coming into the wilderness without a charter, they proceeded to the enactment of laws for the establishment of the courts of justice for their common defense, for the collection of debts, for the punishment of crime, for the restraint of vice. Having no early education, knowing only the meaning of the word "duty," they proceeded to express it in the laws made.

The names of these worthy delegates were: Squire Boone, Daniel Boone, Samuel Henderson, William Moore, Richard Callaway, Thomas Slaughter, John Lythe, Valentine Harmon, James Harrod, Nathan Hammond, Isaac Hite, Azariah David, John Todd, Alexander Spotswood Dandridge, John Floyd, and Samuel Wood.

REBECCA BRYANT BOONE.

The wife of Daniel Boone, born about 1755 in the Yadkin settlement of western North Carolina, and her daughter Jemima, are supposed to be the first white women residents of Kentucky. In 1773, in company with her husband, she set out for their new home. It is believed that no women suffered more hardships or showed more heroism than these two white women, the first to enter Kentucky. This little band was attacked by Indians in the mountains, and six men of the party were killed, among them her eldest son. They took up their home in the Valley of the Clinch River, where they lived until 1775. Daniel Boone had undertaken a surveying trip for the Government extending from tidewater to the Falls of the Ohio, a distance of about eight hundred miles. After attending the Rustic Parliament, he returned to Clinch River and brought his family back to Boonesborough. In February, 1778, Daniel Boone was captured by the Indians while out trying to secure a supply of salt. He was carried north of the Ohio River, and all tidings of him to his family ceased. His wife, of course, supposed he had been killed, and taking her children, she returned to Yadkin, North Carolina. In 1778, Boone escaped and returned to Boonesborough, joining his family the following autumn and bringing them into Kentucky in 1780. In 1782 another son was killed in a massacre by the Indians. Mrs. Boone died in 1813, leaving a record of heroism unequalled by any woman of that time, living as she had, much of her time alone and constantly surrounded by savages, her life and that of her children in constant peril. Kentucky has shown its appreciation of this heroism and her part in the early history of the state by the legislature passing a resolution to bring her remains and those of her husband back to the state and burying them with honor at Frankfort.

KETURAH LEITCH TAYLOR.

Keturah Leitch Taylor, formerly Keturah Moss, was born September 11, 1773, in Goochland County, Virginia. She was the daughter of Major Hugh Moss of the Revolutionary Army. Her father having died in 1784, she, with two sisters, was brought to Kentucky by her uncle, Rev. Augustine Eastin, their mother having married again. While en route to Kentucky, the train of settlers of which they were a part, was attacked by Indians, and many were killed. This was witnessed by Keturah Moss, then only a child of fifteen years. Her early experiences and her courage make her one of the cherished memories of Kentucky, and her descendants are among the well-known names of that state.

SUSANNA HART SHELBY.

Susanna Hart was born in Caswell County, North Carolina, February 18, 1761, and died at Traveler's Rest, Lincoln County, Kentucky, June 19, 1833, aged seventy-two years. She was the daughter of Captain Nathan Hart and Sarah Simpson. The Harts were very wealthy people for those early times. His brother Thomas was the father of Mrs. Henry Clay. The three Harts, Nathan, David and Thomas, formed a company known as Henderson and Company, proprietors of the "Colony of Transylvania in America." This was a purchase from the Indians, and consisted of almost the entire state of Kentucky, but the legislature of Virginia made this transaction null and void, and gave them two hundred thousand acres of land, for which they paid ten thousand pounds sterling, for the important service they had rendered in opening the country. This is the company which first sent Daniel Boone to Kentucky; and he was the pioneer who opened up this country for them. In April, 1784, Sarah Hart was married to Colonel Isaac Shelby, who was afterwards the first governor of the state. He had seen distinguished service in the Revolutionary War, remaining with the army until after the capture of Cornwallis. While on a visit to Kentucky, in 1782, in the fort at Boonesborough, he met Susanna Hart, whose father had just a short time previous been killed by the Indians, leaving her an orphan. Their marriage took place in the stockade fort at Boonesborough. The hardships and bravery which these people showed and endured in the early settling in this part of the country, then a wilderness filled with savages, can hardly be appreciated by the present generation. Fitting tribute to such women should not be neglected, as they went as pioneers blazing the trail of civilization, spreading Christianity, which brought these sections into states, and made life in them possible and peaceful. Susanna Hart was the helpmeet of her husband, and in all the duties which devolved upon the wife and mother of those days—the spinning of the flax, the making of clothing, the entire labor of the home—were to her always a pleasant occupation. She was spoken of as a woman of most pleasing face, quiet and dignified presence, possessing the rare combination of extreme energy and great repose. She seemed a woman who could perform and endure, kind and helpful, a woman who retained to the last that gentle disposition and sweet nature which inspired confidence, of an even temperament, who retained to the last her beauty, and transmitted her charms to her descendants. She was the mother of ten children. Her life left her name one which Kentucky holds dear.

MARY HOPKINS CABELL BRECKENRIDGE.

Was born in February, 1768, and died at Lexington, Kentucky, in 1858, aged ninety years. Her husband, Hon. John Breckenridge, was one of the noted men of Kentucky, and was appointed Attorney-General of the United States at one time. She is spoken of as a woman of great courage and remarkable character, and was the "founding mother" of a worthy and distinguished family. One of her daughters, Mary, married General David Castleman, of Kentucky, and Letitia

Preston married General P. B. Porter, of Niagara Falls. One of her descendants was General Peter A. Porter, who fell in the assault on Coal Harbor. A granddaughter, Margaret E. Breckenridge, the daughter of Dr. John Breckenridge, was known during the Civil War as the "angel of the hospitals." It is reported she once said, "Shall men die by thousands for their country and no woman risk her life?"

HENRIETTA HUNT MORGAN.

Daughter of Colonel John W. Hunt, and sister of Honorable Francis Keys Hunt, of Kentucky, was born in Lexington, Kentucky, in 1805, and died November 15, 1891. She married Governor Calvin C. Morgan, and was the mother of two of Kentucky's famous men, Colonel Calvin M. Morgan and General John Morgan. She had three other sons and two daughters, one of whom was the wife of General Basil W. Duke, and the other of General A. P. Hill.

SUSAN LUCY BARRY TAYLOR.

Was born in Lexington, Kentucky, in 1807, and died at the old family mansion at Newport, Kentucky, December 8, 1881. She was among the first women who, even at the tender age of fifteen, made an appeal in one of her essays at school for the higher education of women. Her children were more or less famous in their own state.

MARY YELLOTT JOHNSTON.

Formerly Mary Yellott Dashiell, was born September 13, 1806, and was a great-niece of the distinguished Governor Winder, of Maryland. She was connected with several of our most distinguished families, the Dashiells, Handys, Harrisons, Hancocks, Bayards, Randolphs, Warder and Percys.

MARGARET WICKLIFFE PRESTON.

Margaret Wickliffe Preston one of the first "granddames" of the olden times, was born in Lexington, Kentucky, in 1819, and was the daughter of Robert Wickliffe, who gave his daughter every advantage which wealth, social position, and education could bring to her. Her husband was appointed minister to Spain, in 1858, and there she made a most favorable impression, by her culture, refinement, and grace of manner. Her conversational powers were always remarkable, and she was usually the center of attraction wherever she appeared. Her daughter married General Draper, of Massachusetts, who served in Congress and then as our minister to Italy, and Mrs. Draper's home in Washington is one of the social centers of to-day.

MARY BLEDSOE.

One of the earliest pioneers of the colonial history of Kentucky. In 1758, Colonel Burd, of the British Army, established Fort Chissel, in Wythe County, Virginia, to protect the frontiers, and advancing into what is now Sullivan County, Tennessee, built a fort near Long Island on the Holston. There was not then a single white man living in the borders of Tennessee. At irregular intervals from 1765 to 1769, pioneer parties came from Virginia and North Carolina, forming settlements and stations. The country was one vast wilderness, its only inhabitants being buffaloes and all kinds of wild game, with the savage Indians making frequent raids, but the newcomers were not daunted by the situation, and here erected cabins, and constructed stockade forts against the attacks by the Indians. In 1769, at Fort Chissel, we find two Bledsoe brothers, Englishmen by birth. They soon pushed farther on into the valley of the Holston. This portion of the county, now Sullivan County, was supposed to be, at that time, within the limits of Virginia. The Bledsoes with the Shelbys settled themselves here in this mountainous region. They suffered the severest privation and the greatest hardships in exploring the regions and establishing their little homes. During the first year not more than fifty families crossed the mountains, but others afterward came until the little settlement swelled to hundreds, and during the Revolutionary struggle, that region became the refuge of many patriots, driven by British invasion from Virginia, the Carolinas, and Georgia, some of their best families seeking homes there. Colonel Anthony Burd, an excellent surveyor, was appointed clerk to the commissioners who ran the line dividing Virginia and North Carolina. In June, 1776, he was chosen to command the militia of the county to repel the invasions and attacks of the savages and defend the frontier. The battle of Long Island, fought a few miles below Bledsoe Station, was one of the earliest and hardest fought battles in the history of Tennessee in those times. In 1779, Sullivan County was recognized as a part of

North Carolina, and Anthony Bledsoe was appointed Colonel, and Isaac Shelby Lieutenant-Colonel of its military forces. Colonel Isaac Shelby, of whom we have spoken heretofore as the surveyor employed by the Henderson-Hart Company, and who was betrothed to Miss Susan Hart, a celebrated belle of Kentucky, was the Lieutenant-Colonel chosen to aid Bledsoe in these military operations. Colonel Ferguson of the British army was at that time giving the settlement great trouble, sweeping the country near the frontier, gathering in all the loyalists under his standard. When the troops went out against the British under Colonel Ferguson, it was necessary that one of the colonial officers remain behind to protect the inhabitants against the Indians, and as Shelby had no family, he was chosen to lead the forces, and Bledsoe to remain and protect the people against the Indians. Shelby took command of the gallant mountaineers, and gave battle at King's Mountain, on the 7th of October, 1780, considered one of the greatest victories of the frontier army. Colonel Bledsoe, with his brother and kinsman, was almost incessantly engaged with the Indians in his laborious efforts to subdue the forests and convert the wilds into fields of plenty. Mary Bledsoe, the Colonel's wife, was a remarkable woman, filled with knowledge and noted for independence of thought and action, of remarkable courage and never hesitating to expose herself to the greatest dangers. At the close of 1779, Colonel Bledsoe and his brothers crossed the Cumberland mountains and were so delighted with the beautiful country and the delightful climate that, on their return, they induced their friends and neighbors, of east Tennessee, to seek new homes in the Cumberland Valley. Although Colonel Bledsoe did not remove his own family there for three years, he was the originator of the first expedition which established the first colony in that part of the country. The labors of Colonel Bledsoe and his brother were indefatigable in protecting this little colony, and Mrs. Bledsoe was always a constant and able assistant to her husband. On the night of the 20th of July, 1788, their home was attacked by Indians, and Colonel Anthony Bledsoe was killed. This sad loss was followed by the death of both of her sons at the hands of the Indians, her brother-in-law, a cousin, as well as many friends and earnest supporters of her husband in his work. Bereft of every male relative, almost, and her devoted friends, Mrs. Bledsoe was obliged to undertake the care and education of her little family and the charge of her husband's estate. Her mind was one of almost masculine strength, and she discharged these duties with remarkable ability. Her death came in 1808, but her life of privation, hardship, and Christian courage has placed her among the pioneer mothers and distinguished women of America.

CATHERINE SEVIER.

Among the pioneers from the banks of the Yadkin in North Carolina who crossed the mountains to seek new homes in the valley of the Holston, was Samuel Sherrill with his family consisting of several sons and two daughters. One of these daughters, Susan, married Colonel Taylor; the other, Catherine became the second wife of General Sevier. With the family of Sherrill came that of Jacob Brown, from North Carolina. These two families were intimately associated, and intermarried later. Colonel Sherrill took an active part with the Bledsoes against the Cherokee Indians, in 1776. In the attack on the fort, one of the men seeking shelter was killed. A story is told of Miss Sherrill, who was distinguished for her nerve and fleetness of foot. When scrambling over the stockade in her effort to gain an entrance to the fort, she found she was being assisted by some one on the other side. The savages were gaining so rapidly and were then so close upon her that she decided she must leap the wall or die. In leaping over, she fell into the hands of her rescuer, Captain John Sevier. This was their introduction. At this time Captain Sevier was a married man, his wife and younger children not having arrived from Virginia. In 1779, his wife died, leaving him ten children, and in 1780, he and Miss Sherrill were married. Not long after their marriage, Colonel Sevier was called to the duty of raising troops to meet the invasion of the interior of North Carolina by the British, and Colonel Sevier took part in the battle of King's Mountain. His brother was killed in this engagement, and one son severely wounded. The second Mrs. Sevier was the mother of eight children—three sons, and five daughters—making a family of eighteen children, to all of whom Mrs. Sevier was equally devoted. The life of her husband was one of incessant action, adventure, and contest, and the history of the Indian wars of east Tennessee and of the settlement of the country, and the organization of the state government, furnish a record of the deeds of his life. Mrs. Sevier's influence was widespread and evenly exerted, and was resultant of good even among the captive Indian prisoners. The Tories gave Colonel Sevier more personal trouble than even the Indians, as they endeavored to confiscate his property, and Mrs. Sevier was frequently obliged to hide her stock of household articles to protect her family against suffering. She is pictured as tall in stature, stately, with piercing blue eyes, raven locks, and firm mouth, of most commanding presence, inspiring respect and admiration. She devoted her entire life to her husband's advancement and career, and the care of her children. Her trust in God and the power of her husband made her decline on all occasions the protection of the nearest fort, and once when urged "to fort," as it was then called, she said: "I would as soon die by the tomahawk and the scalping knife as by famine. I put my trust in that Power who rules the armies of heaven and among the men on the earth. I know my husband has an eye and an arm for the Indians and the Tories who would harm us, and though he is gone often, and for a week at a time, he comes home when I least expect him and always covered with laurels. If God protects him whom duty calls into danger, so will He those who trust in Him and stand at their post. He would stay out if his family forted." This was the spirit of Catherine Sevier. At one time when attacked by the Tories, who demanded her husband's whereabouts in order to hang him to the highest tree in front of his own house, she replied to the man who stood over her with a drawn pistol: "Shoot! shoot! I am not afraid to die, but remember that while there is a Sevier on the earth my blood will not be unavenged." He did not shoot, and the leader of the band said: "Such a woman is too brave to die." And again when they came to rob her smokehouse and carry off all the meat put aside for her family, she took down the gun which her husband always left her in good order, and said: "The one who takes down a piece of meat is a dead man." Her appearance and manner were so unmistakable that she was left unmolested. She was distinguished for her kindness and liberality to the poor; always gentle and loving, but firm and determined when occasion demanded. The mere motion of her hand was enough for her family and servants to understand that her decision was invincible. Her husband was called upon to serve as the Governor of Tennessee and to a seat in the Congress of the United States. These honors were a great gratification and happiness to her, whose belief and trust in the ability and greatness of her husband never diminished one jot or tittle during his entire life. After his death, in 1815, Mrs. Sevier removed to middle Tennessee, and made her home in a most romantic spot on the side of one of the isolated mountains, and here she resided for years alone save for the attendance of two faithful darky servants. The last few years of her life were spent with her son in Alabama, and there she died on the 2nd of October, 1836, aged eighty-two years.

ANNA INNIS.

Mrs. Anna Innis was the widow of Hon. Henry Innis, and the mother of Mrs. John J. Crittenton. She died at Frankfort, Kentucky, May 12, 1851. Her early days, like those of most of the women of her time, were spent in the wilderness but in the society of such men as Clarke, Wayne, Shelby, Scott, Boone, Henderson, Logan, Harte, Nicolas, Murray, Allen, Breckenridge and the heroic spirits of the West.

SARAH RICHARDSON.

Another of Kentucky's eminent daughters, who was the mother of General Leslie Combs, was connected with some of the best families of the early days, and came of good Quaker stock from Maryland. The residence of Mrs. Combs was near Boonesborough. She endured hardships that the women of those times and localities were called upon to endure with much courage.

CHARLOTTE ROBERTSON.

Was the wife of James Robertson, one of the settlers on the Holston River, friend and companion of General Bledsoe. Charlotte Reeves was the second daughter of George Reeves and Mary Jordon, and was born in Northampton County, North Carolina, in January, 1751. Her husband was one of the pioneers who went with Bledsoe to explore the Hudson Valley, and in February, 1780, Mrs. Robertson joined her husband in the new country. This little party consisted of herself and four small children, her brother, William Reeves, Charles Robertson, her husband's brother, her sister-in-law, three little nieces, two white men servants, and a negro woman and child. They were conveyed in two small, frail, flat boats. Captain James Robertson commanded the party traveling by land, driving the cattle and bringing the few belongings of this little expedition. The perils which they encountered and the difficulties which beset them, traveling through an unexplored country, were beyond anything we of the present day can appreciate. When the little band of travelers reached the Ohio River, the ice was just breaking up, the water rising, and everything so discouraging and dangerous to the small boats, that many became so disheartened they bade adieu to their companions, and sought homes in Natchez. The others, led by Mrs. Robertson, and the only two men of the party living, her brother and brother-in-law, lashed the boats together, and Mrs. Johnson, the widowed sister of Captain Robertson, undertook to serve as pilot and manage the steering oar, while Mrs. Robertson and Hagar, the colored servant, worked at the side oars alternately with Reeves and Robertson. By this slow and most laborious process they made their way up the Ohio to the mouth of the Cumberland, and finally reached their destination, landing in April at what is now the site of Nashville. For years after their removal to this new country, they suffered great privations, and were compelled to live most of the time within the shelter of forts, subjected constantly to attacks by the Indians. Two of Mrs. Robertson's sons were killed, and at one time she suffered the horrible experience of seeing brought from the woods the headless body of one of her beloved sons. It is difficult for us to appreciate the nerve-racking danger which these poor settlers endured, when we read that if one went to the spring for a bucket of water, another must stand watch with his ready gun to protect the first from the creeping stealthy Indian hidden in the thicket ready to take off these settlers one by one. How they ever tilled their fields, or raised their crops under such conditions, is little less than a miracle, and what the life of these poor women must have been, when they could not carry on the common duties of domestic life without seeing the stealthy enemy lurking in the bush, is beyond our conception. In 1794, Mrs. Robertson went on horseback into South Carolina, accompanied by her eldest son to bring out her aged parents who had removed to that state with some of their children. Both lived beyond the eightieth year of their lives in peace and comfort in the home of this devoted daughter. Mrs. Robertson was the mother of eleven children, and lived to an advanced age notwithstanding these experiences, which one might think would have shortened her days. Her manners were always modest and unassuming. She was gentle, kind, affectionate, open-hearted and benevolent, of industrious habits and quiet self-denial, an example to all who knew her, and retained her faculties to the close of her life which occurred in her ninety-third year, on June 11, 1843, at Nashville, Tennessee. General Robertson's death occurred in 1814.

JANE BROWN.

Jane Gillespie was born in Pennsylvania about the year 1740. Her father was one of the pioneers of North Carolina. Her early life was spent in the county of Guilford, and two of her brothers, Colonel and Major Gillespie, were noted Revolutionary officers. About the year 1761, Miss Gillespie became the wife of James Brown, a native of Ireland, whose family had settled in Guilford. At the breaking out of the Revolutionary War, her husband gave his services to his country, leaving his wife with a small family of children. During the retreat of General Greene, in 1781, on the Dan and Deep Rivers, Brown acted as pilot and guide for Colonels Lee and Washington, and through his knowledge of the country, contributed not a little to the successful retreat of the American army, by which they were enabled to elude and break the spirit of the army of

Cornwallis. For his services, he received from the state of North Carolina land warrants which entitled him to locate large quantities of land in the wilderness of the mountains. His neighbors made him sheriff of the county, and he was rapidly rising in the esteem of his people. Notwithstanding the fact that his future seemed opening up to brighter and higher things, he realized that he could do more for his family by tearing himself away from these prospects, and he set out on his journey to explore the valley of the Cumberland, taking with him his two eldest sons, William and John, and a few friends. He secured land on the Cumberland River below Nashville. In the winter of 1787, he had returned to Guilford to bring his family into this country. At that time there were two routes to the Cumberland Valley—one down the Tennessee River, and one, the land route, a long and tedious one through the Cumberland gap across the head waters of the Cumberland, Greene, and Barren Rivers. The one down the river was much better when accompanied by women and children, and permitted the transportation of goods, but along the banks of the Tennessee there were many villages of the Cherokee and Chickasaw Indians, with marauding parties of Creeks and Shawnees. Having built a boat in the style of a common flat boat very much like the model of Noah's Ark except that it was open at the top, he entered upon this fearful voyage about the 1st of May, 1788, having on board a large amount of goods, suitable for traffic among the Indians, and his little family and friends. The party consisted of Brown, two sons, three hired men, a negro man (seven men in all), Mrs. Brown, three small sons, four small daughters, an aged woman, and two or three negro women, the property of Brown. Brown had mounted a small cannon on the prow of this boat, and I dare say this was the first man-of-war that ever floated down the Tennessee River. They encountered no trouble until they reached the present site of Chattanooga. Here a party of Indians appeared in canoes, led by a white man by the name of John Vaughn. After pretending to be friendly, and thus gaining admission to his boat through the assurance of this man Vaughn that their intentions were of a thoroughly friendly character, they soon began to throw over his goods into the canoes, break open his chest of treasure, and when Brown attempted to prevent this, he was struck down by an Indian, his head almost severed from his body. They were all taken ashore as captives, Vaughn insisting that these marauders would be punished when the chief arrived. Mrs. Brown, her son George, ten years old, and three small daughters were taken possession of by a party of Creek braves, while the Cherokees were deliberating on the fate of the other prisoners. In one short hour, this poor woman was deprived of husband, sons, friends, and liberty, and began her sad journey on foot along the rugged, flinty trails that led to the Creek towns on the Tallapoosa River. At this time there lived a man named Thomas Turnbridge, a French trader married to a woman who had been taken prisoner near Mobile and raised by the Indians. She had married an Indian brave and had a son twenty-two years old. This son desired to present to his mother some bright-eyed boy as a slave, for according to the savage code of the times, each captive became a slave to his captor. This woman's son was one of the marauding party who had seized Brown's boat, and from the first knew the fate of the party. He tried to induce little Joseph Brown to go with him, but the boy would not; but when the boat landed, he took Joseph to his stepfather Turnbridge, who in good English told the boy he lived near and asked him to spend the night with him. This the poor little frightened fellow consented to do, and while on his way out, he heard the rifles of these savage beasts who were murdering his brothers and friends. Later they came to the Turnbridge house, demanding that the boy be relinquished, and when about to surrender him to the fate of his brothers, the old woman, the wife of Turnbridge, begged for his life, and he was saved only later to be scalped. All of his head was shaved and a bunch of feathers tied to the only remaining lock of hair, his ears pierced with rings, his clothes taken off, and he was supposed to be made one of their tribe. His sisters were brought back by a party of Cherokees, and here they were adopted into different families in this same town with Joseph. From them he learned the fate of his mother, his brother George, and sister Elizabeth. War was now going on between the Indians and the people of Cumberland and east Tennessee. Two thousand warriors, principally Cherokees, were laying waste everything before them in east Tennessee. They had stormed Fort Gillespie, torturing men, women and children, and carrying off Mrs. Glass, the sister of Captain Gillespie. In the spring of 1789, an exchange of prisoners was agreed upon, and a talk held with General Sevier, in which it was stipulated that the Cherokees should surrender all white persons within their borders. When this occurred, young Brown was out on a trading trip, and did not return until all the prisoners had gone up to Running Water. On his return, he was sent also to Running Water, but his little sister would not leave her Indian mother, who had treated her kindly, but Brown finally took her forcibly with him. His eldest sister was claimed by a trader, who said he had bought her with his money. Joseph being unable to redeem her, was obliged to leave her behind. At the conference with the Indians, Brown refused to be exchanged unless his sister was brought in by the Indians, the old chief sent for the girl, and she was brought to Running Water, where on the 1st of May, 1789, young Brown and his sisters were once more restored to liberty. Having nothing and being entirely alone, these three young people were sent to relatives in South Carolina until their mother should be released from captivity

from the Creeks. Mrs. Brown's experiences were full of horror
and agony, a prisoner with a knowledge of her three children
captives among the savages, not knowing what their fate was
to be. She was driven forward on foot many days and nights
over these terrible roads and through this wild country, arriving
at the town of her captors to find herself their slave doomed to
work for a savage mistress, and, to add to her distress, her
little son and daughter were taken to different towns and she
was left alone. At this time Alexander McGillivray, a half-
breed Creek of Scotch descent, was chief of the Muscogee
Indians, and assumed the title of commander-in-chief of the
upper and lower Creeks and the Seminoles, being also the recognized military leader and civil governor of all the Indians of
Florida, Alabama and lower Georgia. He combined the
shrewdness of the savage with the learning of the civilized man.
Mrs. Brown fortunately was taken to a town in which lived the
sister of McGillivray, who was the wife of a French trader by
the name of Durant. She pitied Mrs. Brown, and told her her
brother, the chief of the Creeks, did not approve of his people
making slaves of white women, and advised Mrs. Brown to go
to him. She offered her a horse and saddle, but told her that she
must take them herself. Mrs. Brown being ignorant of the
country, an aged Indian was chosen to act as her guide. At an
appointed hour, Mrs. Brown mounted her friend's horse, and
started in pursuit of her Indian guide, whose demeanor was
that of entire ignorance of her existence. As Mrs. Durant had
told Mrs. Brown, her brother showed the kindest interest in her
story and offered her every protection under his roof. In a few
days her savage master appeared and demanded her return.
Colonel McGillivray informed him she was in his house and he
would protect her. He threatened to kill Mrs. Brown, but
McGillivray persuaded him that a dead woman could do no
work, and finally offered a rifle, powder and lead, some beads

and paint for his wife, which overcame his spirit of revenge, and Mrs. Brown became the ransomed captive of McGillivray. This is a noted instance of the chivalry of the savage chieftain. Here Mrs. Brown taught the Indian women needlework, and they became very fond of her. On a trip to one of the upper Creek towns, McGillivray found Mrs. Brown's daughter, aged eleven years, and purchased her from her master, restoring her to her mother. He also tried to gain possession of her son George, but the Indian who had possession of him had grown very fond of him, and would not surrender him. In November, 1789, Colonel McGillivray arranged for a peace conference at Rock Landing, Georgia, and took Mrs. Brown and her daughter with him and there delivered her to her son William, who had come hoping to hear news of her. After spending some time in South Carolina, she returned to Guilford, at the end of two years only, she had had all these privations and experiences. In 1788, her benefactor, the Creek chieftain, passed through Guilford and paid her a visit. Her brothers offered to pay him any sum for the ransom of Mrs. Brown and the children, but he refused it, and promised to use every effort to restore her son to her. In 1792, a formidable body of Indians, Creeks, Seminoles, and Shawnees invaded the Cumberland Valley, attacking Buchanan Station. Joseph went to the assistance of Buchanan, but the Indians had retreated. What was his astonishment on approaching the scene of action to find his Indian brother lying cold in death. Later on Joseph Brown led a successful campaign against the Indians. His knowledge of the country during his captivity, and the fact that this Indian chieftain had been killed previously, made him well fitted for the position of leader. As they had spared his life, so he spared the lives of the Indian prisoners; and soon after this generous act on his part, his brother, young George Brown, was liberated by the Creeks. In 1812, during the Creek War, a large number of

6

Cherokee Indians offered their services to General Jackson. General Jackson asked Joseph Brown to take command of these Indians, but this he never did. He served as an aid of General Robards in the army, and was a most valuable interpreter and guide. When General Jackson became President, Colonel Brown obtained an allowance from Congress for a part of the property lost by his father in 1788. Mrs. Brown lived to be ninety years of age, having spent one of the most eventful lives, and exhibited the greatest heroism amidst the trials of the women of even that day. Her son George became a noted citizen of Mississippi, and her captive daughter Jane, the wife of Mr. Collinsworth, became well known in Texas where they resided. No history can do adequate justice to the sufferings and heroism of Mrs. Brown and these early pioneers of the Holston and Cumberland Valleys.

ELIZABETH KENTON.

The name of Simon Kenton, one of the early pioneers of Kentucky, is intimately associated with that of Daniel Boone, he being one of the hardy explorers who went into the wilderness of the Alleghany Mountains and spent three years in the wilds near the Kanawha River, until the breaking out of the wars between the Indians and the settlers in 1774, when he tendered his service to his country and acted as a spy. He was captured by the Indians, carried off and the details of his capture form one of the most thrilling stories of these days. He was tied on the back of an unbroken horse and eight times was exposed to what the Indians call "the running of the gauntlet," which consists in giving a man this one chance for his life. He is allowed to run a certain distance, and if he reaches the enclosure selected by the Indians in safety, when all the Indians are shooting at him, he is given his life. He was three times bound to a stake with no prospect of rescue, but suddenly saved through the interference of a friendly Indian. He was at another time saved through the intercession of Logan, the great Mingo chief, and such experiences filled his almost daily life among his savage captors. He afterwards rendered distinguished service under General George Rogers Clark and in the campaign of Wayne. General Kenton's first wife was Martha Dowdon, who lived ten years. Elizabeth, his second wife, was the daughter of Stephen Jarboe, a French settler from Maryland, who had come to Mason County, Kentucky, about 1796, when Elizabeth was about seventeen years of age. A clever story is told of the wooing of Elizabeth Jarboe by General Kenton. She had many admirers, among them young Mr. Reuben Clark, and the race seemed close between young Clark and General Kenton; but the wily hero of so many more perilous experiences cleverly outwitted his young friend Clark by sending him on some important work to Virginia, and in his absence General Kenton secured the prize. They were married in the year 1798 at Kenton's Station. A few months after their marriage they removed to Cincinnati, and later to what was then called the Mad River Country, a few miles north of Springfield, Ohio. Here they had many experiences of a thrilling nature with the Indians. General Kenton's family consisted of five children. He was greatly beloved and had most successful influence with the Indians. His home became the rendezvous of both settlers and Indians, which necessitated incessant toil and privation on the part of Mrs. Kenton. General Kenton had lost a great deal of land in Kentucky through the dishonesty of agents whom he had entrusted with his business, and in 1818 they procured only a small portion of some wild land in Logan County, and again took up their residence in Kentucky. In 1836 General Kenton died. In 1842 Mrs. Kenton returned to Indiana and on November 27 passed away. Her daughter was a Mrs. Parkinson of Dayton, who remembers seeing her mother instruct the Indian wife of Isaac Zain.

SARAH WILSON.

One of the pioneers to remove to the Cumberland Valley was Joseph Wilson, and he, like the others, suffered great hardships and exposure. In the attack made by the Indians on the 26th of June, 1792, upon the blockhouse erected by the settlers, Mrs. Wilson showed her great courage in insisting that her husband should attempt to escape and seek aid from the other settlers, and that he should leave her and her young children, believing the savages would spare them rather than his life. The blockhouse had been set on fire and there were but a few moments left for his escape. He and his son, a young lad of sixteen years, made a rush through the line of their assailants, but Wilson received a wound in his foot which made it impossible for him to go on for relief, and his son went on hoping to obtain a horse from some neighbor. Immediately on the disappearance of her husband, Mrs. Wilson, with her baby in her arms and followed by five small children, walked slowly out of the fort. Her courage made such an impression upon the Indians that the lives of herself and children were spared. All the rest of the inmates of the fort were killed. Young Wilson obtained relief and carried his father to Bledsoe Station. A party of soldiers hastened to the relief of Mrs. Wilson, but she and her children had been carried off as captives into the Upper Creek Nation. Through the efforts of Colonel White, Mrs. Wilson's brother, after twelve months of captivity, she and her family were restored to their homes. One young girl, however, still remained a captive among the Creeks and it was some time later before she was returned to her own people. She had entirely forgotten her own language and every member of her home circle.

SARAH THORPE.

Sarah Thorpe was the wife of Joel Thorpe. They removed from North Haven to Ashtabula County, Ohio, in 1799. An incident is related in the life of Mrs. Thorpe which illustrates the extreme privations to which these early settlers were frequently reduced. In the absence of Mr. Thorpe, who had gone over into Pennsylvania to procure provisions for his family, it is told that Mrs. Thorpe emptied the straw out of her bed to pick it over to obtain what little wheat there was left in it, and this she boiled and gave to her children. Mrs. Thorpe was married three times. Her first husband was killed in the War of 1812, and her last husband's name was Gardner. The first surveying party to enter the Western Reserve arrived on the Fourth of July, 1796. Permanent settlers did not come in until two years later. In 1798 small settlements were found all over the reserve and a little schooner had been built to ply on the waters of Lake Erie. The necessity for the building of a grist mill near the site of what is now the city of Cleveland is believed to be the foundation of that city.

The child of Mr. Kingsberry is believed to be the first white child born in the Western Reserve. The wife of Hon. John Walworth was quite noted among these early settlers. In 1801, it is said, the first ball was given at Cleveland in the log cabin of Major Carter, and here Anna Spofford opened the first school. Mrs. Carter was one of the prominent women of this settlement.

ELIZABETH TAPPEN.

Was the second daughter of Alexander and Elizabeth Harper, and was born February 24, 1784, in Harpersfield, New York. She was fifteen years of age when her parents removed to Ohio, and later became one of the teachers in the school which was opened in the Western Reserve. In 1803, Abraham Tappen was appointed to take charge of this school, and alternately he and Miss Harper taught, which was the beginning of their friendship and resulted in their marriage in 1806. Tappen was employed later as a surveyor and took part in the equalizing of the claims of landholders. They became prominent citizens and Mr. Tappen afterwards became a judge. The little village of Unionville is believed to be built on the site of their first home.

REBECCA HEALD.

The life of this woman is associated with one of the most prominent incidents and horrible scenes of the War of 1812, the massacre at Fort Dearborn, Chicago. Rebecca Heald was the daughter of Captain Wells of Kentucky. In her early life she resided with her uncle, Captain William Wells, whose life was one of the most singular and romantic of the early border days. He was captured by the Miami Indians when but a very small child, and was adopted by the son of Little Turtle, one of the most famous Indian warriors of the day. After living and becoming completely identified with the lives of his captors, he saw and realized the superior power of the white settlers then' fast filling up that section of the country, and he determined to leave his adopted friends and return to his own people, which he did without severing the bonds of friendship then existing. He joined the army of General Wayne, and his services were most conspicuous and valuable through his knowledge of the country and the Indian character. He commanded an organization of spies and fought in the campaign of Wayne until the treaty of Greenville in 1795, which restored peace between the whites and the Indians, when Wells again rejoined his old friends and foster-father, Little Turtle. Captain Wells was chosen to escort the troops from Chicago to Fort Wayne at the time of the outbreak in 1812, and while living there with her uncle, Miss Wells met Captain Heald, and in 1812 Captain Heald was placed in command of the garrison at Chicago, at that time a remote outpost of the American frontier. The communication between the posts at Fort Wayne, Detroit, and Chicago was carried on over an Indian trail with a friendly savage as guide frequently. Opposite the fort which stood at the junction of the Chicago River with Lake Michigan and separated by the river stood the home of Mr. Kinsey. They were the first to have knowledge of the outbreak, which occurred on the night of the 7th of April, 1812. The commander of the fort, Captain Heald, received, on the 7th of August, dispatches from General Hull at Detroit, announcing the declaration of war between the United States and Great Britain. Captain Heald decided upon a plan of action which brought forth the greatest indignation and resentment from his officers and men. He had received orders to distribute all the supplies of United States property equally among the Indians in the neighborhood, and evacuate the post. The officers and men urged upon him the necessity to remain and fortify themselves as strongly as possible, hoping for aid from the other side of the peninsula, but Captain Heald announced that he was going to carry out what seemed to them a foolhardy decision on his part and distribute the property among the Indians and ask them to escort the garrison to Fort Wayne, with the promise of reward for the safe conduct of all, adding that he felt a profound confidence in the profession of friendship on the part of the Indians. This brought on a most unhappy condition of affairs. The troops became almost mutinous, and the Indians set in defiance the restraint which had heretofore been maintained over them. A council with the Indians was held on the 12th of August, none of the officers attending from the fort but Captain Heald. Secret information had been brought that the Indians intended falling upon the officers and murdering them all. Among the chiefs were several who held personal regard for many of the officers and troops in the garrison, and did their utmost to allay the war-like feeling, which was constantly arising and increasing each day among the Indians. On the evening following the last council Black Partridge, a prominent chief, came to the quarters of Captain Heald and said: "Father, I come to deliver up to you the medal I wear. It was given me by the Americans and I have long worn it in token of our mutual friendship, but our young men are resolved to imbrue their hands in the blood of the whites. I cannot restrain them and I will not wear a token of peace while I am compelled to act as an enemy." This should have been enough to allow Captain Heald to appreciate the seriousness of the temper of the Indians, but he went on with his preparation for departure, which was to take place on the 15th. Everyone was ready, reduced to the smallest equipment possible in view of the journey before them. Mr. Kinsey had offered to accompany the troops, intrusting his family to the care of some friendly Indians who had promised to carry them in a boat around the head of Lake Michigan to a place on the St. Joseph River, where they should be joined if the march proved successful. The following morning Mr. Kinsey received word from the chief of St. Joseph's Band that they must expect trouble from the Pottawattamies, urging him to give up his plan to accompany the troops and promising that the boat would be permitted to pass in safety to St. Joseph's, and urged him to go with his family instead, but Mr. Kinsey declined this, believing he might have some influence in restraining the savages. When they reached the point between the prairie and the beach the Pottawattamies took the prairie instead of the beach with the Americans and their purpose was soon evident. They attacked the whites, being about five hundred strong. This little band was soon reduced to about one-third of their number and finally Captain Wells was obliged to surrender, under the agreement that their lives should be spared, and that all should be delivered at one of the British posts to be ransomed later by their friends. Mrs. Heald took an active part in this fight, and through her heroic conduct her life was spared by one of the Indians, who placed her and Mrs. Kinsey and their children in a boat where they were covered with buffalo robes, their rescuer telling the Indians that it contained only the family of Shawneaukee. They were taken back to the home of Mr. Kinsey, closely guarded by the Indians who intended later to take them all to Detroit. After the work of plunder and destruction was complete on the part of the Indians, the fort was set afire. Black Partridge and Wabansee with three others constituted themselves protectors to the family of Mr. Kinsey. Mrs. Heald and Mrs. Kinsey later succeeded in disguising themselves as French women with some of the clothes they found in the house, and were conducted by Black Partridge to the home of Ouilmette, a Frenchman with a half-breed wife, who had been employed by Mr. Kinsey and whose home was near. Only the absolute devotion on the part of Black Partridge saved these women from massacre. Later they were successfully placed in a boat, and under the care of a half-breed interpreter were taken to St. Joseph and later to Detroit under the escort of Chandonnai, a faithful Indian friend, and the entire party with their servants delivered up as prisoners of war to the British commanding officer. General Hull at the surrender of Detroit had stipulated that all American inhabitants should remain undisturbed in their homes, and here Mrs. Kinsey and Mrs. Heald were allowed to peacefully reside. Mr. Kinsey, through anxiety for his family, ultimately joined them and surrendered as a prisoner of war. During the fight of which we have spoken Mrs. Heald received seven wounds. Lieutenant Helm was taken by some friendly Indians to their village of the Au Sable, and then to St. Louis, where he was ultimately liberated. Mrs. Helm accompanied her father's family to Detroit. During the engagement, she had a horse shot from under her. The little remnant of the garrison at Fort Dearborn with their wives and children were distributed among the villages of the Pottawattamies upon the Illinois, Wabash, Rock River and Milwaukee until the spring, when they were taken to Detroit and ransomed. Mrs. Helm, spoken of, was the daughter of Captain Killip, a British officer attached to one of the companies, who in 1794 aided the Indian tribes against the United States Government. On the death of her husband, Colonel Killip, she afterward became the wife of John Kinsey and removed to Chicago, there establishing a thriving trading post among the Pottawattamie Indians. Their daughter married Lieutenant Lina J. Helm, of Kentucky, and is the one spoken of in this account.

ABIGAIL SNELLING.

Was the daughter of Thomas Hunt, a Revolutionary officer and a native of Watertown, Massachusetts. Her father had entered the American army as a volunteer, but soon received his commission as a regular officer and was in the expedition against Ticonderoga, commanded by Ethan Allen, one of the small band who made themselves masters of Crown Point. He was with General Wayne at Stony Point, and in 1794 went with him in the campaign against the Indians. In 1798, he received the promotion to Lieutenant-Colonel, First Regiment Infantry, and was placed in command of Fort Wayne, remaining until the death of Hantramack at Detroit, when Lieutenant-Colonel Hunt succeeded to the command and became the colonel of the regiment and in command of the post at Detroit, afterwards succeeding to that at Mackinaw. Abigail Hunt was but six weeks old when the family arrived at Mackinaw. When she was but seven years of age, her parents left Mackinaw on their way to St. Louis by way of Detroit. On their journey they stopped for a short time at Fort Wayne, where Colonel Hunt's eldest daughter was married to the surgeon of the post, Dr. Edwards. Colonel Hunt took command of the garrison at the mouth of the Missouri, eighteen miles above St. Louis. This was about the time of the Burr conspiracy, and a court-martial was held there to try Major Bruff, who was supposed to be a party to the conspiracy, but who was acquitted. Lewis and Clark arrived at this post from their exploring expedition, causing the greatest excitement and curiosity owing to their costumes made entirely of skins and furs. The captain in one of the companies of Colonel Hunt's regiment at that time was a man by the name of Pike, who afterwards became famous as General Pike, and was selected by the government to explore the upper Mississippi, being absent on this expedition almost two years. In 1809 Colonel Hunt died, and six months later followed the death of Mrs. Hunt. The eldest son resided in Detroit, and after the death of his mother, he removed the family to Waltham, Massachusetts, to reside with their maternal grandfather, Samuel Wellington. This brother later became Colonel Henry J. Hunt. When the War of 1812 was declared, no one among the officers then in the service was more distinguished than one Captain Snelling. When General Hull arrived with his army at Detroit early in July, Dr. Edwards, who had married Colonel Hunt's eldest daughter, joined General Hunt's army at Dayton, and with him was John E.

Hunt, so that the sisters were again brought together. Here Captain Snelling was introduced to Miss Hunt by Major Edwards, and in a very short time they were engaged. On the 13th of August, Miss Hunt was married to Captain Snelling by a chaplain in General Hull's army. Captain Snelling had quite distinguished himself in the fight at Brownstown under General Hull. Three days after their marriage, the British landed at Springwells and Captain Snelling with others was humiliated by having General Hull retire before the enemy, and it is reported that when an aid asked Captain Snelling to help him plant the white flag, he replied with indignation: "No, sir, I will not soil my hands with that flag." General Hull was so panic-stricken that he surrendered the fortress without even demanding terms, and words cannot express the disgust and indignation of these brave soldiers as they stacked their arms to be taken over by the British. Colonel Hunt was permitted to remain in Detroit as a prisoner, accompanied by John Hunt, but Captain Snelling and his family were placed on board a boat which was to convey General Hull and his command as prisoners of war to Eric, where they were turned over to the British guards. Mrs. Snelling and the women were taken care of by the captain of the boat with promises that they should rejoin their husbands at Fort George, but it was some time before they were reunited. One of the strange incidents of war was that a British officer who had been most cruel and unkind to Captain Snelling, whose courteous treatment in contrast to that which he had received, so embarrassed and humiliated him that he apologized, and they became fast friends. Captain Snelling was one of the most unbending patriots, and at one time when the troops were in Montreal, the order was given for hats off in front of Nelson's monument, the guard knocking off the hats of the prisoners, but on an officer attempting such with Captain Snelling he received the quick warning, "At your peril, sir, touch me." Later he received the apology of the officer in question. The married officers were soon paroled and sent to Boston, where Captain Snelling and his wife remained until he was ordered to Plattsburg to join General Hampton's army. Their eldest child, Mary, was born when Mrs. Snelling was but sixteen years of age. Captain Snelling rapidly rose in distinction, and was on the staff of General Izard as Inspector-General, stationed at Buffalo. On peace being declared Snelling was made Lieutenant-Colonel of the Sixth Infantry and ordered to Governor's Island, and later to Plattsburgh, where he remained four years, when the order came to start for the upper Mississippi by way of St. Louis. Their family then consisted of Mrs. Snelling and three children, her youngest sister, and one brother, a graduate from West Point, Lieutenant Wellington Hunt, also a married man. Mrs. Snelling's sister, Eliza N. Hunt, married a man by the name of Soulard, a French gentleman. The following summer, Snelling received his colonelcy and was placed in command of the Fifth Regiment and ordered to relieve Lieutenant-Colonel Leavenworth, who had been promoted to another regiment, and Captain Snelling conducted his regiment to within eight miles of the Falls of St. Anthony, where Fort Snelling, Minnesota, now stands. Enroute he held councils with the Indians of Prairie Little Du Chien, where he found Governor Cass. Their first occupation in their new home was the building of the log barracks and fort which were to form the homes and protection of the regiment and its officers. These rude quarters were papered and carpeted with buffalo robes and here Mrs. Snelling's fifth child was born. It was a two years' struggle before the post was completed. In June, 1823, the first steamboat made its appearance on the upper Mississippi, and caused great excitement among the troops. A French gentleman brought letters of introduction to Mrs. Snelling from friends in St. Louis, being invited by the Colonel to remain as long as it was his pleasure. He found it most agreeable, as Mrs. Snelling spoke French fluently. At one time this post was visited by General Scott, and he ordered the name of Fort St. Anthony, which it then bore, changed to Fort Snelling in approval of Colonel Snelling's labors. In 1825 the family left Fort Snelling and visited Mrs. Snelling's brother, Lieutenant Wellington Hunt, in command at Detroit. In 1826 Captain Thomas Hunt, then residing at Washington, wrote his sister to send her two eldest children to him to be educated, and her eldest daughter, Mary, was sent with Captain and Mrs. Plympton who were going to that city. In 1827, the regiment was ordered to Jefferson Barracks, St. Louis, and during the winter Colonel Snelling went on to Washington on business, and was there when his daughter Mary died, the effects of a cold taken at a ball. As Colonel Snelling was obliged to remain in Washington for some time, Mrs. Snelling with her three children joined him there, and a few months after her arrival Colonel Snelling died. After his death she lived on her farm near Detroit, later removing into the city. In 1841, Mrs. Snelling married Rev. J. E. Chaplain, the grandson of President Edwards, who was appointed principal of one of the branches in the Michigan State Institution. Mrs. Chaplain's son, James Snelling, was with General Worth and took part in the battle of Palo Alto, and other battles under General Taylor. The later years of Mrs. Chaplain's life were spent with her daughter, Mrs. Hazard, in Cincinnati.

MARY McMILLAN.

There were but a few small settlements along the Lakes, and in 1688 Sault Ste. Marie was one of the most prominent French posts and a favorite resort for traders. Michigan had passed from the possession of the French to Great Britain in

1760. The military occupation taking place at the time of the Pontiac war extends through the struggles of the British, Indians and Americans to obtain possession of the country down to the victory of Commodore Perry. Then comes the opening up of the country, followed by the period of agriculture, manufacturing and commerce of to-day. The early French were engaged in the fur trading business, and, under the control of the British, they were allowed to pursue this occupation. During the Revolutionary troubles the peninsula remained in quiet, and the treaty in 1783 included it in the bounds of American territory, and in 1795, after the victories of General Wayne, settlers began to go in and open up the country. In 1810 Mackinaw was the chief trading point. Among these early settlers of the eastern portion of Michigan was Mary McMillan, who with her husband had removed to this new land. In 1813, Mr. McMillan had left his family to take part in the military operations of that time, leaving Mrs. McMillan alone to care for her little family. One day while away from home to secure food, she became nervous over the fate which might have overtaken her little ones in her absence, which anxiety was not ill founded, as they had all disappeared with the entire contents of her house. Being of a courageous nature, she was undaunted by the realization of her fears and followed the Indians to find her children hid in the woods on the opposite side of the river. She suffered many like experiences of terror and anxiety during the absence of her husband. After the war was over, when they were living near Detroit, Mr. McMillan was murdered by Indians and her son, eleven years old, captured. After four months' absence, she obtained the news of his whereabouts and raised the money necessary for his ransom, when he was restored to his mother.

CHARLOTTE CLARK.

Her husband was a commissary officer with the troops who were with Colonel Leavenworth on the upper Mississippi. The daughter of Mrs. Clark was Mrs. Van

Cleve of Ann Arbor, Michigan, and was born while the troops were stationed at Prairie Du Chien. They later resided at Fort Snelling. Mrs. Clark was described as a very handsome woman with unusual intelligence and great charm in conversation. Her son, Malcolm Clark, was a trader among the Indians near Fort Benton in Oregon, and married one of the women of the Black Foot Tribe. His two daughters were educated at Ann Arbor. One of Mrs. Clark's daughters, Charlotte Clark, was Mrs. Gear, the wife of Hezekiah Gear, one of the early pioneers of Illinois, and resided at Galena.

SARAH BRYAN.

Was conspicuous among the early settlers of Michigan as the wife of John Bryan.

SYLVIA CHAPIN.

The wife of Syrena Chapin was considered one of the oldest settlers and pioneers of Buffalo, where Dr. Chapin came with his family in 1805. Her husband was a man very much beloved by the citizens of Buffalo.

MRS. ANDERSON.

One of the early settlers of Plymouth, Wayne County, Michigan.

ELIZA BULL.

Eliza Bull, afterwards Mrs. Sinclair, was also an early pioneer of Michigan.

MARY ANN RUMSEY.

One of the early residents of Ann Arbor, Michigan, the county seat of Washtenaw County. This Indian name signified grand or beautiful, and the Grand River takes its name from this word. The name Ann Arbor was given to this little village by John Allen and Walter Rumsey who came to the settlement in February, 1824, from New York State. Mary Ann Rumsey, the wife of Walter Rumsey, was quite a remarkable character and many interesting stories are told of her own life in these early days. Mr. Rumsey died at Ann Arbor, and his wife afterwards married Mr. Van Fossen, and removed to Indiana. There was another woman who bore the name of Ann quite distinguished in this little settlement to which she came in 1824 with the parents of her husband, James Turner Allen, from Virginia. The local tradition is that to these two women, Ann Allen and Ann Rumsey, the town of Ann Arbor is indebted for the addition of Ann to its name. After the death of Mr. Allen his widow returned to Virginia. Mrs. Allen's maiden name was Barry. Her husband's name was Dr. McCue, a Virginian.

BETTY O'FLANAGAN.

Among the remarkable characters of the early days of Detroit there is mention made of one very unique person, Betty O'Flanagan, who is said to have been one of the followers of Wayne's army. When listening to her reminiscences she often told the young people that she would have been better off had "Mad Anthony" lived.

HARRIET L. NOBLE.

Quite a wave of excitement spread over western New York in 1824, over the opportunities offered in the new country known as Michigan. Among those seized with the mania was Nathaniel Noble, and in January of that year he with his brother and family set out for their new home, joining in Ann Arbor their former friends, John Allen and Walter Rumsey. The deprivations and hardships of the journey are only a repetition of those which we have already given. The town of Dixborough was laid out by Mr. Dix of Massachusetts. Miss Frances Trask was a cousin of Mrs. Dix, and was one of the remarkable characters of this day. She was a noted belle and coquette of the community, possessing fine qualities of heart and real worth; her eccentricities and unfeminine defiance of general opinion often caused great talk and comment among her neighbors. She was a general favorite owing to her wit, force, and happy disposition, among the men and many amusing stories are told of her ready repartee. She was at one time engaged to Sherman Dix, a relative of her brother-in-law, but married a Mr. Thompson, being left quite early a widow. Her nephew by marriage was at one time the Secretary of State in Texas.

MRS. HECTOR SCOTT.

Mrs. Hector Scott is worthy of mention among the early settlers of Michigan. She was the daughter of Luther Martin, the attorney who so successfully defended Aaron Burr. One of the famous beauties of that time was a Mrs. Talbot, who was the daughter of Commodore Truxton.

MRS. MOSELEY.

Mrs. Moseley is also deserving of mention. She was the daughter of the Missionary Bingham, and was said to be the first white child born in the Sandwich Islands.

REBECCA J. FISHER.

Mrs. Fisher gives the following facts regarding her life and harrowing experiences as a daughter of pioneer parents:

"I was born in Philadelphia, Pennsylvania, August 31, 1831, and came to Texas with my parents, Johnstone and Mary Gilleland, and two little brothers, about 1836 or 1837. My father was one of the bravest, most conscientious and active soldiers of the Republic of Texas, and had come home for a few days to look after his family when a cruel death awaited him.

"The day my parents were murdered was one of those days

which youth and old age so much enjoy. It was in strange contrast to the tragedy at its close. We were only a few rods from the house. Suddenly the war whoop of the Comanche burst upon our ears, sending terror to all hearts. My father, in trying to reach the house for weapons, was shot down, and near him my mother, clinging to her children and praying God to spare them, was also murdered. As she pressed us to her heart we were baptized in her precious blood. We were torn from her dying embrace and hurried off into captivity, the chief's wife dragging me to her horse and clinging to me with a tenacious grip. She was at first savage and vicious looking, but from some cause her wicked nature soon relaxed, and folding me in her arms, she gently smoothed back my hair, indicating that she was very proud of her suffering victim. A white man with all the cruel instincts of the savage was with them. Several times they threatened to cut off our hands and feet if we did not stop crying. Then the woman, in savage tones and gestures, would scold, and they would cease their cruel threats. We were captured just as the sun was setting and were rescued the next morning.

"During the few hours we were their prisoners, the Indians never stopped. Slowly and stealthily they pushed their way through the settlement to avoid detection, and just as they halted for the first time the soldiers suddenly came upon them, and firing commenced. As the battle raged, the Indians were forced to take flight. Thereupon they pierced my little brother through the body, and, striking me with some sharp instrument on the side of the head, they left us for dead, but we soon recovered sufficiently to find ourselves alone in that dark, dense forest, wounded and covered with blood.

"Having been taught to ask God for all things, we prayed to our Heavenly Father to take care of us and direct us out of that lonely place. I lifted my wounded brother, so faint and

7

weak, and we soon came to the edge of a large prairie, when as far away as our swimming eyes could see we discovered a company of horsemen. Supposing them to be Indians, frightened beyond expression, and trembling under my heavy burden, I rushed back with him into the woods and hid behind some thick brush. But those brave men, on the alert, dashing from place to place, at last discovered us. Soon we heard the clatter of horses' hoofs and the voices of our rescuers calling us by name, assuring us they were our friends who had come to take care of us. Lifting the almost unconscious little sufferer, I carried him out to them as best I could. With all the tenderness of women, their eyes suffused with tears, those good men raised us to their saddles and hurried off to camp, where we received every attention and kindness that man could bestow.

"I was seven years of age when my parents were murdered. Over seventy years have passed since then, and yet my heart grows faint as that awful time passes in review. It is indelibly stamped upon memory's pages and photographed so deeply upon my heart that time with all its changes can never erase it."

In 1848 Rebecca J. Gilleland married Rev. Orceneth Fisher, D.D., a prominent and distinguished minister of the Methodist Church. For over sixty years they served the church in Texas and California, organizing it in Oregon. Dr. Fisher died in Austin, Texas, some years ago. Mrs. Fisher has been president of many church associations, was Acting President of the Daughters of the Republic of Texas for twelve years, and is even yet in the evening of a long and honored life, surrounded by children, grandchildren and great-grandchildren, the distinguished member or guest of many patriotic clubs and societies.

Early Settlers.

The Pacific Coast Company was founded by John Jacob Astor, of New York, in 1810, to carry on trading operations on the Pacific Coast. These exploring parties started from Astoria, Oregon, and experienced the greatest privations and hardships in these trips, the Indians of that time being most hostile and determined in their opposition against the approach of white settlers. The war between Great Britain and the United States breaking out, the Hudson Bay Company took possession of Astoria, and in 1812 a party of traders under the command of Mr. Reed, accompanied by Pierre Dorian, an interpreter, with his wife and two children started on a expedition into the "Snake Country." For almost a year nothing was heard of this little party, until the following summer, when they arrived at Walla Walla, and the accounts given of the hardships of this tribe and the heroism of Mrs. Dorian hardly have a parallel.

In the summer of 1846 a band of settlers started for California, and their experiences and adventures fill one of the darkest pages of our early history. The party consisted of J. F. Reed, wife and four children; Jacob Donner, wife and seven children; William Pike, wife and two children; William Foster, wife and one child; Lewis Kiesburg, wife and one child; Mrs. Murphy, a widow, with five children; William McCutcheon, wife and one child; W. H. Eddy, wife and two children; Noah James, Patrick Dolan, Patrick Shoemaker, John Denton, C. F. Stanton, Milton Elliott, Joseph Raynhard, Augustus Spiser, John Baptiste, Charles Burger, Baylis Williams, and a man by the name of Smith, one by the name of Antoin, and one by the name of Herring. They were well supplied with wagons, teams, cattle, provisions, arms, and ammunition. On reaching White Water River, on the eastern side of the Rocky Mountains, they were persuaded by one of their party to take a new route to California. This brought upon them the greatest suffering, ultimate disaster and the annihilation of almost the entire little band. Many animals were lost; those which survived were exhausted and broken down. Many of their own party gave up their lives. Thirty days were occupied in traveling forty miles. They were lost in the desert for some time, being without water and almost all of their supplies exhausted. Attacked by the Indians, they lost several of their ablest defenders and many of their animals. They reached the mountains in the most distressed condition. It was then the fall of the year, late in October. On the evening of the 22nd, they crossed the Truckee River the forty-ninth time in eighty miles, and on October 28th they reached Truckee Lake at the foot of Fremont's Pass of the main chain of the Sierra Nevadas. This pass at this point is 9,838 feet high. After struggling to the top of the pass they found the snow five feet deep. Frequent efforts to cross the mountains proved useless, and they found they would be compelled to winter here. They retraced their steps to a lower level and commenced the erection of cabins. On the 21st of November, it is said, six women and sixteen men made an attempt to cross the mountains for provisions. Many of this little band died of starvation. On the 16th of December, another effort was made by a small party on snow-shoes. The records of this little band contain some of the most heartrending stories and revolting details. Cannibalism was forced upon them, and the bodies of many who died were consumed to satisfy those of sterner strength. This camp is known in history as "The Camp of Death." Several men forsook the camp to save their lives and perished of starvation on the mountains. The news of the condition of these emigrants had reached California, and an effort was made on the part of the government to send them relief. Two expeditions failed to cross the mountains, but finally a small party of seven men reached the camp. Fourteen men had died of starvation and others were too weak to even be carried. The annals of human suffering nowhere present a more appalling spectacle than that which greeted the eyes of this little rescuing party. The women seemed to withstand the suffering better even than the men. The names of Mrs. Reed, Mrs. Eddy, Mrs. Pike, are conspicuous for their heroism among those who lived, and among the survivors who ultimately reached California were, Mary Graves, Ellen Graves, Nancy Graves, Viney Graves, Elizabeth Graves, Sarah Fosdick, Georgianna Donner, Elizabeth Donner, Mary Donner, Mrs. Wolfinger, Mrs. Kiesburg, Sarah Foster, Mary Murphy, Harriet Pike, Miriam Pike, Margaret Brinn, Isabell Brinn, Virginia Reed, and Pattie Reed. Throughout the horrible scenes of this disastrous expedition the courage, devotion, and fortitude of the women stand out conspicuously. When the hearts of the stoutest men sank, the unflinching energy of the women was shown. When men became mere brutes, woman's true nobility shone forth and her power of soul over body was proven, and the history of this expedition stands as a memorial to what women may endure and accomplish.

Mrs. Reed's daughter, Mrs. Virginia Reed Murphy, of Springfield, Massachusetts, is very well known. She wrote an interesting account of these experiences of her parents and herself, which appeared in the "Century Magazine."

PIETY LUCRETIA HADLEY.

Mrs. Hadley was the daughter of Major David Smith, by his second wife, Obedience Fort Smith, and was born in Logan County, Kentucky, in April 1807. Her early life was spent in Mississippi and Kentucky. On June 14, 1831, Miss Smith was married to Mr. T. B. J. Hadley of Jackson, Mississippi. Of this union there were five daughters. In 1840 Colonel and Mrs. Hadley moved to Houston, Texas. She was one of the conspicuous figures of Texas.

MIREBEAN B. LAMAR.

Mrs. Lamar was the daughter of a celebrated Methodist minister, John Newland Maffitt, and sister of Fred Maffitt, commodore in the Confederate Navy. She was the wife of the first vice-president and the second president of the republic of

Texas, John Lamar, who had come to Texas from Georgia, his native state, in 1835, rendered conspicuous service in the Battle of San Jacinto; was President Burnet's Secretary of War. Immediately after her marriage, Mrs. Lamar and her husband moved to their plantation near the town of Richmond on the Brazos River. In 1857 General Lamar accepted a mission to one of the American Republics, and while on his visit to Washington to receive his credentials, Mrs. Lamar was greatly admired and became one of the belles of the Capital City. While on this visit she was taken seriously ill and returned to their southern home. After two years' service abroad and on General Lamar's return to Texas he was stricken with apoplexy. During the war she did conspicuous service for her people and will long be remembered by the victims of the lost cause. Her death, October 8, 1871, caused unfeigned sorrow.

MRS. JOHN RAGAN.

Was Miss Molly Ford Taylor before her marriage and was a conspicuous figure among the prominent women of Texas in 1875. She was with her husband when he took his seat for the third time in the House of Representatives. Her home in Texas was Fort Houston near Palestine and was noted for the graceful hospitalities dispensed by its mistress.

MRS. THOMAS J. RUSK.

General Thomas J. Rusk having lost his fortune removed from his native state of South Carolina to Clarksville, Georgia, to practice law. Here he married a daughter of General Cleveland, a prominent man of this section. Forming some business connection, his assistants absconded to Texas with the funds of the corporation and he pursued the fugitives in an attempt to recover the stolen property. This was in 1835, and he followed them as far as Nacogdoches, Texas. Here the whole country was in a state of the wildest excitement. Everything was aflame with the spirit of Revolution. He soon became interested and forgetting everything else took up the cause of the patriots as his own. He joined one of the companies and soon became its commander and from that the leader of the little Republic's undisciplined battalions. He was sent by the people to the memorable convention of 1836 that declared the independence of Texas, and took service under the new government as its first Secretary of War, and as such, stopped Houston's army before Santa Anna and brought on the celebrated Battle of San Jacinto and distinguished himself in this battle so that he has since been considered one of the heroes in the history of Texas. In Houston's administration he was again called into the cabinet, resigning to take a seat in the Texas Congress. He was a conspicuous figure in the Indian warfare against the Caddos and Cherokees and other hostile tribes who gave the settlers at that time so much trouble. When more peaceful conditions prevailed he was appointed chief justice of the Republic, and later resigned and resumed his practice of law. He was in favor of the annexation to the United States and in 1845 was President to the convention which formed the constitution of the then future state of Texas. He was elected to the first legislature and held this position until his death in 1857. General Rusk's career gave Mrs.

Rusk a position of great prominence in her State. She filled with great courage and energy all duties which these positions entailed. Their life on this early frontier showed her to be one of the women of which America is proud and to which we owe the opening up of these new countries which are now such great and glorious states of our Union. Mrs. Rusk was the mother of seven children. She died in 1856, in the forty-seventh year of her age.

MRS. SIDNEY SHERMAN.

Mrs. Sherman's husband was a lineal descendant of Roger Sherman. Her father was married in 1835 and lived at Newport, Kentucky. The cry of distress from Texas reached the ears of young Captain and Mrs. Sidney Sherman and they felt it their duty to go to its assistance. Captain Sherman raised and equipped a company of fifty men and in 1835 embarked for the scene of his future exploits. Mrs. Sherman accompanied the expedition as far as Natchez, but from there she returned to her parents in Frankfort, Captain Sherman continuing on to Texas and arriving there in February, 1836. He took part in the engagement which preceded and led his regiment in the last stand made by the Texans on the San Jacinto. All through these trying days in the early history of Texas, Colonel Sherman bore a conspicuous part. In 1842 he was elected to Congress from his district, and some years later by popular vote Major-General of the Texan Army, and this he held until Texas was annexed to the United States. Colonel Sherman suffered severe losses prior to the war and during that period. His young son, Lieutenant Sidney Sherman, was killed. This so told upon Mrs. Sherman's health that she died in January, 1865.

LUCY HOLCOMB PICKENS.

Mrs. Pickens was one of the famous beauties of Texas. In 1856 she married Colonel Pickens, a member of Congress from South Carolina. In the following year her husband was appointed, by President Buchanan, Minister of the United States to the Imperial court of Russia, and in St. Petersburg she was no less famous as a beauty and remarkably gifted woman than in her own land. In 1860 Colonel Pickens resigned his commission, having been elected Governor of South Carolina, and here Mrs. Pickens discharged with inimitable grace and dignity her duties as the wife of the Governor, and it was said that General Pickens on the twelfth day of April, 1861, at Charleston, took his little daughter in his arms and placed in her tiny hand the lighted match that fired the first gun of the war on Fort Sumter. Mrs. Pickens held all through her life the friendship of the Imperial family of Russia, and on the marriage of their daughter, "Doushka", a silver tea service was sent her by the Imperial family. Mrs. Pickens died some years ago.

MRS. ALEXANDER W. TERRELL.

Mrs. Terrell's home was in Austin. Her husband was Minister to Turkey at one time and she traveled extensively in Europe. Her attractive personality and strength of character made her, before her recent death, one of the conspicuous figures of the prominent women of Texas.

MRS. WILLIAM H. WHARTON.

Was the daughter of Jared E. Groce, who went to Texas in 1821. Their home, Groce's Retreat, on the Brazos River, near the town of Hempstead, is well-known in Texas. Sarah Groce married when quite young William H. Wharton, a brilliant young lawyer, who had gone to Texas from Nashville, Tennessee, in 1829. He was president of the convention in 1833, held to dissolve the bond which united Texas to Mexico, and two years later was in the Texan Army at San Antonio. He was sent to the general consultation of the United States as one of the three commissioners and the following year was accredited to that Government as Minister from the Republic of Texas. Later he was elected to the Senate of the Republic, where he attained distinction. In 1839 his death was the result of an accident. Mrs. Wharton is remembered as one of the most forceful women in the political and social life of Texas, and some of her letters addressed to the prominent public women in the dark days when the prospects of Texan independence was in doubt are filled with a fervor, patriotism and energy worthy of the women in the heroic days of Carthage, and her appeals for the cause of human liberty were not unheeded and she is to-day believed to have been one of the potent powers of that time. Mrs. Wharton died in the late seventies. She had one son, General John A. Wharton, who served throughout the Civil War in the Confederate Army, but was afterward killed. His only daughter died unmarried, so that no direct descendants survive this pioneer woman.

MISS PETERSON.

Among the heroic women of the early days, we find many instances in those who went to California with the settlers. One of these was Miss Peterson, who aided in saving the lives of some miners who were perishing in the mountains of starvation. On being told of their condition by an Indian, she insisted on going to their rescue.

KATE MOORE.

There is a very interesting incident told of the bravery of one Kate Moore who resided on one of the islands in the south. She was brought to America by Grace Darling. Many disasters had overtaken vessels landing at Montauk Point, so upon taking up her residence near by she was constantly on the alert. She so trained her ear that she could tell the difference between the howling of the storm and the cries for help, and thus direct a boat, which she herself had learned to manage, in the darkest night to the spot where these poor, perishing mariners could be found. She was a person of fine education and great refinement, but adapted herself to her father's humble calling, and no night was too dark, nor storm too severe for her hand to be ready to launch her boat and aid in the rescue, and in fifteen years she had personally saved the lives of twenty-one persons.

THE BATTLE OF BUNKER HILL.

Women of the Revolution.

ESTHER REED.

Esther De Bredt was born in the city of London, on the 22nd of October, 1746, and died on the 18th of September, 1780, in the city of Philadelphia. Her thirty-four years of life were adorned by no adventurous heroism, but her self-sacrifice, her brave endurance, and her practical aid during the short years she was permitted to dedicate to the young country in the throes of a great and devastating war, earned for her a place among the women who have helped to form the nation.

Her father, Dennis De Bredt, was a British merchant, and his house, owing to his large business relations with the Colonies, was the home of many young Americans who at that time were attracted by pleasure or business interests to the imperial metropolis. Among these visitors, in or about the year 1763, was Joseph Reed, of New Jersey, who had come to London to finish his professional studies among British barristers (such being the fashion of the times). There the young English girl met the American stranger, and the intimacy, thus accidentally begun, soon produced its natural fruits. The young couple came to America in November, 1770, and from the first, as in all the years of turmoil that came with the war, the English girl, who had been reared in luxury, threw her heart and her fortunes into the conflict in which her husband's country was involved. Under her urging, her husband joined Washington's army, and, inexperienced as he was, he earned military fame of no slight eminence. Washington peculiarly honored him, and the correspondence between Mrs. Reed and the Commander-in-Chief on the subject of the mode of administering to the poor soldiers has been published and is of the greatest interest as showing how the influence of woman was felt even in those times when she is popularly supposed to have been considered "an afterthought and a side issue." Her letters are marked by business-like intelligence and sound feminine common sense, on subjects of which, as a secluded woman, she could have had personally no previous knowledge, and Washington, as has been truly observed, "writes as judiciously on the humble topic of soldiers' shirts, as on the plan of a campaign or the subsistence of an army."

La Fayette refers to Mrs. Reed's efforts in behalf of the suffering soldiers as those of "the best patriot, the most zealous and active, and the most attached to the interests of her country."

All this time, it must be remembered, it was a feeble, delicate woman who was writing and laboring; her husband away from her with the army and her family cares and anxieties daily multiplying. As late as August, 1780, she wrote from her country place on the banks of the Schuylkill, where she had been forced to retreat with her three babies: "I am most anxious to get to town, because here I can do little for the soldiers." But the body and the heroic spirit were alike over-tasked, and in the early part of the next month an alarming disease developed itself, and soon ran its fatal course. Esther Reed died as much a martyr to the cause of her country's liberty as any of General Washington's soldiers who met death on the battlefield.

ELIZA LUCAS.

To have been a genuine "New Woman" in the New World, and a society woman in the highest circles of the Old World, is the somewhat unique distinction of Eliza Lucas, afterwards the wife of Chief Justice Charles Pinckney. She was born on the West Indian Island of Antigua, in 1723, but most of her childhood was passed in England, where she was sent with her two little brothers to be educated. She had barely returned to the Island of Antigua, where her father, Lieutenant Colonel George Lucas, an officer in the English army was stationed, when it became necessary for them to go in search of a climate that would suit her mother's delicate health. Eliza was a girl of sixteen when they finally settled upon South Carolina as a place of residence. The balmy climate of Carolina formed a welcome contrast to the languishing tropical heat they had endured, and Colonel Lucas started extensive plantations in Saint Andrew's parish near Ashley River, about seventeen miles from Charleston.

At the renewal of England's war with Spain, the Colonel was obliged to hurry back to his Island position, and Eliza was left with the care of a delicate mother and a little sister, the management of the house and three plantations. It was a responsible position for a girl of sixteen, but she proved herself a capable, practical, level-headed young woman, doing a woman's work with a woman's shrewdness and tact. She entered upon her agricultural duties with energy and spirit, her plan being to see what crops could be raised on the highlands of South Carolina to furnish a staple for exportation. She thus tried plots of indigo, ginger, cotton and cassava. With her indigo she was especially successful, after many disappointments mastering the secret of its preparation. Her experiments in that crop proved a source of wealth to the Colony; the annual value of its exportation just before the Revolution amounting to over a million pounds, and her biographer quite justly implies that this modest unassuming Colonel's daughter, of almost two hundred years back, did as much for her country as any "New Woman" has done since.

From the time of her coming to Carolina, Eliza Lucas' letters tell the story of her life, and they portray a fullness and usefulness and activity remarkable in so young a girl; they also show a charming, unaffected personality, and are, moreover, a splendid reflection of the living, working and social conditions of the times. In the midst of the busy life she found time to cultivate her artistic tastes. She tells us that she devoted a certain time every day to the study of music, and we find her writing to ask her father's permission to send to England for "cantatas, Weldon's Anthems, and Knollyss' Rules for Tuning." Her fondness for literature, it seems, quite scandalized one old gentlewoman in the neighborhood, who took such a dislike to her books that, "She had liked to have thrown my Plutarch's Lives into the fire. She is sadly afraid," writes the amazed young lady, "that I might read myself mad." All through her letters we catch glimpses of grain fields, pleasant groves of oak and laurel, meadows mingling with young myrtle and yellow jasmine, while to the sweet melodies of the birds she listened and learned to identify each.

There is another sort of music quite different from that of the birds, mentioned now and then in her letters. It is the humming of the fiddles floating down to her through the maze of years in the solemn measures of the minuet, the gay strains of the reel and the merry country dances; for this industrious young daughter of the Colonial days could be frivolous when occasion demanded it and she could trip the dance as charmingly as any city belle. Her letters give vivid pictures of society in Charleston and the festivities at the country seats near her home.

When Miss Lucas went to a party she traveled in a post-chaise which her mother had imported from England, and her escort rode beside her on a "small, spirited horse of the Chickasaw breed." If she went by water she was carried down the dark Ashley River a la Elaine in a canoe hollowed from a great cypress and manned by six or eight negroes, all singing in time to the swing of their silent paddles. It appears there was always good cheer awaiting the guest at the memorable houses along the Ashley River. After the feast, the men lingered over their wine and the women gossiped in the drawing-room until the fiddles began to play. Then the men left their cups, and with laughter, bows and elaborate compliments invited their partners to the dance. Such were the good social times in which Eliza Lucas took part. But, although she enjoyed them and entered into them with spirit, she did not dwell much upon them; she was engaged with more serious matters. She was also very much worried by the dangers of the West Indian campaign, in which her father was engaged, and longed for the war to end. "I wish all the men were as great cowards as myself," she wrote, "it would then make them more peaceably inclined."

Among all the friends she made in the Colony, there was one to whom she could turn for earnest talk, good counsel and fatherly advice. This was Colonel Charles Pinckney. He and Mrs. Pinckney had done much to help the young girl in her early struggle to establish plantations, and at Mrs. Pinckney's death we find Eliza Lucas writing sadly of her personal loss in the event. The story is told that Mrs. Pinckney had once said that rather than have her favorite young friend Eliza Lucas lost to Carolina, she would herself be willing to step down and let her take her place. She probably never imagined that fate would take her so thoroughly at her word. But so it happened. Some time after her death John Lucas sent his son George to Carolina, to bring Mrs. Lucas and the girls back to Antigua to meet him. But Eliza was not destined to make that voyage, and it was her old friend Colonel Pinckney who prevented her departure. He was then speaker of the House of the Colonial Assembly, a distinguished lawyer and wealthy planter, and a

man of "charming temper, gay and courteous manners, well
looking, well educated and of high religious principles," and
when this gentleman offered himself to Miss Lucas the joys
of a single life seemed to lose their charm for her, and she
smilingly agreed to become Mrs. Pinckney the second.
Accordingly on a warm, sunshiny day in May, of the year
1744, she was married to Mr. Pinckney, "with the approbation
of all my friends," as she proudly declared.

The new life brought new responsibilities, for Colonel
Pinckney, or Chief Justice Pinckney, as he came to be, occupied
a high position in the Colony, and his wife's social duties were
not slight.   On many nights the Pinckney mansion was
brilliantly lighted, and the halls and drawing-rooms crowded
with gentlemen in satin coats and knee-breeches, and ladies in
rustling brocaded growns.   But there were other times when the
house was quiet except for the patter of children's feet upon
the stairways, and the echo of children's voices through the
halls.   There were three children—two boys and their pretty
sister, Harriott, who resembled her mother, it is said, fair-
haired and blue-eyed, with a touch of her mother's spirit and
energy.

Then there came a day when Mrs. Pinckney no longer gave
her parties to the people of Carolina, for one March morning, in
the year 1753, Chief Justice Pinckney, the new Commissioner of
the Colony, and his family sailed away and arrived in England
with the springtime.   Five years the Pinckneys remained in
England, living sometimes in London, sometimes in Richmond,
sometimes in Surrey, the Garden County of England, with
sometimes an occasional season at Bath.   The Pinckneys certainly found favor everywhere; even Royalty opened its doors
to them, and they were entertained by the widowed Princess of
Wales and her nine little princes and princesses.   Among them
was the future George III, who, of course, could not know

that his guests would some day be rebels against his sovereignty. But pleasant days in England had to end, and when the war between France and England was renewed, and the English colonies in America became endangered, Justice Pinckney instantly decided to return to Carolina to settle his affairs there. The two boys were left at school in England, and it was a sad good-bye for the mother parting from her sons. Fortunately, she could not know that when she next saw her little boys she would be a widow and they would be grown men.

Her widowhood began soon after her arrival in Carolina. Then there were long sorrowful days when she was, as she expressed it, "Seized with the lethargy of stupidity." But her business ability and her love for her children brought her back to an interesting life, and in time she was able to look after her plantation affairs with the same splendid efficiency of her earlier "New Woman" days. Mrs. Pinckney's last days were clouded with shadows of war. There had always been more or less of war in her life. First in her girlhood it was the Spanish War, which threatened her own home and filled her heart with anxiety for her father; then in later years occurred the terrible Indian raids in which many a brave Carolina soldier lost his life, and finally in her old age, came the American Revolution.

Mrs. Pinckney's position at the beginning of the Revolution was a hard one, for she was, like her own state of Carolina, part rebel and part Tory. Among the English people she numbered many of her dearest friends, and she remembered her fair-haired English mother and her father in his English regimentals, while her heart turned loyally to England and the King. But her boys, in spite of fourteen years in England, were, as their father had been, thorough rebels. Even as a boy at school Tom Pinckney had won the name of "Little Rebel," and in one of Charles Cotesworth Pinckney's earliest portraits he is presented as declaiming against the Stamp Act. When the test came their mother's sympathy went with the cause for which her boys were fighting, naturally making their country her country. And she never regretted her choice. She was rewarded for her brave life by living to see America free and at peace, and her sons most highly respected citizens. And so her old age was happy—happier indeed she declared than her youth had been, for she writes, "I regret no pleasures that I can enjoy, and I enjoy some that I could not have had at an earlier season. I now see my children grown up and, blessed be God, I see them such as I hoped." What is there in youthful enjoyment preferable to this?

CATHERINE GREENE.

Catherine Littlefield, the eldest daughter of John Littlefield and Phebe Ray, was born in New Shoreham, on Block Island, in 1753. When very young she came with her sister to reside in the family of Governor Greene, of Warwick, a lineal descendant of the family, whose wife was her aunt. It was here that Miss Littlefield's very happy girlhood was passed; and it was here also that she first knew Nathaniel Greene. Their marriage took place July 20, 1774, and the young couple removed to Coventry. Looking at that bright, volatile, coquettish girl of this time, no one could dream of her future destiny as a soldier's wife and comrade; nor that the broad-brimmed hat of her young husband covered brows that should one day be wreathed with the living laurels won by genius and patriotism.

But when Nathaniel Greene's decision was made, and he stood forth a determined patriot, separating himself from the community in which he had been born and reared, by embracing a military profession, his spirited wife did her part with enthusiasm to aid and encourage him in his ambition and efforts for the success of the patriots. When the army before Boston was inoculated with smallpox, she voluntarily gave up her beautiful house for a hospital.

When the army went into winter quarters, she always set out to rejoin her husband, sharing cheerfully the narrow quarters and hard fare of a camp, bearing heroically her part in the privations of the dreary winter at Valley Forge, in that "darkest hour of the Revolution." It appears that there, as at home, her gay spirit shed light around her even in such scenes, softening and enlivening the gloom which might have weighed many a bold heart into despondency. There are extant some interesting little notes of Kosciuszko, in very imperfect English, which show her kindness to her husband's friends, and the pleasure she took in alleviating their sufferings.

Mrs. Greene joined her husband in the South after the close of the active campaign of 1781, and remained with him till the end of the war, residing on the islands during the heat of summer, and the rest of the time at headquarters. In the spring of 1783, she returned North, where she resided till the General completed his arrangements for removing to the South. They then established themselves at Mulberry Cove, on a plantation presented to General Greene by the state of Georgia. Mrs. Greene's first impression of southern life and manners are painted in lively colors in her letters to northern friends. The following passage is from one to Miss Flagg:

"If you expect to be an inhabitant of this country, you must not think to sit down with your netting pins; but on the contrary, employ half your time at the toilet, one quarter to paying and receiving visits, the other quarter to scolding servants, with a hard thump every now and then over the head, or singing, dancing, reading, writing or saying your prayers."

After the death of General Greene, she removed with her

8

family of four children to some lands she owned on Cumberland Island, and while occasionally visiting the North in the summer, she continued to look upon the South as her home.

A letter from her about this time gives the incident of Colonel Aaron Burr's requesting permission to stop at her house when he came South after his duel with General Hamilton. She would not refuse the demand upon her hospitality, but his victim had been her friend and she could not receive as a guest one whose hands were crimsoned with Hamilton's blood. She gave Burr permission to remain, but at the same time ordered her carriage and quitted the house; returning as soon as he had taken his departure. This incident is strongly illustrative of her impulsive and generous character.

Her discipline was remarkably strict and none of her children ever thought of disobeying her. Yet, she would sometimes join with child-like merriment in their sports. A friend has related how one day, after the close of the war, passing General Greene's house in Newport, she saw the General and his wife playing "puss in the corner" with the children.

It was while she lived at Mulberry Cove that she became instrumental in introducing to the world an invention which has covered with wealth the fields of the South.

Late in 1792, her sympathies were enlisted in behalf of a young man, a native of Massachusetts, who having come to Georgia to take the place of a private teacher in a gentleman's family, had been disappointed in obtaining the situation and found himself without friends or resources in a strange land. Mrs. Greene and her family treated him with great kindness. He was invited to make his home in her house while he pursued the study of law, to which he had determined to devote himself. At one time a party of gentlemen on a visit to the family spoke of the want of an effective machine for separating the cotton from the seed, without which it was mournfully agreed there could be no more profitable cultivation of this special product of the Southland. Mrs. Greene spoke of the mechanical genius of her young protégé—who was, of course, Eli Whitney—introduced him to the company and showed little specimens of his skill in tambour frames and articles for the children. The result of this introduction to interested men was the equipment of a basement room, into which no one else was admitted, and which was appropriated for the young student's workshop. There he labored day after day, making the necessary tools and persevering with unwearied industry for the perfection of his invention. By spring the cotton gin was completed and exhibited to the wonder and delight of planters invited from different parts of Georgia to witness its successful operation.

Mr. Phineas Miller entered into an agreement with Whitney to bear the expense of maturing the invention and to divide the future profits. He was a man of remarkably active and cultivated mind. Mrs. Greene married him some time after the death of General Greene. She survived him several years, dying just before the close of the second war with England. Her remains rest in the family burial ground at Cumberland Island, where but a few years afterwards the body of one of her husband's best officers and warmest friends—the gallant Lee —was also brought to molder by her side.

CATHARINE SCHUYLER.

Catharine Schuyler was the only daughter of John Van Rensselaer, called the Patroon of Greenbush, a patriot in the Revolutionary struggle, and noted for his hospitality and for his kindness and forbearance towards the tenants of his vast estates during the war. Many families in poverty remember with gratitude the aid received from the daughter of this household. After her marriage to Philip Schuyler, General Schuyler of Revolutionary War renown, she came to preside over the Schuyler mansion in Albany as well as his beautiful country seat near Saratoga, and by her graceful courtesy did much to soften the miseries of the war. Nor was she wanting in resolution and courage; she proved equal to every great emergency. When the Continental army was retreating from Fort Edward before Burgoyne, Mrs. Schuyler herself went in her chariot from Albany to Saratoga to see to the removal of her household goods and gods. While there she received directions from the General to set fire with her own hands to his extensive fields of wheat rather than suffer them to be reaped by the enemy. The injunction shows the soldier's confidence in her spirit, firmness and patriotism, and, as she literally obeyed his commands, proved that "the heart of her husband doth safely trust in her."

This elegant country-seat was immediately after destroyed by General Burgoyne, and it is related how, after the surrender of Burgoyne, General Schuyler being detained at Saratoga, where he had seen the ruins of his beautiful villa, wrote thence to his wife to make every preparation for giving the best reception to the conquered General. It was certainly one of the most picturesque incidents of the war, that the captive British general, with his suite, should be received and entertained by those whose property he had wantonly laid waste. A writer has said in this connection, "All her actions proved that at sight of the misfortune of others, she quickly forgot her own." This delicacy and generosity drew from Burgoyne the observation to General Schuyler, "You are too kind to me, who have done so much to injure you." The reply was characteristic of the noble-hearted host: "Such is the fate of war; let us not dwell on the subject."

Many of the women of this illustrious family appear to have been remarkable for strong intellect and clear judgment, but none lived more brightly in the memories of all those who knew her than the wife of General Philip Schuyler.

Catherine Schuyler died in 1803.

Such instances were exemplified after the Civil War in innumerable instances; conquered vied with the conquerors in magnanimity toward each other.

ELIZABETH SCHUYLER.

In the family Bible of young Philip Schuyler, when a captain under General Bradstreet, the Quartermaster of the English army, appears this entry: "Elizabeth, born August 9, 1757. Do according to Thy will with her." Thus entered into the world Elizabeth Schuyler, afterwards the wife of Alexander Hamilton.

When she was only two months old the frightful massacre of the German Flats occurred and the refugees fled to Albany. In the big barn on the Schuyler estate they found shelter and the little Schuyler babies, Elizabeth and Angelica, had to be set aside while their young mother, Catharine Schuyler, with the other women of the house, helped administer to the needs of the poor destitute people. At this time, too, the town of Albany was filled with rapacious army troops. A detachment of red-coats, under General Charles Lee, lay in the "Indian Field" adjoining the ground of the Schuyler mansion, and they did not hesitate to lay hands on whatever suited their purpose. Aber-crombie, Lee, and kindly, courteous Lord Howe, were all visitors there during this period.

Later, when the defeat of Ticonderoga came, the Schuyler barn again opened its hospitable doors. This time it was con-verted into a hospital and the wounded British and provincial soldiers lay beneath the rafters, fed by the negro slaves and nursed by the women of the Schuyler homestead. So, in the midst of war scenes, Elizabeth Schuyler passed her early child-hood. As the daughter of so worthy and distinguished a man as General Schuyler, she received an education superior to that of most Colonial girls, she with her sisters being sent to New York to school. Afterwards returning to the Schuyler house at Albany, on a memorable afternoon, in October, 1777, she met young Alexander Hamilton, the brilliant aid-de-camp on her father's staff. The friendship so formed between "Betsy" Schuyler and Alexander Hamilton during his short stay in Albany was not destined to end there, although it was a period of almost two years before they met again.

When news of the battle of Lexington came "Betsy" was at Saratoga with the rest of the family. War had begun and in the days that followed she lived in the midst of army talk and army doings, for generals, officers and aids-de-camp were coming and going continually at the Schuyler mansion. But later on, John Schuyler was appointed to Congress and went to live at Philadelphia with his family. The headquarters of the army during the campaign of 1779-80, were at Morristown, some fifty miles from the Schuyler's Philadelphia home, and to Morristown Betsy Schuyler very shortly journeyed to visit her aunt. Headquarters were gay at that time, Washington's household being composed of a brilliant company. Washington and his wife sat opposite each other in the center of the board, and on both sides of them almost continually, were ranged many distinguished visitors. Impetuous young Aaron Burr was of the party, the elegant Baron Steuben and the splendid Duke Lauzun. In this illustrious group of men Alexander Hamilton shone as the bright particular star, and naturally the one of whom Betsy Schuyler saw the most during her visit to Morris-town was Alexander Hamilton As it happened, her stay at Morristown was happily prolonged, her father being invited by the commander-in-chief to come to headquarters as his military adviser. The Schuyler family were soon established at Morristown, and their home became one of the centers of social life, and Hamilton spent most of his evenings there.

On December 14, 1780, Elizabeth Schuyler and Alexander Hamilton were married in the ample and handsome drawing-room of the Schuyler mansion at Albany, where three years before, if reports be true, they had met and loved. Elizabeth Schuyler's story of Colonial days ends with her marriage. The merry, light-hearted Betsy Schuyler became Mrs. Alexander Hamilton, one of the most prominent leaders of official society. She was eminently fitted for her high position. In her father's home she had been accustomed to entertaining great people of the day, and from her mother she had learned the ways of a large and ever-ready hospitality, while her natural grace and ability assured her own success. We may judge how great a lady Betsy Schuyler had become when we read that at the Inaugural Ball the President distinguished Mrs. Hamilton, and one other woman, by dancing with them. She and her husband were included constantly in Washington's dinner and theatre parties.

The Hamiltons were not rich. "I have seen," writes Talleyrand, "one of the marvels of the world. I have seen the man who made the fortune of a Nation laboring all night to support his family." Hamilton, however, was not merely the most brilliant statesman of his day, and his wife was not only a charming society woman. There are glimpses of a beautiful home life set apart from official duties and social obligations. Hamilton's reason for resigning his seat in the Cabinet has become historic. In it we see a proof of his love for his wife and children. In this life of "domestic happiness," for which Hamilton resigned his career as a statesman, Elizabeth Hamilton was a bright and cheerful influence. She entered warmly into her husband's plans and sympathies and heartily into the interests of her children. The sweetness of disposition and kindness of heart which, in her girlhood, had so endeared her to her friends made her relations as wife and mother very beautiful.

The peace and gladness of the Hamilton home were cruelly ended on that fatal July morning, in 1804, when Hamilton lost his life. At his untimely death all America mourned and the terrible sorrow of his family cannot be described. His wife, the "dear Betsy" of his boyhood, survived her husband for fifty, long, lonesome years. When she died, at ninety-seven, a pleasant, sweet-faced old lady, praised for her sunny nature and her quiet humor, a pocketbook was found in her possession. Within it lay a yellow, time-worn letter. It was written on the morning of the duel, and was Hamilton's farewell to his "Beloved Wife."

MARY BUCKMAN BROWN.

The wife of Francis Brown is one of the unsung heroines of the Revolutionary War. She was born in 1740, and died in Lexington in 1824. The only biography of her merely states that she was "small in stature, quiet and retiring, of great refinement and of considerable culture." But the descendants of Mr. and Mrs. Francis Brown are many and they have always been prominent or representative citizens in that part of New England. Her husband traced his descent back to earliest Colonial ancestry in the persons of "John Brown and Dorothy his wife," who came to the New World in 1630. The knowledge of the Lexington Minute Men is such as to show that Francis Brown was a man of great decision of character, and well fitted by nature and training to meet the impending crises of that time. In letters treasured by his descendants we find the highest tribute to the true courage of his wife, and of her heroic conduct, when during the war her house was attacked, and after a hasty concealment of her household treasures, she was obliged to retreat to the woods and care for her children there for several days.

SARAH HULL.

Sarah Hull, the wife of Major William Hull, was one of those women who followed their husbands in the response to the Revolutionary call to arms and partook of their dangers and privations. She was the daughter of Judge Fuller of Newton, Massachusetts, and was born about 1755.

While with the army at Saratoga, she joined the other American women there in kind and soothing attentions to the wives and families of the British officers who were held prisoners, after Burgoyne's surrender. For several years after the close of the war General Hull held the office of Governor of Michigan Territory, and in her eminent station, Mrs. Hull displayed so much good sense with more brilliant accomplishments, that she improved the state of society in this neighborhood, which was at that time a pioneer tract, without provoking envy by her superiority. Those who visited the then wild country about them found a generous welcome at her hospitable mansion, and departed with admiring recollections of her and her daughters.

But it was in the cloud of misfortune that the energy of Mrs. Hull's character was most clearly shown. Governor Hull having been appointed Major-General in the war of 1812, met with disasters which compelled his surrender and subjected him to suspicion of treason. His protracted trial and his defense belong to history. His wife sustained these evils with patient, trustful serenity, believing that the day would come when all doubts would be cleared away, and her husband restored to public confidence. The loss of her son in battle was also borne with the same Christian fortitude, her quiet demeanor and placid face betraying no trace of the suffering that had wrung her heart. Happily she lived to see her hopes realized in the General's complete vindication, and died in 1826, in less than a year after his decease.

SUSAN LIVINGSTON.

Susan, the eldest daughter of William Livingston, Governor of New Jersey at the time of the Revolution, is accredited with two strategic moves against the enemy, which were distinctly clever and which could have been effected only by a woman.

On the 28th of February, 1779, a party of British troops from New York landed at Elizabethtown Point for the purpose of capturing the Governor of New Jersey and annihilating the force stationed in that village. One detachment marched at night to "Liberty Hall," the executive mansion, and forced an entrance. Governor Livingston, however, happened to have left home some hours previously, hence they were disappointed in not securing their prisoner. The British officer demanded the Governor's papers. Miss Livingston, the embodiment of modest and charming young womanhood, readily assented to the demand, but, appealing to him as a gentleman, requested that a box standing in the parlor which she claimed contained her private belongings, should be unmolested. The gallant young British officer, flattered by her appeal, stationed a guard over it, while the library was given over to the soldiers for sacking. They forthwith filled their foraging bags with worthless papers and departed, little suspecting that the box which had been so sedulously guarded contained all the Governor's correspondence with Congress, with the commander-in-chief and the state officers, and that the strategy of Susan Livingston had thus preserved what would have proved a most valuable prize to the plunderers.

Again, when New Jersey was once more invaded by the British, and all the neighboring villages were seen in flames, the Governor's house, the historic "Liberty Hall" in Elizabethtown, was left untouched, and its inmates, the women of the family, the Governor being absent, were treated with the greatest courtesy. The explanation lies in the romantic fact that just as the soldiers were advancing upon the house, one of the British officers received a rose from Miss Susan Livingston as a memento of a promise of protection he had made the fascinating young woman at the time when hostilities merely hung fire.

It was a younger sister of Miss Livingston who figures in the national tapestry as the recipient of the favor of General Washington, as expressed in the following very human note written amid the hardships of that most desolate of all American camps in the Revolution.

"General Washington having been informed lately of the honor done him by Miss Kitty Livingston in wishing for a lock of his hair, takes the liberty of inclosing one, accompanied by his most respectful compliments.

"Camp Valley Forge, March 18th, 1778."

All the letters of Governor Livingston to his daughters

show the sympathy that existed between them, and his confidence in the strength of their Republican principles. His opinions and wishes on all subjects are openly expressed to them, showing how thoroughly women of this period of struggle and stress were taken into partnership, not only, as was necessary, in the dangers, but in sharing the ambition and confidences of the men, when the exigencies of the times demanded that they should know how to fight as well as to pray.

ELIZABETH CLAY.

Elizabeth Clay, the mother of Henry Clay, was born in the county of Hanover, in Virginia, in 1750. Her early education was such as was attainable at that period in the colony. She was the younger of two daughters who were the only children of George and Elizabeth Hudson, and before she was fifteen years old she had married John Clay, a preacher of the Baptist denomination. She became the mother of eight children and Henry Clay was among the elder of these. Her husband died during the Revolution, and some years after Mrs. Clay contracted a second marriage with Mr. Henry Watkins, and in course of time eight more children were added to her family. The cares devolving upon her in the charge of so many children and the superintendence of domestic concerns naturally occupied her time to the exclusion of any participation in matters of public interest. She must, however, have borne her share in the agitations and dangers of the time, in behalf of those who claimed her maternal solicitude and guidance. She died in 1827, having survived most of her children.

DOROTHY HANCOCK.

Mrs. Hancock was one of those who, by her courtesies to the officers and ladies of the British army when Burgoyne was under the convention of surrender, made Cambridge a brilliant center of hospitality and fashion. She was the daughter of Edmund Quincy, of Massachusetts, and was born in 1750. At the age of twenty-four she married John Hancock, one of the great men of the age, and, aided by the lustre of his fortunes, she became a leader in society, filling her station with rare dignity and grace. At her table there might be seen all classes; the grave clergy, the veteran and the gay, the gifted in song, or anecdote or wit. The dinner hour was at one or two o'clock; three was the latest for formal occasions. The evening amusement was usually a game of cards, and dancing was much in vogue. There were concerts, but theatrical productions were prohibited. Much attention was paid to dress; coats of various colors were worn by the men. All of which shows that the new country was capable of a salon and much pretentious social intercourse, notwithstanding the war they had just passed through and the hardships they had endured.

During the life of her husband Mrs. Hancock was of necessity much in the gay world, in which she occupied a position of unusual distinction. After Hancock's death, she married Captain Scott, with whom she passed a less brilliant yet no less happy life. Her later years were spent in seclusion. She was still, however, surrounded by friends who felt themselves instructed and charmed by her superior mind. She went but little into society, yet, whenever she appeared she was received with great attention. La Fayette, on his visit to this country, called upon her and many spoke of the interesting interview witnessed between "the once youthful chevalier and the splendid belle." She died in her seventy-eighth year, a woman of whose brilliant life and beautiful poise her countrymen may well be proud.

MERCY WARREN.

The name of Mercy Warren belongs to American History. In the influence she exercised she was, perhaps, the most remarkable woman who lived during the Revolutionary period. Seldom has one woman in any age acquired such an ascendency over the strongest by mere force of a powerful intellect. She is said to have supplied political parties with their arguments; and she was the first of her sex in America who taught the reading world in matters of state policy and history.

She was the third child of Colonel James Otis, of Barnstable, in the old colony of Plymouth, and was born there, September 25, 1728. The youth of Miss Otis was passed in the retirement of her home, and her love for reading was early manifest. At that period the opportunities for woman's education were extremely limited and Miss Otis gained nothing from schools. Her only assistant in intellectual culture of her early years was Rev. Jonathan Russell, the minister of the parish from whose library she was supplied with books and by whose counsels her tastes were in a measure formed. It was from reading at his advice Raleigh's "History of the World" that her attention was particularly directed to history, the branch of literature to which she afterwards devoted herself. In later years, her brother James, who was himself an excellent scholar, became her adviser and companion in literary pursuits.

There existed between them a strong attachment, which nothing ever impaired. Even in the wildest moods of that insanity with which, late in life, the great patriot was afflicted, her voice had power to calm him, when all else failed.

When about twenty-six, Miss Otis became the wife of James Warren, then a merchant of Plymouth, Massachusetts, and in him she found a partner of congenial mind.

It was during the occasional visits of a few weeks at a time to their farm near Plymouth, which she called "Clifford," that most of her poetical productions were written.

With a fondness for historical studies, and the companionship of such a brother and husband, it is not strange that the active and powerful intellect of Mrs. Warren should have become engaged with interest in political affairs. How warmly Mrs. Warren espoused the cause of her country, how deeply her feelings were enlisted, appears in her letters to the great spirits of that era. This rich correspondence has been preserved by her descendants. It includes letters, besides those from members of her own family,—and letters were dissertations, not a hodgepodge of trivialities in those days—from Samuel and John Adams, Jefferson, Dickinson, Gerry, Knox and others. These men asked her opinion in political matters, and acknowledged the excellence of her judgment. Referring to some of her observations on the critical state of affairs after the war, General Knox writes: "I should be happy, Madam, to receive your communications from time to time, particularly on the subject enlarged on in this letter. Your sentiments shall remain with me."

During the years that preceded the Revolution and after its outbreak, Mrs. Warren's house appears to have been the resort of much company. As she herself says, "by the Plymouth fireside were many political plans discussed and digested." Although her home was in Plymouth, her place of residence was occasionally changed during the war. At one time she lived in the house at Milton, which Governor Hutchinson had occupied. Wherever she was, the friends of America were always welcomed to the shelter of her roof, and the hospitalities of her table. In different passages of her letters to John Adams, the officers with whom she became acquainted are described. The following extract is interesting:

"The Generals, Washington, Lee, and Gates, with several other distinguished officers, dined with us three days since. The first of these, I think, is one of the most amiable and accomplished gentlemen, both in person, mind, and manners, that I have met. The second, whom I never saw before, I think plain in his person to a degree of ugliness, careless even to impoliteness, his garb ordinary, his voice rough, his manners rather morose; yet sensible, learned, judicious, and penetrating; a considerable traveler, agreeable in his narrations, and a zealous, indefatigable friend of the American cause, but much more for a love of freedom and an impartial sense of the inherent rights of mankind at large, than from any attachment or disgust to particular persons or countries. The last is a brave soldier, a high republican, a sensible companion, and an honest man, of unaffected manners and easy deportment."

And La Fayette is praised in this laconic fashion: "Penetrating, active, sensible, judicious, he acquits himself with the highest applause in the public eye, while the politeness of his manners and sociability of his temper insure his welcome at every hospitable board."

Every page from the pen of Mrs. Warren is remarkable for clearness and vigor of thought. Thus, her style is not vitiated by the artificial tastes of the day; yet, her expression is often studiously elaborated, in accordance with the prevalent fashion, and smothered in classic allusion. This is the case in her letters written with most care; while in others, her ardent spirit pours out its feelings with irrepressible energy, portraying itself in the genuine and simple language of emotion. Mrs. Warren kept a faithful record of occurrences during the dark days of her country's affliction, through times that engaged the attention of both the philosopher and the politician. She did this with the design of transmitting to posterity a faithful portraiture of the most distinguished characters of the day. Her intention was fulfilled in her history of the American Revolution. This work exhibits her as a writer in advance of her age. Its sound judgment and careful research, with its vigorous style, give it a high and lasting value. Her portraiture of Mr. Adams gave offense to the great statesman, which, for a time, threatened to interrupt the affectionate relations between the two families. But after a sharp correspondence, it was amicably settled, and as a token of reconciliation, Mrs. Adams sent her friend a ring containing her own and her husband's hair. This is now in possession of one of Mrs. Warren's descendants.

The several satirical dramatic pieces that Mrs. Warren wrote criticising the follies of her day and humorously introducing the leading Tory characters, produced a marked sensation, and a strong political influence is ascribed to the bold and keen satire in these poems.

Her two tragedies, "The Sack of Rome" and "The Ladies of Castile" are more remarkable for patriotic sentiment than for dramatic merit. The verse is smooth and flowing and the language poetical, but often wanting in the simplicity essential to true pathos. The tragedies were, however, read with interest and much praised in after years. Alexander Hamilton writes to the author, "It is certain that in the 'Ladies of Castile' the sex will find a new occasion of triumph. Not being a poet myself, I am in the less danger of feeling mortification at the idea that, in the career of dramatic composition at least, female genius in the United States has out-stripped the male."

Altogether, the literary workmanship and the political influence of Mercy Warren appears an anachronism in time and place, for a new country at war is not supposed to shape its course by literature, and surely the Puritan forbearance had shown little disposition to abide by the counsels of women, though ofttimes acting unconsciously under the influence of some brainy woman, who was too clever to let on that she recognized the conceptions of her fertile brain expressed by some man over whom she had subtle power.

In her last illness, her constant fear was that she might lose her mental faculties as death approached. She prayed effectively to be spared this dreaded condition. To her latest breath her mind was unclouded, and with an expression of thankfulness and peacefulness, she passed to the rest that awaits the faithful Christian, October 19, 1814, in the eighty-seventh year of her remarkably forceful life.

MARY DRAPER.

Mary Draper, who was the wife of Captain Draper of Revolutionary fame, deserves to be classed with Putnam and Stark whose rough-and-ready and instantaneous response to their country's appeal has become a matter of historic tradition. When the news reached Connecticut that blood had been shed, Putnam, who was at work in the field, left his plow in the furrow, and started for Cambridge without changing his coat. Stark was sawing pine logs without a coat; he shut down the gate of his mill and began his journey to Boston in his shirt sleeves. And Mary Draper, from her farm in Dedham, Massachusetts, was not one whit less active in her patriotic zeal. When the first call to arms sounded throughout the land, she exhorted her husband to lose no time in hastening to the scene of action; and with her own hands bound knapsack and blanket on the shoulders of her only son, a stripling of sixteen, bidding him depart and do his duty. To the entreaties of her daughter that her young brother might remain at home to be their protector, she answered that every arm able to aid the cause belonged to the country. "He is wanted and must go. You and I, Kate, have also service to do. Food must be prepared for the hungry; for before to-morrow night hundreds, I hope thousands, will be on their way to join the Continental forces. Some who have traveled far will need refreshment, and you and I, with Molly, must feed as many as we can." This speech has not come down to history with the sententious utterances of great generals and yet it was the basis of homely action that was of inestimable succor in the starting of that terrific struggle for liberty. Captain Draper was a thriving farmer; his granaries were filled and his wife's dairy was her special care and pride. All these resources she made contribute to her benevolent purpose. Assisted by her daughter and the domestic, she spent the whole day and night, and the succeeding day, in baking brown bread. The ovens of that day were suited for such an occasion, each holding bread sufficient to supply a neighborhood. These were soon in full blast and the kneading trough was plied by hands that shrank not from the task.

At that time of hurry and confusion, Mary Draper realized that none could stop long enough to dine, so she prepared to dispense her stores even as the men hurried along to join the army. With the aid of a disabled veteran of the French wars, who had been a pensioner in her family, she erected a long form by the roadside; large pans of bread and cheese were placed upon it and replenished as often as was necessary, while old John brought cider in pails from the cellar, which, poured into tubs, was served out by two lads who volunteered their services. Unquestionably if it had not been for this aid to the weary

9

patriots, many of them, who, under the influence of strong excitement, had started without rations of any sort, would have fallen by the way, exhausted from want of food.

Then, ere long, after the battle of Bunker Hill, came the startling intelligence of a scarcity of ammunition, and General Washington called upon the inhabitants to send to headquarters every ounce of lead or pewter at their disposal, saying that any quantity, however small, would be gratefully received. Now, it is difficult at this day to estimate the value of pewter then, as an ornament as well as an indispensable convenience. The more precious metals had not then found their way to the tables of New Englanders, and throughout the country, services of pewter, scoured to the brightness of silver, covered the board, even in the mansions of the wealthy.

Mrs. Draper was rich in a large stock of pewter, which she valued of course, as an excellent housewife would, but also much of it was precious to her as the gift of a departed mother. But the call of General Washington reached her patriotic heart and she delayed not obedience, thankful only that she was able to contribute so largely to the requirements of her suffering country. Nor was she satisfied with merely giving the material required. Her husband before joining the army had purchased a mold for casting bullets, and Mrs. Draper herself now transformed her platters, pans, and dishes into balls for the guns of the Continental Army. Such was the aid rendered by this woman whose deeds of disinterested generosity were never known beyond her own immediate neighborhood.

Who shall say that such an example of moral courage and self-sacrifice was not equal to the bravest deeds of the soldiers of the Revolutionary War, and that the report of the heroism of Captain Draper's wife exercised a more powerful influence over Captain Draper's men than all of his importuning to them to stand firmly by their guns in the cause of freedom.

MRS. RICHARD CRANCH.

Mary Smith, the elder sister of Abigail Adams, was married in 1762 to Richard Cranch, afterwards Judge of the Court of Common Pleas in Massachuchusetts. In 1775 the family moved from Boston to Quincy, then a part of Braintree, where they continued to reside till 1811. In October of that year both Mr. and Mrs. Cranch died and were buried on the same day: Mrs. Cranch is remembered for the work she accomplished in collecting supplies and clothing for the ragged army in the Revolution. Judge William Cranch was her son.

SABRINA ELLIOTT.

In times of national stress a turn of wit has often done more to strengthen the spirit of a cause than a deed of spectacular resistance. The following anecdote of Sabrina Elliott's wit illustrates the point. Living a widow, and unprotected, her home was raided by the enemy's soldiers, and the British officer in command personally supervised the plundering of her poultry houses. Afterward, in surveying the wreck, she observed straying about the premises an old muscovy drake which had escaped the general search. She immediately had him caught, and mounting a servant on horseback, ordered him to follow and deliver the bird to the officer, with her compliments and to express her grief that in the hurry of departure he had left such an important acquisition behind.

This story, laughed over by grim camp fires, did more to hearten the discouraged American soldiers than hysterical resistance to the enemy on the woman's part could possibly have done.

MARTHA WILSON.

Mrs. Wilson was the daughter of Colonel Charles Stewart, of New Jersey. She was born December 20, 1758, at "Sidney," the residence of her maternal grandfather, Judge Johnston, in the township of Kingwood and county of Hunterdon in that state. This old mansion was at that time one of the most stately and aristocratic of the colonial residences in that section of New Jersey. Constructed while the border settlements of the province were still subject to treacherous visits from the Indian, its square and massive walls and heavy portals were not only an expression of "the pride of life," but had reference as well to protection and defence, and for many years in its earlier use it was not only the stronghold of the wealthy proprietor, his family and dependents, but the refuge in alarm for miles around to the settlers whose humbler abodes were more assailable by the rifle and firebrand of the red men. "The big stone house," as it was designated in the common parlance of the people, was thus long noted as a place of refuge in danger and not less, in later times, as one of redress for wrongs and their punishment, Judge Johnston having been, for more than thirty years previous to the Revolution, the chief magistrate of that section of the colony, holding court on Monday of every week in one of the halls of his dwelling.

Such was the birthplace and home in childhood of Mrs. Wilson, but her girlhood and young womanhood, passed in the home of her father, was in no less beautiful and interesting surroundings. Previous to the Revolution, Colonel Stewart resided chiefly at "Lansdowne," a beautiful property immediately adjoining the estate of his father-in-law; and here, when she was thirteen, her mother having died, Mrs. Wilson already giving proof of mental attainments and maturity of character, entertained for her father the most distinguished men of the day. The hospitality of Colonel Stewart was unbounded. His friend, Chief Justice Smith, of New Jersey, expressed this trait of character in the epitaph upon his tomb: "The friend and the stranger were almost compelled to come in." And it was at his table and fireside in association with the choice spirits in intellect and public influence that his daughter imbibed the principles of patriotism and the love of liberty which entitles her name and character to a prominent place among women of the Revolution.

Colonel Stewart had, by energy of character and enlarged enterprise, secured both private and public influence, and the first breath of the "spirit of '76" which passed over the land fanned into flame his zeal for freedom and honor of his country, which no discouragement could dampen and which no toil, nor danger, nor disaster could extinguish. One of his daughter's strongest recollections was of being told, on his return from the first general meeting of the Patriots of New Jersey for a declaration of rights, an incident relating to himself and highly characteristic of the times. Many of the most distinguished royalists were his personal and intimate friends and when it became evident that a crisis in public feeling was about to occur, great efforts were made by some of those holding office under the crown to win him to their side. Tempting promises of ministerial favor and advancement were made to induce him to at least withhold his influence from the cause of the people, even if he would not take part in the support of the King. Such overtures were in vain, and at this meeting he rose and was one of the first boldly to pledge "his life, his fortune, and his sacred honor," in defence of the rights of freemen against the aggressions of the throne. The attorney-general, approaching and extending his hand, said to him in saddened tones, "Farewell, my friend Charles, when the halter is about your neck, send for me. I'll do what I can to save you." Colonel Stewart eventually became one of the Staff of Washington, as Commissary General of Issues, by Commission of the Congress of 1776.

Thus, Mrs. Wilson, who again became the head of her father's household, when her young husband, Robert Wilson, himself an ardent American adherent, died after barely two years of married life, was given an opportunity for more favorable observation and knowledge of important movements and events than that of any other woman certainly in her native state. Her father, at the head of an important department, from necessity became acquainted with the principal officers of the army, and headquarters being most of the time within twenty or thirty miles of her residence, she not only had constant intercourse in person and by letter with him, but frequently and repeatedly entertained at her house many of his military friends. Among these were Washington, La Fayette, Hamilton, Wayne, Greene, Maxwell, Lincoln, Henry Lee, Stevens, Walter Stewart, Ethan Allen, Pulaski, Butler, Sinclair, Woodward, Varnum, Paul Jones, Cochrane, Craik and many others.

General and Mrs. Washington were several times her guests, and the hospitality which Mrs. Wilson had the privilege thus repeatedly to extend to these illustrious guests was not forgotten by them, but most kindly acknowledged by very marked attentions to Mrs. Wilson's daughter and only child on her entrance into society in Philadelphia, during the presidency of Washington. By personal calls and invitations to her private parties, Mrs. Washington distinguished the young woman by consideration rarely shown to youthful persons.

It was not alone for friends and acquaintances and persons of distinction and known rank that Mrs. Wilson kept open house in the Revolution. Such was the liberality of her patriotism that her gates in the public road bore in conspicuous characters the inscription: "Hospitality within to all American officers and refreshment for their soldiers," an invitation not likely to be allowed to remain a mere form of words on the regular route of communication between northern and southern posts of the army.

From the commencement of the struggle for freedom till its close, Mrs. Wilson was a personal witness and participator in scenes of more than ordinary interest. She was in Philadelphia on the day the Declaration of Independence was made, and made one of a party—embracing the elite of the beauty, wealth and fashion of the city and neighborhood—to be entertained at a brilliant fete given in honor of the event, on board the frigate "Washington" at anchor in the Delaware, by

Captain Reed, the Commander. The magnificent brocade which she wore on the occasion, with its hooped petticoat, flowing train, laces, gimp and flowers, remained in its wardrobe unaltered for years, but was eventually cut up to become the victim of that taste of descendants for turning the antique frocks of grandmammas into eiderdown bedspreads and drawing-room chair covers.

Till the death of Colonel Stewart, in 1800, Mrs. Wilson continued at the head of his family, the wise, benevolent, energetic and universally admired manager of a house proverbial in her native state and extensively out of it, for generous and never changing hospitality. For a period of nearly fifteen years after the death of her father, much of Mrs. Wilson's time became necessarily devoted to the settlement of a large and widely scattered landed estate, and the clearness of judgment, practical knowledge and firmness of purpose and character witnessed in her by much of the finest talent at the bar and on the bench, not only in New Jersey, but in the adjoining states during the legal investigations of claims, titles and references, were such as to secure to her in general estimation a degree of respect for talent and ability not often accorded her sex in that day.

Not long after she had been called to the management of her father's estate, two orphan sons of her brother were left in their childhood to Mrs. Wilson's guardianship and maternal care. A series of letters written by her to one of these adopted sons, while a boy in school and college, have been given to the public, and their deep appreciation of the spirit of youth, and at the same time the inspiring guidance of their text makes them not only a striking exhibition of the fidelity with which she fulfilled her trust, but a contribution to literature.

The marriage of her only daughter and child, in 1802, to John M. Bowers, of Bowerstown, Otsego County, New York, led Mrs. Wilson to change her home from New Jersey to Cooperstown, New York, in which village for a long period afterward she had a home, but eventually she went to live with her daughter at the latter's beautiful home "Lakelands" in the immediate vicinity. Her end in the peaceful prosperity of her country was in marked contrast to her thrilling experiences during its struggle for Independence.

REBECCA MOTTE.

The manorial style of living, together with the slave labor, bred in the South during Colonial times developed a type of *grande dame* such as the more rigorous living in the northern colonies had not evolved at the time of the Revolution. But that the heroic strain existed in the women of social grace and softened loves, as well as in the stern Puritan Mothers, is fully illustrated in the sacrifice and heroism of Rebecca Motte. A few incidents of her life told without the least attempt at ornament show forth the rare energy and firmness of this woman, and her disinterested devotion to the American cause, as no rhetorical encomium could.

In 1758 she married Jacob Motte, one of the wealthiest men of the South and an ardent patriot, but his life was sacrificed early in the struggle for Independence, and having no son to perform his duty to the country, Mrs. Motte showed herself equal to the courage of men together with the dignity and diplomacy of the highest type of womanhood.

At different times during the first part of the war, it was her lot to encounter the presence of the enemy, and, surprised by the British at one of her country residences on the Santee, her son-in-law, General Pinckney, who happened to be with her at the time, barely escaped capture by taking refuge in the swamps. It was to avoid such annoyances that she removed to

"Buckhead," the then new and large mansion house between Charleston and Camden, to be known afterwards as Fort Motte because of the patriotism so strikingly displayed there by this daughter of South Carolina.

A British detachment under McPherson had seized the mansion house and occupied it with a garrison, removing Mrs. Motte, without ceremony, to an old farmhouse on a hill oppo- site the beautiful residence which was her legal home. The American force attempting to dislodge McPherson from this position was under Lieutenant-Colonel Lee and the intrepid Marion, and, receiving orders from General Greene to complete the surrender of McPherson, before he could be re-enforced by General Rawdon, who was proceeding to the Motte Mansion, on his retreat from Camden, they concluded that redoubled activ- ity was imperative. On account of the deep trench and strong and lofty parapet which McPherson had placed about the man- sion, there could be no direct assault attempted, and the only expedient left for compelling the immediate surrender of the garrison was to burn the homestead. This expedient was reluc- tantly resolved upon by Marion and Lee who, unwilling under any circumstances to destroy private property, felt the duty to be much more painful in the present case, since it must be done in sight of the owner, whose husband had been a firm friend to his country, and whose daughter was the wife of a gallant officer, then a prisoner in the hands of the British. Moreover, Lee had made the farmhouse dwelling of Mrs. Motte his quarters, and she, not satisfied with extending hospitality as liberal as possible to the officers of her country, had attended with active benevolence to the sick and wounded of the Ameri- can force. It was thus not without deep regret that the com- manders determined on the sacrifice and that the Lieutenant- Colonel found himself compelled to inform Mrs. Motte of the unavoidable necessity of the destruction of her property.

The smile, however, with which the communication was received gave instant relief to the embarrassed officer. Mrs. Motte not only assented, but declared that she was "gratified with the opportunity of contributing to the good of her country, and should view the approaching scene with delight." Moreover, shortly after, seeing by accident the bow and arrows which had been prepared to carry the balls of blazing rosin and brimstone to the shingled roof of the mansion, Mrs. Motte sent for Lee, and presented him with a bow and its apparatus, which had been imported from India, and was better adapted for the object than those provided.

The scorching rays of the noonday sun had prepared the roof for the conflagration, and, despite the efforts of McPherson's men to tear off the shingles as they caught fire, it soon became evident that the place could not be held against the flames, and the commandant hung out the white flag and surrendered the garrison.

"If ever a situation in real life afforded a fit subject for poetry," remarks one historian, "it was that of Mrs. Motte contemplating the spectacle of her home in flames, and rejoicing in the triumph secured to her countrymen—the benefit to her native land by her surrender of her own interest to the public service."

After the captors had taken possession of the fortified house, McPherson and his officers accompanied the victorious Generals to Mrs. Motte's dwelling, where they all sat down to a sumptuous dinner. Here again the value of their hostess' character shone. She showed herself prepared not only to give up her splendid mansion to insure victory to the American arms, but to do her part toward obliterating the recollection of her loss, and at the same time to remove from the minds of the prisoners the weight of their misfortune.

To her example of dignified, courteous and graceful conduct toward the defeated is doubtless due much of the magnanimity exercised by the visitors towards those who, according to strict rule, had no right to expect mercy. While the mingled party was still at the table, it was whispered in Marion's ear that Colonel Lee's men were even then engaged in hanging certain of the Tory prisoners. Marion instantly hurried from the table, seized his sword and, running with all haste, reached the place of execution in time to rescue one poor wretch from the gallows. With drawn sword and a degree of indignation that spoke more than words, Marion threatened to kill the first man that made any further attempt in such diabolical proceedings. Mrs. Motte's gentle kindness in the face of personal loss had pointed the way to Christian warfare.

When an attack upon Charleston was apprehended, and every man able to render service was summoned to aid in throwing up intrenchments for the defense of the city, Mrs. Motte dispatched a messenger to her plantation, and ordered down to Charleston every male slave capable of work, providing each, at her own expense, with proper implements and a soldier's rations. The value of this unexpected aid was enhanced by the spirit which prompted the patriotic offer.

When, indeed, the British took possession of Charleston, the house in which Mrs. Motte resided was selected as the headquarters of the English colonels in command, but she determined not to be driven out, and with inimitable grace and tact, she continued to preside at the head of her own table in a company of thirty British officers, who may have been disconcerted at being treated as guests, but who certainly could not complain of her hospitality. The duties forced upon her were discharged with exquisite tact, yet she always replied with spirit to the discourteous taunts frequently uttered in her presence against her "rebel countrymen." In many scenes of danger and disaster her fortitude was put to the test, yet, through all, this noble-spirited woman regarded not her own advantage, but always and ever the public good.

Perhaps one of the "biggest little" things Rebecca Motte ever did was the assumption of the responsibility of certain claims against her husband's depleted estate, he having become deeply involved by securities undertaken for his friends. Despite her friends' warning of the apparent hopelessness of such a task, she set about determinedly to devote the rest of her life to the task of honorably discharging those obligations, and steadfast in the principles that had governed all her conduct, she persevered. She procured on credit a valuable body of rice land, then an uncleared swamp, on the Santee, built houses for her negroes, and took up her abode on the plantation. Living in an humble dwelling and sacrificing all her habitual comforts, she so devoted herself with untiring industry to the problem before her that, in spite of the distracted state of the country, following the war, she eventually triumphed over every difficulty, and not only succeeded in paying her husband's debts, but secured for her children and descendants a handsome and unencumbered estate. As her biographer said: "Such an example of perseverance, under adverse circumstances, for the accomplishment of a high and noble purpose, exhibits in yet brighter colors the heroism that shone in her country's peril."

This woman of whom her state and country should be so justly proud, died in 1815 on the plantation on which her long years of retirement since the war had been passed, the seventy-seven years of her splendid life having embraced the most thrilling period of our Nation's life.

SUSANNAH ELLIOTT.

Closely connected with the better-known name and personality of Rebecca Motte, there lies in the memory of South Carolina history a proud recollection of

Susannah Elliott. She was the daughter of Benjamin Smith, for many years Speaker of the Assembly of the province, but left young an orphan and an heiress, she was brought up by her aunt, Mrs. Rebecca Motte, with whom she lived until her marriage. She seems to have absorbed much of Mrs. Motte's spirit of patriotism, and to history she is known principally through an incident that illustrates the effects of this inspiration. This was after her marriage to Colonel Barnard Elliott, when she presented a pair of colors embroidered by her own hand to the second South Carolina regiment of infantry, commanded by Colonel Moultrie, in commemoration of their illustrious bravery during the attack on Fort Moultrie, Sullivan's Island, which took place June 28, 1776. The colors, one of fine blue and the other of red silk, were received from Mrs. Elliott by the Colonel and Lieutenant-Colonel, and a solemn vow registered by the Colonel in the name of the soldiers that they should be honorably supported and never tarnished by a discreditable record of the second regiment. And this pledge was nobly fulfilled. Three years afterwards they were planted on the British lines at Savannah and the two officers who bore them having lost their lives just before the retreat was ordered, the gallant Sergeant Jasper in planting them on the works received a mortal wound and fell into the ditch. One of the standards was brought off in the retreat, and Jasper, having succeeded in regaining the American camp, said in his last moments: "Tell Mrs. Elliott I lost my life supporting the colors she presented to our regiment." The colors were afterwards taken at the fall of Charleston and were deposited in the Tower of London.

Mrs. Elliott was, moreover, most resourceful in her patriotism. While at her plantation called "The Hut," she had at one time some American officers as guests in the house, and when surprised by the sudden approach of the British, she calmly showed them into a closet, and opening a secret door disclosed a large opening back of the chimney known only to herself and contrived for a hiding place. The enemy, convinced that they had cornered their quarry, searched the house thoroughly but unsuccessfully, and failing further in all their attempts to induce Mrs. Elliott to reveal their place of retreat, the officers then demanded her silver. They discovered some mounds of earth not far off and began excavation, although the woman protested against the desecration. To their great chagrin, a coffin was disinterred from the first mound and Mrs. Elliott remarked that it was the grave of one of their countrymen, to whom she had endeavored to give decent burial. On opening the coffin the truth was at once made manifest, and the British soldiers then departed in extreme mortification, so that the silver which was buried close at hand escaped discovery.

Mrs. Elliott was beautiful in person—a fact attested to in her portrait which was, however, defaced by the act of a British soldier, a small sword having been run through one eye—and her face, inexpressibly soft and sweet-looking, yet gives witness to the strength and determination that marked the deeds of her life. The great men fighting for the nation at that time appreciated her worth, and among the papers in the possession of the family is a letter from General Greene to Mrs. Elliott expressive of high respect and regard and offering her a safe escort through the camp and to any part of the country to which she desired to travel.

ANN ELLIOTT.

Ann Elliott, too, the wife of Lewis Morris, won her fame and gave inspiration through a mere incident in her life. She was one of the belles of Charleston, when that city was occupied by the British, and she always insisted upon wearing a bonnet decorated with thirteen small plumes in order to flaunt her devotion to the struggling colonies, and for her patriotic spirit she was called "the beautiful rebel." At one time, while Colonel Morris, to whom she was then engaged, was on a visit to her, the attention of the family was drawn to the windows by an unusual noise and they perceived that the house was surrounded by the Black Dragoons, who had been informed of the young American's presence in the city. The American officer had no time to escape, but Ann Elliott went to one of the windows and calmly presenting herself to the view of the British Dragoons demanded what they wanted. "We want the—rebel," was the reply. "Then go and look for him in the American Army," answered the young girl. "How dare you disturb a family under the protection of both armies?" Her firmness and resolution conquered the day, and the enemy, somewhat confused, departed without pressing their search.

Later in life, Mrs. Lewis Morris received the praise of a prominent American General, who said: "She has ever been one of the most cheering examples of patriotic spirit; the influence of her active, courageous life has been felt deeply among the soldiers."

She died in New York on the 29th of April, 1848, at the age of eighty-six.

BEHETHLAND FOOTE BUTLER.

Behethland Moore was born on the 24th of December, 1764, in Fauquier County, Virginia. Her father, Captain Frank Moore, commanded as lieutenant one of the Virginia troops at Braddock's defeat. Her mother was Frances Foote. About 1768, her parents removed to South Carolina and settled on Little River, in Laurens District, where Captain Moore died two years afterwards. His widow then married Captain Samuel Savage, who in 1774 removed to a plantation just above what was then known as Saluda Old Town. Here Miss Moore and her two brothers, William and George, lived with her mother and stepfather.

On one occasion a band of Tories came to the house of Captain Savage and were taking off a Negro boy, who had been a personal attendant of Miss Moore's father in the Indian Wars. With no thought of risk to herself, she hastened after them to rescue him. The men finally compromised on being shown where the horses were and appropriating certain of them for their use. One horse proving refractory, they ordered the black servant to catch it for them, and when, at Miss Moore's direction, he refused, the Tory swore he would beat the servant for his disobedience, but the intrepid young girl threw herself between them and the grumbling Tory was forced to withdraw the intended violence.

When the Revolutionary War was in progress, it became necessary at one time to convey intelligence of danger to Captain Wallace, who was in command of a small force on the other side of the Saluda River just above her home. No male messenger could be procured, but Miss Moore, then but fifteen years of age, volunteered to undertake the mission. Accompanied by her little brother and a friend named Fanny Smith, she went up the river in a canoe in the middle of the night, gave warning to Captain Wallace and through him to Colonel Henry Lee, and thus a disastrous attack on our feeble troops was averted. The next morning a young American officer, who had been below this point on some reconnoitering service, rode up to the house to make a few inquiries. These were answered by the young lady who apparently appeared as pleasing to the young officer as this handsome fellow in dragoon uniform did to her, for this was the first occasion on which Miss Moore saw her future husband, Captain William Butler. The marriage took place in 1784 and the young people took possession of a small farm near Willing which Captain Butler had inherited.

General Butler was almost constantly engaged in public service, and was necessarily absent from home a great part of the time. In Congress from 1801 to 1814, and commanding the South Carolina forces in Charleston as Major-General during 1814 and 1815, naturally the whole care not only of the large family but of his plantation devolved upon Mrs. Butler. Never were such varied responsibilities more worthily met and discharged. The support of the family depended mainly upon the produce of the small farm and in the energetic toil of wringing profit from the soil. Mrs. Butler evinced a wonderful fertility of resource. Moreover, she superintended her children's education and did what few modern mothers with all their leisure accomplish, impressed upon them the moral point of view which always gives tone to character in after life. "With a singular power of command and stern energy," it has been said of her, "she combined the softest and most womanly qualities. In her it might be seen that a superior mind, rigidly disciplined, may belong to a woman without the development of any harsh or unfeminine lineaments, and that a heart the most tender and affectionate may prompt to all generous charities of life without being allied to weakness."

Her sons did illustrious service for their country and one of them is said to have declared on the occasion of his public honor that he deserved no credit since it had been his mother who instilled in his and his brothers' minds the old Greek idea that they were born but for their country.

DEBORAH SAMSON.

It has been said that in the early days of this Republic "men learned to fight and pray; the women to endure," but there are several instances in the history of the Revolutionary War in which a woman's courage was displayed by the actual adoption of man's work on the battle field. The resolution of Congress is on record in which honorable mention is made of the services of Margaret Corbin, the gunner's wife who took her husband's place when he was killed, at the battle of Monmouth, and did such execution that, after the engagement, she was rewarded with a commission. And there were many other examples, though generally of women who, having suffered incredibly from the spoliations of the enemy, lost patience, and fought manfully for the last loaf of bread or the last bed quilt for their children. But, in one case, the heroism and deeds, exploits and adventures of a woman soldier make her life seem a figment of pure imagination. This was Deborah Samson.

Deborah Samson was the youngest child of poor parents who lived in the colony of Plymouth, in Massachusetts. Poverty was the least of the evils suffered by the unfortunate children and, at length, their parents becoming so degraded that intervention was necessary, they were removed from the destructive influences, and placed in different families. Deborah found a home in the house of a respectable farmer, whose wife bestowed upon her as much attention as was usual in the case of any poor girl "bound out." The friendless and destitute girl was treated kindly, and, in exchange for her work, was provided with clothes and food, but no advantages of education. There was none to teach her, but she seized every opportunity for acquiring knowledge, even borrowing books from the children who passed the house on their way to and from school, and persevered with untiring exertion until she had learned to read quite well. Then, the law releasing her from her indenture, she found a place where, by working one-half time in payment for her board and lodging, she was able to attend the common district school in the neighborhood. In a few months she had acquired more knowledge than many of her schoolmates had done in years.

But the Revolutionary struggle had swept upon the country—the sound of the cannon at Bunker Hill had reached every hearthstone and vibrated in the heart of every patriot in New England, and the zeal which urged men to quit their homes for the battlefield found its way to the bosom of lonely Deborah Samson.

Much effort has been expended by historians and women annalists to extenuate the conduct of this woman who claimed the privilege of shedding her blood for her country, but, after all, it was a most natural decision. It is likely her youthful imagination was kindled by the rumor of the brave deeds possible in that varied war life, and it must be borne in mind, too, that she was alone in the world, with few to care for her fate, and so she felt herself accountable to no human being. Be that as it may, she took the scant twelve dollars she had earned by teaching the district school, and purchased a quantity of coarse fustian and, working at intervals, made up a suit of men's garments—each article as it was finished being hidden in a stack of hay. Having completed her preparations, she announced her intention of going where she might obtain better wages for her labor. The lonely girl departed, but probably only to the shelter of the nearest wood, before putting on the disguise she was so anxious to assume. Her features were animated and pleasing, and her figure, tall for a woman, was finely proportioned. As a man, she might have been called handsome—her general appearance said to have been prepossessing, and her manner calculated to inspire confidence.

She pursued her way to the American army where, in October, 1778, she was received and enrolled by the name of Robert Shircliffe, a young man anxious to join his efforts to those of his countrymen in their endeavors to oppose the common enemy. She was one of the first volunteers in the company of Captain Nathan Thayer, of Medway, Massachusetts, and the captain gave her a home in his family until his company should be ready to join the main army. In performing the duties and enduring the fatigues of military life, her sex passed unsuspected. Accustomed to labor, from childhood, upon the farm and in out-of-door employment, she had acquired unusual vigor of constitution; her frame was robust and of masculine strength, and she was enabled to undergo what a woman delicately nurtured would have found it impossible to endure.

For three years Deborah Samson appeared in the character of a soldier, and during that time the fidelity with which her duties were performed gained her the approbation and confidence of the officers. She was a volunteer in several hazardous enterprises, and was twice wounded, the first time by a sword cut on the left side of the head. About four months after this first wound she was again severely injured, being this time shot through the shoulder. Her first emotion, when the ball entered, she described to be a sickening terror at the probability that her sex would be discovered, but, strange as it may seem, she escaped unsuspected, and soon recovering her strength, was able again to take her place at the post of duty, as well as in the deadly conflict. Unfortunately, however, she was soon seized with brain fever, and for the few days when reason struggled against the disease her sufferings were indescribable, haunted by the terrible dread, as she was, lest consciousness should desert her and the secret so carefully guarded be revealed. She was carried to the hospital with a great number of soldiers similarly stricken, and, her case being considered hopeless, and partly owing to the negligent manner in which all patients were attended, she actually escaped detection for some days. But at length the physician of the hospital, inquiring "How is Robert?" received from the nurse in attendance the answer, "Poor Bob is gone." The doctor went to the bed and, taking the hand of the youth supposed to be dead, found that the pulse was still feebly beating, and attempting to place his hand on the heart, he perceived that a bandage was fastened tightly around the breast. This was removed and, to his uttter astonishment, he discovered in this fever-racked youth, a woman patient.

With prudence, delicacy and generosity of the highest order, this physician, Dr. Binney, of Philadelphia, kept his discovery to himself, but paid the patient every attention, and provided every comfort her perilous condition required. As soon as she could be moved with safety, he had her taken to his own house, where she could receive better care, his family wondering not a little at the unusual interest manifested in this particular invalid soldier.

But, once her health was restored, the physician had a long conference with the commanding officer of the company in which Robert had served, and this was followed by the issuing of an order to the youth, "Robert Shircliffe," to carry a letter to General Washington.

Deborah Samson's worst fears were now confirmed. From the time of her removal into the doctor's family she had misgivings that the doctor had discovered her deception, yet, in conversation, as she anxiously watched his countenance, not a word or look had indicated suspicion, and she had again begun to assure herself that she had escaped. When the order came for her to deliver a letter into the hands of the commander-in-chief, however, she could no longer deceive herself. There was nothing for it but to obey, but when she presented herself at Washington's headquarters she trembled as she had never done before the enemy's fire. When she was ushered into the presence of the chief, she was almost overpowered with dread and uncertainty. Washington noticed the extreme agitation, and bade her retire with an attendant, who was directed to offer the soldier some refreshment while he read the communication of which she had been the bearer.

Within a short time she was again summoned into the presence of Washington. The great man said not a word, but handed her in silence a discharge from the service, putting into her hand at the same time a notice containing advice and a sum of money sufficient to bear her expenses to some place where she might find a home. The delicacy and forbearance thus observed affected her sensibly. "How thankful," she is said to have often explained, "was I to that great and good man who so kindly spared my feelings. He saw me ready to sink from shame; one word from him at that moment would have crushed me to the earth. But he spoke no word, and I blessed him for it." This is an interesting sidelight on the character of Washington, wherein he is shown to have had the fine instinct of tact and sympathy even in his warrior days.

After the war had ended, Deborah Samson married Benjamin Gannett, of Sharon, and when Washington was President she received a letter inviting "Robert Shircliffe," or Mrs. Gannett, to visit the seat of the government. Congress was then in session, and during her stay in the Capital a bill was passed granting her a pension in addition to certain lands which she was to receive, as an acknowledgment of her services to the country in a military capacity. She was invited to the houses of several of the officers and to parties given in the city, attentions which manifested the high esteem in which she was held.

Deborah Samson-Gannett, in the capacity of wife and mother, lived to a comfortable old age, and finally yielded up her soul as any prosaic and worthy matron might, with no hint of mystery nor adventure in her past.

It has been well said: "Though not comparable, certainly, to the 'Prophetess' in whom France triumphed—for the dignity with which the zeal of a chivalrous age and the wonderful success of her mission invested her—yet it cannot be denied that this romantic girl exhibited something of the same spirit of the lowly herdmaid who. even in the round of her humble duties, felt herself inspired to go forth and do battle in her country's cause, exchanging her peasant's garb for the mail, the helmet, and the sword." At least Deborah Samson is a figure of brave strength and intrepid daring in the hour of her country's greatest peril.

MARGARET GASTON.

Heroism and strength of character, which in peaceful times would have remained latent in a serene personality, were often brought forth to shine most illustriously through pressure of cruelty in the Revolutionary War. Such was the case of Margaret Gaston. She was born Margaret Sharpe into a quiet old England household in the county of Cumberland, England, about 1755, and her parents desiring her to have every advantage of education in the Catholic faith, sent her to France when a very young girl. She was brought up in the seclusion and calm of convent life. Her two brothers, however, were extensively engaged in commerce in this country and she came out to visit them. Then began for this retiring, timid young woman, a tumultuous era of New World romance and soul-trying grief. It was during her sojourn that she met Dr. Alexander Gaston, a native of Ireland, of Huguenot ancestry, to whom she was married at Newbern, in the twentieth year of her age. But the happy married life of these two young people was destined to be of brief duration and tragic end.

Doctor Gaston was one of the most zealous patriots in North Carolina, and while his devotion to the cause of liberty won for him the confidence of the Whigs, it also gained him the implacable enmity of the opposite party. At length, so actively expressed was his patriotism and so great was his influence, a price was placed on his head by the loyalists.

On the 20th of August, 1781, a body of Tories entered Newbern, being some miles in advance of the regular troops, who had come by forced marches with a view to taking possession of the town. The Americans, taken by surprise, were driven to capitulation after an ineffectual resistance. Gaston, unwilling to surrender to the foe, hurried his wife and children across the river from their home, hoping to escape with them and proceed to a plantation eight or ten miles distant. "He reached the wharf with his family," the old account runs, "and seized a light scow for the purpose of crossing the river; but before he could stow his wife and children on board, the Tories, eager for his blood, came galloping in pursuit. There was no resource but to push off from the shore, where his wife and little ones stood—the wife alarmed only for him against whom the rage of the enemies was directed. Throwing herself in agony at their feet, she implored his life, but in vain. Their cruelty sacrificed him in the midst of her cries for mercy—and the musket which found his heart was levelled over her shoulder."

It is wonderful that the convent-bred girl did not go distraught, but, instead, a fierce heroic strength seemed to animate her whole being. Even the indulgence of grief was denied to the bereaved wife for she was compelled to exert herself to protect the remains of her murdered husband while her ears rang with the inhuman threats that the "rebel should not even have the rest of the grave." After she had found men brave enough to aid her in carrying the body home, she was obliged to protect the beloved lifeless form from desecration, and by its side she watched constantly until it was deposited in the earth through a midnight burial.

Margaret Gaston was now left alone in a foreign land—both her brothers and her eldest son having died before the tragic taking of her husband. A boy three years of age and an infant daughter demanded all the care and protection she could get for them in the pioneer country. Many women possessed of her sensibility and shrinking nature would have been overwhelmed, but the severe trials only served to develop the admirable energy of her character. She never laid aside the habiliments of sorrow; the anniversary of her husband's murder was kept as a day of fasting and prayer; and to the great object of her life—the support and education of her children, she devoted herself with a firmness and constancy which wrested success despite the most adverse conditions.

When she had finally sent her son to Princeton College, where he was soon bearing away the first honors, it happened that her house and furniture were destroyed by fire, yet her letters to him breathe not one word of the calamity which, with her slender resources must have been severely felt, because she feared he might feel called to abandon his studies and rally to her support. The fact that this son, William Gaston, became a distinguished citizen of the country, was to his mother a sufficient reward for all she had borne with deep piety and stoic reserve.

Those who spoke of Margaret Gaston invariably named her as the most dignified as well as the most devout woman they had ever seen. She survived the husband she had seen murdered thirty-one years, in which time she never made a visit save to the suffering poor. Her home life was yet one of great activity, attending the sick and indigent, and the poor sailors who came to Newbern looked to her as a ministering angel. She passed away in this town where she had stepped from the convent to become a bride.

SARAH BACHE.

Perhaps the best estimate of a woman who might otherwise shine only in the reflected glory of a distinguished father, may be obtained by a private view of her and her work through the eyes of a contemporary. The Marquis de Chastellux in a letter wrote the following description of Mrs. Bache, the daughter of Benjamin Franklin: "After a slight repast, we went to visit the ladies, agreeable to the Philadelphia custom, where morning is the most proper hour for paying visits. We began by Mrs. Bache. She merited all the anxiety we had to see her, for she is the daughter of Dr. Franklin. Simple in her manners, like her respected father she also possesses his benevolence. She conducted us into a room filled with work, lately finished by the ladies of Philadelphia. This work consisted neither of embroidered tambour waistcoats nor of artwork edging, nor gold and silver brocade. It was a quantity of shirts for the soldiers of Pennsylvania. The ladies bought the linen from their own private purses, and took a pleasure in cutting them out and sewing them themselves. On each shirt was the name of the married or unmarried lady who made it and they amounted to twenty-two hundred." To this picture illustrating how a woman of Mrs. Bache's standing found means to aid the struggling country may be added the commendatory words of Marquis de Marbois to Dr. Franklin, in the succeeding year—who speaks thus of the distinguished man's daughter: "If there are in Europe any women who need a model of attachment to domestic duties and love for their country, Mrs. Bache may be pointed out to them as such. She passed a part of the last year in exertions to rouse the zeal of the Pennsylvania ladies, and she made on this occasion such a happy use of the eloquence which you know she possesses, that a large part of the American army was provided with shirts, bought with their money or made by their hands. In her applications for this purpose, she showed the most indefatigable zeal, the most unwearied perseverance, and a courage in asking which surpassed even the obstinate reluctance of the Quakers in refusing."

Such is the outside impression of the worthy and charming daughter of Benjamin Franklin. Her own letters to her father and others show much force of character and an ardent, generous and impulsive nature. When in 1764 her father was sent to Europe in a representative capacity, she writes girlish, light-hearted observations and clever chatter, but in 1777, when the British army's approach had driven her and her young husband from their Philadelphia home, her letters to Dr. Franklin, then sent to France by the American Congress, are strong accounts of events, sound philosophy, and even some correct prophecy on the Nation's future—letters which must have been really helpful to the statesman abroad.

Mrs. Bache lived through stirring experiences, for the Revolution did not spare those of gentle breeding or station. On the 17th of September, 1777, four days after the birth of her second daughter, Mrs. Bache left town, taking refuge at first in the home of a friend near Philadelphia but afterward going up into the state, where they remained until the evacuation of the Quaker City by the British forces. The letters written to her father after her return to the Franklin house which had been used in the meantime as headquarters for Captain Andre, give a splendid picture of the prohibitive prices that existed in the Colonies at this time. "There is hardly such a thing as living in town, everything is so high," she writes. "If I was to mention the prices of the common necessaries of life, they would astonish you. I have been all amazement since my return; such an odds have two years made, that I can scarcely believe that I am in Philadelphia. They really ask me six dollars for a pair of gloves, and I have been obliged to pay fifteen pounds for a common calamanco petticoat without quilting that I once could have got for fifteen shillings."

These prices were owing to the depreciation of the Continental money; it subsequently was much greater. The time came when Mrs. Bache's domestics were obliged to take two baskets with them to market, one empty, to contain the provisions they purchased, the other full of Continental money to pay for them.

It has been said that every woman is a brief for womankind, and surely Mrs. Bache may be considered a composite reflection of the fate of the sheltered woman during the Revolution, and of how they bore their unaccustomed hardships and turned their talents to the benefit of the humble defenders of the nation.

The brilliant Sallie Franklin was born on the 11th of September, 1744. It was on the 29th of October, 1767, that she was married to Richard Bache, a merchant of Philadelphia, and a native of Seattle, in Yorkshire, England; 1807 marks the sad date when the still charming woman was attacked by cancer and removed to the city once more for the benefit of medical attendance. Her disease proved incurable, and on the 5th of October, 1808, she died in the historic house in Franklin Square, where Dr. Franklin had spent his last years.

In person Mrs. Bache was rather above the middle height, and in the latter years of her life she became very stout. Her complexion was uncommonly fair, with much color; her hair brown and her eyes blue like those of her father. Strong good sense, and a ready flow of wit, were among the most striking features of her mind. Her benevolence was very great and her generosity and liberality were apparently limitless. Her friends ever cherished a warm affection for her. It has been related that her father, with a view to accustoming her to bear disappointments with patience, was given to requesting her to remain at home and spend the evening over the chess-board, when she was on the point of going out to some meeting of her young friends. The cheerfulness which she displayed in every turn of fortune proves that this discipline was not without its good effect—also that Benjamin Franklin could teach his own family as well as the public, which has not always been demonstrated in the lives of statesmen.

ELIZA WILKINSON.

A vivid picture of the part borne by many women through Revolutionary trials and privations may be found in the letters of a young and beautiful widow living in the city of Charleston at the time of its occupation by the British under Prevost and the approach of Lincoln to its relief. The period was one of almost continual skirmishing and of harrowing the inhabitants by the British, and the young woman's graphic description of the occurrences makes one no less interested in her personality than in the stirring events of which she writes.

This was Eliza Wilkinson. Her father was an emigrant to America from Wales named Francis Yonge. He took possession of an island some thirty miles south of Charleston, calling it Yonge's Island. Mrs. Wilkinson was his only daughter. She had been married only six months when her husband died, and when the Revolutionary warfare swept down into her section of the country, exciting days came to her in protecting her property and escaping before British invasion and aiding our own wretched soldiers. At one time, when she had taken refuge in an inland plantation, she writes of the distressing condition of refugees passing that way. A large boatload of women and children hurrying for safety to Charleston stayed with them for a day or two and presented a sad spectacle of the miseries brought in the train of war. One woman with seven children, the youngest but two weeks old, preferred venturing her own life and that of her tender infant to captivity at the hands of a merciless foe.

"The poorest soldier," says another letter, "who would call at any time for a drink of water, I would take pleasure in giving it to him myself; and many a dirty, ragged fellow have I attended with a bowl of milk, for they really merit everything who will fight from principle alone; for from what I could learn, these poor creatures had nothing to protect and seldom got their pay; yet with what alacrity will they encounter danger and hardships of every kind."

At another time, two men belonging to the enemy rode up to the house and asked many questions, saying that Colonel McGirth and his soldiers were coming and that the inmates might expect no mercy. The family remained in a state of cruel suspense for many hours. Then, as Mrs. Wilkinson writes to a friend: "The horses of the inhuman Britons were heard coming in such a furious manner that they seemed to tear up the earth, the riders at the same time bellowing out the most horrid curses imaginable—oaths and imprecations chilled my whole frame. 'Where are these women rebels?' That was their first salutation." Nor was the fear of the household unfounded for Mrs. Wilkinson continues: "They plundered the house of everything they thought valuable or worth taking; our trunks were split to pieces and each mean, pitiful wretch crammed his bosom with the contents, which were our apparel." And when Mrs. Wilkinson ventured to beg that just a few articles be left to her, the soldier she addressed, so far from relenting, cast his eyes on her shoes and immediately knelt at her feet but to wrench the buckles from them. "While he was busy doing this," the letter continues, "a brother villain bawled out 'Shares there, I say shares.' So they divided the buckles between them. The other wretches were employed in the same way, taking not only buckles from the other women but ear-rings and rings, and when one protested against surrendering her wedding ring, they presented a pistol at her and swore if she did not deliver it immediately they would fire." But the ready wit of Mrs. Wilkinson appears to have suffered no eclipse even in such dire straits and she closes this letter with a quip: "So they mounted their horses—but such despicable figures! Each wretch's bosom stuffed so full, they appeared to be all afflicted with some dropsical disorder. Had a party of rebels (as they call us) appeared, we should have seen their circumference lessen."

After such unwelcome visitors, it is not surprising that the unprotected women could not sleep or eat. They went to bed without undressing and started up at the least noise, while the days were spent in anxiety. And yet one morning when Mrs. Wilkinson with her eyes fixed on the window—for she was continually on the watch—saw a party of Whigs dragging along seven Royalist prisoners, notwithstanding the injuries she had received from some of these very men, her kind heart relented at the sight of their worn-out condition, and, when the American soldiers had brought one of the Tory officers into her house, she took from her neck the only remaining handkerchief the British marauders had left her and with it bound up a wound in his arm.

The siege and capitulation of Charleston brought the evils under which the land had groaned to their height. Mrs. Wilkinson was in the city at this time and her letters tell of the hardships borne by those in the beleaguered community—the gloomy resignation to inevitable misfortunes and the almost abandonment of hope for relief. Yet with indomitable patriotism, Mrs. Wilkinson's independent spirits would find vent in sarcastic sallies at the enemy's expense. "Once," she writes, "I was asked by a British officer to play the guitar."

"I cannot play, I am very dull," she replied.

"How long do you intend to continue so, Mrs. Wilkinson?"

"Until my countrymen return, sir."

"Return as what, madam, prisoners or subjects?"

"As conquerors, sir."

The officer affected a laugh. "You will never see that, madam."

"I live in hopes, sir, of seeing the thirteen stripes hoisted once more on the bastions of this garrison."

"Do not hope so, but come, give us a tune on the guitar."

"I can play nothing but rebel songs."

"Well, let us have one of them."

"Not to-day—I cannot play—I will not play; besides, I suppose I should be put into the Prevost for such a heinous crime as chanting my patriotism!"

Like many others, Mrs. Wilkinson refused to join in the amusements of the city while in possession of the British but gave her energies to the relief of her friends. The women were the more active when military efforts were suspended, and we learn through Mrs Wilkinson's letters of the many ingenious contrivances they adopted to carry supplies from the British garrison to the gallant defenders of their country. Sometimes cloth for a military coat, fashioned into an appendage to feminine attire would be borne away unsuspected by the vigilant guards whose business it was to prevent smuggling, the cloth afterwards being converted into regimental shape. Boots "a world too wide" for the small feet that passed the sentry in them were often conveyed to the partisan who could not procure them for himself. A horseman's helmet has been concealed under a well-arranged head-dress, and epaulettes delivered from the folds of a matron's ample cap. Other articles in demand for military use were regularly brought away by some stratagem or other. And one can well imagine the cheer diffused about a desolate camp by the visits of women as sprightly and courageous as Mrs. Wilkinson.

The last of her letters of public interest is joyous with congratulations on the glorious victory of Washington over Cornwallis, so that the woman who had lived a brave, helpful life, through the darkest trial of her country, lived to know the glory of its independence and peace.

LYDIA DARRAH.

All who admire examples of courage and patriotism, especially those who enjoy the fruits thereof, must honor the name of Lydia Darrah. In 1777 she was living in Philadelphia—then under British occupation—with her brother. They were both members of the Society of Friends. Their house, selected, perhaps, on account of the unobtrusive character of its inmates, whose religion inculcated meekness and forbade them to practice the arts of war, had been chosen by the superior officers of the British army for private conference, whenever it was necessary to hold consultations on subjects of importance. On the second of December of that year the order to prepare her house for such a meeting concluded with these words: "And be sure that your family are all in bed at an early hour. We shall expect you to attend to this request. When our guests are ready to leave the house, you will be called, that you may let us out and extinguish the fire and candles." This injunction to retire early rang in her ears and, being intensely loyal to her country, the young girl determined that some move of importance was on foot against the Continental army. The evening closed in and the officers came to the place of meeting. Lydia had ordered her family to bed, and herself admitted the guests, after which she retired to her own apartments and threw herself upon the bed without undressing. In a short time she was listening at the keyhole of the room where the officers were assembled. There was a confused murmur of voices, but at length came silence, broken shortly by a voice reading a paper aloud. This proved to be an order for the English troops to quit the city on the night of the fourth and march out in secret to an attack upon the American army, then encamped at White Marsh. The young girl had heard enough. She stole back to her bed and lay there, listening to the beating of her own heart. She feigned sleep and let the officer knock thrice before she pretended to rouse up and go with the men to the door.

She thought of the danger that threatened the lives of thousands of her countrymen and at once determined to apprise General Washington of the danger. In the morning, under the pretense that it was necessary for her to go to Frankfort to procure flour for the household, she set out, stopping first at the British headquarters to secure from General Howe his written permission to pass the British lines. Fully realizing the dangers of her undertaking, she walked the five miles to Frankfort through the snow, and, having deposited her bag at the mill, pressed on toward the outposts of the American Army. At length she was met by an American officer, who had been selected by General Washington to gain information respecting the movements of the enemy. This was Lieutenant-Colonel Craig, and he immediately recognized Lydia Darrah. To him she disclosed the secret, after having obtained from him a solemn promise not to betray her individually, since the British might take vengeance upon her family. The officer took her timely warning to his Commander-in-Chief, and preparations were immediately made to give the enemy a fitting reception. Lydia Darrah pursued her way home through the snow, but with a lighter heart, carrying the bag of flour which had served as the ostensible object of her journey. Her heart beat anxiously as, late on the appointed night, she watched from her window the departure of the army—on what secret expedition bound she knew too well! She listened breathlessly to the sound of their footsteps and the trampling of horses, until they died away in the distance, and silence reigned through the city.

The next morning a sudden and loud knocking at her door brought her face to face with the British officer who had ordered the meeting at her house. His face was clouded and his expression stern.

"Were any of your family up, Lydia," he said, "on the night when I and my brother officers were in this house?"

"No," was the unhesitating reply; "they all retired at eight o'clock."

"It is very strange," mused the officer. "You, I know, were asleep, for I knocked at your door three times before you heard me; yet it is certain that we were betrayed, for, on arriving near the encampment of General Washington, we found his cannon mounted, his troops under arms and so prepared at every point to receive us that we were compelled to march back, without injuring our enemy, like a parcel of fools."

It is not known whether the officer ever discovered to whom he was indebted for the disappointment. None about her suspected the demure Quakeress, Lydia Darrah, of having snatched from the English the anticipated victory.

As for the intrepid woman herself, she went on leading her grave, quiet, subdued life, blessing God for her preservation, and no doubt rejoicing that it had not been necessary to utter an untruth in order to save the defenders of her country a cruel blow.

ELIZABETH MARTIN.

Nowhere in the history of the Revolution do we find greater piety and heroism displayed than in the life of Elizabeth Martin. Her maiden name was Elizabeth Marshall, and, a native of Carolina County, Virginia, she was probably one of the family from which descended Chief Justice Marshall, since of the same neighborhood. After her marriage to Abram Martin she removed to his settlement bordering on the Indian nation, in what was called District "Ninety-six," in South Carolina. The country at that time was sparsely settled, most of its inhabitants being pioneers from other states. Their proximity to the Indians had caused the adoption of some of the latter's savage habits, and for a time life was very crude indeed. Yet this district was among the foremost in sending to the Revolutionary field its hearty and enterprising troops to oppose the British.

At the commencement of the contest Elizabeth Martin had nine children, seven of whom were sons old enough to bear arms. When the first call for volunteers sounded through the land the mother encouraged patriotic zeal in them. "Go, boys," she said, "fight for your country, fight till death if you must, but never let your country be dishonored. Were I a man I would go with you."

At another time when Colonel Cruger, commanding the British at Augusta, stopped with several British officers at her house for refreshment, and one of them asked how many sons she had, she answered, "Eight." To a question as to their whereabouts she replied promptly, "Seven of them are engaged in the service of their country." "Really, Madame," observed the officer sneeringly, "You have enough of them." "No, sir," retorted the matron, "I wish I had fifty."

At the time of the siege of Charleston the sound of the cannon could be heard clearly in that part of the state and Mrs. Martin knew they must come from the besieged city. As report after report reached her ears she became more and more fearful lest each sound might be the knell of her sons, three of whom were then in Charleston. Their wives were with her and shared the same heart-chilling fears. They stood still for a few minutes, each wrapped in her own painful and silent reflections. At length the mother, lifting her hands and eyes toward heaven, exclaimed fervently "Thank God they are the children of the Republic!" Of the seven patriot brothers six were spared through all the dangers of partisan warfare in that region of dark and bloody ground. But the eldest, William M. Martin, was killed at the siege of Augusta, just after he had obtained a favorable position for his cannon by elevating it on one of the towers constructed by General Pickens. It is related that not long after his death a British officer, anxious to gratify his hatred of the Whigs by carrying fatal news of these gallant young men, called at the house of Mrs. Martin and asked if she had not a son in the army at Augusta. She replied in the affirmative. "Then I saw his brains blown out on the field of battle," said this monster, who anticipated triumph in the sight of a parent's agony. The effect of the startling announcement was, however, other than he had expected. Terrible as was the shock and aggrieved by the ruthless cruelty with which her bereavement was made known, no woman's weakness was yet allowed to appear. After listening to the dreadful recital, the only reply made by Elizabeth Martin was, "He could not have died in a nobler cause." The evident chagrin of the officer as he turned and rode away was treasured as a family tradition.

GRACE AND RACHEL MARTIN.

In reviewing the American Revolution, few people have realized how important the daring exploit of those two young women was in averting the British invasion in South Carolina. They were the wives of the eldest sons of the Martin family—all the members of which were distinguished for active service in the cause. While their husbands were at the front they remained with the mother, Elizabeth Martin, herself a prominent figure in the Revolution. One evening intelligence came to them that a courier conveying important dispatches was to pass that night along the road, guarded by two British officers. They determined to waylay the party and even at the risk of their own lives to obtain possession of the papers. For this purpose the young women disguised themselves in their husband's clothes, and being well provided with arms, took their station at the point on the road which they knew the escort must pass. It was late and they had not waited long before the tramp of horses was heard in the distance. It may be imagined with what anxious expectation they awaited the approach of the critical moment, on which so much depended. The stillness of the night and the darkness of the forest must have added to the terrors conjured up by busy fancies. Presently the courier with his attending guards appeared. As they came close to the spot, the disguised women leaped from their covert in the bushes, presented their pistols at the officers, and demanded instant surrender of the party and their dispatches. The men were completely taken by surprise and in their alarm at the sudden attack yielded a prompt submission. The seeming soldiers put the enemy on their parole, and having secured possession of the papers, hastened home by a short cut through the woods. No time was lost in sending the documents by a trusted messenger to General Greene. The adventure had a singular sequel. The bewildered officers thus thwarted in their mission returned by the same road they had come and stopped at the house of Mrs. Martin, asking accommodation as weary travelers for the night. The hostess inquiring the reason for their returning so soon after they had passed, they replied by showing their paroles, saying they had been taken prisoners by two rebel lads. The women rallied them upon their want of courage. "Had you no arms?" was asked. The officers answered that they had arms, but had been suddenly taken off their guard and were allowed no time to use their weapons. They departed next morning having no suspicion that they owed their capture to the very women whose hospitality they had claimed.

HANNAH WESTON.

Hannah Weston, who was a granddaughter of the famous Hannah Dustin, was born in Haverhill, Massachusetts, on the 27th day of November, 1758, and died on the 12th of December, 1856, living very nearly a hundred years. Her father, Captain Samuel Watts, gentleman, received his title as Captain by the royal concession of King George III, on the fourth day of May, 1756, under the hand of Governor Wentworth and Seal-at-Arms of Portsmouth, New Hampshire. In 1775 Hannah Weston was living with her husband and his sister, Rebecca, in a humble cottage in Jonesboro, Maine, with no thought of heroism or fame in the minds of any of the three. But word was brought to Josiah Weston that there was danger threatening their neighbors in Machias, who were about to strike a bold blow against England's tyranny and for American liberty. The people of Machias had erected a liberty pole which was plainly visible to the English warship "Margaretta" lying in the harbor. They had been ordered, in the name of the King, to take down the pole or suffer an attack by the British soldiers from the warship, commanded by Captain Moore. The Americans, under a young man known as Jerry O'Brien, determined to anticipate the attack and a messenger was sent to Josiah Weston's cottage for help and ammunition. Weston rallied a goodly number of men to go to the rescue, but there was little ammunition for them to take with them. As the recruits passed down the road, Hannah Weston sighed, for she believed her husband had gone on an almost desperate venture; there was to be much fighting and the American troops had each hardly enough powder to shoot a partridge. But suddenly a new thought flashed through her brain, and hastily putting on her shawl and bonnet she hastened out of the cottage. At twilight the young woman returned carrying in her arms a bag of something that appeared both bulky and heavy. "Why whatever have you got there?" asked Rebecca Weston, her husband's sister, in a voice that expressed querulous surprise. "Bullets," said Hannah Weston triumphantly. She emptied the bag of its contents. Out they tumbled and clattered—pewter mugs, platters, saucers and all sorts and sizes of spoons before the round-eyed maiden. "Quick, Rebecca!" continued Hannah, "We must melt these and make bullets for the men at Machias." "Machias!" gasped the girl, "Machias is a good sixteen miles away." "Never mind that; they must have ammunition. If there be not time to melt them, these pewter dishes must go as they are."

By the time the first streaks of light were showing under the Eastern sky the two women were ready to start out upon their journey. The pewter platters and spoons were secured in Hannah's strongest pillow-case, which made a burden of forty pounds to be borne over a distance of forest and marsh little traveled save by the Indians and the wolves. Shouldering the pillow-case full of material for ammunition, Hannah Weston, followed by Rebecca who carried a smaller bundle of food, set out upon her perilous enterprise with that confidence in God's protection that animated the women of those dark days with courage and upheld them with fortitude. It was necessary to leave the path at frequent intervals, and the masses of tangled woods and briers rendered progress so slow that the day was far advanced before they had reached one half of the journey's length that lay before them. Rebecca was almost fainting from fatigue, and Hannah, whose courage had

stimulated the younger girl to unwonted exercise, was now given to fear the consequences of a night's exposure in the woods and its attending dangers. She made
the younger woman sit down while she took up her burden and went forward to
explore. After much wandering she at length reached the crest of a knoll, toward
which she bent her faltering footsteps. Looking downward she saw a stretch of land
before her, and not far in the distance a house. Her heart gave a great bound, for
she knew that the humble dwelling lay on the outskirts of Machias. Hurrying
back she aroused the sleeping Rebecca and they headed forward to the cottage which
Hannah had seen from the hilltop. Here they rested until morning, for the kind
inmates declared that they were fit for nothing but their beds. The next morning
they pressed forward, but the sun was high in the sky when the two women made
their way into the little town of Machias, which wore a very bustling and important
expression. The first words which reached their ears were: " 'Margaretta' was
captured by brave Jerry O'Brien and his men, and they say the young English
captain is like to die from a shot fired by Sam Weston."

Hannah Weston heard the news with joy but some disappointment. "We
came to bring this ammunition to the men," she said, "but we have had our pains
for nothing." "No," answered Jerry O'Brien, on hearing this, "This pewter is in
the nick of time, for I warn you before many days be passed the English will be
upon us again. And, Mistress Weston, I promise your bullets shall do good work
when our visitors come." History will tell you that Jerry O'Brien was right. In
the attack by the British which followed, the pewter, which Hannah Weston's midnight journey through the woods had brought, was passed in bullets from the
muskets of the Americans into the ranks of the attackers with bitter and defeating
effect.

A merchant presented Hannah and Rebecca with twelve yards of "camlet,"
which was divided between them and made into two gowns. This was a small
pattern for two gowns, but the fashions of our great-grandmothers' days were very
simple. Girls of our times would turn up their noses at such a gift, but Hannah
and Rebecca Weston were greatly pleased, and for a hundred years their children
and grandchildren and great-grandchildren kept bits of these famous "camlet"
gowns, handing down from one generation to another scraps of the narrow petticoats
and short bodices as their most cherished heirlooms.

During the ninety-eight years of her life this heroine of Machias had seen
much of toil, sorrow and privation. But neither toil nor hardship nor sorrow
quenched her brave spirit or hardened the heart that made this woman always brave
to entreat and ready to help and comfort when danger threatened or sorrow came
near. For many years the grave of this historic woman lay unmarked in the little
sea-coast village of Jonesboro, Maine. Some six years ago her descendants from
all parts of the United States joined their efforts with the people of the remote
town and at last erected a monument fitting to commemorate the brave Hannah
Weston.

SALLIE WISTER.

On the twenty-fifth day of September, 1777, just two weeks after the battle
of the Brandywine, the British Army entered Germantown. On the same day, but

a few miles distant from the place, Sallie Wister, a bright and charming Quaker girl, sixteen years of age, began to keep a sort of journal of her observations and experiences. It was evidently written with the object of keeping her dearest friend, young Deborah Norris, informed of the exciting happenings of this period. But strangely it never reached the hands for which it was intended until years after the death of the writer. It was published as one of the most interesting and valuable records that has come down to us. Its clever descriptions of persons and events, its naive confessions of likes and dislikes, it roguishness and genial good humor and withal its dramatic spirit, make it an extremely illuminating human document. Instances are here depicted which are nowhere supplied by the published records. And this diary of a bright Quaker girl is a historical picture of social conditions in the midst of the most important scenes of the Revolutionary times. In the nine months covered by this account occurred the British capture of Philadelphia, the battle of Germantown, the surrender of Burgoyne, the skirmishes before Washington's intrenchments of White Marsh and the acknowledgment of American Independence by France. All these with many sidelights pass in review before us, over the pages of Sallie Wister's diary. At length when the British had really decamped, and Philadelphia was once more open to its rightful citizens, she exclaims, "The Red Coats have gone, the Red Coats have gone, and may they never, never, never return!"

With this happy cry Sallie's diary closes and our little Quaker, with her humors and follies, vanishes from our sight. Little is known of Sallie Wister's later days. History only tells us that she grew to womanhood, that she became "quite serious" and that she "died unmarried, April 21, 1804." We are left to wonder about the rest. Why did Sallie Wister grow serious and why did she never marry? All sorts of romantic reasons suggest themselves, for the Sallie Wister of her diary was the very girl to have "an interesting story." But we can get no further than surmise, and it is better, perhaps, not to puzzle with what came after, but to think of her always as the light-hearted mischievous Sallie Wister, who though only a little Quaker made a valuable contribution to American history through her diary.

BETTY ZANE.

When Ebenezer Zane of Berkley County, Virginia, pushed his way through the wilderness to the banks of the Ohio River he took with him to a rough-hewn log cabin just above Wheeling Creek not only his wife and family but a younger sister, Betty Zane. This was in 1772, and Betty Zane was then only sixteen years of age. It was a wild spot where the Zane cabin stood and perhaps the little maiden was lonely now and then, but restlessness and discontent were not among the ailments of the girls of Revolutionary days. The fact of surrounding danger and possibility of having to flee from their homes at a moment's notice made them cling all the more closely to the fireside and knit them all the more closely in the bands of family love and life.

Now in the year 1764 the Six Nations of the great Indian Confederacy in the American colonies had made a treaty by the terms of which warfare for a time came to an end. But English folly at last overtook the treaty after ten years of peace—a blunder for which the colonists had to pay dearly. "Cornstalk," the great Indian chief, had been killed by the Whites who suspected him unjustly, and the savages had begun a terrible war on the Virginia border. To protect these frontier settlers, in 1774, under the superintendence of Ebenezer Zane, Fort Henry, at first called Fort Fincastle, was built. The Fort was built in an open space and its main entrance was through a gateway on its eastern side, joining the struggling hamlet of Wheeling which consisted of about twenty-five log houses. It was three years before the Wheeling Creek pioneers had to use their Fort as a place of refuge and defence. Then one day in September, 1777, Sheppard, who was the military commander of Fort Henry, noticed scores of Indians in the neighborhood and felt sure that an attack would be made on the garrison. He ordered the settlers to shut themselves in the block houses within the fortification. Next morning the savages approached, and from the little garrison force of only forty-two fighting men thirteen were led out by Captain Samuel Mason to repulse the Indian attack. From the loopholes of the block house the besieged saw Mason's men cut down one by one until not a white man of the little band of fourteen was left. Reduced now to twenty-six defenders with a force of from three to five hundred Indians hemming them in on three sides, the garrison was in a desperate plight, yet they fought on day after day, always hoping for the help that did not come. And during this time little Betty Zane was running bullets, as were the other women in the fort, and sometimes firing the muskets to relieve the weary men. Then one day the commander stood with white, tight-drawn lips before the dauntless band. The horrible truth must at last come out. The ammunition was nearly exhausted. In a few hours there would not be a bullet for those brave hands to load with. What was to be done? Outside the palisades sixty feet from the fort stood Ebenezer Zane's log. house, and in it was a keg of ammunition. Who would dare risk death from bullets, tomahawks or by torture in the face of five hundred foes. Several men stepped out and offered themselves. But every man's life possessed a hundredfold value that day and it was a hard matter to decide. While the volunteers stood in silence before their leader, Betty Zane laid her hand on the commander's arm. "I will go," she said simply. "You!" he exclaimed in amazement, "Oh no, you're not strong enough or fleet enough, besides . . ." "Sir," said the brave girl firmly, "it is because of the danger that I offer, if I, a woman, should be killed, 'twere not so great a loss as if one of these men should fall. You cannot spare a man, sir. Let me go." And so the matter was settled. The gate was opened and swift as a deer sped the girl out beyond the pickets towards the little log cabin. Courage was the thing most admired by the North American Indians, and as five hundred Wyandottes saw the fleeing figure of the daring girl pass directly before them not a hand was raised to bow or musket. Not a man of them fired at Betty Zane. She passed into the cabin, seized up the keg of ammunition, wrapped her apron about it, and then once more ran the gauntlet of the enemy's fire. And this time there was need for desperate haste, for the Indians guessed her burden and a shower of arrows and shot was sent after her flying figure. But the messengers of death fell harmlessly about her or broke vainly against the walls of Fort Henry as Betty gained the entrance. The great gateway flew open and a dozen strong arms were stretched out to take the precious keg. Women wept and men sobbed as they realized

11

that Betty Zane had saved the fort. The next morning at daybreak Colonel McCulloch marched with a small force from Short Creek to the relief of the garrison and completed the work of its salvation begun by Betty Zane.

MOLLY PITCHER.

Among the true stories of the history of the American nation in the making none touches the blood with a warmer thrill of admiration than that of brave Molly Pitcher, whose heroism on Monmouth field has found lasting record in the pages of American history.

Some time during the middle of the eighteenth century there came to America from Germany an immigrant by the name of John Gurex Ludwig, who settled in the colony of Pennsylvania. Here in the town of Carlisle was born to the wife of John Gurex Ludwig, October 13, 1744, a little daughter, whom he called Mary. The Ludwigs being poor, Mary became a servant girl in the family of Doctor William Irvine, a gentleman living in Carolina. It was while employed in Doctor Irvine's household, no doubt, that "Molly," as she was familiarly known, first learned to love the country of her birth, and there she developed that patriotism and loyalty that was one day to make the humble servant girl a soldier and heroine.

In July, of the year 1769, Molly left the roof of her master, and became the wife of a barber named John Hays. Whether or not Molly filled her husband with warlike ambition is an open question, but, at any rate, Hays was commissioned gunner in Proctor's first Pennsylvania Artillery on the fourteenth day of December, 1775, "changing the peaceful occupation of cutting of hair with shears to the more exciting one of cutting off heads with cannon balls." With a loyalty born of devotion and unselfishness, Molly determined to follow her husband, so when Gunner Hays marched off with Proctor's first, Molly marched with him.

Through the din of battle, the heat of summer and the difficulty of winter the gunner and his wife followed the fortunes
of the American army. But it was not until the retreat of our
forces at Fort Clinton that Molly's first deed of daring became
a by-word in tent and camp. Finding that it was necessary to
leave the enemy in Pennsylvania, Hays started to fire his gun
as a parting salute to the British, but in the rush and confusion
of the moment he dropped his lighted match. There was no
time to lose, and there was danger of being captured, so he did
not stop, but Molly, who was behind him, seized the match from
the ground, ran to the gun, touched it off, and then scampered
down the hill as fast as her legs could carry her, to join the soldiers. This happened some months before the famous battle
of Monmouth.

Down in Monmouth Mountain the people never dreamed
that there would be any fighting in their midst. The murmur
of the sea on one side and the murmur of the pine forest on the
other made a melody of sound that shut out the roar of warfare,
so that the tramp, tramp, tramp of the British army that suddenly aroused them must have been a very great surprise. Sir
Henry Clinton had succeeded to the command of the British
army, with orders to New York and a line of march through
the Jerseys. And so it happened that Monmouth became the
scene of conflict, Washington, with his troops, having pressed
forward to head them off. Halting at a little place called
Allentown, the English commander found the American forces
at his front. He pushed on, however, and on the twenty-
seventh of June encamped at Monmouth Courthouse, on rising
ground, hemmed in on all sides by woods and marshes. General
Washington, with grave deliberation, decided to risk the fight,
and although the battle was heartily contested, the American
army was victorious. That memorable Sunday, the twenty-
eighth of June, 1778, was the hottest day that year. Yet,

through the dust and heat and smoke, Molly, the gunner's wife, carried water to her husband and the soldiers on the field all day. The little spring from which she fetched the water was at the bottom of the hill and, instead of a pail, she brought it in a pitcher, and this was the origin of her name, "Molly Pitcher," among the soldiers—a name that, from that day has become historic. There had been a fierce charge of the enemy's cavalry on Hays' gun, and just as she was returning with a refreshing draught for the almost perishing men, she saw her husband fall, mortally wounded. Rushing forward, she heard an officer say, "Wheel back the gun, there is no one here to serve it!" Checking the blinding rush of tears, Molly threw down her pitcher and seized the rammer of the gun. "I will fire it," she said, and taking her place beside the dead gunner's cannon she filled his place during the rest of the day.

The next day General Greene sent for Molly and brought her up to General Washington, who praised her for her courage, and presented her then and there with the commission of sergeant in the Continental army. As the half-dazed Molly stood before the great General in her soldier's coat and cap cheer after cheer for "Sergeant Molly Pitcher" went up from ten thousand throats. It must have been a stirring picture. Stately Washington and the blood-stained, smoke-begrimed figure of the gunner's wife.

The battle of Monmouth was the only battle of the Revolution in which every one of the thirteen colonies was represented, so Sergeant Molly's heroism is a matter of National as well as local pride. For eight years she did her part in the great struggle and when the war was over she went back to her old home in Carlisle, where she engaged employment as a nurse, and where in later years she kept a little shop. To the soldiers she was always Captain Molly Pitcher and the French officers and soldiers admired the woman soldier so much that whenever she passed their lines her sergeant's cocked hat was always filled with French coins. By a special act of state legislature she was given a pension of eighty dollars a year. There is more than a thrilling story in this woman's life; there is a lesson of loyalty and courage; a lesson of a life not to be spoiled by praise and popularity.

"Oh Molly, Molly with eyes so blue,
Oh Molly, Molly here's to you,
Sweet honor's role will aye be richer
To hold the name of Molly Pitcher."

MARY SLOCUMB.

If a plain, unvarnished narrative of the sayings and doings of the actors in our Revolutionary times—those unknown by name save in the neighborhood where they lived—could by some miraculous means be gathered and published, it would surpass in thrilling interest any romance ever written. And one of the most remarkable chapters of such a volume undoubtedly would be the career of Mary Slocumb. Her maiden name was Hooks and she was born in North Carolina in 1760. When she was about ten years old, her father moved into a region called Goshen, famous for years in North Carolina for the frank simplicity of its inhabitants and for their profuse and generous hospitality. Here were nurtured some of the noblest spirits of the Revolution. The constant presence of the Loyalists and Tories in the neighborhood and their depredations called for vigilance as well as bravery. Sometimes the barn or dwelling of an unfortunate Whig wrapt in flames lighted up the darkness; sometimes his fate was to be hung to a sapling and not infrequently similar atrocities were in like manner avenged upon the aggressors.

Accustomed to hear of such things and inured to scenes of danger, it is not to be wondered at that the gay and sprightly Mary Hooks should acquire a degree of masculine energy and independence with many really manly accomplishments, all of which stood her in good stead in the days to follow when her strength as well as her spirit were tried as the wife of a fighting patriot. Soon after the removal of the family to Goshen, her mother died and in 1777 her father married the widow of John Charles Slocumb, whose eldest son, Ezekiel Slocumb, eventually took her as an eighteen-year-old bride to his large plantation on the Neuse. To prevent and punish the frequent incursions of the Tories, her husband joined a troop of light-horse who, acting on their own responsibility, performed the duty of scouts, scouring the country wherever they had notice of any necessity for their presence. In these prolonged absences, young Mary Slocumb took the entire charge of the plantation. She used to say laughingly that she had done in those perilous times all that a man ever did, except "mauling rails," and to take away even that exception she went out one day and *split a few!*

While her husband was away on one of his excursions, General Tarleton and a large division of the British army took possession of his plantation, and the young wife was torn with anxiety lest Lieutenant Slocumb, who was known to be somewhere in the vicinity, should return to his home all unsuspecting and walk into the enemy's ambush. Yet her conduct betrayed none of this; with splendid dignity, rare in one so young, she received these invaders of her home and she addressed herself immediately to preparing a dinner of much elaborateness for the uninvited guests, but dispatching in secret a messenger to warn the American scouts.

Before the messenger could discover Lieutenant Slocumb's whereabouts in the wood, a party of British soldiers, whom Tarleton had sent out to reconnoiter, blundered upon the American scouters and in the skirmish that ensued, the sounds of which were heard with sinking heart by Mrs. Slocumb, more than half the British company was shot down, and suddenly, before the astonished British officers and the terrified wife, the owner of the plantation dashed into sight in hot pursuit of the retreating Tory who had been in command of the British troop. Mrs. Slocumb's messenger, an old negro, known as "Big George," sprang directly in front of his horse, shouting "Hold on, massa, de debbil here. Look you!" The imprudent young officer at once perceived the peril into which he had ridden. A gesture from his wife indicated the great encampment of some eleven hundred men in occupancy of his plantation and, quick as thought, he dashed down the avenue directly towards the house, calling the few Americans who were with him. On reaching the garden fence—a rude structure formed of a kind of lath and called a wattle fence—they leaped that and the next, amid a shower of balls, crossed a stream at one tremendous leap and scoured away across an open field and were in the shelter of the wood before their pursuers could clear the fence of the inclosure. A platoon had begun the pursuit but the trumpets sounded the recall before the flying Americans had crossed the stream, for the presence of mind and lofty language of the heroic wife had convinced the British Colonel that the daring men who so fearlessly dashed into his camp were supported by a formidable force near at hand. Had Mrs. Slocumb not so diplomatically concealed the truth, and the fugitives pursued, nothing could have prevented the destruction not only of the four who fled but the rest of the pitifully slender company of American scouts on the other side of the plantation.

As Tarleton walked into the house, he observed to the brave woman: "Your husband made us a short visit, madam, I should have been happy to make his acquaintance."

"I have little doubt," replied the wife, "that you will meet again the gentleman and he will thank you for the polite treatment you have afforded his wife!"

The Colonel mumbled an apology that necessity compelled them to occupy her property, but it is worthy of remark that he removed his troops before long and when the British army broke up their encampment at her plantation, a sergeant was ordered by Colonel Tarleton to stand in the door till the last soldier had gone out, to insure protection to a woman whose noble spirit had inspired him with the most profound respect.

The most remarkable occurrence in the career of this patriotic wife was the dream which led to her being the heroine of the battle at Moore's Creek, one of the bloodiest battles of the Revolution. Her husband, now Colonel Slocumb, was accustomed to dwell lightly on the gallant part borne by himself in that memorable action but he would give abundant praise to his associates, and he would add: *"My wife was there."* She was indeed; but the story is best told in her own words. "The troop left from this house with my husband Sunday morning and they got off in high spirits; every man stepping high and light. I slept soundly and quietly that night and worked hard all the next day, but I kept thinking where they got to—how far; when and how many Tories they would meet and all that, I could not keep myself from the study, and when I went to bed at the usual time I could not sleep for it. As I lay—whether waking or sleeping I know not, I had a dream; yet it was not all a dream. I saw distinctly a body wrapped in my husband's guard cloak—bloody—dead; and other dead and wounded all about him. I uttered a cry and sprang to my feet, and so strong was the impression on my mind that I rushed in the direction in which the vision appeared and came up against the side of the house. Seated on the bed I reflected a few moments; then said aloud: 'I must go to him.' I told my woman that I could not sleep and would ride down the road, and although she appeared in great alarm, I reassured her, telling her merely to lock the door after me and look after my little child. I went to the stable, saddled my mare, and in one minute we were tearing down the road at full speed. Again and again I was tempted to turn back. I was soon ten miles from home and my mind became stronger every mile I rode. That I should find my husband dead or dying was as firmly my presentiment and conviction as any fact of my life. When day broke I was thirty miles from home. I knew the general route our little army was to take and followed them without hesitation. Again I was skimming over the ground through a country thinly settled but neither my spirit nor my beautiful nag's failed in the least. We followed the well-marked trail of the troops.

"The sun must have been well up, say eight or nine o'clock, when I heard a sound like thunder which I knew must be a cannon. I stopped still; when presently the cannon thundered again—I spoke to my mare and dashed on in the direction of the fighting, and the shots and shouts now grew louder than ever. The blind path I had been following brought me into the Wilmington road leading to Moore's Creek Bridge a few hundred yards below the bridge, and a little distance from the road were lying perhaps twenty men. They were all wounded. Suddenly I knew the spot; the very trees and the position of the men I knew as if I had seen it a thousand times. I had seen it all night—it was my dream come true. In an instant my whole soul was centered upon one spot, for there, wrapped in his bloody guard-cloak, was, I was sure, my husband's body. I remember uncovering the head and seeing a face clothed with blood from a dreadful wound across the temple. I put my hand on the bloody face, and found it warm, but suddenly an *unknown* voice begged for water. A small camp-kettle was lying near and a stream of water was nearby. I brought it; poured some in his mouth; washed his face and behold it was Frank Cogdell—not my husband. He soon revived and could speak, and as I washed the wound in his head he said: 'It is not that; it is that hole in my leg that is killing me.' I took his knife, cut away his trousers and stocking and found that the blood came from a shot-hole through and through the fleshy part of his leg. I looked about and could see nothing that looked as if it would do for dressing wounds but heart-leaves, so I gathered a handful and bound them tight to the holes, and the bleeding stopped. I then went to the others and dressed the wounds of many a brave fellow who did good fighting long after that day. When the General appeared, he seemed very much surprised and was with his hat in his hand about to pay me some compliment when I interrupted him by asking: 'Where is my husband?' 'Where he ought to be, madam, in pursuit of the enemy. But pray,' said he, 'How came you here?'

"'Oh, I thought,' replied I, 'you would need nurses as well as soldiers. See! I have already dressed many of these good fellows, and there is one'—going to Frank Cogdell and lifting him up with my arm under his head so that he could drink some more water—'who would have died before any of you men could have helped him.'

"'I believe you,' said Frank. Just then I looked up and, my husband as bloody as a butcher and as muddy as a ditcher, stood before me.

"'Why Mary,' he exclaimed. 'What are you doing there? Hugging Frank Cogdell, the greatest reprobate in the army?'

"'I don't care,' I cried. 'Frank is a brave fellow, a good soldier and a true friend to Congress.'

"'True, true, every word of it,' said the General with the lowest kind of a bow.

"I would not tell my husband of my dream that had brought me; I was so happy, and so were all. It was a glorious victory. I knew my husband was surprised but I could see he was not displeased with me. It was night again before our excitement had at all subsided. But in the middle of the night I again mounted my mare and started for home. The General and my husband wanted me to stay until the next morning and they would send a party with me; but no, I wanted to see my child and I told them they could send no party that could keep up with me! What a happy ride I had back. And with what joy did I embrace my child as he ran to meet me."

In these days of railroads and steam, it can scarcely be credited that a woman actually rode alone in the night through a wild, unsettled country, a distance—going and coming—of a hundred and twenty-five miles; and in less than forty hours and without any interval of rest. Yet such was the feat of Mary Slocumb, and such was the altogether natural manner of relating her heroic deed, that it is as a modern woman might speak of having attended a social function of a somewhat exciting nature.

Of course, there are various explanations to be offered for the vision that produced an impression so powerful as to determine this resolute wife upon her nocturnal expedition to the battlefield, but the idea of danger to her husband, which banished sleep, was sufficient to call up the illusion to her excited imagination.

Mrs. Slocumb possessed a strong and original mind, a commanding intellect and clear judgment which she retained unimpaired to the time of her death. Her characteristic fortitude in the endurance of bodily pain—so great that it seemed absolute stoicism—should be noticed. In her seventy-second year she was afflicted with a cancer on her hand which the surgeon informed her must be removed with a knife. At the time appointed for the operation, she protested against being held by the assistants, telling the surgeon: "It was his business to cut out the cancer; she would take care of the arm," and bracing her arm on the table, she never moved a muscle nor uttered a groan during the operation.

At the age of seventy-six, on the sixth of March, 1836, she sank quietly to rest in the happy home on the plantation "Pleasant Green," where all these exciting scenes and stiring events of the Revolution had taken place.

SARAH REEVE GIBBES.

No better picture of the distress and, indeed, the cataclysm that the later campaigns of the Revolution brought into southern life can be offered than the story of the experiences of Sarah Reeve Gibbes. She was married when about eighteen to Robert Gibbes, a man considerably older than herself, but who possessed wealth and was in every case one of those gentlemen of the old school of whom South Carolina has justly made her boast. He had a house in Charleston, which had been the girlhood home of Miss Sarah Reeve, but they both preferred to spend most of the year at his country seat and plantation on John's Island, about two hours sail from the city. This was a splendid place, the various clusters of buildings resembling a settlement rather than one estate, while the beautifully laid-out grounds and shaded walks gave a most inviting aspect, and earned for its large, square, ancient-looking stone mansion the name of "Peaceful Retreat." Here the young wife devoted herself with earnestness to the duties before her. The children that came to them were many and strong, but before they were fully grown she assumed the care of seven orphan children of the sister of Mr. Gibbes, who at her death had left them and their estate to his guardianship. Two other children were before long added to her charge. Then she saw her husband gradually become a chair-ridden invalid with gout, and the management of the estate, with the writing on business it required, devolved absolutely upon Mrs. Gibbes. The multiplied cares involved in meeting all these responsibilities, together with the superintendence of household concerns, required a rare degree of energy and activity, yet the mistress of this well-ordered establishment dispensed the hospitality of "Peaceful Retreat" with such grace that it became famous. Unable by reason of his affliction to take active part in the war, the feelings of Robert Gibbes were nevertheless warmly enlisted on the Republican side and their house was ever open for the reception and entertainment of the friends of liberty. It was doubtless the fame of the luxurious living at this delightful country-seat which attracted the attention of the British during the invasion of Prevost, while the Royal army kept possession of the seaboard about Charleston. A battalion of British and Hessians determining to quarter themselves in so desirable a spot, arrived at the landing at the dead of night, and marching up in silence, surrounded the house.

The day had not begun to dawn when an aged and faithful servant tapped softly at the door of "Miss Gibbes'" apartment. The whisper "Mistress, the redcoats are all around the house," was the first intimation of their danger. "Tell no one, Caesar, but keep all quiet," she replied promptly, and her preparations for receiving the intruders were instantly begun. Having dressed herself quickly she went upstairs, waked several women guests and requested them to dress with all haste. In the meantime the domestics had waked the children, of whom with her own and those under her care, there were sixteen, the eldest being only fifteen years old. Mrs. Gibbes then assisted her husband as was her custom, to rise and dress and had him placed in his rolling chair. All these arrangements were made without the least confusion and so silently that the British had no idea any one was yet awake within the house. The object of all this preparation, by the clever woman, was to prevent violence on the enemy's part, by showing them at once that the mansion was inhabited only by those who were unable to defend themselves. The impressive manner in which Mrs. Gibbes drew the curtain on her pathetic drama produced its effect even on the hardened soldiers. The invaders had no knowledge that the inmates were aware of their presence till daylight, when the heavy rolling of Mr. Gibbes' invalid chair across the great hall toward the front door was heard. Supposing the sound to be the rolling of a cannon, the soldiers advanced and stood prepared, with pointed bayonets to rush in when the signal for assault should be given.

As the door was thrown open and the stately, though helpless form of the invalid was presented, surrounded by women and children, they drew back and, startled into an involuntary expression of respect, presented arms. Mr. Gibbes addressed them, and for a moment the pathos of his words seemed to halt the intended invasion. The British officers, however, soon took possession of the house, leaving the premises to their men, and making no proviso against pillage; so the soldiers roved over the place at their pleasure, helping themselves to whatever they chose, breaking into the wineroom, drinking to intoxication and seizing upon and carrying off the negroes.

Within the mansion, the energy and self-possession of Mrs. Gibbes still protected her family. The appearance of fear or confusion might have tempted the invaders to incivility; but it was impossible for them to treat otherwise than with deference a lady whose calm, quiet deportment commanded their highest respect. Maintaining her place as mistress of the household and presiding at her table, she treated her uninvited guests with a dignified courtesy that insured civility while it prevented presumptuous familiarity. The boldest and rudest among them bowed willingly to an influence which fear or force could neither have secured.

When the news of the occupation of the Gibbes Plantation—no longer, alas! in reality "Peaceful Retreat"—by the British reached Charleston, the authorities dispatched two galleys to dislodge them. The men were given strict instructions not to fire on the house for fear of injury to any of the helpless family, but it could not be known to Mrs. Gibbes that such a caution was to be taken, and as soon as the Americans began to fire, she decided that she must seek a place of safety for her family. The horses being in the enemy's hands, they had no means of conveyance, but Mrs. Gibbes, undaunted and desperate, to secure shelter for her helpless charges, set off to walk with the children and her husband—the latter pushed in his chair by a faithful servant—to an adjoining plantation. A drizzling rain was falling, and the weather was extremely chilly; moreover the firing from the boats was incessant and in a direction which was in range with the course of the fugitives. The shot falling around them cut the bushes and struck trees on every side. Exposed each moment to this imminent danger, they continued their flight with as much haste as possible for about a mile when they were at least beyond reach of the shot.

Having reached the house occupied by the negro laborers on the plantation, they stopped for a few moments to rest, and Mrs. Gibbes, wet, chilled, and exhausted by fatigue and mental anxiety, felt her strength utterly fail and she was obliged to wrap herself in a blanket and lie down upon one of the beds. Then, just when the fleeing party first drew breath freely, thankful that the fears of death were over, it was discovered, on reviewing the trembling group, that a little boy, John Fenwick, was missing. In the hurry and the terror of the flight, the child had been forgotten and left behind. Mrs. Gibbes not being equal to further effort she was obliged to see her little daughter, only thirteen years of age, set out upon the fearful peril of a return journey to the house. The girl reached the house still in possession of the enemy and persuaded the sentinel to allow her to enter. She found the child in a room in the third story, and lifting him joyfully in her arms carried him down and fled with him to the spot where her anxious parents were awaiting her return. The shot flew thickly around her, frequently throwing up the earth in her way, but with something of her mother's intrepidity, she had pushed through in safety.

Some time after these occurrences, when the family were again inmates of their own home, a battle was fought in a neighboring field. When the struggle was over, Mrs. Gibbes sent her servants to search among the slain for her nephew who had not returned. They identified him by his clothes, his face being so covered with wounds that he could never have been recognized. Life was, however, not extinct, and under the unremitting care of his aunt, he eventually recovered.

In after years, Mrs. Gibbes was accustomed to point out the spot where her eldest son when only sixteen years old had been placed as a sentinel, while British ships were in the river and their fire was poured on him. She would relate how, with a mother's agony of solicitude, she watched the balls as they struck the earth around him, while the youthful soldier maintained his dangerous post notwithstanding the entreaties of an old negro servant who hid behind a tree.

So, we, who enjoy the liberty and peace purchased at such fearful cost, cannot fully estimate the sacrifice of the heroines of the Revolutionary War. Sarah Reeve Gibbs exhibited always the same composure and the readiness to meet every emergency with the same benevolent sympathy for all unfortunates.

Mrs. Gibbes had a cultivated mind, and in spite of her many cares, still found leisure for literary occupation. Volumes of her writings remain, filled with well-selected extracts from the many books she read and accompanied by her own comments; also essays on various subjects, poetry, and copies of letters to her friends. Most of her letters were written after the war, and beside expressing the tenderest sensibility and refinement, throw interesting light on the pitiable condition of the southern sections at that time.

During the latter part of her life she resided at "Wilton," the country seat of a friend, "Peaceful Retreat" having become uninhabitable. At "Wilton" she died in 1825, at the age of seventy-nine. Her remains, however, were laid to rest in the family burial ground upon John's Island, the scene of her trials during the days of bloodshed and ruthlessness in the Revolutionary War.

HANNAH CALDWELL.

Not numbered among the heroic, the strong, the dashing or the prominent in the records of the Revolution but held in memory as one of its martyrs, is the name of Hannah Caldwell, whose barbarous murder was perpetrated not as "an act of vengeance upon an individual, but with the design of striking terror into the country and compelling the inhabitants to submission."

So far from producing this effect, however, the crime aroused the whole community to a state of belligerency before unknown. One of the journals of the day says: "The Caldwell tragedy has raised the resolution of the country to the highest pitch. They are ready almost to swear enmity to the name of Britain."

And yet, there was probably no one in all the colonies who was leading a quieter or more peaceful life than Hannah Caldwell. She was the daughter of John Ogden of Newark, and Hannah Sayre, a descendant of the Pilgrims. Her brothers were all stout Whigs, and in 1763 she married the Rev. James Caldwell, pastor of the first Presbyterian church in Elizabethtown (the Elizabeth of to-day), New Jersey, and he was one of the earliest to espouse the cause of this country. Her husband acted as chaplain of the Americans who occupied New Jersey, and his zeal in throwing the influence of his eloquence for the cause of freedom rendered him obnoxious to the enemy, and at length a price was put upon his head. It is said that while preaching the Gospel to his people he was often forced to lay his loaded pistols by his side in the pulpit. The church in which he preached became a hospital for the sick and wounded of the American army and the weary soldiers often slept upon its floor and ate their hurried and scanty meals from the seats of the pews so that worshippers were not infrequently compelled to stand through the service. But even this shelter the British and Tories, because of their anger toward the pastor of the church, determined to destroy, and accordingly it was burned with the parsonage on the night of January 25, 1780. The wife, Hannah Caldwell, fled into the interior of the state with her nine children, but even here there seemed no peace, for a body of Hessian and British troops had landed on the New Jersey coasts and were proceeding to spread devastation and terror throughout the colony. When informed of the enemy's approach, the pastor put his elder children into a baggage wagon which was in his possession as commissary, and sent them to some of his friends for protection. But three of the youngest, with an infant about eight months old, remained with their mother in the house, Mr. Caldwell having no fears for the safety of his wife and young family since he believed it impossible that "resentment could be extended to a mother watching over her little ones." He was called to join the force collecting to oppose the British marauders, and early in the morning, while his wife was handing him a cup of coffee, which he drank as he sat on horseback, he saw the gleam of British arms in the distance, and he put spurs to his horse. What followed is best given in the simple terrible account of the crime. Mrs. Caldwell herself felt no alarm. She placed several articles of value in a bucket and let it down into the well, and filled her pockets with silver and jewelry. She saw that the house was put in order and then dressed herself with care that, should the enemy enter her dwelling, she might, to use her own expression, "receive them as a lady." She then took the infant in her arms, retired to her chamber, the window of which commanded a view of the road, and seated herself upon the bed. The alarm was given that the soldiers were at hand. But she felt confident that no one could have the heart to do injury to the helpless inmates of her house. Again and again she said: "They will respect a mother." She had just nursed the infant and given it to the maid. A soldier left the road and, crossing a space of ground diagonally to reach the house, came to the window of the room, put his gun close to it and fired. Two balls entered the breast of Mrs. Caldwell; she fell back on the bed and in a moment expired.

After the murder Mrs. Caldwell's dress was cut open and her pockets were rifled by the soldiers. Her remains were conveyed to a house on the other side of the road, the dwelling was then fired and reduced to ashes with all the furniture, but the ruthless soldiers evidently desired her death to be known, that such a fate might intimidate the countryside.

Some attempts were made by the Royalist party to escape the odium of the frightful outrage by pretending that Mrs. Caldwell had been killed by a chance shot. The actual evidence, however, sets beyond question the fact that one of the enemy was the murderer and there is much reason to believe that the deed was deliberately ordered by those high in authority.

It seems peculiarly sad that such an end should have been the fate of a woman known as Hannah Caldwell was for her benevolence, serenity and sweetness of disposition, but the memory of this martyr to American liberty will long be revered by the inhabitants of the land, with whose soil her blood has mingled.

REBECCA BARLOW.

Rebecca Barlow was the daughter of Eli Nathan Sanford of Reading, Connecticut. By her marriage to Aaron Barlow she became the sister-in-law of Joel Barlow, the poet, philosopher and politician who, it is believed, owed much of the formation of his mind and character to this wife of his elder brother. Much of his time in early life was spent in the society of this sister-in-law, who was a woman of strong mind, and he has admitted that he wrote the "Columbiad" and other works under her inspiration.

When the stirring scenes of the Revolution began, both brothers felt called upon to act their part. The husband of Rebecca Barlow entering the service of his country was in a short time promoted to the rank of colonel. His military duties requiring long absences from home, the young wife was left in the entire charge of their estate and of their helpless little ones. At one time a rumor came that the British army was approaching and would probably reach her town that very night. The terrified inhabitants resolved on instant flight and each family, gathering together such of their effects as they could take with them, left the village and traveled the whole night to reach the only place of refuge available. Mrs. Barlow could not carry away her children and to leave them was out of the question. She therefore remained to protect them or share their fate in the deserted village. No enemy, however, was near, the groundless alarm having been excited by the firing of some guns below. The story of Mrs. Barlow's heroism in remaining alone in the village when the attack from the British was expected reached the ears of bluff General Putnam, then in command of a brigade of American troops in the vicinity. It is said that feeling a curiosity to make the acquaintance of a woman whose character so met with his strong appreciation, he took a stroll over the fields toward her house, wearing the clothes of a countryman, his ostensible errand being a neighborly request that Mrs. Barlow would be kind enough to lend him a little yeast for baking. Without ceremony he entered the kitchen, where the matron was busily engaged in preparing breakfast, and asked for the yeast. She had none to give, and told him so each time his request was repeated, without stopping her employment to look at the face of her visitor. It was not until after his departure that she was informed by her old black servant who it was who had asked the favor with such importunity. "I suppose," was her remark, "had I known him I should have treated him with rather more civility, but it is no matter now." General Putnam came away from the interview declaring that she was the proper material for the matrons of the infant nation. A few years after the war ended Colonel Barlow with his family removed to Norfolk, Virginia, where he subsequently fell a victim to the yellow fever, and after the burial of her husband and daughter Rebecca Barlow returned to her former home in Connecticut, where she died at an advanced age. Some of her sons have rendered important services to their country as statesmen. The youngest, Thomas, accompanied his uncle Joel, when serving as Minister Plenipotentiary at the court of France, as his secretary, and after the death of his uncle, in the winter of 1813 escorted his wife who had been left in Paris, to America. The remains of the Minister were brought with them and placed in the family vault at Washington.

ANNA BAILEY.

In every sense of the word Anna Bailey may be called a Daughter of the Revolution. At the time of the burning of New London, Connecticut, a detachment of the army of the traitor Arnold was directed to attack Fort Griswold, at Groton, on the opposite bank of the river. This fort was little more than a rude embankment of earth thrown up as a breastwork for the handful of troops it surrounded. Although the garrison defending it, under the command of the brave Colonel Ledyard, stood their ground they were overwhelmed by numbers, and after a fierce and bloody encounter the result was indiscriminate butchery of the Americans. On the morning after this massacre Mrs. Anna Bailey, then a young woman, left her home three miles distant and came in search of her uncle, who had joined the volunteers on the first alarm of invasion and was known to have been engaged in the disastrous conflict. His niece found him in a house near the scene of slaughter, wounded unto death. It was evident that life was fast departing. Perfect consciousness still remained and with dying energy he entreated that he might once more behold his wife and child. Such a request was sacred to the affectionate and sympathetic girl. She lost no time in hastening home, where she caught and saddled the horse used by the family, placed upon the animal the delicate wife, whose strength would not permit her to walk, and taking the child herself, bore it in her arms the whole distance and presented it to receive the blessing of its dying father.

With pictures of cruelty like the scene at Groton fresh in her memory, it is not surprising that Mrs. Bailey during the subsequent years of her life was noted for bitterness of feeling toward the enemies of her country. In those times of trial she nourished the ardent love of her native land and the energy and resolution which in later days prompted the patriotic act that has made her name so celebrated as the "Heroine of Groton." On the 13th of July, 1813, a British squadron appearing in New London Harbor, an attack, evidently the enemy's object, was momentarily expected. The most intense excitement prevailed among the crowds assembled on both sides of the river, and the ancient fort was again manned for a desperate defence. In the midst of the preparations for resistance, however, it was discovered that there was a want of flannel to make the cartridges. There being no time to cross the ferry to New London, Mrs. Bailey proposed appealing to the people living in the neighborhood, and herself went from house to house to make the collection, even taking garments from her own person to contribute to the stock. This characteristic instance of enthusiasm in the cause of her country, together with the impression produced by her remarkable character, acquired for her a degree of popularity which elevated her, as "Mother Bailey," to almost the position of patron saint in her state.

Her maiden name was Anna Marner until she married Captain Elijah Bailey of Groton. Her descendants throughout Connecticut have made a museum of Revolutionary relics from her belongings, but her gift to them has been the inheritance of strong mental faculties and ardent patriotism.

EMILY GEIGER.

In South Carolina, Emily Geiger's ride, though not as dramatic, is accorded all the eulogy of that of Paul Revere, as wrung from New England. It occurred when General Nathaniel Greene was moving his army toward Ninety-six, the most important post in the interior of South Carolina—it being his intention to capture this place if possible. Pursued by the British army under Lord Rawdon, he withdrew northward across the Saluda river. Here he heard that Rawdon's force had been divided and therefore immediately determined to send for General Sumter a hundred miles away, so that together they might make an attack upon the General. But in order to do this a courier must be dispatched quickly, and the journey was a difficult one through forests and across many rivers. By far the greatest hazard, however, lay in the fact that British soldiers guarded all the roads and that a large portion of the people living in that region were Tories. Indeed the difficulty was so great that no man would undertake the mission. At last a girl eighteen years old came to General Greene and offered her services for the desperate enterprise. This was Emily, daughter of John Geiger. The father was a true patriot, but being a cripple, was unable to serve as a soldier, and the daughter was anxious for a chance to have the family do something for the country. She was an expert horseback rider and familiar with the roads for many miles around. At first General Greene refused to send a defenseless girl on such a journey. But she insisted that being a woman she could do it with less peril than any man, and at length the General consented, giving her a letter to General Sumter. The first thing she did was to commit to memory the entire letter. Then she made ready for her journey. Unarmed, without provisions, this young girl bade the General and her friends good-bye and sped away.

She had crossed the Saluda River and was nearing Columbia when she was halted by three of Rawdon's scouts. To their questions she gave evasive answers, and observing that she came from the direction of the American army the scouts arrested her and took her directly to Lord Rawdon. She was not skilled in the art of concealing the truth and the British General became suspicious. Yet having the modesty not to search her himself, he sent for an old Tory matron who lived some distance away, as being more fitted for the purpose. Emily was not wanting in resource. As soon as the door was closed she tore the letter into bits, and one after another she chewed and swallowed the fragments. After a while the matron arrived. But although she ripped open every seam in the girl's garments she could find nothing contraband, and without further questioning Lord Rawdon permitted the girl to continue on her way. He even furnished her a guide to the house of one of her friends several miles distant. When the guide had left her she obtained a fresh horse from her patriot friend and continued her journey through swamp and forest by a circuitous road. The whole night long she rode until daylight, having been fully forty-eight hours in the saddle with the exception of the time lost at Rawdon's headquarters. After a short rest until early morning at the house of another patriot she pushed on. At three o'clock in the afternoon she rode into Sumter's camp, where almost fainting from fatigue and hunger, she delivered the message sent by General Greene. She had not forgotten one word of the letter and recited it from beginning to end as though she were reading it from the written sheet. Scarcely an hour passed before Sumter's army was ready for the march.

Two weeks after her ride of a hundred miles Emily Geiger returned home. She afterwards married a wealthy planter, and it is said that her descendants cherish a pair of ear-rings and a brooch given her by General Greene as well as a beautiful silk shawl presented to her by General Lafayette, when he was in this country in 1825.

ALICE IZARD.

The correspondence of Ralph Izard has been published and he has been acclaimed a great patriot. Few realize, however, how worthy, through her great executive ability, and her aid to him in the days of his invalidism, the wife of this patriot is of sharing his fame. She was the daughter of Peter Delancey, of West-

Engraved by J. Rogers from the Painting by D. M. Carter.

MOLLY PITCHER AT THE BATTLE OF MONMOUTH.

chester. She was married in 1767 to Ralph Izard. Mr. Izard represented his country abroad for many years but during part of the Revolutionary War their home was in Dorchester, South Carolina. An interesting anecdote related of Mrs. Izard illustrates well to what a severe trial the courage of American women was put during this stormy period. Her husband's life was sought by the British because of his ardent support of the cause of the colonies. At one time a number of British soldiers from Charleston invaded their plantation, surrounded the house and demanded that Mr. Izard give himself up. There seemed no way of escape, but his wife hastily concealed him in a clothes-press, while she awaited the entrance of his enemies. The search was instituted, which, proving unsuccessful, the soldiers threatened to fire the house unless he surrendered himself. In their rage and disappointment they proceeded to ransack the house. They fell upon the wardrobe of Mr. Izard and the marauders arrayed themselves in his best coats. Valuable articles were seized in the presence of the mistress of the house, and an attempt was even made to tear the rings from her fingers—all of this being done to draw the fire of her temper and compel her to disclose her husband's whereabouts. But through all the trying scene Mrs. Izard preserved in a wonderful manner her self-control. So calm and dignified was she that the plunderers, doubting the correctness of the information they had received, and, perhaps, ashamed of themselves, withdrew. No sooner were they gone than Mr. Izard made his escape across the Ashley and gave notice to the Americans on the other side of the river of the approach of the enemy. The neighborhood rallied, met the British detachment, and so completely routed them that few of their party returned within their lines to relate the disaster.

After the Revolution Mr. and Mrs. Izard found their estate in a condition of lamentable dilapidation, and they would probably have come, as did many others at that period, to poverty and suffering but for the energy and good management of Mrs. Izard, who soon restored good order and rendered the "Elms," the old family residence, a seat of domestic comfort and liberal hospitality. During her husband's illness, which lasted several years, she was his devoted nurse, while the management of the estate, embarrassed by losses sustained during the war, devolved upon her. She conducted all of his business correspondence, and found time to read to him several hours every day, and notwithstanding these cares each day was marked by some deed of quiet charity. In the faithful preformance of the duties before her and in doing good for others her useful life was closed in 1832, in the eighty-seventh year of her age.

DORCAS RICHARDSON.

Dorcas Richardson, bearing more than her share of the terrible trials which fell to woman's lot in the Revolutionary War, affords a splendid example of the modest heroism and humble, cheerful faith of the women of that time. She was the daughter of Captain John Nelson, a native of Ireland, and was married at the age of twenty to Richard Richardson, with whom she went to live on a plantation on the Santee River in South Carolina. In this home of peace, contentment and abundance she enjoyed all the comforts of southern country life among the pros-

12

perous class until the outburst of that storm, in which the fortunes and happiness
of so many patriots were wrecked. At the commencement of the war her husband
was captain of a company of militia, and when the three regiments of regulars from
South Carolina were raised and officered in 1775 he was made a colonel. But at the
surrender of Charleston he was taken prisoner, and in violation of the terms of
capitulation he was sent to a military station on Johns Island. With the aid of his
wife he made his escape, and returned to the neighborhood of his home, where he
concealed himself in the Santee Swamp. At this time the British troops had
overrun the state, and Colonel Tarleton seized upon the house of Colonel Richardson as a station for his regiment of cavalry. The enemy lived luxuriously on the
abundance of this richly-stocked plantation, but Mrs. Richardson was restricted to
a single room and allowed but a scanty share of the provisions furnished from her
own stores. Even here she exercised great self-denial, that the wants of the one
dear to her might be supplied. Every day she sent food from her own small
allowance to her husband in the swamp, by an old Negro, in whose care and discretion she could trust implicitly. Expecting the seizure of her horses and cattle
by the British she had Colonel Richardson's favorite riding horse sent into the
swamp for concealment. This horse was shut up in a covered pen in the woods,
which had once been used for holding corn—thence his cognomen "Corncrib," a
name which clung to the famous charger through the great battlefields on which
he afterward figured. Mrs. Richardson not only sent provisions to her husband in
his place of shelter but sometimes ventured to visit him, the stolen meetings being,
of course, full of consolation to the fugitive soldier. The British being informed
of Richardson's escape naturally concluded that he was somewhere in the vicinity
of his family, and a diligent search was instituted, scouts being sent in every direction. It was only through the most determined efforts on the part of his wife that
the searchers were frustrated. Not infrequently did the officers, in the most
unfeeling manner boast in the presence of the wife of what they would do to her
husband when they should capture him. On one occasion some of the officers
displayed in the sight of Mrs. Richardson their swords reeking with blood, probably that of her cattle, and told her that it was the blood of her husband whom
they had killed. At another time they said that he had been taken and hanged.
And in this state of cruel suspense she sometimes remained for several successive days unable to learn the fate of her husband and not knowing whether to
believe or distrust the horrible tales brought to her ears. Once only did she deign
the reply, "I do not doubt" she said, "that men who can outrage the feelings of a
woman by such threats are capable of perpetrating any act of treachery and
inhumanity toward a brave but unfortunate enemy. But conquer or capture my
husband if you can do so before you boast the cruelty with which you mean to
mark your savage triumph. And let me tell you meanwhile that some of you, it
is likely, will be in a condition to implore his favor before he will have need to
supplicate or deign to accept yours." This prediction was literally verified in more
than one instance during the remainder of the war.

One day, when the troops were absent on some expedition, Colonel Richardson ventured on a visit to his home, but before he thought of returning to his
refuge in the forest, a patrolling party of the enemy appeared at the gate. Mrs.

Richardson's presence of mind and calm courage were in requisition, and proved the salvation of the hunted patriot. Seeing the British soldiers about to come in, she pretended to be intently busy about something in the front doorway and stood there retarding their entrance. The least appearance of agitation or fear, the least change of color, might have betrayed all by exciting suspicion, but with a self-control as rare as admirable she hushed even the wild beating of her heart, and continued to stand in the way till her husband had time to retire through the back door into the swamp near at hand.

Later Colonel Richardson left his retreat in the woods to go to the aid of General Marion, and together with a handful of men they made several successful sorties on the enemy. The British were not long in discovering that the Colonel had joined the force of Marion, and their conduct toward his wife was at once changed. One and all professed a profound respect for her brave and worthy husband, whose services they were desirous of securing. They endeavored to obtain her influence to prevail on him to join the Royal Army by promise of wealth and honorable promotion. The high-spirited wife treated all such offers with the contempt they deserved and refused to be made an instrument in their hands for the accomplishment of their purpose. She sent constant messages to her husband in his exile assuring him that she and the children were well, and provided with an abundance of everything necessary for their comfort. Thus with heroic artfulness did she conceal the privations and want she was suffering, lest her husband's solicitude for her and his family might tempt him to waver from strict obedience to the dictates of honor and patriotism.

When peace returned to shed its blessings over the land, Mrs. Richardson continued to reside in the same house with her family. Tarleton and his troopers had wasted the plantation and destroyed everything movable about the dwelling, but the buildings had been spared, and Colonel Richardson, who had been promoted for his meritorious service in the field, cheerfully resumed the occupation of a planter. His circumstances were much reduced by the chance of war, but a competence remained, which he and his wife enjoyed in tranquillity and happiness for many years.

Mrs. Richardson died in 1834 at the advanced age of ninety-three. She was remarkable throughout life for the calm judgment, fortitude and strength of mind, which had sustained her in the trials she suffered during the war, and protected her from injury and insult when surrounded by a lawless soldiery.

ELIZABETH FERGUSSON.

Elevated by her talents and attainments to a position of great influence and an intimacy with the great men of her time, Elizabeth Fergusson's life appears to have been darkened by sadness and the cloud of a charge of having attempted by bribery to corrupt a general of the Continental Army. And yet when she died, at sixty-three years of age, there was a wide circle of adherents who believed in her independence and integrity of character. She was born in 1739 and was the daughter of Doctor Thomas Graeme, living in a palatial home in Philadelphia afterward known as the Carpenter Mansion. When she was quite young her mother's death called her to manage her father's house and to preside at the entertainments given for his visitors. Later the mansion became the headquarters of the literary coterie of that day, with Miss Graeme as presiding genius. Her brilliant intellect, her extensive and varied knowledge, her vivid fancy and cutivated taste made her an authority on things literary and political.

It was at one of these evenings that she first saw Hugh Henry Fergusson, a young gentleman lately arrived in this country from Scotland. They were pleased with each other at the first interview being congenial in literary tastes and a love of retirement. Their marriage took place in a few months, notwithstanding the fact that Fergusson was ten years younger than Miss Graeme. Not long after this event Doctor Graeme died bequeathing to his daughter the country seat "Graeme Park," in Montgomery County, which she had always loved. But the happiness anticipated by Mrs. Fergusson in country seclusion and her books was of brief duration. The contentions were increasing between Great Britain and America and finally they resulted in the war for independence. It being necessary for Mr. Fergusson to take part with one or the other, he decided according to the prejudices natural to his birth, and espoused the royal cause. From this time on a separation took place between him and his wife, she feeling unable to look upon the desolations and miseries of her countrymen and have any sympathy with England. In spite of this protested sympathy for the American cause, and her secret acts of charity for the benefit of suffering American soldiers and their wives, she was to be accused of trying to purchase the close of the war for England. It happened in this way: In Philadelphia she met Governor Johnson, one of the commissioners sent under parliamentary authority to settle the differences between Great Britain and America.

He expressed a particular anxiety to have the influence of General Reed exerted toward ending the war, and asked Mrs. Fergusson, should she see the General to convey the idea that provided he could, "comfortably to his conscience and view of things," exert his influence to settle the dispute "he might command ten thousand guineas, and the best post in the government." In reply to Mrs. Fergusson's question as to whether General Reed would not look upon such a mode of obtaining his influence as a bribe, Johnson immediately disclaimed any such idea and said such a method of proceeding was common in all negotiations; that one might honorably make it to a man's interest to step forth in such a cause. In the end Mrs. Fergusson seems to have been persuaded, and she sought out General Reed, who on hearing the proposition brought by her from Governor Johnson made the prompt and noble reply, "I am not worth purchasing; but such as I am, the king of Great Britain is not rich enough to do it."

General Reed laid before Congress both the written and verbal communications of Governor Johnson, withholding, however, the name of the lady. But of course an account of the transaction was also published in the papers of the day and it was useless to attempt concealment of her name; suspicion was at once directed to her and her name was called for by a resolution of the Executive Council of Pennsylvania. Congress issued a declaration condemning the "daring and atrocious" attempts made to corrupt its members and declaring it incompatible with their honor to hold any manner of correspondence with the said George Johnson.

Brilliant Elizabeth Fergusson reaped a harvest of censure and humiliation. In a letter to General Reed, she says: "I own I find it hard, knowing the uncorruptness of my heart to hold out to the public as a tool of the commissioners. But the impression is now made, and it is too late to recall it." And again from her now impoverished estate she writes: "Among the many mortifying insinuations that have been hinted on the subject none has so sensibly affected me as an intimation that some thought I acted a part in consequence of certain expectations of a post or some preferment from Mr. Johnstone to be conferred on the person dearest to me on earth."

And so, a careless political transaction deprived this woman of world-wide knowledge, of marked poetical talent and of a beautiful and benevolent spirit, of all the influence she once wielded so royally. She died at the house of a friend near Graeme Park, on the twenty-third of February, 1801.

ELIZABETH PEABODY.

Elizabeth Smith, better known as Mrs. Stephen Peabody, was the sister of Abigail Adams, and was also remarkable in character and influence. She was born in 1750 and married the Reverend John Shaw, of Haverhill. Her second husband was the Reverend Stephen Peabody, at Atkinson. Like her distinguished sister, she possessed superior powers of conversation, combined with a fine person and polished and courtly manners. Her house at Haverhill was the center of an elegant little circle of society for many years after the Revolution, and the most cultivated and learned from Boston and its vicinity gathered there.

Her correspondence shows her to have been an ardent patriot and advocate for her country. "Lost to virtue, lost to humanity must that person be," she writes to her brother-in-law, John Adams, "who can view without emotion the complicated distress of this injured land. Evil tidings molest our habitations and wound our peace. Oh, my brother! Oppression is enough to make a wise people mad."

Mrs. Peabody's very useful life terminated at the age of sixty-three.

JANE THOMAS.

It is in wild and stirring times that such spirits as Jane Thomas are matured and rise in their strength. She was a native of Chester County, Pennsylvania, and the sister of the Rev. John Black of Carlisle, the first president of Dickinson College. She was married about 1740 to John Thomas, supposed to be a native of Wales, who had been brought up in the same county. Some ten or fifteen years after their marriage Mr. Thomas removed to South Carolina. Their residence for some time was upon Fishing Creek in Chester District. About the year 1762 he removed to what is now called Spartanburg District and built a home upon Fair-forest Creek, a few miles above the spot where the line dividing that district from Union crossed the stream. From being adjutant and captain of the militia, Colonel Thomas was elected to lead the regiment raised in this district. In an engagement with the British early in the Revolution he was taken prisoner and sent to Charleston, where he remained in durance until the close of the war. The district about his home was then continually robbed and pillaged by British invaders. The Whigs were robbed of their horses, cattle, clothing and every article of property of sufficient value to be taken away. In this state of things Mrs. Thomas showed herself a bright example of boldness of spirit and determination. While her husband was prisoner in a local jail before his removal to Charleston she paid a visit to him and her two sons, who were his companions in rigorous captivity. By chance she overheard a conversation between some Tory women, the purport of which deeply interested her. One said to the others, "To-morrow night the Loyalists intend to surprise the Rebels at Cedar Springs." The heart of Mrs. Thomas was thrilled with alarm at this intelligence, for Cedar Springs was within a few miles of her own house, and among the Whigs posted there were some of her own children.

Her resolution was taken at once for there was no time to be lost. She determined to warn them of the enemy's intention before the blow could be struck. Bidding a hurried adieu to her husband and sons she was upon the road as quickly as possible, rode the intervening distance of nearly sixty miles the next day, and arrived in time to give information of the impending danger. The moment this body of Whigs knew what was to be expected a party of consultation was held and measures were immediately taken for defence. So successful were their strategic preparations that when the foe advanced warily upon the supposed sleeping camp sudden flashes and shrill reports of rifles revealed the hidden champions of liberty and the British finding themselves assailed in the rear by the party they had expected to strike unawares gave themselves over to overwhelming defeat. The victory thus easily achieved was due to the spirit and courage of a woman. Such were the matrons of that day! Not merely upon this occasion was Mrs. Thomas active in arousing the spirit of independence among its advocates, and another instance of her intrepid energy is still remembered. Early in the war Governor Rutledge sent a quantity of arms and ammunition to the house of Colonel Thomas to be in readiness for any emergency that might arise. These arms were under a guard of twenty-five men, and the house was prepared to resist assault. When, however, word was brought to Colonel Thomas that a large party of Tories was advancing to attack him, he and his guard deemed it inexpedient to risk an 'encounter with a force so much superior to their own, and they retired, carrying off as much ammunition as possible. Mrs. Thomas was left alone with only two youths and a few women to guard the considerable supply of powder and arms which was necessarily left behind. The Tories advanced and took up their station, supposing the place to be heavily guarded, and demanded the treasure. Their call for admittance was answered by a volley from the upper story which proved most effectual. The old-fashioned batten-door, strongly barricaded, resisted their efforts to demolish it. Meanwhile Mrs. Thomas urged on the youths to continue their fire from the upper windows, she loading their guns as fast as they discharged them. Believing that many men were concealed in the house and apprehending a sally, the enemy retired as rapidly as their wounds would permit, little dreaming that almost the sole defender of the house had been a woman.

Mrs. Thomas was the mother of nine children and her sons and sons-in-law were active in the American service. She thus became liable to some share in the enmity exhibited by the Royalists to another matron against whom the charge, "She has seven sons in the Rebel Army," was an excuse for depredations on her property. If Jane Thomas had but five sons she saw to it that her daughters married men who were both brave and efficient patriots.

Mrs. Thomas was a woman of considerable beauty, with black eyes and hair, fair complexion and a countenance sprightly and expressive. Soon after the close of the war Colonel Thomas and she removed to the Greenville District where they resided until their death.

MARTHA BRATTON.

The year 1780 was a dark period for the patriots of Carolina, and in this time of trial none bore the distress or aided the cause with more courage and sagacity than shrewd Colonel Bratton and his wife. Mrs. Bratton was a native of Rowan County, North Carolina, where she married William Bratton, a Pennsylvanian of Irish parentage, who resided in the York District in the state of South Carolina. Although Charleston surrendered, and General Lincoln and the American army became prisoners of war, the inhabitants of York District were offered British protection if they would swear allegiance to the crown. But almost to a man they refused to give their paroles, preferring resistance and exile to subjection and inglorious peace. Many of them banded themselves together under such men as Colonel Bratton, and harassed the victorious enemy by sudden and desultory attacks. They were unpaid, and depended on their own exertions for everything necessary to carry on the warfare. British officers and troops were dispatched to every nook and corner of South Carolina to banish every Whig with the utmost disregard of conditions, but the largest detachment of these was met and attacked by the party under the command of Colonel Bratton. From that time on a price was set on this patriot's head. It was at this time that the heroism of the wife of Colonel Bratton was nobly displayed. While her husband was at the front one night a British officer rudely entered her house demanding where her husband was.

"He is in Sumter's army," was the undaunted reply. The officer then essayed persuasion and proposed to Mrs. Bratton that she induce her husband to come in and join the Royalists, promising that he should have a commission in the royal service. Mrs. Bratton answered staunchly that she would rather see him remain true to duty and his country even if he perished in the American Army. Enraged at this he sought by violence to get the information that might endanger her husband's safety. He even stood by while one of the common soldiers, seizing a reaping hook that hung near them on the piazza, brought it to her throat with the intention of killing her. She would undoubtedly have died, taking the secret of her husband's hiding place with her to the grave, had not the officer second in command interposed and compelled the soldier to release her.

Mrs. Bratton was then ordered to prepare supper for the British and it may be conceived with what feelings she saw her house occupied by the enemies of her husband and her country and found herself compelled to minister to their wants.

What wild and gloomy thoughts had possession of her soul is evident from the desperate idea, afterwards confessed to, which occurred to her of playing a Roman matron's part and mixing poison, which she had in the house, with the food they had to eat. But her noble nature shrank from such an expedient. She well knew the brave spirit that animated her husband and his comrades, and that her husband would not approve of such a desperate deed. They might even now be tagging the footsteps of this enemy; they might be watching the opportunity for an attack. She would not have them owe to a cowardly stratagem the victory they should win on the battlefield. So, having calmly prepared the repast, she retired with her children to an upper apartment.

After they had eaten, the British officer drew his men to another house about half a mile off to pass the night. They lay in camp about it, the guard keeping negligent watch and little dreaming of the scene that awaited them. Mrs. Bratton had, in the meantime, dispatched a trusted messenger to her husband with word of the position and number of the enemy. He thereupon marshalled his pitiful troop of only seventy-five men and proceeded against the impromptu British encampment attacking it rear and front at the same time. The British officer failed to rally his men, and the spirit and determined fervor of the patriots carried all before them. This victory was due to the presence of mind of one loyal American woman.

About daylight, when the firing had ceased, Mrs. Bratton ventured out, fearful of finding her nearest and dearest among the dead and dying lying about the building, but none of her loved ones had fallen. She opened her house to the wounded of both sides and humanely attended the sufferers in person, giving them indiscriminately, Loyalist and Whig alike, every relief and comfort in her power to bestow. The sequel to this chapter of her courage and resolution is interesting. The leader of the British troops having been slain in the battle, the next officer in command took his place and he was among the prisoners who surrendered to the Whigs. They determined to put him to death. He entreated as a last favor to be conducted to the presence of Mrs. Bratton. She instantly recognized him as the officer who had interfered and saved her life. Gratitude, as well as the mercy natural to woman's heart, prompted her now to intercede for him. She pleaded with an eloquence which, considering the share she had borne in the common distress and danger, could not be withstood. Her petition was granted. She procured the officer's deliverance from the death that awaited him and entertained him in her own house until he was exchanged. There is hardly a situation in romance or dramatic fiction which can surpass the interest and pathos of this simple incident.

Another anecdote is related of Mrs. Bratton. Before the fall of Charleston, when resistance throughout the state was in a great measure rendered impossible by the want of ammunition, Governor Rutledge had sent on a supply to the regiment to enable them to harass the invading army. The portion given to Colonel Bratton was in his absence from home confided to the care of his wife. Some Loyalists who heard of this informed the British officer in command of the nearest station and a detachment was immediately sent forward to secure the valuable prize. Mrs. Bratton was aware that there could be no chance of saving her charge but she resolved that the enemy should not have the benefit of it. She therefore immediately laid a train of powder from the depot to the spot where she stood and when the British detachment came in sight set fire to the train and blew it up. The explosion which greeted the ears of the foe informed them that the object of their expedition was frustrated. The officer in command demanded who had dared to perpetrate such an act, and swore vengeance upon the culprit. The intrepid woman answered for herself: "It was I who did it. Let the consequence be what it will I glory in having prevented the mischief contemplated by the cruel enemies of my country."

Colonel Bratton continued in active service throughout the war, and during his lengthened absences from home he was seldom able to see or communicate with his family. Mrs. Bratton, however, never complained, although herself a sufferer from the ravages of war, but devoted herself to the care of her family, striving at the same time to aid and encourage her neighbors. On the return of peace the husband resumed the cultivation of his farm. Grateful for the preservation of their lives and property, they did everything in their power to the other homes that had been wrecked by death and devastation. Mrs. Bratton died in 1816 and is buried near the scene of her distress and suffering during the war.

MRS. SPALDING.

The wife of a patriot during the Revolution should be sufficient title to a place among the world's heroines. But it is only through the lives of those few whose cases have passed them into the class of super-woman that we call emphasis to the brave spirit which must have upheld them. Of such an embodiment of the spirit of the Revolution was Mrs. Spalding, the wife of one of the patriots who took refuge in Florida, after Colonel Campbell had taken possession of Savannah. In 1778 Mrs. Spalding left her residence with her child when flight became necessary. Twice during the war she traversed two hundred miles between Savannah and St. John's River in an open boat, with only black servants on board, and the whole country a desert without a house to shelter her and her infant son. The first of these occasions was when she visited her father and brothers while prisoners in Savannah; the second, when in 1782 she went to congratulate her brothers and uncle in their victory. At one time she left Savannah in a ship of twenty guns, built in all points to resemble a sloop of war. Without the appearance of a cargo, it was in reality a small merchantman engaged in commerce. When they had been out some days, a large ship, painted black and showing twelve guns on a side, was seen to the windward running across their course. She was obviously a French privateer. The captain announced there was no hope to out-sail her should their course be altered nor would there be wisdom in conflict, as those ships usually carried one hundred and fifty men. Yet he rather thought if no effort were made to shun the privateer the appearance of his own ship might deter an attack. Word of the peril was sent to Mrs. Spalding, who was below, and after a few minutes the captain visited her to find a most touching scene. Mrs. Spalding had placed her children and the other inmates of the cabin in the two staterooms for safety, filling the berths with cots and bedding from the outer cabin. She had then taken her own station beside the scuttle which led from the outer cabin to the magazine, and there she stood ready with two buckets of water. Having noticed that the two cabin boys were heedless she had determined to keep watch herself over the magazine. This she did until the danger was passed. The captain took in his light sails, opened his ports, and stood upon his course. The privateer waited until the ship was within a mile, then fired a gun to windward and stood on her way. The ruse had saved the merchantman. The incident may serve to show the spirit of this woman, who bore her bitter part in the perils of the Revolution.

MARGARET ARNOLD.

Defence as well as eulogy is occasionally necessary in reviewing the names of women who have been prominent in American history. Certainly explanation or investigation of fact is necessary in rightly judging the character of the wife of Benedict Arnold. John Jay, writing from Madrid when Arnold's crime had first become known, says, "All the world here curses Arnold and pities his wife." Robert Morris writes, "Poor Mrs. Arnold! Was there ever such an infernal villain!" But there are others who still believe in her complicity in her husband's plot to betray his country, and point to certain significant sentences in her correspondence with André as denoting that she knew at least something of her husband's treachery. The facts of her life would seem to support the theory that all her sympathy would naturally lie with the Loyalist's cause. She was Margaret Shippen of Philadelphia. Her father, Daniel Shippen, afterwards chief justice of Pennsylvania, was distinguished among the aristocracy of the day. He was prominent after the commencement of the contest among those known to cherish Loyalist principles—his daughters being educated in this persuasion and having their constant associations and sympathies with those who were opposed to American independence. Margaret was the youngest, only eighteen years of age, beautiful, fascinating and full of spirit, she acted as hostess of the British officers while their army occupied Philadelphia. This gay, young creature accustomed to the display of the "Pride of Life" and the homage paid to beauty in high station, was not one to resist the lure of ambition.

Her relatives, too, would seem to have passed their estimate upon the brilliant exterior of this young American officer, without a word of information or inquiry as to his character or principles. One of them writes boastfully in a letter, "I understand that General Arnold, a fine gentlemen, lays close siege to Peggy."

Some writers have taken delight in representing this woman who married Benedict Arnold as another Lady Macbeth, an unscrupulous and artful seductress whose ambition was the cause of her husband's crime. But there seems no real foundation even for the supposition that she was acquainted with his purpose of betraying his trust. She was not the person he would have chosen as the sharer of a secret so important, nor was the dissimulation attributed to her consistent with her character. It is likely, of course, that his extravagance was encouraged by his young wife's taste for display and she undoubtedly exercised no saving influence over him. In the words of one of his best biographers, "He had no domestic security for doing right—no fireside guardianship to protect him from the tempter. Rejecting, as we do utterly, the theory that his wife was the instigator of his crime, we still believe that there was nothing in her influence or association to overcome the persuasions to which he ultimately yielded. She was young, gay and frivolous, fond of display and admiration and used to luxury; she was utterly unfitted for the duties and privations of a poor man's wife . . . Arnold had no counsellor in his home who urged him to the assumption of homely republican principles, to stimulate him to follow the ragged path of a Revolutionary patriot. He fell, and though his wife did not tempt or counsel him to ruin, there is no reason to think she ever uttered a word or made a sound to deter him." This was the judgment of Mr. Reed. Mrs. Sparks and others, who have closely investigated the subject, are in favor of Mrs. Arnold's innocence in the matter. We cannot but have great sympathy at least for the young wife, whose husband was to go down in history as the foremost traitor to his country.

It was after the plot was far advanced and only two days before General Washington commenced his tour, in the course of which he made his visit to West Point that Mrs. Arnold came thither with her baby to join her husband, making the journey in short stages in her own carriage. Near New York she was met by General Arnold, and proceeded up to headquarters. When Washington and his officers arrived at West Point, Lafayette reminded the General that Mrs. Arnold would be waiting breakfast, to which Washington answered, "Ah, you young men are all in love with Mrs. Arnold, and wish to get where she is as soon as possible. Go breakfast with her and do not wait for me." Mrs. Arnold was at breakfast with her husband and his aid-de-camp when the letter arrived which brought to the traitor the first intelligence of André's capture. He left the room, immediately went to his wife's chamber, sent for her and privately informed her of the necessity of his instant flight to the enemy. This was perhaps the first intelligence she received of what had been so long going on, and the news so overwhelmed her that when Arnold went from the room he left her lying in a faint on the floor.

Her almost frantic condition is described with sympathy by Colonel Hamilton in a letter written the next day. "The General went to see her, and she upbraided him with being in a plot to murder her child. She raved, shut the doors and lamented the fate of the infant. All the loveliness of innocence, all the tenderness of a wife, and all the fondness of a mother showed themselves in her frenzied conduct." He, too, expressed his conviction that she had no knowledge of Arnold's plan until his announcement to her that he must banish himself from his country forever. Mrs. Arnold went from West Point to her father's house, but was not long permitted to remain in Philadelphia, the traitor's papers having been seized by direction of the executive authorities and the correspondence with André brought to light. Suspicion rested on her, and by an order of the council, dated April 27th, she was ordered to leave the state and return no more during the continuance of the war. She accordingly departed to join her husband in New York. The respect and forbearance shown towards her on her journey through the country, notwithstanding her banishment, testified to the popular belief in her innocence. It is related that when she stopped at a village where the people were about to burn Arnold in effigy they put it off until the next night. And when she entered the carriage on the way to join her husband all expression of popular indignation was suspended as if respect for the shame she suffered overcame their indignation towards Arnold.

Mrs. Arnold resided with her husband for a time in the city of St. Johns, New Brunswick, and was long remembered by persons who knew her there. She afterwards lived in England, surviving her husband by three years, and died in London in 1804, at the age of forty-three. Little is known of her after the blasting of the bright promise of her youth by her husband's crime and a dreary obscurity hangs over the close of her career. It is to her credit that her relatives in Philadelphia always cherished her memory with respect and affection.

RACHEL CALDWELL.

The history of North Carolina is in many ways identified with the life of the Reverend David Caldwell and his wife Rachel Caldwell. Mrs. Caldwell was the third daughter of the Reverend Alexander Craidhead, the pastor of what was known as the Sugar Creek congregation, and in her early life she had a share in many of the trials and hardships of the Indian War; the attacks of the savages being frequent and murderous, and her home being quite an exposed station. She often said in describing these attacks that as the family would escape out one door the Indians would come in at another. When defeat left the Virginia frontier at the mercy of the savages, Mr. Craidhead fled with some of his people, and crossing the Blue Ridge passed to the more quiet regions of Carolina, where he remained till the close of his life. Rachel married Dr. Caldwell in 1776. He was called the Father of Education in North Carolina, because his celebrated classical school was for a long time the only one of note in the state, and so great was the influence of Mrs. Caldwell in his school that it gave currency to the saying throughout the country, "Doctor Caldwell makes the scholars and Mrs. Caldwell makes the preachers."

Doctor Caldwell's pronounced preaching for freedom, however, made him an object of especial enmity to the British and Tories, and finally a reward of two hundred pounds was offered for his apprehension. This necessitated his going into hiding and leaving Mrs. Caldwell alone and unprotected during those days when every part of the country was subject to all manner of spoliation and outrage. On the eleventh of March the British army was dispatched to the Caldwell plantation and camped there, the officers taking possession of the house. They at first announced themselves as Americans and asked to see the mistress. A servant had ascertained, by standing on the fence and seeing the redcoats at a distance, that they were part of the army of Cornwallis and quickly communicated her discovery to her employer. Excusing herself by saying that she must attend to her child, Mrs. Caldwell returned to the house and immediately gave warning to two of her neighbors who happened to be there so that they escaped through another door and concealed themselves. She then returned to the gate and accused the British soldiers of masquerading as patriots. They openly demanded use of the dwelling for a day or two and immediately took possession, evicting Mrs. Caldwell, who with her children retired to the smokehouse and passed a day with no other food than a few dried peaches and apples. A physician then interfered and procured for her a bed, some provisions and a few cooking utensils. The family remained in the smokehouse two days and nights being in the meantime frequently insulted by profane and brutal language. To a young officer, who came to the door for the purpose of taunting the helpless mother, by ridiculing her countrymen, whom he termed rebels and cowards, Mrs. Caldwell replied, "Wait and see what the Lord will do for us." "If He intends to do anything," roughly answered the officer, "it is time He had begun."

In replying to Mrs. Caldwell's application to one of the soldiers for protection, she was told that she could expect no favors, as the women were regarded as great rebels as the men. After remaining two days the army took their departure from the plantation, on which they had destroyed everything. Before leaving the officer in command gave orders that Doctor Caldwell's library and papers should be burned. A fire was kindled in the large oven in the yard and Mrs. Caldwell was obliged to look on while books, which could not at that time be replaced, and valuable manuscripts, which had cost the study and labor of years, were carried out by the soldiers, armful after armful, and ruthlessly committed to the flames.

The persecution of Doctor Caldwell continued while the British occupied that portion of the state. He was hunted as a felon and the merest pretenses were used to tear him from his hiding-places. Often he escaped captivity or death by what seemed a miracle. At one time when he had ventured home on a stolen visit the house was suddenly surrounded by men, who seized him before he could escape, intending to carry him to their British camp. One or two were left to guard him while the others searched the house for articles of any value. When they were nearly ready to depart Mrs. Caldwell came forward, and with the promptitude and presence of mind which women frequently display in sudden emergencies, stepped behind Doctor Caldwell and leaning over his shoulder, whispered to him as though intending the question for his ear alone, she asked if it were not time for Gillespie and his men to be there. One of the soldiers who stood nearest caught the words and with evident alarm demanded what men were meant. Mrs. Caldwell replied ingenuously that she was merely speaking to her husband. In a moment all was confusion; the whole party was panic-stricken! Exclamations and hurried questions followed in the consternation produced by this woman's simple manœuvre, and the Tories fled precipitately, leaving their prisoner and their plunder. The name Gillespie was a terror to the Loyalists, and this party never doubted that he was on their trail.

Some time in the fall of 1780 a stranger appeared before Mrs. Caldwell's door, faint and worn, asking for supper and lodging for the night. He was bearing dispatches for General Greene and he had imagined that he would be free from danger under the roof of a minister of the Gospel. Mrs. Caldwell longed to offer him shelter, but she was constrained to explain that her husband was an object of peculiar hatred to the Tories and she could not tell the day or hour when an attack might be expected. She said he should have something to eat immediately but advised him to seek some safer place of shelter for the night. Before she finished preparing his meal voices were heard without, with the cries of "Surround the house," and the dwelling was presently assailed by a body of

Tories. With admirable calmness Mrs. Caldwell told the stranger to follow her and led him out by an opposite door. A large locust tree stood close by and the night was so dark that no object could be discerned amid its clustering foliage. She urged the man to climb the tree and conceal himself till the intruders should be absorbed in plundering her house. He could then descend on the other side and trust to the darkness for his safety. The house was pillaged, as she expected, and the man bearing the message so important to his country escaped, to remember with gratitude the woman whose prudence had saved him while undergoing the loss of her own property.

Another little incident, not without humor, illustrates how a woman's intrepidity was sometimes successful in disbanding marauders. Among such articles as the housewife so prizes, Mrs. Caldwell had an elegant tablecloth, which she valued as the gift of her mother. While the Tories on one occasion were in her house gathering plunder, one of them broke open the chest of drawers which contained it and tore out the tablecloth. Mrs. Caldwell seized and held it fast, determined not to give up her treasure. When she found that her rapacious enemy would soon succeed in wresting it from her unless she could make use of something more than muscular force to prevent him, she turned to the other men of the party and appealed to them with all a woman's eloquence, asking if some of them had not wives or daughters for whose sake they would interfere. A small man who stood at the distance of a few feet presently stepped up and with tears in his eyes said that he had a wife, and a fine little woman she was too, and that he would not allow any rudeness to be practiced toward Mrs. Caldwell. His interference compelled the depredator to restore the valued article, and then the tide of opinion turned, and the British soldiers cheered lustily for courageous Rachel Caldwell. After the war Doctor Caldwell resumed his labors as teacher and preacher. He died in the summer of 1824, in the one hundredth year of his age. The wife who had accompanied him in all the vicissitudes of his long life followed him to the grave at the age of eighty-eight. All who knew Rachel Caldwell regarded her as a woman of remarkable character and interest and she is remembered throughout her state with high respect.

CORNELIA BEEKMAN.

In the venerable Van Cortlandt mansion, the old-fashioned stone house erected upon the banks of the Croton River many years previous to the Revolution, Cornelia, the second daughter of Peter Van Cortlandt and Johanna, was born in 1752. Peter Van Cortlandt was Lieutenant-Governor of the state of New York under George Clinton from 1777 to 1795, and was distinguished for his zealous maintenance of American rights. His daughter inherited the principles to which in after life she was so ardently devoted. On her marriage at about the age of seventeen, with Gerard G. Beekman, she removed to the city of New York, where her residence was in the street which still bears her name. Her husband was in mind, education and character worthy of her choice. Not many years of her married life had passed when the storm of war burst upon the land and taught her to share in aspirations for liberty. She entered into the feelings of the people with all the warmth of her generous nature. She even spoke with enthusiasm of an impressive ceremonial procession she witnessed, when the mechanics of the city brought their tools and deposited them in a large coffin made for the purpose and then marched to the solemn music of a funeral dirge and buried the coffin in Potter's Field. They returned to present themselves each with a musket in readiness for military service. Finding a residence in New York impossible in the state of popular excitement she withdrew to the Peekskill Manor House, a large brick building situated two miles north of Peekskill. Here she resided during the war marked as an object of insult by the Royalists, on account of the part taken by her relatives and friends as well as her own ardent attachment to the American cause. At times in the struggle, when portions of the British army were ranging through Westchester she was exposed to their injuries, but her high spirit and strong will contributed to her safety, and supported her through many scenes and trials. One day, when the troops were in the neighborhood a soldier entered the house and walked unceremoniously toward the closet. Mrs. Beekman asked him what he wanted. "Some brandy," was the reply. When she reproved him for the intrusion he presented his bayonet at her breast and with many harsh epithets swore he would kill her on the spot. Although alone in the house except for an old black servant, she showed no alarm at the threats of the cowardly assailant but told him that she would call her husband and send information of his conduct to his officer. Her resolution triumphed over his audacity, for seeing that she showed no fear he was not long in obeying her command to leave the house. Upon another occasion she was writing a letter to her father, when looking out she saw the enemy approaching. There was only time to secrete the paper behind the framework of the mantelpiece, where it was discovered when the house was repaired after the war.

The gist of Mrs. Beekman's contemptuous replies to the enemy under Bayard and Fanning is related by herself in a letter written in 1777. A party of Royalists commanded by those two Colonels paid a visit to her house, conducting them-selves with the arrogance and insolence she was accustomed to suffer. One of them imprudently said to her, "Are you the daughter of that old Rebel, Pierre Van Cortlandt?" She replied, "I am the daughter of Pierre Van Cortlandt, but it does not become such as you to call my father a Rebel." The Tory raised his musket, but with perfect calmness she reproved him for his insolence and bade him begone. He finally turned away abashed.

The illustrations in every page of the world's history of vast results depending upon trivial things finds support in a simple incident in the life of Cornelia Beekman. It would really seem that in the Providence that disposes all human events the fate of a Nation may be found suspended upon this woman's judgment. This is the incident: John Webb, familiarly known as "Lieutenant Jack," who actively served as aid on the staff of the commander-in-chief, was much at her house during operations of the American army on the banks of the Hudson. On one occasion passing through Peekskill he rode up and requested her to take charge of a valise which contained his new suit of uniform and a quantity of gold. "I will send for it whenever I want it," he added, "but do not deliver it without a written order from me or brother Sam." He then threw the valise in at the door and rode on to the tavern at Peekskill, where he stopped to dine. A fortnight or so after this departure Mrs. Beekman saw an acquaintance named Smith, whose loyalty to the Whig cause had been suspected, ride rapidly up to the house. She heard him ask her husband for Lieutenant Jack's valise and Mr. Beekman was about to direct the servant to bring it. Mrs. Beekman, however, demanded whether the messenger had a written order from either of the brothers. Smith replied that he had no written order, the officer having had no time to write one. He added, "You know me, Mrs. Beekman, and when I assure you that Lieutenant Webb sent me for the valise you will not refuse to deliver it, as he is greatly in want of his uniform." Mrs. Beekman often said that she had an instinctive antipathy toward Smith, and by an intuition felt that he had not been authorized to call for the article she had in trust, so she answered, "I do know you very well; too well to give up to you the valise without a written order from the owner or the Colonel." Greatly angered at her statement he turned to her husband urging that the fact of his knowing that the valise was there and its contents should be sufficient evidence that he came by authority. His representations had no effect upon Mrs. Beekman's resolution. Although even her husband was displeased at this treatment of the messenger she remained firm in her denial and the disappointed horseman rode away as rapidly as he had come. Results proved that he had no authority to make the application, and it was subsequently ascertained that at the very time of this attempt Major André was in Smith's house, and had Smith obtained possession of the uniform André would have made his escape through the American lines. Lieutenant Webb confessed that while dining at the tavern that night he had

13

mentioned that Mrs. Beekman had taken charge of his valise, and told what its contents were. Smith had evidently overheard and Major André being of the same stature and form as Lieutenant Jack, the scheme to steal the American officer's uniform as a disguise for the spy had immediately taken form. Lieutenant Webb was deeply grateful to Mrs. Beekman for the prudence which had protected him from the dire result of his own folly, had saved his property, and had prevented an occurrence which might have caused a train of national disasters.

Many of Mrs. Beekman's letters written during the war breathed the most ardent spirit of patriotism. The wrongs she was compelled to suffer in person, and the aggregation of wrongs she witnessed on every side aroused her just indignation. Her feelings were expressed in her many and frequent prayers for the success of the American armies. Although surrounded by peril and disaster she would not consent to leave her home; her zeal for the honor of her family and her country inspired her with the courage that never faltered and caused her to disregard the wrong she so continually had to bear.

The energy of mind which characterized her through life was evinced on her deathbed. Calmly and quietly, bearing much suffering, she awaited the coming of that last enemy, whose nearer and yet nearer approach she announced unshrinkingly to those about her. When it was necessary to affix her signature to an important paper, and being supposedly too weak to write, she was told that her mark would be sufficient, she immediately asked to be raised, called for a pen and placing her left hand on the pulse of her right, wrote her name distinctly. It was the last act of her life. She looked death in the face with the same high resolve and strong will with which she had been wont in her lifetime to encounter losses and terrible enemies. It was the strength of Christian faith which thus gave her the victory over the "King of Terrors."

Early Women of Prominence.

The influence wielded by the women in the early days of our Republic cannot be underestimated. During the colonial period in American history there are some women who shine out conspicuously by their brilliancy and mental attainments. Their influence in public affairs was conceded at that time and appreciated to-day. They were worthy helpmeets of their distinguished husbands and did their part in shaping the affairs of the nation in its infancy and crudity.

In 1749, Mrs. Jeykell was quite a leader socially in Phila-delphia. Mrs. Schuyler, a niece of the first Colonel Philip Schuyler, was born in 1702, and married her cousin, Philip Schuyler. The French Canadian prisoners called her the "Good Lady, Madame Schuyler." She kept a liberal table and had much influence in the primitive society of that day. Miss Tucker, who married William Fitzhugh, and from whom the Fitzhughs in Virginia, Maryland and western New York are descended, was one of the influential women of her time.

The first wife of Governor Page, Frances Burwell, may be mentioned among these. At the time Mrs. Washington visited her husband when commander-in-chief of the Colonial forces, it is mentioned that at a brilliant entertainment given in the camp near Middlebrook, Mrs. Washington, Mrs. Greene, Mrs. Knox and other distinguished ladies were present, form-ing "a circle of brilliants." At the ball given at the Assembly Rooms on the east side of Broadway above Wall Street on the 7th of May, 1789, to celebrate the inauguration of President Washington, the members of Congress and their families were present with the ministers of France and Spain, distinguished generals of the army and persons eminent in the state. Among the most noted ladies were Mrs. Jay, Mrs. Hamilton and Mrs. Montgomery, the latter the widow of the hero of Quebec.

Mrs. Morris, who entertained Mrs. Washington at the time of the President's inauguration in Philadelphia, was a very remarkable woman and became Mrs. Washington's intimate friend. At all of Mrs. Washington's drawing-rooms and official entertainments, Mrs. Morris sat at her right hand, and at all the dinners, both official and private, at which Mr. Morris was present, he was placed at the right hand of Mrs. Washington. The principal ladies of New York at the time the "Republican Court" was established were Mrs. George Clinton, Mrs. Montgomery, Mrs. Knox, Mrs. Robert R. Livingston, of Clermont, the Misses Livingston, Mrs. Thompson, Mrs. Gary, Mrs. McComb, Mrs. Edgar, Mrs. Lynch, Mrs. Houston, Mrs. Provost, Mrs. Beekman, the Misses Bayard, etc. The President received every Tuesday afternoon. Mrs. Washington received from eight to ten every Friday evening and these levees were attended by the fashionable, elegant and distinguished people in society, and it is said Mrs. Washington was careful, in her drawing-room, to exact those courtesies to which she knew her husband was entitled. "None were admitted to the levees but those who had either a right by official station or by established merit and character; and full dress was required of all."

At Mrs. Washington's levees, the President appeared as a private gentleman, with neither hat nor sword, but at his own official levees he wore "his hair powdered and gathered behind in a silk bag. His coat and breeches were of plain black velvet; he wore a white or pearl-colored vest and yellow gloves, and had a cocked hat in his hand, with silver knee and shoe buckles, and a long sword, with a finely-wrought and glittering steel hilt. The coat was worn over this and its scabbard of polished white leather." He never shook hands at these receptions— even with intimate friends—visitors were received with a dignified bow and passed on.

Among the other ladies intimate with Mrs. Washington besides Mrs. Morris were Mrs. Knox, Mrs. Hamilton, Mrs. Powell, Mrs. Bradford, Miss Ross and Mrs. Otis. Mrs. Otis was the wife of the Secretary of the Senate and mother of Senator Harrison Gray Otis. She was remarkable for her beauty and grace of demeanor, wit and powerful intellect, and she was a prominent figure during the administration of Washington. Mrs. Stewart was the wife of General Walter Stewart. Miss Ross was the daughter of Senator Ross, from Pennsylvania. Mrs. Bradford was the only child of Elias Boudinot and married William Bradford, who was afterward Judge of the Supreme Court of Pennsylvania. Their house was one of the noted social centers and they were distinguished for their cordial hospitality.

Mrs. Carroll, was Harriet Chew, daughter of Benjamin Chew, Mrs. Walcott, of Connecticut, was noted for her graceful manners, culture, intelligence and refinement. It is hardly necessary to mention the Carroll family, so well known are they. The family of Charles Carroll had been settled in Maryland ever since the time of James the Second, and Charles Carroll was among the first to sign the Declaration of Independence. His patriotism is illustrated in an incident which was told as having occurred at this time. When he had signed merely as "Charles Carroll," someone remarked: "You will get clear; there are so many of that name"; he added to his signature "of Carrollton," so there should be no question as to which Carroll had sustained the country in its fight for independence.

The wife of Thomas Jefferson was Mrs. Martha Skelton, a rich widow who, at the time of her second marriage, was but twenty-three years of age, of good family, beautiful, accomplished and greatly admired. Their daughter Martha was entrusted to the care of Mrs. Adams when in Paris and made quite an impression abroad. This daughter married Thomas Mann Randolph, of Virginia, who attained to a dignified station in the general government. The daughters of Henry White were greatly admired, their family holding a high position among the loyalists before the Revolutionary War. One of these daughters became Dowager Lady Hayes, and the widow of Peter Jay Monroe.

Another family prominent in the early history of America was the Livingston family, of New York. The original grant of land given to Robert Livingston bears the date of July 22, 1686, and comprised from 120,000 to 150,000 acres on the Hudson River. Philip Livingston, who succeeded to the estate, was born in 1686. He married Catherine Van Brugh, daughter of Peter Van Brugh, of Albany, an old Dutch family. One of her ancestors was Carl Van Brugge, Lieutenant-Governor under Peter Stuyvesant. Philip Livingston was one of the signers of the Declaration of Independence. William Livingston, Governor of New York, was born in 1723, and married Susannah French, of New Brunswick, in 1745, Governor Livingston's political principles were so decidedly republican that he declined to give to his country-seat at Elizabethtown any name more aristocratic than "Liberty Hall." The family of Governor Livingston was a large one. Several daughters and two sons were born to them. One daughter married John Cleve Symmes, another married Mathew Ridley, of Baltimore, another married John W. Watkins, and the last married James Linn. The sister of Governor Livingston, Sarah Livingston, on April 28th, 1774, in her eighteenth year, married John Jay, a young lawyer. Mr. Jay rapidly rose in prominence from the position of Secretary to the Royal Commission for settling the boundary between New York and New Jersey to a member of the New York Provincial Congress and of the Committee of Safety. His constant absence during this trying period of our country's history brought out the splendid heroism and self-sacrifice of his wife, and her letters during this period show cheerfulness, even when heroically enduring the trials and privations and sacrifices demanded by her country. Mr. Jay later was sent to Madrid as Minister to Spain. They were shipwrecked during this voyage and again Mrs. Jay's strong courage was brought to the test. Later, Mr. Jay was associated with Dr. Franklin, Mr. Adams and Mr. Laurens in a commission to open a way for the negotiation of peace between America and England. Franklin and Jay were to arrange the preliminaries. Adams was in Holland, Jefferson in America and Laurens in London, and it is said that Mrs. Jay was almost a participant in these negotiations from her intimate association with the members of the commission.

The scenes and the society amid which Mrs. Jay lived for nearly two years presented a brilliant contrast to the trials and hardships to which she had been subjected by the war at home, as well as to her more retired life during their residence at Madrid. Among the first to congratulate Mrs. Jay on her arrival at Paris were the Marquis and the Marchioness de La Fayette, and the two circles of society where Mrs. Jay was most at home during their stay at Paris were those to be found in the "hotel La Fayette and Franklin," the residences of La Fayette and Franklin. The acquaintanceship of Mr. Jay and Madame de La Fayette ripened into a warm friendship and their letters later were marked by a tone of sincere regard and affection. Mrs. Henry E. Pierrepont, of Brooklyn, a granddaughter of Mrs. Jay, now has in her possession the armchair embroidered by Mrs. Jay's own hands and presented by her to Madame de La Fayette. Mrs. Jay won for America the friendship and regard of many prominent officials of France and persons of influence and note, which, no doubt, aided largely in the success of her husband. In 1784 Mr. Jay returned to America, and we find it said in a memoir: "Her recent association with the brilliant circles of the French capital assisted her to fill with ease the place she was now to occupy and to perform its graceful duties in a manner becoming the dignity of the republic to whose fortunes she had been so devoted." Her husband was appointed Secretary for Foreign Affairs in the Cabinet, and when Mr. Jay was appointed Chief Justice, which carried him into the New England Circuit, Mrs. Jay added fresh laurels to those won for herself and her country. One of her admirers has said of her that "she is entitled to regard on far better grounds than simply as a 'Queen of American Society,' and her memory may be cherished as that of one who exhibited from her youth amid trial and hardship a steadfast devotion to her country."

In point of influence, we find Mercy Warren is conceded to be the most remarkable woman who lived in the days of the American Revolution. She was the daughter of James Otis, of Barnstable, in the old colony of Plymouth. The family of Otis came to this country about 1630, and Mercy was born in 1728, passing her youth in retirement and study. At the age of twenty-six she married James Warren, a merchant. Her interest in political affairs was so great that she maintained a correspondence with many of the leading spirits of the Revolutionary era—Adams, Jefferson, Knox and others. It is said that they not only wrote her, but consulted her in regard to important matters, and during the years preceding the war, Mrs. Warren's house was the resort of the principal figures in history at that time. Washington, Lee, Gates and other distinguished officers were frequently her guests, and this is found at the close of one of her biographies: "Seldom has a woman in any age acquired such ascendency by the mere force of a powerful intellect, and her influence continued to the close of life."

Another prominent family figure in these historical days was Mrs. Knox, an intimate associate of Mrs. Washington and frequently in the camp of the army. Her influence was shown in many ways. She was the comforter of Mrs. Washington during the siege of Yorktown. When the capital was removed to Philadelphia, the home of Mrs. Knox became one of the leading social centers of the capital city. During their stay here they entertained the Duc de Laincourt, Talleyrand, and our great friend, Marquis de La Fayette. She is said to have had a mind of high and powerful cast, dignified manner and calm and lofty spirit. General and Mrs. Washington always paid her the greatest deference and in every way expressed their warm friendship and admiration of her.

The wife of John Hancock, it is said, added luster to his fame. She was a leader of society in the best circles, a daughter of Judge Edmund Quincy and was born in 1748. In 1775, she married John Hancock, then Governor of Massachusetts, afterward president of the First Congress. The strength of her character is shown in an incident worded by one of her biographers. While in Philadelphia, Hancock came to his wife one day and informed her he had a most disagreeable secret to impart to her and that it must be faithfully kept. The secret was that he had received a letter from home stating it had been thought necessary to burn the city of Boston to prevent its falling into the hands of the enemy. All of Hancock's wealth was centered there. He was asked would he be willing to sacrifice this for the good of his country, and he had given his consent. To his wife he acknowledged it would reduce them to absolute want, but his mind was made up and he asked her would she join him in this sacrifice. This she willingly did. When attending a Quaker meeting a few hours afterward, she showed no signs of the painful secret or terrible personal sacrifice which she had just been called upon to make for her country. Fortunately, later it was found unnecessary to carry out this plan and she was spared the realization of her expected fate. This shows the kind of women who lived at this time and what they did for their country.

Mrs. Greene, who was Catherine Littlefield, daughter of John Littlefield, was born on Block Island, in 1753. Her husband was Governor Greene, one of her kinsmen, to whom she was married in 1774. "The incident of her quitting her own house when Aaron Burr claimed her hospitality after his duel with Hamilton, leaving the house for his use, and only returning to it after his departure, illustrates her generous and impulsive character."

Sarah Thompson—the Countess Rumford,—is mentioned as one of the women who exercised great social influence.

Another woman of the official circle in Philadelphia may be mentioned—Mrs. Bingham. She was the daughter of Thomas Willing, and at the age of sixteen, on October 22, 1780, she married William Bingham, who was United States Senator from Pennsylvania. A few years after their marriage they went abroad and spent some years in France where they brought about them a charming circle of the best of the French capital. On their return to America in 1795, the Viscount de Noailles, brother-in-law to La Fayette, was their guest for some time.

Sarah, the only daughter of Benjamin Franklin, was born in Philadelphia, in September, 1744, and married Richard Bache in 1767. She was a prominent figure in the best society and her house was a center for the philanthropic work which the ladies of Philadelphia carried on for the American Army. In 1792, she accompanied her husband to England, later returning and settling on their farm near the Delaware.

Rebecca Franks is mentioned as one of the leaders in

society in Philadelphia in the days of the Revolution. She married Lieutenant-Governor Sir Henry Johnston. General Scott visited her some years later.

Catharine Schuyler was the only daughter of John Van Rensselaer. After the surrender of Burgoyne, he and his suite were received and entertained by General and Mrs. Schuyler, though he had destroyed their elegant country seat near Saratoga. Mrs. Schuyler was remarkable for her vigorous intellect and keen judgment, and many incidents of her heroic spirit have been recorded. Her social influence was widely recognized. Her daughter Elizabeth, who married Alexander Hamilton, has been already spoken of. Mrs. Wilson was one of the most noted women in New Jersey. She was the daughter of Colonel Charles Stewart and born in 1758. In 1776, she married Robert Wilson, a young Irishman, and went with him to Philadelphia to live. She was one of the intimate friends of Mrs. Washington. Mrs. Beekman's home was near Tarrytown. She was a sister of Mrs. Van Rensselaer and her daughter became Mrs. De Peyster. Mrs. Field was the great-granddaughter of Cornelia Beekman and related to the most prominent families in America at that time—the De Peysters, Livingstons, Beekmans, Van Cortlandts and the Van Rensselaers. Miss De Peyster, in 1838, married Mr. Benjamin Hazard Field, a descendant of Sir John Field, the astronomer. Their home in New York was a leading social center.

Among the Charleston, South Carolina, ladies prominent in society may be mentioned the Misses Harvey, three sisters of remarkably beautiful personal appearance. Another was Miss Mary Roupell; also Mrs. Rivington, the widow of a wealthy planter, and Mrs. Richard Singleton, who came from the best Virginia stock and was devoted to the American cause. She is said to have occupied her time by going continually from the city to the interior, gathering reports of the signs of the times, conveying intelligence and sometimes ammunition to friends in the army, or evolving schemes for the relief and deliverance of the city. Another patriotic woman who devoted herself to the American cause was Mrs. Brewton. Rebecca Motte was celebrated for her heroic conduct in giving Lee the bow and arrows to fire her dwelling when it was occupied by the British. She was a daughter of Robert Brewton and was married in 1758, and died in 1815. The name of Mrs. Barnard Elliott is familiar to everyone in South Carolina. She was a Miss Susannah Smith, the daughter of Benjamin Smith, speaker of the Provincial Assembly. She was an orphan and had been brought up by her aunt, Rebecca Motte, whose patriotism is revered to this day. Another prominent woman mentioned is Sabina, the wife of William Elliott. Her youngest daughter, Ann, married Colonel Lewis Morris, eldest son of Lewis Morris, one of the signers of the Declaration of Independence. One of her devoted friends and admirers was Kosciusko. She is said to have saved the life of Colonel Morris when their house was visited by the Black Dragoons. Anna Elliott, daughter of the brave patriot, Thomas Ferguson, labored constantly for her country and ministered to the poor and afflicted, and many were the favors granted at her request by the British when they held Charleston. The mother of John C. Calhoun was Martha Caldwell, whose parents emigrated to Virginia in 1749. She was one of the conspicuous figures of that day.

About the noted women of North Carolina and Kentucky we have already written in the chapter on our pioneer women: Miss Susan Hart, Sarah Bledsoe, Catherine Sherrill, Mrs. Sevier, Sarah Richardson, Charlotte Reeves, who became Mrs. Robertson, Mrs. Kenton, Sarah Sibley, who was Miss Sproat, Mrs. Talbott, Mrs. Sibley, Rebecca Heald, Mrs. Helm, Mrs. Kinsey and others.

MARY WASHINGTON HOUSE—FREDERICKSBURG, VA.

Prominent Women from the Time of Mary Washington.

Mary Washington, the mother of Washington, was descended from an ancient family of note which emigrated from England in 1650, and settled in Lancaster, Virginia, on the Rappahannock River. Mary, the youngest child of her father, Joseph Ball, was born in 1706, at Epping Forest, the family homestead, which he inherited from his father, William Ball, the first emigrant. Joseph Ball was made Colonel by Governor Spotswood in 1710, and known as Colonel Ball, of Lancaster. Five years before that time he executed a will in which is found the following: "I give and bequeath unto my daughter, Mary, four hundred acres of land in Richmond County, in ye freshes of Rappa-h-n River, being part of a patten of 1,600 acres to her, ye said Mary, and her heirs forever." She was then five years old. We also have the Ball coat-of-arms as follows: "The escutcheon has a lion rampant, a coat-of-mail and a shield bearing two lions and a fleur-de-lys. The crest is a helmet with closed visor. Above the lion is a broad bar, half red and half gold. On the scroll which belongs to it are these words: 'Coelumque tueri.' " When Mary was twenty-one her mother died, and she was taken by her brother Joseph, a lawyer of London, to his home near that city in 1728-29. In 1729 she met Augustine Washington, a son of an eminent and wealthy family of illustrious English descent, and described as "a stately and handsome gentleman." In the prime of early maturity, a widower with two little sons, he had come to England to look after an estate left him by his grandfather.   Renewing, it is supposed, a passing acquaintance, he was captivated with Mary Ball and married her.   They returned to this country and to his Westmoreland plantation of Wakefield on the Potomac, where George Washington, their son, was born February 11, 1732.   In 1735 their dwelling was burned to the ground.   Instead of rebuilding upon the site of the old homestead, Augustine Washington removed to his plantation "Pine Grove," in Stafford County, upon the Rappahannock River, opposite Fredericksburg, where he died August 12, 1743, aged forty-nine years.   They took him back to Westmoreland County, and laid him in the family vault at Wakefield, and the widowed mother returning to the home thus suddenly bereft of its honored head, gathered about her the fatherless children and "took up with both hands life as God had made it for her."   Her own five, and the two little lads who had been left to her guardianship, with their several estates, were a burden and responsibility to appall the stoutest heart; but she shrank not from it, and so faithfully and judiciously did she carry the burden, that she won and retained the affection and respect of all till her life's end—turning over, with added value, the shares of her step-sons' property when they arrived at maturity.   We know with what care and judgment she trained her own eldest born for usefulness; how her wisdom and firmness kept him from service on a British man-of-war, and saved him to his country.   The civil engineer of sixteen years of age soon became the brave and successful soldier and officer, and defender and hope and pride of his country—the great General who struggled through eight weary years of war to its triumphant close.   Early in the struggle her son earnestly entreated her to leave her plantation of "Pine Grove," and take refuge in the town for better protection and safety, which she finally but reluctantly did, establishing herself in a snug home near her only daughter, Betty (Mrs. Fielding Lewis),

where during those "weary eight years" she labored incessantly with her servants in making homespun clothing for the
suffering soldiers, herself knitting the stockings. Her big Bible
with its family record of births, marriages and deaths, is now
the precious possession of her descendant, Mrs. Ella Barett
Washington. On "Kenmore," the home plantation of her
daughter, rises a gentle eminence overlooking the valley of
the Rappahannock and the lovely ampitheatre of hills rising
from it, where are clustered a mass of bold rocks sheltered by
fine old oaks looking towards her old home, "Pine Oak." This
spot was a favorite resort for the mother for meditation and
prayer. The hours spent there, her children and grandchildren held sacred, and never intruded upon. It is still
venerated as "Oratory Rock." On August 25, 1789, after a
painful illness, in unfaltering faith, she passed from earth and
was buried at her own request at this spot, sacrcd to her for all
future time unto the Resurrection Morn.

MARTHA WASHINGTON.

Though the life of Mrs. Washington was a changeful one,
and had its full measure of sorrow and joy, it affords little
material for the biographer. Yet, as some one said in writing
about her years ago, none who take an interest in the history of
the Father of this country, can fail to desire some knowledge
of her who shared his thoughts and plans, and was associated
with him in the great events of his life. And, indeed, few
women have been called to move in the drama of existence amid
scenes so varied and imposing; and few have sustained their
part with so much dignity and discretion. In the shades of
retirement or in the splendor of eminent station, she was the
same unostentatious, magnanimous woman. Through the
gloom of adverse fortune she walked by the side of the chief,

ascending with him the difficult path that had opened before him, and at length stood with him on the summit, in the full light of his power and renown.

She was born Martha Dandridge, in May, 1732, and was descended from an ancient family that migrated to the colony of Virginia. Her education was only a domestic one such as was given to women in those days when there were few "female seminaries" and private teachers were generally employed. Her beauty and fascinating manners, with her amiable qualities of character, gained her distinction among all those belles who were accustomed to gather at Williamsburg, at that time the seat of the government.

When but seventeen, Miss Dandridge was married to Colonel Daniel Parke Custis, of New Kent County, where she was born. Their residence, called "The White House," was on the banks of the Pamunkey River, where Colonel Custis became a highly successful planter. None of the children of this marriage survived the mother; Martha, who arrived at womanhood, died at Mount Vernon in 1770, and John died of fever contracted during the siege of Yorktown eleven years later.

Mrs. Custis was early left a widow, in the full bloom of beauty and "splendidly endowed with worldly benefits." As sole executrix she managed with great ability the extensive landed and pecuniary business of the estate. Surrounded by the advantages of fortune and position, and possessing such charms of person, it may well be believed that suitors for her hand were many and pressing.

"It was in 1758," says her biographer, "that an officer, attired in military undress, and attended by a body servant, tall and militaire as his chief, crossed the ferry called William's over the Pamunkey, a branch of the York River. On the boat touching the southern or New Kent side, the soldier's progress was arrested by one of those personages who give the beau ideal of the Virginia gentleman of the old regime,—the very soul of kindness and hospitality," He would hear of no excuse on the part of this soldier, who was Colonel Washington, for declining the invitation to stop at his house. In vain the Colonel pleaded important business in Williamsburg; his friend, Mr. Chamberlayne, insisted that he must dine with him at the very least, and he promised, as a temptation, to introduce him to a young and charming widow who chanced then to be his guest. At last the soldier surrendered, resolving, however, to pursue his journey the same evening. They proceeded to the mansion. Mr. Chamberlayne presented Colonel Washington to his various guests, among whom stood the beautiful Mrs. Custis. It is not a violent presumption to suppose that the conversation at that dinner turned upon scenes in which the whole community had a deep interest—scenes which the young hero, fresh from his early battlefields, could eloquently describe; and one can fancy with what earnest and rapt attention the fair widow listened, and how, "the heavenly rhetoric of her eyes," beamed unconscious admiration upon the manly speaker. The morning passed; the sun sank low in the horizon and the hospitable host smiled as he saw the Colonel's faithful attendant, true to his orders, holding his master's spirited steed at the gate The veteran waited and marvelled at the delay. But Mr. Chamberlayne insisted that no guest ever left his house after sunset, and his visitor was persuaded, without much difficulty, to remain. The next day was far advanced when Colonel Washington was on the road to Williamsburg. His business there being dispatched, he hastened again to the companionship of the captivating widow.

A short time after his marriage, which took place about 1769, Colonel and Mrs. Washington fixed their residence at Mount Vernon. The mansion at that period was a very small building compared with its present extent. It did not receive

14

many additions before Washington left it to attend the first Congress and thence to the command-in-chief of the armies of his country. He was accompanied to Cambridge by Mrs. Washington, who remained some time with him and witnessed the siege and evacuation of Boston, after which she returned to Virginia.

It was not often that the interest taken by Mrs. Washington in political affairs was evinced by any public expression, though an address which was read in the churches of Virginia and published in the Philadelphia paper in June, 1780, as "The Sentiments of an American Woman," was attributed—it cannot be ascertained with what truth—to her pen.

She passed the winters with her husband during his campaigns and it was the custom of the commander-in-chief to dispatch an aide-de-camp to escort Mrs. Washington to headquarters. Her arrival in camp was an event much anticipated; the plain chariot, with its neat postilions in their scarlet and white liveries was always welcomed with great joy by the army and brought a cheering influence, which relieved the general gloom in seasons of disaster and despair. Her example was followed by the wives of other general officers.

It happened at one time while the ladies remained later than usual in the camp on the Hudson, that an alarm was given of the approach of the enemy from New York. The aid-de-camp proposed that the ladies should be sent away under an escort, but to this Washington would not consent. "The presence of our wives," said he, "will the better encourage us to brave defense."

Lady Washington, as she was always called in the army, usually remained at headquarters till the opening of the succeeding campaign, when she returned to Mount Vernon. She was accustomed afterwards to say that it had been her fortune to hear the first cannon at the opening, and the last at the closing of all the campaigns of the Revolutionary War. How admirably her equanimity and cheerfulness were preserved, through the sternest periods of the struggle, and how inspiring was the influence she diffused, is testified in many of the military journals of that time. She was at Valley Forge in the dreadful winter of 1777-78, her presence and submission to privation strengthening the fortitude of those who might have complained and giving hope and confidence to the desponding. She soothed the distresses of many suffering, seeking out the poor and afflicted with benevolent kindness, extending relief wherever it was in her power, and with remarkable grace presiding in the Chief's humble dwelling. In a letter to Mrs. Warren she says: "The General's apartment is very small, but he had a log cabin built to dine in, which has made our quarters much more tolerable than they were at first."

The Marquis de Chastellux says of Mrs. Washington, whom he met at the house of General Reed, in Philadelphia,— "she had just arrived from Virginia and was going to stay with her husband as she does at the end of every campaign. She is about forty, or forty-five, rather plump, but fresh, and of an agreeable countenance." One little incident when she came to spend the cold season with her husband in winter quarters illustrated how those in the humblest sphere regarded her presence. In the quarters there was only a frame house without a finished upper story, and the General desiring to prepare for his wife a more retired apartment, sent for a young mechanic and asked him and one of his fellow-apprentices to fit up a room in the attic for the accommodation of Lady Washington. On the fourth day Mrs. Washington came up to see how they were getting on. As she stood looking round, the young mechanic ventured diffidently: "Madam, we have endeavored to do the best we could; I hope we have suited you." She replied smiling: "I am astonished! Your work

would do honor to an old master and you are mere lads.   I
am not only satisfied, but highly gratified with what you have
done for my comfort." And seventy years later the mechanic
—then an old soldier—would repeat these words with tears
running down his cheeks, the thrill of delight that penetrated
his heart at the approving words of his General's lady, again
animating his worn frame and sending back his thoughts to
the very moment and scene.

At the close of the Revolutionary War when the victorious
General was merged in "the illustrious farmer of Mount
Vernon," Mrs. Washington performed the duties of a Virginia
housewife, which in those days were not merely nominal. She
gave directions, it is said, in every department, so that without
bustle or confusion the most splendid dinner appeared as if
there had been no effort in the preparation. She presided at
her abundant table with ease and elegance and was indeed most
truly great in her appropriate sphere of home. Much of her
time was occupied in the care of the children of her lost son.

A few years of rest and tranquil happiness in the society
of friends having rewarded the Chief's military toils, he was
called by the voice of the nation to assume the duties of its
chief magistrate. The call was obeyed. The establishment
of the President and Mrs. Washington was formed at the seat
of government. The levees of Washington's administration
had more of courtly ceremonial than has been known since, for
it was necessary to maintain the dignity of office by forms that
should inspire respect for the new government. In this elevated station Mrs. Washington, unspoiled by distinction, still
leaned on the kindness of her friends, and cultivated cheerfulness as a study. She was beloved as are few who occupy
exalted positions.

On the retirement of Washington from public life, he prepared to spend the remnant of his days in the retreat his taste

had adorned.   It was a spectacle of wonder to Europeans to
see this great man calmly resigning the power which had been
committed to his hands and returning with delight to his agricultural pursuits.   His wife could justly claim her share in
the admiration, for she quitted without regret the elevated
scenes in which she had shone so conspicuously to enter with
the same active interest as before upon her domestic employments.   Her advanced age did not impair her ability nor her
inclination to discharge housewifely duties.   But she was not
long permitted to enjoy the happiness she had anticipated.   It
was hers too soon to join in the grief of a mourning nation
for the death of Washington—its great Chief and President—
her husband.   From all quarters came tributes of sympathy
and sorrow, and many visits of condolence were paid by the
President and others to her in her bereavement, but in less
than two years she was attacked by a fever that proved fatal.
When aware that her hour was approaching, she called her
grandchildren to her bedside, discoursed to them on their
respective duties; spoke of the happy influence of religion, and
then, surrounded by her weeping family, died as she had lived—
bravely and without regret.   Her death took place on the
22nd of May, 1802.   Her remains rest in the same vault with
those of Washington in the family tomb at Mount Vernon.

MARY A. SITGREAVES.

Among the intimate friends of "Nellie Custis" was Mary A. Sitgreaves, the
second daughter of Colonel Daniel Kemper of the Revolutionary Army. She was
born in New York, April 1774. During the occupation of New York by the
British, her father removed to Morristown, New Jersey. The headquarters of
General Washington were in the neighborhood and through her frequent visits
to the camp Miss Kemper became an intimate friend of Mrs. Washington. During
a visit to her uncle, Dr. David Jackson of Philadelphia, she met in the drawing-
room of the President Honorable Samuel Sitgreaves, a member of Congress, and
they were married June, 1796.

SUSAN WALLACE.

Mrs. Susan Wallace, the mother of Horace Binney Wallace, lived opposite Washington's house in Philadelphia. She was the daughter of Mrs. Mary Binney of Philadelphia, and married John Bradford Wallace, who died in 1849. He was the nephew of Mr. Bradford, the second attorney-general of the United States. Mrs. Wallace was also one of the close friends of Mrs. Washington.

ABIGAIL ADAMS.

The letters of Abigail Adams form a valuable contribution to the published history of our country, laying open as they do the thoughts and feelings of one who had borne an important part in our nation's history. Mrs. Adams' character is worthy of contemplation for all her countrywomen even to-day, for though few may rise to such pre-eminence, many can emulate the sensibility and tact which she combined with much practical knowledge of life, as well as the firmness that sustained her in all vicissitudes.

She was Miss Abigail Smith, the second of three daughters, and was born at Weymouth, November 11, 1744. She was descended from genuine stock of the Puritan settlers of Massachusetts. Her father, the Rev. William Smith, was, for more than forty years, minister of the Congregational Church at Weymouth, and the ancestors of her mother, Elizabeth Quincy, were persons distinguished among the leaders of the church. From the ancestry, it may be inferred that her earliest associations were among those whose tastes were marked by the love of literature. She was not considered physically strong enough to attend school, consequently, the knowledge she evinced in after life was the result of her reading and observation rather than of what is commonly called education, which all the more emphasizes her native talents. The lessons that most deeply impressed her mind were received from Mrs. Quincy, her grandmother, whose beneficial influence she reverently acknowledges in her letters.

Her marriage to Mr. Adams took place October 25, 1764, and she passed the ten years that succeeded, devoting herself to domestic life and the care of her young family. In 1775 she was called to pass through scenes of great distress amid the horrors of war and the ravages of pestilence.

She sympathized deeply with the sufferings of those around her. "My heart and hand," she wrote, "still tremble at the domestic fury and fierce civil strife. I feel for the unhappy wretches who know not where to fly for succor, and I feel still more for my bleeding countrymen, who are hazarding their lives and their limbs." To the agonized hearts of thousands of women went up the roar of the cannon booming over those hills, and many a heart joined in breathing her prayer: "Almighty God! Cover the heads of our countrymen and be a shield to our dear friends."

But in all her anxieties her calm and lofty spirit never deserted her; nor did she regret the sacrifice of her own feelings for the good of the community. During the absence of her husband, when Mr. Adams had been sent as a joint commissioner to France, she devoted herself to the various duties devolving on her, submitting with patience to the difficulties of the time.

After the return of peace, Mr. Adams was appointed the first representative of the Nation at the British court, and his wife went to Europe to join him. From this time Abigail Adams moved amidst new scenes and new characters, yet in all her variety and splendor of life in the luxurious cities of the Old World she preserved the simplicity of heart which had adorned her seclusion at home. In the prime of life, with a mind free from prejudice, her record of the impressions she received is interesting and instructive. Her letters of this period are filled with that delicate perception of beauty which belongs to a poetic spirit.

As was to be expected, neither she nor her husband were exempt from annoyances growing out of the late controversy. She writes to Mrs. Warren: "Whoever in Europe is known to have adopted republican principles must expect to have all the engines of war of every court and courtier in the world displayed against him."

Yet, notwithstanding the drawbacks that sometimes troubled her, her residence in London seems to have been a most agreeable one, and, with the unaffected republican simplicity and exquisite union of frankness and refinement in her manners, she seems to have won her way even in the proud circles of the English aristocracy.

Her letters are a faithful transcript of her feelings, and there is a surprisingly modern note and almost prophetic suggestion in the following observation from one of her letters to her sister: "When I reflect on the advantages which people in America possess over the most polished of other nations, the ease with which property is obtained, the plenty which is so equally distributed, their personal liberty and security of life and property, I feel grateful to Heaven, who marked out my lot in that happy land; at the same time I deprecate that restless spirit and that baleful ambition and thirst for power which will finally make us as wretched as our neighbors." When Mr. Adams, after having returned to the United States with his family, became Vice-President, his wife appeared, as in other situations, the pure-hearted patriot, the accomplished woman, the worthy partner of his cares and honors.

He was called to the Presidency, and the widest field opened for the exercise of her talents. Her letter written on the day that decided the people's choice shows a sense of the solemn responsibility they had assumed, with a truly touching reliance upon Divine guidance and forgetfulness of all thoughts of pride in higher sentiments.

In this elevated position, the grace and elegance of Mrs. Adams, with her charm of conversation were rendered more attractive by her frank sincerity.   Her close observation, discrimination of character and clear judgment gave her an influence which men and women acknowledged.   Her husband appreciated her worth, and was sustained in spirit by her buoyant cheerfulness and affectionate sympathy in the multiplicity of labor which the highest office of his country brought him.

It was hers, too, to disarm the demon of party spirit, to calm agitations, heal the rankling wounds of pride, and pluck the root of bitterness away.

After the retirement of her husband, Mrs. Adams continued to take a deep interest in public affairs.   Her health was much impaired, however, and from this time she remained in her rural seclusion at Quincy.

MARTHA WAYLES JEFFERSON.

Mrs. Martha Wayles Jefferson, wife of the third President of the United States, was born in 1748 in Charles County, Virginia, and died September 6, 1782, at Monticello, the famous country home of Thomas Jefferson, near Charlottesville, Virginia.   Her father, John Wayles, was a wealthy lawyer, who gave his daughter all the advantages of refinement and education which were afforded at this time. Her first husband was Bathurst Skelton, whom she had married at a very early age, becoming a widow before she was twenty.   In January, 1772, she married Thomas Jefferson.   In 1781 Mrs. Jefferson's health became so precarious that her husband refused a foreign mission.   In the autumn of 1782 she died.   She was the mother of five children, three of whom survived her.

MARTHA JEFFERSON.

Perhaps no better reason why the biography of Martha Jefferson is important can be given than the following estimate of her, found in a history of our young Republic: "As a child, she was her father's only comforter in the great sorrows of his life, in matured years she was his intimate friend and companion; her presence lent to his home its greatest charm, and her love and sympathy were his greatest solace in the troubles which clouded the evening of his life." Thomas Jefferson, going, a lonely widower, on his first mission to France, took with him his little girl, "Patsy," as he lovingly called her, and while she was placed in a convent his regular and constant visits to her there brought all the comfort and happiness of life to both of them. She was only ten years old at the time of her mother's death in 1782, but her own sorrow was almost forgotten in the contemplation which was constantly before her of that greater sorrow of her father. She understood it when, one night, she entered her father's room, and found him giving away to a paroxysm of weeping. But her father would not allow her young life to be shrouded in gloom, and later on, when she was sixteen, she entered with him the world of Paris, and was introduced into the brilliant court of Louis XVI. In spite of her youth and her modest, retiring disposition, she was considered a remarkable young woman. She did credit to the excellent education she had received. She was found to be a good elocutionist, an accomplished musician, and one well versed in matters historical. She was not beautiful (and perhaps it is a relief to learn that she was not, after hearing about so many dames and daughters of a by-gone day whose wondrous fairness is forever being told in story and rehearsed in song), but she is reputed to have been "tall and stately" and to have had an interesting rather than a pretty face. Hints of Miss Patsy's good times and of the interesting people whom she met when she was a debutante in the Paris world have come down to us. We read of her acquaintance with the gay and gallant Marquis de La Fayette, who never chanced to meet the daughter of Thomas Jefferson without pausing to exchange a few merry words with her; and of her enthusiastic admiration for Madame de Stael, whom she saw very often in society, and

to whose wonderful conversation she invariably listened atten-
tively.   But Martha Jefferson loved her country and her father
too truly to think of deserting them for the sake of any gallant
of King Louis' court.   Moreover, she knew that in her own
country there was waiting for her some one infinitely superior
to anyone she might meet abroad.   When, in 1789, she and
her father and her sister returned to their beloved Virginia
home, Monticello, she met again this second cousin, Thomas
Mann Randolph, who had been her childhood sweetheart, and
on the 23d of February, 1790, "Miss Patsy," as she was called,
and her cousin Tom were married.   She was happy in her husband, a man, so Jefferson tells us, "of science, sense, virtue, and
competence."   With him she led an ideal family life.   Her
home, at Edgehill, the Randolph estate, from which, in the winter, when the trees were bare, she could see the glimmer of
the white columns of the portico of Monticello, became filled
with a host of little people.   There were twelve in all, five sons
and seven daughters, all equally lovable and interesting in their
mother's eyes.   But the most enjoyable times of Mrs. Randolph's life were the July vacation months when, with the coming of summer, President Jefferson, tired of Washington and
the affairs of state, retired to Virginia and, stopping *en route*
at Edgehill, picked up the whole Randolph family, and carried
them off with him to Monticello.   When Thomas Jefferson
became President, Mrs. Randolph and her sister came from the
obscurity of their Virginia homes, and began their reign in the
White House.   The two sisters took by storm the Capital of
the nation.   For the first time since their girlhood days in
Paris at the court of Louis XVI they became a part of the gay
world.   During that winter at the President's home Mrs. Randolph was very happy entertaining her father's distinguished
guests and taking part in all the gayeties of the Capital.   She
was everywhere admired.   The Marquis de Yrcijo, who was

then Spanish Ambassador in Washington, declared that she was fitted to grace any court in Europe, and John Randolph, of Roanoke, was so impressed with the beauty of her mind and character that years after, when her health was proposed at a gentleman's table in Virginia, at a time when "Crusty John" himself was one of her father's bitterest political foes, seconded the toast with the exclamation, "Yes, gentlemen, let us drink to the noblest woman in Virginia." In the spring that followed this winter of memorable pleasures and excitements Mrs. Randolph, with her young family, withdrew from Washington society, and returned to live in the utmost simplicity at her home at Edgehill. It was a glorious time for Mrs. Randolph when, at last, the adored father returned to her, not as President of the United States, on a hurried visit to his home and family, but as a simple country gentleman, who was never again to be deprived of that domestic peace and harmony for which he had sighed so many years. When he came this time the removal to Monticello was permanent. For the remainder of his life Jefferson and his daughter and his daughter's children lived happily on the summit of the little mountain, in the home that was so dear to them all.

Her father's death and the loss also of his home, which came of the too generous hospitality which always existed at Monticello, broke Martha Jefferson's heart. The troubles that followed her husband's death, and the worries and vexations of poverty found her resigned, almost unmoved. She passed her last days in visiting among her children. It was at Edgehill, the home of her eldest son, Jefferson, that she was best contented, because of the proximity to Monticello. From a window of the room that was always reserved for her she could look up through the trees and across the meadow to Monticello. Here, in sight of the loved home, she lived over again in memory the associations and happiness she had once enjoyed.

DOROTHY PAYNE MADISON.

There are few figures on the canvas of American history that stand out with such undimmed charm as that of beautiful Dolly Madison. Certainly no one of its kerchiefed dames of the early Republic made their public and private life a better example of American womanhood to American girls of the succeeding generation than the bright-eyed Quaker girl-widow, who became hostess of the White House in 1809.

By the chance of a parental visit, it was in the province of North Carolina, under the reign of King George III, that Dorothea Payne was born, on the 12th of May, 1768. By lineage and residence, however, she had a good right to call herself "A Daughter of Virginia," for her parents returned to their Hanover county plantation when she was an infant, and it was at the old school in Hanover that she learned her first lessons. Her grandfather, John Payne, was an English gentleman, who came to Virginia, and married Anna Fleming, a lady of Scottish birth, and who was descended, it is claimed, from the Earl of Wigton, a Scottish nobleman. Her father, John Payne, Jr., married Mary Coles, the daughter of an Irish gentleman from Enniscorthy, County Wexford, Ireland. This Mary Coles was descended from the Winstons, of Virginia, a family known for its aristocratic lineage. Indeed, it is reasonable to suppose that much of Dolly Payne's conversational gift was a legacy from these Winstons. Her mother's uncle, Patrick Henry, the orator, was said to have inherited his talent from his brilliant mother, Sarah Winston, while another cousin, Judge Edmund Winston, was a local celebrity.

Of the three strains of blood, English, Irish and Scotch, that flowed in Dolly Payne's veins, the Irish appears to have predominated. The roseleaf complexion, the laughing eyes, the clustering curls of jet-black hair, the generous heart and persuasive tongue, all these were legacies from the County Wexford ancestors. The "Cousin Dolly" for whom Dolly Payne was named was the lovely Dorothea Spotswood Dandridge, granddaughter of the famous Sir Alexander Spotswood, of Virgina. Curiously enough, this "Cousin Dolly" married two of Dolly Payne's mother's cousins—first, Patrick Henry, and, after his death, when her little namesake was nine years old, Judge Edmund Winston—making a bewildering maze of cousins, as they used to do, and still do, down in Virginia. Dolly Payne's father was a Quaker, and so little Mistress Dolly wore her ashen gown down to her toes and the queer little Quaker bonnets and plain kerchiefs and long cuffs covering her dimpled arms, as prescribed for those of her sex by the decree of the "Friends." But this sober dress was not to her mind, it seems, for we read that she wore a gold chain about her neck, under the folds of her kerchief, a sin which she confessed to the old black "Mammy Rosy," and who, no doubt, after scolding her for such an impropriety, consoled her with an extra allowance of some particularly longed-for dainty.

It was on account of John Payne's religious belief that he set free his negro slaves, sold his plantation, and moved his family to Philadelphia, where he hoped to find more sympathy than was to be had from the Virginia cavaliers. But John Payne found his financial position much embarrassed with the sale of the Virginia plantation, and was, no doubt, glad when a desirable suitor, in the person of young John Todd, a Quaker lad and rising young lawyer, asked for the hand of Mistress Dolly. Mistress Dolly herself was not enthusiastic in the matter, but she finally yielded to her father's desire, and was married to Lawyer Todd on the seventh day of January, 1790, in the Friends' Meeting House on Pine Street. There were no minister, no bridal veil, no wedding music, no dancing, and no drinking the bride's health, nor any of the merrymaking her gay young heart would have liked.   Her wedding must have cost her many a pang in its absence of all gayety and brilliancy.

Dolly's years with her first husband were brief, though happy, and they ended tragically.   Three years later John Todd died of yellow fever, that swept over Philadelphia, and Dolly Todd was left a young widow in poor circumstances, and with one child, Payne Todd, who was in after years to sadden and shadow her life.   She went to live with her mother, then also a widow, in straitened means, who had taken some gentlemen to board.   But Dolly's sunny nature would not let her brood over her grief.   Now, for the first time, she was mistress of herself.   There was no Quaker father or Quaker husband to restrain her in her life of frivolity.   This period of her life was her real girlhood, and that training school for the personal charm and social grace wherein lay the secret of her future greatness.   In about a year after the death of John Todd, Aaron Burr, who had been an inmate of Mrs. Payne's household, introduced the young widow to James Madison, who had already made a wide reputation.   Mrs. Todd wrote to a friend that Mr. Burr was going to bring "that great little Madison" to call upon her.   The "great little Madison" called; in the words of a biographer, "He came; he saw; she conquered." Shortly after this Mrs. Washington sent for Dolly, and questioned her about Madison's attentions, strongly advising the youthful widow to accept him as a husband.   She did so at once, receiving the President's and Mrs. Washington's heartiest congratulations.   Dolly's sister had married George Steptoe Washington, the President's nephew, so there was a connection in the two families, and the second marriage was solemnized at Harewood, the estate of her brother-in-law, on September 15, 1794.   From Harewood they went to Montpelier, Madison's home, in Orange county, Virginia, traveling over a distance of a hundred miles by coach.

It was here, through his wife's influence, that Madison was induced to hold his seat in Congress until the end of the Washington administration, which concluded in 1797. When it ended Dolly Madison lived in Philadelphia, for Madison did not come to take part in national affairs again until Jefferson became President, in 1801, and in the meantime the seat of government had been moved to Washington. Then the man who had framed the Constitution of the United States, and was known as the "Father of the Constitution," was needed, and Jefferson appointed Madison Secretary of State. From this time began Dolly Madison's social reign in Washington. She became, indeed, a power to be reckoned with in political games. For, though she made no effort to mix in the affairs of state, her influence was felt indirectly in matters of great importance.

In 1809, Dolly Madison's husband succeeded Jefferson as President, and she realized her ambition by becoming the first lady of the land. She was equal to the occasion. When shy young youths came to the White House it was she who put them at ease. When aiders of the opposition party grew most bitter, the President's wife was always unfailing in her courtesy and attention to their wives. In her drawingroom opposing elements met, and she smoothed away the friction with one of those rare smiles or a pleasant word. Even during the trying period of the War of 1812, when Madison was torn to distraction by the Peace party, she was the most popular person in the United States. The story of her cutting out Washington's portrait from the frame when the British were about to enter the Capital, does not seem to be quite true; she had the frame broken because it had to be unscrewed, and there was no time to lose, but one of the servants actually did it. It was a sultry August day that the English fleet sailed up the Chesapeake and anchored at the mouth of the Potomac. At sight of the enemy's ships Washington presented a spectacle very much like

MARY WASHINGTON MONUMENT—FREDERICKSBURG, VA.

Brussels had before Waterloo fell. The bewildered crowds were employed in conveying valuables out of the city, and an endless procession of coaches and chaises, with flurried-looking occupants, went streaming out of the Capital. Mr. Madison and his secretaries were at Bladensburg, the field of battle, and his wife was unwilling to leave Washington until he returned. In spite of her great anxiety she kept brave and cheerful, and even planned a dinner party for the night which was to witness the burning of the Capital. She saw one official after another go out of the city, but heroically refused to desert her post and, though the British Admiral sent her the startling word that he would make his bow in her drawing-room, not until a messenger from her husband arrived, crying, "Clear out, clear out! General Armstrong has ordered a retreat!" did she turn her back upon the White House. And even then she took time to save a carriage load of cabinet papers and the White House silver. Then, reluctantly, she took her departure. "I longed, instead," she affirmed with spirit, "to have a cannon from every window."

She barely escaped the marauding British troops, for it was only a few hours later that they entered Washington, and set fire to the Capitol. By the lurid light of that burning building the destroying army marched down Pennsylvania avenue to the White House, where they partook of the wines and viands that had been prepared for Dolly Madison's dinner party. Mrs. Madison, meantime, with her little train of followers, was journeying to meet Mr. Madison, as some penciled notes from him had directed. Of the next few days' wanderings of the President and his wife, which, to us, in our later century, read like a comedy of errors, it can only be said that had President Madison showed the same coolness and judgment as his wife, much of the ridicule to which he was subjected would have been avoided.

15

But in the days of general rejoicing that followed the declaration of peace Mr. Madison's official blunders were forgotten, and Dolly Madison became more popular than ever. The soldiers, returning home from their long service, stopped before her home, "The Octagon," to cheer. Her receptions in this comparatively small house were more brilliant than those of the White House had been. In the gayeties of the "Peace Winter" Dolly framed a memorable epic in the annals of Washington society. James G. Blaine wrote of her: "She saved the administration," and while, perhaps, his praise was too great, she held greater social and political sway than any other woman of her country. In the midst of her greatest social glory she had one great grief. Her son, Payne Todd, the "American Prince," had his mother's charm, but not her nobility.

After Madison's two terms were over he returned again to Montpelier, where he lived until the year 1836, when he passed out of the world in which he had left so lasting an impression.

After his death Dolly Madison returned to Washington, where the remaining twelve years of her life were spent in the house now owned by the Cosmos Club, but which is still called the Dolly Madison Mansion. Here the old lady, now in poverty, for Montpelier had been sacrificed to pay the gambling debts of her unworthy son, lived, still retaining her old popularity, and receiving attention from everybody who resided in or came to Washington. The nation settled a goodly sum upon her, and voted her "A Seat in the House."

When Dolly Madison died, July 12, 1849, her funeral was conducted with pomp that has marked no other American woman's last rites. The President and Cabinet, Senate, Diplomatic Corps, Judges of the Supreme Court, and officers of the Army and Navy, clergy, and all Washington society attended. It was a pageant worth her beautiful life record. In late years her body was removed to Montpelier.

ELIZABETH K. MONROE.

Mrs. Elizabeth K. Monroe, *nee* Miss Elizabeth Kortright, was the daughter of Captain Lawrence Kortright, a former captain in the British army, who had remained in New York after the declaration of peace in 1783, rearing and educating his family of one son and four daughters. One of these daughters married Mr. Heyliger, late Grand Chamberlain to the King of Denmark. Of the other two, one married Mr. Knox, of New York, and the other was the wife of Nicholas Gouverneur, of New York.

James Monroe was a senator from Virginia when New York was the seat of government, and there met Miss Kortright, who is described as tall, graceful and beautiful, with highly polished manners. They were married in New York in 1786, during a session of Congress. Soon after their marriage Philadelphia was chosen as the Capital, Congress adjourning to that city. Senator Monroe and his gifted wife took up their residence in that city. In 1794 he was appointed Envoy Extraordinary and Minister Plenipotentiary to France. With the prestige of his position as a senator and as a person of wealth and with Mrs. Monroe's accomplishments, they were destined to represent their country with great success.

It was while Mr. Monroe was American Minister to France that La Fayette, who had so gallantly fought under Washington for American independence, was taken prisoner by the Austrians and transferred successively from the dungeons of Wesel, Magdeburg, Glatz, Neisse and Olmutz, which differed only in forms of cruelty and horrors which they inflicted upon the defender of liberty in America. La Fayette, suffering in addition, unspeakable mental torture over the knowledge of the incarceration of Madame La Fayette and two of her innocent babes in the prison of La Force, naturally appealed to the American Minister.

The sympathies of Mr. and Mrs. Monroe were equally aroused for their friends. Mr. Monroe determined that something must be done, or that death would soon end the lives of these martyrs to the cause of freedom. Fortunately, the star of destiny of America was rapidly ascending, which enabled her representatives to assume a loftier attitude in their demands for the recognition of the rights of men. Mr. Monroe, intensely aroused, made haste to try to relieve Marquis and Madame La Fayette. Mrs. Monroe co-operated enthusiastically in the plans for their relief, one of which was for Mrs. Monroe to visit Madame La Fayette in prison. With a brave heart, she went to the prison, and was successful in seeing Madame La Fayette, her inhuman captors being afraid to refuse the request of Mrs. Monroe, who was almost overcome with the wretched condition of that brave lady when she was brought into her presence, supported by the guards who watched her day and night. The day Mrs. Monroe called Madame La Fayette had been expecting the summons to prepare for her execution, and naturally was greatly alarmed when a gendarme commanded her to follow him. More dead than alive, she was ushered into the presence of her rescuer. After a few assuring words of encouragement to Madame La Fayette, in tones loud enough for those in her presence to hear, Mrs. Monroe assured the unhappy woman that she would see her on the morrow. Mrs. Monroe departed to speedily assist in the deliverance of her persecuted friend, which was consummated next day. Madame La Fayette left Paris under the protection of an American passport to join her unhappy husband who, through the intervention of George Washington and Napoleon Bonaparte, was also liberated. It was subsequently learned that the very afternoon of Mrs. Monroe's visit Madame La Fayette was to have been beheaded. To the day of her death Mrs. Monroe regarded the saving of the life of Madame La Fayette as her most gratifying achievement.

When Mr. Monroe was Governor of Virginia Mrs. Monroe presided over the executive mansion with so much distinction that she won great popularity. She was eminently fitted to fill the position of First Lady of the Land when her husband succeeded James Madison as President, after the War of 1812. The White House in Washington was not what it is to-day, and Mrs. Monroe's health was poor during their residence there, but one of their pleasures was the entertaining of La Fayette, when he visited the United States in 1824. Their youngest daughter, Maria, was married in the East Room in March, 1820, to her cousin, Samuel L. Gouverneur, of New York.

After the expiration of Mr. Monroe's eight years in the White House, they retired to Oak Hill, their beautiful home, in Loudon county, Virginia, where Mrs. Monroe continued her benevolence and care of those dependent upon her and the unfortunates of the community about them. She died suddenly in 1830, beloved by all who knew her.

LOUISA CATHERINE ADAMS.

Louisa Catherine Adams was born in London, February 12, 1775. Her father, Mr. Johnson, of Maryland, then resided in England. Upon the breaking out of the Revolutionary War he declared his loyalty to the side of the patriots in America, accepting a commission from the Federal government as a commissioner to audit the accounts of all official functionaries of the United States in Europe, and removed his family to Nantes, France. Still in the service of his country after the independence of the colonies had been recognized, he returned to London, where he continued to reside until 1797, faithfully representing his native land. His daughter, Louisa Catherine, had consequently exceptional educational opportunities in her youth.

She first met Mr. Adams in her father's house, in London in 1794. They were married July 26, 1797, in the church of All Hallows, London. Mr. Adams' father became President soon afterwards, and John Quincy was transferred to Berlin, whither he took his accomplished bride, whom, it may be said, was destined to be a conspicuous figure in the highest social circles for the rest of her life. Her career in Berlin, considering the conditions, was so successful that it might at this distance, through the lapse of time, be called brilliant. Mr. Adams returned, with his family, to the United States, and took up his residence in Boston. Mrs. Adams was soon the admired of all admirers, their popularity putting Mr. Adams in the United States Senate from Massachusetts, and they came to Washington for the sessions of the Senate. She was very happy to be near her own family, the Johnsons, of Maryland, as she had been away from them continuously from the date of her marriage. For eight years, during Mr. Jefferson's two terms as President, she enjoyed her life in Washington.

On the accession of Mr. Madison to the Presidency, Mr. Adams was made our first Minister to Russia. It was a great trial to Mrs. Adams to leave two of her children with their grandparents, as it seemed wise to do, with the many unfavorable conditions then existing. They took a third child, and set sail for Boston in August. After a long and perilous voyage, they reached St. Petersburg in October. The rigorous climate, separation from her children, and the trying position as the wife of our first Minister to that autocratic court, brought into action all her powers of endurance, diplomacy and intuition. She was equal to every emergency.

The six years Mrs. Adams spent in St. Petersburg were probably the most eventful in the history of the New World. Napoleon was at the height of his imperial sway. He had the Old World in turmoil, and was threatening Russia. The

War of 1812 between England and the United States broke out meanwhile, cutting off almost completely all communication with her native land, thereby intensifying her anxiety and distress on account of her separation from her children. Mr. Adams was indefatigable in his efforts in behalf of his struggling country, and by his diplomacy, culture, fine talents and loyalty so impressed Emperor Alexander that he offered to be a mediator between England and the United States. Unfortunately, this munificent offer was unsuccessful, but probably opened the way for the Treaty at Ghent, December 24, 1814. Mr. Adams represented the United States at Ghent, and was obliged to leave Mrs. Adams in St. Petersburg while he attended the commission. She had lost a baby born in St. Petersburg, and but for her remarkable courage and admirable character would have been most unhappy and a greater anxiety to her husband, already overburdened with affairs which threatened dire disaster to his country. After the signing of the Treaty she set out for Paris to join Mr. Adams and return to the United States. It was an heroic undertaking to make this long journey with her child and attendants overland through a country recently overrun by contending armies. She often told her experiences, and related incidents which taxed her genius to avoid serious embarrassment and detention. Prudence and tact finally enabled her to reach Paris on the 21st of March, 1815, immediately after the arrival of Napoleon and the flight of the Bourbons. Mrs. Adams appreciated the fact that these events were momentous, but her children were on the sea, and she was impatient to proceed to London to meet them, after being separated from them six long years. On the arrival of Mr. and Mrs. Adams in London, May 25, 1815, Mr. Adams learned that he had been appointed Minister to the Court of St. James. Hence, they again took up their residence in Great Britain, Mrs. Adams, as ever before, supplementing her illustrious husband's high character and wise diplomacy with matchless intelligence, culture and gracious dignity.

Mr. Monroe succeeding Mr. Madison as President of the United States March 4, 1817, appointed Mr. Adams Secretary of State. Hence Mr. Adams and his family made haste to return home, arriving in New York August 6, 1817. Soon afterwards they established themselves in Washington, when, as wife of the Secretary of State, Mrs. Adams exerted a marvelous influence in harmonizing the various personal animosities, political rivalries, jealousies and sectional strife. They commanded the highest respect and confidence from the diplomatic corps, who depend upon the Secretary of State and his family in all matters of an official and social character.

One source of intellectual development of which Mrs. Adams availed herself was the regular correspondence with her father-in-law, the illustrious, brainy ex-President, John Adams. Their letters to each other were very long and interesting, and in them they discussed all subjects—religion, philosophy, politics, national, foreign and domestic affairs, with masterful ability on both sides. Their letters continued until the death of ex-President John Adams, July 4, 1826.

From Secretary of State to the Presidency was a short step for John Quincy Adams. Mrs. Adams' health began to fail soon after their occupancy of the White House. She, however, as far as her strength would admit, continued her matchless hospitality and powerful influence in politics and society. It was Mrs. Adams' great pleasure to have the honor of entertaining General La Fayette in the White House. Lack of space forbids the description this important event deserves, especially the tender leave-taking of the illustrious foreign soldier and friend of America in the darkest hour of her history. No greater honors have ever been paid a distinguished visitor than were heaped upon La Fayette by the grateful American people.

John Quincy Adams was the ablest and most learned man who had ever occupied the Presidential chair up to that time. Mrs. Adams was equally endowed with superior natural talents, nobility of character and rare accomplishments. And while they had appreciated the honors conferred upon them by the people of their beloved country, on account of personal bereavements and the onerous duties of public life they gladly retired to private life on the expiration of Mr. Adams' Presidential term. But they were not destined to enjoy private life long. The people of the Plymouth District insisted upon Mr. Adams representing them in Congress. He took his seat December 31. On account of advancing age they took little part in the gayeties of Washington, living quietly in their own house, on I street. In November, 1846, Mr. Adams suffered a stroke of paralysis, from which he never fully recovered. He, however, continued to discharge his duties, with intervals of protracted illness until the 21st of February, 1848. While in his seat in the House he had a relapse, and after being removed to the Speaker's room he lingered until the 23rd, when he passed away. Mrs. Adams, though very weak and ill, stayed beside her husband, soothing him until the last.

Mr. and Mrs. Adams had four children, three sons and one daughter: George Washington Adams, their eldest, born in Berlin, April 12, 1801; John Adams, born in Boston, July 4, 1803; Charles Francis Adams, born in Boston in 1807; Louisa Catherine Adams, born in St. Petersburg, August 12, 1811, and died there the following year.

After Mr. Adams' death Mrs. Adams returned to Quincy, Massachusetts, where she lived in retirement, surrounded by her children and relatives, until her death, on the 14th of May, 1852. She was buried beside her husband in the family burying place. She is remembered as one of the most remarkable women who has ever graced the White House and other exalted positions as a fine representative American woman.

RACHEL JACKSON.

When, in the year 1789, Andrew Jackson, a tall, red-haired, strong-featured young man, made his appearance in the new settlement of Nashville, Tennessee, he went to live in a boarding house that was kept by a Mrs. Donelson. Mrs. Donelson was a widow. Her husband, who had been a pioneer in the settlement of Nashville, had been killed, by Indians, it was supposed. With Mrs. Donelson lived her daughter, Mrs. Robards, and the society of this lady Jackson found to be the pleasantest feature in his boarding house life.

Mrs. Robards was an interesting woman. She was of the regular pioneer type, such as was often to be met with in the frontier days of our country during the earliest days of the Republic. Courageous, daring, full of life and spirit, she was universally liked as a merry story-teller, a rollicking dancer, a daring horsewoman and, altogether, a most jolly and entertaining companion. She had been a belle among the hearty young woodmen and planters who had gone out with Colonel Donelson to take charge of the frontier region beyond the big salt lake. But it was not to one of those first Nashville settlers that she gave her heart and hand. She married a Kentuckian, Mr. Lewis Robards. The story of this marriage is not a happy one. It is that of a cruel husband and an early divorce, after which she came back to take up her life again in the valley of the Cumberland.

It is not surprising that Andrew Jackson and Rachel Donelson, living in the same house, as they did, subjected to the common peril of hostile Indians and violence and bloodshed, for which this region was noted, congenial in tastes and characteristics, should have grown to love each other. In the year

1791 they were married, and their life together, from their wedding day until the death of Mrs. Jackson, is delightful to contemplate. In 1804 took place the removal to the "Hermitage," an unpretentious little block house that stood in the midst of flourishing cotton fields, and only a few miles from Nashville. And it is with the "Hermitage" that one associates all the pleasantest memories of Andrew Jackson and his wife. They were known as the "King and Queen of Hospitality." No one was ever turned away from their door. We read of times when each of the four rooms, which was all the house possessed, was filled with a whole family, and when the piazza and other places of half shelter about the house were transformed into bunks for the young men and boys of the visiting party.

In spite of its free-and-easy character, life at the "Hermitage" was a very busy affair. Mr. Jackson was a man of many occupations. He was a slave owner, and a farmer, a storekeeper, a lawyer and a soldier. We may imagine that there was much for him to do, and much also for his helpful wife to do. In his absences from home Mrs. Jackson took charge of all things at the "Hermitage," and an excellent manager she made. Unlearned though she was in the lore of schools she was very wise in knowledge of the woods, the fields, the kitchen and the dairy. The simple life in and about the "Hermitage," free from all ceremonies and conventions, was exactly suited to Mrs. Jackson. She was charming in all its phases. But it was different when, as the wife of the "Hero of New Orleans"—Jackson having been made Major General by the National Government—she was to visit the scene of her husband's triumphs. She could not feel at home among the elegantly clothed people of that city, but confessed that she knew nothing of fine clothes and fine manners. The General himself was delighted to have his "Bonny Brown Wife," as Mrs. Jackson was called, with him at headquarters. He was blind to the difference between her and the other women, and he made it evident to all that he thought his wife "the dearest and most revered of human beings," and nothing pleased him so much as regard bestowed on her.

It was rather more than five or six years later that the General was appointed Governor to Florida, and he and Mrs. Jackson, with the two young nephews, one known as Andrew Jackson Donelson, went to live in this region of fruit and flowers. From Mrs. Jackson's pen which, although occasionally stumbling, was an interesting one, we have a picture of the final evacuation of Florida by the Spaniards, and the formal taking possession of the country, Jackson coming in "under his own standard," as he had vowed he would. But, hard as had been Mrs. Jackson's life with all the hardships and adventures of frontier exposure, she was homesick in the midst of the flowers and fruit of Pensacola for her log cabin home in Tennessee. "Believe me," she wrote to her friends at home, "this country has been greatly overrated. One acre of our fine Tennessee land is worth a thousand here." Mrs. Jackson's letters give a true picture of the General's state of mind. "The General is the most anxious man to get home I ever saw," she said. And it was, indeed, General Jackson's desire to return to the adopted son Andrew and his beloved wife Rachel. But though they did return to the "Hermitage" the happy days which again saw Rachel Jackson mistress there were not many. In the year 1824 Jackson was elected United States Senator. During the period of his senatorship the mighty game was played which was to make him chief magistrate of the land. From the time of Jackson's nomination his victory was sure. It is almost impossible to defeat a military hero. His nickname was "Old Hickory," and hickory poles were set up in his honor all over the country. But there are always two sides to an election, and Jackson was made to taste the bitterness of malice and slander as well as the sweetness of glory.   He could endure that aimed at him, but what was directed at his wife he could not endure.   He raged and fumed at the insults that were dealt her with the fiery wrath of an old soldier.   Mrs. Jackson herself was grieved and appalled at the cruel things that were said of her, when into the peace and harmony of her quiet, retired existence there broke as fierce a volley of taunts as ever issued from a political campaign.   When the news of her husband's election reached her at the Hermitage she received it quietly.   "Well, for Mr. Jackson's sake, I am glad," she said.   "For my own part, I never wished it."

The ladies of Tennessee, who were all proud of Mrs. Jackson, were preparing to send her to the White House with the most elegant wardrobe that could be found, and the people of the neighborhood were planning an elaborate banquet in honor of the President-elect.   On the evening before the fete, worn out with the excitement and pain of the contest through which she had been passing, the mistress of the Hermitage died.   Mrs. Jackson was heard to say when she was dying that the General would miss her, but if she lived she might be in the way of his new life.   It was thus that she reconciled herself to leaving him.   Andrew Jackson proceeded to his place at the head of the nation, a lonely, broken-hearted man.   The memory of the wrong that had been done his wife was always present in his mind.   Years after, when he came to die, the clergyman bent over him, asking the last question.   "Yes," said the old general, "I am ready.   I ask forgiveness, and I forgive all—all except those who slandered my Rachel to death."

ANGELICA SINGLETON VAN BUREN.

President Van Buren had been a widower for seventeen years when he was elected President, consequently his daughter-in-law, Angelica Singleton Van Buren, presided over the White House. Mrs. Van Buren, Jr., came from Sumter District, South Carolina. She was educated at Madame Grelaud's Seminary, Philadelphia. In November, 1838, she was married to Major Abram Van Buren, President Van Buren's eldest son, a graduate of West Point, and long an officer of the United States Army. Mrs. Van Buren was a lady of rare accomplishments and graceful manners, and very vivacious in conversation, and was, consequently, very popular in the White House. At the end of President Van Buren's administration Major and Mrs. Van Buren visited Europe. Her uncle, Mr. Stevenson, was then Minister to England, and she and her husband were the recipients of much attention, as London was unusually gay on account of the recent coronation of Queen Victoria. Returning, they resided throughout his retirement with ex-President Van Buren at Lindenwald, and subsequently removed to New York City, where Mrs. Van Buren remained for the rest of her life. Her home was the resort of people of refinement and education. She was most unselfish and self-denying in the distribution of her wealth and influence for the benefit of others. She died December 29, 1878.

ANNA SYMMES HARRISON.

Anna Symmes Harrison, wife of William Henry Harrison, ninth President of the United States, was born the 25th of July, 1775, at Morristown, New Jersey, her mother dying soon after her birth. She was given into the care of her maternal grandparents, Mr. and Mrs. Tuthill, at Southhold, Long Island, at the age of four years. The British were then in possession of Long Island and, notwithstanding her tender years, she realized the danger of the journey. Her father, Hon. John Cleves Symmes, a colonel in the Continental Army, assumed the disguise of a British officer's uniform, that he might accomplish the perilous undertaking of transferring his little daughter from Morristown, New Jersey, to Southhold, Long Island. He did not see her again until after the evacuation of New York, in the fall of 1783. She had most excellent care by her worthy grandparents, who did not neglect to give Anna religious instruction in her earliest childhood. She was also taught that industry, prudence and economy were Christian virtues. She was educated in the school of Mrs. Isabelle Graham, of New York. In 1794 she accompanied her father and stepmother to Ohio, where her father had a small colony of settlers at North Bend, on the Ohio River. Judge Symmes was appointed one of the associate judges of the Supreme Court of the great northwestern territory. His district was a very large one, and frequently while he was attending the courts in his district Anna visited her sister, Mrs. Peyton Short, at Lexington, Kentucky. During one of these visits she met Captain William Henry Harrison, the youngest son of Benjamin Harrison, of Virginia, and later married him. After his service in the army, General Harrison was appointed the first governor of Indian Territory by President Adams, and removed his family to the old French town of Vincennes, on the Wabash, then the seat of government of the Indian Territory. Here he and Mrs. Harrison and their family lived for many years. Mrs. Harrison, through her courteous manners and liberal hospitality as mistress of the Governor's Mansion, won for herself a wide reputation. She resided in the Governor's Mansion through the administration of Adams, Jefferson and Madison, till 1812, when, after the surrender of Hull, Harrison was appointed to the command of the Northwestern army. Mrs. Harrison remained in Vincennes during the absence of General Harrison, when he commanded the army which fought the battle of Prophets Town, Tippecanoe and other engagements. After his victories General Harrison was appointed Major-General of the forces in Kentucky, and removed his family to Cincinnati,where Mrs. Harrison and her children remained while he conducted his campaign against the hostile Indians.   She arranged for the education of her children by private tutors, and herself conducted the entire rearing of her family, displaying the greatest executive ability, loyalty and Christian fortitude, bearing bravely bereavements that came to her through the death of her children and other members of her family.   When, after his election to the Presidency, General Harrison left his home to be in Washington for his inauguration, the 4th of March, 1841, he was unaccompanied by Mrs. Harrison, who was in very delicate health and, through the advice of her physician, did not accompany her husband to Washington.   Consequently, she never presided over the White House.   One month from the day of his inauguration President Harrison died of pneumonia.   Mrs. Harrison was in her home at North Bend, and was overwhelmed for a time by this fearful blow.   She rallied, however, and lived for many years in the old home.   She eventually removed to that of her only surviving son, Hon. J. Scott Harrison, five miles below North Bend, on the Ohio River, where she resided until her death, the 25th of February, 1864, in the 89th year of her age.   She lived to see many of her grandsons officers and soldiers in the Union Army during the Civil War and to predict the elevation of her grandson, Benjamin H. Harrison, to the office of President of the United States, which office had been filled by his grandfather, General William Henry Harrison.

LETITIA CHRISTIAN TYLER.

John Tyler, the tenth President of the United States, succeeded President William Henry Harrison, whose administration lasted only one month.   His first wife was Letitia Christian, daughter of Robert Christian, of Cedar Grove, Virginia. Mr. Tyler and Miss Christian were married on the 29th of March, 1813.   Young Tyler was one of the most prominent rising young lawyers of the state of Virginia.   Their lives were spent surrounded by everything that could contribute to their happiness and popularity.   Mrs. Tyler, to the day of her death in the executive mansion, was noted for her brilliancy of mind, liberal hospitality, wifely and motherly devotion, and was in all respects a lovely, Christian character.   In the various positions occupied by Mr. Tyler Mrs. Tyler was an able helpmeet, and was as well noted for her great beauty of person, grace of carriage, delicate refinement and exquisite taste.   During President Tyler's occupation of the White House there were many distinguished visitors, among them Charles Dickens, Washington Irving, and many others, who were charmed by Mrs. Tyler's gracious manners.   Her children have been the most enthusiastic eulogists of her lovely character and motherly devotion.   She resided in the White House from April, 1841, to September 9, 1842, the date of her death, leaving behind her an imperishable impression as one of the most accomplished women who ever presided in this historic mansion.

JULIA GARDINER TYLER.

President John Tyler married, as his second wife, Miss Julia Gardiner, on the 26th day of June, 1844, at the Church of the Ascension, New York City.   Their wedding was the first instance of the marriage of a President during his term of office.   Miss Gardiner was the daughter of a wealthy gentleman from Gardiner's Island who had come upon a visit to Washington in the winter of 1843, accompanied by his beautiful daughter.   They were invited by Captain Stockton to accompany the President and other friends to Alexandria on the trial trip of a new ship which had been manned by large guns.   On their return, when opposite the fort, an explosion took place which changed the merry party to one of mourning, Miss Gardiner's father being among the number who were killed.   There were a great many lost in this accident. The bodies of the killed were taken to the White House, from which they were conveyed to their last resting places.   The President's marriage to Miss Gardiner took place some months after this disaster.   Mrs. Tyler was a queenly woman and presided over the White House with exceptional grace and acceptability for eight months prior to the expiration of President Tyler's term of office.   On his retirement they repaired to his home in Virginia.   The ex-President died in Richmond, January 17, 1862.   After the Civil War, Mrs. Tyler recevied from Congress a pension which was voted to her in the winter of 1879.   She had suffered great pecuniary losses after the death of her husband, and it was proper that she should receive this recognition of her husband's services to his country.   For many years she resided in Georgetown, D. C., and being a devout Catholic, found it agreeable to be near the Georgetown Convent, where her daughter was educated.   She died in 1889.

SARAH CHILDRESS POLK.

Sarah Childress Polk, nee Childress, daughter of Captain Joel and Elizabeth Childress was born near Murfreesboro, Tennessee, September 4, 1803.   She was educated at the Moravian Institute at Salem, North Carolina.   She was married at the age of nineteen to James Knox Polk, of Murfreesboro.   Mr. Polk was then a member of the legislature of Tennessee and in the following year was elected to Congress, and after serving on the most important committees of the House of Representatives, he was elected speaker, a position for which he was especially fitted.

Mrs. Polk accompanied her husband to Washington every winter and occupied a prominent position in society. Her influence was not only social, but political. She took great pains to inform herself on political affairs, and was deeply interested in all the discussions of the day which in any way affected the welfare of her country. She had lived all her life in the atmosphere of politics and had extensive acquaintance with the public men of the time, and often counseled with her husband on national subjects. They resided at Columbia, Tennessee. She was a member of the Presbyterian Church of that city and was much esteemed for her devotion to her religious duties. Mrs. Polk was the recipient of many testimonials of high esteem from distinguished men, among them she received a copy of verses addressed to her by the eminent jurist, Honorable Joseph D. Story. In 1839 Mr. Polk was elected Governor of Tennessee and removed his residence to Nashville. Mrs. Polk as mistress of the executive mansion exercised a powerful influence in harmonizing the bitterness which then existed between rival parties. In the campaign of 1844, for the Presidency, in which Henry Clay was the idol of the Whig party, and James K. Polk of the Democratic party, there was the greatest excitement. Mr. Polk was elected and inaugurated on March 4, 1845. Having no children, Mrs. Polk devoted all her time to her duties as Lady of the White House, and no other mistress of that stately mansion left a more favorable impression upon the people and society of that day than did Mrs. Polk. It may be said that she maintained the dignity of the President's mansion without assuming the slightest hauteur and much has been said of her attractive manner, queenly bearing and sincere cordiality. The receptions of President and Mrs. Polk were very largely attended and universally enjoyed. Her style of dress was particularly becoming to her. She had very black hair and eyes and a fair complexion and was much given to wearing bright colors and gay turbans. It was with much regret that the social circles of Washington saw Mr. and Mrs. Polk depart from the White House. It was during Polk's administration that we had the war with Mexico and much credit is due to the President and Mrs. Polk in causing the settlement of the difficulties between the United States and Mexico. Mr. Polk, on his retirement from the White House, purchased a house in Nashville, Tennessee, but did not live long in enjoyment of it. After his death Mrs. Polk lived a great many years in this Nashville home, receiving here the homage of all distinguished visitors to the capital of Tennessee. The legislature of that state called upon her in a body every New Year's Day when they were in session. During the confederate days of Nashville, Mrs. Polk received the most distinguished consideration, all general officers, both Confederate and Union, paying their respects to her by calling in person. The writer remembers hearing George Bancroft, the distinguished historian, give a graphic account of his charming visit to Mrs. Polk not long before her death, which occurred in 1891.

MARGARET TAYLOR AND MRS. BLISS (NEE BETTY TAYLOR.)

Upon the ascension of General Zachary Taylor to the office of the Presidency, much solicitude was expressed as to Mrs. Taylor's ability to preside over the executive mansion. General Taylor, when notified of his election to the office, said "for more than a quarter of a century my house has been the tent and my home the battlefield," an expression which was literally true. Notwithstanding this fact he had never lost his regard for the proprieties and refinements of life. Mrs. Taylor had been his constant companion in all of his campaigns on the frontier and during the Florida War. Her experience was really the most extensive in army life of that of any other army woman. She was known as a true American heroine. She had no fear and was never willing to be separated from her soldier husband. These experiences developed the true nobility of her character. She spent much of her time at Baton Rouge and in addition to the responsibilities of her household she devoted herself to plans for the building of churches and establishing of schools, and exercised her influence to quiet the alarm of the people after the battle of Palo Alto and Resaca de la Palma. It was during the war with Mexico that Lieutenant Jefferson Davis was under the command of General Taylor. It was noticed that they were not on friendly terms, and it was afterwards discovered that it was on account of General Taylor's opposition to his attention to his daughter Sarah. The General violently opposed the attentions of army officers to his daughters, on account of the fact that he considered the life of an army officer at that time, fraught with too many hardships for a woman. Lieutenant Jefferson Davis, however, succeeded in winning the affections of General Taylor's daughter and being unable to overcome the father's opposition, the young people ran away and were married, which General Taylor considered a dishonorable thing on the part of Jefferson Davis. Mrs. Davis died soon after her marriage, which sad event made a very deep impression upon the General's and Mrs. Taylor's lives.

General Taylor's brilliant triumphs in Mexico destined him to become the President of the United States, as much as Mrs. Taylor opposed his being a candidate for the Presidency. Upon receiving the news of his election, General Taylor resigned as an officer of the army and it was with much regret that he and his family severed their connection with the service, in which they had spent nearly their whole lives. Mrs. Taylor had no taste for the gayeties of Washington and after the inauguration of President Taylor she withdrew from all participation in social functions and resigned the duties of the mistress of the White House to her youngest daughter, Elizabeth, the wife of Major Bliss, who had served as General Taylor's Adjutant General during the campaign. "Miss Betty," as she was called, was young, vivacious, accomplished and eminently fitted to discharge the duties of mistress of the White House. Mrs. Taylor selected such rooms as suited her simple tastes, and as far as possible resumed the routine that characterized her simple life at Baton Rouge. General Taylor insisted that she should be indulged in exercising her own wishes in these matters, since Mrs. Bliss was thoroughly competent to relieve her mother of distasteful duties. During President Taylor's residency in the White House there were many illustrious men in the Senate and holding other high positions. The rivalries and jealousies in politics reached an alarming height, and as General Taylor was the victim upon whom was visited many attacks and much vituperation, his brave spirit finally succumbed, and he died July 9, 1850, surrounded by his deeply afflicted family.

Accompanied by her daughter Mrs. Taylor obtained a home among her relations in Kentucky, but soon became very unhappy, because of the continued manifestations of sympathy. She removed to the residence of her son near Pascagoula, Louisiana. Major Bliss' death soon followed that of Mrs. Taylor which occurred in 1852, and Mrs. Bliss, childless and alone, sought the seclusion of private life among friends in Virginia.

ABIGAIL FILLMORE.

Mrs. Abigail Fillmore, wife of President Fillmore, was the daughter of Reverend Lemuel Powers, a Baptist clergyman of note. She was born in Stillwater, Saratoga County, New York, March, 1798. Dr. Powers was a descendant of Henry Leland, of Sherburne, England. Mrs. Fillmore's father died while she was in her infancy and she was left to the care of her sainted mother, whose small income led her to seek a home in Cayuga County, and become a teacher, so that she might be able to have her daughter Abigail educated. In her personality Miss Powers commanded the greatest admiration and her exceeding kindness of heart won for her the affection of all who knew her. She was distinguished not only on account of her great beauty, but because of her keen intelligence. She became a teacher, continuing her occupation after her mother's second marriage. She and Mr. Fillmore met in her little home village, he a clothier's apprentice, she a teacher in the village school, and they became engaged. Mr. Fillmore did not long continue in the profession chosen for him by his father, but as soon as possible began the study of law, in which he was most successful. Circumstances compelled him to move to Erie County, and the young people waited three years before their incomes permitted of their marriage, which event was consummated in February, 1826. They established their home in a small house built by Mr. Fillmore's own hands, and here they both worked very hard for the fulfillment of their ambitions. Mr. Fillmore was elected a member of the state legislature in two years after their marriage. At every rung of the ladder which he climbed, Mrs. Fillmore, with her intellectual strength, ceaseless industry and devotion to her husband's interests, contributed materially to his success. In 1830, the Fillmores removed to Buffalo, where they continued their united efforts and aspirations.   Every year added to the name and fame of Millard Fillmore.   Upon his election to the Presidency and their removal to the White House, they found it absolutely devoid of books and other evidences of culture. It was Mr. Fillmore's first duty to secure an appropriation from Congress for a library, and to Mrs. Fillmore belongs the credit of selecting the first library in the White House. Mrs. Fillmore had suffered the loss of a sister just before their removal to the executive mansion and consequently left many of the duties devolving upon its mistress to her only daughter. Although eminently fitted to preside over any social function with unusual grace and dignity, Mrs. Fillmore preferred a retired life and the devotion of her time to the welfare of her family.   She was very proud of her husband's success and has left behind her a remarkable example of motherly and wifely tenderness.   She died at Willard's Hotel, Washington, D. C., March 13, 1852.

MARY ABIGAIL FILLMORE.

Mary Abigail Fillmore, the only daughter of President Fillmore, was, on account of her mother's delicate health, mistress of the White House during President Fillmore's term.   She was a remarkably intellectual young woman, highly educated, and a fine linguist.   Her taste and talent for sculpture was scarcely second to that of her most intimate friend the distinguished Harriet Hosmer, and but for the cutting off of her life by cholera at the age of twenty-two years, she might have become as distinguished as this beloved schoolmate.   She was much admired and attained a national reputation on account of the graceful and acceptable manner in which she presided over the White House.

JANE MEANS APPLETON PIERCE.

Jane Means Appleton, daughter of Reverend Jesse Appleton, D.D., President of Bowdoin College, was born at Hampton, New Hampshire, March 12, 1806.   She was brought up under the most refined, Christian, educational influences.   Unfortunately she was delicate from her childhood and as she grew older her nervous organization became more and more sensitive, but her unselfish disposition prompted her to forget herself in her desire to contribute to the happiness and pleasure of others. Soon after her marriage she was thrown into political society, which was peculiarly attractive to her. She made a deep impression by her intellectual conversation and her comprehension of political questions. Franklin Pierce was a member of Congress when they were married, in 1834, and though she shrank at first from Washington society she soon became very popular. In 1838 Mr. Pierce removed from Hillsboro to Concord, accepting the appointment of Attorney-General in the cabinet of James K. Polk. This seemed to be the beginning of his national reputation, which eventually made him President of the United States. President and Mrs. Pierce had three children. The eldest, a son, was traveling with his parents from Boston to Concord, on January 5, 1852, before Mr. Pierce's inauguration, when by an accident on the Boston and Maine Railroad, the car in which they were sitting was overturned, and although the President-elect and Mrs. Pierce escaped serious injury, their son was killed. Such a bereavement on the threshhold of their occupancy of the White House threw a pall over the festivities attending the inaugural and Mrs. Pierce never rallied completely from this fearful blow. One can imagine the effort that it cost her to go through the official functions of the White House with such a tragedy ever before her. After Mr. Pierce's retirement, in an effort to establish Mrs. Pierce's health, they sailed for Europe to spend the winter in the Island of Madeira, continuing their journey through Portugal, Spain, France, Switzerland, Italy, Germany and England. She never regained full health and died on December 2, 1863, at Andover, Massachusetts.

HARRIET LANE.

Harriet Lane, the niece of James Buchanan, was one of the most attractive, intelligent and gracious women who ever presided over the White House. She had accompanied her uncle and directed his establishment when he was American minister to St. James. Her grandfather, James Buchanan, emigrated from Ireland in the year 1783 and settled in Mercersburg, Franklin County, Pennsylvania, where he married, in 1788, Elizabeth Speer of Scotch-Irish ancestry. James Buchanan, ex-President of the United States, was the eldest son of this marriage. Miss Lane's mother, Jane Buchanan, was the second child. The two children, so near of an age, were boon companions. Jane, this favorite sister, married Elliot T. Lane and Harriet was their youngest child. The mother died when Harriet was but seven years old; her father died two years later, consequently she was at once adopted by her bachelor uncle, James, and was never separated from him for any length of time afterward. When Mr. Buchanan was a member of Congress he brought Harriet Lane from the Pennsylvania home and placed her in the George-town Convent, from which she graduated with the highest honors of that institution, and was so beloved by the nuns that they kept in touch with her as long as she lived. She was a beautiful blonde with a wealth of Titian hair and eyes as soft as those of a gazelle. All her features were cast in a noble mold. She was full of gay spirits and restless activity; always bright and cheerful. She was an omniv-orous reader, whiling away many an hour for her lonely uncle reading aloud to him in her sweet and pure voice. Her administration of her uncle's household in England won for her the admiration and respect of royalty, and the people of England considered her an unusually fine specimen of American womanhood. Having spent so much of her life in the society of the distinguished people with whom her uncle was intimate, she was eminently fitted to become mistress of the White House. The gathering of the war clouds during Mr. Buchanan's administra-tion was not accelerated in any way by Miss Lane, whose cordial greeting, cheer-ful manner and welcome to the White House were extended alike to war represent-atives of all sections of the country. There are people living to-day who cannot forget her fascinating manners and genuine hospitality in the historic White House. It was said that it was hard to "decide between uncle and niece as to which looked the proudest and greatest, the man or the woman, the earlier or the later born," as they stood together at the first reception on the first New Year's Day after Mr. Buchanan's inauguration. One can readily imagine Miss Lane's difficult position, when each day there passed into the White House alternately the bitterest seces-sionists and the strongest unionists before the ultimate clash of arms. It required almost superhuman tact and diplomacy to show no distinction, but Miss Lane was equal to the task.

In 1860, when the Prince of Wales, the late Edward VII, paid a visit to the United States, and was the guest of the President and Miss Lane in the White House, Miss Lane made an indelible impression upon her royal guest by her fas-cinating manner, sincere cordiality and faultless hospitality. Queen Victoria sent her acknowledgment of appreciation of the courtesy extended to the Prince in an autograph letter couched in the strongest expressions of friendship for Miss Lane personally, as well as for the people of the United States, who had received the Prince of Wales with so much honor, and later sent autograph pictures of the royal family, with Miss Lane's name written upon them.

After the close of Mr. Buchanan's administration Miss Lane accompanied her uncle to his beloved "Wheatland," where she remained with him until his death. After that event she spent part of her time in Baltimore, when not visiting friends in other cities. She was married by the Reverend Edward Y. Buchanan in January, 1866, to Henry Elliott Johnston. They went to Cuba and spent a month or two, after which Mr. and Mrs. Johnston took up their residence in Baltimore in the beautiful home which Mr. Johnston had provided with great thoughtfulness, taste and liberality for his bride. Mrs. Johnston regained some of her former cheerfulness and brightness. She seemed very happy as a wife and mother. She had two sons and it seemed that her life was destined to be a happy one. But, alas, for human hope, on the 25th of March, 1881, her son, James Buchanan Johnston, died, and she was again overwhelmed with grief. A few years subsequently the second son died, and also Mr. Johnston, and Harriet Lane Johnston, widowed and childless came back to Washington to spend the remaining years of her life. She was the recipient of distinguished honors by the people of Washington, by whom she was greatly beloved. After her death in 1904 it was found that she had willed her residence in Washington, and endowed it, as a home for dependent women. She also left means to build and endow the National Cathedral School for Boys, at Washington, D. C.

THEODOSIA BURR.

Someone has said of this daughter of Aaron Burr: "With a great deal of wit, spirit and talent, and a face strikingly beautiful she inherited all that a daughter could inherit of a father's courage—she was a realization of her father's idea of a woman." And it is his love for this daughter, so tender and touching, that makes an appeal to our sympathy, however strong condemnation of his public acts may have been.

At the time of her birth in 1784, Burr was a successful young lawyer. Handsome, fascinating, of good family and considerable fortune, he might have aspired to the hand of a Clinton, a Livingston or a Van Rensselaer, but instead he had married a woman ten years his senior, neither rich nor pretty, and a widow with two sons. "The mother of my Theo," he was heard to say in the days when she of whom he spoke had been long dead, "was the best woman and finest lady I have ever known." It was, however, the general opinion that the coming of Theodosia, their only child, was the explanation of the success of the inexplicable marriage. It became Aaron Burr's great ambition to make of this daughter an intelligent and noble woman. One evening a volume entitled "A Vindication of the Rights of Woman," by Mary Wollstonecraft, chanced to come under his notice and he sat up reading it until late in the night. In the spirit of that book he undertook the education of his daughter. He went on the principle that Theodosia was as clever and capable as a boy, and he gave her the same advantages as he would have given a son. This was an unusual principle in the days when Theodosia Burr was a girl, and in her education she may be said to be the first exponent of the college woman in America. Her father himself superintended her education even to the smallest details. From Philadelphia, where he was stationed as United States senator, he sent her fond letters of advice and criticism and at his request she sent him every week a journal of her doings and of her progress in learning.

These are charming pictures we have of Aaron Burr waiting about in the government building for the arrival of the post that should bring the letter or diary directed in his daughter's girlish handwriting; and again seated at his desk in the noisy senate chamber writing a reply to his "Dear Little Daughter," in time to catch the return mail to New York.

While she was still a child in years Theodosia Burr assumed charge of her father's house, and the distinguished men who gathered there were charmed with the little hostess, her playful wit, her self-poise and dignity of manner. In those days, when she was mistress of "Richmond Hill" after her mother's death, she was more than ever the object of her father's thought and love. He continued to superintend her education, and no social duties, no business or pleasure of any sort were allowed to interfere with her advancement of learning. At sixteen she was still a schoolgirl, though her companions of the same age had relinquished all study books and were giving their entire attention to gowns, parties and beaux. And in later years, in spite of her beauty and talents and her high position as the daughter of Aaron Burr, she was delightfully simple and unaffected. Such was the result of sensible education and her own sweet nature. She also had many admirers. We have a hint of them in one of the jovial Edward Livingston's puns that have come down to us. He was Mayor of New York when Miss Burr was one of the ruling belles. One day he took the young lady aboard a French frigate lying in the harbor. "You must bring none of your sparks on board," he warned her in merry raillery, "for we have a magazine here and we shall all be blown up." However, Miss Burr's "sparks" were not long allowed to remain in evidence for there came impetuous young Joseph Alston from South Carolina, who straightway routed his rivals and captured her.

Through all the period of wifehood and motherhood, as in those earlier days when she was his little daughter, his pupil and mistress of his home, she remained the dearest thing in the world to her distinguished father. On the night before his duel with Hamilton his last thoughts before going to the field were of his daughter. To her he wrote: "I am indebted to you for a very great portion of the happiness which I have enjoyed in this life. You have completely satisfied all that my heart had hoped."

News of the duel reached his daughter in her far-away home. Its shadow fell on her with awful blackness. Her father was a fugitive from justice with an indictment of murder hanging over him. Her days of gladness were over, and her days of anxiety and sorrow had begun. She did not see her father for almost a year, but when he did come to her, blackened through many miles of travel in an open canoe, ruined in fortune and repute, he was as welcome as ever he had been in days of his prosperity. His disgrace had saddened his daughter. It had not lessened her love for him nor her belief in him. Her love and her belief were yet to undergo their trial. The duel with Hamilton was but the beginning of Burr's downfall. The Mexican scheme soon followed. In it Theodosia and her husband became involved. When Burr was to be King of Mexico, she was to be chief lady of the court and her husband chief minister and her little son, Aaron Burr Alston, was to be heir presumptive to the throne. But while they talked of a visionary dynasty the President issued his proclamation, and Burr was summoned to appear before the tribunal at Richmond to answer to the charge of high treason.

Throughout the trial Mrs. Alston was at Richmond. Her presence there was a great help to Burr's cause. She was universally admired for her beauty, her ability and her blind faith in her father. Many believed in Aaron Burr because she believed in him. Luther Martin, her father's counsel, had the keenest admiration for the daughter of his client. "I find," wrote one statesman of this time, "that Luther Martin's idolatrous admiration of Mrs. Alston is as excessive as my own, as it is the medium of his blind attachment to her father."

Burr was acquitted, but popular feeling was so strong against him that he was forced to leave America. In the spring of 1808, the year after his trial, he sailed from New York, and his daughter, sick, sorrowful, but as true as ever, left her Carolina home and journeyed north to see him once more before he went, and to bid him good-bye. The night before his departure she spent with him at the house of a loyal friend. Father and daughter were both brave, and in the morning he parted from her and sailed away in the ship that was carrying him from all that he held most dear. The years of Burr's exile were sad years for his daughter. She realized with keen distress the bitterness of his position, and indeed she herself was made to feel some of the odium that was directed against him. She longed earnestly for his return and pleaded eloquently and pathetically with those in authority that her father might be allowed to come back to America. But when in the year 1812 he did come back to New York and his daughter started to join him there, the ship on which she had taken passage went down off Cape Hatteras and not a soul on board was saved. The father and husband waited in agonized expectancy, but at length came the news of her tragic fate. Thus Burr was left alone, but he did not complain. He was silent through his great sorrow. But there were those who remembered him in his last days, a solitary old man walking along the Battery and looking wistfully toward the horizon for ships. The look was a habit he had acquired while waiting for the ship which never brought his daughter.

ELIZABETH PATTERSON BONAPARTE.

Elizabeth Patterson Bonaparte was born in Baltimore, Maryland, February 6, 1785. She was the daughter of William Patterson, who came a poor boy from Ireland to Maryland, where he became a prominent merchant, and one of the wealthiest citizens. She was a beautiful girl of eighteen when she met Jerome Bonaparte at a social gathering in Baltimore, and despite the opposition of her father, a marriage was speedily arranged, the ceremony taking place with all legal formalities on Christmas Eve, 1803, when the groom had just passed his nineteenth birthday. Mr. Patterson's fears that the marriage would be offensive to the First Consul proved to be well grounded. Attempts were unsuccessfully made, through Robert R. Livingston, the American minister at Paris, and through influential persons, to reconcile Napoleon to his brother's marriage. He ordered Jerome to return immediately to France, "leaving in America, the young person in question." Jerome refused to obey and a year was spent in travel and in residence at Baltimore. Meanwhile, Napoleon had proclaimed himself Emperor, and in 1805 Jerome, hoping for a reconciliation with his brother, took his wife to Europe. They reached Lisbon in safety, but there Jerome was arrested and taken to France, his wife not being allowed to land. Her message to the Emperor was: "Madame Bonaparte demands her rights as a member of the Imperial family." She then proceeded to England where a boy was born to her and christened, Jerome Napoleon. The Emperor refused to recognize her marriage, but promised Elizabeth an annual pension of $12,000 provided she would return to America and renounce the name of Bonaparte, which conditions she accepted. She returned to Europe on occasional visits, where she was the center of attraction, winning attention not only from her husband's mother and other members of the family, but also from the Duke of Wellington, Madam de Stael, Byron, and even Louis XVII, who invited her to appear at court, but as she still received a pension from the exiled Emperor she declined. Her husband married Catharine, daughter of the King of Westphalia. He then sent to America for his son, Jerome Napoleon, but Madam Bonaparte refused to give him up, scornfully declining the offer from her husband of a ducal crown with an income of $40,000 a year. The son frequently visited his father's family in Europe, where he was treated as a son and brother. His subsequent marriage with Miss Williams of Baltimore caused his mother great anger. His cousin, Emperor Napoleon III, invited him to France, where he was legitimized and received as a member of the family. He declined a duchy, refusing the condition which demanded the surrender of the name of Bonaparte. On the death of King Jerome in 1860, Elizabeth Patterson, as his American wife, unsuccessfully contested his will. The last eighteen years of her life were spent in Baltimore. She left a fortune of one million, five hundred thousand dollars, to two grandsons, Jerome Napoleon and Charles J. Bonaparte. The latter was secretary of the navy and attorney-general during the administration of President Roosevelt. Madame Bonaparte died in Baltimore on April 4, 1879.

THE MOTHER OF WEBSTER.

Daniel Webster spent his childhood in a log cabin on the banks of the Merrimac in an unfrequented part of New Hampshire. From his mother he received those lessons which formed his mind and character and fitted him for the great part he was to play in public life. She denied herself everything possible that he might go to Exeter Academy and to Dartmouth College. Her faith in his ability for future greatness being so strong, she desired to give him every opportunity for education. To her Webster always gave the credit for his success in life.

Prominent Women Who Have Wielded a Strong Influence for the Good of the Country.

MRS. LOUIS McLEAN.

In the letters of Washington Irving we find Mrs. Louis McLean mentioned as a prominent leader in the fashionable society of Washington city. She was the eldest daughter of Robert Milligan and in 1812 married the son of Alan McLean of Delaware, who was elected to Congress from that state in 1817. In 1827 he was elected senator and in 1829 was sent by President Jackson as minister to England. In 1831 he returned to accept the portfolio of the Treasury in Jackson's cabinet and two years later was made secretary of state. While Washington Irving was on a visit to this country he was entertained at Mr. McLean's home. Irving also mentions a Miss Barney as a great belle and Miss Butt of Norfolk.

CORNELIA VAN NESS.

The niece of Mrs. Van Ness was universally admired and wielded a personal sway in the society of the national Capital in the winter of 1828-29. She was a Miss Cornelia Van Ness, the daughter of Cornelius P. Van Ness who was chief justice and governor of Vermont. Mrs. C. P. Van Ness, who was the sister-in-law of the wife of General Van Ness, occupied a position not less distinguished than that of her sister-in-law. Her husband was the governor of Vermont and she presided over his home sustaining her position with dignity and added an elevating social influence to its political supremacy. Her house was the resort of distinguished travelers from every part of the United States as well as Europe, and here General Lafayette was entertained when he re-visited the United States. She accompanied her husband when he was sent as minister to Spain and made, while there, an enviable reputation for her countrywomen. Their daughter, Miss Cornelia Van Ness, while on a visit to her uncle, General Van Ness of Washington city, became one of the belles of Washington. While with her parents in Madrid she became conspicuous and made a most pleasing impression, receiving marks of honor and personal favor from the Queen. She spoke both French and Spanish with fluency. After twenty months in the Spanish capital, she went to Paris on a visit, and here at the house of Mr. Reeves in the presence of a most distinguished gathering, among them General Lafayette, she was married to Mr. James J. Roosevelt of New York. In September 1831, Mr. and Mrs. Roosevelt returned to the United States and took up their residence in New York City. In 1840 Mr. Roosevelt was elected a member of Congress and the following year, accompanied by his family, he took up his residence in Washington City, and during the winters of 1842-43 Mrs. Roosevelt became prominent in society and they were among the first to introduce a new fashion of entertaining. During Washington's administration very simple forms of entertainment prevailed, and one of the rules for the President, established with the concurrence of Jefferson and Hamilton, was that the President was never to visit anyone but the Vice-President, or even to dine out. Most of the entertaining was done by the President and foreign ministers but in 1842 Mr. and Mrs. Roosevelt brought about a social revolution by frequent and agreeable dinner and evening parties which President Tyler attended as an unassuming guest, and it is related by Mr. Ingersoll in giving an account of social matters in Washington at this time that he had the honor to play a rubber of whist with President Tyler, Lord Ashburton, ex-minister to England. Many letters were written to Mrs. Roosevelt by statesmen of the greatest distinction in American political life on affairs of national importance, which serve to show the high esteem in which she was entertained and the respect for her judgment and opinions in matters wherein women were not supposed (at that time) to have opinions of value. Mrs. Roosevelt for many years was a leader in society in the city of New York. Her entertainments were always marked by splendor and refined taste; her dignified manner, her intellectual conversation gave a charm to the social intercourse wherever she presided. She was a patron of many of the charitable affairs and institutions of New York and she aided conspicuously in the Sanitary Fair held in New York City.

LADY WILLIAM GORE OUSELEY.

Mrs. Roosevelt's sister was also conspicuous in social life. Her husband was Sir William Gore Ouseley, connected with the British legation in Washington in 1829, when they were married. His life as a diplomat to the various European courts and those of South America was interesting. During Lady Ouseley's stay in Washington she took a prominent part in the social life of that city.

MRS. WINFIELD SCOTT.

The wife of General Winfield Scott was a prominent figure in social life. She was a Miss Maria Mayo, the daughter of Mr. John Mayo of Richmond, Virginia. General and Mrs. Scott had seven children.

MRS. MERRICK.

Mrs. Merrick, the wife of Judge Merrick of the District of Columbia was the daughter of Charles Wickliffe and was a leader in the social life of Washington.

MRS. DANIEL WEBSTER.

The wife of Daniel Webster, Caroline Leroy, accompanied her husband in 1839, when he went abroad and was received at the courts of Europe. They spent their winters in Washington, where Mrs. Webster became prominent socially. Mrs. Webster not only shared his wanderings but was a helpmeet in every sense of the word to her distinguished husband both in public and private affairs. She assisted him in his correspondence and Mr. Webster relied on her in all matters where sound judgment and discretion were required. During his secretaryship both under Presidents Tyler and Fillmore she was his efficient aid, at the same time she made his house the center of a brilliant society, drawing about them the finest minds of the century and those of high position in our country's history.

MRS. JOHN J. CRITTENDEN.

Mrs. John J. Crittenden was one of the American women who shared the glory and distinction of her husband, contributing her part as a wife to his success. The ancestors of Mrs. Crittenden were from Albemarle and Goochland Counties, Virginia. Her great-grandfather was General John Woodson, who had inherited from his father a large estate on the James River in Goochland County, called

Dover. He married Dorothea Randolph. One of her sisters was the mother of Thomas Jefferson. Another, Mrs. Pleasants, was the mother of Governor Pleasants of Virginia. Her only brother was Thomas Mann Randolph. A son of Mr. and Mrs. Woodson, Josiah, married his cousin, Elizabeth Woodson, and their daughter, Mary, in 1801, married Dr. James W. Moss of Albermarle County, Virginia, and they were the parents of Elizabeth Moss, who became later Mrs. Crittenden. Elizabeth was born while her parents were living in Kentucky but when quite a young girl they removed to Missouri which had just been admitted as a state to the Union. Their home was for a time in St. Louis, but later her father removed to the town of Columbia in that state. Elizabeth married when quite young a physician, Dr. William P. Wilcox, who was at that time a member of the state legislature. Dr. Wilcox survived but a short time, leaving his wife with two daughters. The eldest, Mary, became the wife of Mr. Andrew McKinley, only son of Justice McKinley of the Supreme Court of the United States. The youngest daughter, Anna, became the wife of Honorable E. Carrington Cabell, a representative in Congress from Florida and son of Honorable William Cabell late Chief Justice of Virginia. In 1832 Mrs. Wilcox married General William H. Ashley, then the only representative in Congress from Missouri. General Ashley was a resident of St. Louis and one of its distinguished citizens. Mrs. Ashley accompanied her husband to Washington immediately after their marriage and at once became the subject of general admiration and the center of a large social circle. Her natural grace, affability, frank cordiality, intellectual cultivation and above all her genuine kindness of heart drew about her those who appreciated such sterling qualities and charming graces. In 1838, General Ashley died and Mrs. Ashley returned to her home in St. Louis. Occasionally she spent her time in Philadelphia and Washington while her children were being educated. She was always a favorite wherever she went and remained unspoilt notwithstanding the attentions and homage lavished upon her. It is said of her she was never known to speak harshly or censoriously of anyone, nor did she ever forget an acquaintance or wound by a change of manner. She was perfectly familiar with all the political issues of the day but never advocated as a partisan either side; always intelligent and fluent in conversation, she never assumed the slightest superiority or seemed conscious that her own opinion or judgment was better than that of others. Her delicate tact and regard for the feelings or the pride of others rendered her an ornament of every social circle. Honorable John J. Crittenden, then attorney general of the United States in Mr. Fillmore's cabinet in 1853, won the heart of this distinguished woman. After Mr. Crittenden's retirement from the cabinet he was returned to the senate, where he remained until his death in 1863. Mrs. Crittenden always accompanied her husband to Washington and it is said the political and diplomatic world flocked about them. Mr. Crittenden's service was during the stormy days which preceded the outbreak of the Rebellion and many were the trials they were called upon to endure. Mrs. Crittenden sympathized deeply with her husband in his efforts to preserve the Union. After Mr. Crittenden's death Mrs. Crittenden remained for a time at Frankfort, Kentucky, and later removed to New York City.

MRS. SLIDELL.

Mrs. Slidell, the wife of the senator from Louisiana, was conspicuous abroad among the ladies devoted to the Confederate cause and her influence in society was remarkable. Mrs. Slidell was Miss Daylond of Louisiana. Her home was on the Mississippi coast.

MRS. DUVALL AND OTHERS.

Another of the brilliant and intellectual women from the South was Mrs. Duvall, the wife of Mr. Duvall, a planter from Louisiana and son of former Chief Justice of Maryland. Among the social queens of the Confederate court in Richmond, Virginia, was Mrs. James Chestnut of Camden, South Carolina, Mrs. Davis and Mrs. Clement Clay. Mrs. Reverdy Johnson was a prominent leader of the society of Baltimore. She was very beautiful and queenly woman and helped greatly to advance the fortunes of her husband. Mrs. Myra Clarke Gaines was another southern woman prominent in the social life in Washington. Her name is familiar to everyone and her romantic history well known. The history of her claim to her father's estates, prosecuted under various discouragements for thirty-five years, and granted in her favor only a few days before her death, is considered one of the most extraordinary cases as well as one of the most interesting, in the annals of American jurisprudence.

LUCY CRITTENDEN.

Miss Lucy Crittenden who was the sister of John J. Crittenden, the distinguished senator, was a woman possessed of superior intellect and extensive social influence. She married Judge Thornton, a member of Congress from Alabama, the first land commissioner of California, and they made their home in San Francisco.

MRS. JAMES W. WHITE.

Among the women who were distinguished for their efforts for charity, for the poor and afflicted, and who wielded a wide influence through her domestic life, and who commands the admiration of all as a wife, mother and friend, may be mentioned Mrs White. Her mother was the daughter of General Whitney, a wealthy land owner. Her father was General Waterman, one of the earliest settlers of Binghamton, New York. Mrs. James W. White's name before her marriage was Rhoda Elizabeth Waterman, and when quite young she married James W. White a young lawyer of Irish descent and a nephew of General Griffin, author of "The Collegians." Mr. and Mrs. White took up their residence in the city of New York in 1834, and this home was known among her friends as "Castle Comfort." Mrs. White considered it her most sacred duty to God and her husband to deepen, purify and increase in her own heart and in his, the conjugal affection which bound them together and which she prized as Heaven's best gift. We regret that this idea and conception of married life is not more general to-day. In 1853 Mrs. White arranged a private concert in Niblo's salon in aid of charity, at which

Madame Sontag sang, and this proved the great fashionable event of the season. In 1856 Mrs. White was solicited by the Sisters of Charity to aid them in the re-building of their hospital, and a meeting of the ladies representing the different Catholic churches was called for the purpose of carrying out Mrs. White's plan for a fair to be held in the Crystal Palace. A storm of opposition greeted this proposal but this did not deter Mrs. White from proceeding with the plan and, though the ladies manifested their opposition to the very hour of the opening of the fair, this great "Charity Fair" cleared thirty-four thousand dollars, a splendid memorial of the indomitable energy, practical wisdom and noble zeal of the ruling spirit of this enterprise. At the close of the fair the sisters urged upon Mrs. White the acceptance of a massive piece of silver as a mark of their gratitude, but she declined the gift and asked that it be disposed of for the benefit of the hospital. In 1859, Mrs. White was president of an association which brought to a successful ending a large fair in aid of the Sisters of Mercy which was held in the Academy of Music. One of Mrs. White's contributions was a large volume, elegantly bound and valued at twenty-five hundred dollars, containing the rarest and most valuable autographs ever collected. The book was drawn in a lottery after a large sum had been raised by the sale of tickets and the fortunate winner presented it to the original donor. Mrs. White carried on during her lifetime an extensive correspondence with the learned, gifted and distinguished persons of this country and Europe, and some have called her "the Sévigné of the United States." Among these correspondents may be mentioned President Lincoln.

MRS. THOMAS ADDIS EMMET AND MRS. DUBOIS.

Among other social leaders prominent in the charitable work of the city of New York may be mentioned Mrs. Thomas Addis Emmet and Mrs. Dubois, who was Miss Delafield, at that time quite a noted artist in sculpture and cameo cutting. Mrs. Emmet was the widow of Thomas Addis Emmet, the son of the distinguished Irish patriot who was a prominent lawyer in New York City. Mrs. Emmet's father was John Thom, of the firm of Hoyt & Thom, noted East India merchants. Mrs. Emmet was a noted leader in the best circles of the metropolis, who devoted much of her time to public and private charities.

CHARLOTTE AUGUSTA SOUTHWICK.

Charlotte Augusta Southwick was the daughter of Jonathan Southwick a successful merchant of New York City. She is descended from some of the distinguished families of the early period of Colonial history, the Washingtons and Elys. Richard Ely came to America in 1660. John Ely was a colonel in the Revolutionary Army and a celebrated physician. In 1770 he commanded Fort Trumbull, having raised and equipped his regiment at his own expense. The eldest son of John and Sarah Worthington was Worthington Ely, the grandfather of Charlotte Southwick. His wife was Miss Bushnell, of Connecticut. Their youngest daughter, Lucretia, was the mother of Charlotte Augusta Southwick, afterward Mrs. Coventry Waddell. Soon after leaving school Miss Southwick married Mr. McMurray who lived but a few months, and later she married Mr. William Coventry Waddell, who was connected with some of the noble families of England. Mr. Waddell held many important trusts under the government and was at the time of their marriage, in an official position. Their residence was at the corner of Fifth Avenue and Forty-seventh Street, called Murray Hill and occupied an entire block. Their summers were passed at Saratoga. Mrs. Waddell's graceful manners, good humor and kindness of heart, added to her intellectual charms and brilliant conversation gave her supremacy in the social circles of New York City and at Saratoga Springs, the fashionable resort of the times. In the monetary crisis of 1857 Mr. Waddell lost his fortune and he was compelled to sacrifice his beautiful home on Murray Hill and they removed to a residence two miles north of Newburg on the Hudson.

ADELICIA ACKLEN.

Mrs. Acklen, the daughter of Oliver D. Hayes, a native of South Hadley, Massachusetts, was a prominent leader in the social life of Nashville, Tennessee. Her mother was Sarah T. Hightower, the daughter of Richard Hightower, of Williamson County. Their daughter Adelicia married when quite young Mr. Isaac Franklin, a planter of Louisiana, who lived but a few years. After his death she married Colonel Joseph Acklen, of Huntsville, Alabama, who also lived but a few years. After his death Mrs. Acklen spent much time in Europe. After her return to this country she married Dr. W. A. Cheatham, making her home in Nashville, where she became noted for her cordial hospitality and her house a resort for the celebrities of that section.

EMILY MASON.

Another distinguished woman of this time was Miss Emily Mason, of Kentucky. Her mother was descended from the Marshall and Nicholson families. Her paternal grandfather and uncle were both United States Senators from that state. Her father, General Mason, moved to Kentucky and here Emily was born in the city of Lexington. Her brother was the governor of the Territory of Michigan and the family followed, residing in the city of Detroit. At the age of seventeen Emily presided over the governor's mansion at Detroit, where she entertained and exercised unlimited sway in the fashionable society of that day. Her sprightly wit and remarkable powers of conversation even at a very early age, gave her a social pre-eminence unrivalled by any woman in the western country. After her brother's death she returned to Virginia and here and in New Orleans she became a celebrity in society. Later in life, after the death of both her parents, she met with severe reverses. Her home was taken from her during the war "for military purposes," during her absence in the North. She was suspected as a Southern spy. Her property was entirely destroyed. She went into the hospital work and devoted her energies to the inmates of the Winder Hospital near Richmond. Here and in the prisons she helped to care for the sick, wounded and dying and after the close of the war she worked indefatigably for the cause of humanity among her own people in the South.

MRS. HILLS.

Mrs. Hills lived for many years in the city of New York where her morning receptions were quite noted. Her great passion was the cultivation of music and the promotion of the best and highest in art. The daughter of Mrs. Hills was Mrs. John Schermerhorn who inherited her mother's talent in music, and it is said that Gottschalk complimented Mrs. Schermerhorn on the playing of his compositions. Mrs. William Schermerhorn, who was also a prominent figure socially, in New York City, was a Miss Cotinet, and gave during the winter of 1867 three of the most splendid receptions ever given in that city.

WIFE OF JUDGE HUNTINGTON OF INDIANA.

Was esteemed as one of the bright ornaments of western society. She was a daughter of Dr. Christopher A. Rudd, a prominent physician of Springfield, Kentucky, who was descendant of the Carroll family of Maryland. Mrs. Huntington's first husband was Clarke Fitzhugh, of Louisville, Kentucky, a nephew of General George Rogers Clarke. While a widow Mrs. Fitzhugh went to Washington with her cousin Mrs. Florida White and became one of the well-known belles of the Capital city. It was during this visit that she met with Honorable E. M. Huntington, then commissioner of the General Land Office in Washington, and they were married soon afterward. Mr. Huntington was an especial friend of President Tyler, who appointed him to the position of Judge of the United States Court in Indiana, and they removed to that state, making their home in Terre Haute, and Mrs. Huntington became the center and leader of social life in that part of the state.

ELLEN ADAIR.

The daughter of Governor Adair, of Kentucky, was noted throughout the Gulf states for her accomplishments and charm and became one of the belles in Washington city in later years. She married Colonel White, of Florida, and was often called Mrs. Florida White in allusion to the state represented by her husband in Congress. After Colonel White's death, while on a visit to New Orleans, she met Mr. Beattie, an Irish gentleman whom she married. Her sister, Mrs. Benjamin F. Pleasants, was well known and greatly admired in Washington city and always took a great interest in public affairs.

PAMELA WILLIAMS.

Was another prominent woman in the social life of Washington. She was born in Williamston, Massachusetts, in 1785, and at eighteen married General Jacob Brown, and they went to reside at Brownsville, in Jefferson County. During their residence in the Capital city their house was the center of a cultivated circle where were welcome the statesmen and scholars, the gifted and distinguished, with the less fortunate who were in need of sympathy and encouragement.

SALLIE WARD.

Among the noted women of Kentucky, whose beauty and influence became world-wide, none was more entitled to distinction than Miss Sallie Ward, of Louisville, Kentucky. The high position of her family, her marvelous personal beauty and fascination of manner, placed her even in her youth among the conspicuously observed wherever she went. Her ancestors came of old Huguenot stock who had fled from France, bringing to the southern states some of the best blood which was infused into our young nation. Major Mattheus Flournoy served with distinction in the war of the Revolution. Afterwards he purchased a country seat in Scot County, Kentucky, where Sallie Ward was born. Her father, Honorable Robert J. Ward, was a man possessed of the highest intellectual qualities and of that high standard of justice and moral integrity which secured for him lasting friendships. At twenty-eight he was elected speaker of the Kentucky Assembly. Mrs. Ward was one of the most remarkable women of the day, distinguished for her personal loveliness and intellectual gifts. To their daughter, Sallie, they gave every advantage of education and moral training, and while reared in the lap of luxury, enjoying everything which wealth could bestow, receiving from society the most flattering homage, Sallie Ward was unspoiled by adulation and grew up an amiable, gracious, attractive woman, well developed in mind and principles. She possessed a remarkable memory and quick perception, which enabled her to acquire foreign languages with readiness. A talented musician and possessing every accomplishment which could add to her natural charms. Every one in Kentucky seemed to take a pride in her loveliness and the fact that she was a native of their state. She was always interested in the various enterprises, patriotic and municipal. White Sulphur Springs, the noted resort of Virginia, has many legends of her beauty and charm. Statesmen, soldiers, foreign diplomats followed in her train but she gave her hand to Dr. Hart, of New Orleans, and in this city she and her husband established a magnificent home, where her sway continued. In her domestic life Mrs. Hart displayed the noble gifts of her true nature. She had but one child—a son—and after her husband's death she devoted herself to the education and rearing of this boy. Perhaps in the United States there has been no woman so flattered and courted, and the fact that she retained the pure simplicity of her character unimpaired, argues a truly elevated mind.

MARCIA BURNS VAN NESS.

One of the most distinguished and charming women, who gave dignity elegance and grace to the social circles of Washington City, was the wife of General Van Ness. She was the daughter of David Burns of excellent family who had inherited a fine estate near the Potomac in the District of Columbia and held the office of civil magistrate. The building now owned by the Daughters of the American Revolution and the building of the American Republics are now situated where was once the magnificent home and estate of General Van Ness. The seat of National Government was removed to Washington, in May, 1802. Miss Burns had returned home from school in 1800, not long before her father's death, and from him she inherited a large fortune. From the very first she was one of the prominent belles of Washington City. It is said Mrs. Madison was one of her intimate friends. At the age of twenty she married Honorable John P. Van Ness, a member of Congress from New York. After their marriage he became a resident of Washington, and their home was one of the most brilliant social centers in the Capital city, Mrs. Van Ness drawing about her the refined and cultivated persons of the day. Chief Justice Marshall, Henry Clay, President Monroe, General Jackson, Mr. Calhoun, Mr. McDuffie, Daniel Webster, Mr. Hayne and many other noted celebrities of that time were on familiar terms with General Van Ness and frequent visitors in his home. The only daughter of Mrs. Van Ness was Ann Albertina, an accomplished, intelligent young woman. Mrs. Van Ness' influence was always for good, and her example noble and elevating; her friendships true and warm. She ever ministered to the sick and suffering; her deeds of charity were unostentatious. Mrs. Van Ness never recovered from the death of her daughter, which occurred soon after her marriage. A lasting monument of Mrs. Van Ness' charity was the establishing of the Washington City Orphan Asylum by her. To this she gave four thousand dollars, besides many small contributions from time to time, and her indefatigable exertions obtaining, with the aid of a few friends, from Congress an Act of Incorporation and a donation of ten thousand dollars for its permanent support. She also gave directions that a legacy of a thousand dollars should be given this institution after her death. Mrs. Madison was the first directress of the institution, but after her departure Mrs. Van Ness was induced to accept this office, which she held until her death, on the 9th of September, 1832, at the age of fifty years. Her husband, General Van Ness was mayor of Washington at the time; and it is said Mrs. Van Ness was the first American woman buried with public honors in Washington. Few women have indeed ever occupied a larger field of usefulness or been more devotedly engaged in the work for humanity than Mrs. Van Ness.

MARY TODD LINCOLN.

Mary Todd Lincoln, the wife of the immortal Abraham Lincoln, was a Kentuckian, and a member of the distinguished family of Todds of Lexington. At the age of twenty-one, on the 4th of November, 1832, she was married to Abrahm Lincoln, who though a prominent lawyer of Springfield, Illinois, gave no evidence of the immortality which he was to achieve. Mr. Lincoln was elected to Congress four years subsequently and took his seat December, 1847. Mrs. Lincoln did not accompany Mr. Lincoln to Washington while he was a member of Congress. They had three sons, Robert T. Lincoln who still survives, and Willie and Thaddeus, the latter better known as "Tad." When Mr. and Mrs. Lincoln came into the White House, war, grim-visaged war, threatened our country. The excitement between the North and South was so intense that Mr. Lincoln came to Washington incognito, Mrs. Lincoln and the children and servants following by another route. Many were the forebodings as to what might be the fate of the President-elect before his inauguration. Mrs. Lincoln's temperament was such that she could not bear the excitement with the repose of a woman of less emotional nature. Of all the criticisms that have been made of Mrs. Lincoln, no one has been unkind enough to accuse her of disloyalty to her husband, or lack of appreciation of his exalted position to which she had been elevated through his election to the presidency, and it is to be regretted that a keener appreciation of the trials to which she was subjected was not then understood. The political excitement and war's alarms were enough, but to these was added the great bereavement of President and Mrs. Lincoln by the death of their beloved second son, Willie, and it is recorded that the mother never afterward entered the room in which he died, or the Blue Room in which his body lay. Mrs. Lincoln's hospitality and generosity were well known, and it is a melancholy thought that just after the close of the Civil War, when they were enjoying the victories of Mr. Lincoln's second election that the tragedy of tragedies occurred and beyond question Mrs. Lincoln never rallied from this unspeakable blow. As soon as she was able to leave, she departed from the White House and went to live with her sister at Springfield, Illinois, where her paroxysms of grief were so overwhelming that those nearest and dearest to her could do nothing to alleviate her sufferings. Her sorrow was greatly increased again by the death of her son "Tad." It was suggested that she travel in

Europe for diversion and resignation by change of scene. Congress, in 1870, voted her a pension of $3,000 a year. After her return to the United States in 1880, she again took up her residence with her sister, Mrs. Edwards, in Springfield, Illinois, but her mind was so unsettled that it was found necessary to place her in a private asylum. Congress increased her pension to $5,000 and added a gratuity of $1,500, so that she might be properly provided for. She paid little attention to anything, her mind seeming to be a blank as to what was going on about her, and on the night of the 15th of July, 1882, she was stricken with paralysis and died on the 16th, and her remains were deposited beside those of President Lincoln and her children in the Lincoln monument vault at Springfield, Illinois.

ELIZA McCARDLE JOHNSON.

Eliza McCardle, wife of Andrew Johnson, was the daughter of a widow. She was a beautiful girl who had had some opportunities of education and was considered quite an advanced scholar. She was married to Mr. Johnson when seventeen years of age and entered with much enthusiasm upon the labor of assisting him in the acquirement of his ambition. He was a poor boy, his chief capital consisting of high aspirations and indomitable energy. While he was struggling with poverty as a tailor his loyal wife knew no abatement in her energy and vigilance in taking advantage of every opportunity to advance her husband's fortunes. They resided in Greenville, Tennessee, near a college, and the intercourse with the students in the college served to keep alive Mr. Johnson's eagerness for the acquisition of an education. Mrs. Johnson being very popular with these young students, they made many visits to their modest but hospitable home where, without knowing it they aided Mr. and Mrs. Johnson in their educational desires. They continued this struggle for many years with more or less success.

Mr. Johnson being a member of the Tennessee legislature at the time of the breaking out of the Civil War he was most active as a Unionist and was subsequently elected to the Senate of the United States. Mrs. Johnson came to Washington in the spring of '61 to be with her husband during the sessions of the Senate. During the rebellion they had very trying experiences, as they were the victims of the vengeance of the Confederates. Through it all, however, Mrs. Johnson managed to command the respect and protection of the officers of the Confederate and Union armies, but Mr. Johnson dared not return to Tennessee. She displayed marvelous ability and diplomacy in her efforts to protect her family. The Convention of 1864 nominated Andrew Johnson for the vice-presidency on the ticket with Mr. Lincoln. In March, 1865, Mr. Johnson left his family in Nashville and came to Washington. The world knows of the assassination of Mr. Lincoln on the 14th of April, 1865, and of the promotion of Mr. Johnson from the vice-presidency to the presidency. It was with many forebodings and little enthusiasm that Mrs. Johnson came to the White House as its mistress. Her health was very much broken and as a result her daughters, Mrs. Patterson and Mrs. Stover accompanied her and were soon installed as the ladies of the executive mansion. Mrs. Johnson was a confirmed invalid, and was unable even to appear at any social function, but Mrs. Patterson and Mrs. Stover were quite equal to the duties of conducting the affairs of the White House. Mrs. Patterson's husband was a member of the Senate and she had been accustomed to the society of the Capital, but it seemed that the shadows which had gathered over the White House after the assassination of Mr. Lincoln were not to be dispelled during Mrs. Johnson's occupancy of the executive mansion. On account of the impeachment trial of Mr. Johnson their last days in the White House were those of intense grief and anxiety. After their return to Greenville, Mr. Johnson became a candidate for the Senate as successor to Mr. Brownlow. He was defeated, but his indomitable will caused him to become a candidate the second time, when he was successfully elected and took his seat at the beginning of the session, December, 1874. He occupied that position during the extraordinary session which followed, when he made a speech of great importance to himself in vindication of his course as President of the United States. This speech was of such a personal character that it is of great doubt whether it should have been made or not. Returning home in midsummer, he was stricken with illness and on the morning of the 31st of July, 1875, he died in the home of his youngest daughter near Greenville, Tennessee.

Mrs. Johnson survived him but six months and died at the home of her eldest daughter, Mrs. Patterson, on the 13th of January, 1876. She was buried beside her husband. Their children have erected a magnificent monument to the memory of Andrew and Eliza Johnson. Mrs. Johnson was a noble woman and lived a life of self-denial and self-sacrifice.

JULIA DENT GRANT.

Julia Dent Grant was a Missourian by birth, being the daughter of Judge Dent, of St. Louis, who resided on a large farm near that city. Here Mrs. Grant spent her girlhood. Her youngest brother, Frederick J. Dent, was appointed to West Point and formed a strong attachment for his classmate, Ulysses S. Grant, who had been appointed to the Military Academy from Ohio: This intimacy caused young Grant to come with his cadet friend young Dent, to St. Louis, when they had their first furlough.   The result of the meeting of young Grant and Miss Dent was their marriage on the 22nd of August, 1848, at Judge Dent's city residence in St. Louis. Through all the trials to which Mrs. Grant was subjected as the wife of a lieutenant in the army in the forties and fifties, she bore herself with much loyalty to her husband and to her children; in fact her devotion to her husband and her children was her most striking characteristic.

When the war of the Rebellion broke out Lieutenant Grant had resigned from the army and was living at Galena, Illinois.   They had four children, three sons and one daughter, and were in reduced circumstances.   Governor Yates in his great dilemma for mustering officers, received from E. B. Washburn a recommendation of Ulysses S. Grant, a citizen of Galena.   The ex-lieutenant of the army made haste to respond to the call of Governor Yates and engaged in drilling the troops at Springfield.   Soon after he was appointed Colonel of the 21st Infantry Volunteer Regiment, in May, 1861, and from that time until his victorious entry into Washington at the close of the war, Mrs. Grant remained with her family except for making an occasional visit to her husband in the field. Through every phase of her husband's brilliant promotion from one high position to another, Mrs. Grant was the same unaffected, sincere, devoted wife, mother and friend.

When General Grant was elected to the Presidency she assumed the duties of Lady of the White House with the same simplicity of manner, sincerity and cordiality that had characterized her whole life.   At no time in the history of the country has any woman who presided over the White House been called upon to conduct more brilliant functions than was Mrs. Grant.   Entering the White House so near the close of the war there were more distinguished visitors to Washington than there have ever been during any administration.   She received royalty and the most illustrious of our country with such genuine hospitality and graciousness as to avoid all criticisms and to win universal admiration.   For eight years she was the first Lady in the Land, and it can be claimed that she made no enemies and was much beloved for her goodness of heart and sympathetic disposition.

At the close of General Grant's administration, in their journey around the world, they were received by the crowned heads of every country, and Mrs. Grant was universally admired for the simplicity of her manner and sincerity of her greeting.   Her absolute devotion to her husband and children has left an example worthy of emulation.   Her faithful vigilance during General Grant's long illness is especially to be admired.

Weary of excitement and of being in the public eye, her children being married and away from her, she sought the National Capital for a home in which to spend her declining years.   She received the continued respect and loving thought of the Nation to the day of her death in 1902.   Her remains rest beside her husband's in the tomb on Riverside Drive, New York.

LUCY WEBB HAYES.

Lucy Webb Hayes was born in Chillicothe, when it was the capital of Ohio.   She was the daughter of Dr. James Webb and the granddaughter of Dr. Isaac Cook.   The Webbs were natives of North Carolina.   Her father died of cholera in 1833, in Lexington, Kentucky, where he had gone to complete the arrangements for sending slaves, whom his father and himself had set free, to Liberia.   After the death of her father her mother removed to Delaware, Ohio, in order to be near the Western University, where her sons were educated.   Mrs. Hayes pursued her studies and recited with her brothers to the college instructors, by whom she was prepared for the Western Female College at Cincinnati, entering that institution at the same time that her brothers entered the medical college. Mrs. Hayes was very fortunate in having a home in Ohio, which was among the first states to advocate the equal education of men and women. She was a great favorite of Rev. and Mrs. T. B. Wilbur, the principals of the college. She was a devout member of the Methodist Episcopal Church, following in that respect closely in the footsteps of her mother. It was while she was a student that she met Rutherford B. Hayes. They were married December 20, 1852. Mrs. Hayes' chief characteristics were her womanly and wifely qualities and devotion to her religion.

Rutherford B. Hayes was a graduate of Kenyon College and of the Cambridge Law School. He practiced law before the Supreme Court of Ohio and established himself at Fremont, Ohio, but subsequently removed to Cincinnati, where he remained for many years. He was made city attorney twice. At the outbreak of the Civil War he volunteered in the 23rd Ohio Regiment (Infantry) and was subsequently made major of the regiment of which General Rosecrans was colonel and the late Stanley Matthews was the lieutenant-colonel. They were assigned to the army of the Potomac. He was four times wounded and served to the close of the war notwithstanding the fact that he was urged to enter politics. Mrs. Hayes spent two summers and a winter taking care of her husband and his soldiers in the field. After his return from the service he was twice elected to Congress, after which he was made Governor of Ohio and they occupied the executive mansion at Columbus. Mrs. Hayes made a national reputation by her pre-eminently social qualities while occupying the executive mansion at Columbus. She seemed to feel that a state or national executive mansion belonged to the people of the state and the nation and she threw open the doors of the executive mansions in Columbus and Washingon on all occasions that it was proper that she should extend their hospitality to the people, or to distinguished visitors from other lands. She worked with earnestness as the wife of the Governor in the interest of the charities of the state, and was one of the most popular women of her day. Mrs. Hayes was probably one of the most highly intellectual and accomplished of the women who have ever graced the White House and was at the same time the most cordial, unaffected and genial. She had been the idol of the soldiers during the war, as well as of the people of Ohio, and when she came to Washington there was great solicitude as to whether she was worthy of her universal popularity, and people waited with impatience for her first reception. Those who attended that reception went away enthusiastic in their praises of her. While she could not be called a beautiful woman, she had a most attractive face, very bright and expressive eyes and beautiful black hair. She had wonderful health and would not admit that she experienced any fatigue, although she gave more receptions and social entertainments than any occupant of the White House.

There were very many illustrious men in this country when President and Mrs. Hayes were in the White House, and it was her pleasure to make everyone feel at home, and few who called to pay their respects failed to go away without singing her praises. The poorest person who sought alms at the White House was not denied some recognition. She was passionately fond of flowers and there was a profusion of flowers in the White House on every occasion. She created a sensation when she decided not to serve wine on the President's table during their residence in the White House. The adverse criticisms made no impression whatever upon her. She would not discuss the subject, but persisted in her decision, and many time since persons have wished that her example might have been followed by her successors. She was very much interested in the missionary cause, and there is in Washington the Lucy Webb Hayes Home for Deaconesses and retired missionaries, which was named in her honor. A life-sized portrait of Mrs. Hayes by Huntington, was placed in the White House by the Temperance Women of this country. No passing of a Mistress of the White House was more sincerely regretted than was that of Mrs. Hayes, and no one has been more sincerely missed since her untimely death at Fremont, Ohio, in 1889.

LUCRETIA RUDOLPH GARFIELD.

Lucretia Rudolph Garfield was the daughter of Zebulon Rudolph, a farmer who resided near Garrettsville, Ohio. He was one of the founders of Hiram College. Her mother was the daughter of Elijah Mason of Lebanon, Connecticut, a descendant of General Nathaniel Greene. She first met her future husband, James A. Garfield, at the Geauga Seminary. They attended this school together until young Garfield entered Hiram College, of which institution he was a graduate. Not long after he entered the college he was called upon to take the place of one of the teachers because of illness. Into his classroom came his school-girl friend, Lucretia Rudolph, whom he considered one of his brightest pupils. She was especially apt in Latin and was so well instructed by Mr. Garfield that twenty years after she prepared her boy in Latin to enter college. After she graduated from Hiram College, she also became a teacher. When Mr. Garfield went to Williams College to finish his education she went to Cleveland to teach in one of the public schools. By that time they were lovers and both studied very hard, believing that there was a great future before James A. Garfield.

Their marriage took place at the house of the bride's parents, November 11, 1858, Mr. Garfield then being President of Hiram College. Their resources were not very great, so they boarded for several years, each year finding them much advanced in worldly goods and reputation.

Young Mr. and Mrs. Garfield resided in Cleveland until 1860, when he was elected to the State Senate and went to Columbus. In 1861, he left the State Senate to become colonel of the 42nd Ohio Regiment. He went into the army a poor man and it was with the money he saved as an officer of the Union Army that his wife bought a house and lot in Hiram, which cost eight hundred dollars. This sum suggests the style of house which was their home until 1870, when, as a member of Congress from the state of Ohio, he came to Washington. Here his salary of $5,000 a year, with the simplicity of living in those days, enabled him to save enough money to give his family a comfortable home in the Capital of the Nation. Through the helpfulness and economy of his unusually intellectual and economical wife they were able to purchase a farm at Mentor, Ohio, which they named Lawnfield, and where was erected the historic house that was so much advertised during the campaign of 1880. This house was designed by Mrs. Garfield and is a fine specimen of architecture. During the war, Mrs. Garfield lived in her home in Hiram and directed the education of her boys, having only the companionship of Mother Garfield. After the battle of Corinth, Brigadier-General Garfield was at home for six months, suffering from malarial fever. On his return to the front he was assigned chief of staff to General Rosecrans and at the battle of Chickamauga won his major-general's star. Before his return home his baby girl died, which caused him very great distress. In 1863, the people of his district elected him to Congress, where he served for eight terms, and was elected to

18

the Senate, and from the Senate, to the Presidency. During all these years Mrs. Garfield was known as the most devoted wife and mother. Her unusual intelligence and education fitted her pre-eminently for the high positions to which her husband was from time to time promoted. She was never in any sense considered a fashionable woman or a devotee of society. Her ambitions were on a higher plane, but no woman ever received more flattering compliments from her husband and those who knew her best, than Mrs. Garfield. The control she had over her emotional nature was manifested during the ordeal through which she passed at the time of President Garfield's assassination and the eighty days of anxiety and suspense before his death. After the President's death she repaired to Mentor and no woman could have conducted herself with greater propriety, dignity and appreciation of her position than did Mrs. Garfield. The fact that her sons have attained prominent positions is as much due to their mother's care and training as to the inheritance of an illustrious name.

MRS. ELIZA GARFIELD.

Mrs. Eliza Garfield, the mother of James A. Garfield, was an admirable illustration of the true nobility of the women of the earlier days of the Republic. Her devotion to the memory of her husband, her struggle for the maintenance and education of her family, her pure Christian character, native generosity and sympathy with those about her, her self-denial, her humility, her pride in her illustrious son, make her a remarkable woman of her time. She is the only mother of a President who ever resided in the White House. The nation was deeply impressed by the honor paid her by her son after he delivered his inaugural address. Embracing her in the presence of the multitude immediately after he had pronounced the last syllable of that wonderful address, was the greatest tribute a son could have paid a mother and does credit alike to the son and the venerable mother. She survived her distinguished son but a few years.

MARY ARTHUR McELROY.

President Arthur, successor to James A. Garfield, had been a widower for many years, and Washington was much concerned as to who would preside over the White House during the presidency of Chester A. Arthur. The continuous stream of visitors through the White House during President Garfield's long illness was so destructive to everything in the executive mansion that it was really almost uninhabitable when President Arthur took the oath of office, and there was much solicitude lest on account of the absence of a lady of the White House, it would be long before it would resume its attractive appearance. They little realized that President Arthur was a man of exquisite taste and perfect knowledge as to the appointments of an elegant home, and in as brief a time as any woman could have directed its rehabilitation, it presented as attractive an appearance as if a magician's wand had been waved in every room of the historic home of the presidents. Re-furnishings, re-decoration and the addition of up-to-date accessories transformed it into a luxurious home before the meeting of Congress in December, 1881. President Arthur had selected his sister, Mary Arthur McElroy, wife of Reverend John E. McElroy, of Albany, New York, to preside over the White House and take charge of his daughter, Nellie, an attractive schoolgirl.

Mrs. McElroy, the youngest of several children of Reverend William Arthur, a Baptist clergymen of Vermont, was born in Greenwich, Washington County, New York. She was educated in the famous school of Mrs. Willard in Troy. Her mother was a most accomplished woman and transmitted many of her virtues and talents to her children. As Mary Arthur, Mrs. McElroy, had every advantage that could be given at that time. She came to the White House well fitted to grace the historic mansion. It can be said without fear of contradiction, that the social entertainments, state dinners, evening receptions and all social functions given at the White House during President Arthur's administration were the most magnificent and enjoyable of any that had ever been given in the White House by any president and the lady presiding. Mrs. McElroy, as the mistress of the White House, distinguished herself by her graciousness, hospitality, cordiality, good taste and geniality. She allowed no one to feel that they were unwelcome or that she felt bored and fatigued by their presence. She drew about her many young people, among them her own daughter and the President's daughter, Nellie, who added much brightness on every occasion. She introduced the custom of serving tea and other refreshments after every reception. The hospitality thus extended seemed to infuse much good feeling and cheerfulness among the guests, and those who were privileged to enter the White House on these occasions. Mrs. McElroy was a devout Christian and attended St. John's Church on Lafayette Square, where President Arthur, also worshipped. Mrs. Haynsworth, another sister of President Arthur, frequently assisted Mrs. McElroy in the distribution of the hospitalities of this lavish administration. She rarely failed to have about her the ladies of the Cabinet and other distinguished women of Washington. Mrs. McElroy was deeply regretted when she ended her reign and took her departure from Washington.

ROSE ELIZABETH CLEVELAND.

It was a curious coincidence that President Cleveland, President Arthur's successor, was, like Mr. Arthur, a bachelor and had to depend upon someone other than a wife to preside over the White House during his first administration. His choice was his sister, Miss Rose Elizabeth Cleveland, a young woman of fine culture, high attainments and superior character, who was destined to fill the position with infinite credit to herself and the women of the nation. Miss Cleveland was the daughter and granddaughter of New England ministers; a sister and sister-in-law of ministers and missionaries. She was the youngest of the nine children of Richard Falley and Anne Neal Cleveland. She was born in Fayetteville, New York. Her parents subsequently removed to Clinton, New York, and she became a student in Hamilton College. From Clinton her father removed to Utica to become the pastor of a church in that city. He did not, however, long survive. Miss Cleveland was too young to appreciate the full measure of this calamity. As the family were poor, they had to give up the parsonage, but the friends of her husband presented Mrs. Cleveland with a small cottage, where she resided until her death. During their life in the cottage the family had a desperate struggle, but through the dignity of character, economy and discretion of their mother, their slender means were eked out so wisely that the children were able to pursue their studies. Mrs. Cleveland was a southerner and had been born and raised in luxury in the city of Baltimore, where Mr. Cleveland was employed as a teacher, and after graduating in the theological department of Princeton College they were married. The young bride little realized the self-denial and self-sacrifice that she must practice as the wife of a young minister, but she loved her husband and during her whole life was an uncomplaining, devoted wife and mother. Rose, the youngest child, was a studious girl and took advantage of every opportunity to acquire an education. After finishing school, Miss Cleveland went as a teacher to Houghton Seminary, when she remained for two years, at the end of which time she accepted the position of principal of the Collegiate Institute at Lafayette, Indiana, after which she taught in private families. When, later, it became necessary for her to remain with her mother, she conceived the idea of lecturing, proposing it to the principal of Houghton Seminary, who accepted the idea with much enthusiasm. Miss Cleveland prepared a course of historical lectures, which were very successful. Her mother died in the summer of 1882. Miss Cleveland was earnestly urged by her brothers and sisters to choose a home among them but remained in Holland Patent, the old home, except when on lecturing tours, until she was invited by her brother Grover to become mistress of the White House. Miss Cleveland was very reserved in manner, thoughtful and dignified, but most cordial in her reception of people in the White House. She came into the White House heralded as an intellectual, cold woman but proved herself to be a most attractive, womanly woman, thoroughly understanding human nature and what was due the callers at White House. She gave many beautiful entertainments, especially for the house guests, of whom she had many. It is said that she was Mr. Cleveland's best adviser during his first term as President, and while she never presumed to express her opinions on official matters publicly, she was prone to council with her brother privately and freely express her opinions on political questions. She had no ambition to become a social leader or to dictate in frivolous affairs, but she was so affable and agreeable and intellectual that she was greatly admired and will be long remembered as one of the most gracious women who presided over the White House.

FRANCES FOLSOM CLEVELAND.

Rose Elizabeth Cleveland presided over the White House most acceptably for about a year, when it was rumored that she was to be succeeded by her brother's bride, and much interest was manifested as to who that fortunate person was to be. It finally developed that it was the beautiful Miss Frances Folsom, of Buffalo, New York, who immediately on her return from Europe, was married to Grover Cleveland, the President of the United States.

Miss Folsom was the daughter of Mr. Cleveland's former law partner, and she was his ward from the time of the tragic death of her father, who was killed in an accident. She had been educated at Wells College and had spent a year in Europe after Mr. Cleveland's election to the Presidency. It was claimed the engagement existed at the time of his election but desiring to spend a year abroad before assuming the grave responsibility of Mistress of the White House, the wedding was not hastened. She was but twenty-two years old at the time of her marriage. On the 27th of May, she arrived in New York from her European sojourn. It was found that unusual preparations were being made in the White House for expected guests. Miss Cleveland, Mistress of the White House, accompanied by Mr. Cleveland's secretary, Mr. Lamont, and his wife, and several of the ladies of the Cabinet, hurried to New York to meet Miss Folsom and her mother on their arrival on the "Noordland" from Antwerp. The party immediately repaired to the Gilsey House where they were soon after joined by the President and the friends who accompanied him. They returned on Monday to Washington, Mrs. Cleveland and her mother going to the White House with the party. They remained as guests until on Wednesday evening, June 3rd, when the President and Miss Folsom were married in the presence of members of the Cabinet and a few friends.   Every detail of the important event was characterized by refinement and dignity.   After their marriage, the President and Mrs. Cleveland went to Deer Park, Maryland, where the cottage of ex-Senator Davis, of West Virginia, had been prepared for their reception.   In a few days they returned to the White House and no mistress of that staid old mansion ever presided with more grace, dignity and genuine hospitality than did Mrs. Grover Cleveland.   Tall and graceful with dark brown hair, worn loosely back from the forehead, the most distinguishing features of her face were her beautiful violet eyes and exquisitely mobile mouth, which imparted to the face a very sweet expression.   As beauty ever paves a way for its possessor, Mrs. Cleveland was admired from the first as a woman of rare attractions.   Her personality was exceedingly agreeable.   She had by nature all acquirements and attained the art of pleasing in an eminent degree.   Mrs. Cleveland displayed at all times wonderful tact and simplicity of manner.   She was not in the least spoiled by the adulation she received.   Ruth, President and Mrs. Cleveland's first child, was born in the White House.   They retired at the end of Mr. Cleveland's first term, to be absent only four years, when she was again installed in the White House as its Mistress for the second time.   It would be a very fault-finding person who could point out any act of Mrs. Cleveland's while she was the Mistress of the White House that could be criticised. When she took her departure for the second time she left behind her many devoted friends and admirers.   No complaint was ever lodged against her as having extended scant courtesy to any visitor entitled to consideration at the National Executive Mansion.

In establishing their private home in Princeton, New Jersey, she at once became popular with the faculty, trustees and students of Princeton College.   Entering at all times heartily into every scheme for the pleasure of the college people, she won their imperishable admiration. Her uniform dignity and the maintenance of her high position as the widow of an ex-President of the United States has been above criticism.

Her good taste in accompanying her children to Europe to give them some opportunities in the old world, and the modesty with which she took up her residence in Geneva to quietly carry out her plans, is worthy of the highest commendation of our American Nation.

CAROLINE SCOTT HARRISON.

Mrs. Harrison was among the most highly educated and accomplished women who ever occupied the White House. Caroline Scott Harrison was born in Oxford, Ohio, October 1, 1832. Mrs. Harrison's ancestors were Scotch, emigrating to America and settling in the Valley of Neshaminy, Bucks County, Pennsylvania, where the village of Hartsville now stands, twenty miles north of Philadelphia. At this place Reverend William Tennent, in 1726, founded the historic Log College, which was the original of Princeton College. Mrs. Harrison's great-grandfather, John Scott, son of the founder of the family in this country, took up his residence in Northampton County, Pennsylvania, and purchased land opposite Belvidere, New Jersey, which is still known as the Scott Farm. During the Revolutionary War he was a quartermaster in the Pennsylvania line. His brother, Matthew Scott, after serving as Captain in the army, moved to Kentucky. Mrs. Harrison's grandfather, Reverend George McElroy Scott, graduated from the University of Pennsylvania in 1793, and studied theology with the President of Princeton College, Reverend Stanhope Smith. His first charge was Mill Creek Church, Beaver

County, Pennsylvania, the first Presbyterian Church of that locality. He occupied the pulpit in 1799. Her father, Dr. John W. Scott, was born in 1800, while his father was pastor of the Mill Creek Church. Descending from an educated ancestry, Mrs. Harrison had superior educational advantages early in life. She graduated in 1852 from Oxford, Ohio, Female Seminary. Benjamin Harrison, her future husband, took his degree at Oxford University in the same town. They were engaged at the time of their graduation, but Mrs. Harrison taught music in Carrollton, Kentucky, for one year before her marriage October 20, 1853, and removed to Indianapolis, Indiana. When the Civil War broke out, Benjamin Harrison decided to enter the army, his wife saying to him "Go and help to save your country, and let us trust in the shielding care of a higher Power for your protection and safe return."

She took great pride in her husband's distinguished service, especially in his heroic deeds at Resaca and Peach Tree Creek, Georgia. She was a woman of strong individuality and deep sympathy for those in distress; she was generous and benevolent to a fault; she was one of the most active workers in the Presbyterian Church and Sunday school and in all patriotic and charitable organizations; she was universally popular. During Senator Harrison's six years in the United States Senate, prior to his election to the Presidency, Mrs. Harrison was one of the best known and universally beloved ladies of the Senate.

When her husband was made President, Mrs. Harrison's experiences had served to fit her for the duties of Mistress of the White House, and no criticism was ever made of her conduct. She recognized the fact that the house belonged to the Nation, but at the same time she made it a home for her family and none of her predecessors made it more attractive for all who cared to visit the White House.   Her receptions and other social functions were charming in every sense of the word.   Her long illness and pathetic death have left a lasting impression upon the Nation.

IDA SAXTON McKINLEY.

The wife of President McKinley was born Ida Saxton on the 8th of June, 1847, in Canton, Ohio.   Her father died just as she was entering upon her young womanhood; her mother having died when she was but a child.   She was therefore, early left an orphan, and lived with her sister.   It was decided that she should go abroad as a diversion from the grief over the death of her father.   Soon after her return, on January 25, 1871, she was married to Major William McKinley, then a rising lawyer and statesman of the town of Canton, Ohio. She had been delicate from her childhood and after the death of the two children born to her she became a confirmed invalid. The world has long since read of the matchless tenderness and devotion and thoughtfulness of her husband, who was rapidly promoted from one high position to another.   She greatly appreciated the attention bestowed upon her but the story of her resignation, gentleness and beautiful character can never be told.   Her most charming characteristic was her perfect sincerity and thoughtfulness for others.

President McKinley had been a member of Congress for fourteen years, Governor of the state of Ohio, and constantly occupied with public affairs before he was nominated for the Presidency of the United States.   Through all of these positions Mrs. McKinley had caused herself to be beloved on account of her amiability, patience and devotion to her husband and those who ministered to her wants.   She was never able to do what she desired in the White House, yet the effort she made was quite remarkable, in the face of her invalidism. The whole world was deeply touched by her sufferings when she was informed of the tragic death of her husband, and no one expected that she would survive as long as she did her husband's loss. Mrs. McKinley died in 1907, and her remains were placed beside those of her illustrious husband in the magnificent monument built by the Nation to perpetuate his memory.

EDITH KERMIT CAROW ROOSEVELT.

The fearful tragedy which made Vice-President Roosevelt President of the United States was so overwhelming in its effect that no one thought of the consequences on society of such a sudden change in the administration, or seemed to give any thought as to Mrs. Roosevelt's fitness for the position of Mistress of the White House.

Fortunately there was no need of anxiety, as Mrs. Roosevelt was reared amidst the luxuries of life and had received every advantage for the cultivation of her superior mind. With a heart full of tenderness and absolutely without guile, Mrs. Roosevelt had little to learn when she assumed the duties of presiding over the White House. She was so well informed on all subjects of which many women are ignorant that she was well equipped to meet the most learned and cultured people of the land. She was so gracious and natural in her manner that she inspired the confidence and admiration of all who met her. She was a devoted wife and mother. She disliked notoriety and was so simple and refined in her tastes that critics had little ground for discussion as to what she did or what she wore. Her aversion to gossip and her reticence more than once silenced would-be detractors. Her influence was ever exerted for true loyalty, freedom and humanity and it can truthfully be said that her departure from the White House was much regretted.

Edith Kermit Carow Roosevelt was born at Norwich, Connecticut, August 6, 1861. She was the daughter of Charles and Gertrude Elizabeth Carow. She was educated at Comstock School, New York. Married Theodore Roosevelt at St. George's Church, London, December 2, 1886. She is the mother of four sons and one daughter.

HELEN HERRON TAFT.

The wife of the President of the United States was born in Cincinnati, June 2, 1861, and is the daughter of John Williamson and Harriet Collins Herron. She was educated at private schools in Cincinnati, and at her home there was married June 19, 1886, to William Howard Taft. Mrs. Taft is a woman of strong character and an equal degree of intensity in her aims; she is sympathetic, straightforward, sincere, with a wholesome contempt for artificial veneers, social shams and the glitter that has no gold behind it. But for impaired health, which beset her shortly after her occupancy of the White House, she would doubtless have made one of the most forceful and brilliant mistresses of the national executive mansion. Mrs. Taft is well and broadly educated, a trained musician and has had every advantage which culture anl travel can give. She has journeyed much, and lived in many lands. She is the mother of three children—two sons, Robert, a student at Yale, and Charles, a schoolboy at Groton, Massachusetts, and of one daughter, Miss Helen Taft, an accomplished graduate of Bryn Mawr, and now her mother's right hand in all social matters.

MRS. JAMES RUSH.

The ideas which Mrs. Otis applied with such charming results in Boston were also applied by Mrs. James Rush, of Philadelphia, to the social life of that city.

She, like Mrs. Otis, "had learned social democracy abroad where American women are still frequently obliged to go to learn it." In spite of our pretended democracy very frequently extreme formality and ridiculous social customs prevail in this country. Mrs. Rush's husband was one of the great physicians of his day, a man of wide cultivation and a great student, and their circle gave Mrs. Rush ample opportunity for the social reforms which she inaugurated. Among the first changes she made was the abolition of the day at home, and instead she established a fashionable hour for promenade, and at this time the walk to the river in the afternoon was quite the fashionable thing of Philadelphia social life.

Mrs. Rush's dinners and receptions were quite affairs of state. She took these gatherings quite seriously and studied to bring together interesting people. Miss Wharton says Mrs. Rush's recipe for making up a party ran: "An ex-president, a foreign minister, a poet, two or three American artists, as many lady authors, a dozen merchants, lawyers, physicians, and others who are there on the simple footing of gentlemen—their wives, who come as respectable and agreeable 'ladies'—fifty young men who are good beaux and dance well, fifty pretty girls without money but respectable, well dressed, lively, charming, are always indispensable at a party."

The effect in a community of such a circle is incalculable. It breaks down prejudices and caste, it starts lines of thought and creates breadth of opinion. There is no activity of a community, political, social, philanthropic, educational, artistic, which does not receive impulses from circles made up as Mrs. Rush did hers on the base of character and achievement, which should be the basis for every social circle of every city of America, at our national Capital particularly.

Mrs. Rush was a graduate of Mrs. Emma Willard's Seminary of Troy, New York. Mrs. Willard herself was a great social leader. The life at her seminary reflected in those years in a rather unusual way the strong social instincts of its great founder, and the effect was felt all over the country as those women went out into the various sections to establish their homes.

MRS. HARRISON GRAY OTIS.

Among the women conspicuous by their leadership during the '40's and '50's, none are more entitled to mention than Mrs. Harrison Gray Otis, of Boston, who, after several years' residence abroad, undertook the task of lifting the social life of Boston from its old ruts of pretentious formality and exclusiveness, breaking up its stiffness and bringing the social life to a more enjoyable and democratic status. Only such an independent and courageous spirit as Mrs. Otis possessed would have dared such an undertaking. Mrs. Otis was the daughter of one of Boston's richest merchants. Her name before her marriage was Elizabeth Boardman, and her husband, Harrison Gray Otis, was a nephew of James Otis and of Mercy Otis Warren. Several years after her marriage she was left a widow with three sons. At this time she became a social leader and it is said among her many admirers were Daniel Webster and Henry Clay. In 1835 she went to Europe to educate her sons, and while there studied and became a ready conversationalist in several languages. The experience of these years in the flexible, lively, stimulating, intellectual circles of Europe had given Mrs. Otis convincing proof of what a woman might accomplish for a community if she handled the social circle with brains and independence. So, on her return to Boston, she set out at once to build up in her home a social circle where naturalness and simplicity should rule. At that time, elaborate heavy dinners were considered the proper social entertainment for elders and balls for the younger set. There was very little informal visiting. Mrs. Otis swept all of this out of the way and ignored functions, banquets and balls, but instead opened her house every Saturday morning and every Thursday afternoon to her own set and many more invited guests. No aspiring worthy young writer, singer or artist of talent who fell in Mrs. Otis's way but was welcome in her circle. A big, wide-awake informal circle was soon about her, and instead of the previous form of entertainment, she substituted simply tea and cakes. No matter what the occasion, "tea and cakes" were all her guests received, and when entertaining even President Fillmore, Lord Elgin and many other dignitaries, tea and cakes were the only refreshment at the affairs given in their honor. But her innovations were founded on good sense and genuine love for people, and therefore they were a success from the beginning. Her book "The Barclays of Boston" embodies her ideas, and is a valuable document on the manners and customs of Boston in her time. The results of Mrs. Otis's stand were altogether beneficent and stimulating. Mrs. Otis's great passion was the life and character of George Washington. On February 22nd her house was always thrown open and she entertained elaborately. It was her work that made that date a legal holiday in Massachusetts and gave the strongest impulse toward making it a national day. It was natural that she should take a leading part in the enterprise of buying Mr. Vernon for a national monument, and the money which completed the purchase of Mt. Vernon was raised by a ball engineered by Mrs. Otis and given in the Boston Theatre on March 4, 1859. She was also one of the leading spirits in the ball to raise the money for the completion of the Bunker Hill Monument. The success of this affair was due largely to a woman—Mrs. Sarah Josepha Hale—the best-known editor at that time among American women.

MRS. JOSHUA SPEED AND MRS. NINIAN EDWARDS.

Mrs. Joshua Speed and Mrs. Ninian Edwards, of Springfield, Illinois, were conspicuous leaders in their home city, the capital of Illinois. They gathered about their table and in their drawing-rooms such men as Abraham Lincoln, Stephen A. Douglas, John J. Hardin, James Shields, the Edwardses, John Stuart, David Davis, and Edward D. Baker, all distinguished men in the history of our country. At this time all the women were interested in politics and national affairs. Throughout all the West, indeed, there flowed an enthusiastic spirit which made up for everything else. The women of the West were a part of the great growth of that country. They felt their responsibility in the westward movement, the obligations which had been laid upon them as wives and mothers, the obligation of establishing homes while their husbands established the towns and cities, of looking after the education of their children while their husbands made the money to pay for these opportunities, and of preserving and developing the morals not only of their children but of their husbands and the men about them.

ELIZABETH PALMER PEABODY.

The persistency and skill of Miss Elizabeth Palmer Peabody, called "The Grandmother of Boston," in keeping an open house for social gatherings was one of the really valuable contributions to the social life of Boston. Her little shop has been called "a kind of Transcendental Exchange," and her home was the same, and it is said she was the first woman in Boston to give a regular evening to her friends, and to the last days of her life she continued these delightful social gatherings.

MRS. BENJAMIN BUTLER.

In many instances the wife of a great man has failed to prove herself worthy even of reflected glory, but the wife of Benjamin Butler was such an active factor in his career, along military as well as civil lines, that she well deserves a biography of her own. I give it, however, in the words of her distinguished husband, as I have taken it from the story of his own life: "In the year 1830, I made the acquaintance of Fisher Ames Hildreth, the only son of Dr. Israil Hildreth, of Dracut, a town joining Lowell on the north side of the Merrimac River. That acquaintance ripened into an affectionate friendship which terminated only with his death thirty years later. Doctor Hildreth had a family of seven children, six being daughters. The son, having invited me to the family gathering of the Thanksgiving feast I there first met Sarah, the second daughter. I was much impressed with her personal endowments, literary attainments and brilliancy of mind. Doctor Hildreth was an exceedingly scholarly and literary man, who was a great admirer of English poets, especially of Byron, Burns and Shakespeare, and had early taught the great poet's plays to his daughter, who in consequence developed a strong desire to go on the stage. Her father approved of this and she appeared with brilliant success at the Tremont Theatre in Boston and the Park Theatre in New York, her talent for the delineation of character being fully acknowledged by all. When our acquaintance began I had never seen her on the stage, her home life being sufficient to attract me. She declined to leave her profession, however, until I had won my spurs in my own profession. But a most cordial and affectionate intimacy existed between us, and in the spring of 1843, I visited her at Cincinnati, Ohio, where she was a star. There we became engaged and we were married on the sixteenth of May, 1844."

Having thus concisely outlined his wife's girlhood and their courtship, the General proceeds with his tribute to her value as the helpmate of a public man: "My wife, with a devotion quite unparalleled," he says, "gave me her support by accompanying me, at my earnest wish, in every expedition in the War of the Rebellion and made for me a home wherever I was stationed in command. She went with me in the expedition to Ship Island after the attack upon New Orleans, where I was exposed to the greatest peril of my life, and only when my ship was hourly expected to go to pieces and when I appealed to her good sense that our children must not be bereft of both parents did she leave me to seek safety on board a gun boat. She suffered great privation and hardships on Ship Island, while we were awaiting the attack of New Orleans.

"In 1864 she went with me to the field and remained with me during most of the campaign of 1864. Thus I had an advantage over most of my brother commanding-generals in the field in having an adviser, faithful, true and cool-headed, conscientious and conservative, whose conclusions could always be trusted. In the more military movements although she took full note she never interfered by suggestion. In other matters all that she agreed to was right. And if there is anything in my administration of affairs that may be questioned it is that in which I followed the bent of my own actions.

"Returning home with me after I had retired to civil and political life, Mrs. Butler remained the same good adviser, educating and guiding her children during their young lives with such skill and success that neither of them ever did an act which caused me serious sorrow or gave me the least anxiety on their behalf. She made my home and family as happy as could be. She took her place in society when in Washington and maintained it with such grace and dignity and loveliness of character that no one ever said an unkind or a disparaging word of her."

Mrs. Benjamin Butler died in Lowell in 1877. Her veracity and strong mental characteristics survived pre-eminently in her grandson, Butler Ames, the son of her eldest daughter, who has for some years represented the district of her birth in the National Congress.

MRS. HENRY D. GILPIN.

Mrs. Henry D. Gilpin was the widow of an eminent man, and had a ruling influence in Philadelphia owing to her intellectual superiority, her culture and refinement. She was the daughter of Dr. John Sibley, a distinguished physician in Louisiana until the close of his life and exercised throughout that state a wide influence. Leaving school at an early date she joined her father in Louisiana and married Josiah S. Johnston, then Judge of the Western District of that state. He was afterwards elected to the House of Representatives and served for three terms in the Senate of the United States. Mr. and Mrs. Johnston resided in Washington and while there their house was celebrated for its hospitality. After the death of Mr. Johnston, Mrs. Johnston became the wife of Honorable Henry D. Gilpin, United States Attorney for the District of Pennsylvania, and whom Mr. Van Buren, after he was elected President called to his cabinet as Solicitor of the Treasury and subsequently to the office of Attorney-General of the United States. Their home in Philadelphia was the resort of distinguished strangers, artists, connoisseurs. The library of Mr. Gilpin was perhaps the largest private collection in America and was bequeathed by him (after his wife's death), to the Historical Society of Pennsylvania. His works of art were left to the Pennsylvania Academy of Fine Arts in Philadelphia and to this collection Mrs. Gilpin added the portraits of Mr. Gilpin and herself. Mrs. Gilpin took a prominent part in the great Sanitary Fair held in Philadelphia; was chairman of the Ladies' Art Committee, which department alone realized thirty-five thousand dollars.

MARY THOMPSON HILL WILLARD.

The mother of Frances E. Willard was born January 3, 1805, near North Danville, Vermont. She was the daughter of John Hill, of Lee, New Hampshire and Polly Thompson Hill. Mary Hill received her early education in the district schools. At that time these schools were largely taught by students or graduates of Dartmouth and Middlebury colleges. When she was twelve years of age her father removed to the Genessee Valley in Western New York, and in a new settlement fourteen miles from Rochester, known as the town of Ogden, Mary spent her early girlhood. At the age of fifteen she taught her first school and continued in the work as a teacher for eleven years. It is said "she possessed in an unusual degree a love for the beautiful, had a poetic faculty, a sweet voice, remarkable gifts in conversation, rare tact, delicacy and appreciation of the best in others." On November 3, 1831, she married Josiah F. Willard, the son of one of her father's neighbors. Four children were born. The second daughter was Frances Elizabeth Willard, who being rather a delicate child, her parents moved to Oberlin, Ohio, to secure for her educational advantages which were offered in that city. The lives of both Mr. and Mrs. Willard were beautiful and well ordered, their children sharing in every interest. They formed a circle for study long before women's clubs were heard of. Mr. Willard's health failing it became necessary for them to move to what was then the territory of Wisconsin, and in 1846 they settled near Janesville, Wisconsin. They soon became the leaders in the church and affairs of the community. The Willards resided in this home for twelve years, and then moved to Evanston, Illinois, near Chicago in order that their daughters might be educated without being separated from their parents and the home life. In 1862 Mary, the younger daughter, died and in 1868 Mr. Willard passed away and in 1878 the son Oliver.

Frances Willard in her early youth wrote these words of her mother. "I thank God for my mother as for no other gift of his bestowing. My nature is so woven into hers that I think it would almost be death for me to have the bond severed and one so much myself gone over the river. I verily believe I cling to her more than ever did any other of her children, perhaps because I am to need her more." "Enter every open door," was her advice to her daughter, and much of the distinguished career of Frances E. Willard was rendered possible through the courage and by the encouragement given her by her mother. Mrs. Willard preserved her mental powers to the last, and died after a brief illness, August 7, 1892, at the age of nearly eighty-eight years. These words were said at her funeral: "She was a reformer by nature, she made the world's cause her own and identified herself with all its fortunes; nothing of its sadness, sorrow or pain was foreign to her. With a genius, a consecration, a beauty and a youth which had outlived her years, a soul eager still to know, to learn, to catch every word God had for her, she lived on, a center of joy and comfort in this most typical and almost best known home in America. She stood a veritable Matterhorn of strength to this daughter. Given a face like hers, brave, benignant, patient, yet resolute, a will inflexible for duty, a heart sensitive to righteousness and truth, yet tender as a child's, given New England puritanism and rigor, its habits of looking deep into every problem, its consciousness full of God, its lofty ideal of freedom and its final espousal of every noble cause, and you and I shall never blame the stalwart heart, well-nigh crushed because mother is gone." Her household name was "Saint Courageous."

MRS. JOHN HAYS HAMMOND.

The wife of this most distinguished mining engineer of the world was born Natalie Harris, the daughter of a Mississippi judge. Miss Harris was married to "the highest salaried man in the world" in 1881, and her early married experiences were sometimes of a very trying sort. To quote her own words: "We have suffered many hardships in common and during my early life at mines I have known what it was to be underfed and cold. I have slept with a baby on my breast, under a cart in the dust of the roads. We have traveled together in every known sort of vehicle—bullock wagon, Cape cart and private pullman— for days at a time my saddle has been my pillow." Mrs. Hammond has always been her distinguished husband's comrade, greatest admirer and best friend. She is the mother of four sons and one daughter. Mrs. Hammond is a brilliant woman and amply fulfils the demands made upon her, whether these take the form of philanthropic effort, as in serving as president of the woman's branch of the National Civic Federation, or high social position as wife of the special ambassador to the coronation of Britain's king. Mr. and Mrs. Hammond make their winter home at the nation's Capital and summer in their magnificent yacht "The Alcodo" or at their seashore residence at Gloucester, Massachusetts.

MRS. CHAMP CLARK.

Genevieve Davis Bennett, wife of Champ Clark, speaker of the House of Representatives, and daughter of Joel Davis Bennett and Mary McClung McAlfee, his wife, was born in Callaway County, Missouri; educated in the public schools and at the Missouri State University, and is a member in good standing of the Presbyterian Church and the Congressional Club. On both sides of the house, Mrs. Clark is descended from colonial ancestors. Her parents were both from Kentucky, her mother being born in Mercer County and her father in Madison County. Both sides of her family took part in the French and Indian War, the American Revolution and the War of 1812. In the Civil War, which divided the states, Mrs. Clark had first cousins on both sides. In one instance, she had two cousins, brothers, who served on different sides of the great struggle.

On her mother's side, Mrs. Clark comes of Scotch-Irish stock. Two of her ancestors, father and son, were at the battle of the Boyne; on her father's side she is descended from the first Colonial Governor of Virginia; collaterally she is descended from George Rodgers Clark and Joseph Hamilton Daviess. Her grandfather, George McAlfee, served in the War of 1812 and was at the Battle of the Thames, fighting in Colonel Dick Johnson's regiment. Her great grandfather, George McAlfee, Sr., was with General George Rodgers Clark in his expedition

19

against the British and Indians, and received for his services a grant of 1400 acres of land from Benjamin Harrison, then Governor of Virginia.

On her father's side Mrs. Clark's great grandmother, Margaret Dozier, wife of Captain James Davis, was the heroine of a dramatic incident during the closing months of the Revolutionary War, which has been handed down by tradition and told in all the histories of Kentucky. Captain Davis had placed his family, consisting of his wife and four children, a negro slave woman and her child, an infant, at the fort (which was under the command of Captain Jesse Davis) while he went with a body of troops under the command of Colonel Floyd, of Virginia, to find and punish a band of marauding Indians for their depredations committed in the neighborhood of Blue Licks. While they were gone, the Indians surprised the fort, killed all the inmates with great slaughter and burnt the fort. Mrs. Davis, Mrs. Clark's great-grandmother, escaped with her infant son, and the negro servant also had the good fortune to escape with her child. Everybody else was killed but the three little Davis girls, Margaret, Rebecca and Martha or (as they were then called Peggy, Becky and Patty). These children, according to tradition were saved on account of their remarkable beauty, the Indians being actuated by the desire to extort a great ransom made them captive. In the meantime, the mother and servant with their children undertook to make their way to the nearest station to get someone to come and rescue her little girls, but they lost their way in the darkness and wandered around and were picked up after three days and taken to the station. The Indians in the meantime had gotten such a start with the children that it was impossible to overtake them. They were taken to Detroit, and kept there for eighteen months under the care of Major DePeyster who was then commandant at the fort; the children were treated with every consideration. Major DePeyster was a man of considerable taste and accomplishments. His wife was childless and conceived a great fancy for little Peggy Davis and her sisters, and was anxious to adopt Peggy who was the oldest and promised her a life of luxury if she would consent, but young as she was she was not to be weaned from her home and country. The children were finally returned to their parents in Madison County, Kentucky, grew up to womanhood and married three brothers, Joseph, Elijah and Moses Bennett, from Maryland, and from them have descended some of the most notable families in America. It is from Peggy Davis who married Joseph Bennett that Mrs. Champ Clark is descended.

BELLE CASE LA FOLLETTE.

Mrs. Belle Case La Follette was born in April, 1859, at Summit, Juneau County, Wisconsin. Her father's name was Anson Case. Her mother was Mary Nesbit. Their home, at the time of Mrs. La Follette's childhood, was in Baraboo, Wisconsin. She attended the public schools of that city and was a graduate later of the State University, winning at this institution in 1879 the Lewis Prize. In 1881 she became the wife of Robert M. La Follette, a lawyer, who had formerly been her classmate at school. Taking an active interest in her husband's career she decided to enter the Wisconsin Law School, where she was admitted in 1883, graduating in 1885. She was the first woman to receive a diploma from that institution. During that year Mr. La Follette was elected to Congress, which prevented Mrs. La Follette from taking up the active duties of the profession which she had chosen. Mr. La Follette's career has been most successful. Having been elected to the United States Senate, he to-day occupies one of the most conspicuous positions as a member of that body. He has forged rapidly to the front by his independent thoughts and ideas, and to-day is the leader of what is known as the progressive element in politics. Their home is in Madison, Wisconsin. Mrs. La Follette has proved herself a most worthy and capable companion for her distinguished husband in his political and professional career. She is generally known in Washington social circles as one of the brainy women of the day. Their daughter, Fola, has entered the theatrical life as a profession.

BERTHA HONORE PALMER.

Bertha Honoré Palmer was born in Louisville, Kentucky, where she passed her childhood, receiving a common school education. She afterward took a course in the Georgetown, D. C. Convent, where she graduated in 1871. Shortly afterward she became the wife of Potter Palmer, the Chicago millionaire, who was many years her senior. Since her marriage she has been a recognized social leader of that city. She is an accomplished linguist, musician and woman of marked executive ability. She was chosen president of the Board of Lady Managers of the Exposition of 1893, and in 1891 went to Europe in the interest of this section and succeeded in interesting many of the prominent women of Europe in the women's department of the World's Fair, and much of the success of this department is due to her work. Since the death of her husband she has spent much of her time abroad, and during the reign of King Edward, of England, occupied a house in London, where she entertained extensively gaining for herself a high position among the social leaders of the most exclusive and royal circles. She keeps her residence in Chicago, Illinois, where her large interests are located.

IDA LEWIS.

Is better known as the "Grace Darling of America." She was born in Newport, Rhode Island, in 1841. Her father was Captain Hosea Lewis, and was keeper of the Lime Rock lighthouse in Newport harbor. She early became her father's assistant in his duties at this station. She made her first rescue when but seventeen years of age, saving the crew of a boat lost in a storm near the lighthouse, and landed them in safety at Fort Adams, when even men did not venture to launch a boat to aid the helpless men. She received from the United

States Government a gold medal, the first ever given to a woman; a silver medal from the Humane Society of Massachusetts, and also one from the Life-saving Benevolent Society of New York, and her home is filled with testimonials in recognition of her heroism.   She is one of the most distinguished examples of American heroism among women.

MARY ELIZABETH LEESE.

Born in Pennsylvania, September 11, 1853. Her father was Joseph P. Clyens and her mother, Mary Elizabeth Murray Clyens. In 1873 she married Charles L. Leese, and has since been a resident of Wichita, Kansas. She took up the study of law, and has been actively engaged in politics of recent years. The political revolution in Kansas brought her to the front and she became prominent as a Populist leader and through her bitter opposition to the re-election of Senator John J. Ingalls. During the campaign of General Weaver, the Populist candidate, she accompanied him and spoke in his interest from public platforms. She has occupied the position of president of the board of trustees of some of the charitable institutions of the state of Kansas, and other public offices. Her items are radical and her cause has been most aggressive, which has brought much criticism upon her methods.

ELIZABETH TILLINGHAST LAWTON.

Elizabeth Tillinghast Lawton, a direct descendant of Elder Pardon Tillinghast, the noted Baptist Divine, was born July 15, 1832, and died March 1, 1904. Mrs. Lawton was one of the most widely known and highly respected residents in Newport County, Rhode Island, and was always prominently identified with the educational progress of Tiverton, Rhode Island. She was one of the first women in the country on a school committee, serving as chairman and superintendent of schools, and for years was the only woman holding the office of superintendent. She was an unusually strong character with a keen intellect which she retained up to the time she was stricken with apoplexy which almost immediately caused her death. It was always said that in all action she showed the marked characteristics of her distinguished ancestor, who succeeded Roger Williams in his labors in the First Baptist Church, Providence.

ELEANOR BOYLE EWING SHERMAN.

Mrs. Sherman was born in Lancaster, Ohio, October 24, 1824. She was descended from a long line of Scotch and Irish ancestors. Her father, Thomas Ewing, was one of the most eminent lawyers of his day and was twice a Senator of the United States and twice a member of a President's Cabinet. Her mother,

Maria Boyle, was a woman of strong character and gentle mien. When a boy of nine years, William Tecumseh Sherman was adopted by Mr. Ewing on account of the strong affection he bore his family, and at the age of seventeen Eleanor Ewing became engaged to young Sherman. They were married May 1, 1850, in Washington, her father, at that time, being a member of President Taylor's Cabinet. Her husband resigned from the army in 1853 to accept a position in a bank in California, and there they went to reside, returning East again in 1857. During the Civil War, not only was Mrs. Sherman's husband fighting for the Union, but her brothers were also in the army. When grave charges and newspaper criticism were brought upon her husband she went personally to Washington and saw President Lincoln and convinced him that matters had been misrepresented to him. She again rose to her husband's defense at the close of the war when he was severely criticised for his part in the terms of the Johnson Treaty. After the war the family resided in St. Louis, where Mrs. Sherman was most conspicuous in her charitable work for the Roman Catholic Church, of which she was a devoted member. In 1869 her husband's promotion to the command of the United States army took the family to Washington, and here they resided until his retirement. Mrs. Sherman organized the Aloysius Aid Society and inaugurated this by a great charity fair held in Washington. She was very sympathetic to those persons without friends in the Capital city. Their family consisted of seven children, two of whom died when quite young. The eldest daughter, Minnie, was married in 1874 to Lieutenant Thomas William Fitch, Assistant Engineer, U. S. N. On May 18, 1879, their youngest son, Thomas Ewing Sherman, entered the Order of Jesuits, and was ordained in July, 1889. Their daughter Eleanor became the wife of Lieutenant Alexander Montgomery Thackara, U. S. N., in 1880. Lieutenant Thackara resigned from the navy and later entered the consular service of the United States and is now Consul General at Berlin. Philemon Tecumseh Sherman, another son, was a member of the New York bar. Rachel Ewing Sherman married in December, 1891, Dr. Paul Thorndyke. Mrs. Sherman died in New York City November 28, 1888, and was buried in St. Louis, where General Sherman now rests beside her.

MARGARET STEWART SHERMAN.

Mrs. Sherman was the only child of Judge Stewart of Mansfield, Ohio. She was well educated. On December 31, 1848, she married John Sherman then a young lawyer of some prominence, a brother of General W. T. Sherman, and later U. S. Senator from Ohio. During President Hayes' term, Senator Sherman was Secretary of the Treasury, and Secretary of State in President McKinley's Cabinet. Mrs. Sherman fulfilled with dignity and credit her part in all the positions of honor to which her husband was called by the people of his state.

CLARA HARRISON STRANAHAN.

Mrs. Clara Harrison Stranahan was born in Westfield, Mass., and in 1879 she became the wife of Hon. J. S. T. Stranahan, of Brooklyn, New York. In all the active career of her husband, both political and municipal, Mrs. Stranahan has been a powerful factor and a recognized leader in the city of Brooklyn. Mr. Stranahan received an unusual mark of esteem from the people of Brooklyn who erected, while he was living, in June 1891, a bronze statue to his honor under the title "First Citizen of Brooklyn."

KATHERINE TINGLEY.

Mrs. Tingley was born in Newburyport, Massachusetts, July 6, 1852. Was descended from one of the early colonial families and was the daughter of James P. and Susan Wescott. She attended the public schools and had private instruction. In 1879 she married T. B. Tingley, an inventor. She is the leader and official head for life of the universal brotherhood of the Theosophical Society throughout the world, "an outer head" of the inner school of theosophy, the successor of Blavatsky. From 1896-7 she conducted two theosophy crusades around the world, established relief work for Indian famine sufferers, and founded the International Brotherhood League and a summer home for children at Spring Valley, New Jersey, in 1897. Her claim for fame rests upon the society and academy, or as she calls it, the School of Antiquity and the Raja Yoga Academies, located at Point Loma and San Diego, California. She has founded three academies for boys and girls in Cuba; was one to organize relief corps in New York, and helped to establish a hospital at Montauk Point, New York, for the sick and wounded soldiers of the Spanish American War. She was quite active in carrying on this humanitarian work in Cuba, where the Government granted her permission to establish hospitals both in Cuba and Manila, P. I. She is the owner of the Isis Theatre in California, and of large properties in California, Sweden, England and San Juan Hill, Cuba. She is the editor of the *Century Path,* a theosophy publication, published at Point Loma, California.

MRS. JULIUS C. BURROWS.

The maiden name of Mrs. Julius C. Burrows, of Michigan, was Frances L. Peck, daughter of Horace M. Peck and Emilia Barnes of best New England stock. She was born in Michigan, and is a graduate of Rockford College, Illinois. Mrs. Burrows was always active in church work and the club life of Kalamazoo, Michigan, until the election of her husband to the United States Senate, which has necessitated her residence in Washington much of the time.

She is a charter member of the national organization of the Daughters of the American Revolution, was vice-president-general of that society, was national president of the Children's Society of the Daughters of the American Revolution, is a member of the Society of Colonial Dames, was president of the National Relief Association organized at the time of the Cuban War, which accomplished much helpful work.

During Senator Burrows' thirty-two years of official life in Washington, Mrs. Burrows has been one of the most influential women in society, charity, and is prominent in all good works.

EMILIE SCHAUMBURG.

Miss Emilie Schaumburg was a Philadelphia social celebrity. Her grandfather, Colonel Bartholemew Schaumburg, of New Orleans, was a ward of the Landgrave of Hesse Cassel, and educated under the auspices of Frederick the Great at the German Military School. He was commissioned an officer in the Grenadier Guards, and was sent to this country as adjutant and aide-de-camp to General Count Donop. Colonel Schaumburg, however, never joined Count Donop, as their vessel became separated from the fleet in a storm and came up the Delaware, anchoring at Newcastle where they learned the nature of the struggle for independence. Preferring to fight for a people struggling for their independence rather than for England they joined General Washington and were incorporated into General Sullivan's German Legion and served loyally under Washington throughout the Revolutionary War. Colonel Schaumburg sacrificed his title and much of his property by espousing the American cause. He was later earnestly solicited by his relatives to return to Germany, but he refused and married a lady who was a descendant of a noted Indian chief of the Lenape Tribe who signed the Treaty of 1685 with William Penn, selling him the large tract of land on which Philadelphia is situated. Miss Schaumburg is the eighth descendant in a direct line from this aboriginal princess, and was born in New Orleans, though she spent most of her life in Philadelphia. The early portion of her education was largely directed by the Honorable H. D. Gilpin. She had the added accomplishment of speaking several modern languages. When the Prince of Wales visited Philadelphia with his suite, he spent the only evening of his stay at the Academy of Music. He was greatly attracted by the beauty of Miss Schaumburg, and it is said that he declared her the most beautiful woman he had seen in America. When the great Sanitary Fair was held in Philadelphia, a play was given in which the principal parts were taken by the leading society people of Philadelphia. The one given under the title "The Ladies' Battle," in which Miss Schaumburg sustained the principal rôle, created a great furore and it was remembered as a piece of acting unrivaled on the American stage. Miss Schaumburg was invited to Chicago when the fair was given there, to take the leading part, and she sustained with credit the great rôle of Peg Woffington. Miss Schaumburg frequently lent her talent to the cause of charity, and became quite well known throughout the United States for her remarkable gifts in this line.

MARY ELIZABETH LOGAN TUCKER.

Mary Elizabeth Logan Tucker, daughter of Major-General and Senator John A. and Mary S. Logan, was born in Benton, Franklin County, Illinois. In personal appearance and disposition she is strikingly like her illustrious father, and has many of his features and traits of character. She was educated at the Convent of the Visitation, Georgetown, D. C., one of the oldest schools in the United States. She was the organizer and founder of the alumnæ of her alma mater, March 3, 1893, and was elected and served as its first president. Mrs. Tucker was married on the twenty-seventh day of November, 1877, in the home of her parents in Chicago, Illinois. Not long after her marriage she removed to Santa Fe, New Mexico. General Logan having secured the appointment of her husband as an officer in the United States army he was ordered to that remote station. Notwithstanding her youth she adapted herself to all the inconveniences of army life which existed twenty-five years ago.

By her keen intelligence, happy disposition, knowledge of human nature, generous hospitality and versatility in originating entertainments, and helpfulness in all efforts for the betterment of conditions and welfare of the army people, and in all emergencies, she won for herself great popularity and the highest esteem of the citizens of Santa Fe and her associates in the army. In 1886 her husband was ordered to Washington, hence it happened they were both with her parents when her distinguished father died. They remained with the widowed mother for eight years. Part of this time Mrs. Tucker was engaged as one of the staff of the *Home Magazine*, then published in Washington, D. C. Her literary career was interrupted by her husband's orders to other posts of duty as an army officer, including the stations of St. Paul, Chicago and Manila, P. I. Mrs. Tucker is the mother of three sons, two of whom are dead. Her youngest son died in Manila, August 5, 1905. Mrs. Tucker is a woman of marked ability, keen perception, and dauntless moral courage. She has traveled extensively, is an omnivorous reader, and has an unusually extensive knowledge of affairs political and otherwise, her perfect taste guiding her aright in the refinements of life. She is deeply interested and ever ready to join in every movement for the uplift of mankind and the advancement of civilization. She is a member of the Society of the Daughters of the American Revolution, Civic Federation and the Society of the Army of the Tennessee, and is to deliver an address before this Society at the meeting, October 11, 1911, at Council Bluffs, Iowa.

MRS. CHARLES EMORY SMITH.

Was the granddaughter of the late Hon. Charles Nichols, United States Minister to The Hague, and great-granddaughter of Benjamin Romaine, at one time second comptroller of New York City. Her husband, Hon. Charles Emory Smith, was at one time United States Minister to St. Petersburg, and afterwards in the cabinets of Presidents McKinley and Roosevelt as postmaster-general.

CAROLINE E. POREE.

Was born in New Orleans, Louisiana, September 30, 1842. One of her ancestors was John Baptiste Poree, Counsel of America, in 1812. She was for thirty-eight years assistant in the Boston Public Library, in charge of the Men's Reading Room, Periodical Department. For many years she has been an assistant in the new Library of Copley Square.

MARY R. WILCOX.

Was the daughter of Hon. John A. Wilcox and Mary Donelson Wilcox. Her mother enjoyed the distinction of being the first child born in the White

House. She is the granddaughter of Major Andrew J. Donelson, Minister to Prussia in 1846, and Mrs. Emily A. Donelson, who presided over the White House during the administrations of Andrew Jackson, her uncle. She was for some years the recording secretary-general of the Daughters of the American Revolution, and is to-day a clerk in one of the departments of the United States Government.

EMILY WARREN ROEBLING.

No American woman is entitled to a higher place in the rôle of honor than Emily Warren as a sister, daughter, wife, mother and gifted woman. At a very early age the noble traits of her character were manifested by her efforts to be helpful in the home of her childhood, especially in her devotion to her brother, Gouverneur Kemble Warren, which continued during his eventful life.

She was born September 23, 1843, at Cold Spring on the Hudson and was one of the eleven children of Sylvanus Warren. Her girlhood was not unlike that of many of the girls of that day. She was educated at the then noted Convent of the Visitation, Georgetown, D. C., where she graduated. The Civil War having broken out in the meantime and her brother, Gouverneur, having risen to the distinction of major-general, and he being in command of the Fifth Army Corps of the army of the Potomac, then in Virginia, Emily was impatient, after her graduation, to visit him in camp. Obtaining permission, she hastened to present herself at headquarters and one can readily imagine the sensation which the appearance of this beautiful, accomplished, enthusiastic, patriotic young woman created. She immediately interested herself in the work offered about her; she cheered the despondent, wrote letters for the sick and carried sunshine into the hospitals and camps. Colonel Washington A. Roebling, the skilled young engineer was then a member of General Warren's staff, and when she returned home she was engaged to be married to this rising young engineer. They were married January 18, 1865, and after the close of the war, Colonel Roebling took his bride to Mulhausen, Thuringen, Germany, his birthplace. Here he was to study European construction and submarine foundations as his father, Colonel John A. Roebling, was at that time working out the problems connected with the building of the Brooklyn Bridge. While at Mulhausen, the only son of Colonel and Mrs. Roebling, John A. Roebling, was born. On their return to this country, Colonel Roebling associated himself with his father in this great engineering work, and in 1869 his father was killed while making the first survey for this work. Then the responsibility of carrying out the plan for this gigantic undertaking fell upon Colonel Roebling and he, through his constant and untiring devotion, ultimately sank under the strain, and became a bed-ridden invalid. At this critical moment, Emily Warren Roebling proved her rare ability, dauntless courage, keen sagacity and true wifely devotion. It was she who stood between her husband and failure. With matchless diplomacy she smoothed out all friction between the municipal authorities, rival engineers, and ambitious men, in addition to ministering to her husband's comfort and relieving his suffering. She filled his mind with hope and kept him hourly informed of the progress of the work, gained by sitting near his bedside, telescope in hand, faithfully reporting to him every step in the progress of the work. So correct were her observations, from their home on Brooklyn Heights, that he was able to write out instructions and plan for the work of the assisting engineers and laboring force. Armed with these drawings, the faithful wife could be seen daily wending her way to the engineers and workmen, explaining to them explicitly and intelligently Colonel Roebling's directions. Few women have ever had higher tribute paid them than was given to Mrs. Roebling, when Honorable Abram S. Hewitt, the orator of the day, on the occasion of the opening of the bridge, in eloquent terms connected the name of Mrs. Roebling with that of Colonel Roebling as deserving equal share in his unparalleled achievement. That the name of her revered brother, Gouverneur Kemble Warren, should not be forgotten, she caused to be erected a magnificent bronze statue to his memory, on Little Round Top, on the Battlefield of Gettysburg. After Colonel and Mrs. Roebling's removal to Trenton, New Jersey, where she spent the last years of her life, she busied herself in assisting Colonel Roebling in arranging a wonderful collection of books, curios, gems and mineralogical specimens and in interesting herself in social, political, philanthropic and patriotic work. She traveled extensively and was presented, in 1896, to Queen Victoria in London and subsequently, at court, in Russia. On her return from this trip, which she made in company with Mrs. John A. Logan, she gave a most interesting illustrated lecture on, "What an American Woman Saw at the Coronation of Nicholas the Second." The proceeds of this she gave to charity. In 1898 she was among the most active members of the Relief Society which did such noble work during the Spanish War, giving her money, time and strength to the hospital work of this association. She was a graduate from the Law School of the New York University in 1899, the subject of her graduating essay being "The Wife's Disabilities." She was chosen as the essayist of her class and had previously won the prize for the best essay written by any member of her class. She was active in the work of the Daughters of the American Revolution, at one time vice-president-general of that organization, and one of the most important and able members of this great woman's organization. She represented the women of New Jersey on the Board of Lady Managers at the World's Columbian Exposition in 1893. Mrs. Roebling was the first vice-president of the Society of Colonial Dames, and a member of the Colonial Daughters of the seventeenth century, Holland Dames of America, the Huguenot Society, honorary official of the George Washington Memorial Association, a member of the Woman's Branch of the New Jersey Historical Society, the New York Historical Society, the Virginia Society for the Preservation of Historical objects and places, the Revolutionary Memorial Society of New Jersey, the Woman's Law Class of the New York University, an officer of the New York State Federation of Clubs and at one time president of the Georgetown Visitation Academy Alumnæ Association. Her literary attainments were of the highest order. Her articles which appeared in the Brooklyn papers in 1882 and 1883, in defense of Colonel Roebling's methods in the construction of the Brooklyn Bridge, were so able that they completely routed his enemies, men who had conspired to defraud him of the glory she had helped him to win in the successful completion of that structure.

Her biography of Colonel Roebling, contributions to the press on philanthropy and economic questions, "The Journal of Reverend Silas Constant," her able defense of her brother, General Warren; reports and lectures written by her, all prove the delicacy of her taste, purity of her mind, earnestness of thought, indefatigable energy, inborn patriotism and unwavering loyalty to her husband and family. Her judgment of men and measures was singularly unerring for a woman; her ambitions were laudable and did credit to her intelligence and noble character. Her death in 1903 was an irreparable loss to her family, the community, the poor and society. In her brief life she accomplished more than has been done by many men.

MRS. JAMES TANNER.

Mero L. White was born at Jefferson, Schoharie County, September 13, 1844, the daughter of Alfred S. and Julia Snyder White. She was educated at the New York Conference Seminary at Charlotteville, New York. At the age of thirteen she passed an unusually brilliant examination and for several seasons thereafter was a very successful teacher of a district school. On November 17, 1866, she became the wife of James Tanner, and in 1869 they moved to the city of Brooklyn, where she continued to live until 1889, then removing to Washington upon the appointment of her husband as United States Commissioner of Pensions, resided there until her tragic death through an automobile accident on June 29, 1904, at Helena, Montana. She left surviving her husband and four children, James Alfred, an attorney-at-law in Philadelphia, Earle White, a captain in the Eleventh Infantry, United States Army, and two daughters, Ada and Antoinette, who reside with their father who is the Register of Wills for the District of Columbia. The mental endowments of Mrs. Tanner were of a very superior order. She was a deep, careful and omnivorous reader of the best literature of her day. Her nature was very sympathetic and at the same time very practical. She possessed to a marked degree executive capacity and force. The misfortune and helplessness of others always appealed to her most strongly. During her twenty years' life in the city of Brooklyn she was a most earnest and efficient worker on the board of directors of the Brooklyn Nursery, one of the most efficient and helpful institutions of its kind in the United States. She was especially interested in the welfare of the old comrades of her husband who survived the Civil War and struck many a blow in their defense and for their help. Thousands of personal appeals made to her by or for those in distress met with instant and helpful action. During the time of the Spanish-American War her ability, resourcefulness, and executive capacity came into full play. She had been allied for years with the national body of the Red Cross and during that struggle she was a member of the executive committee. Her fellow members, recognizing her peculiar fitness, gave her a very free hand and her work was on large lines. Possessing for many years the personal acquaintance and friendship of President McKinley and Secretary of War Alger, she was particularly well situated to do effective work, and many a negligence and much wrong doing was corrected by a quiet word from her to the President or the Secretary, and thousands upon thousands of sick and wounded soldiers were the unknowing beneficiaries of her words and deeds. It would take no small volume to give in full a statement of her work at that time. Besides all this, she took a great interest in legislation putting the rights of womankind on a much more just basis than had hitherto existed. It is owing to her efforts and those of some of her intimates that a law was enacted by Congress which wiped out the hideous monstrosity of a father having power through his will to bequeath away from the control and care of the mother who bore it, a minor child. On June 29, 1906, while accompanying her husband, who was then commander-in-chief of the Grand Army of the Republic, on a tour over the United States, and while being escorted around the city of Helena in an automobile ride, there was an accident, resulting in the upsetting of the machine and the fatal injuring of Mrs. Tanner, who died on the spot forty minutes later. By the personal direction of President Roosevelt and because of the great interest she had always taken in behalf of the veterans of the Civil War, a beautiful plot was assigned to her in the National Cemetery at Arlington alongside of the main thoroughfare, near the auditorium, where, on each recurring Memorial Day, the waves of oratory and music will roll above her last resting place. This seems all the more appropriate by reason of the fact that prior to her time, interment in the National Cemetery of wives or widows of private soldiers had been prohibited. Against this prohibition she had made strong protest, and had secured the kindly and favorable interest of General Robert Shaw Oliver, assistant Secretary of War. After her death General Oliver, while acting Secretary of War, issued the order which annulled the long time prohibition. There her remains were laid to rest on the 5th of July, 1906, and over them her husband's comrades erected a beautiful memorial. With large work, well done on a high plane, her place, as one of those women because of whose living the world is better, is secured for all time.

MRS. LUKE E. WRIGHT.

Wife of the ex-Secretary of War was Miss Kate Semmes, daughter of Admiral Semmes, C. S. N. Mrs. Wright is one of the many charming Southern women who have served in the official social coterie at Washington. Mrs. Wright is an experienced hostess and versatile woman, and wherever her lines have been cast she has taken a leading place in society. Mrs. Wright is the mother of three sons, who were in service during the Spanish-American War; and two daughters, one of whom is Mrs. John H. Watkins, of New York, and the other, Mrs. Palmer.

AMEY WEBB WHEELER.

Mrs. Amey Webb Wheeler was born in Providence, Rhode Island. Her father's name was Henry Aborn Webb; her mother's, Amey Gorham Webb. She is descended from Roger Williams and Gregory Dexter. Married June 24, 1881, Benjamin Ide Wheeler, the distinguished university professor. Mrs. Wheeler lived in Germany for four years; one year at Harvard (1885-6); at Cornell University, 1886-99, and since 1899, at Berkeley, California.

MRS. MARTIN.

The wife of a former instructor in the Harvard Aeronautical Society and later instructor in the Grahame-White School of Aviation in France. Though an Englishwoman she is an American by adoption. She has not only made many flights with her husband in the machine which he designed, belonging to the Harvard Society, but she is now flying in Grahame-White's Baby Biplane, a small copy of the Farman machine.

HARRIET QUIMBY.

Miss Quimby is the first woman to have her own monoplane and take up seriously the science of aviation. She is an enthusiast in this sport and has entered the Moisant School of Aviation at Garden City, Long Island. Several other women have made short flights alone at Mineola, namely, Mrs. E. Edwards, Miss Mary Shea, who was winner of the Bridgeport (Connecticut) post competition and made a flight, on May 14th, of about five miles from the Bridgeport Aerodrome out over Long Island Sound and back.

LILLIE IRENE JACKSON.

Miss Lillie Irene Jackson was born in Parkersburg, West Virginia. She is descended from one of the leading families of the South. Her father, Honorable John J. Jackson, was Federal District Judge in West Virginia for over a quarter of a century, and her grandfather, General Jackson, was connected with the distinguished Stonewall Jackson of Confederate fame. She is one of the leading women of the South in the progressive work of the present time. She was a member of the Board of Lady Managers from the state of West Virginia, at the Columbian Exposition in 1893.

FLORENCE PULLMAN LOWDEN.

Born Florence Sanger Pullman, August 11, 1868, eldest daughter of George M. and Harriet Sanger Pullman. Mrs. Lowden is a woman of rare talents and attainments. Her qualities of head and heart are of the highest order. From the day of her graduation from Miss Brown's school in New York in 1889, she was the constant companion of her father, entering into all of his philanthropic plans with enthusiasm. Since his death she has conscientiously carried out many of his expressed wishes. April 29, 1896, she was married to Frank O. Lowden, a promising young lawyer of Chicago. It would be impossible for any young woman to enter more heartily into all the aspirations of her husband than does Mrs. Lowden, and notwithstanding her youth and the fact that she was the daughter of affluence all her life, she took upon herself the multiplicity of interests that are supposed to devolve upon persons embarking upon the sea of public favor. She nobly seconded every movement made by her husband upon his election to the Congress of the United States, from the day she made her debut into Washington official and social circles to that of Mr. Lowden's retirement, March, 1911, Mrs. Lowden was a decided leader. Her dignified and yet cordial manner, her perfect equipoise under all circumstances, her culture and quick intelligence, won for her the admiration of all who knew her. Mrs. Lowden is the mother of four beautiful children—one son and three daughters—

to whom she is a wonderfully devoted mother, not forgetting meanwhile that her companionship means much to her widowed mother in her invalidism and loneliness.

ELIZA FRANKLIN ROUTT.

Was born in 1842, in Springfield, Illinois, of Kentucky ancestry. Her grandfather, Colonel William F. Elkin, was one of the famous "long nine" that represented Sangamon County in the legislative session of 1836 and 1837. Each of these men were six ·feet tall. Abraham Lincoln was one of these stalwarts, whose efforts that year secured the location of the capital of the state for their county. Her father, Franklin Pickerell was a noted Kentuckian. She was given an excellent education, which was completed by travel and study abroad. When Colonel John L. Routt was second assistant postmaster-general in 1864, he married Mrs. Routt in her uncle's home in Decatur, Illinois, and she became an addition to the social circles of Washington City. In 1875, General Logan secured the appointment of Colonel Routt as territorial governor of Colorado from President Grant. In 1876, Colorado became a state and Colonel Routt was made its first governor and was re-elected. Mrs. Routt was a woman of remarkable ability, strong character and great culture, adding much to the lustre of her husband's administration. She brought up the daughters of Colonel Routt by his first wife, with devotion and care and they were among Denver's most prominent women.

MARY A. WOODS.

Miss Woods, known as "The second Betsy Ross," has charge of the making of the American flags for the United States Navy in the equipment department. Miss Woods was formerly a well-known dressmaker of New York City when she decided to take up this work, and applied for the position at the New York Navy Yard, receiving the appointment of "quarterwoman" in the equipment department, where she has been for more than a quarter of a century. She superintends the cutting of all of the flags, the stripes and stars and every portion which must be most exact. In this bureau is made not only the flags of our own country for use on all our ships and navy yards of the United States, but the flags of other maritime nations. Miss Woods, herself, has taught her assistants all they know of flag-making. In one year 140,000 yards of bunting were used and $70,000 expended in this work by the Government. When our fleet started for the Pacific all the signals were changed, and all the flags had to be altered accordingly—408 in all, and forty-three foreign ensigns. The most complicated flag in existence to-day is that of San Salvador, and the one flag on which the front is not the same as the back is that of Paraguay.

MRS. JOHN S. FORD.

The splendid work done by the Young Woman's Christian Association is well known in every city in the United States. In Youngstown, Ohio, Mrs. John S. Ford, president of the local Young Woman's Christian Association, deserves especial mention for her efforts in raising, during the year 1910, for their home work, the magnificent sum of $182,000. This magnificent result shows what can be done by the energy, perseverance and executive ability of an able woman aided by enthusiastic supporters. Mrs. John S. Ford is the wife of one of the leading business men of Youngstown, Ohio, and one of its conspicuous social leaders.

SALLIE LOGAN.

Mrs. Logan was born Sallie Oliver, April 15, 1853, in Pittsburgh, Pennsylvania. Her father, Thomas Oliver, came to Pittsburgh in 1826. Her mother, Sarah Ann Hancock, came from Louisville, Ketucky, and was a graduate of the famous Female Seminary at Shelbyville, Kentucky. Miss Oliver became a school teacher, having taught a term before she was fifteen years old. She was married to Thomas M. Logan August 27, 1873. Mrs. Logan has been one of the most active women in church work, charities, educational associations and civic organizations for more than thirty years in Jackson County, Illinois. She is a member of the Commercial Club of Murphysboro, Illinois, her residential city, and is also one of the directors of a local bank.

MRS. GEORGE M. PULLMAN.

Harriet Sanger Pullman, widow of George M. Pullman, was born in Illinois. She was the only daughter of James P. and Mrs. Sanger, who were early settlers in Chicago. Mrs. Pullman's mother was a McPherson of stanch Scotch descent.

Miss Sanger was one of the celebrated beauties of the fifties. She married George M. Pullman in 1866, and at once became a social leader in Chicago, taking always an active part in all movements for philanthropy and hospital work. She is probably one of the most consistent and generous contributors to charity of the wealthy women of her residential city. She distributes her benefactions privately, not allowing her left hand to know what she does with her right. She has an aversion to having her good deeds heralded.

Mrs. Pullman has traveled extensively since the death of her husband, but maintains her residence in Chicago, continuing to support many of the benefactions established by her husband. She is a member of the Presbyterian Church. One daughter, Mrs. Frank O. Lowden, lives in Illinois; the other, Mrs. Frank Carolan resides at Burlingame, California.

Women Who Have Had Monuments Erected to Their Memory in the United Statas.

The first of these was Margaret Haugherty, the baker-philanthropist, who left a fortune for the orphans of New Orleans; the next was erected to the memory of a Chippewa

Indian woman in Chicago; the third was to the great temperance leader, Frances E. Willard, which is in the capitol at Washington. The next to be thus honored was a heroine of the Confederate army during the war—Emma Sanson, of Gadsden, Alabama, and the last was placed in the Capital Park, at Birmingham, in honor of the memory of Mary A. Calahan, a school teacher.

Emma Sanson was the daughter of a poor white farmer, living a few miles from Gadsden, in the northern part of Alabama. When General Forrest was in pursuit of General Straight, of the Union Army, in 1864, she piloted him through a pass in the mountains so that he was able to overtake, surpise and capture Straight. The legislature of Alabama voted her a pension for life, and the legislature of Texas gave her a grant of land, while the people of Gadsden and the survivors of Forrest's command erected a monument in her honor. It is a marble figure of a country girl pointing into the distance, and the inscription tells the story. "I will show you the way."

Mary A. Calahan was the principal of a public school, the Powell school, at Birmingham, when a mere village. Many of the prominent citizens of Birmingham were taught by this woman, and she was the best known and most popular and influential woman in that section of the state. She gave her life to education, and had more to do with the molding of the character of the prominent men of to-day in that part of Alabama than any other agency; hence, when she died, a subscription was started and a monument erected to her memory. It is a marble figure, seated with a book in her hand, and it has been suggested that a memorial library shall also be built to the memory of this splendid woman who was so revered by her students.

Women in the Civil War.

BY MRS. JOHN A. LOGAN.

The preparation of this brief introduction to the part of this volume devoted to the women who dedicated their lives to the arduous duties devolving upon the women at home, in the field, and in the hospitals during the Civil War awakens vivid recollections of experiences that time cannot efface.

Residing between the border states of Kentucky and Missouri and in a community composed largely of southern born people, or those whose ancestors were southerners, and whose sympathies were strongly with their kindred south of Mason and Dixon's line, the inevitable horrors of war were greatly enhanced.

Recollections of pathetic scenes sweep over me with all the vividness of yesterday's events—the parting of sweethearts, husbands and wives, parents and their soldier sons; the speedy news which followed their departure of the misfortunes and calamities of war which had overtaken many of them, and all too often of their death from sickness, wounds or on the field of battle; the agony of waiting for the tardy reports after a battle; the scanning of the long lists which appeared in the papers of the casualties after every sanguinary engagement to see if the name of some loved one was among the killed or wounded; the being summoned to houses of mourning because of death in the families of the absent soldiers or sailors, and their efforts to comfort the members of stricken homes who had heard of the death of a husband, father or son far away in the Southland. The memory of the suffering of those left behind and those who had gone to the front comes back with all of its overwhelming force.

The western troops who were in the expeditions up the

20

306 PART TAKEN BY WOMEN IN AMERICAN HISTORY

Tennessee and Cumberland Rivers and subsequently in the siege and capture of Vicksburg, and later in the Atlanta campaign, were our friends and neighbors; their griefs and misfortunes were ours. They rendezvoused at Cairo, and I remember vividly the delicate women who worked as did the brave women of the South, almost night and day, preparing sanitary stores which could not otherwise be obtained, and who later flocked to the hospitals all over the North and South to care for the sick, wounded, convalescent and emaciated soldiers and sailors who, as the war progressed, were being constantly sent North to be restored to health and fitness to return to the service.

It seems only yesterday that I saw dear Mother Bickerdyke carrying in her strong arms poor, sick and, perhaps dying, boys in the hospitals at Cairo. It was in the autumn of 1861, after the battle of Belmont, the first baptism of blood of the volunteers of the West. She had left her home in Galesburg, Illinois, and joined the first troops who were mobilized for the war at Cairo. She was a remarkable woman in many senses— her frame was that of iron, her nerves as steady as a sharp-shooter's, her intellect as quick as an electric spark, her knowledge of human nature phenomenal, her executive ability wonderful, her endurance limitless. In all emergencies, she knew what to do, when and how to act. Her heart was full to overflowing with patriotism and loving kindness. She had the keenest possible intuitions, could detect fraud, deception, disloyalty, dishonesty and hyprocrisy quicker than an expert detective. She was a law unto herself in supporting the cause in which she was enlisted. Neither the general commanding nor any subordinate officer in any way interfered with her. A surgeon whom she had once detected in some questionable conduct appealed to General Sherman. The sturdy old soldier replied: "My God, man, Mother Bickerdyke outranks everybody, even Lincoln. If you have run amuck of her I advise you to get out quickly before she has you under arrest."

Behind the bluff and unceremonious manner she was all love and tenderness in her great mother heart. An unworthy employee of the hospital corps appeared before her one day fully dressed in the clothing of the Sanitary Commission, of which she was in charge. She said nothing, but stepped up to him, unbuttoned the collar, lifted the garments one by one over his head, until he had nothing but the trousers. She then said: "You can, for decency's sake, keep them on until you can run to your tent, take them off, put on your own and send these to me; do you hear me?" A crowd of soldiers stood near her to protect her. Their shouts and jeers were punishment enough for the unhappy culprit. She rarely had occasion to administer rebukes to offenders more than once, as they soon discovered there was no way of escaping her vigilance.

At the head of the women nurses she followed General Logan's command through all the campaigns from Cairo to the grand review in Washington at the close of the war, and was one of the most conspicuous figures in that review. She took charge of the female nurses who from time to time joined her in her heaven-born work of ministering to the soldiers in camp, in the hospitals and on the battlefield. She had her hospital tents and supplies and quartermasters' wagons, which she pushed to the rear of the lines. She paid no more attention to whistling bullets or booming cannon than did the gallant commanders and dauntless army. She nursed thousands and thousands of officers and men, all of whom have called her blessed.

We have included the biographies of all the patriotic, self-sacrificing women of whom we could obtain any data. We regret that it was not possible to include the name of every woman who laid on the altar of her country her best endeavors for the relief of the sufferers from the inevitable calamities of war.

The refugees from the South and the families of the soldiers added to the burdens and hardships of the women at
home more than to the men, as the majority of the able-bodied
men North and South were either in the Army or the Navy.

The author is glad that she has been able to get the biographies of a partial list of the splendid women of the South
who made such heroic sacrifices for the soldiers, sailors and
unfortunates of the Confederacy. The imaginary line which
divided the two sections made no difference in the nature,
womanly tenderness and righteous impulses of the women or
their devotion to their loved ones engaged in the defense of a
cause they believed to be right and just. It would be difficult
to find in history parallels of moral courage, self-denial and
self-immolation equal to that displayed by the women North
and South during the long and bloody Civil War in the United
States.

The women of the South are entitled to credit for a longer
period of endurance through the unspeakable trials during the
years of reconstruction which followed the treaty of peace at
Appomattox, which event ended in a degree the agonies, anxieties and labors of the women of the North.

The experiences of the people of both sections brought out
at a fearful cost all the nobler instincts of their natures, and
inspired them to higher purposes in life and more earnest efforts
for the progress of civilization and Christianity. The few in
both sections who have tried to stand in the way of human
betterment and adaptation to the conditions of the world's
advancement have had to suffer the consequences of their rash-
ness and be dropped from the rolls of the promoters of the
nation's welfare.

Union of interests and union of ambitions for the highest
attainments in Christianity, humanity, education, philanthropy
and national pride have borne rich fruit since the abolition of

slavery and the close of the fratricidal war, and will, doubtless, place the United States in the lead of all Christian nations of the earth.

SNOW HILL, Md., June 23, 1911.

MRS. JOHN A. LOGAN,
    Washington, D. C.

DEAR MRS. LOGAN:

I am sure your book, "The Part Taken by Women in American History," is just what patriotic societies and patriotic homes want.

Not only the women, but the men will read what our fore-mothers did and dared, that the nation might be truly great, and a new spirit of patriotism will be aroused and urge them to better and higher things for the coming generations and for our great and united country.

I congratulate you upon your work.

Sincerely yours,

MARY M. NORTH.

National Patriotic Instructor, W. R. C.

Women Nurses of the Civil War.

INTRODUCTION BY MRS. JOHN A. LOGAN.

The hospitals established by the Empress Helena in the fifth century were an evidence of Christian feeling; and it was the same Christianity and humanity which actuated Margaret Fuller and Florence Nightingale when in Italy and in the Crimean War they nursed the wounded soldiers. That same Christian spirit sent women, young and old, grave and gay, to the hospitals where our "Boys in Blue" needed their assistance. Bravely they wrought, and often bravely they fell by the side of those whom they nursed—martyrs to the cause of liberty as well as the men who fell in the defense of freedom and the Union. Rev. Doctor Bellows, referring to them and their noble work, said: "A grander collection of women, whether considered in their intellectual or moral qualities, their heads or their hearts, I have not had the happiness of knowing, than the women I saw in the hospitals. They were the flower of their sex. Great as were the labors of those who superintended the operations at home of collecting and preparing supplies for the hospitals and the fields, I cannot but think that the women who lived in the hospitals or among the soldiers required a force of character and a glow of devotion and self-sacrifice of a rarer kind. They were the heroines. They conquered their feminine sensibility at the sight of blood and wounds, lived coarsely and dressed and slept rudely; they studied the caprices of men to whom their ties were simply humane—men often ignorant, feeble-minded, out of their senses, raving with pain and fever; they had a still harder service in bearing with the pride, the official arrogance and the hardness or the folly, perhaps the impertinence and presumption, of half-trained medical men, whom the urgencies of the case had fastened on the service. Nothing in the power of the nation to give or to say can ever compare for a moment with the proud satisfaction which every brave soldier who has ever risked his life for his country ever after carries in his heart of hearts; and no public recognition, no thanks from a saved nation can ever add anything of much importance to the rewards of those who tasted the actual joy of ministering with their own hands and hearts to the wants of our sick and dying men."

It, nevertheless, is to our great regret that only the biographies of those nurses whose services were most conspicuous can be included in this volume. In place of the longer mention of each, which would bring this work to unreasonable length, the following list of these brave women is offered.

Mrs. Eliza C. Porter, of the noble band of western women who devoted kind thought and untiring exertion to the care of our country's defenders.

Mrs. John Harris, the wife of a Philadelphia physician, who was at the front all during the war, and who returned home an invalid for the rest of her life from the effects of a sunstroke, received while in attendance on a field hospital in Virginia.

Margaret Elizabeth Breckenridge, who said at the opening of the conflict, "I shall never be satisfied till I get right into a hospital to live until the war is over," and who fulfilled this lofty ambition in her work in the hospitals in and around St. Louis during all the long and bloody conflict.

Mrs. Stephen Barker, wife of the chaplain of the First Massachusetts Heavy Artillery, who went to the front with her husband and, for nearly two years, continued in unremitting attendance upon the regimental hospitals.

Amy M. Bradley who, having gone South to seek her own health, remained during the four years of the war, nursing her fellow-countrymen of the North.

Mrs. Arabella G. Barlow, of New Jersey, sealed her devotion to her country's cause by the sublimest sacrifice of which woman is capable, and after nursing her wounded husband until his death, remained to care for the other soldiers until she died of fever contracted while in attendance in the hospitals of the army of the Potomac.

Mrs. Nellie Maria Taylor who, though living in that part of the country which had borne the rank weeds of secession, proved her loyalty and patriotism in the care of Union soldiers at her own house.

Mrs. A. H. and Miss S. H. Gibbons,
Mrs. E. J. Russell,
Mrs. Mary W. Lee,
Miss Cornelia M. Tompkins,
Mrs. Anna C. McMeens,
Mrs. Jerusha R. Small,
Mrs. S. A. Martha Canfield,
Mrs. E. Thomas and Miss Morris,
Mrs. Shepard Wells,
Mrs. E. F. Wetherell,
Phebe Allan,
Mrs. Edward Greble,
Miss Isabella Fobb,
Mrs. E. E. George,
Mrs. Charlotte E. McKay,
Mrs. Fanny L. Ricketts,
Mrs. John S. Phelps,
Mrs. Jane R. Munsell,
Mrs. Adeline Tyler,
Mrs. Wm. H. Holstein,
Mrs. Cordelia A. P. Harvey,
Mrs. Sarah R. Johnston,
Emily E. Parsons,
Miss Cornelia Hancock,
Mrs. Mary Morris Husband, (Granddaughter of Robert Morris, the great financier of the Revolutionary War).

Katharine Prescott Wormeley,
The Misses Woolsey,
Anna Maria Ross,
Mary J. Safford,
Mrs. Lydia G. Parish,
Mrs. Anna Wittenmeyer,
Miss Melcenia Elliott,
Mary Dwight Pettes,
Mrs. Elmira Fales,
Louisa Maertz,
Mrs. Harriet R. Colfax,
Miss Clara Davis, (afterwards the wife of Rev. Edward Abbott, of Cambridge),
Mrs. R. H. Spencer,
Mrs. Harriet Foote Hawley, (the wife of Brevet Major-General Hawley, late Governor of Connecticut, and afterwards U. S. Senator from Connecticut),
Ellen E. Mitchell,
Miss Jessie Holmes,
Miss Vance and Miss Blackmar,
Hattie Dada,
Susan A. Hall,
Mrs. Sarah P. Edson,
Maria M. C. Hall.

All these women are mentioned as heroic and efficient nurses in "Women's Work in the Civil War," and to that book the reader must be commended for further knowledge of them.

Besides those whose names have been published in books there were many more—school teachers—who spent their vacations in the hospitals, and women who were content to be the angels of mercy to the suffering soldiers, but whose names have not been scattered far and wide, though their labors were appreciated. As someone has said: "The recording angel, thank Heaven, knows them all," and, "their labor was not in vain in the Lord." Surely the women of that portion of the last century given over to the war are women of whom the nation may well be proud, and whose memories should be cherished.

When the war was over there was still work for the women to do in training the freedmen, and especially their children; and the noble women who had been nurses, and many who had not, enlisted in this philanthropic and trying enterprise with the same zeal and self-sacrifice that had been shown by the women in the hospitals. They wrought also among the families of the soldiers and among the refugees who were homeless and destitute while war devastated the land. The niece of the poet Whittier was among them, bearing a name sacred to all lovers of freedom, because John G. Whittier's lyrics had so earnestly pleaded for the freedom of the slaves. Anna Gardner was a teacher of colored children on her native island of Nantucket when the Abolitionists were ostracized. She taught one of the first normal schools ever established for colored girls, and doubtless gave invaluable service in training the negroes of the South to become teachers for their own race.

After long years of silence, the American Tract Society at last gave the meed of praise to Christian effort without regard to race or color, when it published its sketch of Mary S. Peake, a free colored woman, who was the first teacher of her race at Fortress Monroe.

Mrs. Frances D. Gage, a woman of Ohio birth, but of

New England parentage, in her writings dealt powerful blows for freedom, temperance and other reforms. She had lived the life of a philanthropist, and when the war broke out she gave voice and pen to the right, speaking, editing and writing. When the Proclamation of Emancipation was issued she freed herself from other cares, and found her mission among the freed slaves. Four of her own boys were in the Union Army, and in the autumn of 1862 she went, without appointment or salary, to Port Royal, where she labored fourteen months. She returned North in 1863 and lectured on her experiences among the freedmen, rousing others to labor for the welfare of the colored race. Her name will live forever among the noble and faithful women who "remembered those in bounds as bound with them," and who cared for the soldier and the freedman, to whom God had already said: "Well done, good and faithful servant; enter thou into the joy of thy Lord."

Mrs. Lucy Gaylord Powers was another true friend to the soldier and the freedman. Her last active benevolent work was begun in 1863. This was the foundation of an asylum at the capital for the freed orphans and destitute aged colored women, whom the war and the Emancipation Proclamation had thrown upon the country as a charge. But she was in feeble health, and died while on her way to Albany on July 20, 1863.

Maria Rullann, of Massachusetts, proved herself worthy of her kinship to the first secretary of the Board of Education in that commonwealth by her faithful service as a teacher and philanthropist in Helena, Arkansas, and afterward as a teacher in Washington and Georgetown.

Mrs. Josephine Griffin, always an advocate for freedom, was faithful in her nursing during the war, and afterward took charge of the good work in Washington. One of her philanthropic methods was the finding of good places for domestic servants, from time to time taking numbers of them to various northern and western cities, and placing them in homes. The cost of these expeditions she provided almost entirely from her own means, her daughters helping her as far as possible in her noble work.

There were great numbers of other women equally efficient in the freedmen's schools and homes, but their work was mainly under the direction of the American Union Commission, and it is impossible, therefore, to obtain accounts of their labors as individuals. It is all a tale of self-sacrifice and heroism. There were heroic women North and South, and if, as someone has said, "An heroic woman is almost an object of worship," there are many shrines to-day for the devotees of physical and moral heroism to visit in following the history of the good women of the Civil War.

The women of Gettysburg won for themselves a high and honorable record for their faithfulness to the flag and their generosity and devotion to the wounded. Chief among these, since she gave her life for the cause, was Mrs. Jennie Wade, who continued her generous work of baking bread for the army until a shot killed her instantly. A southern officer of high rank was killed almost at the same moment near her door, and his troops hastily constructing a rude coffin, were about to place the body of their commander in it for burial when, in the swaying to and fro of the armies, a Union column drove them from the ground. Finding Mrs. Wade dead, they placed her in the coffin intended for the officer. In that coffin she was buried the next day, followed to the grave by hundreds of tearful mourners, who knew her courage and kindness of heart. The loyal women of Richmond were a noble band, and they never faltered in their allegiance to the flag nor in their sympathy and services to the Union prisoners at Libby, Belle Isle and Castle Thunder. With the aid of twenty-one loyal white men in Richmond they raised a fund of thirteen thousand dollars in gold to aid Union prisoners, while their gifts of clothing, food and luxuries were of much greater value. Moreover, had we space, many pages might be filled with the heroic deeds of noble southern women who believed in the cause for which their husbands stood, and who sacrificed their homes and all that was most dear during the Civil War, and who worked prodigiously trying to contrive ways and means with which to relieve the sufferings which abounded everywhere in the southland. Their improvised hospitals were poorly supplied with the bare necessities for the relief of the sick and wounded. In and out of hospitals, the demands upon the humane were heartrending; but to the very last heroism characterized the women as well as the bravest of the men who fought and died in the cause of the Condederacy.

CLARA BARTON.

BY MRS. JOHN A. LOGAN.

One of the greatest, if not the greatest woman of the nineteenth century, is Clara Barton, who, in a Christmas greeting to her legion of friends, writes: "I would tell you that all is well with me; that, although the unerring records affirm that on Christmas Day of 1821, eighty-four years ago, I commenced this earthy life, still, by the blessing of God, I am strong and well, knowing neither illness nor fatigue, disability nor despondency."

Miss Barton is the daughter of Stephen Barton, of North Oxford Mass., a man highly esteemed in the community in w... dwelt. In early youth he had served as a soldier ral Wayne, the "Mad Anthony" of the early days blic. His boyish years had witnessed the evacuation of Detroit by the British in 1796, and his military training may have contributed to the sterling uprightness of his character and his inflexible will. His daughter Clara was the youngest, by seven years, in a family of two brothers and three sisters. She was early taught that the primeval benediction, miscalled a curse, which requires mankind to earn their bread, was really a blessing. Besides domestic duties and a very thorough public school training, she learned the general rules of business by acting as clerk and bookkeeper for her eldest brother. Next, she betook herself to the district school, the stepping-stone for all aspiring women in New England. She taught for several years in various places in Massachusetts and New Jersey.

One example will show her character as a teacher. She went to Bordentown, New Jersey, in 1853, where there was not and never had been a public school. Three or four unsuccessful attempts had been made to establish one, and the idea had been abandoned as unadapted to that locality. The brightest boys in the town ran untaught in the streets. She offered to teach a free school for three months at her own expense, to convince the citizens that it could be done. They laughed at her idea as visionary. Six weeks of waiting and debating induced the authorities to fit up an unoccupied building at a little distance from the town. She commenced with six outcast boys, and in five weeks the house would not hold the number that came. The commissioners, at her instance, erected a large brick building, and early in the winter of 1853-4 she organized the city free school, with a roll of six hundred pupils. But the severe labor and the great amount of loud speaking required in the newly plastered rooms destroyed her health and for a time destroyed her voice—the prime agent of instruction. Being unable to teach, she left New Jersey about the first of March, 1854, seeking rest, quiet and a milder climate, and went as far as Washington.

A brief summary of her career will show that an ever-ruling Providence had destined her for a higher and nobler work for mankind than the routine duties—noble as they are—of a teacher in the public schools.

While in Washington, a friend and distant relative, then in Congress, voluntarily obtained for her an appointment in the Patent Office. There she continued until the fall of 1857. She was employed at first as a copyist and afterwards in the more responsible work of abridging original papers and preparing records for publication, and the large circle of friends made while so employed was not without its influence in determining her military career.

Thus it happened that at the beginning of the Civil War she was in Washington. When news came that the troops, on their way to the Capital, under Mr. Lincoln's first call for volunteers in 1861, had been fired upon, and that wounded men were lying in Baltimore, she volunteered, with others, to go and care for them. Unconsciously she had entered upon what proved to be her life work, for Clara Barton is to the American battlefield what Florence Nightingale was to the English in Crimea. From April, 1861, to the close of the war, Miss Barton was, by authority of President Lincoln and Secretary Stanton, to be found in the hospitals or wherever soldiers were in need of attention, and soon she was recognized as a woman of great ability and discretion, and could pass in and out at will, where others met with constant hindrances and "red tape." So many of her pupils had volunteered in the first years of the war that at the second battle of Bull Run she found seven of them, each of whom had lost an arm or a leg.

She met the wounded from Virginia, she was present at the battles of Cedar Mountain, second Bull Run, Falmouth, Charleston, Fort Wagner, Spottsylvania, Deep Bottom, Antietam and Fredericksburg, and was for eight months at the siege of Charleston, at Fort Wagner, in front of Petersburg and at the Wilderness. She was also at the hospitals near Richmond and on Morris Island. Neither were her labors over when the war ended. A friend desiring that the world should know her actual connection with the government during this period of strife, as well as throughout her administration as head of the Red Cross, has induced Miss Barton to tell the story in her own inimitable way, and this is what she says:

"When in the four years of this work the military authorities unquestioningly provided me transportation, teams, men and an open way to every field in the service, it had something to do with the government.

"When, at its close, the President, over his own signature, 'A. Lincoln,' informed all the people of the United States that I would, voluntarily, search for the records of eighty thousand missing men, of whom the government nor army had any record, and asked the people to write me, it had something to do with the government."

The editor cannot resist the temptation to insert Mr. Lincoln's letter:

"To the friends of missing prisoners: Miss Clara Barton has kindly offered to search for the missing prisoners of war. Please address her at Annapolis, Md., giving name, regiment and company of any missing prisoner.   A. LINCOLN."

This brought the heartbroken correspondence of the friends of all missing soldiers to her, and placed on the records of the government the names of twenty thousand men who, otherwise, had no record of death, and to-day their descendants enjoy the proud heritage of an ancestor who died honorably in the service of his country, and not the possible suspicion of his being a deserter.

"When, in the search, I learned the true condition of the

dead at Andersonville, and informed the authorities that, through the death records of Dorence Atwater, the graves of the thirteen thousand buried there could be identified, and was requested by the Secretary of War, Edwin M. Stanton, to take an expedition to Andersonville to mark the graves and inclose a cemetery, and did so, it had something to do with the government.

"Without this there could have been no cemetery of Andersonville, which the government now so worthily owns as a gift from our active women of the Woman's Relief Corps auxiliary to the Grand Army of the Republic.

"And when, in this long search for the missing men of the army, carried on at my own cost until I had invested the greater part of my own moderate means and the brave thirty-seventh Congress stepped into the breach and, unsolicited, voted remuneration and aid in the sum of fifteen thousand dollars, and sent it to me with thanks, it had something to do with the government.

"When a few years later, weary and weak from the war-sacked fields of Europe, I brought the germs of the thrice-rejected Red Cross of Geneva, and with personal solicitations from the 'International Committee' sought its adoption, I had very little to do with the government, for it steadily declined to have anything to do with me, or with the cause I brought to it.

"It had been 'officially declined'—books of the State Department were produced to show this—'we wanted no more war,' neither 'Entangling Alliances.'

"Then followed five years of toil, cost and explanations with the people as well as the government to show that the Red Cross could mean neither war nor entangling alliances; and when at length one martyred President promised and a successor made his promise good, and Congress again acted and the treaty was signed, proclaimed and took its place among the foremost treaties of the country, and we became thence-forth and forever a Red Cross nation, it surely had something to do with the government.

"But this treaty covered only the relief of suffering from war, and realizing the far greater needs we might have in the calamities of civil life, I personally addressed the governments through the 'International Committee of Geneva,' asking their permission for the American Red Cross to act in our national calamities, as in war. This request was gravely considered in the congress of Berne, and was granted by the powers as the American Amendment to the International Treaty of Geneva. Inasmuch as it became a law, under which all nations act to-day, it might be said not only to have had something to do with the government but with all governments.

"Later on, when another martyred President requested and opened the way for me to take the Red Cross to the starving reconcentrados of Cuba; and a little later, when war desolated its fields, to take ship, join the fleet, and seek an entrance for humanity, and the highest admiral in the service bade it go alone with its cargo of food to the starving of the stricken city, and Santiago lay at our feet, it might be said it had something to do with the government.

"During the twenty or more years of such efforts was mingled the relief of nearly an equal number of fields of disaster, none of which were unserved, and for which relief, not one dollar in all the twenty years was drawn from the treasury of the United States; the munificence of the people through their awakened charities was equal to all needs."

The fields of disaster were the Michigan forest fires of 1881; Mississippi River floods and cyclone of 1882-3; Ohio and Mississippi River floods of 1884, especially disastrous, requiring relief for thousands of people; Texas famine, 1885; Charleston earthquake catastrophe, 1886; the Mt. Vernon, Ill., cyclone,

21

1888, which swept away almost the entire town, leaving the people destitute and homeless; Florida yellow-fever, 1888; Johnstown disaster, where Miss Barton personally distributed $250,000.00 and spent months laboring in the field for and with the stricken people in 1889; Russian famine, 1892; Pomeroy, Iowa, cyclone, 1893; South Carolina Islands hurricane and tidal wave of 1893-4; Armenia massacres, 1896; Cuban reconcentrado relief, 1889-1900, where Miss Barton and her staff spent months among these absolutely destitute and suffering people before the declaration of war, saving thousands of lives, establishing orphan asylums and hospitals, a work which claimed the highest commendation from Senator Proctor, of Vermont, on the floor of the Senate, after he had visited the island to know positively the conditions; Spanish-American War.

Miss Barton having in 1908 preceded the army and the navy by many weeks on the chartered steamer "State of Texas" loaded with medical, surgical, sanitary and other supplies, was prepared to save many lives before the government had anything ready. Galveston storm and tidal wave 1909, requiring unprecedented strength and courage, patience and expenditure of money.

Miss Barton modestly omits to speak of the innumerable appeals made to her for aid in all directions. The United States Marshal at Key West, Florida, in his dilemma of how to provide for the people on board the captured vessels—many of them aliens, Cubans and some American citizens who had no means of support or for transportation—petitioned Miss Barton for relief until provision could be made for them. Her response was immediate. By her direction, for many days, food, medicine, and all their needs were supplied by Miss Barton until after long official delays the proper authorities finally assumed the responsibilities they should have taken in the beginning.

Miss Barton reached Havana, February 9, 1898. February 14th she was the guest of honor of Captain Sigsbee on board the "Maine," the captain paying her the compliment of reviewing the men. With characteristic thoughtfulness, she placed the Red Cross at the service of Captain Sigsbee, should any of his brave men be sick or need relief. On the night of the 15th of February, the unspeakable calamity of the destruction of the "Maine" occurred. In the early morning of the 16th, Miss Barton and her nurses visited the Spanish Hospital, San Ambrosia, where the brave marines were dying in great numbers. Miss Barton had gone to Cuba to carry out her mission as President of the Red Cross. She was in no way assisted by the government but used her own money. The citizens of Davenport, Iowa, wired her twelve hundred dollars to be used for the reconcentrados. This sum she diverted from its intended purpose and used for the relief of the victims of this unprecedented catastrophe. The official reports of officers of the navy and Secretary of War gratefully thank Miss Barton and the Red Cross workers for their timely service and supplies in the absence of any provision of the government for war or for such a disaster as that of the "Maine."

Miss Barton represented the United States at the International Congress, at Geneva, in 1884; at Carlsruhe, Germany, 1887. At Rome, Italy, in 1890, she was appointed but would not leave her work in Russia at the time of the Russian famine, but did attend the Congress at Vienna, Austria, in 1900.

Miss Barton was decorated with the Iron Cross of Prussia, by Emperor William I and Empress Augusta, in 1871; with the Gold Cross of Remembrance, by the Grand Duke and Grand Duchess of Baden, in 1870; with the medal of International Committee of the Red Cross of Geneva, Switzerland, 1882; with the Red Cross, by Queen of Servia, 1884; with the silver medal by Empress Augusta, of Germany, 1884; with the flag voted by Congress of Berne, Switzerland, 1884; with jewels by the Grand Duchess of Baden, 1884-87; with the diploma of honor from German War Veterans, 1885; with jewels by the Queen of Prussia, 1887; with the diploma of honor from Red Cross of Austria, 1888; with diploma and decoration by the Sultan of Turkey, 1896; with diploma and decoration by the Prince of Armenia, 1896; with diploma and decoration by Spain, 1899; with vote of thanks by the Cortez of Spain, 1899; with vote of thanks by the Portuguese Red Cross, 1900; with resolutions of the Central Relief Committee of Galveston, Texas, 1900; with vote of thanks from the legislature of the state of Texas, 1901; and with the decoration of the Order of the Red Cross by the Czar of Russia, 1902.

Press notices, eulogies, enrolled and engrossed resolutions innumerable, and every other conceivable tribute has been paid her by her own countrymen, who are and were her compatriots and who revere her as the most self-sacrificing, loyal, upright, honorable, patriotic, courageous woman of her time, and as a woman who has known no creed, political or religious, that is not founded upon the Golden Rule and universal humanity to mankind; whose moral courage has been equal for all emergencies, but who is at the same time as guileless and as loving and as tender as a child. Her masterful mind has ever instantly grasped the most subtle schemes of designing persons, but she has turned the other cheek to the cruel thrusts of the envious and ambitious. Her only fault has ever been lack of resentment and self-assertion when injuries have been inflicted. Her motto has been, "Father forgive them; they know not what they do."

Time moves, and at last Clara Barton reached her Gethsemane, and she proved her greatness in the hour of her bitterest trial. She let her detractors have their way, bowed her head and slipped away without a murmur into retirement, unrewarded and uncared for by a great government in whose service she has given the best of her life and her all. And who shall say she is not the greatest woman of the Nineteenth century? Is there another with such a record of noble achievements for humanity? No other woman has appeared, bearing the banner of the Red Cross, and personally ministering to the suffering on the field of disaster, though many calamities have occurred since Clara Barton was driven from the work to which she was divinely called.

MRS. MARY ASHTON RICE LIVERMORE.

Mrs. Livermore was born in Boston, Massachusetts, December 19, 1821. Her father, Timothy Rice of Northfield, Massachusetts, who was of Welsh descent, served in the United States Navy during the War of 1812-1815. Her mother, Zebiah Vose Glover Ashton, was the daughter of Captain Nathaniel Ashton, of London, England. Mrs. Livermore was placed in the public schools of Boston at an early age and was graduated at fourteen, receiving one of the six medals distributed for good scholarship. There were then no high, normal, or Latin schools for girls, and their admission to colleges was not even suggested. She was sent to the Female Seminary in Washington, D. C., where she completed the four-years' course in two, and was then elected a member of the faculty as teacher of Latin and French. While teaching she continued her studies in Latin and Greek, resigning her position at the close of the second year to take charge of a family school on a plantation of southern Virginia, where she remained nearly three years. As there were between three or four hundred slaves on the estate Mrs. Livermore was brought face to face with the institution of slavery and witnessed deeds of barbarism as tragic as any described in Uncle Tom's Cabin. She returned to the North a radical abolitionist and henceforth entered the lists against slavery and every form of oppression. In 1857 the Livermores removed to Chicago, Illinois, where Mr. Livermore became proprietor and editor of a weekly religious paper, the organ of the Universalist denomination in the Northwest, and Mrs. Livermore became his assistant editor. At the first nomination of Abraham Lincoln for the presidency in the Chicago Wigwam in 1860, she was the only woman reporter assigned a place among the hundred or more men reporters.

Out of the chaos of benevolent efforts evolved by the opening of the Civil War in 1861, the United States Sanitary Commission was born. Mrs. Livermore with her friend, Mrs. Jane C. Hoge, was identified with relief work for the soldiers from the beginning. She resigned all positions save that on her husband's paper, secured a governess for her children and subordinated all demands upon her time to those of the commission. She organized soldiers' aid societies;

delivered public addresses in the principal towns and cities of the Northwest; wrote the circulars and bulletins and monthly papers of the commission; made trips to the front to the sanitary stores, to whose distribution she gave personal attention; brought back large numbers of invalid soldiers who were discharged that they might die at home; assisted to plan, organize, and conduct colossal sanitary establishments; detailed women nurses for the hospitals by order of Secretary Stanton and accompanied them to their posts. In short, the story of Mrs. Livermore's work during the war has never been told and can never be understood save by those who worked with her. The war over, Mrs. Livermore resumed the even tenor of her life, took up again philanthropic and literary work, which she had temporarily relinquished. She afterwards left Chicago and returned to pass long years in her home in Melrose, Massachusetts, happy in the society of her husband, children and grandchildren, until her death in 1905. She was ever ready with advice, pen and influence to lend a helping hand to the weak and struggling; to strike a blow for the right against the wrong; to prophesy a better future in the distance, and to insist on a woman's right to help it along.

MOTHER BICKERDYKE.

The following is Mother Bickerdyke's own concise account of her services to the nation: "I served in our great Civil War from January 9, 1861, to March 20, 1865. I did the work of one and tried to do it well. I was in nineteen hard-fought battles in the departments of the Ohio, Tennessee and Cumberland armies. Fort Donelson, February 15th and 16th, was the first battle to which I was an eye witness; Pittsburgh Landing, April 6th and 7th, the second; Iuka, September 20th, the third, and Corinth, October 3rd and 4th, the fourth." But certainly the rising generation, to whom the Civil War is already like a half-forgotten story, should know more of the work of this woman for the sake of the patriotism her whole-souled devotion to country and to suffering humanity teaches. After the surrender of Sumter her heart, which had been burdened with a mother's solicitude for the boys she had sent marching away, could no longer endure the dreadful suspense and still more dreadful confirmation of her fears that met her eye as she glanced over the crowded columns of the papers, and she decided to offer her services at the front. Perhaps no single incident in the life of Mrs. Bickerdyke as well as the following portrays her large-heartedness and the motherly care she felt for the wounded soldiers: The victory had been gained at Fort Donelson, and the glad news carried with it great rejoicing. Meanwhile, the soldiers who had won that victory were suffering more than tongue can tell. Their clothes even froze to their bodies, and there were no accommodations for them, so that many hundreds perished wholly without care. The night grew darker and darker, settling down over the deserted field where the dead still lay awaiting burial. The strange weird silence after such a day produced an indescribable feeling of awe. At midnight an officer noticed a light moving up and down among the dead and dispatched a messenger to see what it meant. The man soon returned and told him that it was Mrs. Bickerdyke who, with her lantern, was examining the bodies to make sure that no living man should be left alone amid such surroundings. She did not seem to realize that she was doing anything remarkable, and turning from the messenger continued her search over that awful field simply through her love for humanity. Her work was felt now on the field of battle, now on board a boat caring for a lot of soldiers in transit, now in the hospital. Thus many phases of a soldier's life came under her observation. One night she was making her usual rounds of the wards, the lights were turned down and many of the soldiers were sleeping, while here and there a restless sufferer counted the lagging seconds and longed for morning. Passing along she administered to each as the occasion demanded until one asked, "Aren't you tired, Mother Bickerdyke?" Not for a moment did she think of claiming sympathy, but replied in her usual brusque way: "What if I am, that is nothing. I am well and strong and all I want is to see you so, too." In September a battle was fought at Iuka, and here Mother Bickerdyke again walked over a blood-stained field to save many a life fast ebbing away for want of immediate aid. She deftly stopped the flow of blood from wounds that must otherwise be fatal. When it became necessary to send the wounded, as far as their condition would permit, to Corinth, Mrs. Bickerdyke not only went with them to alleviate suffering on the painful journey, but did much to prevent waste. Owing to limited time and means of transportation, soiled clothing and things that were not especially needed were to be left behind. But prudent Mother Bickerdyke had all the articles packed closely, and when she saw that they were to be left behind she exclaimed, "Do you suppose that we are going to throw away those things that the daughters and wives of our soldiers have worked so hard to give us? I will just prove that they can be saved and the clothes washed. Just take them along." And the order was obeyed. She was always planning for more and better food for her sick boys. Fresh eggs and milk were supplied in scant quantities and were very poor at that. So just as spring was changing to summer she started upon her famous "Cow and hen mission." Her object was to obtain one hundred cows and one thousand hens to be cared for on an island in the Mississippi near Memphis. As soon as she made her plans known in Jacksonville, a wealthy farmer, aided by a few of his neighbors, gave her the hundred cows and as she proceeded chickens were cackling all about her. She procured the desired one thousand and her arrival at Memphis was heralded by the lowing of cows and the sprightly song of hens. Mother Bickerdyke's cows became a well-known feature on many battlefields. One morning some soldiers in fresh uniforms waited upon her to tender her a review. She smilingly consented, donned her sunbonnet and permitted herself to be stationed on a rudely elevated platform. The fine cows that had supplied them with milk filed past her. Each one had been smoothly curried, her horns polished and her hoofs blackened. The favorites were decked with little flags and a lively march was played as the queer procession filed past. Many of these cows had marched a long distance with the army. They were a treasure to Mrs. Bickerdyke, as she could make custards and other delicacies for her sick soldiers. This boyish prank, "The Cows' Review," was a pleasant incident which she greatly enjoyed. Another incident of her thrift has a touch of humor in it. Though Mrs. Bickerdyke was always neat in her dress she was indifferent to its attractiveness and amid flying sparks from open fires her calico dress would take fire, and was full of little holes. Someone asked her if she were not afraid of being burned. She replied, "My boys put me out." With her clothing in this condition she visited Chicago late in the summer of 1863. The women immediately replenished her wardrobe, and soon after sent her a box of nice clothing for her own use. Some of the articles were richly trimmed, among them two nightgowns. She traded off most of the articles with the rebel women of the place for eggs, butter and other good things for her sick soldiers, but she was soon to go to Cairo, and she thought the night-gowns would sell for more there. On her way, however, in one of the towns on the Mobile and Ohio Railroad she found two soldiers who had been discharged from the hospital before their wounds had healed. The exertion of travel had opened them afresh. They were in an old shanty bleeding, hungry and penni-less. Mrs. Bickerdyke took them at once in hand, washed their wounds, stopped the flow of blood, tore off the bottoms of the gowns and used them for bandages. Then, as the men had no shirts she dressed them in the fine nightgowns, ruffles, lace and all. They demurred a little but she commanded them as their superior officer to obey, and they could only join in the hearty laugh with which she suddenly transformed them into two dandies and sent them on their way.

One of her best known acts is an "interference" that gained for her the title of "General." It was at the time when the Confederates attempted to re-capture Corinth and attack the defense, October 3, 1862. The whole action was rapid and concerted. The Board of Trade Regiment, twelve hundred strong, had marched twenty-four miles to enter the conflict, and only four hundred returned. Toward evening Mother Bickerdyke saw a brigade hurrying forward and learned that they had been marching since noon and were about to join in the struggle. The officer in command was requested to let them rest a few minutes, but refused. So the worn-out men were passing the hospital when a strong voice cried "Halt." Instinctively they obeyed, and attendants began to distribute soup and coffee. Meanwhile their canteens were filled and each received a loaf of bread. "For-ward march," came the order in a very few minutes, and it was found that the time lost was more than compensated for by the renewed courage of the men, who had no other chance to rest until midnight. Mrs. Bickerdyke had given the order to halt herself, when she found no one else would do it. That her interference was deeply appreciated was shown by the many letters and visits she received from these same men at the close of the war. When the army was ordered to Charleston for the grand review, and the soldiers realized that they were soon to meet the loved ones at home, they became as light-hearted as boys, and the march from Louisiana was a joyous one. Mrs. Bickerdyke accompanied them, riding her glossy horse. She wore a simple calico dress and as always a large sunbonnet. She crossed the Long Bridge in advance of the Fifteenth Army Corps and was met by Dorothea Dix and others who came to welcome her to the Capital. This was a triumph such as few women have ever attained, and during the weeks following she was everywhere treated with the greatest respect and consideration. The calico dress and sunbonnet were sold for one hundred dollars, and preserved as relics of the Rebellion. This money she spent at once, "for the boys need so many things." At last war was over. Peace was declared, and the nation awoke to the fact that it had a mighty army on its hands. In a short time that army disappeared in a miracle that has been the wonder of every nation, and Mother Bickerdyke, the most picturesque of all war nurses, retired to the home of her son, Professor J. B. Bickerdyke, in Russell, Kansas, and there in that pleasant retreat came the sunset of her most helpful life.

AMANDA FARNHAM FELCH.

Amanda M. Colburn was born in West Dover, Vermont, November 12, 1833. Her father was a farmer in moderate circumstances and having only one son a share in the outdoor work was often given to the daughter. This early training proved of inestimable value to her in later years when a large reserve of physical strength was so necessary to enable her to endure with comparative ease long marches where hundreds of men were overcome, as during Peninsula, Gettysburg and other campaigns. At about twenty-three years of age she was first married, and it was as Mrs. Farnham that she was so well known in the Army of the Potomac in the summer of 1861. After the war she was married to M. P. Felch. Left alone with her little boy and in poor health she returned to the old home to find the family in great trouble. Henry, her brother, had enlisted in the Third Vermont Regiment, and her parents were in pitiful anxiety for his welfare. The daughter's decision was instantaneous. She left her child with her parents and followed her brother to the front, and enlisted at St. John's July 5, 1861. She was enrolled as a member of the regiment and appointed hospital matron. They were mustered in on July 11th, left the state on the twenty-third, arrived in Charleston on the twenty-sixth and the next day went six miles up the river to Camp Lyon near Chain Bridge. And here began Mrs. Farnham's duty as soldiers' nurse. During the following winter sickness and death from disease assumed such alarming proportions that a special corps of noted physicians was sent for to aid the medical officers then in the field, and with them Mrs. Farnham worked almost constantly. In December, 1861, she was dropped from the pay roll as matron of the third, but she still continued her work, and until the Wilderness campaign in 1864, occupied a different position from any other army nurse. She did not do regular war duty but went from one regiment to another, wherever she was most needed. Day or night, it made no difference, she always responded to the call and would stay until the crisis was passed or death had relieved the patient of his suffering. The day after the battle of Antietam she arrived on the field where everything was confusion and where no supplies were at hand, and immediately went to work among the wounded. Nothing illustrated better the resourcefulness and clear-headedness of this remarkable woman than the surgical operation which she performed in an emergency here. A soldier had been stricken in the right breast by a partly spent ball with force enough to follow around the body under the skin, stopping just below the shoulder blade. As quick as thought, taking the only implement she had, a pair of sharp buttonhole scissors, and pinching the ball up with the thumb and finger she made an incision and pressed the ball out, thus putting on record through feminine resourcefulness the quickest case of bullet probing on record. Living, directing and always alone on the battlefields she had of course many thrilling adventures. Before a battle it became a common thing for soldiers, especially of the Vermont troops, to intrust her with money or other valuables for safe keeping. And it so happened that during the battle of Chancellorsville she had an unusual amount of money, which she carried in a belt on her person, with other keepsakes of value in a handbag. After getting into quarters on the Unionists' side of the river she put up a tent, as it was raining, and for the first time in several nights took off the belt and put it with the bag on the ground under the mattress. Perhaps this was all seen in her shadow on the tent cloth by someone watching for that purpose. She had just fallen asleep when she became conscious that someone was trying to get in. The flap-strings had been strongly knotted and tied tightly around the pole so that plan was abandoned and the robber passed around the tent. Fully aroused, Mrs. Farnham now crept from the blankets and finding her revolver awaited results. Her first thought was to give an alarm, but she knew that the thief could easily escape in the dark and return later. He proceeded with his evil errand, cutting a long slit in the tent to reach through. Up to the time when the knife began its work the brave nurse had not realized how serious was her situation; now she hesitated no longer, but aiming as well as she could in the darkness fired. An exclamation, and the sound of hurried footsteps, were all she heard. The next morning news came that one of the new recruits was sick, having been wounded by the "accidental discharge of a pistol in the hands of a chum," and Mrs. Farnham did not ask to have the case investigated. After the battle of Chancellorsville, when the army had to retreat to its old camp, Mrs. Farnham used to keep a horse and team to take along supplies on the march. When in camp the boys could easily procure for themselves what they needed but on the march they often suffered severely. Such articles as shirts, socks, etc., coffee, sugar, condensed milk and canned goods Mrs. Farnham carried in her wagon and gave where most needed. It is now a simple matter of history that the Sixth Corps marched from Manchester to Gettysburg from daylight until 4 p. m., and it was the greatest feat in marching ever accomplished by any troops under like conditions. Mrs. Farnham went with them most of the way on foot, giving up the spare room on her wagon to worn-out soldiers, who could not find room in the crowded ambulances. She was in Fredericksburg on the ninth of May, 1864, where the weary Union troops were lying, and here for about the first time she was a regular army nurse. Appointed by Miss Dorothea Dix she so remained until discharged in June, 1865. Mrs. Farnham used to tell with quiet humor of her first interview with Miss Dix. From the time she entered the army, Mrs. Farnham had worn a dress similar to that so recently designed for the woman aviator—full pants buttoning from the top of her boots, skirts falling a little below the knees and a jacket with full sleeves. This dress she had on when she called to present her papers of request. Miss Dix glanced at the papers then looked Mrs. Farnham over from head to foot until the situation was becoming embarrassing. Finally she arose, saying: "Mrs. Farnham, the dress you wear is abominable, a most abominable dress, and I do not wish one of my nurses to dress in that manner;

but you came highly recommended and I have long known of your work. But I did not know you wore such a dress. However, you can wear it if you choose." Then she wrote the order for Mrs. Farnham to report at Fredericksburg. From that time until the war closed she was one of Miss Dix's trusted nurses and was charged with duties and commissions at the front that she would trust to no one else. Although they met many times when Mrs. Farnham wore the same dress it was not mentioned again.

HELEN L. GILSON.

Helen L. Gilson, of Chelsea, Mass., had been for several years head assistant in the Phillips School in Boston. But ill health obliged her to leave it. She then went to teach the children of her uncle, Frank B. Fay, Mayor of Chelsea. Mr. Fay from the commencement of the war took the most active interest in the national cause, devoting his time his wealth and his personal efforts to the welfare of the soldiers. Influenced by such an example of lofty and self-sacrificing patriotism, and with her own young heart on fire with love for her country, Miss Gilson from the very commencement of the war gave herself to the work of caring for the soldiers first at home and afterward in the field. When Mr. Fay commenced his personal services with the army of the Potomac Miss Gilson wishing to accompany him applied to the Government superintendent of female nurses for a diploma, but as she had not reached the required age she was rejected. This, however, did not prevent her from fulfilling her ardent desire of administering to the sick and wounded. In June, 1862, she took a position on one of the hospital boats of the sanitary commission just after the evacuation of Yorktown. She continued on hospital boats between White House, Fortress Monroe, Harrison Landing and Washington. She reached the field of Antietam September 18, 1862, a few hours after the battle and remained there and at Pleasant Valley till the wounded had been gathered into general hospitals. In November and December, 1862, she worked in the camps and hospitals near Fredericksburg at the time of Burnside's campaign. In the spring of 1863, she was again at that point at the battle of Chancellorsville and in the Potomac Creek Hospital. Early in 1864, she joined the army at Brandy Station, and in May went with the auxiliary corps of the Sanitary Commission to Fredericksburg, where the battle of the Wilderness was being fought. Amidst the terrible scenes of those dreadful days the perfect adaptability of Miss Gilson to her work was conspicuous. Whatever she did was done well and so noiselessly that only the results were seen. When not more actively employed she would sit by the bedside of the suffering men and charm away their pain by the magnetism of her low calm voice and soothing touch. She sang for them and leaning over them where they lay amidst all the agonizing sights and sounds of the hospital ward, and even upon the field of carnage, her voice would ascend in petition for peace, for relief, for sustaining grace in the brief journey to the other world transporting their souls into the realms of an exalted faith.

As may be supposed Miss Gilson exerted a remarkable personal influence over the wounded and sick soldiers as well as upon all those with whom she was brought in contact. They looked up to her, reverenced and almost worshiped her. She had their entire confidence and respect. Even the roughest of them yielded to her influence and obeyed her wishes. It has been recorded by one who knew her well that she once stepped out of her tent, before which a group of men were fiercely quarreling, having refused with oaths and vile language to carry a sick comrade to the hospital at the request of one of the male agents of the commission, and quietly advancing to their midst renewed the request as her own. Immediately every angry tone was still, their voices were lowered and modulated respectfully; their oaths ceased and quietly and cheerfully without a word of objection they lifted their helpless burden and tenderly carried him away.

It finally became necessary to evacuate Fredericksburg and the wounded were sent away. The steamer with the last of the wounded and the members of the auxiliary corps left just in season to escape the Guerrillas who came into the town. William Howell Reed of Boston, who had been in charge of the auxiliary corps up to this point wrote of this boat passage as follows: "As the boat passed down the river the negroes by instinct came to the banks and begged us by every gesture of appeal not to pass them by. At Fort Royal they flocked in such numbers that a Government barge was appropriated for their use. A thousand were stowed upon her decks. They had an evening service of prayer and song and the members of the corps attended the weird ceremony. When their song had ceased Miss Gilson addressed them. In the simplest language she explained the difference between their former relations with their old masters and the new relations they were about to assume with the Northern people, explaining that labor in the North was voluntary and that they could only expect to secure kind employers by faithfully discharging their duties. This was the beginning of Miss Gilson's work for the negroes. Her crowning labor was in her hospital at City Point after the battle of Petersburg. The wounded from this battle had been brought down rapidly to City Point where a temporary hospital had been provided. There was defective management and chaotic confusion; the men were neglected, the hospital organization was imperfect, and the mortality was in consequence frightfully large. Conditions were deplorable. The stories of their suffering reached Miss Gilson at a moment when her previous labors of the campaign had nearly exhausted her strength; but her duty seemed plain. Her friends declared that she could not survive a repetition of her experiences, but replying that she could not die in a cause more sacred she started out alone. That she succeeded in this great work is nothing short of miraculous. Official prejudice and professional pride had to be continually met and overcome. A new policy had to be introduced. Miss Gilson's doctrine and practice were always instant and cheerful obedience to medical and disciplinary orders without question or demur, and by these methods she overcame the natural sensitiveness of the medical authorities. Moving quietly on with her work of renovation, she took the responsibility of all the changes that became necessary, and such harmony prevailed in the camp that her policy was finally completely vindicated. She even established a hospital kitchen upon her own method of special diet, and here cleanliness, order and system had to be in force in the daily routine. This was accomplished by a tact and energy which sought no praise but modestly veiled themselves behind the orders of officials. The management of her kitchen was like the ticking of a clock—regular discipline, gentle firmness and sweet temper always. Her daily rounds in the wards brought her into personal intercourse with every patient and she knew his special need. At one time nine hundred men were supplied from her kitchen.

This colored hospital service was one of those extraordinary tasks out of the ordinary course of hospital discipline that none but a woman could execute. It required more than a man's power of endurance, for men fainted and fell under the burden. It required a woman's discernment, a woman's tenderness, a woman's delicacy and tact; it required such nerve and such executive power as are rarely united in any woman's character. But Miss Gilson brought all this and more, a woman's sympathy, to her task. As she passed through the wards the men would follow her with their eyes attracted by the grave sweetness of her manner and when she stopped by some bedside and laid her hand upon the forehead and smoothed the hair of a soldier speaking some cheering and pleasant word, tears would gather in his eyes and his lip quiver as he tried to speak or touch the fold of her dress.

These were the tokens of her ministry among the sickest men, and it was not here alone that her influence was felt in the hospital. Was there jealousy in the kitchen? Her quick penetration detected the cause and in her sweet way harmony was restored. Or was there hardship and discontent? The knowledge that she too was enduring the hardship was enough to insure patient endurance until a remedy could be provided. And so through all the war, until after the fierce battles which were fought for the possession of Richmond and Petersburg in 1864 and 1865, she labored steadfastly on through scorching heat and pinching cold, in the tent or upon the open field, in the ambulance or in the saddle, through rain and snow, amid unseen perils of the enemy, under fire upon the field, or in the more insidious danger of contagion she worked on quietly doing her simple part with all womanly tact and skill.

From City Point she went to the hospital at Richmond, and remained there until June, 1865. During the following years she spent some months at Richmond working among the colored and white schools. With declining health, alas, she returned to Massachusetts and died in April, 1868, and was buried in Woodlawn Cemetery, Chelsea. A beautiful monument with an appropriate inscription was erected over her grave by the soldiers, and it is decorated each year by Grand Army posts and Women's Relief Corps.

MARY PRINGLE.
(Mary Breckel)

Mary Pringle was born in Columbus, Ohio, June 11, 1833. She was one of the volunteer nurses to go into the hospital at Quincy, Illinois, at the opening of the war, she also did splendid service in the soldiers' hospital organized on Broad Street, Columbus. She worked from the time the war broke out until sick from overwork, she was obliged to leave the service in July, 1863.

MARY A. LOOMIS.

When the Civil War broke out she was Mrs. Van Pelt living at Coldwater, Mich., and entered the service with her husband who was one of the first of the volunteer soldiers. She was afterwards appointed matron of the war hospital in Nashville, Tenn., and remained there from September, 1862, until January, 1863. She was also at the hospital at Murfreesboro, Tenn., and at Huntsville, Alabama. In all she was in the hospitals only about a year. But the remainder of the time she was in camp or on the march with her husband. Although he had fallen in the battle of Chickamauga in September, 1863, she continued her work of nursing Union soldiers.

EMMA E. SIMONDS.

Mrs. Simonds was appointed a nurse by Mrs. Hoge and Mrs. Livermore under the authority of Miss Dix, on August 26, 1863, and was assigned to work at once in Memphis, Tenn. Miss Dix in speaking of her work has said, "She was one of the most excellent, most charitable and most truthful in all her expressions of any woman I have ever known." At the close of the war she returned to her home at Iowa Falls. In 1873 she moved to Fayetteville, Arkansas, where she resumed her practice as professional nurse. This work she continued until January, 1892. She died in May, 1893.

MARGARET HAYES.

On the seventeenth day of February, 1863, Margaret Hayes left her home in Mendota, Illinois, for Chicago as a volunteer nurse. Arriving there she went to the Sanitary Commission rooms and was received by Mrs. Livermore, who, as she afterwards told the experience, gave her her commission, put up a lunch, gave her a pillow and a small comfortable, as there were no sleeping cars in those days, procured the transportations and started her that same evening for Memphis, Tennessee. She arrived safely and was immediately assigned to the Adams General Hospital, which had just been opened to receive the sick and wounded from Arkansas. A part of the time she had two wards to care for and when she was ordered from this hospital to another position she was given a gold watch by her "Boys," which she always held as one of her choicest treasures. She was Mrs. Maggie Meseroll then, but was called "Sister Maggie" by all the soldiers who loved her for the care and tenderness she had bestowed upon them.

DR. NANCY M. HILL.

Nancy M. Hill, daughter of William and Harriet Swan Hill, was born in Cambridge, Massachusetts. Her forefathers were in the battles of Lexington and Bunker Hill. She was educated in the public schools at West Cambridge, and at Mt. Holyoke Seminary, South Hadley, Massachusetts. There was a great call for educated women to go as nurses in the hospitals at Washington, and Mrs. Hill volunteered her services there in April, 1863, and remained until August, 1865, after the close of the war. She gave her service without remuneration, since the pay of volunteer nurses was to go into a hospital fund to buy extras for the soldiers which the Government did not provide. When the battles of the Wilderness were going on, all hospital supplies and sanitary stores had been sent to the front and there were none in Washington. Mrs. Hill wrote to her mother about it and the letter was read next morning in four churches. Immediately congregations were dismissed and all went home to return to the Town Hall bringing tablecloths, linen and cotton sheets, the best they had. The women and men worked all day long making and rolling bandages and picking lint. Before nine o'clock that night the nurse's letter from the front had resulted in two large drygoods boxes the size of upright pianos packed with stores and on their way to Washington.

After the war hospital closed, Mrs. Hill turned to the study of medicine. Afterwards she became a medical student at the New England Hospital for Women and Children at Roxbury, Massachusetts. She was graduated at the medical department of Michigan University, Ann Arbor, in the year 1874. She then went to Dubuque, Iowa, and opened an office and carried on a large and active practice for years.

ELIZABETH B. NICHOLS.

Mrs. Nichols entered the service of volunteer nurses at the request of her husband, who wished her to join him in Chicago where his regiment had been sent on exchange after having been taken prisoners at Harper's Ferry. Her determination to get to his bedside immediately after reaching Chicago illustrated the pluck and courage which showed all through her career as Government nurse. She reached that city at two o'clock in the morning, it was three miles to Camp Douglas where the soldiers were quartered. Alone and in the darkness she found the gate of the camp enclosure, but it was closed and she was challenged by sentries. It was only by insistent appeal that the officer in charge allowed her to enter and find her husband. She slept while at this hospital in the baggage room on a couple of blankets and a pillow, and worked all of the next day getting the sick of the camp ready to be taken to the city hospital. Subsequently she accompanied her husband to Washington, and from there she marched with the regiment to Fairfax crossing the Long Bridge. After the main body of troops had gone to the stockade camp, she and her husband remained at Fairfax nearly two weeks with nine sick men. The only facilities they had for cooking were a coffee pot, one mess pan, a spider and the fireplace. But they saved the lives of all of their patients. By the time they reached the front the hospital was full of men sick with typhoid fever and other maladies, and Mrs. Nichols passed through scenes which she never forgot. She took what little sleep was allowed her, wrapped in a blanket on a pile of straw. One morning as she was about to enter the hospital the doctor met her with the dreadful news that smallpox had broken out. But so heroic was her effort that out of the eighteen cases which developed only one died. She was also at Gettysburg and later at

Philadelphia, where her husband was very ill. As soon as he recovered sufficiently he was ordered to Washington, where with his wife he prepared the food for the invalid corps camp. They stayed there sixteen months, when her husband was honorably discharged from the army, and they went home to live in well-earned peace.

MRS. A. H. HOGE.

Perhaps among all who labored for the soldiers during the Civil War no name is better known than that of Mrs. A. H. Hoge. She dedicated to the service of her country all that she had to bestow, and became widely known as one of the most faithful and tireless workers; wise in counsel, strong in judgment, earnest in action. She was born in Philadelphia, and was the daughter of George B. Blaikie, Esq., an East India shipping merchant—"a man of spotless character and exalted reputation, whose name is held in reverence by many still living there." Mrs. Hoge was educated at the celebrated seminary of John Brewer, A. M. In her twentieth year she was married to Mr. Hoge a merchant in Pittsburgh, where she lived fourteen years. At the end of that period she moved to Chicago, where she became identified with Mrs. Livermore in her work for the soldiers. Two of her sons entered the army at the very beginning of the war, and she at once began her unwearied personal services for the sick and the wounded. At first she entered only into that work of supply in which so large a portion of the loyal women of the North labored continuously all through the war. The first public act of her life as a sanitary agent was to visit at the request of the Chicago Branch of the United States Sanitary Commission, the hospitals at Cairo, Mound City and St. Louis. The object of these visits was to examine such hospitals as were under the immediate supervision of this branch and report their conditions. This report was made and acted upon and was the means of introducing decided and much-needed reforms into similar institutions.

The value of Mrs. Hoge's counsel and the fruits of her great experience of life were immediately acknowledged. In several councils of women held in Washington she took a prominent part and was always listened to with the greatest respect and attention. When she attended the Woman's Council there in 1862, she was accompanied by her friend and fellow laborer, Mrs. Livermore, and after their return to Chicago they immediately began the organization of the Northwest for sanitary labor, being appointed agents of the Northwestern Sanitary Commission. They devoted their entire time to this work opening a correspondence with the leading women in all the cities and prominent towns of the Northwest. They prepared and distributed great numbers of circulars relating to the necessity of a concentrated effort of the aid societies, and they visited in person many towns and large villages, calling together audiences of women and telling them of the hardships, sufferings and heroism of the soldiers, which they had themselves witnessed, and of the pressing needs of these men, which could only be met by the supplies and work contributed by loyal women of the North. Thus they stimulated the enthusiasm of the women to the highest point, greatly increased the number of aid societies, and taught them how, by systematizing their efforts, they could render the largest amount of assistance to the Sanitary Commission.

By two years of earnest and constant labor in this field these women succeeded in adding to the packages sent to the Sanitary Commission fifty thousand, mostly gifts directly from the aid societies but in part purchased with money given. In addition to this, over four thousand dollars came into the treasury through their efforts.

Early in 1863, Mrs. Hoge, in company with Mrs. Colt of Milwaukee, at the request of the Sanitary Commission, left Chicago for Vicksburg with a large quantity of sanitary stores. The defeat of Sherman in his assault upon that city had just taken place and there was great want and suffering in the army. The boat upon which these women were traveling was, however, seized as a military transport at Columbus and pressed into the fleet of General Gorman, which was just starting for the forks at the mouth of the White River.

General Fiske, whose headquarters were upon the same boat, gave Mrs. Hoge and Mrs. Colt the best accommodations and every facility for carrying out their work, which proved to be greatly needed. Their stores were found to be almost the only ones in the fleet composed of thirty steamers filled with fresh troops, whose ranks were soon thinned by sickness consequent upon the exposures and fatigue of the campaign. Their boat became a refuge for the sick of General Fiske's brigade, and these women had the privilege of nursing hundreds of men during this expedition, undoubtedly saving many valuable lives.

Early in the following spring, and only ten days after her return to Chicago from this expedition, Mrs. Hoge was again summoned to Vicksburg, opposite which at Young's Point the army under General Grant was lying, engaged, among other operations against this stronghold, in an attempt to dig a canal across the point opposite the fortified city. Scurvy was prevailing to a terrible extent among the men, and they were greatly in need of the supplies Mrs. Hoge brought. She remained here two weeks, her headquarters being upon the sanitary boat, Silver Wave. She received constant support and aid from Generals Grant and Sherman and from Admiral Porter who placed a tug boat at her disposal, in order that she might visit the camps and hospitals, which were totally inaccessible in any other way, owing to the impassable character of the roads during the rainy season. Having made a tour of all the hospitals and ascertained the condition of the sick and of the army generally, she returned to the North and reported to the Sanitary Commission the extent of that insidious army foe, the scurvy. They determined to act promptly and vigorously, and these efforts undoubtedly proved the salvation of a good proportion of the troops.

Again the following June she returned to Vicksburg on the steamer, "City of Alton," which was dispatched by Governor Yates to bring home the sick and wounded Illinois soldiers. She remained until shortly after the surrender which took place on the fourth of July, and during this time visited the entire circle of hospitals as well as the rifle-pits where she witnessed scenes of thrilling interest and instances of endurance and heroism beyond the power of pen to describe.

In the two great sanitary fairs that were held in Chicago, the efforts of

Mrs. Hoge were unwearied from the inception of the idea until the close of its successful realization. The admirable conduct of these fairs and the large amounts raised by them are matters of history.

During the continuance of her labors Mrs. Hoge was frequently the recipient of costly and elegant gifts as testimonials of the respect and gratitude with which her work was viewed. The managers of the Philadelphia fair, believing Mrs. Hoge to have had an important connection with that fair, presented to her a beautiful gift in token of their appreciation of her services. During the second sanitary fair in Chicago a few friends presented her with a beautiful silver cup bearing a suitable inscription in Latin, and during the same fair she received as a gift a Roman bell of green bronze of rare workmanship and value as a work of art.

Mrs. Hoge made three expeditions to the army of the Southwest and personally visited and ministered to more than one hundred thousand men in hospitals. Few among the many official workers whom the war called from the ease and retirement of home can submit to the public a record of labors as efficient, varied and long-continued as hers.

MRS. JOHN A. FOWLE.

Of all the women who devoted themselves to the soldiers in the Civil War, perhaps none had a more varied experience than Elida B. Rumsey, a girl so young that Miss Dix would not receive her as a nurse. Undaunted by seeming difficulties she persisted in doing the next best thing, and in becoming an independent nurse she fulfilled her great desire to do something for the Union soldiers. Yet it was not to these alone that her kindly administrations extended, for wherever she saw a soldier in need her ready sympathies were enlisted, little caring if the heart beats stirred a coat of blue or gray.

Miss Rumsey was born in New York City, June 6, 1842, and at the outbreak of the war she was living with her parents in Washington, D. C. She had become engaged to John A. Fowle of Jamaica Plains, Mass., who was employed in the Navy Department at Washington, but devoted all his spare time to philanthropic enterprises. His work and Miss Rumsey's were supplementary from the first. In November, 1861, she began to visit the hospitals and sing to the soldiers who found relief and courage in the tones of her strong sympathetic voice. The "Soldiers Rest" was a name very inappropriately given to a place near the B. & O. R. R. depot, where prisoners were exchanged, or sometimes stayed over night when they had nowhere else to go. Miss Rumsey had a strong desire to see what kind of men had been in Libby Prison, and when the first lot had been exchanged she went down to see them off as they were going home on a furlough. Someone recognized the young lady and called for a song. To gain time and give her a moment's preparation, Mr. Fowle stepped to her side and said, "Boys, how would you like a song?" "Oh, very well, I guess," came the reply in spiritless tones. She sang the "Red, White and Blue." Soon they crowded around her with more interest than they had shown since leaving the prison. At the close of the song they called for another and piled their knapsacks in front of her on the ground.

Standing on this rude rostrum she sang "The Star Spangled Banner." Her natural enthusiasm was intensified by the surroundings, and the desire to inspire the boys with the courage they had all but lost. When she had finished, those prisoners now restored to their former spirits rent the air with cheer after cheer. From this time on her voice hitherto used only for the enjoyment of her friends was devoted to her country.

One of the first things definitely accomplished was the establishment of a Sunday evening prayer meeting in Columbia College hospital. The room where this was held was crowded night after night. The interest steadily increased until the boys often did double duty in order to be present. The soldiers planned what they wanted her to sing from week to week, and she threw into the songs all her great desire to bring the boys back to their former selves and help them feel that they were not forgotten nor alone.

All this time her plans had been assuming outward form. Having received a grant of land from the Government a building was erected and the Soldiers' Free Library founded. Mrs. Walter Baker gave the first hundred dollars and the greater part of the remainder was earned by Miss Rumsey and Mr. Fowle giving concerts, at two of which they had the marine band by order of the President. As far as known this was the first library ever founded by a woman, and that by a mere girl scarcely eighteen years of age. The reading room was modestly fitted up with seats which would accommodate two hundred and fifty persons. It had a melodeon, on which the soldiers practiced at will, and every Wednesday evening regular instruction was given in music and singing by Mr. and Mrs. Fowle. Religious services were conducted by the chaplain twice each Sunday. One room was devoted to the storage of medicine, delicacies, stationery, socks, shirts, etc., and was under the charge of Mrs. Fowle, who filled the knapsack of every convalescent soldier leaving camp from these stores.

The honor paid to Miss Rumsey at the time of her marriage demonstrated the public esteem in which she was held. The ceremony took place in the halls of Congress. A good deal of publicity had been given the affair and the floor and galleries were packed, about four thousand persons being present. The bride, we are told, was dressed in a plain drab poplin, with linen collar and cuffs, and with a bonnet of the same color, ornamented with red, white and blue flowers. A bow of red, white and blue ribbon was fastened upon her breast. After the ceremony had been completed, and the couple were receiving congratulations, a soldier in the gallery shouted, "Won't the bride sing the Star Spangled Banner?" And she did, then and there, in her bridal dress, with never more of fervor in her beautiful voice. President Lincoln had intended to be present, but at the last moment he was detained, and sent a magnificent basket of flowers. On their return from their bridal trip Mr. and Mrs. Fowle resumed their work at Columbia Hospital, but later on they determined to consecrate themselves to the service at the front. Knowing that there would be urgent need and fearful suffering, Mrs. Fowle decided to go to the second battle of Bull Run; so, taking a load of supplies and some four hundred loaves of bread, she and Mr. Fowle started in an ambulance. Having no Government pass it was a hazardous undertaking, and she experienced difficulty in getting through the lines. The last guard peremptorily refused to let her go any farther, when springing from the ambulance, she fell on her knees before him and begged her way through. Thus while Miss Dix and her faithful nurses were detained three miles away, she was inside the lines and ready for action. When almost on the battlefield they came to a little negro cabin and resolved to use it for a hospital. It was a tiny affair, but on opening the door they found that it was already occupied. A terrified crowd of negroes had sought shelter there. Almost wild with fear, they could scarcely obey the order, "Be off," but were soon on their way to Washington. The preparation had not been made any too quickly for almost immediately wounded men began to arrive. The little cabin would hold about fifty, and after Mr. Fowle had done what he could for one patient he was removed and another took his place. When the stores had been distributed Mrs. Fowle determined to go in and help care for the wounded. She found the floor completely hidden with blood, but she entered firmly and helped to bind up fearful wounds until the close of that famous Sunday night when the army retreated. Mrs. Fowle carried to her death a scar on her face as a relic of war time, and its story defines her whole attitude during the Civil War. A large carbuncle, the result of blood poisoning while washing wounds on the battlefield, appeared on her cheek. The doctor said it must be lanced. Having a horror of a knife and with nerves already quivering from the sights around her she did not feel equal to the ordeal. Still knowing it must be done she said, "Let me go over to the Judiciary Hospital and see the boys who have had their arms and legs amputated and I can bear it." A chair was placed in one end of the ward and calmly seating herself she looked for a moment at the long rows of cots then told the surgeon to go on. After the close of the war Mr. and Mrs. Fowle resided in Baltimore.

The Woman's Relief Corps, Auxiliary to the Grand Army of the Republic.

INTRODUCTION BY MARY M. NORTH.

When the war cloud hangs darkly over a land, then is the strength of woman made perfect, and she is ready with the kindly ministrations which can only come from the sympathetic hand of the home-maker—the mother, wife, sister, daughter, sweetheart—the loyal woman.

When the dove of peace had taken its departure from our own fair land, and the boom of cannon was heard upon that fateful day in April, '61, then there arose the need for the kindly ministrations of woman, and as ever, she was ready with a response, and everywhere little bands gathered, or a woman alone did "what she could," for those who had answered their country's call.

Not only did she put her hand to the plow, and start the loom with its many bobbins, harvest the crops which she had laboriously planted and tended, but she also sewed, picked lint, made bandages, and knitted socks and numberless other things for the men and boys at "the front."

Societies sprang up and worked steadily all through the Civil War, and even when peace was declared, many found that their work was not done, for there were maimed and invalid veterans to care for, there were widows and orphans who needed succor, and homes had to be provided for hundreds who had no loved ones to look after them.

With the call of duty ever before them they could not disband, and all over the north, the east, and the west, they were still working when their ability and help were recognized by a veteran who was at the head of the Grand Army of the Republic,—Paul Van Der Voort, commander-in-chief.

An invitation was sent out to all loyal women all over the country to assemble at Denver, July 25, 26, 1883, to perfect a National Order, which should include within its folds loyal women from every state in the Union, who were willing to unite in a fraternity which should be of assistance to the Grand Army of the Republic, in all their works of beneficence.

The National Organization was effected at the Denver meeting, and recognized as the auxiliary of the Grand Army of the Republic in accordance with a resolution by that body passed in Indianapolis, in 1881: "Resolved, That we approve of the project entertained of organizing a 'Woman's National Relief Corps.' Resolved, That such 'Woman's Relief Corps' may use, under such title, the words, 'Auxiliary to the G.A.R.' by special endorsement of the Grand Army of the Republic, June 15, 1881."

They were accepted, and left free to work for the veterans in their own way, which as time has fully proven has been a wise one.

Among those present at the Denver meeting were: Mrs. Florence Barker, Mrs. Kate Brownlee Sherwood, Mrs. Sarah E. Fuller, Mrs. Lizabeth A. Turner, Mrs. E. K. Stimson, Mrs. Emily Gardner, Mrs. J. M. Telford, Mrs. I. S. Bangs, Mrs. Clark, Mrs. McNeir, Mrs. Hugg, and Mrs. Charles.

The officers elected were:

National President, Mrs. E. Florence Barker, Malden, Massachusetts.
National Senior Vice President, Mrs. Kate Brownlee Sherwood, Toledo, Ohio.
National Junior Vice President, Mrs. E. K. Stimson, Denver, Colorado.
National Secretary, Mrs. Sarah E. Fuller, East Boston, Mass.
National Inspector, Mrs. Emily Gardner, Denver, Colorado.
National Chaplain, Mrs. Mattie B. Moulton, Laconia, New Hampshire.
National Conductor, Mrs. P. S. Runyan, Warsaw, Indiana.
National Guard, Mrs. J. W. Beatson, Rockford, Illinois.
National Corresponding Secretaries, Mrs. Mary J. Telford, Denver, Colorado, and Mrs. Ellen Pay, Topeka, Kansas.

At this first meeting it was voted that all loyal women were eligible to membership, and the growth of the organization has shown the wisdom of the vote.

CHARTER MEMBERS, W. R. C.

E. Florence Barker, Malden, Mass.
Sarah E. Fuller, East Boston, Mass.
Lizabeth A. Turner, Boston, Mass.
Helen S. Bangs, Waterville, Me.
Kate B. Sherwood, Toledo, Ohio.
Lenore K. Sherwood, Toledo, Ohio
Mary E. Lanning, Columbus, Ohio
Annie W. Clark, Columbus, Ohio
Lottie M. Meyers, Canton, Ohio
Emma K. McCammon, Carthage, Ohio
Ella McCammon, Carthage, Ohio
Helen M. Santmeyer, Carthage, Ohio
Mary Timmerman, Leipsic, Ohio
Marion A. Gillis, Cleveland, Ohio
Amelia A. Moore, Youngstown, Ohio

Frances S. Runyan, Warsaw, Indiana
Frances Elliott Olney, Warsaw, Ind.
Henrietta Norton, Rockford, Ill.
Jane W. Beatson, Rockford. Ill.
Kate Hobart, Rockford, Ill.
Emily T. Charles, Washington, D. C.
Louise V. Bryant, Washington, D. C.
Lizzie Anderson, Topeka, Kan.
Ellen M. Pay, Topeka, Kan.
Sarah E. Devendorf, Topeka, Kan.
Jennie Fensky, Topeka, Kan.
Emma B. Alrich, Cawker City, Kan.
America Anderson, Denver, Colo.
Olive Hogle, Denver, Colo.
Mary A. Stimson, Denver, Colo.

Mary Jewett Telford, Denver, Colo.
Augusta B. Henderson, Denver, Colo.
Angenette Peavy, Denver, Colo.
Josephine L. Peavy, Denver, Colo.
Frances A. Collar, Denver, Colo.
Julia A. Lynd, Denver, Colo.
Nora McIntyre, Denver, Colo.
Maria F. Gray Pitman, Denver, Colo.
Emily Gardner, Denver, Colo.
Mary A. Ingersoll, Denver, Colo.
Mesdames
    S. O. Ver Plank, Denver, Colo.
    F. A. Driscoll, Denver, Colo.
    H. B. Ayers, Denver, Colo.
    W. H. Savage, Denver, Colo.

Margaret Freeman, Denver, Colo.
Mary E. Lattin, Denver, Colo.
Henrietta F. Mills, Denver, Colo.
Harriet B. Jeffries, Denver, Colo.
Lizzie M. Tarbell, Denver, Colo.
Harriet L. Heard, Denver, Colo.
Mary Berwick, Denver, Colo.
Louise E. Sherman, Colo. Springs, Colo.
Mary L. Carr, Longmont, Colo.

J. F. Lather, Denver, Colo.
C. E. Hanly, Denver, Colo.
S. D. Hunt, Denver, Colo.
H. L. Wadsworth, Denver, Colo.
W. H. Leaverns, Denver, Colo.

The Woman's Relief Corps is now the largest beneficent and patriotic organization of women in the world, their membership at last report being about 166,000.

They have spent in relief for the veteran or his dependent ones since organizing, more than three and a half millions of dollars, and upon their twenty-fifth anniversary, presented the Grand Army of the Republic with $5,000, and every year a gift of $1,000 is made for their permanent fund.

At the last convention of the Woman's Relief Corps the treasurer reported $27,267.18 as the total assets, with no liabilities.

At that convention it was voted, to set aside $3,000 for the Grand Army of the Republic, subject to any call of the commander-in-chief for aid of needy veterans; $2,000 for the aid of army nurses who do not receive pensions, and by reason of advanced age cannot provide for themselves the comforts they need; $1,000 for a memorial tablet at Andersonville Park upon which is to be inscribed the source from which the government received its sacred trust of that hallowed ground.

The Woman's Relief Corps has owned very much valuable real estate, notably Andersonville Park, Andersonville,

Georgia, and the National W. R. C. Home, in Madison, Ohio, but the latter was turned over to the state of Ohio as a gift, several years ago. Last year Andersonville Park was also turned over to the government as a gift free of encumbrance.

The way the Woman's Relief Corps acquired this property is interesting: The department of Georgia Grand Army of the Republic, purchased the old prison site, of the owners, but found that as their number was growing less year by year, and as it required a great deal of money to keep up the place, it would be better for them to offer it to the auxiliary of the Grand Army of the Republic. When the Woman's Relief Corps was in annual session in St. Paul, Minn., in 1896, representatives of the Georgia Grand Army came before them, and offering the old prison, asked them to accept the gift and keep it from desecration. The women accepted it as a sacred trust, and immediately appointed Mrs. Lizabeth A. Turner, of Massachusetts, as chairman of a board to beautify the grounds and make a park of them. A house for a caretaker was needed, and as the women did not want to build it within the old stockade, more land was purchased making the acreage within the enclosure about eighty-seven. A ten-room house was erected, a caretaker installed, and then the tedious process of making a park was begun. Bermuda grass was planted root by root, a pear and pecan orchard set out, and a rose garden planted, with rose bushes sent from almost every state in the Union, and then the desert began literally "to blossom as the rose." Several states were given ground upon which to erect monuments to their sons. These were Massachusetts, Ohio, Michigan, Rhode Island and Wisconsin. Mrs. Turner having died while in discharge of her duty, the Woman's Relief Corps also erected a monument to her memory in the park. This beautiful spot, the mecca for all the country side every Sabbath, and for the nation upon Memorial Day, was last year accepted by the government, and this year upon May 30, the memorial tablet set up by the donors, was unveiled, in the presence of a vast concourse of people, Mrs. Sarah D. Winans, chairman of the Andersonville Board, presenting it to the National President of the Woman's Relief Corps, Mrs. Belle C. Harris, who in turn presented it to the government through Captain Bryant, superintendent of the Andersonville Cemetery. Upon the tablet are the names of the incorporators of the Woman's Relief Corps, Mrs. Sarah D. Winans, Mrs. Jennie E. Wright, Mrs. Kate B. Sherwood, Mrs. Cora Day Yound, Mrs. Mary C. Wentzell, Mrs. Mary M. North, Mrs. Sarah E. Phillips, Mrs. Lizabeth A. Turner, Miss Clara Barton and Mrs. Allaseba M. Bliss. Also the names of the Board of Trustees for 1909-10, Mrs. Sarah D. Winans, Mrs. Abbie A. Adams, Mrs. Allaseba M. Bliss, Mrs. Sarah E. Fuller, Mrs. Carrie R. Read, and the names of the committee on transfer to the government, Mrs. Kate E. Jones, Mrs. Kate B. Sherwood, Mrs. Mary M. North and Mrs. Mary L. Gilman.

The aims and objects of the Woman's Relief Corps are:

"To specially aid and assist the Grand Army of the Republic, and to perpetuate the memory of their heroic dead.

To assist such Union veterans as need our help and protection, and to extend needful aid to their widows and orphans. To find them homes and employment, and assure them of sympathy and friends. To cherish and emulate the deeds of our army nurses, and of all loyal women who rendered loving service to our country in her hour of peril.

To maintain true allegiance to the United States of America; to inculcate lessons of patriotism and love of country among our children and in the communities in which we live; and encourage the spread of universal liberty and equal rights to all.

This organization was the first to introduce the salute to

the flag in the public schools, and to make the observance of Flag Day general, by preparing and carrying out suitable programs.

There are two salutes to the flag taught in the schools, the one for the older scholars being, "I pledge allegiance to my flag and to the Republic for which it stands; one nation indivisible, with liberty and justice for all."

The other is taught the younger pupils, and is, "I give my head and my heart to God and my country, one country, one language, one flag."

The Woman's Relief Corps has been instrumental in having flag laws passed in many states, and through their efforts an appropriation was made by Congress for flags for the school houses of the District of Columbia, the writer of this having made the first draft of the bill which was put in shape by Mrs. Belva A. Lockwood and presented to Congress. Upon the roster of this order are the names of women in the highest walks of life, and any who are loyal and of good moral character are welcome to the ranks of those who are banded together for such patriotic work as that of the Woman's Relief Corps.

Those who have served as National President, National Secretary and National Treasurer since the organization are the following:

NATIONAL PRESIDENTS.	NATIONAL SECRETARIES.	NATIONAL TREASURERS.
E. Florence Barker	Sarah E. Fuller	Lizabeth A. Turner
Kate B. Sherwood	Emma D. Sibley	Lizabeth A. Turner
Sarah E. Fuller	Eleanor B. Wheeler	Lizabeth A. Turner
Elizabeth D'Arcy Kinne	Nellie G. Backus	Lizabeth A. Turner
Emma Stark Hampton	Armilla A. Cheney	Lizabeth A. Turner
Charity Rusk Craig	Hettie M. Nichols	Lizabeth A. Turner
Annie Wittenmyer	Abbie Lynch	Armilla A. Cheney
Mary Sears McHenry	Hannah R. Plimpton	Armilla A. Cheney
Sue A. Pike Sanders	Ella Cobean	Armilla A. Cheney
Margaret Ray Wickins	Flora Preston Hogbin	Armilla A. Cheney

NATIONAL PRESIDENTS.	NATIONAL SECRETARIES.	NATIONAL TREASURERS.
Sarah C. Mink	Sarah E. Phillips	Armilla A. Cheney
Emma R. Wallace	Jennie Bross	Armilla A. Cheney
Lizabeth A. Turner	Harriette L. Reed	Isabelle T. Bagley
Agnes Hitt	Ida S. McBride	Isabelle T. Bagley
Sarah J. Martin	Mary H. Shepherd	Isabelle T. Bagley
Flo Jamison Miller	Mattie Jamison Tippett	Isabelle T. Bagley
Harriet J. Bodge	Charlotte E. Wright	Sarah E. Phillips
Mary L. Carr	Fannie D. W. Hardin	Sarah E. Phillips
Calista Robinson Jones	Mary Ellen Conant	Sarah E. Phillips
Lodusky J. Taylor	Ada E. May	Sarah E. Phillips
Sarah D. Winans	Jennie S. Wright	Isabelle T. Bagley
Fanny E. Minot	Helen McGregor Ayers	Sarah E. Phillips
Abbie Asenath Adams	Mary R. Morgan	Charlotte E. Wright
Carrie R. Sparklin	Belle C. Kimball	Charlotte E. Wright
Kate E. Jones	Eliza Brown Daggett	Charlotte E. Wright
Mary L. Gilman	Maria W. Going	Charlotte E. Wright
Jennie Iowa Berry	Georgia Wade McClellan	Charlotte E. Wright
Belle C. Harris	Ida Wilson Moore	Charlotte E. Wright

Women of the Woman's Relief Corps.

E. FLORENCE BARKER.

First national president of the Woman's Relief Corps. When the Woman's Relief Corps was organized as a national body at Denver in 1883, there was present Mrs. E. Florence Barker of Malden, Massachusetts, who at the time, was president of a large patriotic and benevolent organization of the state, called the Union Board Woman's Relief Corps. This, she with a number of other ladies represented at the Denver meeting. She had long been known for her good works, and had been assiduous in working for the soldiers during the Civil War, and after that, she married Colonel Thomas E. Barker, of the 12th New Hampshire Regiment. After a life spent for the good of others, she passed on to her reward, September 11, 1897.

KATE BROWNLEE SHERWOOD.

Mrs. Kate Brownlee Sherwood, second national president of the Woman's Relief Corps, was one of the organizers, acted as secretary at the first meeting and was elected national senior vice-president at that meeting.

She is an Ohio woman and was one of those who "waited" during the Civil War, while she also worked with her might, for not only the soldier husband, but for all who had gone at their country's call. Her husband is General Isaac R. Sherwood, a member of the House of Representatives of the Congress of the United States. Mrs. Sherwood is without a peer as an executive officer, is gifted with the silver tongue of oratory, and has also been blessed above many in that hers is the pen of a ready writer. She has exceptional literary ability, and her poems are found in nearly all the state libraries. Every schoolboy and girl knows her patriotic poems. She is an indefatigable worker, and will not rest until the last roll is called. Her home is in Toledo, Ohio.

SARAH R. FULLER.

Mrs. Sarah R. Fuller, third national president of the Woman's Relief Corps, was one of those who crossed the continent to help found the organization. During the last year of the Civil War her husband lost his life on Southern soil, and left his wife to raise their little son. Since that time she has been devoted to the work of caring for the veteran and his dependent ones.

The beginning of her service antedates that, however, for early in the war she became a member of the Christian Commission, and early and late, gave her services where they were needed. She is a versatile woman, and has done a great deal with both pen and voice to build up the order she loves so well.

At the meeting in Denver she was chosen national secretary, and at the third convention was elected national president. Her love for the order has not abated, and in her own department she has served in every office. She is life member of the Executive Board of the National Woman's Relief Corps, and is also a member of the Andersonville Park Board. Her home is in Medford, Massachusetts, where she is honored and loved by everyone.

ELIZABETH D'ARCY KINNE.

Mrs. Elizabeth D'Arcy Kinne, fourth national president of the Woman's Relief Corps, was reared in Massachusetts, and lived in the Bay State until after her marriage. When the Civil War broke out, Mr. Kinne was living in California, but came east and joined the second Massachusetts cavalry, and while adjutant of that regiment he met, wooed and won Miss D'Arcy. Mr. Kinne served with Sheridan in the Valley of Virginia until the close of the war, then with his wife went to his western home, where they have resided ever since.

Soon after the organization of the Woman's Relief Corps, Mrs. Kinne saw that it was to be a factor for great good, so entered heartily into its work, and organized a corps in her own city. She helped to raise $1,000 with which to procure bedding and other necessities for the State Soldiers' Home. She also helped to found the home for nurses, soldiers' widows, mothers and orphans, at Evergreen near San Jose. Every veteran finds in Mrs. Kinne a warm friend, and no one asks for help in vain at her door. Her home is in San Francisco, California.

EMMA STARK HAMPTON.

Mrs. Emma Stark Hampton, the fifth national president of the Woman's Relief Corps, is one of the women who revised the beautiful ritual of the order. She is a lineal descendant of Israel Stark of Revolutionary fame, and her father was also Israel Stark. He was associated with the Christian Commission during the Civil War. A brother of Mrs. Hampton lost his life while at the head of his regiment in the battle of the Wilderness. Mrs. Hampton rendered valuable assistance during the war, and since that conflict, her zeal has not relaxed in the interest of those who wore the blue. She is a literary woman, and has long represented the Woman's Relief Corps in the National Council of Women of the United States. Her home is in Detroit, Michigan.

CHARITY RUSK CRAIG.

Mrs. Charity Rusk Craig, the sixth national president of the Woman's Relief Corps, comes of patriotic stock, and has shown her patriotism by her work while a member of this great patriotic organization. She is a woman of fine presence and is gifted in speech.

For a number of years her home was in Viroqua, Wisconsin, but for some time past she has been living in Asheville, N. C.

ANNIE WITTENMEYER.

Mrs. Annie Wittenmeyer, seventh national president of the Woman's Relief Corps, went out as a young woman, in charge of a nurse corps, under orders from Governor Curtin of Pennsylvania, and her name is lovingly mentioned, and her presence fondly remembered by thousands of old soldiers who came under her kindly ministrations in the dark days of the war.

She was not only all through the war, but many times was actually "under the guns." If one thing more than another established her fame, it is that she was the first to think of establishing diet kitchens, and hundreds of soldiers are alive to-day, because of the clean, nourishing food which was provided them under her direction.

It was through her influence that hundreds of army nurses have been pensioned in their old age. She is also well known as a poet, and "I have entered the valley of blessing so sweet," is as well known, as her poem telling,of the miraculous breaking forth of the spring at Andersonville during the Civil War, when "The prisoner's cry rang up to Heaven; God heard and with His thunder cleft the earth, and poured His sweetest water gushing there."

Mrs. Wittenmyer died a few years ago at her home in Sanatoga, Pennsylvania.

MRS. MARY SEARS McHENRY.

Mrs. Mary Sears McHenry, eighth national president of the Woman's Relief Corps, comes of Revolutionary stock, being a direct descendant of Isaac Sears. Her husband was an orderly sergeant during the Civil War, afterwards settling at Denison, Iowa, where he became a prosperous banker. Mrs. McHenry came to the head of the order fully prepared for the duties, having passed through all the chairs in her own department, she therefore made an exceptionally good presiding officer.

SUE A. PIKE SANDERS.

Mrs. Sue A. Pike Sanders, ninth national president of the Woman's Relief Corps, is another who has Revolutionary blood in her veins, but she is not so proud of this, as that she is a patriot herself, and had four brothers in the Civil War, two of whom languished in Andersonville for many months. During the war she was a teacher in Bloomington, Illinois, and made a flag and raised it over her schoolhouse. She also belonged to the Soldiers' Aid Society of that town, and gave through it valuable aid to the cause. Mrs. Sander's home is in Bloomington, Illinois.

MARGARET RAY WICKINS.

Mrs. Margaret Ray Wickins, tenth national president of the Woman's Relief Corps, came to the office from her home on the free soil of Kansas filled with enthusiasm, and after many victories won in the upbuilding of the order in her state. While the Civil War was in progress, she gave her time and services whenever there was need, and when hostilities closed, she was as ever, ready and willing to help those who had stood by the flag.

Mrs. Wickins lives in Paris, Illinois.

MRS. SARAH C. MINK.

Mrs. Sarah C. Mink, eleventh national president of the Woman's Relief Corps, was born in the town of Mayfield, New York, April 7, 1837, and again we record the fact that this woman was of Revolutionary stock, and her patriotism was tested in the time that tried men's souls.

When the Woman's Relief Corps was organized in the state of New York, Mrs. Mink zealously went to work to upbuild the order, and she served as executive in the local organization, and in her department a number of terms. The convention which elected her to the highest office also adopted resolutions advocating the introduction of patriotic teaching in the public schools, and as this was a subject very dear to her heart, she entered into it with all the strength of body and mind, and a grand foundation was laid upon which thousands of patriotic characters have been built. Mrs. Mink was the wife of Major C. E. Mink. She passed away at her home in Watertown, New York, December 3, 1896.

MRS. EMMA R. WALLACE.

Mrs. Emma R. Wallace, twelfth national president of the Woman's Relief Corps, came to the executive's chair fully equipped for the arduous duties of the office, for she had had many years of experience in her own department where she had filled all the chairs, and had been a wise counselor for years. She was saturated with patriotism, for she knew the hardships of the camp, the field, the hospital, having faced them all with her soldier husband when she went to the front a young wife to share the joys and sorrows of the one who had laid his life upon the altar of his country. She brought succor to the sick, and comfort to the dying, and her oldest child was born within sound of the guns, at Natchez. She had a fine judicial mind, and was always appealed to if a knotty question arose in any of the deliberations, and was sure to see the way out. She suffered an apoplectic stroke last year and after lingering, a patient sufferer, passed away in June, 1911, at her home in Chicago, Ill.

MRS. LIZABETH A. TURNER.

Mrs. Lizabeth A. Turner, thirteenth national president of the Woman's Relief Corps, casting aside the superstition of ages, accepted the nomination for national president upon a Friday, and was accorded an unusual honor, for her election was unanimous.

Great things were expected of this thirteenth president, for she was from the pioneer state in the work—the "mother of the order"—Massachusetts, and the twelve months which she served, justified the faith which had been put in her.

Mrs. Turner's home was in Boston. When she was not twenty she was left a widow, and the Civil War coming on while her heart was yet sore from bereavement, she gave her love and devotion to her country, and entered into the work of caring for the soldiers and their loved ones at home, with the same zeal which characterized the efforts of her after life. Before she went out of office, Andersonville Prison was given to the Woman's Relief Corps, to be cared for and made into a park. Mrs. Turner was unanimously chosen chairman of the Andersonville Board, and served faithfully, making the hard ground to be fruitful, and the desert of the stockade to blossom as the rose. She served as chairman of the board until her death, which occurred at Andersonville, while there in the discharge of her duty, April 27, 1907. She was beloved by every member of the order not only in Massachusetts, but all over the United States, and by the Grand Army as well. A beautiful monument at Andersonville has been erected by the Woman's Relief Corps as a testimonial to her worth and work.

MRS. AGNES HITT.

Mrs. Agnes Hitt, fourteenth national president of the Woman's Relief Corps, was born in Greencastle, Indiana, where her parents had removed from Kentucky several years before the war. They were prominent people, and the best folk of the state were visitors in the home, one of the oldest friends being War Governor Morton.

Mrs. Hitt's father and her only brother enlisted as soon as the call came for volunteers, and the father left an arm on the field before Richmond as a proof of his patriotism. Two years after the war the daughter was married to Major Wilber F. Hitt, who, when only twenty was assistant adjutant general of a brigade, and then for meritorious conduct on the field of battle, was brevetted captain and major. Mrs. Hitt is well known for her deeds of charity, and her work for patriotic teaching in the public schools. She and her soldier husband live in Indianapolis, Indiana.

MRS. SARAH J. MARTIN.

Mrs. Sarah J. Martin, fifteenth national president of the Woman's Relief Corps, was born in Wheeling, West Virginia, March 21, 1840. After her education was finished and just before the breaking out of the war, she met and loved George W. Martin, and soon the call to arms came and the boy lover enlisted in the 25th Ohio volunteers, and marched to "the front," with his sweetheart's promise as the beacon to guide him. At the battle of Gettysburg he lost his right arm, but that only bound his sweetheart the closer to him, for she saw that she was needed the more. He offered to release her, but she was faithful and true, and they were married October 24, 1865. They settled in Brookfield, Missouri, and here all her married life was spent. She was always interested in the old soldier and in the principles of patriotism. Nothing was too hard for her to do for her country or its defenders. She passed to her reward April 3, 1900.

MRS. FLO JAMISON MILLER.

Mrs. Flo Jamison Miller, sixteenth national president of the Woman's Relief Corps, came to the responsible office, one of the youngest who had ever presided over the National Organization. She was fitted for her duties by several years of service in her department. Zealous to an amazing degree, she saw the needs for a home for soldiers and soldiers' widows, and expended every effort in realizing the ambition of the women of the order, and rested not until their efforts were crowned with success. Mrs. Miller was among the first to carry patriotic teaching into the public schools, and failed not to speak and write upon the subject, in season and out of season. She is the efficient corresponding secretary of the National Council of Women of the United States, and thus is in touch with many thousands of patriotic and progressive women of this, the woman's century. Mrs. Miller is the daughter of Colonel W. H. Jamison, of Grant's old regiment, the 21st Illinois. Her home is in Wilmington, Delaware.

MRS. HARRIET J. BODGE.

Mrs. Harriet J. Bodge, seventeenth national president of the Woman's Relief Corps, came to the office fully prepared for its duties, and up to the mark in every way. From her earliest recollection she had breathed the air of patriotism, and she had further testified that she was loyal, by marrying one who, when his country called, responded at once, "Here!" She is of Puritan and Revolutionary stock, and her family have shown their patriotism by giving members to every war.

Mrs. Bodge's eldest brother served in the Mexican War, and her youngest in the Civil War. Mrs. Bodge, when Miss Woodward, assisted during the war in work through the Sanitary Commission, and she belonged to a society which antedates the Woman's Relief Corps, the Daughters of the Republic. In 1868 she married George R. Bodge who had served in the Twelfth Connecticut Regiment. Mrs. Bodge was born in Charlton, Massachusetts, but for many years she and Mr. Bodge have made their home in Hartford, Connecticut.

MRS. MARY L. CARR.

Mrs. Mary L. Carr, eighteenth national president of the Woman's Relief Corps, was born in Maine, but has lived for so many years among the towering rock-ribbed mountains of our Western land, that she seems "to the manner born" and partakes of their steadfastness, strength and purity. She was a charter member of the Woman's Relief Corps, and her interest in the order ·has never waned, but time and talents are fully consecrated to its objects. Mrs. Carr comes of loyal stock, and marriage to one of the nation's heroes only proves how deep rooted was her love of patriotism. Colonel Byron L. Carr enlisted the day Fort Sumter was fired upon and fought through the war and towards the last, indeed at the last, lost his right arm at Appomattox. Mrs. Carr is the widow of Colonel Carr. She has been a regular attendant at conventions ever since the National Woman's Relief Corps had its birth in Denver. She stands first when it comes to deciding judicial points. As an orator it would be hard to find her equal. Mrs. Carr lives at Longmont, Colorado.

MRS. CALISTA ROBINSON JONES.

Mrs. Calista Robinson Jones, nineteenth national president of the Woman's Relief Corps was teaching in Chicago when the Civil War broke out. To show her patriotism, she, with two other teachers, sat up all one night to make a flag to throw to the breeze the next day. When the banner was completed they raised it over their school, and so far as is known it was the first flag to be raised over a schoolhouse in Chicago, and perhaps in the state. All through those dark days, she worked with the various societies which had sprung up, and in every way possible showed her loyalty to her country and its defenders. From her entrance into the order which promoted her to its highest office, she worked for all its interests and was faithful in performing all its duties. Mrs. Jones made an excellent presiding officer. Her home is in Bradford, Vermont.

MRS. LODUSKY J. TAYLOR.

Mrs. Lodusky J. Taylor, twentieth national president of the Woman's Relief Corps, was the first to hold that office from the far Northwest. She came before the convention with all the members of Minnesota, both Woman's Relief Corps and Grand Army of the Republic endorsing her, and when she went out of office had lived up to the expectations of all her co-workers, and redeemed every pledge made at the beginning of the administration. Mrs. Taylor was born in Le Soeur, Minnesota, being the daughter of Mr. and Mrs. Patton, who were of New England Puritan stock, and were early pioneers of the North Star State. She has for many years been engaged in promulgating patriotic principles among the children of the schools of her own town and state. Mrs. Taylor lives in Le Soeur, Minnesota.

MRS. SARAH D. WINANS.

Mrs. Sarah D. Winans, twenty-first national president of the Woman's Relief Corps, came to her office fully prepared for her duties by years of ser-

23

vices in her department, and by work before that, for the veteran. From the beginning of the Civil War until its close, she had been assiduous in promoting the work of the Sanitary Commission, and in looking after the comfort of the soldier in the hospital, on the field, and in the camp. When the Woman's Relief Corps was organized, she found that her work was only begun, and that the field had widened, but her shoulder was to the wheel and she asked for no discharge. She made a splendid executive, and when her year was finished found that there was other and more sacred work to do. She was made a member of the Andersonville Prison Park Board, and when the chairmanship was made vacant by the death of Mrs. Turner, what more natural than that she should be asked to fill the vacancy, and right nobly has she fulfilled the trust. Last May 30th, it was her duty and privilege to present a monument and tablet (upon which are memorialized the history of the gift of the park to the Woman's Relief Corps, and their transfer of it to the United States Government) to Mrs. Belle C. Harris, national president of the Woman's Relief Corps, who in turn presented it to a representative of the Government, Captain Bryant. It stands within the stockade at Andersonville. Mrs. Winans is the daughter of a minister, and the wife of a soldier who carries the marks of battle upon his person. Their home is in Toledo, Ohio.

MRS. FANNY E. MINOT.

Mrs. Fanny E. Minot, twenty-second national president of the Woman's Relief Corps, is a native of Barnstead, New Hampshire, but when quite young removed with her parents to Concord, where she has since resided. She is descended from John Pickering, who went from Massachusetts to Portsmouth, N. H., as early as 1633, having originally emigrated from England. In 1874 Miss Pickering was married to James Minot, a veteran of the 140th New York Volunteers, and cashier in the Mechanics Bank in Concord. Mrs. Minot is interested in everything which tends to uplift humanity. She is a member of the Concord Woman's Club, a member of Rumford Chapter of the Daughters of the American Revolution, is much interested in literary and educational matters, and has for many years been officially connected with missionary and charitable organizations of the city. Her home is in Concord, New Hampshire.

MRS. ABBIE A. ADAMS.

Mrs. Abbie A. Adams, twenty-third national president of the National Woman's Relief Corps, came to the office full of honors which had been given her in her own department. She was the first national president which the state had ever had, and the organization had been hard at work in it for twenty-two years. Mrs. Adams made an excellent presiding officer, and there was growth along every line while she was in office. Mrs. Adams is the wife of a veteran, and from her patriotic ancestry, some of whom fought in the Revolutionary War, she became a member of the Daughters of the American Revolution. She is identified with many philanthropies, and is active in church work. An ideal wife and mother, she has such a fine system that everything goes on smoothly and nothing is neglected. Thoroughly imbued with the spirit of patriotism, she has by every means in her power, fostered patriotic teaching in the public schools. Mrs. Adams is a member of the Andersonville Board. Her home is in Superior, Nebraska.

MRS. CARRIE R. READ.

Mrs. Carrie R. Read, twenty-fourth national president of the Woman's Relief Corps, was elected to that office from St. Louis, Missouri, where for twenty odd years she had been identified with the work of the order, having from the first given it the preference over all others. Mrs. Read was born in Maryland. Her father was a minister and a loyal man, and when the soldiers were passing through Baltimore, did all in his power to help them. Her father's brother, Charles H. Richardson, was adjutant in the 9th Maryland Regiment.

During the St. Louis World's Fair, Mrs. Read was chairman of the Woman's Relief Corps Committee. During her administration the Woman's Relief Corps celebrated their silver anniversary by presenting $6,000 to the Grand Army of the Republic. For several years she had made her home in Washington, D. C.

MRS. KATE E. JONES.

Mrs. Kate E. Jones, twenty-fifth national president of the Woman's Relief Corps, had held a number of offices in the National Organization before she was elected to the highest. While she was national patriotic instructor, she worked so energetically, and to such good purpose, that all her assistants were enthused, and the patriotic work went forward with leaps and bounds. She was particularly interested in the preservation of Andersonville, and while she was national president the convention voted to present the beautiful park which the Woman's Relief Corps had made, to the United States Government, as a gift, free and unencumbered. Mrs. Jones was made chairman of the committee, and with the other members never rested until the transfer was made last year at Atlantic City, Congress previously having accepted the gift. Mrs. Jones is a poet, and writer of prose as well. Her home is in Ilion, New York.

MRS. MARY C. GILMAN.

Mrs. Mary C. Gilman, twenty-sixth national president of the Woman's Relief Corps, came to the convention which elected her enthusiastically endorsed by the Grand Army of her state, the Woman's Relief Corps of her state and by hundreds in other states. She had served her own department well and faithfully in minor offices, and in the highest within their gift. As a presiding officer she was unequaled. In the home-life she was without a peer, and in philanthropic work she was ever ready to do her whole duty. As her husband said of her, she had been his right arm ever since she had pledged her loyalty to him, and she was the moving power of the Woman's Relief Corps when she took upon her the responsibilities attached to the office of executive. Mrs. Gilman is the wife of Commander-in-Chief John E. Gilman of the Grand Army of the Republic, a veteran who left his right arm, when a mere boy, upon the bloody field of Gettysburg. Their home is in Boston, Massachusetts.

MRS. JENNIE IOWA BERRY.

Mrs. Jennie Iowa Berry, twenty-seventh national president of the Woman's Relief Corps, came to the executive's chair as one of the younger members of the order, but one who was born among patriotic surroundings, and whose earliest inspirations were those of loyalty to the old flag and our great country, for her father was a soldier, and her mother one of the patriots who kept the home embers aglow, while the breadwinner was fighting for his flag. As she grew, the spirit of her patriotic ancestors possessed her, and when womanhood crowned her, she united her fortunes with the organization which was pledged to care for the nation's defenders and to teach the children to emulate their example. Gifted with fluent speech, she was always ready when called upon to speak a word for the flag she loved, and for its defenders.

She had been honored by her own corps and department, and came to the highest office within the gift of the order, fully prepared to carry on the work which had been given her to do. "Advance" seemed to be the watchword, and truly did the order respond to their chieftain's voice. Mrs. Berry and her husband lived in Cedar Rapids, Iowa.

MRS. BELLE C. HARRIS.

Mrs. Belle C. Harris, twenty-eighth national president of the Woman's Relief Corps, had long been a worker in the order in the Sunflower State, and was well known in the national, when she was elected to fill the highest office within their gift. Nature endowed her with a voice of rare sweetness, and many times at convention, has she been heard in song, to the delight of all, and merited the sobriquet which her friends have bestowed upon her of "The sweet singer of Kansas." But not alone for this is she known. There are other things which appeal to the highest and best, and these she has in a rare degree—firmness, justice, executive ability, charity for all and loyalty to country, flag and friends. Mrs. Harris was born in Pennsylvania, and she married Charles Harris, who was a soldier from Iowa, and past commander of the Grand Army of the Republic, of Kansas. She is rounding out her silver anniversary as a member of the Woman's Relief Corps, and right nobly has she come up to every requirement in that time. At the Convention in Rochester, New York, over which she will this year preside, she will read a report which will go on record as one of the best which has ever been given, for everywhere in the order there are signs of new life and vigor, and the auxiliary of the Grand Army of the Republic is being crowned with the greatest honor and success, a membership almost 166,000 strong, a full treasury, with no liabilities, and having spent in relief since their organization more than three and a half millions of dollars, for the Civil War veterans and their dependent ones.

HANNAH R. COPE PLIMPTON.

Mrs. Hannah R. Cope Plimpton, Woman's Relief Corps worker, was born in Hanover, Ohio, June 30, 1841. She is in a direct line of descent from Oliver

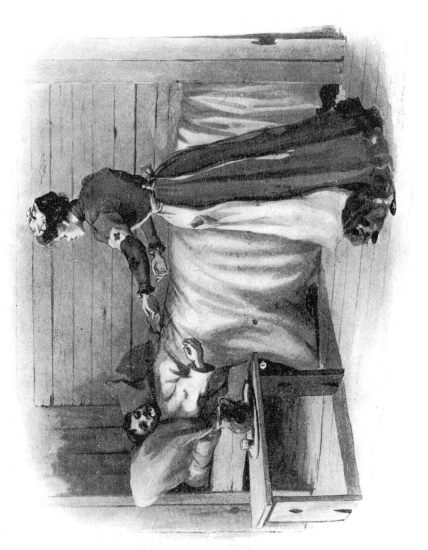

LOUISA MAY ALCOTT AS A HOSPITAL NURSE.

Cope, a Quaker who came to America with William Penn in 1662. After their marriage her parents immigrated to the then "Far West" or eastern Ohio, and Miss Cope became one of the teachers in the public schools of Cincinnati. It was during the spring of 1862, after the battle of Shiloh, when the wounded soldiers were sent up the Ohio River to Cincinnati, and the call was made for volunteers to help take care of them that she, with her mother, responded and did whatever was possible to minister to the needs of the sick and afflicted soldiers, providing such things as were needed in the improvised hospital. Many of the convalescent soldiers were taken into Miss Cope's home, until finally the old orphan asylum was secured and fitted up as comfortably as possible and called the Washington Park Military Hospital. After her marriage to Mr. Silas W. Plimpton, and removal to Iowa, she took an active part in temperance work serving as treasurer and secretary in various societies. At the institution of John A. Logan Corps, No. 56, in March, 1885, with Mrs. McHenry as its president, Mrs. Plimpton became her secretary. The following year Mrs. McHenry was elected as department president, and Mrs. Plimpton as department secretary. In December, 1889, Mrs. McHenry was elected conductor of the John A. Logan Corps and Mrs. Plimpton was her assistant. They both served in that capacity until the national convention held in Boston, in August, 1890, when Mrs. Plimpton was appointed national secretary of the Woman's Relief Corps. And for years she has continued to work for the interests of this patriotic order.

National Association of Army Nurses of the Civil War.

Introduction by Mary M. North.

Out of the throes of battle was born a heroism which fired the breasts of those who proudly wear a badge upon which are the mystic letters "N. A. A. N." and to which every veteran of the Civil War lifts his hat as to something high and sacred. The National Association of Army Nurses of the Civil War is an organization which is held in great esteem, and the badge is worn only by those who left home when "war waged her wide desolation," and braved the dangers of hospital, camp and battlefield, to minister to the wants, and relieve the sufferings of the boys who left home at their country s call and fell victims to the deadly fever, the terrible shot and shell, or some malady of the camp. Eternity alone will reveal how many lives were saved by these devoted women, who, when the mothers, wives or sweethearts were at home, took their places, and with tireless energy and sleepless vigilance, did all in their power to relieve suffering. If the fell destroyer could not be balked, then with the softest touch, the eyes were closed while the watcher thought of the ones at home who would mourn the boy who would never return. It is no wonder that the veteran lifts his hat in deference and reverence to these aged women, and perhaps his thoughts wander to the time, fast approaching, when both shall answer the last "roll call." Watch his eyes grow misty as he thinks of these women who relieved the tedium of the days of suffering and the nights of raving, when fever held him in a relentless clutch. These whispered words of encouragement and hope for the spirit, while also giving attention to the needs of the body. Many a time have their words helped weary ones to a better life. This little band, now numbering one hundred and eighteen, grows fewer as the years glide by, and soon the last one will have ended the march of this organization whose number cannot be increased, for theirs is an association which cannot be recruited. Many of the nurses belong to one or more of the patriotic organizations of women, but as theirs was a distinct work, so they should have a distinct organization. Seeing the need of this, Miss Dix, who had been in charge of the nurses during the war, called the survivors together in Washington, D. C., June 18, 1881, with the result that an organization was effected bearing the title of the Ex-Army Nurses' Association.

Miss Dix was elected president and served until her death, when Dr. Susan Edson was elected to the office and served until failing health compelled her to resign. She was followed by Miss Harriet Dame. The name first selected was changed as being too cumbersome and the name National Army Nurses' Association was chosen, which with a slight transformation is the one borne at present. The National Association was organized in Washington, in 1892, by Mrs. Addie L. Ballou and many others. Mrs. Ballou was elected president. Those who have served as president are: Mrs. Delia B. Fay, Mrs. Fanny Hazen, Miss Cornelia Hancock, Mrs. Ada Johnson, Mrs. Emile Wilson Woodley, Mrs. Clarissa Dye, Mrs. Margaret Hamilton, Mrs. Elizabeth Ewing, Mrs. Rebecca S. Smith and Mrs. Mary E. Robey Lacey, the present incumbent. To become a member of the association, tradition will not do, but there must be documentary proof that the applicant served as a nurse. She must have served at least three months as a regular or volunteer nurse, and her application must be approved by the nearest post of the Grand Army of the Republic. By Act of Congress, all nurses of the Civil War are entitled to burial in National Cemeteries, and several sleep in their "low green tents" in beautiful Arlington. The present officers are: National President, Mrs. Mary E. Lacey, Utah; Senior Vice-President, Mrs. Catherine L. Taylor, N. Y.; Junior Vice-President, Mrs. Hannah J. Starbird, Nev.; Treasurer, Mrs. Salome M. Stewart, Pa.; Chaplain, Miss Hannah U. Maxon, Ohio; deceased; Secretary, Miss Kate Scott, Pa., deceased; Conductor, Mrs. Mary E. Squire, Wis.; Guard, Mrs. Elizabeth Chapman, Ill.; Counselor, Mrs. Rebecca Smith, Minn.; Chief of Staff, Mrs. Lettie E. C. Buckley, Ill.; Surgeon, Dr. Nancy M. Hill, Iowa; Color Bearer, Mrs. Nancy Kripps, Pa. This is the tribute of Rose Terry Cook, to

The Army Nurse.

Give her the soldier's rite!
She fought the hardest fight;
Not in the storm of battle,
Where the drum's exultant rattle,
The onset's maddening yell,
The scream of shot and shell,
And the trumpet's clangor soaring

> Over the cannon's roaring,
> Thrilled every vein with fire,
> And combat's mad desire;
> She fought her fight alone,
> To the sound of dying groan;
> The sob of failing breath,
> The reveille of death;
> She faced the last of foes,
> The worst of mortal woes,
> The solitude of dying,
> The hearts for kindred crying;
> By the soldier's lonely bed
> In the midnight dark and dread,
> 'Mid the wounded and the dead,
> With lifeblood pouring red,
> The cries of woe and fear,
> Rending the watcher's ear,
> The hovering wings of death,
> Fluttered by dying breath,
> There was, her truthful eye,
> Her smile's sweet bravery,
> Her strong word to impart
> Peace to the fainting heart.

Army Nurses of the Civil War, 1861-1865.

Mrs. Mary (Roby) Lacey, president of the National Association of Army Nurses, was born in Plymouth, Massachusetts, and was married to John H. Roby, when only fifteen. Shortly after his marriage he enlisted in the First New Jersey Infantry. He was wounded at the battle of Cold Harbor, and Mrs. Roby took care of him at the United States General Hospital in Philadelphia. The most of her services were rendered in this hospital. Her husband died of his wounds soon after the war, and she later married John E. Lacey. She is now a widow and lives in Salt Lake City, Utah.

Mrs. Catherine L. Taylor, senior vice-president of the National Association of Army Nurses, served as a volunteer nurse from 1862 to 1865. She was for about three years at the United States General Hospital, Davids' Island, New York Harbor. Her home was at Dobbs' Ferry, and with her own team she carried supplies for the sick and wounded, also cared for many families, as well as sending supplies to the soldiers at the front. Mrs. Taylor's home is in New York City.

Mrs. Hannah Judkins Starbird, junior vice-president of the National Association of Army Nurses, enlisted as a nurse August, 1864. She was then Miss Judkins. She was at Carver Hospital, Washington, D. C., and at St. John's

College, Annapolis, where she remained until July '65. She nursed paroled prisoners from Libby, Andersonville and other Southern prisons, poor starved, vermin-infested men with little clothing. Mrs. Starbird lives in Los Angeles, California.

Miss Hannah U. Maxon, late national chaplain National Association of Army Nurses, nursed in the hospital in Gallipolis, Ohio, from the first of the war until its close. For nearly half a century she was a public school teacher in her native town, Gallipolis, and men and women in every walk in life, who came under her influence, call her "blessed." She died at her home, Gallipolis, Ohio, May 26, 1910.

Miss Kate M. Scott, late national secretary National Association of Army Nurses, in the spring of 1861-1862 was with the 105th Pennsylvania Regiment at Camp Jackson, Va., having volunteered in response to a call from Colonel Amos McKnight, for nurses for his soldiers, many of whom were dying from fever and pneumonia. Twice during the winter she, with her associate Miss Ellen Guffy, were quarantined, as the latter had the much dreaded disease. Miss Scott has been identified with the regiment since the war, and was their secretary from 1879-1891. She had been secretary of the army nurses since 1897. She died at her home, Brookville, Penn., in 1911.

Mrs. Salome M. Stewart, national treasurer of the National Association of Army Nurses, was a volunteer nurse, and is known to many who were wounded in the battle of Gettysburg as Miss Sallie Myers. During that battle her father's house was used as a hospital, and she cared for the men there, and at the Roman Catholic Church, the United Presbyterian Church and in Camp Letterman. Her services of three months were entirely voluntary. Her husband was a Presbyterian minister, who died in 1868 of injuries received in the service. He was the brother of a wounded man who died in her father's house. Mrs. Stewart was a teacher in the public schools before the war, has taught for twenty-five years, and is now a substitute teacher in the Gettysburg schools, where she has always resided. She was appointed one of the enumerators of the late census.

Mrs. Mary E. Squire, conductor, National Association of Army Nurses, as Miss Mary Emily Chamberlain, enlisted in Washington Hospital, Memphis, Tennessee, May, 1863, afterwards being transferred to the Officers' Hospital, and then going again to Washington Hospital. In 1861 she went to the Webster Hospital, where she remained until she left the service, June, 1864. Mrs. Squire is 67 years of age and lives in Sheboygan, Michigan.

Mrs. Elizabeth Chapman, guard of the National Association of Army Nurses, served as a volunteer nurse for three months, and then enlisted as a contract nurse, for the balance of the war. Her husband's regiment being in Memphis, and many of the men having measles, she was sent there to nurse them.

She was mustered out in Leighton House Hospital, Keokuk, Iowa, with an honorable discharge. Mrs. Chapman is 80 years of age. Her home is in East St. Louis, Ill.

Mrs. Addie L. Ballou, past national president of the Army Nurses, is a woman well known on the Pacific coast, as author, artist, lawyer and club woman. She is a woman of many talents and indomitable will, for when the earthquake and fire in San Francisco swept away her all, she heroically set to work with the spirit of a young woman to regain her home. At the beginning of the Civil War she offered her services to the Governor of Wisconsin, in which state she was living, and then began work as a nurse in camp of the 32nd Wisconsin regiment, where there were many sick. Later, Surgeon General Wolcott at Milwaukee, commissioned her, and she went with the regiment to Memphis, from there being sent with 255 sick soldiers to Keokuk, Iowa. Again in Memphis she nursed hundreds through a terrible epidemic. She is beloved by every member of the 32nd Wisconsin, and is affectionately referred to as "The Little Mother." She has written a book of poems, "Driftwood." Mrs. Ballou now resides in San Francisco, California.

Mrs. Margaret Hamilton, past president of the Army Nurses, was born in Rochester, New York, October 19, 1840. Her mother dying when the daughter was seventeen, she obtained her father's consent and became a sister of charity, and after due preparation was sent to teach in an orphan asylum in Albany. When the war broke out she wanted to nurse, but the lot did not fall to her until in the spring of 1862 when, with three other sisters, she was sent to Satterlea United States Hospital in Philadelphia, where she cared for the wounded sent up from Chickamauga. She served three years, during which time she fell in love with one of the wounded soldiers, a member of the 19th Maine Volunteers, and left the sisterhood to marry him. Her home life was ideal, and as wife and mother she was a model. Mrs. Hamilton is now a widow and resides in Wakefield, Massachusetts.

Mrs. Fanny Titus Hazen, past president of the Army Nurses, the granddaughter of a soldier of the Revolutionary Army, was born in Vershire, Vermont, May 2, 1840. As was the case with a number of others, when she applied to Miss Dix for an appointment, she was told that she was too young, but because she had two brothers, one seventeen and the other eighteen, in the service, she begged to be allowed to stay and was finally accepted and sent to Columbia Hospital, Washington, where she stayed until it closed, June 27, 1865. From the battle of Cold Harbor, Virginia, her youngest brother was brought to her wounded, and she nursed him until he recovered. Mrs. Hazen lives in Cambridge, Massachusetts.

Mrs. Clarissa F. Dye, past president of the Army Nurses, in 1862, was teaching, but devoted her vacation to field and hospital work in company with Miss Marie McClellan of Germantown, Pa. She was first sent on the steamer

Maine, then Miss Dix gave her a pass to Alexandria, Va. She reached the battlefield of Fredericksburg, ahead of all others, and did hard work among the wounded and dying. In 1863 she nursed in the Second Corps Hospital at Gettysburg, having charge of the Confederate wounded, and from there she went to Rappahannock, carrying supplies from friends in Germantown. She was then Miss Clarissa Jones. After the war she married Mr. John H. Dye of Philadelphia. She is now a widow over 78 years old, and receives no pension. Her home is in Germantown, Pa. Mrs. Dye says she is the only woman who received a medal of honor during the war.

Mrs. Rebecca S. Smith, past president of the Army Nurses, was teaching when an epidemic of diphtheria broke out among the soldiers in 1862. She at once offered her services, began to nurse them, and after that was continuously on duty on battlefields until 1864.

Miss Hannah L. Palmer, past secretary of the Army Nurses, was for nine months on duty at Columbia Hospital, Washington, under the direction of Miss Dix. She is now 84 years of age and resides at Conestoga, New York.

Mrs. Lettie E. Buckley, was enlisted by the Sanitary Commission under her maiden name, Lettie E. Covell, from October, 1863, to June, 1865, at Memphis. She served in hospitals in that Southern city and did excellent work. She is now 74 years of age. Her home is in Chicago, Illinois.

Mrs. Susanna Kripps enlisted in 1863, and served two years and six months. While nursing she was attacked by typhoid fever, which destroyed the hearing of her right ear. She was attended by Dr. Elliott, surgeon in charge of the hospital to which she was attached. She served with the 2nd Pennsylvania Heavy Artillery for five months, then in Capitol Hill Hospital, Washington, Jarvis Hospital, Baltimore, and Hough General Hospital, Alexandria, Virginia. Mrs. Kripps is 69 years old, and seldom misses a convention. She resides in Philadelphia, Pennsylvania.

Mrs. Mary C. Athow went out in February, 1864, as a volunteer nurse under Mrs. Annie Wittenmeyer, and served eighteen months to the close of the war. She was in hospitals at Knoxville, Tenn., Louivsille, Ky., and other places. Mrs. Athow is the widow of a veteran. She is 76 years of age. Her home is in Aurora, Ill.

Mrs. Mary A. Aston was living in Philadelphia when war was declared. Her husband being an invalid, and unable to serve his country, gave his consent for his wife to give as much of her time as possible to alleviating the distress of the sick and wounded in the hospitals of the city. She was a volunteer nurse from September 5, 1862, to August 11, 1865, and was only absent from duty in all that time, two weeks during her husband's last illness and death. Mrs. Aston became deaf by the explosion of a cannon while engaged in the performance of her duties. She is 77 years of age. Her home is in Philadelphia.

Mrs. Belle Alter was Miss Belle Thompson, and served as a volunteer nurse, beginning her work in the Taylor house, which was used as a hospital, in Winchester, Va., September, 1864 and was assigned to duty by the surgeon in charge, Dr. S. Sharpe. She assisted in caring for the wounded from Frohus Hill and Cedar Creek battlefields, until the middle of January, 1865, when she returned home with her brother who was badly wounded. He was Captain Thompson, Company A., 40th Pennsylvania Volunteers. He was a helpless cripple, and she nursed him the two years he lived. Mrs. Alter is 64 years of age, and her home is at Port Royal, Pennsylvania.

Mrs. Elizabeth Baldridge, as Miss Elizabeth Lee, served as a volunteer nurse at Memphis, Tennessee. Mrs. Baldridge is 78 years old, and lives in Pomona, California.

Mrs. Catherine M. Beck, served five months as a volunteer nurse at Fort Leavenworth, Kansas, at which place she was living. She is now 78 years of age and is living at Los Angeles, California.

Mrs. Mary E. Bell enlisted as a volunteer nurse, and her first work was at Covington, Kentucky, assisting her husband, who was in the medical department, in an epidemic of measles.
While the regiment was in camp, smallpox and spotted fever broke out. She also served in a hospital at Jeffersonville, Indiana. Her service extended over three years. She is 70 years old and lives in Albion, Michigan.

Mrs. Helen M. Burnell was a regular nurse under her maiden name of Helen M. Becket. She served two years and six months in the hospital at Memphis, Tenn. She is now 81 years of age. Her home is in Pasadena, California.

Mrs. Mary K. Boyington became a nurse through going to the field of Gettysburg to care for her wounded husband, who was a member of Company L. 105th Pennsylvania Volunteer Infantry. When he was sent to the hospital at York, she accompanied him, and was enrolled as a nurse, serving from July, 1863 to March, 1864, receiving the warm commendation of the surgeons for her services. She is 68 years old and lives in Carner, Okla.

Mrs. Nancy M. Brown, as Miss Nancy M. Nelson, was for eighteen months in West Hospital, Baltimore, and for two years at Gratiot Street Hospital Prison, St. Louis. With her husband after the war she lived in Ashtabula, Ohio, but since his death she has lived with her son in Washington, D. C. Her husband was a veteran. Mrs. Brown is 79 years old.

Mrs. Susan L. Brown was Miss Sue McLaughlin when she answered a call for volunteer nurses sent out by Governor Morton of Indiana. For the nine months she was on hospital boats on the Mississippi River and in hospitals in Memphis. She is very active in all patriotic work, and is the wife of S. C. Brown, past commander of the Grand Army of the Republic of Georgia. Mrs. Brown is 75 years of age and resides with her husband in Fitzgerald, Georgia.

Mrs. M. M. Briggs enlisted in 1861 under Miss Dix, and served for a year in hospitals in St. Louis, and then went to the newly established Harvey Hospital, at Madison, Wisconsin. Mrs. Harvey, wife of the Governor of Wisconsin, herself went to the south and brought from the fields and swamps, one hundred and thirty sick and wounded, and put them in this hospital, where they were tenderly cared for. Mrs. E. O. Gibson was in charge, and Mrs. Briggs' daughters were with her. Mrs. Briggs remained there until the war closed. She is now 91 and is spending her sunset days in the Old Peoples' Home, Elgin, Illinois.

Mrs. Jennie Matthewson Bullard enlisted as a volunteer nurse as Miss Jennie Smole. She afterward married a soldier, and changed her name to Matthewson. From October, 1861, to May, 1865, she served at Savannah, Memphis, Chicago, and Farmington, Miss. From October, 1861 to May, 1862, she was a volunteer nurse, and from the latter date to May, 1865, she was a regular nurse. Mrs. Bullard is 70 years of age. She resides at Desha, Ark.

Mrs. Bell Vorse Clark served from July, 1864, until the close of the war. Her first duty was in the General Hospital, No. 3, in Nashville, Tenn. She stayed at her post until the last man was removed in 1865. She is 77. Mrs. Clark resides in Lewisburg, Penna.

Mrs. Nannie M. Cochran was appointed matron and head nurse of the Simpson House Hospital, Keokuk, Iowa, by Major M. K. Taylor, and served there from November, 1863, until October, 1864. During her stay, there were treated from six hundred to eight hundred wounded. She is 68 years old and lives in Troy, New York.

Mrs. Sarah J. Dumas was Miss Sarah J. Steady, and her first work at nursing was at Sherburn Barracks Hospital, in Washington, D. C., February 14, 1865. She served until December of the same year, when her services being no longer needed, she returned to her home in Vermont.

Mrs. Annie Priscilla Erving (Cilla Zerbe) was a volunteer nurse commissioned by Governor Curtin. During 1861 and 1862 she served at Camp Curtin. While there she and three other nurses gave a picnic on Independence Island to raise money with which to get lint for the wounded. They raised $125. Mrs. Erving also nursed at Gettysburg. She is now 71 years of age. Her home is in Newberg, N. Y.

Mrs. Rebecca E. Frick served in hospitals in Washington, D. C.; Annapolis, Maryland; Winchester, City Point and Hampton Roads, Va. She was a regular nurse, and served two years and six months. She is 87 years old. Her home is in West Conshohocken, Pa.

Mrs. Mary Fryer Gardner, with Misses Scott, Guffy and Allen, served under Colonel McKnight with the 105th Pennsylvania, during the winter and spring of 1861-1862, at Camp Jameson, Va. There being too many for one hospital to accommodate, a division was made, and Miss Fryer and Miss Allen served together; thus they escaped being quarantined twice with smallpox as Miss Scott and Miss Duffy were. Mrs. Gardner is the widow of a veteran. She is 65 years old and resides in Philadelphia, Pa.

Miss Cornelia Hancock is as well known as any of the army nurses, and her service extended from July 6, 1863, to May 23, 1865. She was a volunteer nurse attached to the Second Army Corps of the Potomac. She was at Gettysburg, and so faithful that the soldiers called her the "Battlefield Angel." She remained in the field hospital until the establishment of Camp Letterman, where she worked for a few weeks. Before she left, the soldiers gave her a silver medal as an expression of their appreciation of her services. She is over 70, but as active as at 40. Her home is in Philadelphia, Pa.

Mrs. Julia A. Hibbard served from September 1, 1861, to April 29, 1864. After the battle of Shiloh she was on a floating hospital, serving afterwards in Memphis, Tenn., and in Paducah, Ky. Mrs. Hibbard resides in Peoria, Ill., and is 78 years of age.

Mrs. Joanna Melton was in the service from 1861 to 1864 as a volunteer nurse. She was at Camp Carrington, Lafayette, Indiana, and at Louisville, Ky. She is 76 years of age and resides in Salt Lake City, Utah.

Mrs. Susan Carrie Mills served under her maiden name, Carrie Robinson, for three months. She went to the front under Dr. Crosby, from Concord, N. H., in May, 1861. Her examination being all right, she was enrolled by Miss Dix, in Washington, D. C., and served for three months at Point of Rocks and Harpers Ferry, Va. Mrs. Mills is 71 years of age and resides in Haverhill, Mass.

Mrs. Fannie O. Jackson, as Miss Oslin, served fifteen months in field hospitals, Department of the Cumberland, at Resaca, Big Shanty, Centerville, Vinings Station and Lookout Mountain. She was a regular nurse. She is 76 years of age and lives in Olathe, Kansas.

Mrs. Lydia S. Johnson served from September, 1862, to July, 1865, and was through the epidemic of smallpox from 1863 to 1865. Was in Georgetown, D. C.; Alexandria, Chesapeake and Old Point Comfort, Va. She is 81 years old and lives in Lyndonville, N. Y.

Mrs. Lucy L. Kaiser, as Miss Campbell, served three years in Jefferson Barracks, Missouri, and on hospital steamers. She is 85 and lives in Leland, Michigan.

Mrs. Emeline D. (Tenney) Kingsbury enlisted under Colonel Cushman as a volunteer nurse in the 53rd Illinois Infantry, and served with that regiment until the close of the war. She was in Washington when President Lincoln was assassinated. She served fifteen months. Her home is in Hamilton, Texas.

Mrs. Sarah A. (Plummer) Lemmon was a volunteer in New York City hospitals, giving all of her time before and after school, and on Sundays and holidays. She is 75 years of age and resides in Oakland, California.

Mrs. Jennie (Gauslin) Maish lived in Winchester, Virginia, when the war came, and her father's house was turned into a hospital, which was supported by her own and her father's means. After General Milroy's defeat, she and several loyal ladies were sent to Richmond by Confederate orders, and confined in Castle Thunder. She married Mr. Lewis Maish, a Union soldier, during the war. She is 65 years of age and resides in Stillwater, Minnesota.

Mrs. Mary L. Mannon responded to the call of Governor Morton, of Indiana, in February, 1863, and went to Memphis, where she served until June 4, 1865. She was born in 1843 and resides in Los Angeles, California.

Mrs. Mary B. Maxfield left Peoria, Illinois, November 11, 1863, with the 6th Illinois Cavalry, for Springfield. From there to Paducah, Kentucky, then to Memphis, where she was transferred to Adams Block Hospital. For twenty-two months she served under her maiden name, Miss Kenny. She was commissioned by Mrs. Mary A. Livermore. She is 71 years of age and lives in Kansas City, Kansas.

Miss Adaline Miller served four years. She is 84 years of age and lives in Los Angeles, California.

Mrs. Maria Miller, as Miss Hoppe, served almost two years as a volunteer nurse. She is 64 and lives in Milan, Indiana.

Mrs. Rena L. Miner served as a regular nurse eighteen months.

Mrs. Matilda E. Morris served under Dr. D. W. Bliss in Washington, and also under Dr. Pancoast. She was at Winchester and nursed the wounded after Sheridan's great battle. She served three years. She is 76 years old and lives in Cleveland, Ohio.

Mrs. Jane M. Morton served one year in Nashville, Tennessee. She is 70 and lives in Elgin, Illinois.

Mrs. Mollie C. Mott, as Miss Carnahan, served two years as a volunteer nurse in Tennessee. She is 79 and lives in Elkhart, Indiana.

Mrs. Electa Willard was a volunteer nurse from 1861 until the close of the war. She served in Nashville, Chattanooga and Lookout Mountain, Tennessee. Much of her time was spent in distributing supplies at the front, and also in the various barracks. She is 83 and lives in Detroit, Michigan.

Mrs. Belle Counts served from 1864 to 1865 as a volunteer nurse. She is 71 years of age and lives in Troy, Ohio.

Mrs. Emily J. Cartwright, as Miss Avery, served two years in Cincinnati, Ohio. She is 80 years of age and lives in Brookline, Massachusetts.

Mrs. Clarissa Crossan was Miss Watters. She served two years in Keokuk, Iowa. She is 73 years of age. Her home is in Chicago, Illinois.

Mrs. Sarah B. Cross was born in England, but when her husband entered the service of the United States, she, too, volunteered and served as a nurse, side by side with him, one year and eight months in Lincoln General Hospital, Washington, D. C. She is 71 years of age and lives in Kent, Ohio.

Mrs. Frances D. Daniels was a volunteer nurse and served in hospitals in Vicksburg, Mississippi. She is 68 years of age.

Mrs. Frances A. Dieffenbacker volunteered at a call from Governor Morton, of Indiana, and went to Nashville, Tennessee, then to Murfreesboro, afterwards being detailed as regimental nurse for the 85th Indiana Regiment. She is 76 years of age and resides in Havana, Illinois.

Mrs. Maria O. Eldred, as Miss Olmstead, served over nine months at Falls Church, Virginia. She is 69 years old and resides in Canton, New York.

Mrs. Emily Elmer, then Miss Rowell, was the agent of Miss Dix for over a year, and served in hospitals in Tennessee and in Iowa. She is 70 years of age and resides in Hersey, Michigan.

Mrs. Elizabeth Grass was a regular nurse and served in Missouri and Indiana. She is 69 and lives in S. Fargo, North Dakota.

Mrs. Anna Hahn was a volunteer nurse and served three months. She is now 76 years old and resides in Omaha, Nebraska.

Mrs. Cornelia Harrington served as a volunteer nurse in Tennessee and Kentucky for five months. She is 79 and lives in Dexter, Michigan.

Mrs. Mary F. Hayden, as Miss Strahan, served in Washington, D. C., three months. She is 70 years of age and lives in Roxbury, Massachusetts.

Mrs. Margaret Hayes, who was Miss Maggie Meserolle, served two years and six months in hospitals in Memphis, Tennessee, as a regular nurse. She is 77 years of age and lives in Los Angeles, California.

Mrs. Lauretta H. Hoisington, as Miss Cutler, served thirteen months in hospitals in Chattanooga, Tennessee. She is 85 years of age and resides in Palo Alto, California.

Miss Elizabeth P. Hunt, as Miss Pickard, served three months in Keokuk, Iowa, then contracted smallpox and had to give up. She is 77 years old and resides in Tacoma, Washington.

Mrs. Emily E. (Wilson) Woodley was active in nursing during the cholera epidemic in Philadelphia, and when the war came on was ready for nursing the sick and wounded. She went to the front and enlisted May 29, 1861, and remained until May 26, 1865. She served on the field with the Army of the Potomac, and also in the West. She was lovingly called "Mother Wilson" by the soldiers. She passed away at her home in Philadelphia, May 15, 1908.

Mrs. Elizabeth Wendell Ewing, served from October, 1862, to September, 1863.

Miss Ada Johnson, served from August, 1861, to November, 1865, the longest of any. She was a teacher before the war, and afterwards she taught for thirty years in St. Louis.

Mrs. Delia A. B. Fay, served from the first of the war to the close, marching with her regiment into every battle, and caring for their wounded in the face of shot and shell. She afterwards nursed her blind veteran husband until he died.

Mrs. Anna H. Baker served in a Philadelphia hospital from September 5, 1862, to August 9, 1864.

Mrs. Henrietta S. T. Bunnell served throughout the war, having been commissioned by Governor Curtin, of Pennsylvania. She died in 1910, leaving six children. She had been the mother of twenty-one.

Mrs. Ruth Danforth served from July, 1864, to May, 1865.

Mrs. Mary Jane Fox served six months as a volunteer nurse.

Mrs. Elizabeth L. Fritcher served from July 9, 1862, to June 4, 1863.

24

Mrs. Ann Eliza Gridley, who died in 1909, was the mother of Civil War veterans and of Captain Charles V. Gridley, who was with Dewey at Manila Bay, and was one of the heroes of that battle. Her grandson was also in the navy and was killed by an explosion on his ship in Hampton Roads. Mrs. Gridley was a volunteer nurse with the Army of the Potomac, and served to the close of the war.

Miss Susan Ellen Marsh served nineteen months as a volunteer nurse in Armory Square Hospital, Washington, D. C.

Mrs. Elizabeth Augusta Russell was a volunteer nurse over four years in New York City hospitals.

Mrs. Emaline Phillips served one hundred and sixteen days in the Warren Regimental Hospital, Washington, D. C. She is 70 years of age.

Mrs. Rebecca L. Price, as Miss Pennypacker, served as a volunteer nurse. She did emergency work, going where there was work, and leaving when the need was over. She often carried supplies and books from her home in Phoenixville, Pa. She was also at Wind Mill Point Hospital, Va., Fort Monroe, Gettysburg and Chambersburg. She had a pass from Governor Curtin to go where she was needed. She is 73 years of age. Her home is in Lancaster, Pa.

Mrs. Mary A. Richardson served under her maiden name of Miss Mary A. Ransorn, and went to the hospital at Albany, N. Y., to help Dr. Armsby and Mary Carey, and was enlisted as a nurse by the former, June 2, 1862, serving there six months, when she went to Frederick, Maryland, also serving there six months. She was a regular nurse, serving until discharged, February 21, 1865. She is 76 years of age and resides with her husband at the Soldiers' Home, Vineland, N. J.

Mrs. Alice Carey Risley lived in the South and suffered untold hardships. Through many difficulties, she, then Miss Farmer, with her mother, Mrs. Phoebe Farmer, made her way to New Orleans and commenced the work of caring for the soldiers in Marine University, St. James and St. Louis Hospitals. Mr. Farmer having refused to vote for secession, was obliged to flee from home, and sought safety in New Orleans where his fate was unknown to his family, as they could receive no mail. Mrs. Farmer had been charged with being a spy, and Dick Taylor and his men threatened to hang her. One dark night she and her daughter left their beautiful home, and made their way to the dock, where they were taken aboard a steamer and locked in their cabin by the friendly captain, who landed them in Braspear City. Mrs. Risley served as a nurse from August, 1862, to September, 1865, and like many other devoted women, receives no pension. She is 66 years of age.

Mrs. Ann Maria B. Schram served as a volunteer nurse. Her husband had enlisted, and she, too, wished to serve her country, so the citizens of Amsterdam,

N. Y., assisted her to get to the front. She reported at Fredericksburg, and was assigned by Drs. McKenzie and Haynes to duty in camp outside the city to care for the sick and wounded brought there from South Mountain and Antietam. She served ten months, until her health was impaired by the exposure and hard work, and she was obliged to leave. She received no pay for her services, she says, and not even her board was provided. She receives a pension by special act of Congress. She is 77 years of age and resides in Albany, N. Y.

Mrs. Amanda B. Smythe served seven months. Her husband was in the army, and hearing that he was in the hospital at New Albany, Indiana, she took her year-old child and went to him. She found over three hundred sick and wounded in the hospital, and gave her time to caring for as many as she could. After the recovery of her husband, she went home, but he was afterwards wounded at the battle of Chickamauga, and is still suffering from the wound. They reside at Carrollton, Ohio. Mrs. Smythe is 71 years of age.

Mrs. Mary O. Stevens, as Miss Townsend, was five months at Seminary Hospital, Georgetown, Armory Square and Columbia, Washington, D. C. Mrs. Stevens is now 69 and lives in Peabody, Massachusetts.

Mrs. Annie Bell Stubbs, on account of her youth, was refused by Miss Dix, so she served for one year as a volunteer nurse, and after serving for a short time, because of her faithfulness and ability, Miss Dix sent her testimonials of the highest commendation. After the year was up, she enlisted as a regular nurse, and served over three years, in Harper's Ferry, Acquia Creek, 12th Corps Hospital and after Gettysburg, Chancellorsville and Nashville battles. She is 72 and lives in Merion, Pennsylvania.

Mrs. Helen Brainard Cole was a volunteer nurse in hospitals in Louisville, Washington, Memphis, Nashville and City Point. Mrs. Cole is 70 and resides in Sheboygan Falls, Wisconsin.

Mrs. Maria M. C. Richards was Miss Hall when she served from September, 1861, to May, 1865, as a nurse. She was in the Patent Office, Washington, on the James River transports and camps, in Smoketown Field Hospital after Antietam, and General Hospital, Annapolis, Maryland. She is 74 and resides in Weathersfield, Connecticut.

Mrs. Laura A. (Mount) Newman was, for three years, with her husband's regiment, the 6th Maryland, which was constantly marching or fighting. She was a volunteer nurse, is now 67 years of age and lives in Lafayette, Indiana.

Mrs. Elizabeth Nichols, in 1861, went to nurse her husband, who belonged to the 111th New York Infantry, and stayed with the regiment, and nursed smallpox, diphtheria, fevers and wounds until discharged with her husband. She is 76 and lives in Clyde, N. Y.

Mrs. Rebecca (Lemmon) Oleson was a volunteer nurse from November, 1862, to March, 1865, serving in Tennessee. She is 87 and lives in Sierraville, California.

Mrs. Rebecca Otis went to Missouri with her little son to visit her husband, and seeing how much they needed nurses, stayed on and helped, at the earnest solicitation of Dr. Allen. Her little boy was killed by a log rolling over him while at play, but she tried to drown her sorrow by more assiduous care for the sick and suffering. She continued nursing until the close of the war. She is 86 and resides at Manchester, Iowa.

Mrs. Sarepta C. (McNall) Patterson served for four years in all, as a volunteer. She is 76 and resides at Grand Junction, Colorado.

Mrs. Carrie (Wilkins) Pollard was engaged nearly two years in Tennessee, Kentucky, Indiana and on ships, having been sent out under Mrs. Wittenmyer. She is 68 and resides in Maxwell, California.

Mrs. Mary B. Pollock served as a volunteer nurse two years, mostly in South Carolina. She is 75 years old and resides in San Louis Obispo, California.

Mrs. Malinda A. (Miller) Pratt was seven months at Albany, Indiana, as a volunteer nurse. She is 76 and resides in Lincoln, Nebraska.

Mrs. Maria L. (Moore) Rathnell served over one year as a contract nurse in Camp Dennison, Ohio. She is 76 and lives in Bellefontaine, Ohio.

Mrs. Sarah M. Reading was a volunteer nurse over a year in the General Hospital, Davenport, Iowa. She is 70 and lives in Lowry City, Missouri.

Mrs. Emma A. (French) Sackett was a regular nurse in the hospital at Jeffersonville, Indiana, seven months and twenty-three days. She is 69 and lives in Winterset, Iowa.

Mrs. Mary E. (Webber) Smith served from 1862 to 1865 in Baltimore, Maryland. She is 68 and lives in Lowell, Massachusetts.

Mrs. Sarah J. (Milliken) Sprague served under Miss Dix from 1862 to 1864 in Washington, D. C. She is 82 and resides in Lynn, Massachusetts.

Mrs. Emily P. Spencer went to the front with her husband, who was surgeon of the 147th New York Infantry. She was in all the battles of the Army of the Potomac and was one of the first nurses to reach Gettysburg after the battle, where she remained for several weeks. She cared for General Sickles after he lost his limb. New York selected her as one of the heroines whose effigy in marble should be placed on the grand staircase in the Capitol at Albany.

She was wounded by a spent ball at City Point. The sciatic nerve was injured, and she was crippled for life. She is 92 and resides in Oswego, New York.

Mrs. Susannah Sprague served two years in Kansas as a volunteer nurse. She lives in Denver, Colorado.

Mrs. Cornelia M. (Tompkins) Stanley was commissioned by Miss Dix and served two years and one month in Tennessee and Missouri. ·She is 73 and lives in Gardena, California.

Mrs. Mary E. Stewart, then Mrs. Pearce, was the wife of the surgeon of the hospital in Madison, Indiana. At her own expense she went there and distributed supplies sent by the people of her home town in Ohio, and then nursed the sick, staying seven months in all, under direction of Colonel Grant, who was in charge of the hospital. She resides in Athens, Ohio.

Mrs. Sophia Stephenson served from 1861 to 1865 under Dr. Colham and Dr. B. F. Stephenson, in Ohio, Tennessee and Illinois. She is 75 years of age and lives in Winterset, Iowa.

Dr. Vesta M. Swartz, whose husband was assistant surgeon of the 100th Indiana Volunteers, was a regular nurse and served under Mrs. Wittenmyer for more than a year. She is now 70 years old and resides in Auburn, Indiana.

Mrs. Charlotte Marson Thompson was a volunteer nurse for a short time, then became a regular nurse with pay in Washington, D. C., serving one year. She is 72 and lives in Brodhead, Wisconsin.

Mrs. Pauline Thompson served in Kentucky and in Missouri. She lives in Berwyn, Illinois.

Miss Eliza L. Townsend was a volunteer nurse, serving in Baton Rouge, Louisiana, for eleven months. She is 79 and lives in Portland, Oregon.

Mrs. Laura R. (Cotton) Tyson answered a call for nurses sent out by the Citizens' Hospital, in Philadelphia, in 1862, and remained on duty until the close of the war. Mrs. Tyson is 76 and resides in Chelsea, Massachusetts.

Mrs. Susan (Mercer) Warnock was six months a volunteer nurse in Tennessee. She is 71 and lives in Lockington, Ohio.

Mrs. Lydia L. Whiteman served from the time sick men were left in Philadelphia at the beginning of the war, until the war closed. She relates that after the battle of the Wilderness, she saw a man who had been left for dead at the foot of a tree, and in spite of protests, took him up in the ambulance, and to the hospital and saved his life. He was Colonel Baxter. Mrs. Whiteman was under Miss Dix most of the time. She is 85 and lives in Philadelphia.

Mrs. Cynthia (Elbin) White served in Iowa hospitals for eight and a half months. She is 67 and lives in Lowry City, Missouri.

Mrs. Mary Eleanor Willson was three months a volunteer nurse under Miss Livermore, then was two years with the Army of the Cumberland in the field, in hospitals and on hospital boats on the Mississippi River. She resides in Westgate, California.

Mrs. Leonore (Smith) Wright was commissioned by Governor Morton, of Indiana. She served in Indiana and Tennessee. She is 80 and lives in Terre Haute, Indiana.

Mrs. Lucy A. (Newton) Young served in camps of Vermont soldiers as a volunteer nurse seven months. She is 69 and lives in Johnsbury, Vt.

Mrs. Emily Alder had two brothers in the army and her husband, whom she followed to the front as a nurse. She served six months and then on the Fort Donelson Battlefield was taken so seriously ill that, as the regiment was under marching orders, the surgeon gave her husband four days' leave to stay and see her die. She was spared to care for a disabled husband. She returned home after her illness. She is 71 and lives in Clarion, Iowa.

Mrs. Catherine H. (Griffith) Bengless served about nine months in Philadelphia. At the close of her service, she married Rev. J. D. Bengless, of Pawtucket, Rhode Island. Mrs. Bengless is 75 and resides in Ansonia, Connecticut.

Mrs. Sarah (Chamberlain) Eccleston served one year as volunteer nurse in Tennessee. After the war she became a kindergartner, and in 1868, was called to the Argentine Republic to found its first kindergarten and training school in the Government College, at Parana. Later she was transferred to Buenos Ayres, where she taught until retired on a pension from Argentina in 1904. She is 71 and still lives in the Argentine Republic.

Dr. Nancy M. Hill served in Armory Square Hospital, Washington, until 1865, then went to Dubuque, Iowa, where she settled. She is a native of Massachusetts, but now, at the age of 76, lives in Chicago, Illinois.

Susan E. (Hall) Barry, M.D., began her four years' work of service at Bull Run Battle, and then went wherever needed, finishing her work in Nashville, Tennessee. She had graduated in medicine before going in the army as a nurse. She served under Miss Dix. At the close of the war she married Robert L. Barry and went to Honolulu. She is 85 and lives in California.

Mrs. Rebecca E. Gray was, for two years, in hospitals, on battlefields and on transports. She is 70 and is blind and helpless. Her home is in Brooklyn, New York.

Mrs. Mary Adelaide (Daugherty) Jobes served a year in Tennessee hospitals. She is 71 and lives in Indianapolis, Indiana.

Miss Susan R. Lowell served nearly two years in Tennessee hospitals. She is 79 and lives in Topeka, Kansas.

Miss Adelia Leavitt was a volunteer nurse, serving six months in hospitals in Wisconsin. She is 69 and lives in Oconomawoc, Wisconsin.

Miss Mary A. E. Woodworth served as Miss Mary Keen, from July, 1861, to July, 1865. She was under Miss Dix and was in Georgetown, D. C., and Fort Monroe, Virginia. She is now living in Washington, D. C.

LELIA P. ROBY.

Mrs. Lelia P. Roby, philanthropist and founder of the Ladies of the Grand Army of the Republic, was born in Boston, Mass., December 25, 1848. She was descended from Priscilla Mullens and John Alden of the Mayflower Colony and many of her ancestors were among the revolutionary heroes. She, herself, acted as a regent of the Daughters of the American Revolution, and she has always felt a deep interest in the soldiers who fought in the Civil War. On the twelfth of June, 1886, in Chicago, Ill., she founded the order of the Ladies of the Grand Army of the Republic, which started with twenty-five members but which ten years later numbered fifteen thousand mothers, wives, sisters and daughters of soldiers and sailors who had served in the war of 1861-1865. The members were pledged to assist the Grand Army of the Republic in works of charity, to extend noble aid to brothers in sickness and distress, to aid sick soldiers and sailors and marines, to look after soldiers' orphans' homes and to see that the children received proper situations when they left the homes; to watch the schools and see that the children received proper education in the history of the country and in patriotism. Mrs. Roby's personal activities have covered a wide range and she has secured many pensions for soldiers—herself working long,

countless hours for the good of the survivors of the war. She
was one of four women selected by the Board of Education of
Chicago to represent them before the legislature of the state
to help pass the Compulsory Education Bill, and it was passed
through the fact that a large majority of the legislators were
old soldiers and their affection for Mrs. Roby made voting
for the measure she advocated a pleasant duty. She is the
only woman ever made a member of the Lincoln Guard of
Honor, of Springfield, Ill., an honor conferred on her through
General Sherman, "For her many acts of devotion to the
Martyred President's Memory." She became a member of the
Chicago Academy of Science, was vice-president of the
Women's National Press Association for Illinois, a member
of the Nineteenth Illinois Veteran Volunteer Infantry and also
joined the Society for the Advancement of Women, and the
American Society of Authors. She had the care and over-
sight of supplying the Soldiers' Homes with books and
magazines and periodicals, and she has constantly visited the
homes in various parts of the country, looking after the comfort
of the old soldiers, and when special legislation has been needed
to right their wrongs or give them additional comforts, she has
gone to the state legislatures and to Washington to secure such
enactment. Through her efforts a memorial day was set
apart in the schools for the reading of histories and stories of
the war in preparation for Decoration Day itself. She has
done a good deal of literary work under the pen name of "Miles
Standish," and she has published one large volume entitled
"Heartbeats of the Republic." America has hardly produced
a woman of better courage and patriotism.

MARY COLE WALLING.

Born in Pike County, Pennsylvania, June 19, 1838. She was descended
from the families of Stephen Cole, of Scotland, and Hannah Chase, of England.
During the Civil War she was known as the "Banished Heroine of the South."

Her parents made their home in Cass County, Illinois, where, in 1850, she married Captain F. C. Brookman, of St. Louis, Missouri, who died soon afterwards of yellow fever. Later she married C. A. Walling, of Texas. It is said that in 1863 she was warned by the Vigilance Committee to leave the country within a few hours. Seven of her brothers were in the Union Army, and all lost their lives. She delivered speeches through the North, and on May 10, 1866, the United States Senate passed a resolution permitting her to speak before that body, and there she delivered her argument on "Reconstruction."

HESTER A. DILLON.

Mrs. Hester A. Dillon, wife of Captain Elisha Dillon, is among the most active and patriotic women of the country. Her ancestry runs back many centuries, having been traced to Walgrinus Ridel, Earl of Angouleme and Perigord, a relative of Charles the Bald, King of France.

Her grandfather Ridlon (from Ridel) was in the War of 1812, and was an orderly to General Jackson, at New Orleans. He married a Virginia Davis. Her mother married J. R. Duncan.

Mrs. Dillon was born at Cincinnati, Ohio, October 6, 1845, and named Hester A. Duncan. She was married March 26, 1862, to Captain William J. Dillon, who fell at Shiloh, April 6, 1862. His regiment, the 18th, adopted Mrs. Dillon as its daughter. She is a member of the Methodist Episcopal Church, Woman's Christian Temperance Union and of the Self-culture Class of Benton, Illinois, her place of residence.

Women of the New South.

In her delightful "Reminiscences of a Long Life" Mrs. Sarah Pryor quotes a letter written by her husband, ex-judge Roger A. Pryor, in which occurred the following words: "When I renewed my oath of allegiance to the Union I did so in good faith and without reservation. But as I understand that oath it not only restrains me from acts of positive hostility to the government but pledges me to do my utmost for its welfare and stability. And, while I am more immediately concerned to see the South restored to its former prosperity I am anxious that the whole country may be reunited on the best of common interest and fraternal regard. And this object, it appears to me, can only be obtained by conceding to all classes the unrestricted rights guaranteed them by the laws and by obliterating as speedily and as entirely as possible the distinctions which have separated the North and South into hostile sections."

This letter was written from New York in 1867, and, of course, the rule of conduct outlined in the words here quoted was more difficult to follow when he declared them than it has been in later years. In general, however, it has been followed by all who served the Confederacy in high military and civic station.

And with the women no less than with the men the necessity of accepting the situation and of adjusting themselves to the new conditions made a powerful appeal. This was true of the women and the men who remained in the South, as well as those who immediately after the war sought the larger opportunity for a betterment of fortune which the wealthy and growing North and West offered.

The latter found means of helping the South of which at the outset they did not dream. In the book just named Mrs. Pryor mentions many instances of this sort in her own experience. From her wealthy New York neighbors she brought aid to many poor people, formerly of high position in the South, whom she met in that city. She served on committees which gave entertainments in New York for the endowment of scholarships in Washington and Lee University in Virginia; for the relief of yellow fever sufferers in Florida and Alabama; and for succor to the surviviors of the tidal wave which destroyed Galveston in 1900. But she did not find time to tell about any of this work in books until within the past few years.

The Southern states have produced and are producing many prominent women in all the great fields of activity. They have won a wide reputation for hard, conscientious, intelligent work. In the social scheme of the New South there are no Amelia Sedleys or Dora Spenlows. A great many of them have made their mark national and, some of them, international in literature. Their names—Mrs. Collier Willcox, Mrs. Dolly Williams Kirk, Mrs. Kate Slaughter McKinney, Miss Gertrude Smith, Mrs. Abby Meguire Roach, Mrs. Emma Bell Miles, Miss Maia Pettus, Mrs. Lawrence Turnbull, Mrs. Mary Ware, Miss Lafayette McLaws, Mrs. Ellen Chapeau, Mrs. Carolina Smith Mahoney and Miss Ella Howard Bryan and many others—confront us in the table of contents of the best magazines.

A large number of the writers of the most popular novels of recent times are Southern women. Among these are Miss Ellen Glasgow, Mrs. Amelia Rives Troubetzkoy, author of "The Quick and the Dead" and many other books which have a wide circulation; Mrs. Alice Hegan Rice, well known as the writer of "Mrs. Wiggs of the Cabbage Patch," "Lovey Mary" and many other tales; Mrs. Grace McGowan Cooke, Miss Margaret Prescott Montague, Mrs. Mary Finley Leonard, Mrs. Annie Booth McKinney, Miss Abbie Carter Goodloe, Mrs. George Madden Martin, and Mrs. Danske Dandridge. Mary Murfree who, under the pen-name of "Charles Egbert Craddock," has made every square mile of the mountains in her native Tennessee classic ground to writers of fiction of the higher order; Frances Courtney Baylor has done a similar service for the Blue Ridge and for many of the streams which have their sources in that range. Mrs. Howard Weedon, member of a family of slaveholders for several generations, in addition to her tales and poems on Southern subjects, is a painter of negroes, whose work has attracted wide attention. Mrs. Lucy Meachem Thurston has given us vivid glimpses of Virginia and other parts of the South Atlantic Seaboard. As an illustrator of her own and other novels, poems and sketches, Mrs. Louise Clarkson Whitelock is well known to a large circle of readers. The great-granddaughters of General Isaac

Shelby, the first Governor of Kentucky; Miss Eleanor Talbot Kinkead and Miss Elizabeth Shelby Kinkead are novelists and scholars of reputation, the latter also a lecturer on English literature.

In other branches of literature Southern women are also actively at work. A very good illustrator of that section's readiness and skill with the pen is given by Miss Mildred Lewis Rutherford in "The South in History and Literature," recently published. Miss Rutherford herself is an educator and a writer of educational works. Miss Grace Elizabeth King in her novels has written entertainingly of De Soto, Jean Baptiste Le Moine, founder of New Orleans, and other prominent characters in Southern history. Interesting lives of George Mason and Charles Carroll, of Carrollton, have been written by Miss Kate Mason Rowland. Miss Emily Virginia Mason (recently deceased) sister of John Thomas Mason, first Governor of Michigan, was the author of "Robert E. Lee," and wrote reminiscences of men and things in her native South. Miss Annie Maria Barnes is a well-known writer of histories and biographies, besides being a journalist and active religious worker.

In the intervals between her novels and plays Miss Sarah Barnwell Elliott has found time to write an occasional biography.

To the role of active women journalists the South has made many very creditable contributions. Among them are Miss Martha W. Austin, of New Orleans; Mrs. Sarah Beaumont Kennedy, of Memphis, widow of the late editor of the "Commercial Appeal" of that city; Miss Cally Ryland, of Richmond; Mrs. Annie Kendrick Walker, of Birmingham, Alabama; Mrs. Evelyn Scott Snead Barnett, of Louisville, and Mrs. Helen Pitkin Schertz, of New Orleans. All of these are also workers in other fields, and are prominent in the social life of their respective communities. Mrs. Mary Edwards Bryan, of

Atlanta, who has been on the editorial staff of several journals and magazines of the North and South, is a prolific writer for the leading magazines and the author of many novels, and is a member of several clubs in New York and in the South.

In Marion Harland's "Autobiography," published in 1910, occurred these words, "The idea of reviewing my life upon paper first came to me with the consciousness—which was almost a shock—that of all the authors still on active professional duty in our country I am the only one whose memory runs back to the stage of our national history which preceded the Civil War by a quarter century. I alone am left to tell of my own knowledge and experience when the old South was in debt and in trouble."

But Mrs. Terhune, who was born in Virginia in 1831, must have had a slight lapse of memory when she was penning these words, for Mrs. Pryor, who was born in Virginia in 1830, as already cited in this article, is a living writer, and Mrs. Ruth McEnery Stuart, novelist and clubwoman, who was born in Louisiana long before the Civil War, and who, as the widow of a cotton planter, remembers the old South, and though she has resided in New York in recent years, has been a factor of some influence in the building of the new South. Mrs. Virginia Carolina Clay Clopton, born in North Carolina in 1825, widow of Clement Claiborne Clay, of Alabama, and author of "Memories of Mrs. Clay, of Alabama," or "A Belle of the Fifties," is also still living. Mrs. Myrta Lockett Avary, who resided in Atlanta and who has been actively identified with settlement and charity work for many years, and has been contributor to many magazines and newspapers, and who knows a little of the old South from recollections, is the author of "A Virginia Girl in the Civil War" and "Dixie After the War," and has edited "A Diary from Dixie" and "Letters and Recollections of Alexander H. Stevens." The daughter of Louis T. Wigfall, of

Texas, a senator of the United States and of the Confederacy, wrote a book a few years ago entitled "A Southern Girl in '61," which was widely read.   This is Mrs. Louise Sophie Wigfall Wright, and she resides in Baltimore.   Mrs. Mary Anna Jackson, widow of "Stonewall" Jackson, the distinguished Confederate general author of the "Memoirs" of her husband, was living in Charlotte, North Carolina, until recently.   She, too, like all the other ladies mentioned here, has been prominent in the progressive movements along all lines in the New South. In active educational work, in an executive capacity and as teachers many Southern women are conspicuous.   Miss Julia S. Tutwiler, the president of the Alabama Normal College, at Livingston, was also an active worker in prison reform. Mainly through her efforts the University of Alabama has been opened to the girls of that state.   She is author also of many songs used in Alabama's public schools.   Mrs. Elizabeth Buford, of Nashville, Tenn., is the founder and regent of the Buford College, of that city, and has been connected with other educational institutions of the South.   Mrs. Kate Waller Barrett, of Alexandria, Va., is a well-known sociologist, and is president of the Florence Crittenden Mission, in Washington, D. C.   Miss Mary Kendrick is at the head of the faculty of Sweet Briar College, in the Virginia town of that name.   At Herndon, in that same state, Miss Virginia Castleman is in charge of the music department of the Herndon Seminary, and is the author of many excellent works for young people.   The librarian of the Carnegie Library in Nashville, Tennessee, is Miss Mary Hannah Johnson, who has also organized other libraries in the South.   Among others in the long list of educators in many fields are Miss Margaret Warner Morley, of Tryon, North Carolina; Miss Florence Rena Sabin and Miss Lida Le Tall, of Baltimore; Miss Myra Geraldine Gross, of Emmitsburg, Maryland; Miss Frances Ninno Green and Miss Eliza Frances Ambrose, of Montgomery, Alabama.

In the agricultural field women rarely distinguish themselves. Mrs. Virginia Anne King, however, of Greenville, Texas, has one of the largest stock farms in the world, extending into two or three of the counties of large area of that state, and comprises many ranges and farms, some of them under a high state of cultivation. She has to have many men in her employ. Her name seldom appears in the newspapers, but she is recognized as an important factor in the development of her state and of the Southwest.

Through the "Daughters of the Confederacy" and other orders of this class the women of the South have been doing much for the upbuilding of their localities. In the many national organizations like the "Daughters of the American Revolution" and its twin, the "Colonial Dames," "Daughters of Signers of the Declaration" and many religious and temperance societies of the Southern members have associated themselves with those of the whole country, and have contributed toward making the South better appreciated in the North, and thus minimized sectional passions and tragedies. A strong venture in the same direction is the "Mount Vernon Association," which was founded in 1856, and which, necessarily, includes Southern and Northern women.

Among the Southern women who have been conspicuous in these orders are: Miss Amelia Cunningham, of South Carolina; Mrs. Lizzie Henderson, of Greenwood, Miss.; Mrs. Annie Booth McKinney, of Knoxville, Tenn.; Mrs. Roger Pryor, already mentioned, Mrs. Lawson Peel, of Atlanta; Mrs. Rebecca Calhoun Pickens Bacon, of Charleston; Mrs. Cornelia Branch Stone, of Galveston; Mrs. Andrew W. Dowdell, of Opelika, Alabama; Mrs. George H. Wilson, of Louisville, and Mrs. R. C. Cooley, of Jacksonville, Fla. In the work of reunion Mrs. Virginia Frazer Boyle, of Memphis, novelist, poet and clubwoman, has written "Odes of Jefferson Davis and Abraham Lincoln."

Says Mrs. Myrta Lockett Avary, "True to her past, the South is not living in it. A wonderful future is before her. She is richer than the whole United States at the beginning of the War of Secession. She is the land of balm and bloom and bird songs, of the hand and the open door." In the aggregation of this spirit of hopefulness, courage and progressiveness of the New South the women have indeed been a powerful influence.

SARAH C. ACHESON.

Mrs. Sarah C. Acheson, public-spirited woman of Texas, should be remembered as gratefully by that state as are her ancestors by the nation at large. She was descended on the paternal side from English and Dutch families, who settled in Virginia, 1600, and on the maternal side from Colonel George Morgan, who had charge of Indian affairs under Washington with headquarters at Fort Pitt, and of whom Jefferson in a letter still in possession of the family says, "He first gave me notice of the mad project of that day"—meaning the Aaron Burr treason. Among Mrs. Acheson's ancestors should be mentioned Colonel William Duane, of Philadelphia, editor of the Philadelphia "Aurora" during the Revolution. Mrs. Acheson's girlhood was spent in Washington, Pennsylvania, where she was born February 20, 1844. And there, in 1863, she was married to Captain Acheson, then on General Myer's staff, the marriage taking place when the captain was on furlough with a gunshot wound in the face. He left for the front ten days after, encouraged by his young wife. Doctor and Mrs. Acheson moved to Texas in 1872, and during their residence there Mrs. Acheson has been a moral force, her influence being strongly felt, not only in the city where she resides, but throughout the state. Texas with all the blows which have come to its welfare is a place to bring out heroic deed. Mrs. Acheson has displayed spirit of a kind that the world seldom sees. When a cyclone struck the village of Savoy many of its inhabitants were badly wounded, some were killed, others made homeless. But Mrs. Acheson reached them as speedily as train could take her and she acted as nurse and as special provider for the suffering. She gave three years of active service to the Woman's Christian Temperance Union, and she was state president at a time when a strong leader was greatly needed to guide their bark into a haven of financial safety. The world's progress in social, scientific and religious reform is not only an open but a well-read book to her, and in the evening of her long active life she has become an ardent worker for woman's suffrage.

MARY B. POPPENHEIM.

Miss Mary B. Poppenheim was born in Charleston, S. C., of South Carolina ancestry for six generations on both sides, her forebears having migrated to South Carolina from Bavaria and Ireland prior to the American Revolution.

She was graduated from Vassar College with the Bachelor of Arts degree in 1888, holding the position of vice-president of the entire student body and president of the Art Club at the time of her graduation. Miss Poppenheim made a special study of American History at Vassar College under the direction of Professor Lucy Salmon. Miss Poppenheim organized the Historical Department of the South Carolina Division of the United Daughters of the Confederacy and was historian from 1899-1905, resigning to become state president of the South Carolina Division of the United Daughters of the Confederacy, which office she held from 1905-1907 (limit of term). When historian of the South Carolina Division of the United Daughters of the Confederacy she was one of the compilers and editors of "South Carolina Women in the Confederacy," 2 vols., published by the South Carolina Division of the United Daughters of the Confederacy in 1903 and 1907. Miss Poppenheim was historian of the Charleston Chapter of the United Division of the Confederacy for three years, and was also a member of the Historical Committee of the United Daughters of the Confederacy for three years. She is a charter member of the Vassar Alumnæ Historical Society and was one of the first five women to become members of the South Carolina Historical Society, of which she has been a member since 1899. Miss Poppenheim is chairman of the General United Daughters of the Confederacy Education Committee (organization representing 50,000 women) serving a third term, and also chairman of the South Carolina Division of the United Daughters of the Confederacy Committee, and member of the Board of Directors of the Charleston Chapter of the United Daughters of the Confederacy.

Miss Poppenheim is the literary editor of "The Keystone," the official organ of the club women, and the Daughters of the Confederacy of Virginia, North Carolina, South Carolina, Mississippi and Florida, which position she has held since the establishment of "The Keystone," June, 1899.

Miss Poppenheim organized the Intercollegiate Club of South Carolina, 1899, and has been its president ever since. She is a member of the Ladies' Benevolent Society (organized 1813) and has been its recording secretary since 1896.

A member of the Rebecca Motte Chapter, Daughters of the American Revolution.

A charter member of the South Eastern Branch, Vassar Alumnæ Association.

A charter member of the Vassar Alumnæ Historical Society.

A charter member of the Century Club.

A charter member of the Civic Club.

A charter member of the South Carolina Audubon Society.

A charter member of the Young Women's Christian Association.

On the Board of the Ladies' Memorial Society and Woman's Exchange.

She holds membership in all of these now. Miss Poppenheim was chairman of the Literature Committee of the General Federation of Women's Clubs 1906-1908, and was in charge of the Literature Session of the Boston Biennial.

Miss Poppenheim has written for various magazines along historical lines and has traveled extensively in Europe.

Introduction to Club Section.

BY MRS. C. M. SEVERANCE, "THE MOTHER OF CLUBS."

BELOVED CLUB-WOMEN OF THE COUNTRY:

I rejoice heartily at being in touch with each and all of you, through this friendly introduction—you, who not having seen en masse, I love with sincere regard and affection.

I rejoice unceasingly in the ever-growing acceptance of your new opportunities and duties and in the superb outlook for your future. One of my favorite prophecies is that nothing is impossible to organized womanhood united in aim and effort.

My faith in woman became so great that my zeal took flame, and led me into the early effort toward making my enchanted dream come true on reaching my "Mecca" at Boston in 1855. I felt there best could such a dream come true— as Bronson Alcott assented on his visits to Cleveland, before our family removed to Boston—with the warning, however, that it would not be easy to gather the literary and progressive women from their various circled suburbs and churches. But the hope was still hidden in a warm corner of my heart, and after the Civil War had made many of these women friends and co-workers, who had served their country and homes as valiantly and at as great cost, in sending their husbands and sons to the chances of the battlefield, as their brothers!

The time then seemed ripe for the new venture of comradeship and service through organization. This comradeship and service had hitherto been exercised in efforts outside the home—only in the various sewing circles, Dorcas Societies, study classes and the like—covering some one single, definite purpose; but the idea of discussion and action upon the broader lines of civic interests vitally affecting the home, developed in the organization of the New England Woman's Club—the first in this country—at Boston, in 1868. The Sorosis, at New York, on somewhat the same lines, being founded almost simultaneously, as a result of the refusal of the Men's Press Club to recognize the Women's Press Club of that city on the visit of Dickens to this country. Our well-known and zealous friend, Kate Field, of New York, author and journalist, had visited Boston, and reported our organization as already founded there.

The title of "Mother of Clubs" given to the little book compiled by a sympathetic friend, who had sifted the data and felt warranted in using the title, has been somewhat challenged; but the facts and the records given by Mrs. Croly, in her "History of the Club Movement in America," are its justification; and the innumerable heartfelt acknowledgments by pen and voice of the uplift of club life are a precious benediction to me, and recall the poet's lines:

"What I long to be and was not, comforts me."

Faithfully yours,

(Signed) Madame C. M. Severance.

To the Well-Beloved and Honored Clara Barton.

My Civic Creed.

(In Outline.)

"New occasions teach new duties,
Time makes ancient good uncouth;
We must ever up and onward,
Who would keep abreast of Truth!"

"Governments derive their just powers from
the consent of the governed."

"Taxation without representation is tyranny."

"For the long workday,—
For the taxes we pay,—
For the laws we obey,—
We want something to say,—
By the ballot way,
And without delay!"

"Nothing is impossible to Organized
Womanhood,—united in aim and effort!"

"Why prayest thou on altar stairs
For God to do His will?
Thou art His instrument; go forth,
And thine own wish fulfill.

Till
"The war drums beat no longer,
And the battle flags are furled
In the Parliament of man—the
Federation of the world!"

"Two beside the hearth,
Two in the tangled business of the world—
Self reverencing and reverencing each."

"Love (including justice and peace) is the fulfilling of the
Law."

The Golden Rule is the Biblical and the common sense
panacea for our social ills.

(Signed)   MADAME C. M. SEVERANCE.

Endorsement

FROM MRS. C. M. SEVERANCE.

I honor most heartily the loyalty to womanhood which has prompted our friend, Mrs. John A. Logan, to undertake this chronicle, at the cost of so much strength and energy.

The women who have come into prominence as rulers have had their due records in history—the women of unusual charm, beauty or wit—and woman, as a class, has been sung by the poets from time immemorial. But the achievements of these other women have not been sympathetically recorded—the woman who has given to the world sons whom she nurtured for useful citizenship—given even with heartbreak to the risks of the battlefield which she abhorred; and yielded the daughters of her tenderest love and companionship to the risks of another's ownership and protection, thus serving the state in these invaluable and indispensable ways.

These women are at last seeking the ballot, as the badge of citizenship, and the needed protection of the home and the beloved children when leaving her care for the outside world—so often made cruel under the present competitive system. These women have had mention, but have been suspected and shunned for taking these practical steps towards the broader helpfulness. But let us be of good cheer! Woman is rapidly coming into her fuller heritage, thanks to the braver chronicler, such as Mrs. Logan.

(Signed)   MADAME C. M. SEVERANCE.

Federation of Women's Clubs.

This organization represents 850,000 members. No other organization of women in the world represents such a powerful and active militant movement for social betterment. The

Sorosis of New York and the Woman's Club of Boston have long been rivals in their claim of being the oldest organization in the United States. Each was founded in 1868, but it has been decided that the Ladies' Library Society, of Kalamazoo, Michigan, deserves this honor. It was founded in 1852, and the Minerva Club, of New Harmony, Indiana, was organized in 1859. The Sorosis, however, was the leader of the federation movement and is responsible for broadening the scope of women's club work. The first biennial convention of the General Federation of Women's Clubs was held in Philadelphia, in 1894. Every state in the Union has its state federation, and there are to-day organizations in the Canal Zone and our insular possessions. Almost every one of the five thousand clubs has taken up some measure of active interest. The subject of home economics has been one of the principal issues for club work throughout the United States. Perhaps no other organization in the country represents a greater force for good than the General Federation of Women's Clubs.

Women's Clubs in Cincinnati.

After the Centennial in Philadelphia, in 1876, a few Cincinnati women, enthused by that exhibition of artistic beauty, created a sentiment which resulted in the foundation of the Art Museum Association of Cincinnati, whose object was to bring together collections of art and to form classes in art and handicraft. Ten years later the Art Museum arose in Eden Park, the fruition of continuous and enthusiastic endeavor of a few women who were capable of being inspired, and who possessed the ability and devotion necessary to inspire others.

After the World's Fair in Chicago, Cincinnati women who took an active part in furnishing and the administration of the Woman's Building, came home and were influential in the organization, almost simultaneously, of the Cincinnati Women's Club and the Cincinnati Symphony Orchestral Association. To-day, the club with several hundred members, is the proud possessor of the first Women's Club House in Ohio, whose every line of architecture and decoration expresses the refined taste and broad culture of its members. The Symphony Orchestra is the pride of Ohio as well as Cincinnati.

Arts and Crafts.

About 1893, Mr. Ralph Radcliffe-Whitehead, a wealthy Englishman, who had been a friend of Ruskin, and intimately associated with English arts and crafts leaders, conceived the idea of founding in America an arts and crafts village, in hope of doing something toward making American life less restless, less self-conscious, and less ugly. With this end in view, he bought about 1,200 acres of land on the southern slope of the Catskills, in the town of Woodstock, New York, and christened this tract "Byrdcliffe," and invited all those who desired to carry on artistic pursuits, and at the same time live simply, to come and live in the simple houses which he had built on this tract. Here was established a library, an assembly, a metal shop, and nearly a score of other buildings to be used as studios, shops, boarding houses, and residences. "Byrdcliffe" has produced a distinct type of hand-made decorative furniture. They have done some good metal work and rug weaving. This colony was repeated in the one established in July, 1901, called the Rose Valley Association, chartered as a stock company, with a capital of $25,000, for the purpose of encouraging the manufacture of such articles involving artistic handicraft, as are used in the finishing, decorating, and furnishing of houses. A property was purchased called Rose Valley, located along Ridley Creek, near the city of Moylan, about a dozen miles

392 Part Taken by Women in American History

southwest of Philadelphia, consisting of about eighty acres, which when purchased, was occupied by ruined stone mills and quaint, deserted houses. The mill was transformed into a shop for the making of furniture, and this shop was opened in the spring of 1902. The Rose Valley Association does not manufacture, but extends an invitation and offers an opportunity to accredited craftsmen to work in its shops, under the patronage of its emblem, the emblem to be systematically stamped upon its products, and would be the association's guarantee that the workman has conformed in every item to competent, mechanical, and artistic standards. The Rose Valley furniture is always honest, and often beautiful. Carving is freely indulged in. The aim of this association is to prove that useful things need not be clumsy, and that beautiful things need not be fragile. Hand-weaving, metal-working, book-binding and pottery-making have been practiced at Rose Valley. At old Marblehead, Massachusetts, there is another community established by Dr. Herbert J. Hall, a nerve specialist of this old New England town, who holds the theory that the surest remedy for nerves and invalidism is the practice of a manual occupation which is both useful and aesthetic. These convictions led him to the equipping along the water front of a group of handicraft buildings in which his patients may work. Here artists in clay and ceramics come and some excellent work in silver, precious, and semi-precious stones and enamel has also been done. Artists in oil have gathered about here. Other associations of a similar character have been established in East Ravenswood, Illinois; Syracuse, New York, and East Aurora, New York, and the number of arts and crafts summer schools is rapidly becoming legion. Among the women who have taken an active part in this work may be mentioned, Mrs. Albee, of Pequaket, New Hampshire, and Crawfordville, Indiana; Mr. and Mrs. Douglass Volk, at Center Lovell, Maine; Susan

Chester Lyman, at the log cabin settlement, near Asheville, North Carolina; Mrs. Van Briggle, Miss Laughlin (the two latter being porcelain workers), and Ellen Gates Starr, the noted bookbinder.

The Home Culture Clubs.

Fifteen years ago the university extension movement aroused institutions everywhere to send their teachers out among the people to direct their reading and help them in every way toward mental advancement. Three years before the unversity extension movement, there was organized in Philadelphia an experiment which had its beginning in western Massachusetts. This is what is known as The Home Culture Club. Northampton offered an unusual setting for this enterprise, being a long established New England town, dignified, and always ready for anything in the line of education. Its location especially offered this, being within a radius of a few miles of the best educational institutions of the country—Smith College, said to be the largest woman's college in the world; Mount Holyoke with a long and honorable history; Amherst, one of the best of the smaller colleges; Williston Seminary; the Byrnham School; the Clark Institute for Deaf Mutes, and the New Agricultural College of Northampton. Here Mr. George W. Cable found a most favorable environment when he came from the South to make his home in the North in 1885. With his well-known reputation in literature and intense interest in social and industrial problems, he began to look about for what was most needed in his new neighborhood. He concluded that what had been most detrimental to the rapid progress of democracy was class distinction. In any private effort to elevate the masses of this country, at least, class treatment is out of the question. In breaking down these class distinctions, Mr. Cable proposed to call the home into immediate requisition, and he repeatedly said, "The private home is the public hope," and it was his idea to make the home the beginning and the end of his philosophy of popular education. In the autumn of 1887 he brought a few of his friends together and submitted for discussion a scheme for the organization of a Home Culture Club in every home that would consent, the club to consist of the members of the family and of such neighbors as would come to a weekly meeting in one home or another to read and talk together. From discussion, he went to action, and during the first year there were twenty of these clubs in successful operation in Northampton. A public reading room was opened at a central point to give men and boys habitually on the street a glimpse, at least, of a rudimentary home. Casual reading began to turn into serious study, and classes were formed under direction of the Smith College students, who have always been Mr. Cable's constant helpers. These clubs multiplied throughout the state, and in 1898 they numbered throughout the land ninety-one, and the membership was six hundred and fifty, with a total attendance of nearly fifteen thousand. Since then they have been rapidly increased. Some of them are self-supporting, and some have been the recipients of generous donations from philanthropic people.

Both in the business and educational conduct of the Northampton clubs, Mr. Cable has had almost from the first the valuable help of Mrs. Adelaide Moffatt, the general secretary. At least once a year she visits all the club members in their homes, takes a personal interest in their attendance and keeping up their interest in the work. She has been assisted by a great number of women from Smith College and a council of one hundred and twenty-five women residents of Northampton. Mr. Carnegie generously donated fifty thousand dollars toward the erection of the club house for this work. But while these substantial gifts have come from men, the actual carrying on of this splendid work has been entirely done by women, largely college women, throughout the country, and is only another of the many different avenues of work along educational lines being conducted in this country by our women.

The Washington Travel Club.

The Washington Travel Club was organized in the Strathmore Arms—the home of Mary S. Lockwood, in January, 1880. Judge Lysander Hill, Frank Eastman, Mrs. Sara Dean, Miss Emily Brigham and Mary S. Lockwood, arranged for the first meeting. The officers were to be a "guide," to preside at the meetings; a "courier," whose duty it was to secure speakers and readers; a "journalist," to keep a record of their travels, and an "executive committee" to form the itinerary and choose the subjects for papers, and a music committee. One notable feature of the club in its organization was the determination to have no exercises of a miscellaneous character—no recitations, reading, declarations, or literary fireworks of any kind.

Every Monday night during the winter months, for sixteen years, this club was sustained with unflagging interest. Different countries were selected from year to year, papers read and the addresses given upon all subjects connected with the chosen country.

The home of this club was historic inasmuch as it had been the home of many distinguished people: General and Mrs. John A. Logan, Senator Edmunds, Judge Harlan, Senator Ingalls, Senator Farwell, Governor Boutwell, Thomas B. Reed, Governor Carpenter, of Iowa, Judge Ezra B. Taylor,

Senator Fry, of Maine, and hosts of others, including members and senators.

Among the noted people who entertained the club with instructive papers through these years were: General Logan, George Kennan, Olive Logan, Senor Romero, Dr. Chickering, Hon. A. R. Spofford, Hon. and Mrs. John W. Foster, Mrs. J. C. Burrows, Dr. Charles Knight, Dr. Gregory, Dr. Presbery, Judge Hayden, Professor Burgess, Mr. Fox, Minister to Russia and scores of the literary lights belonging to the club and Washington.

The club's first journeys were through Egypt, where they traveled from near and from far without carriage or car. They went up the Nile, through the plains of Palestine, over the hills of Judea, among the Pyramids of Egypt and into the buried cites of Persia. They were given a fair understanding of the geography, biography, government, military, art, religion, literature, ornamental and practical art, common people and history of the country through which they traveled.

One of the first papers presented while the club was in Egypt was by the late General John A. Logan, upon military art in that country. It was wonderful in research, beautiful in expression and abounded in interesting data. When asked where he got all his information he replied. "I have had no book in my hand but the Bible."

Such experiences only whetted the appetites of the travelers, and the executive committee, guide, and courier then planned the trip for "around the world," which was carried out.

The Woman's National Press Association.

The Woman's National Press Association is the oldest organization of its kind in the world and one of the earliest of women's clubs. The Association is national having members in nearly every state in the Union; also in England and the Philippine Islands.

The first president was Mrs. Emily Briggs, "Olivia." At the close of her term Mrs. M. D. Lincoln was made president, followed by Mary S. Lockwood, Mrs. Hannah B. Sperry, Mrs. E. S. Cromwell, Mrs. Belva A. Lockwood and Mrs. Peeler. The club has a membership of over one hundred. It has had such names among its members as Mrs. Lippincott, "Grace Greenwood"; Miss Mary F. Foster; Mrs. E. M. S. Marble; Mrs. Clara B. Colby; Mrs. E. D. N. Southworth; Mrs. Olive Logan; Miss Clara Barton. Prominent speakers have addressed the association including such names as Hon. Theodore Roosevelt; Dr. William T. Powell, Geologist; Charles M. Pepper; Dr. Sheldon Jackson; C. K. Berryman, Cartoonist; Lillian Whiting; the late Professor Wm. Harkness; Professor Robert T. Hill; Dr. B. L. Whitman; Hon. Frank Mondell; Frank G. Carpenter; Ainsworth R. Spofford; Mrs. May Wright Sewall; Mrs. Ellen M. Henrotin; members of the United States Congress and many prominent journalists. In December, 1894, the Woman's National Press Association issued the call for the formation of a federated organization of Women's Clubs in the District of Columbia.

The Woman's National Rivers and Harbors Congress.

By Mary M. North.

The Woman's National Rivers and Harbors Congress is as truly a patriotic organization as any that exists, for it is built upon the never-dying principle of love of country. The organization came into existence through the efforts of a few women in Shreveport, Louisiana, June 29, 1908. Three women of that city were made officers, Mrs. Hoyle Tomkies, president; Mrs. Frances Shuttleworth, recording secretary, and Mrs. A. B. Avery, corresponding secretary. The object of the organization, which works hand in hand with that of The National Rivers and Harbors Congress, fostered by the leading men of the nation, is to secure for our posterity the conservation of all our natural resources, and in particular to preserve and develop two of the greatest, waterways and forests, for it has been said by an eminent scientist, "no forests, no rivers."

The number of members at the time of organization was seven, and in about a year there was enrolled through individual and club membership, more than twenty-two thousand, and this because the object of the association is so vital. At the first convention held in Washington, D. C., which had a fine representation, The National Rivers and Harbors Congress' Bill was endorsed, which called for an annual appropriation from Congress of fifty million dollars for ten years for waterway improvement, instead of a wasteful policy of appropriating small sums biennially for this purpose. The Woman's National Rivers and Harbors Congress is having conservation taught in the public schools.

At the meeting held last December, in Washington, D. C., the following officers were elected to serve two years: President, Mrs. A. Barton Miller, Charleston, S. C.; First Vice-President, Mrs. Herbert Knox Smith, Washington, D. C.; Second Vice-President, Mrs. F. H. Newell, Washington, D. C.; Corresponding Secretary, Mrs. Elmer G. Laurence, Cincinnati, Ohio; Recording Secretary, Mrs. Mary M. North, Snow Hill, Maryland; Treasurer, Mrs. William Brison, Muscogee, Oklahoma; Auditor, Mrs. H. R. Whiteside, Louisville, Ky.; Vice-Presidents-at-large, Mrs. Hoyle Tomkies, Shreveport, La.; Mrs. E. A. Housman, Brookfield Center, Conn.; Mrs. de B. Randolph Keim, Reading, Pennsylvania.

Alabama:
Mrs. J. W. Hunter,
619 Lauderdale St., Selma.

Arkansas:
Mrs. Marshall H. Patterson,
Augusta.

California:
Mrs. Lovell White,
2245 Sacramento St., San Francisco.

Colorado:
Mrs. D. W. Collins, Pueblo.

Delaware:
Mrs. Geo. W. Marshall, Milford.

Hawaii:
Mrs. B. J. Dillingham,
Honolulu.

Idaho:
Mrs. E. C. Atwood, Hailey.

Illinois:
Mrs. Fred Bowes,
1542 Adams St., West, Chicago.

Indiana:
Mrs. Virginia Sharpe-Patterson,
505 E. Mulberry St., Kokomo.

Kentucky:
Miss Mary Lafon,
1337 Fourth St., Louisville.

Maine:
Mrs. Joseph M. Strout,
83 Pleasant Ave., Portland.

Maryland:
Mrs. Emma D. Crockett,
Pocomoke City.

Massachusetts:
Mrs. Theodore C. Bates,
29 Harvard, Worcester.

Missouri:
Mrs. John H. Curran,
816 Wright Building, St. Louis.

New Jersey:
Mrs. J. E. Sudderley,
11 Columbia Ave., Arlington.

New Hampshire:
Mrs. J. H. Dearborn,
Suncock.

New York:
Mrs. William Cumming Story,
119 E. 19th St., New York City.

North Dakota:
Mrs. J. J. Robson,
Langdon.

North Carolina:
Mrs. E. J. Hale,
Fayetteville.

Oklahoma:
Mrs. Lilah D. Lindsay,
Tulsa.

Oregon:
Mrs. Robert Lutke,
301 N. 24th St., Portland.

Ohio:
Mrs. J. F. Ellison,
2327 Ashland Ave., Cincinnati.

Pennsylvania:
Mrs. Thomas M. Rees,
225 Negley Ave., Pittsburgh.

Rhode Island:
Mrs. Richard Jackson Barker,
The Outlook, Tiverton.

South Carolina:
Mrs. Reid Whitford,
164 Rutledge St., Charleston.

South Dakota:
Miss Marjorie M. Breeden,
910 Euclid St., Pierre.

Tennessee:
Mrs. Eugene Crutcher,
817 Lischey Ave., Nashville.

Texas:
Mrs. J. W. Dosemus,
Bryan.

Virginia:
Miss Katharine Stuart,
719 King St., Alexandria.

Washington:
Mrs. Charles B. Dunning,
1238 South Wall Street, Spokane.

West Virginia:
Mrs. Guy R. C. Allen,
Wheeling.

"The organization has for its object the development of the meritorious waterways and harbors, the preservation of the forests, and the conservation of all the natural resources of the nation. It stands for the establishment by the Federal Government of a definite waterway policy for the improvement of all approved rivers and harbors of the entire country, also for the adoption of such a policy as will secure not only forest reserves, but general forest development." The slogan is "Together for Permanent National Welfare."

Bunker Hill Monument Association.

To women the credit is due for the preservation of historical homes, marking of historical spots, and the completion of many of the works started to commemorate deeds of heroism. Among these should be mentioned the completion of the Bunker Hill Monument. In 1823 the Bunker Hill Monument Association was incorporated and this ended the efforts for this work for two years; then the cornerstone was laid while General Lafayette was on a visit to this country. The material was brought from a granite quarry in Quincy and a railroad had to be built for this purpose—the first in the United States. In 1828 the funds for the work were exhausted and the work stopped, not to be resumed until 1834, and again suspended for lack of funds. In 1839 two gentlemen—Amos Lawrence, of Boston, and Judah Truro, of New Orleans—offered $10,000 if a similar amount would be raised by others. This enlisted the interest and pride of the women of Boston, who proposed to get up a fair for this purpose. The fair was decided upon and was to be held in Quincy Hall, September 5, 1840, and every woman in America was invited to aid, or contribute her work or money. These patriotic women of Boston managed the entire scheme and were rewarded by realizing $30,035.50, and from other sources money came to the association through these women until $55,153.27 was in the treasury of the association and the completion of the monument assured, and to these women we owe Bunker Hill Monument.

JENNIE CUNNINGHAM CROLY.

Mrs. Croly was born in Leicestershire, England, December 19, 1831. Her father, the Reverend Joseph Howes Cunningham, brought his family to the United States when Jennie was about nine years old. The latter was a precocious child and early showed her literary trend in little plays written in childhood. Her first production that was published appeared in the New York Tribune. Her taste for journalism grew rapidly and she filled many important positions on various of the New York newspapers for many years. Her pen name was "Jenny June." Her activity was remarkable and she extended her work to a number of the magazines. She edited and controlled many publications for a great number of years. Early in life she became the wife of David B. Croly, then city editor of the New York Herald, later managing editor of the New York World, and subsequently editor of the Daily Graphic. In all of these publications Mrs. Croly collaborated with her husband. In March, 1868, Mrs. Croly, "Fanny Fern," Alice and Phoebe Cary, Mrs. Charlotte B. Wilbour, Miss Kate Field, Mrs. Henry M. Field, Mrs. Botta and other women met in Mrs. Croly's home in New York and started the famous Sorosis with twelve charter members. This was one of the pioneer women's clubs of America and to Mrs. Croly should be given the credit of its inception. She served for fourteen years as its president. She was among those calling the Woman's Congress in New York in 1866, and again in 1869. She was a member of the New York Academy of Sciences, of the Goethe Club, and vice-president of the Association for the Advancement of the Medical Education of Women. Her home was for many years a center of attraction for authors, artists, actors and cultured persons. Her writings, which continued until her death in 1901, would fill many volumes.

MRS. PHILIP N. MOORE.

The president-general of the Federation of Women's Clubs was born in Rockford, Illinois, and educated at Vassar College, at which institution she pursued a full mathematical and scientific course. The years from 1876 to 1879 she spent in travel and study abroad. Since her marriage she has resided in Kentucky and Missouri. She has been connected and actively interested in the St. Louis Training School for Nurses; is a member of the board of directors of the Providence Association and chairman of their district nurse work from its inception. She is vice-president of the St. Louis School of Philanthropy; is a charter member of the Wednesday Club, and was president of the Missouri Federation from 1901 to 1905; was first vice-president of the General Federation of Women's Clubs from 1904 to 1908. She is intensely interested in the musical growth of St. Louis and assisted in the formation of the Musical Club which brings to St. Louis the best artists in every line and is also devoted to the interests of a larger musical organization, the St. Louis Symphony Society, in which she is an active worker. She has been president of the National Federation of Musical Clubs. Mrs. Moore holds all educational influences to be of the greatest importance; from 1903 to 1907 she was president of the Association of Collegiate Alumnæ and one of the three alumnæ trustees of Vassar College. She was appointed by the board of lady managers of the Louisiana Purchase Exposition, a member of the Superior Jury in which International Jury of Awards the right of membership was given for the first time to a representative of women. A woman of liberal culture and extensive information, she has wielded a large influence in various spheres of women's work. With quiet force and dignity she combines great executive ability and is an effective worker in every movement with which she is identified. She was elected president of the General Federation of Women's Clubs at their meeting, June 1908, in Boston. She traveled extensively in the interests of the federation going even to Panama to visit the clubs of the Canal Zone Federation.

MRS LAWRENCE MAXWELL.

Was born and educated at Ann Arbor, Michigan, meeting her husband, Mr. Maxwell, at the university. Mrs. Maxwell is an ex-president of the Cincinnati clubs and largely identified with the musical interests of Cincinnati. For seven years she has been president of the board of managers of the Widows' and Old Men's Home. Mrs. Maxwell was president of the local biennial board of Cincinnati when the meeting of the General Federation was held in that city in 1911. The success of this board is due largely to the uniform tact and courtesy of Mrs. Maxwell, whose wide club and social experience has been felt not only in Cincinnati but throughout the state. Mrs. Maxwell has a broad view of life and its duties, believing that a woman must prepare herself to reign in her home while dispensing the courtesies and sharing the enjoyments of social life, yet, she still must give a large share of time, strength and interest to the betterment of humanity.

MRS. EDWARD L. BUCHWALTER.

Mrs. Edward L. Buchwalter is one of the best-known club women in the country. She has been identified with the General Federation since the beginning and has attended every biennial. She was born in Ohio but her interests pertaining to women's clubs know no state lines. In 1898 Mrs. Buchwalter was elected a director of the General Federation, serving two terms. She was chairman of the Milwaukee biennial program committee, which for advanced thought has not been surpassed by any biennial program; here civil service reform and the responsibility of women as consumers were first discussed. Mrs. Buchwalter was chairman of the Los Angeles Convention; was a vice-president of the board of lady managers of the Louisiana Purchase Expedition. In 1904 she was elected president of the Ohio Federation, which she had been instrumental in organizing. She has been president of the Springfield Woman's Club. Gifted with a remarkable memory, quick to recognize merit, more critical of herself than others, tireless in her effort to advance the club movement, Mrs Buchwalter plans and executes with the same enthusiasm which has not waned in her twenty years' service.

MRS. ADDISON F. BROOMHALL.

Was elected president of the Ohio Federation in 1909. She has been a worker in the Federation since its organization; has served her state as treasurer,

Federation secretary and chairman of the Convention Advisory Committee. She has been active in library work and for two years was chairman of the Library Extension Committee of the General Federation. Mrs. Broomhall's husband is one of the most brilliant lawyers in Ohio.

MRS. CHARLES H. KUMLER.

Mrs. Charles H. Kumler is a member of the Industrial and Child Labor Committee of the Federation of Women's Clubs; has been active in this line of work for many years, taking a special interest in the organization and development of Noonday Clubs in factories where young women are employed. She did much to create sentiment favoring the regulation of child labor in Ohio. Aside from her club interests she is a well-known collector of antiques and possesses one of the most valuable and varied collections.

MRS. PHILIP CARPENTER.

Mrs. Philip Carpenter, of New York, was born at Rainbow, Connecticut, educated in Mills College, California, and New York University Law School. She is an ex-president of the New York State Federation, president of Sorosis, president of Women Lawyers' Club of New York City, and ex-president of the National Society of New England Women. She was the second woman lawyer to appear in the New York Court of Appeals, and the first to win anything there.

HANNAH KENT SCHOFF.

Mrs. Fredric Schoff, president of the National Congress of Mothers, is the daughter of Thomas Kent of England and Fanny Leonard Schoff of Bridgewater, Massachusetts. Mrs. Schoff is the mother of seven children, and until they were past babyhood she was in no way interested in outside work. She has been president of the National Congress of Mothers almost since its organization, being elected to succeed Mrs. Theodore W. Birney who, together with Mrs. Phoebe A. Hearst, was the founder of the organization. She is also a member of the Society of Mayflower Descendants, Daughters of the American Revolution, New Century Club, Philadelphia, National Education Association, Religious Education Association and the Pennsylvania Juvenile Court and Probation Association.

Mrs. Schoff's interest was aroused in behalf of children from reading of a young child eight years of age being sentenced at the criminal court for burning up the house in which she lived, because she wanted to see the flames, and the engines run. It seemed so dreadful to Mrs. Schoff that she determined to see if there was not something that could be done for these baby criminals, or what was better, do something for the mothers of these babies to aid them in learning their responsibilities as mothers. The first juvenile court in Pennsylvania was held in Philadelphia, June 14, 1901. Mrs. Schoff attended this court. Having previously been appointed probation officer she had investigated the condition of juvenile criminals in Pennsylvania. She found that the state had two reformatories, one in the western and one in the eastern part of the state. There was also a reformatory for boys over sixteen years of age, at Huntington, Pennsylvania.

She found, in the two reformatories, sixteen hundred children comprising waifs, homeless little ones and children accused of the most serious crimes. Men and women contracting second marriages made use of this opportunity to get rid of their existing families and the children, innocent and helpless, were sent to associate with boys and girls of sixteen and eighteen years. Little children were tried in the criminal courts, kept waiting in the cages for criminals, which also housed men and women steeped in crime. There are five hundred children ranging in age from six to sixteen years of age in the Philadelphia County prison, and the same thing existed in every county in the state. There were from two to three hundred children passing through the station houses every month and these were at the mercy of the presiding judge.

Mrs. Schoff appealed to the New Century Club of Philadelphia, presenting the facts she had gathered, which naturally shocked every member of the club. They made haste to organize committees and to urge further investigation as to the conditions affecting children in Philadelphia. Patterning after other states, they succeeded in securing a juvenile court with its merciful provisions and its just judge. While absorbed in this work, Mrs. Schoff became enthusiastic in her work for the betterment of all minors, whether they belonged to the criminal or other classes who were likely to be subjected to demoralizing influences. It would make a volume to describe the work of Mrs. Schoff and her associates. They applied to the National Congress for material and information and made such a thorough investigation of existing laws and the policy of the government and the practice of the courts that the president of the United States heartily approved of the work that had been done. Following this action Mrs. Schoff applied to the National Congress of Mothers to take up this as a special work, believing that the active interest of every auxiliary of the National Congress of Mothers in every community would accomplish more by educating the parents and looking after the children than could be done in any other way.

The present officers of the National Organization are:

Mrs. Frederic Schoff, president.
Mrs. Arthur A. Birney, secretary.
Mrs. W. B. Ferguson, treasurer.

Vice-presidents:

Mrs. David O. Mears.
Mrs. Orville T. Bright.
Mrs. Fred T. Dubois.
Mrs. Edwin R. Weeks.
Mrs. Ray Rushton.

Historian:

Mrs. E. A. Tuttle.

Recording secretary:

Mrs. James S. Bolton.

These ladies, together with the following list of active members of the organization, have done prodigious work in every state in the Union. Mrs.

William T. Carter, of Philadelphia; Mrs. Joseph P. Mumford, of Philadelphia; Mrs. William J. Thacher, of New Jersey; Mrs. Frank De Garmo, of St. Louis; Mrs. B. H. Stapleton, of Mississippi and Miss Sophie B. Wright, of New Orleans. There are many more noble women all over the country, who deserve mention as earnest, effective workers in this holy cause, whom the editor must omit for want of space in this volume.

Mrs. Schoff has been the inspiration of the vital reforms which have been achieved through her leadership and marvelous executive ability.

MRS. S. J. WRIGHT.

President Texas Federation of Women's Clubs 1909-1911.

Mrs. Samuel Johnston Wright (Ione Hervey Wright) is descended, through her maternal grandmother, from a long line of Anglican clergymen—Lord Bishop Hervey of the Court of Henry VIII being the first, descendants of whom coming to America and Virginia in the early days of our country, became Presbyterian ministers.

Mrs. Wright—a woman of high ideals and one who works zealously for the cause not for self aggrandizement—came to Paris, Texas, in 1883 from Leavenworth, Kansas, as the young bride of Captain S. J. Wright, a member of one of the most prominent and influential families of Lamar and Red River Counties, and by her gracious manner and charming personality won friends readily, while her great administrative ability was early recognized. She was elected president of the first Chautauqua Circle organized in Paris, and continued in office for four years till graduating from this Circle in 1894. When the Ladies Auxiliary of the Young Women's Christian Association was founded Mrs. Wright was unanimously made president. She was a charter member of the Lotus Club and has been elected to the highest offices within the gift of this club. In 1903, she was the Lotus president and when the City Federation was formed was chosen president, and by her unfailingly good spirit and agreeable manner of impressing her views, soon made this organization effective for the good of her town. She is now an honorary member of the Twentieth Century Club and an active member of the Quill Club, where only original manuscripts are read and accepted. Not only has Mrs. Wright's home town recognized and appreciated her literary and executive ability, but she has been appointed by several of the state presidents on various important committees, as well as elected to different offices of the State Federation. While a member of the Art Committee during Mrs. Pennybacker's presidency, she gave public art lectures at the different ward schools and aroused great interest in the pictures of the Traveling Art Gallery. As chairman of the Art Committee under Mrs. E. P. Turner she visited by invitation, the adjoining towns, giving lectures on art and creating a widespread interest in the pictures sent out by the Federation. Mrs. Wright gave great impetus to the work of the third district as its president during Mrs. Cone Johnson's administration, and originated in her district the Educational Loan Fund which has so materially aided ambitious young girls. She did effective work as first vice-president with Mrs. Dibrell as president.

Mrs. Wright's varied club experience makes her a strong and most acceptable state president, who keeps in close touch with all the work and advances all good movements. Her address, always dignified and imposing, is courteous; though reserved she is approachable; she is found always in sympathy with every phase of the work which tends to the education, elevation and greater happiness of all mankind.

The impetus given all branches of Federation endeavor during her administration has been evidenced by the large attendance at the district meetings, the excellent reports rendered and the number of new clubs applying for admittance. Mrs. Wright was the first state president to give special attention to the moral and physical welfare of children. In her open letter to club women announcing her candidacy she said:

"This is the century of the child, and thinking, active women are making this more true each succeeding year. What we club women have accomplished along educational lines needs no reviewing here; our work is fostering manual and industrial training in the public schools, and for the founding of free kindergartens throughout the state; our aid in the passage of the Juvenile Court Bill, and in the establishment of an Industrial Training School for Incorrigibles—all of these demonstrate our lines of action favoring the mental, manual and spiritual training of the child. Our fine record made in the cause of parks and school grounds proves our desire for the physical welfare of the child. But we do more. Therefore, club women of Texas, while my plan for the direction of our efforts during the next administration, would, of course, include the accomplishment of any work outlined by preceding administrations and as yet uncompleted, it would also include special endeavor as is the visible outgrowth of what has already been undertaken and which is essential to the highest ideals of our organization—to my mind this directs us to the spread of the gospel of moral and physical training for the child."

At the district meetings all her addresses were on the subject "Present Purposes of the Texas Federation," varying it as the needs of each seemed to require, but always bringing out the thought that her administration stands not only for the perfect and symmetrical education of the child, which means development of brain, hand and heart, but also for social development through the social centre movement, which constitutes the one decidedly new Federation issue for 1909-1911. This movement proposes that the schoolhouse, especially in rural districts, be used as a social centre, becoming the club house, the library, the forum of the community, thus assembling together many of those otherwise isolated, or with no recreative horizon.

Mrs. Wright's administration will be remembered as the one which, through its influence was successful in the passing of an adequate "Child Labor Law" for Texas. Mrs. Wright declares, however, that child idleness is as great a menace to civilization as is Child Labor, and the Federation is now working toward an optional compulsory educational law, the same embodying the industrial feature, as under present conditions in Texas is the only solution of the question.

Her administration has endorsed the Willacy Bill introduced into the senate at the recent legislature, which requires that convicts' dependent families be provided for out of the proceeds of their labor.

AMELIA STONE QUINTON.

Was born near Syracuse, New York, of English ancestry and directly descended from both Pilgrims and Puritan New England stock. Her father was Jacob Thompson Stone, and her mother Mary Bennett Stone. In the early days, her family was intermarried with the Adams family and the son of one was the father of Samuel Adams; another member was aunt to John Adams, the second president of the United States and a great-aunt to John Quincy Adams, sixth president. Mrs. Quinton's early education was acquired in one of the female seminaries of that time. She spent a year as a teacher in a Georgia Seminary, after which she became the wife of the Rev. James F. Swanson, a Christian Minister of that state, whose death occurred within a few years. After this Mrs. Swanson returned north and taught at a female seminary in Philadelphia. During this time she turned to religious and philanthropic work, to which she gave some valuable years. Her first service in this work was among the poor and degraded of New York City. One day of the week she spent in the prison, one in the almshouse, and another in some infirmary or reformatory for women. One service was a weekly Bible class for sailors on shore. Very soon she was invited to go out and represent the Woman's Christian Temperance Union to organize unions and later was elected by the State Woman's Christian Temperance Union as a state organizer. While on a tour in Europe for her health and a rest from her labors, she met Professor Richard Quinton, a native of London and lecturer on historical and astronomical subjects in the institutions of that city. They were married and continued to reside in London for some time. In 1878 they came to America, where Professor Quinton resumed his work, lecturing in Philadelphia, which now became their home. In April, 1879, her friend, Miss Mary L. Bonney, became deeply stirred on the subject of national wrongs to the Indians and enlisted the interest of Mrs. Quinton in this work. Mrs. Quinton had had such large experience in Christian work that she knew how to bring a cause before the people. Miss Bonney agreed to supply the means if Mrs. Quinton would plan and work as the way was opened. She studied up the subject in the libraries, prepared literature and petitions, which she circulated, securing many sympathizers and helpers throughout the United States. The first petition, an enormous roll three hundred feet long, was presented to the Congress of the United States in February, 1880. A society was formed, Miss Bonney was elected president, and the constitution was written by Mrs. Quinton. An executive board was elected, nominated at her request, by pastors of churches, and it became the Indian Treaty-Keeping and Protective Association. Before the end of the year, Mrs. Quinton had secured thirteen associate organizations in five different states. To-day, the Association, now the Woman's National Indian Association, has branches, officers or helpers, in forty states of the Union and more than twenty missions in Indian tribes have been established, and during 1891, missionary work was done in fifteen tribes. In 1884, when Miss Bonney retired from the presidency of the association, Mrs. Mary Lowe Dickinson was elected to that office, which she held for three years, when Mrs. Quinton was unanimously elected president of this association. On one of her tours through the United States, she bore a government commission and did service in behalf of Indian education.

GRACE WILBUR TROUT.

Mrs. Trout was born and educated in Maquoketa, Iowa. Discerning early that certain qualities of voice made her especially fitted for platform speaking, she specialized in that form of study. Her father drilled her, and often said to her, "When you talk, say something." Instead of entering the profession for which she had been prepared, she married George W. Trout, and a few years later they moved to Chicago. Not long afterwards, Mrs. Trout became interested in the Mormon question, writing a story entitled "The Mormon Wife," which received great commendation. Mrs. Trout was at one time president of the Ladies' Auxiliary of the National Club; member of the West End Women's Club; president of the Women's Auxiliary of the Oak Park Club; member of the Nineteenth Century Club of Oak Park; member of the Chicago Women's Club for ten years, and member of the Chicago Chapter of the Daughters of the American Revolution. Is president of the largest Equal Suffrage League in Illinois. She is one of the well-known speakers on the subject of equal suffrage in the Middle West, being thoroughly informed on her subject. Filled with the enthusiasm of it, she presents her theme in a masterly shape.

MRS. NETTIE RANSFORD.

Mrs. Nettie Ransford was born November 6, 1838, in Little Falls, New York. In 1898 she was General Grand Matron of the Masonic Order of the Eastern Star. This order is an organization of the wives and daughters of Masons and affiliates in their charitable work. Her parents were from Scotland. After graduating in 1857 she settled in Nebraska and taught school in Omaha and Fort Calhoun, here, in 1858, she married William T. Ransford, and in 1862 they moved to Laporte, Indiana. She was one of the first women who joined the Order of the Eastern Star, soon after that order was organized in 1872. She was elected Worthy Matron in 1874 and re-elected several times. In 1879 she was elected Grand Matron, being re-elected to this office several times. She was elected Most Worthy General Grand Matron in the sessions of the General Grand Chapter held in Indianapolis in 1879, and was the first General Grand Matron to serve under the changed constitution. Her duties are such that she has traveled throughout the entire General Grand Jurisdiction and has distinguished herself in ways which can only be appreciated and understood by members of this order.

ELIZA HARRIS LAWTON BARKER.

Eliza Harris Lawton Barker, daughter of Moses Turner Lawton and Elizabeth Tillinghast Lawton, was married on October 9, 1873, to Hon. Richard Jackson Barker, a distinguished ex-union officer. Mrs. Barker is a direct descendant of Admiral George Lawton of the Royal Navy, belonging to one of the oldest families of Rhode Island, which was established by George and Thomas Lawton at Portsmouth.

Mrs. Barker completed her education at Vassar College, and probably is the best known woman in Rhode Island in educational and literary circles. She has always been deeply interested in the public school system and was elected twenty-five years ago a member of the school committee of the town of Tiverton. For sixteen years she has been chairman of the school board. She has been historian of the Colonial Dames of Rhode Island, she is an active member of the Daughters of the American Revolution and has been vice-president general of the National Society, to which exalted office she was elected by a large majority at the National Congress of the Daughters of the American Revolution, which was held at Washington, D. C., in April, 1906.

Fourteen years previous she had been an active officer of Gaspee Chapter of Providence, resigning the office of regent to accept the one to which she had been elected. The Gaspee Chapter presented her with a beautiful silver-mounted gavel made from wood taken from the old Gaspee room. She is honorary state regent of Rhode Island and has been made an honorary member of several Rhode Island and Massachusetts Chapters.

In the National Society of the Daughters of the American Revolution, she has filled many prominent places, at one time being chairman of the Magazine Committee, chairman of the Purchasing Committee, a member of the Auditing Committee, member of the Continental Hall Committee, member of the Jamestown Committee, chairman for New England of the Daughters of the American Revolution Exhibit at the Jamestown Exposition. Mrs. Barker was honored by her state by being made hostess at the Rhode Island State Building by the Commissioners of Rhode Island at the Jamestown, Virginia, Exposition.

For four years she was state historian of the Daughters of the American Revolution and was thirteen years chairman of the Gaspee Prize Committee. She is state regent of the Pocahontas Memorial Association and vice-president of the Rhode Island Institute of Instruction. She was one of the chairmen of the Rhode Island Sanitary Relief Association during the Spanish War; was one of the women commissioners of Rhode Island at the Atlanta Exposition.

Among the other various important positions held by Mrs. Barker, she has been a member of the Board of the Woman's College, Brown University, ever since it was founded, vice-president of the Woman's Board of the Union Hospital, secretary of the 13th Congressional District George Washington Memorial Committee. She has been for years actively interested in hospital and other benevolences of Fall River and Tiverton, Rhode Island. She has been especially interested in patriotic education in the public schools and has taken a very active part in every progressive movement in the line of education. She is an exceptional speaker and presiding officer, wields a gifted pen and exercises an incomparable influence for human welfare and progress.

Mrs. Barker is President for Rhode Island of Women's Rivers and Harbors Congress of the United States.

MRS. CHARLOTTE P. ACER BARNUM.

Mrs. Charlotte P. Acer Barnum was born in Shelley Center, Orleans County, New York, in 1865, January 8. Her father was Volney Acer, who was born in Pittsford, Monroe County, New York, and her mother Charlotte Clark Peck, who was born in Tallmadge, Summit County, Ohio. Her mother's ancestors all came from New England, where they had lived for generations. Her father's family settled in Pittsford (7 miles from Rochester) in 1790, and the original farm on which her great-grandfather settled is still in the possession of the family. The Acers were originally from Holland but her great-grandmother was Dorothy Adams, a kin to John, John Quincy and Samuel, as well as to Judge Otis and other early New England settlers.

Mrs. Barnum was graduated from Vassar College in 1886. Since that time she has studied abroad in France and Germany and has done research work in Boston and New York. In 1893 she came to live in Pittsford, her father's old home, where she was married in June, 1907, to Nathaniel C. Barnum, whose ancestors settled in Rochester in 1794.

Mrs. Barnum was for four years secretary of the National Vassar Students' Aid Society and was for ten years the president of the Rochester Branch of the Vassar Students' Aid Society. At present she is treasurer of the Century Club of Rochester, chairman of the committee of the state of New York of the Society of School Patrons of the National Education Association, and on the executive committee of the Society of School Patrons of the National Education Association, representing on the executive committee the Association of Collegiate Alumnæ.

MRS. ELIZABETH LANGWORTHY.

Mrs. Elizabeth Langworthy was born in October, 1837, in Orleans County, New York. Her father was one of the heirs of the Trinity Church property in New York. Her mother was descended from a prominent French family. In 1858 she became the wife of Stephen Langworthy of Dubuque, Iowa, whose parents were among the early pioneers of that state. In 1861 Mr. and Mrs. Langworthy made their home in Monticello, Iowa, and here she was instrumental in founding the public library of that city. Later, in the city of Seward, Nebraska, where their home was established, she served as president of many societies for local improvement and also of the Seward History and Art Club, and it was through her suggestion and instrumentality as a member of the Board of Lady Managers of the World's Columbian Exposition, that the hammer was presented to Mrs. Potter Palmer, then president, with which she drove the last nail in the Woman's Building. Mrs. Langworthy raised the fund for this purpose.

ELIZABETH F. PIERCE.

Miss Pierce is the daughter of the late Charles W. Pierce, a business man of Boston, and a niece of Mrs. J. Ellen Horton Foster, and was born in Boston, Massachusetts. She is noted in her native city for her earnest religious and philanthropic work, especially in the Foreign and Home Missionary Societies of the Methodist Episcopal Church. After the death of her father, she and her mother, Mrs. Foster's sister, removed to Washington. Miss Pierce immediately identified herself with her church, and its wonderful work along many lines. She has been most active as a member of missionary societies, the Daughters of the American Revolution and other patriotic associations. She was elected recording secretary general of the Daughters of the American Revolution, serving as such until 1911, when she was elected chaplain general of that great order.

CATHERINE NOBLES.

Born in New Orleans, Louisiana. Her father, Charles H. Nobles, was a native of Providence, R. I., who moved to New Orleans in early life. Her father was one of the founders of the Howard Association of New Orleans. Was an officer of that body until his death. Mr. Nobles had rendered valuable assistance in the various epidemics that fell upon New Orleans from 1837-1867. Miss Nobles has been prominent in club life in New Orleans and became widely known as a club woman; she served as secretary of the Woman's Club of New Orleans and the Woman's League of Louisiana. In 1892 at a meeting of the General Federation of Woman's Clubs of the United States, held in Chicago, Miss Nobles was elected one of the board of directors.

MRS. HERMAN J. HALL.

Was born in Oneida County, New York, educated in Buffao, New York. Spent much time in travel and study of the history of art. Has made a specialty of Pagan and Christian Symbolism in art and lectures upon these subjects. Founded the League for Civic Improvement and the Art Study Club in 1888, and which now numbers nearly six hundred, the largest of its kind in America. Ex-president of the Woman's Auxiliary and ex-second vice-president, American Outdoor Art League. Ex-chairman Art Committee General Federation Woman's Clubs for first four years of Art Department. Ex-chairman Art Committee Illinois Federation, Woman's Club. Ex-chairman local Exhibition Committee Municipal Art League at Art Institute, Chicago. Honorary member Chicago Outdoor Art League; also Outdoor Art League of San Francisco and founder of the Outdoor Art League of Los Angeles. Member Audubon Park Board, New Orleans, La. Author of "Two Women Abroad" and contributor to various magazines. Most of the work done by Mrs. Hall in the organizing of these various clubs and associations was pioneer work. Her lectures are upon the travels and studies which she has made in the various countries which are subjects of her lectures. She has made a most exhaustive study of the architecture, sculpture, metal work, paintings and prints, porcelains and pottery, textiles, landscape art and flower cult of Japan and China; also the history, agriculture, life and arts of Russia, Spain and other European countries.

MINONA STEARNS FITTS JONES.

Mrs. Jones was born in Abington, Mass., July 5, 1855, of New England ancestry. Her ancestors settled Walpole, Wrentham and Mansfield, Mass. She is the daughter of Dr. I. H. Stearns and Catherine M. Guild Stearns. Attended the New England public schools; New Vineyard, Maine, and Oak Grove Seminary, Vassalboro, Maine, finishing her education at Milwaukee Female College. She studied medicine and assisted her father, Dr. Stearns, in the Milwaukee National Soldiers' Home where he was surgeon. Married Robert C. Fitts, of Leverett, Mass., at Milwaukee, on December 6, 1879. She engaged in business in Milwaukee for six years. She became interested in politics through the street-car strike in Milwaukee in 1896, and was the only woman writer and speaker for the strikers and became converted to woman suffrage at that time and spoke for the populists in their campaign in Wisconsin.

Upon the discovery of rich deposits of mica in Park and Fremont Counties, Colorado, by her son, Roy Fields Fitts, Mrs. Fitts visited Colorado and bought the mines and milling property and began the mining of mica, assisted by her son, who was a boy of eighteen years. Mrs. Fitts returned to Chicago and organized the United States Mica Mining and Milling Company, and was elected secretary and treasurer of same, which position she held for six years. Mrs. Fitts married for the second time, Senator Frank W. Jones, of Massachusetts, May 29, 1905. Mrs. Fitts Jones founded the "No Vote No Tax" League of Illinois. This league was established for the purpose of bringing together all who would refuse to pay taxes until they could vote—since "Taxation without representation is tyranny." Mrs. Fitts Jones is one of the incorporators of the "Public Policy League" of Illinois, and also incorporated the National Race Betterment League, and was elected the first president of this world-wide movement for race betterment.

LUCY GASTON PAGE.

Miss Page, the founder of tne Anti-Cigarette League of America, was well known in Chicago club life and philanthropy, where she founded, several years ago, this work which she carried to New York City, where some of the leading citizens of that metropolis are co-operating with her. We know of no greater field of usefulness or benefit to the human race of the future than the work done by this organization. Investigations on this subject have been started by the interest developed by this organization in many states. The Sage Foundation experts have taken it up in the New York public schools; the Big Brother Movement has also become interested in the importance of this work. It is rapidly commanding the attention of sociologists and philanthropic and home economic workers throughout the country.

LUCINDA H. STONE.

Mrs. Lucinda H. Stone was born in Hinesburg, Vermont, in 1814. Her maiden name was Lucinda Hinesburg. She has always been active in educational work, has founded many women's libraries and has been often called the "Mother of Women's Clubs of the State of Michigan"; taught in several of the well-known educational institutions in that state. In 1840 she became the wife of Dr. J. A. B. Stone, also a teacher. In 1843 they took up their residence in Kalamazoo, Michigan, where Dr. Stone was president of the Kalamazoo College for twenty years. The female department of this institution was under Mrs. Stone's charge for many years. Before the war, Mrs. Stone's home was the resort of the abolitionist and equal suffrage leaders. In 1864 Mrs. Stone gave up her educational work and devoted her time to the organizing of women's clubs and societies for the education of women. Mrs. Stone was the first woman to use her influence toward the admitting of women to the University of Michigan, and for the work which she did in this direction, the University of Michigan, in 1891, conferred upon her the degree of Doctor of Philosophy.

CAROLINE M. SEYMOUR SEVERANCE.

BY MRS. JOHN A. LOGAN.

Mrs. Severance was born in Canandaigua, New York, in January, 1820. She is the daughter of Orson Seymour, a banker of that place. Her mother was Caroline M. Clarke Seymour, who must have been a devoted and wise mother to have reared a daughter of such rare genius as Mrs. Severance. January 12, 1840, Miss Seymour became the wife of Theodoric C. Severance, a banker of Cleveland, Ohio, to which place Mr. Severance took his bride and established their first home. Their five children were born there, their mother devoting her entire time to her husband and children; it was an ideal American home. Mrs. Severance, meanwhile, kept abreast with the progress of the times. Her native talent, active mind and accomplishments made her an authority on the ethics of society. In 1853 she was chosen to give a lecture before the "Mercantile Library Association," the first woman to deliver a lecture before such an association. Her topic was "Humanity; a Definition and a Plea." She made such a brilliant accomplishment that she was obliged to deliver it in many places in the state. "The Woman's Rights Association," of Ohio, prevailed upon Mrs. Severance to arrange the lecture in the form of a tract to be distributed throughout the country. Later Mrs. Severance was appointed to present to the legislature a memorial "asking suffrage and such amendments to the state laws of Ohio, as should place woman on a civil equality with man."

In 1855 Mr. and Mrs. Severance removed to Newton, Mass. The women suffragists of New England were delighted to welcome so brilliant an advocate for the cause of suffrage as Mrs. Severance. She demurred at taking an active part in the work the "Woman's Rights Association" was planning to inaugurate. She preferred to render such service as she could as a member of the committee of the "Theodore Parker Fraternity Association," and to aid in securing a woman lecturer for the course. She earnestly joined her associates in requesting Mrs. Cady Stanton to deliver the course. Mrs. Stanton was, however, unable to accept the invitation of the committee. Mrs. Severance wrote to Mrs. Stanton long afterwards: "I was not able to resist the entreaties of the committee and the obligation that I felt myself under to make good your place, so far as in me lay." Hence she took upon herself the grave responsibility of giving the course of lectures the committee considered of vital importance to the cause of woman's rights. The initial lecture was the first ever delivered by a woman before a Lyceum Association in Boston. Mrs. Severance subsequently in writing to Mrs. Stanton tells of her emotions while delivering the lecture: "I will not tell you how prosy and dull I fear it was; but I know it was earnest and well considered, and that the beaming eyes of dear Mrs. Follen and Miss Elizabeth Peabody, glowing with interest before me from below the platform of Tremont Temple, kept me in heart all through."

Mrs. Severance is a tall, dignified woman, with a handsome face, ever lighted up by her effervescing spirits. Her countenance reflects the brilliancy of her rare intelligence, quickness of thought, and purity of mind and heart. She possesses remarkable conversational powers, and is a most effective and eloquent speaker from the platform. In years gone by she has given "soul-service" in many directions, standing as corresponding secretary for the Boston Anti-slavery Society, as one of the Board of Managers of the Boston Woman's Hospital, and delivering a course of lectures on practical ethics before Dio Lewis' school for girls, at Lexington, Mass. These lectures cover the relation of the young woman to the school, the state, the home and to her own development.

After long and prayerful thought as to how to best utilize "the truth, the goodness, the intelligence of the literary and philanthropic women of New England, and the vast benefits which she foresaw would flow from such a union," in 1868, Mrs. Severance called the sympathetic women together in parlor meetings to talk over her ideas. Their meetings resulted in "the introduction to the world of a new form of social and mental architecture." Mrs. Severance, as founder, "was elected president of the first woman's club in our country—the New England Woman's Club of Boston," and thereby became the "Mother of Clubs" and was the primal force in a movement that has become a stupendous factor in our civilization.

May 30, 1868, in Chickering Hall, the New England Woman's Club was introduced to the world. The noble women who had perfected this beneficent organization were ably assisted and encouraged on that occasion by the addresses of Ralph Waldo Emerson, James Freeman Clarke, Jacob Manning, John Weiss, O. B. Frothingham, Thomas Wentworth Higginson, and Bronson Alcott. The speakers for the club were: Julia Ward Howe and Mrs. E. D. Cheney, who set forth the purposes of the New England Woman's Club so eloquently and comprehensively as to win the endorsement and confidence of the whole assemblage: First, "to organize the social forces of the women of New England"; to establish "a larger home for those who love and labor for the greater human family"; to combine "recreation with the pursuit of wisdom"; to provide "the comforts of the club to the lonely, in city and suburb," and proposed useful work in a registry of women seeking the so-called higher occupations, providing rooms for women who came to Boston for concerts, operas, and lectures.

Among the achievements of the New England Woman's Club has been the establishment of a Horticultural School for women, in which the pupils erected their own greenhouses, painted the buildings, etc.   It was subsequently merged into the "bussey," a department of Harvard.   Caused the passage of the first school-suffrage law, which permitted women to be elected members of the Boston and other school boards. Aided by helpers, the club established the New England Hospital for women and children, which was officered and managed by women, with eminent doctors of the other sex as consulting physicians and surgeons.   In co-operation with Hon. Josiah Quincy, Dr. Bowditch and others, the club joined in the incorporation of a successful Co-operation Building Association, which proved a great assistance to the poor, and furnished an object lesson to the philanthropists of the whole country. Aided by one of its members, "St. Elizabeth" Peabody, the club provided scholarships for studious young women and used its potent influence to promote higher education for women, resulting in the founding of the Girl's Latin School, of Boston.

The club began the agitation and eventually caused the appointment of women police matrons and placed women on the boards of all public institutions.   Homes of detention for women they also secured.

This club also aided the fund of the Egyptian Exploration Society, joined the Archæological Institute of Greece, and abetted the New York Society for the suppression of obscene literature and took an active part in the dress-reform movement.

The club organized classes in English literature, languages, and other higher studies. In 1876, it had classes in political economy, and in 1891 formed a "current topics" class, and secured able lecturers on Political Development, Railroad Laws, Prohibition Laws, George's "Progress and Poverty," Summer's "Obligations of the Social Class," Bryce's "American Commonwealth," Socialism of To-day, Municipal Reform, Rent, The Lobby System, The Silver Question, Food Waste, Prison Reform, The Responsibility of the Employer and Employed, as well as many topics bearing upon the standing of woman and her influence in all departments of human activity. Socially, the club gave many receptions to distinguished visitors and American celebrities, among them: Monsieur Coquerel, Harriet Beecher Stowe, Emily Faithful, Mary Carpenter, Lord and Lady Amberly, Harriet Hosmer, Anne Whitney, Professor Maria Mitchell, Dr. Parsons, the Dante scholar, Professors Pierce, Gould, and Fiske and Rev. Dr. Edward Everett Hale. Thus it will be seen that "the diversity of activities and of sympathy illustrates well the broad purpose and intent of the originators of club-life for American women."

In 1875, Mrs. Severance removed to California with no abatement in her devotion to the cause of woman's rights and the extension of woman's clubs. She was soon actively engaged in the work of organizing woman's rights associations and clubs, and has the satisfaction of seeing many flourishing societies and clubs. She traveled extensively in her early life. Wherever she went, she immediately hunted up persons of note who were interested in the dearest object of her life—woman's rights. Among her many friends in England were: Mrs. Lucas, sister of Jacob and John Bright; Elizabeth Barrett Browning, Florence Nightingale, Mrs. Somerville, Mrs. Jameson, Harriet Martineau, Mrs. Cobbe, Charlotte Robinson and many others.

27

The editor has had the good fortune to know Mrs. Severance and to visit her in Los Angeles, California, in her lovely home, El Nido, which is full of priceless literary treasures and souvenirs of great occasions and honors paid to her as "The Mother of Clubs." She has also been christened the "Ethical Magnet of Southern California." Many contemporary authors have contributed valuable copies of their books suitably inscribed. Arranged in a cabinet are the autographed photographs of her distinguished friends and co-workers, whom she calls her "immortals," including Mrs. Browning, George Eliot, Margaret Fuller, Lydia Maria Childs, Lucy Stone, Frances Dana Gage, Caroline H. Dall, Louisa Alcott, Celia Burleigh, Ednah D. Cheney, and Lucretia Mott. In a corresponding case, are pictures of Junipero Serra, Wendell Phillips, Longfellow, Whittier, James Freeman Clarke, William H. Channing, Lowell, Samuel Johnson, and Charles Sumner. Another rare picture is one of five generations of the Severance family in a group.

Among the most valued are the souvenirs of the celebration of the silver wedding of Mr. and Mrs. Severance, which occurred in 1865. When her literary friends and admirers journeyed from the Middle West and every part of the country to Boston, Mass., to participate in the festivities of the felicitous occasion, they brought tributes of affection in poetry and prose. Of the number, such illustrious names appear, as Isabella Beecher Hooker, Dr. and Mrs. Dio Lewis, Mattie Griffith, Albert G. Browne, Mrs. Satterlee, Mr. and Mrs. Henry Ivinson (sister of Mrs. Severance), the Burrage family of Boston and a host of others. While the letters of regret bore the signatures of such immortals as George Bradburn, Harriet Minot Pitman, James Freeman Clarke and Mrs. Clarke, William Lloyd and Frank Garrison, Dr. Marie Zakrzewska, Rev. Zachos, William H. Avery, Salmon P. Chase,

Theodore Tilton, Grace Greenwood, Truman Seymour, James F. Hall, George Wm. Curtis, Anna Q. T. Parsons, W. W. Story (the artist), General and Mrs. Fremont, Miss Fremont, Lieutenant Frank Fremont and George B. Grinnell.

Mrs. Severance's "Ye Geste Book" is a rare volume, containing innumerable names of those who have paid their respects to this remarkable woman. John W. Hutchinson and his wife, with a record of "fifty-eight years old, thirty-nine years singing and ten thousand concerts," made a visit to Mrs. Severance. Ludlow Patten and wife (nee Abby Hutchinson), Henry M. Field and wife, Helen Hunt Jackson, Captain R. H. Pratt, J. Wells Champney and wife, William J. Rotch, Locke Richardson, Charles Dudley Warner, George W. Cable, Elizabeth B. Custer (widow of General Custer), J. W. Chadwick and wife, John W. Hoyt and wife, Mary A. Livermore, Lucy Stone, Elizabeth Cady Stanton (written in her eighty-seventh year), Rev. William Milburn (the blind chaplain of the Senate), Mrs. A. D. T. Whitney, Edward Everett Hale, Miss Susan Hale, Charlotte Perkins Stetson, Grace Ellery Channing, Rev. J. Minot Savage, Kate Sanborn, Cordelia Kirkland, Ida Coolbrith, Susan B. Anthony, Carrie Chapman Catt, Mrs. E. O. Smith, "Vivekananda," (who wrote, "From the unreal, lead me to the real—from the darkness into light"), Mrs. J. S. Langrana, of Poona, India; Miss Florence Denton, of Kyoto, Japan; Jan Krigo, of Transvaal, South Africa; Henry Demarest Lloyd, who prefaced his autograph with "We can preserve the liberties we have inherited only by winning new ones to bequeath."

Rich beyond compare in experiences which make life worth the living, and the fullness of years of well-doing for all mankind, Mrs. Severance is one of the noblest types of American womanhood. Fascinated by the external youthfulness of her spirits and charming personality, one realizes that age cannot wither.

M. ELEANOR BRACKENRIDGE.

An educational movement coincident with the wonderful awakening of women to a sense of their responsibilities characterized the last decade of the last and the first decade of the present century. A conspicuous leader in this movement, Miss M. Eleanor Brackenridge, of San Antonio, Texas, was a graduate of Anderson's Female Seminary, New Albany, Indiana, Class of 1855. Her girlhood was spent in Jackson County, Texas, where she devoted her energies to ministering to family and friends, even studying medicine and applying remedies for the diseases incident to a new country with much sickness and few physicians. With a burning desire to be helpful to humanity, it was not until 1898 when a club progressive in education and altruistic in scope was planned in San Antonio, that she found her opportunity as president, organizer and leader along her chosen line of work. Her enthusiasm and earnest zeal won the loyal support of her co-workers, to whom she insists the honor of the success of the first department club of Texas belongs. She served as regent for the first seven years of the State College of Industrial Arts for Women, and has served on state and national educational committees of women's clubs, Daughters of the American Revolution and Mothers' Congress. She has educated from three to seven girls yearly in the all-round education, the higher education, or in the profession of medicine. Her interest in humanity naturally makes her an ardent advocate of woman suffrage. With a keen realization of the possibilities of organized womanhood, in a quiet way she has started movements that are far-reaching in their results. A modest, home-loving, conservative, but progressive in thought, she has used her wealth, social position and even accepted offices to encourage the organization of women for the betterment of humanity.

MRS. SARAH PLATT DECKER.

One of the most distinguished clubwomen of the country is Mrs. Sarah Platt Decker, of Denver, Colorado. Mrs. Decker has been very active in the work of the societies to which she belongs, giving her time and strength to the work these clubs have undertaken. She was for some time president of the Woman's Club of Denver, and is considered an authority on the best methods for civic improvement. She has been vice-president and president of the National Federation of Clubs. Her exceptional talent and wonderful executive ability contribute largely to the success of the various clubs of which she is a member.

HELEN VARICK BOSWELL.

Miss Helen Varick Boswell is a Baltimorean, and although, for some years, has been an active worker in the political and later in the industrial and social work taken up by the New York State Federation of Women's Clubs, she is probably to-day best known as the woman selected by President Taft and sent by the United States Government to Panama to look into the social conditions there, and as having founded eight women's clubs on the zone, which are federated and are known as the "Canal Zone Federation of Women's Clubs." This creating

MEMORIAL CONTINENTAL HALL, WASHINGTON, D. C.

Erected by the Daughters of the American Revolution.

of social life through united club effort was much needed in the zone, and it brought the women together and helped to make the history of that place. When Mr. Taft last visited the zone and was the guest of the women's clubs, he was emphatic in his statement that they had been a strong factor in the progress of the work, for they had helped to keep all the people contented, and have done much for the civic betterment of the small communities in which they are at present placed.

Miss Boswell devotes much of her time to the women's department of the Federation and General Federation of Women's Clubs; is chairman of the Industrial and Social Conditions department of that organization. Among the subjects discussed in her lectures and talks before the public in the interest of her work, are: "Social and Political Progress of American Women," "Society and the Criminal," "The Club Woman as a Molder of Public Opinion," "Every-day Life on the Canal Zone."

Miss Boswell comes of Revolutionary ancestors, is prominent in the Daughters of the American Revolution, and is well known in the social and official life of Washington and New York.

The National Society Daughters of the American Revolution.

INTRODUCTION BY MRS. DONALD MCLEAN.

Just twenty-one years ago, in 1890, was organized a national society of women, whose purpose was patriotism and whose deeds now speak for them. To paraphrase the resolution presented for action to and by the Continental Congress, when the flag of our nation was created: "A new constellation was born," in woman's universe, and the stars sing together as they course through an approving heaven. Upon August 9th, 1890, was held the first organizing meeting of the National Society Daughters of the American Revolution. Three women were actually present, and these women, Miss Eugenia Washington (great-niece of General Washington), Mrs. Ellen Hardin Walworth, and Miss Mary Desha, have since been known as the "founders" of the society. A final meeting to complete organization was held October, 1890, and thereafter the society was an accomplished fact. The necessary eligibility to membership consists in direct descent from an ancestor—man or woman—who rendered "material aid" in establishing the independence of the republic. This ancestor may have been a commanding officer, or an humble private with true and proper American spirit. Rank, as such, has no influence in determining the eligibility of an applicant, but genealogical claims must be thoroughly proven, and an applicant must be acceptable to the society. As to the *raison d'etre* of the organization, the constitution states that the objects of this society are:

(1). To perpetuate the memory of the spirit of the men and women who achieved American independence by the acquisition and protection of historical spots, and the erection of monuments; by the encouragement of historical research in relation to the Revolution and the publication of its results; by the preservation of documents and relics, and of the records of the individual services of revolutionary soldiers and patriots, and by the promotion of the celebration of all patriotic anniversaries.

(2). To carry out the injunction of Washington in his farewell address to the American people, "to promote, as an object of primary importance, institutions for the general diffusion of knowledge," thus developing an enlightened public opinion, and affording to young and old such advantages as shall develop in them the largest capacity for performing the duties of American citizens.

(3). To cherish, maintain, and extend the institutions of American freedom, to foster true patriotism and love of country, and to aid in securing for mankind all the blessings of liberty.

As a practical demonstration of patriotism, as a central crystallization of concrete accomplishment, Memorial Continental Hall stands the pre-eminent work of this society. Women conceived the idea and have carried into execution the rearing of a memorial such as the world has never heretofore beheld. A temple to liberty, a mausoleum of memory, and, withal, a building wherein the Daughters of the American Revolution may gather officially for the transaction of business. The society has grown in its twenty-one years of existence, from the three members in attendance at the first meeting to a present membership of eighty thousand. Who could have foreseen such a phenomena of patriotism? Hence the necessity for business offices in addition to a revolutionary memorial. Continental Hall is the trunk from which spring all branches of sentiment and of active work. It is built of white marble and in pure colonial type; it is situated in Washington, the nation's Capital, and is adjacent to the White House and the Washington Monument; its cost, including the land, was half a million dollars; it stands now complete, without and within. The most notable feature of the exterior is the "memorial portico," looking southward down the Potomac; it is semi-circular in shape, and its roof is supported by thirteen monolithic columns memorializing the thirteen original states. The notable feature of the interior is the auditorium, seating two thousand; its walls finished in highly ornate colonial decoration and its roof of translucent glass, in medallion designs, harmonizing with the mural ornamentation. There is a fireproof museum for revolutionary relics, documentary and otherwise, upon one side of the auditorium; upon the other is a library containing volumes chiefly pertaining to historical and genealogical research. Thus it would seem that Memorial Continental Hall, in itself, is the fulfillment of the first clause of the constitutionally stated "objects of the society". Had the National Society Daughters of the American Revolution achieved naught else, the erection of such a monument would justify the existence of the organization and shed lustre upon it. But the society is engaging in other and important activities throughout the country.

"To promote the general diffusion of knowledge" a national committee on patriotic education exists. This committee is broad in scope; it deals with the incoming immigrant and with the native mountaineer; it teaches by lecture and by literature; it encourages scholarships; it presents flags (through the flag teaching the nation's history in one glorious demonstration). Connected with the committees on patriotic education is the "Interchangeable Bureau" for the lectures, with slides illustrating the subject-matter. Frequently these lectures are delivered in various languages to meet the need of the lately landed immigrant. There is an interchange of these lectures from the chairman as fountain-head, throughout all the states. Besides such work, scholarships in perpetuity have been established in certain colleges for women. These scholarships insure a living monument to patriotic educational attainment. One student after another shall reap the benefit, so long as the college endures, and specializing in American history, as the student does, sends out into the world a force of wider and yet wider dominance, through which knowledge is distributed and the ideals of our formative period preserved, while practical results are obtained for the student, who is thus fitted to teach and become self-supporting. From Continental Hall, too, will emanate the true spirit of the "diffusion of knowledge" for lectures on American History will be delivered in its auditorium to the general public. "The acquisition and protection of historical spots" has not been neglected by the society. In many localities throughout the country are valuable properties, replete with revolutionary and historic associations, owned or cared for by the Daughters of the American Revolution. Sites of battles are marked by boulders and by monuments; historic events are recorded by tablets on the walls of churches, courthouses and other buildings; libraries are provided for, the army and navy, and Red Cross nurses have been sent to the front.   A national committee on Child Labor exists and the fruits of its energies are rapidly maturing into beneficent reforms.   The Daughters of the American Revolution have been especially interested and active in the propagation of International Peace Arbitration.   The society took action in its Congress of 1907 looking toward the encouragement of such work, and sent a memorial stating its action to the International Peace Congress being held in New York at the same time. Also, Continental Hall was offered to President Roosevelt for the use of the Japanese-Russian Peace Commission assembled in this country at the President's invitation.

By all these means and many more, does the National Society Daughters of the American Revolution consider that it is fostering "true patriotism and love of country."   That the Government of the United States so regards the work of the organization is argued, in that such Government recognizes the society in the official printing of the latter's annual reports, and the dissemination of them through the Smithsonian Institute.

The first president-general of the National Society Daughters of the American Revolution was Mrs. Benjamin Harrison; she has been succeeded by Mrs. Adlai E. Stevenson. Mrs. John W. Foster, Mrs. Daniel T. Manning, Mrs. Charles W. Fairbanks, Mrs. Donald McLean and Mrs. Matthew T. Scott.

A Word by the President-General D. A. R.

"The Wilds,"
Charlevoix, Mich., July 1, 1911.

My Dear Mrs. Logan:

It gives me great pleasure to learn that you are compiling a book to be known as "The Part Taken by Women in American History," and I am quite sure it will give to women credit which has been withheld from them for their masterful achievements along many lines for the betterment of mankind and the preservation of republican institutions. I am sure that we may in advance congratulate the public upon a volume that will faithfully record and do justice to the history of the women who have been factors, and who have done their full part, in molding that most wonderful product of the age, which we proudly proclaim "Americanism."

The roll call of women who have taken part in the work of the National Society Daughters of the American Revolution is a long and distinguished one. I need not recall to you the names of the six president-generals who have preceded me— Mrs. Harrison, Mrs. Stevenson, Mrs. Foster, Mrs. Manning, Mrs. Fairbanks, and Mrs. McLean. Among those upon whom I have most relied during the two years of my administration are: Mrs. J. Ellen Foster, authority upon abuses of child labor, Mrs. John W. Foster, Mrs. Stevenson, Mrs. McLean, Madame Pinchot, a name synonymous with conservation, Mrs. Dickinson, wife of the Secretary of War, Mrs. Samuel Ammon, Mrs. Alexander Patton, Mrs. John A. Murphy, Mrs. Howard Hodgkins, Mrs. Draper, Mrs. Swormstedt, Mrs. Mussey, Mrs. Orton, Mrs. Edwin Gardner, Jr., all of whom except Mrs. McLean, Mrs. Stevenson and Mrs. John W. Foster—with many others equally able and devoted—have been chairmen of committees and done faithful and zealous work.

In accordance with that law of nature and of Providence, that in this world one sows and another reaps, it is my glorious privilege to have gathered up into one splendid sheaf the results of the labor and devotion of all my greater predecessors in office, as well as of the 87,000 Daughters of the American Revolution, who, by their toils, labors, sacrifices and gifts, have produced the grand results we see in our magnificent memorial building, and in the reports of the inspiring work of state regents and chairmen of national committees presented at the annual Congresses.

It is a source of pride and gratification to me that during my administration Continental Hall has been literally finished and was formally handed over to the society by the architect and contractors in March, 1910. Within the two years not only have all the offices been successfully removed from 902 F. street to the hall, but many magnificent rooms have been furnished in splendid style by different states, and $30,000 of the $200,000 debt paid off, an income for current needs provided and business matters arranged on a satisfactory basis.

With this material advancement, the intellectual and patriotic educational work has kept splendid pace, and the Daughters of the American Revolution are proving worthy descendants of the revolutionary ancestors whose memory and achievements they seek to perpetuate. This they are doing not only by showing their reverential homage for the old flag, but by continuing the work and the traditions of the fathers as a stimulus to this and to coming generations—both American and foreign born—to maintain the high standard of American citizenship, the splendid ideals of American manhood and womanhood we have inherited as a rich legacy from the past, and intend to hand down uncankered to our remotest posterity.

Faithfully,

(Signed) Julia G. Scott.

The Active Incorporation of the Daughters of the American Revolution.

The Daughters of the American Revolution were chartered by an act of the fifty-fourth Congress in 1895. The list of incorporators contains the names of the most conspicuous women of the United States: Mrs. John W. Foster, of Indiana;

Mrs. William D. Cabell, of Virginia; Mrs. Henry V. Boynton, of Ohio; Mrs. A. W. Greely, of Washington, D. C.; Mrs. F. O. St. Clair, of Maryland; Mrs. A. Leo Knott, of Maryland; Mrs. Roger A. Pryor, of New York; Mrs. G. Browne Good, of Washington, D. C.; Miss Mary Desha, of Kentucky; Mrs. Stephen J. Field, of California; Mrs. Thomas Alexander, of Washington, D. C.; Mrs. Rosa Wright Smith, of Washington, D. C.; Mrs. Hugh Hagan, of Georgia; Mrs. John Risley Putnam, of New York; Mrs. G. H. Shields, of Missouri; Mrs. Ellen Hardin Walworth, of New York; Mrs. Marshall MacDonald, of Virginia; Miss Eugenia Washington, of Virginia; Mrs. A. Howard Clarke, of Massachusetts; Miss Clara Barton, of Washington, D. C.; Mrs. Teunis S. Hamlin, of Washington, D. C.; Mrs. Arthur E. Clarke, of New Hampshire; Mrs. Henry Blount, of Indiana; Mrs. deB. Randolph Keim, of Connecticut; Miss Louise Ward McAllister, of New York; Mrs. Frank Stuart Osborne, of Illinois; Miss Marie Devereux, of Washington, D. C.; Mrs. Joshua Wilbour, of Rhode Island; Mrs. W. W. Shippen, of New Jersey; Mrs. N. B. Hogg, of Pennsylvania; Mrs. Clifton C. Breckinridge, of Arkansas; Mrs. Adolphus S. Hubbard, of California; Mrs. Charles E. Putnam, of Iowa; Mrs. Simon E. Buckner, of Kentucky; Mrs. Samuel Eliot, of Massachusetts; Mrs. William Wirt Henry, of Virginia; Miss Elizabeth Lee Blair, of Maryland; Mrs. Julius C. Burrows, Mrs. James McMillan, Mrs. J. A. T. Hull, and Mrs. Joseph Washington.

The charter was signed by Thomas B. Reed, and Vice-President Adlai A. Stevenson, president of the Senate, approved by Grover Cleveland, and certified to by Richard Olney. The board of management was composed of the following prominent women: Mrs. Daniel Manning, of Albany, New York; Mrs. Albert D. Brockett, Alexandria, Va.; Mrs. Russel A. Alger, Detroit, Mich.; Mrs. N. D. Sperry, New Haven, Conn.; Mrs.

John W. Thurston, Omaha, Neb.; Mrs. Horatio N. Taplin, Vt.; Mrs. Marcus A. Hanna, Cleveland, Ohio; Mrs. William W. Shippen, Seabright, N. J.; Mrs. William P. Frye, Lewiston, Me.; Mrs. John N. Jewett, Chicago, Ill.; Mrs. Eleanor W. Howard, Alexandria, Va.; Mrs. Anita Newcomb McGee, Iowa; Mrs. Ellen M. Colton, San Francisco, Cal.; Miss Mary Boyce Temple, Knoxville, Tenn.; Mrs. Charles W. Fairbanks, Indianapolis, Ind.; Miss Mary Isabella Forsyth, Kingston, N. Y.; Mrs. Abner Hoopes, West Chester, Pa.; Mrs. Charles O'Neil, Massachusetts; Miss Anna Benning, Columbus, Ga.; Mrs. Green Clay Goodloe, Kentucky; Mrs. Charlotte E. Main, Washington, D. C.; Mrs. Angus Cameron, La Crosse, Wis.; Mrs. Charles Averette Stakely, Washington, D. C.; Mrs. Albert Akers, Nashville, Tenn.; Mrs. Kate Kearney Henry, Washington, D. C.; and Miss Susan Riviere Hetzel, of Virginia.

To Mrs. Ellen Hardin Walworth, Mrs. Mary S. Lockwood, Miss Mary Desha and Miss Virginia Washington belong the credit of having conceived the idea of the organization of the Daughters of the American Revolution, and as explained by Mrs. McLean, three of these women met together and from this beginning of three the organization has grown to the number of one hundred thousand. The reports of the Daughters of the American Revolution show that the first meeting of the Continental Congress was held at the Church of Our Father, in Washington, D. C., February 22-24, 1892, with Mrs. Benjamin Harrison, the first president of the society, in the chair. The meeting was opened by the Chaplain, Mrs. Hamlin. The work which they have accomplished since that day has occupied the time, thought, and affection of hosts of noble women. Mrs. Harrison, the president-general, made the address of welcome to the delegates on this occasion, which was responded to by Mrs. Clifton R. Breckinridge, of Arkansas. After examining the credentials of the different delegates, they formed a number of committees, who took up their work with much enthusiasm.

CAROLINE SCOTT HARRISON.

Mrs. Caroline Scott Harrison, the first president-general of the Daughters of the American Revolution, and the wife of President Benjamin Harrison, was born in Oxford, Butler County, Ohio, the daughter of John Witherspoon Scott and Mary Scott; granddaughter of George McElroy Scott and Annie R. Scott, and great-granddaughter of Robert Scott, who was a member of the Scottish Parliament, before the union of the crown. Her great-grandfather, John Scott, was commissary general of the Pennsylvania line and rendered efficient service in the Revolutionary struggle for independence. Her father, Dr. John Witherspoon Scott, was a pioneer minister of the Presbyterian Church, and an educator at Oxford, Ohio. He was the president of the well-known Young Ladies' Academy at that place, where his daughters were educated. It was here that Benjamin Harrison, then a student in Miami University, met Miss Caroline W. Scott. They were married at Oxford, October 20, 1853, and removed to Indianapolis, in 1854. Mrs. Harrison's life during her husband's struggles for success as a lawyer, legislator, soldier, and statesman was that quiet homelife which is so characteristic of American homes. During all those years she showed herself the self-sacrificing, self-denying wife and mother. In every position she has filled, whether as the wife of the poor lawyer, the daring soldier, the senator, or the president of the United States, she has displayed rare adaptability. Mrs. Harrison met the demands made upon her as "first lady of the land" with wonderful success. She endeared herself to all who knew her by her unostentatious, natural womanliness. On October 11, 1890, she was unanimously elected as the first president-general of the Daughters of the American Revolution, and took great interest in the organization. During the early difficulties of the society, consequent upon the inexperience of the members and the perplexities of the organization, her advice and good judgment and kindly consideration of the feelings of others materially aided in bringing about a happy solution. At the Continental Congress, in February, 1892, she met delegates from all parts of the country, and by her courtesy and prompt decision, won the hearts of all. A Northern delegate asked one from the South: "What do you think of our Caroline?" "She is simply splendid," came the quick reply, and she voiced the sentiment of all. She was unanimously elected as president-general by a rising vote of the congress. Her patriotic feelings were intense, and the National Society will always have cause to be proud of its first president-general. Mrs. Harrison died October 25, 1892. At a meeting of the Board of Management of the National Society of the Daughters of the American Revolution, held in Washington, D. C., November 16, 1892, the following motion, made by Mrs. Walworth, was passed: "*Resolved*, That to facilitate the collection of a fund of $1,500, for a portrait of Mrs. Harrison, wife of the president of the United States and first president-general of this society, the said portrait to be placed in the White House, the

Board of Management of the National Society, Daughters of the American Revolution, authorize the action of a national committee to be composed of all officers of the National Society, state regents, honorary officers, all of whom will be ex-officio members of the committee; and that the vice-president-general presiding shall be authorized to appoint a chairman and also a treasurer to receive, report upon, and receipt for contributions; and that any surplus moneys collected over and above the amount required for the portrait, shall be appropriated to the permanent fund for the house of the Daughters of the American Revolution, to be erected in Washington, D. C., a project in which Mrs. Harrison had taken an earnest and active interest."

The Board of Management met October 25, 1892, for the purpose of expressing the feelings inspired by the sad dispensation which had deprived the National Society of the Daughters of the American Revolution of its honored president. The following members were present: Mrs. Cabell, Mrs. Kennon, Mrs. Field, Mrs. MacDonald, Mrs. Alexander, Mrs. Boynton, Mrs. Clarke, Mrs. Keim, Mrs. St. Clair, Mrs. Tittmann, Mrs. Cockrell, Mrs. Walworth, Mrs. Hamlin, Mrs. Blount, Mrs. Greely, Mrs. Devereux Miss Desha and Mrs. Rosa Wright Smith. On motion, a committee of three, composed of Mrs. Alexander, Miss Desha and Mrs. Rosa Wright Smith, was appointed to select a suitable floral offering, to be sent to the White House, in the name of the "National Society of the Daughters of the American Revolution."

CATHARINE HITCHCOCK TILDEN AVERY.

Mrs. Avery, founder and regent of the Western Reserve Chapter of the Daughters of the American Revolution, of Cleveland, Ohio, was born December 13, 1844, at Dundee, Michigan. She is the eldest daughter of Junius Tilden and Zeruah Rich Tilden. She received her early education at Monroe, Michigan. Her father died in 1861, and she, with her sister, went to Massachusetts, and was graduated at the State Normal School of Farmingham. On July 2, 1870, she was married to Elroy M. Avery, of Monroe, Michigan. In 1871 Mr. and Mrs. Avery moved to the village of East Cleveland and engaged in public school work, he as superintendent and she as principal of the high school. Mrs. Avery continued in high school work until 1882. As wife, teacher, helper, and friend she has proved her loyalty and wisdom, her benevolence and energy, and both merits and enjoys the admiration and affection of all who know her. Her chapter has been a model in its business and patriotic methods, its enthusiasm, and above all in its historic work.

KATHARINE SEARLE McCARTNEY.

Mrs. McCartney is the regent of the Wyoming Valley Chapter of the Daughters of the American Revolution of Wilkes-Barre, Pennsylvania. Her ancestry is closely associated with the earliest Colonial period. She is descended from five of the Mayflower Pilgrims, viz: William Mullins and wife; Priscilla Mullins, who married John Alden; Elizabeth Alden, the "first Puritan maiden," who married William Pebodie; Elizabeth Wabache, who married John Rogers (John Thomas, of the Mayflower); Sarah Rogers, who married Nathaniel Searle; Nathaniel Searle, Jr., assistant governor of Rhode Island from 1757-62, who married Elizabeth Kennicutt, sister of Lieutenant-Colonel Kennicutt; Constant Searle, killed in the battle of Wyoming, who married Harriet Minor, descendant of Thomas Minor and Grace Palmer; Rogers Searle, who married Catharine Scott; Leonard Searle, who married Lyda Dimock, whose grandfather was a lieutenant in the Revolutionary Army and had charge of Fort Vengeance, a northern frontier of Vermont, and who was a great-grandfather of Mrs. McCartney. She is also descended from Rev. John Mayo, Rev. John Lathrop, Nathaniel Bacon, John Coggeshall, first president of Rhode Island; John Rathbone, who came in the Speedwell in 1620; from Margaret Beach, sister of Governor Winthrop's wife, and wife of John Lake, through daughter Harriet, who married Captain John Gallup; Captain James Avery and other early colonists.

LOUISA ROCHESTER PITKIN.

Mrs. Pitkin is a daughter of Colonel Nathaniel Rochester, of Revolutionary fame, is a member of the New York Chapter and an honorary vice-president of the National Society of the Daughters of the American Revolution, and resides in Rochester, New York. She has reached the golden age of eighty-two years. Her reminiscences of these years are of great interest to her friends and to the Daughters of the American Revolution. She is an aunt of General Rochester, of the United States Army.

SARAH BERRIEN CASEY MORGAN.

Mrs. Thomas Saunderson Morgan, regent of the Augusta Chapter of the Daughters of the American Revolution, is the daughter of Dr. Henry Roger Casey and Caroline Rebecca Harriss Casey; granddaughter of Dr. John Aloysius Casey and Sarah Lowndes Berrien Casey; great-granddaughter of Brigade-Major John Berrien and Wilhamina Sarah Eliza Moore Berrien; great-great-grand-daughter of Lord Chief Justice John Berrien and Margaret Eaton Berrien (niece of Sir John Eaton, of England). Major John Berrien entered the army at the age of seventeen and was made brigadier-major at eighteen. He made the campaign of the Jerseys, was at the battle of Monmouth, and served with General Robert Howe in Georgia and Florida. He was decorated by the hand of Washington with the badge of the "Order of the Cincinnnati," and by him appointed secretary of that society. After the war he was made treasurer of the state of Georgia. He died in 1815, and is buried in Savannah, Ga. Lord Chief Justice John Berrien, the father of Major Berrien, was a personal friend of General Washington, who often shared the hospitality of the chief justice's home at Rock Hill, Somerset County, New Jersey. It was from that home that "The Father of his Country" bade farewell to his gallant band when the war was over. Lady Berrien, the wife of the chief justice, gave her family silver to be melted in order to assist in paying the soldiers of the Revolutionary Army. Washington used the home of Chief Justice Berrien as his headquarters. When offering to have the home repaired, which had suffered by its usage during the war, Lady Berrien declined, saying: "What I have done for my country, I have done." Through Wilhamina Sarah Eliza Moore Berrien, Major Berrien's wife, Mrs. Morgan is descended from Dr. James Weemyss Moore. This Dr. Moore, Mrs. Morgan's great-great-grand-father, was a surgeon of the South Carolina troops under General Gates. Insensible must be the heart and cold the patriotism of one who cannot be touched by such memories as these. Mrs. Morgan has also an honorable ancestry through Dr. James Weemyss Moore, who is descended from the Earl of Weemyss, who was the second son of the Macduff of Shakespeare. Through her grandfather, Dr. Aloysius Casey, Mrs. Morgan is descended from Sir John Edgeworth, of Longworth, Ireland, a cousin of Maria Edgeworth, the noted author.

MARY NEWTON.

For years Mrs. Newton, of Athens, Georgia, has received a pension from the government in virtue of being the only surviving child of John Jordan, who was a Revolutionary hero, and was at Yorktown when Cornwallis surrendered. Mrs. Newton is now eighty-seven years of age, and is remarkable for her activity and much beloved by all who know her.

JANE SUMNER OWEN KEIM.

The family roll of honor in the Revolution contains the names of eighteen heroes in the three collateral lines of Sumner descent from the colonists, some of whom belong to that of Mrs. Keim, including also Robert, the son of her fighting ancestor, Captain John Sumner. Mrs. Keim's paternal great-great-grandfather, Benjamin Owen, born in 1761, at Ashford, Connecticut, fourth descendant from Samuel and Priscilla Belcher Owen, who came to America from Wales in 1685, with their son Josiah, and settled first in Massachusetts and later in Rhode Island, was a captain in the Windham County, Connecticut, militia. The sixth line of Mrs. Keim's Colonial and Revolutionary ancestry, the Palmers, descended from Walter, the settler in the Endicott Colony, through Ruth Palmer, her great-grandmother, were also distinguished for patriotic service in the Revolution. Dr. Joseph Palmer, the father of Ruth Palmer, served as a surgeon in the Continental forces. At the outbreak of the Revolution he was captain of a company from Voluntown for the relief of Boston during the Lexington alarm. Mrs. Jane Sumner Owen Keim was born in Hartford, Connecticut, and educated in the public schools of her native city, graduating in 1862 from the high school, formerly the Latin grammar school, founded in 1636, the second oldest institution of the kind in America. She took a higher course of two years at East Greenwich Seminary, on Narragansett Bay, Rhode Island. She engaged immediately in charitable work in the city of her birth, teaching seven years in the Sixth Ward Evening School, and was active in city mission, Sunday and sewing schools. She also organized, with Miss Fannie Smith, authoress, pianist, and lecturer, and conducted for some years a boys' reading room and Sixth Ward Temperance Society, out of which initial movement sprung the "union for home work," a noble charity in Hartford to-day.   Mrs. Keim has the gratification of knowing that many boys taught by her in charity have become men of prosperous business in several states.   On June 25, 1872, she became the wife of deBenneville Randolph Keim, of "Edgemount," Reading, Pennsylvania, an author and Washington correspondent.   They spent six months in foreign travel.   They visited the localities associated with their ancestral families and nearly all the countries of Europe, extending their journey to Nijni Novgorod, on the Volga.

MRS. ROGER A. PRYOR.

The Southern woman-writer has become, of late years, an important factor in the literary life of New York.   One who is perhaps at present better known in the first circles of society in New York than in literature, as yet, is Mrs. Roger A. Pryor, the lovely wife of Judge Pryor, of the Court of Common Pleas.   Mrs. Pryor is known in New York as the writer of charming and brilliant feuilletons for the most prominent society journal there, but she invariably publishes over a pen-name, so that, outside the circle who penetrated the secret of her nom-de-plume, she is best known as a society woman.   She has also published many sketches and short stories.   "The Story of a Persian Rug" was copied widely in English periodicals, and was the true story of an exquisite Persian carpet that lies before the hearth of her pretty drawing room.   Mrs. Pryor has refused the most flattering offers from editors to write over her own name, for probably there is no one who can write more cleverly and authoritatively on social life in New York than she.   She has no methods of work, writing when she feels the inclination.   Mrs. Pryor was a Southern heiress, born to every imaginable luxury, and never a life looked more hedged in with happiness than hers, yet, when the war wrecked and stranded the fortunes of the family, no bourgeois housewife ever performed heavier duties to a large family, ever sewed more diligently on her children's little garments, than this brave and brilliant woman in that dark period after the war when so many great fortunes were swept away.   Through the efforts of Mrs. Pryor a handsome sum has been added to the Mary Washington Monument Association fund, and this is most gratifying to the Daughters of the American Revolution, as one of the first working objects placed before the Daughters by an early resolution of the society was assistance to be given to this Mary Washington fund.   It is a noble cause, in which women are called upon to honor a woman who displayed high qualities of character under conspicuous circumstances—one who combined tenderness with strength, and dignity with simplicity, as found in the individuality of Mary Washington.   Mrs. Pryor's services to the Society of the Daughters of the American Revolution cannot be compassed in this brief sketch.   She was the first regent of the New York City chapter.   She organized it and led it on to success under trying circumstances.   After serving for over a year she resigned on account of uncertain health, amid the regrets of the chapter.   As vice-president-general of the National Society, and a member of the New York City chapter, she is still active in her efforts for the organization.   Mrs. Pryor's home in New York is a charming place, where, in her artistic drawing-room, the hospitable traditions of her family are maintained, and at her weekly receptions one may meet many agreeable and eminent persons.

DELIA GRAEME SMALLWOOD.

Mrs. Smallwood, vice-regent of the District of Columbia, was born in Lawrence, Massachusetts. Her Revolutionary ancestry is on the side of her mother, whose people have lived in New England for many generations. Her great-grandfather, Dr. James Jackson, for whom the town of Jackson, New Hampshire, was named, was one of the first surgeons of New England. Another ancestor was Joseph Clark, who was one of the men who rowed General Benedict Arnold to the British ship "Vulture" on the morning of his desertion and who refused a command in the British army which was offered him as an inducement to remain on the British side. One of the earliest of Mrs. Smallwood's ancestors in this country was General Hercules Mooney, who came from the north of Ireland in his own boat, "The Hercules," landing at Plymouth, New Hampshire. He was highly educated and became one of the foremost teachers of his day. He served in the early Colonial wars as a British colonel and took part in the capture of Louisburg. At the beginning of the Revolutionary War, however, he united his fortunes with the American colonies, was made a general and figured largely in the northern campaign of that heroic seven years' struggle. Through her father Mrs. Smallwood belongs to the Graemes of Scotland and the Hetheringtons of England. "The Fighting Graemes," as they were called, have served in every English and Scotch war and at the battle of Bunker Hill they were in the British army and stormed the heights which her mother's people were valiantly defending. Mrs. Smallwood's family have always placed a high valuation upon education. Her own was obtained in Boston, where she received the advantages of its splendid public school system in conjunction with private tutoring in music, art, oratory, literature and science, and finally occupied a high position as a teacher in the Boston public schools. For years she has been, conjointly with her husband, principal of the Washington Seminary of the Capital city. Mrs. Smallwood is a public spirited woman, active in the philanthropic work of the city, and she is closely identified with the Young Women's Christian Association as one of its vice-presidents. She is well known as an accomplished teacher, able speaker and an enthusiastic member of the Daughters of the American Revolution. She is tireless in her work in whatever case she champions.

RUTH M. GRISWOLD PEALER.

Ruth M. Griswold Pealer, genealogist of the Daughters of the American Revolution, was born in Dansville, Steuben County, N. J., daughter of Hubbard Griswold, one of the pioneers of western New York, a descendant through an unbroken male line from Edward Griswold, of Kenilworth, England, who settled in Connecticut in 1639.

In early life Ruth Griswold was a student at the Rogersville Union Seminary, near her home, and spent a year at the seminary in Dansville, Livingston County, N. Y. At the age of seventeen she became a teacher in a country school, which occupation she followed until her marriage in 1869 to Philip J. Greene, who was also a teacher of Dansville, N. Y. He died in 1883, leaving her with one son. In 1881 Mrs. Pealer, then Mrs. Greene, was a member of the faculty of the Rogerville Union Seminary as teacher of music. During this period she was also active in grange work of her county.

In 1885 she married Peter Perry Pealer, of South Dansville, N. Y., who in 1890 was a member of the New York State legislature from the first district of Steuben, and later received an appointment as chief of a division in the Government Printing Office, Washington, D. C. Previous to her removal to Washington, Mrs. Peeler had taken an active part in club work and musical circles, having been one of the organizers and president of the literary club in South Dansville. This club was instrumental in securing a free library for the town. Soon after her removal to Washington she became a member of the National Society of the Daughters of the American Revolution and joined "Continental Chapter," of which she became recording secretary. At the Daughters of the American Revolution Congress of 1902, she was elected registrar-general, and re-elected in 1903. In the fall of 1903 she resigned and was elected genealogist of the National Society, which position she still holds.

Mrs. Pealer is also the national registrar of the Daughters of Founders and Patriots of America, serving her fifth term. She is a past-president of the Woman's National Press Association and a past-secretary-general of the National Auxiliary, United Spanish War Veterans, an organization which she assisted in forming soon after the close of the Spanish-American War. For two years she was president of the first auxiliary formed—"Mary A. Babcock, of Washington, D. C."

Work for temperance has also appealed strongly to her and for three years she was president of the West End Union Woman's Christian Temperance Union in Washington, and for years has been the superintendent of the Press on the State Executive Woman's Christian Temperance Union. She is a member of the Washington Colony of New England Women and a member of the Order of the Eastern Star in Canaseraga, N. Y.

Some Real Daughters of the American Revolution.

These women are our nearest links in independence and it is surprising fact that there are one hundred and fifty-eight "Real Daughters" alive to-day (July 4, 1911). Sentiment has impelled the Daughters of the American Revolution organization to provide each "real daughter" with an enduring souvenir to be handed down to posterity, and this memento takes the form of a solid gold spoon properly inscribed. No dues or fees are expected from these survivors, as members of the Daughters of the American Revolution.

The oldest living child of a Revolutionary patriot is

MRS. ILEY LAWSON HILL,

of Lakeport, California, who is over one hundred and three years of age, having been born in Adams County, Ohio, May 5, 1808. Her patriot father, James Lawson, was born in 1760, and was but seventeen years of age when he entered Washington's army, and when the war for our independence was over he fought in some of the Indians wars.

MRS. SAMANTHA STANTON NELLIS.

The next "real daughter" in point of age is Mrs. Samantha Stanton Nellis, of Naples, New York, whose father Elijah Stanton, was one of Washington's bodyguard. She was one hundred and one years of age January 5 last (1911).

MRS. SUSAN S. BRIGHAM.

Mrs. Susan S. Brigham, of Worcester, Massachusetts, won her century goal February 3, 1911, and is the daughter of Ammi Wetherbee, a Massachusetts Minute Man.

Very close indeed to the century mark are Mrs. Jane Newkirk, of Laporte, Indiana, and Mrs. Margaret K. Johnson, of Flemington, Kentucky; also Miss Jeannette Blair, of Madison, New York, who entered upon her ninety-eighth year May 30, 1911. Her father, Seth Blair, enlisted three times during the Revolution.

MRS. MARY ANNE RISHEL,

of Clintondale, Pennsylvania, is the daughter of a Revolutionary veteran, a sister of a veteran of the War of 1812 and the mother of a Civil War veteran. Her father served during five years of the Revolution as a ranger on the frontier. Mrs. Rishel celebrated her ninetieth birthday, March 23, 1911.

Two remarkable women among this group of "real daughters" are the twin sisters, Elizabeth Ann Russell and Julia Ann Demary, of Lake Odessa, Michigan, daughters of John Peter Frank, a patriot of the Revolution.

MRS. EUPHRASIA SMITH GRANGER

in 1909 came to Washington to the annual meeting of the Daughters of the American Revolution as an alternate for her regent.

MRS. MARY ANNE SCOTT,

of Medway, Massachusetts, who was born December 29, 1851, when her father, Thomas Platt, a veteran of the Dorchester Heights Guards was in his eighty-eighth year, is said to be the youngest "real daughter."

Although one hundred and thirty years have elapsed since Cornwallis surrendered, there is still one Revolutionary pensioner upon the government pension rolls, Phœbe M. W. Palmiter, of Brookfield, New York, who entered upon her ninetieth year December, 1911. Her father was Jonathan Wooley, born in Swansea, New Hampshire, August 21, 1759, and died in Vermont, July 21, 1848. He enlisted in the Vermont Volunteers in 1775 at the age of sixteen in Colonel Capron's command and served under Gates and Sullivan. He was present at Saratoga at the surrender of Burgoyne and also took part in the battle at Valley Forge.

LUCY PARLIN.

Almost in sight of Judge's cave, in the home of her son-in-law, near New Haven, Connecticut, lives Mrs. Lucy Parlin, one of the surviving daughters of the heroes of 1776. The father of this venerable lady was Elijah Royce, of Wolcott, Connecticut, who at the age of sixteen enlisted in the Revolutionary Army and served seven years and three months. In the famous battle of Monmouth, New Jersey, he received a severe sabre wound on the face and was left for dead on the field. During the terrible winter at Valley Forge, Corporal Royce was awakened one night by some intruder who was trying to share his scanty blanket. He kicked the unwelcome visitor most lustily, and when daybreak came, to his surprise and chagrin, he saw the familiar features of the Marquis de Lafayette.

MRS. DONALD McLEAN.

"Mrs. Donald McLean, member and vice-president of the New York State Commission to the Jamestown Exposition, and president-general of the Daughters of the American Revolution, was born in Prospect Hall, Frederick, Maryland; and is the daughter of Judge and Mrs. John Ritchie. Her father was judge of the Court of Appeals of Maryland, and served in the National Congress before his elevation to the bench.

"Mrs. McLean's grandfather was Judge William P. Maulsby, and her grandmother, Emily Nelson (for whom Mrs. McLean is named), was the daughter of General Roger Nelson, who was at college, a boy of sixteen, when the Declaration of Independence was signed. He ran away from the university and joined the Revolutionary forces. He was commissioned lieutenant, and afterwards brevetted brigadier-general for conspicuous bravery on the field of battle. Later in life he served in the National Congress, and afterwards was placed upon the bench of his native state.

"Further back in Mrs. McLean's ancestry were Judges Lynn and Beattie, two of the twelve judges known as 'The Twelve Immortals,' who first signed a protest against the British Stamp Act, eleven years before the first battle of the

Revolution.   Lieutenant James Lackland was also an ancestor, as was one of the earlier deputy governors of Maryland, Governor Burgess.

"Mrs. McLean was educated at the Frederick Female Seminary, now known as the Woman's College.   She graduated at the age of fourteen, receiving a diploma.   She continued the study of history, the languages, and music until her marriage and, indeed, has pursued the former ever since.   In 1883 she married Mr. Donald McLean, a lawyer of standing in New York, who has had various distinctions in office conferred upon him by the President of the United States and the Mayor of the City of New York.   Mrs. McLean is the mother of three children.

"From the time of her marriage and removal from Maryland to New York, Mrs. McLean has been interested in social, professional and educational circles of that city.   On learning of the formation of the Daughters of the American Revolution, her interest was immediately aroused, and she became a charter member of the society, and also of the New York City Chapter of that organization, being elected to its regency.   A scholarship in perpetuity has been founded in Barnard College by the New York City Chapter, and named the 'Mrs. Donald McLean Scholarship.'   Mrs. McLean held the office of regent for ten years, until her election, in April, 1905, to the presidency-general of the National Society of the Daughters of the American Revolution.

"The president-general has served as an active commissioner from New York to the Cotton States International Exposition, in 1895, and as an honorary commissioner to the South Carolina Exposition.   She made public addresses at both above-named expositions; also at the Tennessee Exposition, and at the Pan-American Exposition, in 1901, at Buffalo, and at the Louisiana Purchase Exposition, in 1903-04, at St. Louis,—

representing the varied interests of women, education, and the Daughters of the American Revolution. Mrs. McLean was an active commissioner and vice-president of the commission from New York to the Jamestown Exposition. In the president-general's administration a memorial building has been erected by the D. A. R. on Jamestown Island in Virginia, which building is a replica of the old Malvern Hall, and will remain as a permanent 'rest house,' upon the island.

"Mrs. McLean has traveled several hundred thousand miles throughout the states, visiting innumerable cities and towns, making addresses upon patriotic subjects, not only in furthering the work of the Daughters of the American Revolution, but in participation in civic and national patriotic celebrations. She is deeply interested in the work of patriotic education, both for immigrants and Southern mountaineers, as well as in keeping alive a patriotic spirit in all classes of American citizens, and is widely and internationally known as a speaker in patriotic and educational gatherings, and in her interest in the movement for peace by arbitration."

The foregoing sketch of Mrs. Donald McLean was taken from the report of the Jamestown Exposition Commission of the state of New York. Mrs. McLean was the only woman upon that distinguished commission, and this report gives indubitable evidence of the high esteem in which she was held by the commission, and their appreciation of her keen perceptions, rare intelligence, sound judgment, and wonderful executive ability.

It has been the editor's valued privilege to have known Mrs. McLean since the beginning of the twentieth century, and she takes pleasure in adding that among the thousands of gifted women she has met during these years Mrs. McLean is second to none in largeness of heart, brilliancy of mind, quickness of perception, eloquence of speech, marvelous executive ability, genial disposition, sturdiness of purpose, and charming personality. As president-general of the Daughters of the American Revolution she lifted the society out of the chaos into which contentious rivals had dragged it, and placed it in the line of progression and achievement. She made the dream of Continental Hall a possible reality by her skillful financial management. No other woman has received greater honors or worn them more gracefully than has Mrs. Donald McLean, who is among the most faithful of wives, tenderest of mothers, loyal of daughters, truest of patriots, most generous and loyal of friends.

ELLEN HARDIN WALWORTH.

Mrs. Walworth was born in Jacksonville, Illinois, and is a daughter of General John J. Hardin, United States Volunteers, and Sarah Ellen Hardin. She was educated at Jacksonville Academy and by private tutors. She was married at Saratoga Springs, New York, to M. T. Walworth in 1852. She graduated from the Woman's Law Class of the University of New York. She was president and founder of the Art and Science Field Club of Saratoga and founder and ex-president of the Post Parliament, New York, and was one of the first three women nominated and elected to a school board under the New York law admitting women as trustees. She is chiefly prominent as being one of the three founders—with Miss Eugenia Washington and Miss Mary Desha—of the National Society of the Daughters of the American Revolution. She was director general of the Woman's National War Relief Association in 1898, and was at the Field Hospital at Fortress Monroe to meet the first wounded brought from Santiago, with supplies, nurses, etc. She went to Montauk and remained in the Field Hospital there until it closed. She has served on many important committees of the Daughters of the American Revolution. She is the author of "Battles of Saratoga," "Parliamentary Rules," also various monographs.

MRS. MATTHEW T. SCOTT.

Mrs. M. T. Scott, recently re-elected as president-general of the Daughters of the American Revolution, is one of the most charming and interesting personalities in American public life. She is a rare combination of the best that blood, culture and wealth can produce on our continent.

Born in old Kentucky, her ancestry goes back through a long line of the best, bravest and the most distinguished men and women that this country can boast, including such names as that of Lawrence Washington, Colonel Joshua Fry, Augustine Warner, Dr. Thomas Walker, etc.

Her father, the Reverend Lewis Warner Green, was one of the most eloquent and scholarly divines of his generation, and was at one time president of Hampden Sydney College, Virginia, and later of Centre College, Danville, Kentucky. Up to his premature death at the age of fifty-six, he was recognized as one of the intellectual and spiritual leaders of the old South, who by sheer force of brains and character, so largely directed and dominated our national life up to the time of the Civil War. The home life of the youthful Hypatia could hardly have been more propitious for the development of those charms and graces of mind and character, which have gained for her so unique a position in the history of womankind, than was that of the beautiful and accomplished Miss Julia Green.

At the age of nineteen her romantic and sheltered girlhood was brought to an end by her marriage and migration across the almost trackless prairies, to take up her abode among the prairie dogs and rattlesnakes of central Illinois. Here for a score of years she threw herself heart and soul into her self-appointed tasks of inspiring and helping her husband, who rapidly became one of the financial, political and intellectual "master builders" of this great region, and of making her home a center from which radiated countless refining and ennobling influences on every side. The good old Southern way in which these hospitable Kentuckians entertained friends and relatives for weeks and even for months at a time, was for years the talk of the countryside.

On her husband's sudden death in the midst of his brilliant business career, she found herself forced to take his place at the helm, and to concentrate all her thought and attention upon the heavy responsibilities connected with the management of the M. T. Scott estate, one of the largest estates in this the most fertile and influential agricultural region in the world. To the surprise of herself and her closest friends, her sound judgment and careful husbandry soon gained for her the title of "the best business man in central Illinois." Moreover, with that dignity, poise and balance which have always been her distinguishing characteristics, she demonstrated that it is quite possible to be hard-headed without being hard-hearted. For in spite of being a first-class woman of affairs, she never forgot nor allowed others to forget, that first of all she was an old-fashioned Kentucky gentlewoman.

Up to the time of her election to the highest office within the gift of the women of this country, Mrs. Scott had been too completely occupied with her own business interests to devote much time or energy to club matters or public affairs. But in spite of this, her friends had quietly pushed her to the front as much as she would permit, instinctively recognizing her innate capacity for leadership, and for the effective handling of large enterprises.

It is a curious and interesting psychological fact, that at an age when most women don becoming lace caps and retire to the fireplace with their knitting—to watch the procession of life go by—Mrs. Scott, whose previous years had been almost exclusively devoted to her home, her friends and her business interests, should suddenly have launched out on a new, untried and signally tempestuous sea of activity, where she at once assumed a prominent, and very soon, a dominant position.

Mrs. Scott during her incumbency as president-general of the Daughters of the American Revolution has been a surprise to herself and her friends as well as to her enemies. Talents and traits of character which had lain almost dormant for a quarter of a century were aroused to newness of life by the fresh interests aroused and the new duties which were imposed upon her by her high official position.

When she went to Bloomington, Illinois, to attend the "homecoming banquet" given by her friends and neighbors, she made a powerful and polished speech, putting into it all the strength and restrained force of character of which she is capable. A day or two after, a remark was made by an old friend and neighbor, which gave expression to the widespread feeling among those present at the banquet. "I have come to the conclusion," she said, "that though I have known Mrs. Scott for so long and have known her so intimately, I have always underestimated her. I was aware that she was a woman of great ability, but I am free to confess, that I did not think she had it in her to speak as she spoke last night. I did not realize that we had in our midst a woman of such intellectual grasp, and such wonderful personal dignity and strength."

However, the eloquence and literary charm of her speeches are apparent to everyone. What is, perhaps, less generally known and certainly more rare in her makeup, is her largeness, her ability to rise above petty personal considerations, the broad impersonal way she has of treating people and questions that are brought to her attention. For example, when some of her old-time friends have deserted her and joined the ranks of the enemy, she not only has wasted no time nor energy in recriminations and lamentations, but actually has felt no bitterness toward them. The ability to maintain this attitude is very rare among men and almost unheard of among women. It has something about it that is reminiscent of the attitude manifested towards quitters and turncoats by Julius Caesar in Bernard Shaw's "Caesar and Cleopatra" and shows the remarkable mastery of the conscious mind, of the rational element in her nature, over whims, prejudices and ordinary human passions.

The past two years have also proven to be a sort of Indian Summer for the spiritual element in her nature. The old-time ideals which she had learned to love as a girl sitting at her father's feet, the old-time belief in the efficacy of spiritual powers and the reality of spiritual values have again been quickened into life. The long stretch of years during which she was largely engrossed in family affairs and the heavy labors involved in the management of the material interests of herself and her children, was brought to a close when she assumed her present position of moral and intellectual leadership among American women. As a widow and a mother, she did not hesitate to focus all her energies and abilities upon the financial duties and responsibilities which she felt demanded her first attention, but when these affairs having been satisfactorily and successfully attended to, new intellectual and spiritual responsibilities were thrust upon her, the latent moral fires and spiritual enthusiasms of her girlhood burst into sudden flame— the idealistic element in her nature again asserted itself. To her own surprise, as much as that of her friends and family, she threw into her new work not only the practical skill, and trained energy, which had been developed during her long business career, but as well the old moral fervor and the old spiritual outlook, that had been handed down to her as a rich spiritual inheritance from her distinguished father.

In spite of the fact that she has manifested an extraordinary ability as a presiding officer, showing not only a remarkable mastery of parliamentary law, but an even more remarkable mastery of all the complicated and tempestuous situations that have arisen during the various discussions of the nineteenth and twentieth Congresses; and in spite of the fact that her unusual business and executive ability have enabled her to manage all the financial and administrative affairs of the National Society, with a clear head and a firm hand, yet undoubtedly the most distinctive thing about her administration has been her own personality—that subtle combination of the patrician and the idealist, which has enabled her to infuse into the organization so much of her own spirit of refinement, strength and moral fervor.

In nearly all of her speeches, she somewhere and somehow manages to strike the same clear and fearless note of noble aspiration, high purpose, fearless independence and invincible resolve. In her address at the opening session of the nineteenth Continental Congress occurs the following passage which is a fair sample of her literary style and of her conception of the mission of the "Daughters."

"The National Society of the Daughters of the American Revolution had its genesis in the sentiment of 'noblesse oblige.' It is our proud title to distinction that we trace our ancestry back, not to forbears distinguished for the arrogance of wealth, or the supercilious vanity that is based upon a supposed aristocratic blueness in our blood—but one and all of us trace our lineage back to faithful men and women whose splendid distinction it was to have served their country in their time, at the sacrifice of all that was most precious from the material standpoint of life. Ours is an aristocracy of *service*. It is no light responsibility to have become, as we have undertaken to make ourselves, the ambassadors in this twentieth century, of the ruling spirits of the colonies of the last half of the eighteenth century—the time that tried men out and called them to cement with their blood a union of new-born states, setting up for the whole modern world, so startling a conception of political freedom, religious tolerance and social justice."

The Daughters of the American Revolution have since their inception, some twenty-two years ago, selected worthy and distinguished women to wear the badge of supreme authority. Mrs. Benjamin Harrison, Mrs. Adlai Stevenson, Mrs. John W. Foster, Mrs. Daniel Manning, Mrs. Charles Warren Fairbanks, Mrs. Donald McLean and the present incumbent, Mrs. Matthew T. Scott, of Bloomington, Illinois. Mrs. Scott is now well into the third year of her stewardship, and the list of splendid results which may be directly ascribed to her methods is worthy of five times that lapse of time. Like Joshua, she led the cohorts into the land of their desire—the Continental Memorial Hall—and has placed the business affairs of the society on a firm financial basis which will lighten the burden for her successors for all time to come. To build this national hall of fame had been the goal of the society's ambition from the early days of its existence. Every president-general which the Daughters elected labored indefatigably for this end, but it was the keen business acumen, the steady purpose and unflagging labor of Mrs. Scott which made possible so speedy a realization of this hope. Mrs. Donald McLean had by her prompt action in raising the money by mortgage made possible the erection of the hall without the slow, painful method of waiting for the money to be collected. Mrs. Scott took up the work with splendid energy and pushed the lagging forward, closed out every contract connected with the building and planning without one lawsuit or even unfriendly episode with those in charge of the construction. This is a remarkable record in Washington, where even the national government gets entangled in the laws affecting labor and construction. Pushing the work to a speedy termination and taking possession of the Memorial Hall far in advance of the time generally named, Mrs. Scott saved the society a tidy sum in the rental of a great suite of offices. During this same busy juncture of time, she has begun the reorganization of the business affairs of the society in the effort to place it on the same plane as that of other corporate enterprises. The result will be that the society will be saved a considerable amount annually which is to go into the treasury to take up the notes due on the Memorial Hall.

This Valhalla is in an especial way dear to Mrs. Scott, as her sister, Mrs. Adlai Stevenson, who was second and fourth president-general of the Daughters, was the first to crystallize the endeavor to collect funds for its erection. It is unique among the magnificient halls which the national Capital or the country at large possesses. It is the largest and most costly monument ever erected by women in this land or any other, in this era or any past one. It is besides, the first grand monument erected to all heroes who helped to gain American independence, men and women alike. The insignia of the society, the distaff, is pregnant with memories of the noble women who were the ancestresses of those who from the motives of purest patriotism erected the noble memorial. The history and achievements of the Daughters of the American Revolution are written in this hall in letters of bronze and marble. It is a Corinthian temple built of white Vermont marble with a wonderful colonnade, thirteen majestic pillars, typical of the thirteen states which formed the first American union and given by the Daughters from each of these historic commonwealths. Magnificent among the stately buildings which are its near neighbors, the Corcoran Gallery of Art and the Bureau of American Republics, the Memorial Continental Hall is an achievement of which every woman in the land may be proud, because it is the result of the conservation of the vital forces obtainable when worthy women are leagued together.

The interior of the hall has been the object of loving solicitude from the day the foundation stone was laid. It is a rare combination of delicate and graceful symmetry combined with every practical consideration. Over each door and in the ornamental niches may be seen busts of heroes, gifts of states, chapters and of individuals. The beginnings of the nation are plainly written here—George Washington, Benjamin Franklin, Thomas Jefferson, John Hancock, Nathan Hale, John Adams, James Oglethorpe, Edward Hand, Isaac Shelby, John Stark, General Clinton, and Ethan Allen look down benignly on the passersby.

Mrs. Scott's energy and enthusiasm is well attested in the rich and varied decorations of the various rooms. Always ready to encourage and to suggest, the entire hall is now furnished, nearly every pledge made by the members has been redeemed, and the hall stands in completeness, a sign of what the strong purpose and ripe judgment of the present president-general accomplished in little more than two years. Mrs. Scott brought all forces into a mighty effort to this endeavor and she used all means at her command. In a word she gathered, while she might have scattered.

All these material proofs of her success as an executive officer are worthy of all praise, but when the sum total of Mrs. Scott's regime as president-general is computed, it will be found that her best and most useful service has been in the deep and intelligent study which she has given the ideals and aspirations of the society, and her dominant energy in forcing the public to accept them, and not a preconceived, distorted notion. She has elevated the tone of the society; not that she has labored for this end especially, but her dignity and personal worth have eliminated the smaller issues which for a time overpowered the real issues. Mrs. Scott is the first president-general from whom the President of the United States accepted an invitation to open a Continental Congress. The highest officials of the land feel honored when they are requested to appear before the Daughters, and the wives of the loftiest officials now work side by side with the councillors. Those who went before Mrs. Scott solved many a problem and did many a useful and uplifting service to the society, but it remained for her to place the Daughters of the American Revolution before the country as they should be known.   She broke down the bulwark of ridicule and sarcasm which greeted every effort, erected by a sensation-loving press of the country.   She made it plain to those responsible for giving such news to the world that to bear false witness applied to women organized as well as to women individually, and through courteous and gentle means she showed the injustice with which her society had been treated. In this she performed a service for the society greater in the moral sense than the brilliant management of the business affairs is in a material way.

Very recently she has been elected president of the McLean County Coal Company, of Bloomington, Illinois, to succeed the former vice-president, Adlai Stevenson.   The respect and admiration in which she is held by her Illinois neighboring farmers, many of them keen-witted business men, is in itself a tribute which bears testimony to her rating in the realm of great and practical affairs.   Her farms yield a golden harvest, but better is the distinction which she has earned as a stimulus to scientific farming and a factor in the future welfare of her environment.   One of her many wisely beneficent deeds is to send a certain number of her tenants yearly to the Agricultural College of Illinois to prepare themselves for more productive work.

Mrs. Scott has always taken a keen interest in inland water-ways, and she has served on many committees which inquired into that problem which so vitally concerns the future.   She has learned by practical experience the excellent results of con-serving water.   As Father Noah says in that wonderful poem of Jean Ingelow, "With my foot, have I turned the river to water grasses that are fading," she has redeemed a wilderness in the lower counties of Iowa by means of irrigation.

A favorite charity of Mrs. Scott's is to aid the mountain whites in various Southern states, but especially in her home state, Kentucky. Many years ago, she established a school at Phelps, Kentucky, named in honor of her husband, the Matthew T. Scott Institute. Her noble intention is when she rests from the arduous labors connected with the stewardship of the Daughters, to devote her time and energy to arousing the people of this country to their duties towards the poor mountaineers. Mrs. Scott deplores that so much more is given to educate and uplift the Afro-American race than for the poor whites who are left in ignorance and poverty, without hope or ambition. That this phase of our national neglect is now receiving so much attention may be attributed in a large measure to public-spirited women like Mrs. Scott, who by word and deed have set the example of what should be done. She served for many years with eminent success as secretary of the Home Missionary Board of the Presbyterian Church of Illinois, and later as president of the Woman's Club of Bloomington.

Mrs. Scott has written a charming book on her Revolutionary ancestors. This book is intended for her children and grandchildren and has only a limited circulation. It contains some exceedingly interesting facts and ranks among the genealogical records of times remote from written history. Even a meagre list of the famous men and women from whom Mrs. Scott and her sister, Mrs. Stevenson, claim descent, would make a long article. One of the very interesting points, however, is that one of her first American ancestresses was Mildred Warner, aunt and godmother of the "Father of His Country." This hallowed name is perpetuated in the only granddaughter of Mrs. Scott, Mildred Warner Bromwell, daughter of her elder daughter, Letitia, wife of Colonel Charles S. Bromwell, U. S. A.

Since she became president-general of the Daughters of

the American Revolution, historic work has been emphasized and innumerable landmarks have been saved from the decaying tooth of time. She encouraged the marking of the trails followed by the pioneers of the nation, and almost every month some new achievement in this line has been recorded in the annals of the society. The trail of the first adventurers to the Golden West has been marked by the Pueblo Chapter of Colorado; the Natchez trail by the Tennessee Daughters; the Oregon trail by the Daughters of Nebraska. General Harrison's military road has been marked by the Daughters of Ohio and Indiana, and the path of Daniel Boone by the Daughters of the American Revolution of Kentucky. But while urging the marking of historic spots, Mrs. Scott has always urged on the society that deeds are more prolific of results than words, and she deplores that so many believe that patriotism is best expressed by enthusiastic devotion to the past. She gives profound deference to the past, but under her leadership the seventy-six thousand women who compose the National Society Daughters of the American Revolution are endeavoring to obtain exact knowledge of present conditions. Her ambition is that the Daughters shall play an important part in forming public opinion upon certain vital national questions— child labor, the Juvenile Court, patriotic education in all its scope, playgrounds, the observance of a safe and sane July 4th, the preservation of historic spots and records, and the conservation of the national resources in the interest of the future homemakers of the nation. Mrs. Scott's optimistic philosophy put in epigrammatic form is, that there "exists in the heart and mind of every loyal American woman, latent civic and moral sentiment that needs only to be aroused and intelligently focused, in order to make of women one of the most potent and resistless factors for good in the civilization of the twentieth century."

Mrs. Matthew T. Scott is one of the noblest types of American womanhood. Her character in every sense is worthy of emulation by those who come after her.

EUGENIA WASHINGTON.

Miss Washington was born beneath the shadow of the Blue Ridge Mountains near the romantic and historic Harper's Ferry. Her father, William Temple Washington, a graduate of William and Mary College, educated his daughters at home. About 1859 Miss Washington's father moved to Falmouth, opposite Fredericksburg, the Rappahannock flowing between. On this debatable land, between the contending armies of the Civil War, the family suffered all the horrors and all the hardships, and the end showed them deprived of all worldly goods. Mrs. Washington soon died and was followed in a short time by Mr. Washington. Miss Eugenia Washington was offered and accepted an honorable place under the government and made Washington her home until her death. On her mother's side she was descended from Charles Francis Joseph, Count de Flechir, and who served in the War of the Revolution. He was the friend and kinsman of Lafayette. On her father's side she was descended from John Washington who, with his brother Lawrence, settled in the northern neck in Westmoreland County, where the Potomac ran strong and ample and there was easy trade with the home ports of London and Bristol. Descended from such illustrious ancestry on both sides, closely allied with the Father of His Country, George Washington, and of lineal descent from so many who served in the war that made us a nation, it was fitting that Miss Washington should be identified with the organization of the National Daughters of the American Revolution. She was one of the founders and the first registrar. Having served the society as registrar-general, secretary-general and vice-president-general she was, in 1895, made honorary vice-president-general, which high position was for life. She was presented by the society with a magnificent jeweled badge, showing the high appreciation in which she was held and that they recognized in her one of the founders of the great powerful organization. Miss Eugenia Washington died at Washington on Thanksgiving Day, 1900.

MARY DESHA.

Miss Desha was born in Lexington, Kentucky, and was the daughter of Dr. John Randolph and Mary Bracken Desha. She was educated at Sayre Institute and the Kentucky State College at Lexington. She was a teacher in the Kentucky public schools for twelve years, until 1886, when she came to Washington to take a position under the government. This she held until her death in 1910. Miss Desha is most prominent as having been one of the three founders—with Mrs. Ellen Hardin Walworth and Miss Eugenia Washington—of the National Society of the Daughters of the American Revolution. In that society she served in many capacities. She was assistant director of the Daughters of the American Revolution Hospital Corps, which furnished a thousand trained nurses during the Spanish-American War. She was an honorary vice-president-general of the National Society, and served on many of its committees. Miss Desha was a president of the Albert Sidney Johnston Chapter of the United Daughters of the Confederacy, and was parliamentarian of the National Mary Washington Memorial Association and recording secretary of the Pocahontas Memorial Association.

MRS. JOHN W. FOSTER.

Mrs. Foster, president-general of the Daughters of the American Revolution, was born in Salem, Indiana, and is a direct descendant of a line of Revolutionary heroes on both sides of the house. Mrs. Foster is the daughter of the late Rev. Alexander McFerson, her mother being Eliza Reed McFerson, whose nine brothers all became distinguished at the bar, in medicine, or in the army or navy. She graduated at Glendale College, near Cincinnati. Her marriage to Mr. Foster has proved a very happy one. In 1873, four years after the marriage of Mr. and Mrs. Foster, General Grant appointed Mr. Foster minister to Mexico. Their residence at the Mexican capital covered a period of seven years. During this time Mrs. Foster became thoroughly familiar with the language, people, habits and manners of the country. Many of the literary societies of Washington have been beneficiaries of her and her husband's experience and knowledge. From Mexico Mr. Foster was transferred to St. Petersburg, in 1880, by President Hayes. During her stay in Russia, Mrs. Foster spent a part of her time in translating Russian fiction into English. Upon Mr. Foster's return to Washington, he was again urged by President Arthur to accept a mission to Spain, which he accepted in 1884. During a residence there of two and a half years Mrs. Foster mingled in the brilliant court of Alphonso XII. The residence in Washington of Mr. and Mrs. Foster has often been the scene of brilliant social events. Mrs. Foster is a woman who has had personal experience in the working of the various governments of the world. She has seen the glory and pomp of monarchs, emperors and kings, and comes back to the simplicities of a democratic republican government more of an American than ever, believing that her institutions are the making of the grandest people of the earth, for the foundation of her law is for whatsoever things are true, honest, just, pure and of good report.

MRS. CHARLES WARREN FAIRBANKS.

Mrs. Fairbanks was born in the Buckeye State, at Marysville, in Union County. Her father, Judge Philander B. Cole, was one of the prominent men of the Southern shore. He believed in the higher education of women and consequently sent his daughter Cornelia to college. She entered the Wesleyan College in 1868, taking the classical course, and she graduated in 1872. Like many Western girls she was as active in the athletic field and the gymnasium as she was in the historical and literary societies of the college. She was also connected with the college paper of which Charles Warren Fairbanks, one of the students at the college was the editor. Mrs. Fairbanks, as a girl, became familiar with parliamentary law and her early training gave her an excellent basis for her work in later years. Two years after obtaining her degree she became the wife of Charles Warren Fairbanks, her former college editor, and they took up their residence in Indianapolis. Mrs. Fairbanks became the president of the first literary club of the state and was the first woman appointed on the Indiana State Board of Charities. She organized "The Fortnightly Literary Club" and belonged to art and musical societies, all of this in addition to caring for her little family of five children. When Mr. Fairbanks was elected senator from Indiana Mrs. Fairbanks became one of the winter residents of Washington, joined the Washington Club, and founded, together with a number of other progressive and enterprising women, "The Woman's League," to aid and assist the "Junior Republic." During the Spanish War she did an incalculable amount of work for our soldiers, was made president of the Indiana Aid Society to send nurses, hospital supplies and commissary stores to the front. In 1900 Mrs. Fairbanks was elected director of the Federation of Woman's Clubs. One of her chief aims was the promotion of Continental Hall, in which she was actively interested. Another measure that Mrs. Fairbanks strongly advocated during her term as president-general was the commemoration of the historic places of the country which she thought might be made into object lessons in love of country to those who had not had early patriotic training.

MRS. A. LEO KNOTT.

Mrs. Knott is among the earliest members of the Society of the Daughters of the American Revolution, being at the time of its formation, a resident of Washington. She was elected a member of the society on June 19, 1891, having previously attended several preliminary meetings of the society at the residence of Mrs. Cabell. On the 9th of May of the same year she was elected one of the vice-presidents-general. Mrs. Knott claims membership in the society on account of the Revolutionary services rendered by Captain John Phelan, through her mother Mary J. Kienan, nee Mary J. Phelan. Captain Phelan joined the American army at Boston in 1776. He survived the war, being promoted to the rank of captain for gallant services performed during the war and was with the army until it disbanded at Newburg in October, 1783. After the war Captain Phelan engaged in mercantile business in New York. He made a trip to Rio Janeiro in connection with his business. On his return he was shipwrecked, losing the vessel and cargo in which most of his fortune was invested. He removed to Baltimore and established a classical and mathematical school which enjoyed a wide reputation for many years. He died in Baltimore in 1827. Mrs. Knott took an active part in the work of the early building up of the Daughters of the American Revolution. On the retirement of Mrs. Flora Adams Darling from the position which she filled of vice-president-general in charge of the organization of chapters, Mrs. Knott, together with Mrs. John W. Foster and Mrs. H. V. Boynton was appointed by the national board to take charge of that work. In 1891 Mrs. Knott, on her removal to Baltimore, was requested by the national board to accept the position of state regent of Maryland and to undertake the work of establishing chapters in that state. In accordance with that request Mrs. Knott, in 1892, sent out invitations to ladies in Baltimore whom she knew were eligible to membership in the National Society and on March 4th, the Baltimore Chapter was formed at her house. Mrs. Knott appointed Miss Alice Key Blunt regent of the chapter. In 1894 Mrs. Knott resigned the office of state regent of Maryland, and at the succeeding congress was elected one of the honorary vice-presidents-general for life. In 1889, at the urgent request of many of the members of the chapter, Mrs. Knott was elected to the office of regent of the Baltimore Chapter, which has done good work under her regency and has taken a lively interest in the construction of Continental Hall.

SOPHIE WALKER HYNDSHAW BUSHNELL.

The subject of this sketch was born in Henry, Illinois; her father Silas Condict Hyndshaw, coming there from Morristown, New Jersey as a young man. In 1858 he was married to Miss Elizabeth Walker of Cincinnati, Ohio. At an early age Mrs. Bushnell was sent to Monticello Seminary, one of the oldest schools for young women in the Middle West and there she spent four years. During the time she was attending school at Monticello, her parents moved to Norwood Park, a suburb of Chicago, and there in 1878 she was married to Drayton Wilson Bushnell. Mr. Bushnell was a native of Ohio, his ancestors coming there from Connecticut in 1880 and settling on the Western Reserve.

After their marriage Mr. and Mrs. Bushnell went to Council Bluffs, Iowa, and decided to make that place their home. Mrs. Bushnell became much interested in the Daughters of the American Revolution during the first years of the organization but did not identify herself with the society until 1897, when a chapter was formed in Council Bluffs, and she became a charter member. She has served the chapter in various offices, being regent for three years and in office or a member of the board of management constantly since the chapter was organized. She was state historian for two years, state vice-regent for one year and vice-president-general for four years. She is also a member of various other patriotic societies—the Colonial Dames—the Huguenot Society—United States Daughters of 1812 and others. Her line of ancestry through her father embraces many prominent New Jersey, Pennsylvania and New England names; her father having been named for the Hon. Silas Condict of New Jersey, who was a member of the first Continental Congress and speaker of the House; while his great-grandfather, Captain James Hyndshaw, was a distinguished soldier in the French and Indian Wars; a fort near the Delaware Water Gap being named for him in recognition of his service. Her mother (Elizabeth Walker of Ohio) traces her lines to the Walkers, Fosters, Hicks, Millers and many of the old Maryland families; also to the Wiltsees and other Dutch families of New York. When elected to the office of vice-president-general, Mrs. Bushnell suggested to the Daughters of Iowa that they pay for one of the rooms in Memorial Continental Hall, to be called the Iowa Room. This plan met with the approval of the members, and Mrs. Bushnell was made the chairman of the Iowa Room Committee and has held the office until the room has been finished and furnished. Recognizing the good work accomplished in the chapter, the state, and on the national board by a member of their own chapter, the Council Bluffs Daughters had the name of Mrs. Bushnell placed on the roll of honor book in Memorial Continental Hall. Mrs. Bushnell's greatest interest is in her patriotic work, her first love, the Daughters of the American Revolution claiming the most of her attention. She has given to it of her best, and in return it has been her privilege and pleasure to feel that in a small way she has been able to add her "mite" to the growth, development, and great work achieved by this grand society.

MRS. I. C. VANMETER, JR.

Mrs. Pattie Field Vanmeter was an enthusiastic and active member of the National Society of the Daughters of the American Revolution from the earliest days of its organization, having joined in 1890, when a pupil in Mrs. Somer's popular school in Washington, D. C. The tradition of her family lead her to an immense interest in a society which honored Revolutionary sires. She was the daughter of Thomas M. Field, of Denver, Colo., and was born in that city on April 10, 1865. She was graduated from the Denver High School in 1883, and bore off prizes in painting and in elocution. After leaving school in Washington she, with her younger brother and sister visited, in 1887, most of the countries of Europe. On May 4, 1892, she was married to I. C. Vanmeter, Jr., of Kentucky, and they removed to Winchester, Kentucky, where on February 24, 1893, she died.

LUCIA A. BLOUNT.

Mrs. Blount was born in Kalamazoo, Michigan. She was the daughter of Lovett Eames and Lucy C. Morgan Eames, and comes of good Revolutionary stock. Mrs. Blount was educated in Kalamazoo College under Dr. and Mrs. Stone. She lived several years abroad to educate her children. Since her home has been in Washington she helped to organize and was made the president of the Pro-ra-Nata Society, an organization which has taken a front rank in the federated clubs. Mrs. Blount is a charter member of the Daughters of the American Revolution. She has been a vice-president and historian for two years. She has also been identified with several other societies and clubs whose trend is for the betterment of society.

MRS. J. HERON CROSMAN.

Mrs. Crosman has been deeply, lovingly interested in the National Society of the Daughters of the American Revolution from its inception. When the vice-president, first in charge of organization, was sent to form a chapter in New York, initial meetings were held at Mrs. Crosman's house and the proposed members were entertained by her. From these beginnings grew the great army of over four thousand daughters of the American Revolution in New York, the banner state. Mrs. Crosman was the fourth member from New York and her national number is 262. Her distinguished services were fittingly recognzied when in 1900 she was elected vice-president-general to represent the Empire State in the councils of the society. She is a member of the Continental Hall Committee and of the Magazine Committee. Among her ancestors who won renown in Colonial and Revolutionary times is Elihu Hall who served as lieutenant-captain and colonel, receiving his commission as colonel of the Susquehanna battalion in 1778. He was descended from Richard Hall of Norfolk, England, who settled in Cecil County, Maryland. John Harris, another of Mrs. Crosman's colonial forefathers, came from Yorkshire, England, to Philadelphia, where he married Esther Say. Mrs. Crosman was Miss Ellen Hall, daughter of William M. and Ellen Campbell Hall. Mr. J. Heron Crosman, whose wife she is, is a member of an old West Point family. Besides being an honored and beloved Daughter of the American Revolution, Mrs. Crosman is a Colonial Dame, and a promoter of the Society of Children of the American Revolution. A beautiful home life is her crowning inheritance.

ANNA SCOTT BLOCK.

Wife of Colonel Williard T. Block, is a daughter of William P. Scott, and Mary Piper, his wife. Mr. Scott is a descendant of Hugh Scott, who came to America prior to 1720, and settled in Lancaster County, Pa., and whose descendants have had much to do with the making of this country in civil, military, political and industrial affairs. In 1748 some of the Scotts moved from Donegal Church, in Lancaster County, and took up land in Adams County, upon part of the land over which in 1863 the great battle of Gettysburg was fought.

Mrs. Block's ancestor, Rebecca Scott, married Captain James Agnew, who commanded a company of associators in 1756, among whose descendants were Colonel Thomas A. Scott, late president of the Pennsylvania Railroad, also president of the Northern Pacific Railroad, Union Pacific Railroad, Kansas Pacific Railroad and Texas Pacific Railroad, the latter road owned by him, when he sold it to Jay Gould.

Colonel Scott was appointed by President Lincoln assistant secretary of war in 1861, and was placed in charge of all the railroads needed for military operations of the war. Colonel Scott was Mrs. Block's uncle.

Other descendants of Captain Agnew and his wife Rebecca Scott were Dr. D. Hayes Agnew the celebrated surgeon. Another descendant was David A. Stewart, a former partner of Andrew Carnegie, and president of the Carnegie Steel Company.

The great-grandmother of Mrs. Block, Sarah Agnew, was married to Archibald Douglas, a descendant of Lord Douglas of Scotland. Mrs. Block's grandmother, Rebecca Douglas, married Thomas Scott, whose father John Scott was a pioneer in the settlement of Franklin County, Pa., and served in the Revolution.

Mrs. Block's great-grandfather on her maternal side was General John Piper of Bedford County, Pa., who served his state in 1763 as lieutenant in the French and Indian Wars, provincial justice in 1775 and 1776. June 18, 1776, was a member of the provincial conference held in Carpenter Hall, Philadelphia, which conference took steps to form a new government to denounce George III. The conference signed the declaration on June 18, 1776, that the state of Pennsylvania was willing to concur in a vote to the Congress declaring the colonies free and independent states.

Colonel Piper was a member of the convention of 1776, that formed the Constitution of Pennsylvania. In 1776 Colonel Piper was appointed lieutenant-colonel of Bedford County, Pennsylvania, with free military power reporting to the president of the assembly.

In 1777 he was appointed lieutenant of western Pennsylvania. From 1779 to 1783 he represented Bedford County in Supreme Executive Council, and a member from 1785 to 1789 of the general assembly, member of the convention of 1789, and one of the framers of the Constitution of 1790, a justice from 1796 to 1801, a senator from 1801 to 1803, presidential elector in 1797, major-general of state militia in 1801 until his death in 1817.

Upon the organization of the Daughters of the American Revoultion, Mrs. Block was one of the charter members, her number being 337, and a charter member of the Chicago Chapter, her number being three, also a member of the first board of management.

Mrs. Block represented her chapter several times as a delegate at Annual Congress and at the Congress of 1911. She presented before Congress a plan to raise money to pay off the debt on Memorial Continental Hall, and to start a fund for its maintenance by designing a beautiful and artistic certificate that could be sold at one dollar each to every Daughter and descendant. Her plan as suggested by her was so simple, so effective, that it was unanimously adopted by the Congress and Mrs. Block was appointed chairman of a committee to carry out her idea. This she is now employed in doing.

She is a member of the Daughters of 1812, the Second Presbyterian Church of Chicago, and The Woman's Athletic Club of Chicago.

CHARLOTTE LOUISE LAWRENCE.

Mrs. Lawrence, a Daughter of the American Revolution, has the following ancestry: She is a great-granddaughter of Roger Sherman, a signer of the Declaration of Independence, who was her mother's grandfather; the great-granddaughter of Major Morgan, her father's grandfather on his mother's side; the great-granddaughter of Colonel Jonathan Bliss, of Longmeadow, Massachusetts, by her father's grandmother on his father's side, who commanded a Massachusetts regiment of the Continental Line, and a great-great-granddaughter of David Morgan, from her father's grandmother on his mother's side, who was a private in Captain Joseph Hoar's company of Colonel Gideon Bart's regiment of Massachusetts militia, who served in 1782 in the army of Canada.

Mrs. Lawrence, a charter member of the Daughters of the American Revolution, was the daughter of Randolph Morgan Cooley and Maria Louise Stevenson Cooley. She is the wife of George A. Lawrence of New York City.

HELEN MASON BOYNTON.

Mrs. Boynton was born in Cincinnati, Ohio, of Massachusetts parentage on both sides of the house in an unbroken line back to 1630, when Robert Mason came to America from England and settled in Dedham. The family was prominent in civil and military affairs in the colonies. Thomas Mason, son of Robert, was killed by the Indians at the defense of Medfield in 1676. Lieutenant Henry Adams, one of her lineal ancestors was also killed in this massacre. He was the ancestor of Samuel Adams, Revolutionary patriot, John Adams and John Quincy Adams, presidents of the United States. Andrew Hall, her colonial ancestor on her mother's side, was a lineal descendant of Elizabeth Newgate, daughter of John de Hoo Hessett, of England. The Halls were active in the Indian wars, and in the Revolution. Mrs. Boynton's national number is twenty-eight. She has served as vice-president-general in charge of organization, vice-president-general, honorary vice-president-general and librarian-general. In 1871 she married General H. V. Boynton an officer of national reputation in the Civil and Spanish Wars. He received the medal of honor for gallantry in the attack on Missionary Ridge.

LUCY PRESTON BEALE.

Mrs. Beale was elected through the Continental Congress in Washington to the honor of vice-president-general of the Daughters of the American Revolution. She was already well known as a representative for her state to the Colorado Exposition. She is the daughter of the late honorable William Ballard Preston and Lucy Staples Redd and was born in Montgomery County, Virginia, at the old family seat, Smithfield. When it was proposed to reproduce for the Virginia State building at Chicago, facsimiles of the furnishings of the home of Washington, Mrs. Beale was able to save the state some expense by her offer to furnish several counterparts from the household belongings of old Smithfield. She is descended on both sides from distinguished Revolutionary ancestors and in her we find the high courage which grapples with different enterprises, the talent that organizes, the executive force that reaches completion, and the diplomatic instinct that leads all circumstances to the consummation of determined purpose. The office to which Mrs. Beale was called was not of her own seeking, for contented in the happy home of an honored husband, she found all that her true, womanly heart asked, in his devotion and that of her children to which is lavishly added the warmest devotion of a wide circle of friends.

AUGUSTA DANFORTH GEER.

Mrs. Geer, vice-president-general of the Daughters of the American Revolution, was born at Williamstown, Massachusetts. She was the daughter of Keyes and Mary Bushnell Danforth. She is of good Revolutionary stock, being the grandchild of Captain Jonathan Danforth, a soldier at Bunker Hill and Bennington, besides her grandfather, two uncles and ten other relatives who fought at Bunker Hill. Her father served several terms in the state legislature of Massachusetts and was for many years leader of the Democratic party in Berkshire

County. Miss Danforth was married in January, 1856, to Asahel Clark Geer, a lawyer of Troy, New York. She was educated by her brother-in-law, Joseph White, secretary of the board of education of Massachusetts and one of the founders and trustees of Smith College, and for nearly forty years treasurer and trustee of Williams College. She was an excellent scholar, especially proficient in the languages. Mrs. Geer was one of the earliest members of the National Society of the Daughters of the American Revolution and has been unwavering in her devotion to its largest interests.

ELIZABETH HANENKAMP DELAFIELD.

Mrs. Delafield was the daughter of Richard P. Hanenkamp and Agnes C. Jones, his second wife. She was born in Missouri and has resided in St. Louis all her life. On her father's side she is descended from Pennsylvania Dutch, on her mother's side from Virginia ancestry. One of her ancestors was governor of Virginia in 1617. She has been prominent in the work of the Daughters of the American Revolution, having held the offices successively of treasurer and regent of the St. Louis Chapter, vice state regent and state regent of Missouri. At the sixteenth Continental Congress she was elevated to the high position of vice-president-general of the National Society. She was chairman of the Daughters of the American Revolution at the Louisiana Purchase Exposition, where the entertainments arranged by her were a great success. She has served the Daughters well on the Continental Hall Committee, as the liberal contributions from Missouri show. She is a member of the Daughters of 1812, of the Colonial Dames and the Colonial Governors and of many local clubs for betterment. She is the wife of Wallace Delafield, one of the best-known business men of St. Louis and has five children. Mrs. Delafield is a descendant of Peter Humrichhouse. William Jones, who was killed at the battle of Guilford Court House, was another of her ancestors.

MARY STEINER PUTNAM.

Mrs. John Risley Putnam, vice-president-general of the Daughters of the American Revolution, was born in Ohio. Her life until her marriage was mainly spent in her father's country seat, Glendale, fifteen miles out of Cincinnati. Her father, Robert Myers Shoemaker, was one of the most prominent citizens of his state, being a power among railroad men of the country. Mrs. Putnam's mother was, before her marriage, Mary Colegate Steiner, the daughter of Captain Henry Steiner, who served in the War of 1812. Mrs. Putnam is a charter member of the Daughters of the American Revolution and one of its most zealous officers, having been from the first vice-president-general representing the state of New York. Mrs. Benjamin Harrison was an early and long valued friend of Mrs. Putnam, and when the latter came to Washington in the interest of the National Society a warm welcome awaited her at the White House.

MARY KATHARINE JOHNSON.

Mary Katharine Johnson, vice-president-general of the Daughters of the American Revolution, was born in Washington, D. C., and was educated at the

Fulford Female Seminary, Maryland. She is a daughter of the late Mitchel Hervey Millar and Sallie Clayton Williams Millar and the wife of Charles Sweet Johnson, who is a member of the District of Columbia Society of the Sons of the American Revolution. On the paternal side she is descended from John and Jane Millar, born in Scotland, who came to America from Ireland in 1770 and settled in the western part of Pennsylvania; on the maternal side from Pierre Williams, sergeant-at-law, of London, England. Mrs. Johnson has been actively interested in the Society of the Daughters of the American Revolution for many years, having served one year as registrar-general and one year as a member of the National Advisory Board before she was elected vice-president-general.

ALICE BRENARD EWING WALKER.

Mrs. Walker is the widow of John Reed Walker, a lawyer of Kansas City, Missouri, widely known in his profession and in politics. She is the daughter of Ephraim B. Ewing and Elizabeth Ann Allen, his wife. Judge Ewing was born in Todd County, Kentucky, but grew to manhood in Missouri and is identified with its history in many distinguished positions——secretary of state, attorney-general, judge of the Supreme Court and of the Surrogate Court of St. Louis, and was on the supreme bench at the time of his death. His father, Finis Ewing, was born in Bedford County, Virginia, but at an early date he and his brothers went to Kentucky. An old historian says: "The Ewings brought with them the law and the Gospel to Kentucky." Finis Ewing was the founder of the Cumberland Presbyterian Church and was a man of great ability and force of character. In the war of 1812 he served as chaplain on condition that if needed he might use his rifle. He was the intimate and lifelong friend of Andrew Jackson and Thomas H. Benton. Mrs. Walker's mother, Elizabeth Ann Allen, was the daughter of Dr. Thomas Allen and Nancy Watkins, his wife, of Prince Edward County, Virginia. Dr. Allen's father, Charles Allen, was a colonel in the Revolutionary army. On the maternal side her grandfather was Colonel Thomas Watkins, who served under Washington and was personally complimented by him for bravery at Guilford. Mrs. Walker was elected vice-president of the Daughters of the American Revolution in 1903 and re-elected in 1905, both times receiving the highest vote cast by the congress. She served the Elizabeth Benton Chapter of Kansas City, Missouri, as regent three consecutive terms, resigning when elected vice-president-general. Mrs. Walker is identified with the Memorial Continental Hall monument, as a member of that committee. She incorporated the fund for the Missouri room. She has written and spoken much on patriotic subjects, delivering an address on Daughters' Day at the World's Fair and was invited by both Mrs. Fairbanks and Mrs. McLean to respond to the address of welcome. She was elected to represent Missouri at the ceremonies of the Jamestown Exposition, September 19, 1906.

CHARLOTTE EMERSON MAIN.

Mrs. Main was vice-president-general in charge of the organization of chapters. She comes of fine New England stock. On her father's side her ancestry has been traced back to the time of King Henry VI. Mrs. Main's paternal grandmother was a direct descendant of Roger Conant, who was appointed first governor by the Dorchester Company of St. Ann, Endicott being his successor. Mrs. Main's mother, Elizabeth Emerson, belonged to that family which was so prominent in the early educational life of New England, the most widely known member being Ralph Waldo Emerson, whose fame as a thinker is world-wide. Her maternal grandmother was Esther Frothingham, daughter of Major Benjamin Frothingham, the personal friend of George Washington. Mrs. Main has been identified with the Daughters of the American Revolution since 1896, having filled many important offices in the society.

MRS. BALDWIN DAY SPILMAN.

Mrs. Baldwin Day Spilman, vice-president-general of the Daughters of the American Revolution, is a daughter of Senator and Mrs. J. N. Camden, and though born in Wheeling, West Virginia, has always lived in Parkersburg. She was educated at Madam Lefebvre's school in Baltimore. She lived in Washington during her father's service in the United States Senate and traveled abroad, thus acquiring many graces which distinguished her, and which later attracted the fine young lieutenant who became her husband, and which have made her successful in the work which she has undertaken. Mrs. Spilman formed the James Wood Chapter in Parkersburg. In the annual congress in Washington, in April, 1904, she was elected regent of the little mountain state of which all West Virginians are so justly proud. She was later elected to the position of one of the vice-presidents-general of the Daughters of the American Revolution. Mrs. Spilman's Revolutionary ancestor, Captain Cornelius Stimrod, enlisted in the Westchester Militia of New York in 1776 under Colonel Alexander McDougal. He commanded a company of Minute Men in 1782.

MRS. JOHN RITCHIE.

Mrs. Ritchie was elected at the Congress of 1895 state regent of Maryland. She is the widow of the late Honorable John Ritchie, of Frederick City, Maryland, and is the daughter of the late Judge William Pinkney Maulsby, of Maryland, and his wife, Emily Contee Nelson, daughter of Roger Nelson, from whom she derives her eligibility to the Daughters of the American Revolution. She is descended from the legal profession on every side. Her grandfather, General Israel David Maulsby, was one of the most distinguished lawyers of his day, an eloquent and polished orator and a tried public servant, having represented his country in the state legislature twenty-nine times. He was one of the volunteer defenders of the city of Baltimore when it was besieged by the British in 1814, and was one of those who made it possible for the "Patriot Poet" to see the Star-Spangled Banner still waving "in the dawn's early light." His wife was the daughter of John Hall, an officer of the Revolution. Mrs. Ritchie's maternal ancestors came to this country in the latter part of the seventeenth century, locating first in St. Mary's County, Maryland, and later coming up into western

Maryland. The first patent issued to John Nelson was for several thousand acres of land and bears the date of 1725. Mrs. Ritchie was commissioned by the first president-general of the Daughters of the American Revolution, Mrs. Caroline Scott Harrison, regent of the Frederick Chapter. Entering upon the work of its organization with enthusiasm, her efforts were crowned with success. In 1894 she was elected vice-president-general of the society, and in 1895 regent for the state of Maryland. She was a member of the State Committee on Women's Work for the Columbian Exposition of 1893, and did good service in that cause. She was a member of the Academy of Political and Social Science and an active member of the Frederick Historical Society, to whose annals she contributed several papers. She is one of the founders and one of the board of management of the Key Monument Association. She was commissioned by Governor Brown a member of the Maryland Committee for the Cotton States Exposition in Atlanta, Georgia, and was also appointed a member of the Colonial Relic Committee. In her character Mrs. Ritchie manifests the traits to be expected from her inheritance. Courageous, gracious and courtly, she represents the typical Maryland woman. She is distinguished for her patriotic spirit and her zeal has resulted in the establishment of a most prosperous chapter in Frederick. Mrs. Ritchie resides in the old colonial mansion built by her uncle, Honorable John Nelson, the eminent jurist.

MRS. R. OGDEN DOREMUS.

Mrs. R. Ogden Doremus was appointed regent of the New York City Chapter of the Daughters of the American Revolution, January 1, 1892, by the Committee of Safety, and this election was unanimously confirmed by the chapter at its next meeting on May 19, 1892. She was also made corresponding secretary and has been performing the duties of both offices until the present time. Mrs. Doremus, the daughter of Captain Hubbard Skidmore and Caroline Avery Skidmore, was born in the city of New York and educated under the care of the celebrated Madam Mears. She was married in New York to Dr. R. Ogden Doremus, the distinguished professor of chemistry, October 1, 1850. The ceremony took place in the South Dutch Church, corner of Fifth Avenue and Twenty-first Street, the oldest church organization in the city of New York. The original edifice was built by the Dutch within the fortification walls at the Battery. Mrs. Doremus' maternal grandfather, Thaddeus Avery, of Mount Pleasant, Westchester County, New York, was born October 19, 1749, and died November 16, 1836. He was captain of cavalry during the Revolution and at one time paymaster of the Westchester troops. Mrs. Doremus is richly endowed by nature with a graceful and commanding figure, beautiful features, and a brilliancy of complexion rarely seen. Her tact in securing representative audiences, premiums on boxes at the Charity Ball, for the benefit of the Nursery and Child's Hospital (which the revered mother of her husband was instrumental in founding) inaugurated entertainments which continue to be successful to the present time. Never have the receipts been so large as when under her management. In Paris, during the Empire, her receptions were the favorite resorts of our distinguished American colony, and of French scientists and army officers. Here among other celebrities, Mlle. Christine Nielsson sang while yet a pupil. Mrs. Doremus' table at the fair of the Princess Czartoryska, for the benefit of the exiled Poles, attracted American residents in the gay capital. Before the late war she gave efficient aid to the "Metropolitan Fair." During the war, in 1863, she was among the most zealous and indefatigable workers for the sanitary fair, which secured $1,400,000 for the sick and wounded soldiers. Her scientific table, with its marvels of the microscope and other philosophical instruments, always surrounded by the wit and wisdom of the day, added greatly to swell the donations. By a vote for the most popular lady at the French fair, held in New York for disabled soldiers, during the Franco-Prussian War, she was honored with the ambulance decoration of the Red Cross, set with diamonds. Successful performances of the play of "Cinderella" were planned and conducted by her, in 1876, in the New York Academy of Music, for the benefit of the "Women's Pavilion," at the Centennial Exposition held in Philadelphia. She secured the hearty co-operation of the parents and children of our best families. She rendered efficient aid in the performances of pantomimes on the "Mistletoe Bough" and "Sleeping Beauty," at the Academy of Music, for the Mount Vernon fund. She never allowed her charitable and patriotic work to interfere with the duties and responsibilities as a mother of eight children—seven sons and a daughter. Her nursery witnessed her greatest triumphs. She has been for many years a communicant in the South Reformed Church of New York.

MRS. J. MORGAN SMITH.

Mrs. Smith comes of illustrious Colonial and Revolutionary ancestry. She is eligible to membership in the Daughters of the American Revolution through seven different ancestors who served in the Revolutionary War. For ten years she held the state regency of Alabama, and her service, efficient, faithful and enthusiastic, has won for her a high place in the esteem and affection of her "Alabama Daughters." At the sixteenth continental congress Mrs. Smith was made vice-president-general, a distinction which she has well earned, not only by her tireless efforts in her own state, but by labors which have been far reaching and national in their extent. Mrs. Smith is also an honored member of the Pennsylvania Colonial Dames and an officer of the Alabama Colonial Dames.

MABEL GODFREY SWORMSTEDT.

Mrs. Swormstedt is a native of the "Old Bay State" and a graduate of Wellesley College, class of 1890. She was a teacher in the Washington High School for three years and is the wife of Dr. Lyman Beecher Swormstedt. She is the mother of a beautiful daughter eleven years old. She has held several offices in the Columbia Chapter, culminating in the regency. She has been president of the Washington Branch of the Association of Collegiate Alumnæ and corresponding secretary of the Ladies' Aid Association of the Homeopathic Hospital. Mrs. Swormstedt claims six Revolutionary ancestors.

ESTHER FROTHINGHAM NOBLE.

Mrs. Noble is the wife of the Rev. Thomas K. Noble, pastor emeritus of the First Congregational Church of Norwalk, Connecticut. She is a native of

Massachusetts and connected with some of the most prominent New England families. On her mother's maternal side she is a direct descendant of Major Benjamin Frothingham, a personal friend of George Washington and one of the original members of the Order of the Cincinnati. On her mother's paternal side she belongs to the noted Emerson family, that long line of ministers and teachers who have been ever since Colonial times such an important factor in the religious and educational life of New England. On her father's side she is descended from Captain Thomas Bradbury and from Roger Conant, who were among the earliest settlers of Massachusetts. During Mr. Noble's pastorate in Norwalk, Connecticut, she was state vice-regent of Connecticut and regent of the Norwalk Chapter. She is a member of the Daughters of the Cincinnati, the Daughters of Founders and Patriots and the Daughters of 1812, the Mary Washington Memorial Society and the board of directors of the Aid Association for the Blind, and also of the Presbyterian Home for the Aged. She is an honored member of the Society of New England Women and of the National Geographic Society.

ELIZABETH MOORE BOWRON.

Mrs. Bowron is the daughter of Hannah Hoffman Moore and the late Watson Appleby Bowron. She is the wife of Henry Snowden Bowron. She was born in New York City of Dutch and New England descent on her mother's side and of English and New England with two lines from Virginia on her father's side; she is allied with some of the most prominent families. Mrs. Bowron was elected recording secretary of the Mohegan Chapter at its first meeting. Her Revolutionary ancestor was Captain Robert Nichols, of the New Jersey Volunteers, who served throughout the entire war. In 1896 Mrs. Bowron became interested in the work of the National Society of the Daughters of the American Revolution, and as chairman conducted successfully a "Loan Exhibit" to raise funds for Continental Hall. In April, 1897, she formed a chapter of the Children of the American Revolution, and this same year her untiring work as secretary of Auxiliary No. 13 of the Red Cross Society formed by the Mohegan Chapter, contributed largely to its success. In 1900 she became regent of the Mohegan Chapter. The chapter then elected her honorary regent presiding and still continues the word "presiding" as a mark of confidence. Mrs. Bowron, through her interest in genealogy, has personally assisted many in her home chapters and others to qualify for membership in the Society of the Daughters of the American Revolution. She has served on many committees of the society and with Mrs. Charles H. Terry collected the exhibit from ancestry for the Hall of History at the Jamestown Exposition. She is a member of the New York Genealogical and Biographical Society and the Mary Washington Monument Association.

REBECCA CALHOUN PICKENS BACON.

Mrs. Bacon was born near Edgefield Court House, South Carolina. She was the daughter of Governor Francis W. Pickens, a wealthy planter of the South, and she enjoyed all the advantages attendant upon such a life in the ante-bellum days. After a thorough training with governesses she attended a course at the famous Montpelier Institute, presided over by Bishop Elliot of Georgia, where she was graduated with high honors. Having lost her mother when very young, she accompanied her distinguished father to Washington while he was there in Congress, and elsewhere in his political career. In this way she attained unusual accomplishments and became a fine linguist. In 1856 her father was appointed by Mr. Buchanan Minister to Russia, with residence at St. Petersburg, at that time the most brilliant court in Europe. There she married John E. Bacon, secretary of the American Legation at that court, after which they made an extended tour through Europe. Upon the election of Mr. Lincoln she returned to the United States with her husband, who entered the Civil War and served until its close. After the war the family settled in Columbia, South Carolina. In 1884 Mrs. Bacon went to South America, her husband having received from Mr. Cleveland the appointment of Minister to Paraguay and Uruguay. She resided four years at Montevideo, where she acquired a thorough knowledge of the Spanish language. Her letters on South America were widely read and greatly admired. In February, 1893, Mrs. Bacon was elected by the National Board of the Daughters of the American Revolution state regent for South Carolina. No more appropriate appointment could have been made, as in addition to her superior qualifications she is lineally descended on the paternal side from General Andrew Pickens, who ranked with Sumter and Marion as one of the principal leaders in the war for independence. On her maternal side Mrs. Bacon is descended from General Elijah Clarke, of Georgia, and of Revolutionary fame; also Captain Arthur Simpkins, an intelligent and brave officer and staunch friend of his country. Her father's mother was a daughter of Christopher Edward Wilkinson, whose grandfather was Landgrave Joseph Moreton, colonial governor of South Carolina under Charles II, in 1681, and who married the niece of the famous Admiral Blake, of England.

ANNIE WARFIELD LAWRENCE KERFOOT.

Mrs. Kerfoot was the daughter of Otho Williams Lawrence, a lawyer of Hagerstown, Maryland, and his wife, Catherine Murdock Nelson, of Frederick, in the same state. Her maternal grandfather was Brigadier-General Roger Nelson, of Point of Rocks Plantation, Frederick County, who entered the troops of horse under command of Colonel Augustine Washington in 1776, at the age of sixteen years. After the disbandment of the Maryland troops General Nelson read law. Was for six years in the Maryland senate; for a similar period in the National House of Representatives and was subsequently appointed for life judge of the upper district of Maryland. Three granddaughters and five great-granddaughters of General Nelson have become members of the associations of the Daughters of the American Revolution. Among the distinguished lineal ancestors of Mrs. Kerfoot on the maternal side was her great-grandfather, Colonel Joseph Sims, of Prince George County, Justice of the Supreme Court of Maryland, who represented his country in the convention held at Annapolis June 22, 1774, to denounce the English bill closing the port of Boston. Mrs. Kerfoot was born in Hagerstown,

Maryland, in 1829, and was a graduate of St. Mary's Hall, Burlington, New Jersey, having received her diploma during the presidency of its revered founder, Bishop George W. Doane, in 1846. She married, in 1847, Samuel Humes Kerfoot, son of Richard Kerfoot, of Castle Blaney, Monaghan County, Ireland. Mr. and Mrs. Kerfoot removed from Maryland to Chicago in 1848 and have since resided in that city. Their home was burned in the Chicago fire of 1871, with a rare library and very fine collections of paintings and many priceless relics of Revolutionary and Colonial ancestry. Mrs. Kerfoot has inherited in a marked degree the clear mind and sound reasoning powers and unbiased judgment of her distinguished ancestors of the bench and bar. She has the enthusiastic temperament of her cavalier blood, which is united with the moderation of her Quaker forefathers. She is a member of the Executive Committee of the Chicago Chapters of the Daughters of the American Revolution and holds the chairmanship of its Literary Committee and that of the Committee upon Membership, and was elected in February, 1893, state regent of Illinois.

GEORGIA H. STOCKTON HATCHER.

Mrs. Hatcher, regent of the General de Lafayette Chapter, Daughters of the American Revolution, of Lafayette, Indiana, was born in that city July 11, 1864, and is of New Jersey Revolutionary stock. In 1883 she was graduated from the Moravian Seminary for Young Ladies at Bethlehem, Pennsylvania, which is the oldest institution of the kind in this country, the school having been turned into a soldiers' hospital during the Revolution. In 1889 she became the wife of Mr. Robert Stockwell Hatcher, of Lafayette, and after a long residence in France and other European countries returned to her native city. Mrs. Hatcher was commissioned as chapter regent by the national board June 1, 1893, and on April 21, 1894 she organized the General de Lafayette Chapter at Lafayette, Indiana, which is in a flourishing condition, with a membership of twenty-seven enthusiastic daughters.

MRS. WILLIAM WATSON SHIPPEN.

Mrs. Shippen was born in Hoboken, New Jersey, the daughter of George Washington, D. C., and joining the Daughters of the American Revolution in 1896, ancestry extends back in all its lines to the early settlement of this country. She early married William Watson Shippen, of New Jersey. He was always prominent and active in affairs in his native state and she was his coadjutor in all his schemes for its prosperity and progress. She was prominent during the late war in the Sanitary Commission and has always been connected with popular charities. She is a leading member of the Ladies' Club in New York; also a trustee of Evylyn College, the woman's college of New Jersey. When a regent of the Daughters of the American Revolution was to be appointed in New Jersey, Mrs. Shippen was chosen and held office from April, 1891, to February, 1895. In a large measure it is due to her good judgment, patience, perseverance and tact that the organization has been perfected in New Jersey. It is one of the most cleverly and thoroughly organized of all the states. After serving as regent she was unanimously elected one of the vice-presidents-general of the National Society.

MRS. M. E. DAVIS.

Mrs. Davis is a native of Wisconsin. She removed from that state to Washington, D. C., and joined the Daughters of the American Revolution in 1896, being indorsed by and entering through the Columbia Chapter of the District of Columbia. Mrs. Davis has served the chapter as historian, treasurer, vice-regent and regent, and represented it in the Continental Congress as delegate or regent from 1897 until she was elected to fill out the unexpired term of Mrs. D. K. Shute, resigning the office of regent to become treasurer-general. At the Fourteenth Continental Congress she was called upon to succeed herself. No other candidate being brought forward, she was declared the unanimous choice of the congress. Mrs. Davis is of English descent in three lines of ancestors. She also had the honor of receiving and reporting the two largest contributions to the Memorial Continental Hall, that to the Fourteenth Congress being in cash and pledges and amounting to $37,660.32 and that to the Fifteenth Congress being in cash and pledges amounting to $35,654.60.

MRS. JOHN C. AMES.

Mrs. John C. Ames—Minerva Ross Ames—state regent for Illinois, 1909-1910, is a native Illinoisan. Her father, John Ross, of Cumberland County, Pennsylvania, whose antecedents were the same as George Ross, the "signer," and her mother, Elizabeth Hunter Ross, of Indiana County, Pennsylvania, came to Illinois about 1850.

Mrs. Ames comes of patriotic stock, tracing her ancestry back to Revolutionary soldiers both through her father's and mother's line. Her great-grandfather, Lieutenant Hunter (on her mother's side), was a Revolutionary hero. She is also eligible to the Daughters of 1812. Her only brother gave his life for his country in the Civil War. She has perpetuated the patriotic and military spirit by giving a son for service in the Spanish-American War.

Mrs. Ames became a member of the National Society Daughters of the American Revolution many years ago, and has always taken an active part in promoting the welfare of the organization and the patriotic principles for which it stands. During her temporary residence in Chicago she served the Chicago Chapter as its recording secretary and first vice-regent.

Mrs. Ames is possessed of a love and loyalty for the order, a fervent patriotic spirit, a pleasing personality and great executive ability and extended acquaintance throughout the state. She was a member of a "State Park Commission" appointed by Governor Deneen to investigate and report to the legislature several sites suitable for state parks, which resulted in an appropriation by the legislature of funds for buying the historic spot, "Starved Rock," and several hundred acres surrounding it as a state park. She was one of the founders of the oldest and most active literary clubs in her city and has served as its president. She has since her childhood been a member of the Baptist Church. In 1875 she was married to John C. Ames, and coming to Streator a bride she has ever since been a resident of that city. She is a member of the Amor Patriæ Chapter of Streator, Illinois.

MRS. AMOS G. DRAPER.

Mrs. Draper was born in Haverhill, New Hampshire, and is the daughter of Daniel F. Merrill, for many years principal of a large boys' school in Mobile, Alabama, and Luella Bartlett Bell Merrill, of Haverhill, New Hampshire. She was graduated from Mount Holyoke Seminary in 1877 and soon after graduation was married to Professor Amos G. Draper, of Gallaudet College, a national institution, and the only one in the world where deaf mutes can receive a college education. Among the several ancestors through whose services Mrs. Draper claims eligibility to the Daughters of the American Revolution, two, Daniel and Jonathan Weeks, were over seventy years, and one, John Bell, Jr., only sixteen years of age at the time of service. Another, Hon Josiah Bartlett, the last president of New Hampshire and its first governor, was the first member of the Continental Congress to vote for the Declaration of Independence, and the first after John Hancock, the President, to attach his name to that document. Since her marriage Mrs. Draper has lived very quietly, surrounded by her family, but devoting her leisure moments to some of the many historical and benevolent societies of the Capital. She was one of the original members of the Ladies' Historical Society, is the vice-president of the Home Missionary Society in her church, and has for many years been connected with the Homeopathic Hospital and Dispensary. She was for two years regent of the Dolly Madison Chapter, and in that capacity attended the Third and Fourth Continental Congresses of the Daughters of the American Revolution, and by the latter body was unanimously elected treasurer of the society.

MRS. HENRY LEWIS POPE.

Sarah Lloyd Moore Ewing Pope, of the city of Louisville, Kentucky, was appointed regent of Louisville on September 15, 1891, by the president-general of the Daughters of the American Revolution, Mrs. Caroline Scott Harrison. Mrs. Pope is descended from William Moore, of Pennsylvania, who with unfailing loyalty rendered material aid to the cause of American independence as president of the Executive Council of Pennsylvania during the war, Council of Safety and of the Board of War, captain-general of the commonwealth of Pennsylvania. Mrs. Pope was twice married; first, to Nathaniel Burwell Marshall, grandson of Chief Justice John Marshall. On the 11th of January, 1891, when she organized her chapter, it was named the "John Marshall Chapter." Her second husband, Mr. Henry Lewis Pope, is related to the Washingtons. Mr. Pope's father, William Pope, although only seventeen years old, fought during the Revolutionary War. Mrs. Pope's father, Dr. Urban E. Ewing, was also of Revolutionary descent. The Rev. Finis Ewing, the great-uncle of Mrs. Pope, founded the

Cumberland Presbyterian Church. Mrs. Pope, a devoted Episcopalian, is proud of the patriotism and piety of these relations. Adlai Ewing Stevenson former Vice-President of the United States, is a relative of this family. Gently affectionate and stately, Mrs. Pope displays a remarkable strength of character and energy of action for one who has led an easy, luxurious life. Being of natural right one of the queens of social life in the beautiful city of her birth, she has ever exercised other queenly gifts of charity and hospitality that inspire love as well as respect. Her patriotic spirit was warmly aroused at the first inception of the organization of the Daughters of the American Revolution, and her unfailing zeal has resulted in the establishment of a most prosperous and important chapter in Louisville.

MARY McKINLAY NASH.

Mrs. Nash, regent of the state of North Carolina, Daughters of the American Revolution, was born in New Bern, North Carolina, January 2, 1835. She is the daughter of John Pugh Daves and Elizabeth V. Graham Daves. Her paternal ancestor was of England and came to this country about the middle of the seventeenth century, settling first in what is now Chesterfield, Virginia. Her maternal ancestors were Grahams, of Arglyeshire, Scotland. Mrs. Nash was educated at St. Mary's School Raleigh, and at Madam Chegaray's, New York. On August 11, 1858, she was married to Hon. John W. Ellis, who was later made governor of North Carolina. Governor Ellis died while still in office, July 7, 1861. In 1866 she became the wife of James E. Nash, of Petersburg, Virginia, who died in New Bern May 30, 1880. On March 21, 1892, Mary McKinlay Nash was appointed regent for the state of North Carolina, her identity with its interests and history rendering her peculiarly fitted for this honorable position,

MARY MARGARET FRYER MANNING.

Mrs. Daniel Manning can trace her Dutch ancestry back many generations in Holland on her father's side. On her mother's side she traces her ancestry from Robert Livingston, first head of the house of Livingston. She is a woman of pleasing and gracious presence, a sweet and abiding kindness pervading her every act, official or social. She is a leader in social circles at home, but it is in the humanitarian and spiritual side of life, in her church work and in her deeds of charity that the sweetest and truest womanhood is found. She is the daughter of W. J. Fryer, one of the early merchant princes of Albany, and her mother was Margaret Livingston Crofts, granddaughter of Robert Thong 'Livingston. Miss Fryer was the second wife of the late Daniel Manning. They were married in November, 1884, and in March, 1885, he was appointed by Mr. Cleveland Secretary of the Treasury. During the years that Mr. Manning held the portfolio of the Treasury their home in Washington became a center of social and political affairs in Washington. After Mr. Manning's death in 1887 Mrs. Manning continued to spend part of each year in Washington, and has never lost sight of the friendships made there. Her patriotism is shown in her work for the Mohawk Chapter of Albany, of which she was regent. She has done yeoman service on the Continental Hall Committee.   She was admirably adapted to her position of president of the society, to which she was elected by the congress of 1898.

JULIA CATHERINE CONKLING.

Mrs. Roscoe Conkling, founder and first regent of the Oneida Chapter of the Daughters of the American Revolution, was born in Utica, New York, May 4, 1827.   She was the youngest child of Henry Seymour and Mary Ledyard Forman Seymour.   Mrs. Conkling was endowed with rare gifts of personal beauty and most lovable traits of character.   All her early life was spent in Utica.   In June, 1855, she married Roscoe Conkling, who was just beginning his brilliant public career.   During the many winters Mrs. Conkling spent in Washington with her husband, she was frequently mentioned as one of the most graceful and refined women of the administrations of President Lincoln and President Grant, and as possessing a high-bred charm of manner rarely equaled.   The Oneida Chapter of the Daughters of the American Revolution was formed at her house in 1893 with a most gratifying number of eligible applicants, full of zeal and patriotism, present.   Mrs. Conkling died at Utica, New York, October 18, 1893.

MARY ORR EARLE.

Mrs. Mary Orr Earle, corresponding secretary-general of the Daughters of the American Revolution, is the daughter of the late Hon. James L. Orr, of South Carolina.   She was born in 1858, while her distinguished father was Speaker of the United States House of Representatives.   Mrs. Earle's connection with the National Society of the Daughters of the American Revolution is through descent from Robert Orr, a captain of Pennsylvania troops, and dates from the organization of the society in 1890, she having been one of the early vice-presidents and a member of the first national board.   At the congress of 1895 she was elected corresponding secretary-general, which position she has filled with marked ability.   Gifted with rare mental and social qualities, Mrs. Earle has drawn around her a large and cultured circle of friends at the national Capital, where her accomplishments as a linguist are much appreciated in the diplomatic corps.

MRS. OGDEN H. FETHERS.

Mrs. Ogden H. Fethers was born in New York State and educated at Claverock on the Hudson.   Her maiden name was Frances Conkey.   She is a descendant of Elder William Brewster, of Plymouth Colony, and her membership to the Society of the Colonial Dames is through Rev. James Fitch of Connecticut Colony.

On July 15, 1868, she was married in Canton, New York, to Ogden Hoffman Fethers, a well-known and able attorney, of Janesville, Wisconsin.

In 1909, upon the death of Mrs. James Sidney Peck, of Milwaukee, Mrs. Fethers succeeded her as governor of the Society of Mayflower descendants for the state of Wisconsin.   Wisconsin is the only state which has enjoyed having a woman governor of this society.   Mrs. Fethers' name will be long remembered by her song "The Star of Wisconsin," which has been adopted by the Daughters of the American Revolution of Wisconsin for the state song. Mrs. Fethers was state regent of the Daughters of the American Revolution for Wisconsin for four years. From the sale of this song, she has furnished a small room in the Memorial Continental Hall.

Mrs. Fethers has been high in the councils of the Daughters of the American Revolution, having served on some of its most important committees and having done particularly valuable work for the Continental Hall. She is a woman of unusual culture and refinement, of wide travel and an intimate acquaintance with the best literature and art. Mrs. Fethers is a director of Janesville public library, in which she has done work of inestimable value for her city and state. The private library of Mr. and Mrs. Fethers and their collection of valuable works of art are among the finest in the country.

ELIZABETH CAROLYN SEYMOUR BROWN.

Mrs. Brown was born at Linden, Michigan. She is a granddaughter of the late Zenas Fairbank, one of the early and most prominent citizens of that town. She was educated at the University of Michigan, and was an active member of the musical and dramatic societies connected with that institution. She spent several years teaching in the schools of Ann Arbor and Manistee, Michigan, and Duluth, Minnesota. She married Frederick Charles Brown, editor and journalist, and since his death in 1900 has resided in Phoenix, Arizona, and at the present time occupies the position of preceptress at the Arizona State Normal School. Mrs. Brown has been an enthusiastic worker in the Maricopa Chapter. Being a writer of merit and possessing a love for research she made an efficient officer and historian and furnished the chapter with a great deal of interesting data connected with the early history of this section. On her mother's side she is descended from Thomas Dudley and Simon Bradstreet, colonial governors and on her father's side from Mathew Gilbert, also one of the colonial governors.

MARGUERITE DICKINS.

Mrs. Dickins was born in the picturesque valley of the Unadilla in central New York, and had the good fortune to pass her childhood at the home of her grandfather, Squire Noah Ely, a lawyer and influential citizen in his section of the country, and under his careful tuition she acquired a thorough knowledge of the dead languages, which no doubt gave her greater ability to acquire foreign languages, of which she speaks French, German and Spanish fluently Her widowed mother married Mr. C. Francis Bates of Boston and then the scenes of her life were transferred to New York City and Newport, Rhode Island. In the former state she pursued her studies at one of the most famous private schools for young ladies until 1872, when she was taken by her mother to Europe, where she remained three years, visiting the principal capitals and continuing her studies of languages and art. Shortly after her return to the United States she married Commander F. W. Dickins, United States Navy In 1882 she traveled extensively through the south and has given her impressions in a series of letters published in the *Danbury News,* of Connecticut. In 1883 she went with her husband to the South Pacific, living on board the United States steamship "Onward," then stationed at Callao, Peru. The period of two years that was spent in Peru was full of interest due to the war then going on between that country and Chile. Naturally she became interested in the situation in that part of South America. These impressions were published in a series of letters in the *National Republican,* of Washington, D. C. Not long after her return to the United States in 1889, she followed her husband to the east coast of South America where she passed more than two years, visiting principally the countries of Brazil, Uruguay, Argentine and Paraguay, and living on board the United States steamship "Tallapoosa" most of the time. Her perfect knowledge of the Spanish language enabled her to become familiar with the home life of the people and gain much correct information as to their manners and customs, accounts of which she contributed to the *Washington Post.* After her return to the United States she made her home in Washington, D. C., where her husband was stationed on duty. She accompanied her husband on a trip to Japan and her impressions of that country were published in the *Washington Post.* Besides her literary and artistic pursuits, Mrs. Dickins devotes much of her time to missionary work and is prominently connected with many charitable institutions in Washington. She is the well-known author of the delightful volume "Along Shore with a Man of War." At the Continental Congress of February, 1893, she was elected by unanimous vote, treasurer-general of the National Society of the Daughters of the American Revolution. Her work in this important position has been earnest and thorough. She held the unqualified confidence and respect of her associates while her cheering view of life and labor wins for her an affectionate regard. Her many high qualities are exercised with the modest unconsciousness of a sincere purpose and directed by generous culture.

MRS. J. STEWART JAMIESON.

Mrs. Jamieson, registrar-general, entered the society by virtue of the records of two patriots, James Schureman, born in New Jersey, in 1751, and died at New Brunswick, New Jersey, June 23, 1824. Served in the Revolutionary army; was a delegate to the Continental Congress from New Jersey in 1776-1777. and was elected to the first Congress as a Federalist, serving from March, 1789, until March, 1791, and again to the fifth Congress, serving from May, 1797, until March, 1799. Was then chosen United States Senator in place of John Rutherford, serving from December, 1799, until February, 1801, when he resigned. Subsequently became mayor of the city of New Brunswick and was again elected to Congress serving from May 24, 1813, to March 2, 1815. Dr. Melanchthon Freeman of Piscataway township, New Jersey, was a member of the Committee of Observation and surgeon in the state troops, Colonel Forman's battalion, Heard's brigade.

JENNIE FRANKLIN HICHBORN.

Mrs. Hichborn, registrar-general of the Daughters of the American Revolution, is the daughter of Philip Franklin and Mary Bailey Franklin, and was born in southern Vermont. She was educated at Leland and Gray Seminary, Townshend and Glenwood Seminary, Brattleboro, Vermont. At the age of nineteen her attention was called to music, and three years were profitably spent at the Old Boston Music School, after which several years were devoted to church music and teaching the art. Mrs. Hichborn's claim of eligibility to the National Society of the Daughters of the American Revolution is through Captain Comfort Starr, Captain Richard Bailey, Lieutenant Joshua Hyde and Philip Franklin, the second. At the Congress of 1895, she was elected registrar-general of the society. Mrs. Hichborn is the wife of Philip Hichborn, the distinguished chief constructor of the United States Navy. A son and daughter constitute the home circle.

MRS. LA VERNE NOYES.

The subject of this sketch was born in the state of New York, of New England ancestors. When quite young, her parents moved to Iowa. She is a graduate of the Iowa State College, with a record for scholarship which was not equaled for a great many years. When in college, she was president of a literary society. She married La Verne Noyes, also a graduate of the Iowa State College, who later became widely known as an inventor and manufacturer in Chicago. She lives in one of the beautiful homes of Chicago.

For many years her fields of activity have been manifold in literary, social and philanthropic work. She is one of the directors of the Twentieth Century Club and of the Woman's Athletic Club; was, for years, president of the North Side Art Club; has been active in the Woman's Club; has been regent of Chicago Chapter Daughters of the American Revolution, the first chapter organized in the United States, and the largest one, having over 800 members. She is a good writer of verses and an excellent and forceful speaker. During the last Continental Congress, where there were nearly 1100 delegates present, she made the nominating speech for the successful candidate for president-general; a brilliant speech, considered by many the best nominating speech delivered during the Congress. Her felicity and strength as a writer and speaker in this organization made her a vice-president-general, and makes her a strong factor in its management.

In the work of the Daughters of the American Revolution she has been especially active in the Department of Patriotic Education and in the organization of boys' clubs to teach patriotism.

MRS. ROBERDEAU BUCHANAN.

Mrs. Buchanan, a native and life-long resident of Washington City, is the wife of Roberdeau Buchanan, of the Nautical Almanac Observatory. She entered the Society of the Daughters of the American Revolution on February 2, 1892, by virtue of descent from her grandfather, Thomas Peters, who was one of the original twenty-eight men of family and fortune who formed the famous First Troop, Philadelphia City Cavalry, November 17, 1774. He served with great distinction at the battles of Trenton and Princeton, under General Washington. Mrs.

Buchanan was elected to a vacancy on the National Board of Management as registrar-general on December 10, 1894, and at the Congress of 1895 was elected to the office of recording secretary-general.

EMILY TRUE DE REIMER.

Mrs. De Reimer, state chaplain of the District of Columbia, is a Boston woman, educated at Abbot Seminary, Andover, Massachusetts, and the New York Musical Conservatory. She was a teacher at Wilbraham Academy before her marriage. Her father, Dr. Charles De True, a Harvard graduate, was Professor of moral philosophy and belles lettres in Wesleyan University, Middletown, Connecticut. Her mother, Elizabeth Hyde True was one of the early pupils of the famous Emma Willard School at Troy, New York. Through the Hyde ancestry Mrs. De Reimer becomes a Daughter of the American Revolution. Her early life was spent in Boston, Middletown, Connecticut and New York City. Returning to Boston she married Reverend William E. De Reimer and went with him to India and Ceylon. Mrs. De Reimer spent ten years in Asia learning an Oriental language and conducted a Hindoo Girls' School. On her return to this country she lived in Wisconsin, Iowa and Illinois. She started the first Christian Endeavor Society in Iowa and has organized Chautauqua Circles and has taken a great interest in missionary work. After editing a series of Congregational Missionary studies and doing other literary work, she was made a member of the Illinois Women's Press Association. Coming to Washington years ago, she became a Daughter of the American Revolution and was elected chaplain of Columbia Chapter. She has served as state chaplain three times. She has represented the Daughters of the American Revolution at various meetings and congresses of well-known clubs and during the Lewis and Clark Exposition, represented the Smithsonian Institution.

MRS. TEUNIS S. HAMLIN.

Mrs. Hamlin was elected four times to the position of chaplain-general of the Daughters of the American Revolution and was the first to hold this position. Mrs. Hamlin's descent is from Andrew Ward, who was one of the four sent from the Bay Colony to govern Connecticut, having come over the sea with Winthrop. Her great-grandfather, David Ward, entered the first New York Continental Regiment at the age of fourteen, while her great-great-grandfather was killed in the militia during Burgoyne's raid into Vermont. Her grandparents were pioneers in Michigan, where for three generations the "Ward Line" was the great steamboat line on the Great Lakes. Mrs. Hamlin has been very active in Home Mission work, being a vice-president in the Woman's Presbyterian Board of Home Missions. She has been a strenuous opponent of Mormonism and few understand the subject better than she. She is treasurer of the National League of Women's Organizations, and it was due to her that resolutions relative to an amendment of the Constitution of the United States on polygamy was introduced and unanimously passed at a Congress of the Daughters. She was educated in the State Normal School of Michigan, and was a fine parliamentarian and fluent extemporary speaker.

MARY C. BEACH.

Mrs. Beach, corresponding secretary of the Daughters of the American Revolution, comes of Colonial and Revolutionary ancestry. She is a native of New York and is eligible to membership in the Society of the Daughters of the American Revolution on the maternal side through five different ancestors; the Holland Dutch and Huguenot French, who are so closely identified with the history of New York, and on the paternal side from the Scotch-Irish Puritans of New England. She is a member and ex-regent of the Continental Chapter and chairman of the Committee on Neighborhoods, and two classes have been formed in industrial training through her. With the regent of the chapter, she is a frequent attendant at the Juvenile Court and is also greatly interested in the night schools and particularly in the foreign classes, and believes that they deserve the support and co-operation of the Daughters in promoting good citizenship. She was instrumental in forming a new chapter in Telma, Alabama, which was christened "The Cherokee," and at their first meeting she was elected an honorary member.

MARY S. LOCKWOOD.

Mrs. Lockwood is a woman who has done as much as any other woman in this century to elevate her sex and to secure to herself an honorable place in the literary world. Mary Smith was born in Chautauqua, New York. She lost her mother when but four years old, and the tender love of her infancy was lavished on her brother, three years her senior. To him her last book, "The Historic Homes of Washington," is most touchingly dedicated. She is physically slight, but strong and rather below the medium height. She has firmness, strength and executive ability of a high order. An interesting face with character written on the broad brow; and in the deep blue eyes of intellectual sweetness there is mingled a determination of purpose and firm resolve. Her hair, silvered and wavy, shades a face full of kindly interest in humanity. Her voice has a peculiar charm, low-keyed and musical, yet sympathetic and far-reaching. She is friendly to all progressive movements, especially so in the progress of women. Mrs. Lockwood was the founder of the celebrated "Travel Club," which met at her home ever since its formation, on Monday evenings for many long years. In her house was also organized the association of the Daughters of the American Revolution. Mrs. Lockwood was elected historian at the first meeting. She is the author of a text-book on ceramics, and of many bright articles on the tariff written for the best periodicals. She is also the author of "The Historical Homes of Washington." She has been president of the Woman's National Press Club, and she held the position of Lady Manager at Large of the Columbian Exposition and was among the most efficient managers of the Woman's Board, throwing immense labor into the work of classification, and exercising serious responsibilities in the Committee on the Press. We look at her with amazement and wonder, when we see this little woman doing so much and still holding all her faculties in calm, leisurely poise. She certainly demonstrates the possibility of combining business with literature, and both with an active sympathy in social reforms, and all with a womanly grace that beautifies every relation of life.

MRS. JAMES EAKIN GADSBY.

Mrs. Gadsby, historian-general of the Society of the Daughters of the American Revolution, comes of a long line of distinguished ancestry on both sides, who served in Colonial and Revolutionary periods, all of whom settled in Maryland on original land grants. All of her ancestors were of English descent. Mrs. Gadsby entered the society in 1898 for patriotic services in the Spanish American War and assisted Mrs. Dickens in her work for the soldiers' families of the District of Columbia. She also sent supplies of clothing to General Fitzhugh Lee for the hospital he founded at Havana for the destitute women and children. She was a member of the Mary Washington Chapter from 1898 and served as its historian and did special work for Continental Hall. In May, 1907, she resigned from the Mary Washington Chapter and was transferred to the Emily Nelson Chapter. She was appointed by Mrs. Charles W. Fairbanks, a member of the Continental Hall and other committees and was re-appointed by Mrs. Donald McLean. She is a member of the Jamestown and Pocahontas Societies and a member of the Columbia Historical Society. She served as chairman of the Daughters of the American Revolution Press Committee for the District and has been a writer of historical articles for many years and an enthusiast on historical subjects, devoting her time to her office of historian with interest and zeal.

MARY CHASE GANNETT.

Mrs. Gannett, the third historian-general of the Daughters of the American Revolution, is a New England woman by birth and education, her early home having been in Saco, Maine. Her grandfather on the maternal side, Samuel Peirson, entered the Revolutionary Army when very young and after a short period of active service became Washington's private secretary. Her great-grandfather was Major Hill, who served through the war and afterwards held many positions of trust and honor. On the paternal side Mrs. Gannett is descended from General Frye, an officer who distinguished himself at the battle of Louisberg, and as a reward for his services received a grant of the township in Maine which has since borne the name of Fryeburg. Mrs. Gannett was married in 1874 to Henry Gannett. Her husband is one of the leading men in the scientific society of Washington. He is a geographer by profession and has been for many years connected with the United States Geological Survey.

MARIE RAYMOND GIBBONS.

Mrs. Gibbons was born in Toledo, Ohio, but removed with her parents to California when a young girl and her subsequent life was entirely passed on this coast. In 1871 she married Dr. Henry Gibbons, Jr. She was a member of the Society of Colonial Dames of America and of the Order of the Descendants of Colonial Governors, and eligible to the Society of Descendants of the Mayflower, but her special interest was in the Society of the Daughters of the American Revolution. She was the organizer and regent for two years, of the second

Chapter of Puerta del Ora. Mrs. Gibbons was eligible to the Daughters of the American Revolution through several lines, but chooses to found her claim to membership upon the services of Captain Samuel Taylor of Danbury, Connecticut, an ancestor of her father, Samuel Augustus Raymond. When, during the war with Spain, San Francisco became a vast camp and the Red Cross Society was established for the aid of our volunteers, the patriotic instincts and the generous feeling of Mrs. Gibbons at once responded to the call.

E. ELLEN BATCHELLER.

Miss Batcheller was born in Freetown, New York. The founder of her family in America was Honorable Joseph Batcheller who came from England in 1636 with his wife Elizabeth, one child and three servants. Miss Batcheller's father, Charles Batcheller was the personal friend and co-worker with Gerrit Smith and Wendell Phillips. Too old to enter the army at the time of the Civil War, he sent his son, who was a martyr to the cause. Miss Batcheller is also eligible through two grandmothers, Rebecca Dwight and Sarah Norton, to membership in the Mayflower, Colonial Dames and Huguenot Societies, but her chief patriotic work has been with the Daughters of the American Revolution, organizing the General Frelinghuysen Chapter and remaining regent until elected state regent, in which position she was eminently successful, organizing nine new chapters in as many months. Few, if any families have more illustrious members— Whittier, Daniel Webster, Caleb Cushing, General Dearborn, Senators Morrill and Allison and many others. A sister of Miss Batcheller married James Jared Elmendorf, a descendant of Sobieski, King of Poland. Miss Batcheller is a staunch Episcopalian, has traveled extensively in her own country and resides in Somerville, New Jersey.

ELLEN SPENCER MUSSEY.

Mrs. Mussey is a woman esteemed for her knowledge of practical affairs and general business capacity. She was chosen by the District Supreme Court as successor to Mrs. David J. Brewer on the Board of Education for the district. For years was active in the business life of the Capital and a genuine factor in the practice of law at the local bar. Organizer of the Washington College of Law. Member of the Daughters of the American Revolution and state regent of the District of Columbia. Descended from Caleb Spencer, who enlisted from Danbury, Connecticut, under Captain Benedict, in the first call for troops.

MRS. ROBERT A. McCLELLAN.

Mrs. Aurora Pryor McClellan is the daughter of Luke Pryor, who was prominent in public life of Alabama for many years, and in 1880 succeeded George S. Houston, his law partner, as United States Senator from Alabama. Mrs. McClellan's mother was Isabella Harris, a descendant of distinguished Virginia families—the Spotswoods and other well-known families of that state. Mrs. McClellan's father was descended on the paternal side from the Blands, of

Virginia, and through this ancestry from Governor Richard Bennett, of the commonwealth period in the Old Dominion; on his maternal side from Ann Lane, of Virginia, whose mother, Sylvia Perry, was descended from Judge Freeman Perry, of Rhode Island.

Mrs. McClellan is a member of the Daughters of the American Revolution, Colonial Dames and the Order of Descendants of Colonial Governors. She founded a chapter of the Daughters of the American Revolution in Athens, Alabama, and was for four years state vice-regent of the Alabama Daughters of the American Revolution and six years state regent, and is to-day honorary life regent of the Alabama Daughters of the American Revolution.

Mrs. McClellan has devoted most of her time and efforts to securing the adoption of the "Golden Rod" as the national flower. She is to-day second vice-president of the National Flower Association of the United States, and through her personal efforts the National Farmers' Congress adopted this flower in 1890 and recommended its adoption as the national emblem.

Mrs. McClellan is one of the most gifted of Southern women, possessing wonderful executive ability and a strong, clear mind. Her capacity as an original thinker made her a marked woman in the South.

MRS. JOHN H. DOYLE.

Mrs. Doyle was born in Windsor, Connecticut, in 1851. In 1868 she was married to John H. Doyle, of Toledo, Ohio, where her parents moved after the Civil War. Her father served as a surgeon all through the war. Her maiden name was Alice Fuller Skinner. She was the second member to join the Daughters of the American Revolution in Toledo, Ohio, and is now vice-regent of the Toledo Chapter. Mrs. Doyle has always been an enthusiastic and conscientious worker for the Daughters of the American Revolution and in the many philanthropic efforts of Toledo and throughout the state of Ohio. She is a member of the Colonial Dames and one of the board of managers of the Ohio Circle She is also a member of the Colonial Governors Society and has always taken a foremost place in all matters in which she was personally interested and is to-day one of the representative women from the state of Ohio.

MRS. LINDSAY PATTERSON.

Mrs. Patterson is a descendant of the "Fighting Grahams," of Scotland, of whom the Duke of Montrose is the head. Her grandfather, Robert Patterson, fought through three wars, that of 1812, in which he was made captain at nineteen, the Mexican War, in which he was offered the chief command, but refused on account of his devoted friendship for General Scott, and the Civil War. For fifty years he was one of the notable hosts, of Philadelphia. Elizabeth Patterson of Baltimore, who married Jerome Bonaparte, was a distant cousin. General Patterson married Sara Engle, a Quakeress, whose father, when a boy, ran away from home and joined the Revolutionary Army. It is through this ancestor that Mrs. Patterson is eligible to be a Daughter. Her father was Colonel William

Houston Patterson. Mrs. Patterson is a Tennessean by birth, a Philadelphian by residence and a North Carolinian by marriage to Mr. Lindsay Patterson, who is descended from the older branch of the family that settled in Lancaster County, Pennsylvania. Mrs. Patterson is president of the Southern Woman's Interstate Association for the Betterment of Public Schools, vice-president, of the North Carolina Historical Society, vice-president of the Salem Historical Society and president of the County Association for Betterment of Public Schools.

MRS. CHARLES H. DEERE.

Of Colonial ancestors Mrs. Deere has record of sixty-five who were founders and patriots and fighters in the Indian wars. Six of their descendants marched at the first alarm at Lexington. Mrs. Deere is a member of the Memorial Continental Hall Committee of the Daughters of the American Revolution.

MRS. A. L. CONGER.

Mrs. A. L. Conger, widow of Colonel A. L. Conger, of Akron, Ohio, is a woman who has devoted much of her life, time and means to charitable works. She is a member of the Woman's Relief Corps, the Daughters of the American Revolution and other patriotic organizations and has from the beginning of the Civil War, done all that she possibly could in the interest of the soldiers and their families. After the death of Colonel Conger she went to Kirksville, Missouri, and studied osteopathy at the Still Institute graduating with honors. She is an enthusiastic osteopathic physician and spent more than two years in the Philippines, giving her services, time and money to the relief of the soldiers of the Spanish-American War. She was in the field at Iloilo-Iloilo and gave all her time to the hospitals. She is deeply interested in Evangelistic work and has contributed largely to Evangelistic and other charitable work in Akron. She has three sons. Her eldest son, Mr. K. B. Conger, assisted Mr. McAdoo when he built the great New York tunnel. Captain A. L. Conger, Jr., is in the United States Army. Her youngest son is engaged in railroading.

MRS. JOHN MILLER HORTON.

One of the most accomplished and representative women of her native state, the great Empire State of New York, and identified with many interests along patriotic, educational and philanthropic lines. She has achieved not only state, but national fame as well, having faithfully performed the duties of the various offices she has been called upon to assume. Mrs. Horton was Miss Katharine Lorenz Pratt, the daughter of Pascal Paoli Pratt, a prominent banker, financier and philanthropist of Buffalo. Being the eldest daughter, Mrs. Horton shared intimately in her father's ambitions for the welfare of Buffalo, and has continued this work, becoming one of the most prominent factors in the social life and civic welfare of the city of Buffalo.

Mrs. Horton was elected unanimously regent of the Buffalo Chapter,

31

Daughters of the American Revolution, for seven successive years, and through
her duties as regent has been a prominent figure in the national congress each
year of the Daughters of the American Revolution, which meets in Washington.
The Buffalo Chapter is the largest in the New York State organization, and the
second largest in the national organization. It was through her instrumentality
that the New York State Daughters of the American Revolution Conference was
held in Buffalo in 1898, which was one of the most interesting gatherings of
Daughters held outside of Washington. The Buffalo Chapter has the honor of
having on its rolls the names of two real daughters whose fathers served as
soldiers in the Army of the Revolution. It is largely due to the energy and
generosity of Mrs. Horton, as regent of the Buffalo Chapter, that the graves of
over one hundred patriots of the War of Independence, buried in the vicinity of
Buffalo, bear markers to tell of their devotion to the cause of patriotism. The
graves of these heroes were found, all the records restored and the ceremony of
marking these graves and the ritual used in the ceremony being written and the
ceremonies directed by Mrs. Horton.

She has been indefatigable in sustaining an active interest in the patriotic
educational work of her chapter, and during the winter season two illustrated
lectures, weekly, are given to the Italians and Poles of the city of Buffalo on
the history of the United States. The lectures are given in the Polish and Italian
language, at the expense of her chapter. Buffalo Chapter was the pioneer in this
commendable work of educating the foreign element.

Mrs. Horton was appointed on the Board of Woman Managers of the
Pan-American Exposition, at Buffalo, N. Y., and acted as chairman of the com-
mittee on ceremonies and entertainments of the Women's Board of the Pan-
American Exposition. She was also appointed by the Governor of New York,
commissioner to the Charleston Exposition in 1902, and again served on the
Board of Lady Managers of the St. Louis Exposition. She was appointed by
President Francis of the Exposition, and Mrs. Blair, president of the Ladies'
Board, chairman of the Committee on Exposition interests at the National Congress of the Daughters of the American Revolution, held at Washington, Febru-
ary, 1903.

In close touch with all this patriotic work, in New York, there is an
organization known as the Niagara Frontier Landmarks Association, of which
Mrs. Horton is vice-president, a position which she has held since the formation
of the society. The purpose of this society is to mark all important historical sites
along the Niagara Frontier with tablets and monuments. At La Salle was erected
a tablet commemorative of the building, by La Salle, of "The Griffon," the first
boat to navigate the waters of the north; Mrs. Horton drove the stake to mark
the spot, and also unveiled the tablet at the ceremonies held afterwards. Later
on, when a tablet was placed in the Niagara Gorge to mark the spot of the
Devil's Hole Massacre, Mrs. Horton, in the name of the Colonial Dames, unveiled
the tablet. When the site of "Fort Tompkins" was marked by the society, Mrs.
Horton presided over the program and made the principal address, and on the
momentous occasion of placing a tablet to mark the site of the first Court House
of Erie County, it was Buffalo's gifted townswoman who presided, gave the

address and introduced Judge Haight, the last judge to hold a judiciary session in the old house of justice, and other important and prominent lawyers who were speakers—Mr. Herbert Bissell, and others of the Erie County Bar.

And back of all these praiseworthy undertakings for patriotism and civic betterment, is the president of Buffalo City Federation of Women's Clubs. Because the federation's aims are solely to lend a woman's assistance to the civic author-ities wherever it will ameliorate the condition of women and children, Mrs. Horton consented to accept the office of president. During her administration it has brought about the appointment of a woman probation officer, and has estab-lished penny luncheons in some of the public schools of the poorer districts of the city, with hopes of further increasing the number of schools similarly located. Medical inspection for public schools of Buffalo is another excellent philanthropy in which the Federation has been successful in securing, Mrs. Horton having made an appeal in its favor before the Common Council of Buffalo, which did much towards securing the appropriation towards this good work, while it has pledged the sum of $2,000.00 towards a scholarship in the proposed Buffalo Uni-versity Extension for the education of a poor girl, to be won by competitive examination.

At the urgent request of the national officers of the society, Mrs. Horton, in 1904, organized the "Niagara Frontier Buffalo Chapter, National Society United States Daughters of 1812," and was appointed regent. In 1908, Mrs. Horton organized the Nellie Custis Chapter, National Society Children of the American Revolution. Mrs. Horton was appointed president of the national board, and is also vice-president-general of the national society. She is also a member of the following organizations: President of Buffalo City Federation of Women's Clubs; regent of the Buffalo Chapter, National Society Daughters of the American Revolution; Buffalo Historical Society; Buffalo Genealogical Society; Buffalo Twentieth Century Women's Club; Buffalo Society Natural Sciences, honorary member; American Social Science Association; Buffalo Society of Artists; Buffalo Art Students' League; Church Home League; Old Planters' Society of Massachu-setts; Memorial Continental Hall Committee, National Society Daughters of the American Revolution; National and New York State Daughters of the American Revolution Committee on Patriotic Education; National and New York State Committee on Real Daughters who are living descendants of soldiers of the American Revolution; Women's Republican League of New York State; New York State Federation of Women's Clubs; Federation of Women's Literary and Educational Organizations of Western New York; president, Section 2, Army Relief Association; Trinity Church Society, trustee of National Society of Daughters of the Empire State; regent of Niagara Frontier Buffalo Chapter, National Society United States Daughters of 1812; vice-president Niagara Frontier Landmarks Association; vice-president Order of Americans of Armorial Ancestry; director Women's Educational and Industrial Union; director Women's League of New York State; New York State Historical Association; New York Genealogical and Biographical Society; Buffalo Fine Arts Association; vice-president general National Society, Children of the American Revolution; president Nellie Custis Chapter, National Society Children of the American Revolution;

Chautauqua New York Women's Club; Chautauqua Daughters of the American Revoution Circle; Buffalo Society of Mineral Painters; National Society of New England Women, Colony 2; National Society Daughters of Founders and Patriots of America; National Society Colonial Dames of Vermont; National Society Daughters of American Pioneers; National George Washington Memorial Association; National Mary Washington Memorial Association; International Sunshine Society; Eclectic Club of New York; the Entertainment Club of New York; Japanese Red Cross Association; vice-president Erie County Branch of the American National Red Cross Association; National Society of Patriotic Women of America; Rubinstein Club of New York; Minerva Club of New York; chairman Franco-American Committee, National Society Daughters of the American Revolution; chairman Pension Records Committee, National Society of the Daughters of the American Revolution; chairman Magazine Committee, National Society of the Daughters of the American Revolution; Buffalo Peace and Arbitration Society; National Committee and New York City Peace Society; delegate to Peace Congress at Rome, and vice-president National Society United States Daughters of 1812.

WINNIE DAVIS MONUMENT IN "HOLLYWOOD," RICHMOND, VA.
Erected by the Daughters of the Confederacy.

Women of the Confederacy.

In Richmond, when the hospitals were filled with wounded men brought in from the seven days' fighting with McClellan, and the surgeon found it impossible to dress half the wounds, a band was formed, consisting of nearly all the married women of the city, who took upon themselves the duty of going to the hospitals and dressing wounds from morning till night; and they persisted in their painful duty, until every man was cared for, saving hundreds of lives, as the surgeons unanimously testified. When nitre was found to be growing scarce, and the supply of gunpowder was consequently about to give out, women all over the land dug up the earth in their smoke-houses and tobacco barns, and with their own hands faithfully extracted the desired salt, for use in the government laboratories.

Many of them denied themselves not only delicacies, but substantial food also, when, by enduring semi-starvation, they could add to the stock of food at the command of the subsistence officers. I, myself, knew more that one houseful of women, who, from the moment that food began to grow scarce, refused to eat meat or drink coffee, living thenceforth only upon vegetables of a speedily perishable sort, in order that they might leave the more for soldiers in the field. When a friend remonstrated with one of them, on the ground that her health, already frail, was breaking down utterly for want of proper diet, she replied, in a quiet, determined way, "I know that very well; but it is little that I can do, and I must do that little at any cost. My health and life are worth less than those of my brothers, and if they give theirs to the cause, why should not I do the same? I would starve to death cheerfully, if I could feed one soldier more by doing so, but the things I eat can't be sent to camp. I think it a sin to eat anything that can be used for rations." And she meant what she said, too, as a little mound in the churchyard testifies.

Every Confederate remembers gratefully the reception given him when he went into any house where these women were. Whoever he might be, and whatever his plight, if he wore the gray, he was received, not as a beggar or tramp, not even as a stranger, but as a son of the house, for whom it held nothing too good, and whose comfort was the one care of all its inmates, even though their own must be sacrificed in securing it. When the hospitals were crowded, the people earnestly besought permission to take the men to their houses and to care for them there, and for many months almost every house within a radius of a hundred miles of Richmond held one or more wounded men as especially honored guests.

"God bless these Virginia women," said a general officer from one of the cotton states, one day; "they're worth a regiment apiece." And he spoke the thought of the army, except that their blessing covered the whole country as well as Virginia.

'The United Daughters of the Confederacy.

INTRODUCTION BY CORNELIA BRANCH STONE.

It is a privilege accorded me by the author of this work, to write, at her request, a brief introductory to that part of her book which recognizes the organization known as the United Daughters of the Confederacy—a body of Southern women, approximately numbering sixty thousand, and now organized in thirty-one states, the District of Columbia and city of Mexico, Republic of Mexico.

In 1894 the chapters of the Daughters of the Confederacy, which had been previously formed in many of the Southern states met in Nashville, Tennessee, and organized themselves into one general federation, the objects of which are "memorial, historical, benevolent, educational and social, namely to honor the memory of those who served and those who fell in the service of the Confederate states; to record the part taken by the women of the South, in patient endurance of hardships and patriotic devotion during the struggle, as well as their untiring effort, after the war, in the reconstruction of the South; to collect and preserve the material for a true history of the war between the states; to protect and preserve historical places of the Confederacy; to fulfill the sacred duty of charity to the survivors of that war, and to those dependent upon them; to promote the education of the needy descendants of worthy Confederates; and to cherish the ties of friendship among the members of the association."

With such aims and purposes, the women of this organization—worthy daughters of noble sires—have cared for the living veterans, and urged upon the legislatures of the Southern states the payment of pensions and the establishment and maintenance of homes for these old heroes, and for the needy Confederate women. By their own efforts they have erected monuments throughout the South, to commemorate the heroism of the "men behind the guns," and their great leaders—among whom stand high on the scroll of fame, the name of Robert E. Lee, Stonewall Jackson, J. E. B. Stuart and a host of others who have now become, in our re-united country, a common heritage, as types of American courage and valor.

Under a well-organized educational system, much valuable work is being done for the higher education of worthy sons and daughters of needy Confederates by securing scholarships in universities and colleges. Within such sacred effort, no spirit of antagonism or bitterness has entered, for the heart and soul of this organization has lived and had its being in a clearer, purer atmosphere, where loyalty and faithfulness to our common country has had full part; and the youth of our land while being taught to honor and revere these memories, are also instructed in that patriotism, which leads to the highest type of citizenship, and which will give to the service of our country faithfulness and honesty of purpose.

With such inspiration it is not surprising that the women of this organization—heirs of a rich heritage of glorious achievements, calling forth the best qualities of manhood and womanhood—should have in many cases, developed a high order of executive and administrative ability.

MRS. JEFFERSON DAVIS.

It has been said of Mrs. Varina Howell Davis, who was born May 7, 1826, that she was the key of President Davis' career, and certain it is, that while the public life of this celebrated family was in many respects one long storm, their private life was full of peace and sunshine. In the memoirs of her husband, a work of great merit which Mrs. Davis published early in the '90's, we find every evidence of her loving ministrations and their intellectual companionship, during the memorable years of his life, and her children bear testimony that she enabled him more completely to achieve that career which has made his name immortal. The war career of Mrs. Davis is historical, and a cherished memory of those who watched her unfaltering devotion in the dark days, and when overcome by misfortune met the inevitable like a true daughter of noble sires. She was indeed well descended coming from the famous Howell family, whose founder settled in New Jersey. Her grandfather, Governor Richard Howell, was a Revolutionary officer, and her father, William Burr Howell, won distinction under McDonough on Lake Champlain. Mrs. Davis' maternal grandfather, James Kempt, was an Irish gentleman who came to Virginia after the Emmet Rebellion. He was a man of much wealth and moved to Natchez, Mississippi, when Mrs. Davis' mother was an infant. Colonel Kempt organized the Natchez troops and accompanied them during the Revolution. Mrs. Davis' uncle, Franklin Howell, was killed on the "President." Her marriage to Jefferson Davis took place the 26th of February, 1845. When Jefferson Davis died there was ended a most remarkable chapter of national history and domestic devotion. His widow retired to live in absolute seclusion in their pleasant home in Beauvoir, Mississippi, having with her as close companion her daughter "Winny," affectionately known throughout the South as the "Daughter of the Confederacy."

Many anecdotes have come down to us bearing testimony to the mercy and kindness and loyal service of this "Highest Lady of the Southern Land." The following is typical: During the height of the war a minister passing through the streets of Augusta, Georgia, on his round of duty to the sick, called at the hospitals, and encountered a stranger who accosted him thus: "My friend, can you tell me if Mrs. Jeff Davis is in the city of Augusta?" "No, sir," replied the minister, "she is not." "Well, sir," replied the stranger, "you may be surprised at my asking such a question and more particularly so when I inform you that I am a discharged United States soldier, but," (and here he evinced great feeling) "that lady has performed acts of kindness to me which I can never forget. When serving in the Valley of Virginia, battling for the Union I received a severe and dangerous wound. At the same time

I was taken prisoner and conveyed to Richmond, where I received such kindness and attention from Mrs. Davis that I can never forget her; and, now that I am discharged from the army, I wish to call upon her and carry my expressions of gratitude to her and offer to share with her, should she unfortunately need it, the last cent I have in the world."

Mrs. Davis died in 1906.

SALLIE CHAPMAN GORDON.

Just upon the eve of preparation by ex-Confederates a few years ago to celebrate the Fourth of July in a becoming manner and spirit, the sad news was announced of the death of the venerable Mrs. Law, known all over the South as one of the mothers of the Confederacy. She was also truly a mother in Israel in the highest Christian sense. Her life had been closely connected with that of many leading actors in the late war, in which she herself bore an essential part. She passed away June 28, 1904, at Idlewild, one of the suburbs of Memphis, nearly ninety-nine years of age.

She was born on the River Yadkin, in Wilson County, North Carolina, August 27, 1805, and at the time of her death was doubtless the oldest person in Shelby County. Her mother's maiden name was Charity King. Her father, Chapman Gordon, served in the Revolutionary War, under Generals Marion and Sumter. She came of a long-lived race of people. Her mother lived to be ninety-three years of age, and her brother, Rev. Hezekiah Herndon Gordon, who was the father of General John B. Gordon (late senator from Georgia), lived to the age of ninety-two years.

Sallie Chapman Gordon was married to Dr. John S. Law, near Eatonton, Georgia, on the 28th day of June, 1825. A few years later she became a member of the Presbyterian Church, in Forsyth, Georgia, and her name was afterward transferred to the rolls of the Second Presbyterian Church, in Memphis, of which she remained a member as long as she lived.

She became an active worker in hospitals, and when nothing more could be done in Memphis she went through the lines and rendered substantial aid and comfort to the soldiers in the field. Her services, if fully recorded, would make a book. She was so recognized that upon one occasion General Joseph F. Johnston had thirty thousand of his bronzed and tattered soldiers to pass in review in her honor at Dalton. Such a distinction was, perhaps, never accorded to any other woman in the South, not even Mrs. Jefferson Davis, or the wives of the great generals. Yet, so earnest and sincere in her work was she that she commanded the respect and reverence of men wherever she was known. After the war she strove to comfort the vanquished and encourage the down hearted, and continued in her way to do much good work.

MRS. A. BAUM.

Mrs. Baum, late of Irwinton, Georgia, was born near Bingen, Germany. She emigrated to the United States in 1849 and came to Georgia, residing in Savannah one year, when she removed to Irwinton and there married. From 1850 till her death Irwinton was her home. She died October 30, 1910. During the trying times of 1861-1865 she was ever diligent in aiding in every way in her power the cause of the Confederacy, by donating food, clothing and medicines to the soldiers, and by caring for the needy and sick wives and children of the soldiers of her country at the front.

SARAH ANN DORSEY.

Mrs. Dorsey was the daughter of Thomas G. P. Ellis and was born at Natchez, Mississippi. She was the niece of Mrs. Catherine Warfield, who left her many of her manuscripts. In 1853 she married Mr. Samuel W. Dorsey, of Tensas Parish, Louisiana. She established a chapel and school for slaves. Their home was destroyed during the war and they removed to Texas, but afterwards returned to Louisiana, and in 1875, on the death of her husband, made her home at "Beauvoir" and acted as the amanuensis of Jefferson Davis in his great work, "Rise and Fall of the Confederacy." In her will she left this beautiful home to Mr. Davis and his daughter Winnie.

LUCY ANN COX.

On the evening of October 15th, an entertainment was given in Fredericksburg, Virginia, to raise funds to erect a monument to the memory of Mrs. Lucy Ann Cox, who, at the commencement of the war, surrendered all the comfort of her father's home, and followed the fortunes of her husband, who as a member of Company A, Thirteenth Virginia Regiment, served the South until the flag of the Southern Confederacy was furled at Appomattox. No march was too long or weather too inclement to deter this patriotic woman from doing what she considered her duty. She was with her company and regiment on their two forays into Maryland, and her ministering hand carried comfort to many a wounded and worn soldier. While Company A was the object of her untiring solicitude, no Confederate ever asked assistance from Mrs. Cox but it was cheerfully rendered.

She marched as the infantry did, seldom taking advantage of offered rides in ambulances and wagon trains. Mrs. Cox died, a few years ago. It was her latest expressed wish that she be buried with military honors, and, so far as it was possible, her wish was carried out. Her funeral took place on a bright autumn Sunday, and the entire town turned out to do homage to this noble woman.

The camps that have undertaken the erection of this monument do honor to themselves in thus commemorating the virtues of the heroine, Lucy Ann Cox.

CORNELIA BRANCH STONE.

No one can read an account of the daily life in our Southern states during the Civil War without becoming impressed with the fact that the lofty zeal and heroic fortitude of the Confederate women has received too little attention in our literature. A Southern man in his writing has given us a glimpse of the "war women" of Petersburg. "During all those weary months," he says, "the good women of Petersburg went about their household affairs with fifteen inch shells dropping, not infrequently, into their boudoirs or uncomfortably near to their kitchen ranges. Yet they paid no attention to any danger that threatened themselves and indeed their deeds of mercy will never be recorded until the angels report. But this much I want to say of them—they were 'war women' of the most daring and devoted type." The following succinct report of a Confederate general in the midst of the war shows that the women of Winchester were in no wise second in their unselfish fortitude to the women of Richmond, Petersburg and elsewhere. "Its female inhabitants (for the able-bodied males are all absent in the war)," ran the general's brief, "are familiar with the bloody realities of war. As many as five thousand wounded have been accommodated here at one time. All the ladies are accustomed to the bursting of shells and the sight of fighting and all are turned into hospital nurses and cooks." Throughout the whole South, in every city, town and hamlet arose heroines to meet the emergency of war. On first thought it would have been expected that these women, reared in luxury and seclusion, would have become greatly excited and terrified when under fire and amid scenes of actual war, but almost invariably they exhibited a calm fearlessness that was amazing.

But it was after the war, when the contemplation of ruined homes and broad desolation was thrust upon the South, that the real test came. The men met the awful responsibility and their hideous trials with amazing courage, and to the glory of the Southern woman be it said that the women became equal sharers in courage and in work. They have never faltered and never shown any weariness. Those left penniless, who were once wealthy, took up whatever work came to hand. Not a murmur escaped their lips. They cheered each other as they strengthened the energies of the men, and they kept up their work for the Confederate soldiers and keep it up till this day. Memorial associations were organized all over the South. The two great societies of Richmond, the Hollywood, and the Oakwood, each look after thousands of graves, the names of whose occupants are unknown. But probably the most noble work for the support of charity as well as of loyal sentiment has been done through the United Daughters of the Confederacy. A foremost worker in this noble society is Mrs. Cornelia Branch Stone, for several years president of the Texas Division, and whose biography will well illustrate the strength of character and the executive ability for which the leading ladies among Southern womanhood were distinguished.

A wise counsellor, of clear judgment and indefatigable energy, remarkable administrative ability, tact, high literary attainments, loyal to duty, and a gracious and charming personality—these are the characteristics which make Mrs Cornelia Branch Stone one of the most admired and influential women of the South. She has been and is an active worker in every organization which stands for the good of the people and the uplift of mankind.

She was born in Nacogdoches, Republic of Texas, in February, 1840. Her father, Edward Thomas Branch, a native of Chesterfield County, Virginia, went to Texas in the fall of 1835. He enlisted in the army of Texas, under General Sam Houston and participated in the battle of San Jacinto, which victory decided the independence of Texas from the Republic of Mexico. He was a member of the first and second sessions of the Congress of the Republic of Texas, was district and supreme judge of that republic and was a member of the first legislature of Texas. From this distinguished father, Mrs. Stone undoubtedly inherited her keen virile mind, though her mother, Ann Wharton Cleveland, was a woman of rare culture and intellect.

At fifteen years of age Cornelia Branch was married to Henry Clay Stone, a Virginian by birth. After his death in 1887 Mrs. Stone devoted her time to the education of her only son and when he had graduated in medicine she took up her active work in the organization which she has since pursued with such distinctive success. Her first official position was president of the Texas Division of the United Daughters of the Confederacy. While Mrs. Stone was president, the Texas Division increased twenty-six chapters in two years. She served as president-general of the United Daughters of the Confederacy and during that administration she kept in touch through correspondence with all the daughters and the heads of departments, writing every letter with her own hand. Any one reading her decisions and rulings while presiding over this body cannot but realize the excellency of Mrs. Stone's mind.

She was later first vice-president of the Texas Federation of Woman's Clubs, during· which time she was chairman of a committee to secure an amendment to the poll tax law of the state of Texas. The effect of this was to better enforce the poll tax, one-fourth of which is paid to the school fund of Texas, and it was wholly through the efforts of Mrs. Stone that the amendment was carried, increasing the school fund by many thousands of dollars. As chairman for two years of the committee on education in the Texas Federation of Women's Clubs, she contributed many papers on educational interests, secured scholarship in several colleges of Texas and recommended in her report the provision of a fund by the clubs for the maintenance of the beneficiaries of these scholarships when unable to pay board and lodging. She has held offices of trust in the Daughters of the Republic of Texas, and as first vice-president has served as acting president at their convention. Although Mrs. Stone loves the cause represented by the Daughters of the Confederacy and as guiding hand for it gave her best efforts of pen and brain, she is moreover an enthusiastic Colonial Dame and patriotic member of the Daughters of the American Revolution and is known prominently among the womanhood of her state as a Daughter of the Republic of Texas. It was largely through Mrs. Stone's efforts that the name of Jefferson Davis was restored to the tablet on Cabin John's Bridge, near Washington—this great historic arch having been erected while Davis was secretary of war.

While Mrs. Stone was serving as president-general of the Daughters of the Confederacy, affliction laid a heavy hand upon her, through the loss of her only son, Doctor Harry D. Stone, a brilliant and most promising physician, who after the death of her husband had become the very soul and joy of her life. But this did not embitter the strong woman. With her sorrow still upon her heart she took up her work with renewed zeal. When her term of office expired she was known and loved by each of her sixty thousand daughters, and as a token of their appreciation of her sterling worth she was presented with many beautiful and valuable badges, each inscribed with a legend of the esteem and honor in which she was held by the daughters.

A Wayside Home at Millen.

Only a few of the present inhabitants of Millen know that it was once famous as the location of a Confederate Wayside Home, where, during the Civil War, the soldiers were fed and cared for. The home was built by public subscription and proved a veritable boon to the soldiers, as many veterans now living can testify.

The location of the town has been changed slightly since the 60's, for in those days the car sheds were several hundred yards farther up the Macon track, and were situated where the railroad crossing is now. The hotel owned and run by Mr. Gray was first opposite the depot, and the location is still marked by mock-orange trees and shrubbery.

The Wayside Home was on the west side of the railroad crossing and was opposite the house built in the railroad by Major Wilkins and familiarly known here as the Barrien House. The old well still marks the spot. The home was weather-boarded with rough planks running straight up and down. It had four large rooms to the front, conveniently furnished with cots, etc., for the accommodation of any soldiers who were sick or wounded and unable to continue their journey. A nurse was always on hand to attend to the wants of the sick. Back of these rooms was a large dining hall and kitchen, where the weary and hungry boys in gray could minister to the wants of the inner man, and right royally they performed this pleasant duty, for the table was always bountifully supplied with good things, donated by the patriotic women of Burke County, who gladly emptied hearts and home upon the altar of country. This work was entirely under the auspices of the women of Burke. Mrs. Judge Jones, of Waynesboro, was the first president of the home. She was succeeded by Mrs. Ransom Lewis, who was second and last. She was quite an active factor in the work, and it is largely due to her efforts that the home attained the prominence that it did among similar institutions. Miss Annie Bailey, daughter of Captain Bailey, of Savannah, was matron of the home. She was assisted in the work by committees of three ladies, who, each in turn, spent several days at the home.

This home was to the weary and hungry Confederate soldier as an oasis in the desert, for here he found rest and plenty beneath its shelter. The social feature was not its least attraction, for when a bevy of blooming girls from our bonny Southland would visit the home, and midst feast and jest spur the boys on to renewed vigor in the cause of the South, they felt amidst such inspirations it would be worthy to die, but more glorious to live for such a land of charming women. One of our matrons with her sweet old face softened into a dreamy smile by happy reminiscences of those days of toil, care, and sorrow, where happy thoughts and pleasantries of the past crowded in and made little rifts of sunshine through the war clouds, remarked: "But with all the gloom and suffering, we girls used to have such fun with the soldiers at the home, and at such times we could even forget that our beloved South was in the throes of the most terrible war in the history of any country!"

The home was operated for two years or more and often whole regiments of soldiers came to it, and all that could be accommodated were taken in and cared for. It was destroyed by Sherman's army on their march to the sea. The car shed, depot, hotel and home all disappeared before the torch of the destroyer and only the memory, the well, and the trees remain to mark the historic spot where the heroic efforts of our Burke County women sustained the Wayside Home through two long years of the struggle.

Mrs. Amos Whitehead and others who have "crossed the river" were prominently connected with this work; in fact, every one lent a helping hand, for it was truly a labor of love, and was our Southern women's tribute to patriotism and heroism.

OCTAVIA COHEN.

Mrs. Cohen was ninety-three years old on May 30, 1911. During the four years of the war she remained in Savannah, making it her duty to look after the needs of the Southern soldiers, who had been exchanged, and attended them in sickness, and in every way ministered to their comfort.

When Captain Cuyler, who was then ordnance officer, did not have sufficient bullets, she took the leaden weights from her windows, putting wood in their place to support the windows, and with those weights Captain Cuyler made five hundred bullets. She, with her two daughters, Fanny (Mrs. Henry Taylor) and Georgina

(Mrs. Clavius Phillips) made in their home two kegs of gunpowder. She also made and collected clothes, which she sent to Jekyl Island to Captain Charles Lamar, for his men.

Mrs. Philip Phillips was in Washington with her husband, Judge Phillips, at the breaking out of the war. She was sent, under flag of truce, with two grown daughters and younger children to Fortress Monroe, from which place they returned to their home in New Orleans. Later Mrs. Phillips was imprisoned by Ben Butler on Ship Island in the Gulf of Mexico for many months. She devoted time and money to the cause, giving her jewels, even selling them when she had no other money to give.

Her daughters, Fannie, now Mrs. Charles Hill, of Pittsburgh, Pa., and Caroline, now Mrs. Frederic Myers, of Savannah, Georgia, though very young, helped in the care of the sick and wounded.

Miss Martha Levy gave the same support to the cause as did all the loyal women of the South.

Mrs. P. Y. Pember, eighty odd years old, residing at Pittsburgh, Pa., was at the head of the Chimborazo Hospital, Richmond, Va., and did wonderful work with little money, few necessities and volunteer nurses.

These four ladies were all daughters of Mrs. S. Y. Levy, who worked earnestly for her adopted Southland, being an Englishwoman never in America until after her marriage. She lived to be ninety-four years old, and died in Philadelphia, Pennsylvania.

The following names are of women who loved the cause and who fought the battles with their men, whose hearts were torn with the bullets that mowed down the flower and chivalry of the South: Mrs. Isaac Minis, Mrs. Abram Minis, Mrs. Yates Levy, Mrs. Mordecai Myers, Mrs. Levy Myers, Mrs. Solomon Cohen, the Misses Rebecca, Fanny and Cecelia Minis, and Mrs. Theodore Minis.

LETITIA DOWDELL ROSS.

Mrs. Letitia Dowdell Ross, the newly elected president of the Alabama Division of the United Daughters of the Confederacy, is the daughter of the late William Crawford Dowdell, of Auburn, Alabama. Her mother was Elizabeth Thomas Dowdell, a woman prominent and influential in the foreign missionary work of the Methodist Episcopal Church, South and for thirty years president of the Woman's Foreign Missionary Society of Alabama. Mrs. Ross is a niece of the late Colonel James F. Dowdell, who commanded the Thirty-seventh Regiment, Confederate States of America, and for several years before the war was a member of Congress from the East Alabama district. She is also a first cousin of Chief Justice Dowdell, of the Supreme Court, and of the late Governor William J. Samford, of Alabama. Mrs. Ross was given the best educational advantages at home and abroad, having spent some time in Germany as a student, later becoming the wife of B. B. Ross, professor of chemistry in the Alabama Polytechnic Institute and chemist for the state of Alabama. Her husband's work has brought Mrs. Ross into close connection with educational work. She has always taken an active interest in all movements looking to the benefit of the young men of the institutions with which her husband is connected. She enters with interest and enthusiasm into the literary and social life of her home town and is greatly admired for her intelligence and her many amiable and womanly qualities. Mrs. Ross has been prominently associated with the United Daughters of the Confederacy work since the organization of the Admiral Semmes Chapter, of Auburn, and was for several terms its president. She has also held the positions of recording secretary and first vice-president in the state division and frequently has been a delegate to the general convention, United Daughters of the Confederacy. Mrs. Ross is also an active member of the Daughters of the American Revolution.

ADALINE GARDNER.

Mrs. Gardner was born near Bingen in Germany. She emigrated to Georgia in 1849 and removed to Florida in 1853. At the commencement of the war she lived at Fernandina and shortly before its occupation by the Federals removed to Waldo, Florida. While residing at Waldo she did all she could to feed the hungry and relieve the sick and furloughed boys passing her door. In the summer of 1864 the family removed to Savannah, Georgia, where she is still living and is in her ninetieth year.

BERTHA GARDNER.

The daughter of Mrs. Adaline Gardner aided and assisted her mother during the war, from 1860 to 1865, to the best of her ability, although but a young girl at the time, by feeding the hungry and nursing the sick.

SADIE CURRY AND "CLARA FISHER."

In the later years of the war a great many of the wounded soldiers were brought from east and west to Augusta, Georgia. Immediately the people from the country on both sides of the Savannah River came in and took hundreds of the poor fellows to their homes and nursed them with every possible kindness. Ten miles up the river, on the Carolina side, was the happy little village of Curryton, named for Mr. Joel Curry and his father, the venerable Lewis Curry. Here many a poor fellow from distant states was taken in most cordially and every home was a temporary hospital. Among those nursed at Mr. Curry's, whose house was always a home for the preacher, the poor man and the soldier, was Major Crowder, who suffered long from a painful and fatal wound, and a stripling boy soldier from Kentucky, Elijah Ballard, whose hip wound made him a cripple for life.

Miss Sadie Curry nursed both, night and day, as she did others, when necessary, like a sister. Her zeal never flagged, and her strength never gave way. After young Ballard, who was totally without education, became strong enough, she taught him to read and write, and when the war ended he went home prepared to be a bookkeeper. Others received like kindnesses.

But this noble girl had from the beginning of the war made it her daily business to look after the families of the poorer soldiers in the neighborhood. She mounted her horse daily and made her round of angel visits. If she found anybody sick she reported to the kind and patriotic Dr. Hugh Shaw. If any of the families lacked meal or other provisions, it was reported to her father, who would send meal from his mill or bacon from his smoke-house.

In appreciation of her heroic work, her father and her gallant brother-in-law, Major Robert Meriwether, who was in the Virginia army, now living in Brazil, bought a beautiful Tennessee riding horse and gave it to her. She named it "Clara Fisher," and many poor hearts in old Edgefield were made sad and many tears shed in the fall of 1864, when Sadie Curry and "Clara Fisher" moved to southwest Georgia.

Bless God, there were many Sadie Currys all over the South, wherever there was a call and opportunity. Miss Sadie married Dr. H. D. Hudson and later in life Rev. Dr. Rogers, of Augusta, where she died a few years ago.

VIRGINIA FAULKNER McSHERRY.

The subject of this sketch is a woman of strong and attractive personality. She is a member, on both sides, of distinguished families that gave lustre to the society of the Old Dominion, in its palmiest days. Her father was the late Hon. Charles James Faulkner, Sr., who filled many positions of honor and trust, not only in his own state, but under the government of the United States. He represented his country as minister to the court of St. Cloud, with distinguished ability, just prior to the Civil War, coming home at the commencement of the troublous times of 1861, and casting his fortunes with the South. Mrs. McSherry was born in Martinsburg, Virginia, now West Virginia, and spent the greater part of her young life, with the exception of the years she lived with her father's family, in Paris, at her ancestral home "Bodyville," until her marriage to Dr. J. Whann McSherry. Mrs. McSherry's heart was bound up in the Southern Confederacy, in the service of which, her father, her husband, her brothers, and many friends, displayed unswerving fidelity, and immediately after the cessation of hostilities, she devoted her energies to the care of the gallant soldiers, who fought so nobly for the cause they believed to be right and just. Mrs. McSherry organized a chapter of the United Daughters of the Confederacy in her county of Berkeley, which by her energy and exceptional executive ability became a model of efficiency, in caring for the living and keeping bright the memories of the dead. When the West Virginia Division of the United Daughters of the Confederacy was organized, Mrs. McSherry was elected its president, which office she filled with marked ability, until called higher, and at Houston, Texas, in 1909, she was elevated to the highest office in the gift of the organization, that of president-general of the noble band of women, who compose the National Association of the United Daughters of the Confederacy, and was re-elected, at Little Rock, Arkansas, at the succeeding election. Her administration of that exalted office has been eminently acceptable, impartial and just. Her conscientious discharge of her duties has won for her the enviable reputation of having been one of the very best presiding officers that this organization has ever had. She will go down in the history of the United Daughters of the Confederacy, with the plaudit, "Well done, good and faithful servant," and many are the old soldiers of the Confederacy who rise up and call her blessed. Besides being a zealous member of the United Daughters of the Confederacy, Mrs. McSherry is a leader in all good works in her community, and is regarded as a most valuable member of society.

LAURA MARTIN ROSE.

Mrs. Rose is a native Tennesseean. She was Miss Laura Martin, born at Pulaski, Tennessee, in the year 1862, daughter of William M. Martin and Lizzie Gorin Otis. Her grandfather, Mr. Thomas Martin, was born in Albemarle County, Virginia, in 1799, and at the age of ten years moved with his father, Abram Martin, to Sumner County, Tennessee, in the year 1809, when that country was still the happy hunting ground of the Red Man. His ancestors were of Welsh origin, emigrating to Virginia in the early days. Mr. Martin as merchant, planter and banker impressed himself upon the history of Giles County, Tennessee, and left a name revered by all. He was a man of strong intellect, public spirited and noted for his uprightness and charity. Through her mother, a beautiful and brilliant woman, Mrs. Rose claims French descent. The Gorins were descendants of the Huguenots of France, two brothers emigrating to this country and settling in Maryland. John Gorin, her great-great-grandfather, was a revolutionary soldier, moving to Barron County, Kentucky, in 1789. Mrs. Rose was married in 1881 to Solon E. F. Rose, of Pulaski, Tennessee, son of Colonel Solon E. Rose, an eminent Tennessee lawyer. This union brought together two of Tennessee's most prominent families. She is the mother of three children, a daughter and two sons. Her daughter, Lizzie Otis Rose, died some years ago. Her sons, Martin and Solon Clifton, live with their parents at West Point, Mississippi.

Mrs. Rose at the present time enjoys the distinguished honor of being the president of the Mississippi division, United Daughters of the Confederacy. Prior to her election to this high position, she was historian of the division for two years. She did good work along historical lines. She has written several papers of interest and value, namely, "The United Daughters of the Confederacy, Its Objects and Missions," "Arlington, Its Past and Present," "The Ku Klux Klan," giving authentic history of the origin of that famous "klan." Her public work has been along United Daughters of the Confederacy lines, and she has thrown into it all the love and enthusiasm of her nature for her beloved Southland. She has stood for the truth of history, believing that "History is the life of a nation," and has been untiring in her efforts to present in her work the truths of the history of the Southern Confederacy, that "Storm-cradled Nation" that fell.

ANNIE H. BOCOCK.

Mrs. Annie H. Bocock, the second wife of Thomas S. Bobcock, the distinguished Virginia statesman, was a worthy companion during the latter part of his distinguished career. She was the daughter of Charles James Faulkner, who was minister from the United States to Paris at the outbreak of the war.

She is the mother of three children, W. P. Bocock, Mrs. Thomas Carey Johnson and Mrs. Sallie D. Reynolds. She makes her home at Richmond, Virginia; is an active worker in the Daughters of the Confederacy and in all patriotic and philanthropic work of her state and city.

MOLLIE R. M. ROSENBERY.

Mrs. Mollie R. Macgill Rosenbery, of Galveston, Texas, is prominent in the work of the Daughters of the Confederacy and a philanthropist of note in Texas and other states.

MRS. PERCY V. PENNYBACKER.

Mrs. Percy V. Pennybacker, of Texas, is president of the Texas Federation of Women's Clubs, and author of "An Abridged History of Texas," which is used in the public schools of that state. She is a woman of fine attainments, and an easy, ready speaker. She is also a member of the United Daughters of the Confederacy.

MRS. GRANT.

Among other women who have done conspicuous work in the United Daughters of the Confederacy, we mention Mrs. Grant, who is of a distinguished Virginia family, that of Lewis. She is the wife of Chief Justice Grant of the Supreme Court of Missouri. She has done splendid work in her state along educational lines.

KATIE DAFFAN.

Miss Katie Daffan was twice state president of the Daughters of the Confederacy of Texas, and author of "Woman in History," "The Woman on the Pine Springs Road," "Texas Hero Stories," and "Verses and Fables."

ANNIE SIMPSON.

Miss Simpson was a native of Charleston, South Carolina. She was a young woman when the war between the states began. She was heart and soul with the Confederacy and devoted her time, energies and money to the help and needs of the Southern soldiers, nursing the sick and wounded in the hosptials of Charleston and Columbia, South Carolina. At the close of the war, she, with other devoted women, formed the Memorial Association and founded the Confederate Home, both of Charleston, South Carolina. She was secretary of the former, and vice-president and one of the Board of Control of the Home from its formation until her death, at the age of eighty-five, in 1905.

ALICE BAXTER.

Miss Baxter was born in Athens, Georgia, and is the daughter of Andrew Baxter and Martha Williams Baxter. She was graduated with distinction from

Wesleyan Female College, Macon, Georgia, which is the oldest chartered woman's college in the world. Miss Baxter's public work has been almost entirely with the Daughters of the Confederacy of Georgia. She is also a daughter of the American Revolution.

The United Daughters of the Confederacy holds a unique place in history. It is a memorial to the storm-cradled Southern Confederacy, which although a lost cause this organization is notwithstanding a strong and growing one. Its objects are historical, memorial, benevolent, social and educational. Much is accomplished on all these lines, and Miss Baxter in her work for the organization has endeavored to foster all its aims, but her greatest interest has been for the educational uplift of the Georgia people. Miss Baxter has served the organization in various capacities for more than fifteen years, a portion of the time as recording secretary, vice-president, and president of the Atlanta Chapter, at other times as corresponding secretary, vice-president and president of the state. She has for the past four years served the state as president, her term expiring with the State Convention, October 24, 1911. Miss Baxter has builded on the good foundation of her predecessors. There is a handsome $25,000 girls' dormitory attached to the State Normal School, at Athens, which was undertaken during the presidency of Mrs. James A. Rounsaville, continued during that of Miss Mildred Rutherford, and completed after Mrs. A. B. Hull was made state president.

During Mrs. Hull's administration a three-thousand-dollar fund was gathered toward the erection of a girls' dormitory in the Georgia Mountains in honor of Francis Bartow, in connection with the Rabun Gap Industrial School. During Miss Baxter's administration the plans were changed and the fund made the nucleus for a ten-thousand-dollar educational endowment fund, as a memorial to Francis Bartow. This fund is to remain in the hands of the Georgia Division, United Daughters of Confederacy, the interest to be used for education. It has now reached over seven thousand dollars.

It is rare that a woman brings to the duties of a high executive office, so clear a conscientiousness and such absolute devotion to the best that is in the work, as Miss Baxter, the present state president, United Daughters of the Confederacy, of Georgia. The work has developed and grown under her administration, and the part that will last,—the educational part,—has received an impetus and an encouragement, that cannot fail to be productive of results that will continue as long as the division lasts.

A Sketch of the Life of Mrs. Joseph B. Dibrell.

By Hon. A. A. Terrell.

Ella Peyton Dancy was born in the Reconstruction Days and reared on the banks of the Colorado at La Grange, Texas, the plantation where her father settled in 1836, and which is still owned by this youngest child of the Dancy family. She was married in her sixteenth year and has two daughters born of this marriage. Her mother inherited the homestead of her father which was built in Austin, in 1847, in the primitive days of the capital, built by the hands of her grandfather's servants. While yet a very young woman, she and her little daughters removed with her mother, Mrs. Dancy, to Austin where she then entered the University, taking special courses in literature under Mark Harvey Liddell, the noted Shakespearian scholar, who is now editing his Shakespeare under the auspices of Princeton University. She was married to Joseph B. Dibrell, member of the state senate in October, 1899, and is now the mother of John Winfield Dancy Dibrell, born four years after the marriage, now a lad of eight. She lived at Seguin, Texas, Mr. Dibrell's lifelong home until his recent appointment to the Supreme Bench of Texas, when she has again returned to the state capital at Austin, the home of her grandfather and distinguished father who was a member of Congress of the Republic of Texas.

Ella Dancy Dibrell comes of old revolutionary stock. Through her mother's line she descended from Anne Robinson Cockrell, who received distinction in the early days as a leader in establishing the church work in the French Lick where Nashville, Tennessee, is now located. Her father was John Winfield Dancy who descended from the Turners, Dancys and Colonel Masons, in Virginia, and was a direct kinsman of General Winfield Scott, for whom he was named. Being of a romantic nature, soon after leaving his home in Virginia, going to Alabama, he cast his fortune in the Golden West, then the New Republic of Texas.

Mrs. Dibrell is one of the charter members of the American History Club at Austin; member of the Altar Society of St. Davis' Church at Austin; first president of the Shakespeare

Club of Austin, which consists of the University circle almost entirely; organizer of the History Club of San Antonio, the Shakespeare and Civic Improvement Club of Seguin; state president of the Texas Federation of Women's Clubs; state president of the Texas Division of the United Daughters of the Confederacy, during which time the Confederate Woman's Home was begun and completed. She is now Texas regent of the Confederate Museum of Richmond, Va., and Texas director of the Arlington Monument Committee to be erected at Arlington, in Washington, D. C. At one time chairman of the Civic Committee of the General Federation of Woman's Clubs. One of the directors of the Daughters of the Republic of Texas. Mrs. Dibrell secured the first appropriation for a memorial to Stephen F. Austin, and General Sam Houston, by placing statues of these heroes in the national Capitol at Washington and replicas in the state Capitol of Texas, the works of the noted European artist Elizabeth Ney, a grandniece of Marshall Ney, who died in the city of Austin, June 29, 1907. Two years after this artist's death, Mrs. Dibrell purchased her studio and the grounds, on the condition that the valuable property of the artist, the works contained therein would be given to the University of Texas, in accordance with the artist's desire. A debt of many thousand dollars upon the studio prevented the gift being made direct, by this artist friend in whom Mrs. Dibrell has become deeply interested, after her exile from Europe. This is now the uppermost work of Mrs. Dibrell, having formed a Fine Arts Association for the state of Texas, which will have in charge the management of this collection in connection with the board of regents of the University of Texas, and the Fine Arts Association is always to have its home in this building, and this association is given the right to develop a Fine Arts Museum without charge, as a tribute to Texas and her friend, Elizabeth Ney. It was solely through the efforts of Mrs. Dibrell that the works of Elizabeth Ney were brought into prominence in the United States.

The officers of the Fine Arts Association are: Mr. James H. McClendon, president, friend and legal counselor of the artist; vice-presidents, S. E. Mezes, president of the University of Texas, and ex-Governor Joseph D. Sayers; secretary, Mrs. Mary Mitchell; treasurer, Miss Julia Pease, daughter of ex-Governor Pease. Mrs. Dibrell is chairman of the board of directors of this institution and Judge A. W. Terrell, ex-Minister to Turkey (prominent from a political, judiciary and educational standpoint, submitted the legal transfers of the statuary for Mrs. Dibrell to the regents of the University, while he was a member of that body.) During a former administration, the Library Commission bill, which has been conceived and fostered by Mrs. J. C. Terrell, of Fort Worth, Texas, was passed by the legislature, while Mrs. Dibrell as president of the Federation rendered active support and assistance in the passage of the bill which had failed for eight years—four legislatures. Mrs. Terrell was justly accredited the honor of being made the first lady appointed in the Library Commission.

Governor Oscar B. Colquitt of the present administration has appointed Mrs. Joseph B. Dibrell and Mrs. Sayers, wife of ex-Governor Sayers, as the lady members of the State Library Commission. Mrs. Dibrell not only holds this office, but is the Texas regent of Confederate Museum, chairman of the Fine Arts Association Board of Directors, director of the Daughters of the Republic of Texas, Texas regent of Confederate Museum in Richmond, Va., and state secretary of the General Federation of Woman's Clubs. She was elected a member of the University of Texas "Alumni Association" for the splendid services she had rendered to the woman's work of the state and the university. She is one of the directors of the United Charities, has an interest in all humanitarian and philanthropic propositions, as well as an advocator of civic and moral beauty and cleanliness. March 10th has been established in Texas through her influence, while chairman of the General Federation of Woman's Clubs Civic Committee, as clean-up day for this state, and ordered annually by the state health officer. This generally observed day has been adopted by many states.

Mrs. Dibrell stands in the front rank of the women of her state who have achieved the best for Texas, humanity, progress and mankind. She has made a distinct impression upon her race and time, attained by few in any country, and among the "immortals" in her great state, no name will ever reach a higher plane.

Women in the Missionary Field.

Many of these entered upon their work before the modern woman's societies were inaugurated, and had not the inspiration of associates, but were upheld solely by their Christian faith which led them to undertake the work in far distant and heathen lands. Patiently they endured the toil, danger, and loneliness with fortitude and Christian forbearance, dwelling almost universally in unhealthy climates, and frequently in contact with all forms of debasing heathenism.

MRS. ANNE H. JUDSON.

Was born in Bradford, Massachusetts, December 7, 1789, and educated at the Bradford Academy. In her early youth, she was full of pleasure and was of a restless and roving disposition, but the impression made upon her by Bunyan's "Pilgrim's Progress" brought to her the resolution to follow Christian's example, and try to lead a Christian life, and at the age of sixteen an entire change came over her, and she from that time devoted her life to Christian work. She first took up teaching in Salem, Haverhill, and Newberry. At a meeting of one of the associations of the American Board of Foreign Missions in 1810, at Bradford, she met for the first time the young missionary Judson. This resulted in their marriage and their going into the foreign missionary field. They sailed for India the nineteenth of February, 1812, arriving in Calcutta, June 16. Trouble ensuing between the English government and the English missionaries, both Judson and Newall were ordered to return to America. They went to the Isle of

PART TAKEN BY WOMEN IN AMERICAN HISTORY

France, and here labored until June 1st, when they left for
Madras, where they found ample opportunity for their work
among the Burmese. At Ringon, their son was born, the first
white child ever seen by the Burmese. Mr. Judson translated
a portion of the Bible and other religious books into the Burmese language. In 1819, Mrs. Judson removed to Bengal,
without any decided improvement in her condition, finally being
forced to return to England, and ultimately to America, arriving in New York, September, 1822. Here she aroused great
interest in the missionary work among her friends in the various cities which she visited. Her health improving, she
returned to Rangoon, December 3, 1823. Mrs. Judson was
taken prisoner, owing to the feeling incited against foreigners,
but ultimately her husband was released, after she had passed
through the great hardships, a scourge of smallpox and the dir-
est privations, the family were reunited. Mr. Judson was later
rearrested, but the English officers found him such a valuable
assistant that they did everything they could for his comfort,
and when peace was concluded Mr. Judson's property was
restored to him, and the mission placed under the British protection. On October 24, 1826, Mrs. Judson died, beloved and
lamented by both the English and natives of that country.

HARRIET NEWELL.

Harriet Atwood was born at Haverhill, Massachusetts, the 10th of October,
1793. At the age of thirteen, when a student at the academy in Bradford,
Massachusetts, she became strongly imbued with religious thought and took up
religious readings and the study of the Bible during her leisure time, and in 1809
made an open confession of Christianity. In 1811 she met Mr. Newell who was
preparing for missionary service in India. The following year they were married,
and in February, 1812, sailed with Mr. and Mrs. Judson for India. Owing to
trouble between the United States and England they were not permitted to remain
in Calcutta, so sought residence in the Isle of France. Here their little daughter
was born, but lived but a short time, and was soon followed by her mother.
She was then but nineteen years of age.

MARTIA L. DAVIS BERRY.

Mrs. Berry was born in Portland, Michigan, the 22nd of January, 1844. Her father being of Irish and Italian descent, was naturally a firm believer in human rights and her mother was an ardent anti-slavery woman and strong prohibitionist. Her mother was a woman of great advancement and of thought decidedly above the women of her day. After her marriage, Mrs. Berry removed to Kansas and here she organized the first Woman's Foreign Missionary Society west of the Missouri River and was the originator of the woman's club. Was elected to the office of state treasurer of the Kansas Equal Suffrage Association and also placed at the head of the Sixth District of the Kansas Woman's Temperance Union.

ANN LEE.

Founder in America of the sect known as the Shaking Quakers. Was born in Manchester, England, about 1736. Her father was a blacksmith and she was taught the trade of cutting fur for hatters. She was married when quite young and four children were born to her, but all died in infancy. When but twenty-two years of age she was converted to the doctrine of James Wardley, a Quaker who preached against marriage and whose followers, because of the great agitation of their bodies when wrought with religious excitement were called Shakers. She became a teacher of the faith, but in 1770 was imprisoned as a fanatic. While in prison she claimed to have a revelation and declared that in her dwelt the "word" and her followers say, "The man who was called Jesus and the woman who was called Ann are verily two great pillars of the church," and she was acknowledged as a spiritual mother in Israel and is known among her followers as Mother Ann. In 1774 she came to New York with a few of her followers and in the spring of 1776 they settled in Muskayuna, now Watervliet, opposite Troy, where the sect flourishes. With the superstition of those times of course Ann Lee was charged with witchcraft and the Whigs accused her of secret correspondence with the British, her countrymen, because she preached against war. The charge of high treason was preferred against her and in 1776 she was imprisoned in Albany, and later sent to Poughkeepsie with the intention of placing her within the British lines in New York, but she remained a prisoner in Poughkeepsie until 1777, when she was released by Governor Clinton. She returned to her home and the greatest sympathy was awakened for her, which greatly increased her followers. Such a movement of revival followed that the converts came into the sect by thousands. She declared that she judged the dead and no favor could be found except through confession of their sins to her, in fact she became a second Pope Joan; those coming under her spell threw aside all worldly things, pouring their jewels, money and valuables into her hands. She declared she would not die but would be translated into Heaven like Enoch and Elijah, but contrary to this announcement, on the 8th of September, 1784, she did die, but many believed it was not real death.

BARBARA HECK.

The family of Barbara Rukle were driven from their homes on the Rhine by Louis XIV, and sought refuge in Ireland, and there Barbara Rukle was born. When but a young girl of eighteen, she joined the Methodist "Society" which had been established by John Wesley on one of his religious tours some years before. Barbara Rukle was early recognized among her associates as a woman of deep religious thought, a good counsellor, and her greatest treasure was her old German Bible, which she clung to all through her long eventful life. In 1760 she married Paul Heck and they emigrated to the new world and settled in New York. At the house of Philip Embury, a cousin of Barbara, she gathered a few religious people and begged that Philip Embury should preach to them, and this was the germ of the Methodist Episcopal Church in America. Embury proved to be a very devout man and earnest preacher. As the congregation increased Barbara Heck began to entertain the idea of building a church. Captain Webb, a military officer, was one of Wesley's local preachers and had aroused the people by his zeal. Barbara succeeded in interesting him in her project and in 1770 the site for a church on John Street was purchased and the subscription started, Captain Webb subscribing thirty pounds. This list bears the names of the Livingstons, Duanes, Delancys, Leights, Stuyvesants, Lispenards, and the clergy of the day, Auchmuty, Ogilvie, and Englis, and this is supposed to be the first church of the Methodist denomination in America. Embury worked with his own hands on the building and Barbara Heck helped to whitewash the walls. Within a year there were a thousand members in this congregation. During the Revolutionary War, the Heck family emigrated to lower Canada, where they lived near Montreal, finally removing to Augusta, upper Canada, where Barbara Heck died at the age of seventy. She was found sitting in her chair dead with her much-loved Bible in her lap.

ANN ELIOT.

One of the women who took her part in the missionary field was Mrs. Ann Eliot, the wife of Rev. John Eliot who was surnamed "the apostle." His work was among the Indian tribes of New England in the early days of the colonies. Mrs. Eliot not only was an able assistant to her husband in his religious work but she worked as a humanitarian among these savage people. Her skill and experience as a doctor brought her great reputation among these people. She dispensed large charity and salutary medicines. To her is ascribed no small share of her husband's success.

JEMIMA BINGHAM.

Another woman who deserves mention in the missionary work among the Indians during the colonial period was Jemima Bingham, the niece of Eleazar Wheelock, D.D., an eminent missionary among the Indians. In 1769 she married the Rev. Samuel Kirkland who had taken up the missionary work among the Oneida Indians in that section of country where Rome, New York, is now situated. She taught the women and children and by her example and patient work brought about a changed condition among these people. In 1787 the Ohio Company was organized in Boston and built a stockade fort at Marietta, Ohio, called Campus

Martius, and Rev. Daniel Story was sent out as a chaplain. He was probably the first Protestant minister to go into the vast wilderness west of the Ohio River. In this garrison at Marietta was formed one of the first Sunday schools in the United States and its first superintendent and teacher was Mrs. Andrew Lake

SARAH L. SMITH.

Another name worthy of mention is Sarah L. Smith, whose maiden name was Huntingdon. She was born in 1802, and married the Reverend Eli Smith, in July, 1833, going with him to Palestine where her work as a foreign missionary was undertaken. Later she entered the home missionary field and worked among the Mohegan Indians. Through her correspondence with Lewis Cass, secretary of war, she secured the aid of that department in 1832, and a grant of nine hundred dollars was made from the fund appropriated to the Indian department. Five hundred was given for the erection of missionary buildings and before her labors were closed in this field she had the pleasure of seeing a chapel, parsonage, and schoolhouse stand on what she had found a barren waste of land.

The Moravian Missions are well known. The character of the Moravian women seemed peculiarly fitted for missionary work. The enthusiasm of the Slavs was blended with the steadfastness, energy, and patience of the Germans. It was before the middle of the last century that these pious women commenced their work among the North American Indians. The first field of their labors was in Pennsylvania, Bethlehem and Nazareth being the seats of their missionary homes. From here they worked all through Pennsylvania. It is said that the Moravians in their various settlements were surrounded literally with circles of blood and flame, and in November, 1755, the Indians fell upon these poor missionaries and almost entirely destroyed them. Some splendid work was done by the missionaries in Oregon. In 1834 this part of our country was a vast wilderness and here roamed more than thirty different Indian tribes, the only settlements being a few scattered posts of the Hudson Bay Company. Dr. Marcus Whitman and his wife, and Mr. and Mrs. Spaulding were among the first to go into this wilderness and take up the missionary work among them. Mrs. Whitman and Mrs. Spaulding were the first white women to cross the Rocky Mountains. They were followed by Mr. and Mrs. Grey, Mr. and Mrs. Clark, Mr. and Mrs. Littlejohn, Mr. and Mrs. Smith, Mr. and Mrs. Griffin, and Mr. and Mrs. Munger. Those to go later were Mrs. White, Mrs. Beers, Miss Downing, Miss Johnson, and Mrs. Pittman. Dr. and Mrs. White offered their services to the Board of Missions when a call was made in 1836 for volunteers to go into this new field, and they reached their destination from Boston via the Sandwich Islands. They established mission schools for the children and taught them the domestic arts. Later they were joined by others until their party was sixty, all zealously working in this field.

MARY LYON.

Born in Buckland, Franklin County, Massachusetts, February 28, 1797, and died March 5, 1849. She grew up as a simple country girl of that time, learning the household arts of spinning, weaving, netting and embroidery, her school advantages being the most limited, but at the age of twenty she entered Sanderson Academy, at Ashfield, as a pupil. Being imbued with a deep religious spirit, she worked among the pupils for their conversion. Her work spread among the people of Ashfield, Buckland and Derry. Ipswich was the scene of her earliest labors. Until 1790 girls were not admitted to the public schools of Boston, and from 1790 to 1792 they were allowed to attend only in the summer months. There were more than one hundred colleges for young men in the state of Massachusetts, when in 1836 she was granted the first charter for "a school for the systematic higher education of women," Mount Holyoke Seminary. She raised the thirty thousand dollars deemed requisite to obtain this charter. Her purpose was as philanthropic as her impulses were religious, and she sought to increase the usefulness of women as well as to bring them to Christ. During the first six years of her presidency of the seminary, not a graduate or a pupil left the school without a deep religious faith.

Her intense consecration to the spiritual work made her essentially a missionary, and it was her desire to spread the words of Christ through the far distant lands. She organized the first missionary society in Buckland in her early years. She never would consent to receive any salary as president of the seminary, but consecrated all the moneys received, except two hundred and fifty dollars a year, to the missionary work. Hardly a class went out of the seminary which did not have among its number one or two, or even more, missionaries ready for the field. Her monument stands to-day in the grounds of the Mount Holyoke Seminary, and her works live after her. She stands as one of the earliest pioneers for the higher education for women.

MRS. T. C. DOREMUS.

Born in New York, but her parents moved to Elizabeth, New Jersey. She spent her early childhood in that city; in 1821 married a merchant of the city of New York, and returned there to live. Though a communicant of the Reformed Dutch Church, she was a woman of broad religious ideas, and of strong and independent mind. She became an enthusiastic worker in the missionary field. Organizations were formed and had their meetings in her house. In those days there were no facilities for procuring ready-made things to be sent out to the missionary fields, so she organized societies for making garments to be sent to those in the far ends of the earth. She did a great deal of work among the Greeks and Turks, also taking an interest in the missions on the frontier in Canada. In 1859, the Woman's Union Missionary Society was formed, embracing all denominations of Christian women, and working independently of all boards, its direct object being an agency to send out teachers and missionaries to redeem the women of Persia and the East from the degradation in which our missionaries had found them. She worked with untiring energy, giving her time, money and interest to the work, but though devoting her thought and time to this work, she never for one moment neglected her family. She did not allow her work to interfere with her duty to her family of nine children, to whom she was all that a mother could be. Her death in January, 1877, caused widespread sorrow, not only to friends in this land, but to the missionary fields all over the world. Her name has been perpetuated by the Woman's Union Missionary Society in Calcutta, India, by calling their home the Doremus Home.

FIDELIA FISKE.

Born in Shelbourne, Massachusetts, in 1816. She was a graduate of Mount Holyoke Seminary, and a missionary to Persia. She was the first unmarried woman to enter that field. Her work in Oroomia, where the women were fearfully degraded (and it was considered a disgrace for a woman to learn to read) was most earnest and valuable. The poverty and intense prejudice of the people made her task a trying one, but her efforts were crowned with great success. Her work spread in the smaller places of the mountains, and the school which has been established there is a monument to her energy and fearless Christian faith. She returned to America in 1847, and was president of Mount Holyoke Seminary for a brief time, but her health failing, she died July 26, 1864, in her forty-eighth year.

MRS. R. B. LYTH.

She went with her husband, Rev. R. B. Lyth, M. D., to the South Sea missions in 1836, living among the cannibals of the Fiji and Polynesian Islands, and suffering the most frightful experiences and sickening sights among the cannibal tribes of these islands. Nothing but a deep sense of duty and a strong determination to perform it, added to her religious faith, could have made a woman of refinement endure the experiences she was called upon to witness. The incident is told of how she saved the lives of six women out of thirteen, who were killed for a feast of one of these tribes. Braving every danger, she appeared before this cannibal king to beg for mercy and he listened to her pleadings and spared their lives. She lived to see a great work accomplished, the islands Christianized, the Sabbath observed. On September 18, 1890, Mrs. Lyth died.

ANNE WILKINS.

Her work as a missionary was among the people of Liberia, Africa. She was born in 1806 in New York State, of Methodist parents. She sailed for Liberia, June 15, 1837, the first time. She made many trips back and forth on account of her health, dying November, 1857.

MELINDA RANKIN.

Her work among the Mexicans forms a thrilling missionary story. Born in 1811, dying at her home in Bloomington, Illinois, December 7, 1888, she had great faith in the power and ability of women. In 1840 a call came for missionary teachers to go to the Mississippi valley, foreign immigration having brought in a great many Roman Catholics to that portion of the country. Miss Rankin responded

33

to that call, and went to that country, established schools, and gradually pushed her way up the Mississippi. At the close of the Mexican War, through officers and soldiers returning home, she learned a great deal of the condition in Mexico. Her sympathies became so aroused, that she tried to awaken an interest among the people by writing articles on the subject, but gaining no response, she determined to go herself to Mexico and see if she could not do something to help these poor ignorant people. She opened a school for Mexican girls at Brownsville, Texas, on the American side of the Rio Grande, opposite Matamoras, Mexico, there being a large Mexican population in this town. As she was successful she found opportunities for sending hundreds of Bibles and tracts into Mexico through her scholars and their friends. When the Civil War came, she was driven out of her home as she was not in sympathy with the people about her; thus she found shelter in Matamoras, and commenced her direct missionary labors for the Mexican people. Her work took her later to Monterey, one of the largest Catholic cities, and there she established a Protestant mission. As a result of her work, Protestant schools and churches were built, ultimately assuming such proportions that they required regularly ordained ministers. Her health failing in 1872, she returned home and died in 1888.

LYDIA MARY FAY.

She is most affectionately remembered for her work in China. Miss Fay was a native of Essex County, Virginia, but entered the missionary field from Albany, New York, sailing for China, November 8, 1850, the first single woman sent there by the missionary society. She was a remarkable woman, with a most sympathetic heart and well-trained mind, and had a peculiar fitness for the work in that country. She established in her own house in Shanghai a boarding school for boys, and from this she educated teachers and preachers to carry on the work. She taught in the school, attended to all the domestic course, provided the clothing, managed the finances, and at the same time devoted much of her time to the study of the Chinese language. At the close of her twenty-fifth year, she passed this school over to the Episcopal Board. Her efforts developed from this very small beginning into the Doane Hall and Theological School, with president, professors, ten Chinese teachers, and some of her pupils in the Christian ministry. She was always known as "Lady Fay" to her pupils, who were impressed by the purity and simplicity of her Christian life and devotion to their interests After twenty-eight years of hard work, her health failed, and she died October 5, 1878.

MARY BRISCOE BALDWIN.

Born in the Shenandoah Valley of Virginia, May 20, 1811, and died June 21, 1877. Her mother was the niece of James Madison, the fourth president of the United States. She received her education from private tutors. She was a disciple of Bishop Meade of the Protestant Episcopal Church, who greatly influenced her in her religious life. The death of her parents breaking up her home when but twenty years of age, she went to Stanton, Pennsylvania to live. Wearying of fashionable life, she decided to engage in some Christian work. First she became a teacher in a young ladies' seminary, then the call came for her to enter the missionary field, through Mrs. Hill of Athens and the Protestant Episcopal Society. Being a friend of Mrs. Hill, she decided to accept this call, and went into the work in Greece. Dr. and Mrs. Hill were American missionaries who had established a school, and Miss Baldwin joined them as an assistant in this work. She took entire charge of the domestic department, teaching fine sewing and other useful arts. She became so beloved that she was known among her scholars and the people as "Good Lady Mary." Not only did she train these young Greek girls in the domestic arts, but she Christianized them and taught them to be good daughters, wives and mothers. In 1866 when the Christians of Crete revolted against the Turkish government, many impoverished and destitute Cretans fled to Athens. Among these poor people, Miss Baldwin labored with great success. She opened day schools and Sunday schools, feeding them and providing the women and girls with work. For forty-two years she labored among these people. She was buried on a bluff overlooking the Jordan Valley, and these loving people placed over her a tombstone of Greek marble.

MARY REED.

Born in Crooked Tree, Noble County, Ohio, at the age of sixteen years, she entered the missionary field, offering her service to the Foreign Missionary Society of the Methodist Episcopal Church. This was accepted, and she was sent to India by the Cincinnati Branch. On her arrival in India, she was sent to the work in Cawnpore. After four years of successful labor in this field, she was sent to the girls' boarding school in Gonda, but here her health completely broke down, and she was obliged to return home. While convalescing, she noticed a peculiar spot on her cheek, and insisted on having medical books brought to her wherein she could study up her case, and became convinced that she was a victim of leprosy. She insisted on returning to India, and that her mother should not be told of her fatal malady. She hastened to the mission among the lepers in India. At Chandag, she was put in charge of one of the leper asylums, and here she has worked diligently and faithfully among these outcasts, receiving treatment herself. The life she lives among these poor isolated creatures emphasizes the sweet faith she teaches.

EMMA V. DAY.

Mrs. Day was born June 10, 1853, in Philadelphia, and died August 10, 1894, near Lewisburg, Pennsylvania. Her mother died when she was quite an infant, and she was reared by an aunt. In 1874, she was married to Rev. D. A. Day of the Lutheran Mission of Africa for the Evangelical Lutheran Church. On the establishment of their home in Africa, she took upon herself, as her part of her husband's work, the training of the children, and in a short time many of these naked little heathens were transformed into civilized creatures able to take part in the household duties of a Christian home. Being of a peculiarly cheerful and happy disposition, Mrs. Day met with great success in her work among these little people.   Two of Mrs. Day's own children were born in this far away land.   In 1894. Mrs. Day's health became so precarious she returned to America, and in August passed away.

ELIZA AGNEW.

Born in New York City, she did not enter the missionary field until she was over thirty years of age.   Was then sent by the Board of Foreign Missions to Ceylon to work in the Oodooville Boarding School.   Miss Agnew was the first unmarried missionary to arrive in Ceylon, and caused great consternation among the natives.   She never returned to America, but gave her whole life to work among the people of India, and died an old lady in 1883.

MURILLA BAKER INGALLS.

Married at her home in Eastport, Wisconsin, in 1850, and sailed with her husband, a missionary, for Burma, July 10, 1851.   Her husband lived only two years after they were married.   After a visit to America to leave her husband's daughter to be educated, she returned to the work in Burma in 1859.   She had a wonderful power and great influence among the Buddhist priests in spreading the truth of Christianity.   She established Bible societies, distributing tracts in their own language to the French, English, Burmese, Shans, Hindus and Karens.   She opened a library for the benefit of the employees of the railway, and established branch libraries on these lines.   Her work was most valuable among the men who went out into these countries to work for the syndicates building railroads, and also among the native workers.   She and her associates gave lectures, and in every way tried to better the conditions and life of these men.   The various governments represented appreciated her work, and often assisted her.

BEULAH WOOLSTON.

Was born in Vincenttown, New Jersey, August 3, 1828, and died at Mount Holly, New Jersey, October 24, 1886.   She was educated at the Wesleyan Female College in Wilmington, Delaware, where she was graduated with honor in both the English and classic departments.   She taught for some years in this college, and while engaged in this occupation, she took up missionary work, going as a teacher to one of the Chinese missions.   Her sister accompanied her to this field, and their work consisted in organizing and superintending a boarding school for Chinese girls under the Chinese Female Missionary Society of Baltimore.   After twenty-five years of faithful work, she returned to this country in 1883 and died October 24, 1886.

JERUSHA BINGHAM KIRKLAND.

Jerusha Bingham, as a niece of the Rev. Doctor Wheelock, who was deeply interested in missionary work, had her attention early called to the needs of Christian teaching among the Indians.   Later she married Doctor Kirkland, the well-known missionary, and she and her husband had the distinction of being recommended by the Continental Congress as adapted to labor among the Indians, and as alone able to preserve their neutrality toward the war. During the period when the early wars threatened the destruction of the new nation by the aboriginal inhabitants, she worked faithfully with her husband in that arduous and responsible work of pacification. She was the mother of John Thornton Kirkland, who was born at Little Falls, New York, August 17, 1790. When this son had achieved national prominence his biographer wrote, "It was from a mother of distinguished public spirit, energy, wisdom and devotedness that he received the rudiments of his high intellectual and manly resolutions."

MARY ELIZABETH WILLSON.

Born May 1, 1842, in Clearfield County, Pennsylvania. Her father Mr. Bliss, was a very religious man. Her mother Lydia Bliss, a Christian woman. Her only brother was the noted evangelist singer and hymn writer, P. P. Bliss. While Mary Bliss was quite young the family removed to Tioga County, Pennsylvania. When she was fifteen years of age she accompanied her brother into Bradford County, where her brother taught a select school. They made their home with a family named Young, who were very musical, and the daughter of this family gave P. P. Bliss his first lessons in singing, and eventually became his wife. In 1858 Mary Bliss began teaching, and taught until 1860, when she married Clark Willson of Towanda, Pennsylvania. Her brother will be remembered not only through his evangelical work but as the author of "Hold the Fort." He and his wife lost their lives in the terrible railway wreck of Ashtabula Bridge on December 29, 1876. Mr. and Mrs. Willson were urged by a friend, Major Whittle, to assist him in his evangelistic work in Chicago and they accepted this call. Their work as Gospel singers was so successful that they made this their life work. In 1878 Francis Murphy, the apostle of temperance, invited them to aid him in what was known as the Red Ribbon Crusade. They visited the principal cities of the Northern and Southern states and everywhere met with great success. Mrs. Willson was known as the Jenny Lind of sacred melody. In 1882 Mr. and Mrs. Willson spent several months in Great Britain in the Gospel Temperance work and Mrs. Willson's voice was as much admired in England as in her home country. She has written several hymns and sacred songs. Among the most popular are: "Glad Tidings," "My Mother's Hands" and "Papa Come This Way." She was also the author of two volumes of Gospel Hymns and songs entitled "Great Joys" and "Sacred Gems." She contributed words and music to most of the Gospel song books for a number of years.

ALICE BLANCHARD MERRIAM COLEMAN.

Born in Boston, May 7, 1858. All Mrs. Coleman's life has been spent in the old South End of Boston, where she still resides. She was graduated from the Everett Grammar School in 1873 and immediately went abroad with her parents for nine months, spending a large part of the time in London and Paris, and absorbing with great eagerness all that fitted on to the studies of the grammar school, especially the history of England. In September, 1874, she entered Bradford Academy, in Bradford, Mass., the oldest academy in New England for young women, where she had the privilege of being trained by Miss Annie E. Johnson, one of the best-known educators of that time. The four years of boarding school life were marked by the awakening of the missionary spirit and by the resolve to herself to become a foreign missionary. She graduated in 1878, with the expectation of spending one year in the further study of Latin and Greek in order to fit herself for Smith College, but her eyes, already a source of trouble and anxiety, again gave out and all thought of further study or of any life work which would involve language study had to be abandoned.

In the fall of 1879, the Woman's Home Missionary Association (Congregational) was organized in Boston under the leadership of her former principal, Miss Annie E. Johnson. The purpose of the association was the prosecution of educational and missionary work among the women and children of our own land, especially among the alien races and religions. This opened the door for her entrance into the work of home missions which has from that day to this been the main work of her life. At the request of the directors of the association, she visited all its fields of work in 1884 in order to prepare herself to speak of the work among the churches. The trip covered the country as far west as Utah and as far south as Texas, including the work among the Negroes, Indians, Mormons, and pioneer settlements. The next year was spent in visiting the churches and marked the beginning of her platform work.

In 1886, she transferred her denominational relationship to a Baptist church, and at once became a member of the board of directors of the Woman's American Baptist Home Mission Society, thus continuing her activity in home mission work and as a speaker among the churches. Various lines of church work also claimed a considerable share of her time and strength.

On June 30, 1891, Miss Merriam was married to George W. Coleman of Boston. They have had no children and so she has continued in the lines of activity already referred to. In 1891 she became president of the Woman's American Baptist Home Mission Society and held that position until April, 1911, when by the consolidation of the Woman's American Baptist Home Mission Society, headquarters in Boston, and the Woman's Baptist Home Mission Society, headquarters in Chicago, a new national organization was formed having the name of the Boston organization but with headquarters in Chicago. Mrs. Coleman is now the first vice-president of the new organization and president of the New England Branch of the Woman's American Baptist Home Mission Society, the branch being a local organization whose purpose is the holding of inspirational meetings and otherwise fostering the work of the Woman's American Baptist Home Mission Society.

In December, 1906, the Interdenominational Committee of Women for Home Mission Conferences for the East was formed to provide for and to conduct a summer conference in Northfield, Mass. For the first three years, she served the committee as its president, and is still a member of the governing body.

As a result of the formation of similar committees in different parts of the country, the Council of Women for Home Missions was organized in November, 1908, and Mrs. Coleman has served as president of the council from its beginning.

The Home Mission work has brought Mrs. Coleman into a close relationship to the schools and colleges provided for the colored people of the South and she is a trustee of Hartshorn Memorial College, Richmond, Virginia, and of Spelman Seminary, Atlanta, Georgia.

Mrs. Coleman's activities during the last five years in connection with the Ford Hall meetings in Boston and the Sagamore Sociological Conference, which meets each summer at their summer home, have her warmest sympathy and support though she has no official connection with them. Mrs. Coleman has, however, been for several years one of the non-resident workers of the Denison House, a settlement house for women in a district largely populated by Syrians and Italians.

SARAH PLATT HAINES.

Among the names prominent in New York City is that of Sarah Platt Haines, wife of Thomas C. Doremus, who for fifty years was called the "Mother of Missions." She stands as a representative of woman's efforts in missionary labors. She was born in August, 1842. Her father was Elias Haines, and her mother was Mary Ogden. Her grandparents, Robert Ogden and Sarah Platt, had also devoted their lives to missions.

AMELIA ELMORE HUNTLEY.

Mrs. Amelia Elmore Huntley, daughter of Mr. and Mrs. R. T. Elmore, was born in Esopus New York, in February, 1844. Her mother died when she was nine years old. Her father, early in life, moved to Milwaukee, where he became an active member of the Methodist Episcopal Church, occupying many positions of trust including that of delegate to the general conference. He was a successful business man and gave his children every advantage of education, travel, etc.

Mrs. Huntley was educated in a Female College of Wisconsin and was graduated from a Woman's College, at Lima, N. Y. She was married to Rev. E. D. Huntley, in 1867, he being actively engaged in the ministry of the Methodist Episcopal Church. Mrs. Huntley has great genius for organization and is very successful with young people. Having lost her only child in infancy, her arms were empty to aid more fully other lambs of the fold.

For years Dr. Huntley was president of the Lawrence College, Appleton, Wisconsin, and many bright students were led by this devoted couple into lives of Christian consecration and usefulness. She was an active member of the Women's Christian Temperance Union of Wisconsin, where she did fine preventive work and was instrumental in forming reading rooms, night schools, etc. She was a member of the Woman's Foreign Missionary Society from its inception, serving in various official capacities. She has fine executive ability and is a stirring and sympathetic speaker. Her intelligent enthusiasm has inspired many an indifferent and even careless woman into active and valuable membership When Dr. Huntley was appointed pastor of the Metropolitan Memorial Methodist Episcopal Church in Washington, Mrs. Huntley brought her zeal and inspiration on missionary lines into active service there, and to this may be attributed much of the intelligent interest in missions which is shown in that church at the present day.

She served as secretary of the Washington District Association, from which she was called to take the responsible position of the Baltimore branch as corresponding secretary of that society. When the saddest trial of her life came—the sudden death of her gifted husband—she bravely kept on with her work. She was sent a delegate to Edinburgh to the International Conference on Missions in May, 1910.

BELLE CALDWELL CULBERTSON.

Mrs. Belle Caldwell Culbertson, wife of Rev. John Newton Culbertson, of Washington, D. C., was born in 1857, in Wheeling, West Virginia, of Scotch-Irish and English Quaker descent. Her ancestor, James Caldwell, a Scotch Presbyterian, came to America from Ulster, Tyrone County, Ireland, in 1769. He was a defender of Fort Henry (now Wheeling), in which defense, out of 44 men in the fort, 24 were killed and 5 wounded.

She is also a descendant of Honorable Francis Yarnall who emigrated from Worcestershire, England, in 1684, settled in Chester County, Pennsylvania, and in 1711 represented Chester County in its Provincial legislature.

John Jolliff Yarnall, a relative of Mrs. Culbertson, was Perry's first lieutenant in the battle of Lake Erie, and for distinguished gallantry on that occasion he was voted a sword by the legislatures of Pennsylvania and Virginia.

Mrs. Culbertson was graduated from the State Normal School of West Virginia, in 1876. Was valedictorian of her class from the Wheeling Female College in 1877; sailed for Indo-China as a missionary of the Presbyterian Board in 1879, and for two years she was principal of the Harriet House School for Girls in Bangkok, Siam.

In January, 1880, Miss Caldwell married Rev. John Newton Culbertson of the same Board of Missions, and in 1881 returned to America. From 1881 to 1887 Rev. and Mrs. Culbertson served as home missionaries at their own charges in South Dakota, building up a flourishing church in that far western field. From 1887 to the present date Mrs. Culbertson has resided with her family in Washington, D. C., active in every good work for the betterment of humanity. From 1897 to 1905, Mrs. Culbertson served as the efficient president of the Woman's Foreign Missionary Society of the Presbytery of Washington City. She personally organized many societies throughout the large field and under her leadership the society raised an extra gift of $5,000.00 for "The Washington City Memorial Hall," Tokyo, Japan.

In 1906 Mrs. Culbertson was chosen president of the Woman's Interdenominational Missionary Union of the District of Columbia, which honored position she now fills. Mrs. Culbertson has for two years been a correspondent for the religious press and a translator of German, her latest translation "Sunnyheart's Trial" was published December, 1910, in the *Southern Observer*.

Rev. and Mrs. Culbertson have three children living, a son and two daughters.

CARRIE FRANCES JUDD MONTGOMERY.

Church worker and poet. Was born April 8, 1858, in Buffalo, New York. Her father was Orvan Kellogg Judd, and her mother was Emily Sweetland. Her first literary effort appeared in *Demorest's, Young America* and the *Buffalo Courier*. At eighteen she published a small volume of poems. She was imbued with a deep Christian faith and most of her writings are of a religious character. She established a Faith Rest and Home, where sick and weary ones may stay a brief time free of charge. This is sustained by voluntary contributions. She married George Simpson Montgomery, of San Francisco, California, and both she and her husband entered the Salvation Army in 1891.

LILLIE RESLER KEISTER.

Mrs. Lillie Resler Keister was born in May, 1851, in Mount Pleasant, Pennsylvania. Her father was the Rev. J. B. Resler. Her husband was the Rev. George Keister, Professor of Hebrew in the Union Biblical Seminary of Dayton, Ohio. An active worker in the Missionary Association of her church, the United Brethren in Christ. Is a woman of marked executive ability and has delivered lectures for the Women's Missionary Society. In 1880 she was one of the two delegates sent by the Woman's Missionary Association to the World's Missionary Conference in London, England.

MRS. ANGELA F. NEWMAN.

Born December 4, 1837, in Montpelier, Vermont. She taught school at the age of fourteen in the city of her birth. In 1856 she married Frank Kilgour, of Madison, who died within a year. Afterwards she became the wife of D. Newman, a merchant of Beaverdam, Wisconsin. In 1871 they removed to Lincoln, Nebraska. She has held the position of Western secretary of the Woman's Foreign Missionary Society, and lectured on missions throughout the West. In 1883, at the request of Bishop Wiley, of the Methodist Episcopal Church, her attention having been drawn to the condition of the Mormon women, she went to Cincinnati, Ohio, and presented the Mormon problem to the National Home Missionary Society, and a Mormon Bureau was created to push missionary work in Utah, of which she was made secretary. She acted also as chairman of a committee appointed to consider a plan for founding a home for Mormon women who wished to escape from polygamy, to be sustained by the society. The Gentiles of Utah formed a home association, and on Mrs. Newman's recovery from a serious accident she was sent as an unsalaried philanthropist to Washington to represent the interests of the Utah Gentiles in the Forty-ninth, Fiftieth and Fifty-first Congresses, and delivered an elaborate argument before the congressional committees. Two other arguments which she had prepared were introduced by Senator Edmonds in the United States Senate, and thousands of copies of these were issued. Mrs. Newman secured appropriations of $80,000 for this association, and a splendid structure in Salt Lake City was the result of her efforts. She has spoken from pulpits and platforms on temperance, Mormonism and social purity; has long been a contributor to the religious and secular journals; has been commissioned by several governors as delegate to the National Conference of Charities and Corrections. In 1888 she was elected a delegate to the quadrennial General Conference of the Methodist Episcopal Church, the first woman ever elected to a seat in that august body.

MRS. WILLIAM BUTLER.

Mrs. Butler, known as "The Mother of Missions," was the wife of Rev. William Butler, who was commissioned in 1856 to open the mission work for the Methodist Episcopal Church. After passing through the great Sepoy rebellion, in 1857, their headquarters were made at Bareilly, India. After eight years in India, Dr. Butler returned to the United States, and was then sent by his church to the missionary field in Mexico. Mrs. Butler has reached the advanced age of ninety years. She makes her home at Newton Center, Massachusetts.

Mrs. William J. Schieffelin, Miss Grace Dodge, Mrs. Henry W. Peabody, of Boston, chairman of the central committee of the United States for women's foreign misssions; Mrs. Helen Barrett Montgomery, Miss Jennie V. Hughes, of China; Dr. Mary Riggs Noble, Mrs. Joseph H. Knowles, who is chairman of the committee of prayer circles, and secretary of the Methodist Women's Foreign Missionary Society, are all women actively engaged in missionary work. Mrs. Wilfred Grenfell, whose husband is superintendent of the Labrador Medical Mission, was Miss Anna McClanahan, of Chicago, Illinois, and since her marriage has been an able assistant of her husband in his work among these far northern people.

Women as Philanthropists.

DOROTHEA LYNDE DIX (1805-1887.)

In all past ages the weak, the lame, the blind and the insane were supposed to be beyond cure or even help. Only within recent years have the strong strived to help the condition of those they often pitied but more often despised. The insane particularly were often judged as under the control of Satan, and any effort to lessen their sufferings or to improve their condition seemed the same as helping the evil one. In 1730 the first asylum for the humane treatment of these unfortunates was established in England, and in 1750 Benjamin Franklin and others in the New World added a department for demented people in the Pennsylvania Hospital. But little was done for the benefit of the insane, either in this country or in Europe until Dorothea Dix with strong and unyielding purpose began her heroic work in their behalf. She was eminently fitted for the work because she herself had seen only the hard side of life. Her home with her grandparents in Boston was a gloomy, joyless one, and she herself said later in life, "I never knew childhood." Yet, the very hardness of this experience fitted her for her life work. After years of teaching, her mind was opened to the neglect and suffering of weak-minded and insane. It is hard to believe the shocking conditions which existed at that day in the treatment of the insane, the patients being confined in cells with no floor but the earth, no windows, consequently no ventilation. The straw on which th   `~nt was changed once a week, at which time the occup' given their only exercise. Such were the condition found when she visited the prisons, hospitals and retreats in every state this side of the Rocky Mountains. As she gazed at the appalling sight of human beings in cages, closets and cellars, many of them naked, most of them chained, and all of them thrashed into obedience, she realized that a radical and immediate change was necessary. In Providence at last was found a small asylum that gave its patients wise and kind treatment, but it was much overcrowded, and Miss Dix at once resolved to gather the means for enlargement and make the institution an object lesson. She went to the richest man in the city, who was also notoriously close-fisted, and to him she related with her wonderful power of feeling and eloquence the pathos and tragedy of the condition of these benighted souls. To the surprise of everyone the wealthy man listened spellbound, and at length exclaimed: "Miss Dix, what do you want me to do?" "Sir, I want you to give $50,000 toward the enlargement of the insane hospital in your city," replied Miss Dix. "Madame, I will do it," said the rich man, with perhaps the first desire of his life to help suffering humanity, inspired by this young woman. This was the beginning which has changed the whole conditions of the institutions of our country, and started work along the right line for the insane and criminals.

In the Civil War Dorothea Dix offered her services to the Secretary of War as a nurse, and under her direction much was done to improve the hospitals and so relieve the suffering of those sick and wounded. At length, when four-score years old, well worn out with her work, she was invited to make her home in the asylum in Trenton, N. J., one of the many institutions founded by her. Here she was visited by a multitude of friends, while a continual flow of letters from all over the country brought to her the grateful expressions of the many she had aided. She died July 19, 1887, and one of the many prominent men who passed judgment on her work at this time said, "Thus

has died and been laid at rest in the most quiet and unostentatious way the most useful and distinguished woman America
has yet produced."

CAROLINE MARIA SEVERANCE.

Philanthropist. Mrs. Severance was the daughter of
Orson and Caroline M. Seamore. Was born in Canandaigua,
N. Y., January 12, 1820. She was the valedictorian of her
class in 1835, when she graduated from the Female Seminary
at Geneva, N. Y. In 1840 she married Theodoric C. Severance, a banker of Cleveland, where she resided until 1855, then
in Boston, and later in Los Angeles, Cal. She was the founder
and first president of the New England Woman's College, of
Boston, which antedated the well-known Sorosis Club, of New
York, by only a few weeks, and Mrs. Severance is frequently
called the mother of women's clubs in the United States. She
has always been an active worker in woman's suffrage work,
having lectured in various states. Has written several memorials and appeals on this subject, which have been read before
the Woman's Congress. Has founded clubs in Los Angeles
and Santa Barbara; is trustee of the Unitarian Library and
president of the Los Angeles Free Kindergarten Association,
and is one of the most progressive women of the present day
in America. She is now spending the evening of her life in Los
Angeles, Cal.

MARY TILESTON HEMENWAY.

Mary Tileston Hemenway, philanthropist, was born in
New York City, in 1822; daughter of Thomas Tileston, a
wealthy New York merchant. Her husband, a Boston business
man, the owner of extensive silver mines in South America;

acquired a large fortune, and after his death she came into possession of about $15,000,000, thus becoming the richest woman in Boston. During her long life Mrs. Hemenway bestowed much thought and money upon charitable and educational institutions. She gave the sum of $100,000 to found the Tileston Normal School, Wilmington, N. C. In 1876, when the existence of the Old South Meeting House, Boston, was threatened, she gave one-half of the $200,000 necessary to save the historic edifice from being torn down. In 1878 the series of free lectures for children was started at her suggestion in the Old South Church, which continued informally until 1883, when the regular free course of historical lectures for young people was inaugurated. In 1881 she established four annual prizes for High School pupils for the best essays on scientific topics and American history. She also established kitchen gardens, sewing schools, cooking schools and the Boston Normal School of Gymnastics; contributed duly to the support of archæological expeditions and explorations in the Southwest and to the funds of the American Archæological Institute; was the patroness of the "Journal of American Ethnology and Archæology," and gave generously to the Boston Teachers' Mutual Benefit Association. After her death the trustees of her estate conveyed to the state board of education the "Boston Normal School of Household Arts," established by her, and which was subsequently transferred to Farmingham, Mass. She died in Boston, Mass., March 6, 1894.

MARTHA REED MITCHELL.

Was born March, 1818, in Westford, Mass. Her parents were Seth and Rhoda Reed. She was educated at Miss Fiske's School, Keene, N. H., and Mrs. Emma Willard's Seminary, in Troy, N. Y. In 1838 her family removed to what was then the wilds of Wisconsin. They traveled down the Erie Canal and by the chain of Great Lakes, the journey comprising three weeks before they reached their destination, the city of Milwaukee, Wis. Wisconsin was then a territory, and Milwaukee a village of only five hundred inhabitants. In 1841 Martha Reed married Alexander Mitchell, one of the sturdy pioneers of this Western country, and later one of the most prominent men in the state of Wisconsin. Mr. Mitchell amassed great wealth, but neither prosperity nor popularity deprived Mrs. Mitchell of her simple manner and her love and interest in the cause of the less fortunate. Mrs. Mitchell was ever ready with her means and personal efforts in all charitable work of her home city. She organized what is now known as the Protestant Orphan Asylum, and was its first treasurer, and for years she supported a mission kindergarten, where daily nearly one hundred children from the lowest grades of society were taught to be self-respecting and self-sustaining men and women. Art and artists are indebted to her for her liberal patronge. After the Civil War she established a winter home near Jacksonville, Fla., where she brought to great perfection tropical fruit-bearing trees, and many of the rare trees of foreign lands, among them the camphor and cinnamon from Ceylon, the tea plant from China, and some of the sacred trees of India. While here she became interested in the charities of this state, and St. Luke's Hospital stands among her monuments to her charitable work in Florida. Mrs. Mitchell will long be remembered as one of the moving spirits and able women of the early pioneer days in the West. She was one of the vice-regents of the Mt. Vernon Association.

CYNTHIA H. VAN NAME LEONARD.

Was born February 28, 1828, in Buffalo, N. Y. Was a pioneer in many fields of labor which have been invaded by women in this century. She was the first woman to stand behind a counter as a saleswoman, and was a member of the first Woman's Social and Literary Club organized in her city. In 1852 she married Charles E. Leonard, connected with the *Buffalo Express,* and later with the *Commercial Advertiser* of Detroit, Michigan. In 1856 Mr. and Mrs. Leonard moved to Clinton, Iowa, where he published the *Herald.* Mrs. Leonard was active in establishing schools and churches in this little frontier city, and when the war broke out she was foremost in all sanitary work, and assisted in opening the first soldiers' home in Iowa. In 1863 Mr. Leonard moved to Chicago, Ill., where Mrs. Leonard at once became prominent in the fair for the Freedmen's Aid Commission. She organized and was president of the Women's Club of that city, which later was called the Sorosis. Mrs. Leonard and Mrs. Waterman published a weekly paper in the interest of this club. Mrs. Leonard has been very active in shelter work for the unfortunate women of her own city, and through her efforts succeeded in establishing the Good Samaritan Society and the opening of a shelter for the unfortunate class of society. After the Chicago fire she worked constantly for the protection and assistance of these poor women. Mrs. Leonard is the mother of Lillian Russell, the well-known actress, whose name was Helen Leonard. She organized in New York the Science of Life Club. All Mrs. Leonard's daughters are well known and more or less prominent in the musical and theatrical world.

AMANDA L. AIKENS.

Editor and philanthropist. Mrs. Aikens was born in North Adams, Massachusetts, the 12th day of May, 1833. She received her education at Maplewood Institute, Pittsfield, Massachusetts. She married Andrew Jackson Aikens, and moved to Milwaukee, Wisconsin. In 1887 she began to edit the Woman's World, a department in her husband's paper, the *Evening Wisconsin.* During the Civil War she was one of the noted women workers of our country, and it was through her public appeals that the question of the national soldiers' homes was agitated. She raised money in Wisconsin for the Johns Hopkins Medical School in Baltimore, for the purpose of having women admitted on equal terms with men. She took an active interest in all charity and educational work in her state, and must be included among the prominent women up-builders of our country. Mrs. Aikens died in Milwaukee, the 20th of May, 1892.

ELIZABETH DICKSON JONES.

Born in Chicago October 6, 1862. Daughter of William Wallace and Fidelia Hill Norton Dickson. In 1884 married Joseph H. Jones, who has since died. Active in musical work; secretary of the Iowa Humane Society, and in 1904, James Callonan, former president, left the Iowa Humane Society $70,000 conditioned upon her being made secretary for life; was vice-president of the American Humane Society.

JUDITH WALKER ANDREWS.

Philanthropist. Mrs. Andrews was born in Fryeburg, Maine, April 26, 1826, and was educated at the academy in her home town. Her brother, Dr. Clement A. Walker, was appointed in charge of the hospital for the insane in Boston, and Mrs. Walker joined him there to assist in the work in which she was deeply interested. Her work in this line has been of great value. Since 1889, she has been very much interested in the child-widows of India and formed an association to carry out the plans of Pundita Ramabai. Mrs. Andrews and her co-workers are carrying on the management of a school at Puna, India.

HANNAII J. BAILEY.

Philanthropist and reformer. Mrs. Bailey was born in Cornwall-on-Hudson, New York, July 5, 1839. In her early youth she taught school. She became very much interested in the work among the criminal institutions of New England. Her father had been a member of the Society of Friends, and she attended the yearly meeting of this sect. While attending one of these she met Moses Bailey, to whom she was married in October, 1868. In 1882 his death left her with one son, twelve years of age, and her own health very much impaired. She took up her husband's business, an oilcloth manufactory, and also a retail carpet store in Portland, Maine, and carried these on with success, selling them in 1889 most profitably. She is a woman prominently connected with all the missionary societies and the work of her religious faith, the Friends; is a strong advocate for peace, and in 1888 she was made the superintendent of that line of work for the World's Woman's Christian Temperance Union, and has carried on the publishing of two monthly papers, the *Pacific Banner* and the *Acorn*, besides the distribution of a great deal of literature on this subject. She has worked diligently in the interest of a reformatory prison for women in her own state, and her name is found among the first in all philanthropic work for the church and schools and for young men and women who are trying to earn an education.

34

PHOEBE APPERSON HEARST.

Philanthropist.   The wife of Senator George Hearst, of
California, was the daughter of R. W. Apperson, and was born
December 3, 1842.   She was married to George Hearst, June
15, 1862, and their only child is William Randolph Hearst,
editor of the *New York American* and the *San Francisco Examiner,* and a syndicate of papers published in the principal cities
in the United States.   Mrs. Hearst, since her husband's death,
has been very active in philanthropic work.   She established
and maintained in San Francisco free kindergarten classes and
working girls' clubs for several years, and also classes for training kindergarten teachers in Washington City.   The latter were
maintained by her for almost ten years, and from these classes
came the first kindergarten teachers in the public schools of
Washington, D. C.   In Lead, S. D., where she owns much
mining interests, she has established a kindergarten for about
three hundred children.   She gave two hundred and fifty thousand dollars to build the National Cathedral School for girls in
Washington, D. C.   She paid the cost for the plans submitted
by the architects of Europe and America for enlarging the University of California, and erected and equipped in connection
with that university the Mining Building as a memorial to her
husband; has given free libraries to the city of Lead, S. D., and
also to Anaconda, Mont.; was the first president of the Century
Club of San Francisco; vice-president of the Golden Gate Kindergarten Association; regent of the University of California,
and vice-regent for California of the Mount Vernon Association.   Mrs. Hearst is a woman of great ability, and has done
much for the progress and educational improvement and advantages for education, not only in her own state of California, but
in many places of the United States.   She has helped and is
helping to-day in many ways the less fortunate.   She is one of

the conspicuous women of America, and one to whom her country is greatly indebted.

ANNA ELIZA SEAMANS NAVE.

Well-known hospital worker in the Spanish-American War, and author of religious writings; was born at Defiance, Ohio, June 4, 1848; was the daughter of William and Mary Seamans; her husband, Orville J. Nave, was an army chaplain.

MRS. WILLIAM ZIEGLER.

The work done by Mrs. Ziegler for the blind deserves especial mention. Mrs. William Ziegler, of New York, founded and maintained, at an expense of twenty thousand dollars a year the *Matilda Ziegler Magazine for the Blind*. When she established this magazine she expressed the wish that it should never make public the name of the donor, but it was found necessary, to further its benefits, to allow her name to appear. This magazine has a printing plant of double the capacity of any other printing plant for the blind in the world. Five hundred thousand pages a month are printed. Ten blind girls work in the office, earning a dollar and a quarter a day, assembling the sheets for the magazine, which they do as correctly as those who can see. One of these girls is deaf and blind. The proof reader for the magazine is a blind man, a graduate of Columbia College.

GEORGIA TRADER.

Another woman who is doing splendid work for the blind is Miss Georgia Trader, of Avondale, Cincinnati, Ohio, who lost her sight very early in life. The Misses Florence and Georgia Trader, after finishing school, took up this work. They succeeded in establishing classes for the blind in the public schools of Cincinnati, and ultimately established a library with nearly two thousand volumes, from which the books in raised type are loaned to the blind all over the country, and as the government takes books for the blind free through the mails there is no knowing the good this work is doing. Miss Georgia Trader's greatest work has been the establishing of a working home for the blind girls, where she maintains thirteen destitute girls, for whom she furnishes employment in weaving rugs and other artistic work, which finds ready sale. They have purchased the girlhood home of Alice and Phoebe Carey, with twenty-six acres of land, in the suburbs of Cincinnati, and through the co-operation of the Misses Trader's friends they have now established this home on a firm foundation, and will go on with this splendid work.

RUTH HINSHAW SPRAY.

Born in Mooresville, Indiana, February 16, 1848. The wife of Samuel J. Spray, of Indianapolis. Prominent as a teacher in the public schools and work for the protection of children and animals; also of the child labor organizations and in the international peace cause, Woman's Christian Temperance Union, Retail Clerks' Association and other associations for public welfare; is a resident of Salida, Colorado.

KATE WALLER BARRETT.

Born at Clifton, Stafford County, Virginia, January 24, 1858; is the daughter of Withers and Ann Eliza Stribling Waller; graduated in a course of nursing at the Florence Nightingale Training School and the St. Thomas Hospital of London; married Rev. Robert South Barrett in 1876; has long been an active worker in philanthropic work. Is the vice-president and general superintendent of the National Florence Crittenton Mission, of Washington, D. C., and now president of that institution; was a delegate to the convention for the discussion of the care of delinquent children in 1909, vice-president-at-large of the National Council of Women, member of the Mothers' Congress, League of Social Service, Daughters of the American Revolution, National Geographical Society, and is to-day a public speaker and one of the most prominent workers in the philanthropic work of the United States.

HELEN CULVER.

Born at Little Valley, New York, March 23, 1832; was a school teacher in her youth. In 1863 she was matron of the military hospital at Murfreesboro, Tennessee. In 1868 she entered into partnership with her cousin, Charles J. Hull, in the real estate business in Chicago, and dealt largely in properties of that city and of the West. After his death she built and endowed the four Hull biological laboratories for the University of Chicago; was trustee of the Hull House Association from its organization in 1895, and is one of the noted philanthropists of the United States.

ELLA MARTIN HENROTIN.

Born in Portland, Maine, July, 1847; was the daughter of Edward Byam and Sarah Ellen Norris Martin; was educated in Europe, and in 1869 married Charles Henrotin, of Illinois; one of the leading spirits of the women's department of the World's Columbian Exposition in Chicago in 1893; president of the General Federation of Women's Clubs in 1894; was decorated by the Sultan of Turkey in 1893, and also made an "officier de l'Academie" by the French Republic in 1899, and decorated by Leopold II, in 1904; one of the foremost women in public and charitable work in Chicago.

MOTHER MARY ALPHONSA.

Was the daughter of Nathaniel Hawthorne, and in 1871 married George Parsons Lathrop. Both Mr. and Mrs. Lathrop were converts to the Catholic faith. Mrs Lathrop became greatly interested in the cause of those unfortunate people afflicted with cancer, and took up a course of study of this disease and its treatment at the Bellevue Hospital, New York. She worked among the poor and labored assiduously in their homes and in the hospitals. On the death of her husband she established in a house on Cherry street, New York City, a small hospital for these poor unfortunate creatures, who were turned out of other hospitals as incurable, or because they were too poor to pay for treatment. In addition to this, she established a home at Hawthorne, in Westchester County, and an order was formed to aid her in her work under a rule of the Third Order of St. Dominic. This charity is for those who are pronounced incurable, and is known as St. Rose's Free Cancer Hospital, with the country house in Westchester County. To this work Mrs. Lathrop consecrated her life, and entered the order and became its head, under the name of Mother Alphonsa. She has written some poems under the title "Along the Shore," and, with her husband, was the author of "Memories of Hawthorne" and "A Story of Courage."

MRS. GEORGE BLISS.

Is the daughter of Henry H. Casey and Anais Blanchet Casey. She married Mr. George Bliss, a distinguished Catholic lawyer, who was legal adviser of the late Archbishop Corrigan. He was knighted by Pope Leo XIII. In 1897 Mr. Bliss died. Mrs. Bliss' greatest work has been the establishment with other interested persons of the Free Day School and Crèche for French children, located at 69 Washington Square, New York. This school is entirely dependent on the voluntary contributions, receiving no aid from the city treasury. She is vice-president of this association, and is president of the Tabernacle Society, whose headquarters is in the Convent of Perpetual Adoration, in Washington, D. C.

HARRIET L. CRAMER.

Was born in Fond du Lac County, Wisconsin, in 1848; is president and publisher of the *Evening Wisconsin,* which was founded by her hsuband, Hon. William E. Cramer, and of which he was editor until his death. She is the donor of the granite columns in the interior of the Church of Gesu, in Milwaukee, said to be the only columns of this kind in the country, and were placed there at a cost of $20,000. She, with her husband, gave forty acres of ground in Milwaukee County, upon which the house and school of the Good Shepherd are situated. To this institution Mr. Cramer left a large sum of money at his death, and Mrs. Cramer has been constantly adding to this. She is one of the most philanthropic, generous women in the charitable world of America.

MARY L. GILMAN.

Was born in Boston, Massachusetts. Her father, William Lynch, was a wealthy man of North End. In 1870 she married John E. Gilman, a prominent member of the Grand Army of the Republic, and at one time department commander of Massachusetts. Mrs. Gilman is prominent in women's relief corps work and the Ladies' Aid Association of the Soldiers' Home of Chelsea, and the home for destitute Catholic children. She was for some time organist of a church musical society.

FLORENCE MAGRUDER GILMORE.

Was born February 13, 1881, in Columbus, Ohio. Her father was James Gillespie, and her mother Florence Magruder Gilmore. Through her father Mrs. Gilmore is connected with the prominent families of Blaine, Ewing and Sherman, in this country, and, through her mother, with some of the well-known families of Scotland. She is engaged in doing settlement work under Catholic organizations in St. Louis; is a contributor to the *America, Extension, Benzinger's, Messenger of the Sacred Heart, Rosary* and *Leader* magazines.

MRS. RICHARD H. KEITH.

Is the founder of St. Anthony's Infant Home, Kansas City, Missouri.

KATHERINE BARDOL LAUTZ.

Was born in Rochester, New York, in 1842; is the daughter of Joseph Bardol and Mary Reinagle Bardol. Her husband is J. Adam Lautz, of Germany, at the head of the Lautz Soap Manufacturing Company, of Buffalo. She has been president of the St. Elizabeth's Hospital Association for many years; is director of the Working Boys' Home, Women's Educational and Industrial Union, St. James' Mission and Angel Guardian Mission.

MARGARET BISCHELL McFADDEN.

Was born in St. Louis, Missouri, but removed when a child to Winona, Minnesota. Their father was an extensive ship builder of St. Louis. In 1890 she married M. J. McFadden, one of the prominent business men of St. Paul, Minnesota. She has been twice elected president of the Guild of Catholic Women, one of the leading and most powerful religious organizations in the Northwest. She is active in all charitable work, and especially are her interests enlisted in the cause of young girls who are brought before the Juvenile Court, many of whom she has been able to save. Mrs. McFadden is greatly beloved, and is considered one of the prominent women of the Northwest.

SARAH McGILL.

Was born in New York City; is the daughter of James and Ellen McGill. She is a noted linguist, and has made quite a number of translations from the French, Spanish, Italian and German. During her residence in Mobile, Alabama, she was known on account of her splendid charitable work as the "Mother of the Orphans." She and her sister, Mary A. McGill, who is also an author, and active in all charitable work, were instrumental, with their brothers, in founding McGill Institute, in Mobile, and also the McGill Burse, in the American College in Rome, a fund for the education of students for the priesthood, in the Mobile diocese, and a fund for the building of churches. Associated with them in this splendid charity was their brother, Felix McGill. The McGill crypt, beneath the Chapel of the Visitation Convent, is a work of art.

AGNES McSHANE.

One of the founders of the Visiting Nurses' Association, a charitable organization, which works among the poor sick of Omaha. She is the wife of Felix J. McShane, a nephew of the distinguished philanthropist, Count Creighton, the benefactor of Creighton University.

KATHERINE KELLY MEAGHER.

Is president of the graduate chapter of the Visitation Convent Alumnæ Association, treasurer of the Catholic Guild of Women, and prominently identified with the charitable and social clubs of St. Paul, Minnesota. She is the daughter of the late P. H. Kelly, and in 1907 married John B. Meagher.

MARY VIRGINIA MERRICK.

Is the daughter of Richard T. Merrick, a prominent lawyer of Washington, D. C., whose father, William Duhurst Merrick, was a member of the Maryland state legislature, and United States Senator from Maryland from 1838 to 1845. Miss Merrick was the founder of the Christ Child Society of Washington. She began her work by interesting her friends in the preparation of infants' outfits, to be given to the poor on Christmas Day, and in 1900 this little circle was formed into a society. Sewing classes, children's libraries, Sunday school classes were gradually added to the work of relief among the destitute children of Washington City. Articles of incorporation were taken out for the society, and to-day there is a membership of over six hundred of the prominent Catholic women of Washington, which includes many from official and diplomatic circles and the army and navy. There are to-day branches of this society in New York City, Omaha, Worcester, Massachusetts; Chicago, Illinois; Ellicott City, Maryland, and Davenport, Iowa. Miss Merrick is the author of a life of Christ (for children) and translator of Mme. de Segur's life of Christ, also for children.

MARY RICHARDS.

Daughter of Henry L. and Cynthia Cowles Richards; was born in Jersey City, New Jersey, in 1855; charter member and director of the Winchester, Massachusetts, Visiting Nurses' Association, and active in charitable matters of her home city.

MRS. THOMAS F. RYAN.

Was the daughter of Captain Barry, who was the owner of a line of vessels plying between Baltimore and the West Indies. She married Thomas F. Ryan. She and her husband have been generous contributors to many of the charitable institutions and philanthropic work of the church, especially in Virginia. They furnished the interior of the Sacred Heart Cathedral of Richmond, which had been given to the city by her husband, at a cost of $500,000; built the Sacred Heart Church, Washington Ward, and Sacred Heart Cathedral School at Richmond; church and convent at Falls Church, Virginia; contributed to churches at Hot Springs and Harrisburg, Virginia, and Keyser, West Virginia; the chapel at Suffern, New. York, where their summer home is located, and together gave Ryan Hall and a wing to Georgetown University, Georgetown, D. C. She was decorated with the Cross of St. Gregory and made a countess by Pope Pius X for her philanthropic work.

MYRA E. KNOX SEMMES.

Was the daughter of William Knox, a prominent banker and planter of Montgomery, Alabama, and Annie O. Lewis Knox, whose family was related to the Fairfaxes, Washingtons, and other families of Virginia. Her husband was Thomas J. Semmes, a distinguished jurist, prominent in the political affairs of Louisiana, and was a member of the convention in 1861 which passed the articles of secession in the state of Louisiana. Since her husband's death Mrs. Semmes has devoted her life to charity and benevolence, and has erected a magnificent chapel in the Jesuit Church, in New Orleans, in memory of her husband.

ANNE SPALDING.

Was a descendant of the distinguished Spalding family of Morganfield, Kentucky, from which two archbishops have been made. Active in charitable work in Atlanta, Georgia, where her husband, Dr. Robert Spalding, is well known.

SISTER M. IMELDA TERESA (SUSIE TERESA FORREST SWIFT, O. P.)

Was the daughter of George Henry and Pamelia Forrest Paine; was born in 1862; a graduate of Vassar College. Her first philanthropic work was with the Salvation Army. She trained the officers for the organization at the International Training Home, London; established a home for waif boys in London, England, and suggested to General Booth the outline of his work, "Darkest England's Social Scheme"; was the author of many stories and poems written for Salvation Army publications. In 1896 she became a convert to Catholicism, and since has served as assistant editor of the *Catholic World Magazine* and editor of the *Young Catholic*. In 1897 she entered a religious order, and was for a time directress of an orphanage in Havana, Cuba, and directress of the Dominican College of Havana. Since October, 1904, she has served as novice mistress of the Dominican congregation of· St. Catherine di Ricci, of Albany, New York.

CAROLINE EARLE WHITE.

Was born in Philadelphia in 1833. Her father and mother were active opponents of slavery, and he wrote the (new) Constitution of Pennsylvania, and was a candidate for the Vice-Presidency in 1840 on the Anti-Slavery ticket. Mrs. White has devoted nearly her whole life to children and animals. She was one of the women who ably assisted Henry Bergh in the establishment of the Humane Society in New York, and was the founder of the Pennsylvania Society for the Prevention of Cruelty to Animals; also of the Society for the Prevention of Cruelty to Children, of that state; author of "Love in the Tropics," "A Modern Agrippa," "Letters from Spain and Norway," "An Ocean Mystery," and contributor to *Harper's Magazine* and the *Forum;* member of the Society of Colonial Dames.

HELEN MILLER GOULD.

Miss Gould was born in New York, June 20, 1868, daughter of the late Jay and Helen Day Gould; sister of George Jay, Edwin, Howard and Frank Jay Gould. She has been identified with philanthropic work for many years; has made many notable gifts, including: Library building, costing $310,000 to University City of New York, $100,000 to United States Government for war purposes, $10,000 to Rutgers College, $10,000 to Engineering School, University City of New York, $50,000 to the naval branch of the Brooklyn Young Men's Christian Association, and numerous other donations for educational and charitable purposes.

Miss Gould is indeed a unique figure—a wealthy woman, born into the New York smart set, she is yet puritanical, conscientious, modest, loyal, conservative, charitable and utterly indifferent to that phase of society which means a laborious career and a heart-burning competition.

Annually she gives in charity tens of thousands of dollars, and with her liberal inclination in this direction it is well that she is a trained business woman (she has had a good course in law) for each year demands come to her for over two million dollars. She has received requests for everything, from her autograph on a blank slip, to her signature on a thousand dollar check. In one week alone she had 1,303 appeals, amounting to $1,500,000.

One of her sweetest charities is the home for poor children at Lyndehurst, and another at Woodycrest, three miles out of Tarrytown, New York, where she cares for twenty-five little ones. To all these benefactions has she given greatly, and then the half has not been told.

MILDRED A. BONHAM.

Mrs. Bonham was born in Magnolia, Illinois, August, 1840. In 1847 her parents removed to Oregon, and in 1858 she married Judge B. F. Bonham, of Salem, Oregon. In 1885 Judge Bonham was made consul-general to British India, and the family removed to Calcutta. Her letters, under the pen name of "Mizpah," had wide circulation in the Oregon and California papers. She did some splendid work among the women of India, and succeeded in raising $1,000 to found a scholarship for these women in one of the schools of this country.

KATHARINE BEMENT DAVIS.

Katharine Bement Davis was born in Buffalo, New York. Her parents were Oscar B. Davis and Frances Bement. They moved to Dunkirk, New York, when she was two years old. She was educated in the Dunkirk public schools, but moved to Rochester, New York, while she was in the high school, and graduated from the Rochester Free Academy. She returned to Dunkirk, New York, as a teacher of chemistry and physics in the high school, and taught there several years before she entered Vassar College, where she graduated in 1892. The year following her graduation she went to New York, where she taught sciences in the Brooklyn Heights Seminary in the morning, and studied chemistry at Columbia University afternoons and Saturdays.

In the spring, summer and fall of 1893 she conducted an experiment under the auspices of the New York State commission for the World's Fair, called "A Workingman's Model Home." The house was built and furnished to illustrate what a workingman could do in New York State, outside of New York City, who was earning $600 a year. Here she had a real family living, and gave demonstrations of the bill of fare which such a family could have.

In the fall of 1893 she went to Philadelphia as head worker in the College Settlement. After four years there she went to the University of Chicago as a fellow in the Department of Political Economy. In 1888-1889 she held the European fellowship of the New England Women's Educational Association, studying in Berlin and Vienna. Returning to this country, she took her doctor's degree at the University of Chicago in the Departments of Political Economy and Sociology in the spring of 1900.

At this time the New York State Reformatory had been incorporated, and was in process of construction. The board of managers, of whom Mrs. Josephine Shaw Lowell, of New York, was one, and whose president is, and was, Mr. James Wood, of Mt. Kisco, were on the lookout for someone to accept the superintendency. They wanted someone who would conduct the institution along new lines, and not one who was institution trained. Through Mrs. Lowell Mrs. Davis became interested in the plan, and in the fall of 1900 accepted the superintendency, and has been in that position ever since.

Mrs. Davis has been a lecturer on penology, particularly as concerns women in the New York School of Philanthropy, since its organization. Happening to be in Sicily on a six-months' leave in the winter of 1908-1909, at the time of the Messina earthquake, she acted as agent for the American Red Cross in Syracuse, Sicily, helping to organize relief work. She received medals, both from the American and Italian Red Cross for this service. At the International Prison Congress, held in Washington in 1910, she was elected to preside over the section on children. It is not customary to elect women to these positions, but it was done on this occasion as a recognition of the important part that American women take in matters of penology.

MARTHA BERRY.

Miss Martha Berry is one of the most prominent women to-day in the philanthropic work in the South, and one who deserves conspicuous mentior for her personal efforts and what she has accomplished in her splendid work for the benefit of the children of the mountaineers of Georgia, who are so isolated and so shut out from every opportunity of education. The beginning of the Martha Berry Industrial School, to which only the poor are eligible, was the result of Miss Berry's efforts to interest a few of the mountain children who strayed into a simple cottage which she had built on the mountain side, near her father's home. The Bible stories and tales from Grimm which she told them brought them frequently together. A year later four mountain day schools were established. Through them Miss Berry realized that the only salvation of these mountain children lay in training them in a home school, where strict discipline and industrial training would go hand in hand with book learning. So she built her own school, a ten-room building. Her first two scholars were boys whom she had found in a cabin far out in the hills, boarding themselves and paying two dollars a month tuition to an old broken down schoolmaster who was teaching them the Greek alphabet, though they couldn't read or write. She took these boys under her charge, promising them a literary and industrial education at fifty dollars a year, including their board, with the privilege of working their way through school. This was in January, 1902. The school opened with one building and five pupils, two teachers and about thirty acres of forest land. Their industrial equipment consisted of an old horse, one small plough, two hoes, a rake, two axes and a mallet. To-day Miss Berry's buildings and equipments represent an investment of two hundred thousand dollars. More than a thousand boys have come to this school and gone back to the mountains to help reclaim their people from the ignorance and superstition into which they had fallen. A girls' school has also been established in connection with this, and there are in it fifty girls. Miss Berry has raised thirty-five thousand dollars every year to keep the work going. Hundreds of boys and girls of the mountain districts of Georgia, Tennessee, Alabama and Virginia are pleading to enter this school. Nothing but the lack of a generous support prevents Miss Berry from extending her work in this much-needed field.

ELECTA AMANDA JOHNSON.

Mrs. Electa Amanda Johnson was born in Wayne County, New York, in November, 1838. She was descended from a distinguished Revolutionary family on her father's side, and an old Knickerbocker family on her mother's side. In 1860 she married A. H. Johnson, a lawyer of Prairie du Chien. She was one of the founders of the Wisconsin Industrial School for Girls, and has been selected by the governor of Wisconsin several times to represent the state on the questions of charity and reform.

IRMA THEODA JONES.

Mrs. Irma Theoda Jones was born March 11, 1845, in Victory, New York. Mrs. Jones' maiden name was Andrews, and her family were among the early pioneers of western New York, who later removed to Rockford, Illinois. Her work is among women's clubs and the temperance union; she is also a contributor to various newspapers. In 1865 she married Nelson B. Jones, a prominent citizen of Lansing, Michigan. In 1892 she became editor of the Literary Club Department of the *Mid-Continent*, a monthly magazine published in Lansing.

CORA SCOTT POND.

Was born March 2, 1856, in Cheboygan, Wisconsin. Her father was born in Maine, and her mother in New Brunswick. She was a second cousin, on her father's side, of General Winfield Scott. Her father was a successful inventor of machinery and booms for milling and logging purposes, and one of the early pioneers in Wisconsin. After her graduation from the state university she taught music, and at this time became interested in the woman's suffrage and temperance movements, and was invited by Mrs. Lucy Stone to help organize the state for woman's suffrage. Although intending to teach, she took upon herself this work, and organized eighty-seven woman's leagues in Massachusetts, speaking in public and raising money to carry on the work in that state for over six years. In 1887 she organized a woman's suffrage bazaar, and raised over six thousand dollars. While teaching in the Conservatory of Music in Boston she contributed sketches of Shakespeare, Dickens and other authors. She originated a dramatic entertainment called the National Pageant, which she gave with great success for the benefit of the various societies of women in Massachusetts. She was intimately associated with Mary A. Livermore, and aided and assisted her in her Boston work. Mrs. Pope traveled through the country, giving the National Pageant for local societies, and raised many thousands of dollars for charitable purposes. In Chicago, in one night's performance, given in the Auditorium, sixty thousand dollars were cleared. While here she met and married John T. Pope, who assisted her in her work.

MARGARET CHANLER.

The philanthropy of Miss Chanler has been almost equal to that of Miss Gould, and she has strewn with a lavish hand many blessings upon the poor and needy. During the Cuban War she volunteered as a nurse to the soldiers, serving faithfully in that inhospitable climate. She has been very modest in the manner in which she has disbursed many thousands of dollars for the comfort and salvation of the indigent of New York City and elsewhere. Her charity is broad and enters many avenues.

ELIZA GARRETT.

The name of Eliza Garrett will ever be remembered with gratitude by Biblical students and the Methodist Church throughout the world. Her original name was Eliza Clark, and she was born near Newburg, New York, March 5, 1805. In 1825 she married Augustus Garrett. Their early married life was filled with frequent change, they having made their home in New York City, Cincinnati,

New Orleans and Mississippi. While on their voyage down the Mississippi River they lost a daughter with cholera; later, they lost a son, their only surviving child.

In 1834 Mr. Garrett moved to Chicago, and became one of the prominent men and early pioneers of that city. After Chicago became a city Mr. Garrrett was elected mayor. In December, 1848, his death occurred. Mrs. Garrett became possessed of one-half the entire estate. Of a strong religious faith, her influence was always exerted for a Christian life and Christian principles. She was always benevolent, and now decided to carry out her desires to aid in some educational enterprise. She believed the future of the church and country demanded a thorough intellectual training for the young under the auspices of Christianity. She realized that ministerial education was by no means receiving a corresponding share of attention, and that for various reasons it was not likely soon to be provided for in the ordinary way. To this, therefore, she directed her thoughts. She saw in her own church (Methodist) a growing denomination of Christians, then numbering seven hundred thousand communicants, and requiring for its ordinary pastoral care not less than five thousand ministers, while the claims made upon it for missionaries throughout the United States and distant lands were unlimited. Besides, it was lamentably true that many who were engaged in ministerial work left it prematurely, unable, with an imperfect preparation, to bear up under its weighty responsibilities. The want of an institution which should provide for ministerial students ample libraries and all appropriate apparatus of thorough and extended study, in which teachers of ability and experience would be ever ready to welcome, guide and instruct those desiring to profit for such opportunities, was badly felt. After due reflection and investigation, Mrs. Garrett decided to found such an institution. Her will, executed December, 1853, gave, after some personal legacies, more than one-third of her estate—"all the rest and residue— that is to say, the rents, issues, profits and proceeds thereof," to the erection, furnishing and endowment of a "theological institution for the Methodist Episcopal Church, to be called the Garrett Biblical Institute." Said institution was to be located in or near Chicago, and was to be perpetually under the guardianship of the church.

This will, also, with a wise reference to the distant future, contained this proviso: "In case at any time the said trust property, the rents, issues and proceeds thereof, shall exceed the amount necessary to build, fit, furnish, endow and support said Biblical institute as aforesaid, I direct and devote the surplus to accumulate, or otherwise to be invested for accumulation, for the erection within the city of Chicago, or its vicinity, of a female college, as soon as my said executors, the survivors or survivor of them, or the trustees of said trust property, as herein provided, shall deem the same adequate therefor; the said female college to be under the same control and government, and the trustees to be elected in the same manner, and to possess the same qualifications as are provided for said Biblical institute."

At the time when Mrs. Garrett's will was executed, it was not supposed by herself or her friends that the benevolent designs she contemplated could be accomplished from the avails of her estate for some years to come. Her property had been rendered, by fires, mostly unproductive, while it was to some extent incumbered with debts. At this point a fact should be stated most honorable to her name and highly illustrative of her Christian self-denial. So anxious was Mrs. Garrett to disincumber her estate of its liabilities at the earliest possible period and make it available to carry out her pious and benevolent designs that, for several years, she would only accept four hundred dollars per annum for her support, and nearly half of that she devoted to religious uses. There are probably few who would have been as self-denying under such circumstances. The providence of God did not allow designs so wise and so essential to the welfare of His Church to remain long undeveloped. The friends of the Church became interested to have the measure proposed carried into operation at the earliest moment possible. A beautiful site had just been selected for the Northwestern University on the shore of Lake Michigan, twelve miles north of Chicago, and it was resolved to erect at the same place a temporary building for the Biblical institute. Through the agency of the Rev. P. Judson, the building was promptly constructed; so that in January, 1855, a temporary organization of the institute was effected, under charge of the Rev. Dr. Dempster. It was arranged that this organization should be supported independent of the estate for a period of five years. Meantime, a charter for the permanent institution was secured from the legislature of the state in full accordance with Mrs. Garrett's wishes.

In the autumn of 1855, from a state of perfect health, Mrs. Garrett was stricken down with mortal disease, and after a few days of suffering was called to her reward on high. On Sunday evening, the 18th of November, she was in her place at church, and on Thursday, the 22d, she died.

"Only a few years have passed away since the death of Mrs. Garrrett, and already the seed planted by her hand is producing fruit—an earnest of a glorious and endless harvest. The institution which her liberality endowed, and which, it was feared, might have to struggle for a time with opposition and prejudice, was only a few months after her decease formally accepted and sanctioned by the general conference, the highest judicatory of the Church. The Bishops, the highest officers of the Church, were apppointed a board of council for the institution, and under their advice it has been permanently organized. It is now in efficient operation, and has already given the earnest of widespread and continued usefulness in the Church."

MME. SLAVKO GROUITCH.

Mme. Grouitch, wife of the Servian Charge d'Affaires at the Court of St. James, London, England, was formerly Miss Mabel Gordon Dunlop of West Virginia, whose father was a prominent railroad man of the early days in Virginia and later in Chicago, Illinois. Mme. Grouitch when quite a young girl became interested in the study of archæology and ethnology, to which her father was greatly devoted. After studying at the Chicago University for several years, she went to Athens to revel in the ruins and collections of Greece. While a student in Athens she met her husband, a member of a distinguished family of Servia, who was at that time Attaché of the Servian Legation in Paris, where their marriage occurred. Since her marriage Mme. Grouitch has devoted herself to the work of up-lifting the women of Servia. The University at Belgrade admits girls, but in Servia a girl may not go away from home or into the street unchaperoned, and it is for these girls and to teach the girls of the people scientific culture and domestic arts that Mme. Grouitch and certain noble women of Belgrade determined to found a boarding school in the city of Belgrade. The wives of the representatives of the Servian Government at the various courts of Europe are helping Mme. Grouitch to raise the money for this work. Mme. Grouitch's niece was educated in Belgrade and went from that University to England and took high rank in mathematics, met the senior wrangler at Oxford and vanquished him. Mme. Grouitch is particularly anxious to establish an agricultural course for girls in connection with the University of Belgrade, for the reason, as she says, often where a son cannot be spared to go and study agriculture, because the sons must enter the army, a daughter could be spared and then return to her home and teach the family what she had learned. Among the Servian peasants the women work with the men in the fields. Servian land has great possibilities. Tobacco, for instance, is so fine that Egypt takes Servia's entire output but the farming methods are very primitive. Another thing which these women plan to do is to re-awaken interest in the national needle work. Everybody knows the wonderful embroidery for which Servian women have always been noted, but in the last thirty years Servia has been flooded with cheap things from other countries and art has declined. Mme. Grouitch says the Servians are the cleanest people she has ever known; nothing can be taught them as to housework and sanitation. Eighty girls from the provinces are now studying in Belgrade and boarding at this home established by Mme. Grouitch and her associates. The Servian Government has given the land for the school and the building is under construction. Mme. Grouitch has raised a large sum of money from her friends in this country. She is a gifted, cultured and charming woman, one in which America can feel a pride at having her represent her country in the various parts of Europe to which her husband's official positions may call him.

JANE LATHROP STANFORD.

PHILANTHROPIST AND SOCIAL LEADER.

Mrs. Jane Lathrop Stanford was born in Albany, New York, August 25, 1825. Mrs. Stanford is well known as the wife of Leland Stanford, of California. During the early years of Mr. Stanford's struggle and varying fortunes, she proved herself a worthy helpmeet and is one of the type of American women produced by the early days of California's mining history. Mrs. Stanford's public career commenced when Mr. Stanford was elected governor of California in 1861. Mr. Stanford occupied different positions of prominence and was finally elected United States Senator from his state, California. After the death of their only child, Leland Stanford, Jr., Mrs. Stanford and her husband erected to the memory of this boy the university which bears his name. The "Leland Stanford, Jr., University"—at Palo Alto, their country seat, situated about thirty miles from San Francisco. Not a building of this great university was erected without Mrs. Stanford's advice and wishes being consulted. She erected at her own individual expense a museum which contained works of art and a most valuable collection of curios gathered during their tours in foreign lands. Much of this was lost at the time of the great earthquake a few years ago.

The entire estate of Mr. Stanford and that of his wife at her death were left to endow this great university. Mrs. Stanford was a generous friend to the many charitable institutions of San Francisco. Though a woman of such strong personality, she had one of the tenderest hearts and the deepest sympathy for those in trouble. To such women the Pacific coast owes much of its development and growth. Mrs. Stanford's death occurred in 1905.

MRS. M. A. HUNTER.

Mrs. M. A. Hunter, widow of Commodore Hunter of the navy, founded the first home for orphans in the state of Louisiana, and perhaps in the South. In 1817 a vessel loaded with emigrants arrived at New Orleans, who were fatherless and motherless owing to the loss of their parents by cholera during the voyage. Mrs. Hunter was then a prominent social leader, but a most charitable, sympathetic woman. She gathered these poor little orphans into her own home until a place could be found for them. A wealthy merchant and planter offered a temporary home and took upon himself the work of erecting a suitable building as an asylum for orphan children, but it was through the interest aroused by Mrs. Hunter and her efforts in this work that the institution exists to-day.

D. A. MILIKEN.

Mrs. D. A. Miliken, of New Orleans, founded a memorial hospital for white children at the cost of $150,000, in memory of her husband, and left it handsomely endowed.

WILLIE FRANKLIN PRUIT.

Born in Tennessee in 1865. Her parents' name was Franklin, and they moved to Texas at the close of the Civil War. She is prominent in the city of Fort Worth, Texas. Most of her poems have been published under the pen name of "Aylmer Ney." In 1887 she married Drew Pruit, a lawyer of Fort Worth; has been engaged in many public and charitable enterprises for civic betterment. Vice-president of the Woman's Humane Association of Fort Worth and through her efforts a number of handsome drinking fountains were placed about the city for the benefit of man and beast.

MARY ELIZABETH BLANCHARD LYNDE.

Was born December 4, 1819, in Truxton, New York. Her father was Azariel Blanchard, and her mother, Elizabeth Babcock. She was the widow of the eminent lawyer, Hon. William P. Lynde. Governor Lucius Fairchild appointed her a member of the Wisconsin Board of Charities and Reforms when he was governor of that state. She was active in the work for the advancement of women and a member of this association and greatly interested in the Girls' Industrial School of Milwaukee.

SARAH ANN MATHER.

Was born March 20, 1820, in Chester, Massachusetts. She was the wife of Rev. James Mather, and of Puritan ancestry. She was at one time principal of the Ladies' Department and professor of modern languages in Western University, Leoni, Michigan. After the close of the war and before the United States troops were withdrawn from the South, she went among the freedmen as a missionary and brought to bear all her powers upon this work, sacrificing her health and investing all of her available means in the work of establishing a normal and training school for the colored youth in Camden, South Carolina. Her interest in this work brought about the necessity of her becoming a public speaker in order to arouse the interest of others. She organized the Woman's Home Missionary Society of the Methodist Episcopal Church, and through her efforts a model home and training school was established in Camden, South Carolina, and the school is sustained by this society. She is the author of several works, among them "Young Life," "A Hidden Treasure" and "Little Jack Fee."

MRS. RUSSELL SAGE.

Mrs. Sage, before her marriage to Russell Sage, on November 24, 1869, at Watervliet, New York, was Miss Margaret Olivia Slocum. She was born in Syracuse, N. Y., September 8, 1828, and was the daughter of Joseph and Margaret Pierson Jermain Slocum. Mrs. Sage has always devoted her life and means to charity. She has never had any inclination or taken any part in the social life of New York, preferring to do her part toward the cause of humanity. She was president of the Emma Willard Association; is a member of the Society of Mayflower descendants and Colonial Dames. Since the death of her husband, in 1906, she has given one million dollars to the Emma Willard Seminary, of Troy, N. Y.; one million to Rensselaer Polytechnic Institute; $115,000 to a public school at Sag Harbor, L. I.; ten millions to be known as the Sage Foundation for Social Betterment; $350,000 to the Y. M. C. A. of New York; $150,000 to American Seamen's Friend Society; $150,000 to Northfield (Massachusetts) Seminary; $300,000 to Sage Institute of Pathology of City Hospital on Blackwell's Isand; $250,000 to a home for Indigent Women; $100,000 to

Syracuse University.   These represent only her public gifts, while her private and individual charities and gifts to relatives and friends are manifold.

The purposes of the Sage Foundation Fund are broad and generous and will be of lasting benefit to the men and women of to-day and to those of the future in the work of uplifting the unfortunate and aiding helpful men and women to do their part in the work of the human race in the building of our nation. The Russell Sage Foundation was incorporated under the laws of the state of New York in the month of April, 1907.   The endowment consists of the sum of $10,000 donated by Mrs. Russell Sage.   The purpose of the Foundation, as stated in its charter, is "the improvement of social and living conditions in the United States of America."   The charter further provides that "It shall be within the purpose of said corporation to use any means which, from time to time, shall seem expedient to its members or trustees, including research, publication, education, the establishment and maintenance of charitable and benevolent activities, agencies and institutions, and the aid of any such activities, agencies or institutions already established."

In a letter addressed to the trustees in April, 1907, Mrs. Sage further defines the scope of the Foundation and its limitations as follows: "The scope of the Foundation is not only national, but it is broad.   It should, however, preferably, not undertake to do that which is now being done or is likely to be effectively done by other individuals or other agencies.   It should be its aim to take up the larger, more difficult problems, and to take them up so far as possible in such a manner as to secure co-operation and aid in their solution."

Among the other activities to which the Russell Sage Foundation has contributed financial aid are the National Red Cross, the President's Homes Commission and the Child-Saving Congress in Washington.   Some idea of the scope of the Foundation's activities may be gained from the following titles of a few of its publications:

The Standard of Living Among Workingmen's Families in New York City.

Medical Inspection of Schools.

Laggards in Our Schools.

Correction and Prevention. Four volumes.

Juvenile Court Laws in the United States: Summarized.

The Pittsburgh Survey. Six volumes.

Housing Reform.

A Model Tenement House Law.

Among School Gardens.

Workingmen's Insurance in Europe.

The Campaign Against Tuberculosis in the United States.

Report on the Desirability of Establishing an Employment Bureau in the city of New York.

Wider Use of the School Plant.

The above statement of some of the activities of the Foundation is not inclusive or complete, nor is it intended to be. It is only illustrative. The Foundation has never published a complete report of all of its activities.

GEORGIA MARQUIS NEVINS.

Miss Nevins, the superintendent of the Garfield Memorial Hospital and president of the Graduate Nurses' Association, District of Columbia, was born in Bangor, Maine. She was reared in Massachusetts, and educated in public and private schools. In 1889, she entered the Johns Hopkins Training School for Nurses, and was a member of the first class graduated from that school. She served one year as the first head nurse appointed. Miss Nevins became superintendent of nurses in the Garfield Memorial Hospital School, Washington, D. C., in 1894. She was appointed superintendent of the hospital in 1908. She is an active member of the National and International Nursing Societies, of the Red Cross Nursing Service, of the American Hospital Association, and for years president of the Graduate Nurses Association of the District of Columbia.

Woman Suffrage.

INTRODUCTION BY MRS. JOHN A. LOGAN.

In preparing sketches of the heroic women who have fought the battles and won the victories of the woman suffragists of the United States one is deeply impressed by the similarity in heroism, steadfastness of purpose, indefatigable industry, conscientious convictions and determination of these noble women and the women of the Revolution of 1776. The women of those trying days were sustained by their convictions on the subject of human rights, and with the suffragists the movement was started as a revolt against what they considered cruel injustice toward the supposed weaker sex, and because women had not equal rights under the laws of which men were the authors and administrators. From the early days of the Republic and the persecution and cruel decisions of judges and jurors, American women have kept alive a righteous resentment over the discrimination against them in a Republic that pretended to be founded upon principles of equal justice for all mankind before the law. The smouldering fires of indignation were fanned into a flame by such courageous women as Lucy Stone, Elizabeth Cady Stanton, Susan B. Anthony, Caroline M. Seymour Severance and a host of remarkable women who have enlisted in the cause of equal rights for women. It would take volumes to list their achievements by causing the enactment of laws in every state in the Union, lightening the burdens of women and in securing protection for them against all forms of injustice. Mrs. C. E. Lucky, president of the Knoxville, Ky., Equal Suffrage League, has recently summed up some of the work of the woman suffragists in so graphic a form that it is herewith submitted:

"Woman suffrage is a very live issue in the world at present, and though voted down in many places it refuses to remain quiescent. In five states in our country—Wyoming, Utah, Idaho, Colorado and Washington—the entire franchise is granted to women. School suffrage for women prevails in twenty-nine states and territories. In Australia, New Zealand, Iceland, Finland and the Isle of Man, women have been granted equal political rights. All suffrage except the right of vote for members of Parliament has been granted in England, Ireland, Scotland, Wales, Denmark and Sweden. Norway has granted equal political rights to women, with the exception of a slight property qualification. In Canada the same privileges have been bestowed on unmarried women and widows, while nearly all the Canadian provinces grant municipal suffrage to women. Now, what are the resulting benefits of equal suffrage? In America the states having full or partial school suffrage for women have less than one per cent. of illiteracy. (Tennessee, by the way, has 14.2 per cent.) In Colorado and some other equal suffrage states, since women have been voting, there have been established: A state industrial school for girls, parents' and truant schools, compulsory education, compulsory examination of eyes, ears, teeth and breathing capacity of children, a law giving teachers equal pay for equal work, and a law pensioning teachers after a certain number of years. All these good results have come because mothers and teachers have had the ballot. Equal suffrage has helped the home life, since there is not a department of the home that is not touched by politics. It has widened all forms of charity and philanthropy, increasing their efficiency a hundred-fold. Colorado and the other suffrage states have established a splendid pure food law, a law raising the age of consent to eighteen, the indeterminate sentence for persons convicted of crime, compulsory factory inspection, the making of fathers and mothers joint heirs of deceased children, a reform in the registration laws and passing of the referendum, initiative and recall, state traveling libraries and the local option laws, thus enabling many towns and counties to go dry. Instead of thinking less of their homes and children, women who vote consider them more, and work harder for them. Let us turn again to the question of education. The per capita for school expenditure in Massachusetts is $4.96; Pennsylvania, $3.52; Virginia, $1.07; North Carolina, sixty-six cents; Georgia, ninety-seven cents; Colorado, $5.08. Equal suffrage wherever tried has given the best laws for the protection and rescuing of young girls, boys and children. It has improved the legal condition of women, giving them just control over their property, and mothers equal rights over their children (in many states the mother is not regarded as the parent of the child, which can be willed away from her even before it is born.) The ballot has benefited the working women, cutting down their hours of hard, brutal labor and providing more sanitary surroundings in their places of employment. Women have wonderfully improved political life, which has become higher and cleaner because they vote. Women support reforms and candidates, and public officers are looking more carefully to their record and moral standing. The fate of the mayor and chief of police of Seattle is a fine instance of the way women will vote against moral and official corruption. We need not expect the millennium to come because of equal suffrage, but through it already changes for the better have been made in legislation and in public ideals, and the same subtle feminine influence that is felt in the home makes the home exert itself in the political life, rendering moral considerations superior to mere partisanship. 'The women of Denver have elected me, and made possible the juvenile court,' said Judge Lindsay, and we know that Democrats and Republicans united in his cause—the cause of children. But there is another and, what we might term, the indirect benefit resulting from equal suffrage. This is the influence of public life and its great responsibilities upon women themselves. In exercising the rights and duties of citizenship they read and discuss questions of real importance. Their lives widen out, they have enlarged sympathies and higher standards of life for themselves and their country. They acquire an intense wish to be of real use in the world, and they now know how to work, and are at last given the power to work with individual freedom and independence. The testimony of the most distinguished men and women is that the results of equal suffrage are good. Norway says: 'Nothing but good, nothing but purity has come from suffrage.' New Zealand says: 'If again brought to the question, not two men would be found to oppose.' The same witness comes from all the lands beyond the seas, while in our country the distinguished Judge Ben Lindsay says: 'We have in Colorado the most advanced laws of any state in the Union for the care and protection of the home and the children. I believe I voice the general impression when I say we owe this condition more to woman suffrage than to any other cause. The results of woman suffrage have been so altogether satisfactory that it is hard to understand how it encounters opposition in other states. I never heard a criticism directed against woman suffrage that ever worked out in practice, or, if it did, was not equally applicable to male suffrage.' As briefly as may be I would like to base on these facts an appeal for votes for women. I say nothing of the right to vote. That is a self-evident truth. One writer says: 'All powers of government are either delegated or assumed, and all assumed powers are usurpations.' Since women never gave men such powers they are usurpations; they are tyranny. Taxation without representation is another form of oppression. Why is it tyranny for men and not for women? Why should women, the mothers who bear and care for and train the children, teachers who give education and noble purpose in life, business women who work hard to support themselves and others dependent on them, why should these find themselves legal nonentities? Women are under the laws, governed and punished by them, let them have a voice in the legislation. The ballot will take them out of the company of idiots and convicts, and make them the equals of husbands and sons. It will bring equal pay for equal work, give the women the power to work for the conservation of children, the best asset of the state. These are vital questions, with which women are peculiarly fitted to deal. Men lose, the world loses, if opposition to equal suffrage prevents the intelligent co-operation of the sexes. Lincoln says: 'No man is good enough to govern another without the other's consent.' Certainly no man or body of men is good enough to arbitrarily make laws that, without their consent, control the other class of human beings known as women. Roosevelt says: 'Our nation is that one among all the nations of the earth, which holds in its hand the fate of the coming years.' Oh, men, for sixty-two years we have sought from you our right to stand by your side in helping to make our country the greatest, the best governed in the world. We have asked for bread, and you have given us a stone. We have asked for justice, and you prate of chivalry and generosity. Cease to praise us like angels and disfranchise us like idiots. Oh, women! let us combine our forces and join the great movement that alone will give us real power, that will bind all women into one solid phalanx, and make it one of the most impressive and irresistible forces of the present day."

History of Woman's Suffrage Organization.

HARRIET TAYLOR UPTON.

It is seldom that there is a time when a single reform question alone is before the people. There are often many, and it is not until the agitation is over and the question settled that we realize they were all a part of a great whole.

Women, as well as men, were interested in the questions which led up to the war. Northern women took part in the agitation for the abolition of slavery and were among the best and most convincing speakers.

The name of Abby Kelly Foster was known throughout the North, as was that of Lucretia Mott. It was but natural when the World's Abolition Convention was called in London in 1840 that women should be elected delegates to that body. Lucretia Mott, a Quaker preacher of refinement, culture, brain power and influence, was one of these delegates. Henry Stanton, another delegate, had brought with him his bride, Elizabeth Cady, and as these two, with the other women, repaired to the gallery, and there listened to the debates on the question in which they were so vitally interested, they grew more and more incensed each day.

William Lloyd Garrison, probably the most powerful man of the Abolition movement, was delayed in transit, and when he arrived and found that the women delegates had been denied seats he refused to take his place on the floor. He knew the part they had played in the abolition cause, and he believed in justice and equality for all human beings, women as well as slaves.

The action of the men delegates showed clearly to Mrs. Mott and Mrs. Stanton the place the world set apart for them, and they resolved that, upon their return to America, they would make a public demand for the proper recognition of women.

There were then no such easy ways of traveling or communication as there are now. Mrs. Mott's attention was still on the slave, and Mrs. Stanton's on her little family, whose members came close together, and it was not till eight years later, in 1848, that they carried out their determination and called the first woman's rights convention at Seneca Falls, Mrs. Stanton's home. This convention, as is generally supposed, was not called for the consideration of political rights. In fact, at that time it was the least thought of, personal rights, property rights, religious rights were demanded. In fact, there was much opposition to including political rights, and but for Elizabeth Cady Stanton that clause would have been left out.

The storm of ridicule which burst forth as soon as these reports were issued by the press frightened many of the women, but a few held fast. To their bravery, foresight and conviction is due the fact that to-day women vote in Wyoming, Colorado, Utah, Idaho and Washington upon exactly the same terms as men vote. They vote for all officers, from the lowest to the president, and can hold any office to which they can be elected.

Susan B. Anthony did not attend that convention; in fact, she rather doubted the wisdom of calling it. However, she seldom missed another throughout her long life, her last being at Baltimore in 1906. During all those years she gave her life to the political enfranchisement of women. In the early days, Mrs. Stanton not being able to leave her family, Miss Anthony would go to her home, help with the work and the care of her babies, while she wrote an argument suitable for the legislators, and then, armed with this, Miss Anthony would appear before that legislature and make her demands. In this way these two women caused to be changed most of the old New York laws under which women were not much more than chattels.

The friendship between Mrs. Stanton and Miss Anthony was one of the most beautiful, strongest and purest of which history writes. Together they worked for a great cause with perfect love and understanding for nearly fifty years. They supplemented each other, and their joint work was powerful.

A little later than the 1848 convention Lucy Stone, a gentle, strong, able, conscientious woman, who had completed a course of study at Oberlin, began to agitate the question of woman's rights, and it was under her direction that a convention was called in March, 1850. Lucy Stone was not at all like Mrs. Stanton in character, except they were both radicals, but Lucy Stone exercised more influence among progressive women of New England than any woman of her time. Their memory is still greatly cherished. These two women, together with Miss Anthony, were the real leaders of the women suffragists, and this trinity is the one which married women should remember, since through them they procured their property rights. To these women should the 6,000,000 working women turn with thankful hearts, since they were the first to demand equal pay for equal work.

Susan B. Anthony was the best known of the three; in fact, she was the figure of her century. Born of well-to-do parents, well educated, capable, loving and charitable to a fault, optimistic and generous, self-effacing, of undoubted will, she saw only a sex in a position in which it could not develop itself, and she fought for its freedom. No one woman had as many friends as she had, because no one woman had ever loved so many people as she had. She was not an orator in its common sense, and yet probably she, in her lifetime, addressed more people than any other American woman. She was at ease with the lowest and the highest, and worked for fifty years without salary, that the women of the United States might have a weapon to fight their own battle. She was the greatest woman of them all.

Delegates to the World's Abolition Convention in 1840:

Lucretia Mott	Mary Grew
Sarah Pugh	Ann Green Phillips
Abby Kimber	Emily Winslow
Elizabeth Neal	Abby Southwick

Prominent Suffragists.

The biography of every officer, great or small, in the nation's army would be a prodigious task, but hardly less is that of giving in detail the work of every American woman actively interested in reform movements. It would take volumes to give at length the work of all the women now interested in the enfranchisement of women and in the temperance field. There was a time in our history when the question of women's suffrage, unless it threatened the immediate community in which we lived, was a matter to which the majority of us in America, whether men or women, were, if not indifferent, still somewhat neutral. Now, I think it would be safe to say the majority have the most ardent convictions *pro et contra.* It is, therefore, with such deep regret that I find it possible to offer at length only the biographies of the pronounced leaders in suffrage and temperance, that I have appended merely a roll-call of notable names. Even this, I fear, can only approximate the number of women dedicating their lives to the work of their sex.

Among those who have done distinguished work for suffrage we find such names as these:

Mrs. Jean Brooks Greenleaf, successor to Lillie Devereux Blake as president of the New York State Woman Suffrage Association.

Mrs. Elizabeth Boynton Barbert, who succeeded in inducing the Republicans of Iowa to put into their state platform a purely women's plank, thus being the first woman to design a women's plank and secure its adoption by a great political party in a great state.

Mrs. Rebecca N. Hazard, who, as early as 1867, formed the Woman Suffrage Association of Missouri.

Mrs. Eliza Trask Hill, one of the active leaders in the

battle for school suffrage for women in Massachusetts, and later editor of a paper, which is cared for by a stock company of women.

Mrs. Mary Emma Holmes, the earnest and brilliant worker who represented the National American Suffrage Association in the World's Fair at Chicago in 1893.

Mrs. Mary Seymour Howell, who has lectured in behalf of women's suffrage in many of the towns and cities of the North and West, as well as repeatedly pleaded the cause of woman before committees of state legislatures and of Congress.

Mrs. Josephine Kirby Williamson Henry, who has lectured and labored and stood for office in a state where the popular prejudice is against "Women's Rights."

Mrs. Sarah Gibson Humphreys, of Louisiana and Kentucky, who has served on a board of road directors, a unique position for a woman in the South, and has worked all her public life to secure the vote for women.

Mrs. Jane Amy McKinney, who, as president of the Cook County Equal Suffrage Association, effectively furthered the cause in Illinois.

Mrs. Theresa A. Jenkins, daughter of one of the pioneers of Wisconsin, herself became a pioneer as a champion of suffrage in the literary field over that portion of the country, and even farther West. In April, 1889, she contributed to the "Popular Science Monthly" a striking paper, entitled "The Mental Force of Women." She became Wyoming correspondent of the *Women's Tribune,* the *Union Signal* and the Omaha *Central West.* She was a recognized power in Wyoming in bringing about the absolute recognition of the equality of the sexes before the law.

Mrs. Laura M. Johns, of Kansas, was six times president of the State Suffrage Association in that state, and her great work was the arrangement of thirty conventions beginning in

Kansas City in February, 1892, and held in various other important cities of the state, and for these meetings she secured such speakers as Rev. Anna H. Shaw, Mrs. Clara H. Hoffman, etc.

Mrs. Cora Scott Pond Pope was invited by Mrs. Lucy Stone to help organize the state of Massachusetts for women suffrage, and continued the work, organizing eighty-seven women suffrage leagues, arranging lectures, speaking in the meeting, and raising the money to carry on the state work for six years. In 1887 she organized a Woman Suffrage Bazaar, which was held in the Music Hall in Boston for one week, and which cleared over six thousand dollars. In 1889 she originated the National Pageant, a dramatic arrangement of historic events, to raise more money for state work for suffrage. This pageant, given in Hollis Street Theatre, May 9, 1889, played to a crowded house, at two dollars a ticket, and over one thousand dollars was cleared at a single matinee performance. Afterwards it was produced in other large cities of the country with equal success. In the Chicago Auditorium, at the time of the Exposition, in one night six thousand, two hundred and fifty dollars was cleared.

Mrs. Lizzie B. Read dedicated her marked ability as a journalist to the suffrage cause, becoming publisher of a semi-monthly journal called the "Mayflower," and devoted to temperance and equal rights. She worked up for this paper a subscription list reaching into all the states and territories. Later, when her marriage to Dr. Read had taken her to Algeria, Iowa, she published the paper *Upper Des Moines,* into which she infused much of women's rights. She also published a series of articles on the status of women in the Methodist Church, and later became associate editor of the *Women's Standard,* of Des Moines. While residing in Indiana she was vice-president of the State Women's Suffrage Society and president of the Iowa State Society.

Mrs. Marrilla M. Ricker's success at the bar and as a political writer has demonstrated so conclusively the intellectual quality of women that her advocacy of female suffrage has influenced as only a concrete object lesson can.

Mrs. Martha Parmelee Rose's writings on the sewing women and on other laboring questions brought to light the frauds and extortions practised upon her sex without the vote.

Mrs. Elizabeth Lyle Saxon, of New Orleans, has literally spent her lifetime carrying out a promise made to her father on his deathbed, "Never to cease working for unfortunate women so long as her life should last." For years she has been in demand as a lecturer on universal suffrage, temperance, social purity and kindred subjects. Her keen, logical and yet impassioned style of oratory fairly takes her audiences by storm, and has won for her a national reputation as a public speaker. Her great work, however, has always been for the most degraded and downtrodden of her sex.

Mrs. Rosa L. Segur, though born in Hesse, Germany, came to the United States when a child, and when quite young began contributing stories and sketches to the Toledo *Blade,* always expressing herself a staunch supporter of movements in favor of women's suffrage. To her belongs much of the credit for obtaining the repeal of obnoxious laws in regard to the status of women in the state of Ohio.

Mrs. Mary Barr Clay is the daughter of Cassius M. Clay, a noted advocate for freedom and the emancipation of the slave in a slave state. Through her sympathy with his views, his daughter gained the independence of thought and action necessary to espouse the cause of women's political and civic freedom in that same conservative community.

Mrs. Estelle Terrell Smith's famous "Mothers' Mass Meetings," held in the large city hall in Des Moines, have accomplished much good, especially in banishing from her city disreputable posters, cigarettes, cards and other evils. Through those meetings a bill regulating the property rights of women was drafted and presented to the state legislature.

Mrs. Cornelia Dean Shaw is a woman alert in all the movements of the enfranchisement of women, and a tower of strength to the Woman Suffrage Association in Ohio and Illinois.

Miss Mary Crew has preached the rights and equality of women from her pulpit in the Unitarian Church, since in that church there is no distinction based on sex.

Mrs. Adeline Morrison Swain, of Iowa, was, for her prominence in the women's suffrage cause in 1883, unanimously nominated by the Iowa State Convention of the Greenback party for the office of superintendent of public instruction. Being one of the first women so named on an Iowa state ticket, she received the full vote of the party. In 1884 she was appointed a delegate, and attended the national convention of the same party, held in Indianapolis, Ind., to nominate candidates for president and vice-president. Mrs. Swain was, moreover, for many years editor of the *Woman's Tribune.*

Mrs. Minnie Terrell Todd is one of Nebraska's staunchest woman suffragists, is also a member of the State Board of Charities, and prominent in every reformative and progressive movement.

Mrs. Anna C. Wait is editor of the *Beacon,* a reform paper started by her in Lincoln, Kan., in 1880, and every page is devoted to prohibition, woman's suffrage and anti-monopoly. To her more than to any other person does the cause of woman's enfranchisement owe its planting and growth in Kansas.

Mrs. Caroline McCullough Everhard is a public-spirited daughter of Ohio, who proved herself well equipped for the office of president of the Ohio Women's Suffrage Association. She had the honor of organizing the Equal Rights Association of Canton, Ohio, the home of the martyred President McKinley.

Mrs. Ellen Sulley Fray is an adopted daughter of the United States who, after marriage had brought her to America, formed suffrage clubs in several different states and in Canada, and became one of the district presidents of the Ohio Women's Suffrage Association.

Mrs. Miriam Howard Du Boise wrote brilliant arguments arguing for the cause while vice-president for the Georgia Women's Suffrage Association.

Mrs. Martha E. Sewell Curtis, descended from Chief Justice Samuel Sewell, of witchcraft fame and, on the mother's side, from Henry Dunster, first president of Harvard College, has delivered brilliant lectures at the meetings of the Women's National Suffrage Association in Boston, proving her worthy of her distinguished ancestors. For years she edited a weekly woman's column in the *News,* of Woburn, Mass., and was president of the Woburn Equal Suffrage League.

Mrs. Emma Smith Devoe distinguished herself in a brave fight for suffrage in South Dakota, making her home in Huron headquarters of the workers throughout the state.

Mrs. Priscilla Holmes Drake, a lifelong friend of Lucretia Mott, worked with Robert Dale Owen during the Indiana Constitutional Convention of 1850-57 to remove the legal disabilities of women, and before the sections of this instrument, which worked such benefit to women, were presented to the Assembly, they were discussed line by line in Mrs. Drake's parlor.

Mrs. Eleanore Munroe Babcock is well known throughout the East for her work in organizing in New York State.

Mrs. Emma Curtis Bascom, descendant of Miles Standish, is a charter member of the association for the advancement of women in Massachusetts, and for many years was one of its board of officers. When her husband, a professor at Williams

College, was deprived of the use of his eyes during a long period, she shared his studies and rendered him every assistance in reading and writing. This training she has found of great advantage in her work for women suffrage in her state.

Mrs. Emma Beckwith was a candidate for the mayoralty of Brooklyn. The campaign, of ten days' duration, resulted in her receiving fifty votes, regularly counted, and many more thrown out among the scattering, before the *New York Tribune* made a demand for the statement of her vote. Mrs. Beckwith afterwards compiled many incidents relating to that novel campaign in a lecture, which she used with telling effect from the suffrage platform.

Mrs. Marietta Bones, daughter of the noted Abolitionist, succeeded in making the social question of temperance a political question in Dakota.

A further roll-call of noted women suffragists includes the names of Mrs. Adelaide Avery Clafflin, Mrs. Electa Noble Lincoln Walton, Mrs. Frances Dana Gage and Miss Matilda Josslyn Gage.

LUCY STONE.

Of Lucy Stone, Mrs. Stanton says: "She was the first speaker who really stirred the nation's heart on the subject of woman's wrongs. Young, magnetic, eloquent, her soul filled with the new idea, she drew immense audiences, and was eulogized everywhere. She spoke extemporaneously." Her birthplace was West Brookfield, Mass., and she was born August 13, 1818. The family came honestly by good fighting blood, her great-grandfather having been killed in the French and Indian War and her grandfather having served in the War of the Revolution and afterwards was captain of four hundred men in Shays' Rebellion. Her father, Frances Stone, was a prosperous farmer and a man of great energy, much respected by his neighbors, and not intentionally unkind or unjust, but full of that belief in the right of men to rule, which was general in those days, and ruling his own family with a strong hand. Although he helped his son through college, when his daughter Lucy wished to go he said to his wife, "Is the child crazy?" and she had to earn the money herself. For years she taught district schools, teaching and studying alternately at the low wages then paid to women teachers. It took her till she was twenty-five years of age to earn the money to take her to Oberlin, then the one college in the country that admitted women. In Oberlin she earned her way by teaching during vacations, and in the preparatory department of the college, and by doing housework in the ladies' boarding hall, at three cents an hour. Most of the time she cooked her food in her own room, boarding herself at a cost of less than fifty cents a week. At her graduation we have the first hint of the stand she was to take for woman's rights. Graduating with honors, she was appointed to write a commencement essay, but finding that she would not be allowed to read it herself, but that one of the professors would have to read it for her (the young women in those days not being allowed to read their own work in public) she declined to write it. After her return to New England she discovered her ability as a speaker, and her first woman's rights lecture was given from the pulpit of her brother's church, in Gardner, Mass., in 1847. Soon after she was engaged to lecture for the Anti-Slavery Association. It was still a great novelty for a woman to speak in public, and curiosity attracted great audiences. She always put a great deal of woman's rights into her anti-slavery lectures, and finally when Powers' "Greek Slave" was on exhibition in Boston the sight of the statue moved her so strongly that in her next lecture there was so much woman's rights and so little anti-slavery that Rev. Samuel May, who arranged her lectures, said to her, "Lucy, that was beautiful, but on the anti-slavery platform it will not do." She answered, "I know it, but I was a woman before I was an Abolitionist, and I must speak for the women." Accordingly, it was arranged that she should lecture for woman's rights on her own responsibility all the week and should lecture for the anti-slavery society on Saturday and Sunday nights. Her adventures during the next few years would fill a volume. She arranged her own meetings, putting her own handbills up with a little package of tacks which she carried and a stone, picked up in the street. Of course, woman's rights was still considered a subject for ridicule when not the object of violent attack. One minister in Malden, Mass., being asked to give a notice of her meeting, did so, as follows: "I am asked to give notice that a hen will attempt to crow like a cock in the town hall at five o'clock to-morrow evening. Those who like such music will, of course, attend." At a meeting in Connecticut one cold night a pane of glass was removed from the church window and a hose inserted and Miss Stone was suddenly deluged from head to foot. She wrapped a shawl about her, however, and went on with her lecture. At an open air meeting in a grove on Cape Cod, where there were a number of speakers, the mob gathered with such threatening demonstration that all the speakers slipped away, till no one was left on the platform but Miss Stone and Stephen Foster. She said to him, "You had better go, Stephen, they are coming."

He answered, "Who will take care of you?" At that moment the mob made a rush and one of the ringleaders, a big man with a club, sprang up on the platform. Turning to him without a sign of fear she remarked in her sweet voice, "This gentleman will take care of me." And to the utter astonishment of the angry throng he tucked her under one arm and holding his club with the other, marched her through the crowd. He then mounted her upon a stump and stood by her with his club while she addressed the mob upon the enormity of their attack. They finally became so ashamed that, at her suggestion, they took up a collection of twenty dollars to pay Stephen Foster for his coat, which they had rent from top to bottom.

In 1855 she became the wife of Henry B. Blackwell, Thomas Wentworth Higginson, then the Unitarian Pastor, performing the ceremony. She had protested against the marriage, particularly the taking of the husband's name by the wife as a symbol of her subjection to him and of the merging of her individuality in his, and as Ellis Gay Loring, Samuel E. Sewell and other eminent lawyers told her that there was no law requiring a wife to take her husband's name she retained her own name with her husband's full approval and support.

In 1869, with William Lloyd Garrison, George William Curtis, Julia Ward Howe, Mrs. Livermore and others, she organized the American Woman Suffrage Association and was chairman of its executive committee during the twenty years following, except during one year when she was its president. She took part in the campaigns in behalf of Woman Suffrage Amendments, submitted in Kansas in 1867, in Vermont in 1870, in Colorado in 1877 and in Nebraska in 1882. For over twenty years she was editor of the *Woman's Journal.* The following eloquent appeal from her faithful, fearless pen, appearing in that magazine during the presidential activities of Centennial Year, gives a characteristic glimpse of her ardor for woman's rights. "Women of the United States, never forget that you are excluded by law from participation in the great question which at this moment agitates the whole country —a question which is not only who the next candidate for president will be, but what shall be the policy of the government under which we live for the next four years. . . . But have you ever thought that the dog on your rug and the cat in your corner has as much political power as you have? Never forget it, and when the country is shaken, as it will be for months to come, over the issue, never forget that this law-making power states every interest of yours. It states your rules to a right in your child. You earn or inherit a dollar and this same power decides how much of it shall be yours and how much it will take or dispose of for its own use. Oh, woman, the only subjugated one in this great country, will you be the only adult people who are ruled over! Pray for fire to reveal to you the humiliation of the unspeakable laws which come of your unequal position." Lucy Stone died in Dorchester, Mass., the 18th of October, 1893.

ELIZABETH CADY STANTON.

Mrs. Elizabeth Cady Stanton was the daughter of Judge Daniel Cady, and Margaret Livingston Cady, and was born November 12, 1816, in Johnstown, New York, not far from Albany. A noted Yankee once said that his chief ambition was to become more noted than his native town. Whether this was Mrs. Stanton's ambition or not, she has lived to see her historic birthplace shrink into mere local repute while she herself has been quoted, ridiculed, abused and extolled into national fame.

She took the course in the academy in Johnstown and then went to Mrs. Emma Willard's Seminary in Troy, New York, where she was graduated in 1832. In the office of her father, Mrs. Stanton first became acquainted with the legal disabilities of women under the old common law, and she early learned to rebel against the inequity of law, which seemed to her made only for men. When really a child she even went so far as to hunt up unjust laws with the aid of the students in her father's office and was preparing to cut the obnoxious clauses out of the books supposing that that would put an end to them, when she was informed that the abolition of inequitable laws could not be thus simply achieved. But she devoted the rest of her life in an effort toward the practical solution of women's rights. She has said that her life in this village seminary was made dreary in her disappointment and sorrow in not being a boy, and her chagrin was great when she found herself unable to enter Union College, where her brother was graduated just before his death.

In 1837, in her twenty-fourth year, while on a visit to her distinguished cousin, Gerrit Smith, at Peterboro, in the central part of New York State, she made the acquaintance of Henry Brewster Stanton, a fervid young orator, who had won distinction in the anti-slavery movement, and in 1840 they were married. They immediately set sail for Europe, the voyage, however, being undertaken not merely for pleasure and sightseeing, but that Mr. Stanton might fulfill the mission of delegate to the World's Anti-Slavery Convention, to be held in London, in 1840.

There Mrs. Stanton met Lucretia Mott and learned that there were others who felt the yoke women were bearing as well as herself. It was with Mrs. Mott that she signed the first call for a woman's rights convention and when she was once asked, "What most impressed you in Europe?" she replied, "Lucretia Mott." Their friendship never waned, and they worked together for reform all the long years after that meeting.

Mrs. Stanton and her husband removed to Seneca Falls, N. Y., and it was in that town, on the 19th and 20th of July, 1848, in the Wesleyan Chapel that the first assemblage known to history as a woman's rights convention was held. Mrs. Stanton was the chief agent in calling that convention. She received and cared for the visitors; she wrote the resolutions of declaration and aims, and she had the satisfaction of know-ing that the convention, ridiculed throughout the Union, was the starting point of the woman's rights movement, which is now no longer a subject of ridicule. Judge Cady, hearing that his daughter was the author of the audacious resolution, "That it is the duty of the women of this country to secure for them-selves their sacred right to the elective franchise," imagined that she had gone crazy, and he journeyed from Johnstown to Seneca Falls, to learn whether or not her brilliant mind had lost its balance. He tried to reason her out of her position but she remained unshaken in her faith that her position was right.

The practice of going before a legislature to present the claim of woman's cause has become quite common, but in the early days of Mrs. Stanton's career it was considered unusual and sensational. And yet, with the single exception of Mrs. Lucy Stone, a noble and gifted woman, to whom her country-women owe affectionate gratitude, not merely for eloquence that charmed thousands of ears, but for her practical efforts in abolishing laws oppressive to her sex, I believe that Mrs. Stan-ton appeared oftener before state legislatures than any of her co-laborers. She repeatedly addressed the legislature of New York at Albany and on these occasions was always honored by the presence of a brilliant audience, and never failed to speak with dignity and ability. In 1854, when she first addressed the New York legislature on the rights of married women, she said, "Yes, gentlemen, we the daughters of the Revolutionary heroes of '76, demand at your hands the redress of our grievances, a revision of your state constitution and a new code of laws." At the close of her grand and glowing argument, a lawyer who had listened to it and who knew and revered Mrs. Stanton's father, shook hands with the orator and said, "Madam, it was as fine a production as if it had been made and pronounced by Judge Cady, himself." This, to the daughter's ears, was sufficiently high praise.

In 1867 she spoke before the legislature and Constitutional Convention of New York, maintaining that during the revision of its constitution the state was resolved into its original elements and that citizens of both sexes therefore had a right to vote for members of the convention. In Kansas, in 1867, and Michigan, in 1874, when those states were submitting the woman suffrage question to the people, she canvassed the state and did heroic work in the cause. From 1855 to 1865 she served as president of the national committee of the suffrage party. In 1863 she was president of the Woman's Loyal League. Until 1890 she was president of the National Woman's Suffrage Association. In 1868 she was a candidate for Congress in eighth congressional district of New York and in her address to the electors of the district she announced her creed to be: "Free speech, free press, free men and free trade." In 1868, the *Revolution* was started in New York City and Mrs. Stanton became the editor, assisted by Parker Pillsbury. She is joint author with Miss Susan B. Anthony of the "History of Woman Suffrage."

Religious and worshipful by temperament, she cast off in her later life the superstition of her earlier, but she never lost her childhood's faith in good, and her last work was the "Woman's Bible," a unique revision of the Scriptures from the standpoint of women's recognition. She is said to have declared that she would willingly give her body to be burned for the sake of seeing her sex enfranchised, and when this desire of her heart is gratified, her name will be gratefully remembered by those who fought for the emancipation of womankind.

Mrs. Stanton died in New York, October 26, 1902. Her family consists of five sons and two daughters, all of whom are gifted.

SUSAN B. ANTHONY.

Susan B. Anthony, according to Mrs. Stanton, was born at the foot of the Green Mountains, South Adams, Massachusetts, February 15, 1820. Her father, Daniel Anthony, was a stern Quaker; her mother, Lucy Read, a Baptist, but being liberal and progressive in their tendency they were soon one in their religion. In girlhood years Miss Anthony attended Quaker meetings with aspirations toward high-seat dignity, but this was modified by the severe treatment accorded the father, who, having been publicly reprimanded twice, the first time for marrying a Baptist, the second for wearing a comfortable coat with a large cape, was finally expelled from "meeting" because he allowed the use of one of his rooms for the instruction of a class in dancing, in order that the youth might not be subjected to the temptations of a liquor-selling public house.

Miss Anthony's father was a cotton manufacturer, and the first dollar she ever earned was in his factory, for, though a man of wealth, the idea of self-support was early impressed on all the daughters of the family. Later, after their removal to Rochester, she became a teacher and fifteen years of her life were passed in teaching school in different parts of the state of New York. Although superintendents gave her credit for the best disciplined schools and the most thoroughly taught scholars in the county, yet they paid her eight dollars a month, while men received from twenty-four to thirty dollars. After fifteen years of great labor and the closest economy she had saved but three hundred dollars. This experience taught her the   woman's rights. She became an active member   York State Teachers' Association and in their   made many effective pleas for higher wages   cognition of the principle of equal rights for women in all the honors and responsibilities of the association. The women teachers from Maine to Oregon owe Miss Anthony a debt of gratitude for the improved conditions they hold to-day.

Miss Anthony had been from a child deeply interested in the subject of temperance. In 1847, she joined the Daughters of Temperance, and in 1852 organized the New York State Women's Temperance Association, the first open temperance organization of women. Of this Mrs. Elizabeth Cady Stanton was president. As secretary, Miss Anthony for several years gave her earnest efforts to the temperance cause, but she soon saw that woman was utterly powerless to change conditions without the ballot and from 1852 she became one of the leading spirits in every women's rights convention, and was acting secretary and general agent for the suffrage organization for many years. She left others to remedy individual wrongs while she devoted herself to working for the weapon by which she believed women might be able to do away with the producing causes. She used to say she had "no time to dip out vice with a teaspoon, while the wrongly adjusted forces of society are pouring it in by the bucketful." From 1857 to 1866 Miss Anthony was also an agent and faithful worker in the anti-slavery cause. She has, moreover, been untiring in her efforts to secure liberal legislation, now enjoyed by the women in the state of New York.

The most harassing, though probably the most satisfactory, enterprise Miss Anthony ever undertook was the publication for three years of a weekly paper, *The Revolution*. This formed an epoch in the woman's rights movement and roused widespread interest in the question. Ably edited by Elizabeth Cady Stanton and Parker Pillsbury, with the finest intellects of the nation among its contributors, and rising immediately to a recognized position among the papers of the nation, there was no reason why it should not have been a financial success, save that Miss

Anthony's duties kept her almost entirely from the lecture field. After three years of toil and worry, and the accumulation of a debt of ten thousand dollars, Miss Anthony set bravely about the task of earning money to pay the debt. Every cent of this was duly met from the earnings of her lectures.

The most dramatic event of Miss Anthony's life was her arrest and trial for voting at the presidential election of 1872. Owing to the mistaken advice of her counsel, who was unwilling that she should be imprisoned, she gave bonds which prevented her taking her case to the Supreme Court, a fact she always regretted. When asked by the judge, "You voted as a woman did you not?" She replied, "No sir, I voted as a citizen of the United States." The date and place of trial being set, Miss Anthony thoroughly canvassed her county so as to make sure that all of the jurors were instructed in citizens' rights. And yet, at the trial, after the argument had been presented, the judge took the case out of their hands, saying, "It is a question of law and not of fact," and he pronounced Miss Anthony guilty, fining her a hundred dollars and costs. She said to the judge, "Resistance to tyranny is obedience to God, and I shall never pay a penny of this unjust claim," and she gloried in the fact that she never did.

Miss Anthony was always in great demand on the platform, and she had probably lectured in every city that can be marked. She made constitutional arguments before Congressional Committees, and spoke impromptu to assemblies in all sorts of places. Whether it was a good word in introducing a speaker, or a short speech to awaken a convention, or the closing appeal to set people to work, or, again, the full hour address of argument or helpful talk at suffrage meetings she always said just the right thing and never wearied her audience. A fine sense of humor pervaded her arguments, and often by *reductio ad absurdum* she disarmed and won her opponents.

Moreover, a wonderful memory which carried the legislative history of each state, the formation and progress of political parties, the parts played by prominent men in our national life, and whatever has been done the world over to ameliorate conditions for women, made Miss Anthony a genial and instructive companion while her unfailing sympathy made her as good a listener as talker. The change in public sentiment toward woman suffrage was well indicated by the change which came in the popular estimate of Miss Anthony. Where once it was the fashion of the press to ridicule and jeer it came to pass that the best men on the papers were sent to interview her. Society, too, threw open its doors, and into many distinguished gatherings she carried the refreshing breadth of sincerity and earnestness. Her seventieth birthday, celebrated by the National Woman's Suffrage Association, of which she was vice-president at large, from its formation in 1869 until its convention in 1892, when she was elected president, was the occasion of a spontaneous outburst of gratitude, which is without any doubt unparalleled in the history of any living woman. Miss Anthony is truly one of the most heroic figures in American History, and her death in 1906 was the occasion of national sorrow.

ISABELLA BEECHER HOOKER.

Mrs. Isabella Beecher Hooker was the first child of the second wife of Doctor Lyman Beecher, the illustrious preacher of New England, and was born February 22, 1822, at Litchfield, Connecticut.

Individually and collectively, the Beecher family is considered the most remarkable in the United States, each member of it having been the possessor of a commanding talent, great energy and force of character and great gifts of the highest order. Isabella Beecher inherited her personal beauty from her mother and her great individuality came to her from her father. She married John Hooker, of Hartford, Connecticut, in 1841, and he was a descendant in the sixth generation of Thomas Hooker who founded the city of Hartford. He was a man of note in his day, a famous theologian, earnest patriot and an enlightened statesman. Mrs. Hooker kept pace intellectually with her husband, accompanying him in his theological researches and speculations, learning from him much of his profession and making a study of the phases and evolution of the law that governed the United States. She thus became an earnest and profound student of social, political, and religious questions, and when she adopted the idea that women should be allowed to vote as a fundamental right she at once, in characteristic style, began to do all she could to bring about the great reform. She considered women's suffrage the greatest movement in the world's history, claiming that the ballot would give women every social and intellectual, as well as political, advantage. She wrote and lectured, and studied and explained the doctrine of equal suffrage for women for thirty years. She was at the front of this and other reform movements, going cheerfully through the ridicule and abuse that fell to the lot of earnest agitators and reformers. During several seasons she held a series of afternoon talks in Boston, New York and Washington, and at these assemblages she discussed political economy and other topics. When well along in life she published a book entitled "Womanhood—Its Sanctities and Fidelities," which treated of the marriage relation and of the education of children to lives of purity in a courageous yet delicate way. It attracted wide attention and brought to her many earnest expressions of gratitude from intelligent mothers. For many years she held the office of vice-president for Connecticut, in the National Women's Suffrage Association, and in the yearly conventions of the organization in Washington, D. C., she delivered a number of able addresses. In the International Council of Women in 1888 in the session devoted to political conditions, she delivered an address on the "Constitutional Rights of the Women of the United States," and gave an unanswerable presentation of the subject. In 1878 she took a leading part and acted as spokesman before the committee of Congress upon a petition asking for legislation in favor of the enfranchisement of women. One of her later efforts in behalf of women was in the Republican National Convention in Chicago, where, in company with Miss Susan B. Anthony, she prepared an open letter reviewing work of women, claiming that they had earned recognition and ending with a powerful plea that the convention would include women in the term "citizens."

When Mr. and Mrs. Hooker celebrated their golden wedding on August 5, 1891, the celebration took place in City Mission Hall, in Hartford, Senator Joseph R. Hawley acting as master of ceremonies. The whole city turned out to honor the venerable couple, whose fame shed a luster on the place they called home. Many prominent persons attended the reception, the judges of the Supreme Court of Connecticut going in a body to tender their respects. The National American Women's Suffrage Association was represented by Susan B. Anthony, Mrs. Mary Seymour Howell, Mrs. Rachel Foster Avery, Miss Phebe Couzins, and many others. Mrs. Hooker's long life was one of zealous toil, heroic endurance of undeserved abuse and exalted effort. She died in 1907, but her name stands for one of the best known exponents of the claims of the women of America who desire the right to vote.

ZERELDA GRAY WALLACE.

A self-made woman in every sense of the word, was Mrs. Zerelda Gray Wallace, reformer and suffragist. She was born in Millersburg, Bourbon County,

Kentucky, August 6, 1817, the daughter of John H. Sanders and Mrs. Polly C. Gray Sanders. Her father was of South Carolina descent and her mother was of the Singleton family. She was the oldest of five daughters and received as good an education as could be had in the Blue Grass region schools of those early days. At a sale of public lands in Indianapolis, then the frontier, her father purchased his homestead and after leaving Kentucky his daughters had only limited opportunities for education. Mrs. Wallace, however, assisted her father in his practice and became interested in medicine. She educated herself by reading works on hygiene, mental philosophy and other subjects, and was acquainted with many prominent men. In 1837 she became the wife of Honorable David Wallace, soldier and jurist and then lieutenant-governor of Indiana. In 1837 he was elected governor of the state and in 1840 he went to Congress as a Whig. During his term Mrs. Wallace spent some time in Washington with him, ever urging him to vote against the Fugitive Slave Law, and she shared all his reading in law, politics and literature. At the time she married, Mr. Wallace was a widower with a family of three sons, and six children were born to them. This large family Mrs. Wallace reared, carefully cultivating their particular talents and developing all their powers in every way. All her living children have succeeded in life. Her husband's children by the first wife included General Lewis Wallace, the soldier, scholar, statesman and author of the immortal "Ben Hur," and General Wallace never referred to her as "stepmother," but always as mother. She was one of the first of the women crusaders, and joined the Women's Christian Temperance Union, in which she did much valuable service. She spoke before the Indiana legislature in advocacy of temperance, and was soon after lecturing before them in favor of women's suffrage. As delegate to temperance conventions she addressed large audiences in Boston, Saratoga Springs, St.Louis, Detroit, Washington, Philadelphia and other cities. She lived to a splendid old age, her physical and intellectual powers unimpaired, and recently died in Indianapolis surrounded by her children and grandchildren.

AMELIA BLOOMER.

The ridicule of the press has often dimmed a worthy name and such seems to have been the case with Mrs. Amelia Bloomer, who was born May 27, 1818. An insignificant myth of American history lies in the supposition that Mrs. Bloomer originated the garment to which her name was attached in ridicule, but which has become one of the commonest words in the English language. Mrs. Bloomer was not the originator of the style, but adopted it after seeing it worn by others and introduced it to the public through her paper. But, be that as it may, Mrs. Bloomer's life and work is no subject for the cartoonist; she should be ranked among the foremost workers for the betterment of her sex in America. The facts of her life substantiate this. It was in 1840 that she first appeared in public life as an advocate for temperance reform. The study of that question soon led her to understand the political, legal, and financial necessities and disabilities of women, and having seen the depth of the reform needed she was not slow to espouse the cause of freedom in its highest, broadest, most just sense. At that early day no woman's voice had yet been heard from the platform pleading the rights or wrongs of her sex, so Mrs. Bloomer employed her pen to say the thoughts she could not utter. She wrote for the press over various signatures, her contributions appearing in the *Water Bucket, Temperance Star, Free Soil Union* and other papers. On the first of January, 1849, a few months after the inauguration of the first Women's Rights Convention, she began the publication of the *Lily*, a folio sheet devoted to temperance and the interests of women. That journal was a novelty in the newspaper world, being the first enterprise of the kind ever owned, edited and controlled by a woman and published in the interests of woman. It was received with marked favor by the press and continued a successful career of six years in Mrs. Bloomer's hands. In the third year of the publication of her journal Mrs. Bloomer's attention was called to the neat, convenient and comfortable, if not esthetic costume afterwards called by her name. The press handed the matter about and commented more or less on this new departure to fashion's sway until the whole country was excited over it, and Mrs. Bloomer was overwhelmed with letters of inquiry. Many women adopted the style for a time, yet under the rod of tyrant fashion and the ridicule of the press they soon laid it aside. Mrs. Bloomer herself finally abandoned it after wearing it six or eight years, but the grotesque caricature remained forever attached to her name.

In 1852 Mrs. Bloomer made her debut on the platform as a lecturer, and in the winter of that year, in company with Susan B. Anthony, she visited and lectured in all the principal cities and towns of her native state, from New York to Buffalo. At the outset her subject was temperance, but temperance strongly spiced with the wrongs and rights of women. In 1849 Mr. Bloomer was appointed postmaster of Seneca Falls, and on receipt of the office he at once appointed Mrs. Bloomer his deputy. Upholding her theory of woman's brain equality with man's she soon made herself thoroughly acquainted with the details of the office, and discharged such duties throughout the four years of the Taylor and Fillmore administration. In the winter of 1853 she was chairman of the committee appointed to go before the legislature of New York with petitions for a prohibitory liquor law, and she continued her work throughout the state, lecturing on both temperance and woman's rights and attending to the duties of her house and office until the winter of 1853-1854, when she moved to Mt. Vernon, Ohio. Here she continued the publication of the *Lily* and was also associate editor of the *Western Home Visitor* a large literary weekly paper published in that place. In the columns of *The Visitor,* as in all her writings, some phase of the woman question was always made her subject. At the same time that she was carrying on her literary work she visited and lectured in all the principal towns and cities of the North and West, going often where no lecturer on women's enfranchisement had preceded her. In January, 1854, she was one of the committee to memorialize the legislature of Ohio on a prohibitory liquor law. The rules were suspended and the committee received with mock respect and favor, but the same evening the legislature almost in a body attended a lecture given by her on women's right of suffrage. In the spring of 1855 Mr. and Mrs. Bloomer removed to Council Bluffs, Iowa, making it their permanent home. Mrs. Bloomer intended henceforth

37

to rest from her public labors, but this was not permitted to her. Calls for lectures were frequent, and to these she responded as far as possible, but was obliged to refuse to go long distances on account of there being at that day no public conveyance except the old stage coach. In the winter of 1856, Mrs. Bloomer, by invitation, addressed the legislature of Nebraska on the subject of woman's right to the ballot. The Territorial House of Representatives shortly afterwards passed a bill giving women the right to vote, and in the council it passed to a second reading, but was finally lost for want of time, the limited session drawing to a close and the last hour expiring before the bill could come up for final action. Mrs. Bloomer took part in organizing the Iowa State Suffrage Association, and was at one time its president. Poor health eventually compelled her to retire from active work in the cause. She died on the thirtieth of December, 1894.

LILLIE DEVEREUX BLAKE.

Both the parents of Mrs. Lillie Devereux Blake were descended from the Reverend Jonathan Edwards, D.D., so her inclination to reform might have been a matter of direct inheritance. But the vehicle she used for her preaching was much milder than the invectives of her distinguished ancestor. She was born in Raleigh, North Carolina, August 12, 1835, but was brought to New Haven, Connecticut, by her widowed mother that she might have every advantage of education. She took the Yale college course with tutors at home, and continued her studies until after she was married in 1855 to Frank Q. Umsted. When in 1859 he died leaving her a widow with two children she had already begun to write; one of her first stories, "A Lonely House," having appeared in the *Atlantic Monthly*. A novel, "Southwold" had also achieved its success. The large fortune she had inherited was sadly impaired and it was necessary that the young widow begin to work in earnest, writing stories, sketches and letters for several leading periodicals. In 1862 she published a second novel "Rockford" and afterwards several romances. It was not until 1869, after her second marriage to Grenfill Blake, a young merchant of New York, that she became actively interested in the women's suffrage movement. In 1872 she published a novel called "Fettered for Life," designed to show the many disadvantages under which women labor. In 1873, she made an application for the opening of Columbia College to young women, and as an argument she presented a class of qualified girl students. The agitation then begun by Mrs. Blake eventually led to the establishment of Barnard College. In 1879 she was unanimously elected president of the New York State Woman Suffrage Association, and she held that office for eleven years. She has also lectured a great deal, but being a woman of strong affection and marked domestic tastes, her speaking out of New York has been done almost wholly in the summer when her family was naturally scattered. Her lectures printed under the title of "Woman's Place To-Day," had a large sale. Among the many reforms in which she has been actively interested has been that of securing matrons to take charge of women detained in police stations. As early as 1871 Mrs. Blake spoke and wrote on this subject but it was not until 1891 that public sentiment was finally aroused to the point of passing a law enforcing this much-needed reform.

The employment of women as census-takers was first urged in 1880 by Mrs. Blake. The bills giving seats to saleswomen, ordering the presence of a woman physician in every insane asylum in which women are detained and many other beneficent measures were presented or aided by her. In 1886 Mrs. Blake was elected president of the New York City Women's Suffrage League and throughout this office she attended conventions and made speeches in most of the states and territories besides addressing committees of both houses of Congress and the New York and Connecticut legislatures.

A graceful and logical writer, witty and eloquent as a speaker, Mrs. Blake has proved herself a charming hostess, her weekly receptions through the season in New York having been for many years among the attractions of literary and reform circles.

DOCTOR MARY E. WALKER.

Because of her determination to wear male attire, Doctor Mary Walker has been made the subject of abuse and ridicule by people of narrow minds. The fact that she persists in wearing the attire in which she did a man's service in the army blinds the thoughtless to her great achievements and to her right to justice from our government. It should be remembered that she is the only woman in the world who was an assistant army surgeon; that she was the first woman officer ever exchanged as a prisoner of war for a man of her rank, and that she is the only woman who has received the Medal of Honor from Congress and a testimonial from the President of the United States.

She belongs to a family of marked mental traits and was as a child distinguished for her strength of mind and her decision of character and grew up an independent young woman, attending medical college in Syracuse, New York, and New York City. When the Civil War broke out she left her practice and went to the front and served the Union army in a way that in any other country would have caused her to be recognized as a heroine of the nation. Of all the women who participated in the scenes of the war, Doctor Walker was certainly among the most conspicuous for bravery and for self-forgetfulness. She often spent her own money and she often went where shot and shell were flying to aid the wounded soldiers. Her bravery and services in the field were rewarded by a medal of honor, and she draws a pension from the Goverment of exactly eight dollars and fifty cents a month, a half pension of her rank, in spite of the fact that she really deserves the highest recognition of the Government and the public for her patriotic services in the army.

Doctor Walker has always been prominent and active in the women's suffrage and other reform movements. She was among the first women who attempted to vote and did vote, who went to Congress in behalf of women's suffrage and who made franchise speeches in Washington. In 1866-1867 she was in Europe and directed and influenced ten thousand woman to vote in the fall of 1869, but her public activities were practically ended by an injury caused by slipping and falling, and which resulted in lameness. She retired to the old family homestead in Oswego County, New York, her last known residence.

MAY WRIGHT SEWALL.

Mrs. May Wright Sewall's life work has been founded on the conviction that all avenues of culture and usefulness should be opened to women, and that when that result is obtained the law of natural selection may safely be trusted to draw women to those employments, and only those to which they are best fitted. This is the theory she has striven to propagate in her educational work as well as on the suffrage platform.   Born in Milwaukee, Wisconsin, May 27, 1844, she is descended on both sides from old New England stock and her father, Philander Wright, was one of the early settlers of Milwaukee.   Miss Wright entered the Northwestern University in Evanston, Illinois, and was graduated in 1866.   She received the Master's Degree in 1871.   After an experience of some years in the common schools of Michigan she accepted the position of principal of the Plainwell High School and later was principal of the High School in Franklin, Indiana. From that position she was called to the Indianapolis High School as teacher of German, and subsequently engaged to work in English literature.   That was in the year 1874, and since that date she has resided in Indianapolis.   In 1880 she resigned her position in the Indianapolis High School, receiving the unprecedented compliment of a special vote of thanks for her conspicuous and successful work. In October of the same year she became the wife of Theodore L. Sewall and Mr. and Mrs. Sewall opened a classical school for girls making the course identical with the requirements of the Harvard entrance examinations   A private school for girls, which made Latin, Greek and mathematics through trigonometry a part of its regular course, was then a novelty in the West, but the immediate success of this girls' school showed that the public was quick to appreciate thorough work in the education of girls.   This school established by Mr. and Mrs. Sewall now has an annual enrollment of several hundred pupils.   In spite of all her public work for suffrage and civic welfare Mrs. Sewall continues to give much time to the details of supervising her school.   The girls in the school are taught to dress plainly and comfortably, to which end they wear a school uniform, and above all they are encouraged to believe that all departments of knowledge are worthy of their attention and of right ought to be open to them.

About the time of her removal to Indianapolis, Mrs. Sewall became prominent in various lines of women's work.   She soon became known as a lecturer and as a delegate to conventions called to the interest of higher education of women and the promotion of the cause of women's equality before the law.   She edited for two years a women's column in the Indianapolis *Times,* and she has written largely in the line of newspaper correspondence.   She is the author of the Indiana chapter in the "History of Women's Suffrage," edited by Miss Anthony, Mrs. Stanton and Mrs. Gage, and of the "Report on Women's Industries in Indiana," "Work of Women in Education in the Western States" and of many slighter essays.   Her first public appearance in the reform work outside of local letters was as a delegate from the Indianapolis Equal Suffrage Society to the Jubilee Convention in Rochester, New York, in 1878.   Since that time she has been one of the mainstays of the cause of women's advancement and has enjoyed the fullest confidence and unqualified support of its leaders.   She has delivered addresses before most of the suffrage organizations all over the country and also before committees of the Indiana legislature, committees of the United States Senate, and the National Teachers' Association. In 1889 Mrs. Sewall was the delegate from the National Women's Suffrage Association and from the Women's National Council of the United States to the International Congress of Women assembled in Paris by the French Government in connection with the Exposition Universelle. In that congress she responded for America when the roll of nations was called and later in the session gave one of the principal addresses, her subject being, "The National Women's Council of the United States." Her response for America, which was delivered in French, was highly praised for its aptness and eloquence, by M. Jules Simon, who presided over the session.

Mrs. Sewall's writings and addresses are characterized by directness, simplicity and strength. Her extemporaneous addresses are marked by the same closeness of reasoning, clearness, and power as her written speeches and they display a never-failing tact. She is conspicuously successful also as a presiding officer, a position in which she has had a long and varied experience.

THE REVEREND ANNA H. SHAW.

Mrs. Anna H. Shaw was born in New Castle-on-Tyne, England, on the fourteenth of February, 1847. Her descent is interesting as illustrating the force of heredity. Her grandmother refused to pay tithes to the Church of England and year after year allowed her goods to be seized and sold for taxes. She sat in the door knitting and denouncing the law while the sale went on in the street. Her granddaughter evidently inherited from that heroic ancestor her sense of the injustice of taxation without representation. Mrs. Shaw's parents came to America when she was four years old, and after living four years in Massachusetts they moved to the then unsettled part of Michigan where the young girl encountered all the hardships of pioneer life. She was, however, a child of strong individuality and those pioneer days were an inspiration to her. She may be said to have been self-educated, for her schooling consisted in making herself master of every book and paper that fell in her way. At fifteen years of age she began to teach, remaining a teacher for five years. When about twenty-four years old, despite her descent from a family of English Unitarians, she became a convert to Methodism and joined the Methodist Church. Her ability as a speaker was soon recognized, and in 1873 the District Conference of the Methodist Church in her locality voted unanimously to grant her a local preacher's license. This was renewed annually for eight years. In 1872 she had entered Albion College, Michigan, and in 1875 she entered the theological department of the Boston University, from which she graduated with honor in 1878. She worked her way through college and while in the theological school she was constantly worn with hard work, studying on weekdays and preaching on Sundays. At length when her health was becoming seriously impaired a philanthropic woman offered to pay her the price of a sermon every Sunday during the remainder of her second year if she would omit the preaching and take the day for rest. That help was accepted and afterwards when Miss Shaw was earning a salary and wished to return the money she was bidden to pass it on to aid in the education of some other struggling girl, which she did. She often says that when she was preaching those Sundays while in college she never knew whether she would be paid with a bouquet or a greenback. After graduation she became pastor of a church in East Dennis, on Cape Cod, where she remained seven years. She had been asked there merely to supply their pulpit until they secured a regular minister, but they were so well satisfied that they made no further effort to obtain a pastor and for six years she preached twice every Sunday in her own church in the morning, and in the afternoon in the Congregational Church. During her pastorate in East Dennis she applied to the New England Methodist Episcopal Conference for ordination, but though she passed the best examination of any candidate that year, ordination was refused her on account of her sex. The case was appealed to the general conference in Cincinnati in 1880 and the refusal was confirmed. Miss Shaw then applied for ordination to the Methodist Protestant Church and received it on the twelfth of October, 1880, being the first woman to be ordained in that denomination. But her remarkable mind was never satisfied, and she sought still further to break down the limitations sex had placed upon her, so she supplemented her theological course with one in medicine and receiving the degree of M.D., from the Boston University. But becoming more and more interested in practical reform she finally resigned her position in East Dennis and became a lecturer for the Massachusetts Woman Suffrage Association.

After entering the general lecture field and becoming widely and favorably known as an elegant speaker on reform topics, she was appointed national superintendent of franchise in the Women's Christian Temperance Union. Soon after, however, at the urgent request of leading suffragists, she resigned this office and accepted in place, that of national lecturer for the National American Women's Suffrage Association, of which, in 1892, she was elected vice-president at large.

Her old parishioners at times have reproached her for no longer devoting herself to preaching the Gospel but she replies that in advocating the franchisement of women, the temperance movement and other reforms, she is teaching applied Christianity and that she exchanged the pulpit where she preached twice a week for the platform where she may preach every day and often three times on Sunday.

She is indeed one of the most eloquent, witty and popular speakers in the lecture field. Her face is very beautiful, even in its aging lines, and she is possessed of the most remarkable personal magnetism, a magnificent voice and great power of pointed argument. Much of her strength and force and thought of expression are believed to result from the experiences of her pioneer life in Michigan, and her power of moving audiences from the touch of humanity which came to her while practicing medicine in the city of Boston. She is believed to be the first woman to have the double distinction of the titles Reverend, and M.D. Her family were opposed to her studying for the ministry, on the ground that she would be a disgrace to them if she persisted in such an unheard of course, but it may be added that her career has effectually reconciled them to that "disgrace."

Dr. Shaw has spoken before many state legislatures and several times before committees in both houses. Her appearance in Washington as presiding officer of the Woman's Suffrage Convention in 1910 made many converts to the cause of equal suffrage from the ranks of national legislators. In appearing before the joint committee of senators and representatives and in the open-air meetings, in which she was the moving spirit on this occasion, her splendid characteristic of keen humor and ready wit enabled her to carry her points where logic alone would have failed.

HELEN M. GOUGAR.

A naturally gifted woman and supported by an unflinching enthusiasm for the right, about the richest possession any cause can have! Such has been the record of Mrs. Helen M. Gougar, author and woman suffragist, born in Litchfield, Mich., July 18, 1843. At forty years of age her head was prematurely whitened by a bitter and hard-fought attempt to weaken her power in political circles by defamation, but the battle over and her enemies completely vanquished, she went on to contest heroically, fighting for what she believes to be the right and patriotic cause to a higher civilization. In this battle she decided forever the right of women to take an active part in political warfare without being compelled to endure ridicule or defamation. Her special work in reforms lies in legal and political lines and constitutional law, and statistics she quotes with marvelous familiarity when speaking in public. Mrs. Gougar is the author of the law granting municipal suffrage to women in Kansas, and the adoption of the measure was wholly due to her efforts. She proved the correctness of her theory by redeeming Leavenworth, the largest city in the state at that time, from slum rule by the votes of women. The success which has attended this law in the interest of political honor and exaltation of public service is well known. As a writer she has a concise, direct and fluent style. For many years she was a contributor to the Chicago *Inter-Ocean*, and no better evidence of her ability and enthusiasm could be found than the high esteem in which she was held by the management of that old Republican organ.

BELVA ANN LOCKWOOD.

In the summer of 1884 Mrs. Belva Ann Lockwood was nominated for the presidency of the Equal Rights party in San Francisco, California, and this was the first step toward giving woman suffrage a similar recognition to that accorded the male vote. In 1888 she was renominated by the same party in Des Moines, Iowa, and on this occasion awakened the people of the United States as never before to the consideration of the right of suffrage for women. The notoriety given to her by these bold movements called forth much censure; nevertheless, in a history of what women have done for the United States, Mrs. Lockwood's life should figure prominently. She was born in Royalton, Niagara County, New York, on the 24th of October, 1830. Her parents' name was Bennett, and they were of the farming class in moderate circumstances, so their daughter was educated first in the district school, and later in the academy of her native town. At fourteen years of age she taught the district school in summer and attended school in winter, continuing that strenuous regime until she was eighteen, when she became the wife of a young farmer in the neighborhood, Uriah H. McNall. Her husband died in April, 1853, leaving one small daughter who, later in life, became Mrs. Lockwood's principal assistant in her law office. As Belva Ann McNall, a young widow, she entered Genesee College, in Lima, New York, and was graduated therefrom with honor on the 27th of June, 1857. She was immediately elected preceptress of Lockport Union School, and here she ruled with efficiency and success for four years, leaving there to become proprietor of the McNall Seminary, in Oswego, New York. At the close of the Civil War Mrs. McNall came to Washington, and for several years had charge of Union League Hall, meanwhile taking up the study of law. On the 11th of March, 1868, she became the wife of the Rev. Ezekiel Lockwood, a Baptist minister, who, during the war, was chaplain of the Second D. C. Regiment. Doctor Lockwood died in Washington, D. C., on the 23d of April, 1877, and three years later we find Mrs. Lockwood taking her second degree of A.M., in Syracuse, New York. In May, 1873, she had graduated from the National University Law School, of Washington, D. C., and after a spirited controversy about the admission of women to the bar she was admitted to the bar of the Supreme Court, the highest court in the district. She at once entered into the active practice of her profession, and accomplished over twenty years of successful work. For about thirteen years of that time Mrs. Lockwood was in court every court day, and engaged in pleading cases in person before the court. In 1875 she applied for admission to the Court of Claims, and was refused, on the ground, first, that she was a woman and, second, that she was a married woman. The contest was a bitter one, sharp, short and decisive. But, undiscouraged, Mrs. Lockwood had her application for admission to the bar of the United States Supreme Court renewed. That motion was also refused, on the ground that there was no English precedent for the admission of women to the bar. Again, nothing daunted, she drafted a bill admitting women to the bar of the United States Supreme Court, secured its introduction into both houses of Congress, and after three years of effort, aroused influence and public sentiment enough to secure its passage in June, 1879, and two months later, on the motion of the Honorable A. G. Riddle, Mrs. Lockwood was admitted to the bar of that august tribunal, the first woman upon whom the honor was conferred. After the passage of the act Mrs. Lockwood was notified that she could then be admitted to the Court of Claims. This honor she accepted, and had for many years before that court a very active practice. There is now no Federal Court in the United States before which she may not plead. In later years, however, she has confined her energies more especially to claims against the government. She has even made an argument for the passage of a bill before the committees of the Senate and the House of Congress, and in 1870 she secured a bill giving to the women employees of the Government, of whom there are many thousands, equal pay for equal work with men. At another time she secured the passage of a bill appropriating $50,000 for the payment of bounties of soldiers and mariners, heretofore a neglected class. During Garfield's administration, in 1881, Mrs. Lockwood made application for appointment as minister to Brazil, but these negotiations were terminated by the unfortunate death of the President.

Mrs. Lockwood is interested, not only in equal rights for men and women, but in temperance and labor reforms, the control of railroads and telegraphs by the Government, and in the settlement of all difficulties, national and international, by arbitration instead of war. In the summer of 1889, in company with the Rev. Amando Deyo, Mrs. Lockwood represented the Universal Peace Union at the Paris Exposition, and was there delegated to the International Congress of Peace in that city, which opened its sessions in the Salle of the Trocadéro, under the patronage of the French government. She made nearly all the opening speeches, and later presented a paper in the French language on international arbitration, which was well received. In the summer of 1890 she again represented the Universal Peace Union in the International Congress in London, and here she presented a paper on "Disarmament." Before returning to the United States Mrs. Lockwood took a course of university extension lectures in the University of Oxford. She was elected for the third time to represent the Universal Peace Union, of which she was then corresponding secretary, in the International Congress of Peace, held in November, 1891, in Rome. Her subject in that gathering was "The Establishment of an International Bureau of Peace."

Mrs. Lockwood now lives in retirement in Washington, D. C., but her appearance upon a woman suffrage platform is always greeted with applause. Mrs. Lockwood has always been a student, and one of the most valuable acts of her career was when she became prime mover in the university extension course in this country.

CARRIE LANE CHAPMAN CATT.

Mrs. Carrie Lane Chapman Catt, for some years one of the most active and prominent workers for women's suffrage in the United States, was born in Ripon, Wisconsin, on the 9th of January, 1859. Her maiden name was Lane. While yet a child her parents moved to northern Iowa, where her youth was passed. In 1878 she entered as a student the scientific department of the Iowa Agriculture College, and was graduated therefrom in 1880 with the degree of D.S. She was an earnest student, and attained first rank in her class. For three years she devoted herself to teaching, first as principal of the high school in Mason City, Iowa, from which position she was soon promoted to city superintendent of schools in the same place In 1885 she became the wife of Leo Chapman, and carrying out her ideas of the wife as economic helpmate she entered into partnership with him as a joint proprietor and editor of the Mason City *Republican*. Within a year Mr. Chapman died. Disposing of her paper, Mrs. Chapman went to California where, for a year, she was engaged in newspaper work in San Francisco. In 1888 she entered the lecture field, and for some time spoke only in lecture courses, but the cause of women's enfranchisement soon enlisted her warmest sympathies, and she accepted a position as state lecturer for the Iowa Women's Suffrage Association. Since that time all her energies have been devoted to the cause, and her earnest, logical eloquence has won her many friends. At every convention of the national association she has been called upon as a speaker. As the work for the cause in America has expanded and the suffrage army has grown, Mrs. Catt has come to be more and more acknowledged as one of its generals. Her health having suffered from her constant devotion to the cause, she has gone abroad. She said, on sailing, that it was her purpose to study the possibilities and status of equal suffrage in all of the countries throughout which she passed on her tour of the world, and it is safe to conclude that her deep, powerful voice will be heard in advocacy of the cause as often as possible.

In 1890 she became the wife of George W. Catt, civil engineer of New York City. Her home is in Bensonhurst-by-the-sea, on Long Island.

RACHEL FOSTER AVERY.

The father of Mrs. Avery was J. Heron Foster, editor of the *Pittsburg Dispatch,* and her mother was a native of Johnstown, New York, the birthplace of her Sunday school teacher and lifelong friend, Elizabeth Cady Stanton. From this heredity it might have been forecasted that the daughter would develop a strong, quick mentality and an advocacy for the independence of her sex. Mrs. Avery was born in Pittsburgh, Pennsylvania, December 30, 1858. When she was still a child Mrs. Stanton lectured in Pittsburgh, and shortly after a suffrage meeting was held in the Foster home, and a society was formed, of which Mrs. Avery's mother was made vice-president. Thus the young girl grew up in an atmosphere of radicalism and advanced talk, and she became a suffragist from conviction, as well as by birthright. In 1871 the family, consisting of her mother, her sister and herself, the father having died shortly before, moved to Philadelphia, where they at once identified themselves with the Citizens' Suffrage Association in that city. When about seventeen years old Miss Foster began to write for the newspapers, furnishing letters weekly from California, and afterwards from Europe, to the Pittsburgh *Leader.* In the winter of 1879 she attended the eleventh convention of the National Women's Association, and this determined her career. With characteristic promptitude she began to plan the series of conventions to be held in the West during the summer of 1880, and in the spring of 1881 she planned the series of ten conventions in the different states, beginning at Boston. In 1882 she conducted the Nebraska Amendment campaign, with headquarters in Omaha. But perhaps the act which best illustrated her ability to propagate the cause was when she engaged Governor John W. Hoyt, of Wyoming, to give a lecture in Philadelphia on "The Good Results of Thirteen Years' Experience of Women's Voting in Wyoming," had the lecture stenographically reported, collected the money to publish twenty thousand copies, and scattered them broadcast over the state of Pennsylvania. In February, 1883, Miss Foster sailed for Europe with Susan B. Anthony, and by reason of her superior linguistic attainments she served for ears and tongue in their journey through France, Italy, Switzerland and Germany. Miss Foster's management of the International Council of Women, held in Washington, D. C., in February, 1888, under the auspices of the National Women's Suffrage Association, was the crowning effort of her executive genius. The expenses of this meeting made a grand total of fourteen thousand dollars, the financial risk of which was assumed beforehand by Miss Anthony, supported by Miss Foster.

Her marriage to Cyrus Miller Avery took place November 8, 1888, the Reverend Anna H. Shaw assisting in the ceremony. But she continued her suffrage work even more ardently, and for years held the office of corresponding secretary of the National Suffrage Association and of the National and the International Councils of Women. Mrs. Foster Avery is, moreover, a philanthropist in the broadest sense, giving constantly from her independent fortune to reforms and charities.

HARRIOT STANTON BLATCH.

Mrs. Harriot Stanton Blatch is the brilliant daughter of Mrs. Cady Stanton, who was one of the founders of the Woman's Suffrage Organization. Her father's name was Henry Brewster Stanton and her grandfather was Daniel Cady, a noted lawyer who, after serving a term in Congress, became a judge of the Supreme Court of New York.

Mrs. Blatch is now one of the leading spirits in the woman's suffrage movement in this country and president of the Woman's Political Union of 46 East Twenty-ninth Street, New York City. She is a woman of great strength of character and marked ability which has brought her to the front rank in this great wave of suffrage which is sweeping over our country.

Mrs. Blatch was the organizer of the league for Self-supporting Women which has to-day 19,350 members. It is a league of working women of New York City and has affiliated with it such divisions of organized labor as The Typographical Union, The Pipe-Caulkers' Union, The Painters' and the Bookbinders' Union. For several years Mrs. Blatch has devoted much of her time to amalgamating women workers and teaching them the value of the franchise. The national suffragists count their greatest gain to be the working women and the college women, who for many years held aloof from each other in suspicion and conservatism, but in the past few years both classes, for various reasons, now are united against tyranny or taxation without representation and for the advancement and rights of women.

ELLEN C. SARGENT.

Mrs. Ellen C. Sargent, of San Francisco, has just died of old age at the house of her son, George C. Sargent, a lawyer. Mrs. Sargent has been for many years one of the great women of California, broad-minded, interested in all progressive work, most of all in woman suffrage, and always optimistic. She lived in Washington many years while her husband, Hon Aaron A. Sargent, was senator from California, and was a regular attendant at National Suffrage Conventions. She and Susan B. Anthony were very close friends and often visited each other and always were in correspondence. When her husband was minister to Germany, she accompanied him to Berlin, and on their return to California lived in Nevada City and in San Francisco. She had the advantages of New England birth, of Washington society, foreign travel, and a fortune, but she was at all times unassuming, helpful, sympathetic and regarded with deepest esteem and fondest affection by all of her friends. Mrs. Sargent was president of the California Equal Suffrage Association during the campaign of 1896, and the campaign headquarters was in her house. Miss Anthony was her guest during a large part of the time. While suffrage has been her first thought, she has always seen the relation of other movements toward suffrage and has distributed much literature on peace, direct legislation and other related work.

AMALIA BARNEY SIMONS POST.

Mrs. Amalia Barney Simons Post, like so many others of the women suffragists can boast of ancestors who were prominent in early American History. Thomas Chittenden, the first governor of Vermont, was one of her ancestors and several were officers in the Revolutionary War, and in the army and navy in the war of 1812. Mrs. Post's father was William Simons and her mother Amalia Barney. Both parents were stern in integrity and patriotism and of great strength of character. In 1864, in Chicago, Miss Simons became the wife of Morton E. Post. She with her husband crossed the plain in 1866, settling in Denver, Colorado and later moving to Cheyenne, Wyoming. Mrs. Post's life in Wyoming was closely identified with the story of obtaining and maintaining equal political rights for Wyoming women, and to her perhaps more than to any other individual is due the fact that the women of Wyoming have to-day the right of suffrage. In 1871 Mrs. Post was a delegate to the Women's National Convention in Washington, D. C., and before an audience of five thousand people in Lincoln Hall she told of women's emancipation in Wyoming. In the fall of 1871 the Wyoming legislature repealed the act granting suffrage to women, but Mrs. Post by a personal appeal to Governor Campbell induced him to veto the bill. To Mrs. Post he said, "I came here opposed to women's suffrage but the eagerness and fidelity with which you and your friends have performed legal duties when called upon to act has convinced me that you deserve to enjoy those rights." A determined effort was made to pass the bill over the governor's veto, and a canvass of the members showed that the necessary two-thirds majority could probably be secured by the narrow margin of one vote. With political sagacity equal to that of any man Mrs. Post decided to secure that one vote. By an earnest appeal to one of the best educated men she won him to its support and upon the final ballot being taken upon the proposal to pass the bill over the governor's veto that man, Senator Foster, voted "no," and women's suffrage became a permanency in Wyoming. From 1880 to 1884, Mrs. Post, whose husband was delegate to Congress during that time, lived in Washington and by her social tact and sterling womanly qualities she made many friends for the cause of women's suffrage among those who were inclined to believe that only the radical or immodest of her sex desired suffrage. For twenty years Mrs. Post was vice-president of the National Women's Suffrage Association. In 1890, after equal rights to Wyoming women had been secured irrevocably by the constitution adopted by the people of the new state, Mrs. Post was made president of the committees having in charge the statehood's celebration. On that occasion a copy of the state constitution was presented to the women of the state by Judge N. C. Brown, who had been president of a Constitutional Convention which adopted it, and Mrs. Post received the book in behalf of the women of the state.

Women Reformers.

GRACE ALEXANDER.

Miss Alexander, temperance reformer, was born in Winchester, New Hampshire, the 26th of October, 1848, and was the daughter of Edward and Lucy Catron Alexander, whose parents were among the early Puritan settlers. Miss Alexander taught school after graduating, and then accepted a position in the Winchester National Bank; finally became the cashier, and in 1881 when the incorporation of the Security Savings Bank took place, Miss Alexander was the first woman to be given the position of treasurer of a banking corporation. She is an earnest worker in Sunday schools, temperance societies and other religious organizations.

FANNIE B. AMES.

Mrs. Ames was born at Canandaigua the 14th of June, 1840, and is a noted industrial reformer. She was a student in Antioch College when Horace Mann was its president. Her first work was in the military hospitals during the war. She was married in 1863 to Reverend Charles G. Ames, a minister of Philadelphia, and here she took up the work of organized charity, becoming one of the state visitors to the public institutions of Pennsylvania. She was president of the New Century College, of Philadelphia, one of the most influential women's colleges of this country. Her lectures and writings have been full of force and most salutary in their effect. In 1891 she read a paper entitled "Care of Defective Children" before the National Council of Women and was appointed by Governor Russell factory inspector in Massachusetts.

ROSA MILLER AVERY.

Mrs. Avery was born in Madison, Ohio, the 21st of May, 1830. In September, 1853, she married Cyrus Avery, of Oberlin, Ohio. While living in Ashtabula, Ohio, she organized the first anti-slavery society of that time in that section of the country, and though only two years before the war there was not a clergyman in the place who would give notice of this meeting. During the war she wrote constantly for the various papers and journals of that day on the union and emancipation, being obliged to use a male signature in order to gain attention. Her pen-name signed to her later writings was "Sue Smith." These were on social questions and things helpful to young people. After removing to Chicago she took up the work of social purity and equal suffrage and has written many able articles for the *Chicago Press* on these subjects.

LUCRETIA MOTT.

One of the most famous characters of American womanhood was born at Nantucket, January 3, 1793. Her father was a sea captain; her mother, one of those energetic, sensible, cheerful women of that day and time. As an illustration of the amusements of the children in that simple home, one writer says of Mrs. Coffin, Lucretia's mother, that it was her custom to say to her daughters: "Now after you have finished knitting twenty bouts you may go down in the cellar and pick out as many as you want of the smallest potatoes, the very smallest, and roast them in the ashes." The family moved to Boston when Lucretia was but twelve years of age and she received her primary education at a public school, which her father felt was more in accordance with the democracy of our country. Later she attended the Friends' Boarding School, at Nine Partners, New York. James Mott, her cousin, attended this same school and here their friendship began. At fifteen, Lucretia was appointed an assistant teacher in this school, and she and Mr. Mott took up the study of French together. When she was eighteen and James Mott twenty-one, they were married and went to reside at the home of Lucretia's father in Philadelphia. Mr. Mott assisted Mr. Coffin in his business. The war of 1812 came on and destroyed Mr. Coffin's business, and the death of Captain Coffin soon thereafter brought great suffering upon the family. James Mott endeavored to do what he could for their support, but his business venture proved also a dismal failure and Lucretia Mott decided to open a school, which commenced with four pupils and soon increased to forty. Mr. Mott's prospects also had improved and the family were placed in more cheerful and satisfactory surroundings. Lucretia Mott's family were Quakers and about the time she was twenty-five her natural religious tendency compelled her to give up work as a teacher, and she began the close study of the Bible. At this time she had four children, but the care of her house did not prevent her becoming a diligent student. Her husband, James Mott, was now prospering in a cotton business, and so luxuries had been added to the necessities of the home, which gave her more time for her work and she was enabled to go to the different Quaker meetings and speak. She had always been deeply interested in the question of slavery and on December 4, 1833, when a convention met in Philadelphia for the purpose of forming The American Anti-Slavery Society, Lucretia Mott was one of four women to brave criticism and social ostracism as friends of the then despised abolitionists. She spoke at this meeting with great earnestness and power and immediately after the Philadelphia Female Anti-Slavery Society was formed with Mrs. Mott chosen as its president. The women were so unused to the proper methods of organization and conduct of a woman's society that they were obliged to call a colored man to the chair to assist them. We all have read how these anti-slavery lecturers suffered. Some were even tarred and feathered. In New York and Philadelphia houses were burned, church windows broken, and threats were being made to destroy the home of Mr. and Mrs. Mott, but amidst all this frenzy Mrs. Mott remained placid and unruffled even when the mob threatened her with personal violence. In 1839 the World's Convention was called in London to discuss the slavery question, and among the delegates sent from this country were James and Lucretia Mott, Wendell Philips and his wife, with others. On their arrival in London they were amazed to find that no women were to be admitted as delegates. This seemed a death blow to Mrs. Mott's work, but the friendship of William Lloyd Garrison was here shown when he refused to take part in the convention and sat in the gallery with the women. Mrs. Mott was shown the greatest honors, entertained by the Duchess of Sutherland, Lady Byron, Carlyle expressing for her the greatest admiration. She had made frequent public speeches and addresses while in England and aroused the greatest interest in the work. Soon after their return to this country she spoke before the legislatures of New Jersey, Delaware, and Pennsylvania; called upon President Tyler and discussed the slavery question with him. She was greatly interested in the question of suffrage for women, total abstinence, and national differences settled by arbitration instead of war, which after all these years is now so popular in our country. She felt greatly the difference in women's pay for the same work done by men. In 1848 Mrs. Mott, with Elizabeth Cady Stanton and some other noble women of that time, called the first women's suffrage convention held in this country at Seneca Falls, New York. Her home became the rendezvous of the enthusiasts and earnest workers in these various lines, and black as well as white were welcome guests. She aided the escaped slaves and took up the cause of injustice freely. All this multitude of labor was carried on in addition to the duties of her home and to her children, which were always most conscientiously performed. In 1856 it became necessary to change their home from the city into the country, as Mrs. Mott had become much worn with care, and they established the residence, which was known far and wide as "Roadside." In 1861 Mr. and Mrs. Mott celebrated their golden wedding, she being at that time seventy years of age but still active and interested in the cause of humanity. Lucretia Mott passed the latter years of her life near Philadelphia, where in 1880 she died.

MARY A. LIVERMORE.

Mrs. Livermore was one of the great characters and remarkable women developed by the few years prior to the Civil War, and her name is always associated with the great work of the Sanitary Commission of which she was the head and leader. She was born in Boston, December 19, 1821. Her people were Welsh and she was reared under the strictest Calvinistic faith. Mr. Rice, her father, was a man of strong character. The family consisted of five children younger than herself, and even as a child she was imbued with a great religious faith. When but twelve years of age she became anxious to do something in order to earn money to contribute her part toward the support of the family and, as she said, not to have her father work so hard for all of them. She took up the trade of dressmaking, which at that time could not be considered one giving much financial return, as she was paid but thirty-seven cents a day. She was always eager to learn and hungered for an education. In this she met great encouragement from Doctor Neal, their minister, who assisted her to go to the Charlestown (Massachusetts) Female Seminary. While there one of the teachers died, during Mary's first term, and she was asked to fill the vacancy. She accepted at once, studying at night in order to fit herself for the position, and when but twenty years of age she had taught two years as a governess on a Virginia plantation and had returned to the family with the sum of six hundred dollars. At this time she was asked to take charge of the Duxbury High School, which she did. Her sister had died and the family were in great sorrow. Their minister at this time was Rev. D. P. Livermore who became interested in her reading and mental advancement and soon became fascinated with her personality, and when she was twenty-three they were married.

She became his assistant in the editing of the *New Covenant,* a religious paper published in Chicago, where they made their home. They had three children. In 1861 when the war broke out and the slavery question was one which everyone was discussing, Mrs. Livermore was deeply affected by the evidence of the case. She was in Boston when Mr. Lincoln's call for seventy-five thousand men was responded to and she was so affected by the hardships which she knew were facing them and the agony and distress of the women left at home, that she felt it her duty to see if there was not some work that she and the women of this country could do to help in this dreadful struggle. A meeting for women was called in New York City, which resulted in the formation of an aid society, which was to send assistance to the soldiers and their families. They sent a delegate to Washington to inquire if there was not some work which the government would let the women undertake, but they were told they were not wanted. This only added fuel to the flame of their desire to undertake what they knew would be needed of the women, and soon the United States Sanitary Commission was organized for working in hospitals, looking after camps, and providing comfort for the soldiers. Branches were formed in ten large cities. The northwestern branch was put under the direction of Mrs. Livermore and Mrs. A. H. Hoge. Supplies began to come in to these loyal women from all parts of the country, and Mrs. Livermore was sent to Washington to talk with President Lincoln about the work, and while he told her that "by law" no civilian, either man or woman, would be allowed to act officially, personally he was in favor of anything which would help the women to do their duty to their country. Mrs. Livermore's first work was after the battle of Fort Donelson. There were no hospitals. The poor wounded and sick had to be hauled in the rough Tennessee wagons, many dying before they reached St Louis. At the rear of the battlefields the sanitary commission took up its work. They kept the men supplied with hot coffee and soup; they furnished supplies for the sick; they helped care for those in the hospitals, nursing and working personally among them and many a poor fellow closed his eyes in death in Mrs. Livermore's arms. This commission expended about fifty million dollars, and the women raised the largest proportion of this. It is said each battle cost the commission about seventy-five thousand, and the battle of Gettysburg, one half million. Mrs. Livermore when not on the field, went about the country making appeals to the people for money and supplies to be sent to their own boys at the front. At one time the need of money was so great that Mrs. Livermore decided to have a fair in Chicago. This was one of the famous charitable efforts during the war. Fourteen of Chicago's largest halls were hired, and the women assumed an indebtedness of ten thousand dollars. The

MARY A. LIVERMORE

FRANCES WILLARD

ANNA E. DICKINSON

SUSAN B. ANTHONY

DISTINGUISHED WOMEN ORATORS.

City Council and Board of Trade of Chicago advised the abandonment of the project, but Mrs. Livermore and her loyal supporters went bravely on and every hall was filled with things to be sold, and supplies for the men. Instead of twenty-five thousand, which they hoped to raise, the women cleared one hundred thousand dollars. This was followed by others in Boston, New York, Cincinnati, and Philadelphia. In New York one million dollars was raised, and in Philadelphia two hundred thousand more than that raised by New York. Mrs. Livermore was asked to make a tour of the hospitals and posts on the Mississippi River, and all officials and military officers were ready now, not only to lay down the bars of red tape and army regulation but glad to welcome this noble woman who had done so much and showed such remarkable executive ability and willingness to aid in lessening the suffering necessary. Her labors cannot be justly estimated and the American people owe to her and to Clara Barton, of the Red Cross, a debt which cannot be cancelled. She was the author of several books, one "What Shall We Do With Our Daughters," and "Reminiscences of the War." She died in 1905.

Sociologists.

MARGARET DREIER ROBBINS.

Born in Brooklyn. The daughter of Theodore and Dorothea Dreier. She is the founder of the Woman's Municipal League of New York; president of the New York Association for Household Research; president of the New York Woman's Trade Union League in 1905; member executive board of Chicago Federation of Labor since 1908; member of committee on industrial education, American Federation of Labor; member of executive committee, Illinois section, American Association for Labor Legislation, and prominent in all labor and social organizations for many years.

CORINNE STUBBS BROWN.

Born in Chicago, 1849. Teacher in the public schools of Chicago and married Frank E. Brown. Is a student of social problems and socialist of some prominence. President of the Illinois Women's Alliance for the purpose of obtaining the enactment and enforcement of factory ordinances and compulsory educational laws. An active worker in the study of economic and social questions among the clubs.

GABRIELLE MULLINER.

Lawyer and social reformer of New York. Is using her efforts to procure separate trials for women.

HELENA STUART DUDLEY.

Born in Nebraska, in 1858. Daughter of Judson H. and Caroline Bates Dudley. Teacher of biology and chemistry in the Packer Collegiate Institute at

38

one time. Became head worker of the college settlement work in Philadelphia; also of the Denison House College settlement in Boston since 1893.

MRS. ROBERT CARTWRIGHT.

Chairman of the public safety committee of the city of New York. Originated and caused to be placed the electric signs at elevated railway stations indicating the next stop; also the signs in the cars of the Interborough Rapid Transit Company, giving the names of the subway lines and their destination. It is believed that these have prevented thousands of accidents and hundreds of thousands of tourists from boarding the wrong trains.

DIANA BELAIS.

Active worker in the reform concerning the treatment and care of disabled and overworked animals. Finding the Society for the Prevention of Cruelty to Animals did not entirely accomplish the work she desired—was not far-reaching enough—she framed the bill and caused it to be presented to the legislature at Albany, New York, and for two years she struggled for the passage of this bill and ultimately was successful in her efforts, and to-day the agents of the society are invested with full police power and have brought about a wonderful change in the humane treatment of animals and the sanitary conditions for them. But the greatest of Mrs. Belais' municipal achievements lies in her splendid crusade against the horrors of vivisection, and she is now engaged in trying to accomplish her ideas through legislative measures and ordinances in the cities.

MRS. A. M. PALMER.

President of what is known as the Rainy Day Club and organizations to rectify the short weights and false measurements. It was said that the city of New York, according to authorized statements, lost one million dollars yearly on short-weighted package goods. All devices for fraud resorted to by merchants and dealers were to be brought to account. She has been joined in this work by Mrs. William Grant Brown, of New York.

ELEANOR M. WHALEY.

Interested in the cleansing of cities under the Municipal Woman's League.

LAURA B. HERTZ.

Chairman of the Civic Committee of California's Women's Clubs. Mrs. Hertz was born in San Francisco, November, 1869, and received a high school education in Santa Barbara. She married Louis Hertz in March, 1891, after having taught school for several years. Mrs. Hertz's work and activities are for the betterment of all civic conditions, moral, physical and educational. Especially is she interested in work for the young. She was elected president of the Council of Jewish Women, serving in this position for two years, after which she was elected a delegate to the triennial council, which met in Chicago in 1905. For two years past, she has been chairman of the Sabbath school committee, and inaugurated an international union Thanksgiving service conducted by the children of all the Jewish Sunday-schools of San Francisco. Mrs. Hertz is at present the chairman of the Department of School Patrons of the National Education Association, and is at the head of the entertainment for the Jewish Chautauqua Assembly, meeting in San Francisco.

MARGARET SMYTH McKISSICK.

Mrs. Margaret Smyth McKissick was born in Charleston, South Carolina, and is proud of her Maryland, Virginia, as well as South Carolina, colonial and revolutionary ancestry. She has one son, about nineteen years old, and it has been largely her interest in him that has led to her interest in the industrial schools of South Carolina

She has been vice-president for two years, president for two years of the State Federation of Women's Clubs, and for the last four years has been chairman of the Department of Forestry and Civics.

Mrs. McKissick oversees the educational system, carries baskets to the families at the Christmas season and generally guards the welfare of employees and their families in some of the mill villages of South Carolina. Mrs. McKissick follows in her work the methods inaugurated by her father, Captain Ellison A. Smyth, at Pelzer, South Carolina.

MARTHA PARMELEE ROSE.

Mrs. Rose was born March 5, 1834, in Norton, Ohio. Her father, Theodore Hudson Parmelee, was one of the founders of the Western Reserve College, and went with the early colony to Ohio, in 1813. He was educated under Lyman Beecher and accepted the views of Oberlin, which opened its doors to women and the negro. Here Miss Parmelee obtained her education, graduating in 1855. While teaching in a seminary in Pennsylvania, she became the wife of William G. Rose, a member of the legislature of that state; an editor and lawyer. In 1864 Mr. and Mrs. Rose removed to Cleveland, Ohio, where Mr. Rose was later the mayor of the city. Mrs. Rose became intensely interested in the poor and destitute, especially the sufferings of the poor sewing women as a result of the frauds and extortions practised upon them. Through lectures and reports of the Royal Commission of England on the training schools of that country and the manual training schools of France and Sweden, she succeeded in arousing the press and business men of the city to the necessity for the establishment of a training school in Cleveland, which was accomplished. She has written a book entitled, "Story of a Life of Pauperism in America," many articles on the labor question and kindred topics. She reviewed Mrs. Field's "How to Help the Poor"; many of her suggestions were accepted by the associated charities of Cleveland. She helped to form the Woman's

Employment Society, which gave out garments to be made at reasonable prices and sold to home missions. She was at one time president of the Cleveland Sorosis, aiding materially the success of this woman's club. She is known as a patron of art.

ANNA BYFORD LEONARD.

Mrs. Anna Byford Leonard was born July 31, 1843. She was the daughter of a well-known physician and surgeon of Chicago, Illinois, who was the founder and president of the Woman's Medical College of Chicago, and devoted his life and his work to the cause and diseases of women. In 1889 Mrs. Leonard was appointed sanitary inspector, the first woman to be appointed to that position. Through her efforts and those of five other women, who were aiding her in this splendid work, the eight-hour day was enforced, which provides that children under fourteen years of age shall not work more than eight hours a day. Through Mrs. Leonard's efforts seats were placed in stores and factories for the relief of girls employed in these places; and through her efforts, also, schools have been established in some of the stores to give the children employed two hours of schooling a day. Many of these girls whose first labors were those of cash girls were unable to write their own names. In 1891 Mrs. Leonard was made president of the Women's Canning and Preserving Company, which she brought to great success. She is entitled to a place among the distinguished business women of this country as well as among cultured and prominent social leaders and representative American women.

JANE ADDAMS.

Miss Addams was born at Cedarville, Illinois, September, 1860. She is the daughter of the late Hon. John H. and Sarah Weber Addams. Studied abroad for two years and later in Philadelphia. Opened a social settlement department known as Hull House, in Chicago, in 1889, in connection with Miss Ellen Gates Star and of this she has since been the head. Was inspector of streets and alleys for three years in the neighborhood of Hull House. Has done a wonderful work in sociology and is to-day recognized as one of the foremost women in this country in her line of work. She has written and lectured on social and political reform.

Miss Addams has been ranked the foremost living woman in America to-day, as having done the most for womankind and, for that matter, for human kind. This modest, unassuming little woman has proven a power in Chicago, which political corruption and vicious ignorance could not withstand. She has matched kindness with kindness, craftiness with craftiness until ward bossism fell before her. A lifelong sufferer from spinal trouble, she has already accomplished a work in Chicago and sent forth a worldwide influence for social and industrial betterment which many a strong man might be proud to call his life work. What Miss Addams has accomplished in Chicago cannot be told briefly, but here are a few of the things she has done: Through Hull House she has provided a place where nine thousand men, women and children go to take sewing, millinery and dancing lessons; drink coffee; paint pictures; to mould clay; a place where they have free access to library, club rooms, day nursery, kindergarten, children's playgrounds, labor bureau, medical dispensary, ideal bakery, diet kitchen, visiting nurses, social, educational and industrial clubs for all ages and purposes. She has cleaned up one of the filthiest and most corrupt districts in Chicago. She has replaced in the heart of this district an ill-kept and filthy stable with an art gallery and a children's playground; she has done this for about two thousand children whose only playground was the street. She has made a long and vigorous fight against druggists who sold cocaine to children; against the spread of typhoid fever by personal inspection of four thousand tenements; against tuberculosis among the rear-tenement dwellers; for new factory laws, and in all of these cases she has won out. She has co-operated with the Juvenile Courts. She has established public baths, free reading rooms, better public and home sanitation and cleaner streets. She has established a model apartment house with twelve model apartments. She maintains a visiting kindergarten by means of which children too crippled to attend school are visited in their homes and instructed by trained kindergarten teachers, and yet the half has not been told.

IDA WHIPPLE BENHAM.

Mrs. Benham was born near Ledyard, Connecticut, on the 8th of January, 1849, and was the daughter of Timothy and Lucy Ann Geer Whipple. The 14th of April, 1869, she married Elijah B. Benham, of Groton, Connecticut. She inherited from her Quaker father and mother a desire for peace, and lectured on this and the subject of temperance. Is a director in the American Peace Society, and a member of the Universal Peace Union, and has always taken a conspicuous part in all peace conventions. Has contributed poems to the *New York Independent, Youths' Companion, St. Nicholas,* and other prominent periodicals.

CLARISSA CALDWELL LATHROP.

Miss Clarissa Caldwell Lathrop was born in Rochester, New York, and died September, 1892 in Saratoga, New York. She was the daughter of the late General William E. Lee Lathrop. Her prominence came from her remarkable experience. She was confined and unlawfully imprisoned in the Utica State Asylum for twenty-six months through a plot of a secret enemy to put her out of existence. She managed at last to communicate with James B. Silkman, of New York, a lawyer who, like herself, was confined in the same asylum under similar circumstances. He succeeded in obtaining a writ of *habeas corpus* in December, 1882. Judge Barnard of the Supreme Court pronounced her sane and unlawfully incarcerated. Miss Lathrop felt she owed it to her own sex to take her case before the legislature of New York State, and demand reform in this direction, but she was unsuccessful in two efforts and found herself penniless and facing the necessity of her own support. After several efforts in most humble capacity, she became a court stenographer and ten years after her release wrote her book, the story of her own prison experiences, entitled "A Secret Institution." This book led to the formation of the Lunacy Law Reform League, in 1889, a national organization with headquarters in New York City, of which Miss Lathrop became the secretary and was the national organizer.

MRS. ARCHIBALD HOPKINS.

Mrs. Archibald Hopkins, president of the District of Columbia Association of the Civic Federation, was Charlotte Everett Wise, born June 7, 1857 in Cambridge, Massachusetts. She was the daughter of Captain Henry A. Wise, United States Navy, and Charlotte Brooks Wise, the granddaughter of Edward Everett and Charlotte G. Everett, of Boston, Massachusetts. Mrs. Hopkins has always been active in the charitable and philanthropic work of Washington. She is one of the original members of the Civic Federation and as president of the local organization of the city of Washington has done some splendid work in the effort to ameliorate the condition of the employees of the government. Many surprisingly unsanitary and unwholesome conditions have existed and the local organization has gained the attention of the chiefs of the various departments and Congress for the betterment of surroundings and the rectifying of injustices.

ELIZABETH GERBERDING.

Mrs. Elizabeth Gerberding is the leader of the fight for municipal reform in the city of San Francisco. To the women who took a part in this great revolt against graft the men owe much. Mrs. Gerberding was born in a little mining town in California in 1857. Her parents moved to San Francisco when she was but eight years of age. Soon after an early marriage she was thrown on her own resources, and for some years made her living and educated her children by teaching. This struggle brought out and developed in her the courage she has shown throughout the great war for civic righteousness in San Francisco. In 1894 she married Albert Gerberding, coming in close connection with those who were afterwards in the forefront for public weal. Mr. Gerberding's father was the owner and publisher of *The Bulletin,* the paper which in the early days helped to put down the lawlessness of organized theft and which to-day represents the public feeling which has brought to San Francisco a decent government. Mrs. Gerberding succeeded in getting representative women to show by their presence at the trials of these officials the stand of the best element of society. A League of Justice was formed. Mrs. Gerberding became the only woman member of the executive committee. On her own initiative she formed the Woman's League of Justice which soon had a membership of five hundred. This became a strong auxiliary in the graft prosecution; the value of their moral support to those engaged in the prosecution was incalcuable.

Of Mrs. Gerberding's active work for the betterment of San Francisco, this is but a part. She formed the California women's Heney Club of San Francisco, and as president made it a real power for good. This organization became the Woman's Civic Club of San Francisco.

Immediately there was new work for this club to do. On a trip east, Mrs. Gerberding discovered that an active propaganda was afoot to defeat the Hetch Hetchy water project on the ground of the preservation of natural resources. Persons had even succeeded in getting the Federation of Woman's Clubs to pass resolutions against the grant.

Mrs. Gerberding went back to San Francisco and persuaded the Century Club, the oldest woman's club on the Pacific coast, to withdraw in protest from the federation. The women of San Francisco are in a great fight for pure water.

Since her husband died in 1902, leaving her comfortably provided for, Mrs. Gerberding has been militant for her city. She loves San Francisco as only the native Californian can. The men who have fought the good fight for San Francisco know how often she has poured the balm of her sympathy upon their wounds and filled them with renewed energy and courage.

ADA M. BITTENBENDER.

Mrs. Bittenbender, lawyer and reformer, was born in Asylum, Bradford County, Pennsylvania, August 3, 1848. Her father's family were partly of New England and partly of German stock; her mother, of New England. Her father served all during the Civil War, and died soon after its close. Mrs. Bittenbender's maiden name was Ada M. Cole. In 1874 she entered as a student of the Pennsylvania State Normal School, from which she was graduated in 1875. After graduating, she was elected a member of the faculty and taught one year. She then entered the Froebel Normal Institute in Washington, D. C., and graduated from this institute in 1877. The day on which she graduated she was called to her Alma Mater as principal and accepted the position, teaching for one year, when illness prevented her continuing her work. In 1878 she married Henry Clay Bittenbender, a young lawyer of Bloomsburg, Pennsylvania, and a graduate of Princeton College. Soon after their marriage they moved to Osceola, Nebraska. Mrs. Bittenbender taught school for a short time. In 1879, Mr. Bittenbender bought the *Record* published in Osceola. Mrs. Bittenbender was engaged as editor and served in this capacity for three years, making an able, fearless, moral, temperance newspaper of this journal. Mrs. Bittenbender strongly opposed the granting of saloon licenses. When the Nebraska Woman Suffrage Association was organized in 1881, she was elected recording secretary. She with others secured the submission of the woman suffrage amendment to the constitution in 1881. The following year she was elected president of the association. In 1881 she became the editor of the *Farmers' Alliance* paper, started in Nebraska. While editing the *Record* she read law with her husband, and in 1882 passed an examination and was licensed to practise. She was the first woman admitted to the bar in Nebraska. She became her husband's law partner, and for many years the firm existed under the name of H. C. and Ada M. Bittenbender. She secured the passage of the scientific temperance instruction bill and the tobacco bill; secured a law giving the mother the guardianship of her children equally with the father, and several other laws beneficial to women. She was the author of the excellent industrial home bill which was enacted by the Nebraska legislature in 1887. At the International Council of Women, held in Washington, D. C., in 1888 she addressed the council on "Woman in Law." She represented the Woman's Christian Temperance Union at the national Capital for many years in urging legislation in the interest of temperance. In 1888 she was admitted to practise in the Supreme Court of the United States, and elected an attorney to the International Woman's Christian Temperance Union, which she held for some time. She is the author of the chapter on "Woman in Law" in "Woman's Work in America" and the "National Prohibitory Amendment Guide." It is through her efforts and by her untiring devotion to the cause that much of the beneficial legislation for temperance and the protection of women and her interests have been obtained.

HELEN MAROT.

Is an industrial reformer and worker in social economics. Miss Marot has been engaged in the work of social economics for the past sixteen years. Her first efforts in this direction was the forming of a small center for the use of all sorts and conditions of people interested in economic problems in Philadelphia, her native city. In this work she was assisted by Dr. David G. Brinton. Books and pamphlets were collected and a reading-room and gathering place for the discussion of these problems was opened. While this center was in active operation, lectures were delivered by Sidney Webb, of England, Ramsay MacDonald, M.P., and men from the Pennsylvania University. During the existence of this circle Miss Marot compiled a handbook of labor literature which was most favorably received by bibliographers as well as sociologists. This was a selected and classified bibliograph of the more important books and pamphlets in the English language at the time of its publication of 1897. In 1900 Miss Marot, in connection with Miss Caroline L. Platt, made an investigation and report of the manufacture of men's clothing in Philadelphia. The part referring to ready made clothing was published by the United States Industrial Commission. The part relating to the manu- facture of custom made clothes was published by the Pennsylvania Consumers' League and the Journeyman Tailors' Union. This was the first exposure of conditions under which the latter class of clothing is made. After this Miss Marot made some investigations in New York and in 1903 was asked to investigate conditions under which children worked for the New York Child Labor Com- mittee which was just then being formed. The investigation led to the enactment of laws formulated by her associates and herself which placed New York in the lead in child labor reform. This was the beginning of the child labor campaign throughout the country now led by the National Child Labor Committee. At this time Miss Marot's health broke down and she was forced to lay aside her work for over a year; she was then called to Philadelphia to take the secretaryship of the Pennsylvania Child Labor Committee. This committee made an extensive investigation of child labor and began a legislative campaign which resulted in the passing of a fine piece of legislation but which was declared unconstitutional on a slight technicality raised by those interested in vitiating the law. Miss Marot realized that the only method of eventually destroying this evil was in better educational facilities and new economic conditions. She left the Pennsylvania Committee and returned to New York to work with the New York Public Education Association. She was urged to accept the secretaryship of the Woman's Trade Union League of New York City, and gave up her educational work to acecpt this responsible office and to-day there is a membership of over fifty-two thousand in this league.

Miss Marot and her associates, who are largely college girls and students of social questions in sympathy with the cause of organized labor, aided and managed the strike of woman shirt-makers in New York last year, when forty thousand of these women united, formed a union and declared a strike. This was settled by their employers ultimately coming to a recognition of their claims and it was settled on a basis of increased pay and a recognition of their union. Miss Anna Morgan, the daughter of J. P. Morgan, was one of the moving spirits in aiding these women to obtain their rights. After the strike was over, about three thousand of the workers were still out of employment. It remained for the practical mind of Miss Morgan to make provision for these girls. Miss Morgan proposed to establish by subscription a shirtwaist factory which should be a model in every sanitary and architectural respect and operated under strictly union con- ditions and finally to have a profit-sharing system. Their first order was from Wellesley College—a thousand waists to be made by their special pattern.

MRS. ISAAC L. RICE.

Mrs. Isaac L. Rice, organizer of the Anti-noise Society, was born in New Orleans, Louisiana, May 2, 1860. Is the daughter of Nathaniel and Annie Hyne-Barnett and is the wife of Isaac L. Rice, a prominent lawyer of New York City. On her mother's side, Mrs. Rice descended from Elias Hyneman, a native of Holland who came to this country in the eighteenth century. Mrs. Rice received a classical and musical education and also completed a course at the Woman's Medical College of the New York Infirmary in New York City, where she took her degree of M.D., in 1885, but soon after this she was married and abandoned the plan of practising her profession. Her home is one of elegance and distinction on the Riverside Drive, overlooking the Hudson River in the city of New York. The situation of her home brought to her attention as one of the sufferers the unnecessary noise of the river craft which rendered her days uncomfortable and her nights sleepless. The long distance signalling indulged in by tugs on their way up and down the river, their shrieking sirens, even when two miles away from the pier, became insufferable. At one time Mrs. Rice planned to sell her house and move to a quieter neighborhood, but learning that the inmates of the hospitals along the East River were sufferers from these same river noises and that no attempt had been made to obtain relief for them, she then determined to devote herself to this work. She had hitherto been unaccustomed to any public effort, having lived a quiet, domestic, home life. To convince the most sceptical of the extent of the nuisance, Mrs. Rice had careful records made on various nights of the number and duration of the whistle blasts, engaging for this purpose law students from the Columbia University, their reports being duly attested. From these it was learned that almost three thousand blasts could be noted in one locality during a period of eight hours, from ten p. m. to six a. m. She recognized the fact that this whistling was not called for either by statute or emergency requirements and that it could be dispensed with by having watchmen on their piers and by a system of like signals. She contended, furthermore, that this unnecessary whistling was not only a general public nuisance, but a grave menace to health; that it was also a detriment to navigation, because it covered or rendered difficult to distinguish, those signals which were necessary or demanded by law, from the unnecessary and that in justice to all they ought to be immediately suppressed. She gathered data from all of the municipal institutions exposed to noise and from every one came the plea for relief. All of this testimony was corroborated by the most eminent physicians in New York. She appealed to the municipal and state authorities, but in vain, as they contended that it was a local nuisance on a federal waterway, and therefore, the municipal authorities had no right to act. Therefore, it was stated there was nobody in the United States who had the right to regulate the size of a boat whistle or to forbid useless handling of the same. After a year's constant effort Congressman Bennett succeeded in having a law passed through Congress, giving authority to the Board of Supervising Inspectors to punish unnecessary whistling. Mrs. Rice then decided to organize a society composed of representative men in the various cities of the United States to abate one of the gravest ills of city life—unnecessary noise. She has succeeded in interesting in this work

Archbishop Farley, Bishop Greer, the commissioner of health, the president of the Academy of Medicine, the president of Columbia University, the College of the city of New York and the New York University, the late Richard Watson Gilder and the late Mark Twain and William Dean Howells, and many other distinguished physicians, educators and public men. Europe has also taken up the work in the most encouraging manner. Germany, Austria, Holland, Denmark, Sweden and England now have organizations, and the appeal of this society in many of the cities has brought about the granting of "quiet zones" around city hospitals. Mrs. Rice has organized also a children's society, in which Mark Twain took a great interest and was at the time of his death its president. The latest phase of Mrs. Rice's work is to form a national committee of the governors of all the states in order to make this movement country-wide. This work and great movement instigated by the persistency and perseverence of one woman entirely unaided is acknowledged to be one of the most revolutionizing reforms of the century, and Mrs. Rice's courageous perseverence and ceaseless efforts denote a character worthy of the widest emulation. Mrs. Rice is a refined, cultured woman, an accomplished musician and linguist and occupies a high social position in the city of New York. She is a woman of literary ability and has contributed to many of the leading magazines.

MARY VAN KLEECK.

Miss Van Kleeck is a social reformer and economic worker. Secretary of committee on women's work of the Russell Sage Foundation. Miss Van Kleeck was born June 26, 1883, in Glenham, New York. She is the daughter of Eliza Mayer, whose father, Charles F. Mayer, was a prominent lawyer of Baltimore, Maryland. Her father was the Rev. Robert Boyd Van Kleeck, of Fishkill-on-the-Hudson, New York. She graduated from Smith College in 1904, and since then has been engaged in social work, holding the following positions: During the summer of 1904, secretary, Sea Breeze, the fresh air home of the New York Association for Improving the Condition of the Poor; from 1905 to 1907 she was holder of the joint fellowship of the Smith College Alumnæ Association and the College Settlements Association, during which time the subjects of investigation were overtime work of girls in factories and child labor in the New York City tenements. The results of the first investigation were published in *Charities and the Commons*, October 6, 1906, and the report of the second appeared in *Charities and the Commons*, January 18, 1908. From 1907 to 1909 Miss Van Kleeck was industrial secretary of the Alliance Employment Bureau in charge of the investigations of women's work. In 1909 she was secretary of the committee on women's work of the Russell Sage Foundation, continuing the investigations begun at the Alliance Employment Bureau and undertaking others. The subjects of investigation have been women's work in the bookbinding trade in New York, makers of artificial flowers, and working girls in public evening schools in New York. Miss Van Kleeck has also supervised an investigation of the working girls in the millinery trade carried on by Miss Alice P. Barrows, a member of the same staff.

ELSA DENISON.

Miss Denison was born May 17, 1889, in Denver, Colorado. She is the daughter of Dr. Denison and granddaughter of Henry Strong, of Chicago, the well-known philanthropist. She was graduated in Bryn Mawr in June, 1910, and immediately volunteered as a worker in the New York Bureau of Municipal Research and has spent all her time in that important work since her graduation. This one of the most important progressive movements was started in New York by an organization to be known as the New York Bureau of Municipal Research, whose object is an investigation as to the benefit derived from the co-operation of educational associations, women's clubs, boards of trade, and charities with the public schools in the matters of medical and dental examinations, school nurses, sanitary improvements, new buildings, recreation and playgrounds, decorations, industrial training, kindergartens, changes in school laws, relief of the needy, instructions in civics and many other things which will be conducive to the welfare of the children destined to be the men and women of the near future. In reply to their circulars begging for information the bureau has had many interested responses and volunteer workers. Miss Denison, though but twenty-two years of age, has been one of the most effective workers under the bureau and will make a report in September that will be valuable to the bureau in forming plans for further activities. Miss Denison chose the problem of "Civic Co-operation with the Public Schools," because of her patriotic conviction that "upon the wise education of the child to-day depends the efficiency of the citizen of to-morrow." To have that education the best, every citizen must take an active interest in the schools of his community.

MRS. CHARLES S. THAYER.

Mrs. Thayer is the present head of the college settlement in New York. Before her marriage, in 1904, she was Miss Mary Appleton Shute. Mrs. Thayer is a graduate of Smith College.

Among other women prominently connected with settlement work and social investigation may be mentioned Mrs. C. B. Spahr, of Princeton, New Jersey; Miss Jean Gurney Fine, Miss Elizabeth Williams, Miss Maud Miner and Miss Mary B. Sayles, who are all graduates of Smith College. Other Smith women who are prominent in literature are Miss Anna Hempstead Branch, Miss Fannie Harding Eckstorm, Miss Olivia Howard Dunbar, Miss Zephine Humphrey, Miss Anna Chapin Ray, Miss Ella Burns Sherman and Miss Fannie Stearns Davis.

Catholic Women in America.

The Founding of the Georgetown Convent, the Oldest School for Girls in America.

The foundress of the Georgetown Convent, Georgetown, D. C., the first Visitation house in America, was Miss Alice Lalor, known later in religion as Mother Teresa. She was born in Queen's County, Ireland, but her parents removed to Kilkenny where her childhood and early youth were spent. Her tender piety and bright and charitable character won the affection and regard of every one around her, and especially of her pastor, Father Carroll. When at the age of seventeen she received the sacrament of confirmation from Bishop Lanigan, he was attracted also by her modesty, and having instituted with Father Carroll a confraternity of the Blessed Sacrament at Kilkenny, he named Alice Lalor as its first president or prefect. She soon resolved to consecrate herself to God, and was permitted to make the vow of virginity, although complete renunciation of the world could not be made because there was no convent in the neighborhood. One of Alice Lalor's sisters married an American merchant, Mr. Doran, who was desirous that his wife should have the companionship of Alice in her new transatlantic home for a while. Alice, now thirty-one years of age, agreed to go with them, but promised Bishop Lanigan that she would return in two years to aid in forming the religious community so long contemplated. She sailed from Ireland with her sister in the winter of 1794. Among the passengers on the sailing vessel were Mrs. McDermott and Mrs. Sharpe, both widows. During the long voyage, they formed an intimate friendship with Alice and expressed the desire which they had long felt to enter the cloistered life and agreed that when they landed they would go to confession and communion and take the priest, whomsoever might be their confessor, as their spiritual director. They landed in Philadelphia, and the priest whom they found and accepted as their director was, happily, Father Neale. These three devout women brought so unexpectedly to his feet from beyond the sea were the women destined to co-operate with him in founding the community of his vision which he had never ceased to hope that he might realize. Although Alice Lalor felt bound by her promise to return to Ireland, Father Neale saw the greater service she could render to religion in America and offered to release her from her promise to return to her native land. Miss Lalor, Mrs. McDermott and Mrs. Sharpe settled in Philadelphia, hired a house and lived in community. Mrs. Sharpe had her daughter with her, a child of eight years. Suddenly the yellow fever broke out and Father Neale narrowly escaped death. Alice Lalor and her companions remained persistently in the path of danger, ministering to the pest-stricken people. In the winter of 1798-99, Father Neale was ordered to Georgetown as president of the Jesuit College. He sent for the three devoted religious converts and domiciled them for a time with three Poor Clares, who being driven from France to this country by the Revolution of 1793 had set up a little convent not far from the college. The Poor Clares attempted to keep a school as a means of support, but their poverty was so extreme and their life so rigorous that not many scholars applied. These women, poor and barefooted according to their rules, came of noble blood and had been born and reared to luxury. Alice Lalor and her two friends boarded and taught in this convent, but it soon became apparent that the austere rule of St.

Clare differed widely from that they wished to adopt, and was uncongenial to the times and needs of the locality. Father Neale, therefore, bought a house and land nearby and installed them in it. Thus was begun by these three ladies an establishment and school which has become famous in America and from which many of her most noted women have graduated. In 1800 Father Neale was consecrated Coadjutor to Archbishop Carroll and continued as president of the Georgetown College. It is not known when Bishop Neale decided to place these devoted women under visitation rules. This little group increased to five members all of whom were known round about as "The Pious Ladies," their only appellation for many years. Mrs. Sharpe who was known as Sister Ignatia, their principal teacher, after a sudden illness died. In 1804 the Poor Clares returned to France, and Mother Teresa (Alice Lalor) was able to buy the house and land which the Poor Clares had occupied. In 1808, Bishop Neale's term as president of the college ended and he took a dwelling close to the convent, which made it possible for him to supervise closely these new daughters of a still unformed community, whom he was endeavoring to train for a monastic life. It is said that in 1812 their buildings were in a state of total disrepair, the monastery a forlorn-looking house containing six rooms, and in 1811, it is said, Sister Margaret Marshall "succeeded by her energy and the toil of her own hands in lathing and plastering the assembly room." There remains scarcely a vestige of these primitive structures to-day. For a while this was the only Catholic institution of the kind in the United States where the daughters of Catholics might become well grounded in the principles of their religion. The first nine years only four members joined "The Pious Ladies," these were: Sister Aloysia Neale, Sister Stanislaus Fenwick, and Sister Magdalene Neale, and a lay sister, Mary. In 1808 Miss Catherine Ann

Ridgen joined the order and was chosen as Mother Teresa's successor. The mother house at Annecy had been suppressed during the French Revolution, and was not restored until 1822. The other houses in Europe were unwilling to send a copy of the constitutions to Georgetown, because this community had not been founded in the usual way by professed members of the order. The whole undertaking, in short, was looked upon as irregular, and it was believed that Rome would never approve of Bishop Neale's little community. Although schools were opened by Mrs. Seton in Baltimore and one at Emmitsburg Bishop Neale would not consent to abandon his scheme. A rich lady living in Baltimore, who had been educated with the Ursuline nuns in Ireland, heard of the embarrassments at Georgetown, and offered her means and influence to the Archbishop for the benefit of "The Pious Ladies," if they would consent to transform their house into an Ursuline convent. These plans were laid before Bishop Neale, who politely and respectfully thanked this generous and excellent lady for her liberality, but stated he would never consent to the proposed change. The Archbishop, seeing how invincible was Bishop Neale's purpose to continue on the lines he had already laid down, told the good Bishop that he would give him power to do what he could, but he must expect no help from him. One day in examining the books which they found in the little library purchased from the Poor Clares, they found on the title page of one of the books the name of St. Francis de Sales and the word "Visitation." This volume, on examination, proved to contain the rules of the Visitation Order, which they had sought so long and so ardently prayed for. This is believed to have been in about 1809 or 1810, or perhaps a little later. And now, having the rules of the Order, they had but to decide upon their dress. Bishop Neale decided to let them wear the Teresian costume, and wrote to his brother Charles, at

Port Tobacco to send him a model of it from the convent there. A large doll, fully dressed in the habit of the Order, was forwarded to the Bishop. This convent at Port Tobacco was a Carmelite house, so while the costume adopted provisionally at this time was Carmelite, it was changed by the Bishop; the white bandeau of the Teresian Carmelites was replaced with the black, and in this respect, at least, the Georgetown sisters were able to conform to Visitation requirements. Having gained this much, the Bishop, undismayed by those doubts and tremors which beset even some of his loyal co-workers, resolved to admit the sisters to simple vows. This was done on the feast of St. Francis de Sales, January 29, 1814. The secluded life of this community, with its constant, patient, obscure struggles and peaceful joys, was threatened with destruction by the war of 1812 and in 1814, when a formidable movement was begun against the Capital city by Cockburn and General Ross, and the battle of Bladensburg was fought. The sisters were greatly alarmed by the rapid advance of the enemy and the burning of the Capitol, which they witnessed from the upper windows of their monastery. They, however, were spared. In 1815 Archbishop Carrol died at the age of eighty years, and Bishop Neale succeeded him in his high office, becoming the Archbishop of Baltimore. The Archbishop received authority for the admission of his beloved sisters to solemn vows, and the date he fixed upon was the Feast of Holy Innocents, December 28, which was the one hundred and ninety-fourth anniversary of the death of St. Francis de Sales. The three who were chosen for admission first were the oldest members, Alice Lalor, Mrs. McDermott, and Henrietta Brent, who were known, the first as Sister Teresa, Sister Frances, and Sister Agnes, Sister Teresa (Alice Lalor) was appointed Superior; Sister Frances (Mrs. McDermott), the second assistant, and Sister Agnes (Henrietta Brent) Mistress of Novices.

Bishop Neale said in establishing the school that it was founded "to teach the female youth of America," and truly did he prophecy and plan, for hither came the best of the "female youth of America" for many years, and to-day some of our most distinguished women claim the Georgetown Convent of Visitation as their Alma Mater.

In the period just before the war-days, there came to the academy the two daughters of Senator Ewing, of Ohio (the first secretary of the Department of the Interior). One of them, Ellen Ewing, afterwards married General William Tecumseh Sherman. Here also was educated Harriet Lane Johnston, niece of President Buchanan, who gained social distinction at the Court of St. James while her uncle was United States Minister there, and afterwards gracefully conducted for him the social functions of the executive mansion, as one of the most charming in all the line of "ladies of the White House." Another graduate, famous for her exceptional beauty, as well as for her social leadership in Washington, was Adelaide Cutts, who married Stephen A. Douglas, the brilliant rival of Abraham Lincoln for presidential honors. Mrs. Douglas long after her first husband's death, became the wife of General Robert Williams, United States Army.

General Joseph E. Johnston, eminent afterwards among Confederate military chieftains, found his wife in a Visitation graduate, Miss McLain, a daughter of Secretary McLain. Another pupil, Teresa Doyle, married Senator Casserly; and Miss Deslonde, of Louisiana, who studied here, became Mrs. General Beauregard. The following account of the students of the institution is compiled from "A Story of Courage; Annals of the Georgetown Convent of the Visitation of the Blessed Virgin Mary."

"Among others who graduated before the war were Marion Ramsay, who became Mrs. Cutting, of New York; the daughters of Judge Gaston, of North Carolina; the daughters of Commodore Rogers; Eliza and Isabella Walsh, the daughters of the United States Minister to Spain; Minnie Meade, a sister of General Meade, who became the wife of General Hartman Bache, United States Army; Albina Montholon, daughter of the French Minister and granddaughter of General Gratiot, United States Army; Kate Duncan, of Alabama, who married Dr. Emmet, of New York; the daughters of Commodore Cassin; the Bronaugh sisters, one of whom married Admiral Taylor; the Carroll sisters, one of whom became the Baroness Esterhazy, of Austria; the daughters of Senator Stephen Mallory, of Florida; the daughter of Senator Nicholson, of Tennessee, afterwards Mrs. Martin, who became principal of a leading seminary in the South; Katie Irving, a grandniece of Washington Irving; the daughters of Major Turnbull; Mary Maguire, who became the wife of General Eugene Carr. Of the daughters of Mrs. Bass, of Mississippi, afterwards wife of the Italian Minister, Bertinatti, one married a foreign nobleman. Madeleine Vinton became the wife of Admiral Dahlgren; Emily Warren became Mrs. Roebling, the wife of the builder of the Brooklyn bridge, who herself completed the great work when her husband had been stricken with illness. Nancy Lucas, who married Doctor Johnson, of St. Louis, sent five daughters to the convent, as did also Major Turner. General Frost sent five representatives, one of whom married Philip Beresford Hope, son of the distinguished member of Parliament. Adele Sarpy, who became Mrs. Don Morrison, a pupil herself, later on sent her three daughters. Ellen Sherman Thackara and Rachel Sherman Thorndyke, daughters of General Sherman, followed in their mother's footsteps at Georgetown. Myra Knox became Mrs. Thomas J. Semmes, of New Orleans. Ada Semmes, who married Richard Clarke, the historian, with her sisters, one of whom was Mrs. Ives were also pupils here.

Among other leading Southern families represented at the school at this time were the Floyds of Virginia and the Stephenses of Georgia.

"Of those who have graduated since the war are: Bertha and Ida Honore; the former Mrs. Potter Palmer, who was brought prominently before the country as the president of the Board of Lady Managers of the World's Columbian Exposition. Her sister became the wife of General Frederick D. Grant, formerly United States Minister to Austria, now a general in the United States Army. Blanche Butler, the daughter of General Benjamin F. Butler, became the wife of Governor Ames, of Mississippi, and Mary Goodell married Governor Grant, of Colorado. Harriet Monroe, of Chicago, who wrote the ode for the Columbian World's Fair, graduated in 1879, having for her classmates Adele Morrison, of St. Louis, now Mrs. Albert T. Kelly, of New York; Ella Whitthorne, of Tennessee, now Mrs. Alexander Harvey, of Baltimore, and Miss Newcomer, of Baltimore who, as Mrs. H. B. Gilpin, annually presents a medal for music to the school. Mary Saunders, the daughter of ex-Senator Saunders, of Nebraska, as the wife of Russell Harrison, the ex-President's son, graced the White House by her presence during Benjamin Harrison's administration. Mary Logan Tucker, the daughter of the soldier and statesman, General John A. Logan, now wields as a journalist a pen as trenchant as was her father's sword.

"The portraits of Emma Etheridge, of Tennessee, the daughter of Honorable Emerson Etheridge, and Josephine Dickson, of Missouri, which adorn the walls of the convent parlor, are those of two young ladies noted for their beauty. The former is now Mrs. John V. Moran, of Detroit, and the latter Mrs. Julius Walsh, of St. Louis; Estelle Dickson studied art in Paris.

"Among other pupils were Pearl Tyler, daughter of

President Tyler; Gertrude and Jessie Alcorn, the daughters of Senator Alcorn, of Mississippi; Romaine Goddard, daughter of Mrs. Dahlgren, who became the Countess von Overbeck; Irene Rucker, who become the wife of General Philip H. Sheridan; Constance Edgar, now the Countess Moltke Huitfeldt, daughter of Madam Bonaparte and granddaughter of Daniel Webster; Mary Wilcox, granddaughter by adoption of General Andrew Jackson. Ethel Ingalls, daughter of ex-Senator Ingalls, has reflected credit on the academy by her literary work; her younger sister, Constance, followed her at the school, together with Anna Randall Lancaster, and her sister Susie, daughters of the late Samuel J. Randall; the five daughters of the late A. S. Abell, of Baltimore, and Jennie Walters, daughter of W. T. Walters of the same city.

"Miss Early and Miss Ould were two gifted Southern ladies who are remembered at the school. Miss E. M. Dorsey, also, a bright and winning story-writer, whose 'Midshipman Bob' is well and favorably known to young readers, is one of the later graduates."

Even this partial list of some among those who have received their training at Georgetown Convent in knowledge, morals, manners and the conduct of life, is at first rather surprising by reason of the high rank and average of the women educated here. Yet on second and deeper thought it will appear to be only a reasonable result of so much patient labor, lofty endeavor, unselfish effort, and devout studiousness, offered day by day for a century, with no other thought than that of contributing to the glory of God and the blessing of the human race, in whole and in particular.

The annals of this illustrious institution, which celebrated its Centennial in 1899, must, we think, place one fact very clearly before the minds of all thoughtful and observant readers, and that is, the marked degree of individuality characterizing the members of such a body as the Georgetown Convent of the Visitation.

This we trust has been demonstrated by such definite examples as the steadfast endurance and guiding hope of Mother Teresa Lalor; the virgin self-reliance and bravery of Sister Margaret Marshall; the firm executive quality of Mother Agnes Brent and other Superiors; the gentle, tactful rule of Mother Juliana Matthews; the vivacious and exquisitely trustful, spiritualized personality of "Sister Stanny" (Sister Stanislaus) who was the daughter of Commodore Jacob Jones, United States Navy, who captured the British war-sloop "Frolic," for which act he received the thanks of Congress, a reward of $25,000.00 and a gold medal; the enthusiasm for astronomical study of Sister Genevieve White, who was a sister of the late Judge White, of New York, and niece of Gerald Griffin, the famous Irish poet, and her sister, dear Sister Teresa, in the midst of bodily suffering; the grand, sturdy serviceableness of Sister Joseph Keating, who was of noble French descent; the delicate, skillful housekeeping and responsive charity of Mother Angela Harrison, or the perfect meekness of Sister Mary Emmanuel Scott, daughter of General Winfield Scott; Sister Bernard Graham, daughter of Honorable George Graham, who was a very remarkable business woman; Sister Eulalia Pearce; Sister Mary Austin, who was a wife and the mother of five children when she presented herself for her vows in the Order. She was received and became a nun—her husband a Jesuit priest—and two of her children were brought up by the mother of Father Fenwick and three by the Sisters of the Convent in which she was a nun. Among those of later date who are affectionately remembered by the present generation of graduates and scholars are: Sister Mary Loretto King, long the able directress of the school and a woman of wonderful executive ability, strength of character and mental qualities possessed by few of her sex; Sister Paulina Willard; Sister Loyola Leocadia, a gifted woman and to whom we are indebted for the collecting and preparation of the Annals of the Convent, now in book form.   Sister, now Mother Fidelis, is the last of that type of women noted for their great executive and mental strength which have put their stamp on the women they sent out into the world to become forces in the progress of their sex, going on in America to-day; Sister Benedicto, with her gentle spirit and marked artistic talents, has developed the talents of those of the students who came within her care, among whom many are to-day well known in the world of art and owe to her their first creditable work.   It might be mentioned that Madame Yturbide found a refuge in this Convent after the tragic death of her husband, the self-proclaimed president of Mexico, who was shot on his return from exile.   She wore the garb of a nun and her daughter became a novice and is buried with the sisters here.   These are but a few, among the larger few, whom we have sketched in this book, and all, taken together, are only instances of the traits and capacities of numberless other sisters. They show that not only may there be pronounced individuality among the members of a religious order, but also a wide variety of development, under the uniform garb and the equal submission to a common rule and discipline.

The alumnae of the Georgetown Convent of Visitation was organized by Mary Logan Tucker, daughter of General John A. Logan, a graduate of the Georgetown Convent of Visitation, who was elected its first president, March 3, 1893.

Prominent Catholic Women in America.

Mrs. Frances Tiernan, novelist, whose pen name is "Christian Reid," was a daughter of Colonel Charles F. Fisher of the Confederate Army.   Her girlhood home was in Salisbury, North Carolina, to which she returned on the death of her husband, James M. Tiernan, of Maryland.   Among the thirty or more stories which have made famous her pen name "Christian Reid," are "A Daughter of Bohemia," "Valerie Aylmar," "Morton House," "Heart of Steel," "Cast for Fortune," and "A Little Maid of Arcady." Mrs. Tiernan has received a Laetare medal from Notre Dame University, Indiana.

Miss Grace Charlotte Mary Regina Strachan, educator, social worker and writer, is the daughter of Thomas F. Strachan, a Scotch Presbyterian, but entered the Catholic church, of which her mother was a devoted member. She was educated in Buffalo, New York, first, at Saint Bridget's and later at the Buffalo State Normal School and she has taken several New York University extension courses. Since 1900 she has been superintendent of the public schools of New York, and is well known for her philanthropic work in the Young Women's Catholic Association of Brooklyn, where she has taught free classes. Miss Strachan has also been most active in promoting the cause of equal pay for equal work and is interested in all Catholic charities. She has contributed several articles and stories to the *Delineator* and has traveled in this country and abroad, having been granted an audience with Pope Pius X. She is president of the Interborough Association of Women Teachers and a member of many other organizations.

Georginia Pell Curtis was born in New York City, February 19, 1859, and although of Protestant parentage and educated at a Protestant school she was afterwards converted to the Roman Catholic Church, and has since been a constant and brilliant contributor to all the publications devoted to the interests of that church. Her writings have appeared in the *Ave Maria*, the *Catholic World*, the *Messenger*, the *Magnificat*, the *Messenger of the Sacred Heart, Donahoe's*, the *Rosary*, and the *Pilgrim*. She is also the editor of "Some Roads to Rome in America," and the "American Catholic Who's Who." She comes justly by her ready, facile mental qualities and her ability for logical work, coming from distinguished ancestry along Colonial and Dutch lines; on the maternal side Miss Curtis is a granddaughter of Thomas Hill, known on the stage as Thomas Hillson, an English actor of the old Park Theatre, New York, who numbered among his intimate friends, Junius Brutus Booth, John William Wallack, and Washington Irving. Other lineal ancestors of whom Miss Curtis is justly proud were Peter Vandewaker, keeper of the city gate at the foot of Wall Street, New York, in the eighteenth century, and Jacobus Vandewaker, mayor of New Amsterdam, in 1673.

Mrs. Edwin F. Abell, daughter of the late Frank Laurenson, a noted merchant of Baltimore. She married the late Edwin F. Abell, son of Arunah S. Abell, founder of the *Baltimore Sun*. Mr. Abell, succeeded his father as editor of the *Sun*, and under this guidance it remained as it had always been one of the most efficient and influential journals in the United States, and in its columns all affairs of interest and benefit to the Catholic Church in America have always been given just and dignified treatment.

Madam Marie Louise Alband, was born at Chambly, near Montreal, in 1852, and was the daughter of Joseph Lajeunesse, a musician. Musical ability was early evidenced in the daughter and at the age of fifteen she had finished her education at the Sacred Heart Convent in Albany, New York, and had become organist at the Church of the Sacred Heart in New York City. Later she studied in Paris and Milan under distinguished musicians, eventually making her debut in Messina, in 1870. Her success, which established her as a famous singer, was achieved in the Royal Italian Opera in London, in 1870. Since then her voice has been heard in opera and sacred music by great audiences in America and England.

MOTHER O. C. D. AUGUSTINE.

She was the daughter of the late Samuel Tuckerman. She entered the Religious Order of the Carmelites, in Baltimore, in 1893, and for three years was Superior of the Carmelite Monastery, in Roxbury, Boston, having been one of the founders of this order. In 1908 a branch of the order was established in San Francisco on the estate of Robert Louis Stevenson, and Mother Augustine was placed in charge, where she has remained ever since.

LAURA ELIZABETH LEE BATTLE.

Was born January 26, 1855, and is a descendant of the celebrated Lees of Virginia. Has been active in the work of building Catholic Churches in Michigan and North Carolina.

KATE WALKER BEHAN.

Was the daughter of William Walker, a prominent citizen of New Orleans, Louisiana. She married General William J. Behan. Is president of the ladies auxiliary of the Good Shepherd, for Magdalenes, one of the most prominent Catholic Societies of New Orleans; also president of the Ladies' Confederated Memorial Association and president of the Jefferson Davis Monument Association, and chairman of the civic department of the Women's League of New Orleans.

MARY ELIZABETH THOMAS BLOW.

Was born May 27, 1863 at Cape Elizabeth, Maine. One of her father's ancestors, Isaiah Thomas, was the publisher of the first Bible in New England. One of her mother's ancestors, General Timothy Pickering, was president of the war board in Revolutionary time, Secretary of State, and Postmaster-General under Washington. She is the wife of Major William N. Blow, 15th Infantry, United States Army.

ROSALIE B. DE SOLMS BOND.

Was the daughter of Sidney J. de Solms and Maria del Carmen de Solms. She was born November 26, 1843, in Philadelphia, Pennsylvania. Is one of the founders of the Catholic Guild, now the Dominican House of Retreat; member of the association of Perpetual Adoration and Work for Poor Churches, and other societies. The de Solms family is one of the most distinguished Catholic families of Philadelphia and Mr. de Solms presented to the Cathedral, in Logan Square, the painting of the "Crucifixion" which is over the main altar.

JOSEPHINE HALE BOYLE.

Was the daughter of Joseph P. Hale, of San Francisco, California. Her husband enjoys the distinction of being heir-presumptive to the Earldom of Cork.

MRS. PETER ARRELL BROWNE.

Was born April 14, 1834, and is the daughter of Thomas Parkin and Julianna M. Scott, of Baltimore. In 1860 she married P. A. Browne, Jr., who was the son of Peter Arrell and Harriet Harper Browne, of Philadelphia, and in 1861 they removed to Baltimore. Mr. Browne was a prominent lawyer of Maryland and auditor of the Superior Court, of Baltimore. Mrs. Browne's father was also a distinguished lawyer being chief judge of the Supreme Bench of Baltimore City, and a member of the Maryland legislature in 1861, and with others was imprisoned for refusing to take the oath of allegiance to the United States.

ANNA ELIZABETH BRYAN.

Was one of the most prominent women of the South, being the daughter of the late Admiral Raphael Semmes. Is prominent in Catholic charitable work of her home city, Memphis, Tennessee.

EMMA WESTCOTT BULLOCK.

Is the widow of Jonathan Russell Bullock, who was formerly judge of the United States District Court of Rhode Island She is a member of the national patriotic societies of the country, The Colonial Dames, Descendants of Colonial Governors, Society of the Mayflower, etc.; hereditary life member of the National Mary Washington Memorial Association.

SUZANNE BANCROFT CARROLL.

Is a graddaughter of Honorable George Bancroft, the historian of the United States. Her husband is the son of John Lee Carroll, of Ellicott City, Maryland. The family emigrated to Maryland, in 1688, and have been conspicuous in the history of the United States. One of his ancestors, Charles Carroll, of Carrollton, was a signer of the Declaration of Independence. He took a prominent part in the Independence Movement and was a member of the Convention of Maryland chosen to frame the constitution; also a member of the first Congress of the United States in 1777, and of the board of war, and a senator from Maryland. Mrs. Carroll lives in Paris, France.

MOTHER PRAXEDES CARTY, (SUSAN CARTY).

Was born at Rawnsboy, County Cavan, Ireland, and entered into the novitiate of the Loretta Sisters in 1874. She was Superior of the convent in Bernalillo, New Mexico; also Las Cruces, New Mexico; Florissant, Missouri, and Loretta Heights, near Denver. In 1896 she became Mother Superior of the whole order of the Society of the Sisters of Loretta at Loretta, Kentucky. She has made several trips to Rome in the interests of this order and was elected Mother-General in 1904. The order is now known as the Sisters of Loretta at the Foot of the Cross, and her title is Superior-General of this order.

MARGARET ELIZABETH CASEY.

Was born December, 1874, in Beatrice, Nebraska. Active in the ladies' auxiliary, Ancient Order of Hibernians. Was secretary in 1900 of the law class of the Kansas State University.

MRS. JAMES BLANCHARD CLEWS.

Is the granddaughter of the late Honorable Charles Nichols, at one time minister to The Hague. Her husband, J. B. Clews, is a nephew of Henry Clews of the firm of Henry Clews and Company, bankers of New York City. She is active, and has been for several years, in all Catholic charitable work.

ZOE DESLOGE COBB.

Was born in Potosi, Missouri, December 18, 1850. Is president of the Children of Mary, Sacred Heart Convent, and also president of the ladies' auxiliary, St. Louis Obstetrical Dispensary.

EDYTHE PATTEN CORBIN.

Mrs. Corbin, the wife of General Henry C. Corbin, United States Army, was one of the most prominent social leaders of Washington before her husband's death, and by her kindliness, charm, and practical sense endeared herself to the army. She is the daughter of Edmund and Anna Statia Patten, of California, who were pioneers of the Pacific coast, and belonged to that circle of early settlers the Mackays, Fairs, and Crockers, who made their fortunes in the gold fields of that state. Mrs. Corbin and her sisters were educated in a convent in Paris. She is a most accomplished conversationalist, speaking French, German, and Italian fluently, and is to-day one of the charming women of Washington, D. C.

ANNA McLANE CROPPER.

Was born March 11, 1859, in Portsmouth, New Hampshire. Is the daughter of Allen and Ariadne Knight McLane. Her family were prominent in the army, navy, and diplomatic service of the United States. Her father's father, Louis McLane, was a member of Congress, Senator, Secretary of the Treasury, Secretary of State under General Jackson, and Minister to England. Her own father was a graduate of the Naval Academy, but resigned in 1850, and was for many years president of the Pacific Mail Steamship Company. She is prominent in the Society of Colonial Dames.

MOTHER ANTONINA O. S. D. FISCHER.

Before entering sacred order her name was Mary Ann Fischer, and she was born in Bavaria, Germany, November 22, 1849. Is the daughter of John and

Mary Ann Fischer. She was a member of the Dominican Order for thirty-four years. In 1902 she went with seven Sisters to Great Bend, Kansas, and founded the Mother House and novitiate of the Sisters of St. Dominic.

STELLA M. HAMILTON.

Daughter of Mr. and Mrs. Charles W. Hamilton, and was born in Omaha. Is prominent in social work of that city, and active member of the Christ Child Society.

JULIA CARLIN HARDIN.

Was born in Carrollton, Green County, Illinois. Her ancestors were prominent among the early settlers of Illinois. She married John A. Hardin, of Louisville, Kentucky, who died in 1884.

MRS. FRANCIS T. HOMER.

Is the daughter of George W. and Jennie Webb Abell, and granddaughter of A. S. Abell, the well-known founder of the *Baltimore Sun.* In 1902 she married Francis T. Homer, of Baltimore.

LOUISE FRANCES HUNT.

Was born in Paris, France, in 1837. Is the daughter of John T. and Anne Maria Hyde Adams, and the wife of William H. Hunt, Secretary of the Navy under President Garfield, and Minister to Russia under President Arthur

MRS. GEORGE MERRIAM HYDE.

Is the daughter of the late Oliver Prince Buel, of New York, and granddaughter of General Charles Macdougall. Her mother was a member of the well-known family of Hillhouse and of Bishop Atkinson's family. Mrs. Merriam is now Sister Mary of the Tabernacle.

ELIZA LE BRUN MILLER JOYCE.

Was born in Ohio, April 5, 1840. Her father, Thomas Miller, in that year came to Ohio from Bronwnsville, Pennsylvania. Her mother's (Margaret T. Wilson) father, Thomas Wilson, Mrs. Joyce's grandfather, was obliged to leave Ireland in the rebellion of 1798, forfeiting his property, which was restored to him forty years later. She is regent for Trinity College, Washington, D. C., and on the board of mangers of several charitable institutions. Active in organizing charitable societies in the church.

ANNE LEARY.

Was born in the city of New York of Irish parentage, and is a sister of the late Arthur Leary. She is one of the most prominent social leaders of

New York City and Newport and much beloved for her generous charity and her great accomplishments. She was created a countess by Pope Leo XIII in recognition of her services to the church. She spends much of her time abroad.

ADELE LE BRUN.

Was the daughter of Napoleon Le Brun, of New York, the well-known architect. She was instrumental and conspicuous in bringing to this country the Society of the Helpers of the Holy Souls, which had been founded in France by Mère Marie de la Providence. The house for this order was opened in May, 1892, and she has made the extension and the furtherance of the good works of this order her life work.

MARGARET McCABE.

Was born in 1846 in Cincinnati, Ohio. Founded the Sacred Heart Home for Working Girls and the Boys' Home in Cincinnati, and prominent in the building of the Church of the Sacred Heart of that city.

MARCHIONESS SARA McLAUGHLIN.

Created a marchioness by Pope Pius X in 1908, in recognition of her benefactions in the interest of religion. She is the widow of the late political leader, Hugh McLaughlin.

MOTHER EUTROPIA McMAHON.

Superior of the Sisters of Charity, of Nazareth, Kentucky, to which she was elected in 1909, having been previously Superior of the Presentation Academy at Louisville.

SISTER JOSEPHINE O. S. D. MEAGHER.

Was born in 1841 in County Tipperary, Ireland, and emigrated to this country in 1852. She and her sister both entered the order of St. Dominic at Springfield, Illinois. In 1873 Sister Josephine was placed in charge of a little band of religious people and sent to Jacksonville, Illinois, to establish an independent community, over which she presided for fifteen years. In 1908 they celebrated the fiftieth anniversary of her entrance into religious life.

REBECCA NEWELL MORISON.

Was born in Rhode Island, and is the widow of H. G. O. Morison. It is said the "Knownothings" tried to burn the convent in New England where she was staying to "rescue her from the Popish Nuns."

MARGARET O'BRIEN.

Assistant librarian, Omaha Public Library. Is the daughter of the late General George Morgan O'Brien, United States Army.

MARY SEMMES ORRICK.

Is a descendant of the distinguished Admiral Raphael Semmes, U. S. N., and the widow of Dr. Nicholas C. Orrick, of Kenton, Massachusetts.

MARIE MARTIN PALMS.

Is the wife of F. L. Palms, of Detroit, Michigan, and was born in New Orleans, Louisiana. Is the president of the Weinman Catholic settlement.

MRS. THEOPHILE EMILY CARLIN PAPIN.

Was born in Carrollton, Illinois, and is the daughter of William and Mary Goode Carlin. In 1865 she married Theophile Papin, great-grandson of Pierre de Laclède Ligueste, the founder of St. Louis. Some of her ancestors left Ireland in the Revolution of 1798 and settled in Virginia, eventually going with a colony to Illinois. An uncle, Thomas Carlin, was governor of Illinois from 1838 to 1842 and founded the town of Carrollton. Mrs. Papin is prominent as an active worker in the charitable work of the Catholic church in St. Louis and in the social life of that city.

KATHERINE LAUGHLIN PFOHL.

Was born in Buffalo, New York, in 1867. Is the daughter of John M. and Mary A. Whalen Laughlin. Her grandfather on her mother's side was one of McMahon's Irish Regiment and was killed at Spottsylvania Court House. Her granduncle was Bishop Marrom of Kilkenny, Ireland. In 1887 she married George W. Pfohl, whose ancestors came to this country with Lafayette. Mrs. Pfohl is the director of the Working Boy's Home of the Sacred Heart; also St. Elizabeth's Hospital Association, and St. Mary's Infant Asylum. Is president of the O. M. I. Parish Aid Society, Holy Angels Church, and vice-president of the St. James Mission and of the Catholic Women's Club.

MRS. ANDREW WELSH, SR.

One of the generous benefactors of the Catholic Church, having given $100,000 to St. Ignatius College, California, and later $50,000 to Santa Clara College near San Francisco.

MOTHER MARY DE SALES (WILHELMINA TREDOW).

Was the daughter of William Tredow of Vienna, and the Princess Clementine of Saxe-Coburg. Is the director of the Bradford Park Academy, Ursuline Nuns, located in Bedford Park, New York.

ELIZABETH A. SETON.

Founder and first Superioress of the Sisters of Charity. Elizabeth Ann Bayley was born in New York City, the 28th of August, 1774, and was the daughter of Dr. Richard Bayley, a distinguished American physician. Her mother died when she was but three years of age. Miss Bayley was brought up in the doctrines and practices of the Protestant Episcopal Church, to which her parents belonged. At the age of twenty she became the wife of William Seton, a merchant of New York City, whose early life had been spent in Leghorn. About the beginning of the year 1800, Mr. Seton's affairs became much embarrassed from the consequences of the war and other vicissitudes incident to trade. Mrs. Seton rose to the necessities of the occasion. She not only cheered him by her unfailing courage, but aided him in the arrangement of his affairs. Mrs. Seton was the mother of five children. Her influence was not only confined to her own family circle, but she sought wherever it was possible to draw the hearts of others to the consideration of their true welfare. So zealous was she in this respect that she and another relative were frequently called the Protestant sisters of charity. In 1801, Mrs. Seton's father, Dr. Bayley, died, but although her father had married a second time, Mrs. Seton was very devoted to him during his entire life. In 1803 Mr. Seton's health became so precarious that they resolved upon visiting Italy. Owing to many calamities and a form of contagion and sudden illness among her children, and the extreme kindness and devotion of the Catholic friends of Mr. and Mrs. Seton, she was brought under the influence and lived in the atmosphere of the Roman Catholic Church, and ultimately she became a convert to this faith. While away she was in constant correspondence with Father Cheverus, and owing to the counsel and advice of Bishop Carroll she ultimately, on Ash Wednesday, March 14, 1805, presented herself for acceptance in the Church of St. Peter's, New York City. She was received into the church by Rev. Matthew O'Brien. Mrs. Seton being anxious to exert her influence for the benefit of her own family and others, opened a boarding house for young boys who attended school in the city. May 26, 1806, Mrs. Seton was confirmed by Bishop Carroll in the presence of her devoted friend, Mr. A. Filicchi, her husband's former friend of Leghorn. Through Mrs. Seton's zeal she brought her sister-in-law, Cecelia Seton, into the circle of the Roman church and her sister Harriet joined Mrs. Seton when she went to Baltimore, and here she collected around her a band of religiously inclined young women. Mrs. Seton decided upon establishing an order for the care and instruction of poor children. Mr. Cooper, a convert and student of St. Mary's for the priesthood, was anxious to devote his property to the service of God. The clergy were consulted on this occasion and the city of Emmitsburg, Maryland, was fixed upon as full of moral and physical advantages for a religious community. The title of Mother had already been gladly given everywhere to Mrs. Seton. One lady after another came gathering about her in fervor and humility offering themselves as candidates for the new sisterhood. A conventual habit was adopted, which was afterwards changed to that worn by the Sisters of Charity and under the title of Sisters of St. Joseph, a little band was organized under temporary rules. At the end of July, Mother Seton and the whole of her community, now ten in number, besides her three daughters and her sister-in-law, removed to a little farmhouse on their own land, in St. Joseph's Valley, which was to be their own home. In 1811, measures were taken to procure from France a copy of the regulations in use among the Daughters of Charity founded by St. Vincent de Paul, as it was intended that St. Joseph's community should model itself upon the same basis. All during this time, Mrs. Seton had continued her devotion as mother to her own children, and she says, in writing to a friend, "By the law of the church I so much love, I could never take an obligation which interfered with my duties to the children, except I had an independent provision and guardian for them, which the whole world could not supply to my judgment of a mother's duty." This and every other difficulty in the adoption of the rules was, however, at length arranged by the wisdom of Archbishop Carroll, and in January, 1812, the constitutions of the community were confirmed by the Archbishop and Superioress of St. Mary's College in Baltimore. In 1820 Mrs. Seton's health failed, and her lungs became so seriously affected that medical attendance gave her no hope of recovery. Her death occurred January 4, 1821. 1821.

MARY HARDEY.

As we trace the lineage of Mother Mary Aloysia Harley we turn to one of the brightest pages in the history of America. It records the eventful day when under the leadership of Leonard Calvert a company of English Catholics sailed from their native land to lay the foundation of civil and religious liberty in the new world. Among these high-souled pilgrims was Nicholas Hardey, a man of undaunted courage and of unflinching fidelity to his faith. Another, the grandfather of Mary Hardey, came in direct line from this loyal son of the mother church and was well-known in the colonial times throughout Maryland and Virginia. He lived near Alexandria and was an intimate friend of George Washington. Frederick William Hardey was the third son of Anthony Hardey and inherited the winning qualities of his father. In 1800, he married Sarah Spalding. The year 1803 is noted in the history of America as the year of the Louisiana Purchase. When this

40

last territory came into the United States, a tide of emigration flowed steadily for a number of years in the direction of the Gulf of Mexico. Among the pioneers from Maryland was Mr. Charles Anthony Hardey, who fixed his residence in lower Louisiana. The young Republic of America after separating from the mother country, entered at once upon a life of intense energy, and the church was not the last to feel the inspiration of freedom. Before the close of the eighteenth century the orders of Carmel and the Visitation were established in the United States. The first decade of the nineteenth century saw the birth of Mother Seton's congregation in Maryland, and about this time two religious communities sprang up in the newly settled regions of the far West, the Lorettines and the Sisters of Nazareth in Kentucky. A little later came the Daughters of St. Dominic. On the Atlantic coast, the Ursulines had founded convents in New York and Boston. In 1815, when Bishop Dobourg was appointed to the See of New Orleans, his first care was to provide educational advantages for the children of his vast diocese; hence when in Paris, he made application to Mother Barat for a colony of nuns. He had been silently preparing among the Daughters of the Sacred Heart an apostle for the American mission in the person of Mother Phillipine Duchesne. On the fifteenth of December, 1804, Mother Barat accompanied by three nuns arrived at Sainte Marie and took possession of it in the name of the Sacred Heart. Mme. Duchesne was anxious to undertake the work for the church in the new field and far off regions of America. After fourteen years of waiting, her earnest desires were realized. She was accompanied by Mme. Octavie Berthold, who was born a Calvinist, her father having been Voltaire's private secretary. Mme. Eugenie Audi entered the Society of the Sacred Heart in Paris, and offered herself for the mission of the Sacred Heart in America. Two lay sisters were chosen to accompany this little band of missionaries, and on the 29th of May, the anniversary of the Feast of the Sacred Heart, they landed on the shores of America about sixty miles below New Orleans. After their arrival they determined to join the Ursulines in St. Louis, arriving there August 21, 1818, where they established a school about fifteen miles out of the city. The wife of Mr. Charles Smith, a relative of the Hardey family, who had left Maryland in 1803 to make Louisiana his home, built the first Catholic church in New Orleans, and one of their plans was the establishment of a school at Grand Cateau which was the home of Mary Hardey. Proposal for this foundation was in due time accepted by Mother Barat and the organization entrusted to Mme. Audi. In October, five pupils were received, one of whom was Mary Hardey. Here she spent the early years of her education, and during this time her thoughts were turned to a religious life which met with the hearty approval of her mother, but her father, while not approving did not oppose her in her plans, and on September 29, 1825, she entered upon her training for religious orders, receiving the religious habit on the 22nd of October, 1825. About sixty miles from New Orleans, on the left bank of the Mississippi, lie the farm lands associated with the pathetic story of the Arcadian exiles and glorified by the charm of Longfellow's magical pen. These woodlands are embalmed with memories of the gentle Evangeline. Not far from these smiling scenes, in the midst of a devout Catholic population, the Society of the Sacred Heart founded its third convent in America. The Abbé Delacroix, curé of the small town of St. Michael, appealed to Mother Duchesne to establish a convent in his parish, and it was decided that Mother Audi was the only one who could carry on the work. She entered upon it assisted by some novices, among them being Mary Hardey, who was then not yet sixteen. On the 23rd of October, 1825, they bade farewell to their relatives and friends, and on the 20th of November, took possession of their new convent. Mme. Hardey profited so well by the training she received and made such progress in humility and self-renunciation that her period of noviceship was abridged, and she was admitted to her first vows, March, 1827. May, 1827, Mme. Matilda Hamilton, assistant superior of the School of St. Michael died. Like Mme. Hardey to whom she was related, Mme. Hamilton sprang from one of those English Catholic families who sought liberty on the shores of the Chesapeake. Her father left Maryland in 1810 for upper Louisiana. In those days the advantages of education in this part of the world were very great. After taking her first vows, Mme. Hamilton was sent to Cateau and later accompanied Mother Audi to St. Michael, where her death occurred. In 1832, the Convent of St. Michael counted two hundred inmates. In the spring of 1832, the Asiatic cholera appeared for the first time in America, having been carried to Quebec. The pestilence turned southward, advancing with the current of the Mississippi, along whose borders it mowed down thousands of victims. During the next spring the contagion swept over Louisiana, and the Convent of St. Michael was included in its destructive course. Mme. Audi and Mme. Aloysia Hardey stood valiantly by this little community and remained at their post of duty. After Mother Hardey's service as superior at this convent, she was appointed superior of the Convent of New York. Her work in Louisiana was the beginning of a long and eventful career in labors for the church in various institutions which were established throughout the country. She assisted in the foundation of orders in Halifax, Nova Scotia and Buffalo, New York. In 1846, she established a convent in Philadelphia. In 1847, she purchased the Cowperthwaite estate, ten miles from Philadelphia, and established a school known as Eden Hall, and confided it to the care of Mother Tucker, mistress-general of Manhattanville. The two foundations of Halifax and Buffalo made heavy demands on the community of Manhattanville. Among the many foundations organized by Mother Hardey, there is probably none more interesting in history than that of Detroit. In 1852, Mother Hardey established a free school in New York City for the instruction of poor children. The Manhattanville School owes its establishment and organization to her. In 1863, she began labors for the church in Cuba, establishing a boarding school for girls in Sancto Spiritu, Cuba. At one time when it was decided that Mother Hardey should leave Manhattanville and be succeeded by another superior this met with the earnest disapproval of Archbishop McCloskey, and a letter was received from Mother Barat at the head of the order in France written to Archbishop Hughes promising that she would never withdraw Mother Hardey from Manhattanville. In addition to this she organized parochial schools and many of the prominent educational institutions of the church in existence to-day. She was the instrument of the church for the foundation in Cincinnati. At the time of the memorable and terrible conflagration in Chicago in 1871, Mother Hardey organized bazaars in all her houses and sent the proceeds to be distributed to the most needy sufferers. When the terrible days of 1871 had drawn to a close, Mother Hardey was appointed assistant-general and deputed to visit the convents in North America, which required several months, as at this time they numbered twenty-five houses. After this service, she was permanently transferred to Paris to give to Mother Goetz the benefit of her experience and judgment in determining matters of importance to the church. Mother Goetz's death occurred January 4, 1874. She was succeeded by Mother Lehon as superior-general and her first act as such was to send Mother Hardey to America to attend to business matters for the Manhattanville property.

It was during this visit to America that she established the Tabernacle Society in connection with the sodality of the Children of Mary.   In 1876, after her return to France, she was sent by the mother-general to visit the convents of Spain. Fifty years of labor, zeal, and devotedness to the good of others is the record of this noble woman. In September, 1877, when the superiors from sixty houses in the various parts of the world met for the purpose of a spiritual retreat, Mother Hardey requested that she be permitted to return to America with some of the visiting superiors owing to her failing health, and on the 20th of October, the little party sailed for New York. On the 18th of July, she sailed on her return journey to France.   She accompanied Mother Lehon on several tours to various convents in Belgium, England and Italy.   In 1882, she was again sent to New York for the purpose of saving the Manhattanville property, the encroachments of the city threatening its very existence.   While in America on this mission, she experienced a severe illness, and it was doubtful whether she would be able to make the return voyage, but on February 18, 1884, she sailed for France, very weak and at the risk of her life.   Although she never regained her health, gradually failing physically, she remained mentally strong until the very last.   On Thursday, the 17th of June, 1886, at the age of seventy-six, she died, after sixty years and ten months' service for her church. Thus ended the life of one of the most remarkable women in America in labors for the advancement of education and religion.

The Jewish Women of America.

Though woman's activity in communal affairs has been great and potent, its record is one of work so modestly performed that while fully appreciated, there are but few records to be procured on so important a topic. While men have sacrificed property and even life itself for the faith of their fathers, yet some of the most dramatic cases of self sacrifice and devotion on American soil were cases of Jewish women during the colonization of South America, Mexico and this country and during the wars for our independence and the abolition of slavery. To this day the Spanish and Portuguese congregation of New York shows its gratitude to the women who gave substantial aid in effecting the building of the first synagogue erected in that city in 1730. In this manner their names have been preserved and all honor is due to Abigail Franks, Simha de Torres, Rachel Louiza, Judith Pacheco, Hannah Michaels and Miriam Lopez de Fonseca. Jewish immigrants continued to come from Spain and Portugal as late as 1767 and in Georgia they were among the earliest settlers of that colony in 1733. Another distinct group were the early German Jews in America, and to this group belongs the Shetfall family. In 1740 the British government passed an act for the naturalization of foreigners in the American colony and it is remarkable that a large number of Jewish women availed themselves of this act. In Jamaica no less than forty names appear, several of them doubtless related to many of our old American families. Among these Esther Pereira Mendes, Leah Cardoza, Esther Pinto Brandon and similar names. In colonial society prior to the Revolution, several Jewish women

(631)

took a prominent part and not a few were numbered among the belles of that day.

Among these may be mentioned several ladies of the wealthy and influential Franks family; Abigail Franks married Andrew Hamilton, of Philadelphia. Phila Franks, in 1750, married General De Lancy and their New York home was one of the pretentious mansions of the day and later became the Fraunces Tavern and was the very building in which George Washington delivered his farewell address. A daughter of Joseph Simon, of Lancaster, married Dr. Nicholas Schuyler, subsequently one of the surgeons in the Revolutionary War. Sarah Isaacs, the daughter of a patriot soldier, married outside of her own religion and her son was John Howard Payne, the noted composer of "Home, Sweet Home." Among these Rebecca Frank deserves special mention. She was born of wealthy parents gifted with a ready wit and rare personal beauty, and had access to the most exclusive circle of colonial society. Her grandfather was the sole agent for the British kings for the Northern colonies while her father was the king's agent for Pennsylvania, which readily explains why this family, like so many of the colonial aristocracy, took the king's side in the Revolutionary struggle. Rebecca Franks is mentioned as one of the queens of beauty at the Meschianza, a splendid fete given to General Howe before leaving Philadelphia in 1778. She married Colonel, afterwards General, Sir Henry Johnson. Many distinguished Americans visited her in her English home, among these being General Winfield Scott. Her death occurred in 1823. The great majority, however, were staunch adherents of the patriot cause and several Jewish women figure in Revolutionary history. Among the women of the South are the names of Mrs. Judy Minis and her daughter. The wife of a Revolutionary soldier, she was heart and soul in the cause. A strict observer of Jewish ritual, she prepared the meals for Jewish soldiers taken prisoners by the British, after the fall of Savannah. Her intense patriotism so disturbed the British commander, that for a time he ordered each woman to remain in her house, but finally, owing to their constant communication and assistance to the patriots, Mrs. Minis and her daughter were ordered to leave the town; they accordingly went to Charleston, of which place the husband was one of the patriot defenders.

In Westchester County we meet another patriotic Jewess, Esther Etting Hays, the wife of David Hays, also a Revolutionary soldier. When Tarleton with a party of British raided the village of Bedford in 1779, Tory neighbors entered the house where Mrs. Hays was lying upon a sick bed with a new-born infant. They demanded information, which she was supposed to possess, concerning the patriot plans, on her refusal to comply the house was set afire. The mother and child were saved only by faithful negro servants, who conveyed them to a shelter in the wood.

Among the noble examples of Jewish womanhood at this period were Mrs. Moses Michael Hays, of Boston, and Mrs. Reyna Touro, who, in a Puritan community, with hardly any Jewish associations, brought up their children as observant Jews, Judah Touro and his brother becoming the great communal workers of the next generation.

The beginning of the nineteenth century finds women taking a more active part, by their organization of benevolent and charitable institutions. The most prominent name at this period is that of the noblest daughter American Judaism has produced, Rebecca Gratz, who was born in Philadelphia in 1781. Like Rebecca Franks, she, too, was born to wealth and social position; she too moved in the most exclusive society and possessed, like her, beauty, grace and culture. She, too, might, doubtless, have made a match as brilliant, as distinguished as her namesake, but, unlike her, she was a devout Jewess. Writers have hinted that it was her devotion to her faith that was the sole cause of her remaining unmarried. Her beauty, refinement and wealth of noble qualities, made her beloved by all who knew her, so that we may well look upon her as the ideal American lady and Jewish woman.

Miss Gratz had been the close friend of Matilda Hoffman, Washington Irving's first and only love. Her charm and nobility of character so deeply impressed the great American author, and so enthusiastically did he describe them to his friend, Sir Walter Scott, during his European trip, that the latter is said to have found in her the character he so beautifully depicted as the Rebecca in "Ivanhoe." Among her intimate friends were some of the leading statesmen and writers, Henry Clay and Sully, the artist, among others. This noble woman from the start took a keen interest in every charitable endeavor. Her name is inseparably associated with every benevolent movement in Philadelphia during the first half of the nineteenth century.

In 1819 two Jewish women, Mrs. Aaron Levy and Miss Hannah Levy, happened to witness a case of distress in a Jewish family, and at once resolved to call upon other ladies for aid. Their appeal led to the formation of the Female Hebrew Benevolent Society of Philadelphia, in which Miss Gratz at once took a leading part. In 1838 she organized the first Hebrew Sunday School in America, and to it devoted her best efforts. She appealed to the ladies of other cities as well, and thus led to the establishment of similar institutions in New York and Charleston.

As early as 1850 Rebecca Gratz advocated a society to take care of Jewish orphans. Her appeal was finally answered in the organization of the Jewish Foster Home in 1855. She was also active in the Ladies' Hebrew Sewing Society and the

Fuel Society. Nor were her labors entirely of a sectarian character. As early as 1801 she was secretary of the Female Association for the relief of women and children, and in 1815 one of the founders of the Philadelphia Orphan Asylum, winning from the gentile world the highest admiration and sincere regard. Her death occurred in 1869, and her memory well deserves to be kept fresh by the Jewish women of America for all time.

With Rebecca Gratz were associated three other women who deserve to be mentioned on this occasion. All of them were women of refinement and social standing, thoroughly American by ancestry and intensely devoted to their race and faith. As Leroy-Beaulieu well put it, it is only those Jews who do stand for their race and faith who gain the respect and friendship of the Christian world. The ladies to whom I refer were Mrs. Anna Allen, Miss Louisa B. Hart and Miss Ellen Phillips. They were among the founders of the Hebrew Sunday School and the Jewish Foster Home, and, like Miss Gratz, took a warm interest in all charitable enterprises. Miss Hart was born in 1803 at Easton, Pennsylvania, and to her belongs the credit of founding the Ladies' Hebrew Sewing Society. Miss Phillips was the granddaughter of Jonas Phillips, a Revolutionary soldier, and at her death in 1891 bequeathed over $100,000 to the charities in which she was interested. Mention should also be made of Mrs. Matilda Cohen (1820-88), a member of the Woman's Centennial Commission in 1876, and Mrs. Rebecca C. I. Hart (also of Revolutionary ancestry) who, for thirty years, was president of the Hebrew Benevolent Society. Did time permit, extended notice should also be given to the names of Mrs. Florence, Miss Pesoa, Mrs. Binswanger, of Philadelphia, of the Moises, and Miss Lopez, of Charleston, Mrs. Pricilla Joachimsen, of New York, the founder of the Hebrew Sheltering Guardian Society, Mrs. Simon Borg, and many others.

Within the past thirty years the Jewish women have done wonderful work in the various fields of charitable endeavor throughout the Union. The societies organized by them are far too great in number, even to be enumerated within the scope of this paper. Much less is it possible to give the names of the noble women who have labored so diligently in behalf of those institutions. Many of them are fortunately here to-day, and we hope will continue to labor in their noble work for many years to come.

In law and medicine some of the earliest to break down the prejudice against women in the professions, were Jewish women. On the stage are the names of Pearl Eytinge and her sister Rose, who appeared with Booth. In art you can point to Miss Katherine Cohen, the gifted pupil of St. Gaudens, who has exhibited her sculptures at the Paris Salon. In the realms of education some of the best private schools during the first half of the nineteenth century were conducted by Jewish women, like Miss Harby and Miss Moise. Since the establishment of the public school system, hundreds of Jewish women have won the admiration of the communities throughout the country for their work as teachers, while in this city the first female assistant superintendent appointed by the Board of Education is a Jewess well known to all, not only as an educator, but as a devoted worker in every department for the betterment of the Jewish community.

Quite a number of names have appeared in the realm of letters. Not to mention contemporaries, we may point to Rebekah Hyneman as a poet of no mean ability, and to Penina Moise, a gifted writer, both in prose and verse, the author of "Fancy's Sketch Book" and a contributor to various magazines. Her hymns have for many years been chanted throughout the synagogues of the South. Unfortunately few bright rays came into her life, a life which had much of misery and sorrow, closing with years of total blindness. Miss Charlotte Adams has written an appreciative sketch of her, and I know of no sentiment more pathetic than the last words of Penina Moise, "Lay no flowers on my grave. They are for those who live in the sun, and I have always lived in the shadow."

Jewish Women's Work for Charity.

Theodore Roosevelt once paid the following tribute to Jewish citizenship:

"I am glad to be able to say that, while the Jews of the United States, who now number more than a million, have remained loyal to their faith and their race traditions, they have become indissolubly incorporated in the great army of American citizenship, prepared to make all sacrifices for the country either in war or peace, striving for the perpetuation of good government and for the maintenance of the principles embodied in our constitution. They are honorably distinguished by their industry, their obedience to law, and their devotion to the national welfare."

And Simon Wolf, in his notable volume, "The American Jew, as Patriot, Soldier and Citizen" gives the names of nearly eight thousand Jews who served, on both sides, in the Civil War. It is after all in the grand fabric of Jewish charity, whose broad expanse extends throughout the land, that the Jewish people and pre-eminently the women, have been able to prove themselves patriots and worthy citizens. Indeed in the field of philanthopic efforts the Jewish citizens of America may unhesitatingly claim to have built for themselves monuments more numerous and larger by far than their proportionate share, and their forces have been directed not to saving souls by a chance or creed but by bettering the conditions of human existence. The ideal of the Jewish religion—the universal fatherhood of God and the direct responsibility of every human being to the Maker of all—has steadfastly been upheld. But in the Jewish charity, as in such work under the direction of no other religious body, its forces have not been exerted in striving to make good the seeming shortcoming of the divine nature, but in striving to make good the essential shortcomings of our human nature, by alleviating the distresses arising from the constitution of society and by lessening the sufferings that are inevitably incident to the conditions of life. To this end the American Jewish citizens have organized a widely diversified system of relief for the sick and needy, and while so doing have not restricted their efforts within denominational bounds but have opened their doors and stretched out their hands towards all humanity. And not alone in dealing with conditions that are inseparable from the social system, but also in dealing with such as are removable, in educating and lifting up those of the community who are in need of fostering care and in furthering the spread of intelligence, have the Jewish women been unceasingly active in their charitable organizations.

Moreover, it was remarked in the recent political campaign of the Jewish voters, "Their quiet critical analysis of political nostrums is most disheartening to the district leaders of Tammany Hall," and the Jewish women in their careful investigation, their sound sense and their zeal to instill and foster independence in every invidual should be an inspiration and not a discouragement to the women of wealth and careless thought who rush into hysterical benevolence.

How efficient the efforts of these Jewish charity workers has been is amply demonstrated by a glance at public charitable institutions. In the House of Refuge on Randall's Island there were found, according to a recent official report, only two hundred and sixty Jewish boys and girls. In the Juvenile Asylum there were two hundred and sixty-two Jewish children under sixteen years of age committed for various misdemeanors. Compared with the entire Jewish population of New York City this number is insignificant, and the ratio will probably be found to be considerably lower than in the general population. Furthermore, the records of the department of charities in the city of New York showed that out of the Jewish population approximating seven hundred thousand in greater New York, in the almshouse in Blackwell's Island there were only twenty-six pauper Jews, of whom the majority were blind, idiotic, or possessed of some peculiar defect, which prevented admission to existing Jewish charitable institutions.

And there is no indiscriminate alms-giving among Jewish charity workers. The work of the United Hebrew Charities of New York is typical of similar Jewish organizations throughout the United States, and it is organized and run as accurately and scrupulously as any large business house. It is in their auxiliaries to these organizations that the Jewish women have accomplished a work which richly deserves mention in an account of what women are doing for America's welfare. The sisterhoods in various districts co-operate with the United Hebrew Charities. They give material relief, have developed day nurseries, kindergartens, clubs and classes of various kinds, employment bureaus, mothers' meetings and in fact have become social centers for the poor of their neighborhoods. Since a large percentage of the distress which is met with is occasioned by illness, medical relief of all kinds has been organized, each district as a rule, having its physician and its nurse.

The Home for Aged and Infirm at Yonkers, New York, is managed by well-known philanthropists but all the kitchen utensils, linen and all household articles are provided by a Ladies' Auxiliary Society composed of twelve hundred members.

Of all the problems which confront the average charity

organization, possibly the most perplexing is the one of the family where the mother must be wage earner. The kindergarten and the day nursery have done something to solve the problem, but the Chicago Women's Aid, an organization of Jewish women for literary and philanthropic purposes, has thrown much light on the most creditable way of helping these women. This society has for three seasons supported a workroom for women. The workroom is in charge of a paid superintendent but the members of the society take an active part in the executive and personal service departments. Work is provided for about five months each year during the winter, and the rooms are within walking distance of Hull House, thus being convenient for women who wish to leave their young children at the Hull House Day Nursery. The hours are from nine a. m. to twelve m. and from one to four p. m. The superintendent is assisted by one permanently employed cutter and several who work part of the time. In extreme cases work is supplied at home, but it is preferred to have the women come to the workroom. All sorts of garments are made, the workers receiving seventy-five cents a day. The beneficiaries of the workroom are such women as would ordinarily be entitled to the benefits of relief societies, especially the United Hebrew Charities, but in this way, by requiring them to give at least a partial equivalent for what they get, their self-respect is retained even though the charities are in reality helping them. It has proved far superior to the old-time method of unconditional giving, tending to keep them away from relief agencies and is in many ways a most wholesome substitute for alms. It gives those who ordinarily spend their days in dingy unclean tenements an opportunity to leave the crowded quarters for seven hours a day, to breathe purer air, to learn the value of cleanliness, and to live in an atmosphere of cheerfulness and refinement. And this is far from being the only successful experiment by the Jewish women of America.

In Philadelphia, besides the main bureau of the United Hebrew Charities, various organizations of women have been formed as auxiliary to the United Charity, such as the Ladies' Auxiliary Committee, the Ladies' Volunteer Visiting Committee, and the Personal Interests Society, whose activity has aided to a great degree in mitigating the suffering among the Russian Jews. Another of the older charities of Philadelphia, the Esrath Mashim, or Helping Women, is to be noted in this regard. This society was organized in 1873 in aid of lying-in women at their homes, and after the year 1882 devoted its effort chiefly to the needs of the refugee immigrants from Russia. In 1891 the demands on this charity as on all others grew beyond the confines of the organization, and the society was reorganized as the Jewish Maternity Association, establishing a hospital known as the Maternity Home, which has grown to be one of the large charitable institutions. A training school for nurses was added in 1901, and at the same time a branch of the work inaugurated at Atlantic City as the Jewish Seaside Home for invalid mothers and children. This splendid work has enlarged immensely in the more recent years. In Philadelphia, too, we find a loan society conducted by Jewish women, which makes loans without interest to deserving persons in amounts of from five dollars to twenty-five dollars, repayable in installments.

So we find in every city these evidences of the intense vitality of the Jewish women's spirit for uplifting unfortunates. We find Jewish women on the committees for improved housing in the congested sections of our cities. We find Jewish women serving on the boards of trade schools, figuring in the organization of bureaus and federations of the United Hebrew Charities, opening public baths for the poor and investigating tirelessly the conditions of health and sanitation among them. It is with great regret that we are obliged to curtail the list of individual endeavor, for certainly many of the names of the

41

Jewish women of America belong on the honor roll of her womanhood:

There is Mrs. Joseph Pulitzer, a niece of Jefferson Davis, whose benevolences are famed; Kate Levy, well-known worker for health and sanitation in Chicago; Henrietta Szold, secretary of the Jewish Publishing Society of America, with others too numerous to mention.

SADIE AMERICAN.

The splendid work done by Miss American should be the pride not only of her own race, but of all American women. She was born in Chicago, March 3, 1862, and educated in the public schools of that city. She has been a frequent speaker at clubs and conventions on the subject in which she is so deeply interested, philanthropy, civic and educational subjects; has occupied the pulpits in synagogues and churches; was secretary of the Congress of Jewish Women at the World's Fair in 1893; one of the founders of the Council of Jewish Women, 1893, an organizer of many sections of this association, and its executive secretary in 1893; president of the New York section, Council of Jewish Women; speaker and delegate representing Council of Jewish Women at the International Congress of Women; also at the Atlanta Exposition, 1896; London, 1899, Speaker Vacation Schools; Berlin, 1904, Toronto, 1909, Speaker Playgrounds; Chairman of the Press Committee of Council of Jewish Women, 1899-1904. Jewish Societies: Was instrumental in the formation of the Jewish Study Society, 1899, and later in the formation of the Union of Jewish Women Workers, England. Assisted in the formation of the Bund Judischer Frauen, Berlin, 1904. Council of Women of the United States. Member of the Executive Committee of the Council of Women of the United States since 1898. Speaker

Triennial Council of Women of the United States, 1895, 1898, 1902. Committee on Peace Propaganda, Council of Women of the United States, 1899-1904. Chairman Committee on Immigration and Emigration 1911. Federation of Women's Clubs. Speaker at Biennial of General Federation of Clubs, Denver, 1896. Member of Industrial Committee, New York State Federation of Women's Clubs, 1905. Speaker on Playgrounds at the General Federation of Women's Clubs, Boston, 1908. Woman's Municipal League. Director Woman's Municipal League New York City, 1901. Chairman of Woman's Municipal League Tenement House Committee, 1902-1903. Member Executive Committee Intermunicipal Association for Household Research, 1904. Consumers' League: Vice-president, 1898-1899 and director, 1899, Illinois Consumers' League. President of Consumers' League of New York State, 1901-1905. Member Executive Committee National Consumers' League, 1901-1906. Chicago Activities: Club Leader Maxwell Street Settlement, Chicago, 1894-1898. Teacher Sinai Temple Sunday School, Chicago, 1894-1899. Member Executive Committee, Civic Federation of Chicago, 1895-1899. Founder Vacation Schools, Chicago, 1896. President League for Religious Fellowship, Chicago, 1896. Founder and Chairman Permanent Vacation School and Playground Committee of Chicago Women's Clubs, 1896-1900. Member of Executive Committee of South Side District Bureau of Charities, Chicago, 1896-1899. Director Cook County League of Women's Clubs, 1897-1898. Member of committee in Chicago which drew and secured the passage of the Illinois Juvenile Court Law. Member of Executive Committee of Committee of One Hundred to revise laws regulating education in Illinois, 1897-1898. Member Executive Committee and one of the founders at the call of the Governor, Army and Navy League of Illinois during the Spanish-American War, 1898.

National Association of Charities and Corrections. Speaker
National Association of Charities and Corrections, 1895.
Member of Committee on Neighborhood Improvement,
National Association of Charities and Corrections, 1903. Play-
ground Association of America: One of the founders of
Playground Association of America. Member of Executive
Committee and Secretary of Board of Directors. Chairman of
Committee on Playgrounds in Institutions, 1908. Public
Education Association: Member of Committee on night school
and Social Centers, Public Education Associations, New York
City, 1899-1903. National Educational Association: Member
of Executive Committee, Department of Women's Organ-
izations, 1907. Delegate to the National Education Association,
Department of Superintendents, Washington, 1908. Delegate
Department of Women's Organizations, National Educational
Association, Washington, 1908. Delegate to Department of
Women's Organizations, National Education Association,
Cleveland, 1908 and Denver, 1909. International Congress on
Tuberculosis: Delegate and speaker at the International Con-
gress on Tuberculosis, Washington, 1908. Immigrant Aid:
Member of Executive Committee of societies co-operating to
secure United States' women inspectors to protect girls coming
in first and second class cabins since 1903. Founder and chair-
man of the Committee on Immigrant Aid, Council of Jewish
women. Publications: Reports of Council of Jewish Women.
Articles on Vacation Schools and Playgrounds, among them
two in the *Journal of Sociology,* University of Chicago,
November, 1898, and January, 1899. Reports of Vacation
Schools and Playground Committee, Chicago Woman's Club,
1897-1899. Plan of Work Committee on Immigrant Aid,
Council of Jewish Women. Many fugitive lectures and articles
on social subjects.

Miss American is particularly proud of founding the

vacation schools and playgrounds in the city of Chicago. These, Colonel Parker of Chicago stated, "could hardly have gone forward without her; that the method and conduct was so unique he considered it epoch making in education." While vacation schools were first started on philanthropic lines in New York City, these schools in Chicago were purely educational, and were conducted under a Board of Education of the best educators and social service workers of that city, and this work has since been incorporated in the schools of Chicago. To-day vacation schools and playgrounds are common, but when Miss American started this work in 1897, in Chicago there was neither literature nor activity on the subject in the sense of its being a great movement and hers was really the pioneer work in this direction. One of the special features of these schools was that provision was made for the deaf, the dumb and the blind. A school for these unfortunates was conducted in a summer camp. In 1900, while Miss American and her mother were en route to New York to establish a home, she met with a severe railroad accident and since that time her health has been such that her activities and the great work that she has accomplished in these various lines has been conducted from her home. Miss American is at present greatly interested in vacation schools and welfare work for the blind, among the Jews in the city of New York and has organized a national association and work has been commenced in New York, Pittsburgh and Cincinnati. Another problem which has been forced upon her attention is the question of the care and provision for the Jewish immigrant girl and she has organized a committee on immigration aid which follows every Jewish immigrant girl who comes to this country, no matter what her destination and this has aroused a general interest in that of other immigrant girls which has been taken up by other philanthropic societies. Long before the white slave traffic appalled the country, Miss American had been doing work in the interest and protection and saving of these young women. She was a delegate to the International White Slave Convention and has been active in associations which are aiding the individual work and work done by the government in this question. Miss American attended the conference on children called by President Roosevelt and did splendid work in the interest of the illegitimate child. The Lakeview Home for wayward girls and unmarried mothers was founded by Miss American in the city of New York. The varied and important character of Miss American's charitable work has not received, thus far, the appreciation which it so justly deserves. In future generations, hundreds of thousands will enjoy the benefits of work of which she has been the initial spirit, and which never could have been brought to realization without her energy and ability.

ROSE SOMMERFIELD.

Rose Sommerfield taught in the public schools of Baltimore from 1889 to 1899. Actively interested in the First Grade Teachers' Association, helping to shape its policy. Inaugurated the first Mothers' Meetings held in public schools of Baltimore. Interested in Jewish and non-Jewish philanthropic and educational institutions as a volunteer worker. Helped to organize the Daughters of Israel and the Baltimore Section of the Council of Jewish Women, being the first secretary of both organizations. Also a Day Nursery, First Jewish Working Girls Club and the Maccabeans, an association of men who interested themselves in work among Jewish boys. Organized a free Sabbath school for Jewish children. Principal of the elementary school of the Kitchen Garden Association, also of the evening school for adult immigrants. A director and assisted in organizing the Young Men's Hebrew Association of Baltimore. Taught Jewish Sabbath school. Helped to organize first home for Jewish working girls in the United States. Gave model lessons in Hebrew at the Summer Assembly Jewish Chautauqua. Also appointed critic of lessons given at first Summer Assembly. Wrote articles on "Truancy in Public Schools" for Maryland State Conference of Charities, "Charity Organization" for first Triennial of Council of Jewish Women, in which Federation of Charities was urged and a school of philanthropy advocated. "Homes for Working Girls" for National Conference of Jewish Charities meeting in Philadelphia and many articles on educational and philanthropic subjects. In 1899 went to New York and organized the Clara de Hirsch Home for Working

Girls and its Trade Classes, also organized the Clara de Hirsch Home for Immigrant Girls, the Welcome House Settlement, the Model Employment Bureau, and helped to reorganize the Hebrew Sheltering and Immigrant Aid Society and the Virginia, a non-sectarian Working Girls Hotel. Was on the first committee of the Lakeview Home for Girls, chairman of the committee on philanthropy of the National Council of Jewish Women, secretary of the Monday Club of New York, vice-president of the Jewish Social Workers of New York, and secretary of the Jewish Social Workers, Section of the National Jewish Conference of Charities. Assisted in organizing the Wage Earner's Theatre League, and a member of its executive committee.

REBECCA GRATZ.

Miss Gratz was born in Philadelphia, Pennsylvania, March 4, 1781, died in Philadelphia, Pennsylvania, August 29, 1869. She was one of the most distinguished women of her day of the Jewish race in this country. She was one of a family of thirteen children; her father Michael Gratz, a wealthy East India merchant, married Miriam, daughter of Joseph Simon, of Lancaster Pennsylvania, the best known and most respected Hebrew in the state. The names of Joseph Simon, Michael Gratz and Bernard Gratz, his brother, were signed to the "Non-importation Act," the forerunner of the Declaration of Independence which was drafted by Thomas Jefferson in the house then owned by the Gratz brothers. Their signatures with many others of the family may also be seen on the first list of seat holders (1782) of the Congregation Mikve Israel (Hope of Israel) one of the oldest Jewish Congregations in the United States. The Gratz home was the center of refinement, culture and hospitality, with the sweet Jewish setting of family affection. Washington Irving delighted "to roost in the big room." Henry Clay, Fanny Kemble and many others met there the best and most cultivated society of Philadelphia. Rebecca had every advantage of education and her friendships were largely among Christians. A most romantic and life-long attachment was formed with her beautiful schoolmate Maria Fenno. Though there were no railroads or steamboats in those days, intercourse by stage between New York and Philadelphia was frequent and upon one of these visits to the former city Maria married Judge Ogden Hoffman, a widower, and most accomplished gentleman with children older than herself. One, a young daughter, Matilda, was the only love of Washington Irving, who was then pretending to study law in her father's office, but Judge Hoffman did not approve of his suit and the lovers were very unhappy. Consumption developed in Matilda Hoffman and Rebecca Gratz and Washington Irving nursed the poor girl until her death. After this Irving went abroad, traveling extensively, he visited Abbotsford, and there told Scott the story of Rebecca Gratz, her personal charm, strength of mind and her steadfastness to her faith. She had a few years before this refused on account of her faith, to marry a young man who was considered a most suitable match, sacrificing her inclination to follow what she considered her duty. In 1817, when "Ivanhoe" was published Scott sent a copy to Irving saying, "How do you like your Rebecca now?" In 1817 the ladies of Philadelphia opened the first Philadelphia Orphan Asylum. Rebecca Gratz was chosen secretary and served in this capacity for forty-eight years. In 1835, when past the age when most people think their work is finished, she being then fifty-six years of age, she founded the first Sunday school for Jewish children, over which she presided for twenty-five years. This school, in the last year of her service, numbered four thousand pupils, it having opened with but five. In 1855 Miss Gratz started a Jewish Foster Home. Her long experience on the board of the Philadelphia Asylum enabled her to found the infant home, and though she lived to see it well established she could hardly anticipate its present usefulness as a modern institution. She was connected with every movement for bettering the condition of the poor and the sick of the city among her people. When the unfortunate Civil War occurred she was over eighty, but she stood firm and true to her country. Her one thought was for a united land with no North, no South, no East, no West. Rebecca Gratz lived long past the Psalmist's age, but she never lost her wonderful appearance, her charm of manner, her interest in good works, and above all, her devotion to the Jewish faith.

JULIA SCHOENFELD.

Miss Schoenfeld was born in Bellaire, Ohio, of German-Jewish parentage. Her father was born in Germany and migrated when a very young man to this country. Her mother was born in Frederick, Maryland, the daughter of German parents. When Miss Schoenfeld was a few months old her parents moved to Columbus, Ohio, and engaged in mercantile enterprises, but meeting with reverses, the family moved to Meadville, Pennsylvania, which was chosen for their home on account of its educational advantages. It was a college town with musical schools, where children could be given opportunities at a small cost. Miss Schoenfeld was graduated from the public schools of Meadville and entered Allegheny College in 1894, being graduated in 1897. She decided to study medicine and entered the Woman's Medical College at Toronto, Canada, but her father objecting to her being a professional woman she gave up her work. While at school in Toronto, the family moved to Johnstown, Pennsylvania. On Miss Schoenfeld's return, she was appealed to in the interest of the work for a settlement in the Jewish district in Pittsburgh and was requested to undertake the establishment of this institution. She was then but twenty-one years of age, but filled with a desire to work for others. She offered her services to those interested in the movement and the Columbian Council Settlement developed from this small beginning. After three years' residence at the settlement, which was located in the heart of the Ghetto, Miss Schoenfeld left on account of ill health and returned to Johnstown. This was in 1902. At this time Miss Schoenfeld organized the Civic Club of Johnstown. This being an industrial center, iron mills and mines have brought to the community thousands of foreigners, for whom her efforts were made.

The first work this club undertook was the establishment of the Juvenile Court. Miss Schoenfeld, during the first year, served as volunteer probation officer; she also helped in the establishment of vacation schools and playgrounds. Her successor at the Columbian settlement remained but a year and she was again called to serve in the work in Pittsburgh, where she remained a year. Later an opportunity offered to study vacation and amusement resources of working girls in New York City by the committee who had organized themselves for that purpose. In 1908 Miss Schoenfeld left for New York and as a result of her work there is in New York to-day the best legislation that has ever been enacted in regard to licensing and regulating dancing academies, public amusement parks, etc. In 1911 Miss Schoenfeld received her degree of M.A., from Columbia University. She has spent much time in the study of the immigrant question and its relation to the protection of girls in this country, and as secretary of the committee on immigrant aid of the Council of Jewish Women she has developed the protective bureau for girls. She has visited many cities, studying the work done in each along the lines of philanthropic and social endeavor; attended many conferences in this country and abroad. While in London in 1907, she made a close study of the Toynbee Hall and University Settlement. She has been an active worker on the state committee and state confederation of Women's Clubs, also in the Consumers' League and with other state and national organizations for the improvement of working conditions among women and children. She has written many articles for the press and addressed many of the prominent clubs of the country relative to the work in which she has been such a valuable worker and adviser. She is considered to-day one of the prominent women in the philanthropic work of our country and a valued representative of the able women of her race.

ANNIE NATHAN MEYER.

Simon Wolf gives in his "Jew as an American Citizen, Soldier and Patriot," the names of nearly eight thousand Jews in the Civil War. There has been made, unfortunately, no such muster of the Jewish women who have shown such public spirit for the good of American citizenship. But near the head of such a roll call would appear the name of Mrs. Annie Nathan Meyer, author and worker for the advancement of women. She was born in New York City in 1867, the daughter of Robert Weeks Nathan. She belongs to a prominent Jewish family and is a cousin of the late Emma Lazarus. She was educated at home in her childhood and afterward entered the School for Women, a branch at that time of Columbia College. She was one of the first to enter the women's course when it was opened in Columbia College in 1885, and eventually she became one of the founders of Barnard College, affiliated with Columbia College, and the first women's college in New York City. After this institution had received full sanction and recommendation at the hands of the faculty of the brother college she became one of the trustees and at the same time edited "Women's Work in America," a volume containing the result of three years earnest work and research. She married Dr. Alfred Meyer of New York, in 1887. Mrs. Meyer is opposed to women's suffrage, unless the franchise be restricted by laws providing for educational qualification. It is her theory that legislation should follow in the footsteps of education. She is a gifted woman, a poet and essayist, though most of her activities have been expended in philanthropic reform and charitable work. Her home is in New York City.

MRS. CAESAR MISCH.

At fourteen years of age organized and taught a Sabbath school in Pittsfield, Massachusetts, a community too small to support a Rabbi. She was the first president of the Providence Section Council of Jewish Women; has been auditor and chairman of religious school. Commander of National Council of Jewish Women; president of various charitable societies; member of board of directors Providence Society for Organizing Charity; member board of managers Providence District Nursing Association; member Sex Hygiene Committee of Rhode Island State Conference of Charities; first woman appointed on Providence Playground Committee, having been appointed by both Republican and Democratic mayors, and having entire charge of purchasing all the supplies. Chairman of North End Free Dispensary, which she organized under auspices of Providence Section, Council of Jewish Women. Has lectured in various cities and has written newspaper articles on Jewish topics and on White Slave Traffic. Has written a "Children's Service" for use in the synagogue and compiled a book of "Selections for Homes and Schools."

ROSE MORDECAI.

Prominent Jewish woman. Miss Mordecai says of herself, that she is simply Miss Rose Mordecai "without either romance or mystery, but one who loves his fellow men." She was born in Washington, D. C., February 14, 1839. Her father was Major Alfred Mordecai, Sr., a distinguished officer of the old army before the war, who resigned in preference to fighting in the Civil War, opposed to the idea of brother against brother. He went to reside in Philadelphia where Miss Mordecai, with two sisters, kept a private school for forty years. Her father was an intimate friend of Mr. W. W. Corcoran the great philanthropist, of Washington, and Miss Mordecai now resides in the Louisa Home, established by Mr. Corcoran. Her mother's aunt was Miss Rebecca Gratz, the noted Jewish beauty of Philadelphia, whose beautiful character is believed to have been portrayed by Sir Walter Scott in his Rebecca of Ivanhoe.

BERTHA RAUH (MRS. ENOCH)

Bertha Rauh was born June 16, 1865, at Pittsburgh, Pennsylvania. Daughter of Samuel Floersheim and Pauline Wertheimer. Educated in the Pittsburgh public schools. Graduated 1884 with second honor degree, Pittsburgh Central High School. Married Enoch Rauh, president Milk and Ice Association, and of the Juvenile Court Aid Society; vice-president Ladies' Auxiliary, Gusky Orphanage; member of board, Columbian Council School Settlement; board of visitation for institutions in state of Pennsylvania; visiting board of the Pittsburgh and Allegheny Free Kindergarten Association; Civic Club of Allegheny County and of Permanent Civic Committee of Pittsburgh. Member Juvenile Court Committee of the Juvenile Court Association of Allegheny County. Chairman finance committee and member advisory board, Soho public bath. Was member of board of

Humane Society of Pittsburgh and Allegheny, and of ladies' auxiliary of the Allegheny General Hospital. Organizer and leader of reading circle, in existence nine years, for study of literature. Articles: "The Advantages of the Higher Education"; "A Trip up the Allegheny Valley"; "Benefits of the Sunday Concerts"; "A Tribute to Christopher Lyman Magee"; "Justice to the Jew"; "Reform in Confirmation"; "Woman's Place on Judaism," in local papers. Her address is 5837 Bartlett Street, Pittsburgh, Pa.

GRACE P. MENDES.

Was born at St. Croix, Danish West Indies. Her father was Jacob Osino De Castro and an active Confederate. When New Orleans fell he fled to Mobile, Alabama. Her mother was Hannah De Sola. Miss De Castro was educated in the public schools of New Orleans, Louisiana. Married Reverend Isaac P. Mendes, an Englishman. She labored shoulder to shoulder with her husband for twenty-seven years, working in the interest of the Jewish people in Savannah and gave them a standing second to none in the South. She has been president of the Savannah Section of the Council of Jewish Women since its organization in 1895, and is affiliated and does active work in the following organizations: First vice-president of the Ladies' Hebrew Benevolent Society; honorary president of the Savannah Branch of the Needle Work Guild; second vice-president of the Association for the Education of Georgia Mountaineers; treasurer of the committee on Health and Sanitation; a member of a committee of the Associated Charities; one of the Georgia Joint Committee of the Department of School Patrons of the National Educational Association and honorary president of the Temple Guild of "Mickve Israel" Congregation.

BERTHA KAHN ELKERS.

Mrs. Elkers was born in New York City in 1863. Parents were Israel and Sarah Kahn, both natives of Germany, and of the Hebrew race. They with their family moved to California in 1877. Mrs. Elkers was married in Oakland to Albert Elkers of Sacramento in 1882. They have two sons, both graduates of the University of California. At the beginning of the Spanish War, in April, 1898, Mrs. Elkers founded the Sacramento Red Cross branch. Was its president from 1898 to 1908. Sacramento raised about $12,000 in money, food and supplies for the Red Cross work during the few months of the war. The Galveston disaster also received the attention of this branch and it did much to help the refugees from the earthquake and fire of 1906, which visited San Francisco. Mrs. Elkers was on the California State Red Cross Board from 1898 to 1904, and she is a charter member of the Saturday Club, 1893, one of the largest musical clubs in the United States, having a membership of fourteen hundred. She has done active musical work (piano), and has served on its board since 1894, and was president of the same from 1901 to 1905; honorary president since 1907. Assisted in starting four other musical clubs—Pacific Musical Society of San Francisco, Fresno Musical Club, Auburn and Berkeley, and is honorary member of the two first named. She has been treasurer of the Hebrew Women's Benevolent Society for twenty-three years; secretary for the women's auxiliary of Congregation B'nai Israel for past five years; is one the board of the Sacramento City Mission; member of Home of the Merciful Saviour; Young Woman's Christian Association; Society for Homeless Children; San Francisco Auxiliary to Hebrew Orphan Asylum; Tuesday Club; Museum Association; Golf Club and has been on the board of the University of California Extension work. Her husband, Albert Elkers, is a native of Sacramento, where they have continued to reside.

Women as Temperance Workers.

FROM MRS. SARAH D. LA FETRA,

PRESIDENT WOMAN'S CHRISTIAN TEMPERANCE UNION, DISTRICT OF COLUMBIA.

"I am especially glad to know that you are writing this book, to do justice to the women workers for the benefit of mankind, as heretofore not enough has been said or written of women's achievements.

Very cordially yours,

SARAH D. LA FETRA."

FRANCES ELIZABETH WILLARD.

In the Capitol at Washington, a statue of Frances E. Willard stands in the great circle of honor to represent the prairie state of Illinois, and in the great circles of reformers gathering through all ages, her place is forever secure. The early home life of Frances Willard was pre-eminently Christian. Her father, Josiah F. Willard, was a descendant of Major Simon Willard, of Kent, England, who, with Reverend Peter Bulkeley, settled in Concord, Massachusetts, less than fifteen years after the landing of the Pilgrims at Plymouth. Major Willard was a man of great force of character and of distinguished public service and his descendants included many men and women who inherited his talents with his good name.

Inheriting many of the notable gifts of both parents and of more remote ancestors, Frances Willard grew up in an atmosphere most favorable to the development of her powers. Early in her life her parents moved to Oberlin, Ohio, that the father might carry out a long cherished plan of further study

(653)

and that the family might have the advantages of intellectual help and stimulus. But in May, 1846, Mr. Willard's health demanded a change of climate and life in the open. He moved his family to Wisconsin, then a territory, and settled on a farm, near the young village of Janesville. Miss Willard wrote many years afterward of their pioneer life here on a farm, half prairie, half forest, on the banks of the Rock River. She says that her career as a reformer had its root and growth in the religious character of the family in this log cabin neighborhood. Their abode was named Forest Home, and in the earlier years without what a Yankee would call "near neighbors" the family were almost entirely dependent upon their own resources for society. Mrs. Willard was poetical in her nature and she made herself at once mentor and companion to her children. The father, too, was near to nature's heart in a real and vivid fashion of his own. And so the children, reared in a home which was to their early years a world's horizon, lived an intellectual and yet a most helpful life. Miss Willard enjoyed entire freedom from fashionable restraint until her seventeenth year, clad during most of the year in simple flannel suits, and spent much of the time in the open air, sharing the occupations and sports of her brothers. Her first teachers were her educated parents; later an accomplished young woman was engaged as family teacher and companion for the children. Her first schoolmaster was a graduate of Yale College. At the age of seventeen she, with her sister Mary, was sent from home to school, entering Milwaukee Female College, in 1857. She completed her education at the Northwestern Female College, in Evanston, Illinois. After several years of teaching, her soul was stirred by the reports of the temperance crusade in Ohio during the winter of 1874, and in this she felt she heard the divine call of her life work. Of all her friends, no one stood by her in her wish to join the crusade except Mrs. Mary A.

Livermore who sent her a letter full of enthusiasm for the new line of work, and predicted her success therein. In the summer of 1874, while in New York City, a letter reached her from Mrs. Louise S. Rounds, of Chicago, who was identified there with the young temperance association. "It has come to me," wrote Mrs. Rounds, "as I believe, from the Lord, that you ought to be our president. We are a little band without money or experience, but with strong faith. If you would come, there will be no doubt of your election." So it happened that Miss Willard turning from the most attractive offers entered the open door of philanthropy in the West. Within a week she had been made president of the Chicago Woman's Christian Temperance Union. For months she carried on this work without regard to pecuniary compensation, many a time going without her noon-day lunch downtown, because she had no money, and walking miles because she had not five cents to pay for a street car ride. Yet she declared that period the most blessed of her life so far, and that her work baptised in suffering grew first deep and vital, and then began to widen. With the aid of a few women she established a daily gospel meeting in Lower Farwell Hall for the help of the intemperate, and her gospel talks came to be in demand far and wide. Every dollar earned by writing or lecturing not needed for current expenses was devoted to the relief of the needy or to the enlargement of her chosen work. The Chicago Woman's Christian Temperance Union from that day of small things in the eyes of the world, has gone on and prospered until now it is represented by a wide range of established philanthropy.

Miss Willard continued wielding a busy pen, speaking in Chautauqua, addressing summer camps in New England and the Middle States, and in 1876, while engaged in Bible study and prayer, she was led to the conviction that she ought to speak for women's ballot as a protection to the home from the tyranny of drink, and in the autumn, in the national convention, in Newark, N. J., disregarding the earnest pleadings of conservative friends, she declared her conviction in her first suffrage speech. She originated the motto, "For God and home and native land." This was first the motto of the Chicago Union. It was then adopted by the Illinois State Union; in 1876 beame that of the National Union, and was adapted to the use of the World's Union in Faneuil Hall, Boston, Mass., in 1891, then becoming, "For God, and home and every land." Miss Willard was one of the founders of the National Woman's Temperance Union Paper, *Our Union* in New York, and of the *Signal,* the organ of the Illinois Union. These, in 1882, were merged in the *Union Signal* which is now one of the most widely circulated papers in the world.

In the autumn of 1877 she declined the nomination of the presidency of the National Woman's Christian Temperance Union, but she accepted it in 1879, when she was elected in Indianapolis, Ind., as the exponent of a liberal policy including state rights for the state societies, representation on a basis of paid membership and the advocacy of the ballot for women. At that time no Southern state except Maryland was represented in the national society and the total yearly income was only about $12.00. In 1881 Miss Willard made a tour of the Southern states, which reconstructed her views of the situation and conquered conservative prejudice and sectional opposition. Thus was given the initial impetus to the formation of the home protection party which it was desired should unite all good men and women in its ranks. During the following year Miss Willard completed her plan of visiting and organizing every state and territory in the United States, and of presenting her cause in every town and city that had reached a population of ten thousand. She visited the Pacific coast, and California, Oregon, and even British Columbia, were thoroughly organized, anu more than twenty-five thousand miles of toilsome travel enabled her to meet the national convention, in Detroit, Michigan, in October, 1883, to celebrate the completion of its first decade with rejoicing over the complete organization of the Woman's Christian Temperance Union in each one of the forty-eight sub-divisions of the United States, Alaska not then included.   In 1885 the national headquarters were removed from New York to Chicago and the White-Cross movement was adopted as a feature of the work of the national union. Because no other woman could be found to stand at the helm of this new movement, Miss Willard did so.   No other movement of the work developed so rapidly.   A great petition for the better legal protection of women and girls was presented to Congress with thousands of signatures.   Mr. Powderly, chief of the Knights of Labor, through Miss Willard's influence, sent out ninety-two thousand petitions to local assemblies of the Knights to be signed, circulated and returned to her.   Through the efforts of the temperance workers the same petition was circulated and presented for legislative action in nearly every state and territory.

The sacrifices which Miss Willard has so freely made for this work were repaid to her in abundant measure.   She was called by Joseph Cook the most widely known and best-beloved woman in America, and the widespread influence of the Woman's Christian Temperance Union, in England, Canada and America is an imperishable monument to her place among the great of the world.

The end of the career of Francis Willard, so far as her earthly life was concerned, was as truly religious as the great days of her power.   As she lay upon her last bed of sickness after a hard day, she suddenly gazed intently on a picture of the Christ directly opposite her bed.   Her eyes seemed to meet those of the compassionate Saviour and with her old eloquence, in the stillness, she said:

"I am Merlin, and I am dying,
But I'll follow the gleam."

And a little later she said to the friends who gathered about her, "Oh, let me go away, let me be in peace; I am so safe with Him. He has other worlds, and I want to go." And so still following the Christ gleam with a brave heart and a courageous step, the dauntless soul went on to follow her Lord to all worlds, whithersoever He may lead her.

ANNIE ADAMS GORDON.

Miss Annie Adams Gordon, vice-president of the National Women's Christian Temperance Union and honorary secretary of the World's Women's Christian Temperance Union, is one of the most unique figures in the temperance reform of to-day. Miss Gordon came into the work with Miss Willard. In 1877 when Miss Willard was conducting a women's meeting for Mr. Moody, there was no one to play the organ. An earnest appeal was made and after waiting some moments, a young girl stepped forward and offered, saying. "As no one volunteers, I will do the best I can." This was Annie Gordon. Miss Willard was so attracted by her modesty and sweet nature that she persuaded her to come to her as private secretary, and thus began her work in the Women's Christian Temperance Union of this country.

Miss Gordon was born in Boston but early in her childhood her family removed to Auburndale, one of the suburbs of the former city. She was educated by a course in the Newton High School, Mount Holyoke College and Lasell Seminary. The many and varied offices held by Miss Gordon indicate the breadth of her view and the wide scope of her abilities, and identified with the interests of the Women's Christian Temperance Union almost from its inception, she has conserved and served these interests with love and loyalty. Loyalty may be said to be the crowning virtue of her character, a character possessing many of those sterling qualities which we have come to regard as the birthright of the native-born New Englander.

Through her extensive travels on behalf of the Women's Christian Temperance Union, Miss Gordon has acquired an added breadth and culture which make her equally at home in social and official life. As honorary secretary of the World's Women's Christian Temperance Union, Miss Gordon enjoys almost a world-wide reputation, but it is as "the friend of the children" that she is best known on both sides of the Atlantic.

As general secretary of the World's Loyal Temperance Legion (the branch of the organization work devoted to the boys and girls of this and other countries), Miss Gordon has made a large place for herself in the hearts and lives of the world's young people. She has written quite a number of musical compositions for this work and her "Marching Songs" in particular have been a conspicuous factor in popularizing the work of the Loyal Temperance Legion. By the terms of Miss Willard's will, Miss Gordon was made, in conjunction with Lady Henry Somerset, her literary executor. By request of the general officers of the National Women's Christian Temperance Union, she undertook to prepare a biography of Miss Willard and in a very short space of time she gave to the world "The Beautiful Life of Frances E. Willard." She has written several pieces of prose and poetry and contributed to the work "Questions Answered; a Manual of the Loyal Temperance Legion work," "Marching Songs for Young Crusaders" Nos. 1, 2, 3 and 4, "The White Ribbon Birthday Book," "The Y Song Book," and "The White Ribbon Hymnal." Her style is terse and strong.

Miss Gordon is altogether a strong, well-poised, gentle and lovable woman, and has made for herself a noble place in the world's work. Willard Fountain, which stands at the entrance of Willard Hall, in Chicago, is the embodiment of her own thought and work. The money for its erection was raised by having the children give their dimes and sign total abstinence pledges on red, white and blue cards, which were used to decorate the Women's Christian Temperance Union rooms at the Columbian Exposition.

She was Miss Willard's constant companion during the last years and especially the last weeks of Miss Willard's life. The life use of Rest Cottage, at Evanston, Ill., was given to Miss Gordon by Miss Willard, but she has never used it as a source of income to herself, but has held the gift as a sacred trust, keeping the property in order, and providing a caretaker, so that tourists and friends of the Women's Christian Temperance Union may visit the rooms and home made sacred by Miss Willard.

LILLIAN M. N. STEVENS.

Mrs. Lillian M. N. Stevens, national president of the Woman's Christian Temperance Union, was born in Dover, Me., and has always made her home within the borders of the Pine Tree state. Like so many women of the New England states, Mrs. Stevens' first public work was in the schoolroom as a teacher, but she early left this sphere and at the age of twenty-one married Mr. M. Stevens, of Stroudwater, at that time a charming little suburb of Portland, Me. Born a prohibitionist, Mrs. Stevens early began her temperance activities and the following data holds an interest for all: "Mrs. Stevens first met Miss Willard at Old Orchard, Me., in the summer of 1875, and there aided in the organization of the State Woman's Christian Temperance Union, of which she was elected treasurer. She held this position for three years.

"For many years Mrs. Stevens was reckoned as Neal Dow's chief coadjutor, and since his death she is recognized throughout the state as the leader of the prohibition forces. Indeed, in the well-fought battle of 1884, which placed prohibition in the state constitution, Mrs. Stevens won for herself a fame as organizer and agitator hardly second to Neal Dow himself. Some of the triumphs of the Maine Woman's Christian Temperance Union under her leadership have been the raising of the age of protection to sixteen years, a strong Scientific-Temperance-Instruction law, and the constitutional amendment to which we have already referred."

Mrs. Stevens, in addition to her temperance work, is prominently identified with many other reform and philanthropic movements of her city and state. She is one of the chief promoters of the Temporary Home for Women and Children in Portland and the State Industrial School for girls. She represented the state of Maine on the board of lady managers at the World's Columbian Exposition. To the executive ability essential to successful administration, Mrs. Stevens adds rare gifts as a speaker. Socially as well as officially, she has won recognition from some of old England's noblest houses and her home is the gathering place for the multitude of her co-laborers, her many friends and the philanthropic people of the city of Portland.

MRS. WOOD-ALLEN CHAPMAN.

Mrs. Wood-Allen Chapman, born at Lakeside, near Toledo, Ohio, is the only daughter of Dr. Mary Wood-Allen, the noted lecturer, author and editor. She attended various schools, including what is now known as Lake Erie College, and the Ann Arbor High School, from which she graduated in 1895. The following fall she entered the University of Michigan. Being unable, because of threatened ill-health, to finish the year's work, she accompanied her mother on a trip and made her first appearance on the lecture platform. Two years of college followed, when failing health on the part of her mother called her from her studies to take up the duties of acting editor of the magazine owned and edited by her mother, then known as "The New Crusade," still being published under the name of "American Motherhood." With this she remained associated both in the business management and editorially until her marriage, in 1902, to Mr. William Brewster Chapman, of Cleveland, Ohio.

For several years following this event her home was in northern Michigan, from whence she began to contribute to such periodicals as *The Congregationalist, The Ladies' World, The Union Signal, The Christian Endeavor World,* etc.

In 1905 New York City became her home and she at once joined The Woman's Press Club, The Mother's Club, The Woman's Forum, The Pen and Brush Club, and The American Society of Sanitary and Moral Prophylaxis. In August, 1905, her only child, a son, was born. In October, 1907, she was appointed national superintendent of the Purity Department of the Woman's Christian Temperance Union. In this capacity she wrote a large number of articles and leaflets, including her book "The Moral Problem of the Children." In April, 1910, she became editor of a department in the *Ladies Home Journal,* and in June of the same year, was appointed associate superintendent of the Moral Educational Department of the Woman's Christian Temperance Union. This position, however, together with her national superintendency she resigned in the spring of 1911 on account of threatened ill-health, and in order to devote herself more exclusively to her literary work.

SARAH DOAN LA FETRA

Mrs. Sarah Doan La Fetra, temperance and missionary worker, was born in Sabina, Ohio, June 11, 1843. She is the daughter of Rev. Timothy and Mary

Ann Custis Doan, her mother being of the Virginia Custis family. In early youth, religious truths made a deep impression on her mind and heart, and at sixteen she was converted and became an active member of the Methodist Episcopal Church. She improved every opportunity for study in the public schools and prepared herself in the Normal School of Prof. Holbrook in Lebanon, Ohio, for teaching. She taught in a graded school in Fayette County, Ohio, for some time before her marriage with George Henry La Fetra, of Warren County, Ohio. Three sons were born to them, the youngest dying in infancy.

Mrs. La Fetra was a charter member of the Woman's Christian Temperance Union, of the District of Columbia, was the treasurer for some time, and from 1885 served as president for eight years. She was one of the founders of the Florence Crittendon Hope and Help Mission in Washington. All local missionary work has had her sympathetic support. She presided for years over a temperance hotel in the heart of the nation's Capital, and not only did she make it attractive but successful financially.

She is connected with the Metropolitan Memorial Methodist Episcopal Church. She has at various times been president of the Woman's Foreign Missionary Society and of the Ladies' Association. She is the vice-president of the Washington District, Association for Foreign Missions. A recent honor has been conferred on her by the Baltimore branch of the Woman's Foreign Society in voting to erect a building at Bidar, India, to be called "The Sarah D. La Fetra Memorial," in recognition of her effective labors in that society.

Mrs. La Fetra possesses a warm heart and generous public spirit, so that it has been said of her "every woman's work is made lighter by coming in touch with her." She is an intensely patriotic woman and the historic Metropolitan Methodist Church, so well known as the church of Grant, Logan and McKinley, is supplied with beautiful flags largely through her efforts.

FRANCES E. BEAUCHAMP.

Mrs. Beauchamp, reformer and lecturer, was born in Madison County, Kentucky, in the home of her paternal ancestor, General Samuel Estill, and was of the fifth generation born on the old farm which was taken up from the Commonwealth of Virginia by his progenitors. She was an only child, of a highly imaginative temperament and spent her childhood in dreamland. Trees, flowers and animals became sentient beings with a vivid personality, among which she moved and conversed. Hours were daily given to this imaginative existence and but for the fact that her parents were intensely practical and insisted on regular habits and a systematic performance of the tasks assigned, she would probably have gone through life a visionary, and not the highly sensitive, keenly responsive, and eminently practical woman that her mature years have given to her day and generation. She attended a private school in Richmond, Kentucky, until her ninth year and established herself at the head of her classes, being prominently expert in mathematics. She was devoted to her teacher, the Reverend R. L. Breck, and was deeply grieved when her parents removed her from this school to Science Hill, Shelbyville, Kentucky. Her education covered the English branches, music and French. She was graduated from this institution in her sixteenth year and was to have been finished abroad, but instead married during the year, J. H. Beauchamp, a rising young lawyer, who ever shared her ambitions and encouraged her work. She has been devoted to her church and a local philanthropist from her youth. In 1886 she joined the Woman's Christian Temperance Union, and in the fall of that year was made corresponding secretary of the State Union. The following year she was appointed superintendent of juvenile work for Kentucky. In 1894 she was made one of the recording secretaries of the National Woman's Christian Temperance Union, and in 1895 was elected president of the Kentucky Woman's Christian Temperance Union, which office she is ably filling at the present time. She is a speaker of rare quality, uniting eloquence and force in a logical presentation of facts.

JENNIE McKEE GRANDFIELD.

Mrs. Jennie McKee Grandfield, the wife of the first assistant postmaster general, was born in Troy, Missouri. Her father, Hon. A. V. McKee, a distinguished lawyer of Troy and a member of the Missouri Constitutional Convention, died in 1884. Her mother, who is still living, was Miss Clara Wheeler, daughter of Captain Wheeler, a graduate of the United States Military Academy at West Point, who served with distinction in the Seminole and other Indian wars. Miss McKee attended the public schools of Troy and was graduated from the Troy Collegiate Institute in 1884. She was a noted belle in a town famed for its beautiful women. On December 23, 1885, she married Charles P. Grandfield and returned with him to Washington, where he was employed in the post office department, and they have since resided in the Capital city.

Mrs. Grandfield has taken an active interest in church work ever since, and at present is a member of the Gurley Memorial Presbyterian Church. Many years ago she joined the Woman's Christian Temperance Union and has been an active worker in that organization. At present she is treasurer of the District of Columbia Branch of the Woman's Christian Temperance Union. She is also a prominent member of the Daughters of the American Revolution, and is regent of her chapter in that association. Mrs. Grandfield is possessed of a fine personal presence and is universally beloved by all who know her.

She has two charming daughters. The elder, Mrs. Clara C. White, is the wife of Mr. H. F. White, an attorney-at-law in Cambridge Springs, Pennsylvania. The younger daughter, Miss Helen, was graduated from the Central High School of Washington in June, 1911.

LELIA DROMGOLD EMIG.

Lelia Dromgold Emig, eldest daughter of Walter A. and Martha Ellen Shull Dromgold, was born near Saville, Perry County, Penna. Left motherless at the age of nine, her father moved to York, Pa., where he has since engaged in extensive manufacturing business.

In 1890 she accompanied members of the Young Women's Christian Temperance Union on a Flower Mission visit to the county jail and became interested in temperance reform.

In 1894 she was married to Clayton E. Emig, an attorney-at-law, of Washington, D. C. Here she immediately became associated with the District Woman's Christian Temperance Union and has served as a local president, general secretary of work and state corresponding secretary; and has written several temperance leaflets of merit.

Mrs. Emig is active in church and rescue mission work and is a member of the Daughters of the American Revolution, tracing her ancestry to the following patriots of the Revolutionary War: John Hench, Jacob Hartman, Zachariah Rice, Nicholas Ickes, John Hartman, Frederick Shull, Thomas Donally and Abigail Rice, of Pennsylvania.

"The Dromgold family in America" is her latest published contribution to genealogy.

In 1909 she organized a Society of Children of the American Revolution, which was named by Mrs. William Howard Taft in honor of her distinguished ancestor, Thomas Welles, the fourth colonial governor of Connecticut. The society has 100 members and includes many of the official families of Washington.

Mrs. Emig is the mother of three daughters, Evelyn, Gladys, and Lelia, who are enthusiastic followers in her philanthropic work.

MAUD CLARK HARVEY.

Mrs. Maud Clark Harvey, Sunday school and missionary worker, was born in Plattsburg, New York, August 8, 1865, and is the daughter of Judge George Lafayette and J. Ann Walling Clark, and is the sister of Dr. Nathaniel Walling Clark, now the efficient superintendent of the Italian mission work of the Methodist Episcopal Church, Rome, Italy. This fact may possibly serve to accentuate Mrs. Harvey's interest in foreign missions.

She was educated in the public and high schools of Plattsburg and was married to Evert Lansing Harvey, of Boonville, N. Y., on June 10, 1890. Coming to reside in Washington, D. C., they connected themselves with the Metropolitan Memorial Methodist Episcopal Church, of which Mr. Harvey is recording steward. They have two sons, George Lansing and Walling Evert, who are both students at Wesleyan University, Middletown, Conn., of which institution their uncle, John Cheeseman Clark, is president of the board of trustees.

Mrs. Harvey is district secretary of the Woman's Foreign Missionary Society of Washington District and superintendent of the young people's work of the Baltimore Branch; she teaches a large class of young men in the Sunday school and is recording secretary of the Ladies' Association. She is a Daughter of the American Revolution and is possessed of a fine personal presence and great repose of spirit.

SUSAN LUCRETIA DEWHIRST.

Mrs. Susan Lucretia Dewhirst, missionary worker and organizer, was born in Washington, D. C., on February 19, 1876, and is the daughter of Mary Katherine and Junewell Simonds Hodgkins. Her father was a cousin of Justice Salmon P. Chase. She was educated in the public schools of Washington, graduating in 1892. She is possessed of a deeply sympathetic nature and a philanthropic spirit.

Connecting herself in early life with the Metropolitan Memorial Methodist Episcopal Church, she became engaged in Sunday school, Epworth League and other church activities. For years she has been the efficient president of one of its missionary societies, "The World Wide Circle," and has been highly successful in raising funds for the support of orphans, Bible women, etc., in foreign lands. She has been acting treasurer of the Washington District Woman's Foreign Missionary Society for some years, and is the statistical secretary for the Baltimore branch of that association.

She was married to William Sherman Dewhirst, of Illinois, in 1897, he having connected himself with government service in Washington, D. C. He is a steward of the Metropolitan Church. They have one son, twelve years of age.

Mrs. Dewhirst is a daughter of the American Revolution and recording secretary of "Our Flag" Chapter. She has fine financial ability and is a welcome ally in every good work.

THERESA A. WILLIAMS.

Mrs. Theresa A. Williams, temperance worker and philanthropist, was born September 22, 1853, in Detroit, Michigan, and is the daughter of J. A. and Martha Hepburn Riopelle. She is descended on her mother's side from the Clements of New England, through whom she has common ancestry with Frances E. Willard, and on her father's side with the well-known French family of Riopelles, of Detroit.

She was blest with a liberal education and a broad and generous public spirit. She was married to Henry E. Williams on November 15, 1876, residing for many years in Washington, D. C. Mr. Williams is assistant chief of the United States weather bureau and has always been in the fullest accord with her temperance and philanthropic work. Mrs. Williams is prominently connected with the Woman's Christian Temperance Union of the District of Columbia, which she joined in 1882, and is official parliamentarian for that body. She is president of Chapin Union, its pioneer auxiliary, and was for many years district treasurer. She was so efficient that an article printed in the daily papers giving a sketch of the officers who planned the great national convention of 1900 called her the "Sherman Financier." She served for ten years as treasurer of the National Missionary Association of the Universalist Church of which society she is now the president.

EMMA SANFORD SHELTON.

Mrs. Emma Sanford Shelton, president of the Woman's Christian Temperance Union, of the District of Columbia, was born in Westmoreland County, Va., in 1849. She was the daughter of Julia Ellis Bibb and Charles Henry Sanford, a lawyer residing at Montrose, the county seat.

She was educated in the public schools of Washington, and in October, 1872, was married to Charles William Shelton, of Boston, Mass. They have one son, Arthur Bentley Shelton.

Mrs. Shelton has been connected with the Woman's Christian Temperance Union, of the District of Columbia from the time of its organization in 1874. As superintendent of narcotics, she was instrumental in securing the passage by Congress of a law prohibiting the sale of cigarettes and tobacco to minors under sixteen years of age. While working for this law, she secured petitions in its favor signed by nearly every physician in the city, the superintendent of public schools, all the supervising principals and nearly every teacher, as well as by pastors of all denominations. The petitions were ordered printed by the United States Senate and attracted such attention and created such an interest on the subject, that the bill prepared by her was speedily reported by the senate committee with favorable recommendations, and became a law.

Mrs. Shelton was recording secretary of the District of Columbia Woman's Christian Temperance Union for more than twenty years, and for several years was the assistant national superintendent of the department of legislation. When, in 1901, it was decided by the District Union to secure a building of its own, the matter was placed in the hands of a board of trustees, of which Mrs. Shelton was made financial secretary. The building, 522 Sixth Street, which is the Woman's Christian Temperance Union Headquarters, was purchased and entirely paid for within eight years by money raised almost entirely by the members of the organization under the efficient leadership of the president of the board of trustees.

Mrs. Shelton has been for many years an active member of the Vermont Avenue Christian Church, a teacher in the Sunday school, and was for several years president of the board of Deaconesses of that church. She is a vice-president of the Interdenominational Missionary Union of the District of Columbia, and also represents her denomination in the Interdenominational Council of Women for Christian and Patriotic Service, whose headquarters are in New York City. She has recently been appointed on the advisory board of the Washington Seminary for young ladies.

Mrs. Shelton has developed great ability as a leader in temperance and other Christian work, and has the peculiar genius of being able to secure the hearty co-operation of her associates in carrying out the plans formulated by herself and other leaders in the movements in which she is interested for the uplift of humanity.

MARGARET DYE ELLIS.

Mrs. Margaret Dye Ellis, daughter of Dr. Clarkson and Margaret Dye, was born in the city of New York. Her parents, who were members of the Anti-Slavery Society, were foremost also in benevolent and philanthropic endeavor. At the age of eighteen years, Margaret married Jonathan T. Ellis, a business man of New York but a native of Maine, and during their forty odd years of married life, in every possible way did he second his wife's efforts for the betterment of the world.

Four children were born to them, two of whom with their father have passed on. During 1873-1874, Mrs. Ellis with her family were sojourning for a time in California. The great "temperance crusade," which had started in Ohio, found its way to the Pacific coast, and Mrs. Ellis, with other women, united in a movement to bring about better conditions in that western state. Upon their return to New Jersey in 1876, she identified herself with the Woman's Christian Temperance Union of that state, and in 1880 was elected corresponding secretary of the state union, a position she held for fifteen years. In 1895 she was appointed legislative superintendent for the National Woman's Christian Temperance Union, a position she still holds. For sixteen years she has spent her winters, or the time during the sessions of Congress at Washington, D. C., looking after the interests of temperance legislation. Mrs. Ellis has done much platform work, also, having spoken at Chautauquas, conventions, etc., in nearly every state in the union. Mrs. Ellis was appointed by President Taft as delegate to the Thirteenth International Non-Alcoholic Congress which met at The Hague in September, 1911, an official certificate from the department of state making her a representative of this government.

ELLA ALEXANDER BOOLE.

Mrs. Ella Alexander Boole was born at Van Wert, Ohio, where she attended the graded and high schools, after which she entered the University of Wooster at Wooster, Ohio, being graduated in the classical course in 1878. Her record in college was second in her class of thirty-one, twenty-eight of whom were young men, and she was awarded the first prize in the Junior Oratorical Contest. After her graduation, she served as assistant in the high school in her native town for five years and in 1883 was married to the Rev. William H. Boole, an honored member of the New York East Conference of the Methodist Episcopal Church.

Her interest in the temperance work began at the time of the Crusade when as a schoolgirl she came in touch with that mighty movement. Her platform work began in 1883 and since that time she has been actively engaged in the prosecution of religious, temperance and philanthropic work. She has served New York Woman's Christian Temperance Union as an officer since 1885, having been elected corresponding secretary, first vice-president, secretary of the Young Woman's Branch, and in 1898 was elected president of the state. In 1903 she was elected secretary of the Woman's Board of Home Missions of the Presbyterian Church, United States of America, and her active leadership in home missionary work was felt not only in that church but in Interdenominational home missionary endeavor. In 1909 she was again elected president of New York State Woman's Christian Temperance Union, which position she still holds.

As a member of the Woman's Press Club, chairman of the Woman's Anti-Vice Committee of New York City, president of the Allied Forces for Civic and Moral Betterment in the state of New York, and of many important committees in philanthropic work, she is well known among literary people and her platform experience has extended all over the nation.

ELLA HOOVER THACHER.

Mrs. Ella Hoover Thacher is of old Holland and English descent. She taught school when she was fifteen and one-half years old; was prepared for college, but too young to enter; married at 17; began her temperance work when only five years old; joined church at twelve years of age; taught a Sunday school class of three little children when eleven years of age; moved to Florence, New Jersey, after her marriage and with the help of her husband, organized a Sunday school there, from which a church grew, with an attendance of more than 600 people. They organized settlement work—cooking, sewing classes, boys' and girls' clubs, evangelistic work and helpers in work with boys in library; began Woman's Christian Temperance Union work with children of the town and a Woman's Christian Temperance Union followed; was elected county president of Burlington County Woman's Christian Temperance Union in 1893; made national superintendent of soldiers' and sailors' work; made world's superintendent of soldiers' and sailors' work; has traveled all over the United States and many foreign countries in interest of this department; visited every National Soldiers' Home and many State Homes; organized Christian Temperance Unions. Over 10,000 soldiers and sailors in forts, barracks, navy yards and on the large battle-ships and cruisers have pledged against strong drink through her influence; many of these are filling places of trust in the business world to-day. Some of them are preaching the Gospel of Christ.

Mrs. Thacher has been sent by the World's Woman's Christian Temperance Union to Mexico where President Diaz became interested in the work; also sent to Cuba and the Bahama Islands. Visiting government reservations while the canteen was in them, she learned of the dreadful havoc it was making and traveled extensively telling the people of the country of its dreadful wickedness; also arousing her own organization which, with other temperance societies and the Christian people of the nation, helped in the abolishing of the curse.

For twenty-five years she was treasurer of an associational Woman's Foreign Missionary Society; is connected with the National Congress of Mothers and is on many local boards of philanthropic societies. For years she was the only woman on the executive board of the New Jersey State Red Cross Society, having been instrumental in its organization.

MARY HARRIS ARMOR.

Mrs. Mary Harris Armor of Eastman, Georgia, was called "The Southern Joan of Arc." She is state president of the Woman's Christian Temperance Union and has electrified the whole community, North and South with her match-less eloquence, her unanswerable logic, and her magnetic personality, as she has gone from city to city pleading the cause of prohibition. Mrs. Armor is credited with being the main factor in the passage of the state prohibitory law for Georgia, and she is now in constant demand as a speaker at Chautauquas and all over the country. Mrs. Armor's chief claim to distinction, aside from her platform work, is the fact that she raised a subscription of $7,000.00 in a single evening, for the work of the National Woman's Christian Temperance Union. One who was present at that memorable meeting, said: "A panic was on, the banks had closed down. Everyone who had money had it glued to the bottom of his pocket. When the little Georgia woman announced that she was going to raise $5,000 before she sat down, everybody smiled. She made no speech but talked simply, but the appeal went to the hearts of every one present. She was pleading passionately for her people, she was a Joan of Arc calling on her countrymen to rise, buckle on the sword and defend themselves. She was eloquent, formidable, tragic. Her humor would steal a smile from the lips of grief; she was malevolent and objurgatory against her enemies; she was strong in her rhetorical efforts and intensity. Chaste, eloquent and moving a marvelous woman truly!" She said all that 5,000 people could stand and $7,000 was raised. Mrs. Armor is in demand all over the country to speak for temperance and philanthropy.

EDITH SMITH DAVIS.

Mrs. Edith Smith Davis is of English descent and was born and bred near the childhood home of Frances E. Willard in Wisconsin. Milton College, Lawrence University, and Wellesley College contributed to her education. From Lawrence University she received the degree of A.B., A.M. and of Litt. D. After taking post-graduate work at Wellesley College, she taught English literature for three years in Clark University. In 1884 she was married to the Reverend J. S. Davis, D.D., and began her active work in the Woman's Christian Temperance Union. In this organization she has held a great variety of offices and departments, aiding as much by her pen as by her voice. She is the author of a number of books, and has constantly written for the press. Her business ability was manifested when she aided in the raising of three hundred thousand dollars for the endowment of her "Alma Mater." After the death of Mrs. Mary Hunt in 1905, Mrs. Davis was elected to the superintendency of the Department of Scientific Temperance Instruction and Scientific Temperance Investigation of the Woman's Christian Temperance Union. During the five years that she has held this position she has been sent at a delegate to the Anti-Alcoholic Congress held at Stockholm in 1907, to London in 1909, and to The Hague in 1911. Mrs. Davis considers her most important work to be the incorporation of courses of study in the higher schools, the publication of the "Temperance Educational Quarterly," and the holding of prize essay contests in the public schools.

SUSAN HAMMOND BARNEY.

Mrs. Barney, evangelist, was born in Massachusetts. In 1854 she married Joseph K. Barney, of Providence, Rhode Island. She was the founder of the Prisoners' Aid Society of Rhode Island. Has done work with the Woman's Foreign Missionary Society and was the first president of the Rhode Island Woman's Christian Temperance Union. Is an evangelist of note, and was largely instrumental in making prohibition a constitutional enactment in Rhode Island in

1886; and also to her is due the securing of police matrons for the station houses of large cities. She has been one of the helpful women in America to the cause of her sisters.

JESSIE WILSON MANNING.

Author and lecturer. Was born October 26, 1855, in Mount Pleasant, Iowa. An active worker and eloquent speaker on literary subjects and for the cause of temperance.

TEMPERANCE LEADERS.

Mrs. Mary Osburn, born in Rush County, Indiana, July 28, 1845, while matron and teacher of sewing and dressmaking in the New Orleans University accomplished much as superintendent of the Woman's Christian Temperance Union among the colored people throughout Louisiana.

Mrs. Mary Jane Walter is secretary of the department of evangelistic work in the Woman's Christian Temperance Union of Iowa, and co-worker with J. Ellen Foster. She has attended many conventions, notably one in which the Woman's Christian Temperance Union of Iowa withdrew from auxiliaryship with the national association, because of its opposition to the political women's Christian temperance work.

Mrs. Mary Brook Allen's remarkable executive talent in reform and philanthropic work, combined with all the grace of a born orator, have made her such a power in the work for temperance that she has received the unqualified praise of such noted men as Doctor Heber Newton and Doctor Theodore Tyler.

Miss Julia A. Arms, to her the white ribbon and the silver cross were the symbols of life and her short life was crowned with the success of her brilliant work as editor of the Woman's Christian Temperance Union Department in the Chicago *Inter-Ocean* and as editor of the *Union Signal.*

Mrs. Ruth Allen Armstrong, as national superintendent of heredity for the Woman's Christian Temperance Union, issued leaflets and letters of instruction to aid in the development of the highest physical, mental and spiritual interest in those of her sex. Her lectures on heredity and motherhood were the first public instruction issued by the Woman's Christian Temperance Union and their effect for social purity has been tremendous. They carried convictions that for the highest development of manhood and womanhood, parentage must be assumed as the highest, the holiest, and most sacred responsibility entrusted to us by the Creator.

Mrs. Lepha Eliza Bailey, whose girlhood was passed in Wisconsin when that part of the country was an almost unbroken wilderness, afterwards became a lecturer of national repute upon temperance and women's suffrage. In 1880 Mrs. Bailey was invited to speak under the auspices of the National Prohibition Alliance. She responded and continued to work in the East until that society disbanded, and finally merged with the prohibition party, under whose auspices she worked for years over the temperance field.

Mrs Frances Julia Barnes, who in 1875 became associated with Frances E. Willard, in conducting Gospel temperance meetings in lower Farwell Hall, Chicago, was afterwards given charge of the young women's department of the National Woman's Christian Temperance Union. Later she was made superintendent of the world's Young Women's Christian Temperance work and during every year she traveled extensively giving addresses and organizing new local unions. She was one of the most effective organizers that the cause of temperance had in the early days.

Mrs. Josephine Penfield Cushman Bateman is one of the most devoted missionaries in the cause of temperance, for years managing the interests of the Woman's Christian Temperance Union at Asheville, North Carolina. When she was sixty-one years old, but with the same ardor for temperance as burned in her heart at the opening of the temperance crusade, twenty years before, made a lecture tour of every state and territory and through the Hawaiian Islands. She traveled sixteen thousand miles and gave three hundred lectures. She has also published a long line of valuable leaflets on temperance.

Mrs. Mary Frank Browne is the author of an interesting temperance book, "Overcome," portraying the evils of fashionable wine drinking and intemperance. In 1876 she organized the San Francisco Young Women's Christian Association, and it was through her efforts that the first free kindergarten among the very poorest people was established. Later she assisted in organizing the California Woman's Christian Temperance Union, of which she served as president for many years.

Mrs. Caroline Buell, the daughter of an itinerant minister, knew the trials of hard living and high thinking pertaining to that life and came out of it to work for temperance with her character developed on ruggedly noble lines. She entered heartily into the work, and her sound judgment, her powers of discrimination, her energy and her acquaintance with facts and persons made her at once a power in the temperance association. For many years she was reëlected as corresponding secretary of the National Woman's Christian Temperance Union.

Mrs. Sarah C. Thorpe Bull, wife of the late Ole Bull, the famous violinist, was long the superintendent of the department of sanitary and economic cooking in the National Woman's Christian Temperance Union. Mrs. Bull was largely instrumental in securing the monument to Ericsson on Commonwealth Avenue, Boston. Her home was for years in Cambridge, Mass.

Mrs. Helen Louise Bullock gave up her profession of music, in which she had achieved some prominence, to become a practical volunteer in the work for suffrage and temperance. In 1889 she was appointed national organizer of the Woman's Christian Temperance Union and in that work went from Maine to California, traveling 13,000 miles in one year. During the first five years of her work she held over twelve hundred meetings, organizing a hundred and eight new unions and securing over ten thousand new members, active and honorary.

Mrs. Emeline S. Burlingame was the acknowledged leader in the securing of a prohibition amendment to the constitution of Rhode Island in 1884. In 1891 Mrs. Burlingame resigned the presidency of the Rhode Island Woman's Christian Temperance Union and was elected National Woman's Christian Temperance Evangelist and made her tour over the country addressing large audiences on the various phases of temperance work.

Miss Julia Colman originated the Temperance School that marked a new departure in the temperance work among children, using text-books, tracts, charts and experiments. For fifteen years she was superintendent of literature in the Woman's National Temperance Union.

Mrs. Anna Smeed Benjamin, of Michigan, is one of the best known orators in the cause of temperance. She was a logical, convincing, enthusiastic speaker, with a deep powerful voice and urgent manner, which made her a notable presiding officer. She was also a skilled parliamentarian and became superintendent of the national department of parliamentary uses in the Woman's Christian Temperance Union. The drills which she conducted in the white ribboners' "School of Methods" and elsewhere were always largely attended by both men and women.

Mrs. Sarah Hearst Black bore the labor of self-denial incident to the life of a home missionary's wife in Kansas, Nebraska and in Idaho, and achieved a splendid work of organization as president of the Woman's Christian Temperance Union in Nebraska.

Miss Alice Stone Blackwell, daughter of Lucy Stone and Henry B. Blackwell, has come forward in the cause of temperance, as is shown in the small weekly paper of which she is the editor. This is called *The Woman's Column* and is also largely devoted to suffrage.

Mrs. Ellen A. Dayton Blair, of Iowa, as national organizer in the temperance cause, visited nearly every state and territory as well as Canada, and is a member of nearly every national convention.

Mrs. Ann Weaver Bradley has done notable work for temperance in Kansas and Michigan. From young womanhood she has had an inherent hatred for the destroying agents in narcotics, and has done splendid work for the cause, being especially fitted for it by her gifts of persistence, thoroughness of research and her love of humanity.

Mrs. Martha McClellan Brown worked strenuously as organizer of the National Prohibition Alliance and made her husband's newspaper the vehicle of a vigorous warfare against the liquor traffic. Later, her husband and she were appointed to the presidency and vice-presidency of Cincinnati, Wesleyan College, which offered them a field for propagating ideas of temperance in the young minds brought under their control.

CYNTHIA S. BURNETT.

Miss Cynthia S. Burnett passed her early life in Ohio, but her first "White Ribbon" work was done in Illinois, in 1879, later answering calls for help in Florida, Tennessee, Ohio and Pennsylvania. In 1885 she was made state organizer of Ohio, and the first year of this treaty she lectured one hundred and sixty-five times, besides holding meetings in the daytime and organizing over forty unions. Her voice failing, she accepted a call to Utah as teacher in the Methodist Episcopal College, in Salt Lake City. While living there she was made territorial president of the Woman's Christian Temperance Union, and eight unions and fifteen loyal legions were organized by her. Each month one or more meetings were held by her and the work was further indorsed in a column of a Mormon paper which she edited. Later, she spent a year as state organizer in California and Nevada, and for these efficient services in the West she was made a national organizer in 1889. She spends the evening of her life as preceptress of her Alma Mater, which has become Farmington College.

Mrs. Mary Towne Burt began her work for temperance with the first crusade in Ohio and continued without intermission for many years. In March, 1874, she addressed a great audience in the Auburn Opera House on temperance and immediately afterward was elected president of the Auburn Woman's Christian Temperance Union, holding the office two years. She was a delegate to the first national convention held in Cleveland, Ohio, 1874, and was eventually promoted in the organization until she was made managing editor of the *Woman's Temperance Union,* the first official organ of the national union. In 1877 she was elected corresponding secretary of the national union, retaining the position for three years, and during that term of office she opened the first headquarters of the national union in the Bible House, New York City. In 1882 she was elected president of the New York State Union and during the years of her presidency it increased from five thousand to twenty-one thousand members, and from a hundred and seventy-nine to eight hundred and forty-two local unions.

Mrs. Matilda B. Carse, whose young son was run over and instantly killed by a wagon driven by a drunken man through the streets of Chicago, was brought by this tragedy to register a vow that until the last hour of her life she would devote every power of which she was possessed to annihilate the liquor traffic. She has been president of the Chicago Central Woman's Temperance Union since 1878. To Mrs .Carse is due the credit of establishing the first creche in Chicago, known as the Bethesda Day Nursery. Besides this, several other nurseries, two free kindergartens, two gospel temperance unions, the Anchorage Mission, a home for erring girls; a reading room for men, two dispensaries for the poor and two industrial schools have been established through Mrs. Carse's energetic management, and these charities are supported at a cost of over ten thousand dollars yearly. Mrs. Carse personally raised almost the entire amount and yet she has never received any compensation whatever for her services to the public. She founded the Woman's Temperance Publishing Association and in January, 1880, the first number of the *Signal* was published. This was a large sixteen page weekly paper and two years later when *Our Union* was merged with it, it became the *Union Signal,* the national organ of the society. In this publishing business Mrs. Carse started the first stock company composed entirely of women as no man can own stock in the Woman's Temperance Publishing Association. Mrs. Carse was president and financial factor of this association from its inception. The great building, the national headquarters of the Woman's Christian Temperance Union, is a monument to her life work.

Mrs. Clara Christiana Chapin, prominent member of the Woman's Christian Temperance Union, in Nebraska, wrote much for the press on women and temperance questions. An Englishwoman by birth, Mrs. Chapin's life work has been of great benefit to America, her pen and personal influence aiding materially in the securing of the temperance, educational and scientific law for the state in which she lived.

43

Mrs. Sallie F. Chapin, has always been a firm believer in prohibition as the sole remedy for intemperance. In the Woman's Christian Temperance Union she was conspicuous for years, serving as state president and she did much to extend that order in the South where conservatism hindered it for a long time. In 1881 she attended the convention in Washington, where she made a brilliant reply to the address of welcome on behalf of the South. A forceful and brilliant writer, she was at one time president of the Women's Press Association of the South. In the Chicago Woman's Christian Temperance Convention in 1882 when the Prohibition Home Protection Party was formed, she was made a member of the executive committee and by pen and voice she popularized that movement in the South.

Mrs. Louise L. Chase, in 1886, represented her state of Rhode Island, in the national convention of the Woman's Christian Temperance Union, in Minneapolis, Minn. In 1891 she was elected state superintendent of scientific instruction in the schools of Middletown, R. I.

Mrs. Elizabeth Coit, of Ohio, a well-known humanitarian and temperance worker throughout the West. During the Civil War she was a member of the committee of three appointed to draft the constitution of the Soldiers' Aid Society. She was chosen president of the first Woman's Suffrage Association organized at Columbus and for many years served as treasurer of the Ohio Woman Suffrage Association.

Mrs. Cordelia Throop Cole, of Iowa, took a most conspicuous part in the temperance crusade of her state, riding many miles on her lecture trips to meet appointments with the mercury twenty degrees below zero, and sometimes holding three or four meetings at different points within twenty-four hours. In 1885 she was made the Iowa superintendent of the White Shield and White Cross work of the Woman's Christian Temperance Union. Her earnest talks to women were always a marked feature of her work and later her published leaflets "Helps in Mother Work" and "A Manual for Social Purity Workers" have been of admirable effect.

Mrs. Emily M. J. Cooley began her temperance work in 1869, and when once awakened to the extent of the liquor evil she became one of its most determined foes. Although grown white-haired in the service is an indefatigable worker in the cause of prohibition. She served for years as state organizer in Nebraska and some time as national organizer speaking in every state in the Union. She did long service as president of the Second District Woman's Christian Temperance Union, of Nebraska.

Mrs. Mary A. Cornelius, despite the cares of motherhood and the responsibilities of her position as a pastor's wife, found time and energy to act for years as president of the Woman's Christian Temperance Union, of Arkansas. While leading an effort for prohibition in her state her life was threatened by the desperate element in the capital of Arkansas and personal violence attempted. Still she persevered, her pen never idle. Poems, numerous prose articles and voluminous newspaper correspondence testified to her industry and enthusiasm in the temperance cause.

Mrs. Mary Helen Peck Crane delivered addresses on several occasions before the members of the New Jersey legislature when temperance bills were pending and she greatly aided the men who were fighting to secure good laws. At the

Ocean Grove camp meeting, as the pioneer of press work by women, she gave valuable service and her reports for the *New York Tribune* and the *New York Associated Press* during the last ten years of those great religious and temperance gatherings at that noted Mecca of the Methodist Church, are models of their kind. She led the life of a sincere Christian, and died December 7, 1891, after a short illness contracted at the national convention of the Woman's Christian Temperance Union.

Mrs. Emma A. Cranmar of Wisconsin has lectured on literary subjects and on temperance in many of the cities and towns of the Northwest. An earnest worker in the white ribbon movement, with which she has been connected for years, she served with great efficiency as president of the South Dakota Woman's Christian Temperance Union.

Mrs. Lavantia Densmore Douglas has shown during her long life such ardent enthusiasm and untiring zeal in her work for prohibition that it made her name in her own community of Meadville, Pennsylvania, a synonym for temperance. She became a member of the Women's Christian Temperance Union and for many years was president of the Meadville Union. Arriving home from a trip to Europe on the twenty-third of December, 1873, the day of the great woman's crusade, and finding Meadville greatly aroused, she went immediately to the mass meeting that had been called and effected the temperance organization, which under one form or another has existed up till the present time.

Miss Cornelia M. Dow is the youngest daughter of Neal Dow, almost the original temperance reformer in the United States, and it is most natural that the greater part of her time should be given to works of temperance. For years she was officially connected with the Woman's Christian Temperance Union of Portland, Maine. She was president of the Union in Cumberland County, one of the superintendents of the state union as well as one of the most effective vice-presidents. Her mother died in 1883 and Miss Dow became her distinguished father's housekeeper and companion up to the time of his death.

Mrs. Marion Howard Dunham, of Iowa, entered upon the temperance field in 1877 with the inauguration of the red ribbon movement in her state, but believing in more permanent effort she was the prime mover in the organization of the local Woman's Christian Temperance Union. In 1883 she was elected state superintendent of the Department of Scientific Temperance and held the office for four years lecturing to institutes and general audiences on that subject most of the time. She procured the Iowa State Law on the subject in February, in 1886. When the Iowa State Temperance Union began to display its opposition to the national union she came to be considered a leader on the side of the minority who adhered to the national and when the majority in the state union seceded from the national union October 16, 1890, she was elected president of those remaining auxiliary to that body. She spends a large part of her time in the field lecturing on temperance, but is interested in all reforms that promise to better the system and condition of life for the multitudes.

Mrs. Edward H. East, of Tennessee, has spent much of her time and money in the cause of temperance. When the prohibition amendment was before the people of Tennessee she was active in the work to create sentiment in its favor.

A large tent that had been provided in the city as a means of conducting Gospel services she had moved to every part of the city. For a month she procured for each night able prohibition speakers. She was a delegate to every national convention after her first appearance in 1897.

Mrs. Lucie Ann Morrison Elmore, of West Virginia, was always a pronounced friend to all oppressed people, especially the colored people of the United States. She is an eloquent and convincing speaker on temperance and after coming to live in Englewood, N. J., she held several important editorial positions and she used these opportunities to present to the public her belief in freedom, quality and temperance.

Mrs. Rhoda Anna Esmond was married, and fifty-three years of age when first the influence of the woman's crusade of the West reached Syracuse, N. Y., where she was living, and she helped organize a woman's temperance society of four hundred members. Henceforth her life was devoted to the cause. She was made a delegate to the first state Woman's Christian Temperance Union Convention held in Brooklyn in February, 1875, with instruction to visit all the coffee houses and friendly inns in Brooklyn, New York, and Poughkeepsie, to gather all the information possible for the purpose of opening an inn in Syracuse. The inn was formally opened in July, 1875. As chairman of the inn committee she managed its affairs for nearly two years with remarkable success. In the first state Woman's Christian Temperance Union Mrs. Esmond has been made chairman of the committee on resolutions and appointed one of a committee on "Memorial to the State Legislature" and many other offices were tendered her in the state and national associations. In 1889 she resigned the presidency of her local union having held that office nearly six years, and she then devoted herself to her duties as state superintendent of the Department of Unfermented Wine, to which she gave her most earnest efforts for many years.

Mrs. Harriet Newell Kneeland Goff entered the temperance lecture field in 1870, and has traveled throughout the United States, Canada, New Brunswick, Nova Scotia, Newfoundland, England, Ireland, Scotland and Wales, speaking everywhere and under various auspices. In 1872 she was made a delegate by three societies of Philadelphia, where she then resided, to attend the prohibition convention in Columbus, Ohio, and there she became the first woman ever placed upon a nominating committee to name candidates for the presidency and vice-presidency of the United States. Through her presence and influence at that time was due the incorporation of woman suffrage into the platform of the prohibition party. She then published her first book (Philadelphia, 1876), "Was it an Inheritance?" and early the next year she became traveling correspondent to the New York *Witness,* besides contributing to *Arthur's Home Magazine,* the *Independent* and other journals. In 1880 she published her second book of which six editions were issued in one year. Her third volume (1887) was, "Who Cares?" Early in 1874 she had joined and lectured in several states for the Woman's Temperance Crusade. She became a leader in the organization and work of the Woman's Christian Temperance Union of Philadelphia, and was a delegate therefrom to the first national convention of the Woman's Christian Temperance Union, in Cleveland, Ohio, and again from the New York Union to the convention in

Nashville, Tennessee in 1887. Her special work from 1886 to 1892 was for the employment of police matrons in Brooklyn, N. Y., then her place of residence. For this she labored long, drafting and circulating petitions, originating bills, interviewing mayors, commissioners, councilmen, committees of senate and assembly, and individual members of those bodies in behalf of the measure, and by personal observations in station houses, cells, lodging rooms, jails and courts she substantiated her every argument, and as a result she procured such amendments of the law as would place every arrested woman in the state in the care of an officer of her own sex. Mrs. Goff is probably one of the most effective reform workers who ever fought for women's benefit in America.

Mrs. Jennie T. Gray, though of Quaker descent, became a zealous worker and a zealous speaker in the cause of temperance. Her greatest work was in the Woman's Temperance Union of Indiana, her home state, but she has traveled extensively, and in all her travels from ocean to ocean and from gulf to lake she endeavored to carry the strongest possible influence for temperance, often finding suitable occasions for advocating her claim in a most convincing way.

Miss Elizabeth W. Greenwood, already devoting her life to philanthropic work, when the Woman's Temperance Crusade opened she found her sympathies at once enlisted for the cause and she became conspicuous in the white ribbon movement, not only throughout New York State, but throughout the country. When scientific temperance instruction in the New York schools was being provided for, Miss Greenwood did important work with the legislature as state superintendent of that department. She served as national superintendent of juvenile work, and she was for years president of the Woman's Christian Temperance Union in Brooklyn, where she did splendid work as lecturer and evangelist. In 1888 she was made superintendent of the evangelistic department of the National Woman's Christian Union, and in 1889 she visited Europe, and there continued her reform methods.

Mrs. Eva Kinney Griffith was lecturer and organizer of the Wisconsin Woman's Temperance Union for seven years. Her illustrated lectures won her the name of "Wisconsin Chalk Talker." She wrote temperance lessons and poems for the *Temperance Banner* and the *Union Signal*. She published a temperance novel "A Woman's Evangel" (Chicago, 1892), having already put out a volume named "Chalk Talk Handbook" (1887), and "True Ideal," a journal devoted to purity and faith studies. In 1891 she moved to Chicago where she became a special writer for the *Daily News-Record,* and afterwards an editor on the Chicago *Times,* and by this means she made public her views on temperance.

Mrs. Sophronia Farrington Naylor Grubb during four years of the Civil War was one of those who gave time and strength in hospital, camp and field, and finally when the needs of the colored people were forced upon her attention she and her sister organized a most successful freedman's aid society. At the close of the war she returned to St. Louis, and here as her sons grew to manhood, the dangers surrounding them as a result of the liquor traffic, led Mrs. Grubb to a deep interest in the struggle of the home against the saloon. She saw there a conflict as great and needs as pressing as in the Civil War and she gradually concentrated upon it all her powers. In 1882 she was elected national superintendent of the work among foreigners one of the most onerous of the forty departments of the national organization of the Woman's Christian Temperance Union and by her effort and interest she brought that department up to a thoroughly organized, wide-reaching and flourishing condition. She published leaflets and tracts on all the phases, economic, moral, social and evangelistic of the temperance question and in seventeen languages. At the rate of fifty editions of ten thousand each, per year, these were distributed all over the United States. She established a missionary department in Castle Garden, New York City, through which instructions in the duties and obligations of American citizenship were given to immigrants in their own tongue as they landed. She also served long as president of the Kansas Woman's Temperance Union.

Mrs. Anna Marie Nichols Hammer's connection with the work of the National Woman's Christian Temperance Union was as superintendent of three departments, work among the reformed, juvenile work, and social or parlor work. In all these branches she was eminently successful. She was also vice-president of the Woman's Christian Temperance Union for the state of Pennsylvania, and ranked high as a clear, forceful and ready speaker.

Mrs. Sarah Carmichael Harrell was a member and the secretary of the educational committee among the World's Fair managers of Indiana. Her greatest work was the origination and carrying to successful completion the plan known as the "Penny School Collection Fund of Indiana" to be used in the educational exhibit in the Columbian Exposition. From this work came to her the idea of temperance work among school children, and she was made superintendent of scientific temperance instruction for Indiana, and was moreover responsible for the enactment of a law to regulate the study of temperance in the public schools.

Mrs. Mary Antoinette Hitchcock was living with her husband, Rev. Alfred Hitchcock, in Kansas, when the Civil War cloud hung over the country, and being imbued by nature and training with Union and anti-slavery sentiments, she was all enthusiasm for the cause and ready to lend her aid in every way possible. At that time many of the leaders passed through their town to Osawatomie to form the Republican party and she housed and fed fifty of them in one night, among them Horace Greeley. Later in her life having moved to Fremont, Nebraska, where her husband accepted a pastorate, she became an enthusiastic member of the Woman's Christian Temperance Union, and impressed with the idea that a state organization was necessary for its lasting influence she, in 1874, started the movement that resulted in the state organization. She was called to Sioux City, Iowa, on account of the death of her cousin, George G. Haddock, the circumstances of whose untimely murder at the hands of a drunken ruffian caused general indignation and horror. Over his lifeless body she promised the sorrow stricken wife to devote the remainder of her life to the eradication of the terrible liquor evil, and she fulfilled her promise. She accepted the state presidency of the Nebraska Temperance Union and for years traveled continually over the state, organizing unions and attending conventions.

Mrs. Emily Caroline Chandler Hodgin was one of the leaders in the temperance crusade of Terre Haute, Indiana, in 1872, and was a delegate to the convention in Cleveland, Ohio, where the crusading spirit was crystallized by the organization of the Woman's Christian Temperance Union. After that she began work of organizing forces in neighboring parts of the state. She became president of the Woman's Christian Temperance Union in her own county and secretary of the State Temperance Association, and she has greatly aided the cause from the lecture platform, for though a member of the Society of Friends, she availed herself of the freedom accorded to the speaker in meeting.

Mrs. Jennie Florella Holmes began her public work at the beginning of the Civil War in 1861, by giving good service to the Soldier's Aid Society of Jerseyville, Ill. Earnest and untiring in her advocacy of the temperance cause and all equal political rights for women, on her removal, at marriage, to Tecumseh, Nebraska, she immediately allied herself with these elements and in the winter of 1881 she became a member of the first woman's suffrage convention held in that state and labored for the amendment submitted at that session of the legislature. She was chairman of the executive committee of the state suffrage society from 1881 to 1884. In 1884 she was elected president of the State Woman's Christian Temperance Union, which office she held for three years. She was elected delegate-at-large from Nebraska to the National Prohibition Party Convention held in Indianapolis in 1888, and in her ardent love for the cause she considered this the crowning honor of her laborious life. She remained, however, with all her love for the temperance cause an active member of the Woman's Relief Corps and was sent a delegate to the Woman's Relief Corps Convention held in Milwaukee in 1889. She died in her home in Tecumseh the twentieth of March, 1892.

Mrs. Esther T. Housh became a prominent temperance worker in 1883 but she had done editorial work in the periodical *Woman's Magazine* published by her son in Brattleboro, Vermont, and when she attended the national convention in Detroit, she was immediately elected press superintendent of the Woman's Christian Temperance Union. She held that position until 1888, instituting the *National Bulletin* which averaged eighty thousand copies a year. In the national conventions in Nashville and New York she furnished a report of the proceedings to a thousand selected papers of high standing. In 1885 she was elected state secretary of the Vermont Woman's Christian Temperance Union and was given editorial charge of *Our Home Guards*, the state organ. Her literary work has been of the most valuable character for the cause.

Mrs. Mary H. Hunt, after a careful study of the sentimental, religious, and legal phases of temperance reform became convinced that if the nation were to develop on a high plane the liquor evil must be abolished by the wide dissemination of actual knowledge concerning the nature of the effects of alcohol upon the body and mind of man. She felt she must reach the children through the medium of the public schools. To reach the public schools with authority to teach, she must have behind her the power of the law, and her plan of operation she decided must include direct attack upon legislation, and to secure an influence over legislation there must be a demand from the people. Miss Hunt laid her plan before the National Woman's Christian Temperance Union and there was created an educational department of which she became the national superintendent. By an appeal to the American Medical Association in their annual meeting of 1882, she secured a series of resolutions from that body concerning the evil nature and effects of alcoholic beverages. These resolutions were made the text for her successful appeals before legislative bodies. She superintended this work in the Woman's Christian Temperance Union of the world, bringing the people to see the need of compulsory temperance education. Her work meant years of journeying from state to state addressing audiences almost continually, but it also meant victory in thirty-five states, in the national military and naval academies and in all Indian and colored schools under national control. It meant the creation of a new school of literature, the revision of old text-books, and the actual creation of new ones covering the entire course of instruction concerning the welfare of the body. All in all Miss Hunt's work has been of extremely practical benefit to the cause of temperance.

Mrs. Henrica Iliohan was born in Vorden, province of Gelderland, kingdom of the Netherlands, but the love of liberty and independence seemed to have been instilled in her from birth, and when she had come to America and was obliged to earn her living, the disability of sex became of more and more importance as she thought and studied over her situation. In trying to read English she noted for the first time an article on woman suffrage in the Albany *Journal.* In 1871, when Mrs. Lillie Devereux Blake addressed the assembly and asked the question: "Whom do you think, gentlemen of the committee, to be most competent to cast a ballot, the mother who comes from the fireside or the father who comes from the corner saloon?" Mrs. Iliohan again pondered deeply. This was a query that struck home to this young foreign woman, living at that time in Albany, and she made inquiries as to why women did not and could not vote in this land of the free. Very much interested she read all that was accessible on the subject and when, in 1877, the first Woman's Suffrage Society of Albany was organized she became an earnest member. With the remembrance of woman's share in the brave deeds recorded in Dutch history, she gained courage and enthusiasm and began to express her views publicly. Her first appearance on the lecture platform was a triumph. She was a foreigner no longer, but an American woman working for the rights of all American women. Encouraged by many she gained in experience and became one of the acknowledged leaders of the society. She was elected four times a delegate from her society to the annual convention in New York City and worked during the session of the legislature to obtain the consideration of that body. Mrs. Iliohan has also done some good work in translation. "The Religion of Common Sense," from the German of Professor L. Ulich, was one of her valuable contributions. In 1887 she moved to Humphrey, Nebraska, and thereafter became identified with Nebraska and the subjects of reform in that state and as she had done in the East, she endeared herself to the leaders and to the public.

Mrs. Ella Bagnell Kendrick, of Hartford, Connecticut, has always been an earnest advocate of temperance. When in 1891 her husband became a business manager of the *New England Home,* one of the leading prohibition newspapers of the country, she accepted the position of associate editor and through the columns waged a systematic campaign against all liquor traffic. She was an efficient member of the Woman's Christian Temperance Union and served through several terms as assistant secretary of the Hartford Prohibition Club.

Mrs. Ada Miser Kepley, inheriting strong anti-slavery principles from both maternal and paternal ancestors, this intense hatred of slavery took with her the form of hatred for the bodily slavery to alcoholic drink. And although she studied law and later was ordained a minister in the Unitarian denomination, Mrs. Kepley will be best remembered for her work for the abolition of alcoholic drinking and of the laws which tended to perpetuate that evil habit. In her law practice she made a specialty of exposing the hidden roots of the liquor trade in her town and county of Illinois. Through the paper *Friend at Home* which she edited, her readers learned who were the granters, grantees, petitioners and bondsmen for all the liquor shops there. She and her husband built in Effingham, Ill., "The Temple," a beautiful building which was made the headquarters for the Woman's Christian Temperance Union, prohibition and general reform work.

Mrs. Narcissa Edith White Kinney found her place in the white ribbon ranks in the fall of 1880, bringing to the work the discipline of a thoroughly drilled student and successful teacher. Her first relation to the Woman's Christion Temperance Union was as president of the local union in her town, Grove City, Pennsylvania, and next of her own county, Mercer, where she built up the work in a systematic way. She did an immense amount of thorough effective work, lecturing, writing and pledging legislatures to the hygiene bill, for she had made herself a specialist in that department after much study in regard to the best method of teaching hygiene to the young. In 1888 she was sent to assist the Woman's Christian Temperance Union of Washington State in securing from the legislature the enactment of temperance laws, and, under her persuasive eloquence and wise leadership, the most stringent scientific temperance laws ever enacted were passed by a unanimous vote of both houses, also in spite of the bitter opposition of the liquor trade a local option bill was passed submitting to the vote of the people the prohibition of liquor traffic in each precinct. Miss White assisted in that campaign and had the gratification of seeing prohibition approved by a majority vote. After her marriage she came to reside permanently in Astoria in Oregon, and she liberally supported the Chautauqua movement for temperance in that state.

Mrs. Janette Hill Knox, in 1881, was elected president of the New Hampshire State Woman's Christian Temperance Union, and as the responsibilities connected with that office drew her out from the quieter duties of home to perform those demanded by her public work, her executive ability developed and the steady and successful growth of the Woman's Christian Temperance Union during the years she held office bore testimony to the strength of her work. Her re-election year by year was practically unanimous.

Mrs. Mary Torans Lathrop was licensed to preach in Michigan in 1871, and was laboring as an evangelist when the woman's crusade swept over the state. She took an active part in the crusade, was one of the founders of the Woman's Christian Temperance Union, and in 1882 was made president of the state union of Michigan. Gradually her work became that of organization and she labored in various states as a strong helper in securing scientific instruction laws, in Michigan, Nebraska and Dakota amendment campaigns. In 1878 she secured the passage of a bill in the Michigan legislature appropriating thirty thousand dollars for the establishment of the Girls' Industrial Home, a reformatory school in Adrian, Michigan. Mrs. Lathrop's lectures have always been successful and she is equally at home on the temperance platform, on the lecture platform, or at the author's desk. Her memorial ode to Garfield was widely quoted and her brilliant oratory won for her the title "The Daniel Webster of Prohibition."

Mrs. Olive Moorman Leader, on her marriage in 1880, going to live in Omaha, Nebraska, immediately identified herself with the active work for the temperance cause. She introduced the systematic visiting of the Douglas County jails and she was one of the first workers among the Chinese, being first state superintendent of that department. For twelve years she was identified with the suffrage cause and an adherent and devout believer in the efficacy of Christian Science.

Mrs. Harriett Calista Clark McCabe, in April, 1874, wrote the constitution of the Woman's Temperance Union of Ohio, which was the first union organized. After serving the union for nine years she withdrew from public life but in time yielded to earnest persuasion to aid in the National Woman's Indian Association, and then in the Woman's Home Missionary Society, becoming the editor of *Woman's Home Missions* the official organ of that society.

Mrs. Caroline Elizabeth Merrick, wife of Edwin T. Merrick, chief justice of the Supreme Court of Louisiana at the time of the Civil War, began her work for the Woman's Christian Temperance Union at a time when the temperance cause was widely agitated in the South, though its reception on the whole was a cold one. She was for many years state president for Louisiana. She has written extensively on the subject but her chief talent was impromptu speaking and she developed into a very successful platform orator, holding an audience by the force of her wit and keen sarcasm. Her sympathies were also aroused upon the question of woman's suffrage and for years she stood comparatively alone in her ardent championship of the cause. She was the first woman in Louisiana to speak publicly in behalf of her sex. She addressed the state convention in 1879, and assisted in securing an article in the constitution making all women over twenty-one years of age eligible to hold office in connection with the public schools. It required considerable moral courage to side with a movement so derided in the South at that time, but Mrs. Merrick never faltered in her work for the emancipation of women; moreover, she always took active part in the charitable and philanthropic movements of New Orleans, her native city.

Mrs. Mary Clement Leavitt after being prominent in New England temperance work for years was elected president of the Woman's Christian Temperance Union of Boston, and national organizer of the society. In 1883 she accepted from the president of the National Woman's Christian Temperance Union, Miss Willard, a roving commission as pioneer for the temperance union which was organized in that year. Thenceforth Mrs. Leavitt's work has been without parallel in the records of labor in foreign missions and for temperance. When volunteers were asked for a canvas of the Pacific Coast states she was the first one to answer, and she was also the first to go abroad in the interests of the new organization. The association offered to pay her expenses but she decided not to accept it. She bought her ocean ticket with her own money and in 1883 sailed from California for the Sandwich Islands. In Honolulu the Christians and white ribboners aided her in every way, and after organizing the Sandwich Islands she went on to Australia where she promptly established the new order. Leaving Australia she visited all the other countries of the East and completed her tour over all the lands in the European continent. She organized eighty-six Woman's Christian Temperance Unions and twenty-three branches of the White Cross, held over one thousand, six hundred meetings, traveled nearly a hundred thousand miles and had the services of two hundred and twenty-nine interpreters in forty-seven languages. After her return to the United States in 1891, she published a pamphlet, *The Liquor Traffic in Western Africa*. During her great tour of the world she never in seven years saw a face she knew and only occasional letters from her enabled the home workers to know where she was laboring.

Mrs. Addie Dickman Miller, while teaching at Philomath College in Philomath, Oregon, where her husband was also a professor, the temperance movement in that state became a critical issue and she and her husband identified themselves with the cause. Mrs. Miller indeed gave up teaching and devoted herself to the work of the Woman's Christian Temperance Union. After moving to Portland, Oregon, and while caring for her children, she found time to serve several terms as president of the Portland Temperance Union arraying the motherhood of the city against the evil of intemperance. Besides her platform work she for years edited the woman's department in the *West Shore*, a Portland periodical. She also published "Letters to Our Girls" in an Eastern magazine—a series of articles containing many valuable thoughts for the young women to whom they were addressed.

Mrs. Cornelia Moore Chillson Moots knew the state of Michigan in its pioneer days, her parents taking her there in 1836. Abigail Chillson, the grandmother, went with them and as the new settlements were without preachers this elderly woman and ardent Methodist even supplied the itinerary by preaching in the log cabins and the schoolhouses of the early pioneers. Mrs. Moots' father was a temperance advocate also and staunch anti-slavery man, and the Chillson home was often the refuge of the slave seeking liberty across the line. With such inheritance and under such influence it was only natural that Mrs. Moots should become a forceful evangelist herself. After years of activity in exhorting and organizing new branches, a new field opened to her as a temperance worker and like her father she turned her force into the broad channel of temperance reform. She served many terms as state evangelist in the Woman's Christian Temperance Union and in spite of her radical views on temperance, equal suffrage and equal standard of morals for men and women, she was one of the most popular and most beloved speakers in the cause.

Miss Ellen Douglas Morris was reared according to the strictest sect of the Presbyterians and never dreamed of becoming a public speaker, until happening to attend a district convention of the Woman's Christian Temperance Union in Savannah, Missouri, where she was teaching, the state president believed she saw the latent power in the quiet looker-on and said to the local union, "Make that woman your president." After great entreaty on their part and great trepidation on hers this was done. The next year saw her president of the district, which she quickly made the pioneer of the state. When a state's secretary was needed Miss Ellen Morris was unanimously chosen and installed at headquarters. Her success in every position she held in the Woman's Christian Temperance Union was due to the careful attention she gave to details and the exact fulfillment of her service.

Mrs. Josephine Ralston Nichols, a popular lecturer, was attracted to the temperance movement by an address delivered in Maysville, Ky., her home, by Lucretia Mott. She was soon drawn into the movement and added to her lectures a number devoted to temperance. The scientific aspect of the work received her special attention and some of her lectures have been published by the Woman's Temperance Publishing Association. Her greatest triumphs, however, have been won in her special department as superintendent of the exposition department of the National Woman's Christian Temperance Union, where she worked for years, beginning in 1883. In state and county fairs all over the country she aided the women in making them places of order, beauty, and sobriety instead of scenes of disorder and drunken broil. In many cases she entirely banished the sale of intoxicants either by direct appeal to the managers or by securing the sole privilege of serving refreshments and in all cases banners and mottoes were displayed, and cards, leaflets and papers and other literature given away. So general was the satisfaction that several states passed laws prohibiting the sale of intoxicating drinks on, or near the fair grounds. In 1885 the Woman's Christian Temperance Union of Indiana made her its president, but she continued her practical work for the national society, extending and illustrating knowledge of the aims of the cause.

Mrs. Martha B. O'Donnell's work for temperance was accomplished through the society of Good Templars. It was most effective and she became president of the Woman's Christian Temperance Union of her county in New York State. Having long been identified with the independent order of Good Templars she began in 1868 the publication of the *Golden Rule,* a monthly magazine in the interest of this order. In 1869 she was elected one of the board of managers of the Grand Lodge of the state of New York. In 1870 she was elected grand vice-templar and was re-elected in 1871. At her first attendance in the right worthy grand lodge of the nation she was elected right grand vice-templar. Interested deeply in the children she was the moving spirit in securing the adoption of the "Triple Pledge" for the children's society connected with the order. She had charge of introducing the juvenile work all over the world. Her activity in this direction led her to visit Europe as well as many parts of the United States and always with success. Late in her life she became president of the Woman's Christian Temperance Union of her own county and passed many quiet years at her home in Lowville, New York.

Mrs. Hannah Borden Palmer, of Michigan, accompanied her husband to the front in the Civil War, camping with his regiment until the muster-out in September, 1865, and returning home she was elected president of the Woman's Christian Temperance Union of Dexter, Michigan. Under her guidance this union organized a public library and reading room in the town. It was mainly through her efforts, too, that a lodge of Good Templars was organized in Boulder.

Colorado, where her husband's business had called him. Her love for children induced her to organize a Band of Hope which grew to an immense membership. During that time she was, moreover, presiding officer of the Woman's Christian Temperance Union of Boulder. Yet another move in her life brought her fresh opportunity for temperance work. In Buffalo, New York, she united with the Good Templars, serving as chaplain, vice-councillor, and select councillor. Her council sent her as its representative to the grand council in February, 1890, and on her introduction into that body she was made chairman of the committee on temperance work and was elected grand vice-councillor, being the first woman to hold that position in the jurisdiction of New York. In the subsequent sessions of the grand council in February, 1891, and February, 1892, she was re-elected grand vice-councillor, being the only person ever reëlected to that office.

Mrs. Florence Collins Porter's early surroundings were those incidental to the new country, her father, Honorable Samuel W. Collins, being one of the early pioneers in Aroostook County, Maine. Later she left the little town of Caribou, where she had been writing for newspapers and periodicals, since she was fifteen years of age, and in Ohio she became greatly interested in public temperance reform with considerable success as a lecturer. At the formation of the non-partisan Woman's Christian Temperance Union in Cleveland, Ohio, she was chosen national secretary of literature and press work and in that capacity she worked for many years.

Miss Esther Pugh of Ohio, early became interested in moral reforms and she was one of the leaders in the crusade joining the Woman's Christian Temperance Union in its first meetings. She was an officer of the Cincinnati Union from the beginning, giving the best years of her life to the work. She was publisher and editor of *Our Union* for years, and her management as treasurer of the national society repeatedly aided the organization in passing through financial difficulties. She traveled on temperance work through the United States and Canada, lecturing and organizing unions by the score. She was called "The Watch-dog of the Treasury."

Mrs. Lulu A. Ramsey of South Dakota is exceptionally broad in her aims and charities, and a firm believer in woman's power and influence, yet for the field wherein to exert her best energies and benevolences, she chose the Woman's Christian Temperance Union. She was for years president of the local union, took an active part in the work of her district for which she filled the office of corresponding secretary and which selected her as its representative in the national convention in Boston, in November, 1892. Her ambition was to found an industrial school which should be so broad and practical in its aims and methods that each pupil should be self-supporting while there and leave the institution as master of some occupation. For years she labored to organize such a school and make it the special charge of a National Woman's Christian Temperance Union.

Mrs. Mary Bynon Reese came to Alliance, Ohio, just before the breaking out of the temperance crusade, and led the women of the city to a prohibition success. While lecturing in Pittsburgh and visiting the saloons with the representative women of the place, she was arrested and with thirty-three others imprisoned in the city jail, an event which aroused the indignation of the best people and made countless friends to temperance. After the organization of the Woman's Christian Temperance Union, she was identified with the state work of Ohio as lecturer, organizer and evangelist. She was the first superintendent of the Department of Narcotics and in 1886 she was made one of the national organizers and sent to the North Pacific Coast, where her work was very successful. She afterwards made her home a few miles from Seattle, which city became her headquarters as state and national organizer.

Mrs. Anna Rankin Riggs has won many honors in the white ribbon army, her principal field being Portland, Oregon. On her coming to the Northwest, Portland had no home for destitute women and girls and in 1887 the Portland Temperance Union, under the auspices of Mrs. Riggs and a few noble women, opened an industrial home. The institution was kept afloat by great exertion and personal sacrifice until it was merged into a refuge home and incorporated under the laws of the state. Mrs. Riggs was almost continuously in office as president of the Oregon Woman's Christian Temperance Union. In 1891 she started the *Oregon White Ribbon* which proved a successful publication. A prominent feature of her work in Oregon was a school of methods which proved an inspiration to the local unions in their department work. Mrs. Riggs has also represented Oregon at conventions and was president of the International Chautauqua Association for the Northwest Coast.

Mrs. Ellen Sergent who has held the highest office open to a woman in the order of Good Templars, was a member of the board of managers of the first state Woman's Christian Temperance Union, established in Syracuse, N. Y., and was one of a committee sent from that convention to appeal to the Albany legislature for temperance laws. But for all these honors she is best remembered in the white ribbon ranks for her children's stories on temperance. These were published in the *Sunday School Advocate* and *Well Spring*, and are delightful and poetic as well as instructive.

Mrs. Jennie E. Sibley of Georgia showed such courage in temperance work that she gained a reputation throughout the land. It has been said of her that "She worked with her hand, her purse, her pen, her eloquent tongue, with all the force and ferver of a crusader, and the most purifying and regenerating results followed her efforts in every field."

Mrs. Henneriette Skelton's name was associated in the minds of thousands of German citizens of the United States of her time as one of the most indefatigable workers in the cause of temperance. Born in Giessen, Germany, she with her brothers emigrated parentless to America. The energy and zeal with which she devoted her life as a young woman to temperance work were recognized by the national executive board of the Woman's Christian Temperance Union and she was appointed one of its national organizers. In that capacity she traveled all over the United States, lecturing both in English and her native tongue and leaving behind her local unions of women well organized and permeated with earnestness. For a time she edited the temperance paper known as *Der Bahnbrecher,* besides writing three books published in the English language, "The Man Trap," a temperance story, "Clara Burton," and "The Christmas Tree," a picture of domestic life in Germany. Her platform efforts were marked by breadth of thought, dignity of style and the very essence of profound conviction.

Mrs. Emily Pitt Stevens devoted her life to educational and temperance work on the Pacific Coast. She started an evening school for working girls; she organized the Woman's Co-operative Printing Association, and edited the *Pioneer*, a woman's paper produced entirely by women on the basis of equal pay for equal work. She was aided by prominent men in placing the stock of the company and through it she exercised great influence in advancing the cause of women in California. After the organization of the Woman's Christian Temperance Union in California she labored earnestly in that society. She contributed to the columns of the *Bulletin, Pharos,* and *Pacific Ensign,* and served as state lecturer. She joined the prohibition party in 1882 and she led the movement in 1888 to induce the Woman's Christian Temperance Union to endorse that party. As far back as 1874, she instituted the Seaman's League in San Francisco, and in 1875 the old Seaman's Hospital was donated by Congress to carry on the work, and the institution became firmly established. The inception of this splendid work together with many other California reforms in those days was from the mind of Mrs. Stevens.

Mrs. Lillian M. N. Stevens of Maine, co-worker with Neal Dow for the prohibition of liquor traffic, her first attempt as a speaker was made in Old Orchard, Maine, when the Woman's Christian Temperance Union for the state was organized. This movement fired her soul with zeal and she threw her whole heart into reform work. She was treasurer of the Maine union for the first three years of its existence and then was made its president. She was also one of the secretaries of the National Woman's Christian Temperance Union and corresponding secretary for Maine of the national conference of charities and corrections, treasurer of the National Woman's Council of the United States and was one of the commissioners of the World's Columbian Exposition in Chicago is 1893. She was one of the founders of the temporary home for women and children near Portland and one of the trustees of the Maine Industrial School for Girls. In all these manifold lines of work she proved herself an honorable daughter of a state noted for its distinguished sons.

Mrs. Eliza Daniel Stewart, a leader in all movements, whose purpose was the happiness and upholding of humanity, in 1858 became a charter member of a Good Templar Lodge organized in her town of Piketon, Ohio, and she remained a warm advocate of the order for the rest of her life. She delivered her first public temperance address before the Band of Hope in Pomeroy, and continued thereafter to fight for the temperance cause with voice and pen. When the boom of cannon upon Sumter was heard she devoted her time to gathering and forwarding supplies to the field and hospital, and at length she went South herself, to aid in the hospital work. She remained at the front during the Civil War and became convinced that in the appetite for drink that had come to so many of the soldiers the country was fostering a foe even worse than the one which the soldiers had conquered by force of arms. On the twenty-second of January, 1872, she delivered a lecture on temperance in Springfield, which was her first step into crusade movements. Two days later a drunkard's wife prosecuted a saloon keeper under the Adair law and Mrs. Stewart, called Mother Stewart since the war, going into the courtroom, was persuaded by the attorney to make the opening plea to the jury. And to the consternation of the liquor fraternity, for it was a test case, she won the suit. It created a sensation and the press sent the news over the country. Thereafter Mrs. Stewart was known to the drunkard's wives, if not as attorney, at least as a true friend and sympathizer in their sorrows and they sought her aid and counsel. Her next case in court was on the sixteenth of October, 1873, and a large number of the prominent women accompanied her to the courtroom. She made the opening charge to the jury, helped examine the witnesses, made the opening plea, and again won her case amid great excitement and rejoicing. Next, in order that the intensity of interest already awakened should not die down, Mrs. Stewart, with the co-operation of the ministers of the city, held a series of weekly mass meetings which succeeded in keeping the interest at white heat. On the second of December, 1873, she organized a woman's league that was the first organization ever formed in what came to be known as the Woman's Christian Temperance Union work. Soon after she went to a saloon in disguise on Sunday, bought a glass of wine and had the proprietor prosecuted and fined for violating Sunday ordinance. That was an important move because of the attention it called to the open saloon on the Sabbath. Then the world was startled by an uprising of women all over the state in a crusade against the saloons, and Mother Stewart was kept busy in addressing immense audiences and organizing and leading out bands through her own and other states. She was made president of the first local union of Springfield, formed January 7, 1874. The first county union ever formed was organized in Springfield in 1874 with Mother Stewart as president. In June, 1874, the first state union was organized in her state, her enthusiastic labors throughout the state contributing duly to that result. In the beginning of the work Mrs. Stewart declared for legal prohibition and took her stand with the party which was working for that end. In 1876 she visited Great Britain by invitation of the Good Templars. There she spent five months in almost incessant work, lecturing and organizing associations. A great interest was awakened throughout the kingdom, her work resulting in the organization of the British Woman's Temperance Association. In 1878 she was called to Virginia and there introduced the Woman's Christian Temperance Union and the blue ribbon work. Two years later she again visited the South and introduced Woman's Christian Temperance Union work in several of the Southern states organizing unions among both the white and the colored people. Age and overwork necessitating rest, she wrote, "Memories of the Crusade," a valuable and interesting history, also "A Crusader in Great Britain," an account of her work in that country. Her long work finished, though still young of heart, she passed her last years in Springfield, Ohio.

Mrs. Anna Elizabeth Stoddard going South in 1883 to engage in Christian work she stayed for several years, laboring in various parts of that country along lines of reform. Always an advocate of temperance she had united at an early age with the Good Templars in Massachusetts, and had occupied every chair given a woman in that association, but feeling a desire for more practical aggressive work against the liquor traffic she severed her connection with the order and gave her energies to the Woman's Christian Temperance Union, just then coming to the front. It was this reform that she actively espoused in the South, organizing in different parts Woman's Christian Temperance Unions and Bands of Hope. Having been located in Washington, D. C., for a year or more she was led to establish a mission school for colored children, to whom she taught the English branches, with the addition of work in an industrial department. Later she returned to Boston, Mass., where her labors were numerous and her charities broad and noble. She believed that "To oppose one evil to the neglect of others is not wise or Christian."

Miss Missouri H. Stokes, while in charge of the Mission Day School in Atlanta, and very successful in that missionary field, found herself drawn into the crusade for temperance which invaded even the South. She became a member of the first Woman's Christian Temperance Union organized in Georgia, and in 1881 was made secretary, going in 1883 to be corresponding secretary of the state union organized that year. She worked enthusiastically in the good cause, writing much for temperance papers and she was for years the special Georgia correspondent of the *Union Signal*. She took an active part in the struggle for the passage of the local option law in Georgia, and she made a most valiant attempt to secure from the state legislature scientific temperance instruction in the public schools, a state refuge for fallen women, a law to close the barrooms throughout the state, and she fought on for these acts of legislation for years despite the fact that she and her co-workers were everywhere met with the assertion that all these measures were unconstitutional. After being a conspicuous figure in the temperance revolution in Atlanta, Mrs. Stokes made several successful lecture tours in Georgia paying her expenses from her own slender purse and never allowing a collection to be taken in one of her meetings.

Mrs. Lucy Robins Messer Switzer is one of the most prominent temperance workers which Washington Territory, now State, has ever known. In 1882 she was appointed vice-president of the Woman's Christian Temperance Union for Washington Territory, and before Miss Willard's visit in June, and July, 1883, she had organized unions in Spokane Falls, Waitsburg, Dayton, Olympia, Port Townsend and Tacoma. She arranged for the eastern Washington convention in Cheney, the twentieth to the twenty-third of July, 1883, and she acted as president for the Eastern Washington State Union, then formed, for many years. Her work in the campaign of 1885-1886 for scientific instruction and local option and constitutional campaigns for prohibition are matters of record, as representing arduous work and wise generalship. She traveled thousands of miles in the work, having attended the national conventions in Detroit, Philadelphia, Minneapolis, Nashville, New York, Chicago and Boston. She was active during the years from 1883 to 1888, when women had the ballot in Washington, voting twice in territorial elections and several times in municipal and special elections. She wrote many articles in forceful and yet restrained style on all the phases of woman's temperance work and woman's suffrage, and it is safe to conclude that the present equal suffrage law in Washington State was made easier of accomplishment through the earlier works of such strong, thoughtful women as Mrs. Switzer.

Mrs. Eliza J. Thompson was early led into temperance work both by her own inclination and by the influence of her father, the late Governor Trimble of

44

Ohio. In her youth she accompanied her father to Saratoga Springs, New York, to attend a national convention and was the only woman in that meeting. On the twenty-third of December, 1873, in her own town, Hillsborough, Ohio, she opened the temperance movement that in a few weeks culminated in the Woman's Temperance crusade, and the great success of that movement as it swept from city to town throughout the state is accorded to Mrs. Thompson.

Mrs. Anna Augusta Truitt was one of those who marched, sang and prayed with the crusaders in that remarkable movement in Indiana, and she remained a faithful worker in the Woman's Christian Temperance Union. President of the Delaware County Woman's Christian Temperance Union for many years, she was selected by the union to represent them in state and district meetings, as well as in the national conventions. Her addresses, essays and reports proved her a writer of no mean talent. She was an advocate of woman's suffrage, believing that women's votes would go far towards removing the curse of intemperance. In the Woman's Christian Temperance Union she adhered always to the principle of non-partisan, non-sectarian work, and in spite of various hostile attacks she fought on until the temperance union in her city of Munsey, Indiana, was so strongly established, and so influential that no criticism nor persecution could turn the workers she left in the field from their path of duty.

Mrs. Mary Evalia Warren, for many years prominent in temperance reform, was a member of the Woman's Christian Temperance Union from its first organization and she had a field of her own for propagating the work at Wayland University, Beaver Dam, Wisconsin, where she had furnished money to erect a dormitory for girls called the "Warren Cottage." She joined the Good Templars' order in 1878 and filled all the subordinate lodge offices to which women usually aspire, and as grand-vice-templar she lectured to large audiences in nearly all parts of the state.

Mrs. Lucy H. Washington was a leader in the crusade movement, and when temperance organization was sought in her town of Jacksonville, Illinois, in response to the needs of the hour she was brought into public speaking. Her persuasive methods, Christian spirit, and her eloquence made her at once a speaker acceptable to all classes. Her first address in temperance work outside her own city was given in the Hall of Representatives in Springfield, Illinois. Commendatory press reports on this led to repeated and urgent calls for further lecture work and opened the door of service which was never closed during her life. During succeeding years she was in various official capacities largely engaged in Woman's Christian Temperance Union work giving addresses in twenty-four states and extending her labors from the Atlantic to the Pacific. In the great campaigns for constitutional prohibition in Iowa, Kansas, Maine and other states she bore a helpful part and in difficult emergencies, when great interests were imperiled, her electric utterances often produced a decision for victory. Her temperance hymns have been sung throughout the country.

Mrs. Margaret Anderson Watts, always a deep thinker on the most advanced social and religious topics, occasionally published her views on woman, in her political and civil relations. She was the first Kentucky woman who wrote and advocated the equal rights of women before the law. During the revision of the constitution of Kentucky she was chosen one of six women to visit the capital, and secure a hearing before the committees on education, and municipalities, and on the Woman's Property Rights Bill then pending. When the woman's crusade movement was initiated she happened to be living in Colorado where business affairs called her husband for several years, but her sympathies were with the women of Ohio who formed the Woman's Christian Temperance Union and as soon as she returned to Louisville she joined the union there. She worked actively in various departments of that organization, her special work being given to scientific temperance instruction in the public schools. In this and in many benevolences for her city Mrs. Watts accomplished much positive good.

Mrs. Delia L. Weatherby, inheriting the same temperament which made her father an abolitionist, became an active worker in the order of Good Templars. She could endure no compromise with intemperance and in the various places she lived she was always distinguished as an advanced thinker and a pronounced prohibitionist. She was a candidate on the prohibition ticket in 1886, for county superintendent of public instruction in Coffey County, Kansas, and she was elected a lay delegate to the quadrennial meeting of the South Kansas Lay Conference of the Methodist Episcopal Church in 1888. In 1890 she was placed in nomination for the office of state superintendent of public instruction on the prohibition ticket. In 1890 she was unanimously elected clerk of the school board in her home district. She was an alternate delegate from the fourth congressional district of Kansas to the national prohibition convention in 1892, and also secured the same year for the second time by the same party, the nomination for the office of public instruction in her own county. All this experience in political life greatly enhanced her value as a member of the white ribbon army, in which cause she has always been prominent. She was president of the Coffey County Woman's Christian Temperance Union for several years and as superintendent of the Press Department of the Kansas Woman's Christian Temperance Union, and state reporter for the *Union Signal* she proved herself one of the strongest women that this enterprising state has ever given to the temperance cause.

Miss Mary Allen West of Galesburg, Illinois, was a wise practical leader of the temperance cause. When the Civil War came she had worked earnestly in organizing women into aid societies to assist the Sanitary Commission, and after the war she accomplished a remarkable piece of editorial work, editing in Illinois the *Home Magazine,* which was published nearly one thousand miles away in Philadelphia, but later she left pen and desk for active work in the temperance cause. When the woman's crusade sounded the call of woman, the home and God against the saloon her whole soul echoed the cry, and after the organization of the Woman's Christian Temperance Union had been effected she became an earnest worker in its ranks, giving efficient aid in organizing the women of Illinois and becoming their president. In that office she traveled very extensively throughout Illinois and became familiar with the homes of the people. It was that knowledge of the inner life of thousands of homes that made her work for temperance direct, practical and efficient. She was often called upon to help in the editorial labors of Mrs. Mary B. Williard, the editor of the *Signal,* published in Chicago, and later whom it had been merged with our *Union,* into the

Union Signal and Mrs. Willard gone to Germany to reside, the position of editor-in-chief was given to Miss West who moved to Chicago to accept it. As editor of that paper, the organ of the National and the World's Woman's Christian Temperance Union, her responsibilities were immense but they were always carried with a steady hand and an even head. She met the demands of her enormous constituency with a remarkable degree of poise. A paper having a circulation of nearly one hundred thousand among earnest women, many of them in the front rank of intelligence and advancement of thought and all of them on fire with an idea, needs judicious and strong, as well as thorough and comprehensive editing. This the *Union Signal* under Miss West has had and the women of the Woman's Christian Temperance Union repeatedly, in the most emphatic manner, endorsed her policy and conduct of the paper. Soon after she went to Chicago some women of that city, both writers and publishers, organized the Illinois Woman's Press Association, its avowed object being to provide a means of communication between women writers and to secure the benefits resulting from organized efforts. Miss West was made president and filled the position for several consecutive terms. Her work in that sphere was a unifying one. She brought into harmony many conflicting elements and helped to carry the association through the perils which always beset the early years of an organization. She had an unusual capacity for vicarious suffering; the woes of others were her woes and the knowledge of injustice or cruelty wrung her heart. That made her an effective director of the protective agency for women and children, but the strain of that work proved too great and she stepped outside its directorship, although remaining an ardent upholder of the agency. Miss West in 1892 visited California, the Sandwich Islands, and Japan in the interests of temperance work. She died in Kanazawa, Japan, first of December, 1892.

Mrs. Dora V. Wheelock of Nebraska was one of the earliest women temperance workers of that state. In 1885 she became an influential worker for the Woman's Christian Temperance Union, serving for several years as local president in Beatrice, and three years as president of the Gage County Union. She was state superintendent of press work and reporter for the *Union Signal* for Nebraska. She has written much, her articles appearing in the *Youth's Companion, Union Signal* and other publications, and in every way she has accomplished all that a variously gifted woman might, as one of the advance guard in the cause of temperance.

Mrs. Mary Bannister Willard, sister-in-law of Francis Willard, was called to assume the editorship of the *Signal,* the organ of the Illinois Woman's Christian Temperance Union and during years of successful work for it she displayed remarkable ability both in the editorial sanctum and as organizer and platform speaker. The *Signal* under her leadership came quickly to the front and it was said that no other paper in America was better edited. But Mrs. Willard's health had become impaired from the constant strain of overwork and with her two daughters she went to Europe. In the autumn of 1886 she opened in Berlin, Germany, her American Home School for Girls, unique in its way and which for years she managed on the original plan with much success. It combined the best features of an American school with special advantage in German and

French and the influence and care of a refined Christian home. In the years of her residence in Europe Mrs. Willard's gifts and wide acquaintance have ever been at the service of her countrywomen and she stood there as here as a representative of the best phases of total abstinence reform.

Mrs. Alice Williams during years of suffering and invalidism read, studied and thought much on temperance subjects, and when restored to health the Woman's Christian Temperance Union was formed in her state of Missouri. She became an active local worker. In 1884 she went with her husband to Lake Bluff, Ill., to a prohibition conference there. At the request of Missouri state president, Mrs. Williams' voice was first heard from the platform in a two minutes' speech. She was appointed superintendent of the young woman's work in Missouri and was called to every part of the state to speak and organize. She always commanded large audiences and her lectures presented the truth of the temperance question and social purity in an unusually strong, yet not offensive manner.

Mrs. Jennie Fowler Willing's father was a Canadian "patriot," who lost all in an attempt to secure national independence, and was glad to escape to the States with his family to begin life again in the New West, so that this inherited love of freedom and a mixture of heroic English, Scotch and Irish blood in her veins, naturally brought Mrs. Willing to the fore when the great temperance crusade swept over the land. For several years she was president of the Illinois State Woman's Temperance Union, and with Emily Huntington Miller she issued the call for the Cleveland convention, presiding over that body in which the National Woman's Christian Temperance Union was organized. For a few years she edited its organ now the *Union Signal*. Mrs. Willing was drawn into public speaking by her temperance zeal and soon found herself addressing immense audiences in all the great cities of the country. As an evangelist she held many large revival services with marked success, and after moving to New York City in 1899, her life was as full of good works as it would seem possible for any human being's to be. She was interested in foreign mission work conducting her evangelistic services, was superintendent in an Italian mission and the bureau of immigration with its immigrant girls' homes in New York, Boston and Philadelphia. Her English sturdiness, Scotch persistence, and Irish vivacity, her altogether usefulness made her an ideal type of an American woman.

Mrs. Annie Wittenmyer, although originally famous for her work in the Women's Relief Corps, has done no less efficient service for the temperance cause. When the Civil War broke out she became Iowa's volunteer agent to distribute supplies to the army and was the first sanitary agent for the state, being elected by the legislature. She received a pass from Secretary of War Stanton, which was endorsed by President Lincoln and throughout the Civil War she was constantly in the field ministering to the sick and wounded in the hospital and on the battlefield. She was personally acquainted with the leading generals of the army and was a special friend of General Grant and accompanied him and Mrs. Grant on the boat of observation that went down the Mississippi to see six gunboats and eight wooden steamers run the blockade. While in the service she introduced a reform in hospital cookery known as the special diet kitchens, which was made a part of the United States Army system and which saved the lives of thousands of soldiers who were too ill to recover on coarse army fare. But after the war she turned to temperance work with the same courage and zeal that kept her coolly working even while under fire during the war. She was the first president of the Woman's Christian Temperance Union, in Iowa, and beginning without a dollar in the treasury she won the influence of the churches and the support of the leading people until her efforts were crowned with success. She established the *Christian Women*, in Philadelphia, and was editor for eleven years. She also contributed lectures, articles in periodicals, and a numerous collection of hymns to the cause of temperance.

Mrs. Mary Brayton Woodbridge was one of the most prominent women in the Ohio temperance movement. She joined the Woman's Christian Temperance Union and filled many important offices in that organization. She was the first president of the local union in her own home town, Ravenna, then for years president of her state union, and in 1878 she was chosen recording secretary of the National Woman's Christian Temperance Union, a position which she filled with marked ability. Upon the resignation of Mrs. J. Ellen Foster, in the St. Louis National Woman's Christian Temperance Union Convention, in October, 1884, Mrs. Woodbridge was unanimously elected national superintendent of the department of legislation and petition. Her crowning work was done in conducting a constitutional amendment campaign. She edited the *Amendment Herald,* which gained a weekly circulation of a hundred thousand copies. From 1878, she was annually reëlected recording secretary of the national union. She was secretary of the World's Woman's Christian Temperance Union and in 1889 attended the world's convention in England. She died in Chicago, Illinois, October 25, 1894.

Mrs. Caroline M. Clark Woodward entered the field of temperance in 1882 as a temperance writer and she proved herself a consistent and useful worker for the cause. In 1884 she was elected treasurer of the Nebraska Woman's Christian Temperance Union and in 1887, vice-president at large of the state. In 1887 she was appointed organizer for the National Woman's Christian Temperance Union and was twice reappointed. In the Atlanta convention she was elected associate superintendent of the department of work among railroad employees. She was a member of each national convention of the Woman's Christian Temperance Union, including the memorable St. Louis convention of 1884. She was a delegate to the national prohibition party convention in 1888, held in Indianapolis and as a final and well-earned honor she was nominated by that party for regent of the state university of Nebraska and led the state ticket by a large vote.

The roll call of temperance workers in America further includes: Mrs. Mary L. Doe; Mrs. Martha M. Frazier; Mrs. Elizabeth P. Gordon; Mrs. Clara Cleghorn Hoffman; Mrs. Eliza B. Ingalls; Mrs. Lide Meriweather, well known for her work to obtain constitutional prohibition in Tennessee; Mrs. Ann Viola Neblett, indefatigable worker for temperance in Greenville, South Carolina, and the first woman in her state to declare herself for woman suffrage over her own signature in public print, which was an act of heroism and might have meant social ostracism in the conservative South; Mrs. Sarah Mariah Clinton Perkins, Mrs. Laura Jacinta Rittenhouse, of Illinois; Miss Mary Scott, an earnest advocate in Canada, whose writings on temperance have had wide circulation among our Woman's Christian

Temperance Unions; Miss Mary Bede Smith, state reporter of Connecticut for the *Union Signal;* Mrs. Mary Ingram Stille, to whose efforts the success of the first Woman's Christian Temperance work in Pennsylvania was largely due; Mrs. Lydia H. Tilton; Mrs. Harriett G. Walker, one of the first to take up the work of the Woman's Christian Temperance Union and to whom Minneapolis is indebted for the introduction of police matronship; Mrs. Mary Williams Chawner Woodey, who was for years president of the Woman's Christian Temperance Union in North Carolina, and who made notable addresses in several state conventions.

Woman's Work for the Blind.

There are eighty public libraries which have embossed literature for circulation, and there are also many state commissions and associations for the welfare of the blind. The Misses Trader, of Cincinnati, Ohio, have accomplished wonders through their Library Society for the Blind and their Clovernook Industrial Home for the Blind. (Miss Georgie Trader is without sight.)

Mrs. Andrew Cowan, of San Francisco, Cal., organized an auxiliary for the blind before the disastrous earthquake in that city, and had a delightful library, where books were circulated and entertainments and readings given by volunteers.

The work in Dayton and Cleveland, Ohio, was started by ladies, and the Women's Educational and Industrial Union, of Boston, began the work which is now done by the Massachusetts Commissioners. Mrs. Hadder, of Brookline, Mass., did splendid work in this connection. Mrs. Fairchild and Miss Chamberlin and Miss Goldthwaite and Miss Trader, of the New York State Library, are well known in this work. Miss Bubier (blind) of the Lynn, Mass., Library, and Beryl Ghuhac, of the Brookline Library (also blind), are among the well-known women workers. Matilda Zeigler, of New York City, spends more than $25,000 annually on the fine publication which she founded, with Mr. Walter G. Holmes as managing editor, for the benefit of the blind. Miss Winifred and Miss Edith Holt, of the New York Association for the Blind, have done some particularly good work in the New York Association for the Blind, Department of Blind Home Teachers. Mrs. Laborio Delfino, formerly Miss Emma R. Neisser, is in charge of the

Library for the Blind connected with the Free Library, of Philadelphia, and the Pennsylvania Home Teaching Society and Library for the Blind. The Aid Association for the Blind of Washington, D. C., was organized about 1898 by Mrs. Hearst and Mrs. John Russell Young, the latter being its first president. At present Mrs. Charlotte Emerson Main is president.

Mrs. Rebecca McManes Colfelt and her late mother, Mrs. James McManes, have given large sums of money to pay the blind for copying books into English braille for the Library of Congress, and these ladies, by their generosity and interest in this work, made it possible for Miss Giffin, late librarian for the blind, Library of Congress, Washington, D. C., to be sent as a delegate to the International Congress held in Brussels in 1902; that held in Edinburgh, in 1905; at Manchester in 1908; Vienna in 1910, and Cairo, Egypt, in 1911. During these various trips Miss Giffin has visited schools and institutions and libraries for the blind in all the principal cities of Great Britain, Europe, Oriental Europe and Egypt. Miss Giffin has aroused the interest of prominent people in Washington to the immediate necessity of rescuing this library from ultimate destruction. Mr. Thomas Nelson Page has been made president of an organization, and Miss Giffin the director, with the hope of interesting friends all over the country to aid in this splendid work. There are eighty thousand blind in the United States, 82 per cent. beyond the school age, and two-thirds of them are dependent for their sole recreation on books. This movement is American in its spirit, and thoroughly in accord with the practice of our government. We have always prided ourselves on recognizing the rights of every class of citizens, and no woman has done a greater and more needed work better and more unselfishly than has Miss Giffin.

LAURA DEWEY BRIDGMAN.

Miss Bridgman was born in Hanover, N. H., December 21, 1829, and died in South Boston, Mass., May 24, 1889. When but three years of age she lost, through scarlet fever, her sight and hearing, becoming a blind deaf mute. In 1837 she was placed in the Institution for the Blind in Boston. Here Dr. S. G. Howe was director. He developed a special system of training for her, and in a short time she had acquired a considerable vocabulary, and so successful was the course of training used by Dr. Howe in her case that she became well known throughout the country, and this was successfully applied in the cases of other similarly unfortunate persons.

ETTA JOSSELYN GIFFIN.

Librarian for the blind; formerly in the Library of Congress, Washington, D. C. In 1897 Miss Giffin was appointed assistant librarian in the Library of Congress by John Russell Young, librarian at that time. A number of blind citizens had made a personal appeal to the librarian for a reading room, which was granted, and Miss Giffin placed in charge. When the new building was opened to the public, October 1, 1897, a room for the blind was appropriated and everything done to adapt this room to the use of the blind. So much interest was immediately shown by all visitors to the new library that it was decided by Mr. Young to collect not only books, music, maps and periodicals, but also devices for reading tangible print, guides for keeping pencil and pen in straight lines, games and every device for instructing and entertaining the blind. One of the important things which was commenced by Mr. Young was the collection of the reports from schools and institutions for the blind in American and foreign countries, also books on the care of the eye and the prevention of blindness, and all books concerning the education and employment of the blind. The idea was to build up a special library on all subjects connected with the blind and that most important organ, the eye, which was and would have been in the future most helpful to the blind of the district and those all over the country, and even of international use. Unfortunately, Mr. Young could not be spared to carry out his splendid ideas. This collection has been removed by the present librarian, but the effort is now being made to have it returned to the Library of Congress, where it is more accessible and will be properly cared for and continued and enlarged. Miss Giffin is now actively at work endeavoring to accomplish this end. As the literature in tangible print is limited it was decided on the opening of the reading room in the new library to have oral readings by sighted volunteers for one hour daily, and Mr. Young invited Thomas Nelson Page, F. Hopkinson Smith, Henry Van Dyke, and many others of prominence to read, and, if possible, give an address to the blind. Miss Giffin was particularly active in bringing about and conducting these delightful entertainments.

HELEN ADAMS KELLER.

Miss Keller was born at Tuscumbia, Ala., June 27, 1880. She is the daughter of Captain Arthur H. and Kate Adams Keller, and is descended, on her father s side, from Alexander Spottswood, colonial governor of Virginia, and through her mother is related to the Adams and Everett families of New England. Helen Keller has been deaf and blind since the age of nineteen months, as a result of illness. She was educated by Miss Ann M. Sullivan (now Mrs. Macy) from the beginning of her education to the present time. She entered Radcliffe College in 1900, graduating with the degree of A.B. in 1904.

She was formerly a member of the Massachusetts Commission for the Blind, and is a member of advisory boards for the various societies for the blind and deaf. She has contributed articles in the *Century Magazine, Youth's Companion,* and has written "The Story of My Life" and "The World I Live In," etc.

Miss Keller stands forth as a shining example of overcoming almost insurmountable obstacles. To-day she is a well-educated, keen-minded, cultured woman, equally enthusiastic over a walk in the woods or a sail on the water as over the treasures of Homer and Shakespeare. She converses in two or three languages, and writes as many more. She counts among her friends the most eminent contributors to the intellectual life of the day, and her own literary efforts compare favorably with those of women possessed of all their faculties.

In the face of what she has had to overcome Miss Keller's achievements are marvelous. She is one of the most remarkable American women of our day.

Christian Science.

MARY BAKER EDDY.

BY ALFRED FARLOW.

Mrs. Mary Baker Eddy was born at Bow, N. H., a few miles distant from Concord, the Capital City of the state. Her home commanded a charming view of the picturesque valley of the Merrimac River. She was the daughter of Mark and Abigail Ambrose Baker. Her great-grandfather was Captain Joseph Baker, among her ancestors were Captain Joseph Lovewell and General John Macneil, of Revolutionary fame. Her father was a well-to-do farmer and gave his daughter Mary all the school privileges that his neighborhood afforded. Besides school advantages, Mary Baker's educational opportunities were enhanced by private tutors, among whom were Rev. Enoch Corser, of Sanbornton Bridge Academy, and Professor Dyer H. Sanborn, the author of Sanborn's grammar.

In her youthful days Mrs. Eddy wrote both prose and poetry which were acceptable for publication in the periodicals of their day. Letters written to members of her family in her early girlhood, which have recently been published in *Munsey's Magazine,* give evidence of her close observation and depth of thought, as well as of her piety. These letters show that peculiar fondness for her home and the members of her family which is always in evidence in a deeply spiritual nature.

Samuel B. G. Corser, A.M., her boyhood friend, referred to her as the "brightest pupil" in his father's class, and declared that, "intellectually and spiritually, she stood head and shoulders above any girl in the community," that "she discussed philosophical and religious subjects" with his father which were oftentimes too deep for his comprehension.

In 1843 she was united in marriage with George W. Glover, a contractor and builder of Charleston, N. C. Mr. Glover was at one time a member of the governor's staff, and thus received the title of colonel. He was a man of large affairs. The records of Charleston show that between 1839 and 1844 he transferred thirteen pieces of real estate, while two were transferred to him in that city. Most of his property, however, consisted of slaves, which Mrs. Eddy was unwilling to own, and which she allowed to go free after Colonel Glover's death. During her early widowhood Mrs. Eddy earned some means by her pen. She possessed advanced ideas, and found ready acceptance for her writings with progressive thinkers.

At the early age of twelve she had pronounced religious opinions, some of which conflicted with those of her father and his co-religionists, notably a disbelief in the doctrine of eternal punishment. She contended that if her brothers and sisters, none of whom had made any public profession of religion, but all of whom were honorable, trustworthy and commendable citizens, were to be debarred from the heavenly estate, she wished to remain outside also. While wrestling over this religious problem she became ill. In her book, "Retrospection and Introspection," she states that on this occasion her mother "bathed" her "burning temples," bade her "lean on God's love, which would give" her "rest, if" she "went to Him in prayer, as" she "was wont to do, seeking His guidance." She further states, "I prayed; and a soft glow of ineffable joy came over me * * * * the 'horrible decree' of predestination—as John Calvin rightly called his own tenet—forever lost its power over me. When the meeting was held for the examination of candidates for membership, I was, of course, present. The pastor was an old-school expounder of the strictest Presbyterian doctrines. He was apparently as eager to have unbelievers in these dogmas lost, as he was to have elect believers converted, and rescued from perdition; for both salvation and condemnation depended, according to his views, upon the good pleasure of infinite Love. However, I was ready for his doleful questions, which I answered without a tremor, declaring that I could never unite with the church, if assent to this doctrine was essential thereto * * * * To the astonishment of many, the good clergyman's heart also melted, and he received me into their communion, and my protest along with me." Mrs. Eddy continued a member of the Congregational Church until after she organized a church of her own.

It was in 1866, after many disappointments and sorrows which culminated in invalidism, that she met with an accident while living in Lynn, Mass. As a result she found herself in a critical condition, and in her extremity her thoughts turned to God, and, as she afterwards more fully realized, she thus came in touch with the divine influence, and was instantly healed. This experience caused her to ponder upon the subject of spiritual healing. She was impressed that what she had experienced on the momentous occasion above mentioned might be repeated in all cases of sickness and disorder, if mortals could but understand how to approach the infinite Spirit. For the next three years she made a constant study of this subject, searched the Scriptures night and day, and finally arrived at the conclusions which, in 1875, she set forth to the world in her text-book, "Science and Health, with Key to the Scriptures." She attached the name "Christian Science" to her teaching, and at once began to put her ideas to a practical test by healing the sick. The propaganda of her system of thought was effected by the circulation of her book and also by the personal instruction which she gave to those who sought it. In 1879 she established the Christian Science Church, of which the name was afterwards changed to First Church of Christ, Scientist. This, the mother church of the denomination has at the present time a membership of tens of thousands, and it has branch churches in all parts of the United States and in many foreign countries. In this dissemination of her healing apprehension of Truth, Mrs. Eddy has contributed very largely to the health, happiness and general well being of mankind.

Christian Science is founded upon the Scriptural declaration that God is Spirit, Mind, Truth, Love, Good; that man is made in God's own image and is, therefore, spiritual, and not material, a point which accords with the generally accepted truism that "like begets like," and that, in accordance with the Master's teaching, "the flesh (matter) profiteth nothing," material sense is false, a deception which will vanish from consciousness through spiritual awakening. This teaching of Christian Science does not mean that the universe is unreal, but that it is not what it seems to be to uneducated human thought, to that quality of understanding which does not perceive objects from the spiritual viewpoint. Christian Science teaches that when one has attained to that spiritual perfection which St. Paul denominated "the measure of the stature of the fullness of Christ," the creations of God will be recognized as spiritual, and will appear infinitely more wonderful and beautiful than are the projections of our present material concept of being. This corrected view of man and the universe, the Christ-idea, destroys the false foundation of human woe and thus heals the sick. Christian Science reforms the sinner by destroying his false belief of life, substance and intelligence in matter, and of pleasure or benefit in sin, and thereby removes the incentive to do wrong.

Mrs. Eddy was an indefatigable worker. Although her books brought her a liberal income she spent relatively little money on herself, her whole aim in life being to advance the cause of Christian Science and to do good. She made her church the principal legatee of her fortune. She was an eloquent and fluent speaker, an inspiring teacher and a brilliant and convincing conversationalist.

In the early part of her life as leader of the Christian Science Church, she resided in Boston, Mass. In 1889 she removed to Concord, N. H., where she resided until 1908, when she returned to Boston, taking up her residence in the beautiful suburb of Chestnut Hill, where she remained until her demise, December 3, 1910.

Mrs. Eddy was not only much beloved by her own followers, but was highly respected by the community at large, and on the event of her passing away the newspapers of the country spoke in appreciative terms of the character which she had attained and of the good which she had accomplished.

SUE HARPER MIMS.

Mrs. Mims was one of the most prominent women in the Christian Science movement in America, and a social leader of Atlanta, Ga. She was born in Brandon, Mass., May, 1842, and was the daughter of the late Colonel William C. Harper and Mrs. Mary C. Harper. Her father was a lawyer of great learning and distinguished ability. She became the wife of Livingston Mims in 1866, one of the most prominent business men of Atlanta, a gentleman of aristocratic lineage and culture. For many years he was president of the Capital City Club, by which President and Mrs. Cleveland were entertained while on a visit to that city. Mrs. Mims gathered about her a circle of literary, artistic and musical people, exerting a wide influence for intellectual and ethical culture. She is a devoted follower of Mrs. Eddy, and has been one of the prime movers and teachers of Christian Science in the South.

45

Women Educators.

EMMA WILLARD.

Emma Willard, born in Berlin, Conn., in February, 1787, was one of the women whose names received votes for a place in the Hall of Fame. Her biographer, Dr. John Lord, in summarizing her claim for immortality in the hearts of her fellow-citizens, declares that her glory is in giving prominence to the cause of woman's education. In this cause she rendered priceless service. When we remember the institution she founded and conducted; the six thousand young women whom she educated, many of them gratuitously; when it is borne in mind the numerous books she wrote to be used in schools and the great favor with which these books have generally been received; when we think of the zealous energy in various ways which she put forth for more than half a century to elevate the standard of education of her sex, it would be difficult to find a woman who, in her age or country, was more useful or will longer be remembered as both good and great. Not for original genius, not for immortal work of art, not for a character free from blemishes and blots, does she claim an exalted place among women, but as a benefactor of her country and of her sex. In this influence she shed luster around the home, and gave dignity to the human soul.

Emma Willard was deeply religious, and never lost sight of the highest and noblest influence in her educational work. Beautiful hymns which she composed were sung by her pupils in the "Troy Female Seminary," of which, for many years, she was the head.

An interesting occasion in her life occurred in connection with a visit of General La Fayette to this country in 1825. His services in the cause of American Independence, in upholding the constitutional liberty in France and his mingled gallantry and sentiment early gave him prominence and fame, and made him an idol of the American people.

All this feeling Mrs. Willard had nobly imbued in the verses with which she celebrated this distinguished visitor's coming to her school in Troy. The young women of her school sang this poem before General La Fayette, who was affected to tears by this reception, and at the close of the singing said: "I cannot express what I feel on this occasion, but will you, madame, present me with three copies of those lines to be given by me as from you to my three daughters?"

Emma Willard was a woman of loftiest patriotism, and her "National Hymn" deserves at least equal appreciation with Doctor Smith's "Columbia." Her prose displays uncommonly strong mental powers and endowments. She published a large book or treatise on the motive powers which produce a circulation of the blood, which gained her great praise both at home and abroad. In 1849 she published "Last Leaves From American History," giving a graphic account of the Mexican War, and later appeared her "History of California" and a small volume of poetry.

In Emma Willard's case the promise of the Psalmist, "That the righteous shall bear fruit in old age," was splendidly realized. To the close of her long and useful life she maintained her youthful vivacity, her enthusiasm of spirit and her power of work. Every Sunday evening she gathered around her hospitable board her children, grandchildren and great-grandchildren, as well as her friends, and heard them repeat passages of Scripture. This was a habit of many years. Beautiful were those family reunions, but the most beautiful thing among them was the figure of the benignant old lady. Entering into every subject of interest with the sympathy of youth, she received from all the profoundest reverence and respect.

She died April 15, 1870, at the age of eighty-three. A distinguished educator said of her at the time of her death, "In the fullness of age she approached the termination of life with the calmness, Christian philosophy and faith of a true believer." The place of her death was the old seminary built at Troy where, half a century before, she had founded an institution which was an honor to the country, and where she taught the true philosophy of living and dying—works done in faith made practical in works.

MARY LYON.

While still very young, Mary Lyon, who was afterwards to become the foremost woman in America in the mental and spiritual training of young girls, wrote a letter to her sister revealing not only the strength of her thought and the intensity of her patriotism, but the deep bed rock of Christian faith which undergirded all her thinking. "This day," she wrote, "completes half a century since the Declaration of Independence. How interesting must be the reflections of those few who remember that eventful day. Who on the face of the earth fifty years ago could have expected such results? It is true that Washington and almost all Americans who lived in the days of Washington hoped for independence, but did they look forward to this time and expect such a nation as this? Must not all believe that self-promotion comes neither from the east nor from the west nor from the south, but God is the Judge who putteth down one and setteth up another. Must not all exclaim, 'This is the finger of God!'" This same spirituality of her mind was made manifest later in her influence over all those whom she taught. As time went on and Mary Lyon became more and more intrenched in her life work of teaching, her spiritual life deepened and her activities were intensified in two or three very important ways. She was deeply imbued with the importance of instruction in Bible truths, and in the conversion of her pupils, and more and more impressed with the importance of loyalty and self-sacrifice for the promotion of foreign missions. I think she was the pioneer in what is now quite common in Christian colleges—a definite laboring for the conversion of students as an important part of the college work. It was her custom to write to Christian friends in all parts of the country and enlist their prayers for the spiritual condition of her school. She had wonderful faith in prayer, and the results justified her faith. Mary Lyon's power in developing Christian character in her pupils lay in the fact that she not only lived a Christian life herself, but regularly taught it to her pupils. Her manner was simple; there was not the slightest pretense of speaking for effect or trying to speak eloquently, but her intense faith and earnestness made her a powerful speaker. Doctor Hitchcock, at one time president of Amherst College, says that the vividness with which she evidently saw and thought the truths she was telling was only second to her power. If she ever had a fleeting doubt of the certainty of future retribution that doubt was never known or suspected by her most intimate friends. The foundations of faith never wavered. The principles of the Christian religion seemed interwoven in the fibres of her soul. The world to come was as present to her thoughts as this world to her eyes. Her confidence in God was as simple and true as a child's in its mother.

Mary Lyon had broad and noble ideas concerning the necessity for the education of woman and the possible bless-

ings that would come from it to the world.   One one occasion,
when she was under the strain of great effort to obtain needed
help for Mt. Holyoke Female School (the institution of which
she was the founder is now known as Mt. Holyoke College)
she wrote a letter to a leading minister, in the course of which
she said: "Woman elevated by the Christian religion was
designed by Providence as the educator of our race.   From her
entrance into womanhood to the end of her life this is to be her
great business.   By her influence not only her friends, her
scholars and her daughters are to be affected, but also her sons,
her brothers, the young men around her, and even the elder
men, not excepting her father and his peers.   Considering the
qualifications which the mothers in our land now possess is
there not a call for special effort from some quarter to render
them aid in fitting their daughters to exert such an influence
as is needed from this source in our infant Republic, on our
Christian country?"   Such a letter would not seem daring now,
but it took a prophetess to write it twenty years ago.   Miss
Lyon's work in behalf of foreign missions was so immense that
it can only be referred to in this short sketch of her life.   So
many missionaries went out from her seminary that worldly
families became afraid to send their daughters there to school
lest they should give themselves to Christian work.   After her
death, in 1849, one writer suggested the breadth of her missionary work in these words, "Is she missed?   Scarcely a state
in the American Union but contains those she trained.   Long
ere this, amid the hunting grounds of the Sioux and the villages
of the Cherokees the tear of the missionary has wet the
page which has told of Miss Lyon's departure.   The Sandwich
Islander will ask why his white teacher's eyes dim as she reads
her American letters.   The swarthy African will lament with
his sorrowing guide, who cries, 'Help, Lord, for the Godly
ceaseth!'   The cinnamon groves of Ceylon, and the palm trees

of India overshadow her early deceased missionary pupils, while those left to bear the heat and burden of the day will wail the saint whose prayers and letters they so prized. Among the Nestorians of Persia, and at the base of Mount Olympus will her name be breathed softly as the household name of one whom God hath taken."

SOPHIA SMITH.

Sophia Smith, educationist, was born in Hatfield, Massachusetts, August 27, 1796, daughter of Joseph and Lois (White) Smith, granddaughter of Lieutenant Samuel and Mary (Morton) Smith, and of Lieutenant Elihu White; niece of Oliver Smith, philanthropist, and first cousin once removed of Benjamin Smith Lyman, geologist. Her early education was extremely meagre. She attended school in Hartford, Connecticut, in 1810, for three months, and in 1814 was for a short time a pupil in the Hopkin's Academy, Hadley, Massachusetts. She was an extensive writer, and in 1861 inherited a large fortune ($450,000) from her brother, Austin Smith. In later years she conceived the idea of building a college for women, defined the object and general plan of the institution, appointed the trustees and selected Northampton, Massachusetts, as its site. The college, which bears her name, and which was the first institution for the higher education of women in New England, was opened in September, 1875, with L. Clark Seelye as president. Miss Smith bequeathed for the founding of the college, $365,000 and also $75,000 for the endowment of Smith Academy, at Hatfield, Massachusetts, where she died, June 12, 1870.

MARY L. BONNEY RAMBAUT.

Miss Bonney was born June 8, 1816, in Hamilton, Madison County, New York. Her father was a farmer in good circumstances. Her mother had been a teacher before her marriage. Religion and education were prominent in their thoughts and directed the training of their son and daughter. Miss Bonney was a pupil for several years of the Female Academy in Hamilton and also under Mrs. Emma Willard, in Troy Seminary, at that time the best institution for young ladies in this country. Her father's death occurred when she was quite young, obliging her to take up the profession of teaching. In 1850 she decided to establish a school of her own and provide a home for her mother. In connection with Miss Harriette A. Dillaye, one of the teachers in Troy Seminary, and a friend of her earlier days, she founded the Chestnut Street Seminary, located for thirty-three years in Philadelphia and later, in 1883, enlarged into the Ogontz Seminary, in Ogontz, Pennsylvania, one of the famous schools for girls in the United States. Here, for nearly forty years, Miss Bonney presided. Her attention was first attracted to the cause of the Indians through a newspaper article in regard to

Senator Vest's efforts to have the Oklahoma lands opened to settlement by the whites. It was at this time Miss Bonney formed the friendship with Mrs. A. S. Quinton, and these two women began their task of aiding in righting the wrongs done by the government to the Indians. Miss Bonney gave freely from her own income to this cause. She became the first president of the society and devoted the latter years of her life to this work. While in London, in 1888, as a delegate to the World's Missionary Conference, Miss Bonney met and married Rev. Thomas Rambaut, D.D., LL.D., a friend of many years and also a delegate to the conference. Mrs. Rambaut died in 1900.

LOUISE POLLOCK.

With all the time and attention now given to the study of psychology in America it is interesting to review the career and work of a pioneer in this line of work. Mrs. Pollock was born in Erfurt, Prussia, October 29, 1832. Her father, Frederick William Plessner, was an officer in the Prussian army, but retiring from active service was pensioned by the emperor and devoted the rest of his life to literary labors. He seems to have taken special delight in directing the education of this young daughter, who at an early age showed a marked preference for literary pursuits. On her way to Paris, where she was sent at the age of sixteen to complete her knowledge of French, she made the acquaintance of George H. Pollock, of Boston, Massachusetts, whose wife she became about two years later in London. Her own five children started her interest in books treating of the subject of infant training, hygiene and physiology, and in 1859 she first became acquainted with the philosophy of the kindergarten by receiving from a German relative copies of everything that had been published upon the subject up to that time. Her first work as an educator was naturally enough in her own family, but her husband being overtaken by illness and financial reverses, Mrs. Pollock turned her ability to pecuniary account and began her literary work in earnest. Executing a commission from Mr. Sharland, of Boston, she selected seventy songs from German melodies for which she wrote the words; then she translated four medical works, a number of historical stories, besides writing for several periodicals. In 1861 her "Child's Story Book" was published and among the kindergarten works which she received from Germany was a copy of Lena Morganstern's "Paradise of Childhood," which she translated in 1862, into English. She had become so enthusiastic over adopting the kindergarten system in her own family that she sent her daughter Susan to Berlin, where she took the teacher's training in the kindergarten seminary there. In 1862, upon the request of Nathaniel T. Allen, principal of the English and Classical School, of West Newton, Massachusetts, Mrs. Pollock opened a kindergarten in connection therewith, the first pure kindergarten in America. During 1863, she wrote four lengthy articles on the kindergarten, which were published in the *Friend of Progress*, New York, and were the earliest contributions to kindergarten literature in this country. In 1874, Mrs. Pollock visited Berlin for the purpose of studying the kindergarten system in operation there, and upon her return to America she moved her family to the City of Washington where her "Ledroit Park Kindergarten" was opened, and her series of lectures to mothers was commenced. The sixty hygienic and fifty-six educational rules which she wrote in connection with those lectures were afterwards published in the *New England Journal of Education*. Other works from her pen are: "The National Kindergarten Manual," "The National Kindergarten Songs and Plays" and her song book, "Cheerful Echoes." In 1880 through President Garfield, she presented a memorial to Congress, asking an appropriation to found a free national kindergarten normal school in Washington. But, although it was signed by all the chief educators of the country, it was unsuccessful. Then she turned from Congress to Providence and with better success, for after giving a very profitable entertainment in 1883, the "Pensoara Free Kindergarten," with the motto, "Inasmuch as ye have done it to the least of these, ye have done it unto me," was opened. In order to raise the necessary funds for its continuance a subscription list was started at the suggestion of Mrs. Rutherford B. Hayes, who during her life was a regular subscriber. In connection with that kindergarten, Mrs. Pollock had a training class for nursery maids in the care of young children, and in San Francisco, Boston, Chicago and other places, nursery maids' training classes were soon opened upon the same plan. Mrs. Pollock with her daughter was for years at the head of the National Kindergarten, a kindergarten normal institute for the training of teachers, hundreds of whom went out to fill positions throughout the country.

MARY LOWE DICKINSON.

Mary Lowe Dickinson was born in Fitchburg, Massachusetts, in 1839. "We read of all-round women. They are of two kinds. There is the little all-round woman, smooth and small, like a bird's egg, holding infinite unfolded possibilities that never had the proper warmth and brooding for adequate development. And there is the other all-round woman, big as the world, with all sorts of excrescences and deficiencies, mountains and valleys of character, with rivers of thought and seas of sympathy, and forests of varied feeling crowned with abundant leaves for the healing of the nations, and with plains of experience and deserts of sorrow, and inside a burning heart of love that penetrates all, and now and then shows itself in some volcanic outburst that reveals the real passion and fervor of its inward life. And yet, with all this infinite variety, the all-round nature holds all in such true balance and poise, develops in such fine proportion, as never to seem to be all sympathy or all sense, or anything but a rounded and symmetrical whole."

Perhaps if the writer of the above paragraph had dreamed that the day would come when her own words would be chosen as perhaps the most fitting description of her own development she would have hidden them, as she has hidden most of her best thoughts, from the world.

From a primary school in a Massachusetts country town, the step to the head assistant principal's place in the Hartford Female Seminary brought her to the opening of Vassar, which occurred in her twenty-fourth year. The lady principal chosen to be the mother of Vassar was sixty years old. From among the younger educators of that day, it was proposed that this teacher should take, in the new college, the vice-principal's or elder sister's place. But an opportunity opening for three years of life and study abroad with one of her own pupils, the teaching was interrupted, to be resumed with still greater eagerness after three years of travel and student life in the great European centers. After one year as principal of what was then one of the most flourishing of New York City boarding schools, came the marriage with John B. Dickinson, a prominent banker of New York, and after that the social and philanthropic life which was interrupted only by periods of European travel until her husband's death.

Being recognized as one who had watched the development of every new educational movement, the opportunities to put personal touch upon one institution after another came to this busy woman's life. Boards of trustees conferred with her in reference to plans; philanthropists desiring to found educational institutions, and heads of schools and colleges, sought her co-operation, and invited her to aid in the development of their work. One after another, many institutions of prominence for the education of girls invited her to a place on their faculty. Wellesley, the Woman's College of the Northwestern University, Lasalle Seminary, Vassar, the Universities of Denver and Southern California, invited her to positions of honor and trust. Having made a specialty of the study of literature, keeping abreast constantly of the changes and advancement made in that department both in American and European colleges and universities, Mrs. Dickinson was quite ready when the opportunity offered to undertake the chair of literature in the University of Denver, Colorado. Here for two years she worked earnestly, especially for the advancement of young Western womanhood, which she insisted was the coming womanhood of our day. The work involved many outside demands, much lecturing upon literary and philanthropic topics, and heavy responsibilities, under which her health gave way; but the work had been so well done that the board of trustees continued to hold her position open for her. When return to that altitude was impossible, she was honored by the board of trustees, who named the chair of literature for her. Of this chair they made her emeritus professor, conferring upon her also a lectureship in English.

In the lecture field, one of Mrs. Dickinson's strong characteristics has been the combination of womanliness that never rants, with the earnestness that never fails to present the truth as she sees it with uncompromising directness and power. Much of her speaking has been before educational and philanthropic societies, in colleges and schools and before literary and historical clubs. She has been too busy a woman for much distinctive club life, but she is a member of the Barnard, Patria, and several other clubs.

Aside from her general interest in the development of all phases of woman's education and the special interest in the study of literature, no one subject has more engrossed her attention than that of education in citizenship. So far as possible, she has tried to avoid representing the work of organizations, believing that individual influence over individuals was the surest basis of help. Nothwithstanding this preference for individual labor, she has at one time been secretary of the Bible Society, one of the oldest organizations in New York; the superintendent of a department of higher education in the Woman's Christian Temperance Union; the president of the National Indian Association; the general secretary from its beginning of the International Order of the King's Daughters and Sons, and she is now an honorary president—having served as president for several years—of the

National Council of Women of the United States, an organization composed of twenty national societies, whose aggregate membership numbers more than half a million women.

Nor have the educational and philanthropic phases made the entire life of this working woman. Her work has been threefold. Teaching in schools or living a life crowded more or less with women and girls to whom she was teaching some one thing or another that they needed most to know; giving instruction or lecturing in schools and putting her hand to the wheel in charitable societies, there has been another life of work, in which the amount of labor done would have sufficed alone, it would seem, to fill one busy life.

Never fancying herself possessed of any special talent, nevertheless, when the fortune went and troubles came, Mrs. Dickinson turned to account the use of her pen, a facility in the use of which had marked her from a child. After her misfortunes, she began scattering about, at the solicitation of her friends, bits of verse written at one time or another.

Mrs. Dickinson's first book was a gathering up of these little verses, which made a home for themselves in the hearts of many people, and made a way for the author to such fields of journalistic work as would have kept her busy without her other tasks. From that time until this she has been an active writer along all journalistic lines. Never believing in her own talent, always saying that if she had any genius or great ability she would never have needed the spur of necessity, holding steadily to her early resolution never to write anything that should harm or belittle human nature, she pursued the work of reviewer, novelist, poet, biographer, essayist, and educator, never permitting her name to be used if by any means it could be avoided. Thus, enormous amounts of work that have issued from this pen were never recognized as her own. She wrote for the cause which interested her, for the object to be obtained. Her first novel, "Among the Thorns," was an expression of her thought as to the responsibilities of wealth and the best methods for alleviating the woes of the poor. "The Amber Star," printed first in England, and reprinted in America, deals with the problem of waif-life and the question of caring for dependent and orphan children. "One Little Life" is the expression of her thought as to the true significance of The King's Daughters' character and work in the world. Various smaller works have been issued from her pen, one called "Driftwood," including fifteen or twenty of the smaller stories, of which she has given the world more than three hundred, but few of which, however, appeared under her own name. These stories, short or long, reveal unquestionably the true story-teller's gift. The power of characterization, the power of making the individuals live the tale out before one's eyes, the unquestioned plot power, have long ago had their recognition, and opened the way for whatever work in this direction her busy life can do. Her latest novel, "Katherine Gray's Temptation," is said to be the strongest analytical work and the best character-study that has yet appeared from her pen.

CAROLINE HAZARD.

Caroline Hazard, educator, was born at Oakwoods, Peace Dale, Rhode Island, June 10, 1856, daughter of Rowland and Margaret (Rood) Hazard, granddaughter of Rowland Gibson and Caroline (Newbold) Hazard and of the ninth generation from Thomas Hazard, the founder of the town of Newport, Rhode Island.   She was liberally educated primarily in a private school, and for ten years as a member of a class of twenty women conducted by Professor Jeremiah Lewis Diman, D.D., of Brown University.   She was elected president of the board of trustees of the South Kingston High School; maintained the kindergarten in Peace Dale; was president of a King's Daughters circle in Peace Dale and became a member of the "Society of Colonial Dames."   She also is listed as organizing the Narragansett Choral Society in 1889, and instituted free Sunday afternoon concerts held in the Hartford Memorial Building, Peace Dale.   This building was erected as a memorial to her grandfather, Rowland Gibson Hazard.   During her tour of the old world 1876-77, she added to her knowledge of political economy, art and literature.   In 1899 she was elected president of Wellesley College, Wellesley, Massachusetts, as successor to Mrs. Julia J. Irvine.   She was elected a member of the Rhode Island Historical Society and of the New England Historical and Genealogical Society.   The University of Michigan conferred upon her the degree of M.A., and Brown University the degree of Litt.D., in 1899.   She published "Memoirs of Professor J. Lewis Diman" (1886); "College Tom"; "A Study of Life in Narragansett in the Eighteenth Century by his Grandson's Granddaughter," (1893); "Narragansett Ballads, with Songs and Lyrics," (1894); and "The Narragansett Friends' Meeting in the Eighteenth Century," (1899); she also edited philosophical works of her grandfather, Rowland Gibson Hazard, (1899); and contributed to magazines.

LOUISE KLEIN MILLER.

Miss Louise Klein Miller was born in Montgomery County, Ohio.   When she was two years old, the family moved to Miamisburg, Ohio, where she attended the village school.   Inefficient and uninteresting teachers gave direction and color to her whole life.   At times they were so deadly dull she "took to the woods" and there from the Great Teacher she learned the songs and nesting habits of the birds, the color of the butterflies' wings, when and where the first spring flowers bloomed and was unconsciously absorbing the great truths Nature has in store for those who love her.   The training at Central High School, Dayton, Ohio, organized the knowledge she had been accumulating from original sources.   After graduation, she attended the Normal School and taught in the city schools.

In 1893 she went to the Cook County Normal School, where she came under the influence of Colonel Parker and Mr. Jackman, who were the exponents of rational nature study.   After a post-graduate course, she went to East Saginaw, Michigan, as supervisor of nature study in the schools and assistant in the training school.   This position was occupied for two years, when she was called to fill a similar position in Detroit, Michigan, and remained there four years.

During the summer months she taught at the Bay View, Michigan Summer School, and with Doctor John M. Coulter, of Chicago University, studied the evolution of plants under the most favorable conditions.   At Cornell University, Professor L. H. Bailey gave a more practical direction to her work in agriculture and horticulture. Here she studied forestry, geology, entomology, chemistry, and other subjects which are fundamental in the work she was later to pursue.

From Cornell University she was called to Briarcliff Manor, New York, where some of the millionaires of New York City had established a School of Practical Agriculture and Horticulture. Later she was called to Lowthorpe, a school of horticulture and landscape gardening for women, Groton, Massachusetts. This afforded an opportunity for study at the Arnold Arboretum.

The work of the children of the Village Improvement Association, of Groton, was placed under her direction and she began school gardens. After two years at Groton, she went to Cleveland, Ohio, where she occupies her present position. She established school gardens and the Board of Education created the position of curator of school gardens and appointed her to fill the position which is unique, being the only one of its kind in the country. The duties are to supervise the school gardens, give illustrated lectures on gardening in the public schools, extend the home garden work, arrange for autumn flower shows and superintend the improvement of school grounds. Under her leadership, this school garden work is recognized as being among the best in the country. The influence of her work in the city is marked. Each school yard and garden has become a radiating center for civic improvement. Disease breeding and fly breeding places have been cleaned up and the city made more sanitary and more beautiful. Children are being taught the yielding capacity of a small plot of ground, succession of crops and harmonious color effects; they are becoming interested in gardening and many are seeking the suburb and country life. She has always emphasized the physical, mental and moral influence of this work in the fresh air and sunshine.

Miss Miller is a lecturer of wide experience, appearing at Chautauquas, before Civic Associations, Women's Clubs, Teachers' Associations in many parts of the United States and Canada. She is the author of "Children's Gardens," a "Course in Nature Study for the Pennsylvania Schools," and is also contributor to many magazines.

She is interested in all movements for the constructive upbuilding of humanity; is Fellow of the American Association for the Advancement of Science; member of the Executive Board of the American Civic Association; vice-president of the National Plant, Flower and Fruit Guild; vice-president of School Gardening Association of America; and honorary member of the Iowa State Audubon Society.

LUELLA CLAY CARSON.

Miss Carson was born in Portland, Oregon, March 12, 1856. Is the daughter of John Crosthwaite and Elizabeth Talbot Carson. Graduated from one of the private schools of Portland, receiving a state diploma in 1888 and a life diploma in 1890. Studied in Boston at one of the schools of expression of that city; Harvard College; University of Chicago; University of California, and Cambridge, England. Was preceptress of the Taulatin Academy and Pacific University; vice-president of the Couch School, Portland, Oregon; professor of rhetoric and elocution, English literature, American literature, and dean of women of the University of Oregon;

president of Mills College, California since 1909. Is the author of "Public School Libraries," and "A Reference Library for Teachers of English," "Handbook of English Composition," and is one of the conspicuous educators of the country.

SARAH PLATT DECKER.

President of the Woman's College of Denver and ex-president of the General Federation of Woman's Clubs. One of the most important women in the country.

HESTER DORSEY RICHARDSON.

Born in Baltimore. Is the daughter of James Levin and Sarah Ann Webster Dorsey. Married Albert Leverett Richardson January 27, 1891. Has written on Maryland history and is engaged in historical and genealogical research. Represented the Executive Department of Maryland in the historical work at the Jamestown Exposition in 1907. Was the founder of the Woman's Literary Club of Baltimore; member of the Colonial Dames; historian of the Baltimore Chapter Daughters of the American Revolution; incorporator of the Maryland Original Research Society and was secretary of the General Federation of Women's Clubs from 1901 to 1905.

ANN LOUISE WOLCOTT.

Was born in Providence, Rhode Island, May 25, 1868. Student at Wellesley College. At one time principal of Wolfe Hall, Denver, Colo. Founder of Wolcott's School, Denver. A member of the Archæological Institute of America; also of the State Forestry Association of Colorado, Colonial Dames, National Congress of Mothers, and prominent in the school of American Archæology. One of the leading educational women of the West.

KATHERINE ELIZABETH DOPP.

Born at Belmont, Wisconsin, March 1, 1863. Daughter of William Daniel and Janet Moyes Dopp. Student of the schools of Wisconsin and of the University of Chicago. Principal and teacher in several of the normal schools of Wisconsin and Illinois. Principal of the Training Department of the State Normal School, Madison, South Dakota, in 1896, and of the training department of the Normal School of the University of Utah in 1898. Instructor in Correspondence Study Department of Philosophy since 1902; lecturer in Educational Extension Division since 1894 of the University of Chicago. Has written several educational works, industrial and social histories, "The Tree Dwellers," "The Early Cave Men," and "The Later Cave Men," articles and reviews in educational and sociology journals.

FLORENCE AMANDA FENSHAM.

Born in East Douglass, Massachusetts, May 25, 1861. Daughter of Hon. John and Sarah Alice Fensham. Student of the Chicago Theological Seminary,

Mansfield College, and at Oxford and Cambridge, England and Edinburgh. Teacher in the American College for Girls in Coustan, Turkey, in 1893. Was professor of Biblical literature and dean until 1905, and instructor in Christian Instruction of the Chicago Theological Seminary in Chicago from 1906 to 1909, and dean of the training school for women in Chicago since October, 1909.

MARY ELIZABETH LITCHFIELD.

Born at Jamaica Plain, Massachusetts, May 9, 1854. Daughter of Lawrence and Sarah Minot Litchfield. Author of "The Nine Worlds; Stories from Norse Mythology."

ELLA LYMAN CABOT.

Born in Boston. Daughter of Arthur Theodore and Ella Lowell Lyman. Graduated from Harvard College in 1904, and took a special course in logic and metaphysics. Married in 1894 to Richard Clark Cabot. Teacher of ethics in private schools and member of the State Board of Education, many reform associations, council of Radcliffe College, Massachusetts Society Civic League and German Educational Department of the Boston Woman's Municipal League. Has written books entitled "Every-Day Ethics," "Teachers' Manual of Ethical Training," and other educational works.

NINA ELIZA BROWNE.

Born at Erving, Massachusetts, October 6, 1860. Daughter of Charles Theodore and Nancy Smith Brown. Assistant librarian of the Columbia University Library, New York, also the State Library; librarian of the Library Bureau, Boston, in 1893; assistant secretary, then secretary, of the publishing board of the American Library Association, and the Massachusetts Free Public Library Commission. Is a compiler and bibliographer of Hawthorne; editor of the catalogue of graduates and non-graduates of Smith College.

MARY DANA HICKS PRANG.

Born in Syracuse, New York, October 7, 1836. Daughter of Major and Agnes Amelia Livingston Johnson Dana. Took a post-graduate course at Harvard; also student of the school of music and fine arts of Boston. Married in 1856 to Charles S. Hicks, who died in August, 1858. Married to Louis Prang, April, 1900, who died June 14, 1909. President of the Social Art Club, of Syracuse, and director of the Prang Normal Art classes. Contributor to various art and educational journals. In connection with John S. Clark and Walter S. Perry, wrote "The Prang Complete Course in Form Study and Drawing," "Form Study without Clay," "The Prang Elementary Course in Art Instruction," "Suggestions for Color Instruction," "Art Instruction for Children in Primary Classes," and many books on drawing and art for use in the schools. Is active in teachers' associations, prison work, suffrage associations, art leagues, and women's educational associations.

AMY MORRIS HOMANS.

Born at Vassalboro, November 15, 1848. Daughter of Harrison and Sarah Bliss Bradley Homans. Prominent educator. Principal of the Hemenway School and McRae and Chadbourn private school; in charge of the educational work founded by the late Mrs. Mary Hemenway from 1877 to 1909. Organized and directed the Boston Normal School of Household Arts, Boston School of Gymnastics; director of Hygiene and Physical Education in Wellesley College since 1909.

MARY AUGUSTA SCOTT.

Daughter of Abram McLean and Julia Anne Boyer Scott. Has received degrees from Vassar and Cambridge, England; student in Romance languages at Johns Hopkins, and the first woman fellow of Yale, Ph.D., 1894. Professor of English language and literature at Smith College. Author of "Elizabethan Translations from the Italian." Editor of "Operative Gynecology," by Dr. Howard A. Kelly, "Walter Reed and Yellow Fever," by Dr. Kelly, "Bacon's Essays," and contributor to the *Dial* for many years. Writer of reviews and criticisms in literature for academic journals, American and foreign.

ELLEN BLISS TALBOT.

Born in Iowa City, Iowa, November 22, 1867. Daughter of Benjamin and Harriet Bliss Talbot. Professor and head of the department of philosophy of Mount Holyoke College. Author of "The Fundamental Principles of Fichte's Philosophy." Contributor to philosophical and psychological journals and reviews.

MARY VANCE YOUNG.

Born in Washington, Pennsylvania, May 22, 1866. Daughter of John Seavers and Jane Vance Young. Was instructor of the Romance languages of Smith College; professor of Romance languages at Mount Holyoke College since 1901; Officier d'Académie, French Government; member of the Modern Language Association of America; Société Amicale Gaston, Paris, and author of Molière's "Kunst Komödien," also an Italian grammar.

KATHERINE COMAN.

Born at Newark, Ohio, November 23, 1857. Daughter of Levi P. and Martha Seymour Coman. Was professor of economics since 1900 at Wellesley College; author of "The Growth of the English Nation," "History of England," "History of England for Beginners," "Industrial History of the United States" and other books.

ELLEN HAYES.

Born in Granville, Ohio, September 23, 1851. Daughter of Charles C. and Ruth Wolcott Hayes. Was lecturer and writer on astronomy and other scientific subjects; professor of mathematics, applied mathematics and astronomy since 1904 of Wellesley College. Author of "Elementary Trigonometry," "Algebra," "Calculus with Applications," etc.

MARY EMMA WOOLLEY.

Born in South Norwalk, Connecticut, July 13, 1863. **Daughter of Rev.** Joseph J. and Mary E. Ferris Woolley. Was instructor and associate professor of Bible history for several years in Wellesley College. President of Mount Holyoke College since 1900. Member of the Board of Electors for the Hall of Fame; member College Entrance Examination Board. Director of the Woman's Educational Industrial Union of Boston. Member of the Executive Committee of the American School Peace League; vice-president of the American Peace Society. Member of the Moral Educational Board of Ethical-Social League; vice-president of the National Consumers' League; trustee of the American International College; vice-president of the Third National College Playground Association of America; member of the Advisory Committee American Scandinavian Society; member of Hellenic Travelers Club; Rhode Island Society for Collegiate Education of Women; Salem Society for Higher Education of Women; Daughters of the American Revolution; member of the Sorosis; Boston College; Northeast Wheaton Seminary Club; Pawtucket Woman's Club; Springfield College Club, and Lyceum of London, England.

SARAH LOUISE ARNOLD.

Born in Abington, Massachusetts, February 15, 1859. Daughter of Jonathan and Abigail Noyes Arnold. Taught in the public schools of Massachusetts, New York, and Minneapolis. Dean of Simmons College since 1902. Author of books for teachers, "Stepping Stones to Literature," "Reading: How to Teach It," "Waymarks for Teachers."

ELEANOR COLGAN.

Enjoys the distinction of having had conferred upon her by the Pope, for her excellent work among the Italian children of this country, the order of Knighthood of the Church and the Papacy, and is the first woman in America entitled to wear the gold cross of the order. She is an instructor in the Brooklyn Training School for Teachers.

MARY BERNARDINE CORR.

Was born October 3, 1858, in Dubuque, Iowa. Is a teacher in the Boston Grammar and Normal Schools, and is a contributor to the *Sacred Heart Review* and *Donahoe's Magazine.*

46

MARY ISABEL CRAMSIE.

Was born in Friendsville, Pennsylvania, May 5, 1844. President for ten years of the Sacred Thirst Total Abstinence Society. Superintendent of the Catholic division, Newsboys' Sunday School for some years; secretary of the Diocesan Union for many years, and organized one of the first total abstinence societies for boys and girls under twenty years of age. Is the author of poems and has written for the *Catholic World,* the *Northwestern Chronicle* and local newspapers.

MARY HICKEY DOWD.

Was born at Manchester, New Hampshire, January 22, 1866. Daughter of John and Mary Joy Hickey, and in 1889 married Dr. John F. Dowd. Taught in the public schools of Massachusetts and New Hampshire. Delivered lectures on her travels in England. Associate editor of the *Guidon* for years, and author of "Life of Rt. Rev. Denis Bradley." Contributor to the various Catholic journals.

MOTHER KATHERINE DREXEL.

Daughter of Francis A. Drexel of the well-known Philadelphia family. She early became interested in the welfare of the Indians and negroes, and through Bishop O'Connor of Omaha she was lead to the founding of the community for these people and became its first superioress. She was for a while with the Sisters of Mercy in Pittsburgh, but gave her entire fortune to the new order which she had founded. The first novitiate of this order was located temporarily at the Drexel homestead at Torresdale, Pennsylvania, and she established also a boarding school and home for colored children at St. Elizabeth's, Cornwells, in 1892, and a boarding school for Pueblo Indians in Santa Fe, New Mexico, in 1894; an industrial boarding school for colored girls at Rock Castle, Virginia, in 1899; a boarding school for Navajo Indians in Arizona, in 1903, and an academy for the higher education of colored girls in Nashville, Tenn., in 1905, with a preparatory annex school in 1906, and a day school for colored children at Carlisle, Pa. The order which Mrs. Drexel established is known as the Sisters of the Blessed Sacrament, of which she is at present superioress.

REV. MOTHER MARY AGNES HINES.

Was born in Avon, New York. Is of French and German ancestry. In 1869 she entered the Order of the Sisters of St. Joseph, in Rochester, N. Y., being received into the order in 1871. She is a woman of most remarkable character, notable business ability, and a great talent for art. She was made assistant superior in 1882. Through her active efforts the Nazareth Convent and Mother House, and the academy were gradually enlarged; a Nazareth Normal School, the community's house of studies, was erected.

The Nazareth Hall and Preparatory School for boys under twelve years of age, the St. Agnes Conservatory of Music and Art, the Home for the Aged, and St. Joseph's Hospital in Elmira, all owe their existence to Mother Agnes' untiring efforts and interest in the cause of education. The schools of this sisterhood are under the regents of the University of New York, and many of their teachers have had their course of instruction in the art centers of Europe.

MOTHER IRENE (LUCY M. T. GILL).

Was born in Galway, Ireland, March, 1858. Her father, Joshua Paul Gill, was secretary of the Galway branch of the Bank of Ireland, and came to this country in 1864. In 1876 Miss Gill entered the Ursuline Convent and was later transferred to the Convent of St. Teresa, New York City, where for twelve years she was teacher and principal of the parish school. From this school many of the teachers in the public schools in New York City have graduated. In 1893 she was made superior of the community and established the Normal School at Teresa's Academy.

SISTER MARY JULIA (ELIZABETH ANN DULLEA).

Was born April 8, 1886, in Boltonville, Wisconsin. Her father and mother were natives of Ireland. Sister Julia has spent her life in teaching in Catholic schools. Is a writer of prose and poetry. She is an accomplished musician and linguist. Is very active in work for children, especially in the advancement of their physical, mental, and spiritual interests.

MATILDA THERESA KARNES.

Was born in Rochester, New York. Daughter of James Karnes of Middleton, England, and his wife, Ellen Brady, a native of Ireland. She taught industrial drawing and later astronomy, algebra, geometry, trigonometry, and is head teacher of the mathematical department in the high schools of Buffalo, New York. For many years Miss Karnes' classes in English composition have won the medals offered by the Sons of the Revolution for original essays on Revolutionary subjects. Miss Karnes is the first vice-president of the Buffalo Women's Civil Service Reform Association, a subject to which she has given much study. Also on the committee of the Buffalo Humane Society. Is president of the Catholic Women's Saturday Afternoon Club, a literary, musical, and social organization of the Catholic women of Buffalo.

ELIZABETH BLANEY McGOWAN.

Daughter of James D. Blaney and Mary A. McCourt Blaney. Her grandfather was Colonel Patrick McCourt of the British Army. She taught in the grammar school of Buffalo for years. Was a member of the board of managers of the Pan-American Exposition, and organizer of the Ladies' Catholic Benevolent Association.

ELIZA MARIA GILLESPIE.

Eliza Maria Gillespie, educator, was born near West Brownville, Pa., February 21, 1824. She removed with her parents to Lancaster, Ohio, while quite young, and was educated by the Sisters of St. Dominic at Somerset, Perry County, and at the Convent of the Visitation, Georgetown, D. C. Thomas Ewing, Secretary of the Treasury under Harrison, was her godfather, and James Gillespie Blaine, Secretary of State, under Garfield, was her cousin. While in Europe she was a leader of society and with Ellen Ewing, afterward wife of General W. T. Sherman, collected large sums of money for the aid of the sufferers from the famine in Ireland, adding to the fund by their tapestry, handiwork and magazine stories, which they wrote in collaboration. She was received into the congregation of the Sisters of the Holy Cross in 1853 under the religious name of Mother Mary of St. Angels and made her novitiate in France, taking her vows from Father Moreau, founder of the order of the Holy Cross. She returned to America in 1855 and was made Superior of the Academy of St. Mary's, Bertrand, Michigan, which in 1856 was removed to Terre Haute, Indiana, where it was known as St. Mary of the Immaculate Conception, and she became the Mother Superior of the Sisters of the Holy Cross. She obtained for the institution the shelter from the legislature and added to the immediate curriculum of the Academy, foundation for a professor's conservatory of music. She multiplied academies of the order to the number of thirty and upwards in different parts of the United States. When the Civil War called for nurses in the army, she left her home, organized at Cairo, Ill., the headquarters, enlisted a corps of sisters, established temporary and permanent hospitals and used her influence at Washington to further the comfort of the sick and wounded soldiers and with the help of her corps she cooked gruel and even fed the moving army as well as those detained in the hospital. Her labors broke down her health, and at the close of the war she was an invalid. The order in the United States was separated from the European order in 1870, and she was made Mother Superior, filling the office two terms, when she retired to become Mistress of Novices. She contributed to the Catholic periodicals, notably war sketches for the *Ave Maria*. She died at the Convent of the Holy Cross, Notre Dame, Indiana, March 4, 1887.

JANE KELLEY ADAMS.

Was born in Woburn, Massachusetts, October 13, 1852. She has always been active in the educational work of her city and state. Was one of the founders of the Woburn Home for Aged Women, president of many clubs and societies, and chairman of the Equal Suffrage League. Was president of the school board and is active among the various societies of college women in the cities near Boston.

SUSAN LINCOLN MILLS.

Was born November 18, 1826, at Enosburg, Vermont. Daughter of John and Elizabeth Tolman. A graduate of Mount Holyoke Seminary and one of the

teachers under Mary Lyon, its founder. She accompanied her husband, Cyrus
T. Mills, D.D. to Ceylon, and they were both engaged in educational work in
Batticotta College of that country. In 1865 they moved to California and opened
as a college for girls what had been one of the oldest Protestant schools of that
state, and in 1885 this was the only college for women in California, known as
Mills College, of which Mrs. Susan Lincoln Mills was president.

CLARA BRADLEY BURDETT.

College woman and active worker in women's club organizations, and federa-
tions, and in philanthropic work. First president of the California Federation of
Women's Clubs, and first vice-president of the General Federation of Women's
Clubs. Was the builder and donor of the Pasadena Maternity Hospital, trustee
of the Polytechnic Institute of Pasadena, California, vice-president of the finance
committee of the Auditorium Company, Los Angeles; member of the Social
Science Society, Archæological Institute of America, and National Geographic
Society. Lectures on educational and social questions. She was born in Bloom-
field, New York, July 22, 1855. Daughter of Albert H. and Laura C. Bradley.
Married N. Milman Wheeler Burdett in 1878.

CATHERINE ESTHER BEECHER.

Author and educator. Was born in Easthampton, Long Island, September
6, 1800, and died in Elmira, New York, May 12, 1878. She was the oldest child
of Lyman B. and Roxanna Foote Beecher. Her early education was received
from her mother and a devoted aunt. When but nine years of age her parents
removed to Litchfield, Conn. She early began to write and was a frequent contributor to the *Christian Spectator* under the initials C. D. D. Some of her
poems interested one of the young professors of mathematics in Yale College,
whom she later married. Her life was greatly saddened by his death. He
perished in a storm off the Irish coast. She opened, with her sister, a select
school in Hartford, Conn. Soon it became a question for the proper housing of
the many students which applied for admission and her friends of Hartford
assisted her in the purchase of the land and the erection of the buildings for the
Hartford Female Seminary. Miss Beecher became its principal and they opened
with a corps of eight assistant teachers. One of her writings "Suggestions on
Education" attracted attention and brought additional interest in the Hartford
Seminary. She wrote an arithmetic which she used as one of her own text-
books; also a text-book, "The Mental Philosopher." Later when her health broke
down, she and her sister removed to Cincinnati and opened a school. Her later
years she devoted to authorship and has written quite a good many books on
domestic economy and other subjects, which are used as text-books in schools.

GERTRUDE S. MARTIN.

Gertrude S. Martin occupies the novel and interesting position of "adviser
of women" at Cornell University, and as such is in a measure responsible for the

physical, moral and social development of 400 young women. She realizes the responsibilities and possibilities of her task and regards every girl in the University as a daughter, or a sister, to be cared for and directed in the path that will lead to the greatest happiness and usefulness in life.

ESTELLE REEL.

Miss Estelle Reel is a woman who has done a great work in the United States. She was for many years superintendent of the Indian schools established by the United States Government in the various states. The fact that she served under different secretaries of the Interior Department and Commissioners of Indian Affairs is a guarantee that her work was satisfactory. Miss Reel is a practical woman, possessed of great executive ability and business capacity. She traveled many miles on horseback and endured hardships in the conscientious pursuance of her duties. After finishing her education in St. Louis and the East, Miss Reel was obliged to go to Wyoming for her health. Here she became a teacher and the climate proved all she had desired. She was a resident of Laramie County, the largest county of that state and its political center. During the absence of one of her friends, who was county superintendent, Miss Reel felt it her duty to look after her friend's interests, and so impressed were the political leaders of that section by her ability that Miss Reel was nominated for county superintendent, which was her introduction into politics. Her campaign was made solely on the school question in that section of the country. She was elected by a large majority and re-elected. During her services as county superintendent of Laramie County she brought about many improvements in the school system. Every school was comfortably housed and conditions were brought up to a much higher standard. She was then named for state superintendent of schools and was the first woman to occupy this position in any state of the union. She became very much interested in the leasing and disposition of the state school land with the object of securing a good school fund. The result of her efforts in this direction was that the state of Wyoming in a few years enjoyed a most satisfactory school fund and the best possible system of schools. Her duties as state superintendent took her all over the state. Many of these journeys were made on horseback. Her work in this position brought her to the attention of the officials when the Indian schools were established. They believed she would bring practical common sense into the management of these schools, an important factor in the education of the Indian. Her work has proven most satisfactory to the government. Miss Reel believed in a practical education and the Indians were first taught English, then industrial training as well as education from books. She was equally popular with her "charges," who frequently requested her to take entire care of their children. Miss Reel left the government service June 30, 1910, to marry Mr. Curt L. Meyer, of Toppenish, Washington.

NELLIE O'DONNELL.

Born June 2, 1867, in Chillicothe, Ohio. Her father was a native of Auburndale, Mass., and her mother of Brookline, Mass. They removed when

Miss O'Donnell was but a child, to Memphis, Tenn. Miss O'Donnell was a teacher in the public schools of that state and was elected superintendent of public schools for Shelby County, Tenn. When elected, there were but 148 schools in the county. She has increased the number and brought them to the high standard of the present day.

HELEN ALMINA PARKER.

Was born in Salem, Oregon. Is a near relative of Commodore Oliver H. Perry. Her family is one of patriots; her grandfathers fought entirely through the Revolutionary War, and her father and only brother were in the Union Army during the Civil War. Her mother was one of the active leaders in the great temperance crusade. She is widely known as a philanthropist, having organized the first home for the friendless in Nebraska and was for many years state president of the same. Through her efforts a home was established in Lincoln. She was graduated from the Northwestern University, Evanston, Illinois, in 1885, and immediately entered upon her work as teacher and reader, and for years occupied the chair of oratory and dramatic art in the Cotner University of Lincoln, Nebraska.

ELEANOR LOUISE LORD.

Miss Lord, dean (1907) of the Goucher College, a girls' educational institution of Baltimore, Md., is the daughter of Mr. and Mrs. Henry Clay Lord, of Malden, Mass. She is a graduate of Smith College, and was at one time a teacher there. She pursued a course of study at Cambridge University, England, and was the holder of a scholarship given by the Boston Women's Educational and Industrial Union in 1894. She received in 1898, at Bryn Mawr College, the Ph.D. degree. Miss Lord was for four years a professor at the Goucher College. She is a member of the American Historical Association and the author of several valuable historical works. As a college educator, trained especially in the needs and essentials which aid the modern education of the girl, Miss Lord has had an experience which admirably fits her for the position which she now holds.

ELIZABETH POWELL BOND.

Mrs. Bond was born in Clinton, New York, January 25, 1841. Is dean of Swarthmore College. Daughter of Townsend and Catherine Macy Powell. Her mother was a descendant of the "Goodman Macy" of whom Whittier writes. In 1660, he was driven from his home on the mainland to the Island of Nantucket. Mr. and Mrs. Powell made their home at Ghent, New York, and here Elizabeth spent her youth. She commenced her work as a teacher when but fifteen years of age in a Friends' school in Dutchess County. She taught in the different schools of the neighborhood, and at one time had a school in the home of her parents. She was connected with the abolition movement and the work done by the anti-slavery leaders. She taught gymnastics in Boston, and was in 1865 appointed instructor of gymnastics in Vassar College. About 1866, Miss Powell married Henry H. Bond, a lawyer of Northampton, and with him edited the *Northampton Journal*. After her husband's death in 1881, she returned to Florence, Massachusetts, and devoted herself to the education of her son, gathering about her a class of children. Later she accepted the position of matron in Swarthmore College, and in 1891, that of dean of this well-known school. She has written tracts on social purity, and has lectured quite extensively.

EDNA CHAFFEE NOBLE.

Born August 12, 1846, in Rochester, Vt. After a course in elocution under Professor Moses True Brown, of Boston, she was invited to the chair of oratory in the St. Lawrence University, where she taught until her marriage to Dr. Henry S. Noble. Her most important step was the opening of the training school of elocution and English literature in Detroit, Mich., in 1878. This proved a most fortunate venture. Aside from her work in the one school, her personality has been felt in the schools which she founded in Grand Rapids, Mich., Buffalo, N. Y., Indianapolis, Ind., and London, England.

ANNE EUGENIA FELICIA MORGAN.

Was born October 3, 1845, in Oberlin, Ohio. Her father, Rev. John Morgan, D.D., was one of the earliest professors in Oberlin College. Miss Morgan's mother was a Leonard of New Haven. The Leonard family removed to Oberlin in 1837. Miss Leonard married during her sophomore year at Oberlin College, Professor John Morgan, and graduated in 1866. In 1869 she received the degree of M.A. from this same institution. For three years she conducted in New York and Newark, N. J., classes in philosophy and literature, devoting considerable time to music and the study of harmony with her brother, the distinguished musician, John Paul Morgan, at that time director of music in Trinity Church, New York. In 1875 she taught Greek and Latin in Oberlin College. In 1877 she accepted an appointment to teach in the classical department of Vassar. In 1878 she was appointed to the professorship of philosophy in Wellesley College. In 1887 Professor Morgan published a small volume entitled "Scripture Studies in the Origin and Destiny of Man." Her little book entitled "The White Lady" is a study of the ideal conception of human conduct in great records of thought and is a presentation of lecture outlines and notes on the philosophical interpretation of literature.

SARAH F. COLES LITTLE.

Was born March 6, 1838, in Oberlin, Ohio. Daughter of Professor Henry Coles of Oberlin Theological Seminary. Her mother, Alice Welsh, a woman of superior character and education, was for several years principal of the ladies' department of Oberlin College. Her education was obtained in Oberlin, from which college she graduated in 1859, with the degree of B.A. After graduating she taught school for several years. In 1861 she was principal teacher in the

Wisconsin School for the Blind at Janesville, Wisconsin, of which Thomas H. Little was superintendent. In 1862 Mr. Little and Miss Coles were married. On the death of her husband in February, 1875, Mrs. Little was chosen by the board of trustees as his successor. At this time no other woman in the United States was in charge of so important an institution as the Wisconsin School for the Blind, and during her superintendency it was one of the best managed institutions of the country, and Mrs. Little is recognized as a leading educational authority in this particular line of work. Mrs. Little was a zealous Christian and thorough Bible student. One of her daughters was a missionary, and on the opening of the Oberlin Home for Missionary Children in 1892, Mrs. Little assumed charge. In this school the children of missionaries are educated.

FLORENCE RENA SABIN.

Dr. Florence R. Sabin, associate professor in the Johns Hopkins Medical School, is the only woman professor in that institution and is a distinguished physiologist. She was born in Central City, Colorado, November 9, 1871, and is the daughter of George Kimball and Rena Miner Sabin. Received her degree of B.S. from Smith College in 1893, and that of M.D. at the Johns Hopkins University in 1900. She is the author of several works, among them being "An Atlas of the Medulla and Mid-Brain." Dr. Sabin has written articles for medical journals and magazines on medical and anatomical subjects.

JANE SHERZER.

Was a graduate of the University of Michigan; has been a student of languages in Paris, Jena and Munich; she studied for three years in the Berlin University taking the degrees of M.A. and Ph.D., in English, German, old Scandanavian and Philosophy, and is one of the very few women who have attained to the great scholastic distinction of winning the Doctorate of Philosophy at Berlin.

HELEN ALMIRA SHAFER.

Was born September 23, 1839, in Newark, New Jersey. Her father was a clergyman. He gave his daughter a thorough and liberal education. She graduated from Oberlin College in 1863. In 1865 she became a teacher of mathematics in the public schools at St. Louis. Mrs. Shafer ranked as the most able teacher in her line at that time and was one of the most potent educational forces in the city of St. Louis. In 1877 she was called to Wellesley College as professor of mathematics filling this chair until 1888, when she was elected president of Wellesley. In 1878 Oberlin College had conferred upon her the degree of A.M. and in 1893 that of LL.D. As president of Wellesley College she manifested an executive ability and faculty for business quite as marked as her talents as a teacher. At the time of her death, January 20, 1894, she was considered one of the most prominent and successful college administrators.

ELIZABETH PALMER PEABODY.

Was born May 16, 1804, in Billerica, Mass. Her sister, Sophia, became the wife of Nathaniel Hawthorne, and her sister Mary, the wife of Horace Mann. She succeeded Margaret Fuller as a teacher of history in Mr. Olcott's school. She was among the earliest advocates of female suffrage and higher education for women and aided Horace Mann in founding a Deaf Mute School. Among her personal acquaintances were Emerson, Thoreau and other prominent men of the day. Her literary productions include "Aesthetic Papers," "Crimes of the House of Austria," several works on kindergarten study and circulars on education, "Reminiscences of Dr. Channing," "Last evening with Alston" and other papers. The latter years of her life she was partially blind; during these years she wrote a little, but the loss of her sight and increasing infirmities made all literary effort difficult. She was one of the most conspicuous persons in the famous literary and educational circles of Boston. Miss Peabody's death occurred in Jamaica Plains, Boston, June 3, 1894.

HELENA THERESA FRANCESCA GOESSMANN.

Daughter of Charles Anthony Goessmann, the well-known scientist. Was born at Syracuse, New York. Received degrees from the Ohio University. Was the organizer and first president of the Woman's Auxiliary Catholic Summer School, Cliff Haven, New York. Head of the department of history, Notre Dame College, Baltimore, from 1897 to 1899; head of the department of Catholic higher education, New York, from 1904 to 1907. Has lectured in the United School of New Orleans and the Summer Catholic Schools, and lectured before non-sectarian organizations on education and culture in New England. She has written a number of songs and books on philanthropic Christianity. Contributor to the press and magazines of the United States, but is known principally through her lectures. After her father's death, she was elected professor of English in the State College of Massachusetts, at Amherst.

LIDA ROSE McCABE.

Was born in Columbus, Ohio. Was at one time at the Sorbonne in Paris; also at Columbia University and Oxford University. She has written a number of books, "Occupation and Compensation of Women," etc. Was the author of the second act of the "Vanderbilt Cup," and is a contributor to the *Popular Science Monthly, Lippincott's McClure's, Cosmopolitan, St. Nicholas, Outlook, Bookman,* and *Town and Country.* Paris correspondent of the American Press Association and the *New York Tribune.* Has written extensively of Alaska, spending several months along the Siberian coast and visiting points of this far Northland. Made an extensive study of the life of General Lafayette. Is a lecturer on art and travel and was the second woman to lecture before the New York Historical Society on a most interesting subject to American women, Mme. De Lafayette, America's half-forgotten friend. Opened an ethical lecture course to women at St. Xavier's College.

JULIA GORHAM ROBINS.

Granddaughter of Samuel Parkman, of Boston, and also a descendant of Colonel Thomas Crafts, who is distinguished for having read the Declaration of Independence from the balcony of the State House. She was born in Boston, Massachusetts, and educated in that city. Author of "Lectures on Greek Sculpture and Archæology," and is a contributor to some of the Catholic publications of the day.

ELIZABETH W. RUSSELL LORD.

Was born in Kirtland, Ohio, April 28, 1819. Her parents were natives of Massachusetts and prominent among the early settlers of the Western Reserve. She was a student of Oberlin College, and in 1842 became the wife of Asa D. Lord, M.D. In 1847 Dr. Lord removed to Columbus, Ohio, and established the first graded school in that state, and Mrs. Lord was the first principal of the first high school, to be opened in Ohio. Dr. Lord later assumed charge of the Institution for the Blind, a work in which he was greatly interested. In 1868 he was induced to go to New York State to organize the State Institution for the Blind. Mrs. Lord aided her husband in all this work, and met with great success in teaching the adult blind to read. It is believed she has taught more blind persons to read than any other teacher in the country, probably in the world. On the death of Dr. Lord in 1875, Mrs. Lord was unanimously made superintendent of the institution which Dr. Lord had so successfully organized. Later Mrs. Lord became assistant principal of the women's department of Oberlin College, which position she has held for some years. She has given liberally from her means for all charitable and educational institutions. Her best gift was that in 1890 of $10,000 to Oberlin College, to build, with the aid of other friends, the "Lord Cottage" for the accommodation of young women. Mrs. Lord may be regarded as one of the noble women of America.

LUCY ANN KIDD.

Mrs. Lucy Ann Kidd was born June 11, 1839, in Nelson County, Kentucky. Her father, Willis Strather Thornton, was a descendant of an old English family and one of the early residents of Virginia. She was at one time president of the North Texas Female College, in Sherman, Texas, being the first woman in the South to hold such a position.

CLARA E. SMITH.

Was born in Northford, Conn., as were seven generations of her ancestors before her. In 1902 she received the degree of B.A. from Mount Holyoke College, having previously taught for several years in the State Normal School at Bloomsburg, Pennsylvania. In 1904 she received the degree of Ph.D. from Yale University for work done in mathematics. Her thesis on "A Theorem of Abel and its Application to the Development of Functions in Terms of Bessels' Functions" was pulished in the *Transactions of the American Mathematical Society* for January, 1907. Since 1908 she has been an instructor in mathematics at Wellesley College.

GRACE CHARLOTTE MARY REGINA STRACHAN.

Was born in Buffalo, New York. Daughter of Thomas F. and Maria Byrne Strachan. Has taken several degrees at the New York University. Is superintendent of the public schools of New York, and well known for her philanthropic work in the Young Women's Catholic Association of Brooklyn, teaching classes free. Is an ardent worker in the Association for Equal Pay for Equal Work; contributor to the *Delineator*, and is president of the Interborough Association of Women Teachers of Brooklyn and New York City.

VIRGINIA C. GILDERSLEEVE.

Virginia C. Gildersleeve was born in New York City, October 3, 1877, and prepared for college at the Briarly School, and graduated from Barnard College in 1899. In 1900 she received the degree of A.M. from Columbia University, and that of Ph.D. in 1908. During the years from 1900 to 1907, and from 1908 to 1910, she was instructor in the department of English, Barnard College, Columbia University. In 1910 she was promoted to the rank of assistant professor of English, and in 1911 made dean of the College. Virginia C. Gildersleeve is the author of "Government Regulations of the Elizabethan Drama," and has contributed articles to several of the leading magazines.

MARY MORTIMER.

Born December 2, 1816, in Trowbridge, England, and died in Milwaukee, Wisconsin, July 14, 1877. In 1849 she taught in a private school in Ottawa, Illinois. While Miss Catherine Beecher was on an educational tour in the West she became acquainted with Miss Mortimer's power as a teacher, and persuaded her to take up with her some educational plans on which she was then engaged. In 1850 she began this work in a school which Miss Beecher had purchased in Milwaukee, Wis., and adapted to her plans, and which was later known as the Milwaukee College. This school met with remarkable success and foremost in its faculty was Miss Mary Mortimer. In 1886 she was made principal, a position which she held until 1874. After her retirement from active work she gave courses of lectures on art and history to classes of women in Milwaukee Wis., Elmira, N. Y., Auburndale, Mass., and St. Louis, Mo. She was instrumental in founding the Industrial School for Girls in Milwaukee and a leading spirit in organizing the Woman's Club of Milwaukee, but her chief monument is the Milwaukee College to which she devoted the best years of her life. In this College Mrs. M. B. Norton has placed a memorial to Miss Mortimer in the establishment of the Mary Mortimer Library.

ELLEN FITZ PENDLETON.

Is the president of Wellesley College. She was formerly the dean of Wellesley College and acting president for some time. Miss Pendleton was born at Westerly, Rhode Island, August 7, 1864. Her father is Enoch Burrows and her mother Mary E. Chapman Pendleton. She graduated in the class of 1886 at Wellesley and taught for many years in the department of mathematics before assuming the office of dean.

ELLA FLAGG YOUNG.

One of the most noted educational women in America to-day, being president of State Editors' Association of Illinois, the school board of Chicago, having won this latter distinction over several men who had long served as public school teachers, took her degree of A.B., and later, her Ph.D., at the University of Chicago. She is the daughter of Theodore and Jane Flagg. A graduate of the Chicago High School and the Chicago Normal School; was married to William Young in 1868; has been teacher since 1862, her first position being District Superintendent of Schools; professor of educational work in the University of Chicago; Principal of the Chicago Normal School; Superintendent of the schools of Chicago; member of the State Board of Education for Illinois. One of the colleges composed of women principals of the elementary schools is named the Ella Flagg Young College. President of the Illinois State Teachers' Association, and editor of the *Educational Bimonthly;* has written several important papers on school work.

MARY FRANCES FARNHAM.

Miss Mary Frances Farnham was born in South Bridgton, and was the daughter of the late William and Elizabeth (Fessenden) Farnham. After the death of her parents, in her early childhood, the late John Putnam Perley became her guardian and his house her home.

In 1863, after private study at home, she entered Bridgton Academy, of which the late Charles E. Hilton was principal. Here she spent two years in fitting for Mount Holyoke, and was graduated with honor from that well-known institution in 1868. Returning to South Bridgton, Miss Farnham spent several years of quiet usefulness in the home of her childhood. It was during these years that she served the town most faithfully as a conscientious member of the school committee, a superintendent of schools from 1887 to 1890. During the latter year the opportunity came to her which resulted in her accepting the vice-principalship of the Bloemhof School, in Stellenbosch (thirty miles from Cape Town), Cape of Good Hope. This is a large boarding and day school for the daughters of European colonists and, under government supervision, prepares pupils for higher examinations and degrees of the University of the Cape of Good Hope. In addition to school duties much time was spent in working on the flora of the Cape and Stellenbosch districts of Cape Colony.

Leaving Africa in 1888 and visiting the Island of St. Helena, on the way to Europe, she traveled extensively in that continent, remained a long time in London, and reached the United States the same year.

We next find Miss Farnham in the capacity of preceptress and teacher of English and history in Burr and Burton Seminary, Manchester, Vt.; then she accepted a similar position in the Forest Park University, St. Louis, Mo. Four years as preceptress of Fryeburg Academy, Fryeburg, Me., followed, which brought her to 1895. While occupying these last three positions Miss Farnham was brought into contact with a very large number of boys and girls, and had the great privilege of training many for extended courses of study, as well as for business life.

In 1895-96 she was a student at Radcliffe College, Cambridge, Mass. In addition to general work in colonial and United States history (also in literature and sociology), Miss Farnham has been carrying on a research course under the direction of Dr. Hart, in connection with the Historical Seminary, on documentary history of Maine. The result is a more complete set of documents from original sources conferring territory or jurisdiction than has yet been made. The work has been done in the archives of Maine and Massachusetts, the Harvard, Boston and Athenaeum Libraries. These studies were supplemented by courses at the Harvard Summer School, and by continued research work the following year.

In September, 1897, Miss Farnham came to the Pacific University, Forest Grove, Ore., as dean of women and instructor in English literature; in 1901 she was made full professor. Under the titles of "Farnham Papers," "Documentary History of Maine," second series, the Maine Historical Society published in two volumes the result of Miss Farnham's researches.

Miss Farnham is a Daughter of the American Revolution; for twelve years a member of the Young Women's Christian Association Board of Oregon, and until the establishment of the Territorial Board of the Pacific Northwest; for fourteen years vice-president of the missionary boards of the Congregational Church of Oregon; is a director of the Oregon Audubon Society of Oregon; for eight years secretary of the Civic Improvement Society of Forest Grove; in the work of the Oregon Federation of Women's Clubs, Miss Farnham is vice-chairman of the trustees of the Scholarship Loan Fund; she is also the club representative of the Department of School Patrons of the National Educational Association, and is chairman of the joint committee for Oregon; she had a place on the programme of that department at the recent convention in San Francisco—a discussion of the topic, "The Co-operation of Informed Citizens."

Women in Professions.

MARY GARARD ANDREWS.

Mrs. Andrews was born in Clarksburg, W. Va., March 3, 1852. Is a Universalist minister. Left to struggle with the adverse elements she developed a strong character and overcame many difficulties and acquired such education as she had wished. In Hillsdale College she completed the English Theological course, and during this time she had charge of two churches, preaching twice every Sunday for three years. For five years she was in charge of the Free Baptist Church, but she severed her connection with this faith and united with the Universalist Church. She has been a close student and active worker. Since her marriage she has made Omaha her home.

MARTHA WALDRON JANES.

Mrs. Martha Waldron Janes was born in Northfield, Michigan, in June, 1832. Her father, Leonard T. Waldron was a native of Massachusetts. Her mother, Nancy Bennett, was a native of New York. She educated herself by doing housework at $1.00 a week. She was converted when very young, and by her religious zeal and exhortations became so conspicuous that many considered her mentally unsound. In October, 1852, she married John A. Sober, who died November, 1864, leaving her with two young children. In 1867 she married her second husband, H. H. Janes, and though she had preached for some time from the pulpits of the Free Baptist Church she was not regularly ordained until 1868, being the first woman ordained in that conference. She was actively engaged in the work of women's suffrage and temperance.

MARY C. JONES.

Mrs. Mary C. Jones was born November 5, 1842, at Sutton, N. H. Her husband moved to the Pacific Coast in 1867. They ultimately made their home in Seattle, Washington, where she preached her first sermon in August, 1880, in the First Baptist Church of that city. She was recognized as a minister and supplied the pulpit in the absence of the regular minister. In 1882 she became permanent pastor of the First Baptist Church; later that of the First Baptist Church of Spokane at that time the second largest church in the state of Washington. For some years she has been engaged in evangelical work. Mrs. Jones is the founder of the Grace Seminary and School for Girls in Centralia, Wash. She has been the founder and organizer of several churches throughout the state and has done splendid work for religion in this new country.

(736)

ANTOINETTE BROWN BLACKWELL.

Mrs. Blackwell was born in Henrietta, Monroe County, New York, May 20, 1825. Daughter of Joseph Brown, of Thompson, Conn. and Abby Morse, of Dudley, Mass. Her ancestors belonged to the early English colonists of New England. When but sixteen years of age, she taught school in order to pay for a collegiate course. She was a graduate of Oberlin College. In 1848 she published her first essay in the *Oberlin Quarterly Review.* After she had completed her theological course, she found she could not obtain a license, but she preached wherever an opportunity offered, and gradually all obstacles melted away, and in 1852, she became an ordained pastor of the Congregational Church in South Butler, Wayne County, New York. In 1856 she married Samuel C. Blackwell. Her life as a preacher, lecturer and writer has been a busy and useful one. She is the author of "Studies in General Science," "A Market Woman," "The Island Neighbors," "The Sexes Throughout Nature" and "The Physical Basis of Immortality."

FLORENCE E. KOLLOCK.

Miss Florence E. Kollock was born January 19, 1848, in Waukesha, Wis. Daughter of William E. Kollock and Anne Margaret Hunter Kollock. Her first work was in the missionary field at Waverley, Iowa, in 1875. Later she removed to Blue Island, Ill., then to Englewood, where she has since made her home. Her first congregation was in Englewood. There meetings were held in the Masonic Hall until through the efforts of Miss Kollock a church was built. She is recognized as a woman of great ability as an organizer in various branches of church work. She is the possessor of wonderful personal magnetism. In her preaching she has gathered about her a large circle. During one of her vacations she established a church in Pasadena Cal., which is now the largest Universalist Church on the Pacific Coast. She is prominent in all reformatory and educational work, the woman's suffrage and temperance movements.

MARY LYDIA LEGGETT.

Miss Mary Lydia Leggett was born April 25, 1852, in Sempronius, New York. Daughter of the Rev. William Leggett and Freelove Frost Leggett. In 1887 she was ordained in the Liberal Ministry in Kansas City, Mo. She built and dedicated a church in Beatrice, Neb., of which she was the minister until 1891, when she became pastor of a church near Boston. This church in Green Harbor, Mass., was founded by the granddaughter of the statesman, Daniel Webster, whose summer home was in this quaint little town on the old Plymouth shores. Miss Leggett has in her study the office table on which the great orator wrote his famous speeches.

ESTHER TUTTLE PRITCHARD.

Born January 26, 1840, in Morrow County, Ohio. Her father, Daniel Wood, was a minister. Her husband, Lucius V. Tuttle, was a volunteer in the Civil

47

War, and died in 1881. In 1884 Mrs. Tuttle was chosen by the Woman's Foreign Missionary Board to edit the Friends' *Missionary Advocate,* which was published in Chicago. Here she married Calvin W. Pritchard, editor of the *Christian Worker,* and became proprietor of the *Missionary Advocate,* which, in 1890, she presented to the Woman's Foreign Missionary Union of Friends. She was well known as a teacher of the English Bible in the Chicago Training School for the City, Home and Foreign Missions, and as superintendent of the Systematic-giving Department of the National Woman's Christian Temperance Union.

ANNA WEED PROSSER.

Born October 15, 1846. An invalid for many years, she believed her recovery due to prayer, and immediately entered upon her evangelical work in gratitude for her restored health. She worked for some time under the Woman's Christian Temperance Union, ultimately establishing a mission of her own, known as the Old Canal Street Mission, in Buffalo, of which she took charge and was assisted in this work by reformed men whom she had saved from lives of sin. After ten years spent in ministry among the poor and unfortunate class, she entered the general evangelical work and became president of the Buffalo Branch of the National Christian Alliance.

MARIAN MURDOCH.

Was born October 9, 1849, in Garnaville, Iowa, and is one of the successful ministers of that state. Her father, Judge Samuel Murdoch, was a member of the territorial legislature of Iowa, also of the state legislature, a judge of the District Court and is well known throughout the state. She was educated in the Northwest Ladies' College, at Evanston, Ill., and the University of Wisconsin. On deciding to take up the ministry she entered the School of Liberal Theology in Meadville, Penna., in 1882, receiving her degree of D.D. in 1885. Her work in the ministry began while she was yet a pupil. After completing her course, she was called to the Unity Church of Humbolt, Iowa, and later to the First Unitarian Church in Kalamazoo, Mich. Later she took a course of lectures at Oxford, England. Miss Murdoch is essentially a reformer, preaching on questions of social, political and moral reform.

CAROLINE BARTLETT CRANE.

Mrs. Crane was born at Hudson, Wis., August 17, 1858. Daughter of Lorenzo D. and Julia A. Bartlett. She married Dr. Augustus Warren Crane in 1896. Was first a teacher and newspaper writer and editor, then became a minister, her first charge being All Souls' Church, Sioux Falls, S. D., which she held for three years. She organized the new creedless institution, the "People's Church," but resigned her pastorate in 1889. Has since been engaged in social and sanitary surveys of cities, but has also found time to lecture, teach and preach.

CORA BELLE BREWSTER.

Miss Brewster was born September 6, 1859, at Almond, New York. She was one of the students of the Northwestern University. Later she removed to Baltimore, Maryland, and began the study of medicine. In 1886, she graduated from the College of Physicians and Surgeons, of Boston. Completing her course, she returned to Baltimore, and formed a partnership with her sister, Flora A. Brewster, M.D., and in 1889 they began the publication of the *Baltimore Family Health Journal.* This was later changed to the *Homeopathic Advocate and Health Journal.* In 1890 she was elected gynecological surgeon to the Homeopathic Hospital and Free Dispensary, of Maryland. She has achieved marked success as a medical writer, surgeon, editor and practicing physician.

HANNAH E. LONGSHORE.

Was born in Montgomery, May, 1819. She was among the first women to practise medicine in this country. Her father Samuel, and her mother Paulina Myers were born in Bucks County, Pennsylvania, and belonged to the Society of Friends. When but a small child her family removed to Washington, District of Columbia. After her marriage to Thomas E. Longshore she made her home in Philadelphia and here read medicine with her brother-in-law, Professor Joseph S. Longshore. Her death occurred in 1901.

JENNIE DE LA MONTAGNIE LOZIER.

Physician and president of the Sorosis Club, of New York City, where she was born. Her father was William de la Montagnie, Junior. Her ancestors were Huguenot French. She is a graduate of Rutger's Female Institute, now Rutger's Female College, which conferred upon her in 1891 the degree of Doctor of Science. She received a very thorough and liberal education and traveled extensively after leaving school. When but nineteen years of age she was instructor in the languages and literature of Hillsdale College, Hillsdale, Michigan, and was later chosen vice-principal of the women's department of this college. In 1872 she married Doctor A. W. Lozier, of New York City. Her interest in medicine was brought about through her mother-in-law, Doctor Clemence S. Lozier, who was founder and for twenty-five years dean of the New York Medical College and Hospital for Women. Mrs. Lozier graduated from this college after her first child was born and was made professor of psysiology in that institution serving also on the hospital staff. Before retiring from her professorshp she was invited to address the Sorosis Club on physical culture. She soon became a member and prominent in the councils of this club. She is a cultured woman, brainy, broad-minded, and forceful speaker. She served on the various important committees of the Sorosis Club, and in 1891 was elected president of this organization and re-elected in 1892. In this year she was sent as a delegate to the council of the Women's Federation of Clubs held in Chicago, reading before this gathering an able paper on "Educational Influences of Women's Clubs." In 1889 she was sent to represent the New York Medical Club and Hospital for Women in the International Homeopathic Congress in Paris, before which she read a paper in French on the "Medical Education of Women in the United States." She has been the president of the Emerson and Avon Clubs. Was a member of the Association for the Advancement of Women and also the "Patria Club." She has read papers of great merit before the various literary and reform associations of New York City and the United States. She always speaks for the liberal and thorough education of women not only in art and music but also in chemistry, social economics, psychology, pedagogy, and physiology. Mrs. Lozier has exerted a wide influence among the club women of this country and occupies a commanding position in the fields open to women for advancement in social, literary and general culture.

ANNA LUKENS.

Was born in Philadelphia, October, 1844. Her family were residents of Plymouth, Pennsylvania, and belonged to the Society of Friends. She was graduated from the Woman's Medical College of Pennsylvania, in 1870. Was a member of the class attending clinics in the Pennsylvania Hospital, November, 1869, when the students from the Woman's Medical College were hissed by the male members of the clinic. Miss Lukens and a Miss Brumall led the line of women students who passed out of the hospital grounds amid the jeers and insults of the male students, who even threw stones and mud at them, but these brave women were not discouraged by such conduct and might be considered to have blazed the way for other women who to-day enjoy the privilege. In 1870, Miss Lukens entered the Woman's Hospital of Philadelphia, as an interne and in 1871 she began to teach in the college as an instructor in the chair of physiology. In 1872 she taught pharmacy in the college by lectures and practical demonstrations in the dispensary of the Women's Hospital. She was the first woman to apply for admission to the Philadelphia College of Pharmacy. Not meeting with much encouragement, owing to the opposition which existed at that time against all women taking up this vocation, she entered the College of Pharmacy in New York City, and took a course in analytical chemistry in the laboratory of Dr. Walls. In 1873 she became attending physician of the Western Dispensary for Women and Children, and at some portions of the time paid the rent for this dispensary out of her own pocket in order to keep up the work. In 1873 she was elected a member of the New York County Medical Society. In 1877 she was appointed assistant physician in the Nursery and Child's Hospital of Staten Island, assuming entire charge of the pharmaceutical department. In 1880 she was appointed resident physician of the Nursery and Child's Hospital. Two papers which she read before the Staten Island Clinical Society were published in the *New York Journal* and copied in the *London Lancet* and received favorable notice by the *British Medical Journal*. In 1884 she went abroad for study in children's diseases in the principal hospitals of Europe, and later opened an office for private practice in the city of New York. She was elected consulting physician of the Nursery and Child's Hospital of Staten Island, and a fellow of the New York State Medical

Society. Was appointed in 1876, one of the vice-presidents of the New York Committee for the Prevention and State Regulation of Vice. She is a member of the Sorosis Club, and is considered a woman of marked executive ability for hospital administration. Her work is of a high standard and she occupies a conspicuous position for a woman in the profession which she has chosen.

DOROTHEA LUMMIS.

Was born in Chillicothe, Ohio, November, 1860. Her father was Josiah H. Rhodes, of Pennsylvania Dutch stock, and her mother, Sarah Crosby Swift was descended from a New England Puritan family. Although a successful student of music in the New England Conservatory of Music, in Boston, in 1881, she entered the musical school of Boston University and graduated with honor in 1884. In 1880, she married Charles F. Lummis, and in 1885 removed to Los Angeles, California, where she began the practice of medicine. She has served as dramatic editor of the *Los Angeles Times* and also musical editor and critic on that journal. She was instrumental in the formation of a humane society which was brought about through her observations of the neglect and cruelty to the children of the poor, and Mexican families, visited in her practice. She is a writer for *Puck, Judge, Life, Women's Cycle, San Francisco Argonaut,* and the *Californian,* as well as contributing many important papers to the various medical journals of the United States.

MARY PUTNAM JACOBI.

Dr. Mary Putnam Jacobi was born in August, 1842, in London, England, daughter of George B. Putnam, the well-known publisher. Her parents returned to this country when she was quite young and she was educated in Philadelphia, taking a course in the Women's Medical College of that city; afterwards taking a course at the New York College of Pharmacy, being one of the first women graduates of that institution. She was the first woman to be admitted to the Ecole de Médecin in Paris, and received the second prize for her thesis. On her return to America she immediately took up the work of having women students placed on the same footing with men and received on these terms in all medical societies. In 1872 she read before the American Journal Association an able paper, the first ever given by a woman. In 1873 she married Doctor Abraham Jacobi, a distinguished physician and specialist of New York City. After her marriage she was known by the name of Doctor Putnam-Jacobi. For many years she held the chair of therapeutics and materia medica of the Woman's College of the New York Infirmary and was afterwards professor in the New York Medical College. Mrs. Jacobi, in 1874, founded an association for the advancement of the medical education of women and was its president for many years. She has written much on medical and scientific subjects. Doctor Putnam-Jacobi takes front rank among the women of America, as her knowledge of medicine and its allied sciences is profound and accurate and she has won a distinguished position for herself among physicians and specialists of note.

HARRIET B. JONES.

Miss Harriet B. Jones was born June, 1856, in Ebansburg, Pennsylvania. She is of Welsh ancestry. Appreciating the necessity for women physicians, after her graduation from the Wheeling Female College she went to Baltimore, to take a course as a medical student there, and graduated with honors from the Women's Medical College, in May, 1884. Wishing to make nervous diseases her specialty she accepted the position of assistant superintendent of the State Hospital for the Insane in Weston, West Virginia. In 1892 she established in Wheeling a private sanatorium for women and nervous diseases. She is an active worker in the temperance cause.

ANNA M. LONGSHORE POTTS.

Born April 16, 1829, in Attleboro, Pennsylvania. She was one of the class of eight brave young Pennsylvania Quaker girls graduating from the Woman's Medical College of Philadelphia, in 1852. This was the first college in which a woman could earn and secure a medical degree and at the time mentioned, when Miss Longshore graduated, they were received with faint applause from their friends and marks of derision from the male medical students. In 1857, she became the wife of Lambert Potts, of Langhorne, Pennsylvania. After removing to Michigan, she made a tour of the Pacific coast, New Zealand, Sidney, New South Wales, England and the United States lecturing on the prevention of sickness.

ANN PRESTON.

Born December, 1813, in West Grove, Pennsylvania, and died in Philadelphia, April 18, 1872. She was a daughter of Amos and Margaret Preston, members of the Society of Friends. When the Woman's Medical College of Pennsylvania was opened in 1850, Miss Preston was among the first applicants for admission and graduated at the first commencement of the college. She remained as a student after graduation and in the spring of 1852, was called to the vacant chair of physiology and hygiene, of this college. She lectured in New York, Baltimore and Philadelphia on hygiene. Miss Preston and her associates obtained a charter and raised funds to establish a hospital in connection with the college, and when it was opened she was made a member of its board of managers, its corresponding secretary and its consulting physician, positions which she held until her death. In 1866 Doctor Preston was elected dean of the faculty. In 1867, she was elected a member of the board of corporators of the college. During the twenty years of her medical practice she saw the sentiment towards women physicians gradually become more liberal, until they were admitted to hospital clinics with men.

ELIZABETH BLACKWELL, M.D.

The first woman physician in the United States was born in England, February 3, 1821, but her father brought his family to New York when she was eleven years old. After five or six years in that city, his business failed and he moved to Cincinnati. He had been there but a few weeks when he died, leaving a widow and nine children in very embarrassed circumstances. Elizabeth, who was his third daughter, together with her two oldest sisters opened a Young Ladies' Seminary and supported the family. Finding a better opportunity for private teaching in South Carolina, she went there in 1845, teaching music and French in a few wealthy families, while she read medicine with Doctor Samuel H. Dickson, of Charleston. After two or three years of hard labor in South Carolina, and about two years more devoted to the study of medicine in Philadelphia and Geneva, New York, she received her medical diploma. In receiving it from the head director, she replied, "I thank you sir. With the help of the Most High it shall be the effort of my life to shed honor upon this diploma." Nor was this resolution in vain. Elizabeth Blackwell may be said to be the dean of the corps of splendid women physicians in the United States, and few if any have exceeded her in conscientious skill.

FLORA L. ALDRICH.

Mrs. Aldrich was born in Westfield, New York, October 6, 1859. Her ancestors were among the early Dutch settlers of the Hudson Valley. Her maiden name was Southard, but little is known of her family. Her great-grandfather only remembered that his name was Southard and that he was stolen from a port in England. She married Doctor A. G. Aldrich, of Adams, Massachusetts, in 1883, and this resulted in her immediately taking up the study of medicine and surgery. Later removing to Minnesota, she graduated from the Minnesota Medical College and took post-graduate courses in many of the best schools of the country.

SARAH B. ARMSTRONG.

Miss Armstrong was born in Newton near Cincinnati, on July 31, 1857. She was educated in the schools of Cincinnati and later in Lebanon, Ohio, where the family made their home. At sixteen she became a teacher. She received the degree of B.S., in 1880, from the Lebanon University and the highest honors in a class of sixty-six members. She later became a teacher in this school and while engaged in this work, obtained her degree of B.A. and later that of M.A. In 1886 she took her first degree in medicine and was appointed physician to the college. Later she spent some time in New York taking a course in the hospitals of that city. She inherits the love for the profession from her great-grandmother who was the first woman to practice medicine west of the Alleghany Mountains. Miss Armstrong possesses a very fine voice and has also literary talents.

ALICE BENNET.

Miss Bennet was born in Wrentham, Massachusetts, January 31, 1851. She taught in the district schools in her early youth but took up the study of medicine in the Woman's Medical College of Pennsylvania, from which she graduated in March, 1876. Spent one year as an interne in the New England Hospital, of Boston. After graduating, engaged in dispensary work in the slums of Philadelphia. In 1876 she pursued a course of scientific study in the University of Pennsylvania, from which she received her degree of Ph.D., in 1880, and that year she was elected superintendent of the department for women of the State Hospital for the Insane, in Norristown, Pennsylvania. The placing of a woman in charge was without precedent and the results were awaited with anxiety by the public and the profession. At the end of twelve years the hospital was acknowledged to be the leading institution of the kind in the state, if not in the country, and this experiment has been the cause of this course being adopted by other states and the question is being very generally agitated as to whether this should not be generally adopted. When Miss Bennet entered upon this field of her labors she had but one patient and one nurse. More than two thousand, eight hundred and seventy-five insane women have been cared for, and in 1892 there was a force of ninety-five nurses under her. She is a member of the American Medical Association, of the Pennsylvania State Medical Society, of the Montgomery County Medical Society, of which she was made president in 1890; of the Philadelphia Neurological Society, of the Philadelphia Medical Jurisprudence Society, and of the American Academy of Political and Social Science. She has several times delivered the annual address on mental diseases before the State Medical Society and was appointed by Governor Pattison, of Pennsylvania, as a member of the board of five commissioners to erect the new hospital for the insane of the state.

MARTHA GEORGE RIPLEY.

Born November 30, 1843, in Lowell, Massachusetts. She married William W. Ripley, June 25, 1867, and removed to Boston, where she entered the Boston School of Medicine, in 1880. At her graduation in 1883 she was pronounced by the faculty one of the most thorough medical students who had ever received a diploma from the university. Soon after she settled in Minneapolis, Minnesota, and founded the Maternity Hospital. Mrs. Ripley was always deeply interested in the cause of woman's suffrage, and in 1883 she was elected president of the Minnesota Woman's Suffrage Association, serving as such for six years.

CLARA HOLMES HAPGOOD NASH,

Was born January 15, 1839, in Fitchburg, Massachusetts. Was the daughter of John and Mary Anne Hosmer Hapgood. Her mother belonged to the same family of Hosmers from which Harriet Hosmer, the noted sculptor was descended. Soon after her marriage in 1869 to Frederick Cushing Nash, of Maine, she began the study of law and in 1872 was admitted to the Supreme Judicial Court of Maine, being the first woman admitted to the bar, in New England.

KATE PIER.

Was born June 22, 1845, in St. Albans, Vermont. Her father was John Hamilton and her mother's maiden name was Meakinn. Mrs. Pier gave the name of Hamilton to each of her three daughters. In 1866 she became the wife of C. K. Pier, of Fond du Lac, Wisconsin. She has accomplished what we believe no other woman in this country has—she made lawyers of herself and her three daughters. Mrs. Pier began her legal life by managing the large estate left by her father so successfully that other business of a like character was attracted to her. She was made court commissioner at one time and has enjoyed a successful professional career. She has accomplished much for women in her work before the legislature of her state in looking after bills in the interest of women.

ALICE PARKER.

Miss Alice Parker was born in Lowell, Massachusetts, April 11, 1864, and was the daughter of the well-known Doctor Hiram Parker, of Lowell, Massachusetts. She was admitted to the Massachusetts bar, in 1890. Miss Parker published an interesting series of articles in the *Home Journal,* of Boston, under the title of "Law for My Sisters," of great value to women. They contained expositions of the law of marriage, widows, breach of promise, wife's necessaries, life insurance, divorce, sham marriages and names. She is the author of many amendments before the Massachusetts legislature affecting the property rights of women, and has made it her special work to procure such legislation at each session as will accomplish this end.

MYRA BRADWELL.

Lawyer and editor. Mrs. Bradwell was born in Manchester, Vermont, February 12, 1831. Daughter of Eben and Abigail Willey Colby. When quite young, her parents removed to New York City, and when she was about twelve years of age, to Chicago. In 1852, she married James B. Bradwell, whose father had been one of the leading pioneers of Illinois. She studied law in her husband's office. Passing the required examination, she was the first woman in America to ask to be admitted to the bar, but was refused on the grounds of being a married woman. This only added indignation to her desire, and she never ceased her efforts until this disability was removed, and finally received a certificate based upon her original application, and was the first woman to be admitted to the Illinois Bar Association. She was the editor of the first legal paper published in the Western states, known as the Chicago *Legal News,* and she remained its manager and editor until her death. The legislature of Illinois gave her a special charter for this paper, and it became a valuable medium for the publication of legal notices. Mrs. Bradwell drew up the bill making the law giving to married women their own earnings, and its passage was secured by her efforts in 1869. The work of editing and managing her paper became so arduous that her husband, Judge Bradwell, retired from the bench to assist her in this work. She was always prominent in all charitable and philanthropic work of her home city—Chicago. She was a member of several of the prominent associations for literary and philanthropic work. Both of her children, a son and daughter, were admitted to the bar.

ELLA FRANCES BRAMAN.

Mrs. Braman was born March 23, 1850, in Brighton, now a part of Boston, Massachusetts. In 1867 she was married to Joseph Balch Braman, a member of the Boston bar. She commenced her life as a lawyer by assisting her husband, and proved so competent that he decided to ask for her appointment as commissioner for different states, and acted as such during her husband's absence. On their removal to New York City, she became a full partner with her husband.

ELLA KNOWLES.

Miss Ella Knowles was born in 1870 in New Hampshire. When quite young she gave dramatic readings. In 1888 she took up the study of law in the office of Judge Burnham, of Manchester, New Hampshire. In 1889 she went to Iowa as a teacher of French and German and taught through the West for a number of years. While a resident of Helena, Montana, she finished her law course. In 1889 she was admitted to practice before the Supreme Court of Montana. In 1890 she was admitted to practice before the District Court of the United States and also before the Circuit Court of the United States. In 1892 she was named for attorney general of Montana, by the Alliance Party She is regarded as a woman of great ability, tact and courage and is well known throughout the Northwest.

NELLIE BROWN POND,

Born May 7, 1858, in Springfield, Massachusetts. Her maiden name was Nellie Frank Brown. Mrs. Pond stands in the front rank of the women of America who have made their mark upon the platform. Her father was Doctor Enoch Brown, an eminent physician of Springfield, Massachusetts. The family moved to New York City, where her father died when Mrs. Pond was quite young. Later they became residents of Boston, and it was here that Mrs. Pond's dramatic talent became known when through friends she was induced to become a member of the Park Dramatic Company, and appeared for the first time as Margaret Elmore in "Love's Sacrifice," achieving an immediate success. She remained with the company during that season, her great dramatic talent securing for her extensive popularity, and winning recognition from many prominent professionals. Mrs. Thomas Barry, then leading lady of the Boston Theatre, became greatly interested in her and through her exertions, Mrs. Pond appeared upon the Lyceum platform, and for many years she continued her dramatic readings. In 1880 she became the wife of Ozias W. Pond, of Boston, the well-known manager of musical and literary celebrities.

MARY E. MILLER.

Miss Miller, a distinguished woman lawyer of Chicago, is a farmer's daughter, and was born on a Michigan farm, in Calhoun County, December 28, 1864. Her early education was obtained in a country district school. She afterwards attended the Marshall High School, and graduated in the Latin course. She then attended the Michigan State Normal School located at Ypsilanti, from which she graduated in 1886. The following year she taught school at Portland, Michigan. The next summer she entered the office of the county clerk, of Calhoun County, and there learned to use the typewriter. In the winter of 1888, Miss Miller went to Chicago, and entered a shorthand school, and in the following autumn took a position as stenographer and typewriter with A. C. McClurg & Co., publishers, remaining with them until the following spring. She followed the occupation of a stenographer until 1894, occupying places during that period in the offices of some of the most prominent lawyers in the city of Chicago.

Miss Miller began the study of law about the 1st of October, 1893, attending the Chicago College of Law, from which college she received her diploma in June, 1896, being admitted to the bar at that date. She afterwards took a postgraduate course in law, and received the degree of B.L., from the Lake Forest University. She commenced the practice of law about the 1st of July, 1895, and opened her office in Chicago.

It is something to have earned a $30,000 fee, but what Miss Mary E. Miller has done for the poor is of far more importance to the public. Miss Miller, who has been practising law in the Chicago courts for thirteen years, received her largest fee for winning a suit in behalf of the heirs of a millionaire and secured a court order for the immediate distribution of $3,000,000. It was a triumph that attracted attention to her, but what she considers her real success at the bar was in a suit in which she received no fee whatever. Miss Miller possesses a high sense of eternal justice of right, and when she discovered that the Illinois courts had deprived the poor of their rights of "a day in court," she forthwith took up the cause of the pauper and fought to restore to him equal rights before the law with the rich. The case which brought her into the white light was a petition for mandamus, compelling the judge to examine the relator, and certain documents presented by her, and to determine whether she could sue as a "poor person" under the Illinois statutes. The judges of the Superior Court had enacted a rule regulating suits brought under the statute as poor persons, whom the rule styled "paupers," which was so burdensome and oppressive both to the lawyer and the client, that it was naturally impossible to comply with it conscientiously. The rule worked to the benefit of the corporations, traction companies, and others against whom personal injury suits were brought, as it deprived many of the opportunity of going into court. Miss Miller won her case for the "poor person," and the Supreme Court held the unjust rule null and void, overruling the law enacted by the eleven judges of the Superior Court. Miss Miller thereupon brought suit for her client, a "poor person," and won damages of $1,000, the verdict, however, was set aside and a second trial called.

Miss Miller's fee in this case was less than nothing, her client being a poor negress, born a slave, but the suit established the right of so-styled "poor persons" to fight in court for their right against the rich. "It restored," says Miss Miller, "the rights of the poor to sue, a right of which the court had shamelessly deprived them."

She has always been very much interested in procuring suffrage for women, and has devoted more or less time to that purpose. For a short time in 1896 she published a little suffrage paper in Chicago. For a number of years she was also connected with various women's clubs, but has dropped her membership in all save the Chicago Political Equality League. She is the organizer of Cook County for the Illinois Equal Suffrage Association, and has devoted considerable time to that work.

Through her acquaintance obtained in the suffrage work, she became interested in the Norwegian Danish Young Women's Christian Home, and is now vice-president of the executive committee which has this home in charge. The home was instituted for the purpose of furnishing Norwegian and Danish servant girls in Chicago a safe, clean, and attractive residence. There is also connected with it a free employment bureau, which investigates the applications for servant girls by employers and ascertains whether they are desirable and safe positions. By this means it is hoped to save numerous girls from white slavery, as they are frequently lured into dens through the employment agencies.

Miss Miller has spoken for suffrage in the automobile tours through Illinois, and at the parlor and hall meetings in the city of Chicago.

J. ELLEN HORTON FOSTER.

For many years the figure of Mrs. J. Ellen Horton Foster was a familiar one in Washington. Familiarity did not, however, dull the respect and honor which the women of the Capital felt for her. Born in Lowell, Massachusetts, November 3, 1840, the daughter of Reverend Jotham Horton, a Methodist Minister. She was educated in Lima, New York, and subsequently moved with her parents to Clinton, Iowa, where in 1869 she became the wife of E. C. Foster, a lawyer. She studied law and was admitted to the bar of the Supreme Court, of Iowa, in 1872, being the first woman to practice before that court. She followed the legal profession for years, at first practicing alone but subsequently forming a partnership with her husband.

Her fame as a lawyer in Iowa has been equaled by her work for temperance, the Methodist Church, Home and Foreign Missions, Philanthropy, Education, Patriotism and other great reforms. She joined the temperance workers with such ardor that when her home in Clinton, Iowa, was burned it was suspected that it was the work of enemies of the temperance cause.

As a member of the Woman's Christian Temperance Union she has been able to give the most valuable service in the legislative department of that organization. Her legal knowledge enabled her to direct wisely the movements for constitutional amendments in many states, aimed to secure the prohibition of the sale and manufacture of alcoholic liquors. Maintaining as she did that no organization has the right to prejudice the rights of its members to any other organization for any purpose, these views led her to affiliate with the non-partisan league, and she served that body for several years as corresponding secretary, having her office in Boston, Massachusetts. In 1887 she visited Europe, where she rested and studied the temperance question. After her return from England, she moved to Washington City and rapidly became prominent in public affairs. She was sent by Secretary Hay, with Clara Barton, as a delegate to the International Congress of the Red Cross. She was an official member of the Taft party to the Philippines, and then went on to other lands to visit branches of the Foreign Missions of the Methodist Church. Her last appointment was to investigate the conditions of women and children workers, and the condition of the Federal prisons. She succeeded in causing a special wing ror women to be established in the Leavenworth penitentiary. She continued her activities in the cause of humanity until the day of her death, August 11, 1910.

BELL A. MANSFIELD.

Mrs. Bell A. Mansfield was the first woman admitted to the practice of law in the United States. She was admitted to the bar in 1868 in the state of Iowa. Her death occurred August 1, 1911, at the home of her brother, Judge W. J. Babb, of Aurora, Illinois. She was in her sixty-fifth year at the time of her death.

ELLEN SPENCER MUSSEY.

Born at Geneva, Ohio, in 1850. Was the daughter of Platt R. Spencer, (the author of the Spencerian system of writing,) and Persis Duty Spencer. She read law in the office of her husband, General Mussey, whom she married June 14, 1871. She established the Washington College of Law for Women in 1899. In 1893 she was first admitted to the bar and practiced law even before her husband's death. Was counsel for some of the foreign legations, and several national, patriotic, and labor organizations. She secured the passage of the bill through Congress giving mothers in the District of Columbia the same right to their children as their fathers and giving married women the right to do business and to control their own earnings, and also an appropriation for the first public kindergarten in the District of Columbia. She was one of the founders of the National Red Cross, a member of the Legion of Loyal Women, ex-vice-president-general Daughters of the American Revolution, and is now a member of the Board of Education of Washington, District of Columbia.

Artists.

Looking back over the field of art for the past five centuries, one cannot fail to be impressed by the exceeding scarcity of men and women who have attained enduring eminence as painters of portraits.   Though in every exhibition of current work numerous portraits are shown, few are found worthy of prominent preservation, and the painters who can be counted upon for worthy productions can equally be enumerated.   One of those who to-day holds pre-eminence is Cecilia Beaux.   Comparison is often made between her work and that of Sargent. Most critics think her work is more studied but equally strong.

CECILIA BEAUX.

Cecelia Beaux is a dramatist in her studies of character and her art is probably more subtle and more various than that of any woman painter who has devoted her life to portraiture. Her work is modern in every way.   Her handling is broad and strong.   Many of her touches seem most accidental, while they are of the highest art.   Miss Beaux is one of those painters who seem to have arrived almost abruptly on a plane of exceptional accomplishment.   Few better works has she produced than those exhibited at the Paris Salon in 1896, which took the French critics by storm, and brought her the honor of Associate Membership in the Societe Nationale des Beaux-Arts.   Her portraits of the daughters of Mr. Richard Watson Gilder and the portrait of Mr. Gilder were considered of masterly interpretation.   There is one portrait wherein Miss Beaux actually created personality.   This was her portrait of John Paul Jones, which was presented by the Class of 1881 to the United States Naval Academy at Annapolis.

GERTRUDE O'REILLY.

Daughter of James William O'Reilly, a member of the famous O'Reilly family identified with Irish Nationalism.   Her great-uncle, Father Eugene O'Reilly, was one of the first promoters of the Irish revival, being the author of the Gaelic dictionary, and a catalogue of the Ancient Manuscripts. Her mother, Susan MacDonell, was the only daughter of Colonel Alexander MacDonell, member of a famous Irish family. Miss O'Reilly has won great success in decorative work and applied design, being a student of the South Kensington School, and has received several awards and prizes for leather work design and painting, as well as a special prize for the studies from the ancient Irish manuscript. These she obtained at the great Irish festival, Oireacthais, which is held in Dublin under the auspices of the Gaelic League. In 1900 Miss O'Reilly became first superintendent of the house founded by the Dominican families in Dublin for a residence house for the business girls in that city. She opened a branch house, and originated and established a summer home, managed a large non-residential club in connection with this house, and edited a magazine called *The Star* for the girls. In 1905 while spending the summer in the county of Galway, she did some splendid work among the fisher folk of this section in the line of hygiene and the betterment of their condition. She has acted as honorary secretary for the Galway Branch of the Irish Industrial Association. In 1907 she came to America and has since contributed to the daily press of this country and the leading magazines.

ALICE CORDELIA MORSE.

Was born June 1, 1862, in Hammondsville, Jefferson County, Ohio. After a common school education she took her first lessons in drawing in an evening class started by the Christian Endeavor Society of Doctor Eggleston's Church. That little class of crude young people was the beginning of the art education of some of the noted competitors to-day in New York Art Circles. Miss Morse submitted a drawing from this class to the Woman's Art School, Cooper Union and was admitted for a four years' course, which she completed. Entering, later, the studio of John La Farge, the foremost artist of stained class designing in this country, she studied and painted with great assiduity, under his supervision. Later she sent a study of a head, painted on glass, to Louis C. Tiffany and Company, which admitted her into the Tiffany studio to paint glass and study designing. While there, she was a successful contestant in several designs for book covers, which aroused interest in this comparatively new art in this country, and she decided to take up this field of designing. She made many covers of holiday editions and fine books for well known publishing houses. This she has carried on in connection with glass designing, until her name is familiar to the designing fraternity and the annual exhibitors in the New York architectural League. She was the designer of the glass window in the Beecher Memorial Church, of Brooklyn.

ISABEL ELIZABETH SMITH.

Miss Isabel Elizabeth Smith was born in Clairmont County, Ohio, in 1845. After studying abroad for three years, Miss Smith opened a studio in Washington, District of Columbia, where she met with marked success, painting portraits of many prominent persons. She has won quite an enviable reputation as a miniature painter and is now doing work on the Pacific coast.

ROSINA EMMETT SHERWOOD.

Mrs. Rosina Emmett Sherwood was born in New York, December 13, 1854. She was a twin sister of Robert Temple Emmett, direct descendant of Thomas A. Emmett, the Irish Patriot She studied under William M. Chase; also in Paris. Her first work was on china, followed by illustrations of juvenile books. In 1884 she illustrated Mrs. Burton Harrison's "Old Fashioned Tales." She is a member of The American Society, and a member of the Society of American Artists. In 1887 she married the son of Mrs. John Sherwood.

CARRIE M. SHOFF.

Mrs. Carrie M. Shoff was born in Huntington, Indiana, April 2, 1849. She invented a method of manufacturing imitation limoges, largely used in the manufacture of advertising signs and in cheaper wares.

EUGENIA SHANKLAND.

Is a member of the "Order of the Visitation" in Wilmington, Delaware, and is the daughter of Manning R. Shankland. She is an artist of some note, painting a number of fine altar pieces for several of the churches of the Capital City, and her copy of Washington, in the room of the vice-president at the United States Capitol, has attracted much attention.

ELLEN HARDIN WALWORTH (THE YOUNGER).

Was born at Saragota Springs, New York, October, 1858. Was the Daughter of Mansfield Tracy Walworth. She was a student of art, conducting classes in sketching, and was principal of St. Mary's Academy, Albany, from 1888 to 1890. Author of "An Old World as Seen Through Young Eyes," "Lily of the Mohawks," "Life and Sketches of Father Walworth," and other works.

JENNIE WILDE.

Is the daughter of Judge R. H. Wilde a distinguished newspaper writer and jurist of New Orleans, her native city. She was a student of designing and painting in some of the foremost art schools of Europe. Is a contributor to Northwestern periodicals and devotes her time to art and journalism. Owing to her creative ability and inventive genius as an artist, Miss Wilde has been invited by the Carnival Society of New Orleans to design the tableaux and many of the spectacular effects used during the Mardi Gras festival each year in New Orleans.

AMALIA KUSSNER COUDERT.

Is a miniature painter. Born March 26, 1873, in Terre Haute, Indiana. Daughter of Lorenz Kussner. Married July 3, 1900, in New York City, to Charles

Dupont Coudert. In 1896 went to London and painted the portrait of the King (then the Prince of Wales) and many of the prominent people of England. In 1899 was summoned to Russia to paint portraits of the Emperor and Empress and of the Honorable Cecil Rhodes, in Africa.

MRS. WILLIAM HENRY HORNE.

Mrs. William Henry Horne was born at Eliot, Maine, the daughter of Lizzie Young and John Harrison Mathes. She was educated in Portsmouth and Boston, and studied art in Boston, New York and in the studio of W. D. Tenney, with whom she painted for twenty years.

Mrs. Horne is the vice-regent of the John Paul Jones Chapter Daughters of the American Revolution, member of the Twentieth Century Club of Boston, The Fathers' and Mothers' Club, The Copley Society, and is a well-known artist of Boston and New York, where her work is frequently exhibited.

CANDACE WHEELER.

Thirty years ago, with a handful of bright, eager New York girls, Mrs. Wheeler started the School of Decorative Art, turning out needle and embroidery work as artistic as fingers could make it. No other work was done by this school until a paper firm in New York offered a $2,000 prize for original wall paper designs. Up to this time no wall paper patterns were made in this country; even our calico designs were made in England. Mrs. Wheeler and her girls decided to compete for this prize. When the exhibition took place, they found that of all the designs offered theirs were the only American patterns exhibited, and they were hung by themselves. A day or two later information came to the School of Decorative Art that they had won the entire award of $2,000.

Mrs. Wheeler founded the famous Onteora Club, where she wrote the greater part of "Principles of Home Decorations," and other books bearing on art. Mrs. Wheeler was the artistic genius of the Woman's Building of the Columbian Exposition, and her daughter, Mrs. Keith, painted the ceiling in the library of that building. Pupils of this School of Decorative Art are scattered all over the country. One of the best painters now, is a pupil of this school, Miss Jean B. Stearns. Her specialty is Italian art.

EMMA SCHOLFIELD WRIGHT.

Mrs. Emma Scholfield Wright, of Pueblo, Colorado, was born in Hunslet, near Leeds, England, in 1845, and came to America when very young. She was married in 1878 to Henry T. Wright of Morgan Park, Illinois, and is the mother of four children. She lived in Minneapolis, Minnesota, from 1881 until 1897, when she removed to Chicago. Since 1902 her home has been in Pueblo.

She is prominent as an artist, and while her first work was in oils, it is her work in ceramics, which gives her the position she occupies in the world of art. Her work is notable for its fine feeling, for color values and harmony, and in

48

illusive shadings and blendings. Her designing is wonderful, enabling her to put into form her color schemes.

Her first original work was exhibited at the World's Columbian Exposition in 1893, and received the highest award for original design and coloring. The following year she exhibited at Chicago, where her work was so different from the rest of the exhibit, that it attracted instant and marked attention from art critics and art writers. Each year following her exhibit was larger and finer, and art critics recognizing the fact that she had opened up a new thought in decorative art, her work won full and complete recognition.

Mrs. Wright is not the student of any school, and all that she has accomplished is the result of her genius, and her untiring work and continuous study, carried on for the most part in her own home.

One of the notable examples of her work is seen in the decoration of the Colorado Fuel and Iron Company's hospital at Pueblo. The decoration includes eight panels filled with life-size portraits, done on tiling in monochrome, of some of the great workers connected with the history and development of the healing art.

She has exhibited her work at the Chicago, Buffalo and St. Louis expositions, and at art exhibitions the country over. The honors and awards taken by her where she has exhibited are many, and she is always spoken of in the highest terms of praise by the art critics. They all say of her work, that it is absolutely original in design, and beautiful in color, and some of them do not hesitate to pronounce her among the greatest of American decorators in ceramics.

FLORENCE MACKUBIN.

Born in Florence, Italy. Daughter of Charles Nicholas, of Maryland, and Ellen M. Fay Mackubin. Painter of miniatures, and exhibitor at all of the large expositions. Selected by Governor Smith and the Board of Public Works of Maryland, in 1900, to paint the portrait of Queen Henrietta Maria (after whom Maryland was named), to be hung in the State House. This was executed in a copy of the portrait by Vandyck, in Warwick Castle, England. Also painted the portrait of Governor Lowndes, to be hung in the executive chamber in the Maryland State House; the portrait of Professor Basil Gildersleeve, for the University of Virginia, and a miniature of Cardinal Gibbons; and portraits of the first and second Barons of Baltimore, founders of Maryland.

SUSAN HALE.

Born in Boston, December 5, 1833. Daughter of Nathan and Sarah Preston Everett Hale. Artist in water colors. Exhibitor of landscapes in Boston and New York. Author of "Life and Letters of Thomas Gold Appleton"; also "Family Flight," Series of Travels for Young People. She wrote in connection with her brother, Edward Everett Hale.

RHODA CARLETON MARIAN HOLMES NICHOLLS.

Born in Coventry, England; daughter of William and Marian Holmes; studied at Bloomsburg Art School, and at the Circle Artistic, Rome; married to

Burr H. Nicholls, in 1884; exhibited at the Royal Academy, London, Dudley Gallery, London; also in Rome, Turin, Milan, and all current American exhibitions. Received Queen's Scholarship London; medal at Prize Fund Exhibition New York; medal at Boston Biennial Exhibition, Chicago World's Fair, 1893; medal at Charleston Exposition, at the West Indian and Interstate Exhibition Nashville, at the Pennsylvania Art Exposition, St. Louis Exposition; represented in Boston Art Club, Boston Museum of Art; illustrated (in collaboration) Powell's Venetian Life; is author of articles in the *Art Exchange, Art Amateur and Keramic Studio;* member of the National Arts Club, New York; was vice-president for nine years of the Water Color Club, of New York; member of the American Society of Miniature Painters, Pen and Brush Club, Woman's Art Club, (of which she is a member of the Art Committee), Art Club, of Canada, Nineteenth Century Club. Her address is 913 Seventh Avenue, New York City.

EMILY MARIA SCOTT.

Born at Springwater, New York; daughter of Thomas Lawrence and Almira Spafard; studied at the National Academy of Design, and at the Art Students' League, in New York, and in Paris under Raphael Collin. Married to Charles Scott, in 1860; exhibited at the Paris salon in 1886, and Paris Exposition in 1911. Appears in all the current exhibitions and expositions held in the United States. Received gold medal at Atlanta Exposition; honorable mention at the Pan-American Exposition in 1901; represented in the Erie Public Library; vice-president New York Water Color Club; member of American Water Color Society and National Arts Club, New York.

CHARLOTTE B. COMAN.

Mrs. Coman was born in Waterville, New York; studied in Paris under H. Thompson, and Emille Vernier; exhibited in Paris Salon, St. Louis World's Fair, and various exhibitions in the United States. Received bronze medal at the California Mid-winter Exposition, prize at Woman's Art Club, member of New York Water Color Society, Art Workers' Club and Women's Art Club. "A French Village" exhibited at the Paris Exposition in 1878, "Near Fontainebleau," "Sunset at the Seaside" exhibited in Boston in 1877, "On the Borders of the Marne," and "Peasant Home in Normandie," are among her best works.

VIOLET OAKLEY.

Born in Jersey City, New Jersey, 1874; studied at the Art Students' League in New York, Pennsylvania Academy of Fine Arts under Howard Pyle; in Paris, under Raphael Collin and Aman Jean; has exhibited extensively throughout the United States; received gold medal for illustrations, St. Louis Exposition, 1904; also medal for mural decoration at the St. Louis Exposition; gold medal of honor at the Pennsylvania Academy in 1905; is represented in the Pennsylvania Academy of Fine Arts; member of the Society of Illustrators, New

York Water Color Club, fellowship of the Pennsylvania Academy of Fine Arts, Philadelphia, Philadelphia Water Club, and Plastic Club, of Philadelphia.

ELIZABETH NOURSE.

Those who have closely followed the history of American art will be interested in the principal facts of Elizabeth Nourse's life. She is a descendant of an old Huguenot family who settled in Massachusetts some two or three hundred years ago. She was born in Cincinnati, Ohio. At the age of thirteen she showed such remarkable talent for painting that she attended the School of Design in that city. Her father losing his fortune, at the time of her parents' death, she found herself confronted by the necessity of earning money to undergo the course in art which she had so long desired. After school hours she taught design and decorated the walls in the homes of Cincinnati's wealthiest citizens.

After completing her four years' course in the School of Design, she was offered a fine position there as teacher of drawing, but having more ambitious projects in her mind, she refused this position. Aided by her sister, she accumulated $5,000 and this, with the little rescued from their father's estate, insured them a living abroad for several years. When some of the young artists of Paris founded the Societe Nationale des Beaux-Arts, Miss Nourse decided to send her pictures to this new salon where they were received with acclamation. Three years later she was made an associate. A sincere student of nature, Miss Nourse paints only what she sees, but hers is the vision of a noble soul, which pierces through conventionalities to the poetry and beauty that underlies all life. Her pictures are not portraits of models, but types of human character; all nature appeals to her, and some of her most beautiful pictures are landscapes of Brittany, and bits of the old forest of Rambouillet.

The art of Elizabeth Nourse has been influenced by no other painter. Years of study in Paris have broadened her technique. Her brush work has become more firm, her color more beautiful, but the character of her painting remains unaltered. In the work of Miss Nourse, is shown the broad, human sympathy of a strong woman who believes in art not only for art's sake but for the sake of humanity which it can uplift and spiritualize.

ANNA LEA MERRITT.

In the front rank of our noted women painters stands Anna Lea Merritt, who is as well known in England as in her own country. She was not taught in schools, and to this fact is probably attributable the great individuality conspicuous in her works. She belongs to no particular religion in art, and attended no school or class, but diligently attended Mr. Marshall's lectures on anatomy, a subject to which she devoted much attention and study. She had a few lessons from Professor Legros and from Mr. Henry Merritt, whom she afterwards married; also from Mr. Richmond, R.A., and from Mr. William Roxall, R.A.

Much of Mrs. Merritt's work has been in portraiture. She did some decorative pictures for the Woman's Building, Chicago World's Fair, and later frescoed St. Martin's Church, at Chilworth. Mrs. Merritt was at one time a member of the Painters' Etchers' Society, and has exhibited many original etchings.

ANNIE C. SHAW.

Born at Troy, New York, 1852; lived for some years in Chicago studying art under H. C. Ford; in that city she was elected an associate of the Chicago Academy of Design, in 1873, and an academician, in 1876, the first woman upon whom the distinction has been conferred. Among her paintings are "On the Calumet," "Willow Island," "Keene Valley," "Ebb Tide on the Coast of Maine," "Head of a Jersey Bull," "The Return from the Fair" and "Illinois Prairie." She has exhibited in Chicago, Boston. New York and the Centennial Exposition.

EMILY SARTAIN.

Born in Philadelphia; daughter of John and Susan Sartain; studied engraving under her father; also at the Pennsylvania Academy of Fine Arts in Philadelphia; and under Christian Schuessele; and in Paris under E. Luminais; exhibited at the Paris Salon and in all prominent exhibitions of the large cities of the United States; received medal for oil painting at the Centennial Exhibition, Philadelphia, 1876; the Mary Smith Prize at the Pennsylvania Academy of Fine Arts; medals for engravings at the Atlanta Exposition and Pan-American Exposition; member of the International Bureau of Awards, the Art Department of the Chicago World's Fair, chairman of Artists' Committee officially in charge of Pennsylvania State Building, Chicago World's Fair; art delegate to the International Congress of Women in London, in 1899; afterward delegate to represent the United States at International Congress on Instruction in Art, Paris, 1900, and Berne, Switzerland, 1904; member of the Advisory Committee, Art Section, St. Louis Exposition, 1904; for many years was the only woman mezzotint engraver in the world; has been principal of the Philadelphia School of Design for Women since 1886; president of the Plastic Club, Philadelphia, and vice-president of the Fellowship of the Pennsylvania Academy of Fine Arts, Philadelphia.

HARRIET SARTAIN.

Born in Philadelphia; daughter of Henry and Maria Sartain; studied at the Philadelphia School of Design for Women exhibited in the Pennsylvania Academy of Fine Arts, Philadelphia Art Club, New York Water Color Club, American Water Color Society, Chicago Art Institute, Chicago World's Fair, St. Louis Exposition; instructor of drawing and water color in the Philadelphia School of Design for Women since 1893; director of the Art Department of Swarthmore College 1902; instructor in art at Pocono Pines Assembly, summer schools at Naomi Pines, Pennsylvania; member of the Plastic Club, of Philadelphia and alumnæ of the Philadelphia School of Design for Women.

MARY L. MACOMBER.

Born at Fall River, Massachusetts, August 21, 1861; daughter of Frederic W. and Mary W. Macomber; studied at the Boston Museum of Fine Arts and under Dunning, Duveneck, Crowningshield and Grundmann. Exhibited at The Hague, Carnegie Institute, Chicago Art Institute, Chicago World's Fair, St Louis Exposition; National Academy of Design, Society of American Artists, Pennsylvania Academy of Fine Arts, Boston Art Club, Copley Society; received Dodge Prize at the National Academy of Design, honorable mention at the Carnegie Institute, medal at Massachusetts C. M. Association, 1895; medal at Atlanta Exposition, 1895; is represented in the prominent collection at the Boston Museum of Fine Arts. Her work, accompanied by articles, has been reproduced in the *New England Magazine* and other current periodicals. Member of the Copley Society, Boston.

KATHARINE AUGUSTA CARL.

Born in Louisiana; daughter of Francis Augustus Carl, Ph.D., LL.D., and Mary (Breadon) Carl. She was graduated from the State College, of Tennessee, at Memphis, with the degree of M.A., and afterward studied art in Paris under Bouguereau, Jean Paul Laurens and Gustave Courtois. She first exhibited in the Paris Societe des Artists Francais, in 1887, received honorable mention from that society in 1890, and was made an associate of the Societe Nationale des Beaux Arts, Paris, in 1894. Miss Carl is a painter of portraits and figure paintings, and has painted many notable subjects, among whom was the late Empress Dowager of China. The Empress Dowager conferred upon her the orders of officer of the Double Dragon and the Manchu Flaming Pearl. She wrote and illustrated an account of her life in the Imperial Palace, of China, which was published under the title of "With the Empress Dowager of China." Miss Carl is a member of the International Society of Women Artists, London; Societe Nationale des Beaux Arts, Paris, and of the Lyceum Clubs, of London, and Paris.

MARIA LONGWORTH STORER.

Mrs. Bellamy Storer was born in Cincinnati, in March, 1849. She studied especially music and drawing when she was a child, and is greatly interested in everything that could help to educate and enlighten other people in both these arts. The Cincinnati musical festivals grew out of a conversation with Mrs. Storer's friend, Theodore Thomas, when he was visiting her in Cincinnati, in 1872. She asked him why they might not unite together all their choral societies, and he bring his orchestra and create a great festival organization. He liked the idea very much and under his great leadership they had musical festivals in Cincinnati which have never been surpassed by any in England or Continental Europe. In 1876 she was much interested in the exhibition of pottery and porcelain at the Philadelphia Centennial Exposition, and became anxious to have a place of her own to make experiments in native clays. After working for a while in a pottery where granite ware was made she started, in 1879, a pottery of her own in an old schoolhouse she owned on the banks of the Ohio River. She named the pottery "Rookwood," after their country place. The first kiln was drawn in February, 1880. For ten years after that she worked there almost daily, selecting shapes and artistic designs. Her decorators were usually young men and women who had been students at the art school, an institution in which her father, Joseph Longworth, was much interested, and to which he gave an endowment of three hundred thousand dollars. Mrs. Storer was given the patent for the using of a colored glaze over colored decoration and the Rookwood pottery of that time was dipped in a very thick deep yellow glaze, which gave a rich tone to every color underneath it, like the varnish of an old master. This ware obtained a gold medal at the Paris Exposition of 1889. In 1891 Mrs. Storer's husband was elected to the House of Representatives and, on leaving Cincinnati, she gave the Rookwood pottery to her friend, Mr. William Watts Taylor, who had been business manager for four years and had put the pottery on a paying basis. In her time it was rather an expensive luxury costing her about two thousand dollars a year more than it brought in.

EVELYN LONGMAN.

Has recently come into prominence through the execution of work for Wellesley College. She has already done some of the handsomest bronze work in this country. Her work for Wellesley is a set of bronze doors and transoms for the Wellesley Library Building, in memory of the late Professor Eben Norton Horsford, who died in 1893. Miss Longman's education was acquired entirely in America, chiefly at the Chicago Art Institute. Most of her works have been portrait busts and works of a similar nature. Three years ago, however, she made her first bronze doors, and the circumstances surrounding her first selection for her first commission, placed her at once as the most successful young woman worker in bronze in America. This commission, she received through competition held for a pair of bronze doors and a transom for the entrance to the chapel at the United States Naval Academy, at Annapolis. It was open to all American sculptors and conducted under the auspices of the National Sculpture Society. A jury of five men was selected to pick the winning design. The identity of the competitors was kept strictly a secret and the judges had no means of knowing whose work they were considering. Miss Longman won the award by unanimous decision on the first vote, over thirty-seven competitiors. She is rapidly forging to the front as an artist in bronze. She is a member of the American Numismatic Society, the American Federation of Arts, and the National Sculpture Society, and is one of the few women associates of the National Academy of Design.

MRS. WILLIAM ASTOR CHANLER.

Mrs. Chanler has recently become prominent in art circles in New York as a sculptor of more than ordinary ability. Two of her works were recently accepted by the jury of the National Academy of Design and exhibited at their spring exhibition. Mrs. Chanler is a pupil of Victor Salvator, of Macdougall Alley, the Latin quarter of New York.

SALLY JAMES FARNHAM.

Sally James Farnham, artist and sculptor. Her father was Colonel Edward C. James; her mother, Sarah Perkins. Mrs. Farnham is descended from a long line of soldiers and jurists on one side and sailors on the other. She was born and reared in Ogdensburg, New York. She gave no indication in her early youth of the wonderful talent she possessed. She never received what is ordinarily considered essential to ultimate success, art education. She was not a student in Paris or Rome nor did she show any special taste for drawing or for things artistic during her school days. She was simply a descendant of a cultured race and lived among people of strong artistic tendencies; enjoyed the advantage of extensive foreign travel, becoming familiar with the masterpieces of ancient and modern sculpture. Unconscious of possessing any talent in this line, while convalescing after a severe illness, her husband brought her some modeling wax, in the hope that it could help her to while away a period of enforced inactivity. From this she fashioned a recumbent figure of great beauty and delicacy, representing Iris, "Goddess of the Rainbow." This she executed, in the absence of modeling tools, by the use of the surgical instruments loaned her by the attending physician and the finished result was most charming. The fact that this first effort possessed the technique and finish usually found in the works of the trained and experienced artists, gave rise to the feeling among those who saw Mrs. Farnham's work, that a great future was before her. Her first portrait work was in bronze, a full length figure. This was followed by a bust which is a fine example of the sculptor's skill. Then followed the spirited bronze called "Cowboy Fun." This group is vibrant with life.

The Great Neck Steeple Chase Cup was modeled by Mrs. Farnham, and is considered one of the most artistic pieces of this kind ever produced. Mrs. Farnham's most ambitious effort is the soldiers' and sailors' monument in Ogdensburg, her birthplace. Mrs. Farnham's work for the government has met with great praise from artists and laymen. She did the frieze in the council room of the building of the Pan-American Republics, at Washington, and also designed the medal which was given Mr. Carnegie by the government, in appreciation of his gift of a large sum of money toward this building as a contribution toward the efforts for peace. There is an originality in her work which gives it strength and vitality. Mrs. Farnham is destined to become one of the noted artists and sculptors in this country.

ANNE WHITNEY.

Born in Watertown, Mass., in 1821. Descended from early New England colonists. Her first work was a portrait bust of her father and mother. Her first ideal work was her conception of Lady Godiva, which was exhibited in Boston. This was followed by "Africa," a colossal statue. The "Lotus-Eater" was her next work. After this she spent five years of study in Europe during which time she executed "The Chaldean Astronomer," and "Roma." After her return to America the State of Massachusetts commissioned her to make a statue in marble of Samuel Adams the Revolutionary patriot, for the National Gallery in Washington, and one in bronze for Adams Square in Boston. She went to Rome to execute this commission. Since these works she has executed a sitting statue of Harriet Martineau, of heroic size, for Wellesley College, and another ideal statue of Lief Erikson, the young Norseman who, A.D. 1000 sailed into Massachusetts Bay. Miss Whitney has made many fine medallions, fountains and portrait busts, among the latter, one of President Stearns of Amherst College, President Walker of Harvard, Professor Pickering of Harvard, William Lloyd Garrison, Honorable Samuel Sewall of Boston, Mrs. Alice Freeman Palmer, ex-president of Wellesley College, Adeline Manning, Miss Whitney's friend, Harriet Beecher Stowe, Frances E. Willard, Lucy Stone, Mary A. Livermore and others.

VINNIE REAM HOXIE.

Was born in Madison, Wisconsin, September 25, 1847. Is the daughter of Robert Lee and Lavinia McDonald Ream. Studied art in Washington, and afterwards in Paris under Bonnat. Her first work of note was a statue of Abraham Lincoln under commission from Congress. This was done from life, and later she executed the statue of Admiral Farragut, another commission from the government through an act of Congress, and this statue now adorns Farragut Square in Washington. She has done many ideal figures: "Miriam," "The West," "Sappho," "The Spirit of the Carnival," a bust of Mary Powell, now in the state hall of Brooklyn, portraits and medallions of General George B. McClellan, Thaddeus Stevens, General Sherman, Ezra Cornell, General John C. Freemont, T. Buchanan Read, E. B. Washburn, Horace Greeley, Peter Cooper, also Cardinal Antonelli, Pére Surgeon, Franz Liszt, Gustave Dore, and is now engaged on a heroic statue of Governor Samuel J. Kirkwood a commission from the state of Iowa, which is to be placed in the rotunda of the National Capitol. In 1878 Vinnie Ream married Richard Leveridge Hoxie of the United States army.

HARRIET G. HOSMER.

This famous American sculptor stands out in strong relief among those women of America who have attained distinction in this art. Miss Hosmer was born in Watertown, Mass., October 9, 1830. Her mother died when she was quite young, and a sister also dying with the mother's disease, consumption, Dr. Hosmer determined that Harriet should develop physically before any great effort was made toward her education. Her early life was accordingly spent in the woods and fields about their home and on the Charles River, which flowed near. She grew up like a boy. She was an eager reader and so her education was largely of self-made manner and opportunity. In the first school in which she was placed her brother-in-law, Nathaniel Hawthorne, was principal, but he did not hesitate to write her father, that he could do nothing with her, and she was placed in the care of Mrs. Sedgwick, who had a school at Lenox, Berkshire County. Mrs. Sedgwick was a woman of great tact and breadth of mind, so she soon won Harriet's confidence, and she remained under Mrs. Sedgwick's care for three years. In her early youth she had shown a great fondness for modeling her pets and treasures of the field, and so was permitted to take up lessons in modeling, drawing, and anatomical studies in Boston. She applied to the Boston Medical School for a course of study in anatomy, but her admittance was refused on account of her sex. Later she gained admission to the Medical College of St. Louis, and Professor Macdowell spared no pains to give her every advantage. The life-size medallion which she cut of Professor Macdowell on the base of his bust done by Clevenger, is treasured up to this day by that college. While in St. Louis, she made her home with the family of a former friend and companion at Lenox, Wayman Crow, who proved a most valued friend, and who gave her the order for her first statue when she went to Rome as a student. On her return home Dr. Hosmer fitted up a studio for her and she did Canova's "Napoleon" in marble for her father. Her next work was an ideal bust of Hesper. Then she asked her father to permit her to go to Rome to study, as she wished to make this her life work, and on November 12, 1852, Dr. Hosmer and she arrived in Europe. She desired especially to become a student for a time under John Gibson, the leading English sculptor, and when he saw the photographs of her "Hesper," he consented to take her as a pupil, and for seven years she worked under his direction and encouragement. She copied the "Cupid" of Praxiteles, and "Tasso" from the British Museum. Her first original work was "Daphne," then she produced her "Medusa." These were both accepted in Boston in 1853, and were much praised by Mr. Gibson. She also had the gratification of receiving words of approval from Rauch, the great Prussian sculptor, whose work of the beautiful Queen Louise at Charlottenburg is one of the famous pieces of sculpture of modern times. Later she did for Mr. Crow, "OEnone," and later "Beatrice Cenci," for the St. Louis Mercantile Library. Her father having lost his property and no longer being able to bear the expense of her studies, she determined to support herself by her own work. She took some modest apartments and disposed of all her luxuries and plunged into her work, the results of which have added to her fame. One of her pieces of work was entitled "Puck." This she duplicated for many crowned heads and distinguished people of many of the Continental countries. She did an exquisite figure upon the sarcophagus of the sixteen-year-old daughter of Madam Talconnet, who died in Rome. Her statue of Zenobia, Queen of Palmyra, was considered one of her greatest works. It was exhibited in Chicago at the Sanitary Fair in behalf of the soldiers, and from its exhibition Miss Hosmer received five thousand dollars. While on a visit to this country in 1860, she received an order from St. Louis for a bronze portrait statue of Missouri's famous statesman, Thomas Hart Benton, which was unveiled May 27, 1868, in Lafayette Park by Mrs. John C. Fremont, the daughter of Benton. For this work Miss Hosmer received the greatest praise and a substantial remuneration of ten thousand dollars. Orders now crowded upon her. Her "Sleeping Faun" is an exquisite piece of work, and was exhibited at the Dublin Exposition in 1865. Her "Siren fountain," executed for Lady Marian Alford, is one of her most artistic productions, and for many years prior to her death she was engaged in preparing a golden gateway for Ashridge Hall, England, ordered by Earl Brownlow. She did the statue of the beautiful Queen of Naples, for which she received royal praise and approval. Harriet Hosmer has placed the name of American women high among the sculptors of modern times. Her death in 1908 was a loss to the artistic world.

ELIZABETH NEY.

One of the famous artists of this country, and a worthy follower of Harriet Hosmer, enjoys deserved fame as a sculptor. She studied under Bauch and opened a studio after his death in Berlin, where her works received the warmest praise and admiration. Some of her more conspicuous works are the statues of Mitscherlich, Jakob Grimm, and other celebrities. She was summoned to the Royal Court of Hanover, where she did "The Blind King," "Joachim the Violinist of Arcady," "Stockhausen the Singer," and the gloomy features of the great philosopher Schopenhauer, and later a statue of Garibaldi. While in Munich, she did much of the ornamentation of the interior of some of the public buildings. She executed busts of Liebig and Wohler, which now adorn the Polytechnic School of Munich. She did also what was considered by Emperor William a remarkable bust of Bismarck. This was accepted in the Paris Exposition of 1868, and Mrs. Ney's name is justly placed among American sculptors.

GERTRUDE WHITNEY.

This distinguished young sculptress is the daughter of the late Cornelius Vanderbilt, and the wife of Harry Payne Whitney, of New York. She studied abroad, and has executed a number of marbles and bronzes for public places, notably, the fountain for the Pan American Building, Washington, D. C.

FLORENCE FREEMAN.

Born in Boston in 1836; she received her earliest instruction in sculpture from Richard S. Greenough. In 1861 she went to Italy with Miss Charlotte Cushman, remaining a year in Florence under the instruction of Hiram Powers. In 1862 she removed her studio to Rome where she spent the rest of her professional life. Among her most important works are a bust of "Sandalphon," bas-reliefs of Dante and the sculptured chimney piece representing "Children and the Yule Log, and Fireside Spirits," which was exhibited at the Centennial Exhibition in Philadelphia, 1876 and received honorable mention.

ENID YANDELL.

Born in Louisville, Kentucky, October 6, 1870; is the daughter of Lunsford P. and Louise Elliston Yandell; educated at Hampton College; received degree of B.A. in Louisville, Ky.; exhibited at the Paris Salon since 1895, and has appeared in all of the current exhibitions of the United States; received Designer's Medal at the Chicago World's Fair, where she did a great deal of work for the

Women's Building; Medal at the Tennessee Centennial, Pan-American Exposition, St. Louis Exposition; member of the National Sculpture Society, National Arts Club, Municipal Art Society, and National Historical Preservation Society of New York City.

One of the remarkable features of Miss Yandell's career is the brief period of time in which she has made her reputation. Thirteen years ago she was a member of the Art Students' League. The most imposing product of Miss Yandell's genius is the heroic figure of Athena, which stood in front of the reproduction of the Parthenon at the Nashville Exposition. It is the best figure ever designed by a woman.

MISS AVIS HEKKING.

Born in New York City, daughter of J. A. Hekking, the well-known landscape painter, who came to America at an early age. Miss Hekking's great-great-grandfather was sergeant-major under General Putnam, and served through the Revolutionary War, distinguishing himself in the battles of Trenton and Princeton. Her family are all artists, several of her brothers have won worldwide reputations as violoncellists.

Miss Hekking studied in Paris under Pourtois Debat-Ponson and Blanc; became a pupil of M. Langé. Later she accompanied her parents to Florence, Italy, where she worked in her father's studio, painting several portraits and historical pictures. In her leisure hours she wrote plays. Of late years she has worked steadily at painting and literature and sends, annually, a picture to the Fine Arts Exhibition in Florence.

JULIE RIVE KING.

Madame Julie Rive King was born October 31, 1857, in Cincinnati. Her mother, Mrs. Caroline Rive, was a cultured musician and pianist, being a teacher of these arts. At quite an early age, Julie became a remarkable piano player, appearing in concerts. After studying in New York she returned to her home and created great excitement by her remarkable performances as an artist. In 1873 she went to Europe to study under Liszt, appearing in public in Leipsic and other cities, where the musical world ranked her among the great pianists of the day. She won a brilliant triumph in all the great cities of Europe. Owing to the sudden death of her father, who was killed in a railway accident, she returned to the United States and very soon after this married Frank H. King. She made a tour of this country in concert, establishing her reputation as the greatest pianist in the United States at that time. In 1884, owing to failure in health she retired from the concert stage and devoted her life to teaching.

MRS. ALOYSIUS LOUIS APFELBECK (MARIE LOUISE BAILEY).

Was born in Nashville, Tennessee, October 24, 1876. She was the daughter of Dr. Patrick H. Bailey. She received from the Shah of Persia, in 1902, the Persian medal for art and science, sharing with Mme. Modjeska the distinction of being the only women in the world to receive this honor. She has also a medal for art from the Court of Coburg, and the honor of "Imperial Chamber Virtuoso" from Austria, and from the Emperor Francis Joseph, the Elizabethan medal for Art and Science, and the Golden Order of Merit of the Cross and Crown. These distinctions have been rarely conferred upon foreigners. She is the wife of Captain A. L. Apfelbeck, of the Austrian army.

CAROLINE KEATING REED.

Born in Nashville, Tenn. Is the daughter of Colonel J. M. Keating, a newspaper man of prominence in that city; was a pupil of Emile Levy; studied in New York under S. B. Mills and Madame Carreno; took lessons from Mrs. Agnes Morgan and subsequently from Richard Hoffman and Joseffy; is a successful teacher of music in Memphis; always giving free lessons to one or two pupils, as her contribution to charity and the advancement and aid of her own sex; has written a primer on technique for beginners.

JULIA ELIDA DICKERMAN.

Julia Elida Dickerman, daughter of Charles E. and Ellen Louise Dickerman, was born in Carbondale, Illinois, February 21, 1859. In 1869 Miss Katie Logan—a relation and adopted daughter of General and Mrs. Logan—who possessed a fine soprano voice which had been highly cultivated by the best teachers of Philadelphia and New York, came to Carbondale to reside in General Logan's family, and at the earnest solicitations of friends, among them Mr. and Mrs. Dickerman, gave lessons to a few young girls in vocal and instrumental music. Elida Dickerman was one of her pupils. Miss Logan soon discovered that Elida Dickerman had musical talents of the highest quality, and was exceedingly proud of the progress of her young pupil, who so faithfully and indefatigably mastered every lesson she gave her. She discovered that Elida's voice had a wide range and if properly trained would win her an enviable reputation. At the age of thirteen she was taken to New Haven, Conn., to school, and to study music. Here her musical education was pursued until, as a young lady, she returned to Southern Illinois to practice her chosen musical profession. As a teacher, soloist and organist she has ever since been well known throughout Illinois and the Middle West. She married Charles A. Sheppard, a merchant of Carbondale.

Since the establishment of the Southern Illinois State Normal University, in Carbondale, Mrs. Sheppard has had charge of the musical department of the University.

GERALDINE FARRAR.

Born February 28, 1882, at Melrose, Massachusetts. Is the daughter of Sydney and Henrietta Barnes Farrar. Musical education was completed in Paris and Berlin. Made her debut at the Royal Opera House in Berlin, October 15, 1901, as Marguerite in Faust. Has been a member of the Metropolitan Opera Company since 1906.

LILLIAN NORDICA.

Madame Lillian Nordica, born Lillian Norton, was born in Farmington, Maine, and spent her early life in Boston where her family lived, on account of the educational advantages for their daughters. Madame Nordica's voice was never seriously considered until after the death of her next older sister, Wilhelmina.

On the death of her sister, Madame Nordica's mother transferred her interest and ambition to the one whose talent had until then gone unrecognized. At the age of thirteen she entered the New England Conservatory of Boston with a scholarship. Her teacher, John O'Neill, was so severe and exacting that Madame Nordica was the only scholar remaining of the class at the end of the four years' course. During this period of study she secured an engagement as soloist at the Temple Street Church in Boston. Her first appearance was as soloist with Gilmore's band, giving two concerts a day and touring through the country. Following this American tour, she went with the band for concerts in Ireland and Paris, and by the end of this tour she had saved enough money for a course of study in Italy under San Giovanni of Milan, who coached her for her debut as Violetta in Verdi's "La Traviata."

Madame Nordica has always prided herself on her American birth, and the affection in which her American admirers have always held her was shown in the presentation to her of a magnificent diamond tiara, at the Metropolitan Opera House in New York some years ago, as a tribute of affection.

EMMA WIXON NEVADA.

Born in 1861, in Nevada City, California. Her maiden name was Emma Wixon, and in private life she is known as Mrs. Palmer. Her stage name was taken from her native town. She received her education in the schools of Oakland, and San Francisco, Cal., and Austin, Texas. In 1877 she went to Europe to study for the operatic stage. In 1880 she accepted an offer from Colonel Mapleson, to sing in Italian Opera and made her debut in "La Sonambula," in London, England, and was at once ranked with the queens of the operatic stage and recognized as a star of the first magnitude. She repeated her triumphs in Paris and in a tour in the United States also in Portugal, Spain, and a most successful season in Italy.

CLARA LOUISE KELLOGG.

Clara Louise Kellogg was born July 12, 1842, at Sumterville, S. C. Her father was the well-known inventor, George Kellogg, and her childhood was spent in Birmingham, Conn. In 1860 she made her debut in the Academy of Music in "Rigoletto," and in 1864 she appeared as Marguerite in Gounod s "Faust," making a remarkable success, and was considered the greatest impersonator of that rôle ever seen in this country. After this brilliant success Miss Kellogg went to London, and appeared at her Majesty's Theatre and at the Crystal Palace the same year. In 1868 she toured the United States in concert under Max Strakosch. In 1869 she sang Italian Opera in New York City, and for three years enjoyed a great triumph. She then organized her own company, singing in English. In 1876 she organized another opera company, and appeared as Aida and Carmen. After this she again sang in concert throughout the country for several years. In 1880 she accepted an engagement in Austria to sing in opera, and here she sang in Italian with a company of German singers. Later the tour was extended to Russia and she sang with marked success in St. Petersburg. She was the first American artist to win recognition in Europe. Having amassed quite a fortune on the stage, she retired in 1889. She became the wife of Carl Strakosch.

MME. SELMA KRONOLD.

Was born in Cracow, Poland. Received her musical education at the Royal Conservatory of Music in Leipsic, where she won the Mendelssohn prize, and at the age of seventeen was engaged by Anton Seidl to sing Wagnerian rôles. Is a grand opera singer of note both in Europe and America. In 1904 she retired from the stage and organized and founded the Catholic Oratoria Society and is to-day a director of this society and of the free vocal classes for men and women in connection with it.

JESSAMINE POLAK (BARONESS VON ELSNER.)

Was born at Burlington, Iowa, in 1869. Daughter of Baron Hugo Bongenslav von Elsner, member of an ancient, noble family of Silesia, and Amanda Kate Dimmett, whose family was among the early settlers of Bloomington, Illinois. Baroness Von Elsner has been a concert singer both in this country and in Europe.

MARIE VAN ZANDT.

Born in Texas, October 8, 1861. Daughter of Mrs. Jennie Van Zandt, the well-known singer, whose father was Signor Antonio Blitz. Miss Van Zandt was trained by her mother, as she had early displayed strong musical tendencies. In 1873 she and her mother went to London, where she studied. Adelina Patti took a personal interest in her training. Later she studied in Milan, Italy, and made her operatic debut in Turin in 1879. In 1880 she appeared in London in

Her Majesty's Opera Company, winning success. In 1881 she appeared in Paris in the Opera Comique in "Mignon" and sang there for four seasons. She sang in many of the principal cities of Europe, enjoying a pronounced musical success in her own country and was ranked as one of the foremost sopranos of her time. Miss Van Zandt married Petrovich Tzcherinoff in 1898, and has now retired from the stage.

ANNIE LOUISE CAREY.

One of the noted singers produced by America. She was born in Wayne, Maine, October 22, 1842. Daughter of Dr. Nelson Howard and Maria Stockbridge Carey. Studied under Lyman Wheeler of Boston, and Giovanni Corsi, Milan, Italy, making her debut in Italian opera in Copenhagen. Was afterward a member of the opera company under Strakosch, singing the principal contralto rôles in grand opera both in America and Europe. In 1882 she married Charles Monson Raymond, a banker of New York City, and retired from the stage.

EMMA ABBOTT.

Born in Chicago in 1850. Her father being a music teacher encouraged her musical gift and gave her lessons on the guitar and in singing. At the age of thirteen she taught the guitar with success. Her education was acquired in the public schools of Peoria, Illinois. At sixteen she joined the Lombard Concert Company of Chicago and traveled with them through Iowa, Illinois, and Wisconsin, but at the end of the tour found herself friendless and moneyless. She then undertook a tour by herself and with a guitar she started out alone and gave concerts in Michigan and other states finally reaching New York City, where she gave concerts in the hotel parlors to meet her expenses, but she failed to gain any notice and returned to Chicago discouraged by her failure. She gave a concert in Toledo, Ohio, to recuperate her fortune, and at this concert as a guest was Clara Louise Kellogg, who, recognizing Miss Abbott's merit, gave her money enough to go to New York with a letter to Professor Errani. In 1870 she began her lessons under this noted teacher and filled an engagement to sing in the choir of Dr. Chapin's church, for which she received fifteen hundred dollars a year. In 1872, the congregation of this church raised ten thousand dollars to send her to Europe. She went to Milan and studied with San Giovanni, afterwards to Paris and studied under Wartel, also with Delle Sadie, making a successful debut, and during her stay had gained the friendship of Baroness Rothschild. She married Eugene Wetherell, who was a member of Dr. Chapin's church, and had followed her to Europe, where they were secretly married. On her return to the United States in 1876, she organized an opera company with C. D. Hess, appearing in the famous rôle of Marguerite at the Park Theatre in Brooklyn, New York. She gained in public admiration constantly and ultimately amassed a large fortune. She is among the first famous American singers, and we can well be proud of her as a woman and an artist. She died in Ogden, Utah, January 4, 1891.

SARAH HERSHEY EDDY.

Daughter of the late Benjamin and Elizabeth Hershey; was born in Lancaster, Penn., and educated in Philadelphia, where she received her musical training and made her debut as a singer. She sang for some years in a church choir. Her voice breaking down, she devoted herself to the study of the piano and in 1867 went to Europe and settled in Berlin, where she studied harmony, score-reading, piano playing under Professor Stern, and singing under Miss Jennie Mayer and others of the best known teachers and artists of Germany.

After three years she studied in Italy under some of the best Italian masters, both in music and language. Later she went to London where she took a course in oratorical work with Madam Sainton-Dolby. In 1871 she returned to America, and for several months gave private lessons in New York City, when she was called to Pittsburgh to fill the post of professor in the vocal department of a female college. In 1875 she went to Chicago, and with W. S. B. Matthews founded the Hershey School of Musical Art. The success of this school attracted students from all over the United States. Mr. Clarence Eddy was eventually made director of this school and in 1879 he married Miss Sarah Hershey. Under their joint management the school continued to prosper until the duties became so exacting that both resigned and devoted themselves to teaching in private classes. In 1887 Mrs. Eddy was elected a member of the Board of Examiners in the Vocal Department of the American College of Music, and in 1893 she was made vice-president of the Woman's Musical Congress at the World's Fair in Chicago, and was one of the Examining Committee of Musical Competition, of which Theodore Thomas was the presiding officer. In 1895 Mrs. Eddy retired from her profession and has since lived in Paris.

COUNTESS MARIO VENTURINI.

Was born in New York City where her father, Edward Otto Stern, a naturalized American, was Russian Vice-Consul and a great financier. While Vice-Consul, Mr. Stern married Maltide Druilhet, daughter of Jules Antoine and Emma A. Druilhet, of New Orleans. Miss Stern's maternal great-grandfather was proprietor of St. James Parish, New Orleans. At the beginning of the Civil War in 1861, her maternal grandfather, Jules Antoine Druilhet, better known as Captain Druilhet, was the youngest captain of the Louisiana volunteers. He equipped a regiment of St. James Parish at his own expense and was under orders of Jones, Jefferson and Beauregard.

Madam Druilhet, the mother of Countess Mario Venturini, was an accomplished pianist, and her salon was for many years the musical center of New Orleans. Left a widow a few years after her marriage, Mrs. Stern left America and went to live in Belgium where her home was the center of the best artists of the country. Surrounded by such associations during her childhood, Miss Stern early developed artistic tastes which eventually became the ruling passion of her youth. Miss Stern made her social debut at the Court of Brussels, where she was presented by the United States American Minister, Honorable Bellamy

49

Storer. Miss Stern gave up her social career to enter the Academie Julien to pursue her studies in art. While here she became very much interested in the American students, young girls studying art in Paris. On the 9th of November, 1903, Miss Stern married Count Mario Venturini.

ETHEL ATWOOD.

Miss Atwood was born in Fairfield, Maine, September 12, 1870. Is a musician of note in orchestral work. In Boston she formed the Fadette Ladies' Orchestra, which was soon in such demand that she made this her profession. She studied prompting, and is to-day considered one of the best prompters, and the only lady prompter in the United States.

MARGARET RUTHVEN LANG.

Born in Boston, November 27, 1867. Daughter of Benjamin Johnston Lang and Frances Morse Burrage Lang. Was a student of the violin under Louis Schmidt, Drechsler and Abel of Munich; Composition, with Victor Gluth of Munich; Orchestration under Chadwick of Boston and Macdowell. Is a composer of music for the pianoforte, solos, songs, choruses and orchestral works. Her work, "Dramatic Overture," has been performed by the Boston Symphony Orchestra, and her "Witichis" was performed several times in Chicago under the leadership of Theodore Thomas. She is one of the most prominent musical composers of America.

Actresses.

CHARLOTTE CUSHMAN.

It may be said of Charlotte Cushman that she was one of those strenuous, noble souls who would have dignified and vitalized, as with the vitality of a man, any calling into which it might have pleased Fate to place her, and that she would have left the world better for her presence. For this mental pertinacity, as we might call it, we can credit the sturdy Puritan stock from which she was descended.. The best blood of New England, the blood which has made both martyrs and honest, hopeless bigots ran through her veins. Her father was a respected merchant of Boston, and it was in that city that Charlotte Saunders Cushman was born, July 23, 1816. Her strongest characteristics were her imitative power and her wonderful voice. It was this voice that was soon to aid her in the struggle for existence. Her father was unfortunate in business, and Charlotte began the study of music, and subsequently sang in a Boston church choir, and she was urged to continue the cultivation of her voice and not to waste time in the mere drudgery of teaching. And thus it came about that Miss Cushman became the pupil of James G. Maeder (afterwards the husband of Clara Fisher), and made her appearance under his instruction in April, 1835, as the Countess Almaviva, in the "Marriage of Figaro," the performance taking place at the Tremont Theatre, and was considered a triumph for Miss Cushman. Visions of future operatic achievements filled her mind, when suddenly her voice failed, from overtraining, and through this apparent misfortune Miss Cushman was led to the stage, and through Caldwell, the theatrical manager, of New Orleans, she was given a part to appear on the stage. Her first appearance was as Lady Macbeth, in a benefit performance in that city. Of herself at that time Miss Cushman says: "I was a tall, thin, lanky girl, about five feet, six inches in height." Her rendition of the part was satisfactory, both to the audience and manager. For three years, from September, 1837, to September, 1840, she was at the Park Theatre, New York, playing various parts. This, no doubt, was a fine experience for her just at this time, and she came out of this ordeal a true actress, who was not afraid to play Romeo, Portia, Lady Macbeth, Joan of Arc, Belvidera, in "Venice Preserved," Roxana, in "The Rival Queens," and many other characters. Her greatest achievement has always been believed to be Meg Merrilies. It was said of her first appearance in this part, "There was an uncanny charm, a wealth of picturesqueness and, at the same time, a depth of senile feeling in her portraiture that stamped it at once with the mark of inspiration." No one who ever saw Meg Merrilies will ever forget its terrible effectiveness. After leaving Park Theatre, she played male characters for some time. It was her professional association with Macready during the seasons of 1843 and 1844 that provided the stepping-stone for which Miss Cushman had been groping. After he witnessed her performance of Lady Macbeth he showed a sympathy for this aspiring woman which was of inestimable value to her.

Owing to the encouragement given her by Macready Miss Cushman determined to go to England, and although at the time it seemed rash the end justified the risk. One writer says of her debut in England: "Since the memorable first appearance of Edmund Kean, in 1814, never has there been such a debut on the boards of an English theatre." Miss Cushman returned to America in 1870, and on November 7, 1874, took her farewell of the New York stage in Lady Macbeth, at Booth's Theatre. Her last appearance of all as an actress, although not as a reader, was made in Boston, May 15, 1875, as Lady Macbeth. In the autumn of this year she made her residence in Boston, where she passed away on February 18, 1876.

MAUDE ADAMS.

Born at Salt Lake City, Utah, November 11, 1872. Daughter of Annie Adams, a celebrated actress in the United States. She made her first appearance on the stage when but an infant of nine months, in "The Lost Child." As a little girl she made a great success as Little Schneider in "Fritz," with the late J. K. Emmett. She made her first appearance on the New York stage in 1888, in "The Paymaster." On February 4, 1889, she played Louisa, in "The Highest Bidder," and was next engaged for the Bijou Theatre, where she appeared March 5, 1889, as the minister's sister, in "A Midnight Bell." In 1890 she played Evangeline at Proctor's Twenty-third Street Theatre, and on October 21, 1890, appeared as Dora, in "Men and Women." November 16, 1891, she played Nell, in "The Lost Paradise." Her next appearance was at Palmer's Theatre as leading lady with John Drew, in 1892, making a great success in the part of Suzanne, in "The Masked Ball." She continued to play with Mr. Drew until 1897. She was promoted to the rank of "star" by Charles Frohman in 1897, and made her first appearance in New York in that capacity at the Empire Theatre on September 27, when she appeared as Babbie, in "The Little Minister." She has played this part many hundred times since. This was followed by Mrs. Hilary, in "Mrs. Hilary Regrets," which she played with John Drew. At the Empire Theatre, on May 8, 1899, she appeared for the first time as Juliet, in "Romeo and Juliet," with great success. In 1900 she appeared as the Duke of Reichstadt, in "L'Aiglon," and in 1901 as Phoebe Throssell, in "Quality Street," one of her greatest successes. This was followed by Pepita, in "The Pretty Sister of Jose," and on November 6, 1905, she appeared at the Empire Theatre, New York, in what has been one of her greatest successes, as Peter Pan, in Barrie's play of that name. She played in this for two years, relieved by performances of "Quality Street," "L'Aiglon" and "The Little Minister." In September, 1907, she commenced another tour with "Peter Pan." In 1908 she appeared in "The Jesters." Miss Adams is probably the most popular actress on the American stage today. "The fountain head of her personality is nun-like and virginal. Like an instrument of fine silver, she sounds her pure, rare notes in the key of the ideal and celestial, and is content with the response which they waken."

ETHEL BARRYMORE.

Daughter of the late Maurice Barrymore and Georgie Drew-Barrymore, and niece of the well-known actor, John Drew. She was born in Philadelphia, August 15, 1879, and made her first appearance on the stage on January 25, 1894. At the Empire Theatre, New York, during the autumn of 1894 she played the part of Kate Fennell, in "The Bauble Shop," with her uncle, John Drew, in the leading part. She has appeared in "The Imprudent Young Couple," "The Squire of Dames," Priscilla, in "Rosemary," and on May 15, 1897, made her debut in England as Miss Kittridge, in "Secret Service," with W. H. Gillette. She was then engaged by the late Sir Henry Irving for the Lyceum Company, going on a tour with this company, playing the part of Annette, in "The Bells." On her return to London she appeared at the Lyceum, January 1, 1896, as Euphrosine, in "Peter the Great." She then returned to America, and her next appearance was at the Garrick Theatre, October 24, 1898, as Madeleine, in "Catherine," with Annie Russell. She appeared later in "His Excellency, the Governor," and was promoted to the rank of "star" by Charles Frohman, making her first appearance as such in "Captain Jinks of the Horse Marines." Since then she has appeared as Angela Muir, in "A Country Mouse"; Kate Curtis, in "Cousin Kate"; Sunday, in the play of that name; Gwendolyn Cobb, in "The Painful Predicament of Sherlock Holes"; Nora Helmer, in "A Doll's House"; Mrs. Grey, in "Alice Sit-by-the-Fire," and in 1894 returned to London, and appeared as Cynthia, in a play by that name, by H. H. Davies. This was followed by another season of "Alice Sit-by-the-Fire," "Captain Jinks of the Horse Marines," Mrs. Jones, in "The Silver Box," and in September, 1907, she started on a tour with a new play entitled "Her Sister," written by Clyde Fitch. She is the wife of R. Griswold Colt.

MINNIE MADDERN FISKE.

Was born in New Orleans December 19, 1865. She was educated in the convents of Cincinnati and St. Louis. Has been on the stage practically all her life, playing under her maiden name of Minnie Maddern, achieving great success all over the United States. She first appeared at the early age of three as the Duke of York, in "Richard III"; at the age of fifteen was a "star." She made her first appearance on the New York stage at Wallack's Theatre, July 11, 1870, in the part of Little Fritz, in "Fritz, Our German Cousin," with the late J. K. Emmett. In 1871 she appeared in "Hunted Down," at Niblo's Garden. Since then she has played in "Chicago Before the Fire," "King John," "Fogg's Ferry," "Caprice," "In Spite of All" and "Featherbrain." In 1890 she left the stage on the occasion of her marriage with Harrison Grey Fiske, but after an absence of four years she appeared in 1894 as the heroine, in "Hester Crewe," a play written by her husband. She has played the part of Nora Helmer, in "A Doll's House," with great success; has appeared in "Frou-Frou," "The Queen of Liars" and her own play, "A Light From St. Agnes." One of her greatest successes was as Tess, in "Tess of the D'Urbervilles." Since 1898 she has appeared in "A Bit of Old Chelsea," "Love Finds the Way," "Little Italy" and "Becky Sharp." At the Manhattan Theatre, of which her husband became the lessee and manager, she appeared in 1901 in "Miranda of the Balcony" and "The Unwelcome Mrs. Hatch." Her performance of Mary, in "Mary of Magdala," created a profound impression. In 1906 she appeared in a new play, "The New York Idea," which was one of Mrs. Fiske's greatest successes. In 1907 she appeared as Rebecca West, in Ibsen's "Rosmersholm." Mrs. Fiske is a remarkably gifted woman. Not only is she a fine actress, but she is, as well, a stage manager, and has directed the production of most of the plays produced at the Manhattan Theatre during her husband's tenancy. She is also the author of the following plays: "The Rose," "A Light From St. Agnes," "The Eyes of the Heart," and "Not

Guilty." She has also collaborated with her husband in "Fontenelle."

MAXINE ELLIOTT.

Was born at Rockland, Maine, February 5, 1871. She was educated at the Notre Dame Academy, Roxbury, Mass., and made her first appearance on the stage at Palmer's Theatre, New York, November 10, 1890, as Felicia Umfraville, in "The Middleman," with E. S. Willard, when Mr. Willard made his debut on the American stage. She also played with him in "John Needham's Double," taking the part of Virginia Fleetwood." She has appeared in "A Fool's Paradise," "Judah," "The Professor's Love Story," "The Prodigal Daughter," "The Voyage of Suzette," "Sister Mary," "London Assurance," "Diplomacy," "A Woman of No Importance," and "Forget-Me-Not," and in January, 1895, she was a member of the late Augustin Daly's Company, at the Daly Theatre, in New York, in "The Heart of Ruby," "The Two Gentlemen of Verona," "Nancy and Company," "The Honeymoon," "A Midsummer Night's Dream," and "The Two Escutcheons." Her first appearance in London was made at the Daly Theatre, July 2, 1895, as Sylvia in "The Two Gentlemen of Verona"; and she also played during this engagement in "A Midsummer Night's Dream". In 1896, she appeared at the Fifth Avenue Theatre as Eleanor Cuthbert in "A House of Cards." In 1896 she was married to Nat Goodwin, and accompanied him on a tour to Australia. She appeared in "A Gilded Fool," "An American Citizen," "In Mizzoura," "Nathan Hale," and "The Cowboy and the Lady." She appeared at the Duke of York's Theatre, London, June 5, 1899, in the last mentioned part. At the Knickerbocker Theatre, New York, in 1900, she appeared in "When We Were Twenty-one," and in 1901, as Portia in "The Merchant of Venice." At the Comedy Theatre, London,

September, 1901, she played in "When We Were Twenty-one." In 1902, she toured the United States in "The Altar of Friendship." In 1903, she appeared as a "star" for the first time under the management of Charles B. Dillingham, in "Her Own Way," which after touring several cities in the United States was produced at the Lyric Theatre, London, in 1905. In August, 1905, she played "Jo" Sheldon in "Her Great Match," and was seen at the Criterion in this part later. In 1907, she again appeared in London at the Lyric Theatre as Mary Hamilton in "Under the Greenwood Tree," returning to the United States and appearing at the Garrick Theatre, December 25, 1907.

GERTRUDE ELLIOTT.

Is the sister of Maxine Elliott, and the wife of Johnston Forbes-Robertson, the great English actor. She made her first appearance in 1894 with Rose Coghlan's company, in "A Woman of No Importance." She played with her sister for some time and made her first appearance on the London stage in "The Cowboy and the Lady" at the Duke of York's Theatre, June 5, 1899. In 1900 she was engaged by Forbes-Robertson, and played Ophelia in "Hamlet," Carrot in the play of that name, and Judith Anderson in "The Devil's Disciple." On December 22, 1900, she married Forbes-Robertson, and since then has played in London with the exception of a brief tour in the United States in 1906. Since that time she has played with her husband at the Savoy Theatre, London.

MARGARET MATHER.

Was born in Tilbury, near Montreal, Canada, in 1862, but is an American by adoption. She is of Scotch descent. In 1868 her family left Canada and settled in Detroit, Michigan. Later Margaret was sent to New York to live with one of her brothers, who assumed charge of her education. In 1880, this brother died, and she was left dependent upon her own efforts. This opened up an opportunity for her to satisfy her desire to go upon the stage and she made her debut as Cordelia in "King Lear" with such marked success that she attracted the attention of Manager J. M. Hill, who made a contract with her for six years' engagement, opening as Juliet, August, 1882, in a theatre in Chicago, scoring an immediate success. She then played in all the principal cities of the United States appearing in the Union Square Theatre in New York City in her famous role of Juliet. Her repertoire includes, Rosalind, Imogene, Lady Macbeth, Leah, Julia, Peg Woffington, Mary Stuart, Gilbert's Gretchen, Pauline, Julianna, Barbie's Joan of Arc, Nance Oldfield, Medea, and many other leading parts. In 1887 she became the wife of Emil Harberkorn, leader of the Union Square Theatre orchestra.

JULIA MARLOWE.

Was born in the Village of Caldbeck, England, in 1865. She was christened Sarah Frances Frost. Though her family name was Brough, on entering the theatrical profession she took the name of Julia Marlowe. In 1872 her family came to the United States and settled in Kansas, finally removing to Cincinnati, where Miss Marlowe received her early education in the public schools. Her first appearance on the stage was in 1874, when but nine years of age in "Pinafore." This was followed by children's parts in "Rip Van Winkle," and in 1879 she made a tour with a company headed by a Miss Dowe. Owing to the illness of a member of this company, she was called upon unexpectedly to take the part of a page in "Romeo and Juliet," which she did with such marked indications of talent that for the next four years she was placed under Miss Dowe for study. In October, 1887, she made her debut in New York City as Parthenia in "Ingomar" winning a triumph at once. She afterwards appeared as Viola in "Twelfth Night" and her success soon led her to enter the ranks as a star and she made a tour, appearing in "Ingomar," "Romeo and Juliet," "Twelfth Night," "As You Like It," "The Lady of Lyons," and the "Hunchback," taking the leading female rôles in these plays. Ill health compelled her retirement for several years, but since her recovery she has continued her successes. Her art is of a high standard. She appears in her various rôles true to life and without visible effort. In 1894 she married Robert Taber, her leading man, and for a number of years they managed together their own company. Julia Marlowe's greatest work has been her "Juliet," being recognized as the best "Juliet" on the stage to-day.

MRS. D. P. BOWERS.

Mrs. Bowers, whose maiden name was Crocker, was born in Stamford, Connecticut, March 12, 1830. She was the daughter of William A. Crocker, an eminent Episcopal clergyman, who died when Mrs. Bowers was six years of age. Her first appearance took place at the Park Theatre in July, 1846, as Amanthis, and while playing this engagement she married David P. Bowers, March 4, 1847. After their marriage, Mr. and Mrs. Bowers went to Baltimore, where they remained for nearly four years. March 11, 1847, Mrs. Bowers appeared in Philadelphia as Donna Victoria in "A Bold Stroke for a Husband," at the Walnut Street Theatre. In 1848 she made her first appearance as Pauline in "The Lady of Lyons," in the Arch Street Theatre, remaining here for many years, a great popular favorite. In 1857 her husband died. Mrs. Bowers retired from the stage for some time but appeared again in Philadelphia, December 19, 1857, at the old Walnut Street Theatre. March 4, 1859, she leased the Academy of Music, in Philadelphia, and played a short season. Soon after this she married Dr. Brown, of Baltimore, who died in 1867. Mrs. Bowers made her debut in England, September, 1861, as Julia in "The Hunchback," in Sadler's

Wells Theatre, and made a wonderful impression. She soon succeeded Mrs. Charles Young at the Lyceum and was pronounced a decided acquisition to the London stage. She returned to this country August 17, 1863, and played at the Winter Garden, New York.

MARY GARDEN.

Was reared in Chicago, Illinois. Completed her musical education in Paris, making her debut there in 1891. Is now one of the great operatic stars of the present day. She is recognized by critics, universally, as second to no one on the operatic stage in the dramatic rendition of the parts she has taken.

CLARA MORRIS.

Was born March 17, 1850, in Cleveland, Ohio. Her mother was a native of Ohio, and her father, of Canada. Her father died when she was quite an infant, leaving the mother to support a family of young children. Clara undertook to support herself by caring for young children in families. Mr. Ellsler, the theatrical manager, engaged her to do miscellaneous child work about his theatre when but eleven years old. She soon attracted attention by her intensity in her work and gradually climbed the ladder from her first occupation to the rank of leading lady. In 1868-1869 she played a successful season in Cincinnati, and at its close went to New York City and accepted an offer of forty dollars a week from Augustin Daly, making her debut in that city as Anne Sylvester in "Man and Wife." She has appeared in many other of the more exacting emotional characters and in each and all she is a finished, powerful, perfect and impassioned actress. Her own sufferings, from an incurable spinal malady, have made her success all the more remarkable. In 1874 she became the wife of Frederick C. Harriott, but always retained her maiden name, "Clara Morris," on the stage. Among her most distinct successes were "Camille," "Miss Multon," "The New Magdalen," "L'Article 47" and "Renee."

MARGARET MARY ANGLIN.

Was born April 3, 1876, in Ottawa, Canada, and is the daughter of Honorable T. W. Anglin, formerly speaker of the Canadian House of Commons. She was educated at convents in Toronto and Montreal, and received her dramatic training from the Empire School of Dramatic Acting, in New York City, and in 1894 made her debut on the stage in "Shenandoah." She has played leading parts in the Shakespearean dramas, has acted with Sothern, Richard Mansfield, in "Cyrano de Bergerac," her latest effort was in "The Awakening of Helena Richie."

ELEANOR ELSIE ROBSON BELMONT..

Came to America when a child from England. She entered upon her professional career when but eighteen years of age, appearing as Marjory Knox in "Men and Women." Her greatest success has been Zangwill's plays, "Merely Mary Ann," and later she added to this by her performance in "The Dawn of a To-morrow." On February 12, 1910, she married August Belmont.

MAUDE FEALEY (MRS. LOUIS E. SHERWIN.)

Was born in Memphis, Tennessee, March 4, 1886. Her mother was on the stage for many years, and now conducts the Tabor School of Acting in Denver, Colorado. Augustin Daly discovered Miss Fealey. He made a five years' engagement with her. She played as leading lady with William Gillette for many years. While in England with this company, E. S. Willard made an engagement with her and she played in his company for some time. She has played with R. N. Johnson, but the most important engagement of her career was as leading lady with Sir Henry Irving, playing the rôles formerly taken by Ellen Terry. In 1907 Miss Fealey married Louis E. Sherwin, dramatic critic of the *Denver Republican.*

GRACE KIMBALL (MRS. M. D. McGUIRE.)

Was born in Detroit, February 18, 1870. Has played in one of Frohman's companies in the Lyceum Theatre, the Garden Theatre, Madison Square, and several of the leading New York companies. In 1897 she married M. D. McGuire, a prominent New Yorker and retired from the stage temporarily.

MABEL TALIAFERRO (MRS. FREDERICK W. THOMPSON.)

Was born in May, 1887, in New York City. Entered upon her stage career when a mere child. Has played in various well-known companies, and created the rôle of Lovey Mary in "Mrs. Wiggs of the Cabbage Patch." Miss Taliaferro married F. W. Thompson, a theatrical manager, in October, 1906, and has since starred in her own company.

CORINNE KIMBALL.

Miss Corinne Kimball was born in 1873 in Boston, Massachusetts. She was well known by her stage name of "Corinne." She was the daughter of Mrs. Jennie Kimball, who was herself an actress and theatrical manager. Her first appearance on the stage was at a baby show held in Horticultural Hall, in Boston. She met with success, and exhibiting marked talent she obtained an engagement in light opera, singing in the "Mascot," "Olivet," "The Chimes of Normandy" and "The Mikado.

JENNIE KIMBALL.

Mrs. Jennie Kimball was born in New Orleans, Louisiana, on the 23rd of June, 1851. She appeared first at the Boston Theatre in 1865. After the success made by her daughter Corinne in "Pinafore," Mrs. Kimball retired from the stage herself and became her manager. She was interested in several theatres. She was a woman of remarkable business ability. She personally superintended all of the work connected with the theatre and the companies in which she was interested; wrote her own advertising matter and superintended the work of the scenic artists, occupying a unique position among women.

SIBYL SANDERSON.

Was born in 1865 in Sacramento. She was the daughter of the late Judge S. W. Sanderson, Chief Justice of the Supreme Court of California. In 1884 she went to Europe to study and at different times renewed her musical studies under several of the great teachers. Massenet predicted a brilliant career for her. She made her debut February 6, 1888, in Amsterdam. She was selected by Massenet to create the rôle of Esclairmonde and sang that opera one hundred times the first year. In November, 1890, she made her debut in Massenet's "Mignon" in Brussels, appearing in London, England, in 1891. She ranked with the greatest singers, and was always a great favorite with the American public. She died in 1903.

MARY ANDERSON NAVARRO.

Madame Navarro is one of the most accomplished actresses and gifted women America has ever produced. She was born in Sacramento, California, July 28, 1859. Her maiden name was Mary Antoinette Anderson. Her parents were of foreign descent. She soon decided to make the stage her profession, and neither the discouragements of her parents or friends deterred her from her purpose. On witnessing the performance of Edwin Booth as "Richard the Third," she gave a repetition of this in her own home, which so impressed her parents that a private performance was given before her friends, and here she achieved her first success. She was a student at the Ursuline Convent, in Louisville, and was given private lessons in music, dancing and literature with a view of training her for her dramatic career. Charlotte Cushman advised her to study under Vanderhoff, in New York, and ten lessons from this dramatic teacher were·her only real training; the rest she accomplished for herself, which makes her the more notable. On the 27th of November, 1875, she made her first appearance as Juliet, in the Macaulay Theatre, Louisville, Kentucky. She won a most pronounced success.

After this she had no more difficulties to overcome. She was welcomed everywhere, and everyone was now willing to acknowledge her great talent and natural genius as an actress. Her dignity and high standard as a woman, gave her a most enviable social position, which she has held all through her life. In 1879 she made her first trip to Europe. In 1880 she received an offer to play at the Drury Lane Theatre, London, but declined it fearing she was not quite equal, as yet, to such heights of fame, also refusing an engagement at the London Lyceum, but in 1885 she accepted an offer at the Lyceum in "Parthenia." Her triumph was instantaneous. From this time on during her entire stage career she knew nothing but success until her name was placed at the head of American actresses of her day. In 1889 she was obliged to retire from the stage owing to a severe illness, and in 1890 withdrew permanently to the sincere regret of every American citizen. Soon afterward she married M. Antonio Navarro, a citizen of New York. They have lived, ever since their marriage, in England, where her social position is second to none.

ADA C. REHAN.

Miss Rehan is one of the most noted artists of her adopted country. All of her honors having been earned in the United States, Americans rank her among the distinguished artists of this country. Miss Rehan was born in Limerick, Ireland, April 22, 1859. Her name is Crehan and was accidentally misspelled in a telegram, when she adopted it as her stage name, and by it she will ever be known. Her parents came to the United States in 1864, and settled in Brooklyn, where Ada was a pupil of the common schools of that city until fourteen years of age. At this time a company was playing Byron's "Across the Continent" in Newark, New Jersey, and Ada was asked to take the place of one of the members of the company who was ill. This was the beginning of her professional career, as her family decided after this performance to have her study for the stage. In 1874 she played in "Thoroughbred" in New York, hardly winning notice. She then played in support of Edwin Booth, Adelaide Neilson, John McCullough, Mrs. D. P. Powers, John T. Raymond and Lawrence Barrett, playing Ophelia, Desdemona, Celia, Olivia and other Shakespearean rôles. In 1878 while she was playing in "Katherine and Petruchio," in the city of Albany, New York, Augustin Daly met her and asked her to join his company, and in 1879 she made her first appearance in Daly's Theatre as Nellie Beers in "Love's Young Dream" and Lou Ten Eyck in "Divorce." She immediately took the position of leading lady, which she held until Daly's death. In 1888 the Daly Company went to England, where she achieved the most remarkable success on record, it is stated, in London. She ranks as one of the most intelligent and talented comedians of the age. Her best work has been in the female Shakespearian rôles.

ALICE NIELSEN.

Was born in Nashville, Tennessee. Daughter of Erasmus I. and Sarah A. Nielsen. Received her musical education in San Francisco where she sang later in one of the local theatres, her first appearance being at Oakland, California, as Yum Yum in "The Mikado." In 1896 she attracted the attention of the "Bostonians" then playing in San Francisco, and was engaged by them, taking the rôle of Annabel in "Robin Hood." Has sung nearly all the principal parts which this opera company gave: "Maid Marion," "The Serenade," "The Fortune Teller," and starred in "The Fortune Teller." Later she studied for grand opera in Rome, and has sung in several grand operas both in Europe, and this country, touring the United States in 1906-1907 with the Boston Opera Company.

ROSE MELVILLE SMOCK.

Was born in Terre Haute, Indiana, January 7, 1873. Daughter of Rev. Jacob and Caroline Puett Smock. Created the rôle of Sis Hopkins in 1893, and has starred in this character in her own company since 1899.

AGNES BOOTH.

Was born in Sydney, Australia, October 4, 1846. Daughter of Captain Land and Sara Rookes. Commenced her stage career as a dancer when but a small child. Her first husband was Harry Perry, an American actor who died in 1863. Her second was Junius Booth who died in 1883, and later she married John B. Shoeffel. She made her first appearance in New York in 1865, and soon thereafter became the leading lady in the company of Edwin Forrest.

GENEVIEVE WARD.

Was born March 27, 1833, in New York. She is the granddaughter of Gideon Lee. Genèvieve Ward was her stage name. Her maiden name was Lucia Geneviva Teresa. Her fine voice attracted the attention of Rossini who trained her in music. She had a most successful career as a singer, and having lost her voice through diphtheria she won equal success as an actress. In 1882 she started in a tour of the world. Later became manager of the Lyceum Theatre, London, and in 1888 she retired from the stage.

Lecturers.

NANCY H. ADSIT.

Mrs. Adsit was born in Palerma, New York, May 21, 1825. She was the first woman to enter the insurance field in this country, and, as far as is known, in the world. She was possessed of an unusual combination in a woman—great literary ability and excellent business sense. At the age of thirteen she assumed charge of her own affairs and her future education. Some of her early writings aroused great antagonism, and her identity was withheld by her editor and not until many years later did she acknowledge their authorship. On the death of her husband, Charles Davenport Adsit, of Buffalo, in 1873, Mrs. Adsit assumed entire charge of his business and general insurance agency. After a most successful career in this line, she sold the business and resumed her writing. She contributed to the London Art Journals, writing a most interesting series of articles for them on "The Black and White in Art" or "Etching and Engraving." This brought demands from her friends for lectures, or parlor talks, on art, and she began the course of classes for study. For many years she has delivered these lectures in the principal cities of the United States and her name is prominently connected with art education both in this country and abroad.

JANET ELIZABETH RICHARDS.

Is a lecturer on current topics. Born at Granville, Ohio; is the daughter of William and Helen Ralston Richards. Her mother was a cousin of Judge Salmon P. Chase. Was educated at the Convent of the Sacred Heart, Torresdale, Pennsylvania. Was a writer on the *Washington Post;* and in 1895, she organized classes on current topics to which she lectures every Monday morning in Washington, D. C., also has large classes in New York, Philadelphia, Richmond and other cities. She lectures also on travel and literature. Her class in Washington is composed of the wives of the officials and social leaders. She is an able, gifted woman who has taken a conspicuous part in the literary life and field of the Capital city, and in the patriotic societies, being a charter member of the Daughters of the American Revolution, one of the members of the Women's League, National Geographic Society, and Audubon Society. She was at The Hague during the Peace Conference in 1907. Contributor to the magazines, and an active member of the Christ Child Society.

EMILY MULKIN BISHOP.

Mrs. Bishop was born in Forestville, New York, November 3, 1858. After leaving school she taught, as many others have done, before starting on her professional career. In 1884 she became the wife of Coleman A. Bishop, editor of *Judge,* and later they went to Black Hills, South Dakota, to live. She was made superintendent of the public schools at Rapid City, South Dakota, the first woman to be so honored in that territory. She had made the study of Delsarte a specialty and became a lecturer on that subject and was invited to establish a Delsarte department in the Chautauqua assemblage of New York, which she has made a great success. Out of this has grown the demand for her to lecture on this subject before the public. She has published a book, "American Delsarte Culture"—and is to-day recognized as one of the noted editors and authors on this subject in the United States.

50

ELIZABETH SHELBY KINKEAD.

Was born in Fayette County, Kentucky. Daughter of Judge William B. and Elizabeth De La Fontaine Shelby Kinkead. Lecturer before the Chautauqua Assemblies, and on literature before the State College of Kentucky, and author of "The History of Kentucky."

MRS. E. H. STEVENS.

Mrs. E. H. Stevens was born in Louisiana. Her maiden name was Herbert. For some years she was librarian of the Agriculture Department, of Washington. She is the widow of a graduate of West Point. For many years she occupied the position of translator at the desk known as "Scientific Translations" in the Patent Office. During her occupancy of the different positions she has held under the government, she has frequently contributed to the press.

MINERVA PARKER NICHOLS.

Was born May 14, 1863, in Chicago, is a descendant of John Doane who landed in Plymouth, in 1630, and took an active part in the government of the colony. Seth A. Doane, the grandfather of Mrs. Nichols was an architect and went to Chicago when it was an outpost and trading settlement among the Indians. Her father, John W. Doane, died in Murfreesborough, Tennessee, during the Civil War, being a member of an Illinois Volunteer Regiment. Being obliged to support herself, she gave her time to the cultivation of her talent for architecture, which she had inherited from her grandfather. She studied modeling under John Boyle, and finally entered an architect's office as draftsman. Later she built the Woman's New Century Club, in Philadelphia. Besides her practical work in designing houses, she has delivered in the School of Design, in Philadelphia, a course of lectures on Historic Ornament and

Classic Architecture. Among some of her important commissions was one for the designing of the International Club House, known as the Queen Isabella Pavilion, at the World's Columbian Exposition, Chicago, in 1893. She was among the first women to enter the field of architecture and some of the homes in the suburbs of Philadelphia attest to her ability and talent in this line. In December, 1899, she married Rev. William J. Nichols, a Unitarian clergyman.

LOUISE BETHUNE.

Mrs. Bethune was born in Waterloo, New York, in 1856. Her mother's family came to Massachusetts in 1640. Her father's ancestors were Huguenot refugees. In 1874 Miss Blanchard graduated from the Buffalo High School, and her attention having been attracted to the study of architecture, she soon took this up seriously. She traveled and studied and taught for two years, before taking the architectural course in Cornell University. In 1876 the offer of a position as draftsman made her relinquish her intention of college study, as she found a most valuable library in her employer's office which was at her service. In 1881 she was able to open her own office and thus became the first woman architect in the United States. The partnership formed with Robert A. Bethune resulted in her marriage to him, and they have continued their work together, having erected many public buildings in Buffalo and other cities. She is a member of the Western Association of Architects, and is the only woman member of the American Institute of Architects. In 1886 she organized the Buffalo Society of Architects, out of which has grown the Western New York Association. She and her husband were very active in securing the passage of the Architects' Licensing Bill, which was intended to enforce a rigid preliminary examination and to place the profession on a higher plane. Since Mrs. Bethune entered this profession as its woman pioneer, there have been several others who have taken it up and gained distinction.

LOUISA DOW BENTON.

Mrs. Benton was born in Portland, Maine, March 23, 1831, and is the daughter of Neal Dow, and Cornelia Durant Maynard. On December 12, 1860, she married Jacob Benton, of Lancaster, New Hampshire, who was later a member of Congress, and they spent four years of their life in Washington, D. C. She became a confirmed invalid from rheumatism, being unable to walk, and lost almost the entire use of her hands, but possessed such fortitiude and courage that even this did not prevent her from study, and she learned to read Italian, Spanish, German, Greek, and Russian without any instruction. Then she took up Volapük, and is well-known as a Volapük scholar. Has carried on correspondence with several linguists in Europe and associations for the spreading of this language.

FRANCES BENJAMIN JOHNSTON.

Miss Johnston has made a reputation for herself in photography and photographic illustrations, particularly of public places and men and women prominent in official and social life of Washington; has done work for the railroads in illustrating folders of scenery in the West and Northwest. Born at Grafton, West Virginia, January 15, 1864; daughter of Anderson D. and Frances Benjamin Johnston; studied in Paris at the Julien Academy; also charter member of the Washington, D. C. Art Students' League; exhibited at the Chicago World's Fair, Paris Exposition, Pan-American Exposition, St. Louis Exposition; received gold medal at the Paris Exposition in 1900; was decorated by the French Academy in 1904; is a member of the Photo Club of Paris, New York Camera Club and the Washington Camera Club.

Playwrights.

At the organization of the Women's Playwright Club, of New York City, there were forty women eligible for admission. This vocation for women is especially an American institution. In no other country are there so many who have obtained recognition in a field where the compensation is the same for women as for men. The New Theatre when opened made its bow to the public with a play from the pen of an American woman.

Mary Hunter Austin, the newest woman dramatist, has spent the greater part of her life in the West, and many of her plays deal with the border life.

Margaret Mayo is another successful playwright, who was the author of "Baby Mine" and "Polly of the Circus," two of the biggest New York successes. In private life Miss Mayo is the wife of Edgar Selwyn, a successful writer and playwright of distinction. He is the author of "The Country Boy."

Kate Douglas Wiggin, whose writings we are all familiar with, dramatized her "Rebecca of Sunnybrook Farm."

Charlotte Thompson made a most successful dramatization of "The Awakening of Helena Richie," in which Margaret Anglin starred.

Another successful playwright is the author of "The Nest Egg"—Anne Caldwell, who has been an actress, opera singer, musician, composer, magazine and newspaper writer.

The music of "The Top of the World" is her composition. position.

Another talented writer of plays is Rida Johnson Young, who in five years has successfully produced "Brown of Harvard," "The Boys of Company B," "Glorious Betsey," "The Lottery Man," as well as two plays for Chauncey Olcott. One of the New York successes, "Naughty Marietta," was written by her, Victor Herbert writing the music. Mrs. Young is the wife of Mr. James Young, leading man, who has appeared with E. H. Sothern. He was formerly a newspaper man on the staff of a daily newspaper of Baltimore, Md. Mrs. Young before her marriage was Rida Johnson.

Lottie Blair Parker is another successful professional woman, whose husband, Harry Doel Parker, attends entirely to the production and the leasing of her plays. "Way Down East," written in 1897, is still being played throughout the country. "Under Southern Skies" is another one from her pen. Among others by this same author are "A War Correspondent," "The Lights of Home," a dramatization of "The Redemption of David Corson," a number of one-act plays, and a novel entitled "Homespun."

Miss Alice Ives, the author of "The Village Postmaster," has done every phase of literary work, art criticisms, music notes, deep articles for the *Forum* and similar magazines, as well as some light verse. She has written ten plays. "The Village Postmaster" was on the road for ten successive seasons. Miss Ives wrote a clever one-act play, a satire on women's clubs, introducing all the famous women characters of popular plays. She is the first vice-president of the Society of Women Dramatists, to which all these playwrights belong.

The pioneer playwright of her sex is Miss Martha Morton. Some dozen years ago, the *New York World* offered prizes for the cleverest scenarios to be submitted under assumed names. It was a general surprise when a woman secured one of the prizes. This successful person was Miss Morton. Some of the most distinguished American actors have appeared in her plays, the best known of which are, "Brother John," "His Wife's Father," and "A Bachelor's Romance." Miss Morton was the first vice-president of the Society of Dramatic Authors. Off the stage she is Mrs. Herman Conheim, and is one of the most popular dramatists in New York City.

Another successful prize winner, who ultimately made this her profession, was Mrs. Martha Fletcher Bellinger, a graduate of Mount Holyoke. The title of her scenario was "A Woman's Sphere."

Mrs. Mary Rider Mechtold, also a college woman and successful winner of newspaper prizes, wrote her first plays when she was still a student at the Chicago University. She is the author of a clever play, "The Little Lady."

The thousand-dollar prize offered by the Shakespeare Memorial Theatre in England a year or two ago was won by an American woman, Josephine Preston Peabody. The contest for the best play in English verse dealing with a romantic subject was won by a graduate of Radcliffe. It is said that this college has long been famous for its unusually clever plays, in which its students take part.

Beulah Dix is also a graduate of Radcliffe. She was author of "Hugh Gwyeth." She collaborated with Evelyn Greenleaf in a number of successful plays, "The Rose o' Plymouth Town," and "The Road to Yesterday."

Another Radcliffe graduate, who has become a successful playwright, is Agnes Morgan, who wrote "When Two Write History."

Another is Rebecca Lane Hooper. Miss Hooper not only stages these performances herself, but has often played comedy roles.

The exception to the rule of directors for theatrical performances, which are usually men, is Miss Edith Ellis, author of "Mary Jane's Pa," one of the most successful plays produced. She began her career as a child actress. She is one of the few successful stage managers, and has frequently strengthened lines in places and made a possible success from what seemed an inevitable failure.

Rachel Crothers is another who supervises much of the rehearsing of her own plays. She began her authorship of plays while a teacher in the Wheatcroft School of Acting. Among her plays are "The Coming of Mrs. Patrick," "Myself Bettina," and "The Inferior Sex," which were written for Maxine Elliott. "The Man on the Box" was dramatized by Grace Livingston Furniss, who with the late Abby Sage Richardson dramatized "The Pride of Jennico." Since then she has written a number of other plays, including, "Mrs. Jack," "The Colonial Girl," and "Gretna Green."

Frances Hodgson Burnett writes her books and then dramatizes them. This she has done most successfully in the case of "Little Lord Fauntleroy," "The Little Princess," "A Lady of Quality," "That Lass o' Lowries," "The Pretty Sister of José," and "The Dawn of a To-morrow."

Harriet Ford has successfully dramatized many books, among them: "The Gentleman of France," "Audrey," and with Mr. Joseph Medill Patterson, she wrote the most successful play of last season (1910-1911), "The Fourth Estate." This play brought forth more favorable comment and discussion from the press than any other produced.

Miss Mary Roberts Rinehart has written three plays, two of which were in co-authorship, "Double Life," "The Avenger," and "Seven Days." Her husband, Dr. Stanley Rinehart, contributed to "The Avenger," and Avery Hapgood to "Seven Days." This was one of the season's successes.

Two successful playwrights, Pauline Phelps and Marion Short, have formed a partnership and turned out a number of most successful plays. Miss Phelps, a country girl, deals with life in the country, and Miss Short, with city life and its problems. Their greatest success is "The Grand Army Man," in which David Warfield starred last season. They are also the authors of "The Girl from Out Yonder," "At Cozy Corners," "Sweet Clover," the latter used largely for stock companies.

Anne Warner's "Rejuvenation of Aunt Mary" is familiar to everyone.

Frances Aymar Matthews, as well as being a successful dramatist, is a writer of poetry and books. One of her plays, "Julie Bon Bon," was starred by Clara Lipman.

Among others that may be mentioned are: Cora Maynard, Kate Jordan, and Mrs. Doremus.

MARY W. CALKINS.

Miss Calkins is head of the Department of Philosophy and Psychology at Wellesley College. She was born in Hartford, Connecticut, in 1863, and is the daughter of Wolcott and Charlotte Grosvenor Whiton Calkins. Miss Calkins is a graduate of Smith College of the Class of 1885, where she received the degrees of A.B. and A.M. She has written several books on psychology and numerous monographs and papers on psychological and philosophical questions.

VIDA D. SCUDDER.

Miss Scudder is to-day professor of English at Wellesley College and a well-known writer on literary and social topics. She was born in Southern India, December 15, 1861, and is the daughter of David Coit and Harriet L. Dutton Scudder. She received the degree of A.B. at Smith College in 1884 and that of A.M. in 1889, graduated at Oxford and Paris, and was the originator of the College Settlement in New York City. She is the author of "The Life of the Spirit in Modern English Poets," "Social Ideals in English Letters," "Introduction to the Study of English Literature" and "Selected Letters of Saint Catherine," and was the editor of Macaulay's "Lord Clive," and also of the introduction to the writings of John Ruskin, Shelly's "Prometheus Unbound," works of John Woolman and Everybody's Library.

HANNAH ADAMS.

Miss Adams is believed to be the first woman in the United States to make literature a profession. She was born in Medfield, Massachusetts, in 1755, and died in Brookline, Mass., November 15, 1832. She was the daughter of a well-to-do farmer, of good education and culture. In her childhood she was very fond of writing and a close student, memorizing the works of Milton, Pope, Thomson, Young and others. She was a good Latin and Greek scholar and instructed divinity students who made their home in her family. In 1772, her father losing his property, the children were forced to provide for themselves. During the Revolutionary War, Miss Adams had taught school and after the close of the war she opened a school to prepare young men for college, which was very successful. She wrote quite extensively. One of her books, "A View of Religious Opinions" appeared in 1784, and passed through several editions in the United States and was also published in England and became a standard work. In 1799 she published her second work, "A History of England," and in 1801 "Evidences of Christianity." In 1812, her "History of the Jews" appeared, being followed by "A Controversy with Dr. Morse," and in 1826 "Letters on the Gospels." She spent a quiet, secluded life, and it is said her only journeys were trips from Boston to Nahant and from Boston to Chelmsford. Notwithstanding the many books which she published, her business abilities seemed to have been very limited and in the last years of her life she was supported by an annuity settled upon her by three wealthy residents of Boston. She was buried at Mount Auburn, being the first person buried in that beautiful cemetery.

LYDIA MARIA CHILD.

Lydia Maria Francis was born in Medford, Massachusetts, February 11, 1802. Her ancestor, Richard Francis, came from England in 1636 and settled in Cambridge, where his tombstone may be still seen in the burial ground. Her paternal grandfather, a weaver by trade, was in the Concord fight. Her father, Convers Francis, was a baker, first in West Cambridge, then in Medford, where he first introduced the article of food still known as "Medford crackers." He was a man of strong character and great industry. Though without much cultivation he had an uncommon love of reading and his anti-slavery convictions were deeply rooted and must have influenced his child's later career. He married Susanah Rand, of whom it is only recorded that "She had a simple, loving heart and a spirit busy in doing good." They had six children of whom Lydia Maria was the youngest. While her brother Convers was fitting for college she was his faithful companion, though more than six years younger. They read together and she was constantly bringing him Milton and Shakespeare to explain so that it may well be granted that the foundation of Miss Lydia's intellectual attainments was laid in this companionship. Apart from her brother's help the young girl had, as was then usual, a very subordinate share of educational opportunities, attending only the public schools with one year at the private seminary of Miss Swan, in Medford. In 1819 Convers Francis was ordained for the first parish, in Watertown, and there occurred in his city, in 1824, an incident which was to determine the whole life of his sister. Doctor G. G. Palfrey had written in the *North American Review*, for April, 1821, a "Review" of the now forgotten poem of "Yamoyden," in which he ably pointed out the use that might be made of early American History for the purpose of fictitious writing. Miss Francis read this article at her brother's house one summer Sunday morning. Before attending afternoon service she wrote the first chapter of a novel. It was soon finished and was published that year, then came "Hobomak," a tale of early times.

In juding of this little book it is to be remembered that it marked the very dawn of American imaginative literature. Irving had printed only his "Sketchbook"; Cooper only "Precaution." This new production was the hurried work of a young woman of nineteen, an Indian tale by one who had scarcely even seen an Indian. Accordingly "Hobomak" now seems very crude in execution, very improbable in plot and is redeemed only by a sincere attempt at local coloring.

The success of this first effort was, however, such as to encourage the publication of a second tale in the following year. This was "The Rebels; The Boston before the Revolution, by the Author of Hobomak." It was a great advance on its predecessor, and can even be compared, favorably, with Cooper's Revolutionary novels.

In October, 1828, Miss Francis married David Lee Child, a lawyer of Boston. In that day it seemed to be held necessary for American women to work their passage into literature by first completing some kind of cookery book, so Mrs. Child published in 1829 her "Frugal Housewife," a book which proved so popular that in 1855 it had reached its thirty-third edition.

The "Biographies of Good Wives" reached a fifth edition in the course of time as did her "History of Woman," and in 1833 Mrs. Child was brought to one of those bold steps which made successive eras of her literary life—the publication of her "Appeal for that Class of Americans called Africans." It was just at the most dangerous moment of the rising storm of the slavery question that Mrs. Child wrote this and it brought down upon her unending censure. It is evident that this result was not unexpected for the preface to the book explicitly recognizes the probable dissatisfaction of the public. She says, "I am fully aware of the unpopularity of the task I have undertaken; but though I expect ridicule and censure, I cannot fear them. Should it be the means of advancing, even one single hour, the inevitable progress of truth and justice, I would not exchange the consciousness for all Rothschild's wealth or Sir Walter's fame." These words have in them a genuine ring; and the book is really worthy of them. The tone is calm and strong, the treatment systematic, the points well put, the statements well guarded.

It was the first anti-slavery work ever printed in America and it appears to be the ablest, covering the whole ground better than any other. During the next year she published the "Oasis," also about this time appeared from her hand the "Anti-slavery Catechism" and a small book called "Authentic Anecdotes of American Slavery."

While seemingly absorbed in reformatory work she still kept an outlook in the direction of pure literature and was employed for several years on "Philothea," which appeared in 1836. The scene of this novel was laid in Greece, and in spite of the unpopularity that Mrs. Child's slavery appeal had created it went through three editions.

In 1841 Mr. and Mrs. Child were engaged by the *American Anti-Slavery Standard,* a weekly newspaper published in New York. Mr. Child's health being impaired his wife undertook the task alone and conducted the newspaper in that manner for two years, after which she aided her husband in the work, remaining there for eight years. She was a very successful editor. Her management proved efficient while her cultivated taste made the *Standard* pleasing to many who were not attracted by the plainer fare of the *Liberator*. During all this period she was a member of the family of the well-known Quaker philanthropist, Isaac T. Hopper, whose biographer she afterwards became. This must have been the most important and satisfactory time in Mrs. Child's whole life. She was placed where her sympathetic nature found abundant outlet and earnest co-operation. Here she also found an opportunity for her best eloquence in writing letters to the *Distant Courier*. This was the source of "Letters from New York," that afterwards became famous. They were the precursors of that modern school of newspaper correspondence in which women now have so large a share, and which has something of the charm of women's private letters.

Her last publication, and perhaps her favorite among the whole series, appeared in 1867—"A Romance of the Republic." It was received with great cordiality and is in some respects her best fictitious work. In later life Mrs. Child left New York and took up her abode in Wayland, Massachusetts. She outlived her husband six years and died October 20, 1880.

ALMIRA LINCOLN PHELPS.

There were but two among all the early distinguished literary women of America who had the honor of being members of the American Association for the advancement of science, and these two women were Maria Mitchell and Almira Lincoln Phelps,—one from the North and one from the South. Mrs. Phelp's father, Samuel Harte, was a descendant of Thomas Hooker, the first minister of Hartford and founder of Connecticut. She was the youngest child and was born in Berlin, Connecticut, in 1793, educated at Pittsfield, Massachusetts, and later married to Simeon Lincoln, editor of the *Connecticut Mirror*, in Hartford. She was early left a widow with two children. Finding the estates of both her husband and father insolvent, she took up the study of Latin and Greek, the natural sciences, art of drawing and painting, in order to perfect herself for the work which she had in comtemplation, namely, the education of the young. She was a student under Miss Willard for seven years. In 1831, she married Honorable John Phelps, a distinguished lawyer and statesman of Vermont. In 1839 she accepted a position at the head of the female seminary at West Chester, Pennsylvania. In 1841 she and her husband established the Patapsco Female Institute of Maryland. Pupils came to them from all parts of the West and South. In 1849 she was again left a widow. In 1855 her daughter's death so saddened her that she resigned her position and removed to the city of Baltimore. Her best known works are: "Lectures on Botany," "Botany for Beginners," "Lectures on Chemistry," "Chemistry for Beginners," "Lectures on Natural Philosophy," "Philosophy for Beginners," "Female Students," "A Fireside Friend," "A Juvenile Story," "Geology for Beginners," "Translation of the Works of Benedicte de Saussure," "Progressive Education," with a mothers' journal by

Mrs. Willard and Mrs. Phelps, "Ada Norman, or Trials and Their Uses," "Hours with My Pupils," and "Christian Households." She probably had as much to do with the education of the young of this country as any woman, her works having been largely used in the schools.

SARAH BUELL (MRS. DAVID HALE).

Author and magazine editor, was born in Newport, New Hampshire. When a young girl, the first regular novel she read was "Mysteries of Udolpho," which, noting it was written by a woman, awakened in her an ardent desire to become an author herself. Her first work, however, was a small volume of fugitive poetry; then "Northward," in two volumes. Her first novel was issued in 1827. Afterwards she was given charge of the editorial department of the *Lady's Magazine*, then published in Boston. In 1837 the *Lady's Magazine* united with the *Lady's Book*, published by Godey, in Philadelphia, and in 1841 Mrs. Hill removed to that city editing the double magazine. She has written a large number of books. The most notable of these are "Sketches of American Character," "Traits of American Life," "Flora's Interpreter," "The Lady's Wreath," a selection from the familiar poets of England and America; "The Way to Live Well and be Well While You Live," "Grosvenor," "Alice Ray," a romance in rhyme; "Harry Guy," "The Widow's Son," a story of the sea; "Three Hours or Vigils of Love," and other poems, and, finally, "Woman's Regret."

LYDIA HUNTLY SIGOURNEY.

Born in Norwich, Connecticut, September 1, 1791, and died in Hartford, Connecticut, June 10, 1865; was the daughter of Ezekiel Huntly, a soldier of the Revolution. It is said that she wrote verses at the age of seven. She taught a private girls' school in Hartford for five years, and in 1815 published her first volume "Moral Pieces in Prose and Verse." In 1819 she became the wife of Charles Sigourney, a gentleman of literary and artistic tastes, a resident of Hartford. After her marriage she devoted herself to literature. She wrote forty-six separate works, besides two thousand articles, which she contributed to about three hundred periodicals. She was a favorite poetess in England and France, as well as in her own country. Mrs. Sigourney was always an active worker in charity and philanthropy. Her best known works are "Letters to Young Ladies," "Pocahontas, and Other Poems," and "Pleasant Memories of Pleasant Lands."

LUCRETIA MARIA DAVIDSON.

Lucretia Maria Davidson was born in Plattsburg, New York, September 27, 1808, and was the daughter of Dr. Oliver Davidson, a lover of science. Her mother, Margaret Davidson, whose maiden name was Miller, came of a good family and had received the best education that times afforded at the school of the celebrated Scotch lady, Isabella Graham, in New York City. The family of Miss Davidson lived in seclusion. Their pleasures were intellectual. Her mother suffered for years from ill health. Miss Davidson was delicate from infancy. When eighteen months old, she suffered from typhus fever which threatened her life. Her first literary acquisition indicated her after course. Her application to her studies at school was intense. Her early poems were of great merit. While devoting her time and attention to her invalid mother, she wrote many beautiful poems, the best known of which is her "Amir Khan" and a tale of some length called "The Recluse of Saranac." "Amir Khan" has long been before the public. Its versification is graceful and the story of orientalism beautifully developed and well sustained; as a production of a girl of fifteen it is considered prodigious. Many of her poems are addressed to her mother. "The Fear of Madness" was written by her while confined to her bed and was the last piece she ever wrote. The records of the last scenes of Lucretia Davidson's life are scanty. Her poetical writings which have been collected amount in all to 278 pieces of various length. The following tribute paid her by Mr. Southey is from the London *Quarterly Review,* whose scant praise of American productions is well known. "In these poems ("Amir Khan," etc.) there is enough of originality, enough of aspiration, enough of conscientious energy, enough of growing power to warrant any expectations, however sanguine, which the patron and the friends and parents of the deceased could have formed." Her death occurred August 27, 1825, in Plattsburg, New York.

JULIA WARD HOWE.

Few women of America enjoy greater fame than Julia Ward Howe, the author of the "Battle Hymn of the Republic." She can be classed as an essayist, poetess, philanthropist, and public speaker. She was born in New York City, May 27, 1819. Her parents were Samuel and Julia Cuttler Ward. She included among her ancestors some of the descendants of the Huguenots, the Marions of South Carolina, Governor Sam Ward of Rhode Island, and Roger Williams, the apostle of religious tolerance. Her father being a banker and a man of means gave her every advantage of education and accomplishment. In 1843 she married Dr. Samuel Gridley Howe, and they spent some time abroad. In 1852 she published her first volume of poems; in 1853 a drama in blank verse, and during the war other works and patriotic songs. In 1867 while she and her husband were visitors in Greece they won the affection and gratitude of the people by aiding them in their struggle for national independence. In 1868 she took an active part in the suffrage movement. She preached, wrote and lectured for many years. She died in the summer of 1910, but her fame will ever be linked with the "Battle Hymn of the Republic."

LOUISA M. ALCOTT.

No name is more beloved among the girls of America of former days and present ti........ ....n that of Louisa May Alcott, the author of "Little Women," a .... heart of every American girl. Miss Alcott was born in Ger-........lvania, November 29, 1832. Her parents were charming, culti-........r father, Amos Bronson Alcott, became a teacher. He taught in

Boston for eleven years, Margaret Fuller being one of his assistants. The atmosphere of the Alcott home was always one of culture and refinement, though their life was one of extreme simplicity. Whittier, Phillips, Garrison, Mrs. Hawthorne, Emerson, Thoreau and Oliver Wendell Holmes were frequent guests. Louisa was the eldest child, full of activity and enthusiasm, constantly in trouble from her frankness and lack of policy, but enjoying many friends from her generous heart, and it has not been difficult to recognize the picture of herself in the character of Joe in "Little Women." In this little home in Concord were enacted many of the scenes, sports and amusements pictured in Miss Alcott's stories. At sixteen she began to teach school, having but twenty pupils, and to these she told many of the stories which were later woven into her books. Her restless disposition gave her many occupations; sometimes she acted as a governess, sometimes she did sewing, and again writing. At nineteen she published one of her early stories in *Gleason's Pictorial*. For this she received five dollars. Later appeared "The Rival Prima Donna," and though she received but ten dollars for this, the request from the editor for another story was more to her than a larger check would have been. Another story appeared in the *Saturday Evening Gazette*. This was announced in the most sensational way by means of large yellow posters which spread terror to Miss Alcott's heart. Finding, however, that sensational stories paid, she turned them out at the rate of ten or twelve a month. But she soon tired of this unstable kind of fame, and she began work upon a novel which appeared under the name of "Moods" but was not a success. At this time the Civil War broke out. She offered herself as a nurse in the hospitals and was accepted, just after the defeat at Fredericksburg. After a time she became ill from overwork and was obliged to return home, and in 1865 published her hospital sketches, which made it possible for her to take a rest by a trip to Europe. Here she met many of the distinguished writers of her day. In 1868 her father submitted a collection of her stories to her publishers who declined them, and asked for a single story for girls, which was the occasion for the writing of "Little Women." It was simply the story of herself and her three sisters and she became at once famous. Girls from all over the country wrote her. When "Little Men" was announced, fifty thousand copies were ordered in advance of its publication. Among her other stories are those entitled, "Shawl Straps," "Under the Lilacs," "Aunt Jo's Scrap-Bag," "Jack and Jill," and the greatest after "Little Women," "An Old-Fashioned Girl." Most of her stories were written in Boston and depict her life in Concord. Miss Alcott's devotion to her sex made her a strong supporter of the women's suffrage movement, no one has done more for the women of her own generation than she. The pleasure which her books have given, and will ever continue to give, make her one of the most beloved of our American literary women. Miss Alcott died in Boston, March 6, 1888.

MARY VIRGINIA TERHUNE.

Mrs. Terhune is more familiar to the public under the pen name of "Marion Harland." She was born December 21, 1831, in Amelia County, Virginia, her father Samuel P. Hawes, having removed there from Massachusetts. In 1856 she was married to Rev. E. P. Terhune, and since 1859 has lived in the North, but her stories have dealt largely with Southern life. She wrote her book "The Story of Mary Washington" to get funds to aid in the effort to erect a monument to the mother of Washington, which was unveiled on May 10, 1894. She has been a most industrious writer. Among her works are "Alone," "Nemesis," "The Hidden Path," "Miriam," "Husks," "Husbands and Home," "Sunnybank," "Helen Gardner's Wedding Day," "At Last," "The Empty Heart," "Common Sense in the Household." Her novel "Sunnybank" was very severely criticised by Southern editors, when it appeared soon after the Civil War. Mrs. Terhune's younger brothers were in the Confederate Army.

Mrs. Terhune has three children, with all of whom she has collaborated ii literary work.

ELIZABETH STUART PHELPS WARD.

Mrs. Ward was born in Andover, Massachusetts, August 31, 1844, and inherited literary talent from both of her parents. Her mother was the writer of a number of stories for children, and her father, Rev. Austin Phelps, a professor of sacred rhetoric in the Theological Seminary of Andover, was the writer of many lectures which in book form have become classics and to-day are accepted text-books. At the age of thirteen Mrs. Ward made her first literary venture in a story which was accepted by the *Youths' Companion*. Her first novel, "Gates Ajar," 1869, met with unprecedented success. In 1888, she married Rev. Herbert D. Ward, and with him has written several novels, the most important of which are, "The Last of the Magicans," "Come Forth," "A Singular Life," and what she regards as her most important work, "The Story of Jesus Christ," which appeared in 1897. Some of Mrs. Ward's books are, "Ellen's Idol," "Up Hill," "A Singular Life," "The Gipsy Series," "Mercy Glidden's Works," "I Don't Know How," "Men, Women and Ghosts," "The Silent Partner," "Walled In," "The Story of Avis," "My Cousin and I," "The Madonna of the Tubs," "Sealed Waters," "Jack, the Fisherman," "The Master of Magicians," and many sketches, stories and poems for magazines.

FRANCES HODGSON BURNETT.

Was born in Manchester, England, November 24, 1849. Her father was a well-to-do merchant. He died when she was but ten years old. Soon after his death the family removed to Tennessee to reside with an uncle. They settled in Knoxville, but her uncle having lost everything by the war, they made their home in the country and experienced the greatest poverty. Her mother's health failed under these trying conditions, and she died about two years after. Frances Hodgson obtained a position as school teacher, receiving her pay in flour, bacon, eggs and potatoes. She had early shown much talent in story writing, and at thirteen she wrote quite a creditable story, which her sister insisted on sending to a publisher. The only difficulty in the way of accomplishing this was how to procure the necessary postage, and a basket of wild grapes was sold by these

DISTINGUISHED WOMEN POETS.

two girls to pay for the mailing of the manuscript to *Ballou's Magazine.* As the publisher did not wish to pay for the printing of the story, which he had complimented in his letter to Frances, it was returned and sent to *Godey's Ladies' Book,* and from this source she received her first remuneration. Later she became a regular contributor to *Peterson's Magazine* and the publication of "Mrs. Carruther's Engagement" and another story entitled "Hearts and Diamonds" fixed the author's vocation. In 1873, she married Swan Moses Burnett. They had two children, the heroes of "Little Lord Fauntleroy," Mrs. Burnett's most famous story. The one named Lionel died in Paris, Vivian was the little Lord Fauntleroy of her story. "That Lass o' Lowrie's," "Pretty Polly Pemberton," "The Fair at Grantley Mills," "A Fair Barbarian" and "A Lady of Quality," are some of Mrs. Burnett's novels. Among her plays are: "Little Lord Fauntleroy," "The First Gentleman of Europe" and "A Lady of Quality." Her work has brought to Mrs. Burnett quite a handsome fortune. She now makes her home in England.

SARAH ORNE JEWETT.

Was born in South Berwick, Maine, on September 3, 1849. Her father was Dr. Theodore Herman Jewett, a physician, and her mother was the daughter of Dr. Perry of Exeter, also a prominent physician of that section of New England. Most of the characters and life of the people in her story have been taken from the simple New England life about the little village of Berwick. She frequently went about with her father on his errands of mercy and through these was enabled to gain much data for her stories. Her father was the hero of "A Country Doctor" from her pen. She first wrote short stories for the *Atlantic Monthly,* and it is said was but fourteen years of age when she wrote "Lucy Garron's Lovers." Her first great success was "Deephaven" which appeared in 1877. Lowell and Whittier were among her friends and admirers as a writer. Whittier attended the Friends' meeting in Berwick, and it was here Miss Jewett met him. The old sea-faring life of these New England towns has been preserved to us by Miss Jewett. Her grandfather was a sea captain, and in his home she met and enjoyed the companionship and heard the tales of this old sea captain's friends. Miss Jewett died in 1909.

MRS. BURTON HARRISON.

Was before her marriage Constance Cary, of Virginia, and on her father's side she is descended from Colonel Miles Carey of Devonshire, England, who emigrated to America and settled in Virginia about the middle of the seventeenth century, and during the rule of Sir William Berkeley was one of the king's council. Her father, Archibald Cary, of Cary's Brook, Virginia, was the son of Virginia Randolph, who was the ward and pupil of Thomas Jefferson and sister of his son-in-law, Thomas Mann Randolph. Her mother was the youngest daughter of Thomas Fairfax, Baron of Cameron, who resided upon a large plantation in Fairfax, Virginia. It is said Mrs. Harrison inherits her

51

literary taste from her grandmother on her father's side, Mrs. Wilson Jefferson Cary, who was herself a writer, and whose father's writings exerted quite an influence over Thomas Jefferson. Mrs. Harrison's first story was written when she was but seventeen years of age. The Civil War brought an end to her literary aspirations and the loss of her home necessitated her mother and herself living abroad for some years. After her return to this country she married Burton Harrison, a prominent member of the New York Bar. Charles A. Dana was a great friend of Mrs. Harrison and gave her the agreeable task of editing "Monticello Letters," and from this she gleaned the matter which was the basis of her story, "The Old Dominion." Some of the stories that she has written are: "Helen of Troy," "The Old-Fashioned Fairy Book," "Short Comedies for American Players," a translation; "The Anglomaniacs," "Flower-de-Hundred," "Sweet Bells Out of Tune," "A Bachelor Maid," "An Errant Wooing," "A Princess of the Hills," "A Daughter of the South." Mrs. Harrison resides in New York, and is still busy with her pen.

MARY N. MURFREE.

"Charles Egbert Craddock."

For several years of her early literary life both publishers and public were in ignorance of the fact that she was a woman. She was born at Grantsland, near Murfreesborough, Tennessee, in 1850, at the family home, which had been inherited from her great-grandfather, Colonel Hardy Murfree, a soldier of the Revolution, who, in 1807, had moved from his native state of North Carolina to the new state of Tennessee. Miss Murfree's father, William Law Murfree, was a lawyer, and her mother, Priscilla Murfree, was the daughter of Judge Dickinson. The family suffered greatly from the effects of the war. Mary Murfree had poor health but began to write of the people she found about her in the Tennessee mountains, and her novel, "In the Tennessee Mountains" appeared in the *Atlantic Monthly* and was supposed to have been written by a man. When Mr. Howells assumed the editorial chair in the *Atlantic Monthly* office he requested further contributions from Charles Egbert Craddock, and a series of excellent stories from her pen were published: "Where the Battle was Fought," "The Prophet of the Great Stony Mountain," "The Star in the Valley," "The Romance of Sunrise Rock," "Over on Tother Mounting," "Electioneering on Big Injun Mounting," "A-Playing of Old Sledge at Settlement," "Adrifting down Lost Creek," which ran through three numbers of the *Atlantic*, "Down the Ravine," a story for young people. It was possible for Miss Murfree to cover her identity in her *nom de plume*, for her style of writing and even her penmanship were masculine and she appreciated the fact that, at that time, men in the literary world had a great advantage over women writers. No one was more surprised than her own publishers at the discovery that Charles Egbert Craddock was a woman. Her great skill lies in vitalizing the picturesque characters who are the subjects of her stories.

ANNA KATHARINE GREEN ROHLFS.

Was born in Brooklyn, New York, on November 11, 1846, and was thirty-two years of age when her famous story, "The Leavenworth Case" was published. Her father was a famous lawyer, and from him she is supposed to have gained the knowledge which she had in handling the details of this story. It was questioned for some time, although her maiden name, Anna Katharine Green, was signed to the story, whether it was possible that this story could have been written by a woman. She was a graduate of the Ripley Female College in Poultney, Vermont, and received the degree of B.A. In her early days she wrote poems, but her fame has come from her detective stories. "The Affair Next Door," "The Filigree Ball," and other stories from her pen are well known. In November, 1884, she became Mrs. Charles Rohlfs.

MOLLY ELLIOT SEAWELL.

Miss Seawell's uncle was an officer in the United States navy before the Civil War, and served in the Confederate Army with distinction during the entire war. From him she heard the tales of our early navy which gave her inspiration to write her nautical sketches. Some of these are "Decatur and Somers," "Paul Jones," "Midshipman Paulding," "Quarter-deck," "Fo'c'sle," and "Little Jarvis," the latter winning the prize of five hundred dollars for the best story for boys offered by the *Youths' Companion*, in 1890. She was a constant reader of Shakespeare, Rousseau and other writers. Byron, Shelley, Thackeray, Macaulay, Jane Austen, Boswell's "Johnson" all formed a part of her home education. In 1895, she received a prize of $3,000 from the *New York Herald* for the best novelette, "The Sprightly Romance of Marsac." Her "Maid Marian" is a well-known and an amusing story of the Knickerbocker element of New York.

AMELIA E. BARR.

Among the foremost of American writers is Amelia Barr. She was born in Ulverston, Lancashire, England, in 1831. Her maiden name was Amelia Edith Huddleston. Her father was the Reverend Doctor William Henry Huddleston, and her first introduction into the literary field was when she served as a reader to her father. She was educated in Glasgow and in 1850 married Robert Barr, a Scotchman, and four years later they came to this country. They made their residence in several states, in New York, the South and West, finally settling in Austin, Texas. In 1867, the yellow fever was epidemic in Austin. Mr. Barr became famous through his work among the Indians and white settlers of this city. Doctors and nurses dying on all sides, he gave up his life in his unselfish devotion to poor suffering humanity. Mrs. Barr lost not only her husband but three sons in this terrible epidemic, and after it was over she returned to New York City. Her first literary venture was brought out through the kind personal interest of the editor of the *New York Ledger*, Mr. Robert Bonner, and was a story published in the *Christian Union*. She did all kinds of literary work, wrote advertisements, circulars, paragraphs and verses. Her first great success came in 1885 in the publication of "Jan Vedder's Wife." Three other books followed: "Scottish Sketches," "Cluny MacPherson," and "Paul and Christina," but none equalled "Jan Vedder's Wife." "The Bow of Orange Ribbon" is a delightful picture of New York in provincial days, as is "The Maid of Maiden Lane." One of her later books, "The Lion's Whelp," a story of Cromwell's time, is considered one of her strongest books.

MARY E. WILKINS FREEMAN.

Was born in Randolph, Massachusetts, in 1862. Her father was a native of Salem, and was a descendant of Bray Wilkins of good old Puritan stock. Her mother was a Holbrook, one of the old families of Massachusetts. The family early removed to Brattleboro, Vermont, and with Mr. J. E. Chamberland she wrote "The Long Arm" for which they received a two thousand dollar prize offered by a newspaper. Like many other writers she was largely influenced by the people about her and associated with her early life and that of her family. Barnabas, one of the characters in her story, "Pembroke," was drawn from Randolph. Losing her father and mother and sister, she returned to Randolph and took up her residence. Her story "A Humble Romance" was considered by Phillips Brooks the best short story ever written. In 1893, she wrote a play, "Giles Corey, Yeoman" a drama of the early Puritan days. "The Heart's Highway" is another of her stories of Colonial times, and "The Portion of Labor." In 1902 she married Dr. Charles Manning Freeman, of Metuchen, New Jersey, where she now resides.

ALICE FRENCH.

"Octave Thanet."

Miss French took a *nom de plume* to hide her identity, there being an unmistakably masculine tinge in many of her writings. Her real name is Alice French, she was born in Andover, Massachusetts, March 19, 1850. Her father was George Henry French, a man of important business connections and comfortable means. The family were descended from Sir William French who settled in Massachusetts in the seventeenth century, and one of his descendants took part in the Revolutionary War, receiving the name of the "Fighting Parson of Andover." Miss French's grandfather on her mother's side was Governor Marcus Morton, and some of her ancestors were numbered among those who came to this country in the Mayflower. Miss French is a graduate of Vassar College. Her first story was printed in *Godey's Magazine*. Her story entitled "The Bishop's Vagabond," published in the *Atlantic Monthly*, in 1884, was the beginning of her substantial literary fame. Her story "Expiation" is considered very strong, as is "Knitters in the Sun."

KATE DOUGLASS WIGGIN (MRS. RIGGS.)

Her family were people of prominence in church and politics and at the New England Bar. She was born in Philadelphia and educated in New England, transplanted to California, and returned again to the Atlantic coast. Her first article appeared in *St. Nicholas* and was written at the age of eighteen. This she wrote while studying kindergarten work under the celebrated Marshall in California. After the death of her stepfather, she taught in the Santa Barbara College and organized the first free kindergarten west of the Rocky Mountains. Soon after the successful establishment of this work, she was married to Mr. Samuel Bradley Wiggin, a talented young lawyer. She gave up her work in the kindergarten but continued to give lectures. One of the stories written at this time was the story of "Patsy," which she wrote to obtain money for the work in which was so much interested, to be followed by "The Birds' Christmas Carol," written for the same purpose. After removing to New York, in 1888, she was urged to offer these two books to an eastern publisher, and Houghton, Mifflin and Company reprinted them in book form, and they met with remarkable success. "The Birds' Christmas Carol" has been translated into Japanese, French, German and Swedish, even being put into raised type for the blind. Her story "Timothy's Quest" met with great success as also "Polly Oliver's Problem." Mr. Wiggin's death soon after they left San Francisco necessitated her taking up the kindergarten work in the East with great energy. She does much of her work at her old home in Maine, and many of the scenes and descriptions in the "Village Watch Tower" were taken from this neighborhood. In 1895 she married Mr. George Christopher Riggs, and has spent much of her time since then in England. "Penelope's English Experience" is a story of her own experiences among her English friends, as were those of "Penelope's Irish Experiences," "Penelope's Progress in Scotland" which followed a period of her life in these countries.

GERTRUDE ATHERTON.

Was born in Rincon Hill, a part of San Francisco, in 1857. Her mother was the daughter of Stephen Franklin, a descendant of one of the brothers of Benjamin Franklin. His daughter was quite famous in California as a beauty. She married Thomas L. Horn, a prominent citizen of San Francisco from Stonington, Connecticut, and a member of the famous Vigilant Committee. The daughter Gertrude was educated in California and married George Henry Bowen Atherton of Menlo Park, California, a Chilian by birth. Her first story, "The Randolphs of Redwoods," was published in the *San Francisco Argonaut,* but among her many stories perhaps the best known is "Senator North." Her story of the life of Alexander Hamilton under the title "The Conqueror" is considered her best work.

JOHN OLIVER HOBBES (MRS. CRAIGIE.)

Mrs. Pearl Mary Theresa Craigie was born in Boston, Massachusetts, November 3, 1867. Her mother's maiden name was Laura Hortense Arnold. Her father was John Morgan Richards, the son of Reverend Doctor James Richards, the founder of Auburn Theological Seminary, of New York. She received her early education from tutors, later studying in Paris, and then in London. She was an enthusiastic student of classical literature, and through the advice of Professor

Goodwin, she took up literature as a profession. In 1887, she was married to Mr. Reginald Walpole Craigie of a well-to-do English family. "Robert of Orange" was one of her early and most notable books. Mrs. Craigie did some writing for the stage and one of her plays, "The Ambassador," was considered very good. Her story "Love and Soul Hunters," has not been excelled by any of her contemporaries.

LILIAN BELL.

Was born in Chicago in 1867, but spent her early years in Atlanta. Daughter of Major William Bell, an officer of the Civil War. Her grandfather, General Joseph Warren Bell, was a Southerner, but sold and freed his slaves before the war, brought his family North to Illinois. He organized the Thirteenth Illinois Cavalry. Her first literary work was "The Expatriates." Probably her best known book is "The Love Affairs of an Old Maid." In 1893 she married Arthur Hoyt Bogue of Chicago. They now make their home in New York City, where Mrs. Bogue is still engaged in literary work under her maiden name.

RUTH McENERY STUART.

Mrs. Stuart was born at Avoyelles Parish, Louisiana, the daughter of a wealthy planter. Her family had always been slave holders and her life was spent on a plantation where she gained her familiarity and knowledge of the negro character. She was educated at a school in New Orleans where she remained after her marriage in 1879 to Alfred O. Stuart, a cotton planter, and her early life was spent near their plantation in a small Arkansas town. Her first story was sent by Charles Dudley Warner to the *Princeton Review* in which it appeared, and the second was published in *Harper's Magazine*. Her stories are of the lazy life of the creoles and the plantation negroes. They give a true picture of a peculiar race of people fast disappearing in the South. They are largely dialect stories. Since her husband's death Mrs. Stuart has resided in New York City and here most of her literary work has been done. "Moriah's Mourning," "In Simpkinsville," "A Golden Wedding," "Charlotta's Intended," "Solomon Crow's Christmas Box," "The Story of Babette," "Sonny," "Uncle Eph's Advice to Brer Rabbit," "Holly and Pizen," are some of her well-known stories. Charles Dudley Warner says, "her pictures of Louisiana life both white and colored are indeed the best we have."

ANNA FARQUHAR BERGENGREN.

Mrs. Bergengren was of Scotch-English ancestry, her people coming to America in Lord Baltimore's time and settling in Maryland, near Baltimore. She was born December 23, 1865, near Brookville, Indiana, her father being a lawyer, a member of Congress, and during her life in Washington, she obtained the material for her book called "Her Washington Experiences." Her father's death made her determine upon a career for herself and she chose a musical education, but her health failed while studying in Boston, and she was ultimately obliged to give up singing, in which she had already attained fair success. Her story "The Singer's Heart" expressed her professional ambitions. "The Professor's Daughter" was published in *The Saturday Evening Post* and was very popular. "Her Boston Experiences" appeared in a magazine and ultimately in book form. Her book, "The Devil's Plough," is a story of the early French missionaries of North America. In January, 1900, she was married to Ralph Bergengren, a Boston Journalist, and has continued her literary labors.

PAULINE BRADFORD MACKIE HOPKINS.

Mrs. Hopkins is a writer of historical fiction. For two years after her graduation from the Toledo High School she was engaged as a writer on the *Toledo Blade*. She soon abandoned this for a literary career, and most of her stories have appeared in magazines and newspapers. "Mademoiselle de Berny" and "Ye Lyttle Salem Maide" were, after most trying experiences with publishers, printed in book form. "A Georgian Actress" was written in Berkeley, California, where Mrs. Hopkins had gone with her husband, Dr. Herbert Müller Hopkins, now occupying the chair of Latin in Trinity College, Hartford, Connecticut. Here she also wrote two novels of Washington life during the Civil War. Mrs. Hopkins was born in Connecticut in 1873. Her father, Rev. Andrew Mackie, was an Episcopal clergyman and a very scholarly man, from whom she inherited her literary talent.

MARY JOHNSTON.

The publication of "Prisoners of Hope" brought, in 1898, a new star into the literary firmament, and instantly made Mary Johnston's name famous. At the time of the publication of her first novel Miss Johnston was but twenty-eight years of age. She was born in Buchanan, Virginia, November 21, 1870. Her great-great-great-grandfather, Peter Johnston, came to Virginia early in the Eighteenth Century and was a man of wealth and influence. He donated the land on which the Hampden Sidney College now stands, and Peter, his eldest son, rode in "light-horse," Harry Lee's legion and was the father of General Joseph E. Johnston. Her family numbered among its members some of the most distinguished men of the early Virginia history. "Prisoners of Hope" was hardly more famous than her second book, "To Have and To Hold." The latter established a record of sales among books unprecedented for any work by an American woman. Her latest novel is "The Long Roll," a story of the Confederacy during the war.

ELLEN ANDERSON G. GLASGOW.

Miss Glasgow is a Virginia writer who has become a member of the literary life of the New South. "The Descendant," "The Phases of an Inferior Planet" and "The Voice of the People" are among her best works. She was born in Richmond, Virginia, April 22, 1874, and lived the greater part of her life at the family home. Her father was a lawyer, and the majority of her male ancestors were either lawyers, judges or men of literary tastes and talents.

BERTHA RUNKLE.

One of the most famous novels of the past few years was "The Helmet of Navarre," and was written, when its author, Bertha Runkle, was a little over twenty years of age. One of the most remarkable facts in this connection is that the authoress had never seen the shores of France, in fact had seldom been beyond the boundaries of New York State. Miss Runkle was born in New Jersey, but in 1888 she and her mother moved to New York City. Her father, Cornelius A. Runkle, a well-known New York lawyer, was for many years counsel for the *New York Tribune,* and her mother, Lucia Isabella Runkle, had been, previous to her marriage, an editorial writer on the same paper, in fact she was the first American woman to be placed on the staff of a great Metropolitan daily. In 1904 Miss Runkle married Captain Louis H. Bash, United States Army. She is very fond of outdoor life and spends much of her time in such sports as golf, riding, driving and tennis.

HARRIET BEECHER STOWE.

In the little town of Litchfield, Connecticut, on June 14, 1811, one of the most famous literary women, Harriet Beecher Stowe, was born. She was the seventh child of her parents. Rev. Lyman Beecher and Roxanna Beecher. Her father was an eminent divine, but her early childhood days were filled with the privations of great poverty. When Harriet Stowe was but five years of age, her mother died and she went to live for a short time with her aunt and grandmother, until Mr. Beecher's second marriage. At twelve years of age she was sent to the school of Mr. John P. Brace, a well-known teacher, where she soon began to show a great love for composition, and one of her essays, "Can the Immortality of the Soul be Proved by the Light of Nature," was considered quite a literary triumph, and won great admiration from her father who was ignorant of its authorship. Her sister Catherine went to Hartford, Connecticut, where her brother was teaching, and decided she would build a female seminary that women might have equal opportunities with men. She raised the money and built the Hartford Female Seminary, and Harriet Beecher at the age of twelve attended her sister Catherine's school. She soon became one of the pupil teachers. Mr. Beecher's fame as a revivalist and brilliant preacher took him to Boston, but his heart was in the temperance work and he longed to go West. When called to Ohio to become president of Lane Theological Seminary at Cincinnati he accepted, and perhaps we owe to this circumstance Harriet Beecher Stowe's famous book "Uncle Tom's Cabin." In 1836, Harriet married the Professor of Biblical Criticism and Oriental Literature in that seminary, Calvin E. Stowe. At this time the question of slavery was uppermost in the minds of Christian people. In 1850 the Beecher family and the Stowes moved to Brunswick, Maine, where Mr. Stowe had accepted a professorship at Bowdoin College. The fugitive slave law was in operation and the people of the North seemed lacking in effort. Mrs. Stowe felt she must do something to arouse the people on this question, and we are told that one Sunday while sitting in church the picture of Uncle Tom came to her mind. When she went home she wrote the chapter on his death and read it to her two sons, ten and twelve years of age. This so affected them that they burst into tears. After two or three more chapters were ready she wrote to Dr. Bailey, her old friend of Cincinnati days, who had removed his press to Washington and was editing the *National Era* in that city. He accepted her manuscript and it was published as a serial. Mr. Jewett of Boston feared to undertake the work in book form, thinking it too long to be popular, but Uncle Tom's Cabin was published March 20, 1852, as a book. In less than a year over three hundred thousand copies had been sold. Congratulations came from crown heads and the literary world. In 1853, when Professor Stowe and his wife visited England no crowned head was shown greater honor. Other books followed from her pen on her return to America, her husband having taken a position as Professor of Sacred Literature in the Theological Seminary at Andover, Massachusetts. Her other works are: "Sunny Memories of Foreign Lands," "Dread," an anti-slavery story; "The Minister's Wooing," "Agnes of Sorrento," an Italian story; "Pearl of Orr's Island," a New England coast tale; "Old Town Folks," "House and Home Papers," "My Wife and I," "Pink and White Tyranny," but none has added to the fame of her great work, "Uncle Tom's Cabin." This book has been translated into almost all the languages. The latter years of Mrs. Stowe's life was spent between her home among the orange groves of Florida, and her summer residence in Hartford, Connecticut. On her seventy-first birthday her publishers, Houghton Mifflin & Company, gave her a monster garden party in Newton, Massachusetts, at the home of Governor Claflin. Poets, artists, statesmen, and our country's greatest men and women came to do her honor, and when her life went out at Hartford, Connecticut, July 1, 1896, we lost one of the famous women of America.

HELEN HUNT JACKSON.

She was born in Amherst, Massachusetts, October 18, 1831. Her father, Nathan W. Fiske, was a professor of languages and philosophy in the college of that town. When twelve years of age both her father and mother died, leaving her to the care of her grandfather. She entered the school of Rev. J. S. C. Abbott of New York. At twenty-one she married a young army officer, Captain, afterward Major, Edward B. Hunt. They lived much of their time at West Point and Newport. Major Hunt was killed in Brooklyn, October 2, 1863, while experimenting with a submarine gun of his own invention. After a year abroad and a long illness in Rome, she returned to this country in 1870. In her first small book of verses she was obliged to pay for the plates when they appeared, and it was only after years of hard work that she succeeded in her literary career. Her health becoming somewhat impaired, she moved to Colorado, and here in 1876 she married Mr. William Sharpless Jackson, a banker and cultured gentleman. They made their home at Colorado Springs, and it became one of the attractions of the place, her great love for flowers beautifying her surroundings. Here she wrote her first novels, "Mercy Philbrick's Choice" and "Hetty's Strange History," also, later "Ramona," but her strongest work was brought about through her intense interest and indignation over the wrongs of the Indians inflicted upon them by the white race. She advocated education and christianization of the race rather than their extermination. Leaving home, she spent three months in New York in the Astor Library gathering facts and material for her "Century of Dishonor." When published she sent a copy to each member of Congress at her own expense to awaken interest in her favorite theme, and this resulted in her being appointed special commissioner with Abbott Kinney, her friend, to examine and report on the condition of the Indians in California. She went into the work with enthusiasm and energy and the report was most exhaustive and convincing. In the winter of 1883, she began to write her famous novel, "Ramona," and we quote her own language when she says of it "I put my heart and soul into it." The book enjoyed wonderful popularity not only in this country but in England. In June, 1884, a fall caused a long, severe and painful illness. She was taken to Los Angeles, for the winter, but a slow malarial fever followed and she was removed to San Francisco and on the evening of August 12, 1885, she died. Her two works "Ramona," and "The Century of Dishonor" will ever preserve her name among the famous literary women of America. "The Century of Dishonor," has placed her name among the up-builders of our nation. She was buried near the summit of Cheyenne Mountain, four miles from Colorado Springs, a spot of her own choosing, and which is to-day one of the shrines of America.

THE CARY SISTERS.

The Cary sisters stand out as the most prominent poetical writers of the state of Ohio. Alice Cary was born April 26, 1820, on the farm of her father, situated within the present limits of Mount Healthy, Ohio. In 1832, the family moved to a larger residence near their former home, and it was christened "Clover Nook." Alice Cary had only the advantages of ordinary school education, but began early in life to contribute literary compositions, and at the age of eighteen, her first poetical adventure, "The Child of Sorrow," to the *Sentinel and Star*, a universalist paper of Cincinnati. Gradually her reputation spread and she contributed to many papers, among them, the *National Mirror* of Washington, D. C., the editor of which, Dr. Bailey, was the first to consider her writings worthy of pecuniary reward. In 1848, her name appeared first among the female poets of America, and in 1850, a small collection of poems by Alice and Phoebe Cary made their first appearance. Horace Greeley and John G. Whittier were among the warm friends and literary admirers of the Cary sisters. In 1860, Alice moved to New York City, and on February 12, 1870, she died.

PHOEBE CARY.

Was born September 4, 1824, in the old homestead at Clover Nook, Hamilton County, Ohio. Her writings were noted for their sincerity and sweetness. Her gifts were hardly inferior to those of her sister, Alice, whom she outlived but one year and a half, dying July 31, 1871.

ALICE WILLIAMS BROTHERTON.

Daughter of Alfred Baldwin Williams and Ruth Hoge Johnson Williams, was born at Cambridge, Indiana, her parents removing to Cincinnati, Ohio, when she was quite young. Her education was received mainly from the grammar and high schools of Cincinnati. She was married October 18, 1876, to Mr. William Ernest Brotherton of that city. She has been a constant contributor to newspapers and magazines, a prominent college woman, and has devoted much time to essays and writings on Shakespeare, delivering lectures before women's colleges and dramatic schools.

EDITH MATILDA THOMAS.

Was born in Chatham, Ohio, August 12, 1854. Daughter of Frederick J. Thomas and Jane Louisa Sturges Thomas, both natives of New England, her great-grandfather being a soldier in the Revolutionary War. The family lived for a short time at Kenton, Ohio, and also at Bowling Green, where her father died in 1861. Soon after this, her mother and sisters moved to Geneva, Ohio, where Edith received her education at the Normal Institute. She taught for a short time in Geneva, but soon decided to make literature her profession. She had, while a student, contributed to the newspapers, and her first admirer was Helen Hunt Jackson, who brought her to the attention of the editors of the *Atlantic Monthly* and *Century*. In 1888, Miss Thomas moved to New York City, making her home on Staten Island, and has devoted her entire time to literature, being a frequent contributor to the prominent magazines of the day.

ALICE ARCHER SEWALL JAMES

Daughter of Frank Sewall, an eminent Swedenborgian divine, and Thedia Redelia Gilchrist Sewall, and was born at Glendale, Ohio, in 1870, where her father was in charge of a church. The family removed to Urbana, Ohio, that year, and Doctor Sewall became president of Urbana University. Here Alice received her early education. At sixteen, she studied in the art schools of Glasgow, Scotland, traveling later on the Continent. In 1899, her home was in Washington, D. C., and here she met Mr. John H. James, a prominent attorney of Urbana, Ohio, whom she married. As an artist, Mrs. James' work has received much favorable comment and honors from the New York Architectural League, the Philadelphia Academy of Art, the Chicago World's Fair, the Expositions of Atlanta and Nashville, and at the Salon, Paris. Her illustrative work is of a high order, and she has contributed designs to the *Century Magazine, Harper's Monthly*, and the *Cosmopolitan*. She is hardly less noted as a poet than as a painter, and has published several volumes of verses. She was the authoress of the "Centennial Ode" of Champagne County, Ohio.

MARGARET JUNKIN PRESTON.

Daughter of Rev. Dr. Junkin, the founder of Lafayette College in Pennsylvania, was born in Philadelphia in 1820. Her father moved to Virginia in 1848, and became the president of Washington College in Lexington, now known as the Washington and Lee University. He was succeeded in this position by Robert E. Lee. In 1857, Miss Junkin married Professor J. T. L. Preston, one of the professors of the Virginia Military Institute. Mrs. Preston belonged to a very noted family of the South, her brother being General Stonewall Jackson, who was also one of the professors of this famous college of the South. A few years prior to her death, she removed to Baltimore, her son being a prominent physician and surgeon of that city, and here she died March 28, 1897. She was a great admirer of the Scotch writers and produced some valuable literary work in verse and prose, which appeared in the magazines and journals of the day. she also published five volumes of poems. "Her Centennial Ode" for the Washington and Lee University was considered a very notable production. Much of her writings were of a religious character, and all breathed a very pure, simple and sweet nature.

MARGARET FULLER. (MARCHIONESS D'OSSOLI.)

Margaret Fuller was a woman of most eccentric genius and great mental powers. She was born May 23, 1810, the daughter of Timothy Fuller, Esq., of Cambridge, Mass. In very early life Miss Fuller was put to the study of classical languages and showed wonderful power of acquisition. She then turned to living tongues and before she reached a mature age she was accounted a giant of philological accomplishments. Indeed she poured over the German philosophers until her very being became imbued with their transcendental doctrines. She was the best educated woman in the country and devoted her life to raising the standard of woman's intellectual training. To this effect she opened classes for women's instruction in several of the larger towns of New England.

Her first publication was a translation of Goethe's "Conversation," which appeared in 1839. In the following year she was employed by the publisher of the "Dial," at whose head was Ralph Waldo Emerson, and she aided in the editorship of that journal for several years. In 1843 Miss Fuller moved to New York and entered into arrangement with the publishers of the *Tribune,* to aid in its literary department. This same year she made public her best literary effort, her "Summer on the Lakes," a journal of a journey to the West.

MARTHA JOANNA LAMB.

Mrs. Martha Joanna Lamb was born on August 18, 1829, at Plainfield, Massachusetts. She was at one time considered the leading woman historian of the nineteenth century. She is a life member of the American Historical Association and a Fellow of the Clarendon Association of Edinburgh, Scotland. Was editor of the *Magazine of American History* for eleven years. Her father was Arvin Nash and her mother was Lucinda Vinton. Her grandfather, Jacob Nash, was a Revolutionary soldier. The family is an old English one and to it belong the Rev. Treadway Nash D.D., the historian, and his wife, Joanna Reade, and to her family belongs Charles Reade, the well-known novelist. The ancestors of the Reade family came to America in the "Mayflower." Mrs. Lamb made her home at different times at Goshen, Massachusetts, Northampton and Easthampton. In 1882 she became the wife of Charles A. Lamb, and became conspicuous in charitable work in the city of Chicago, in which they resided from 1857 to 1866. She was an active worker after the great fire of 1863. In 1866 the Lambs made their home in New York City. Mrs. Lamb had always been a woman of remarkable mathematical talent and training. In 1879 she prepared for *Harper's Magazine* a notable paper translating to unlearned readers the mysteries and work of the Coast Survey. She has written a remarkable history of the city of New York, in two volumes, which was pronounced by competent authorities to be the best history ever written on any great city in the world. The preparation of this work required fifteen years of study and research. The list of Mrs. Lamb's works is long and distinguished, among them many historical sketches. Some titles are: "Lyme, a Chapter of American Genealogy"; "Chimes of Old Trinity," "State and Society in Washington," "The Coast Survey," "The Homes of America," "Memorial to Dr. Rust" and the "Philanthropist;" several sketches for magazines, "Unsuccessful candidates for the Presidential Nomination," sketch of Major-General John A. Dix, "Historical Homes in Lafayette Place," "The Historical Homes of Our Presidents." It is said that Mrs. Lamb wrote upwards of two hundred articles, essays and short stories, for weekly and monthly periodicals, but her greatest work was her "History of the City of New York," which is a standard authority and will be throughout all time. Mrs. Lamb died in 1893.

EMMA D. E. N. SOUTHWORTH.

Emma D. E. Nevitt was the eldest daughter of Captain Charles Nevitt, of Alexandria, Virginia. Was born in Washington, D. C., December 26, 1819. The family was descended from those of high rank in England and France. Her people had emigrated to this country in 1632, and were conspicuous in the American Revolution. Her father served at the head of a company in the War of 1812, receiving a wound from which he never recovered. At the age of forty-five, Captain Nevitt married his second wife, a young girl of but fifteen years and removed to Washington, where they leased a large house said to have been occupied at one time by General Washington. Mrs. Nevitt, after Captain Nevitt's death, married the second time, her husband being Joshua L. Henshaw of Boston, and to him Mrs. Southworth says she is indebted almost entirely for her education. Among her early writings is "The Irish Refugee," which was accepted by the editor of the *Baltimore Saturday Visitor*, who so encouraged the young writer that she wrote "The Wife's Victory." A few of her early stories were printed in the *National Era* of Washington City, its editor engaging her as a regular writer for that paper. She then commenced her third novel "Sibyl's Brother, or The Temptation," and in 1849 "Retribution" was published by Harper Brothers, and in five years after its appearance she had written "The Deserted Wife," "Shannondale," "The Mother-in-Law," "Children of the Isle," "The Foster Sisters," "The Courts of Clifton," "Old Neighbors in New Settlements," "The Lost Heiress" and "Hickory Hall." Her prolific pen was latterly engaged exclusively for the *New York Ledger*. In 1853 Mrs. Southworth moved to a beautiful old home on the heights above the Potomac in Georgetown, and this became the rendezvous of distinguished people from all parts of the country. Here, in what was known as Prospect Cottage, Mrs. Southworth spent the last years of her life, dying there June 30, 1899.

MADELEINE VINTON DAHLGREN.

The wife of the distinguished Admiral Dahlgren was born in Gallipolis, Ohio, about 1835. She was the only daughter of Samuel F. Vinton, who served with distinction as a member of Congress for some years. At an early age she became the wife of Daniel Convers Goddard, who left her a widow with two children. On the 2nd of August, 1865, she became the wife of Admiral Dahlgren, and three children were born of this marriage. Admiral Dahlgren died in 1870. Her first contributions to the press were written in 1859 under the signature "Corinne." She also used the pen-name "Cornelia." Her first book was a little book entitled "Idealities." She made several translations from the French, Spanish and Italian languages, among them, "Montalembert's Brochure," "Pius IX," and the philosophical works of Donoso Cortes from the Spanish. These translations brought her many complimentary notices and an autographed letter from Pope Pius IX, and the thanks of the Queen of Spain. She was also the author of a voluminous biograph of Admiral Dahlgren and a number of novels including, "The South-Mountain Magic," "A Washington Winter," "The Lost Name," "Lights and Shadows of a Life," "Divorced," "South Sea Sketches," and a volume on "Etiquette of Social Life in Washington," and quite a number of essays, reviews, and short stories for the leading papers and periodicals of the day. She was a woman of fine talent and a thorough scholar, and in the social circles of Washington of which she was a conspicuous figure, she was considered a literary authority, and the Literary Society of Washington, of which she was one of the founders, had about the only "Salon" ever in existence in Washington. Her house was the center of a brilliant circle of official and literary life of the Capital city. In 1870-1873 she actively opposed the movement for female suffrage, presenting a petition to Congress which had been extensively signed asking that the right to vote should not be extended to women. Mrs. Dahlgren was a devout Catholic, and was for some time president of the Ladies' Catholic Missionary Society of Washington, and built a chapel at her summer home on South Mountain, Maryland, near the battlefield, known as St. Joseph's of the Sacred Heart of Jesus.

EMILY LEE SHERWOOD.

Mrs. Sherwood was born in 1843, in Madison, Indiana, where she spent her childhood. Her father, Monroe Wells Lee, was a native of Ohio; her mother, of the state of Massachusetts. At the age of sixteen she entered the office of her brother, who published the *Herald* and *Era*, a religious weekly paper in Indianapolis. Here she did most creditably whatever work she was asked to do in the various departments of this paper. At the age of twenty she became the wife of Henry Lee Sherwood, a young attorney of Indianapolis, and later they made their home in Washington, D. C. Mrs. Sherwood became one of the most prominent newspaper correspondents of the Capital city. She sent letters to the various papers over the country and was a contributor of stories and miscellaneous articles to the general press. In 1889 she became a member of the staff of the *Sunday Herald*, of Washington, D. C., and contributed articles also to the *New York Sun* and *World*. She is an all-round author, writing in connection with her newspaper work, books, reviews, stories, character sketches, society notes and reports. She published a novel entitled "Willis Peyton's Inheritance"; is an active member of the Daughters of the American Revolution, National Press League and the Triennial Council of Women.

JULIA HOLMES SMITH.

Born in Savannah, Georgia, December 23, 1839. On her mother's side, her grandfather was Captain George Raynall Turner, United States Navy. She was educated in the famous seminary of Gorman D. Abbott, and after graduating, married Waldo Abbott, eldest son of the historian, John S. C. Abbott. Mrs. Abbott was the organizer and first president of the Woman's Medical Association, the only society of its kind in America. In 1889 she contributed to the *New York Ledger* a series of articles on "Common Sense in the Nursery." She was at one time the only woman who contributed to the Arndts System of Medicine.

MARY STUART SMITH.

Mrs. Mary Stuart Smith was born at the University of Virginia, February 10, 1834. Was the second daughter of Professor Gessner Harrison and his wife, Eliza Lewis Carter Tucker. In 1853 she became the wife of Professor Francis H. Smith, of the University of Virginia. Besides original articles, her translations from the German for leading periodicals form a long list. She is a most pleasing writer for children.

MARY ELIZABETH SHERWOOD.

Mrs. Mary Elizabeth Sherwood was born in Keene, New Hampshire, in 1830. Her father, General James Wilson, served as a member of Congress from New Hampshire. Her mother, Mary Richardson, was well known for her great beauty and fine intellect. Mrs. Sherwood was a woman of strong personality and distinguished appearance. While living in Washington she became the wife of John Sherwood and soon obtained a prominent place among literary people. She was a contributor to all the leading magazines of the day, a writer of several well-known novels, among them, "A Transplanted Rose," "Sweet Briar," and "Royal Girls and Royal Courts," but is best known for her books on etiquette, being considered an authority on that subject. During Mrs. Sherwood's residence abroad she was prominent in the literary circles of · Europe. In 1885 she gave readings in her New York home for the benefit of the Mt. Vernon Fund. Mrs. Sherwood was active in many of the charities of New York City, and through her pen raised sums of money for many in which she was interested. Mrs. Sherwood died in 1903.

KATE BROWNLEE SHERWOOD.

Mrs. Kate B. Sherwood was born in Mahoning County, Ohio, September 24, 1841. Of Scotch descent, her maiden name was Brownlee. Before graduating from the Poland Union Seminary, she became the wife of Isaac R. Sherwood, afterward General Secretary of the State, and at present Congressman from Ohio. Her husband was the owner and editor of the *Canton Daily News Democrat.*

She has always taken an active interest in all public and philanthropic questions for the soldiers and her state. While her husband served his first term in Congress, she was correspondent for the Ohio papers, and at one time contributed to the columns of the *National Tribune,* Washington, D. C., published for the benefit of the Grand Army of the Republic and the soldiers of the country.

Mrs. Sherwood has done valiant work for her state and the Woman's Relief Corps, being one of the founders of the latter organization. She was at one time its national president; organized the Department of Relief and instituted the National Home for Army Nurses in Geneva, Ohio.

In her earlier years she was well known by her very melodious voice and frequently sang at meetings of military organizations. There is no woman better known or whose ability is more universally conceded or who wields a wider influence in the organizations of women for the advancement of her sex and the progress of our country.

EVA MUNSON SMITH.

Mrs. Eva Munson Smith was born July 12, 1843. She was the daughter of William Chandler Munson and Hannah Bailey Munson. Her mother was a direct descendant of Hannah Bailey of Revolutionary fame, who tore up her flannel petticoat to make wadding for the guns in battle.

Mrs. Smith has made a collection of sacred compositions of women under the title "Women in Sacred Song." She has written quite a number of musical selections.

AMELIE RIVES. (PRINCESS TROUBETZKOY).

Princess Troubetzkoy was born in Richmond, Virginia, August 23, 1863, but her early life was passed at the family home, Castle Hill, Albermarle County. She is a granddaughter of William Cabell Rives, once minister to France and who wrote the "Life of Madison." Her grandmother, Mrs. Judith Walker Rives, left some writings entitled "Home and the World" and "Residence in Europe." Amelie Rives was married in 1899 to John Armstrong Chanler, of New York. Her most conspicuous story was. "The Quick and the Dead." She wrote "A Brother to Dragons," "Virginia of Virginia," "According to St. John," "Barbara Dering," "Tanis" and several other well known stories. Her first marriage proved unhappy and she was divorced, and has since married Prince Pierre Troubetzkoy, a Russian artist, and continues her literary work.

GRACE ELIZABETH KING.

Miss King was born in New Orleans, in 1852, and is the daughter of William W. and Sarah Ann King. She has attained a distinguished reputation as the writer of short stories of Creole life. Among them are: "Monsieur Mottee," "Tales of Time and Place," "New Orleans, the Place and the People," "Jean Baptiste Lemoine, Founder of New Orleans," "Balcony Stories," "De Soto and His Men in the Land of Florida," "Stories from the History of Louisiana."

ELIZABETH WORMELEY LATIMER.

Mrs. Elizabeth Wormeley Latimer was born in London, England, in July, 1822. Her father was Rear Admiral Ralph Randolph Wormeley of the English navy, and her mother was Caroline Preble, of Boston, Massachusetts. In 1842 she was a member of the family of George Ticknor, of Boston, and her first literary work was the appendix to Prescott's Conquest, of Mexico. Her father's death occurred at Niagara Falls, in 1852. In 1856 Miss Wormeley married Randolph Brandt Latimer and they later made their home in Howard County, Maryland. Mrs. Latimer's works have been quite numerous. Among them are "Cousin Veronica," "Amabel," "My Wife and My Wife's Sister," "A Chain of Errors," and "France in the Nineteenth Century." Mrs. Latimer died in 1904.

MARY A. RIPLEY.

Was born January 11, 1831, and was the daughter of John Huntington Ripley and Eliza L. Spalding Ripley. The Huntington family was very prominent in New England, one of its members, Samuel Huntington, signed the Declaration of Independence and Articles of Federation. On her mother's side Miss Ripley is descended from a distinguished French Huguenot family. She taught school in Buffalo for many years and contributed letters, articles on questions of the day and short poems. Her poems are characterized by sweetness and vigor. Her articles attracted much attention and exerted a wide influence. In 1867 she published a small book entitled "Parsing Lessons for School Room Use," which was followed by "Household Service," published under the auspices of the Woman's Educational and Industrial Union, of Buffalo. Her health failing, she resigned her position and removed to Carney, Nebraska, where she took an active part in every good work of that state, and was later made state superintendent of Scientific Temperance Instruction in the public schools and colleges of Nebraska.

EMMA WINNER ROGERS.

Was a native of Plainfield, New Jersey. She is the daughter of Reverend John Ogden Winner and granddaughter of Reverend Isaac Winner, D.D., both

52

clergymen of the Methodist Episcopal Church. For six years she was the corresponding secretary of the Woman's Home Missionary Society of the Detroit Conference and later honorary president of the Rock River Conference, Woman's Home Missionary Society. She is specially interested in literary work on the lines of social science and political economy and has been a contributor on these subjects to various papers and periodicals. ˙She has written a monograph entitled "Deaconesses in the Early and Modern Church." Mrs. Rogers is a woman of marked ability and specially endowed with strong logical faculties and the power of dispassionate judgment. She is of the type of American College women who, with the advantage of higher training and higher education, bring their disciplined faculties to bear with equally good effect upon the amenities of social life and the philanthropic and economic questions of the day. She is the wife of Henry Wade Rogers, of Buffalo, New York, dean of the Law School of the University of Michigan, and later president of the Northwestern University of Evanston, Illinois. As the wife of the president of a great University her influence upon the young men and women connected with it was marked and advantageous. Mrs. Rogers has left an impress upon the life of her times that is both salutary and permanent.

ELLEN SARGENT RUDE.

Born March 17, 1838, in Sodus, New York. Her mother died when she was an infant. Educated in the public schools of Sodus and Lima, New York. She became the wife of Benton C. Rude, in 1859. She won a prize for a temperance story from the *Temperance Patriot.* Some of the choicest poems of the "Arbor Day Manual" are from her pen.

GRACE ATKINSON OLIVER.

Born in Boston, September 24, 1844. In 1869 she became the wife of John Harvard Ellis, the son of Reverend John E. Ellis, of Boston, who died a year after they were married. She was for some years a regular contributor to the *Boston Transcript.* In 1874 Mrs. Ellis spent a season in London and while there met some of the members of the family of Maria Edgeworth, who suggested her writing the life of Miss Edgeworth. This she did, and the book was published in the famous old corner book store in Boston, in 1882. In 1879 she became the wife of Doctor Joseph P. Oliver, of Boston. Subsequently she wrote a memoir of the Reverend Dean Stanley, which was brought out both in Boston and London. Mrs. Oliver is a member of the New England Woman's Press Association and the New England Woman's Club; vice-president of the Thought and Work Club, in Salem, and a member of the Essex Institute, in Salem. Mrs. Oliver died in 1899.

ELIZABETH MARTHA OLMSTED.

Born December 31, 1825, in Caledonia, New York. Her father, Oliver Allen, belonged to the family of Ethan Allen. In 1853 she became the wife of John

R. Olmsted, of LeRoy, New York. The Olmsteds were descended from the first settlers of Hartford, Connecticut, and pioneers of the Genesee Valley, New York. Her poems were well known during the war, and appeared in the newspapers and magazines of that period.

MARY FROST ORMSBY.

Was born in 1852 in Albany, New York. Her family connections included many distinguished persons. She opened a school known as the Seabury Institute, in New York City, a private school for young women. She has been active in reforms and movements on social and philanthropic lines. Mrs. Ormsby is a member of the Sorosis Club also of the American Society of Authors, Woman's National Press Association, an officer and member of the Pan Republican Congress and Human Freedom League, a member of the executive committee of the Universal Peace Union and in 1891 was a delegate from the United States to the Universal Peace Congress, in Rome, Italy. Writer of short stories and a contributor of articles to various publications.

REGINA ARMSTRONG NIEHAUS.

Was born in Virginia, March 4, 1869. Daughter of Thomas J. and Jane Ann Welch. Married Charles Henry Niehaus, in 1900. Has contributed poems, stories and critiques to leading New York magazine since 1896, also to *The Studio,* London.

MARIA I. JOHNSTON.

Mrs. Maria I. Johnston was born in Fredericksburg, Virginia, May, 1835. Her father was Judge Richard Barnett, of Fredericksburg, who later removed to Vicksburg, Mississippi, and here Mrs. Johnston was a resident during the terrible forty days' siege of that city during the Civil War. That experience was made the subject of her first novel, "The Siege of Vicksburg." She was a contributor to the *New Orleans Picayune, The Times Democrat* and to the *Boston Women's Journal.* Since the death of her husband, Doctor W. R. Johnston, Mrs. Johnston has supported herself by her pen. She has educated her children, one son, a graduate of Yale, becoming a Judge of the Circuit Court of Montana. She was editor at one time of *St. Louis Spectator,* a weekly family paper. She has made her home in St. Louis, Missouri, for some time.

CORNELIA JANE MATTHEWS JORDAN.

Mrs. Cornelia Jane Matthews Jordan was born at Lynchburg, Virginia, in 1830. Her father was Edwin Matthews and her mother, Emily Goggin Matthews. Her parents dying when she was young, she was brought up by her grandmother. In 1851 she married F. H. Jordan, a lawyer of Luray, Virginia. She is the author of many poems and some quite stirring lyrics of the Civil War. Her book of poems entitled "Corinth, and other Poems," published after the surrender was seized by the military commander of Richmond and suppressed. She has published a volume entitled "Richmond, Her Glory and Her Graves." Has also contributed many articles to magazines and newspapers, the best of which are "The Battle of Manassas," "The Death of Jackson and Appeal for Jefferson Davis." She is a member of the Alumni of the Convent of the Visitation, Georgetown, District of Columbia, her Alma Mater.

RUTH WARD KAHN.

Mrs. Ruth Ward Kahn was born in August, 1870, in Jackson, Michigan. She is a contributor to magazines and local newspapers. She is one of the youngest members of the Incorporated Society of Authors, of London, England. She is a member of the Authors' and Artists' Club, of Kansas City, and the Women's National Press Association.

MAREA WOOD JEFFERIS.

Mrs. Marea Wood Jefferis was born at Providence, Rhode Island, and is a descendant of William Brewster, of Mayflower fame. Her father is Doctor J. F. B. Flagg, a distinguished physician, who is well known through his work on anesthetics, and to whom is justly due the credit of making them practicable in the United States.

Her grandfather, Doctor Josiah Foster Flagg, was one of the early pioneers in dental surgery in the United States. Mrs. Jefferis' first husband was Thomas Wood; her second husband, Professor William Walter Jefferis, distinguished scientist and mineralogist. Mrs. Jefferis has published a volume of verses in memory of her daughter, the proceeds of which she has devoted to charity. She is a prominent resident of Philadelphia and is actively interested in all charitable work.

LUCY LARCOM.

Miss Lucy Larcom was born in Beverley, Massachusetts, in 1826. Her father died when she was but a child. In her early life Miss Larcom worked in the factories in Lowell, Massachusetts, and in her books "Idyls of Work" and a "New England Girlhood" she describes the life in these places. During her work she had constantly before her text-books to further her education, and in 1842 the operatives in the Lowell mills published a paper known as the *Offering*. Miss Larcom became one of the corps of writers for this paper and in it appeared many of her first poems; also verses and essays which were afterwards collected and published in book form. Miss Larcom holds an honored place among the women poets of America. Among her earliest contributions to the *Atlantic Monthly* was the "Rose Enthroned" which was attributed to Emerson, as it was published anonymously. "A Loyal Woman's Party" attracted considerable attention during the Civil War; also her poems entitled "Childhood's Songs." She was at one time a teacher in one of the young women's seminaries of Massachusetts. She was also a contributor to *Our Young Folks,* and at one time was the associate editor and later the editor of this periodical. She also collected and published in two volumes a compilation from the world's greatest religious thinkers, under the title of "Breathings of the Better Life." She was the author of a number of religious works. Her death occurred in Boston, April 17, 1893.

JOSEPHINE B. THOMAS PORTUONDO.

Was born in Belleville, Illinois, November 23, 1867. Her grandfather was William H. Bissell, the first Republican Governor of Illinois. Writer of short stories and contributor to *Benziger's Magazine* and the *Catholic Standard and Times.*

MARY F. NIXON ROULET.

Author, journalist, musician, art critic, and noted linguist. On her father's side she is descended from a distinguished English family who were prominent in the Revolution of 1812. On her mother's side, the family were prominent in Connecticut, and fought in the Revolutionary War. She was born in Indianapolis, Indiana, and educated in Philadelphia. She married Alfred de Roulet, B.S. and M.D. She is the author of several books, "The Harp of Many Chords," "Lasca and Other Stories," "The Blue Lady's Knight," "St. Anthony in Art," books on Spain, Alaska, Brazil, Greece, and Australia, also Japanese Folk and Fairy Tales, Indian Folk and Fairy Tales, and a contributor to the *Ladies' Home Journal, The Messenger, The Catholic World, The Rosary, New York Sun, New York World, Boston Transcript* and *Ave Maria.* Secretary of the Illinois Women's Press Association.

MARGARET ELLEN HENRY RUFFIN.

Was born in Alabama and is the daughter of Thomas Henry, of Kilglas, Ireland, who was a prominent merchant and banker of Mobile, Alabama. Her mother was a cousin of Archbishop Corrigan, of New York. One of her ancestors was the last Spanish Governor of Mobile. In 1887 she married Francis Gildart Ruffin, Jr., of Richmond, Virginia, who was the son of Francis G. Ruffin auditor of the state of Virginia for many years, and a great-great-grandson of Thomas Jefferson, and related to almost all the prominent families in Virginia, the Randolphs, Harrisons, Carys, Fairfaxes, and others. Mrs. Ruffin has written several books, one of which, "The North Star," a Norwegian historical work, was translated into the Norwegian language for the schools of that country, and she had the honor of receiving the congratulations of the King and Queen of Norway for this work; also having her name mentioned among the writers of consequence by the Society of Gens de Lettres, of Paris, in the Bibliotheque Nationale and given acclaim by the department of Belles Lettres of the Sorbonne, University of Paris, after receiving the degree of Doctor of Literature. Is the author of a small volume of poems entitled, "Drifting Leaves," and a story in verse, "John Gildart." Is a contributor to the magazines and papers of both the secular and religious press.

MARGARET LYNCH SENN.

Was born in 1882 in Chicago. Was the wife of a distinguished surgeon of that city, the late Doctor William Nicholas Senn. Mrs. Senn after her husband's death presented to the Newberry Library, of Chicago, the *cygne noir* edition number one of H. H. Bancroft's "Book of Health" in ten massive volumes. She is a contributor to the *Rosary Magazine* and *Times*.

HELEN GRACE SMITH.

Daughter of General Thomas Kilby Smith and was born in December, 1865, at Torresdale, Pennsylvania. Contributor of poems to various magazines, *The Atlantic Monthly, Lippincott's, The Rosary, Catholic World* and other religious papers.

MARY AGNES EASBY SMITH.

Was born in Washington, District of Columbia, February, 1855, when her father, Honorable William Russell Smith, was serving as a member of Congress from Alabama. Writes under the pen-name of Agnes Hampton. Has written sketches for several newspapers. In 1887 she married Milton E. Smith, editor of the *Church News*. Is the author of romances, poems, sketches, which have appeared in her husband's paper, and also *Donahoe's Magazine, The Messenger of the Sacred Heart,* and other church publications. Wrote some of the sketches which appeared in the "National Cyclopedia of Biography." Is at present one of the expert indexers of the Agricultural Department.

ALICE J. STEVENS.

Editor of *The Tidings,* Los Angeles, California. She was born March 10, 1860. Was at one time notary public for Los Angeles County. Was also engaged in the real estate business prior to becoming editor of *The Tidings.* Is a contributor to *Harper's, Sunset, Overland,* and *Los Angeles Times Magazine,* also edited the Children's Department, of the *Tidings* for a number of years. Is conspicuous in patriotic and philanthropic work.

MARY FLORENCE TANEY.

Was born at Newport, Kentucky, May 15, 1861. Her father, Peter Taney, was a grand-nephew of Roger B. Taney, chief justice of the United States. Her mother, Catherine Alphonse Taney, was descended from a distinguished Maryland family which came to this country with Lord Baltimore, in 1632. Miss Taney has been a teacher, president of a commercial college, newspaper correspondent, private secretary, and assistant editor of the *Woman's Club Magazine.* Has written an operetta, the state song of Kentucky, and has contributed to the well-known Catholic magazines.

CAROLINE WADSWORTH THOMPSON.

Was born in 1856 in New York City. Married Charles Otis Thompson, whose mother was a great-granddaughter of General Israel Putnam and daughter of Lemuel Grosvenor, of Boston. Her grandfather on her father's side was John Wadsworth, of New York. The wife of her maternal grandfather, Howard Henderson, was of French descent and her great-grandfather was one of the original signers of the Louisiana Purchase. Mrs. Thompson is a contributor to the *Ave Maria, Benziger's,* and *Sacred Heart Review,* and is a prominent woman socially and in the charitable works of the Catholic Church.

FRANCIS FISHER TIERNAN.

Is the daughter of Colonel Charles F. Fisher, of Salisbury, North Carolina. Married James M. Tiernan, of Maryland. Mrs. Tiernan is a writer of note and some of her novels, under the pen-name of "Christian Reid," are "A Daughter of Bohemia," "Valerie Aylmer," "Morton House," "The Lady of Las Cruces," and a "Little Maid of Arcady," and many others.

ELEANOR ELIZABETH TONG.

Daughter of Lucius G. Tong, at one time professor in the Notre Dame University. She is a descendant of William Tong, one of the Revolutionary heroes, and related also to Archbishop Punket. She is the author of the new manual of Catholic devotions under the title, "The Catholics' Manual, a New Manual of Prayer."

HONOR WALSH.

Associate editor of the *Catholic Standard and Times.* Is related to Daniel O'Connell and is the wife of Charles Thomas Walsh, of Philadelphia. She has charge of the home and school page of the *Young Crusader.* Is the author of "The Story Book House," and contributor to the *New York Sun, Youth's Companion, Benziger's, Donahoe's, The Rosary, Irish Monthly* and other publications of the Roman Catholic Church.

PAULINE WILLIS.

Was born in 1870, in Boston, Massachusetts. Daughter of Hamilton and Helen Phillips. Was a direct descendant on her mother's side, of Reverend George Phillips, of Watertown, Massachusetts, who came to this country in 1630 in Governor Winthrop's Massachusetts Colony from Norfolk, England. The descendants of this Doctor Phillips were the founders of the Phillips' Academy, at Andover, Massachusetts. Miss Willis is the author of "The Willis' Records, or Records of the Willis Family of Haverhill, Portland, and Boston"; also a memoir of her late brother, Hamilton Willis, and is a contributor to the Catholic and secular press, and active worker in the charitable works and the foreign missions of the Roman Catholic Church.

CELIA LOGAN.

Was born in 1840, in Philadelphia, Pennsylvania. When quite young she filled a highly responsible position as critical reader of manuscripts in a large publishing house of London. While here she was a regular correspondent of the *Boston Saturday Evening Gazette* and the *Golden Era* of San Francisco, and was well-known as a writer of short stories for magazines in the United States and England. After the war, on her return to America, she became associate editor of the *Capital*, Don Piatt's paper published in Washington, District of Columbia. She did a great deal of translating from French and Italian. She was a writer of plays, the first of which was entitled "Rose," followed by "An American Marriage." In one of her plays Fay Templeton made her appearance and won success as a child actress. She wrote several stories and arranged and adapted from the French several plays. Her first husband was Minor K. Kellogg, an artist. After his death she married James H. Connelly, an author. She died in 1904.

HARRIET M. LOTHROP.

Was born June 22, 1844, in New Haven, Connecticut. She is best known under her pen-name "Margaret Sidney." Daughter of Sidney Mason Stone and Harriet Mulford Stone, and is connected with some of the most distinguished of the Puritan families. Her genius for writing began to develop early and the products of her pen have had wide circulation and enjoyed an enviable reputation. She is the author of the well-known "Five Little Pepper Stories," stories for children and young people. Mrs. Lothrop has written many books. Her story, "A New Departure for Girls" was written for those who are left without the means of support with the object of having them see their opportunities. In October 1881, she married Daniel Lothrop, the publisher and founder of the D. Lothrop Company. Their home at Wayside, in Concord, New Hampshire, is well-known, having been the home of Nathaniel Hawthorne. Mr. Lothrop's death occurred March 18, 1892, and since that time Mrs. Lothrop has devoted herself entirely to literary work, the education of her daughter, and to the patriotic societies of which she is a member. She is the originator and organizer of the children's society known as the "Children of the American Revolution," to instill and encourage a spirit of patriotism in the children of America whose mothers are members of the Daughters of the American Revolution. Mrs. Lothrop is a woman of remarkable ability, fine literary talent, and possessed of unusual business qualifications. She is the author of "Polly Pepper's Chicken Pie," "Phronsie's New Shoes," "Miss Scarrett," "So as by Fire," "Judith Pettibone," "Half Year at Bronckton," "How They Went to Europe," "The Golden West," "Old Concord; Her Highways and Byways," etc. She is the author of many short stories which have been published in various periodicals for children and young people of the United States.

FRANCES LAWTON MACE.

Was born January 15, 1836. Her poems have appeared in the *New York Journal of Commerce*. At the age of eighteen she published her famous hymn, "Only Waiting," in the *Waterville Mail*, which has been rated as a classic. In 1855 she became the wife of Benjamin L. Mace, a lawyer of Bangor, and they later removed to San Jose, California. In 1883 she published a collection of poems in a volume entitled "Legends, Lyrics, and Sonnets," and later one entitled "Under Pine and Palm."

CALLIE BONNEY MARBLE.

Was born in Peoria, Illinois. Daughter of Honorable C. C. Bonney, a late noted lawyer of Chicago. She has inherited from a legal ancestry great mental strength. She has published two prose works, "Wit and Wisdom of Bulwer," and "Wit and Wisdom of Webster," and has made many translations of Victor Hugo's shorter works. She has written poems, sketches, stories for periodicals, and quite a number of songs which were set to music. She dramatized the "Rienzi" of Bulwer. She married Earl Marble, the well-known editor, art and dramatic critic, and author.

VELMA CALDWELL MELVILLE.

Writer of prose and poetry. Was born July 1, 1858, in Greenwood, Wisconsin. Her mother's maiden name was Artlissa Jordan. Her father lost his life before Petersburg during the Civil War. She is the wife of James E. Melville, a well-known educator and prohibitionist. She was at one time editor of the Home Circle and Youths' Department of the *Practical Farmer* of Philadelphia, and the Hearth and Home Department of the *Wisconsin Farmer*, of Madison, Wisconsin. She has been one of the most voluminous writers in current publications that the Central West has produced.

DORA RICHARDS MILLER.

Was born in the Island of St. Thomas, Danish West Indies. Her father, Richard Richards, was descended from a noted English family. Through her mother, she was descended from the family of Hezekiah Huntington, of Connecticut. On the death of her father, and on account of many losses through insurrection of the natives and hurricanes, to which this island was subject, her mother removed to New Orleans. In 1862 she became the wife of Anderson Miller, a lawyer from Mississippi, and went to Arkansas to reside. Troubles resulting from the war caused the breaking up of her family, and some of their experiences during the siege of Vicksburg are recounted in her articles published in the *Century Magazine*, entitled "Diary of a Young Woman During the Siege of Vicksburg," and "Diary of a Young Woman in the South." After her husband's death she taught in the public schools, and ultimately was appointed to the chair of science in the Girls' High School of New Orleans. During all this time she was a contributor to the local press. In 1886 her war diary was published in the *Century*, and attracted great attention. In 1889, she wrote, in conjunction with George W. Cable, "The Haunted House on Royal Street." She has written also for *Lippincott's, Louisiana Journal of Education* and *Practical Housekeeper.*

CLARA JESSUP MOORE.

Poet, novelist and philanthropist; was born February 16, 1824, in Philadelphia, Pennsylvania. Her mother's family name is found in the Doomsday Book compiled in 1086. She is of distinguished ancestry, and descended from some of the prominent families of Virginia, Massachusetts and other states of the Union. One of her ancestors was lieutenant in King Phillip's War, and many of the prominent men of pioneer days are among Mrs. Moore's ancestors. She became the wife of Bloomfield Haines Moore, of Philadelphia, Pa., in October, 1842. After her marriage her home in Philadelphia became the resort of literary people, among them some of the most gifted authors of the day, and at this time she began her literary work. In 1855 she was widely known as a writer of prose and poetry, and her name appears in "Hart's Female Prose Writers of America." She is the author of a long list of novels and short stories. She did splendid work on the Sanitary Commission during the war, being corresponding secretary of the Women's Pennsylvania Branch. She also organized the special relief committee, which took such an active part in hospital work during the Civil War, a non-sectional organization. After the war Mrs. Moore resumed her literary work, and has given from the proceeds of her labors liberally to works of charity. One of her articles, which appeared in *Lippincott's Magazine* in 1873, under the title "Unsettled Points of Etiquette," drew upon her much unfavorable comment. In 1873 she published a revised edition of "The Young Lady's Friend," and in 1875 a collection of verses, followed by many others; one "On Dangerous Ground" reached its seventh edition, and was translated into Swedish and French. It is eminently a book for women. She at one time maintained her residence in London, England, which was a center for literary and scientific men and women of the day.

E. PAULINE JOHNSON.

E. Pauline Johnson was born in Brant county, Ontario, at the city of Brantfort. Her father, George Henry Martin Johnson, was head chief of the Mohawks. Her mother, Emily S. Howells, an English woman, was born in Bristol, England. Her paternal grandfather was the distinguished John "Sakayenkwaeaghton" (Disappearing Mist) Johnson, a pure Mohawk, and the speaker of the Six Nation Council for forty years. During the War of 1812 he fought for the British. His paternal great-grandfather, Tekahionwake, was given the name of Johnson by Sir William Johnson, hence the family name which they now use. Mrs. Johnson is a writer of verse and a contributor to many of the leading papers in Canada and the United States, of the latter the *Boston Transcript.*

GENIE CLARK POMEROY.

Born in April, 1867, in Iowa City, Iowa. Her father, Rush Clark, was one of the early pioneers of Iowa, her mother, a teacher, who died when Mrs. Pomeroy was born. When Genie Clark was eleven years old she went to Washington, D. C., to be with her father during his second term in Congress. While at school in Des Moines, Iowa, she met Carl H. Pomeroy, a son of the president of the Callaman College, whom she married. After their marriage Mr. Pomeroy took the Chair of History in this college. In 1888 they moved to Seattle, Washington, and here Mrs. Pomeroy made her first literary venture, contributing to prominent papers of the Pacific coast. She is best known as a poet, though she has written quite a number of short stories and essays.

IDORA M. PLOWMAN MOORE.

Born in 1843, near Talladega, Alabama. She was known by the pen name of "Betsy Hamilton." She was the daughter of the late General Wm. B. McClellan and Mrs. Martha Robey McClellan. General McClellan was a graduate of West Point, and before the Civil War commanded the militia troops of the counties of Talladega, Clay and Randolph, in Alabama. When quite young Miss McClellan became the wife of a brilliant young lawyer, Albert W. Plowman, of Talladega, who died a few years after their marriage. Later, Mrs. Plowman married Captain M. V. Moore, of Atlanta, Georgia, who was on the editorial staff of the *Atlanta Constitution,* and they made their home in Auburn, Alabama. "Betsy Hamilton" was the author of innumerable dialect sketches of the old-time plantation life, life in the backwoods among the class denominated as "crackers." She wrote for the *Constitution* and the *Sunny South.* At the personal request of Mr. Conant, the editor of *Harper's Weekly,* several of her sketches were illustrated and appeared in that magazine. The late Henry W. Grady was a warm prsonal friend of Mrs. Moore, and aided in bringing her talent before the world and making the "Betsy Hamilton" sketches familiar in England as well as this country.

ELLEN OLNEY KIRK.

Mrs. Ellen Olney Kirk was born November 6, 1842, at Southington, Connecticut. Her father, Jesse Olney, was at one time state comptroller, and is the well-known author of a number of text books, particularly so as the author of a geography and atlas, a standard work in the American schools for many years. Her mother was a sister of A. S. Barnes, the New York publisher. Her first work was a novel, entitled "Love in Idleness," which appeared as a serial in *Lippincott's Magazine* in 1876. She has written a great deal since then. Since her marriage her home has been in Germantown, Pa., and the scenes of two of her books are laid in the region surrounding this city. One of her most noted books is entitled "The Story of Margaret Kent." Among her other books may be mentioned "Queen Money," "The Daughter of Eve," "Walfred," "Narden's Choosing" and "Ciphers."

ADELINE GRAFTON KNOX.

Mrs. Adeline Grafton Knox was born in Saccarappa, February 8, 1845. Her father was the Rev. Mark Grafton, a Methodist clergyman of New England, where she passed her early life. At the beginning of the Civil War her father held a pastorate in Albany, New York, and later one in Washington, D. C., while serving as a member of the House of Representatives. Miss Grafton began her literary career in 1860, publishing a few stories and sketches under a fictitious name in the *Republican,* of Springfield, Massachusetts. In 1874 the novel "Katherine Earl" ran as a serial in *Scribner's Monthly;* another, "His Inheritance," in the same magazine. In 1889 she wrote a novelette, which appeared in book form under the title of "Dorothy's Experience." In this year Miss Grafton became the wife of the Honorable Samuel Knox, a distinguished lawyer of St. Louis, Missouri.

AGNES LEONARD HILL.

Born in Louisville, Kentucky, January 20, 1842. Daughter of Dr. Oliver Langdon and Agnes (Howard) Leonard. Writer for newspapers of Chicago and other cities. Has done evangelical work. In 1896 was assistant pastor of St. Paul's Universalist Church, Chicago. In 1905 was pastor of the Congregational Church, Wollaston, England. Has written on religious subjects.

MARY HANNAH KROUT.

Born in Crawfordsville, Indiana, November 3, 1857. Daughter of Robert K. and Caroline (Brown) Krout; sister of Caroline Krout; was the associate editor of the *Crawfordsville Journal* in 1881, and the *Terre Haute Express* in 1882; served ten years on the staff of the Chicago *Inter-Ocean;* was correspondent from Hawaii, New Zealand, Australia and England; writer of syndicate letters for daily papers; also several books on Hawaii; prepared for publication the autobiography of General Lew Wallace in 1906.

SARA LOUISA VICKERS OBERHOLTZER.

Born May 20, 1841, in Uwchlan, Pennsylvania. Her father, Paxon, and her mother, Anne T. Vickers were cultured Quakers. Among her best-known odes was "The Bayard Taylor Burial Ode," sung as Pennsylvania's tribute to her dead poet at his funeral services in Longwood, March 15, 1889. She is very much interested in the study of natural history, and has been considered a naturalist of some prominence; has one of the finest collections of Australian bird skins and eggs in the United States, and has given much attention to the work of introducing school savings banks into the public schools, also aided in instituting the University Extension movement; is prominent in the Woman's Christian Temperance Union.

ANNA CAMPBELL PALMER.

Born in Palmyra, New York, February 3, 1854. She has written a number of poems, which have appeared in the principal magazines; is also a successful author of fiction, biography, etc.

FANNIE PURDY PALMER.

Was born July 11, 1839, in New York City. Daughter of Henry and Mary Catherine Sharp Purdy; descended on her father's side from Captain Purdy, of the British army, who was killed in the battle of White Plains. Her literary contributions have been to the *Home Journal, Putnam's Magazine, Peterson's Magazine* and others. In 1862 she married Dr. William H. Palmer, surgeon of the Third New York Cavalry, accompanying him to the seat of war, and there continuing her literary work by short stories and poems for *Harper's* and the *Galaxy,* and letters to various newspapers. Since the war she has been prominently identified with measures for the advancement of women and the various educational and philanthropic movements. From 1884-1892 she was president of the Rhode Island Women's Club and director of the General Federation of Women's Clubs. She has taken special interest in popularizing the study of American history, having herself prepared and given a series of "Familiar Talks on American History," as a branch of the educational work of the Woman's Educational and Industrial Union. She is keenly alive to the importance of the higher education of women, is secretary of a society organized to secure for women the educational privileges of Brown University, and in 1892 all of its examinations and degrees were open to women.

HELEN WATERSON MOODY.

Was born in Cleveland, Ohio, May 17, 1860; did newspaper work on the Cleveland *Leader* and *Sun,* and was assistant professor of rhetoric and English in the University of Wooster until 1889, when she accepted a position on the staff of the New York *Evening Sun.* Mrs. Moody is best known for her articles which appeared in the *Sun* under the heading "Woman About Town," a title created for her, and under which she wrote in a semi-editorial manner a column every day. Her husband, Winfield S. Moody, Jr., is also a journalist.

HELEN JAMES DOLE.

Born in Worcester. Daughter of William Montgomery and Frances Fletcher Bennett. Translator of Victor Hugo's "Ninety-Three," Theuriet's "Abbe Daniel," Pierre Loti's "Iceland Fisherman," Theuriet, "Rustic Life in France," Rostand's "Cyrano de Bergerac," also orations of Marat, and many other French books.

EDITH WHARTON.

Mrs. Edward Wharton, best known to American story readers as Edith Wharton, author of "The House of Mirth," has a summer home at Lenox, Massachusetts, which is the scene of many gatherings of notable people. As Miss Edith Jones, and afterwards as Mrs. Edward Wharton, she held an enviable position in New York's best society, but of late she has practically given up living in the metropolis, and divides her time between Lenox and Paris. In the French capital

Mrs. Wharton's literary and social success has been phenomenal. The French are the most exclusive people, socially, in the world, but they have opened their doors to Mrs. Wharton in appreciation of her many gifts. The author of "The House of Mirth" speaks French as fluently as a native, and in that language writes regularly for *Le Revue des Deux Mondes.* Some of Mrs. Wharton's other works of fiction are "The Valley of Decision," "Sanctuary" and "The Fruit of the Tree."

MARY JOHNSON BAILEY LINCOLN.

Born at Attleboro, Massachusetts, July 8, 1844. Daughter of Rev. John Milton and Sarah Morgan Johnson Bailey. In 1865 she married David A. Lincoln, at Norton, Massachusetts, who is now deceased; is a writer and lecturer on domestic science, and was the first principal of the Boston Cooking School; culinary editor of the *American Kitchen Magazine* in 1893; is now a noted lecturer on cookery in the seminaries of the large cities of the United States; author of the "Boston Cook Book," "Peerless Cook Book," "Carving and Serving," and other works on domestic science.

EDITH DOWE MINITER.

Born in Wilbraham, Massachusetts, May 19, 1869. Daughter of William Hilton and Jennie E. Tupper Dowe. In 1887 married John T. F. Miniter, now deceased. In 1890 was city editor of the *Manchester Press,* the only woman editor of a daily in New England. In 1895-6 she was editor of the *Boston Home Journal,* and was the first woman president of the National Amateur Press Association. In 1888 she wrote an article for the *Boston Globe,* entitled "How to Dress on $40 a Year," which created widespread notice and discussion.

CHARLOTTE PORTER.

Born in Towanda, Pennsylvania, January 6, 1859. Daughter of Dr. Henry Clinton and Eliza Betts Porter; has edited, in conjunction with Helen A. Clarke, "Poems of Robert Browning," "Browning's Complete Works," and "Mrs. Browning's Complete Works," "The Pembroke Edition of Shakespeare," and is sole editor of the "First Folio Edition of Shakespeare"; author of "Dramatic Motive in Browning's 'Strafford,'" "Shakespeare's Studies," and has contributed poems to the *Atlantic, Century, Outlook, Poet-Lore,* and other periodicals.

HELEN ARCHIBALD CLARKE.

Born in Philadelphia. Daughter of Hugh Archibald and Jane M. Searle Clarke; lecturer on mythology in Philadelphia, also on literary topics; has edited, in connection with Charlotte Porter, the "Poems of Robert Browning," "Clever Tales," from the French, Russian and Bohemian; "Browning's Complete Works," and a folio edition of Shakespeare; author of "Browning's England," "Browning's Italy," "Longfellow's Country," "Child's Guide to Mythology," "Ancient Myths in Modern Poets," in conjunction with Charlotte Porter; "Browning's Study Programmes," "Shakespeare Studies—Macbeth," and is also a composer of music and songs; writer of articles, essays and reviews on poetry, and one of the founders of the American Musical Society.

ANNA ELIZABETH DICKINSON.

Who is an author, playwright, actress, philanthropist and public speaker. She was born in Philadelphia, October 28, 1842. Her parents were Quakers and she was educated at the Friends' Free School. She began her public career by speaking on slavery and temperance. In 1861 she was given a position in the United States Mint, in Philadelphia but was removed because of the charges against General McClellan, which she made in a public address. In 1864 she donated to the Freedman's Relief Society a thousand dollars, the proceeds of one lecture. In 1876 she made her first appearance on the stage in a play from her own pen, called "A Crown of Thorns." She tried other parts, but her career met with disaster. Her principal success has been in the lecture field. She is the author of "A Ragged Register of People, Places and Opinions."

ADA CELESTE SWEET.

Author and business woman. Daughter of Gen. Benjamin J. Sweet, a lawyer and distinguished officer of the Civil War. She was born in Stockbridge, Wisconsin, February 23, 1853. Miss Sweet is one of the most noted women in America. At the age of sixteen she was the assistant to her father who was at that time United States pension agent in Chicago, and afterwards first deputy commissioner of Internal Revenue. Upon her father's death, in January, 1867, President Grant appointed Miss Sweet United States pension agent in Chicago. She has disbursed many million dollars annually making a most remarkable record as a business woman, and has installed many valuable reforms, reduced the work of her office to a system, which the government gladly recognized and approved by installing the same in all other pension offices in the United States. In 1885 she resigned this office to engage in business for herself. She was for two years literary editor of the *Chicago Tribune,* and since 1888 has maintained an office as United States claim attorney, and during this time has done considerable literary and philanthropic work. She was the founder of the ambulance system for the Chicago police.

MARTHA GALLISON MOORE AVERY.

Is the daughter of A. K. P. Moore, and on her father's side is descended from Irish, Scotch and Dutch ancestry; on her mother's, from English. Her people have always been distinguished in the various conflicts for freedom which have taken place in this country. Major John Moore, of Bunker Hill fame, was one of her kinsmen, and her grandfather, General Samuel Moore, was conspicuous in state affairs. Mrs. Avery's first active part in public life was as a charter member of the First Nationalist Club of Boston, which claimed among its members such distinguished personages as Edward Everett Hale and Mary Livermore. She later became a socialist, and was director of the Karl Marx class, which taught the economics of socialism, and this later became the Boston School of Political Economy. She is an acknowledged authority on philosophy, history and economic theories. She wrote, in conjunction with David Goldstein, one of her students, a book entitled "Socialism" and "The Nation of Fatherless Children." She has lectured and written constantly in the interests of socialism for many years. She is at present head of the Boston School of Political Economy. Having become a convert to the Roman Catholic faith, she is to-day one of the most eloquent speakers and writers against the socialistic movement; is a contributor to the *National Civic Federation Review, Social Justice,* and is at work on a book entitled "Twenty-Five Socialists Answered"; also a work on the "Primal Principles of Political Economy."

CAROLINE M. BEAUMONT.

Is the daughter of Joseph I. Beaumont, of St. Paul, Minnesota; is a writer on the *St. Paul Dispatch,* and founder of the Guild of Catholic Women.

MARY AXTELL BISHOP.

Was born January 19, 1859, in Galena, Illinois, and is the daughter of the Rev. Charles Axtell. Her mother was one of the descendants of the Campbells, who took a prominent part in the settlement of Virginia. In 1884 she married General J. W. Bishop. She was the first president of the Guild of Catholic Women, and founder of the Altar Guild of the Cathedral of St. Paul, Minnesota. She has written several poems and some clever prose.

FLORENCE L. HOLMES BORK.

Was born in Bracken County, Kentucky, October 29, 1869, and is a collateral descendant of Patrick Henry. She has written for magazines and papers short stories, sketches and poems since she was thirteen years of age; was private secretary to John M. Crawford, of Cincinnati, when minister to St. Petersburg. In 1902 she married George L. Bork, of Buffalo, whose aunt is Mother Severine, Superior of three institutions of Sisters of Notre Dame de Providence. She is a member of many prominent clubs and charitable organizations and societies, the Federation of Women's Clubs and the Catholic Women's Clubs. She writes principally under the pen name of Alice Benedict.

ANNA ELIZABETH BUCHANAN.

Was born in Trinity, Newfoundland, in 1836, and was the daughter of Rev. David and Elizabeth Roper Martin. She was a direct descendant of Thomas Moore, who suffered martyrdom during the reign of King Henry VIII of England. Her husband was a missionary in Newfoundland, acting also as physician. Mrs. Buchanan for some years conducted a publication, *The Voice of the Deaf,* for deaf mutes, and also was the founder of a mission in England, and contributor to the *Catholic World.* She was a convert to Roman Catholicism.

LELIA HARDIN BUGG.

Author of "The Correct Thing for Catholics," "The Prodigal's Daughter," "Correct English" and "The People of Our Parish." She took a special course in philosophy and modern languages at Trinity College, Washington, D. C.

MARY GILMORE CARTER.

Was born in 1867 in Boston, Massachusetts, and was the daughter of Patrick S. Gilmore, the famous band leader. Her husband was John P. Carter, a prominent business man of New York City. Mrs. Carter is the author of a book of verse and a novel entitled "A Son of Esau," and "Songs from the Wings"; is a contributor to the *Catholic World, The Coming Age, Frank Leslie's* and many other magazines and periodicals.

EMMA FORBES CAREY.

Was born in Boston Massachusetts, October 10, 1833. She is descended from English ancestry, one of whom, Sir William Carey, was mayor and sheriff of Bristol, England in the reign of Henry VIII. Miss Carey has devoted her life for twenty-five years to the needs of the unfortunate inmates of prisons. She is a contributor to the *Catholic World, The Young Catholic* and the *Ave Maria.*

CAROLINE ELIZABETH CORBIN.

Was born November 9, 1835, in Pomfret, Connecticut. Some of her ancestors on her mother's side came over from England in the *Mayflower*, and those of a later generation founded the city of Pomfret. In 1861 she married Calvin R. Corbin, and they removed to Chicago, Illinois. She is the author of quite a number of books, among which are "Our Bible Class and the Good that Came from It," "Rebecca, or a Woman's Secret," "His Marriage Vow," "A Woman's Philosophy of Love," etc. At one time she was president of the Chicago Society for the Promotion of Social Purity and president of a society opposed to the extension of suffrage to women.

MARY CATHERINE CROWLEY.

Daughter of J. C. and Mary Cameron Crowley, and was born in Boston, Massachusetts. She is descended from Scotch ancestry; editor of the *Catholic Mission Magazine* and *The Annals of the Propagation of the Faith* since 1907; author of "Merry Hearts and True," "Happy-Go-Lucky," "A Daughter of New France" and other short and historical stories. She was one of the historians on the "Memorial History of Detroit," and is considered an authority on the early history of that city, and suggested and brought about the erection of a memorial tablet to Mme. Cadillac, the first white woman of the Northwest; is a contributor to the *Catholic World, Ave Maria, St. Nicholas, Wide-Awake, Ladies' Home Journal, The Pilot, Donahoe's* and other magazines.

53

MARGARET DEANE.

Was born July 22, 1831, in New York City; was a public school teacher in the city of New York from 1846 to 1848, and later in San Francisco, California; author of books for children; for ten years was grand president of the Catholic Ladies' Aid Society of San Francisco. Her husband was the late James R. Deane.

ADELAIDE MARGARET DELANEY.

Was born in Philadelphia, Pennsylvania, in 1875; assistant at the University Settlement, and collector of data for the Bureau of Child Labor in New York City; editor of the Woman's Department of the *Philadelphia Record;* has lectured on the Catholic attitude in social work; author of a series of lectures on "Jottings of a Journalist in England, France and Ireland"; contributor to *Ladies' Home Journal* and active advocate of Home Rule for Ireland and suffrage for women.

AGNES CATHERINE DOYLE.

Was born in Boston, Massachusetts, and is the daughter of Edward and Margaret Keating Doyle; is reference librarian in the Boston Public Library; assisted in editing a contribution to the bibliography of the United States navy, compiled by Charles T. Harbeck; author of the "History of the Winthrop School, of Boston"; reviser of a list for finding genealogies of towns and local histories in the public library of Boston; has contributed articles on current topics to magazines and newspapers.

MARTHA CLAIRE DOYLE.

Born in Boston, June 16, 1869. Daughter of Henry and Anne Lande Mac-Gowan. In 1896 she married James R. Doyle. Is the author of "Little Miss Dorothy," "Wide-Awake," "Jimmy Sutor and the Boys of Pigeon Camp," "The Boys of Pigeon Camp; Their Luck and Fun," and "Mint Julep," a story of New England life.

MARY EMILIE EWING.

Was born in Cincinnati, Ohio, November 13, 1872. Her husband was a relative of Mrs. W. T. Sherman, wife of the distinguished general, and also of Edgar Allan Poe. Mrs. Ewing contributes to the religious press of Cincinnati and Chicago and has written some creditable poems.

LYDIA STIRLING FLINTHAM.

Author and lecturer; was born on the family plantation in Cecil County, Maryland. Her family were of English ancestry, and came to New Castle, Delaware, in the early days of our country's history. Miss Flintham is a lecturer on English composition and literary topics; has written many stories, and has for several years been the editor of the juvenile department of the *Good Counsel Magazine,* contributor to *Donahoe's, Rosary, Metropolitan, Catholic World* and other Catholic magazines.

MARY CRAWFORD FRASER.

Was born in Rome, Italy, in 1851. Daughter of Thomas Crawford, the sculptor, and Louise Ward, who was the niece of the late Julia Ward Howe and sister of Marion Crawford. In 1873 she married Hugh Fraser, who was sent on a diplomatic mission to Japan, Vienna and other foreign countries. Mrs. Fraser is the author of a number of books, some of which are "A Diplomatist's Wife in Many Lands," "The Brown Ambassador" and "The Splendid Porsena."

HELEN HAINES.

Daughter of John Ladd Colby, a physician of New York, where she was born. She married Charles Owens Haines, of Savannah, Georgia, who was a railroad builder and manager; has contributed short stories, some of which are entitled "Caper Sauce," "The Crimson Rambler," to the *American Magazine* and *Scribner's Magazine.*

EDITH OGDEN HARRISON.

Daughter of Robert N. Ogden, and the wife of Carter Henry Harrison, mayor of Chicago, Illinois, who occupies the unique position of having been elected five times mayor of Chicago and his father before him was also five times mayor of that city. Mrs. Harrison is the author of "Prince Silverwings," "The Star Fairies," "The Moon Princess," "The Flaming Sword," "The Mocking Bird," "Biblical Stories Retold for Children," "Cotton Myth," "Polar Star" and other short stories.

ELIZABETH JORDAN.

Was born May 9, 1867, in Milwaukee, Wisconsin. Daughter of William Francis Jordan and Marguerita Garver Jordan. Soon after her graduation she accepted a position on the staff of the New York *World,* with which she was connected for ten years as interviewer and writer on questions of the day, doing some of the "biggest features" of the *World.* While engaged in this work she wrote her first story, "Tales of the City Room," which was suggested by her experiences as a reporter and editor. She made quite an extensive investigation of the tenement conditions in New York, and wrote of them under the title, "The Submerged Tenth." Later, she made a study of sociological conditions in London and Paris, which furnished material for other books. In 1900 Miss Jordan became one of the editors of *Harper's Bazar,* a position which she holds at the present time. She is the author of "Tales of the Cloister," a convent story; "Tales of Destiny," "May Iverson—Her Book," "Many Kingdoms," and author in "The Whole Family," written in conjunction with William Dean Howells, Henry James, Henry Van Dyke, Elizabeth Stuart Phelps, Alice Brown and others. She took a special course at the Sorbonne, in Paris, in 1902, and in 1903 she received the blessing of the pope, Leo XIII, for her services in literature.

MARGARET H. WYNNE LAWLESS.

Was born at Adrian, Michigan, July 14, 1847. Daughter of John and Jane Meehan Wynne. After graduating from school she taught for several years, and in 1873 married Dr. James T. Lawless, of Toledo, Ohio, where she has since made her home; has contributed to the *Catholic World, Ave Maria, Rosary Magazine, Pilot, New World,* and conducted the children's department for a number of years of the *Catholic Universe;* has also contributed to *Frank Leslie's Weekly, Demorest's, American Magazine, Lippincott's, Golden Days, Detroit Free Press* and *Travelers' Record.* Both she and her husband have been active workers in the cause of Catholic education and the development of Catholic charitable, literary and socialistic societies and institutions. Mrs. Lawless incorporated and took out a charter for the Catholic Ladies of Ohio, the first insurance and benevolent society for women in the United States, and was for six years secretary of this organization.

ELIZA O'BRIEN LUMMIS.

Daughter of William and Anne O'Brien Lummis, and was born in New York City; was one of the prominent members of the Society of the Children of Mary, and founder of the People's Eucharistic League, an organization in connection with the Catholic Cathedral of New York City, and one of the largest Catholic organizations of New York. She assisted in organizing the Corpus Christi Reunion for Men; was instrumental in the installation of the Fathers of the Blessed Sacrament in the Church of Jean the Baptiste, and in the establishment of the first public throne of exposition in New York. She founded, edited and published the *Sentinel of the Blessed Sacrament,* a Eucharistic monthly and the organ of the Priests' Eucharistic League; is also the founder of the Society of the Daughters of the Faith. Miss Lummis is the author of "Daughters of the Faith," "A Nineteenth Century Apostle," several poems and magazine articles dealing with the questions of the day. She is one of the leading Catholic women of the United States.

MARY JOSEPHINE LUPTON.

Was born in County Down, Ireland; is an associate editor of the *New World,* Chicago; translator of "The Child of the Moon" and "The Task of Little Peter," from the French, and is a contributor to the *Rosary Magazine,* the *New World* and *Church Extension.*

COUNTESS SARAH MARIA ALOISA SPOTTISWOOD MACKIN.

Was born at Troy, Missouri, July 29, 1850, and was the daughter of James H. Britton, at one time mayor of St. Louis. She comes of Revolutionary stock her great-grandfather having commanded the man-of-war *Tempest* in the American Revolution. Her husband James Mackin, was at one time state treasurer of New York. Mrs. Mackin was created a countess by Pope Leo XIII. She is the author of "A Society Woman on Two Continents," "From Rome to Lourdes," and has contributed to the *Revue de la Papauté et les Peuples.*

SISTER MARY MAGDALENE (SARAH C. COX)

Daughter of James Cox, of Philadelphia, Pennsylvania; Mother Superior for several terms at the Convent of the Visitation, Wilmington, Delaware, and translator of devotional and religious works.

MARY E. MANNIX.

Born May 17, 1846, in New York City. Her father, Michael Walsh, was one of the early pioneers of the West, settling in Cincinnati, Ohio many years ago. He did much for the establishment of the Catholic Church in the West particularly in the city of Cincinnati. She married John B. Mannix, a succcessful Catholic lawyer of San Diego, California. Mrs. Mannix's first writings in verse and prose appeared in the *Catholic World*, and were followed by others in various Catholic magazines. She has written sketches, reviews, stories for children, and made some most commendable translations in prose and verse from the French, German and Spanish She is a contributer to the leading Catholic journals of the day; has written a "Life of Sister Louise," Superior of the Sisters of Notre Dame, of Namur, in Cincinnati, and also lives of other sisters of the various orders. She is a well-known writer of children's stories.

ELIZABETH GILBERT MARTIN.

Was born December 21, 1837, at Albany, New York, of Revolutionary ancestry. She married Homer D. Martin, a landscape painter; is the author of "Whom God Hath Joined," and translator of St. Amand's "Women of the French Salons" and other books.

NORMA GERTRUDE McCHESNEY.

Was born March 28, 1876, in Marysville, Kansas. On her father's side she is descended from Highland Scotch ancestry, and through her mother is connected with the famous Choate family, of which Rufus and Joseph Choate are members. She is also a relative of George W. Cable; is a teacher of piano music and contributor to the *London Tablet, St. Peter's Net, The Lamp* and *Rose Leaves.*

ELLA McMAHON.

Sister of the late General M. T. McMahon, of New York, and sister-in-law of Rear Admiral F. M. Ramsay, United States Navy; translator of "Golden Sands," "Little Month of May" and devotional works, and is also a contributor to Catholic magazines.

MARY ANTONIO GALLAGHER MERCEDES.

Who is known under the pen name of "Rev. Richard W. Alexander"; is a Sister of Mercy in the diocese of Pittsburgh. Her parents were among the early settlers of eastern Pennsylvania, and were descendants of the Hookey and Drexel families. She became a Sister of Mercy at the age of eighteen; was treasurer of the extensive community of Pittsburgh, and later became a teacher in St. Xavier's, Beatty, Pennsylvania, where she is at present. She is the author of several books and plays for girls, used in many of the convent schools throughout the world; is a contributor to the *Ave Maria, The Missionary, Catholic Standard and Times.*

MARY ALOYSIA MOLLOY.

Author of a concordance to the Anglo-Saxon version of "Bede's Ecclesiastical History" and articles on the "Celtic Revival and Pedagogical Subjects," "Word Pairs—A Comparative Study of French and English," and "Rhetorical Structure."

JEAN ELIZABETH URSULA NEALIS.

Is the daughter of John Wilkinson, a distinguished engineer, and was born in Frederickton, New Brunswick. One of her ancestors was the founder of the city of Portland, Maine; author of "Drift," a volume of poems, and contributor of poems and stories to Catholic publications.

KATHERINE A. O'MAHONEY.

Born in Kilkenny, Ireland. Daughter of Patrick and Rose O'Keeffe. She married Daniel J. O'Mahoney; teacher in the Lawrence High School, and lecturer on literary and historical subjects; founded, published and edited the *Catholic Register,* and was contributor to the *Boston Pilot,* the *Sacred Heart Review, Donahoe's Magazine* and magazine of *Our Lady of Good Counsel;* prominent in the women's branch of the Irish Land League; founder and president of the Aventine Literary Club and of the Orphans' Friends' Society, of Lawrence County; organizer of a division of the Ladies' Auxiliary, Ancient Order of Hibernians, and was its president for five years, and also president of the Essex County Auxiliary; organizer and first president of the St. Mary's Alumnæ Association, vice-president of the Lawrence Anti-Tuberculosis League; author of "Catholicity in Lawrence," "Faith of Our Fathers," a poem; "Moore's Birthday," a musical allegory; "Famous Irish Women," and a collection of Hibernian odes. Mrs. O'Mahoney was among the first Catholic women to speak in public in New England, and has delivered her lectures in many of the cities. Some of these are entitled "A Trip to Ireland," "Religion and Patriotism in English and Irish History," "Mary, Queen of Scots, and Joan of Arc," "An Evening with Milton," an illustrated lecture on "Paradise Lost;" "An Evening with Dante" and "The Passion Play of Oberammergau."

SALLIE MARGARET O'MALLEY.

Was born in Centreville, Wayne County, Indiana, December 8, 1862, and is the wife of the distinguished and well-known poet and writer, Charles J. O'Malley. She is a descendant of the noted Claiborne called the "Scourge of Maryland," and also of the noted Hill family, of Virginia, her father being a cousin of A. P. Hill, called "Fighting Hill." Her mother was Sallie Rogers Ragland Wilson, a descendant of James Wilson, who was one of the signers of the Declaration of Independence. Mrs. O'Malley has illustrated many of her husband's poems, and is a composer of music, and has written quite a number of songs. She is also author of several novels, among them "The Boys of the Prairie," "An Heir of Dreams."

MARY BOYLE O'REILLY.

Was born in Boston, Massachusetts, May 18, 1873; was prison commissioner for Massachusetts at one time and trustee of the Children's Institution Department of Boston; founder of the Guild of St. Elizabeth; contributor to the *Catholic World*, *Harper's Magazine* and *New England Magazine;* is editorial writer for the *Boston Transcript;* prominent in many of the philanthropic associations of Boston and the state of Massachusetts.

ELEANOR R. PARKER.

Was born in Bedford, Kentucky, March 2, 1874. Daughter of William and Eliza Reordan Parker. Her family was prominent in North Carolina. Her mother was a writer of some distinction, and one of the pioneers in the movement for domestic science; was one of the editors of the *Woman's Home Companion* for several years. She is a contributor to *Donahoe's, New Orleans Times-Democrat, Good Housekeeping, Woman's Home Companion,* and is the editor of the women's page in the *Western Watchman.*

HARRIET PRESCOTT SPOFFORD.

Born in Calais, Maine, April 3, 1835, but her parents removed, when she was quite young, to Newburyport Massachusetts which has since been her home. Her father was Joseph N. Prescott. Her essay on Hamlet when she was a student in the school at Newburyport attracted the attention of James Wentworth Higginson, who interested himself in her career. Both of her parents became helpless invalids, which made it necessary for her to early take up a literary career, and she began by contributions to the Boston papers. In 1859 her story of Parisian life, entitled "In a Cellar," brought her into immediate prominence in the literary world, and the editor of the *Atlantic Monthly*, James Russell Lowell, was so impressed by her ability that from that day she was a well-known contributor of both prose and poetry to not only the *Atlantic Monthly*, but the chief periodicals of the country. In 1865 she married Richard S. Spofford, a lawyer of Boston. Among her works are "Sir Rohan's Ghost," "The Amber Gods," "The Thief in the Night," "Azarian," "New England Legends," "Art Decoration Applied to Furniture," "The Marquis of Carabas," "Hester Stanley at St. Mark's," "The Servant Girl Question" and "Ballads About Authors."

AUGUSTA J. EVANS WILSON.

Mrs. Wilson won literary fame as the author of "Beulah." She was born near Columbus, Georgia, in 1836. Her family lived for a short time in Texas, and later in Mobile, Alabama, and here in 1868 she married L. M. Wilson. Her first novel was "Inez," which met with only moderate success, but in 1859 "Beulah" appeared, and she won instantaneous literary fame. During the war she published "Macaria," and it is said that this book was printed on coarse brown paper, and copyrighted by the Confederate States of America. It was dedicated by her to the soldiers of the Southern army. It was seized and destroyed by the Federal officers, but was subsequently reprinted in the North, and met with a large sale. After the war Mrs. Wilson removed to New York City, and here she published her famous book, "St. Elmo." This was followed by one hardly less popular, "Vashti," later, one entitled "Infelice," and "At the Mercy of Tiberius." Mrs. Wilson died in 1909.

LOUISE CHANDLER MOULTON.

Mrs. Moulton was born in Pomfret, Connecticut, April 5, 1835. She early began to contribute to periodicals under the name of "Ellen Louise," and was but nineteen years of age when she published her first book, entitled "This, That, and the Other." In 1855 she married William U. Moulton, a publisher of Boston. After her marriage she wrote short stories for magazines, and is the author of a novel, "Juno Clifford." From 1870 to 1876 she was the literary correspondent of the New York *Tribune,* and also contributed a weekly letter to the *Sunday Herald,* of Boston; wrote letters during her travels abroad from London and Paris for American newspapers. In 1877 she edited two volumes of verse, "Garden Secrets" and "A Last Harvest." She is especially fortunate in her stories for children. Mrs. Moulton died in 1908.

SARAH MORGAN BRYAN PIATT.

Born in Lexington, Kentucky, August 11, 1836. Her grandfather, Morgan Bryan, was a relative of Daniel Boone and one of the earliest settlers in the state of Kentucky. He emigrated from North Carolina with Boone's party and his "station," near Lexington, known as "Bryan's Station," was one of the principal points of attack by the Indians who invaded Kentucky from the Northwest in 1782. Mrs. Piatt's early childhood was passed near Versailles, where her mother, Mary Speirs, who was related to the Stocktons and other early Kentucky families, died when Mrs. Piatt was but eight years of age. She was placed by her father in the care of her aunt, Mrs. Boone, in Newcastle, where she received her education. George D. Prentice, the editor of the *Louisville Journal,* was an intimate friend of the family, and through his paper Mrs. Piatt's poems first received recognition. On June 18, 1861, she became the wife of John James Piatt, and went with her husband to reside in Washington, D. C. In 1867 they removed to Ohio, and lived on a part of the old estate of General W. H. Harrison, in North Bend. In 1886 she published a volume of poems in London, and others followed in the United States, among them "The Nests at Washington, and Other Poems," "A Woman's Poems," "A Voyage to the Fortunate Isles," etc. Mrs. Piatt contributed to many of the leading magazines of that time. In 1882 Mr. Piatt was sent to Ireland as consul of the United States at Cork, and while residing there Mrs. Piatt brought out other volumes of poems, "In Primrose Time," "A New Irish Garland," "An Irish Wildflower." Her writings have been most complimentarily mentioned in both England and Ireland.

HARRIET STONE MONROE.

Author of the ode for the World's Columbian Exposition in Chicago. She is also a contributor of articles for newspapers and writer on art and literary criticism for the magazines. Miss Monroe was born in Chicago, September 23, 1860. Her father was Honorable H. S. Monroe, a lawyer of distinction in Chicago. She was a graduate of the Academy of the Visitation in Georgetown, D. C.

SARAH JANE LIPPINCOTT.

Better known as "Grace Greenwood." A writer of stories for children, and former editor of *Little Pilgrim*. She was born in Pompey, New York, September 23, 1823, and spent her early youth in Rochester, but in 1842 the family removed to New Brighton, Pennsylvania. She married Leander K. Lippincott, of Philadelphia, in 1873. Although during her early youth she had written verses and short stories, it was not until 1844 that her first publication appeared under her *nom de plume*, "Grace Greenwood." She lectured, and was also a contributor and correspondent for several newspapers. She was the author of several books, the titles of some of which are "Greenwood Leaves," "History of My Pets," "Volume of Poems," "Recollections of My Childhood," "Haps and Mishaps of a Tour in Europe," "Mary England," "Forest Tragedy, and Other Tales," "Stories and Legends of Travel," "History for Children," "Stories From Famous Ballads," "Stories of Many Lands," "Stories and Sights in France and Italy," "Records of Five Years," "New Life in New Lands," and her best-known poem, "Ariadne." Mrs. Lippincott died in 1905.

MARIE LOUISE GREENE.

Miss Greene was born in Providence, Rhode Island. She received the degree of A.B. from Vassar in 1891; has done special work in American history in Yale College. She is a student and writer on gardening and New England history. She is the author of "The Development of Religious Liberty in Connecticut," "Among School Gardens," etc.

DELIA LYMAN PORTER.

Mrs. Porter was born in New Haven, Connecticut; graduate of Wellesley College; has been an active worker among the factory girls of New Haven and Beloit, Wisconsin, and through her efforts the bill for the apppointment of a woman deputy factory inspector for the state of Connecticut was passed by the legislature of that state in 1907. She was appointed by the governor as a member of the committee to name this inspector.

ELLA WHEELER WILCOX.

Mrs. Wilcox was born at Johnstown Center, Wisconsin, in 1855; married Robert M. Wilcox in 1884; has been a contributor to magazines and newspapers for many years; has written many beautiful poems, and is ᴓne of the prominent writers of today.

KATHERINE PYLE.

Miss Pyle was born in Wilmington, Delaware, and has written stories in prose and verse of much charm.

BERTHA G. DAVIS WOODS.

Mrs. Woods was born in Penn Yan, New York, in April, 1873. She is a contributor to magazines, newspapers of poems and short stories.

FLORENCE AUGUSTA M. BAILEY.

Mrs. Bailey was born in Locust Grove, New York, August 8, 1863. Sister of Clinton Hart Merriam. Has written much on bird life in America. Is a member of the American Ornithologists' Union, and the Biological Society of Washington.

ROSE HARTWICK THORPE.

Mrs. Thorpe is the author of the well-known poem, "Curfew Must Not Ring To-night." Was born in Mishawaka, Indiana, July 18, 1850. Is the wife of E. Carson Thorpe. Has written many other poems, but none has added to the fame which she earned by the writing of the poem mentioned. Lives in San Diego, California.

GRACE GALLATIN SETON.

Mrs. Seton is a writer and book designer. Is the wife of Ernest Thompson Seton. Has done a great deal of work on newspapers, both in this country and in Paris. In 1897 took up the work of designing covers, title-pages, and general work for make-up of books. President of Pen and Brush Club, Music-Lovers' Club, and librarian of the MacDowell College. Has made quite a name for herself in literature as well, having written "Nimrod's Wife," "A. B. C. Zoo Sketches," serial stories, and songs.

HARRIET HANSON ROBINSON.

Born in Boston, February 8, 1825. Daughter of William and Harriet Browne Hanson. Was one of the girls employed in the factories of Lowell who wrote for the Lowell *Offering,* showing ability and higher intelligence. Married in 1848 William S. Robinson, a journalist, who wrote under the pen-name of "Warrington," and died March, 1876. Mrs. Robinson is the author of the "Warrington Pen-Portraits," "Massachusetts in the Woman Suffrage Movement," a woman suffrage play, and other writings.

HARRIETTE LUCY ROBINSON SHATTUCK.

Born in Lowell, Massachusetts, December 4, 1850. Daughter of William Stevens and Harriet Hanson Robinson. In 1878 married Sidney Doane Shattuck, of Malden, Massachusetts. Was assistant clerk of the Massachusetts House of Representatives in 1872, being the first woman to hold such a position. Has written several books.

ESTELLE MAY HURLL.

Born in New Bedford, Massachusetts, July 25, 1863. Daughter of Charles W and Sarah S. Hurll. In 1908 married John C. Hurll. Teacher of ethics at Wellesley College from 1884-91. Author of books on art, including "Child Life in Art," "The Madonna in Art," and books on Rembrandt, Michael Angelo, "Greek Sculpture," "Titian," "Landseer," "Correggio," "Tuscan Sculpture," "Van Dyck," "Portrait and Portrait Painting."

JENNETTE LEE.

Born in Bristol, Connecticut, November 10, 1860. Daughter of Philemon Perry and Mary Barbour Perry. In 1896, married Gerald Stanley Lee. At one time was a teacher of English at Vassar College, and also of English in the College for Women, Western Reserve University. Professor of English language and literature in Smith College since 1904. Author of several books, a few of which are "Kate Wetherell," "A Pillar of Salt," "The Son of a Fiddler," and many other sketches and short stories.

JULIA ARABELLA EASTMAN.

Daughter of Rev. John and Prudence D. Eastman. Associate principal of Dana Hall, Wellesley. Author.

MARY FRANCES BLAISDELL.

Born in Manchester, New Hampshire, April 20, 1874. Daughter of Clark and Clara M. Blaisdell. The author, in conjunction with her sister, Etta A. Blaisdell MacDonald, of several books for children: "Child Life in Tale and Fable," "Child Life in Many Lands," "Child Life in Literature," "The Child Primer," "The Blaisdell Spellers," "The Child Life Fifth Reader," and stories for children.

CAROLINE VAN DUSEN CHENOWETH.

Born near Louisville, Kentucky, December 29, 1846. Daughter of Charles and Mary Huntington Van Dusen. Married Col. Bernard Peel Chenoweth, who was United States Consul at Canton, China, and died while occupying this position. Mrs. Chenoweth settled his affairs with the government and received recognition from the United States and the Chinese government as vice-consul. Was professor at one time of English literature in Smith College; also lecturer on history and English literature. Author of "Child Life in China," "School History of Worcester," and other historical books. Contributor to various magazines and reviews.

ANNIE RUSSELL MARBLE.

Born in Worcester, Massachusetts, August 10, 1864. Daughter of Isaiah Dunster and Nancy Maria Wentworth Russell. In 1890, married Charles Francis Marble, of Worcester, Massachusetts. Author of "Thoreau—His Home, Friends and Books," "Books in Their Seasons," "Heralds of American Literature," and has edited other books.

ALICE ELINOR BARTLETT.

Writer under the pen-name of "Birch Arnold." Born in Delavan, Wisconsin, September 4, 1848. Daughter of J. B. and Sophronia E. Braley Bowen. Wrote for many years on the Chicago newspapers. Now engaged in general literary work, besides writer of verse.

CHARLOTTE FISKE BATES.

Writer under the pen-name of "Mme. Rogé." Born in New York, November 30, 1838. Daughter of Hervey and Eliza (Endicott) Bates. In 1891 she married M. Adolph Rogé, who died in 1896. Author of poems. Editor of the "Longfellow Birthday Book," "Cambridge Book of Poetry and Song," and aided Mr. Longfellow in compiling "Poems of Places."

MARY JOANNA SAFFORD.

Was born at Salem, Massachusetts. Daughter of Samuel Appleton and Frances Parker Safford. Is a contributor of original articles, poems, and translations to magazines. Is considered one of the best translators of German stories, and has translated a great many of these for magazines and periodicals. She makes her home in Washington, where she is considered one of the prominent literary women of the Capital City.

JOSEPHINE McCRACKIN.

Mrs. McCrackin came to America from Prussia in 1846. Writes for a great many newspapers. Was the instigator of the movement in behalf of conserving the redwoods of California, and founded the Ladies' Forest and Song-Bird Protective Association. Was the first woman member and fourth vice-president of the California Game and Fish Protective Association. Active in the

Humane Society, member of all protective societies of California, and the Woman's Press Association. A prominent Roman Catholic.

LAURA CATHERINE SEARING.

Mrs. Searing was born in Somerset, Maryland, February, 1840. In her childhood she lost her hearing and power of speech through illness. Educated at the Deaf Mute University of Missouri and at the Clark Institute, Northampton, Massachusetts, where she regained to quite a degree her power of speech. Married a prominent attorney of New York, Edward W. Searing, in 1876. Has been a correspondent on many of the prominent newspapers, doing this work for the *Missouri Republican* during the Civil War. Is one of the American authors now residing in Santa Cruz, California.

LA SALLE CORBELL PICKETT.

Mrs. Pickett is the widow of General George Edward Pickett, C. S. A., who was a conspicuous figure in the Battle of Gettysburg, September 15, 1863. Since her husband's death she has occupied a position in one of the departments in Washington, and has done considerable editorial and literary work in the form of short stories, poems and special articles. Has lectured on patriotic subjects, and has written sketches of Abraham Lincoln, Jefferson Davis, Lee, Jackson, and Grant.

ANNIE JENNESS MILLER.

Mrs. Jenness Miller, while an advocate of dress reform, is so in a much more reserved form than that advocated by the followers of Mrs. Bloomer. She was born in New Hampshire, but resided in Boston prior to her marriage in 1884. Before her marriage Mrs. Miller had won considerable fame in Massachusetts as a woman of letters. Then, as a young and beautiful woman, highly cultured, she took up with energy, combined with good judgment, the question of dress reform, or, as she has stated it, the principles and character of artistic dressing. With other prominent leaders in the dress reform movement she went upon the platform to voice her theories and views. She lectured in all the leading cities of the United States to crowded houses, and had the unusual experience of being invited over and over again to the same place. She was one of the owners of a magazine published in New York and devoted to the æsthetics of physical development and artistic designs for frocks, and containing articles by the best writer on all topics of interest to women. The influence of her work through this magazine was widely acknowledged. She is the author of "Physical Beauty," and of "Mother and Babe," the latter a work which furnished information and patterns upon improved plans for mothers' babies' wardrobes. All the progressive and reformatory movements of the day appealed to her, and have had her support and sympathy. She now lives in Washington, D. C., where she has large real estate interests.

CYNTHIA WESTOVER ALDEN.

Mrs. Alden's grandfather was Alexander Campbell, founder of the Camp-
bellites, and her father, who was a noted geologist and expert miner, was a
descendant of the Westovers of Virginia, who settled early in 1600 near the site
where Richmond now stands. Her mother died when Mrs. Alden was so young
that she has no memory of her, but from her earliest girlhood she accompanied
her father on all his prospecting tours from Mexico to Canada. Naturally, from
these early surroundings she became an expert shot and horsewoman, and she
also acquired an intimate knowledge of birds and flowers, the habits of wild
animals, and many other secrets of nature. She was born in Iowa, in 1858, but
her education was gained in whatever place she and her father happened to be,
and was the result of his companionship as much as anything else, until she went
to the State University of Colorado. After graduating there she took a four-year
course in a commercial college, where she was considered a skilled mathematician,
and after going to New York this practical side of her nature asserted itself, and
she took the civil service examination for custom house inspector. She was
promptly appointed, and with her usual force and energy began to learn French,
German, and Italian. She acquired a general knowledge of languages which placed
her, in an incredibly short time, on speaking terms with most of the immigrants
of all nationalities coming to her shore. When Commissioner Beattie came into
the Street Cleaning Department of New York City he appointed her his private
secretary, she being the only woman, up to that time, who had held a position by
appointment in any of the city departments. During the illness of the Commissioner, for several weeks, she managed successfully the force of the entire department. Many Italians were on the force, and for the first time in their experience
they could air their grievances at headquarters in their own language. As a
further illustration of her active mind she invented a cart for carrying and
dumping dirt, for which the Parisian Academy for Inventors conferred upon her
the title of Membre d'Honneur with a diploma and a gold medal. She was joint
author of a book entitled, "Manhattan, Historic and Artistic," which was so
favorably received that the first edition was exhausted in ten days. She afterwards became a newspaper writer and secretary of the Womens Press Club of
New York City. Her latest work is one of tender benevolence, having organized
a Shut-in Society, by which bed-ridden and chair-ridden invalids correspond with
one another through her medium, and try to make of their pitiful lives a Sunshine
Society.

ISABELLA MACDONALD ALDEN.

Whose *nom de plume* is "Pansy," was born in Rochester, New York, November 3, 1831. Her pen name was given her by her father because she picked all
of the treasured blossoms from a bed grown by her mother. She wrote stories,
sketches, compositions, and these were first published in the village papers. She
wrote her first real story to compete for the prize offered for the best Sunday
School book, and gained her aim. "Helen Lester" was the first volume to appear
signed by the well-known name of "Pansy." Some of her books are "Esther

Reid," "Four Girls at Chautauqua," "Chautauqua Girls at Home," "Tip Lewis and His Lamp," "Three People," "Links in Rebecca's Life," "Julia Reid," "The King's Daughter," "The Browning Boys," "From Different Standpoints," "Mrs. Harry Harper's Awakening." Mrs. Alden was always deeply interested in Sunday School and primary teaching. She was prominently identified with the Chautauqua movement, and most of her books appear in the Sunday School libraries of the United States. She was married to Rev. G. R. Alden in 1866, and is as successful a pastor's wife as she is an author. Mrs. Alden is the mother of a very gifted son, Prof. Raymond Macdonald Alden.

MARY COOLIDGE.

Mrs. Coolidge was born at Kingsbury, Indiana, October 28, 1860. Daughter of Prof. Isaac Roberts and Margaret Jane Roberts. Obtained a degree from Cornell in 1880, one from Leland Stanford in 1882. Her first husband was Albert W. Smith, of Berkeley, California; her second, Dane Coolidge. She served as a teacher of history in the Washington high school, also of Miss Nourse and Miss Robert's school of the Capital; also in private schools in Cincinnati, one of the board of examiners of Wesleyan College, Professor of Sociology of Stanford University, and one of the research assistants in the Carnegie Institute of Washington; also in the research work of San Francisco Relief Survey. Contributor of various articles on sociology and economics to the various magazines of our country. Has written on Chinese immigration and other subjects of public interest. Is considered one of the able women writers and thinkers of the country.

GRACE McGOWAN COOKE.

Mrs. Cooke was born at Grand Rapids, Ohio, September 11, 1863. She is the daughter of John E. and Melvina J. McGowan. Married William Cooke, of Chattanooga, Tennessee, February 17, 1877, and was the first woman president of the Woman's Press Club of Tennessee. Her writings are among the best known of our country. Among them are "Mistress Joy," "Return," "Hulda," "A Gourd Fiddle," "Their First Formal Call," and many contributions to the best magazines.

ALICE McGOWAN.

Miss McGowan is a sister of Grace McGowan Cooke, and was born at Perrysburg, Ohio, December 10, 1858. She was educated at the public schools of Chattanooga. In 1890, desirous of procuring literary material, she rode alone through the Black Mountain regions of North Carolina to her home in Chattanooga a distance of one thousand miles. Her stories are among the best of modern fiction, and include "The Last Word," "Judith of the Cumberlands," and "The Wiving of Lance Cleaverage."

OLIVE THORNE MILLER.

Is the most distinguished woman writer and lecturer on ornithology in this country. She was born in Auburn, New York, June 25, 1831. Daughter of Seth Hunt Mann and Mary Holbrook Mann. Married in 1854 to Mr. Watts Todd Miller. The lists of her books are numerous and valuable, especially to children in the study of bird life, and include, "Little Folks in Feathers and Fur," "Little Brothers of the Air," "True Bird Stories," and "The Bird, Our Brother."

ELIZABETH BISLAND WETMORE.

Mrs. Wetmore was born in Camp Bisland, Fairfax Plantation, Teche County, Louisiana, in 1863. Her family was one of the oldest in the South, and like all such, lost all their property in the Civil War, which necessitated Miss Bisland's supporting herself and members of her family. Having shown some talent for writing, she took up journalism, and her first sketches were published when she was but fifteen years of age, under the name of B. L. R. Dane. She did considerable work for the New Orleans *Times-Democrat* and became literary editor of that paper, but the field not being wide enough she removed to New York to work on the newspapers and periodicals of that city. She was soon offered the position of literary editor of the *Cosmopolitan Magazine,* and while occupying this position she made her famous journey around the world, attempting to make better time than that made by Nellie Bly, who undertook the journey for the *New York World.* This brought Miss Bisland's name conspicuously before the public, and in 1890 she went to London, England, in the interest of the *Cosmopolitan,* writing for that magazine letters from London and Paris which were favorably received. She collaborated with Miss Rhoda Boughton in a novel and a play, and is the author of several books. In October, 1891, she became the wife of Charles W. Wetmore, of New York City.

HELEN BIGLOW MERRIMAN.

Born in Boston, July 14, 1844. Daughter of Erastus B. and Eliza Frances (Means) Biglow. Author and artist.

FANNIE HUNTINGTON RUNNELLS POOLE.

Born at Oxford, New Hampshire. Daughter of Rev. Moses Thurston and Fannie Maria Baker Runnells. Book reviewer for *Town and Country,* and author of "Books of Verse."

ELLEN A. RICHARDSON.

Born at Portsmouth, New Hampshire, August, 1845. Daughter of Oren and Ann H. W. Bragden. Married in 1870, A. Maynard Richardson, of Boston. Founder and also first president for three years, and now honorary president of the George Washington Memorial Association, founded for the purpose of promoting a national university. Organized also the Home Congress; was founder of the Massachusetts Business League; one of the judges of art on the board of awards of the Chicago Exposition and the Atlanta Exposition. Is the head of the cabinet department of art and literature of the National Council of Women of the United States, and represented this organization in Berlin in 1904. Founded and edited the *Woman's Review;* also edited booklets on Home for the Home Congresses; *The Business Folio;* has edited the home department of the *Boston Commonwealth;* a contributor to magazines and a reviewer to *The Arena.*

MARY ALDEN WARD.

Born in Cincinnati, March 1, 1853. Daughter of Prince W. and Rebecca Neal Alden, and a direct descendant of John and Priscilla Mullins, of Plymouth colony. Prominent and active in women's club work. Editor of *Federation Bulletin,* national official publication of the General Federation of Woman's Clubs, and author of a "Life of Dante," "Petrarch; a Sketch of His Life and Work," "Prophets of the Nineteenth Century," and "Old Colony Days."

LILIAN WHITING.

Born at Niagara Falls, New York, October 3, 1859. Daughter of Hon. Lorenzo Dowe and Lucia Clement Whiting. Literary editor, *Boston Traveler;* editor of the *Boston Budget,* and author of "The World Beautiful," "From Dreamland Sent," a book of poems, "A Study of the Life and Poetry of Elizabeth Barrett Browning," "A Record of Kate Field," "The World Beautiful in Books," "Boston Days," "Florence of Landor," "The Outlook Beautiful," "Italy, the Magic Land," "Paris the Beautiful," etc.

KATE TANNATT WOODS.

Born in Peekskill, New York. Daughter of James S. and Mary Tannatt. Married George H. Woods, a prominent lawyer and officer on General Sherman's staff. Has done editorial work on *Harper's Bazar, Ladies' Home Journal, Boston Transcript, Globe and Herald,* and several magazines. Active worker in women's clubs of Massachusetts. One of the original officers and first auditor of the General Federation of Woman's Clubs. Founder of the Massachusetts State Federation of Woman's Clubs, and the Thought and Work Club of Salem, Massachusetts. Has written quite a number of stories on New England life, and also stories of New Mexico.

HANNAH AMELIA DAVIDSON.

Born in Campello, Massachusetts, October 29, 1852. Daughter of Spencer Williams and Mary Packard Noyes. In 1878 married Charles Davidson. Student and teacher of Sanskrit. Teacher of Greek, Latin, and English history, and principal of the Minneapolis Academy at one time. Taught history and English in the Belmont School, California. Student and graduate of the University of Chicago in economics, history and politics. Lecturer on literature, art in fiction, and the drama for Wellesley and Mount Holyoke colleges. Author of "Reference History

54

of the United States," "The Gift of Genius," author and publisher of "The Study Guide Series," also "Study Guide Courses." Edited with aids to study and critical essays, "Riverside Literature Series," "Silas Marner," "Vicar of Wakefield," "House of Seven Gables," "Vision of Sir Launfal," "Irving's Sketch Book," and "Franklin's Autobiography."

HELEN MARIA WINSLOW.

Born in Westfield, Vermont. Daughter of Don Avery and Mary S. Newton Winslow. Writer for papers and magazines. Editor and publisher of *The Club Woman*. Writer of short stories. Editor and publisher annually of the *Official Register* of the Directory of Woman's Clubs of America.

MARY REBECCA FOSTER GILMAN.

Born in Worcester, Massachusetts, in 1859. Daughter of Dwight and Henriette P. B. Foster. Married in 1887, Rev. Bradley Gilman. Critic on the *Springfield Republican* and *Suburban Life*. Author of "The Life of St. Theresa," in series of famous women, "The Pilgrim's Scrip," a collection of wisdom and wit of George Meredith. Edited Mrs. Fawcett's "Life of Queen Victoria." A contributor to magazines and periodicals.

HARRIET ELIZA PAINE.

Writer under the name of Eliza Chester. Born at Rehoboth, Massachusetts, May 5, 1845. Daughter of Dr. John Chester, and Eliza Folger Paine. Author of "Bird Songs of New England," "Chats with Girls on Self Culture," "The Unmarried Woman," and editor of the "Life of Eliza Baylies Wheaton."

ANN EMILIE POULSSON.

Born at Cedar Grove, New Jersey, September 8, 1853. Daughter of Halvor and Ruth Ann Mitchell Poulsson. Graduate of the kindergarten normal class. Teacher in School for Blind, of South Boston; joint editor of the *Kindergarten Review*. Author of "Nursery Finger Plays," "Child Stories and Rhymes," "Love and Law in Child Training," "Holiday Songs."

SARAH PRATT GREENE.

Born at Simsbury, Connecticut, July 3, 1856. Daughter of Dudley Boston and Mary Paine McLean. July, 1887, married Franklin Lynde Greene, now deceased. Her book, "Cape Cod Folks," which appeared some twenty years ago, made quite a stir and entitled her to literary prominence. She has since written "Some Other Folks," "Towhead," "Last Chance Junction," "Moral Imbeciles," "Flood Tide," and many other stories published in book form and has contributed short stories largely to *Harper's Magazine* and other publications.

ELEANOR HABAWELL ABBOT COBURN.

Born in Cambridge, Massachusetts, September 22, 1872. Daughter of Rev. Edward and Clara Davis Abbot. In 1908 she married Dr. Fordice Coburn, of Lowell, Massachusetts. In October, 1905, won the thousand dollar prize offered by Collier with her story, "The Sick Abed Lady," and again in 1907 with one entitled "The Very Tired Girl," and in Howell's selections of the best short stories these are mentioned. Has been a contributor to magazines.

MARY MAPES DODGE.

For many years editor of *St. Nicholas,* and through this magazine she endeared herself to the youth of America. Mrs. Dodge was a native of New York City, where she was born January 26, 1838. Her father was Professor James J. Mapes, one of the first promoters of scientific farming in the United States When quite young, she married William Dodge, a lawyer of New York, and after his death took up the vocation of literature as a means of educating her two sons. At first her writings were short sketches for children, a volume of which was published in 1864 under the name of "Irvington Stories." This was followed by "Hans Brinker, or the Silver Skates." She was engaged with Harriet Beecher Stowe and Donald G. Mitchell as one of the editors of *Hearth and Home,* conducting the children's department of that journal for several years. From this she became editor of *St. Nicholas* in 1873, and continued in that position until her death in 1905. Her famous story, "Hans Brinker," has been translated into Dutch, French, German, Russian and Italian. She also published a number of other volumes of prose and poetry and contributed to the principal magazines of the country, the *Atlantic, Harper's* and the *Century.*

SUSAN ARNOLD ELSTON WALLACE.

Was born December 25, 1830, at Crawfordsville, Indiana. Her maiden name was Susan Arnold Elston. In 1852 she became the wife of General Lew Wallace, famous as the author of "Ben-Hur." During the Civil War she was frequently in camp with the general, and she aided in nursing the wounded. After the war General Wallace practiced law at Crawfordsville, their home. Mrs. Wallace was called upon to occupy high social positions, through the appointment of General Wallace to various offices under the government. From 1878 to 1881 he was governor of New Mexico and from 1881 to 1885 he was United States Minister to Turkey. General Wallace was the intimate friend of the Sultan, and Mrs. Wallace was granted many privileges not formerly given to foreign women. In 1885 they returned to their home, and General Wallace resumed his practice of law and his literary work. Mrs. Wallace was a frequent contributor to papers and magazines for many years. The best known of her poems are "The Patter of Little Feet." Among her books are "The Storied Sea," "Ginevra," "The Land of the Pueblos" and "The Repose in Egypt." Mrs. Wallace devoted a great deal of her time to charitable and philanthropic work, and her home was always a social and literary center. Mrs. Wallace died in 1907.

GEORGINA PELL CURTIS.

Georgina Pell Curtis, daughter of Alfred Leonard and Maria Elizabeth (Hill) Curtis, was born in New York city, February 19th, 1859. At the age of seven years she lost her hearing and was educated at the Fort Washington, N. Y., Deaf and Dumb Institute, and by private tutors. At the age of thirteen she was sent to St. Mary's Protestant Episcopal School, New York, where she remained until her graduation at the age of seventeen. At this school she was the only deaf pupil. For five years after graduation she studied art and worked under different masters, and had almost decided to adopt art as a profession when it was suggested to her that she should try and write. This she thought quite impossible, but was urged so strongly that she made the attempt, and succeeded.

In the meantime, she had joined the Roman Catholic Church, and it is as a Catholic writer that she is best known. She has written for all the best Catholic magazines and has brought out three books—"Trammellings," a collection of short stories of which she is the author; "Some Roads to Rome in America," and "The American Catholic Who's Who," of which she is the editor. Miss Curtis is lineally descended on the paternal side from Peregrine White, the first child born in the Mayflower colony.

The first edition of the "American Catholic Who's Who" appeared in 1911, and the editor hopes to bring it out every year or two, making it a permanent record of prominent American Catholics in the United States, Canada and Europe.

EMMA LAZARUS.

A prominent Jewish educator has recently said, in speaking of his people in America, "We cannot boast such a poet as Heine, a soldier in the intellectual war of liberation which has freed European thought from its mediæval shackles, but there did bloom amongst us the delicate flower of Emma Lazarus' work." And, indeed, it is to be doubted whether poetic feeling and the strength of this young writer's work has been excelled by any other American author.

Emma Lazarus was born in New York City, July 22, 1849, and despite the fact that death came to her just as she had reached her prime she had gained a place and made a mark in literature far above the achievements of many eminent lives well rounded by age. She was the daughter of Moses Lazarus, a well-known merchant of New York, and received a literary education under private tutors. Her attainments included Hebrew, Greek and Latin and modern languages. Even in her childhood she was noted for her quickness and intelligence and her text-book education she herself broadened by her reading on religious, philosophical, and scientific subjects until she became a profound thinker. Her literary bent displayed itself when at seventeen years of age she published a volume of poems, "Admetus," which at once attracted attention by the remarkable character of the work and which brought her many flattering notices.

In 1874 she produced her first important work, "Alide," a romance founded on the episodes in the early life of Goethe. Some translations from Heine that followed were even more successful in making her known. In 1880 was begun the publication of the work to which she had for some time addressed herself, upon the position, history and wrongs of her people. This first book was called "Sons of the Semite" and opened with a five-act tragedy called "The Dance of Death," dealing with the stories of Jewish persecution in the fifteenth century. She wrote for the *Century* a number of striking essays on Jewish topics, among which were "Russian Christianity vs. Modern Judaism," "The Jewish Problem," and "Was the Earl of Beaconsfield a Representative Jew?" Her work also includes critical articles on Salvini, Emerson and others. In the winter of 1882, when many Russian Jews were flocking to New York City to escape Russian persecution, Miss Lazarus published in the *American Hebrew* stories and articles solving the question of occupation for the newcomers. Her plan involved industrial and technical education, and the project was carried out along that line. Her last work was published in the *Century* in May, 1887. It was a series of poems in prose entitled "By the Waters of Babylon," and the attention it excited and the admiration accorded it were general, here as well as across the Atlantic. Miss Lazarus died November 19, 1887. There was no art to which she did not respond with splendid appreciation—music, painting, poetry and drama—she felt keenly, intelligently and generously the special charm of each. For moral ideas she had the keenness of her race. She had, too, that genius for friendship which so few fully understood. That such a nature should have formed close ties of intellectual sympathy with men of the character of Emerson, in America, and Browning, in England, is not a matter of surprise.

ELLEN BLACKMAR BARKER.

Mrs. Barker writes under the name of Ellen Blackmar Maxwell. She was born at West Springfield, Pennsylvania. Her first husband, Rev. Allen J. Maxwell, died at Lucknow, India, in 1890. Wrote "The Bishop's Conversion," "Three Old Maids in Hawaii," and "The Way of Fire." Her second husband is Albert Smith Barker.

MARY CLARE DE GRAFFENRIED.

Miss De Graffenried was born in Macon, Georgia, May 19, 1849. Collector of statistics for the Bureau of Labor of the United States. Has collected data on industrial and sociological subjects in the United States, Belgium and France. Has contributed to magazines on these subjects.

ELLA LORAINE DORSEY.

Miss Dorsey was born in Washington, D. C., March 2, 1853. Daughter of Lorenzo and Anna Hanson Dorsey. Is a graduate of the Visitation Convent, Georgetown, D. C. For many years special correspondent for Washington, Chicago, Boston, and Cincinnati papers. Indexer and Russian translator, Scientific Library, United States Department of the Interior. Is a member of the advisory board of Trinity College, the Catholic college for the higher education of women in the United States, located in Washington, D. C. Member of the Daughters of the

American Revolution, Colonial Dames, and other patriotic societies. Has contributed able articles to the magazines and has written many stories, among them "Midshipman Bob," "The Two Tramps," "The Taming of Polly," "Pickle and Pepper," "Pocahontas," "The End of the White Man's Trail."

JENNIE GOULD LINCOLN.

Mrs. Lincoln is the daughter of the late Judge George Gould of the New York Court of Appeals and the wife of Dr. Nathan Smith Lincoln, of Washington, D. C., now deceased. She is the author of quite a number of short stories and a contributor to magazines. Is one of the prominent society women of Washington who have made a name for themselves in the literary field.

MARY SMITH LOCKWOOD.

Mrs. Lockwood was born at Hanover, New York, October 24, 1831. The daughter of Henry and Beulah Blodgett Smith. In September, 1851, she married Henry C. Lockwood. She was one of the founders of the D. A. R., Commissioner-at-Large of the World's Fair in Chicago, and was the first historian-general and is the vice-president for life of the D. A. R. Prominent member of the Woman's Suffrage Club, Historical Association, Woman's Press Union, one of the committee which prepared the history of women's work at the Chicago Exposition, and is the author of several books, "Historic Homes of Washington," "Handbook of Ceramic Art," "Story of the Records of the D. A. R.," one of the editors of the *D. A. R. Magazine,* and edits the D. A. R. reports to Smithsonian Institution.

IDA TREADWELL THURSTON.

Mrs. Thurston is known by her pen name, "Marion Thorne." She has written several stories, among them "The Bishop's Shadow," "Boys of the Central," "A Frontier Hero," and many other excellent stories for boys.

EDITH ELMER WOOD.

Mrs. Wood was born in Portsmouth, New Hampshire, September 24, 1871. Daughter of Commodore Horace Elmer, U. S. N., and Adele Wiley Elmer. Is the wife of Capt. Albert Norton Wood U. S. N. Mrs. Wood was the founder and first president of the Anti-Tuberculosis League of Porto Rico, which maintains hospitals and sanitariums for indigent patients and conducts a campaign on the isle against this dread disease. She has written several stories and contributed to the leading magazines and newspapers.

MYRTA LOCKETT AVARY.

Mrs. Avary was born in Halifax, Virginia. Is prominent in fresh air and settlement work in the various cities, and engaged in sociology and historical work in the South. Has served on the editorial staff of several high-class magazines and written for syndicates and the religious press on sociology and stories of tenement life, also stories of the Civil War, and edited "Recollections of Alexander H. Stephens," etc.

AMY ALLEMAND BERNARDY.

Though born at Florence, Italy, January 16, 1880, Miss Bernardy is conspicuous for her work in this country. She has been professor of Italian at Smith College, contributor to various magazines and newspapers, and prominently identified with emigration and immigration study movement in Italy and the United States, and is the author of several books in Italian.

URSULA NEWELL GESTEFELD.

Born in Augusta, Maine. Founder of the system of new thought known as the Science of Being, and instructor for the Exodus Club, organized in Chicago in 1897, which became later the Church of New Thought and College of the Science of Being. She was the first pastor of this church and head of the college. She has written several works on this subject and has a large following of students.

FLORENCE HUNTLEY.

Mrs. Huntley was born at Alliance, Ohio. Daughter of Rev. Henry and Charlotte Trego Chance. Editor of the *Iowa City Republican* in 1901. Now engaged on a series of writings on the system of science and philosophy intended to connect the demonstrated and recorded knowledge of ancient spiritual schools with the discovered and published facts of the modern physical school of science. Has written several books, among them "Harmonics of Evolution," "The Great Psychological Crime," "The Destructive Principle of Nature in Individual Life," and "The Constructive Principle of Individual Life," etc.

KATE FISHER KIMBALL.

Miss Kimball was born at Orange, New Jersey, February 22, 1860. Daughter of Horace and Mary D. Kimball. Has been editor of the *Round Table* of the Chautauquan Assembly since October, 1899, and has written the reports of that circle for general circulation.

AMELIA GERE MASON.

Mrs. Mason was born in Northampton, Massachusetts. The daughter of Frederick and Ruth Sheldon (Warner) Gere. Spent seven years in Europe gathering material for books in foreign libraries. The titles of some of her books are "The Women of the French Salons," "Women in the Golden Ages." Has also contributed to magazines.

ELIZA RUHAMAH SCIDMORE.

Miss Scidmore was born at Madison, Wisconsin, October 14, 1856. Her parents being missionaries in Japan and China, Miss Scidmore has spent much of her time in Japan and many of her writings are stories of that country. She first became conspicuous as a writer in the *St. Louis Globe-Democrat*, writing letters from Washington over the signature, "Ruhamah," and by her pen name she is best known. She has written on Alaska, Java, China, India, and her work is reliable and her style fascinating. She spends much of her time in Washington.

M. SEARS BROOKS.

Mrs. Brooks was born in Springfield, Massachusetts. Her family, the Tuttles, of Hertfordshire, England, settled in New Haven, Connecticut upon a tract of land now occupied by Yale College, and this tract remained in their family for more than a century. Her grandfather was one of Anthony Wayne's men at the storming of Stony Point. Presidents Dwight and Woolsey, of Yale, are descendants of her family; also Prescott, the historian, and other noted people. Mrs. Brooks is the author of poems, essays, and short stories which have appeared in the newspapers and magazines of the country.

KATHARINE G. BUSBEY.

Mrs. Katharine G. Busbey was born in Brooklyn, New York. Graduated from Smith College, Northampton, Massachusetts, in 1885. Was married in 1896, and has lived in Washington since that date.

Her father, Horace Graves, was a lawyer; her mother, a college president; her uncle, a college professor.

Mrs. Busbey wrote "The Letters from a New Congressman's Wife," published in a popular magazine. The publisher said they were good and wanted to use her name, but she decided that they should go anonymously to test their value— fearing these stories would be attributed to her husband, who was in the center of the Washington political maelstrom, and people might say she acted only as his amanuensis. She was right. The stories were popular and when a year later the same magazine printed a story by Katharine G. Busbey, author of "Letters from a New Congressman's Wife," she received many letters from all parts of the country and many compliments from public men who had enjoyed those letters. In 1908 she went to England to prepare a report for the United States Bureau of Labor on the conditions of women in English factories, and while in London received a proposition to write for a London publisher a book on "Home Life in America." That book was published in 1910, and it received extended and favorable reviews in all the great literary papers and the dailies. Many of the reviewers did not know the author, but credited her with information, industry and cleverness in handling the subject.

In the past year she has had stories in the *Saturday Evening Post, Harper's Magazine, The Sunday Magazine, Good Housekeeping,* and other magazines here and in England.

Mrs. Busbey is a college bred woman who came back to literature after she had served her country as a mother, and is destined to achieve a brilliant success in the literary world.

ALICE MAY DOUGLAS.

Born in Bath, Maine, June 28, 1865. Daughter of Joshua Lufkin and Helen Lauraman Harvey Douglas. Writer of Sunday School lessons for the primary department in Sunday School journals. Active worker in the missionary societies of the Methodist Church. Delegate to the Boston Peace Congress. Founder of the Peace Makers' Band, and the author of several volumes of verse and songs, also stories and booklets. Contributor to magazines and religious papers.

LAURA ELIZABETH RICHARDS.

Born in Boston, February 27, 1850. Daughter of Samuel Gridley and Julia Ward Howe. Author of sketches and many short stories, letters and journals of Samuel Gridley Howe and the life of Florence Nightingale for young people. Married Henry Richards, of Gardiner, Maine, June 17, 1871.

ELIZA HAPPY MORTON.

Born July 15, 1852, in Westbrook, a former suburb of Portland, Maine. Daughter of Wilson and Eliza Hannah Phenix Morton. Teacher of geography in the normal department of the Battle Creek College, Michigan, at one time. Has written several books on geography such as "Chalk Lessons for Geography Classes," "Potter's Elementary Geography," "Potter's Advanced Geography," also teachers' editions of both works, "Morton's Elementary Geography," "Morton's Advanced Geography," "Thought; Its Origin and Power," many songs and hymns, one of well-known songs entitled "The Songs My Mother Sang."

MARY BRADFORD CROWNINSHIELD.

Daughter of Judge John Melancthon and Sarah Elizabeth Hopkins Bradford. A descendant from Gov. William Bradford, of the Plymouth colony. In July, 1870, married A. Schuyler Crowninshield, who died in May, 1908. Has written several stories, among them "A Romance of the West Indies," "Where the Trade Wind Blows," "All Among the Light-Houses," "The Light-House Children Abroad," "San Isidro," and "The Archbishop and the Lady."

ELLA MAUDE MOORE.

Born at Warren, Maine, July 22, 1849. Daughter of Samuel Emerson and Maria Copeland Smith. In 1872 married Joseph E. Moore, of Thomaston, Maine. Her great claim for conspicuous mention among the famous literary women of the United States is the poem known as "The Rock of Ages," which, it is said, was written hastily on the inside of an old envelope, but which is to-day one of the famous hymns used in almost all of the Protestant churches and is without doubt the most popular. She has written stories for girls for newspapers and magazines; also songs.

MARIE LOUISE MALLOY.

Born in Baltimore. Daughter of John and Frances (Sollers) Malloy. Now dramatic editor and editorial writer and humorist of the *Baltimore American* over the signature "Josh Wink." Author with Creston Clark of "The Ragged Cavalier."

ELAINE GOODALE EASTMAN.

Born at Mount Washington, Massachusetts, October 9, 1863. Daughter of Henry S. and Dora H. (Read) Goodale. In 1891 married Charles A. Eastman. In her early youth wrote verses, in connection with her sister. From 1883 to 1891 was teacher and supervisor of Indian schools and has written magazine and newspaper articles on Indian life and character and the education of Indian children.

ADELAIDE S. HALL.

Born in Westmoreland, New York, November 2, 1857. The daughter of Schuyler and Susan Waldo Wade Hall. Contributor to magazines on topics of art and travel. Curator of the Chicago Gallery of Fine Arts and lecturer on art topics.

SOPHIA MIRIAM SWEET.

Born in Brewer, Maine. Daughter of Nathaniel and Susan Brastow Sweet. At one time associate editor of the *Wide Awake*. Writer of short stories and juvenile books.

ABBIE FARWELL BROWN.

Born in Boston. Daughter of Benjamin F. and Clara (Neal) Brown. Educated at Radcliffe College. At one time one of the editors of the *Young Folks' Library*. Author of books on animals, flowers, birds and other subjects. Writer of stories for children. Contributor to magazines and newspapers. Editor of the *Library for Young People*.

EMMA ELIZABETH BROWN.

Born in Concord, New Hampshire, October 18, 1847. Daughter of John Frost and Elizabeth (Evans) Brown. Writer and illustrator. Has written the lives of Washington, Grant, Garfield, Oliver Wendell Holmes, James Russell Lowell and other noted persons. Is the author of many other books of prose and verse, and is a contributor to magazines.

KATE LOUISE BROWN.

Born in Adams, Massachusetts, May 9, 1857. Daughter of Edgar M. and Mary T. Brown. Contributor to magazines and juvenile publications. Is the author of children's songs and music for the kindergarten.

ANNIE PAYSON CALL.

Born in Arlington, Massachusetts, May 17, 1853. Daughter of Henry E. and Emily (Payson) Call. Teacher of nerve training. Author of works entitled "Power Through Repose," "The Freedom of Life," "A Man of the World" and "Nerves and Common-Sense."

MARGARETTA WADE DELAND.

Born in Allegheny, Pennsylvania, February 23, 1857. In 1880 married Lorin F. Deland, of Boston. Author of the well-known novel, "John Ward, Preacher," "The Old Garden and Other Verses," "Philip and His Wife," "Florida Days," "Sydney," "The Story of a Child," "The Wisdom of Fools," "Mr. Tommy Dove and Other Stories," "Old Chester Tales," "Dr. Lavender's People," "The Common Way," "The Awakening of Helena Richie," which has become as famous as John Ward, Preacher," and has been dramatized.

MARY ELIZABETH DEWEY.

Born in Gloucester, Massachusetts, October 27, 1821. Daughter of Orville and Louisa (Farnham) Dewey. Author of "Life and Letters of Catherine Sedgwick," and "Autobiography and Letters of Orville Dewey."

MRS. GEORGE SHELDON DOWNS.

Born at Wrentham, Massachusetts, June 5, 1843. Daughter of Edward A. and Malvina Ware Forbush. Writer of fiction in serial stories and books under the pen name of "Mrs. Georgie Sheldon." Among them, "A Brownie's Triumph," "A True Aristocrat," "Betsy's Transformation," "Gertrude Elliot's Crucible."

FANNIE MERRITT FARMER.

Born in Boston, March 23, 1857. Daughter of John Franklin and Mary (Watson) Farmer. Principal of Miss Farmer's School of Cookery since 1892. Author of many works on domestic science, among them "The Boston Cooking School Cook Book," "Food and Cookery for the Sick and Convalescent."

ANNIE ADAMS FIELDS.

Born in Boston, June 6, 1834. Daughter of Dr. Zabdiel Boylston and Sarah May (Holland) Adams. In 1854 married James Thomas Fields, of Boston, who died in 1881. Has written "Memoirs of James Fields," "Whittier; Notes of His Life and Friendship," "Authors and Friends," "Nathaniel Hawthorne," "The Singing Shepherd," and other poems.

EDNA ABIGAIL FOSTER.

Born in Sullivan Harbor, Maine. Daughter of Charles W. and Sarah J. Dyer Foster. Contributor to journals and magazines. Editor at one time of *The Household;* also associate editor of the *Youth's Companion* since 1901, and the author of several stories.

ELIZABETH LINCOLN GOULD.

Born in Boston. Daughter of Charles Duren and Sarah Bell (Wheeler) Gould. Contributor to *Youth's Companion.* Author of a play from Louisa M. Alcott's "Little Men"; also one from "Little Women"; the stories, "Little Polly Prentiss," "Felicia," and "Felicia's Friend," and others.

EDITH GUERRIER.

Born in New Bedford, Massachusetts, September 20, 1870. Daughter of George Pearce and Emma Louisa Ricketson Guerrier. Head resident of Library Club House, Boston. Author of "Wonderfolk in Wonderland," and other folklore stories.

MARY BRONSON HARTT.

Born in Ithaca, New York, March 23, 1873. Daughter of Prof. Charles Frederick and Lucy Cornelia Lynde Hartt. Her father was a professor of Cornell

University. She is a contributor to the *World's Work, Scribner's, Century, Youth's Companion,* and *Boston Transcript.*

MARGARET HORTON POTTER.

Born in Chicago, May 20, 1881. Daughter of R. N. W. and Ellen Owen Potter. Married John D. Black, of Chicago, January 1, 1902. Her book, "The Social Lion," published in 1899, created quite a sensation. It has since been followed by others: "Uncanonized," "The House of De Mailly," "Istar of Babylon," "The Castle of Twilight," "The Flame-Gatherers," "The Fire of Spring," "The Princess," "The Golden Ladder," etc.

ELIZABETH ARMSTRONG REED.

Born in Winthrop, Maine, May 16, 1842. Daughter of Alvin and Sylvia Armstrong, who were both prominent educators. She is the only woman whose work has been accepted by the Philosophical Society of Great Britain. Contributor to *Encyclopedia Americana,* and *Biblical Encyclopedia.* Author of "The Bible Triumphant," a book on Hindu literature, and also others on the literature of Persia, ancient and modern, "Primitive Buddhism; Its Origin and Teachings," etc.

LIZZIE E. WOOSTER.

Born in Stubenville, July 24, 1870. Daughter of Charles C. and Nannie Cullom Wooster. Has been engaged in the authorship and editing of school books since 1896, and is her own publisher, establishing her own firm under the name of Wooster and Company. She is the author of reading charts, primers, arithmetics, primary recitations, "First Reader," "Elementary Arithmetic," "Wooster's Combination Reading Chart," "Wooster Sentence Builder," "Wooster Number Builders," "The Wooster Readers," and other well-known school books.

MADELINE YALE WYNNE.

Born at Newport, New York, September 25, 1847. Daughter of Linus Yale, Jr. (inventor of the Yale lock), and Catherine Brooks Yale. Was a student of art in Boston Art Museum and in New York. Pupil of George Fuller. Has originated and developed an interesting specialty in hand-wrought metals. Is a contributor to many of the magazines. Author of "The Little Room," and other stories.

MARY BLATCHLEY BRIGGS.

Mrs. Briggs was born in Valparaiso, Indiana, January 1, 1846. She served for eleven years as assistant secretary, superintendent, and reporter for the press, and manager of county, state and inter-state fairs. She has written a volume of poems. She served on the executive committee, Board of Lady Managers of the World's Fair.

REBECCA RUTER SPRINGER.

Mrs. Rebecca Ruter Springer was born in Indianapolis, Indiana, November 8, 1832. Daughter of Rev. Calvin W. Ruter, a prominent clergyman of the Methodist Episcopal Church, and was educated in the Wesleyan Female College in Cincinnati, Ohio.

In 1859 she married William M. Springer, a noted lawyer of Illinois, and afterwards Congressman for several terms from that state. Mrs. Springer passed much of her life in the Capital City, and no woman was more beloved nor more conspicuous through her abilities and charm of manner. Mrs. Springer wrote several books of verse and two novels, entitled "Beechwood" and "Self," and a volume of poems under the title "Songs of the Sea." Mrs. Springer's death occurred in 1904.

B. ELLEN BURKE.

Was born in Lawrence County, New York, in 1850. Her husband was Charles A. Burke, a lawyer of Malone, New York. In 1896, she organized the Teachers' Institutes for the instructors in Catholic schools, and teachers were brought together from all the states. Her assistants were among the ablest Catholic teachers of the country. She originated and improved the methods of teaching in the Sunday Schools. Has given talks and lectures at the Catholic summer schools of Madison, and Detroit, Michigan, and also the Catholic winter school of New Orleans. In 1889 she accepted the position of editor for the Catholic publishers, D. H. McBride and Company, and in 1900 published the *Sunday Companion*, a periodical for young Catholics, and on the retirement of these publishers from business, she bought the paper and has since been its owner and editor. She has published also a Catholic monthly called *The Helper*, intended for teachers and parents. Has written and compiled a set of readers for Catholic schools and two geographies. Is a prominent contributor to other periodicals beside her own. She taught the first "Method Class," and started the New York Normal School for Catechists, the faculty of which now numbers twenty-eight.

MARGARET MARY BROPHY HALVEY.

Was born in Queens County, Ireland, in the early sixties. Her father's family came to Ireland at the time of Henry II, in 1192, and her mother was one of the first Catholics in her family since the Reformation. In 1884 she married Timothy Frederick Halvey, founder of the first Gaelic School in New York, Chicago, Philadelphia, and Buffalo, and originator of Robert Emmet Day (March 4) She was active during the World's Fair and Social Science Exhibit, introducing the Irish industries, particularly the lace exhibit. Was the first woman secretary of the Catholic Historical Society, and secretary and co-founder of the Woman's Auxiliary Board. Author of poems and short stories. Is one of the officers for the Anti-Vivisection Society; also the Woman's Pen Society, Society for the Prevention of Cruelty to Animals, and president of the Ladies' Land

League, branch secretary of the Ladies' Aid Society for Widows and Orphans. Makes her home in Philadelphia, Pennsylvania.

SARAH MOORE.

Newspaper artist; journalist. Special writer and illustrator on the staff of the *Detroit News*. Is the daughter of Charles B. Moore and was born in Detroit.

ANNIE LAURIE WILSON JAMES.

Mrs. Annie Laurie Wilson James was born in Louisville, Kentucky, November, 1862. She occupies a very unique position among women, having been considered an authority on the heredity of horses, and horse pedigrees. In 1888 she went to California on a business trip and while there became assistant editor and manager of *Breeder and Sportsman*, published in San Francisco. In 1888 she married R. B. James, of Baker County, Oregon, and has made her home there for many years.

EMILY L. GOODRICH SMITH.

Mrs. Emily L. Goodrich Smith was born in the old Hancock House, Boston, Massachusetts, June 1, 1830. She was the oldest daughter of the Hon. S. G. Goodrich, who was well known as "Peter Parley." Her mother was Miss Mary Boote. She was educated abroad and while living in Paris in 1848 she witnessed the terrors enacted during the reign of Louis Philippe. Her father was consul in Paris, and their house was constantly filled with terror-stricken foreigners, who found their only safety under the protection of the American flag.

Returning to the United States, in 1856, she became the wife of Nathaniel Smith, of Connecticut, a grandson of the famous Nathaniel Smith, one time Chief Justice of Connecticut. She has written many stories and verses for magazines, her letters during the war were widely read and copied. She was one of the founders of the Chautauqua Literary Circle and a vice-regent of the Mt. Vernon Association for Connecticut.

SOPHIA BRAEUNLICH.

Mrs. Braeunlich was born July 2, 1860, in Bethpage, Long Island. After the death of her husband, she was left without resources. She took a business course at the Packard Business College in New York, and on her graduation obtained the position of private secretary to the editor of the *Engineering and Mining Journal*, and president of the Scientific Publishing Company. She displayed such ability and mastered so fully the technical details of the paper, that finally she attended the meetings of the American Institute of Mining Engineers as representative of the editor, and when Mr. Rothwell resigned this position, Mrs. Braeunlich was elected to the vacancy and became the business manager of the entire establishment. She assisted the government in obtaining data for the statistics in regard to the collection of gold for the Eleventh Census. She is described as "a woman of strong character, with an instinctive clearness of vision ascribed to women, with the sound judgment of a man."

MARIA MORGAN.

Widely known as Middy Morgan, was born November 22, 1828, in Cork, Ireland, and died in Jersey City, N. J., June 1, 1892. Miss Morgan occupied a unique position among American professional women. She was the daughter of Anthony Morgan, a landed proprietor. In 1865 her father died, and the eldest son succeeding to the entire estate, the other children were left dependent. Maria and a younger sister went to Rome, Italy, and there, owing to her wonderful horsemanship and knowledge of horses, which she had gained on her father's estates in Ireland, she was engaged by Victor Emmanuel, King of Italy, to select the horses for his Horse Guards and take the supervision of his stables, a position which she filled with credit, and to the entire satisfaction of the King. After five years spent in this service, she decided to come to the United States, and on her departure, was presented with valuable jewels in recognition of her service. She bore letters of introduction to Horace Greeley, James Gordon Bennett, and Henry J. Raymond, and was immediately employed by the *New York Tribune,* the *Herald,* and the *Times* to write articles and do live-stock reporting, also for the *Turf, Field and Farm* and the *Live Stock Reporter.* In addition, she wrote the pedigrees and racing articles for the *American Agriculturist.* At one time she was in charge of the Pennsylvania Railroad station at Robinvale, New Jersey, and during this time made three trips to Europe; her first on a cattle boat. After her return she wrote a series of articles on the treatment of cattle on ocean steamers, which resulted in the bettering of conditions and more humane treatment.

AGNES REPPLIER.

Miss Agnes Repplier, of Philadelphia, received March 5, 1911, the Laetare medal, annually awarded by the University of Notre Dame (Indiana) to a lay member of the Catholic Church in the United States, who has performed conspicuous work in literature, art, science, or philanthropy—the highest honor conferred by this University. Miss Repplier's work has extended over a period of a quarter of a century, and she is considered to be an essayist without peer in this country. Of her, Dr. Howard Furness, the critic, says, "She has revived an art almost lost in these days, that of the essayist. There is no form of the essay she has not touched, and she has touched nothing she has not adorned." In 1902 the University of Pennsylvania conferred on her the degree of Doctor of Letters. Agnes Repplier was born in Philadelphia, April 1, 1857, her parents being Joseph and Eliza Jane Repplier, of French extraction. She is the author of "Books and Men"; "Essays in Miniature," etc.

AUBERTINE WOODWARD MOORE.

Musical critic, translator, and lecturer. Was born September 27, 1841, near Philadelphia. She wrote under the pen name of "Aubertine Forestier." She contributed articles to the Philadelphia papers on the resources of California, and published translations of several novels from the German. Also translations of music and original songs. In 1877 she published "Echoes from Mist-Land," or more fully "The Nibelungen Lay Revealed to Lovers of Romance and Chivalry," which is a prose version of the famous poem, and was the first American translation of that work which received favorable comment, not only in this country but in England and Germany. She is a well-known Scandinavian translator and is a pioneer in the translation of the Norway Music Album, a valuable collection of Norwegian folk-lore songs, dances, national airs and compositions for the piano. In December, 1887, she became the wife of Samuel H. Moore. Mrs. Moore is considered an authority on the musical history and literature of the Scandinavians, and a collection of her writings in that field would form the most valuable compendium of Scandinavian lore to be found in the English language. She has done valuable work in making Americans familiar with Norwegian literature and music. She has been invited to give evenings on this subject before the various clubs of this country, notably the Sorosis, of New York, and the Woman's Club, of Boston. She is unexcelled as a translator of the poetry of the Norwegian, French, and German writers, and her translation of Goethe's "Erl King" has been considered the finest ever made.

FRANCES G. DAVENPORT.

Miss Davenport studied history at Radcliffe College (Harvard Annex), from which college she received the degrees of B.A. and M.A.; at Cambridge University, England, and at Chicago University. From the last-named institution she received the degree of Ph.D. (in 1904). She taught history at Vassar College during the year 1904-1905, and since 1905 has been an assistant in the Department of Historical Research in the Carnegie Institution of Washington. Until she became connected with the Carnegie Institution, she worked in English Economic History, and published two books and several articles in that field. Of these, the principal one was a book on "The Economic Development of a Norfolk Manor." Since her connection with the Carnegie Institution began, she has compiled in collaboration, with Professor C. M. Andrews, a "Guide to the Manuscript Materials for the History of the United States to 1783, in the British Museum, Minor London Archives, and the Libraries of Oxford and Cambridge." Has published in the American Historical Review (1909) an article on "Columbus's Book of Privileges," and has been and is now engaged in compiling and editing a collection of "Treaties relating to the territory now included within the United States, to which the United States was not a party."

SUSAN HUNTER WALKER.

Mrs. Walker was born in Banff, Scotland, and received her early education in private schools of Scotland and England. She is the daughter of the late James Hunter, M.A., for quarter of a century rector of the Banff Academy, a school which prepared youths for the University of Aberdeen, Scotland. Mr.

55

Hunter came to this country in the early eighties and engaged in literary work. Among other valuable work he accomplished was the editing of the Supplement to Worcester's Dictionary, and was chief translator and collaborator in the preparation of the "History of All Nations," of Flaathe, of which the late Professor John Henry Wright, of Harvard University, was editor-in-chief.

Miss Hunter remained in school in England for some years after the establishment of her family in Virginia, near the United States Capital. She continued her education under private teachers in this country until she became assistant editor of *Book News*, Philadelphia. This position she held for three years, resigning it to come to Washington to assist Mrs. John A. Logan in the conduct of *The Home Magazine*, of Washington. She was associated with Mrs. Logan in this capacity for several years, and when Mrs. Logan resigned her position as editor of the *Home Magazine* she took up the work, holding it until 1906.

In 1904 Miss Hunter married Rev. Albert Rhett Walker, of South Carolina, rector of the Episcopal Church at Fairfax Court House, Virginia. Mr. Walker died in 1910, and Mrs. Walker has returned to Washington to resume the work relinquished in a great measure upon her marriage. She has for many years been a regular contributor to the general press, writing for *The Christian Herald, The Christian Endeavor World, The Congregationalist, The Epworth Herald, The Churchman, Human Life,* and for many of the best metropolitan newspapers.

MAUD ANDREWS OHL.

Was one of the best known newspaper writers of the United States, being for many years correspondent for the *Atlanta Constitution*, which her husband represented in Washington, and other newspapers of the country. She was born December 29, 1862, in Taliaferro County, Georgia. Her maiden name was Maud Andrews. She spent her early childhood in the home of her grandfather, Judge Andrews, in Washington, Georgia. Her husband, J. K. Ohl, is now in China on special work for some of the leading New York dailies.

EMMA HUNTINGTON NASON.

Was born August 6, 1845, in Hallowell, Maine. Poems for children of larger growth have appeared over her signature in the leading periodicals. She has also written a series of valuable art papers as well as translations from the French and German.

EDITH R. MOSHER.

Edith R. Mosher, born on a farm near Centerville, Michigan, is the daughter of Josephus and Lida Stebbins Mosher. When a child she attended the district schools and, later, moved to the village of Centerville, where she graduated from the High School at the age of 16; she then entered the state normal school, where she took the literary and scientific course and graduated at the age of 18, with a life certificate to teach in the state of Michigan, and immediately began teaching in the public schools. While teaching in the kindergarten and primary grade in Grand Rapids, she studied kindergarten methods with the late Mrs. Lucretia Willard Treat. Having had considerable instruction in drawing at the State Normal School, and having a natural, ready talent for it, she was constantly called upon to do blackboard decorating, and to illustrate science lessons, throughout the school building. In connection with this work, she became impressed with the necessity for finding easy, accurate illustrations of the every-day blossoms and leaves of our trees, which so readily lend themselves to board illustrating and interesting science lessons, and began to realize the vast importance of the forest as a great educational influence upon the growth and upbuilding of humanity. From her somewhat varied experience in the different grades, she grew profoundly conscious of the significance of the early impressions upon the plastic mind of the child, and knowing how children love nature, she believed that it should be the constant study of the teacher to bring into the schoolroom as much of nature and nature suggestions as can be appreciated, thus to fill child life with pure wholesome thought from the overflowing well-spirit of nature, and ideally mold child character.

It was while standing before a blackboard in the schools of Grand Rapids, preparing a science lesson suggested by a small peach branch, which one of the pupils had brought, with only the scientifically accurate, but unattractive outlines from a book on botany and some pictured cards, that there came over her a startling realization of the entire lack of any book really useful to teachers in this kind of instruction, which she believed to be fundamental, and she registered a vow to supply this need in the form of a series of books to be used in the school room. With this object in view she resigned and went to Washington, D. C., to obtain a position in the government, and there carry on her work with the better facilities offered by the Congressional Library. In Washington, she again took up literary work in the George Washington University, and has continued to carry on studies along educational lines, taking a summer course at Harvard University in 1909.

In the meantime the "Tree-Study" books planned in the Grand Rapids school room were growing. A transfer had been obtained to the Forest Service as the best place to perfect this work, which was followed by special permission from the Forester, Mr. Gifford Pinchot, to attend the Yale University Summer School, which is not a co-educational institution.

The work of compiling and illustrating the first book on "Fruit and Nut-Bearing Trees" was finished in 1907, and was followed in 1909 by "Our Oaks and Maples," and "Our Cone-Bearing Trees." The urgent demand of the publisher and others interested in the work resulted in five more of the series in 1910, under the titles of "Fruit Studies"; "Our Queenly Maples"; "Our Kingly Oaks"; "Studies of Nut-Bearing Trees"; "Studies of Evergreens"; a book entitled "Twenty Forest Trees," is now being prepared.

JEANNETTE LEONARD GILDER.

Was the daughter of the late Reverend William H. and Jane Nutt Gilder; the sister of the late Richard Watson Gilder, and was born at St. Thomas Hall, at Flushing, New York. Was associated for some time with her brother, Richard

Watson Gilder, in the editorial department of *Scribner's Monthly*, now the *Century*. Literary editor and afterwards dramatic and musical critic of the *New York Herald* from 1875 to 1880. In 1881, in connection with her brother, Joseph B. Gilder, started *The Critic*, now *Putnam's Magazine*, of which she is associate editor. Was for many years correspondent of the *Boston Saturday Gazette* and the *Boston Evening Transcript*, also the London Academy, and New York correspondent for the Philadelphia *Press* and *Record*. Regular correspondent of the *Chicago Tribune*. Has written plays and stories for magazines. Is the author of "Taken by Siege," "The Autobiography of a Tomboy," "The Tomboy at Work." Edited "Essays from the Critic," and "Representative Poems of Living Poets" and "Pen Portraits of Literary Women" and "Authors at Home."

HELEN HINSDALE RICH.

Born June 18, 1827, on her father's farm in Antwerp, Jefferson County, New York. She is known as the poet of the Adirondacks. At twelve years of age she wrote verses and was proficient in botany. Being obliged to read the debates in Congress aloud to her father, the speeches of Henry Clay and Daniel Webster made her an ardent patriot, and a deeply interested politician. She was the first woman in Northern New York to embrace Woman Suffrage, and lectured during the Civil War for the Union Cause. Among her writings, her "Madame de Stael" has the endorsement of eminent scholars as a literary lecture. She excels in poems of the affections.

MARY ALICIA OWEN.

Was born January 29, 1858, in St. Joseph, Missouri. Daughter of James A. Owen, a lawyer and writer on finance, and Agnes Jeannette. After several years of successful newspaper work she turned her attention to short stories and became a contributor to many of the leading periodicals; later turned her attention and devoted herself to the collection of the curious and romantic myths and legends of the Mississippi Valley. Her most notable success has been the discovery of the Voodoo stories and ritual. Her papers on this subject were read before the American Folk Lore Society at one of its annual meetings in Philadelphia, also before the Boston Folk Lore Society and the International Folk Lore Congress in London, England. She has prepared books on the Voodoo magic and the myths of the rubber devil.

ABBY HUTCHINSON PATTON.

Was born August 20 1829, in Milford, New Hampshire. She was well known as Abby Hutchinson, being a member of the well-known Hutchinson family, whose gift of song made them famous. Mrs. Patton came of a long line of musical ancestors, especially on the maternal side. In 1839 she made her first appearance as a singer, in her native town. On this occasion the parents and their thirteen children took part. In 1841, with her three younger brothers, she began her concert career. They sang in the autumn and winter, devoting the spring and summer to their farm, while their sister pursued her studies in the academy. In 1843 the Hutchinson family visited New York City, and the harmony of their voices took that city by storm. The Hutchinsons were imbued with a strong love for liberty, and soon joined heart and hand with the abolitionists, and in their concerts sang ringing songs of freedom. These singers were all gifted as song writers and musical composers. In 1845 they visited England, finding warm welcome among such friends as William and Mary Howitt, Douglas Gerald, Charles Dickens, Harriet Martineau, Hartley Coleridge, Mrs. Tom Hood, Eliza Cook, Samuel Rogers, Mrs. Norton, George Thompson and John Bright. Charles Dickens honored them with an evening reception in his home. After one year in Great Britain the family returned to America. On February 28, 1849, Abby Hutchinson became the wife of Ludlow Patton, a banker of New York City, and after her marriage she sang with her brothers only on special occasions. After Mr. Patton's retirement from active business in 1873, they spent several years in travel abroad, during which time Mrs. Patton was a frequent contributor to the American newspapers. She composed music for several poems, among which the best known are "Kind Words Can Never Die," and Alfred Tennyson's "Ring Out Wild Bells." Mrs. Patton was always actively interested in the education of women. Her death occurred in New York City November 25, 1892.

KATE SANBORN.

Is a native of New Hampshire, and was the daughter of Professor Sanborn, who occupied the chair of Latin and English literature, at Dartmouth College, for nearly fifty years. Miss Sanborn is a descendant of Captain Ebenezer Webster, the eminent Revolutionary hero, and grand-niece of Daniel Webster. Her literary talents were developed by her father, who privately instructed her in the regular college course, and at eleven years of age she was a contributor to the *Well-Spring,* and at seventeen supported herself by her pen. She became an instructor in elocution at the Packer Institute at Brooklyn, and for five years filled the chair of English literature at Smith College. Miss Sanborn was the originator of Current Event classes in many of the literary clubs, and now so common in every city of the United States in the form of Curent Topics classes. Among her best-known works are "Adopting an Abandoned Farm," and "Abandoning an Adopted Farm," "Witty Records" of her original ideas regarding farming, which she put into practice upon an abandoned farm which she purchased near Boston. Some of her other books are "Home Pictures of English Poets," "A Truthful Woman in Southern California," "Vanity and Insanity; Shadows of Genius," "Purple and Gold," "Grandmother's Garden," and "My Literary Zoo." She has been instrumental in gathering and publishing a valuable historical work on New Hampshire. Few women are so versatile and have reached superiority in so many lines of work as has Miss Sanborn. She is teacher, reviewer, compiler, essayist, lecturer, author, and farmer, and is famous for her cooking and housekeeping.

MRS. MARGARET ELIZABETH SANGSTER.

Was born February 22, 1838, in New Rochelle, New York. Her maiden name was Margaret Elizabeth Munson. In 1858 she married George Sangster.

She was a regular contributor to many of the leading magazines and periodicals, gradually drifting into editorial work, and in 1871 became the editor of *Hearth and Home*. In 1873 she assumed an editorial position on the *Christian at Work*. In 1879 she became a member of the staff of the *Christian Intelligencer*, serving as assistant editor until 1888. In 1882 in addition to her other editorial work she edited the *Harper's Young People*, then just starting. In 1890 she became the editor of *Harper's Bazar*. During all these busy years she has written poems of a high order, stories, sketches, essays, editorial comments, criticisms and everything connected with her work in the various editorial positions which she has occupied. Her published books are "Manual of Missions of the Reformed Church in America," "Poems of the Household," "Home Fairies and Heart Flowers," and a series of Sunday School books.

MRS. CYNTHIA MORGAN ST. JOHN.

Was born in Ithaca, New York, October 11, 1852. She was the only daughter of E. J. Morgan and Anne Bruyn Morgan. In her early youth she showed a passionate love of nature and devotion to the poetry of Wordsworth. Her one pre-eminent interest in a literary way has been in the writings of that great poet. She was a member of the English Wordsworth Society and a contributor to its meetings. She has collected the largest Wordsworth library in this country, and it is said to be the largest in the world, containing all the regular editions, complete American editions, autograph letters, prints, portraits, sketches, and relics associated with the great poet. The chief fruit of her life-long study of the poet has been her "Wordsworth for the Young." In 1883 she became the wife of Henry A. St. John, of Ithaca, New York.

CATHERINE MARIA SEDGWICK.

Born December 28, 1789, in Stockbridge, Massachusetts, and died near Roxbury, Massachusetts, July 31, 1867. She was a daughter of Theodore Sedgwick, a well-known lawyer of Boston, who died January 24, 1813. She received a thorough education, and after her father's death started a private school for young women, which she continued for fifty years. During this time she contributed to the literature of the day. Her first novel, "A New England Tale," was published in 1822. She then brought out "Redwood," which was translated into French and other foreign languages. Her translator attributed this work to J. Fenimore Cooper. This was followed by "The Traveler," "Hope Leslie, or Early Times in Massachusetts," "Clarence," "A Tale of Our Own Times," "Home," "The Linwoods, or Sixty Years Since in America," "Sketches and Tales," "The Poor Rich Man and the Rich Poor Man," "Live and Let Live," "A Love Token for Children," "Means and Ends; or Self-Training," "Letters from Abroad to Kindred at Home," "Historical Sketches of the Old Painters," "Lucretia and Margaret Davidson," "Wilton Harvey and Other Tales," "Morals of Manners," "Facts and Fancies," and "Married or Single?" In addition to her school and novel work, she edited and contributed to literary periodicals and wrote for the annuals. Her work in these lines fills several large volumes.

ABBIE C. B. ROBINSON.

Was born September 18, 1828, in Woonsocket, Rhode Island. Her father, George C. Ballou, was a cousin of Rev. Hosea Ballou and of President Garfield's mother. Her mother's maiden name was Ruth Eliza Aldrich. In 1854 she became the wife of Charles D. Robinson, of Green Bay, Wisconsin, who was the editor of the *Green Bay Advocate* and at one time Secretary of State for Wisconsin. Mrs. Robinson was as famous for political wisdom as her husband. She assisted him in editing the *Advocate*. Owing to failing health, gradually her husband's duties fell upon Mrs. Robinson, and ultimately she assumed them all, including not only the editorial department, business management, but also a job department, bindery and store. Her husband's death occurred four years later, and in 1888 she broke down under these exacting demands and was obliged to retire from the paper. Under all these trying conditions she won for herself the enviable position of a woman of force and ability, animated by the highest and purest motives, and was known as an easy, graceful and cultured writer and astute politician.

EMILY HUNTINGTON MILLER.

Was born October 22, 1833. Graduate of Oberlin College. In 1860 became the wife of John E. Miller. Mr. Miller was principal of the academy in Granville for a number of years, and afterwards professor of Greek and Latin in the Northwestern College, then located in Plainfield. In connection with Alfred L. Sewell, she published *The Little Corporal,* which, after the great fire in Chicago, was merged into *St. Nicholas.* Mr. and Mrs. Miller moved to St. Paul, where Mr. Miller died in 1882. Mrs. Miller published a number of sketches and stories, and has been a constant contributor of short stories, sketches, serials, poems, and miscellaneous articles to newspapers and magazines, and earned a reputation by her work on *The Little Corporal.* She has been conected with the Chautauqua Assembly since its commencement, and was at one time president of the Chautauqua Club. She was elected in 1898 president of the Woman's College of the Northwestern University in Evanston, Illinois. Her published literary works include fifteen volumes. She has been equally successful as a writer, educator, temperance worker, and journalist.

FANNIE RUTH ROBINSON.

Born September 30, 1847, in Carbondale, Pennsylvania. Graduated at the age of seventeen and received the degree of M.A. from Rutgers College, New York. Most of her poems appeared in *Harper's Magazine* between the years of 1870 and 1880. A poem on Emerson, published after his death in the *Journal of Philosophy,* is considered one of her best. She is, at present (1898) preceptress of Ferry Hall Seminary, the Woman's Department of Lake Forest University, Lake Forest, Illinois.

ITTI KINNEY RENO.

Born Nashville, Tennessee, May 17, 1862. Daughter of Colonel George Kinney, of Nashville. In 1885 she became the wife of Robert Ross Reno, son of the late M. A. Reno, Major of the Seventh United States Cavalry, famous for the gallant defense of his men during two days and nights of horror from the overwhelming force of Sioux Indians, who the day before had massacred Custer's entire battalion. Mrs. Reno's first novel, "Miss Breckenridge, a Daughter of Dixie," proved most successful and passed through five editions. Her second book, "An Exceptional Case," likewise met with great success.

HESTER DORSEY RICHARDSON.

Born January 9, 1862, in Baltimore, Maryland. Daughter of James A. Dorsey and Sarah A. W. Dorsey, both of old representative Maryland families. She is known under the pen name of "Selene," and her "Selene Letters," which appeared in the *Baltimore American*, attracted wide attention. A letter from her pen helped to rescue the Mercantile Library from an untimely end. She organized the Woman's Literary Club of Baltimore, laying the foundation of a controlling force in the intellectual and social life of her native city.

EMILY TRACEY Y. SWETT PARKHURST.

Born in San Francisco, California, March 9, 1863, and died there April 21, 1892. She was the daughter of Professor John Swett, a prominent educator of California, known as the "Father of Pacific Coast Eduaction," and author of many educational works of wide use in the United States, England, France, Norway, Sweden, Denmark, and Australia. Miss Swett became the wife of John W. Parkhurst, of the Bank of California, in 1889. She has contributed largely to the magazines and papers of the Pacific Coast. Her literary work includes translations from Greek, French and German and some finished poems of high merit. She dramatized Helen Hunt Jackson's novel "Ramona."

ELIZA J. NICHOLSON.

Born in 1849 in Hancock County, Mississippi, and died February 15, 1896. Contributor to the *New York Home Journal* and other papers of high standing under the pen name of "Pearl Rivers." When asked by the editor of the *New Orleans Picayune* to become literary editor of that paper, a newspaper woman was unheard of in the South. She was not only the pioneer woman journalist of the South, but became the foremost woman editor. In 1878 she became the wife of George Nicholson, then manager, and afterwards part proprietor, but Mrs. Nicholson, up to the day of her death, shaped the policy of the paper.

MARY FRENCH SHELDON.

Mrs. Sheldon was born in 1846, in Pittsburgh, Pennsylvania. She is a great-great-granddaughter of Isaac Newton, and her ancestors include many notable men and women. Her father was an engineer of high standing in Pittsburgh. Her mother, Mrs. Elizabeth French, was a well-known spiritualist. Mrs. Shelden was twice married. Her second husband, E. S. Sheldon, died in the summer of 1892. She was educated as a physician, but never practised. She published one novel and a translation of Flaubert's "Salambo." In 1890 she determined to travel in Central Africa to study the women and children in their primitive state. She was the first white woman to reach Mt. Kilima-Njaro, traveling with one female attendant and a small body of natives. She has published an interesting account of this trip in a volume on Africa entitled, "To Sultan."

CHARLOTTE PERKINS GILMAN.

Charlotte Perkins Gilman, writer on social philosophy, and questions of sociology, was born in Hartford, Connecticut, July 3, 1860. Daughter of Frederic Beecher and Mary A. Fitch (Westcott) Perkins, and great-granddaughter of Lyman Beecher. In 1884 she married C. W. Stetson, and on June 11, 1900, she was married to George H. Gilman, of New York.

In 1890 she began lecturing on ethics, economics and sociology, writing on these subjects for magazines and papers. She is especially identified with the work for the advance of women and the labor question; is a member of the American Academy of Political and Social Science, American Sociology Association, and League for Political Education. Among her writings are: "Women and Economics," "In This Our World," "The Yellow Wallpaper," "Concerning Children," "The Home, Its Work and Influence," "Human Work."

Mrs. Gilman's philosophy is dynamic; it is essentially one of hope, courage, joy; and it is for America of to-day. W. D. Howells pronounces her short story, "The Yellow Wallpaper," a psychological masterpiece. Her sociological works have been translated into many languages. She now publishes, edits and writes entirely a magazine, *The Forerunner*.

MARIETTA HOLLEY.

Miss Marietta Holley is most affectionately remembered by her pen name of "Josiah Allen's Wife." She was born at Ellisburgh, Jefferson County, New York, and is the daughter of John M. and Mary Tabro Holley. Her best known works are: "My Opinions and Betsy Bobbett's," "Samantha at the Centennial," "My Wayward Partner," "The Mormon Wife" (a poem), "Miss Richard's Boy," "Sweet Cicely," "Samantha at Saratoga," "Samantha Amongst the Brethren," "Samantha in Europe," "Around the World with Josiah Allen's Wife," "Samantha at the St. Louis Exposition," "Samantha on Children's Rights," "The Borrowed Automobile."

Frances Willard said of Miss Holley: "Brave, sweet spirit, you don't know how much we all love you. No woman has more grandly helped the woman's cause."

MRS. FRANK LESLIE.

Was born in 1851 in the city of New Orleans, Louisiana. Her maiden name was Miriam Florence Folline. She became the wife of Frank Leslie, the New

York publisher, who died in January, 1880. This name, Frank Leslie, was the name used in signing his articles written for the London press, his real name being Henry Carter. When he came to the United States he assumed legally the name of Frank Leslie. Miss Folline was engaged in literary work on the *Ladies' Magazine,* and through the illness of one of its literary editors, Miss Folline succeeded to the position. After the death of her husband, she continued the publication of his periodicals and brought success out of what seemed failure at the time of her husband's death. She is an extensive traveler and prominent socially.

HULDA BARKER LOUD.

Was born in the town, which is now Rockland, Massachusetts, September, 1844. In 1884 she undertook to publish and edit the paper established in her own town, which was called the *Rockland Independent,* of which she has long remained the editor and chief and sole proprietor, superintending the business department and job printing as well as occupying the editorial chair. This paper has been made the vehicle of her reforms—social and political. In 1887 she represented the Knights of Labor in the Women's International Council held in Washington, and spoke before the Knights of Labor and the Anti-Poverty Society. She frequently addresses associations and woman suffrage organizations, and is conspicuous in this line of work.

LUCY A. MALLORY.

Was born February, 1846, in Roseburg, Oregon. Her father, Aaron Rose, was an early settler of this state, and for him the name of Roseburg was given to one of the leading towns. Miss Rose's early life was spent in the wilds of this new country surrounded by Indians. She became the wife of Rufus Mallory, who was at one time a member of Congress of the State of Oregon, and one of the most successful lawyers in the Northwest, and member of the firm to which Senator Dolph belongs. In 1874 the old slavery prejudice was still so strong in the State of Oregon that some forty-five negro children were prevented from attending the Salem public school, and no white teacher would consent to teach them even in a separate school, although a public fund was set apart for this purpose. Mrs. Mallory volunteered to instruct these children in the face of the ridicule heaped upon her. After three years of personal effort on the part of Mrs. Mallory, and her example of duty to the public, these children were admitted to the white schools, and all opposition disappeared. Mrs. Mallory used the public money which she drew as salary for this work as a fund for the purchase of a printing plant, and started a monthly magazine known as the *World's Advanced Thought,* in which she was assisted in the editorial department by Judge H. M. McGuire. This magazine has a circulation among many advanced thinkers and workers in every portion of the civilized world. Mrs. Mallory's home is in Portland, Oregon.

MARY EDWARDS BRYAN.

Born in Florida, Georgia, in 1844. Daughter of John D. and Louisa Critchfield Edwards. Wrote for Southern papers and was editor of the *New York*

Bazar, and also of the *Half-Hour Magazine,* two New York publications. Return-ing to the South, she is now on the staff of *Uncle Remus' Home Magazine.* Is a member of the Sorosis Club of New York, and several of the women's press clubs of the United States.

MARY AILEEN AHERN.

Born near Indianapolis, Indiana. Teacher in the public schools of Penn-sylvania and Assistant State Librarian in 1889 and State Librarian in 1893. In 1896 she organized and has since edited *The Public Library,* a library journal. Has lectured before several colleges and library schools and associations. Fellow of the American Library Institute, organized the Indiana Library Association, member of the Illinois Library Association, Chicago Library Club, American Peace League, National Association of Charities and Corrections, and is prominent in library work throughout the country.

EMMA ELLA CARROLL.

Emma Ella Carroll, military genius, was born in Somerset County, Mary-land, August 29, 1815; daughter of Thomas King Carroll, Governor of Maryland. When but three years of age she would listen with great gravity to readings from Shakespeare. Alison's History and Kant's Philosophy were her favorites at eleven, Coke and Blackstone at thirteen. Her literary career began early in life when she contributed political articles to the daily press. In 1857 she published "The Great American Battle," or "Political Romanism," and in the year 1858, "The Star of the West," a work describing the exploration and development of our Western territories. In 1858 she rendered valuable assistance in electing Thomas H. Hicks, Governor, and her influence held Maryland loyal to the Union. She freed her own slaves and devoted tongue and pen to upholding the Union. In July, 1861, when Senator Breckenbridge made his speech in favor of secession, Miss Carroll issued a pamphlet in which she refuted each of his arguments, and a large edition was published and circulated by the War Department. Her ability was recognized and she was requested by the government to write on topics bearing on the war. She published in 1861 "The War Powers of the Government," and for her next pamphlet "The Relation of the National Government to the Revolted Citizens Defined," President Lincoln furnishing the theme. In the fall of 1861 Mr. Lincoln and his military advisers had planned a campaign to extend operations into the Southwest, opening the Mississippi to its mouth. Miss Carroll, at the suggestion of government authorities, personally investigated the scene of the proposed operations, and made a study of the topography of the country, and reported that the Tennessee River and not the Mississippi was the true key to the situation. Her explanatory maps and invaluable geographical and topographical information resulted in her plan being adopted, and the land and naval forces were massed on the Tennessee. Fort Henry, Fort Donelson, Bowling Green, Pittsburgh Landing and Corinth, one after another fell into the hands of the Federals. Missouri was saved, and Kentucky and Tennessee brought back into the Union. She also suggested the final plan adopted by the War Department, resulting in the capture of Vicksburg, which opened the way to the North. It was deemed wise at the time to keep secret the fact that this capmaign had been conceived by a civilian and a woman. Mr. Lincoln's death prevented his acknowledgment of the credit, and though Miss Carroll had ample documentary proof of the validity of her claim, which was acknowledged by several of the Congressional Military Committees to be "incontrovertible," no further action was taken in the matter, and Miss Carroll was dependent for support in her declining years upon her sister, a clerk in the Treasury Department at Washington. The above facts will be found in her life, by Sarah Ellen Blackwell, by whom she is called a genius. She died February 17, 1894.

MARIA MITCHELL.

Miss Mitchell was born on the island of Nantucket, August 1, 1818, and was one of ten children, her parents, William and Lydia Mitchell, living in one of the simple homes of this quaint New England spot. Her father had been a school teacher, her mother, Lydia Coleman, was a descendant of Benjamin Franklin, whose parents were Quakers. She was one of the pupils in her father's school, and by him led into the great love of nature which opened up for her the opportunity for her great talents, and to this we are indebted for what she has given to astronomy. He gave Maria the same education which he gave his boys, even the drill in navigation. At sixteen she left the public school, and for a year attended a private school, but being deeply interested in her father's studies, and the study of mathematics, at seventeen she became his helper in the work which he was doing for the United States Government in the Coast Survey. This brought to their home Professor Agassiz, Bache and other noted men. Mr. Mitchell delivered lectures before a Boston society, of which Daniel Webster was president, but scientific study and work at that time brought little money to the family coffers. One sister was teaching for the munificent sum of three hundred dollars a year. Maria felt she must do her part toward adding to the family income, so accepted a position as librarian of the Nantucket library, her salary for the first year being sixty dollars, and seventy-five for the second, and for twenty years she occupied this position, her salary never exceeding one hundred dollars a year. This gave her great opportunity for study, which no doubt reconciled her to the poor pay. On a night in October, 1847, while gazing through the telescope, as was her usual custom for the love of the study, she saw what she believed to be an unknown comet. She told her father, and he at once wrote to Professor William C. Bond, Director of the Observatory at Cambridge, notifying him of the fact, merely asking a letter of acknowledgment in order to please Maria. It was promptly acknowledged that she had made a new discovery, and Frederick VI, King of Denmark, having six years before offered a gold medal to whoever should discover a telescopic comet, awarded this medal to Miss Mitchell, the American Minister presenting her claims at the Danish Court. She was soon gratified by seeing her discovery referred to in scientific journals as "Miss Mitchell's comet." She assisted in compiling the *American Nautical Almanac,* and wrote for scientific periodicals, but she could not content herself with the small opportunities afforded her in this New England village. In 1857 she went abroad to see the observatories of Europe. The learned men of Great Britain welcomed her. She was entertained by Sir John Herschel, and Lady Herschel, Alexander Von Humbolt, Professor Adams, of Cambridge, Sir George Airy, the astronomer royal of England, who wrote a letter of introduction for her to Leverrier of Paris. Later she visited Florence, Rome, Venice, Vienna, and Berlin, where she met Encke. After a year of such triumphs she returned to Nantucket. In 1860 her mother died and the family removed to Lynn to be nearer Boston, where she could pursue her work under better conditions. Miss Mitchell received at this time five hundred dollars a year from the government for her computations. About this time Matthew Vassar was founding and equipping the woman's college that now bears his name. After the observatory of this institution was completed there was but one person mentioned or desired by the patrons and students to be placed in charge, and this was Maria Mitchell. Miss Mitchell moved to the college and made it her home. In 1868, in the great meteoric shower she and her pupils recorded the details of four thousand meteors and gave valuable data of their height above the earth. She gave valuable observations on the transit of Venus, has written on the satellites of Saturn, and on the satellites of Jupiter. She died on June 28, 1889, and was buried in the little island village, where most of her life had been passed.

ALICE D. LE PLONGEON.

Was born December, 1851, in London, England. Her father's name was Dixon, and her mother was Sophia Cook. She married Dr. Le Plongeon, whose extensive travels in South America and Mexico, for the purpose of studying the ancient manuscripts preserved in the British Museum, so interested her that she accompanied him to the wilds of Yucatan. The work done here by Dr. and Mrs. Le Plongeon is well-known all over the world. For eleven years they remained here studying the ruins of that country. Much of the work, and many of the discoveries were made by Mrs. Le Plongeon. They made many hundred photographs, surveying and making molds of the old palaces to be used as models, but the greatest achievement was the discovery of an alphabet by which the American hieroglyphics may be read, something before considered impossible. Though of English birth they have made their home for many years in Long Island, and have written many articles for magazines and papers and published a small volume, "Here and There in Yucatan"; also one "Yucatan, Its Ancient Palaces and Modern Cities," and in order to make ancient America better known to modern Americans, Mrs. Le Plongeon has lectured upon this subject very extensively, and in recognition of her labors the Geographical Society of Paris placed her portrait in the album of celebrated travelers.

GRACIANA LEWIS.

Was born near Kimberton, Chester County, Pennsylvania, October, 1821. Daughter of John Lewis and Esther Lewis. They were descended from Quaker stock, her father's ancestors coming to this country in 1682. Her mother was the oldest child of Bartholomew Fussell and Rebecca Bond Fussell. Bartholomew

Fussell was a minister in the Society of Friends. Her father died when she was but three years old and her mother supported the family by teaching. Miss Lewis' greatest work has been in the field of natural history. She prepared a "Chart of a Class of Birds," also "A Chart of the Animal Kingdom," "Chart of the Vegetable Kingdom," "Chart of Geology with Special Reference to Paleontology." Microscopic studies, including frost crystals and the plumage of birds, as well as the lower forms of animal and vegetable life. She also issued a pamphlet showing the relation of birds to the animal kingdom. In 1876 she exhibited in the Centennial Exposition a model along with her chart of the Animal Kingdom, which caused commendation from Prof. Huxley and other prominent naturalists. One of her pamphlets, "The Development of the Animal Kingdom," was published by Professor Mitchell and extensively circulated among scientific people. In 1870, Miss Lewis was elected a member of the Academy of Natural Science, Philadelphia. Is also honorary member of the Women's Anthropological Society of America and the various scientific societies of Rochester and Philadelphia. Active in the Woman's Christian Temperance work and many of the forestry associations.

LAURA A. LINTON.

Scientist. Was born April, 1853, at Alliance, Ohio. Daughter of Joseph Wildman Linton and Christiana Craven Beans. Her father's family were Quakers, and her mother was descended from a prominent Dutch family of Pennsylvania. Her parents moved to Minnesota in 1868, where she received her education. She was at one time professor of natural and physical science in Lombard University of Galesburg, Illinois. She assisted Professor S. F. Peckham in the preparation of the monograph on petroleum for the reports of the Tenth Census of the United States. She is a member of the American Society for the Advancement of Science and the Association for the Advancement of Women.

FLORA W. PATTERSON.

Born at Columbus, Ohio, September 15, 1847. Daughter of Rev. A. B. and Sarah Sells Wambaugh. Was three years at Radcliffe College, Harvard University, and assistant at Gray Herbarium. Was appointed assistant pathologist in 1896; now mycologist in charge of pathology and mycology collections and inspection work of Bureau of Plant Industry, United States Department of Agriculture. Member of the Geological and Biological Societies of Washington, the Botanical Society of America, and has contributed articles on these subjects. Is assistant editor of *Economic Fungi*.

MARY JANE RATHBUN.

Born at Buffalo, New York, June 11, 1860. Was employed by the United States Fish Commission from 1884 to 1887, and since 1887 in the United States National Museum, and is now assistant curator of the division of marine invertebrates. Member of the Washington Academy of Science, American Society of

Naturalists, American Society of Zoologists, author of various papers in Proceedings of the U. S. National Museum.

HARRIET RICHARDSON.

The daughter of Charles F. E. Richardson and Charlotte Ann Richardson. Received the degree of A.B. from Vassar College in 1896. One of the collaborators of the Smithsonian Institute. Member of the Washington Academy of Science, Biological Society of Washington; has contributed to "Proceedings of the United States National Museum" and other publications. Has written "Monographs on Isopods of North America."

MARY ALICE WILLCOX.

Born in Kennebunk, Maine, April 24, 1856. Daughter of William H. and Annie Holmes Goodenow Willcox. Teacher in the normal and public schools, and professor of zoology in Wellesley College since 1883. Author of "Pocket Guide to Common Land Birds of New England," and various articles on zoological subjects.

CLARA A. SMITH.

Miss Clara A. Smith, instructor of mathematics in Wellesley College. She has recently been elected a Fellow of the American Association for the Advancement of Science, partly because she solved a problem in mathematics which has puzzled college professors for more than a century.

LUCY EVELYN PEABODY.

Born in Cincinnati, January 1, 1865. Was instrumental in securing the passage of an act by Congress setting aside the Mesa Verde Park in Colorado as a national park which includes the most interesting ruins of cliff-dwellers in America. Owns a famous collection of Abraham Lincoln relics and data. Prominent in scientific work.

ADELAIDE GEORGE BENET.

Was born in Warner, New Hampshire, November 8, 1848. Daughter of Gilman C. and Nancy B. George. Taught several years in the public schools of Manchester, New Hampshire. Married Charles Benet, of Pipestone City, Minnesota, in 1887. She is a botanist of distinction.

ELLEN CHURCHILL SEMPLE.

Born in Louisville, Kentucky, in 1863. Daughter of Alexander Bonner and Emerine Price Semple. Graduate of Vassar, and student at Leipzig. Her special field of work is the study of the influence of geographical conditions upon the development of society. She is a member of the Association of American

Geographers, and a contributor of scientific articles to journals both in America and England. Has written on American history and its geographical conditions.

LOUISE M. R. STOWELL.

Born in Grand Blanc, Michigan, December 30, 1850. Daughter of Seth and Harriet Russell Reed. Taught microscopy and botany in the Univeristy of Michigan, and in 1878 married Charles Henry Stowell. Appointed a member of the board of trustees for the Girls' Reform School by the President, for the District of Columbia, and also member of the board of trustees of the public schools of the District of Columbia in 1893. Author of "Microscopical Structure of Wheat," "Microscopic Diagnosis." Is editor and writer in scientific work.

KATHERINE JEANNETTE BUSH.

Born in Scranton, Pennsylvania, December 30, 1855. Was assistant in the zoological department of Yale University. Was a member of the United States Fish Commission for several years and assisted in revising Webster's dictionary, which is now published under the title of "Webster's International Dictionary." Author of several zoological works. Writer of scientific journals, and is one of the noted scientific women of America.

ELLEN HENRIETTA RICHARDS.

Was born December 3, 1842, in Dunstable, Massachusetts. She graduated from Vassar College in 1870, then took a scientific course in the Massachusetts Institute of Technology, Boston, graduating in 1873. She remained in that institution as resident graduate, and in 1875 married Professor Robert Hallowell Richards, the metallurgist. In 1878 she was elected instructor in chemistry and mineralogy in the woman's laboratory of that institute. She has done much to develop the love of scientific studies among women, and is the pioneer in teaching the application of technical knowledge and principles to the conduct of the home to the women of the United States. Mrs. Richards is the first woman to be elected a member of the American Institute of Mining Engineers and is a member of many scientific associations. Among her published works are "Chemistry of Cooking and Cleaning," "Food Materials and Their Adulterations," "First Lessons in Minerals." In 1887, with Marion Talbot, she edited "Home Sanitation." Mrs. Richards is a profound student and a clear thinker. Her work is without equal in its line.

ANNIE SMITH PECK.

In recent years, Miss Peck's achievements as the foremost woman mountain climber of the world has dimmed her creditable efforts as archæologist, but it was in that work that she started her career. Born in Providence, Rhode Island, her early education was received at its high and normal schools. After graduating from the University of Michigan in 1878, having distinguished herself in every branch of study, whether literary or scientific, Miss Peck engaged in teaching, spending two years as professor of Latin in Purdue University. In 1881 she took her master's degree, mainly for work in Greek. Going abroad in 1884 she spent several months in study in Hanover, Germany, and then another period in Italy, devoting herself especialy to the antiquities and passing the summer in Switzerland, mountain climbing. In 1885-1886 she pursued the regular course of study in the American School of Classical Studies in Athens, Greece, and also traveled extensively in Greece, visiting Sicily, Troy, Constantinople, in search of buried antiquities. Immediately after her return home she occupied the chair of Latin in Smith College, later going over the country with a lecture course in Greek archæology and travel. She has since added lectures describing her exploits in reaching the world's highest peaks. When engaged in these expeditions, Miss Peck wears a man's costume, and more often than not the men who accompany her have fallen out and abandoned hope of reaching the goal while she, a woman, has pressed on and planted the flag on the summit. She has climbed more of the highest mountains in South America than any living man. Her lectures have always attracted wide notice and received hearty commendation, both from distinguished scholars and from the press. In addition to her more solid acquirements, Miss Peck also possesses numerous and varied accomplishments; she is a profound classical scholar and accomplished musician.

ALICE CUNNINGHAM FLETCHER.

Was born in Boston in 1845. Was the author of the plan of loaning small sums of money to aid Indians to buy land to build houses for themselves, and active in securing land to the Omaha tribe.

Under this act was appointed special agent to allot the Omaha tribe and also appointed by the President, special agent for the Winnebago tribe in 1887. Is ex-president of the Anthropological Society of Washington. Did work in this connection for the Chicago Exposition. Is holder of the Thaw fellowship and officer in the Archæological Institute of America. Has written on Indian life and song and many papers on anthropology and ethnology. One of the famous women scientists of America.

MATILA COXE STEVENSON.

Is a woman of whom the American woman can be proud. Her work among the Indians and her book on that subject is considered one of the most remarkable books of to-day written by a woman. Daughter of Alexander H. Evans and Maria Coxe Evans, and was born in St. Augustine, Texas, but her parents moved to Washington in her infancy. She is a cousin of Robley D. Evans, U.S.N., familiarly known as "Fighting Bob." She married James Stevenson April 18, 1872, who was then an assistant to Professor Hayden, the first chief of the Geological Survey. Mrs. Stevenson accompanied her husband in his work of exploration in the Rocky Mountains, studying under him and receiving special instruction from him. She accompanied him on the first expedition which went to Zuni. New Mexico, in 1879, for the Bureau of Ethnology, and assisted him in the wonderful collection of implements, ceramics, and ceremonial objects which were procured for the United States National Museum. She was placed on the staff of the Bureau of Ethnology of the Smithsonian Institution after the death of her husband in 1889. She returned to Zuni and made a study of the mythology, philosophy, sociology, and vocabulary of these Indians, making a special study of their ceremonies, traditions, and customs. She explored the cave and cliff ruins of New Mexico, visiting and living for sometime among each of the Pueblo tribes of New Mexico. She and her husband were received into the secret organizations of these peoples. She spent from 1904 to 1910 studying the Taos and Tewa Indians, giving her special attention to their religion, symbolism, philosophy, and sociology; also to the edible plants of the Zunis, and their preparation of cotton and wool for the loom. She was selected to be one of the jury on the Anthropological Exposition at the Chicago Exposition in 1893. Is a member of the Anthropological Society, and is the author of "Zuni and Zunians," "The Religious Life of the Zuni Child," "The Sia," "The Zuni Indians," "Esoteric Articles and Ceremonies," etc. Until recently Mrs. Stevenson made her home in Washington, but she has now established for herself a home in New Mexico, where she spends her summers and continues her research work for the government.

MRS. C. H. HAWES.

Mrs. C. H. Hawes, of Hanover, New Hampshire, the well-known archæologist, was born in Boston, October 11, 1871. She is the daughter of Alexander and Harriet Fay Wheeler Boyd. She received the degrees of A.B. and A.M. from Smith College, and was a student of the School of Classical Studies of Athens, Greece, from 1896 to 1900. On March 3, 1906, she was married to Charles H. Hawes, M.A., of Cambridge, England. Mrs. Hawes served as a nurse in the Greco-Turkish war in 1897, and also in our war with Spain in 1898 at Tampa, Florida. From 1900 to 1905 she was instructor in archæology at Smith College. Mrs. Hawes has carried on her own excavations in Crete, and in 1900 excavated houses and tombs of the Geometric Period (900 B.C.). In 1904 she excavated a Minoan town, at Gournia, Crete, for the American Exploration Society of Philadelphia. Mrs. Hawes has been decorated with the Red Cross by Queen Olga of Greece, for her services during the Greco-Turkish war. She is a distinguished writer on archæology and kindred subjects. Among her best known works are "Gournia, Vasiliki and Other Prehistoric Sites on the Isthmus of Hierapetra, Crete," and "The Forerunner of Greece." She is a contributor to the *American Journal of Archæology*.

Inventors.

The evolution of the woman lawyer, physician, bookkeeper, stenographer, journalist, artist, teacher, writer, etc., from the ill paid farm household and factory drudge of the earlier part of the century, is one of the signal triumphs of modern civilization. But women's rapid advance in these lines of progress has been splendidly supplemented by the parallel advance of the woman inventor. That queer turn for original, utilitarian mental progress has probably always been woman's capability as well as man's, but woman's recognition in this field was slow to come.

For years many of woman's inventions were patented under men's names, and although the first patent to a woman was issued as far back as 1809, to Mary Kies for straw weaving with silk or thread, it was not until the great Centennial Exposition, in Philadelphia in 1876, when articles ranging from a dish washer to a mowing machine were exhibited among women's inventions, that there came a realization, not only of women's ability to invent, but woman's right to hold patents in her own name. As early as the sixties the largest foundry in the city of Troy was run to manufacture horseshoes, turning them out one every three seconds, and while the machine which did this work was invented by a woman the manufactory was carried on under a man's name. The best improvement upon Doctor Franklin's discovery of an iron-lined fire-place, for purposes of heating, was a stove invented by a woman, but the patent was taken out in a man's name. Another woman invented the attachment to the mowing machine whereby the knives are thrown out of gear whenever the driver leaves his seat, thus lessening the liability to accident. But though this feature is embodied in the later mammoth machines, she received no credit, the patent not being taken out in her name. The first large establishment in this country for the manufacture of buttons, the Williston's, was due to a woman, though it was run under a man's name.

The inventor of the seamless bag was Miss Lucy Johnson, who died near Providence, Rhode Island, August 22, 1867, aged seventy-eight. It was in 1824 that "she wove seven pairs of seamless pillow-cases and received a premium at the fair held in Pawtucket in October of that year." Those pillow-cases are supposed to have been the first seamless bags ever made, but ignorant of the value of her invention Miss Johnson took no steps to secure a patent, and while her mode of weaving has since been engrafted on the power loom and patented, yielding a fortune to the patentees, Miss Johnson spent the closing years of her life dependent upon friends and the charity of her native town.

The self-fastening button is a woman's invention, the machine for making satchel-buttoned paper bags was a woman's invention and a very important one, having been long tried for by men without success. Most of the designs for carpets, oil-cloths, calico and wall papers were women's work from the beginning, as were also designs for the embossing of paper, monograms, etc., but for this work little was credited to them, for the reason that women had not come into their own in the industrial world. However, after women became heads of establishments and came to own manufactories as well as to have designed the work done in them, and, above all, when woman had come to win recognition for her mental equality with man, inventions patented in women's names multiplied with astonishing rapidity.

From a report from the clerk of the Patent Office curious details in regard to women's inventions may be gleaned. Though the second patent issued to a woman named Mary Brush in 1815 was for a corset, the patents to women have come to embrace all articles from dress improvers to submarine telescopes, and although to a certain extent it might still be said of women's work along this line, as has been remarked of the male inventor, "the road to wealth is paved with the inventor's bones," still a few women have realized large fortunes from their inventions. A California woman invented a baby carriage which netted her over fifty thousand dollars, and an Illinois woman invented a portable house, which can be carried about in a cart or expressed to the seashore, with folding furniture and a complete camping outfit, and from this she gains a good annual income. A woman in Pennsylvania has invented a barrel-hooping machine which brings her twenty thousand dollars a year. Two California girls are the inventors of a snow plow to be attached to the cow catcher of an engine, and the proceeds from this have well repaid the time and ingenuity given to perfecting their patent. A Maryland woman has distinguished herself by many inventions and among them was the eyeless needle now used so largely by surgeons. Though the sewing-machine was invented by a man there have been some fifty improvements made by women, and these have proved very profitable inventions. The geographical distribution of the inventive talent is also interesting. Most of the women inventors of the country live in New England and the middle states, few patents having been taken out by Southern women.

Quite a number have come from the West. Massachusetts has more inventive women than any other part of New England.

While women have been more or less conspicuous in the fields of literature and education of all countries, from the early history to the present day, we can feel an especial pride in our women inventors. It would be impossible, in this work, to give a complete list, we therefore have selected the more prominent, particularly those who have made inventions along unusual lines for women, mechanical devices and improvements on implements which are not for feminine use but for the benefit of man. We also give short biographies of a few of the most conspicuous women in this line.

The last patent extended under the Act of Congress of March 2, 1861, was that of Henrietta H. Cole, fluting machine.

The first patent found granted to a woman was that to Mary Kies, Killingly, Conn., straw weaving with silk and thread.

Among the patents granted prior to 1836 are found the following:
July Planten, Philadelphia, Pa., foot-stove.
Elizabeth H. Bulkley, Colchester, Conn., shovels, scythes, spades, etc., of cast steel and iron.

The following are some of the inventions made by women. The patents upon these have all expired:

Brush for cotton gins, car couplings (several), combined plow and harrow, construction of railroad tracks, ginning cotton, gate for railway tracks, grain clipping machines, grain scouring machines, wheat cleaning machines, mining machines, separating tin from other metals, paving blocks (several), fire escapes, ladders for fire extinguishing apparatus, fire-proof doors or shutters, nozzle for oil-cans, overflow indicator, snow plow, stage scenery, machine for printing peripheries of spools, etc., hydrocarbon furnaces, road cart, snow shovel and scraper, machine for laying wall-paper, transfer apparatus for traction cable cars.

Martha P. Jewett, Evansville, Indiana, composition of matter to be used for the purpose of fluxing metals.
Alice M. Jayne, Bradford, Pa., mail-binder.
Sarah E. Peeples, Washington, D. C., insulated pipe joints or couplings.
Rebecca T. Swenning, Los Angeles, Cal., process of preparing backgrounds on pile fabric.
Julia B. Mathews, Portland, Maine, hot-air registers.

List of Prominent American Women Inventors.

Zina A. Beecher, Marysville, Ohio, attachment for cultivators.
Eliza J. Bentinck and J. A. Renner, Galveston, Texas, digging machine.
Lucy A. Corning, Rockford, Ill., baling press.
Adeline Widmayer, New York, N. Y., dumping wagon.
Annie H. Chilton, Baltimore, Md., combined horse detacher and brake.
Elina M. Wright, Hartford, Conn., forming decorative panels.
Mary L. McLaughlin, Cincinnati, Ohio, method of decorating pottery.
Ora Orr, Westport, Cal., combined child's carriage and cradle.
Sarah A. Reinheimer, Winchester, Ind., barrel tapping and emptying device.
Dell M. Hawes, Ortonville, Minn., pneumatic tire.
Margaret E. Knight and A. B. Harrington, South Framingham, Mass., window frame and sash.
Florence M. Carr, Chicago, Ill., ornamental grill work.
Eliza Wilcox, Ashley, Mich., carpet stretcher.
Ada V. Goltermann, New York, N. Y., fire escape.
Rena M. Howe, Scranton, Pa., closure for bottles or jars.
Rebecca H. Hayes, Galveston, Texas, cooking stove.
Simon W. and Clara A. Kinney, St. Louis, Mo., steam cooking utensil.

Hiram A. and Maria Benedict, New York, N. Y., gridiron or broiler.

Margaret E. Jehu, Estherville, Iowa, apparatus for cooking, baking, etc.

Kate L. Brewster, Kearney, Nebr., collapsible cover supporting frame for dough receptacles.

Therese R. Fischer, Baltimore, Md., skewer for closing fowls.

Susana Ilgen, Miles City, Mont., ventilated can cover.

Priscilla M. Burns, St. Louis, Mo., flour sifter with reversible bottom and cover.

Alice A. Whipple, Providence, R. I., portable foot warmer, etc.

Helen A. Robinson, Clymer, N. Y., preserving jar.

Ida L. McDermott, Baird, Texas, preparing fruit for canning or preserving.

Jennie D. Harvey, Wilkes-Barre, Pa., mayonnaise mixer.

Mary M. Harris, Chicago, Ill., refrigerator.

Harriet W. R. Strong, Los Angeles, Cal., method of and means for impounding debris and storing water.

Mary M. Vogt, Rochester, N. Y., device for teaching vocal music.

Sallie T. Andrus, Aurora, Ill., combination trunk, bureau and writing table.

Anna Dormitzer, New York, N. Y., chair for washing windows.

Ariette Baird, Riverhead, N. Y., combined baby tender and crib.

Virginia C. Baltzell, Madison, Wisconsin, apparatus for hanging and adjusting window curtains.

Fannie A. and E. N. Gates, Fitchburg, Mass., water-heating system.

Agnes McFadyen, Lincoln, Nebr., heating and ventilating apparatus for buildings.

Harriet Carter, Brooklyn, N. Y., composition of matter for saving fuel.

Augusta R. Isaacs, New York, N. Y., fire box and grate for ranges, stoves or heaters.

Mary F. Bishop, Bridgeport, Conn., hot-water heating device.

Julia Strong, Brooklyn, N. Y., exercising machine.

Fannie M. Garies, New York, N. Y., instrument for chiropodists' use.

Helen A. Blanchard, New York, N. Y., surgical needle.

Ida M. Hemsteger, Chicago, Ill., protector for blisters, poultices, etc.

Lizzie Lane, Dunellen, N. J., electrical head clamp for relieving pain.

Nancy L. Turner, Washington, D. C., motor.

Geo. B. and Amy F. Robinson, Colorado Springs, Colo., variable driving gear.

Julia Samson, Salt Lake City, Utah, portable binder for sheet music, etc.

Frances Higbie, Brooklyn, N. Y., music stand.

Albina E. and J. Edson Goodspeed, Boston, Mass., pump.

Elizabeth V. Vanvorce, Madison, Wisconsin, pipe connection.

Margaret E. Knight, South Framingham, Mass., numbering mechanism.

Alice A. Whipple, Providence, R. I., apparatus for sanding railway tracks.

Marguerite Maidhof, New York, N. Y., car fender.

Minnie McPhail, Taunton, Minn., car coupling.

Emma A. Streeter, N. Y., and B. W. Nichols, Herkimer, N. Y., spike.

Mame Lester, Logansport, Ind., attachment for unloading box-cars.

Mary E. Cook, Amity, Oregon, railway car stove.

Margaret A. Wilcox, Chicago, Ill., car heater.

Sarah B. Walker, Castle Rock, Col., ornamental screen.

Mary E. Hall, Boston, Mass., hemstitching attachment for sewing machines.

Elizabeth Calm, New York, N. Y., cloth-winding attachment for sewing machines.

Anna H. Clayton, Louisville, Ky., motor for sewing machines.

Katy Fenn, Chicago, Ill., multiple record.

Anna M. Parks, Albany, N. Y., punching machine.

Marie L. Fuller, New York, N. Y., mechanism for the production of stage effects.

Margaret De Witt, Kansas City, Mo., face-steaming appliance.

Mary V. Seidell, Washington, D. C., hair curler.

Eleanor M. Smith, Baltimore, Md., toy or doll house.

Lizzie C. Cozens, Philadelphia, Penna., trunk.

Mary F. Blaisdell, Franklin, Maine, combined trunk and couch.

Rebecca E. Hooper, San Francisco, Cal., guide shield for typewriting machine.

Mildred M. Lord, Milwaukee, Wis., washing machine.

Josephine G. Cochrane, Shelbyville, Illinois, dish cleaner.

Georgiana Ferguson, Mount Vernon, New York, window cleaner.

Frances S. Dowell, Eureka Springs, Arkansas, wire clothes line.

Alice A. Pyle, Richmond, Va., carpet-cleaning apparatus.

Oriella I. Littell, Washington, D. C., cleaning and polishing compound.

Mary Tucek, New York, N. Y., method of producing garment patterns.

Louise Schaefer, Oneida, N. Y., method of and apparatus for making patterns.

Libbie A. Call, Oshkosh, Wis., measure for laying off dress charts.

Annie L. Faestel, Milwaukee, Wis., tailors' drafting device.

Helen K. Ingram, Jacksonville, Florida, railroad cars.

Mary D. Wiedinger, Chicago, Illinois, window-guards.

Maria R. Hirsch, Milwaukee, Wisconsin, commutator brushes.

Lizzie B. Fleming, Pierce City, Missouri, wheel-cleaners.

Mary Louisa Campbell, Noyan, Province Quebec, Canada, hammer guard for fire-arms.

Sallie S. Pharr, Marshallville, Georgia, planter.

Alida M. Marcoux, Milford, Mass., filling replenishing looms.

Charlotte R. Manning, Meriden, Conn., method of finishing metal articles.

Margaret A. Mack, Cleveland, Ohio, carriage-pole protector.

Nancy May Ingle, Chetopa, Kansas, air-cooling fans.

Sarah E. Ball, Ritchey, Will Co., Ill., weeder.

Bertha and Mary E. Baumer *et al.*, Troy, Ohio, horse releasing devices.

Cora L. Jones, Stoughton, Mass., rolling toys.

Minnie Averill, Joplin, Missouri, toy bee hive.

Abelina C. Asczman, Chicago, Ill., nozzles for fire-extinguishers.

HELEN AUGUSTA BLANCHARD.

Was born in Portland, Maine. Owing to the death of her father, she found it necessary to turn her inventive genius and talent into a means of livelihood, and in 1876, established the Blanchard Over-seam Company, of Philadelphia, from which other industries have sprung. One of her inventions is the Blanchard over-seaming machine, which is for sewing and trimming at the same time of knitted fabrics; also crocheting and sewing machines. These machines are used largely in manufactories, and are considered among the most remarkable mechanical contrivances of the day.

BETSEY ANN STEARNS.

Mrs. Betsy Ann Stearns was born in Cornish, New Hampshire, June 29, 1830. Her maiden name was Goward. As a child she entered the weaving mills of Nashua, saving her money from her labors to educate herself. June 5, 1851, she married Horatia H. Stearns, of Ackton, Massachusetts. Mrs. Stearns is well known for her dress-cutting invention, which was awarded the highest prize in the Centennial Exposition in Philadelphia, 1876. She organized the Boston Dress-Cutting School, with branches in other states, and now the Stearns's tailor method for cutting ladies' and children's clothes is in common use.

Women in United States Government Departments.

The women who have occupied the positions of experts in the various departments of the United States Government have made for woman remarkable records. Many of these women come from the finest families of our country. Many of their ancestors were identified with the early society and important history of America. The first woman employed by the United States Government was Miss Jennie Douglas. During the war General Spinner persuaded the secretary of the Treasury, Salmon P. Chase, to employ women in that department to cut and trim the treasury notes, and Miss Douglas was the first woman to be employed on this work. Among those who entered the work in that early day was Mrs. Helen L. McLean Kimball. Mrs. Kimball is dean of the government women, as she enjoys the record of the longest service of all the women workers under the United States Government. She is the widow of a Civil War officer who was killed in the field, and shortly after his death she took up her duties in the Treasury. Mrs. Kimball is considered one of the most valued employees of this department, and is a most popular, intellectual woman, who has endeared herself to all her associates. For more than twenty years Mrs. Kimball was chief of the Treasury library, which she helped to build up and make valuable. Later she became a file clerk in the office of the comptroller of the currency. Following close upon the record of Mrs. Kimball is that of Miss Sarah F. Hoey, who has counted money for over forty-four years, and during this long period handled billions of dollars which found their way to the redemption department of the United States Treasury. Mrs. W. A. Leonard is frequently spoken of as the most remarkable woman in the United States Government. She was appointed in 1864, and her work as chief counterfeit detector in the treasurer's office is well known. She has been called "The Female Sherlock Holmes." Mrs. Leonard has just retired from the service after over forty years' work.

Miss Mabel Hatch, who was for many years in the Patent office as clerk to the commissioner, was one of the highest salaried women in the government at one time. Miss Hatch has made a remarkable record for a woman in that, with but a few days' exception, she has never lost a day from her office.

Mrs. Angeline D. Ware held a very responsible position also in the Patent office for more than a quarter of a century. Mrs. Ware is a woman of great refinement and gentle birth. In her young womanhood she moved in the first circles of Ohio society. Her brother was Governor Dennison, the "war" governor of Ohio, and a member of Lincoln's Cabinet. Her husband was one of the first lawyers of Ohio, and after his death it became necessary that Mrs. Ware should support herself, which she has done with cheerfulness and credit to herself and satisfaction to the government for many years.

Miss Caroline C. Kirkland, who reached four-score years

in 1908, has been employed in the Patent office for over a quarter of a century.

Miss Frances R. Lybrand, of Ohio, has a record of nearly thirty years in the Patent office as an expert examiner in the civil engineering division.

Mrs. Mary Fuller, sister of Mrs. Vinnie Ream Hoxie the well-known sculptress, has been chief librarian in the library of the Department of the Interior for over thirty-five years.

Miss Amelia Tyler has been in the service of the United States Government for over thirty-five years. She is a special patent examiner and passes expert judgment on patents for tilling the soil and other agricultural purposes and appliances.

Miss Emma A. McCully is employed in the internal revenue service. Miss McCully's grandfather was Captain Nathaniel Haraden, who served on the "Constitution"—Old Ironsides—in the war with Tripoli, and in recognition of his service, was appointed lieutenant in the navy, and afterward made commandant of the United States Navy, and assigned to duty in the navy yard at Washington. Miss McCully's most valued possession is his commission signed by James Madison. Her grandmother was an intimate friend of Dolly Madison, and Miss McCully's family were identified with the foremost of America's early social and official life.

Two other women who deserve honorable mention for their work in the service of the government for more than a quarter of a century are Miss H. L. Black and Miss Caroline C. Pennock, who are employed in the office of the comptroller of the currency. Miss Columbia McVeigh is employed in the internal revenue service as file clerk, where she has been for many·years.

Mrs. Brewster, the wife of Attorney-General Brewster who was a member of the Cabinet of President Arthur, met her husband while he was obtaining evidence for a case he was prosecuting as district attorney, in the Treasury department, where she was employed for many years before her marriage. She fulfilled her part as the wife of a Cabinet official with dignity and grace, adding much to the popularity and esteem of her distinguished husband and the social life of Washington at the time of his service as a Cabinet minister. Mrs. Brewster was the daughter of Robert J. Walker, who was secretary of the Treasury under Buchanan.

Miss Stoner, niece of General Spinner, was among the first women appointed in the Treasury department by Secretary Chase, when women were given these positions, to take the place of the men called into service at the outbreak of the War.

The Misses Taney, daughters of Chief Justice Taney, were among the capable women who served for many years in the departments of the government.

There are many others who deserve mention, but these are the most prominent in their length of service.

LIZZIE E. D. THAYER.

Miss Lizzie E. D. Thayer was born October 5, 1857, in Ware, Massachusetts. She occupied an unusual position for a woman—that of train dispatcher. Since 1878 she has been employed in the various offices of New England as a telegraph operator. In 1889 she entered the service of the New London Northern Railroad, and on the resignation of the train dispatcher, whose assistant she had been for a year, she was appointed to the office, and filled the position satisfactorily.

Women in Business.

NETTIE L. WHITE.

Born near Syracuse, New York. She is descended from old Revolutionary stock of Massachusetts. About 1876 she began her first regular work with Henry G. Hayes, one of the corps of stenographers with the House of Representatives, Washington, D. C., at a time when very few women were engaged in practical stenography in Washington. She was engaged in this work for thirteen years. After several years of the most difficult work in the Capitol, she desired to work as official stenographer for one of the Congressional Committees and decided upon the Committee on Military Affairs, of which General Rosecrans was the chairman. Her first work was a report on heavy ordance which was being made to the committee by General Benet. When finished her report was accepted by the committee, and she had no furthr difficulties to overcome because she was a woman. Miss White served with Clara Barton in the Red Cross work for the relief of the flood sufferers in Johnstown, and while here she received her appointment to the Pension Bureau as an expert workman gained through civil service examination.

MARY AVERILL HARRIMAN.

Wife of the late Edward Henry Harriman, the great railroad magnate. She takes a position among men through her ability as a business woman. During her husband's life she was his constant adviser and shared in all his great enterprises. He frequently spoke of the regard which he had for her judgment and ability, and after his death it was found that his will in a few simple words had placed most of his great estate in her hands, and directed that she should have control and management of more than one hundred million dollars. Mrs. Harriman was the daughter of a wealthy financier of Rochester, New York, and before her marriage her name was Mary Averill. The management, not only of this vast estate, is in the hands of Mrs. Harriman, but the completion of their home at Arden, on the crest of the Ramapo Hills, an estate half in New York and half in New Jersey, of forty-six thousand acres. Mr. Harriman wished to give employment to the country people and he had laid out this estate on the most extensive plans. This is being carried out in strict accordance to his wishes. Mrs. Harriman is essentially a woman of sound common sense and judgment. The tasks that confront her she is handling with energy and courage. She is devoting much of her time to the shaping of the career of her only son, Walter, a student at Yale, whom his father had already apprenticed to the railroad.

(893)

INA SHEPHERD.

Miss Ina Shepherd, of Birmingham, Alabama, is the only woman who holds the place of secretary to a clearing-house association in this country. She has held this position for the city of Birmingham for over five years, handling the clearings of eight banks, amounting to between ten and fifteen million dollars a month. She is a fine musician and a most accomplished woman.

THE GILLETT SISTERS.

One of the most noted, cultivated and clever families of women in Illinois is that of the late John Dean Gillett and his wife, Lemira Parks Gillett, of Elkhart, Illinois, who were among the oldest settlers of Logan County (1842). The family consists of seven daughters, who were reared in the lap of luxury up to the day of their father's death. At that time each took charge of the estate left her by her father, and has since managed it personally in an intellectual, business-like and successful manner. As girls, these daughters were carefully educated along classical lines, their only business training having been that given by their father. It is therefore somewhat unusual that they should one and all have taken upon themselves the care of their vast estates, and with the result that to-day each personally directs her entire estate and business interests in the most successful manner.

The eldest daughter, Emma Susan Gillett, educated in New Haven, Connecticut, was married in 1867, when quite young, to Hiram Keays, of Bloomington, Illinois. She was left a widow after three years of married life, with one son, Hiram G. Keays. In 1873 she married Richard J. Oglesby, three times elected Governor of Illinois, and once to the United States Senate. The issue of the second marriage was three sons and one daughter. Her second son, John Gillett Oglesby, was elected Lieutenant-Governor of Illinois at the age of twenty-nine, being the youngest Lieutenant-Governor ever elected in the state.

Mrs. Oglesby came into her inheritance after Governor Oglesby had retired from politics, and within a quarter of a mile of the village of Elkhart, Illinois, erected her beautiful home called "Ogleshurst." For seven years she lived there, organizing and putting into shape her property, and since the death of her husband, Governor Oglesby, she has lived in Rome, Italy, her home being one of the most interesting and she being one of the most popular entertainers of the American colony at Rome.

The second daughter, Grace Adeline Gillett, Jacksonville, Illinois, was married in 1885 to Hon. Stephen A. Littler of Springfield, Illinois, one of the most indefatigable political workers of the day. Their handsome and well appointed home was the scene of many magnificent banquets given by Mr. Littler to his political friends. Mrs. Littler's presence, personal charm and grace of manner, as well as her beauty, won her many friends. Her love and personal care and munificent gifts to the suffering infants and children of her tenants, and the working classes about her, won for her the love, respect and admiration of all those fortunate enough to be within her sphere of influence. Mrs. Littler lived only a few years after her father's death to enjoy her share of his fortune, but up to that time was interested in keeping her consignment of the cattle, so well known as the "Shorthorn Herd of John Dean Gillett" up to its well-known reputation, farming and leasing her lands, raising oats, corn, wheat and clover. At her death she left her estate not only intact, but greatly increased in value.

The third daughter, Nina Lemira Gillett, was educated in a convent, and is one of the best read women of her time—a woman of fine business ability who, after placing her land and property in shape, turned her attention and time to the buying of stocks and bonds, being clever enough in the panic of 1903 to throw her enormous savings which she had in readiness to invest, into stocks and bonds at the opportune moment, holding them several years and disposing of the same, thereby realizing a handsome profit, thus showing her ability to be as great in financial foresight as in farming. She has also made a great success socially and financially in Paris, where she now resides. She has circled the globe more than once in her extensive travels, and is a fluent French and Italian scholar.

Katherine Gillett Hill, fourth daughter of the late John Dean Gillett, was educated in a convent at Springfield, Illinois, and was married in 1874 to James E. Hill, a cousin of the late John A. Logan. To them four children were born, two sons and two daughters, the two sons living to manhood and one daughter to womanhood. Edgar Logan Hill, the eldest son, is a graduate of Massacnusetts Institute of Technology, and holds a prominent position with the American Steel & Wire Company, at Worcester, Massachusetts. John Dean Gillett Hill is a graduate of Harvard Law School, and Lemira Gillett Hill is a graduate of Miss Chamberlain's School in Boston.

Mrs. Gillett Hill, at the death of her father, took entire charge of her farming lands, not even requiring the assistance of an overseer. She has for twenty years managed as capably and as systematically as any business man her five thousand acres of farm land in and about Lincoln, Illinois, having about fifty tenants under her supervision. She is a woman of varied qualifications and interests, being artistic and musical, a splendid mother and likewise is greatly interested in the woman suffrage movement. Farming with her is not amateurish, and not the fad of a rich woman, but with Mrs. Gillett Hill it is at once an art and a science, and a very remunerative business, which has made her one of the best known farmers in America. She is none the less womanly for her business capabilities. From her childhood she has been a fine horsewoman, and having been gifted with a beautiful voice, she has done much charitable work with her musical voice. With her fine intellect, she has become a writer of some note and is withal a splendid entertainer, possessing great natural wit and repartee. She has been much sought after in the social world. Mrs. Gillett Hill in the year 1910 purchased a charmingly artistic home in Washington, and this home, once a studio, has proved to be one of the most unique and picturesque residences in the city.

Amaryllis T. Gillett, fifth daughter, was educated in Kenosha, Wisconsin. During her school years she devoted herself to the study of history particularly, and was always a referee for dates and historical events. She held in trust the money presented by her mother, Lemira Parke Gillett, to the Library at Elkhart, Illinois, and selected and bought all of the books for this library for about twenty years. After superintending her farms in and about the town of Cornland for many years, she removed to the City of Washington, in 1908, and bought up a great deal of real estate, building handsome houses and selling them at a great profit. With keen foresight she realized that real estate at the capital was sure to advance. Miss Gillett is one of the prominent women of Washington, and entertains lavishly in her handsome home during the winter season. She is a member of the best clubs of Washington, viz: Chevy Chase Club, Archæological Club, Aviation Club and the Riding Club, and was elected Librarian-General of the Daughters of the American Revolution at the last National Congress, on the ticket with Mrs. Matthew T. Scott, President-General. By the latter, she has been placed on many special commissions to further the improvement of the grounds and surroundings of Memorial Continental Hall.

Jessie D. Gillett is the sixth daughter of John Dean Gillett. A woman who runs a 3000-acre farm, takes a prominent part in the management of a National Bank and is the founder of a public library, which she presented to the village of Elkhart, Illinois, in memory of her mother, in addition to being a shrewd financier, and expert stock grower and an accomplished horse-back rider—all of which is Miss Jessie D. Gillett—has taken a long step in the direction of proving that no nook or corner of what was once the exclusive domain of man is now secure against feminine invasion. After taking hold of "Crowhurst," her home farm, located near the village of Elkhart, Illinois, she soon showed the surrounding farmers what a woman could do with a farm, and the result has caused her male competitors not only to envy, but also to adopt many of her improvements. "Crowhurst" is now one of the most inviting and attractive country residences in the middle west. Miss Gillett believes that if one would be a successful farmer the latest and most progressive agricultural principles must be applied. She has converted this once old-fashioned farm into a model producing possession, and her surroundings are of the most up-to-date character. Her lands being tilled and drained in the best manner known to-day, she produces crops that are seldom equalled in the state; she makes a great specialty of corn and her farm has been made famous in this, the great corn-belt of Illinois. Added to her ability as a farmer, Miss Gillett's personality is most charming. She is a very beautiful woman, with great tact and a most fascinating manner; is one of the women the state of Illinois may well be proud of.

Charlotte Gillett Barnes was seventh and youngest daughter. She inherited her property when quite young, and married the following year, 1891, Dr. William Barnes, one of the most-noted surgeons of central Illinois. Her beautiful home is in Decatur, Illinois, where she interests herself most enthusiastically in musical circles.

Mrs. Barnes' land lies in and about the cities of Elkhart and Mt. Pulaski. She inherited a talent for describing lands and could repeat off-hand and without notes, rapidly and without error, proper descriptions of her lands that numbered up into the thousands of acres.

While an interested and enterprising business woman, she has let music be her principal work in life, and her talent for music has made her one of the most noted pianists of the Middle West. She has two children, Gillette Joan Barnes and William Barnes.

ELLEN ALIDA ROSE.

Born June 17, 1843, in Champion, New York. In December, 1861, she married Alfred Rose, and in 1862 they moved to Wisconsin, where her life has been spent on a farm near Broadhead. She is one of the first and most active members of the Grange. Through Mrs. Rose's efforts and the members of the National Grange Organization, the anti-option bill was passed. She was a prominent member of the Patrons of Industry and by her voice and pen has done much to educate the farmers in the prominent reforms of the day, in which the advancement of women is one which has always claimed her first interest. Mrs. Rose has been an active worker in the Woman's Suffrage Association, and in 1888 was appointed District President of that organization.

MARY A. SAUNDERS.

Born January 14, 1849, in Brooklyn, New York. Her father, Dr. Edward R. Percy, settled in Lawrence, Kansas, where he became so interested in the study, growth and culture of the grape and the manufacture of wine, that he gave up his practice as a physician. Miss Percy became the wife of A. M. Saunders. Being left a widow after two years with a child to support, she endeavored to earn her living as an organist in one of the churches in Lawrence, Kansas. While on a visit to her husband's relatives in Nova Scotia, she decided to return to New York and pursue her musical studies. At this time her attention was drawn to a new invention, the typewriter. She was introduced to G. W. N. Yost, the inventor of typewriters, who promised that as soon as she could write on the typewriter at the rate of sixty words a minute he would employ her as exhibitor and saleswoman. In three weeks she accomplished this task, and in January, 1875, was given employment with the company and was one of the first women to step into the field at that time occupied solely by men. She assisted in arranging the first keyboard of the Remington typewriter, which is now the keyboard, with slight alterations, used on all typewriters. Mrs. Saunders traveled as the general agent of this company throughout the West and inaugurated the use of the first typewriter in St. Louis, Cincinnati, Chicago, Indianapolis, Detroit and other cities. Later she resigned from this position and became corresponding clerk in the Brooklyn Life Insurance Company. While here she studied stenography and two years later, when the head bookkeeper died she applied for the vacancy, which was given her at an advanced salary, she attending to all the correspondence, bookkeeping, examination of all policies and had charge of the real estate accounts. In 1891 the Yost Typewriter Company, Limited, of London, England, was about to be formed. They offered her a fine position with them in London, as manager and saleswoman, which she accepted. Her position as manager of a school enrolling more than one hundred pupils gave her ample scope to carry out her long-desired scheme of aiding women to be self-supporting in the higher walks of life, and she was able to secure positions for men and women. At the expiration of her contract she returned to New York to undertake the management of the Company's office in that city.

MARY SOPHIE SCOTT.

Born October 17, 1838, in Freeport, Illinois. Her father Orestes H. Wright, was a native of Vermont, her mother, Mary M. Atkinson, of England. In 1863 Miss Wright became the wife of Colonel John Scott, of Nevada, Ohio. In 1875 she was invited to collect and exhibit the work of Iowa women at the Centennial Exhibition at Philadelphia. Later she performed a like service for the Cotton Exposition in New Orleans. Her most useful work was the publication of her book "Indian Corn as Human Food."

MARY D. LOWMAN.

Was born January, 1842, in Indiana County, Pennsylvania. In 1866 she became the wife of George W. Lowman, and removed to Kansas. In 1885 she served as Deputy Register of Deeds in Oskaloosa, and was elected mayor of that city in 1888, with a Common Council composed entirely of women and they were again re-elected in 1889. During her administration the city was freed from debt and many public improvements were brought about.

MISS C. H. LIPPINCOTT.

Was born September, 1860, at Mount Holly, New Jersey. In 1891 she entered a new field for women, opening a seed business and issuing a circular which in two years brought her twenty thousand orders. She originated the plan of stating the number of seeds contained in each packet, which compelled all prominent seed houses to follow her example.

IDA HALL ROBY.

Was born March 8, 1867, in Fairport, New York. She graduated from the Illinois College of Pharmacy in the Northwestern University of Evanston, Illinois. Her father's death occurred one year before she graduated, which necessitated her providing for her own support. Having a natural fondness for chemistry, she held a position in a drug house for several years, then started a pharmacy in Chicago, attending the college on alternate days. She is the first woman to graduate from the Pharmaceutical Department of that institution, and has won a unique reputation as a successful woman in a line of business generally left to man.

ANNIE WHITE BAXTER.

Mrs. Baxter was born in Pittsburgh, Pennsylvania, on the second of March, 1864. After graduating from the public schools in 1882, she went to work as an assistant in the County Clerk's office of Jasper County, Missouri. She performed these duties with such satisfaction to everyone that in 1885 she was appointed and sworn in as Deputy Clerk of the County Court, with authority to affix the clerk's signature and the county seal to all official documents, and performed other official acts. The duties of this office embraced the tax levy and extension in a county of five hundred thousand people, the custody, computation and collection of interest on public school funds of over two hundred and twenty-five thousand dollars, keeping of the accounts and making settlements with the State Treasurer, State Auditor, County Treasurer, County Collector, and of the County township officers entrusted with the collection and custody of State and County revenues, the keeping of the records, and the executing of the acts and orders of the County Court. She was found equal to all of these arduous labors and demonstrated so high a standard of mental ability, that she was soon appointed and qualified as principal deputy. At the time of her marriage in 1888, she withdrew from all public work, but owing to the ill health of the County Clerk she was persuaded to again resume the duties and in 1890 was nominated for County Clerk by the Democrat County Convention and was elected in what had always been a strong Republican district. She was the first woman in the United States elected by the people and qualified under the law to fill the office of the Clerk of Court. Notwithstanding her long occupancy of public office she is a modest, refined and retiring woman, and has the respect and admiration of all those who know her.

ELLA MARIA BALLOU.

Miss Ballou was born in Wallingford, Vermont, November 15, 1852. She was educated in the Wallingford schools and commenced life as a teacher, but finding the compensation for women in this vocation so small, she took up the study of shorthand and became so proficient that she went into the courts and wrote evidence and arguments until she became noted among attorneys, and in 1885, upon the numerous applications of the Rutland County Bar, Judge W. G. Veazey in the Supreme Court of that state appointed her Official Reporter of the Rutland County Court. She was the first woman to hold such a position in the state of Vermont, and it is believed, in the United States. She has done some work in the line of literature, but her particular claim to distinction is in the line of her profession.

MRS. L. H. PLUMB.

Mrs. Plumb was born June 23, 1841, in Sand Lake, New York, but has been a resident of Illinois since 1870. Her husband was a prominent business man and politician of Illinois, at one time a member of the Legislature of that State. Her husband's death occurred in 1882, when Mrs. Plumb took the active management of his large estate. She was elected vice-president of the Union National Bank of Streator, Illinois, of which her husband had been president for years. In 1890 she moved to Wheaton, Illinois, to give greater advantages of education to her children. Mrs. Plumb is a woman of liberal education, sound business judgment, great tact and wide experience in practical affairs. She has always been one of the foremost workers for the cause of Temperance in her state, being one of the charter members and originators of the Temperance Hospital in Chicago, Illinois.

ELLA MAYNARD KELLY.

Miss Ella Maynard Kelly was born in 1857 in Fremont, Ohio. She began telegraphy at the age of fourteen, having been given charge of a night office in Egg Harbor on the Lake Shore Railroad. Here for four years she worked as a railroad operator and was responsible for the safe running of the trains on that road. Later, she was engaged in commercial telegraphy in Atlantic City, N. J., Detroit, Michigan, and Washington, D. C., and in the Western Union Office in Columbus, Ohio. She has won unique rank as a woman distinguished in active telegraphy in the United States, and had charge of the first wire of the Associated Press circuit. She was the first woman to use the vibrator in the telegraph service.

HARRIET WHITE FISHER.

Harriet White Fisher was born in Crawford County, Pennsylvania. Daughter of Oscar A. and Hannah Fisher White. Her first American ancestor was Peregrine White, whose parents were passengers on the Mayflower in 1620, from whom the line of descent is traced through his son, who married Frances Clark.

In London, July 20th, 1898, she was married to Clark Fisher, who was formerly chief engineer in the United States Navy, afterward proprietor of the Eagle Anvil Works, Trenton, New Jersey. During the first year of her married life, Mrs. Fisher was engrossed in social duties. She first became interested in her husband's factory during a severe illness of her husband, and her interest continued after his recovery and return to the factory, so that before and after his death she was conversant with many of the business details. On October 8, 1902, Mrs. Fisher and her husband were injured in a railroad wreck which occurred at Menlo Park, as a result of which Mrs. Fisher was in the hospital for months, and the doctors were unanimous in the opinion that she would never again be able to walk, and, in fact, for weeks it was thought that she could not live. Her husband, Clark Fisher, died as a consequence of the injuries he received at that time, and it was while she was partially paralyzed and unable to leave her bed that she continued the management of the Fisher & Norris business, and kept it going until she was able to walk without the aid of crutches. Afterward, through the help of able physicians, she regained the use of her limbs, so that now one would scarcely believe that she had passed through such an ordeal, and except for the injury to her back and spine, she would perhaps forget it herself.

At her husband's death, instead of turning the plant over to the care of a manager, she herself took up the reins and has become one of the best-known business women in the United States. The Eagle Anvil Works are now, and always have been run under the firm name of Fisher & Norris. Mrs. Fisher is the only woman member of the National Association of Manufacturers. She is a member of the Geological Society, the Numismatic Society and of the Civic Federation. She has received a large amount of notice from the newspapers on account of her recent trip around the world in an automobile, which successful trip brought forth hundreds of press notices the world round. She was royally entertained on this trip, and has written a book since her return, giving a full account of her experiences, which book is called "A Woman's Tour in a Motor." Her business necessitates her living in Trenton, New Jersey, during part of the year, but she spends the summer months in her beautiful Villa Carlotta, Brio, on Lake Como, Italy.

MRS. WILLARD A. LEONARD.

Mrs. Leonard, who was for forty-seven years an expert for the United States Government in detecting counterfeit money in the United States Treasury Department, has just retired, owing to ill health, at the age of seventy-one years. She is a woman of strong character, who has devoted the best years of her life to the government, and has done this to educate and place well in life her only son, Major Henry Leonard, United States Marine Corps, who lost his arm at the siege of Pekin during the Boxer troubles.

As chief of counterfeit detectors, Mrs. Leonard's position in the Treasury Department was one of the most exacting in the service. For thirty-five years thousands of dollars a day passed through her hands, bills and bank notes of suspicious appearance, and during that time not a mistake has occurred. She left the service with a clean record. Mrs. Leonard was the "court of last resort." According to the system in the department, should the make-up of a thousand dollar bill arouse suspicion, it would be forwarded to the counterfeit detecting division. Here it passed under the scrutiny of one of the detectors. Should the subordinate be in doubt regarding the genuineness of the bill, it was passed on to Mrs. Leonard.

She was born in Perry County, Pennsylvania. Mrs. Leonard was a wife, a mother and a widow in less than two years. Her first husband was killed during the Civil War. In 1864 she came to Washington and was given a position in the Treasury under General Spinner, Lincoln's Secretary of the Treasury. Later, she married Hiram D. Leonard, of New York, also employed in the Treasury Department. Mr. Leonard died soon after, of wounds received in the war.

MARGARET V. KELLY.

Miss Margaret V. Kelly holds a position in the office of the Director of the Mint in the United States Treasury Department, and draws one of the largest salaries paid a woman by the government. She is third in rank in the big mint establishment presided over by George E. Roberts. She has been for many years in the office of the Director of the Mint, and recently Secretary MacVeagh designated Miss Kelly as Acting Director in the absence of Mr. Roberts and Mr. Preston. This is the first time her position has been officially recognized, she being placed on an absolutely equal footing with her chief.

CHARLOTTE FOWLER WELLS.

Born August 14, 1814, in Cohockton, New York. Her father, Horace Fowler, was an able writer. Her brothers, O. S. and L. N. Fowler were among the first to study and believe the doctrines of Gall and Spuzsheim, and to develop an interest in the science of phrenology. Their sister Charlotte became deeply interested in this subject, teaching the first class in phrenology in this country, and joining her brothers in New York City they established the Fowler-Wells Publishing House. O. S. Fowler entered the lecture field, and L. N. Fowler established a branch of their house in London, leaving Charlotte to manage the large and complicated business in New York. In 1844 she became the wife of Samuel R. Wells, one of the partners in their business. On her husband's death, in 1875, she was left sole proprietor and manager, and later when this business was made a stock company, she was its president. She was vice-president and one of the instructors of the American Institute of Phrenology, which was incorporated in 1866. She was one of the founders and later one of the trustees of the New York Medical College for Women, which was founded in 1863.

HARRIETTE M. PLUNKETT.

Harriette M. Plunkett was a pioneer in the work of sanitary reform in the United States. She was born Harriette Merrick Hodge, February 6, 1826, in Hadley, Massachusetts, and this town, though a community of farmers, had the unusual advantage of an endowed school, "Hopkins Academy," which afforded exceptional opportunities to the daughters of the town, and there Miss Hodge received her early education. Her great interest in sanitary matters did not develop until after she became the wife of Honorable Thomas F. Plunkett, who in 1869 had a very important share in the establishment of the Massachusetts State Board of Health, the first state board established in this country. Mrs. Plunkett became convinced that if the women of the country would inform themselves what sanitary reform was needed in housing and living, and see that it was put in practice, there would be a great saving and lengthening of lives, and making lives more effective and happy during their continuance. To promote that cause she wrote many newspaper articles, and in 1885 published a valuable book, "Women, Plumbers, and Doctors," containing practical directions for securing a healthful home, and though interrupted in her work by the necessity of reading the studies of a college course to her son, who had become totally blind, this accomplished, she at once resumed her pen and returned to subjects of sanitation, though at the same time producing other articles, educational, æsthetic, and political, for various magazines and journals. One article, on the increasing longevity of the human race, entitled, "Our Grandfathers Died Too Soon," in the *Popular Science Monthly*, attracted wide attention. Her great interest in the prevention and healing of diseases also brought her before the public, and she is probably most widely known in connection with the establishment and growth of a cottage hospital in Pittsfield, Mass., called the House of Mercy, started in 1874, and of which she was the president. It was the first one of its clas to be supported by contributions from all religious denominations in the country. Mrs. Plunkett always spoke of her own work with extreme modesty, remarking at one time. that she merely belonged, "to the great army of working optimists."

ALZINA PARSONS STEVENS.

The history of Mrs. Stevens, industrial reformer, born in Parsonfield, Missouri, May 27, 1849, is, in many of its phases, an epitome of women's work in the labor movement in this country during her life. Mrs. Stevens fought the battle of life most bravely. When but thirteen years of age she began work as a weaver in a cotton factory. At eighteen years of age she had learned the printer's trade, at which she continued until she passed into other departments of newspaper work. She was compositor, proofreader, correspondent, and editor. In all these positions she acquitted herself well, and it was in the labor movement that she attracted public attention. In 1877 she organized the Working Women's Union of Chicago, and was its first president. Removing from that city to Toledo, Ohio, she threw herself into the movement there and was soon one of the leading members of the Knights of Labor. Later, she was instrumental in organizing a Women's Society, the "Joan of Arc Assembly, Knights of Labor," and was its first master workman, who went from that body to the district assembly. In 1890 she was elected district master workman, becoming the chief officer of a district of twenty-two local assemblies of knights. She represented the district in the General Assemblies of the hour and the conventions held in Atlanta, Denver, Indianapolis, and Toledo. She represented the labor organizations of Cleveland, Ohio, in the National Industrial Conference in St. Louis, Missouri, in 1892, and in the Omaha Convention of the People's Party that same year. She was always an ardent advocate of equal suffrage, and a capable organizer and untiring worker for the cause. For several years she held a position on the editorial staff of the *Toledo Bee,* later became sole owner and editor of the *Vanguard,* a paper published in Chicago, in the interests of economic and industrial reform through political action.

CASSIE WARD MEE.

Much has been written in recent years of the relative rights and wrongs of capital and labor. But there have been few people who could discuss in private or from the platform these matters in an unprejudiced way. Yet such a platform speaker was Mrs. Cassie Ward Mee, labor champion. She was born in Kingston, Ontario, Canada, October 16, 1848. Her parents and ancestors belonged to the Society of Friends, and many of them were prominent accredited ministers of the society. She came with her husband, Charles Mee, to the United States in 1882 and settled in Cortland, N. Y., where she gained considerable prominence by her writings. She first appeared on the public platform in the cause of temperance. It was in August, 1885, that she first spoke on the labor question. On the twelfth of August, 1886, she addressed ten thousand people on Boston Common, and she received a splendid illuminated address from the Knights of Labor, in token of their appreciation of an address made by her in March, 1887. After lecturing extensively among the miners of Pennsylvania, she finally settled to her life work, which is the education of the members of that powerful organization, "The Knights of Labor."

EVA McDONALD VALESH.

Born of Scotch-Irish parentage, in Orono, Maine, September 9, 1866, Mrs. Valesh's interest in the welfare of working women sprang from her own experience. After leaving school she learned the printer's trade, and here she had supplied to her object lessons to prepare her for the work before her. She was employed on the *Spectator,* and in due time she became a member of the Typographical Union, and by a chance recommendation from the district master workman of the Knights of Labor of Minnesota, she secured a position on a newspaper and began the writing and working which was to occupy the rest of her life. A shop girl's strike was in progress, and many of the girls who were engaged in making overalls, coarse shirts, and similar articles, applied to the Ladies' Protective Assembly, Knights of Labor, into which Miss McDonald had been initiated but a short time. So, while not personally interested in the strike, she attended all the meetings of the strikers and repeatedly addressed them, urging the girls to stand firm for wages which would enable them to live decently. This strike was only partially successful, but it opened an avenue for the talent of the young agitator. In March, 1887, she began a series of letters on "Working Women" for the *St. Paul Globe,* which were continued for nearly a year and attracted wide attention. She began to make public speeches on the labor question, about that time making her maiden effort in Duluth, 1887, when not quite twenty-one years of age. After the articles on the "Working Women of Minneapolis and St. Paul" ceased she conducted the labor department of the *Globe,* besides doing other special newspaper work. She continued her public addresses, and was a member of the executive committee that conducted the street car strike in Minneapolis and St. Paul in 1888, and subsequently wrote the history of the strike and published it under the title of "The Tale of Twin Cities." During the political campaign of 1890 she lectured to the farmers under the auspices of the Minnesota Farmers' Alliance, and she was elected state lecturer of this society on the first of January, 1891, going on the 28th of the same month to Omaha, where she was elected assistant national lecturer of the Minnesota Farmers' Alliance. Her marriage to Mr. Frank Valesh, a labor leader, occurred in 1891. During later years Mrs. Valesh had turned her attention more especially to the educational side of the industrial question, lecturing throughout the country for the principles of the Farmers' Alliance and in the city for trade unions. By invitation of President Samuel Gompers, she read a paper on "Women's Work," in the National Convention of the American Federation of Labor, in Birmingham, Alabama, December, 1891, and was strongly recommended by that assembly for the position of general organizer among the working women. Her strong, sane point of view has been kept before the public through her editorship of an industrial department for the *Minneapolis Tribune,* and through her occasional magazine contributions on industrial matters.

JEANNETTE DU BOIS MEECH.

Daughter of Gideon du Bois, was born in Frankford, Pa., in 1835. She is well known as an evangelist, who married a Baptist clergyman. Her work as an industrial educator is as practical and effective as that wrought by any other educator in America. In 1869, during her husband's pastorate in Jersey Shore, Pennsylvania, she opened a free industrial school in the parsonage with one hundred scholars, boys and girls. She provided all the materials and sold the work when it was finished. In 1870 a larger opportunity to develop her ideas came to her when her husband was chosen superintendent of the Maryland State Industrial School for Girls. Afterwards in 1887, Mrs. Meech was appointed by the trustees of the High School of Vineland, N. J., to superintend a department of manual education where the boys were taught to make a variety of articles in wood and wire work, and the girls to cook and make garments. This was the first introduction of industrial education into public schools. In March, 1891, the South Vineland Baptist Church granted Mrs. Meech a license to preach, and thereafter she held a number of meetings on Sunday evenings in Wildwood Beach, N. Y., and in Atlantic City. She had held aloof from temperance up to this time, but realizing from her work at these shore resorts the great increase of intemperance she joined the Woman's Christian Temperance Union in 1889, and she was made superintendent of narcotics the first year. Two years later she received an appointment as national lecturer for the Woman's Christian Temperance Union, and she continued in active service, at the same time maintaining her interest in industrial education, as well as supporting her family by a successful business career.

LUCY STEDMAN LAMSON.

In defiance of the tradition of women's inefficiency in money and business matters, the career of Miss Lucy Stedman Lamson stands out as a woman educator and business woman. Born in Albany, N. Y., June 19, 1857; in 1886 she was graduated from the state normal school in Albany, N. Y., and in the following years she studied with special teachers in New York City. In September, 1888, she accepted a position in the Annie Wright Seminary, Tacoma, Washington, but during 1888-89, much excitement prevailed in regard to land speculations, and Miss Lamson borrowed funds and purchased city lots, which she sold at a large profit. In March, 1889, she filed a timber claim and a pre-emption in Skamania County, Washington, and in June, at the beginning of her summer vacation from school, she moved her household goods to her pre-emption and, accompanied by a young Norwegian woman, began the six months' residence required by the government to obtain the title to the land. Having complied with the law and gained possession of the timber claim and pre-emption, Miss Lamson sold both at an immense advantage, investing the proceeds in real estate. On this, as Tacoma advanced, she also realized handsomely, and the home of this shrewd business woman became one of the landmarks in that prosperous, western city.

MINNA E. SHERMAN.

Among the names of the many remarkable women which America has produced must be enrolled that of Mrs. Minna E. Sherman, the owner and manager of eleven hundred acres of land in California. She came in possession of her original farm in rather a unique way. Her father, becoming disgusted with the Raw Hide Mining Company's affairs in which he held stock, one day, in a fit of anger, threw the stock certificates into the fire. Minna rescued these, and later, when this mine was developed and paying, her father received as his share fifty-four thousand dollars, on the presentation of the certificate which had been rescued by his daughter. He very generously divided this between his two daughters, each receiving twenty-seven thousand dollars. With this sum, Minna Sherman purchased an unimproved ranch of 688 acres in the San Joaquin Valley of California. To this she has constantly added from her profits until now her farm exceeds eleven hundred acres. On this ranch she has a herd of the finest Holstein cattle, sixty head of blooded Percherons, a piggery of registered Berkshires, twenty-five hundred rose bushes in thirty varieties, forty acres of olive groves; magnificent vineyards. It is said that her vineyards yield the palm to no ranch in California, whether managed by man or woman. Assisting her are two school teachers—Miss Austin and Miss Hatch.

Mrs. Sherman's practical common sense has proven her greatest aid and brought about her wonderful success. She has frequently gone in direct opposition to the advice given her by men of experience. Her first venture in this connection was the bringing of sixty head of Arizona cattle to her ranch when the prices about her were prohibitive for dairy cows. She sent to Arizona, paid but twelve dollars a head, and eventually established one of the finest milk ranches in that part of California from these cattle. In other ways she has proven that practice is far better than theory, and has frequently demonstrated also that the theory held by some of her masculine neighbors are absolutely incorrect. She manages personally this great farm, demanding the best results from each crop. She owns none but the best animals and plants none but the best seeds, trees, and shrubs.

Mrs. Sherman lectures before farmers' institutes and on demonstration trains, is a member of the State Agricultural College faculty, contributes largely to horticultural and agricultural publications, and takes an active part in the work of California's women's clubs. She was but twenty-five years of age when she began this work, and now is an attractive, interesting woman, of middle life, who has always insisted that the mental side is the side in which to put one's best efforts.

VIVIA A. MOWAT.

Mrs. Vivia A. Mowat deserves mention as one of the self-made women of America. She has demonstrated her ability by the success which she made of a small farm in the San Joaquin Valley, California. On this she has grown the grapes which have established for her a large raisin business. The women of this valley are among the controllers of this product in our country.

JESSIE WATERHOUSE.

Is president of the Women's Association of Retail Druggists. Other officers are: Mary S. Cooper, Gertrude Gammon, Winifred B. Woodrow.

INDEX

PAGE

Abell, The Misses 613
Abbot, Emma 768
Abell, Mrs. Edwin F. 616
Acheson, Sarah C. 384
Acklen, Mrs. 260
Adair, Ellen 261
Adams, Abbie Asenath 354
Adams, Abigail 214
Adams, Hannah 793
Adams, Mrs. John Quincy 229
Adams, Jane Kelly 724
Adams, Maud 772
Addams, Jane 596
Adsit, Nancy H. 784
Agnew, Eliza 516
Ahern, Mary Aileen 875
Aikens, Amanda L. 528
Albani, Marie Louise 616
Alcorn, Gertrude 613
Alcorn, Jessie 613
Alcott, Louisa M. 798
Alden, Cynthia May Westover 846
Alden, Isabella MacDonald 846
Alder, Mrs. Emily 374
Aldrich, Flora L. 743
Alexander, Grace 389
Alexander, Mrs. Thomas 428
Alger, Mrs. Russell A. 428
Alkers, Mrs. Albert 429
Allan, Phebe 312
Allen, Anna 635
Allen, Mrs. Guy R. C. 399
Allen, Mary Brook 670
Allerton, Mary 33
Allerton, Mary (Norris) 32
Allerton, Remember 32
Alphonsa, Mother Mary 532
Ambrose, Eliza Frances 382
American, Sadie 642
Ames, Fannie B. 589
Ames, Mrs. John C. 469
Anderson, Mrs. 95
Andrews, Judith Walker 529
Andrews, Mary Garard 736
Andrus, Sallie T. 887
Anglin, Margaret Mary 779
Anthony, Susan B. 570
Apfelbeck, Mrs. Aloysius Louis
  (Marie Louise Bailey) 764

PAGE

Armor, Mary Harris 668
Arms, Julia A. 670
Armstrong, Ruth Allen 670
Armstrong, Sarah B. 743
Arnold, Margaret 186
Arnold, Sarah Louise 721
Asczman, Abelina C. 888
Aston, Mary A. 363
Atherton, Gertrude 805
Atwood, Ethel 770
Atwood, Mrs. E. C. 399
Augustine, Mother O. C. D. 617
Austin, Martha W. 380
Austin, Mary Hunter 789
Austin, Sister Mary 614
Avary, Myrta Lockett 381
Averill, Minnie 888
Avery, Mrs. A. B. 398
Avery, Catherine Hitchcock Tilden. 431
Avery, Martha Gallison Moore 831
Avery, Rachel Foster 586
Avery, Rosa Miller 589

Babcock, Elenora Munroe 561
Bache, Sarah 150
Bacon, Rebecca Calhoun Pickens.383-466
Bailey, Ann 64
Bailey, Anna 174
Bailey, Annie 495
Bailey, Florence Augusta M. 842
Bailey, Hannah J. 529
Bailey, Lepha Eliza .... .670
Baird, Ariette 887
Baker, Anna H. 369
Baldridge, Elizabeth 364
Baldwin, Mary Briscoe 514
Ball, Sarah E. 888
Ballou, Addie L. 362
Ballou, Ella Maria 899
Baltzell, Virginia C. 887
Bangs, Mrs. I. S. 342
Barbert, Elizabeth Boynton 556
Barker, Eliza Harris Lawton 408
Barker, Ellen Blackmar 853
Barker, Florence E. 347
Barker, Mrs. Richard Jackson 399
Barker, Mrs. Stephen 311
Barlow, Arabella G. 311
Barlow, Rebecca 173

(909)

	PAGE
Barnes, Annie Maria	380
Barnes, Frances Julia	670
Barnett, Evelyn Scott Snead	380
Barney, Susan Hammond	669
Barnum, Charlotte P. Acer	409
Barr, Amelia	803
Barrett, Kate Waller	382-532
Barry, Susan E. (Hall) M. D.	374
Barrymore, Ethel	.773
Bartholemew, Elizabeth	54
Bartlett, Alice Elinor	844
Bartlett, Caroline Julia	738
Barton, Clara	316-387
Bascom, Emma Curtis	561
Bass, The Misses	611
Batcheller, E. Ellen	479
Bateham, Josephine Penfield Cushman	671
Bates, Charlotte Fiske	844
Bates, Mrs. Theodore C.	399
Battle, Laura Elizabeth Lee	617
Baum, Mrs. A.	491
Baumer, Bertha and Mary E.	888
Baxter, Alice	501
Baxter, Annie White	898
Bayard, The Misses	196
Baylor, Frances Courtenay	379
Beach, Mary C.	477
Beale, Lucy Preston	460
Beatson, Mrs. J. W.	342
Beauchamp, Frances E.	.662
Beaumont, Caroline M.	832
Beaux, Cecilia	750
Beck, Catherine M.	364
Beckwith, Emma	562
Beecher, Catherine Esther	725
Beecher, Zina A.	886
Beekman, Cornelia	190
Beekman, Mrs.	203
Beers, Mrs.	511
Behan, Kate Walker	617
Belais, Diana	594
Belmont, Eleanor Elsie Robson	779
Bell, Lillian	806
Bell, Mary E.	364
Bellinger, Martha Fletcher	791
Benedict, Maria	887
Benedicta, Sister	615
Benet, Adelaide George	879
Bengless, Mrs. Catherine H. (Griffith)	374
Benham, Ida Whipple	598
Benjamin, Anna Smeed	672
Bennet, Alice	743
Benning, Anna	429

	PAGE
Bentinck, Eliza J.	886
Benton, Louisa Dow	788
Bergengren, Anna Farquhar	806
Bernardy, Amy Allemand	855
Berry, Jennie Iowa	356
Berry, Martha	539
Berry, Martia L. Davis	509
Bethune, Louise	787
Bickereyke, Mother	326
Bidford, Dorthy	31
Billington, Ellen (or "Elen")	34
Billington, Helen	31
Bingham, Jemima	510
Bingham, Mrs.	202
Binswanger, Mrs.	633
Bishop, Emily Mulkin	785
Bishop, Mary Axtell	832
Bishop, Mary F.	887
Bittenbender, Ada M.	599
Black, Miss H. L.	891
Black, Sarah Hearst	672
Blackmar, Miss	312
Blackwell, Antoinette Brown	737
Blackwell, Elizabeth	742
Blair, Elizabeth Lee	428
Blair, Ellen A. Dayton	672
Blaisdell, Mary F.	888
Blaisdell, Mary Frances	843
Blake, Lillie Devereux	578
Blanchard, Helen A.	889
Blatch, Harriot Stanton	587
Bledsoe, Mary	69
Bliss, Mrs. George	533
Block, Anna Scott	458
Bloomer, Amelia	576
Blount, Mrs. Henry	428
Blount, Lucia A.	457
Blow, Mary Elizabeth Thomas	617
Bocock, Annie H.	500
Bodge, Harriet J.	352
Bonaparte, Elizabeth Patterson	253
Bond, Elizabeth	727
Bond, Rosalie B. De Solma	617
Bones, Marietta	562
Bonham, Mildred	537
Boole, Ella Alexander	667
Boone, Rebecca Bryant	67
Booth, Agnes	783
Booth, Elizabeth	36
Borg, Mrs. Simon	635
Bork, Florence L. Holmes	832
Boswell, Helen Varick	420
Bowers, Mrs. D. P.	778
Bowes, Mrs. Fred	399
Bowron, Elizabeth Moore	466

	PAGE
Boyington, Mary K.	364
Boyle, Josephine Hale	617
Boyle, Virginia Frazer	383
Boynton, Helen Mason	460
Boynton, Mrs. Henry V.	428
Brackenridge, M. Eleanor	420
Bradford, Dorothy (May)	32
Bradford, Mrs. William	197
Bradley, Amy M.	311
Bradley, Ann Weaver	672
Bradwell, Myra	745
Braeunlich, Sophia	863
Braman, Ella Frances	746
Brandon, Esther Pinto	631
Brandt, Molly	49
Bratton, Martha	183
Breckenridge, Mrs. Clifton C.	428
Breckinridge, Margaret Elizabeth	311
Breckenridge, Mary Hopkins Cabell	68
Breeden, Marjorie M.	399
Brent, Henrietta	609
Brent, Margaret	43
Brewster, Cora Belle	739
Brewster, Flora, A.	739
Brewster, Kate L.	887
Brewster, Mary	32
Brewster, Mrs.	891
Bridgman, Laura Dewey	698
Briggs, Emily (Olivia)	397
Briggs, Mary Blatchley	862
Briggs, Mrs. M. M.	365
Bringham, Susan S.	437
Brinn, Isabell	101
Brinn, Margaret	101
Brigham, Emily	395
Brison, Mrs. William	398
Bryan, Anna Elizabeth	618
Bryan, Ella Howard	379
Bryan, Mary Edwards	380-874
Bryan, Sarah	95
Brockett, Mrs. Albert D.	428
Bronaugh, The Misses	611
Brooks, M. Sears	856
Broomhall, Mrs. Addison F.	402
Brotherton, Alice Williams	811
Brown, Abbie Farwell	859
Brown, Elizabeth Carolyn Seymour	473
Brown, Corinne Stubbs	593
Brown, Emma Elizabeth	859
Brown, Jane	76
Brown, Kate Louise	859
Brown, Martha McClellan	672
Brown, Mary Buckman	120
Brown, Nancy M.	364
Brown, Susan L.	364
Browne, Mary Frank	671
Browne, Nina Elizabeth	719
Browne, Mrs. Peter Arrell	618
Bubier, Miss	696
Buchanan, Anna Elizabeth	832
Buchanan, Mrs. Roberdean	475
Buchwalter, Mrs. Edward L.	402
Buckley, Lettie E. C.	363
Buckner, Mrs. Simon E.	428
Buell, Caroline	671
Buell, Sarah (Mrs. David Hale)	797
Buford, Elizabeth	382
Bugg, Lelia Hardin	833
Bulkley, Elizabeth H.	886
Bull, Eliza	95
Bull, Sarah C. Thorpe	671
Bullard, Jennie Matthewson	365
Bullock, Emma Westcott	618
Bullock, Helen Louise	671
Bunnell, Henrietta S. T.	369
Burdett, Clara Bradley	725
Burke, E. Ellen	862
Burlingame, Emeline S.	671
Burnell, Helen M.	364
Burnett, Cynthia S.	672
Burnett, Frances Hodgson	800
Burns, Pricilla M.	887
Burr, Theodosia	251
Burrows, Mrs. Julius	294
Burrows, Mrs. Julius C.	428
Burrows, Mrs. J. C.	396
Burrs, Ann	30
Burwell, Frances	195
Burt, Mary Towne	673
Bush, Katherine Jeannette	880
Bushnell, Sophie Walker Hyndshaw	457
Butler, Behethland Foote	142
Butler, Mrs. Benjamin	286
Butler, Blanch	612
Butler, Mrs. William	522
Cabell, Mrs. William D.	428
Cabot, Ella Lyman	719
Calahan, Mary A.	304
Caldwell, Anne	789
Caldwell, Hannah	172
Caldwell, Rachel	188
Calkins, Mary W.	793
Call, Annie Payson	859
Call, Libbie A.	888
Calm, Elizabeth	888
Cameron, Mrs. Angus	429
Campbell, Mary Louisa	888
Canfield, S. A. Martha	312
Carey, Alice	810

PAGE

Carey, Annie Louise 768
Carey, Emma Forbes 833
Carey, Phoebe 810
Cardoza, Leah 631
Carl, Katharine Augusta 758
Carpenter, Mrs. Philip 403
Carr, Florence M. 886
Carr, Mary L. 353
Carroll, Emma Ella 875
Carroll, Suzanne Bancroft 618
Carroll, Mrs. 197
Carroll, The Misses 611
Carse, Matilda B. 673
Carson, Luella Clay 717
Carter, Harriet 887
Carter, Mary Gilmore 833
Cartwright, Emily J. 368
Cartwright, Mrs. Robert 594
Carty, Mother Praxedes (Susan
  Carty) 618
Carver, Katherine 31
Cary, Mrs. 196
Casey, Margaret Elizabeth 619
Cassin, The Misses 611
Castleman, Virginia 382
Catt, Carrie Lane Chapman 585
Chamberlin, Miss 696
Chanler, Margaret 540
Chanler, Mrs. William Astor 759
Chapeau, Ellen 379
Chapin, Clara Christiana 673
Chapin, Sallie F. 673
Chapin, Sylvia 95
Chapman, Elizabeth 361
Chapman, Mrs. Wood-Allen 661
Charles, Mrs. 342
Chase, Louise L. 673
Chenoweth, Caroline Van Dusen.. 843
Child, Lydia Maria 794
Chilton, Annie H. 886
Chilton, Mary 34
Chilton, Mrs. 34
Chippewa Indian Woman 303
Churchill, Sarah 36
Clares, The Three Poor 608
Clark, Bell Vorse 365
Clark, Mrs. Champ 289
Clark, Charlotte 94
Clark, Mrs. 342-511
Clarke, Mrs. Arthur E. 428
Clarke, Mrs. A. Howard 428
Clarke, Helen Archibald 830
Clay, Elizabeth 123
Clay, Mary Barr 559
Clayton, Anna H. 888
Clendennin, Mrs. 51

PAGE

Cleveland, Frances Folsom 277
Cleveland, Rose Elizabeth 275
Clews, Mrs. James Blanchard 619
Clinton, Mrs. George 196
Clopton, Virginia Carolina Clay ... 381
Cobb, Zoe Desloge 619
Coburn, Eleanor Habawell Abbott.. 851
Cochran, Nannie M. 365
Cochrane, Josephine G. 888
Cockrell, Mrs. 431
Cohen, Katherine 636
Cohen, Matilda 635
Cohen, Octavia 496
Coit, Elizabeth 674
Colby, Clara B. 397
Cole, Cordelia Throop 674
Cole, Mrs. Helen Brainard 371
Cole, Henrietta H. 885
Coleman, Alice Blanchard 517
Coleman, Merriam 517
Colfax, Harriet R. 312
Colgan, Eleanor 721
Collins, Mrs. D. W. 399
Colman, Julia 671
Colton, Ellen M. 429
Coman, Charlotte B. 755
Coman, Katherine 720
Conkling, Julia Catherine 472
Cook, Mary E. 888
Cooke, Grace McGowan 379-847
Cooley, Emily M. J. 674
Cooley, Mrs. R. C. 383
Coolidge, Mary 847
Cooper, Emma L. 755
Cooper, Humility 34
Corbin, Caroline Elizabeth 833
Corbin, Edythe Patten 619
Corey, Martha 37
Cornelius, Mary A. 674
Corning, Lucy A. 886
Corr, Mary Bernardine 721
Coudert, Amalia Kussner 752
Counts, Belle 368
Cowan, Mrs. Andrew 696
Cox, Lucy Ann 492
Cozens, Lizzie C. 888
Craddock, Charles Egbert (Mary N.
  Murfee) 802
Craig, Charity Rusk 349
Cramer, Harriet L. 533
Cramsie, Mary Isabel 722
Cranch, Mrs. Richard 131
Crane, Caroline Bartlett 738
Crane, Mary Helen Peck 674
Cranmar, Emma A. 675

Critcher, Mrs. Eugene 399
Crittenden, Mrs. John J. 256
Crittenden, Lucy 258
Crockett, Mrs. Emma D. 399
Croly, Jennie Cunningham 401
Cromwell, Mrs. E. S. 397
Cropper, Anna McLane 619
Crosman, Mrs. J. Heron 457
Crossan, Clarissa 368
Crothers, Rachel 792
Crowley, Mary Catherine 833
Crowninshield, Mary Bradford 858
Culbertson, Belle Caldwell 520
Culver, Helen 532
Cunningham, Amelia 383
Cunningham, Mrs. 51
Curran, Mrs. John H. 399
Curry, Sadie 498
Curtis, Georgina Pell 616-852
Curtis, Martha E. Sewell 561
Cushman, Charlotte 770
Cutts, Adelaide 610

Dada, Hattie 312
Dahlgren, Madeleine Vinton 814
Daffan, Katie 501
Dandridge, Mrs. Danske 379
Danforth, Ruth 369
Daniels, Frances D. 368
Darrah, Lydia 154
Davis, Clara 312
Davis, Edith Smith 669
Davis, Mrs. Jefferson 488
Davis, Katherine Bement 538
Davis, Mrs. M. E. 469
Davidson, Lucretia Maria 797
Davenport, Frances G. 865
Day, Emma 515
de Fonseca, Miriam Lopez 631
De Graffenried, Mary Clare 853
De Reimer, Emily True 476
De Sales, Mother Mary (Wilhel-
    mina Tredow) 622
de Torres, Siraha 631
De Witt, Margaret 888
Dean, Sara 395
Deane, Margaret 834
Dearborn, Mrs. J. H. 399
Decker, Sarah Platt 420-718
Deere, Mrs. Charles H. 481
Delafield, Elizabeth Hanenkamp ... 461
Delaney, Adelaide Margaret 834
Deland, Mararetta Wade 859
Delfino, Mrs. Laborio 696
Demary, Julia Ann 437
Denison, Elsa 604

Dennis, Mrs. 51
Desha, Mary 453
Deslonde, Miss 610
Devereux, Marie 428
Devoe, Emma Smith 561
Dewey, Mary Elizabeth 859
Dewhirst, Susan Lucretia 664
Dibrell, Mrs. Ella Dancy 502
Dickerman, Julia Elida 765
Dickins, Marguerite 473
Dickinson, Anna Elizabeth 831
Dickinson, Mary Lowe 713
Dickson, Estelle 612
Dickson, Josephine 612
Dieffenbacker, Frances A. 368
Dillingham, Mrs. B. J. 399
Dillon, Hester A. 377
Dix, Beulah Marie 791
Dix, Dorothea Lynde 523
Dix, Miss 358
Dodge, Grace 522
Dodge, Mary Mapes 851
Doe, Mary L. 694
Dole, Helen James 829
Donner, Elizabeth 101
Donner, Georgiana 101
Donner, Mary 101
Dopp, Katherine Elizabeth 718
Doremus, Mrs. R. Ogden 464
Doremus, Mrs. T. C. 512
Doremus, Mrs. 793
Dormitzer, Anna 887
Dorsey, Ella Loraine 853
Dorsey, E. M. 613
Dorsey, Sarah Ann 491
Dosemus, Mrs. J. W. 399
Douglas, Alice May 857
Douglas, Jennie 889
Douglas, Lavantia Densmore 675
Dow, Cornelia M. 675
Dowd, Mary Hickley 722
Dowdell, Mrs. Andrew W. 383
Dowell, Frances S. 888
Downing, Miss 511
Downs, Mrs. George Sheldon (Mrs.
    Georgie Sheldon) 860
Doyle, Agnes Catherine 834
Doyle, Mrs. John H. 480
Doyle, Martha Claire 834
Doyle, Teresa 610
Drake, Pricilla Holmes 561
Draper, Mrs. Amos G. 469
Draper, Mary 128
Drexel, Mother Katherine 722
DuBoise, Miriam Howard 561
Dubois, Mrs. 259

58

PAGE

Dudley, Ann 35
Dudley, Helena Stuart 593
Dumas, Sarah J. 365
Duncan, Kate 611
Dunham, Marion Howard 675
Dunlevy, Mary 55
Dunning, Mrs. Charles B. 399
Duvall, Mrs. and others 258
Dye, Clarissa 362

Earle, Mary Orr 472
Early, Miss 613
East, Mrs. Edward H. 675
Eastman, Elaine Goodale 858
Eastman, Julia Arabella 843
Eaton, Sarah 34
Eccleston, Mrs. Sarah (Chamber-
    lain) 374
Eddy, Mary Baker 701
Eddy, Sara Hershey 769
Eddy, Mrs. 101
Edgar, Constance 613
Edgar, Mrs. 196
Edson, Sarah P. 358
Edwards, Mrs. Ninian 285
Eldred, Maria O. 368
Eliot, Ann 510
Eliot, Mrs. Samuel 428
Elkers, Bertha Kahn 651
Elliott, Ann 142
Elliott, Anna 204
Elliott, Mrs. Barnard 204
Elliott, Gertrude 777
Elliott, Maxine 776
Elliott, Melcenia 312
Elliott, Sabina 204
Elliott, Sabrina 131
Elliott, Sarah Barnwell 380
Elliott, Susannah 140
Ellis, Edith 791
Ellis, Margaret Dye 666
Ellison, Mrs. J. F. 399
Elmer, Emily 368
Elmore, Lucie Ann Morrison 676
Emig, Lelia Bromgold 663
Emmet, Mrs. Thomas Addis 259
Erving, Annie Pricilla (Cella
    Zerbe) 365
Esmond, Rhoda Anna 676
Esther, (Queen of Pamunkey) 18
Etheridge, Emma 612
Ewing, Elizabeth Wendell 369
Ewing, Ellen 610
Ewing, Mary Emilie 834
Evans, Martha 52
Everhard, Caroline McCullough ... 560

PAGE

Eytinge, Pearl 636
Eytinge, Rose 636

Faestel, Annie L. 888
Fairbanks, Mrs. Chas. Warren 454
Fairchild, Mrs. 696
Farham, Mary Frances 733
Farmer, Fannie Merritt 860
Farnham, Sallie James 760
Farrar, Geraldine 766
Fay, Lydia Mary 514
Feasley, Maude (Mrs. Louis E.
    Sherwin) 780
Fenn, Katy 888
Fensham, Florence Amanda 718
Fenwick, Sister Stanislaus 607
Ferguson, Georgiana 888
Fergusson, Elizabeth 179
Fethers, Mrs. Ogden H. 472
Fidelis, Mother 615
Fields, Annie Adams 860
Field, Mrs. Stephen J. 428
Field, Mrs. 203
Fillmore, Abigail 247
Fischer, Mother Antonina O. S. D.. 619
Fischer, Therese R. 887
Fisher, Harriet White 900
Fisher, Rebecca J. 96
Fiske, Fidelia 513
Fiske, Minnie Maddern 774
Fleming, Lizzie B. 888
Fletcher, Alice Cunningham 881
Flintham, Lydia Sterling 834
Florence, Mrs. 635
Floyds, The 612
Ford, Harriet 792
Ford, Mrs. John S. 302
Forest, Mistress 30
Fosdick, Sarah 101
Foster, Edna Abigail 860
Foster, Mrs. John W. 454
Foster, J. Ellen Horton 748
Foster, Mary F. 396
Foster, Sarah 101
Forsyth, Mary Isabella 429
Frank, Abigail 631
Frank, Rebecca, ... 632
Franklin, Sarah 202
Franks, Rebecca 202
Fraser, Mary Crawford 835
Fray, Ellen Sulley 561
Frazier, Martha M. 694
Freeman, Florence 763
Freeman, Mary E. Wilkins 804
Frost, The Misses 611

PAGE

Frye, Mrs. William P. 429
Fuller, Margaret (Marchioness D'-
  Ossoli) 812
Fuller, Marie L. 888
Fuller, Mary 891
Fuller, Mrs. 31

Gadsby, Mrs. James Eakin 478
Gage, Frances D. 313
Gannett, Mary Chase 478
Garden, Mary 779
Gardner, Adaline 498
Gardner, Anna 313
Gardner, Bertha 498
Gardner, Emily 342
Gardner, Mary Fryer 366
Garfield, Eliza 274
Garfield, Lucretia Rudolph 272
Garies, Fannie M. 887
Garrett, Eliza 540
Gaston, Margaret 149
Gaston, The Misses 611
Gates, E. N. 887
Gates, Fannie A. 887
Geer, Augusta Danforth 460
Geiger, Emily 175
George, Mrs. E. E. 312
Georgetown Convent, Founding of
  the 615
Gerberding, Elizabeth 599
Gesterfeld, Ursula Newell 855
Ghuhac, Beryl 696
Gibbes, Sarah Reeve 169
Gibbons, Mrs. A. H. 312
Gibbons, Marie Raymond 478
Gibbons, S. H. 312
Gilder, Jeannette Leonard 867
Gildersleeve, Virginia C. 732
Gilman, Mary C. 355
Gilpin, Mrs. Henry D. 287
Gilson, Helen L. 331
Gillespie, Eliza Maria 724
Gillett, The Sisters 894
Gilman, Charlotte Perkins 873
Gilman, Mary L. 533
Gilman, Mary Rebecca Foster 850
Gilmore, Florence Magruder 534
Glasgow, Ellen 379
Glasgoy, Ellen Anderson G. 807
Glass, Mrs. 52
Goessmann, Helena Theresa Fran-
  cesca 730
Goff, Harriet Newell Kneeland .. 676
Goldthwaite, Miss 606
Golterman, Ada V. 886
Good, Mrs. G. Browne 428

Good, Sarah 37
Goodell, Mary 612
Goodloe, Abbie Carter 379
Goodloe, Mrs. Green Clay 429
Goodspeed, Albina E. 887
Goodspeed, J. Edison 887
Gordon, Anna Adams, ... 658
Gordon, Elizabeth P. 694
Goring, Maria W. 368
Gougar, Helen M. 583
Gould, Elizabeth Lincoln 860
Gould, Helen Miller 537
Graham, Sister Bernard 614
Granger, Euphrasia Smith 437
Grant, Julia Dent 267
Grant, Mrs. 501
Gratz, Rebecca 647
Graves, Elizabeth 101
Graves, Ellen 101
Graves, Mary 101
Graves, Nancy 101
Graves, Viney 101
Gray, Jennie T. 677
Greble, Mrs. Edward 312
Greeley, Mrs. A. W. 428
Green, Frances Ninno 382
Greene, Cathrine 112
Greene, Maria Louise 841
Greene, Ruhama 60
Greene, Sarah Pratt 850
Greene, Mrs. 202
Greenleaf, Jean Brooks 556
Greenwood, Elizabeth W. 677
Grenfell, Mrs. Wilfred 522
Grew, Mary 555
Grey, Mrs. 511
Gridley, Anna Eliza 370
Griffin, Etta Josselyn 698
Griffin, Josephine 314
Griffin, Mrs. 511
Griffith, Eva Kinney 677
Gross, Myra Geraldine 382
Gross, Sarah B. 368
Grouitch, Mme. Slavko 542
Guerrier, Edith 860

Hadder, Mrs. 696
Hadley, Piety Lucretia 101
Hagan, Mrs. Hugh 428
Hahn, Anna 368
Haines, Helen 835
Haines, Sarah Platt 519
Hale, Mrs. E. J. 399
Hale, Susan 754
Hall, Adelaide S. 858
Hall, Mrs. Herman J. 411

PAGE

Hall, Maria M. C. 312
Hall, Mary E. 888
Hall, Susan A. 312
Halvey, Margaret Mary Brophy.... 862
Hamilton, Margaret 362
Hamilton, Stella M. 620
Hamilton, Mrs. 195
Hamlin, Mrs. Teunis S. 476
Hammer, Anna Maria Nichols 678
Hammond, Mrs. John Hays 289
Hampton, Emma Stark 348
Hancock, Cornelia 366
Hancock, Dorothy 123
Hancock, Mrs. John 201
Hanna, Mrs. Marcus A. 429
Harby, Miss 636
Hardey, Mary 625
Hardin, Julia Carlin 620
Harland, Marion 381
Harrell, Sarah Carmichael 678
Harriman, Mary Averill 893
Harrington, A. B. 886
Harrington, Cornelia 368
Harris, Belle C. 356
Harris, Mrs. John 311
Harris, Mary M. 887
Harrison, Anna Symmes 238
Harrison, Mrs. Burton 801
Harrison, Caroline Scott 279-430
Harrison, Edith Ogden 835
Harrison, Mother Angela 614
Hart, Louisa B. 635
Hart, Rebecca C. I. 635
Hart, Susan 204
Hartt, Mary Bronson 860
Harvey, Cordelia A. P. 312
Harvey, Jennie D. 887
Harvey, Maud Clark 664
Harvey, The Misses 203
Hatch, Mabel 890
Hatcher, Georgia H. Stockton 468
Haugherty, Margaret 303
Hawes, Mrs. C. H. 882
Hawes, Dell M. 886
Hawley, Harriet Foote 312
Hayden, Mary F. 368
Hayes, Ellen 720
Hayes, Lucy Webb 269
Hayes, Margaret 334
Hays, Esther Etting 633
Hays, Mrs. Moses Michael 633
Hazard, Caroline 715
Hazard, Rebecca N. 556
Hazen, Fanny Titus 362
Heald, Rebecca 85
Hearst, Phoebe Apperson 530

PAGE

Hearst, Mrs. 697
Heck, Barbara 509
Hekking, Avis 764
Hemenway, Mary Tileston 525
Hemsteger, Ida M. 887
Henderson, Lizzie 383
Henrotin, Ella Martin 532
Henry, Josephine Kirby Williamson 557
Henry, Kate Kearney 429
Henry, Mrs. William Wirt 428
Hertz, Laura B. 594
Hetzel, Susan Riviere 429
Hibbard, Julia A. 366
Hichborn, Jennie Franklin 474
Higbie, Frances 887
Hill, Agnes Leonard 828
Hill, Eliza Trask 556
Hill, Iley Lawson 436
Hill, Dr. Nancy M. 334
Hills, Mrs. 261
Hines, Rev. Mother Mary Agnes... 722
Hirsch, Maria R. 888
Hitchcock, Mary Antonette 678
Hitt, Agnes 351
Hobbes, John Oliver (Mrs. Craigie) 805
Hodgin, Emily Caroline Chandler.. 678
Hoffman, Clara Cleghorn 694
Hoge, Mrs. A. H. 336
Hogg, Mrs. N. B. 428
Hoisington, Lauretta H. 369
Holley, Marietta 873
Holmes, Jennie Florella 679
Holmes, Jessie 312
Holmes, Mary Emma 557
Holstein, Mrs. Wm. H. 312
Holt, Edith 696
Homans, Amy Morris 720
Homer, Mrs. Francis T. 620
Honore, Bertha 612
Honore, Ida 612
Hooker, Isabella Beecher 573
Hooper, Rebecca E. 888
Hooper, Rebecca Lane 791
Hoopes, Mrs. Abner 429
Hopkins, Mrs. Archibald 598
Hopkins, Constance (or Constantia) 33
Hopkins, Damaris 33
Hopkins, Elizabeth 33
Hopkins, Pauline Bradford Mackie 807
Horne, Mrs. William Henry 753
Horton, Mrs. John Miller 481
Hosmer, Harriet G. 761
Housh, Esther T. 670
Housman, Mrs. E. A. 398
Houston, Mrs 196
Howard, Eleanor W. 429

	PAGE
Howe, Julia Ward	798
Howe, Rena M.	886
Howell, Mary Seymour	557
Hoxie, Vinnie Ream	761
Hubbard, Mrs. Adolphus S.	428
Hubbard, Mary	36
Hugg, Mrs.	342
Hughes, Jennie V.	522
Hull, Mrs. J. A. T.	428
Hull, Sarah	120
Humphreys, Sarah Gibson	557
Hunt, Elizabeth P.	369
Hunt, Louise Frances	620
Hunt, Mary H.	679
Hunter, Mrs. J. W.	399
Hunter, Mrs M. A.	544
Huntley, Amelia Elmore	519
Huntley, Florence	855
Huntington, Mrs. E. M.	261
Hurll, Estelle May	843
Husband, Mary Morris	312
Hutchinson, Anne	37
Hyde, Mrs. George Merriam	620
Hyneman, Rebekah	636
Ilgen, Susana	887
Iliohan, Henrica	680
Ingalls, Constance	613
Ingalls, Eliza B.	694
Ingalls, Ethel	613
Ingalls, Murilla Baker	516
Ingle, Nancy May	888
Ingram, Helen K.	888
Innis, Anna	75
Irene, Mother (Lucy M. T. Gill)	723
Irving, Katie	611
Isaacs, Augusta R.	887
Isaacs, Sarah	632
Ives, Alice	790
Izard, Alice	176
Jackson, Fannie O.	366
Jackson, Helen Hunt	809
Jackson, Lillie Irene	301
Jackson, Mary Anna	382
Jackson, Rachel	234
Jacobi, Mary Putman	741
James, Alice Archer Sewall	811
James, Annie Laurie Wilson	863
Jamieson, Mrs. J. Stewart	474
Janes, Martha Waldron	736
Jay, Mrs.	195
Jayne, Alice M.	886
Jefferis, Marea Wood	820
Jefferson, Martha Wayles	217
Jehu, Margaret E.	887

	PAGE
Jenkins, Therese A.	557
Jewett, Mrs. John N.	429
Jewett, Martha P.	886
Jewett, Sarah Orne	801
Jeykell, Mrs.	195
Joachimsen, Pricilla	635
Jobes, Mrs. Mary Adelaide	375
Johns, Laura M.	557
Johnson, Ada	369
Johnson, Lady Arabella	35
Johnson, Electa Amanda	539
Johnson, Eliza McCradle	265
Johnson, E. Pauline	826
Johnson, Lucy	883
Johnson, Lydia S.	366
Johnson, Mary Hannah	382
Johnson, Mary Katharine	461
Johnson, Miss	511
Johnston, Frances Benjamin	788
Johnston, Harriet Lane	610
Johnston, Maria I.	819
Johnston, Mary	807
Johnston, Mary Yellott	69
Johnston, Sarah R.	312
Jones, Calista Robinson	353
Jones, Cora L.	888
Jones, Elizabeth Dickson,	529
Jones, Harriet B.	742
Jones, Irma Theoda	539
Jones, Mrs. Judge	495
Jones, Kate E.	355
Jones, Mary C.	736
Jones, Minona Stearns Fitts	411
Jordan, Cornelia Jane Matthews	819
Jordan, Elizabeth	835
Jordan, Kate	793
Joyce, Eliza Le Brun Miller	620
Judson, Anne H.	507
Juggins, Elizabeth	51
Kahn, Ruth Ward	820
Kaiser, Lucy L.	366
Karnes, Matilda Theresa	723
Keating, Sister Joseph	614
Keim, Adelaide	772
Keim, Mrs. DeB. Randolph	398
Keim, Jane Sunner Owen	433
Keister, Lillie Resler	521
Keith, Mrs. Richard H.	534
Keller, Helen Adams	699
Kellogg, Clara Louise	767
Kelly, Ella Maynard	901
Kelly, Margaret V.	901
Kendrick, Mary	382
Kendricks, Ella Bagnell	680
Kennedy, Sarah Beaumont	380

PAGE

Kenton, Elizabeth 82
Kepley, Ada Miser 681
Kerfoot, Annie Warfield Lawrence 467
Kidd, Lucy Ann 731
Kies, Mary 883
Kiesburg, Mrs. 101
Kimball, Corinne 780
Kimball, Grace 780
Kimball, Helen L. McLean 889
Kimball, Kate Fisher 855
King, Grace Elizabeth 380-817
King, Julia Rive 764
King, Sister Mary Lorelto 614
King, Virginia Anne 383
Kingsbury, Emeline D. (Tenney).. 367
Kinkead, Eleanor Talbot 380
Kinkead, Elizabeth 380
Kinkead, Elizabeth Shelby 786
Kinne, Elizabeth D'Arcy 348
Kinney, Clara A. 886
Kinney, Narcissa Edith White 681
Kirk, Dolly Williams 379
Kirk, Ellen Olney 827
Kirkland, Caroline C. 890
Kirkland, Jerusha Bingham 516
Knight, Margaret E. 886
Knott, Mrs. A. Lee 455
Knowles, Ella 746
Knowles, Mrs. Joseph H. 522
Knox, Adeline Trafton 827
Knox, Janette Hill 681
Knox, Myra 611
Knox, Mrs. 201
Kollock, Florence E. 737
Kripps, Nancy 363
Kronold, Mme. Selma 767
Krout, Caroline Virginia 828
Krout, Mary Hannah 828
Kumler, Mrs. Charles H. 403

Lacey, Mary E. Roby 360
La Fetra, Sarah Doan 661
La Follette, Belle Case 290
Lafon, Mary 399
Lalor, Alice 605
Lamar, Mirabean B. 101
Lamb, Martha Joanna 812
Lamson, Lucy Stedman 904
Lane, Harriet 249
Lane, Lizzie 887
Lancaster, Anna Randall 613
Lancaster, Susie 613
Lang, Margaret Ruthven 770
Langworthy, Elizabeth 410
Larcom, Lucy 820
Lathrop, Clarissa Cladwell 598

PAGE

Lathrop, Mary Torans 681
Latimer, Elizabeth Wormeley 817
Lawrence, Charlotte Louise 459
Laurence, Mrs. Elmer G. 398
Lautz, Katherine Bardol 534
Law, Sallie Chapman (Gordon) ... 490
Lawless, Margaret H. Wynne 836
Lawton, Elizabeth Tillinghast ... 292
Lazarus, Emma 852
Leader, Oliver Moorman 682
Leary, Anne 620
Leavitt, Miss Adelia 375
Leavitt, Mary Clement 682
Le Brun, Adele 621
Lee, Ann 509
Lee, Jennette 843
Lee, Mary W. 312
Leese, Mary Elizabeth 292
Leggett, Mary Lydia 737
Lemmon, Sarah A. (Plummer) 367
Leocadia, Sister Loyola 615
Leonard, Anna Byford 596
Leonard, Cynthia H. Van Name .. 527
Leonard, Mary Finley 379
Leonard, Mrs. Willard A. 901
Le Plongeon, Alice D. 877
Leslie, Mrs. Frank 873
Lester, Mame 887
Levy, Mrs. Aaron 634
Levy, Hannah 634
Levy, Kate 642
Lewis, Graciana 877
Lewis, Ida 291
Lewis, Mary 36
Lewis, Mrs. Ransom 495
Lincoln, Jennie Gould 854
Lincoln, Mary Johnson Bailey 830
Lincoln, Mary Todd 263
Lincoln, Mrs. M. D. 397
Lindsay, Mrs. Lilah D. 399
Linton, Laura A. 878
Lippincott, C. H. 898
Lippincott, Sarah Jane 841
Lippincott, Mrs. (Grace Green-
  wood) 397
Litchfield, Mary Elizabeth 719
Littell, Oriella I. 888
Little, Sarah F. Coles 728
Littlejohn, Mrs. 511
Livermore, Mary A. 591
Livermore, Mary Ashton Rice 325
Livingston, Mrs. Robert R. 196
Livingston, Susan 121
Livingston, The Misses 196
Lockwood, Belva Ann 397-583
Lockwood, Mary Smith 854

PAGE

Lockwood, Mary S. 395-477
Logan, Celia 824
Logan, Olive 396
Logan, Sallie 303
Longman, Evelyn 759
Longshore, Hannah E. 739
Loomis, Mary A. 334
Lopez, Miss 631
Lord, Eleanor Louise 727
Lord, Elizabeth W. Russell 731
Lord, Mildred M. 888
Lothrop, Harriet M. 824
Loud, Hulda Barker 874-875
Louiza, Rachel 631
Lowden, Florence Pullman 301
Lowell, Miss Susan R. 375
Lowman, Mary D. 898
Lozier, Jennie de la Montagnie ... 739
Lucas, Eliza 106
Lucas, Nancy and daughters 611
Lukens, Anne 740
Lummis, Dorothea 741
Lummis, Eliza O'Brien 836
Lupton, Mary Josephine 836
Lutke, Mrs. Robert 399
Lybrand, Frances R. 891
Lynch, Mrs. 196
Lynde, Mary Elizabeth Blanchard 544
Lyon, Mary 511-708
Lyth, Mrs. R. B. 513

McAllister, Louise Ward 428
McCabe, Harriett Calista Clark... 682
McCabe, Lida Rose 730
McCabe, Margaret 621
McCartney, Katharine Searle 431
McChesney, Norma Gertrude 837
McClanahan, Anna 522
McClellan, Mrs. Robert A. 479
McComb, Mrs. 196
McCrakin, Josephine 844
McCully, Emma A. 891
McCutcheon, Mrs. 99
McDermott, Ida L. 887
McDermott, Mrs. 605
McElroy, Mary Arthur 274
McFadden, Margaret B. 534
McFadyen, Agnes 887
McGee, Anita Newcomb 429
McGill, Sarah 534
McGowan, Alice 847
McGowan, Elizabeth Blaney 723
McHenry, Mary Sears 349
McKay, Charlotte E. 312
McKinney, Annie Booth 383
McKinley, Ida Saxton 281

McKinney, Mrs. Jane Amy 557
McKinney, Kate Slaughter 379
McKissick, Margaret Smyth 595
McLain, Miss 610
McLaughlin, Marchioness Sara 621
McLaughlin, Mary L. 886
McLaws, Lafayette 379
McLean, Mrs. Donald 438
McLean, Mrs. Louis 254
McMahan, Mother Eutropia 621
McMahon, Ella 837
McManes, Mrs. James 697
McMeens, Anna C. 312
McMillan, Mrs. James 428
McMillan, Mary 93
McNeir, Mrs. 342
McPhail, Minnie 887
McShane, Agnes 535
McSherry, Virginia Faulkner 499
McVeigh, Columbia 891

MacComber, Mary L. 758
MacDonald, Mrs. Marshall 428
Mace, Frances Lawton 825
Mack, Margaret A. 888
Mackin, Countess Sarah Maria
 (Aloisa Spottiswood) 836
Mackubin, Florence 754
Madison, Dolly 221
Maertz, Louisa 312
Magdalene, Sister Mary (Sarah
 O. Cox) 837
Maguire, Mary 611
Mahoney, Caroline Smith 379
Maid, Mrs. Carver's 31
Maidhof, Marguerite 887
Main, Charlotte Emerson 462-697
Maish, Jennie (Gauslin) 367
Mallory, Lucy A. 874-875
Mallory, The Misses 611
Malloy, Marie Louise 858
Manning, Charlotte R. 888
Manning, Jessie Wilson 670
Manning, Mary Margaret Fryer ... 471
Mannix, Mary E. 837
Mannon, Mary L. 367
Mansfield, Bell A. 749
Marble, Annie Russell 844
Marble, Callie Bonney 825
Marble, Mrs. E. M. S. 397
Marcoux, Alida M. 888
Marlowe, Julia 778
Marot, Helen 600
Marsh, Susan Ellen 370
Marshall, Mrs. George W. 399
Marshall, Sister Margaret 607

	PAGE
Martin, Elizabeth	156
Martin, Elizabeth Gilbert	837
Martin, Mrs. George Madden	379
Martin, Gertrude S.	725
Martin, Grace	157
Martin, Rachel	157
Martin, Sarah J.	352
Martin, Susan	37
Martin, Mrs.	31
Martin, Mrs.	300
Mary, Sister	607
Mason, Amelia Gere	855
Mason, Emily	260
Mason, Emily Virginia	380
Mather, Margaret	777
Mather, Sarah Ann	545
Mathews, Julia B.	886
Matthews, Frances Aymar	793
Matthews, Mother Juliana	614
Maxfield, Mary B.	367
Maxon, Hannah U.	361
Maxwell, Mrs. Lawrence	402
Maynard, Cora	793
Mayo, Margaret	789
Meade, Minnie	611
Meagher, Katherine Kelly	535
Meagher, Sister Josephine O. S. D.	621
Mechtold, Mary Rider	791
Mee, Cassie Ward	903
Meech, Jeannette Du Bois	905
Melton, Mrs. Joanna	366
Melville, Velma Caldwell	825
Mendes, Esther Pereira	631
Mendes, Grace P.	651
Mercedes, Mary Antonio Gallagher	837
Meriwether, Lide	694
Merrick, Caroline Elizabeth	682
Merrick, Mary Virginia	535
Merrick, Mrs.	256
Merriman, Helen Bigelow	848
Merritt, Anna Lee	756
Meyer, Annie Nathan	649
Michaels, Hannah	631
Miles, Emma Bell	379
Miliken, Mrs. D. A.	544
Miller, Adaline	367
Miller, Mrs. A. Barton	398
Miller, Addie Dickman	683
Miller, Annie Jenness	845
Miller, Dora Richards	825
Miller, Emily Huntington	871
Miller, Flo Jamison	342
Miller, Louise Klein	716
Miller, Olive Thorne	847
Miller, Maria	367
Miller, Mary E.	747
Mills, Susan Carrie	366
Mills, Susan Lincoln	724
Milton, Joanna	367
Minis, Judy and daughter	632
Mink, Sarah C.	350
Minot, Fanny E.	354
Mins, Sue Harper	705
Minter, Desire	31
Minter, Edith Dowe	830
Misch, Mrs. Caesar	650
Mitchell, Ellen E.	312
Mitchell, Maria	876
Mitchell, Martha Reed	526
Moise, Penina	636
Moises family	635
Molloy, Mary Aloysia	838
Monroe, Harriet	612
Monroe, Harriet Stone	841
Montgomery, Darrie Frances Judd	520
Montgomery, Helen Barrett	522
Montgomery, Mrs.	195
Montague, Margaret Prescott	379
Montholon, Albina	611
Moore, Aubertine Woodward	864
Moore, Clara Jessup	826
Moore, Ella Maude	858
Moore, Idora M. Plowman	827
Moore, Kate	104
Moore, Mary	50
Moore, Mrs. Phillip N.	401
Moore, Sarah	863
Moody, Helen Waterson	829
Mooris, Ellen Douglas	683
Moots, Cornelia Moore Chillson	683
Mordecai, Rose	650
More, Ellen	32
Morgan, Agnes	791
Morgan, Anne Eugenia Felicia	728
Morgan, Henrietta Hunt	69
Morgan, Sarah Berrien Casey	432
Morgan, Mrs. Wm.	51
Morley, Margaret Warner	382
Morison, Rebecca Newell	621
Morris, Clara	779
Morris, Matilda	367
Morris, Mrs.	196
Morrison, Adele	612
Morse, Alice Cordella	751
Morton, Eliza Happy	857
Morton, Jane M.	367
Morton, Martha	790
Mosher, Edith R.	866
Moseley, Mrs.	96
Mott, Lucretia	590
Mott, Mollie C.	367
Motte, Rebecca	139

PAGE

Moulton, Louise Chandler 840
Moulton, Mattie B. 342
Mowat, Vivian A. 907
Mullens, Alice 33
Mullens, Priscilla 33
Mulliner, Gabrielle 593
Munger, Mrs. 511
Munroe, Elizabeth 227
Munsell, Jane R. 312
Murdoch, Marian 738
Murfree, Mary 379
Murphy, Mary 101
Mussey, Ellen Spencer 479-749

Nash, Mary McKinley 471
Nash, Clara Holmes Hapgood 744
Nason, Emma Huntington 866
Navarro, Mary Anderson 781
Nave, Anne Eliza Seamans 531
Neale, Sister Aloysia 607
Neale, Sister Magdalene 607
Nealis, Jean Elizabeth Ursula 838
Neblett, Ann Viola 694
Neisser, Emma R. 696
Nellis, Samantha Stanton 437
Nevada, Emma Wixon 766
Nevins, Georgia Marquis 547
Newcomer, Miss 612
Newell, Mrs. F. H. 398
Newell, Harriet 508
Newman, Angela F. 521
Newman, Mrs. Laura A. (Mount) 371
Newton, Mary 433
Ney, Elizabeth 763
Nicholas, Josephine Ralston 684
Nicholls, Rhoda Carleton Marian
    Holmes 754
Nichols, Elizabeth B. 335
Nichols, Minerva Parker 786
Nicholson, Eliza J. 872
Nicholson, Miss 611
Niehaus, Regina Armstrong 819
Nielsen, Alice 783
Noble, Edna Chaffee 728
Noble, Esther Frothingham 465
Noble, Harriet L. 96
Noble, Dr. Mary Riggs 522
Nobles, Catherine 411
Nordica, Lillian 766
North, Mary M. 309-398
Norton, Minerva Brace 732
Nourse, Elizabeth 756
Noyes, Mrs. LaVerne 475
Nurse, Rebecca 37

PAGE

O'Brien, Margaret 621
O'Donnell, Martha B. 684
O'Donnell, Nellie 726
O'Flanagan, Betty 95
O'Mahoney, Katherine A. 838
O'Malley, Sallie Margaret 838
O'Neil, Mrs. Charles 429
O'Reilly, Gertrude 750
O'Reilly, Mary Boyle 839
Oakley, Violet 755
Oberholtzer, Sara Louisa Vickers .. 828
Ohl, Maud Andrews 866
Oleson, Mrs. Rebecca (Lemmon).. 372
Oliver, Grace Atkinson 818
Olmsted, Elizabeth Martha 818
Ormsby, Mary Frost 819
Orr, Ora 886
Orric, Mary Semmes 622
Osborne, Mrs. Frank Stuart 428
Osborne, Sarah 37
Osburn, Mary 670
Otis, Mrs. Harrison Gray 284
Otis, Rebecca 372
Ould, Miss 613
Ouseley, Lady William Gore 256
Owen, Mary Alicia 868

Pacheco, Judith 631
Page, Lucy Gaston 412
Paine, Harriet Eliza 850
Palmer, Anna Campbell 828
Palmer, Mrs. A. M. 594
Palmer, Bertha Honore 291
Palmer, Fannie Purdy 829
Palmer, Hannah Borden 684
Palmer, Hannah L. 363
Palmiter, Phoebe M. W. 437
Palms, Marie Martin 622
Pamunkey, Queen of 18
Papin, Mrs. Theophile Emily Car-
    lin 622
Parish, Lidia G. 312
Paris, Mrs. (Tituba) 36
Parker, Alice 745
Parker, Helen Almina 727
Parker, Lottie Blair 790
Parkhurst, Emily Tracey Y. Sweet 872
Parks, Anna M. 888
Parlin, Lucy 438
Parsons, Emily E. 312
Patterson, Flora W. 878
Patterson, Mrs. Lindsay 480
Patterson, Mrs. Marshall H. 399
Patterson, Mrs. Sarepta C.
    (McNall) 372

PAGE

Patton, Abby Hutchinson 868
Pay, Ellen 342
Peabody, Elizabeth 181
Peabody, Elizabeth Palmer 286-730
Peabody, Josephine Preston 791
Peabody, Lucy Evelyn 879
Peake, Mary S. 313
Pealer, Ruth M. Griswold 435
Pearce, Sister Eulalia 614
Peck, Annie Smith 880
Peel, Mrs. Lawson, ... 383
Peeler, Mrs. 397
Peeples, Sarah E. 886
Pendleton, Ellen Fitz 733
Pennock, Miss Caroline C. 891
Pennybacker, Mrs. Percy V. 501
Perkins, Sarah Mariah Clinton ... 694
Pesoa, Miss 635
Peterson, Miss 104
Pettus, Maria 379
Pfohl, Katherine Laughlin 622
Pharr, Sallie S. 888
Phelps, Almira Lincoln 796
Phelps, Mrs. John S. 312
Phelps, Pauline 792
Phillips, Ellen 635
Phillips, Emaline 370
Phipps, Lady 37
Piatt, Sarah Morgan Bryan 840
Pickens, Lucy Holcomb 103
Pickett, La Salle Corbell 845
Pier, Caroline Hamilton 745
Pier, Harriet Hamilton 745
Pier, Kate 745
Pier, Kate Hamilton 745
Pierce, Elizabeth F. 410
Pierce, Jane Means Appleton 248
Pike, Harriet 101
Pike, Miriam 101
Pike, Mrs 101
Pitcher, Molly 162
Pitkin, Louisa Rochester 432
Planten, July 886
Plimpton Hannah R. 356
Plumb, Mrs. L. H. 899
Plunkett, Harriette M. 902
Pocahontas 19
Polak, Jessamine 767
Polk, Sarah Childress 242
Pollard, Mrs. Carrie (Wilkins) 372
Pollock, Louise 712
Pollock, Mrs. Mary B. 372
Pomeroy, Genie Clark 826
Pond, Nellie Brown 746
Poole, Fannie Huntington Runnells 848
Pope, Cora Scott Pond 540

PAGE

Pope, Mrs. Henry Lewis 470
Poppenheim, Mary B. 384
Poree, Caroline E. 296
Porter, Charlotte 830
Porter, Delia Lyman 841
Porter, Eliza C. 311
Porter, Florence Collins 685
Portundo, Josephine B. Thomas ... 821
Post, Amalia Barney Simons 588
Potter, Margaret Horton 861
Potts, Anna M. Longshore 742
Poulsson, Ann Emelie 850
Powell, Mrs. 197
Powers, Lucy Gaylord 314
Prang, Mary Dana Hicks 719
Pratt, Mrs. Malinda A. 372
Preston, Ann 742
Preston, Margaret Junkin 811
Preston, Margaret Wickliffe 69
Price, Rebecca L. 370
Pringle, Mary (Mary Breckel) ... 333
Pritchard, Esther Tuttle 737
Prosser, Anna Weed 738
Provost, Mrs. 196
Pruit, Willie Franklin 544
Pryor, Mrs. Roger A. 434
Pryor, Sarah 377
Pugh, Esther 685
Pulitzer, Mrs. Joseph 642
Pullman, Mrs. George M. 303
Putnam, Ann 36
Putnam, Mrs. Charles E. 428
Putnam, Mrs. John Risley 428
Putnam, Mary Steiner 461
Pyle, Alice A. 888
Pyle, Katherine 842

Quimby, Harriet 301
Quinton, Amelia Stone 407

Rambaut, Mary L. Bonney 711
Ramsay, Lula 685
Ramsay, Marion 610
Ransford, Nettie 408
Rathbun, Mary Jane 878
Rathnell, Mrs. Maria L. 372
Rauh, Bertha 650
Read, Carrie R. 355
Read, Lizzie B. 558
Reading, Mrs. Sarah M. 372
Reed, Caroline Keating 765
Reed, Elizabeth Armstrong 861
Reed, Esther 105
Reed, Pattie 101
Reed, Virginia 101
Reed, Mrs. 101

PAGE

Reel, Estelle 726
Rees, Mrs. Thomas M. 399
Reese, Mary Bryon 685
Regan, Mrs. John 102
Rehan, Ada C. 782
Reinheimer, Sarah A. 886
Reno, Itti Kinney 872
Repplier, Agnes 864
Rice, Alice Hegan 379
Rice, Mrs. Isaac L. 602
Rich, Helen Hinsdale 868
Richards, Ellen Henrietta 880
Richards, Janet Elizabeth 784
Richards, Laura Elizabeth 857
Richards, Mrs. Maria M. C. 371
Richards, Mary 535
Richardson, Dorcas 177
Richardson, Ellen A. 848
Richardson, Harriet 878
Richardson, Hester Dorsey 718-872
Richardson, Mrs. Mary A. 370
Richardson, Sarah 75
Ricker, Marrilla M. 559
Ricketts, Fanny L. 312
Rigdale, Mrs. 31
Rigden, Catherine Ann 608
Riggs, Anna Rankin 686
Rinehart, Mary Roberts 792
Ripley, Martha George 744
Ripley, Mary A. 817
Rishel, Mary Anne 437
Risley, Alice Cary 370
Ritchie, Mrs. John 463
Rittenhouse, Laura Jacinta 694
Rives, Amelie (Princess Troubet-
skoy) 379-816
Rivington, Mrs. 203
Roach, Abby Mequire 379
Robbins, Margaret Dreier 593
Robertson, Charlotte 75
Robins, Julia Gorham 731
Robinson, Abbie C. B. 871
Robinson, Amy F. 887
Robinson, Fannie Ruth 871
Robinson, Harriet Hanson 842
Robinson, Helen A. 887
Robson, Mrs. J. J. 399
Roby, Ida Hall 898
Roby, Leila P. 375
Roebling, Emily Warren 297
Rogers, Emma Winner 817
Rogers, The Misses 611
Rohlfs, Anna Katherine Greene.... 803
Roosevelt, Edith Kermit Carow.... 282
Rose, Ellen Alida 897
Rose, Laura Martin 500

PAGE

Rose, Martha Parmelee 559-595
Rosenberry, Mollie R. Macgill..... 501
Ross, Anna Maria 312
Ross, Letitia Dowdell 497
Ross, Miss 197
Roulet, Mary F. Nixon 821
Roupell, Mary 203
Rouse, Rebecca 60
Routt, Eliza Franklin 302
Rowland, Kate Mason 380
Rucker, Irene 613
Rude, Ellen Sargent 818
Ruffin, Margaret Ellen Henry 821
Rullann, Maria 314
Rumsey, Mary Ann 95
Runkle, Bertha 808
Runyan, Mrs. P. S. 342
Rush, Mrs. James 283
Rusk, Mrs. Thomas J. 102
Russell, Elizabeth Ann 437
Russell, Elizabeth Augusta 370
Russell, Mrs. E. J. 312
Rutherford, Mildred Lewis 380
Ryan, Mrs. Thomas F. 536
Ryland, Cally 380

Sabin, Florence Rena 382-729
Sacajawea 20
Sackett, Mrs. Emma A. 372
Safford, Mary J. 312
Safford, Mary Joanna 844
Sage, Mrs. Russell 545
Samson, Deborah 143
Samson, Julia 887
Sanborn, Kate 869
Sanders, Sue A. Pike 350
Sangster, Margaret Elizabeth 869
Sansom, Emma 304
Sargent, Ellen C. 587
Sarpy, Adele, and daughters 611
Sartin, Emily 757
Sartin, Harriet 757
Saunders, Mary 612
Saunders, Mary A. 897
Saxon, Elizabeth Lyle 559
Schaefer, Louise 888
Schaumburg, Emilie 295
Schertz, Helen Pitkin 380
Schram, Mrs. Anna Maria B. 370
Schoenfeld, Julia 648
Schoff, Hannah Kent 403
Schuyler, Catherine 115
Schuyler, Elizabeth 117
Schuyler, Mrs. 203
Scidmore, Eliza Ruhamah 856
Scudder, Vida D. 793

PAGE

Scott, Emily Maria 755
Scott, Mrs. Hector 96
Scott, Kate M. 361
Scott, Mary 694
Scott, Mary Anne 437
Scott, Mary Augusta 720
Scott, Mary Sophie 898
Scott, Mrs. Matthew T. 441
Scott, Sister Mary Emanuel 614
Scott, Mrs. Winfield 256
Scott, Mrs. 52
Searing, Laura Catherine 845
Seawell, Molly Elliot 803
Sedgwick, Catherine Maria 870
Segur, Rosa L. 559
Seidell, Mary V. 888
Semmes, Ada, and sisters 611
Semmes, Myra E. Knox 536
Semple, Ellen Churchill 879
Senn, Margaret Lynch 822
Sergent, Ellen 686
Seton, Elizabeth A. 623
Seton, Grace Gallatin 842
Severance, Caroline Maria 525
Severance, Caroline M. Seymour... 413
Sevier, Catherine 72
Sewall, May Wright 580
Shanklan, Eugenia 752
Sharpe-Patterson, Virginia 399
Sharpe, Mrs. 606
Shattuck, Harriette Lucy-Robinson. 843
Shaw, Rev. Anna B. 581
Shaw, Annie C. 757
Shaw, Cornelia Dean 560
Shelby, Sarah 59
Shelby, Susanna Hart 68
Sheldon, Mary French 872
Sheldon, Susan 36
Shelton, Emma Sanford 665
Shepherd, Ina 894
Sherman, Eleanor Boyle Ewing 292
Sherman, Margaret Stewart 293
Sherman, Ninna E. 906
Sherman, Mrs. Sidney 103
Sherwood, Emily Lee 814
Sherwood, Kate Brownlee 347-816
Sherwood, Mary Elizabeth 815
Sherwood, Rosian Emment 752
Shetfall, family 631
Shields, Mrs. G. H. 428
Shippen, Mrs. William Watson.....468
Shoff, Carrie M. 752
Short, Marion 792
Shuttleworth, Frances 398
Sibley, Jennie E. 686
Sigourney, Lydia Huntley 979

PAGE

Simon, Miss 632
Simonds, Emma E. 334
Simpson, Annie 501
Singleton, Mrs. Richard 203
Sitgreaves, Mary A. 213
Skelton, Henneriette 686
Slidell, Mrs. 258
Slocumb, Mary 165
Small, Mrs. Jerusha R. 312
Smallwood, Delia Graeme 435
Smith, Mrs. Charles Emory 296
Smith, Clara A. 879
Smith, Clara E. 731
Smith, Eleanor M. 888
Smith, Emily L. Goodrich 863
Smith, Eva Munson 816
Smith, Gertrude 379
Smith, Mrs. Herbert Knox 398
Smith, Isabel Elizabeth 751
Smith, Julia Holmes 815
Smith, Mrs. J. Morgan 465
Smith, Mary Agnes Easby 822
Smith, Mary Bede 695
Smith, Mrs. Mary E. (Webber).... 372
Smith, Mary Stuart 815
Smith, Rebecca S. 363
Smith, Rosa Wright 428
Smith, Sophia 711
Smock, Rose Melville 783
Smythe, Amanda 371
Snelling, Abigail 89
Sommerfeld, Rose 646
Southwick, Charlotte Augusta 259
Southworth, Emma D. E. N. .. 397-813
Spalding, Anne 536
Spalding, Mrs. 185
Sparks, Ruth 58
Sprague, Mrs. Sarah J. (Milliken). 372
Sprague, Mrs. Susannah 373
Speed, Mrs. Joshua 285
Spencer, Mrs. Emily P. 372
Spencer, Mrs. R. H. 312
Sperry, Hannah B. 397
Sperry, Mrs. N. D. 428
Spilman, Mrs. Baldwin Day 463
Spofford, Harriet Prescott 839
Spray, Ruth Hinshaw 531
Springer, Rebecca Ruter 861
Sproat, Sarah W. 62
Squire, Mary E. 361
St. Clair, Mrs. F. O. 428
St. John, Cynthia Morgan 870
Stakeley, Mrs. Charles Averette ... 429
Standish, Rose 31
Stanford, Jane Lathrop 543
Stanislaus, Sister (Sister Stanny).. 614

PAGE

Stanley, Mrs. Cornelia M. (Thompkins) 373
Stanton, Elizabeth Cady 566
Stearns, Betsey Ann 889
Stephenses, the 612
Stephenson, Mrs. Sophia 373
Stevens, Alice J. 822
Stevens, Alzina Parsons 903
Stevens, Emily Pitt 687
Stevens, Lillian M. N. 687
Stevens, Mrs. Mary O. 371
Stevenson, Mrs. Adlai 448
Stevenson, Matilda Coxe 881
Stewart, Eliza Daniel 687
Stewart, Mrs. Mary E. 373
Stewart, Salome M. 361
Stewart, Mrs. 197
Stille, Mary Ingram 695
Stimson, Mrs. E. K. 342
Stoddard, Anna Elizabeth 688
Stokes, Missouri H. 689
Stone, Cornelia Branch 383-492
Stone, Lucinda H. 412
Stone, Lucy 562
Storer, Maria Longworth 758
Story, Mrs. William Cumming 399
Stowe, Harriet Beecher 808
Stowell, Louise M. R. 880
Strachan, Grace Charlotte Mary Regina 616-732
Stranahan, Clara Harrison 293
Streeter, Emma A. 887
Strong, Harriet W. R. 887
Strong, Julia 887
Strout, Mrs. Joseph M. 399
Stuart, Katharine 399
Stuart, Ruth McEnery 381-806
Stubbs, Mrs. Annie Bell 371
Sudderley, Mrs. J. E. 399
Surriage, Agnes 36
Swain, Adeline Morrison 560
Swartz, Dr. Vesta M. 373
Sweet, Ada Celeste 831
Swenning, Rebecca T. 886
Swett, Sophia Miriam 859
Switzer, Lucy Robins Messer 689
Swormstedt, Mabel Godfrey 465
Szold, Henrietta 642

Talbot, Ellen Bliss 720
Taliaferro, Mabel 780
Tall, Lida Lee 382
Taft, Helen Herron 283
Taney, Mary Florence 822
Taney, the Misses 892
Tanner, Mrs. James 299

PAGE

Taplin, Mrs. Horatio N. 429
Tappen, Elizabeth 85
Taylor, Betty (Mrs. Bliss) 244
Taylor, Catherine L. 360
Taylor, Kiturah Leitch 67
Taylor, Lodusky J. 353
Taylor, Nellie Maria 311
Taylor, Susan Lucy Barry 69
Taylor, Mrs. Zachary 244
Telford, Mrs. J. M. 342
Temple, Mary Boyce 429
Teresa, Sister 605
Teresa, Sister M. Imelda (Susie Teresa Forrest Swift O. P.)... 536
Terhune, Mary Virginia 799
Terhune, Mrs. 381
Terrell, Mrs. Alexander W. 103
Thacher, Ella Hoover 668
Thackara, Ellen Sherman 611
Thanet, Octave (Alice French) 804
Thayer, Mrs. Charles S. 604
Thayer, Lizzie E. D. 901
Thomas, Edith Matilda 811
Thomas, Mrs. E. 312
Thomas, Jane 181
Thomas, Mrs. 51
Thompson, Caroline Wadsworth ... 823
Thompson, Charlotte 689
Thompson, Mrs. Charlotte Marson. 373
Thompson, Eliza J. 689
Thompson, Mrs. Pauline 373
Thompson, Sarah 202
Thompson, Mrs. 196
Thorndyke, Rachel Sherman 611
Thorpe, Rose Hartwick 842
Thorpe, Sarah 84
Townsend, Miss Eliza L. 373
Thurston, Ida Treadwell 854
Thurston, Mrs. John W. 428
Thurston, Lucy Meachem 379
Tiernan, Mrs. Frances (Christian Reid) 615
Tiernan, Frances Fisher 823
Tingley, Katherine 294
Tinker, Mrs. 31
Tilley, Bridget (Van der Velde) .. 34
Tilley, Elizabeth 34
Tilley, Mrs. 31
Tilton, Lydia H. 695
Tittman, Mrs. 431
Todd, Minnie Terrell 560
Tomkies, Mrs. Hoyle 398
Tompkins, Cornelia M. 312
Tong, Eleanor Elizabeth 823
Touro, Reyna 633
Trader, Mrs. Georgie 531

PAGE

Trader, Misses 696
Trout, Grace Wilbur 408
Truitt, Anna Augusta 690
Tucek, Mary 888
Tucker, Mary Logan 295-612
Tucker, Miss 195
Turnbull, Mrs. Lawrence 379
Turnbull, the Misses 611
Turner, Lizbeth A. 351
Turner, Nancy L. 887
Tuttle, Diana H. 886
Tutweiler, Julia S. 382
Tyler, Adeline 312
Tyler, Amelia 891
Tyler, Julia Gardiner 241
Tyler, Letitia Christian 240
Tyler, Pearl 612
Tyson, Mrs. Laura R. 373

Van Buren, Angelica Singleton 237
Valesh, Eva McDonald 904
Van Kleeck, Mary 603
Van Meter, Mrs. I. C., Jr. 457
Van Ness, Cornelia 255
Van Ness, Marsia Burns 262
Vanvoce, Elizabeth V. 887
Van Zandt, Marie 767
Venturini, Countess Mario (Char-
    lotte Stern) 769
Vinton, Madeline 611
Vogt, Mary M. 887

Wade, Jennie 315
Wait, Anna C. 560
Walker, Alice Brebard Ewing 462
Walker, Annie Kendrick 380
Walker, Harriett G. 695
Walker, Mary 36
Walker, Dr. Mary E. 579
Walker, Sarah B. 888
Walker, Susan Hunter 865
Wallace, Emma R. 350
Wallace, Susan 214
Wallace, Susan Arnold Elston 851
Wallace, Zerelda Gray 575
Walling, Mary Cole 376
Walsh, Honor 823
Walsh, the Misses 611
Walter, Mary Jane 670
Walters, Jennie 613
Walworth, Ellen Hardin 441-752
Ward, Elizabeth Stuart Phelps 800
Ward, Genevieve 783
Ward, Mary Alden 849
Ward, Sallie 262
Ware, Angeline D. 890

PAGE

Ware, Mary 379
Warner, Anne 793
Warnoch, Mrs. Susan (Mercer) ... 373
Warren, Emily 611
Warren, Mary 36
Warren, Mary Evalin 690
Warren, Mercy 124-200
Wharton, Mrs. William H. 104
Washington, Eugenia 453
Washington, Mrs. Joseph 428
Washington, Lucy H. 690
Washington, Martha 207
Washington, Mary 205
Washington, Virginia 429
Waterhouse, Jessie 907
Watts, Margaret Anderson 690
Weatherby, Delia L. 691
Webster, Mrs. Daniel 256
Webster, the Mother of 254
Weedon, Mrs. Howard 379
Wells, Charlotte Fowler 902
Wells, Mrs. Shepard 312
Welsh, Mrs. Andrew, Sr. 622
West, Mary Allen 691
Westmore, Elizabeth Bisland 848
Weston, Hannah 158
Wetherell, Mrs. E. F. 312
Whaley, Eleanor M. 594
Wharton, Deith 829
Wheeler, Amey Webb 300
Wheeler, Candace 753
Wheelock, Dora V. 692
Whipple, Alice A. 887
White, Caroline Earle 537
White, Mrs. Cynthia (Elbin) 374
White, Sister Genevieve 614
White, Mrs. James W. 258
White, Mrs. Lovell 399
White, Nettie L. 893
White, Susanna 33
Whitehead, Mrs. Amos 496
Whitelock, Louise Clarkson 379
Whiteman, Mrs. Lydia L. 373
Whiteside, Mrs. H. R. 398
Whitford, Mrs. Reid 399
Whitney, Anne 760
Whitney, Gertrude 763
Whiting, Lillian 849
Whitthorne, Ella 612
Widmayer, Adeline 886
Wiedinger, Mary D. 888
Wiggin, Kate Douglas (Mrs. Riggs) 804
Wilbur, Mrs. Joshua 428
Wilcox, Mrs. Collier 370
Wilcox, Eliza 886
Wilcox Ella Wheeler 842

PAGE

Wilcox, Margaret A. 888
Wilcox, Mary 613
Willcox, Mary Alice 879
Wilcox, Mary R. 296
Wilde, Jennie 752
Wilkinson, Eliza 152
Willard, Electa 368
Willard, Emma 706
Willard, Frances E. 288
Willard, Frances Elizabeth 653
Willard, Mary Bannister 692
Willard, Mary Thompson Hill 288
Willard, Sister Paulina 615
Williams, Alice 693
Williams, Pamela 261
Williams, Theresa A. 665
Willing, Jennie Fowler 693
Willis, Pauline 823
Wilson, Augusta J. Evans 839
Wilson, Mrs. George H. 383
Wilson, Martha 131
Wilson, Mrs. Robert 203
Wilson, Sarah 84
Winans, Sarah D. 353
Winslow, Elizabeth 32
Winslow, Helen Maria 850
Wister, Sallie 159
Wittenmeyer, Anna 349
Wittenmyer, Annie 693
Wolcott, Ann Louise 718
Wolfinger, Mrs. 101
Wood, Edith Elmer 854

PAGE

Woodbridge, Mary Brayton 694
Woodey, Mary Williams Chawner.. 695
Woodley, Mrs. Emile Wilson 369
Woods, Bertha G. Davis 842
Woods, Kate Tannatt 849
Woods, Mary A. 302
Woodsey, the Misses 312
Woodward, Caroline M. Clark 694
Woodworth, Miss Mary A. E. 375
Woolley, Mary Emma 721
Wooster, Lizzie E. 861
Wormeley, Katharine Prescott 312
Wright, Elina M. 886
Wright, Mrs. Leonore (Smith) 374
Wright, Emma Scholfield 753
Wright, Louise Sophie Wigfall ... 382
Wright, Mrs. Luke E. 300
Wright, Mrs. S. J. 405
Wynne, Madeline Yale 861

Yandell, Enid 763
Young, Ella Flagg 733
Young, Mrs. John Russell 697
Young, Mrs. Lucy A. 374
Young, Mary Vance 720
Young, Rida Johnson 790
Yturbide, Madame 615

Zane, Betty 160
Zeigler, Matilda 696
Ziegler, Mrs. William 531

American Women: Images and Realities
An Arno Press Collection

[Adams, Charles F., editor]. **Correspondence between John Adams and Mercy Warren Relating to Her "History of the American Revolution," July-August, 1807.** With a new appendix of specimen pages from the **"History."** 1878.

[Arling], Emanie Sachs. **"The Terrible Siren": Victoria Woodhull, (1838-1927).** 1928.

Beard, Mary Ritter. **Woman's Work in Municipalities.** 1915.

Blanc, Madame [Marie Therese de Solms]. **The Condition of Woman in the United States.** 1895.

Bradford, Gamaliel. **Wives.** 1925.

Branagan, Thomas. **The Excellency of the Female Character Vindicated.** 1808.

Breckinridge, Sophonisba P. **Women in the Twentieth Century.** 1933.

Campbell, Helen. **Women Wage-Earners.** 1893.

Coolidge, Mary Roberts. **Why Women Are So.** 1912.

Dall, Caroline H. **The College, the Market, and the Court.** 1867.

[D'Arusmont], Frances Wright. **Life, Letters and Lectures: 1834, 1844.** 1972.

Davis, Almond H. **The Female Preacher, or Memoir of Salome Lincoln.** 1843.

Ellington, George. **The Women of New York.** 1869.

Farnham, Eliza W[oodson]. **Life in Prairie Land.** 1846.

Gage, Matilda Joslyn. **Woman, Church and State.** [1900].

Gilman, Charlotte Perkins. **The Living of Charlotte Perkins Gilman.** 1935.

Groves, Ernest R. **The American Woman.** 1944.

Hale, [Sarah J.] **Manners; or, Happy Homes and Good Society All the Year Round.** 1868.

Higginson, Thomas Wentworth. **Women and the Alphabet.** 1900.

Howe, Julia Ward, editor. **Sex and Education.** 1874.

La Follette, Suzanne. **Concerning Women.** 1926.

Leslie, Eliza. **Miss Leslie's Behaviour Book: A Guide and Manual for Ladies.** 1859.

Livermore, Mary A. **My Story of the War.** 1889.

Logan, Mrs. John A. (Mary S.) **The Part Taken By Women in American History.** 1912.

McGuire, Judith W. (A Lady of Virginia). **Diary of a Southern Refugee, During the War.** 1867.

Mann, Herman. **The Female Review: Life of Deborah Sampson.** 1866.

Meyer, Annie Nathan, editor. **Woman's Work in America.** 1891.

Myerson, Abraham. **The Nervous Housewife.** 1927.

Parsons, Elsie Clews. **The Old-Fashioned Woman.** 1913.

Porter, Sarah Harvey. **The Life and Times of Anne Royall.** 1909.

Pruette, Lorine. **Women and Leisure: A Study of Social Waste.** 1924.

Salmon, Lucy Maynard. **Domestic Service.** 1897.

Sanger, William W. **The History of Prostitution.** 1859.

Smith, Julia E. **Abby Smith and Her Cows.** 1877.

Spencer, Anna Garlin. **Woman's Share in Social Culture.** 1913.

Sprague, William Forrest. **Women and the West.** 1940.

Stanton, Elizabeth Cady. **The Woman's Bible** Parts I and II. 1895/1898.

Stewart, Mrs. Eliza Daniel. **Memories of the Crusade.** 1889.

Todd, John. **Woman's Rights.** 1867. [Dodge, Mary A.] (Gail Hamilton, pseud.) **Woman's Wrongs.** 1868.

Van Rensselaer, Mrs. John King. **The Goede Vrouw of Mana-ha-ta.** 1898.

Velazquez, Loreta Janeta. **The Woman in Battle.** 1876.

Vietor, Agnes C., editor. **A Woman's Quest: The Life of Marie E. Zakrzewska, M.D.** 1924.

Woodbury, Helen L. Sumner. **Equal Suffrage.** 1909.

Young, Ann Eliza. **Wife No. 19.** 1875.